# THE HANDBOOK OF EVALUATION RESEARCH

# THE SOCIETY FOR THE PSYCHOLOGICAL STUDY OF SOCIAL ISSUES (SPSSI)

## Editorial Advisory Committee

Donald T. Campbell, *Northwestern University*

Isidor Chein, *New York University*

Jacob Cohen, *New York University*

Howard Davis, *National Institute of Mental Health*

Ward Edwards, *University of Michigan*

Nathan Gage, *Stanford University*

Terence Hopkins, *Columbia University*

Hylan Lewis, *Brooklyn College of the City University of New York*

Peter Rossi, *Johns Hopkins University*

M. Brewster Smith, *University of California, Santa Cruz*

Lauren Wispé, *University of Oklahoma*

As Division 9 of the American Psychological Association, SPSSI began as and continues to be a unique organization. From its very beginning in 1936 it established as the nexus of its concern the application of behavioral science research to the major social dilemmas of modern man; war, poverty, intergroup prejudice, urban stress, industrial strife, and other problems. Implicit in this concern was the compelling assumption that science could not be value free; that in its desire to ameliorate the ills of modern society its systematic research endeavors would have political and social consequences as well as scientific ones. Lewin was right when he stated that research should be socially useful as well as theoretically meaningful, but this could only occur if the researchers involved conceptualized, organized, and directed their investigations with this end in mind.

Excerpt from 1972 Presidential Message by
Harold M. Proshansky

*Volume 2*

# *Handbook*
## of
# *Evaluation*
# *Research*

*Edited by*

**MARCIA GUTTENTAG**
*Harvard University*

*and*

**ELMER L. STRUENING**
*Columbia University*

 SAGE Publications    Beverly Hills  •  London

Copyright © 1975 by Sage Publications, Inc.

All rights reserved. No part of this book may be reproduced or utilized in any form or by any means, electronic or mechanical, including photocopying, recording, or by any information storage and retrieval system, without permission in writing from the publisher.

*For information address:*

SAGE  PUBLICATIONS, INC.
275 South Beverly Drive
Beverly Hills, California 90212

SAGE PUBLICATIONS LTD
St George's House / 44 Hatton Garden
London EC1N 8ER

Printed in the United States of America

International Standard Book Number 0-8039-0429-0

Library of Congress Catalog Card No. 74-15764

THIRD PRINTING

CAMROSE LUTHERAN COLLEGE
LIBRARY

H
62
H 2454/18,137
VOL. II

# CONTENTS

# I
# PREFACE

*1*

# THE HANDBOOK: ITS PURPOSE AND ORGANIZATION

## MARCIA GUTTENTAG

*Harvard University*

and

## ELMER L. STRUENING

*Columbia University*

### THE RELATIONSHIP BETWEEN PROGRAM CONTENT
### AND EVALUATION TECHNIQUES

A basic premise of the Handbook is that evaluation research has a number of distinctive aspects, not the least of which are the context within which it is performed and the content of the program being evaluated. Choices of the conceptual framework for the evaluation, decisions about specific evaluation methodologies, and even the timing of data gathering and analyses should be closely linked to the content and context of the program under evaluation.

Evaluations must be useful. This second volume of the Handbook is organized around the principle that the evaluation researcher cannot use any simple cookbook of methodologies applicable to all evaluations. Rather, an intimate understanding of the special evaluation requirements of each distinctive type of program and every unique setting is required. Too many evaluations which disregard context lie gathering dust on shelves while critical decisions about programs are made despite evaluation findings. An evaluation that is useful and used must be conducted with a lively recognition of the distinctive content of the program being evaluated, and the formal and informal context within which the program occurs.

A serious look at the actual substance of the program being evaluated can prevent some of the obvious but oft repeated evaluation failures of the past.

For example, although it seems too obvious to mention, it is important to know whether a program actually exists. Federal agencies are often inclined to assume that, once a cash transfer has taken place from a government agency to a program in the field, a program exists and can be evaluated. Experienced evaluation researchers know that the very existence of a program cannot be taken for granted even after large case transfers have taken place. Early evaluation of Title I programs in New York City provide an illustration of this problem. Funds from this program went to schools with a large percentage of poor and minority pupils. Evaluators for the program began by simply visiting a number of schools with Title I funds. To their surprise, they learned that in some of the schools teachers were not aware the program existed. In other schools they could find no evidence of any special programs designed for the target population. Wisely, the evaluators refused to pursue the evaluation beyond this point. Obvious though it may seem, evaluations continue without either raising or answering the primary question: "Does the program exist?" This error could not arise if evaluation researchers looked carefully and seriously at program content before decisions about evaluation research methods were made.

Another key problem surfaces repeatedly in evaluation research. It is simply: When can data be aggregated across individual programs? Many serious policy blunders have been made on the basis of national programs which have been incorrectly aggregated across sites. The question is: "Where is the program the same, and where is it different?" When a program occurs in different places, and with different populations, similarity cannot be assumed, even if it is a useful federal fiction. Even when two programs are funded under the same federal title, they may be more dissimilar than similar. The most serious policy errors have been made with program differences, and the interaction between these differences and population characteristics, have been obscured by the aggregation of national data. It is reasonable to predict that, if program differences are ignored, national evaluations will show that overall program effects are negligible. The biases in resulting policy decisions are the direct effects of faults in evaluation methods. These data aggregation errors could be avoided if evaluation researchers paid careful and close attention to the actual content of each individual program being evaluated, especially when national outcomes are studied.

As another illustration of the importance of attention to program content, recently a number of evaluations have tested hypotheses that there would be no differences between experimental and control populations. These hypotheses are derived from the prediction of critics that the programs might well have major negative effects, for example, negative income tax, Manhattan bail evaluations. When, however, the evaluations were designed so that *no* differences were predicted, the interpretation of outcomes was ambiguous. There was no way, for example, to determine whether (a) the programs had so negligible an effect that there were no differences at all between experimental and control populations, or (b) the programs had positive effects but few major negative ones. This ambiguity in inference occurred because the programs were *assumed* to have the effects intended. The ambiguity in interpretation could have been avoided if close attention had been paid to the actual content and processes of the programs and positive effects had been evaluated and not assumed. The evaluation researcher must examine whether a program has any effects *at all* in addition to determining whether the program has negative effects.

The three examples above are just a few illustrations of how critical it is that the evaluation researcher thoroughly familiarize himself with what a program is and does, what the characteristics of recipients of a program are, and how the content of a program shifts or remains stable over a period of time.

In recognition of the importance of the context and content of programs, this second volume of *The Handbook of Evaluation Research* focuses on evaluations in context. Several content areas, their special problems, and the evaluation methodologies applicable to them are presented and discussed.

Part II of this volume includes two chapters which present the political, ethical, and human aspects of the evaluation of human service programs. The two chapters in Part III are a methodological discussion and critical analysis of cost-benefit approaches to evaluation. In Part IV, mental health programs are examined in detail. The eight chapters in this section cover as many different aspects of evaluation in the variety of contexts within which mental health programs are found.

In Part V, three other major program content areas are analyzed. These are: early childhood intervention programs, public health programs, and new careers programs. In each of these chapters, evaluation research methodologies are presented in terms of the unique issues and problems characterizing each content area.

In Chapter 2 of this volume, Gurel wisely and carefully describes the general characteristics of the many contexts within which human service program evaluation occurs. He identifies the four parties which have different goals and viewpoints in most human service evaluation. Then he considers four critical issues that lie at the heart of organizational realities and the powerful but subtle effects they exert on the design and implementation of evaluation. He focuses particularly on the bureaucrat-scientist, or manager-evaluator interaction, and the conflicts and differences in goals between the two. This rounded view of the structural and interpersonal constraints and requirements of evaluation research sets the stage for a consideration of the relationship between program content and evaluation methodologies.

The Sjoberg chapter clarifies the larger political, ethical, and conceptual context within which evaluation research is conducted. A number of the taken-for-granted norms of research are critically reexamined, and the political and ethical commitments of researchers are explored. This penetrating analysis of the sociology of knowledge which underlies evaluation research and researchers leads Sjoberg to a fundamental critique of the ethical assumptions and principles which are usually unspoken in such research. Sjoberg presents an alternative in "countersystem analysis," a form of dialectical reasoning.

Implicit or explicit cost-benefit analysis is part of nearly all evaluation efforts. It is frequently the aspect of evaluation which is most directly linked to the actual choices made by decision makers. What are the conceptual problems in cost-benefit analysis and the assumptions that underlie its use? The Rothenberg chapter explores the meaning of benefits and costs and the complex presumptions that underlie value criteria. His incisive analysis of theoretical issues in cost-benefit approaches reveals their economic, social, and methodological assumptions. Moral as well as measurement issues are considered. The Levin chapter carefully discusses costs and how they can be ascertained and measured. A number of specific examples provide cogent illustrations. The measurement of effectiveness is also thoroughly treated. Effectiveness measures for multiple outcomes and the distribution of effects among different populations are discussed and clearly illustrated. A critical review of cost-benefit health studies is included. Both the Levin and the Rothenberg chapter are essential reading for evaluation researchers who are planning to use cost-benefit methods and for program administrators whose programs will be subject to these approaches.

In the fourth part of this volume, we focus in detail on one content area: evaluations of mental health programs. This part is intended to serve as an illustration of the multiple perspectives required to understand and proceed effectively with evaluation in any major program area. Each of the eight chapters in this part integrates evaluation methodologies into a distinctive setting, context, and/or content of a mental health program.

The Sainsbury chapter provides a plan for the evaluation of community mental health programs, including a number of specific illustrations of such evaluations conducted in England. Sainsbury considers the collection of data, including the selection and definition of variables, and the use of Case Registers and other indices and measures which form a part of such evaluations. Emphasis is given to issues of reliability and validity in the measurement of outcomes. Analyses of data and the application of findings are fully explained and illustrated.

The evaluation contract, following the PSAR:EC model, is the subject of the Pratt and Canfield chapter. This special approach to evaluation is presented in its entirety including the theoretical and methodological rationale. Lawton and Cohen provide an excellent methodological presentation of how to conduct organizational studies of mental hospitals. Included in their chapter are the results of their own studies of mental hospitals and a focused, comprehensive review of other work. Lawton and Cohen carefully consider all the variables that can be used in such studies and provide the methodologies relevant to their use. In these evaluations, they discuss the assessment of quality and the coupling of longitudinal multivariate designs, closing with what should be included in a model design.

Consumer feedback in the measurement of effectiveness of mental health programs, is the subject of the Ellsworth chapter. This is a frequently overlooked, but extremely important, source of data in the analysis of mental health programs. As part of the Ellsworth chapter, the PARS-I, II, and III scales, developed as measures of community adjustment, are presented and discussed. Another type of mental health evaluation, that of residential treatment programs for disturbed children, is discussed by Durkin and Durkin. This careful, comprehensive chapter provides a critical analysis of all the significant evaluations in this area. Process evaluation, systems evaluation, and the research models which underlie them are considered. The authors propose a model for the evaluation of residential treatment programs for disturbed children which can overcome the problems in earlier studies. The terms and concepts used in the model and methods for its application are described.

The Brandon chapter explores the use of social area analysis as method for evaluating a community mental health program in a large metropolitan area. From the operationalization of the goals of the federal legislation to the use of these goals as hypotheses in social area analysis, every step in the approach is fully described. The methods employed in the New York City social area analysis are specified. This new and promising method for studying community mental health programs is presented in its entirety.

The Rabkin and the Kreisman and Joy chapters cover two important and frequently neglected aspects of evaluation of mental health programs. Rabkin considers the extensive research on attitudes toward mental illness and the measures and methods that have been used to study such attitudes. Her chapter is a useful supplement for the evaluation of any mental health program. Kreisman and Joy focus on another powerful contextual variable in the evaluation of mental health programs, the family as a reactor.

The final section of this volume begins with a comprehensive chapter by Bronfenbrenner which considers a number of evaluations made of the effects of early intervention programs on children. The chapter is an excellent illustration of the potential power of secondary analyses. Bronfenbrenner reanalyzes many evaluation studies of early intervention effects. These reanalyses lead to a number of unusual and provocative conclusions. The chapter is of interest from many points of view, not the least of which is its illustration of how the combination and integration of a number of primary evaluations can yield fresh insights when they are reanalyzed in a secondary analysis.

Bice and Eickhorn review evaluations of public health programs and discuss what has happened in the implementation of such evaluations. The Grant and Grant chapter thoroughly and incisively covers methods of evaluation for new careers programs.

In any one volume, it is impossible to cover all distinctive methods of evaluation research which are appropriate in every substantive content area. This volume has emphasized evaluation in mental health programs, and has presented several chapters which illustrate evaluation methods in other important content areas.

## ACKNOWLEDGMENTS

*The Handbook of Evaluation Research* would have been impossible without the dedicated work of the editorial planning committee for the Handbook, established by the Society for the Psychological Study of Social Issues. Members of the committee included Isadore Chein, Jack Cohen, Howard Davis, Nate Gage, Peter Rossi, M. Brewster Smith, and Edward Suchman. Before Professor Suchman's untimely death, he had strongly influenced the contents of the Handbook and would also have been a contributor to it. We want to thank members of the planning committee and many others who have spent so much time reading manuscripts and advising the co-editors. We are deeply grateful for their efforts.

The book would not have been possible without the support of a contract from the Mental Health Services Branch of the National Institute of Mental Health. Funds from this contract made it possible to sustain so large an endeavor over several years. The initial planning of the work was made possible by a small grant from the Society for the Psychological Study of Social Issues and funds from the Advanced Projects Research Agency. APRA funds were returned in accordance with the wishes of the editorial planning committee.

Our warm thanks go to Joanne Breiner and Mattie Jones for their heroic and successful efforts in the accurate typing of so many manuscripts. The following people, who worked in the indexing and proofreading, also deserve commendation: Wendy Willson Legge, Janis Anderson, Lionel Cuffie, Laurence Morrow, George Pollack, Ellen Stotsky, Sharon Stotsky, and Wanda Koltz. We are deeply indebted to them. Our thanks to John Martin for his help in furthering the project.

# II

# POLITICS AND VALUES IN EVALUATION RESEARCH

# 2

# THE HUMAN SIDE OF EVALUATING HUMAN SERVICES PROGRAMS: PROBLEMS AND PROSPECTS

## LEE GUREL

*American Psychiatric Association*

### PROLOGUE

Increasingly in recent years, evaluation has been viewed as an integral and essential, even if often neglected, part of a wide range of service programs funded by public monies. Program evaluation was obviously not invented in the middle of the twentieth century, but one need only look at the mushrooming evaluation literature to see how the field has expanded in the last 10 to 15 years. This rapid growth coincides historically with the emphases on rationalized decision-making associated with the early years of Robert McNamara's tenure in the Department of Defense. These emphases were subsequently formalized throughout the federal government by the (then) Budget Bureau's October 1965 Bulletin # 66-3 requiring agencies to implement the Planning, Programming and Budget system, an essential element of which was the requirement that program effectiveness and efficiency be evaluated in cost-benefit terms. While the specifics of the Bureau of the Budget directive became obscured under the Nixon administration, the pressures for institutionalizing program evaluation have, if anything, increased. Given ever-present shortages of funds available for human services, continuing pressures for intensified evaluation of public service programs are almost a certainty.

Paralleling the growth of evaluation activity, there has been a not unexpected proliferation of the evaluation literature. However, it was not long ago that students of evaluation ventured forth with little more than Suchman's now almost classic

AUTHOR'S NOTE: Separate parts of this chapter have been presented on three previous occasions: Invited Address to the Third Annual Research Seminar, South Florida Chapter of the National Association of Social Workers, Miami, April 1971; Presidential Address, Division of Psychologists in Public Service, Division 18 of the American Psychological Association, at its annual meeting, Honolulu, September 1972; and Invited Address to the 25th Annual Institute on Hospital and Community Psychiatry, Miami Beach, September 1973.

and somewhat elementary monograph (Suchman, 1967) and a general admonition from their mentors that evaluators need clear statements of program objectives and support from top management. Evaluation has proven to be much more complicated than that, and what are examined in this chapter are some of those complications still inadequately covered in the existing literature. These aspects of the evaluation process have to do, not with technical and methodological issues, but with the organizational context, the structural constraints and requirements, and, most of all, the interpersonal interactions which influence program evaluation efforts. The thesis presented here is that these issues have the most profound consequences for the success or failure of evaluative activity. My hope is that readers who are or who become involved in evaluation studies will be forewarned as to the problems and be better prepared to resolve those that can be resolved or to at least defuse those for which there is simply no good solution.

Most of the material in this chapter derives from a 15-year experience in evaluation of several parts of the Veterans Administration's program of medical care, especially its program of psychiatric care. However, I would not lead the reader on a retrospective odyssey had my reading and contacts with evaluators in other fields not convinced me that the principles and examples to be cited are by no means unique and, in fact, have considerable generalizability. Nor do I intend to bore the reader with either an apologia for mistakes I as an evaluator have made or with hostile criticism of program managers with whom I once worked. Rather, what I hope to demonstrate is that the problems of evaluation discussed here are not to be interpreted as evidence that program managers are "the bad guys" who embody evil, while program evaluators are "the good guys" who embody virtue. Those of us who are evaluators often act as though we had a moral imperative to search out truth, and we not infrequently regard those who hinder our quest as malevolent—or worse. What I hope to illustrate is that program managers and evaluators alike are simply human beings made of flesh and blood, that they are, therefore, imperfect humans, and that their seemingly imperfect behavior can be better understood through examining their social roles, their personal characteristics, and the situational demands and constraints acting on them.

## PARTICIPANTS IN EVALUATION

We can distinguish at least four parties to any attempt at evaluation of human services programs. First, there is the sponsoring authority which legitimates or authorizes or orders the provision of services. This can be a board of directors, the Congress, a state legislature, the (now) Office of Management and Budget, or whatever. Let me point out in connection with material in the next section that it would be a mistake to neglect the fact that these kinds of sanctioning bodies possess the real life-or-death power over both service programs and their evaluation and that, because program managers are exquisitely responsive to them, sponsoring authorities can and often do figure centrally in evaluation efforts.

Next, there is the program administrator or executive, or, as I shall refer to him here, the program manager. And, of course, just as there are levels of programs nested within programs and corresponding levels of evaluation, so, too, there can be several levels of program managers. A third group which can strongly affect the outcome of evaluative activity are the program staff who operate or execute the program and who are often the source of the evaluator's data. Finally, the fourth party to any evaluation effort is the evaluating agency, be it a person or a group of people assembled into an evaluation staff.

There can be other concerned parties, of course, depending on the particular situation: program clients, outside commercial interests, the news media, consultants, and the like. The four I have identified seem to me to be universally present in any evaluation effort. All four figure in the discussion that follows, but we will be primarily concerned with the program manager and the program evaluator, since it is my thesis that it is their divergent characteristics, plus the nature of their interaction and the context in which it occurs, which most centrally affect the outcome of program evaluation.

## THE CONTEXT FOR EVALUATION

Looking first at the context within which manager and evaluator interact, I will call attention to four considerations: (1) the conflicting superordinate organizational goals to which the program manager and the program evaluator subscribe, (2) the stereotype of scientific omnipotence, (3) the extension of rigorous evaluation to areas of public service only recently considered exempt from external scrutiny, and (4) the recourse to evaluation as a panacea for programs in failing health. Even just listing these four issues should serve to establish the point that evaluation efforts are necessarily launched into troubled waters.

### Commitment to Conflicting Organizational Goals

Any number of students of organization have noted that, whatever its stated and unstated goals, every organization has two superordinate sets of goals. One has to do with stability and survival; the other has to do with growth and change. And the two always operate to a significant degree to pull the organization in different directions. The important point here is that program managers tend to identify themselves primarily with the organization's stability, while the evaluator is necessarily identified with the forces of innovation which pose a threat to stability.

This seemingly obvious point assumes special significance in the evaluation of public service programs, since most of them are conducted or sponsored by hierarchical, bureaucratic, governmental agencies. Almost by definition, the supervisory echelons to which evaluators report, whether the evaluators are from within or from without an agency, are comprised of people committed to organizational stability. An important concern of management is with not making waves, with not rocking the boat. In contrast, evaluation is necessarily a force which leads to disequilibrium, no matter how minimal or transitory. Seen in this light, a medical analogy seems quite appropriate. The organizational body which serves as unwilling host to the evaluation is in much the same position as the human body when its homeostatic equilibrium is disrupted by an unwelcome pathogen against which it must mobilize its various defenses. So, too, will the forces committed to organizational equilibrium seek to resist the intrusion of agents identified with change.

As an aside, it might be noted that, if John Gardner is correct in arguing that the survival of organizations and social institutions depends on self-renewal through growth and change (Gardner, 1963), then the process described is indeed ironic. However, the irony of it does not alter the problem of organizational resistance to evaluation, nor does it eliminate the need for evaluators to understand its relevance for introducing an evaluation program.

## Stereotype of Scientific Omnipotence

A second consideration has to do with the extent to which our society over-estimates the ability of science and technology to solve any and all problems. A September 1973 editorial in *Science* reported a Harris poll indicating the great confidence which the public has in scientists—greater confidence, in fact, than in the Supreme Court, the Congress, and the executive branch! After all, we live in an age when men walk on the moon, when people are kept alive by mechanical kidneys and hearts, when laser beams are used to guide bombs and to do eye surgery—all this in the less than 50 years since Lindbergh's crossing of the Atlantic seemed incredible. Surely, if given the resources, social scientists would be able to help eliminate poverty, to teach Johnny to read, to improve our mental health, to design more responsive political institutions, and so on. Obviously, any such expectations are doomed.

The dramatic accomplishments of the physical sciences notwithstanding, the social and behavioral sciences do not have even the beginnings of a technology to improve substantially the quality of our lives, even if the resources for such efforts were suddenly to become available. Nevertheless, the optimistic aura persists, and program managers, like others in the society, tend to share such views. It has been my experience that, as a result, many managers entertain a more or less unrealistic set of expectations for what evaluators can help them accomplish, the extent of their erroneous perception varying with the extent to which the evaluator is credentialed as a scientist.

## Evaluating the Previously Unevaluated

A third portent of future difficulty lies in the fact that, historically speaking, the whole notion of formal evaluation has been totally foreign to most human services programs. We need only consider the degree to which organized medicine has fought bitterly to forestall attempts at evaluating the quality of medical care. And what is true for medicine has been equally true for many other service programs and institutions: prisons, educational programs, churches, training programs for the disabled or disadvantaged, and the like. There was never any question but what such institutions and their programs did "good" things and provided useful services; the idea was simply not entertained until fairly recently that one could and should determine whether the programs and the services were accomplishing what they were supposed to accomplish.

Nor is it sufficient to say that evaluation is novel and therefore abstractly threatening to those involved in these kinds of activities. The threat is much more real and immediate. Two facets of this threat merit explication.

The first of these, no matter how dimly perceived, is that evaluation may address itself to the most basic assumptions on which programs and the professional lives of their operators are based. Suppose, for example, that rigorous evaluation of mental health practices consistently failed to confirm benefits commensurate with the resources expended. Where would such a finding leave practitioners? Or, in the field of education, it is one thing for an evaluator to contrast the effectiveness of teaching techniques A and B. But suppose that, over a number of evaluations, it is ultimately established that, not only are techniques A, B, and C through Z essentially equivalent, but that none of them achieves stated educational goals—or achieves them to any greater degree than is accomplished by letting children loose on the streets. Picture, if you will, the terror which would strike into the hearts of thousands of schoolteachers. Better yet, let your mind play with the possibilities of evaluating church programs!

My examples are admittedly more than a little strained, but the issue is one of enormous significance. Mental health practitioners do not just offer mental health services, and teachers do not just teach. They believe in mental health and in education, often in a particular set of theories or methods, for example, psychotherapy a la Jung or free expression a la Summerhill. Many of the services only recently confronted with the prospect of evaluation are built on sets of assumptions and personal philosophies deriving from the accumulated biases and preconceptions which pass for conventional wisdom. In certain areas, such as mental health services, this assumptive framework can command emotional commitments as compelling as a set of religious beliefs. Only the most intrepid of program managers and service providers could be expected to be other than hostile to an inquiry which could conceivably render totally meaningless their personal and professional investments in these assumptive frameworks.

A second kind of threat inherent in evaluation may be more immediate but is no less profound in its impact. Simply stated, evaluation poses a serious threat to whatever degree of power the program manager may exercise. Whether through guile or through naivete, the evaluator may seek to pass off his work as a neutral activity intended only to develop knowledge for knowledge's sake. However, program managers, especially if they have clawed their way up the administrative ladder, are not likely to be taken in by the evaluator's assurances, no matter how innocently offered. They recognize that information and knowledge are not neutral quantities once they enter into the public domain. Knowledge is power. Depending on whether the information is withheld and, if disseminated, how and where it is disseminated, information can be made to serve political ends. The inherently political nature of evaluation has been dealt with at length in another chapter. The point here is that most program managers are probably well aware that they can use evaluation results to suit their own political ends and their own attempts to hold power—and that these results could just as easily be made to serve the opposing political ends and power needs of subordinates and supervisors, to say nothing of a host of potential critics and competitors.

## Evaluation as Panacea

The three considerations just noted serve, it seems to me, as a backdrop for practically any evaluation. A fourth issue, somewhat related to the second, appears to be widely prevalent, but it is by no means as universal.

It was noted above that the social and behavioral sciences do not possess sufficiently precise technology for grappling with the urgent societal problems which daily diminish and complicate the quality of our lives. It is commonly argued that this observation was one of the sobering lessons to come out of the attempt to implement President Lyndon Johnson's plans for the Great Society. However, the lack of experience, skills, and tools did not stop attempts to resolve social problems. People operated programs as best they knew how, the limitations of the available tools notwithstanding. In retrospect, it is now easy to understand why some programs soon found themselves in trouble; but, for present purposes, we are not concerned with performing a postmortem on specific Great Society programs. These situations serve only as a paradigm for the more general instance of programs operating without adequate know-how and therefore running into various difficulties. Programs for delivering mental health services have for decades now illustrated this phenomenon. The point is that, lacking technologically sound expertise, human services programs are doomed to being beset at times by massive problems of one kind or another.

All too frequently, it is precisely when the program is in trouble, particularly when the trouble is a threat to program funding, that the evaluator is called in. Whether or not the problem is specifically financial, the pressures for evaluation in such instances usually come from outside the program management and operators, not uncommonly from a critical and dissatisfied sponsoring authority. It takes little imagination to visualize the chilly reception evaluation and the evaluator will receive from program managers under these circumstances.

The history of the VA's Psychiatric Evaluation Project and its several reorganization-bred successors is instructive as an illustration of how program evaluation is called on when programs are in trouble. Out of nine major evaluation studies, one was generated by the evaluation group itself, and one came from elsewhere in the agency. The others all had their origins in pressures and queries which were conveyed with varying amounts of criticism and/or congressional or Budget Bureau threats of financial reprisal. One study, for example, was largely in response to a Bureau of the Budget attack on what was then the very costly cornerstone of the agency's plans for delivery of institutional psychiatric services. On another occasion, the agency received a rather innocuous query about one of its programs from a prestigious—but probably powerless—group at the level of a presidential commission. My own later contact with the originator of the inquiry convinced me it was just that, an inquiry, and that it carried no covert message of criticism. In the meantime, however, the agency had undertaken several defensive actions, one of which was to mount a large-scale evaluation of the program. On still another occasion, a powerful congressional critic unleashed a withering attack on a program activity in which several levels of management took considerable—and, as it turned out, unjustified—pride; the agency response was again a hastily mounted evaluation study.

Because they are instructive in several respects, these illustrations will be referred to again in connection with a discussion of the need for evaluators to understand what groups are pushing for the evaluation and what their motivations are for doing so. For the present, the major point of these examples is that evaluation is often management's begrudging response to threat. What is not so apparent and what may perhaps be even more important here, is that, no matter how the evaluation may itself be feared and unwelcome, a self-deluding feeling can be generated that the program will now somehow be made well. It is as though the medical specialist has now been called in and will be bringing with him a cureall or another "magic bullet."

Such a false hope is all the more likely if the evaluator had to oversell the evaluation proposal and its potential benefits to managers of the jeopardized program. He may even have believed sincerely that he was going to be of great help in getting the program off the hook! The program operators and management are in turn only too willing, under the circumstances, to accept the evaluator's promises as a ray of hope that the program, no matter how moribund, is going to weather its crisis and be made whole again. This is not to say that such feelings displace the program staff's feelings of threat and suspicion at being, as they may perceive it, "investigated." The point is that all of these feelings will coexist in one big, churning knot of ambivalence toward the evaluation and evaluator.

Having identified these four considerations, it should be apparent that the stage upon which the program manager and the program evaluator will interact is structured in ways that predispose that interaction to serious conflict, as each plays out his respective hopes, anxieties, suspicions, ambivalences, and unrealistic expectations. Some additional considerations more specific to the context of mental health program evaluation are dealt with below.

## SOME CHARACTERISTICS OF MANAGERS AND EVALUATORS . . .

Having considered the milieu within which they interact, it is instructive to look at some of the background, personal, and role characteristics of managers and evaluators. Given limitation of space, I shall present a composite picture, hoping to capture and reflect salient group features without doing too much violence to the individual. Of necessity, some managers and evaluators better fit the generalized image than do others, and it is recognized that there are exceptions to the overall characterization. Let me first make clear, however, that I do not consider here as evaluators persons who do not derive from some kind of scientific or technical background and who have not had specific, even if minimal, training in evaluation methodology; it is true that persons with administrative or managerial backgrounds sometimes function on an ad hoc basis as program evaluators, but they are excluded from consideration here.

### . . . and How They Differ

An attempt to assemble some of the characteristics of managers and evaluators produces an interesting result. It soon becomes apparent that one can practically go down the two sides of a sheet headed with their names, and, whatever characteristic is listed on one side, one can almost invariably list on the other side an essentially polar opposite of that characteristic. As I shall specify in more detail, the point to be noted in the discussion to follow is the extent to which program managers and program evaluators are simply cut out of different kinds of cloth.

Several ways in which managers and evaluators differ have already been alluded to. Most important of these was that managers are necessarily identified with program survival and preserving the status quo, while evaluators are more closely identified with innovation and changing the status quo. As a corollary, the one approaches analysis and evaluation in terms of their potential for program defense, while the other views them in terms of program assessment and appraisal. Both may say sincerely that they want the facts that evaluation can yield, but it should be recognized that they may want them for very different reasons.

Also, the program manager (unless he is some kind of out-and-out fraud) believes deeply in the validity and worth of his program, its possible flaws notwithstanding, and he is vitally involved in seeing that the program succeeds. The evaluator usually has no such commitment to the values and ultimate success of the program; if anything, he approaches the program with a thoroughly ingrained skepticism, and, not infrequently, with an attitude of cynicism toward human service programs in general.

There is, however, one interesting exception to the evaluator's skepticism. He is probably as deeply committed to an ethic of evaluation and to his role as manager of an evaluation program as the manager is to the operating program. So we have a situation of quid pro quo. On the one hand, the manager's commitment is met with skepticism toward the operating program; on the hand, the evaluator's commitment is met with ambivalence toward the evaluation program.

## Bureaucrat vs. Scientist

The differences just noted flow naturally from differences in role. There is another major set of differences between manager and evaluator. These, it seems to me, flow equally naturally from the fact that the one—and it is unfortunate that pejorative terminology is necessary, but it best communicates my conceptual framework of the differences—is a bureaucrat, and the other is a scientist.

The program manager is a "company man" or, to use Whyte's now popular phrase, an "organization man." He is unswervingly loyal to the organization, denies even to himself its faults, and is so strongly identified with it that his own personality becomes submerged in it. He derives security from his identification with the organization and looks to it as his primary source of personal advancement and recognition. When need be, he can be counted on to subordinate his own interests, and even his personally held principles, to what he perceives as the interests of the organization generally and "the management team" specifically.

The evaluator, on the other hand, most often identifies himself as a scientist and an individualist. Not infrequently, he delights in a few iconoclastic swipes at the petty stupidities which seem to abound in any organization. He looks for recognition, less from his associates in the organization, and more from his associates in the professional groups with which he identifies. To obtain such recognition, he seeks to contribute to the expansion of knowledge in his professional field, usually by publishing in the professional literature. My own experience has been that the evaluator's taking time for publication can be particularly annoying to a program manager concerned with the immediate utility of evaluation results for program and organizational defense; the latter very much resents the evaluator's use of time and other resources for activities not clearly and immediately related to organizational goals as he perceives them.

On the other hand, the evaluator can be as frustrated as the manager is resentful over his inability to communicate with his peers. However, the problem goes beyond just journal publication. The more central issue is what constitutes an adequate completion and wrap-up of a study. For the manager, since the evaluation effort is only one of many activities to which he attends, completion can be a series of progress reports which establishes the probable trend of the final results. I have even known managers to be content with just a memorandum or with a brief verbal report. How formal a wrap-up the manager requires is in large part a reflection of his involvement with the evaluation effort, an issue considered in more detail below. His investment, however, can never match that of the evaluator for whom doing the evaluation was a major commitment. Thus, the evaluator will ordinarily want to surround his report of findings with all the fanfare and elaborate packaging possible as evidence of both his personal accomplishment and the importance of the completed work. In a word, he wants reinforcement.

Aside from the intrinsic rewards of the work itself, evaluators tend to derive satisfaction from either the impact of their work on programming or from the recognition of their professional peers, depending on the balance between their identifications with the organization and with their profession. A manager who is content with a verbal report which he stores as information somewhere in the back of his head cuts the evaluator off from both these sources of satisfaction.

Pursuing the matter a step further, let us suppose the evaluator is administratively responsible to the manager. (Although what is to be described could as easily occur if manager and evaluator were both responsible to a supervisor who shared the manager's views.) The manager can operationalize his satisfaction with minimal reporting by assigning the next evaluation effort long before the preceding one is completed to the evaluator's satisfaction. Over a period of time, evaluators thus amass yellowing books of computer output and file drawers full of obsolescent data for addressing no-longer-relevant questions. The mountains of paper are matched by the mammoth frustration well known to psychologists as the Zeigarnik Effect, the annoyance and frustration of not being able to complete something one is very much involved in.

Also in connection with publication, what will be terribly distressing to most managers I have known or heard about is the possibility that the evaluator, committed as he is to an ethic of full and complete disclosure of data, may publicly say something to put the program in an unfavorable light. It makes no difference that the evaluator may be accurate in his analysis and have mountains of data to support his conclusions. To go public with what could be construed as criticism—and what organization cannot be legitimately criticized?—is perceived by the faithful "company man" as whistle-blowing, a "crime" of awesome proportions

(Branch, 1971). No matter the evaluator has published or wishes to publish in some obscure journal. Whatever might possibly rebound to make the organization look bad is seen as an attack. Which, of course, it is, in the sense that the highlighting of imperfections erodes a structure which the manager is committed to defend and to which he has pledged his loyalty. That is, the manager perceives attack because what is being undermined by even the mildest constructive criticism is not just a program or organization, but a set of values, a source of security, and whatever else the program means to the manager as a person.

The latter point was illustrated for me by the reception accorded a paper presented at an annual, predominantly intra-VA conference of mental health researchers and practitioners. On prior occasions, I had reported a study, or some manageable piece of it, much as I would deliver a research paper to an audience of other psychologists: rationale, hypotheses, subjects, procedure, and so on. On the occasion in question, I presented an overview of several years of group effort and several lines of evidence which strongly suggested that the programs evaluated had a number of shortcomings and were generally not achieving the levels of effectiveness publicized by program managers.

Responses to my "disclosures" fell pretty much into two discrete categories, and these were associated with two different role-types. Some very positive, even enthusiastic, reactions came from people who were not centrally involved in the program and who did not figure importantly, or even at all, in the power hierarchy which managed the programs. On the other hand, the nature of the response from the management in-group is best conveyed by its leader's comment that, "I hear you offended some of the boys down in [meeting site] ; I'm sorry I couldn't be there because some of them were pretty upset." The manager's immediate subordinates were less direct. One suggested that, "The paper was OK, but it would have been nice if you had had some brightly colored charts to go with the talk." The paper was equally OK with another subordinate, except that he "sort of wished [I] had gone more into presenting the data"—which, of course, was exactly what had had little impact on several previous occasions. Still another simply wondered, "How many friends did you lose out there today?"

Without going into other evidence on which I based my interpretation of these comments, I believe that what was being expressed by these several program managers was distress that a program with which they were closely identified had been, as they perceived it, not just evaluated, but attacked. Worse yet, the so-called attack had been made publicly (having been picked up and distributed by one of the wire services). While most evaluators are likely to be generally aware of the kinds of sensitivities described here, I have not known them to appreciate fully the depth of feeling involved and the extent to which mere criticism may be interpreted as an attack on activities the manager holds dear. What to the evaluator is nothing more than reporting the facts can be seen by the manager as anything from malicious sabotage to vicious assault.

## Sciencing Around

Another facet of the bureaucrat-scientist conflict of values can be seen in the manager's growing impatience with what he describes as the evaluator's "sciencing around," a set of behaviors which the evaluator sees as a necessary search for precision. The program manager is willing to settle for whatever is good enough for a given job; he is, to use the title of a perfectly delightful book, a "satisficer" (Levin, 1970). Not only is the program manager not committed to the evaluator's goal of scientific accuracy, he sees the never-ending search for precision as so much lost time and wasted effort.

The preceding is not meant to imply that there is something wrong with the program manager's views of what evaluation should be. If blame were to be assigned, an objective assessment might more often determine that it is the evaluator who is at fault. Whereas both serve themselves, the program and the organization, the evaluator, to the extent that he identifies himself as a scientist, also sees himself as serving the so-called broader scientific community. Consequently, the evaluator often tends to perceive what he was hired to do and what he is doing as being research. Whether deliberately or inadvertently, he loses sight of the critical distinctions between research and evaluation and thinks of himself as doing something he describes as evaluative research. Whatever it is called, it may or may not possess the policy and decision-making implications which are the sine qua non of evaluation on which the program manager rightfully insists. Whether the activity meets criteria of scientific respectability, a matter of great concern to the evaluator, will ordinarily matter very little to the manager. What does matter to the manager is that the evaluation be done quickly and that it have implications for planning and administrative action. Such implications are, of course, the hallmarks that distinguish evaluation from research, but the distinction is frequently overlooked by the researcher-turned-evaluator or the evaluator-would-be-researcher.

A list of motivational and personal differences between the manager and evaluator is easily extended. The manager is politically sensitive; the evaluator's orientation toward rules and internal political machinations borders on cavalier dismissal— again, an attitude not likely to endear him to the program manager. The one clearly values conformity, the other nonconformity. The one is a doer, a man of action; the other is far more contemplative and deliberate.

I would add only one final point here, and that concerns the person trained in some scientific field, who does some evaluation, and who later becomes an administrator. Depending on the amount of time spent in administrative roles, my experience has been that such a person more nearly resembles the program manager than he does the evaluator. While this may seem like a minor, or even irrelevant, point, it will be seen to be of significance in the concluding discussion on prospects for the future.

## THE MANAGER-EVALUATOR INTERACTION

And so the stage is set, the actors in place, and the interaction of manager and evaluator begins. In order for there to be any chance of their mounting a successful evaluation, I believe that this interaction necessarily starts off as impossibly frustrating and demanding to the point of being exhausting—or so the initial contacts are likely to be experienced. For purposes of discussion, we can identify four separate areas of potential friction.

## Identifying Program Objectives, Rationale, and Procedures

To begin with, the evaluator must pin the manager down to specific and detailed answers to a list of questions not unlike those that newspaper reporters are taught to ask: who, what, when, where, how, and how much. What are the program objectives, both immediate and ultimate; for what target population; what changes are anticipated as indication that the objectives have been met; when and how will changes be manifested; what kinds of activities are supposed to produce those changes; how much change; how are program activities intended to produce change to be conducted; where and for what length of time; with how much and what kinds of resource inputs?

It is not just that such questions are embarrassing in the sense that they highlight deficiencies in the program planning process—and there almost have to be such deficiencies, since most human service programs are hastily mounted or have grown Topsy-fashion over time. The problem is that they are extremely difficult questions, the first question—the issue of program objectives—being the most difficult of all. Yet the evaluator cannot proceed with the design of a meaningful evaluation unless he has the answers; one cannot operationalize objectives into criterion measures, for example, until one knows those objectives.

Short of a separate paper, it is difficult to convey adequately the extent of mutual frustration and antagonism that can be generated by trying to elicit from program managers an organized statement of the program's ultimate objectives, the major operating goals, the subgoals, the relation of program activities to achieving subgoals, and how some goals, once achieved, will become activities to achieve higher goals. Program managers seem to get fixated at either listing off detailed activities of the program, or, at the other extreme, they offer some vague super-objective, such as helping people to lead more useful lives.

Some of my evaluator associates have speculated that the difficulty of obtaining statements of objectives reflects the influence of covert goals as primary but unstated objectives. The notion is that managers wittingly or otherwise have hidden agendas which are not made explicit in planning the evaluation—as, for example, the real objectives of methadone treatment having to do with cutting down on street crime rather than with rehabilitating heroin addicts. Such explanations may possess some limited validity, especially to the extent that enhancing the prestige and influence of special interest groups constitutes a hidden agenda. However, my own experience suggests that nothing quite so sinister is operating. In fact, rather than anything remotely Machiavellian, I have been impressed with the extent to which program officials simply do not think in the kinds of terms that recognize the pervasive influence of program objectives on program operation and evaluation. Admittedly, I have not dealt extensively at the very apex of agency management, but, at several levels of management below that, I have found an enormous preoccupation with getting started and moving off, with very little awareness that going somewhere necessarily implies having a series of intermediate destinations leading to an ultimate destination and some plans about the mechanics of the trip. (It should be a great boon to evaluators if the present-day emphasis on management by objectives takes root and replaces management by expediency, otherwise known as flying by the seat of the pants!)

## Motivations for Evaluation

Let us assume that the evaluator has managed to obtain answers to the questions posed above, and goes to his office to design the evaluation. That would be most unfortunate if it implied that the evaluator neglected to explore thoroughly the motivations which led to plans for an evaluation. More than any other step in the whole process of planning and executing an evaluation, it is this failure to explore the background of and the motivations for the evaluation that explains for me why so many evaluation projects eventually falter along the way, why so many conflicts develop between manager and evaluator, and, ultimately, why the results of evaluation studies, rare though they may be, have so little impact on programming.

The evaluator too often pays only the most cursory attention to finding out who wants what, why they want it, how much they are willing to invest to get it, and what they plan to do with it when they have it. The possible effects of this neglect can be staggering. Probably the most far-reaching of these is a gross mismatch between the scope of the evaluation and the issues it is intended to address. In particular, it is possible to mount an extensive and costly evaluation for the flimsiest and the most irrelevant of reasons. Again, the history of the VA Psychiatric Evaluation Project (PEP) referred to earlier is instructive on this point.

Although not a party to the initial planning of the venture, my review of memoranda after I joined the group suggested to me a euphonious phrasing for describing PEP's origins: that the initial PEP study of mental hospital effectiveness developed out of a unique confluence of budgetary and professional interest in the outcomes achieved by modern psychiatric treatment methods. I liked the phrase and used it often in various presentations describing the study. At the time, I was only vaguely aware that "unique confluence of budgetary and professional interests . . ." might be a euphemism for (1) the Bureau of the Budget pressuring the VA to justify in terms of documented improvement in patient outcomes the higher operating costs of its newer mental hospitals, (2) program managers already convinced that higher costs were justified doing little more than just going along with an evaluation whose only conceivable outcome was confirming that more money bought better treatment results, and (3) researchers, one of whom would probably head the proposed evaluation, arguing for opposite strategies of evaluation which not accidently coincided with their respective preexisting research interests.

Thus was mounted a multi-year, multi-million dollar project employing 25 to 30 full-time mental health professionals and 15 to 20 clerks and technicians, and requiring the occasional data collection efforts of hundreds of treatment staff. It was not until some years later, while talking with several of those since-relocated managers—in some instances even their replacements had been replaced—that I fully realized how little investment these managers had had in the evaluation. Not only did each have his/her own idea of the project's original purposes, but none of them was really very clear on what those purposes were. The senior program official ultimately responsible for the new program emphasis was perhaps an exception; he was quite clear as to what the evaluation was all about. His question to me was, "What ever happened to that study they started about the time I left that was supposed to prove I had made the right decision [in initiating the program]?"

The lessons to be learned from even this one bit of history are enough to fill another chapter of this volume. For present purposes, I will simply repeat that mounting an evaluation requires the most thoroughgoing kind of planning and, specifically, an intensive scrutiny of the motivations of the parties involved. This by no means implies that there is anything sinister about the participants' reasons for initiating the evaluation and that they should be made to undergo "third-degree" questioning. Viewed negatively, all that is being advanced is the admonition that one avoid through better planning the kind of evaluation that nobody wants: the evaluation that ends up addressing the wrong questions, in the sense of questions in which managers are not really interested; the evaluation that is actually a research project in disguise and does not have a built-in assurance that policy implications will be forthcoming; the evaluation whose financial and other resource costs are out of all proportion to the importance of the issues being addressed; the "quick-and-dirty" look-see which tries to answer questions that can only be answered satisfactorily by a much more intensive effort.

General rules of thumb are risky, but I have found it useful to think of the time requirements for an overall evaluation effort as being roughly divisible into thirds: as much time for planning and tooling up as for data collection and an equal amount of time for analysis and reporting. And it is in the very first planning stages that the kinds of questions listed earlier must be explored—all the way from who wants what kinds of information from the study to how that information will be of value and what differences it will make to somebody to have it. Typically, the pressures to get underway with the evaluation are almost irresistable, and they not infrequently reinforce one another. The evaluator, the manager, and the sponsoring authorities may have different reasons for haste, but they all want to see something get started. Too often, the something that gets started is different from the kind of effort that would be wanted by all the concerned parties if the evaluation were adequately planned. The point can be illustrated by another bit of PEP history mentioned earlier.

What was described as an innocuous request for information from a prestigious group came to the VA during the period when data were still being collected for the first PEP study. Nevertheless, there was little choice but to proceed with new data collection. Top VA management had determined that its best course in responding to the inquiry was the familiar stalling technique of we-can't-reply-yet-because-we're-studying-the-problem. The study that was subsequently—albeit quickly—initiated came down the chain of command in the usual fashion. Only four or five steps on the administrative level were involved. However, by the time the evaluation staff started work on the evaluation plan, the lack of any real managerial commitment to the study had been lost sight of. To make matters worse, the evaluation staff, motivated by their own research interests and reinforced by research-minded consultants, expanded the study plan into something they felt would be more scientifically challenging. In this case, the evaluators ended up answering questions that nobody but they themselves had asked.

Are the instances recounted above only atypical, idiosyncratic anecdotes? Obviously, I am convinced that they are not or I would not be citing them. Each of us has to answer in terms of our own experience and our exposure to the experience of others. As stated, I have been impressed often enough and strongly enough by the problem of unclarified and dissimilar motivations that I accord it unquestioned first place among the possible reasons so much evaluation effort comes to naught.

Two final points by way of postscript. I have had enough exposure to other situations that I can state categorically that the examples cited are by no means unique to the Veterans Administration or to the federal bureaucracy. Except that I am familiar with them only in a consultant role, comparable situations from state government settings could just as well have been described; it is only through the exercise of great restraint that I have refrained from recounting in detail one such chilling sequence which almost ended in an evaluation whose scope required resources several times greater than that of the operating program.

The second postscript echoes a point made at the outset. Although the reader is free to conclude otherwise, I would still maintain that there are no real villains in the incidents cited. However, if responsibility for these and similar misadventures were to be fixed, I would more likely fault the evaluator than the manager. Managers know that evaluation is "good." They come to the evaluator for whatever it is that evaluation can offer to the solution of management problems and without really knowing what it is they are getting into. And, where this is true, instead of being responsive to the manager's need for instant information and a limited inquiry yielding a narrowly restricted set of answers, the evaluator derides the manager's limited purposes and imposes his own preconception that more central issues should be more extensively investigated. Deliberately or otherwise, the evaluator also manages to frame the broader inquiry he would prefer to pursue in ways more likely to yield information of general professional interest. The manager's naivete and haste offer an alluring snare in which evaluators are seemingly only too willing to become entrapped.

## Demands on Operating Staff

One of the inevitable results of expanding an inquiry is an increase in the evaluator's demands on the operating staff, and this constitutes a third area in which manager and evaluator can interact in mutually stressful ways. The position of staff has to be understood as one where they probably know little about the relation of the evaluation to future conduct of the program. Any little knowledge or interest they may have could hardly be interpreted as commitment by even the most sanguine observer. What the staff perceive most clearly is that extra work is being required of them in the form of interviews, or rating scales, or special arrangements of some kind. The point to be noted is that the program manager is sooner or later going to be caught in the middle between operating staff and evaluator. Either staff will complain that too much is being required on top of their—as they see it—vastly more important regular duties, or the evaluator is going to complain that he is not getting the staff cooperation he needs and would the program manager please do something about it.

It might be argued that staff participation need not become a source of difficulty in the manager-evaluator interaction if (1) the staff are adequately involved in planning the evaluation, (2) their participation is recognized and rewarded, and (3) they receive feedback about the course of the evaluation. Such may well be true, and, on general principles, I strongly endorse any moves in these directions. But I am unaware of any positive examples where these efforts have actually eliminated problems of staff cooperation (excluding from consideration research-like studies originated by the staff or worked out with them as a mutual endeavor, a quite different situation). Earlier, problems that could be resolved were distinguished from those that could only be ameliorated; adequately rewarding service staff for collecting evaluation data is one of those problems for which I know of no truly effective solutions.

Implied in what has gone before, but meriting separate attention, is a fourth area in which the manager-evaluator interaction may result in conflict. Evaluation can quite legitimately encompass the gamut from a set of observations and a narrative description of the program to full-blown pre-post comparison of randomly assigned experimentals and controls. As a general rule, the more rigorous the design, the more the evaluator will need to pressure the manager to operate the program in ways required by the design and, more critically, to refrain from program changes that might tend to invalidate the evaluation. It should be obvious that what the evaluator really requires and what he is implicitly asking for when he wants to do a highly rigorous evaluation is that he be given control of the conduct of the program. Whether or not he should have control and whether or not the manager could agree to such an arrangement is immaterial for our purposes. The important point is that the mere presentation of the situation is enough to open a Pandora's box full of impossible, conflict-laden problems: the withholding of services from otherwise eligible clients, management accountability for program success, redistribution of power, the necessity of midstream changes to correct program deficiencies, and so on. Some writers have even gone so far as to suggest that dilemmas such as these render inappropriate the use of rigorous methodologies in evaluating large-scale public service programs. Personally, I tend to disagree with such views, but the fact remains that, given the usual preference of the evaluator, plus the somewhat naive desire of the manager that the evaluation be very scientific, the use of more rigorous methodologies and the attendant problems of program control constitute another major source of potential conflict in the manager-evaluator interaction.

Up to this point, then, the discussion has dealt with (1) how the context within which evaluation of public service programs is conducted militates against the success of the evaluation venture, (2) how the potential for failure is reinforced by the disparate personal and role characteristics of evaluators and managers, and (3) how the interaction of evaluator and manager in mounting and conducting the evaluation is fraught with potential conflict.

There is no guarantee, even under the best of circumstances, that evaluation results will have some payoff in terms of being utilized to improve a program. But, as a general rule, the more difficulties of the kinds discussed here, the less the likelihood of the evaluation findings having any impact.

## SOME THOUGHTS ON THE FUTURE

This chapter was introduced with the view that, as long as a service program is funded by public monies, there will always be pressures for evaluating it. As Klerman (1974) recently pointed out, that assumption is all the more valid in 1974 in view of the country's deepening economic retrenchment and political conservatism. With the prospect of increased public pressures for evaluation as a backdrop, the discussion has focused on some relatively unrecognized issues whose explication should help further the institutionalizing of program evaluation as a routine, ongoing part of program operations. While the content was in many ways ample grounds for pessimism about the future of evaluation, the intent was not to argue that the enormous difficulties attending evaluation cannot be overcome.

In fact, one basis for optimism resides in the very fact of increasing public pressures. As the notion of accountability at all levels of service delivery takes hold, there is no direction in which to move except for evaluation to gain acceptance as an integral part of program operation. At many points in the chapter, we spoke of an evaluation project or an evaluation effort or an evaluation study. The fact of the matter is that evaluation is at this point in time still very much an on-again, off-again kind of activity. As pressures increase, there will be no choice but for evaluation to be instituted as a continuing part of service delivery systems.

One facet of this inevitability is particularly relevant to the content of this chapter. The discussion has stressed problems and pitfalls in the expectation that clarification will lead to correction. If left to their own devices, I am confident that managers and evaluators would slowly learn to be more accommodating to one another and would eventually learn to work more productively together. One of the bases for that faith derives from what was noted about evaluators-turned-managers. What this observation seemed to indicate was that situational determinants play a critical role in producing the kinds of characteristics displayed by both managers and evaluators. Such an interpretation is, of course, consistent with a much larger body of social psychological research now coming into prominence, such as the mock prisoner research and the pseudo-patient studies. To the extent that their behaviors are situationally determined, and to the extent that the situation changes in the directions indicated, it is probably not overly optimistic to hope for a more effective collaboration between manager and evaluator than has characterized their interaction to date.

## SUMMARY

In summary, then, what has been presented here is a series of considerations in support of the view that the major barriers to successful evaluation are not technical and methodological, though these are certainly important and worthy of further effort, but are rather the structural constraints and requirements and the interpersonal relationships which characterize the evaluation endeavor. It is paradoxical that influences which are in many respects somewhat irrational should assume so important a role in a venture which, in origin and intent, represents the height of rationality. However, this has been the nature of my experiences with the evaluation enterprise, and I have presented them with the hope that being fore-warned will help in mounting more successful evaluation projects in the future.

## REFERENCES

Branch, T. Courage without esteem: Profiles in whistle-blowing. *Washington Monthly,* 1971, 3 (3): 23-40.

Gardner, J. W. *Self-Renewal: The Individual and the Innovative Society.* New York: Harper & Row, 1963.

Klerman, G. Current evaluation research on mental health services. *American Journal of Psychiatry,* 1974, 131: 783-787.

Levin, A. *The Satisficers.* New York: McCall, 1970.

Suchman, E. A. *Evaluative Research: Principles and Practice in Public Service and Social Action Programs.* New York: Russell Sage Foundation, 1967.

# 3

# POLITICS, ETHICS AND EVALUATION RESEARCH

## GIDEON SJOBERG

*University of Texas*

The more one delves into the massive literature on evaluation research, the more cognizant one becomes of the deep-seated ethical and political implications of the social scientist's efforts, whether direct or indirect, to evaluate the performance of individuals or the programs of on-going organizations. The political and ethical dilemmas are especially troublesome in the evaluation of experimental programs.

An examination of the relevant literature has persuaded me of the need for a far more disciplined and critical analysis of evaluation research than is currently available. Suchman, in his summary work, *Evaluative Research* (1967), analyzes the problems in a well-reasoned and balanced manner, yet "brackets" many of the key political issues and overlooks the central ethical dilemmas involved in this kind of research. So too, Hyman and his associates (1962, 1967), who rank among the leading methodologists concerned with evaluation in sociology, skirt the fundamental ethical and political problems associated with their own work. Although a number of social scientists have in recent years become sensitive to various ethical and political aspects of the research process, they have not incorporated the issues involved into their methodology or, more narrowly, into their methodology for evaluation research (e.g., Caro, 1971).

Much of the failure to grasp the implications of political and ethical issues stems from the social scientist's limited, even distorted, conception of the research process. Typically methodologists have no means of incorporating relevant ethical and political issues into a research design. Because of this situation, I shall briefly outline a counterorientation toward the dominant methodological perspectives in social science. Such will then lay the basis for an analysis of the impact of political and ethical factors upon evaluation research and for my presentation of an alternative approach to the evaluation of the performance of individuals and of projected social programs.

## A REORIENTATION TOWARD METHODOLOGY

Although there are basic similarities in the nature of the scientific method in the natural and the social sciences, there are essential differences in the nature of reality in the natural and social realms. The two involve different relationships between the researcher and his subject matter, and this calls for different kinds of research procedures. Thus, although we subscribe to the principle of the unity of science on the abstract level, we reject the notion that the actual research procedures employed in the natural and in the social sciences are or can be the same.

The unrealistic view of the research process adhered to by most social scientists and philosophers of science has hindered the advance of research methodology and the social scientist's ability to cope with the problems that confront him in actual practice. The conceptualization of the scientific process as expressed in most treatises on social research makes it impossible to grapple with the political and ethical issues that arise (Sjoberg and Nett, 1968), especially in the area of evaluation research.

### Social Research as a Social Enterprise

If we are to deal with the inadequacies of the traditional formulations, it is essential to recognize that social research is a social enterprise. And although the social scientist's actions differ in some fundamental respects from those in everyday life, the scientific method nevertheless consists of a system of rules or norms created by and sustained by scientists. Such norms relate to those procedures for the collection and analysis of data, all refined for the purpose of acquiring "objective knowledge" about the social order.

If we conceptualize social research as a social enterprise, we can more readily recognize that the scientist is a variable in the research design. Indeed it is empirically demonstrable that the scientist's political commitments or ideology and his ethical orientations enter to some degree into the formulation and execution of the research design.

We must remember that the scientist, while he is a member of a broader community of scholars, also belongs to the social order, particularly a nation-state and various subsystems therein. The scientist carries over, unwittingly or not, many of his general social commitments into the research situation. Although a social researcher may, through reflective consciousness, be able to objectify his (her) political and ethical commitments, and even reduce their impact upon the research process, no scholar can fully eliminate their impact upon her (his) work.

Too frequently the political and ethical commitments of the researcher are taken for granted. Most contemporary social scientists are unaware of their ethical orientation, one that emphasizes the "public interest" and accepts the nation-state as the source of the "ultimate good." Even when scholars adhere to other ethical principles, the impact of the latter upon the research design is typically not explicated or acknowledged.

The role of political factors is more readily discerned. The political constraints upon research in particular have come dramatically to light in recent years. Certainly social scientists must expect to encounter opposition to their activities in any democratic order, and the constraints upon their actions when they carry out research in other societies is far more pronounced. Still, most methodologists have not incorporated the political variable into their research design.

A number of psychologists, Orne (1962) and Rosenthal (1966) among them, have documented the impact of the experimenter's beliefs and values upon the outcome of "controlled" experiments. Rosenthal, for one, seems to assume the impact of the experimenter can be controlled through more carefully designed experiments. While the impact of the researcher may be reduced through ingenious experiments, the control of ethical and political contingencies through carefully designed experiments is unfeasible in most research situations, if for no other reason than such experiments, calling as they do for purposive manipulation of subjects or organizations, are incompatible with many democratic ideals and with the interests of particular power groups. More generally, there are many kinds of social issues that can not be studied via careful experimental designs.

After examining the activities of social researchers, I am forced to conclude that most treatises on research methods propound ideal norms which often have no, and at best only a vague, relationship to what occurs in practice. The actual norms adhered to by the researcher may even be at odds with the ideal ones. Or there are areas of social research where the norms have not yet been explicated. Many of these gaps result from a failure to recognize the relationship of the researcher to the research design.

We need to be particularly concerned with explicating the practical, taken-for-granted, norms of research, For example, Lazarsfeld and Rosenberg (1955: 15), when discussing the selection and construction of indicators, speak of the speculative phase of this task. They fail to recognize that, even in this so-called speculative phase, they and others adhere to certain general rules in the selection of indicators. Researchers typically select indicators that are compatible with or acceptable to the dominant power orientation within the society or subgroup being investigated. Thus Lazarsfeld and Thielens, in their study *The Academic Mind* (1958), developed indicators for ranking colleges and universities in American society that reflect criteria associated with the high-status universities, not low-status ones. Recognition of such a norm, or guiding principle, is essential if we are to analyze the indicators that are employed in research projects.

We can clarify our methodological orientation by contrasting it with that set forth, for instance, by Denzin (1970). In the last chapter of his book, Denzin acknowledges the impact of political and ethical factors upon the research process. Yet he follows the format of detailing the idealized pattern of how research should be conducted and then viewing the ethical and political factors that distort this ideal design. With this perspective, Denzin, like so many other methodologists, is unable to demonstrate how the differing political and ethical commitments of researchers can lead to different research designs, the use of varying procedures for collecting data and divergent modes of analysis. Our conceptualization makes it possible to view the political and ethical commitments of scholars as an integral element of the formulation of particular research strategies.

The research process is far more complex than has been depicted by scholars (cf.

Smith, 1969). Typically there is a kind of "circular causation" that results in the emergence of the final design. The format—statement of the problem, collection of the data, and analysis of the results—is typically imposed upon the research process in an ex-post-facto manner. In practice, the researcher's political and ethical orientation and the broader social constraints placed upon him are such that the procedures for collecting data feed back upon the first stages of the design; so too the type of analysis affects the choice of research procedures; and so on. Changes in strategy during the course of the research project typically lead to a revision of the overall design. The picture of the research process, as idealized in print, is generally a crude approximation to actuality.[1]

### Theory Construction

Research is necessarily carried out within some particular theoretical framework. But the question of theory and its meaning has been the subject of widespread debate, despite the efforts in recent years to oversimplify and mechanize the mode of theory construction (e.g., Stinchcombe, 1968).

Two broad traditions with respect to theory building exist in social science (Sjoberg and Nett, 1968). One school of thought focuses upon the assumptions scholars make about human nature and social reality and how these lead to different interpretations of the social order. These assumptions, which Gouldner (1970) calls "domain assumptions," deal with such matters as whether the individual or the collectivity should be the basic unit of analysis, whether a social order is basically oriented toward tension and conflict or whether it is oriented toward consensus, whether the actors in a social system are "rational" or whether they are "irrational," whether they are oriented toward self-interest or toward altruism. Wallace (1969) has offered one classification of these assumptions and has shown, through illustrative readings, how they are central for an understanding of why sociologists interpret social life in very different ways.

The second tradition in theory building emphasizes the logical form of inquiry. Most social scientists today have been heavily influenced by the natural sciences. As such, most research is oriented toward the testing of hypotheses, notably the statement of relationships between variables. Ideally these hypotheses or propositions should be derived from a complex set of axioms or postulates. Thus those scholars oriented toward this perspective tend to uphold the logico-deductive model as the one toward which the scientist should strive, although most social scientists work with less than ideal norms, even with propositions that form a loose system.

But the logico-deductive model is only one of the logical systems employed by social scientists. The logic of analogy and that of the dialectic are two other significant forms. Moreover, there is a relationship between some of the researchers' domain assumptions and the logical forms they employ. Thus scholars who utilize the logic of analogy fit existing or emerging social patterns into preexisting categories. This is the basis of legal reasoning with its emphasis upon precedent (Berman, 1968); so too, sociologists such as Goffman (1959) use the categories of the theater for interpreting everyday life. This logical orientation has a "conservative" bent to it. Those who examine the relationship among variables, either in relative isolation or in the context of some logico-deductive system, rely upon the categories of the system, but these categories are modified in light of empirical tests. Popper (1962: 5-7, 34-37) seems to have been correct when he equated the logico-deductive method with a commitment to political liberalism. The logic of the dialectic, especially as we employ it, is oriented toward building new categories and thus is associated with a more critical, though optimistic, view of human nature and social reality. Certain implications of the relationships of the domain assumptions and the logic of inquiry should become clearer in our analysis of evaluation research.

## Toward a Critical Perspective

We have argued that the research process is a social enterprise and that political and ethical factors affect the structure of the research design, and we have sought to delineate the nature of theory construction. Our conception of the researcher as a variable in the research design and our view of theory construction are inter-related in several respects. For one thing, the scientist's ethical and political orientations are a part of his domain assumptions, which in turn are related to the logical structure the scientist employs.

Our methodology makes it possible to explicate some of the taken-for-granted assumptions in evaluation research. That various assumptions about human nature and reality—notably political and ethical ones—markedly affect the methods of evaluation and how these in turn are associated with the researcher's logic require explication. Much of the debate over evaluation research, as with most research efforts, is muddled by the failure to clarify the different assumptions held by scholars as they formulate the research design and carry out their projects.

Herein I adopt a modified sociology-of-knowledge orientation. I am employing this perspective as a means of "exposing" some of the assumptions that underlie evaluation research. Some ethnomethodologists have also sought to uncover "tacit assumptions" about the social order, including the world of scientists, but for them this unmasking process seems to have become an end in itself. Methodologists must probe still further: they must seek out alternative solutions to research problems, including those faced in evaluation research, and thus strive to attain relative transcendence over the ethical and political issues that permeate the research enterprise.

## THE NATURE OF EVALUATION RESEARCH

Evaluation is implicit in all social orders. A society's status or stratification system rests upon some form of evaluation. Men and women are evaluated in one way or another throughout their entire lifetime. And this evaluation process is fraught with tensions and dilemmas. Nowadays university students in the United States are claiming the right to evaluate or grade their professors while simultaneously arguing that formal grading of themselves as students should be abolished. Thus, "Who should evaluate whom?" and "What indicators should be employed in the process?" are questions that cannot be disassociated from the structure within organizations, as well as that within the society at large.

Evaluation research, in contrast to social evaluation more generally, has taken on far more restricted meaning. Hyman and his associates (1962) limit their attention to those forms of evaluation that involve fact-finding regarding the results of planned social action. Suchman (1967) defines evaluation as the determination of the results attained by some activity designed to accomplish a particular value or objective. He then argues that the scientific method is the most promising means for determining the relationship of the stimulus to the objective.

This narrowing of the scope of evaluation research has been fostered by events of the 1960s, when social scientists were asked to judge the effectiveness of various programs or policies designed to change segments of the social order, for example, the poverty program. But to limit our attention to evaluation of the negative or positive impact of planned social intervention is too restricted a focus for our purposes.

Social scientists evaluate activities or programs that have been under way for years in order to assess the impact of certain variables (such as size and morale of personnel) upon different organizations' abilities to attain a stated goal or goals. In addition we must take account of the manifold efforts of scholars to develop and refine testing and measurement devices for use in evaluating clients or organizational personnel as well. These instruments can be administered and interpreted by others than the social scientists who devised them.

Our rather broad conception of evaluation is, we believe, in keeping with the activities of social scientists. And this perspective makes it easier to understand the manifold relationships of politics and ethics to evaluation research.

## THE SOCIAL CONTEXT OF EVALUATION RESEARCH

Not only has evaluation research been furthered by recent social forces within modern society but changes in the social structure and the value system that stem from the shift from an industrial to a postindustrial order will have widespread repercussions upon it in the years ahead.

If we look back over the past several decades, we find that the increased bureaucratization of modern society has been associated with a rising interest in evaluation research. Even today, after substantial criticism on both theoretical and empirical grounds, Weber's conception of bureaucracy, with its emphasis upon rationality, remains a dominant image of how industrial-urban life is and should be organized.

The bureaucratic model rests upon the principle of dominance or hierarchy. Although various positions in the structure are interrelated in complex ways, the overall pattern is one of superordination and subordination. It is within this context of dominance that the notion of universalism is applied in, say, the selection and promotion of personnel. It is within this context that the principle of rationality is applied. In practice, however, persons in positions of power determine what is "rational": they select what to them seems to be the most efficient means for attaining the goal in question (e.g., Sjoberg, Brymer, and Farris, 1966).

If we can judge by the results, notably the greatly increased affluence of modern industrial society, the organizational revolution has proved to be highly effective in the economic sphere. Fewer and fewer workers are needed to produce a given amount of goods. At no period in history has humankind experienced such a high standard of living where so many are freed from the contraints of production in order to survive. Although a sizable sector of the population remains near the subsistence level, the relatively great expansion of affluence in the past several decades has been the most striking feature of highly industrialized nations such as the United States and a number in Western Europe.

Some credit for this affluence must be given to the increased knowledge that economists have acquired concerning the functioning of the economic system. Although they quarrel among themselves, they have formulated conceptual tools that have perceptibly furthered economic and industrial growth. Moreover, the application of their ideas rests in part upon the accumulation of more and more factual knowledge about the economic order. Policy makers rely upon numerous economic indicators to make decisions, and these indicators in turn require that vast amounts of data be collected.

Associated with this movement toward the rationalization of an economy dominated by big business, big labor, and big government, we have witnessed a marked shift in the nature of the labor force. Automation, in particular, has led to a decreased need for blue-collar workers in the manufacturing sector, and the increased affluence has facilitated a sharp increase in the size of a service-oriented labor force. Fuchs (1968) speaks of the United States as the first service economy.. More and more segments of the economy have become oriented toward providing services in the areas of health, education, and welfare. In turn, large-scale educational, health, and welfare organizations, through which the expanded services are dispensed, have become part of the American scene in the past few decades.

Many of the issues surrounding evaluation research have arisen out of studies of the service sector. Researchers in the vanguard of the "social indicator movement" have been developing indicators for health, education, and welfare activities to enable them to measure the impact of various policy decisions upon the kind of social services provided (e.g., Bauer, 1966; Gross, 1969). So too, we have witnessed the rise of the PPB (planning, programming, and budgeting system) within the federal government (e.g., Shultze, 1968). Instituted by Hitch and his associates in the Department of Defense, this orientation has been adopted as a means of rationalizing the expenditures of funds in health, education, and welfare. The movement toward the PPB system has been fostered by economists who have sought to apply some of the broader principles used to measure efficiency in the production sector to the service sector.

Although the widely heralded PPB system has been promoted as a means for attaining greater efficiency in the allocation of resources, this system and the use of social indicators are efforts to make the persons who dispense funds accountable for their actions to both politicians and the public at large. Politicians, in particular, want "hard data" by which to evaluate the effectiveness of programs that are becoming increasingly costly. Thus evaluation research has two functions: judging the effectiveness or efficiency of programs and providing some basis for holding those who spend public funds on particular programs accountable for their decisions.

However, scholars who advocate the increased use of social indicators, as well as evaluation research more generally, have typically overlooked various fundamental issues. At the very time when efforts are being made to ensure that bureaucracies in the areas of health, education, and welfare function efficiently, these bureaucracies have come under severe attack for over-concern with efficiency and system maintenance at the expense of their clients' interests or welfare. During the 1960s the welfare state developed to the point where its basic contradictions became apparent. Now key segments of the population have come to challenge openly the manner in which these organizations have been attaining their goals. Thus the relevance of the phrase "the crisis of institutions" (White and Sjoberg, in press).

The proponents of evaluation research simply have not grappled with the dilemmas inherent in modern bureaucratic systems, for example, the fact that bureaucracy, with its emphasis upon hierarchy and efficiency, runs counter to the demands for equality and justice (Sjoberg, Brymer, and Farris, 1966). How is it possible to provide equality of opportunity in a system that is hierarchically oriented? Indeed, many of the measurement devices used in the evaluation of clients have been oriented toward the maintenance of hierarchy. The proponents of particular evaluation efforts have failed to recognize the contradictions in the programs they are evaluating.

One reason for this lack of recognition is that most social scientists, in line with Weber's bureaucratic model, have carried out their research in accordance with the principle that scarcity, not plentitude, is the central problem in modern society. Although I am well aware that the problem of scarcity remains an urgent one for many Americans, the United States is nevertheless moving toward the stage where economic affluence is theoretically possible for a vast sector of the populace.

Evaluation researchers have become captives of Weber's bureaucratic model in still other ways. To achieve efficiency one needs to have well-defined goals. Evaluation researchers frequently complain about the ambiguity, vagueness, or multiplicity of goals in the programs they evaluate. But they fail to recognize the objective possibility that vagueness, ambiguity, and multiplicity of goals are essential if *client-centered* bureaucracies, in contrast to organizations that are oriented to the production of goods, are to satisfy the legitimate demands and interests of their clients.

A considerable body of research and social analysis suggests that client-centered organizations tend to require goals that are multiple and ambiguous. Contemporary client-centered bureaucracies, patterned as they are upon production-oriented systems, are too rigid and inflexible to attain the goals for which they were created. Many of the political and ethical issues in evaluation research grow out of the fact that the organizational structures which researchers take for granted have been under severe attack and must be reordered if a viable postindustrial order is to emerge. This fundamental change cannot be accomplished through application of traditional evaluation procedures.

## THE POLITICAL IMPLICATIONS OF EVALUATION RESEARCH

A number of scholars have argued that evaluation research is fundamentally a political enterprise. In justifying this position, Cohen contends that "Evaluation is a technique for measuring the satisfaction of public priorities; to evaluate a social action program is to establish an information system in which the main questions involve the allocation of power, status, and other public goods" (Cohen, 1970: 232). It follows that if we are to objectify the political dimension of evaluation research, we must understand the ideological orientation of the researcher, as well as the political constraints imposed upon him.

As suggested above, evaluation researchers typically take the structural constraints of the system they are evaluating for granted. This holds even when evaluation is used as a basis for reform or manipulation. Moreover, researchers generally align themselves with the dominant groups in the system. Although we are not committed to the notion of a homogeneous elite in America, there are marked differences between the advantaged and the disadvantaged, and the vast majority of social scientists side with the former rather than the latter. Such a "system orientation" influences the evaluation of all programs, notably experimental ones. To clarify these issues we can examine some of the functions of current evaluation research.

### Evaluation as a Means of Reform and Manipulation

One of the best-developed intellectual rationales for evaluation research as a means for reform is set forth by Janowitz (1966: viii) in his foreword to Street et al., *Organization for Treatment: A Comparative Study of Institutions for Delinquents:*

> ... this research follows the "enlightenment" model ... it focuses on developing a fundamental understanding of the institution jointly by both the social scientists and professional practitioners. In the enlightenment model, there is a continuity of interest and interaction between the researcher and the practitioner.

Janowitz (1966: ix) goes on to state:

> As the authors shared their findings with the executives, the most pervasive impact was to develop in the executive an understanding of the extent to which they were operating with a deficit of information and of how they could ... develop more information about their own inmates and organizations.

In this instance, a stimulas had been introduced, that is, information about the system which was shared with executives, and then a follow-up study was initiated.

The principle underlying this approach was to assist the executives of these organizations to move from a custodial to a treatment model for delinquents. The authors of this study were concerned with delineating the conditions necessary to create and maintain a precarious social structure, the treatment-oriented correctional institution. In this reform model of evaluation research, the emphasis was upon working through the power structure for modification of institutions for delinquents.

Evaluation research can also be used for manipulation of organizational personnel or clients (although what may be reform and manipulation may depend upon the actor's definition of the situation). Unfortunately there is a paucity of data concerning instances where evaluation procedures have been used by leaders of organizations for manipulating personnel (cf. March, 1965). Because the goals of health, education, and welfare organizations are often ambiguous and even contradictory, administrators are in a position to advance certain goals at the expense of others while at the same time sustaining an image of fairness and universality. "Objective measurement instruments" provide the means for attaining universalism. But even "hard data" are not immune to diverse interpretations.

The use of evaluation instruments in academia, notably for judging teaching effectiveness, provides opportunities for manipulation. My own observations, conversations with persons in different academic settings, and incidental comments in the literature, all suggest that these instruments can and do serve the political ends of administrators.

Administrators of educational institutions, even under ideal conditions, must weigh a number of different criteria in making judgments about who is or is not a good teacher. Almost all teacher evaluation instruments utilize a variety of criteria as "indicators" of good teaching (e.g., McKeachie, 1969). Etzioni and Lehman (1969), in analyzing the problems inherent in the use of indicators, rightly speak of "fractured measurement." By this they mean that no one indicator can capture the "meaning" of a concept such as good teaching. Thus we must rely upon multiple indicators. What Etizioni and Lehman fail to grasp is that the indicators employed are not always consistent with one another. Indeed some concepts, such as good teaching, may embody implicit contradictions.

Who is a good teacher? One who appeals to a few especially talented students and who can stimulate them where others cannot? Or the teacher who tries to reach the widest spectrum of students possible? And how should we evaluate the teacher whose primary aim is the "recovery" of possible "failures"? In addition, what about the teacher who is thought to perform poorly in the classroom but who is effective in communicating with students on a personal level and, indeed, dedicates long hours to them outside the formal classroom situation? Because evaluation forms stress classroom performance, this person falls outside the generally accepted teaching model as defined by the key indicators on most measurement instruments. We must recognize that there have been a variety of teaching models from Socrates to the present day and that the measurement of what is good teaching takes place within a relatively circumscribed framework (cf. McKeachie, 1963).

Given the fact that what is good teaching can be defined in various ways, measurement instruments can be used as rationalizations for administrative decisions. If a teacher is considered to have an abrasive personality or if he is a controversial political figure, it becomes rather easy for an administrator to select particular items on a measurement test—say, the finding that a teacher did not spend sufficient time in his office—and, by an arbitrary weighting procedure, to devalue the teacher overall.

More generally, as indicated above, administrators are in a position to push forward certain models of teaching, such as the consensus model wherein the professor appeals to a large number of students rather than to a selected few. In a variety of subtle ways the administrator can interpret and manipulate findings about teacher evaluation to suit his purposes, especially in situations where it is difficult to hold the administrator accountable for his actions.

### Evaluation as a Means for Sustaining Power or Structural Arrangements

Although this category overlaps with the above, our emphasis here is different. Measurement instruments, developed for evaluating either the organization's personnel or its clients, are also utilized by the leadership within bureaucracies to sustain themselves as well as the broader class and power alignments.

With respect to the formulation of social indicators, used as the basis for evaluations, Biderman (1966: 131) writes:

> The greater the organization, self-awareness, and political power of interest groups, the more likely we are to find statistical and other systematic indicators relating to the social and economic conditions and trends that these groups believe affect their welfare.

> Furthermore, it is more than likely that the indicators will reflect the dominant ideological orientations of the most powerful and articulate groups affected by the phenomena measured.

Add to this the fact that evaluation is often carried out by persons in positions of some power, and that they help in deciding upon the indicators to be employed, and we can more readily understand why, for example, the accreditation of Parsons College became a cause célèbre. Koerner, after reviewing the evaluation of Parsons College by the North Central Association of Colleges and Secondary Schools, observes that, although there were many reasons for disaccrediting Parsons College, "most of the errors and weaknesses of which Parsons was guilty from 1955 to 1967 can be found today in more institutions in good standing than Parsons' critics would care to admit" (Koerner, 1970: 214). A double standard was evoked because Parsons College and its president had become too controversial. President Roberts' avowed goal of having a college reap financial rewards by teaching the rejects of other colleges and universities was a threat to the established order within higher education.

The relationship of evaluation to political considerations is by no means a simple one. Biderman (1966), in his highly useful essay on social indicators, analyzes at some length the Uniform Crime Reports, which have perhaps been the most significant noneconomic indicator in American society. These reports have been the basis for formulating policy and for evaluating the results of policy decisions in the area of "law and order."

Nevertheless, these statistics are the product of a complex and decentralized bureaucratic system. Any revision in the indicators would entail some changes in the administrative system of the agencies that "generate" these data. Moreover, Biderman contends that the Uniform Crime Reports have a built-in basis for inflating the crime rate over time. For example, a theft involving $50.00 or more is still recorded as a larceny, a major crime, even though economic inflation has greatly decreased the purchasing value of this amount.

Actually the problem of the Uniform Crime Reports relates back to Biderman's observation concerning the relationship of indicators to the power structure. Such acts as murder, forcible rape, robbery, aggravated assault, burglary, larceny, and auto theft (the so-called major crimes) are associated with the lower rather than the middle and upper classes. A typical white-collar crime such as embezzlement simply does not appear in the index of major crimes.

Biderman suggests that the validity of the Uniform Crime Reports is so questionable that we might be better off with no crime indicators at all. Certainly the implications that these indicators have for reinforcing the class and power arrangements must constantly be kept in mind.

But it is in the economic and educational arena that indicators or measurement instruments have the most transparent implications for class and power relationships. Economic indicators, such as that reflecting the cost of living, have been subject to considerable debate. Special interest groups have sought to gain an economic advantage by having indicators defined so as to favor them.

Moreover, if we judge by patterns in the educational sphere in recent years, we can look forward to an increased hostility by many groups in America to the indicators and measurements that have been employed as screening devices from elementary through graduate school. These instruments play a major role in sustaining existing class and power arrangements.

Psychologists have shown considerable sensitivity to the attacks against their instruments (e.g., Anastasi, 1967). The critics range from some intellectuals to members of minority groups who reason that the tests discriminate against them. Unfortunately, many of the justifications for psychological tests have not dealt with the manner in which these have supported the privileged groups in society. Anastasi, while cognizant of some of the issues involved, fails to grasp the central relationship between testing and social structure. Tests and measurements are intimately related to the needs of bureaucracies. The latter's more privileged members have a stake in sustaining the use of certain kinds of tests and measurements. Thus Anastasi, for instance, does not consider the possibility that if the "culturally deprived" are to advance, we must do more than resocialize individuals; we must change the structure. It is not possible to overcome the problem faced by minorities simply by working with individuals. Many blacks, Chicanos, and other minorities are quite rational when they call for structural change and for abolition of the measuring instruments that support present arrangements.

In line with this reasoning, the recent questioning of SAT scores, which have for some time been utilized as a crucial screening device for entrance into many colleges and universities, is highly informative. The Report of the Commission on Testing (1970) has indicated that there are a variety of skills and knowledge that are related to education and are meaningful to the broader society—for instance, leadership and aesthetic talent—and which fall outside the scope of the SAT instrument. This Commission's views support our own perspective. With the rise of an affluent society, alternative modes of academic success can be tolerated, and moreover it becomes essential to take into account a wide variety of social and intellectual skills. The SAT requires fundamental revisions because it is associated with a power structure and mobility system that has come under attack.

We can expect similar criticisms of the Graduate Record Examination to arise. It is ironic that many social science departments continue to accept GRE scores so uncritically even when the available evidence raises serious questions about their validity as a predictor of academic success. I would suggest that the GRE has served to restrict the recruitment of persons with diverse talents into graduate schools. This instrument, like the SAT, has been oriented toward a narrow conception of education that is not in keeping with the emerging postindustrial order.

## Experimental Programs and Evaluation Research

Nowhere is the tendency to sustain the status quo more clearly dramatized than in the evaluation of experimental social programs. We hypothesize that the overriding pattern is for the dominant bureaucratic structures, or the existing power arrangements, to impose their indicators upon experimental programs. This in turn undermines the very efforts to formulate viable alternatives.

Ward and his associates (1967) suggest that innovation prison reform systems typically are not judged to be successful. However, they do not seem to explore the full range of reasons for their findings. One that they overlooked is that new programs were judged by traditional categories or indicators. Therefore, through a kind of self-fulfilling prophecy, innovative efforts do not suceed. Innovation calls not only for new programs but for new modes of evaluation.

The efforts to evaluate the poverty programs of the 1960s bear mute testimony to the difficulties researchers encounter when evaluating fledgling social experiments. The efforts to provide means for compensatory education for the socially disadvantaged serve as a case in point. More specifically we can consider the Head Start program which was the pearl of the Office of Economic Opportunity's program.

The Head Start program was an effort to provide compensatory education for disadvantaged children. And it was subjected to extensive evaluation. For within the OEO there existed the Office of Research, Plans, Programs, and Evaluation, a product of the social pressures for evaluation discussed above. Thus there was a built-in structural support for evaluation of the Head Start program, and this ultimately led to a study by the Westinghouse Learning Corporation (Ohio University), which carried out an ex-post-facto examination of this experiment (e.g., Williams and Evans, 1969).

There are several significant aspects to the Westinghouse study, which concluded that the Head Start program had little, if any, impact upon the educational progress of the children involved. For one thing, the Westinghouse researchers, while recognizing that the Head Start program had numerous objectives, focused upon the cognitive and affective dimensions of the children's success. The supporters of the evaluation effort argued that this particular set of indicators did not deny the multiplicity of goals; they maintained that cognitive improvement was the primary goal of Head Start and moreover was an activity which reflected the success of other activities (Williams and Evans, 1969: 124). This argument is in keeping with our earlier contention that evaluators tend to impose a unidimensional framework upon a multidimensional world. But this orientation reflects only one way of evaluating educational success. After all, one conclusion of the Westinghouse study was that the parents of Head Start enrollees reported substantial participation in the activities of educational centers. The increased involvement of parents in the educational process could have had considerable long-run impact upon their children's educational attainment, although their participation might have had no real consequence for the Head Start program.

Actually, scholars generally agree that the methodology employed in this research effort deviated markedly from the ideal norms for social research. The nature of the research design—with the lack of an effective control group, the nature of the sample, and the admitted lack of reliability and validity of the indicators (they were used because they were the "best available")—makes it difficult to interpret the meaning of the results. Yet, after the proper apologia, the researchers drew some rather definitive conclusions as to the program's lack of success.

But it would be surprising, on theoretical grounds alone, to have found major cognitive improvement in children who had spent a year or less in the Head Start program. The utilization of traditional categories for measuring educational achievement, plus the diversity of the social order and the factors that impinge upon a child's socialization and learning patterns, would lead one to hypothesize that such a program as Head Start would have little, if any, significant impact upon educational improvement. To break the cycle for the educationally disadvantaged would take more than a modest effort. The assumptions about learning and about the child's relationship to the school and the broader society by the Head Start officials and by the Westinghouse researchers are open to serious question.

The arguments concerning compensatory programs in education, including that of Head Start, took a somewhat different twist in the debate resulting from Jensen's study of IQ tests (1969). Jensen contended that there is a basic difference between the IQ of blacks and that of whites. He reasoned that compensatory education, and he cited various experimental programs, has not been (and will not be) able to overcome the differences resulting from an inherently genetic basis. By resting his case upon differences in the nature of human nature, Jensen provided an ideological justification for the maintenance of existing structural arrangements.

Numerous social scientists have severely criticized Jensen's work. In the main their criticisms reflect the way in which assumptions about the nature of human nature affect the interpretation of data. The measurement of intelligence, even as Jensen defines it, is still a sociocultural process, although he seeks to explain the sociocultural differences in terms of genetic variables.

Stinchcombe (1969), whose criticism of Jensen rests heavily upon domain assumptions that are congruent with my own, contends that the social environment is highly complex, not as undifferentiated as Jensen suggests. Stinchcombe singles out one of Jensen's findings—that IQ scores for blacks are somewhat higher than for whites in early childhood and that these shift afterwards—and argues that it is the more complex environment of the white children that leads them, as they grow older, to acquire cognitive skills greater than those of children in the black community.

Overall the debate about the Head Start program and Jensen's judgment about compensatory education underscore the difficulties of evaluating any efforts that deviate from traditional patterns. These difficulties have in turn led practitioners to make political adjustments with respect to the formulation of social experiments. One pattern consists of "creaming." In order to demonstrate that a new program is worthy of support, administrators select those clients who are most likely to succeed. Thus, in an experiment on the social impact of housing subsidies in Boston (Tilly, Feagin, and Williams, 1968: 118), we find that the persons to be subsidized were screened in such a manner as to help ensure the success of the experiment. Still other means will continue to be employed by supporters of new experiments if they are to circumvent evaluations that are "biased against" innovation.

## ETHICS AND EVALUATION RESEARCH

When examining the relationship of ethics to social research, social scientists have typically dealt with this problem without explicit recognition of the ethical commitments that inform their actions, a pattern related to our thesis that methodologists have not incorporated the fact that the researcher is a variable in the research design.

Elsewhere Vaughan and I (1971) have argued that, taking a world view, the dominant ethical orientation of social scientists has been associated with the categories or value orientations of their particular nation-states. When social scientists reason that ethical commitments are private concerns or that professional associations should, in the name of value neutrality, refuse to take public stands on issues affecting humankind, they tacitly accept the nation-state as a given and come to work within its guidelines. More narrowly, social scientists frequently identify with the large-scale bureaucratic organizations that either support or are supported by the nation's legal framework. Up to a point a scientist can justify his loyalty to an organization or the nation-state. But system loyalty, if it becomes an end in itself, poses serious difficulties for any scholar.

We must recognize that the products of scientific endeavor have been used both for good and for ill. The results of the natural scientists' efforts were employed in Nazi Germany to commit the crime of genocide against the Jews and in the United States to bomb Hiroshima and Nagasaki. In Nazi Germany loyalty to the system became the dominant ideology for justifying the acceptance of the acts of inhumanity against the Jews.

One major step in overcoming some of the ethical dilemmas facing social scientists is to recognize the implications of the fact that science is a human enterprise. Science, if it is to survive, must be predicated upon respect for human dignity. The legal-rational principle, which Weber saw as the basis of legitimacy for the central activities of modern society, is too nation-state specific. We cannot define the idea of human dignity within the context of any one nation-state but only in terms of some transnational category. The emphasis upon human dignity is consistent with, in fact built into, a major premise of the scientific method, namely, that scientists are concerned with the general rather than the particular.

At this point, we are confronted with the problem of defining "human dignity." We must proceed beyond those philosophers or social scientists who stress survival and biological needs; we must emphasize the unique feature of men and women, their sociocultural environment. We define human dignity in terms of people's ability to pursue alternative courses of action, to have available to them significant structural choices. The idea of alternatives, when defined in terms of significant structural choices, stresses the actors' ability to control their own destinies, at least to some degree. Freedom is not to be equated, as is done by a number of sociologists, with mere adherence to norms. Such an assumption would permit one to argue that Hitler's Germany and Stalin's Russia were lands of the free. Nor is freedom to be equated with psychological freedom for self-actualization without regard to the needs of other persons. Human dignity is especially enhanced when humans are free to participate in the construction of structurally meaningful choices. Such can only be attained where there is a built-in tension between the individual and the group or subgroups and the broader society. Only then can scholars look beyond their commitment to the system in which they live.

In light of the aforementioned ethical orientation, it is possible to reanalyze the orientation of most evaluation research. It has been social-system, or more generally nation-state, oriented, and within this context social scientists have too frequently accepted the power structure's definition of what is right and what is wrong. This has made it difficult for social scientists to deal adequately with the notion of human dignity not only for persons in other sociocultural settings but also for the powerless within the researcher's own nation-state.

Our perspective leads us to challenge at least two commonplace commitments of social scientists. One is that enunciated by Moynihan: "The role of social science lies not in the formulation of social policy, but in the measurement of its results" (1970: xxix). Moynihan's argument, even when qualified somewhat, still leaves the researcher committed to system categories, to the acceptance of the power groups, and, more narrowly, the administrative apparatus, definition of right and wrong. It is ironic that Moynihan, who has been committed to developing policy at the highest levels in Washington, has in effect relegated other social scientists to a position where they should not challenge his enunciations.

Still another viewpoint of social scientists needs to be reexamined if one accepts our orientation toward ethics. Some writers, such as Becker (1963, 1967), state that researchers can stand on only one side at a time, and moreover, that they should typically be committed to defending the underdog. Gouldner (1968) has charged that mere identification with the underdog does not lead one to challenge the structure that keeps the disadvantaged in their place. Moreover, Becker's thesis (1963: 172-173) that a social scientist can align himself only with one group at a time makes it impossible for the evaluation researcher to seek some means for transcending the structural hiatus between the privileged and the underprivileged.

Researchers must do more than accept the categories of the system when they carry out their evaluations. They cannot unquestionably accept the categories of the underprivileged if they are to carry out their role effectively. In order to think in terms of significant alternatives, researchers must first adopt a critical perspective. The function of criticism is underscored in the field of mental health. In the late fifties and early sixties, we witnessed a number of evaluations of mental health programs; but these were often carried out with an uncritical acceptance of the society's (and power groups') definition of what is normal. The psychiatrists Szasz (1961) and Laing (1960) and the sociologist Scheff (1966) have, each in his own way, raised questions as to who really is mentally ill. These scholars, as critics, have questioned the very goals of those organizations that treat the "mentally ill." To the degree that such a scholar as Szasz is correct in his stance, the label of mental illness does much to degrade humankind. It confines human beings within social cages from which they find it difficult, if not impossible, to escape. In many instances researchers involved in the evaluation of mental health programs have helped to place locks upon these cages. It is in this sense that the "liberal model" espoused by Janowitz (1966), with its emphasis upon the use of evaluation as a basis for modifying correctional institutions for juvenile delinquents, can be called into question. It is conceivable that many of the so-called delinquents in the institutions he studied should not have been labeled as delinquents at all.

But criticism alone will not advance the cause of human dignity. We must formulate research orientations that emphasize the development of alternative structural arrangements that transcend some of the difficulties inherent in the present-day social order.

## TOWARD A NEW EVALUATION METHODOLOGY

We have sought to explicate some of the taken for granted assumptions in present-day evaluation research. We have reasoned that the political and ethical orientations of social scientists have led them to work within system categories, often those defined by the power groups.

The ethical and political dilemmas in most evaluation research are magnified during periods of rapid change. Researchers, reasoning via the logic of analogy, implicitly assume that the categories of the emerging postindustrial, post-welfare order are analogous to the categories of the traditional industrial-urban one, which is dominated by bureaucracies oriented toward the efficient use of scarce resources.

We have suggested that social criticism becomes an essential ingredient of evaluation research. Consider the field of family planning. Here evaluation studies have been mainly concerned with analyzing the effectiveness of various family planning programs in reducing population growth (e.g., Berelson and others, 1966). But as Kingsley Davis (1967, 1970) has suggested, this orientation is woefully inadequate. Davis contends that if we are to resolve the major population problems facing the modern world, we must restructure the family system so that people will be motivated to have fewer children. Although Davis does not indicate just how we might restructure the family, the existing programs for controlling population growth, and by implication those that have been subjected to evaluation studies, are doomed to failure.

But we must proceed beyond criticism to a more constructive form of analysis. Our approach to evaluation research is based upon what we term "countersystem analysis," a form of dialectical reasoning (Sjoberg and Cain, 1971). A countersystem is a negation of and logical alternative to the existing social order (or social structure) in question and is therefore a kind of "utopian model."

Social scientists are able to construct a number of countersystems with respect to any given social arrangement. They vary according to the assumptions about the social order that are taken as givens. Thus, Fanon (1965) negated the modern industrial-urban order and constructed a countersystem that excluded industrialization and urbanization. Still other countersystem (or utopian) models have been constructed upon the premise that industrialization and urbanization should be sustained, though with the proviso that major elements of the social structure be remade.

Countersystem analysis provides social scientists with some distinct methodological advantages. One of these is that they can employ the countersystem as a standard for evaluating the on going order. The latter does not have to be evaluated on its own terms. And new programs need not be seen simply as deviations from the on-going order; they are also deviations from the ideal order.

To be sure, we must be wary of reifying, as many radical thinkers are prone to do, the countersystem model. Many intellectuals have constructed utopian dreams and then have assumed that these should automatically become a reality. Moreover, there is the danger that a utopian model itself may embody serious limitations. Our own orientation is that both the categories or standards of the system and those of the countersystem are essential in evaluating programs of social action.

At this point, it is possible to suggest an application of our framework to the realm of education, to evaluation of the success of graduate school programs and of college teachers. The evaluations of graduate programs, be these on the university or the departmental level, and to a somewhat lesser degree the evaluations of teachers, have emphasized uniformity (unidimensionality) and the dominant success indicators of the broader society. Too frequently scholars and administrators judge graduate school programs in terms of the publication record of the faculty and their students.

In contrast to the emphasis upon uniformity and success, a countersystem approach would emphasize those programs that help students avoid failure and would place a premium upon faculty and students developing a variety of intellectual and social commitments, not solely those measured by publications. As a utopian dream this countersystem would be difficult, if not impossible, to implement. But it does present a standard by which to evaluate traditional or experimental programs. Moreover, in an affluent, postindustrial order, many elements of the countersystem model may not only be realizable but also essential for meeting the demands and potentialities of the emerging order.

Consider the many activities in which graduate schools could engage. Students could not only be educated to become successful scholars, but they could utilize graduate education as a basis for an avocation. Intellectual pursuits might provide many persons with more meaning in life than presently stems from most leisure-time activities. Graduate schools could also stress the education of persons for policy posts or for upgrading schools and colleges that teach the disadvantaged. And so on.

We could also set forth a variety of criteria for defining good teaching as well, criteria that are typically unmeasured by present-day instruments. How many instruments, for example, include criteria by which administrators or colleagues could positively value a teacher who helps students avoid failure? There are still other criteria mentioned earlier in this essay that do not currently form part of evaluation efforts.

One objection to our proposal is: How would it be possible to eliminate poor graduate programs or ineffective teachers? One could not do so by employing the standards of the countersystem per se. But it certainly seems reasonable to expect that we should begin evaluating graduate programs and teachers not only in terms of their successes but also in terms of the casualties of their efforts. Is it not feasible, indeed necessary, to balance off the successes against the failures and rule out those programs or teachers where the ratio of failure to success is too great?

A number of graduate schools and graduate departments have taken a degree of satisfaction in the failures they produce. A good deal of folklore in sociology concerns programs where in times past few students could overcome the hurdles. Some programs during the 1960s kept many students around but permitted few of them to graduate. The striking negative features of this kind of educational activity have not received the serious attention they deserve. When evaluating programs in terms of the number of failures versus the number of successes we, of course, should take into account the efforts toward prescreening of candidates. A program that accepts persons who are defined by society as "high risks" should not be evaluated on the same basis as one that carefully prescreens its students. To reiterate: a just evaluation of a program should balance off its negative features against its positive ones.

A somewhat similar evaluation effort could be carried out with respect to teaching. It should be possible to establish a rather broad range of socially meaningful indicators. Then we could weigh the negative against the positive features of teachers' activities, and it should be possible to establish outer limits where the contributions of particular teachers are outweighed by the casualties that result from their actions. In practice it is easier to cope with a system's teachers than with its programs. Students can more readily move from one teacher to another than from one school to another.

However one may view my countersystem orientation,[2] and only a brief sketch of its implications is provided here, I am convinced that, because of the deepseated impact of political and ethical factors upon evaluation research, more attention must be given to formulating alternative methodologies (cf. Scriven, 1967; Weiss and Rein, 1969). The emphasis upon experimental designs (cf. Suchman, 1967; Rossi, 1969), although these are useful under certain conditions, often seems misplaced. The deviations from the ideal norms of the experimental design, resulting from the impact of the researcher upon the research process, are usually so marked as to cast doubt upon the results. In addition, experimental designs lead researchers to analyze innovative programs in terms of the control group. This in effect means that researchers employ system variables without benefit of a counter-system perspective. My concern is not with de-emphasizing research but with placing it within a broader perspective and avoiding undue reliance upon technical virtuosity.

## CONCLUSIONS

Some recapitulation and integration of our argument is in order. Our discussion began with an analysis of the researcher's role in the research design. Thus far methodologists have been unwilling to make the major leap of reconceptualizing the research design so as effectively to take account of social factors that structure the research from its inception on through the analysis of the findings. Once this is done, the research process becomes more complex and problematic than books on research methods would have us believe.

We also briefly discussed theory building, which has at least two significant dimensions: the logical structure (or form) and the assumptions about human nature and social reality. The relationship between the researcher as a variable in the research design and our conception of theory building is most clearly seen when we recognize the impact of the researcher's assumptions about human nature and social reality upon the research process. In discussing evaluation research we have attempted to illustrate how researchers typically accept the power structure as given and thus come to align themselves, unwittingly or otherwise, with the dominant groups in the system. They have typically accepted the indicators determining success defined by the dominant groups in the society, as well as the latter's definitions of the "public good" or the "national interest" as standards for evaluating social programs.

Although researchers necessarily must work within a societal or nation-state context, they also have a responsibility to science and to the principle of human dignity to recognize the broader political and ethical implications of their efforts. The tendency of the "social indicator school" to over-identify with the dominant groups within the nation-state raises serious questions that must be honestly faced.

I have suggested one means of avoiding the dilemmas of research evaluation: the use of countersystem analysis. This logical orientation, if properly employed, offers researchers one means of transcending the inherent tension between the advantaged and the disadvantaged in a society and, just as important, between the advantaged and the disadvantaged on a global scale. It is unfortunate that evaluation researchers become so locked into their own framework that they do not attempt to understand the implications of their efforts, not just for the programs they seek to evaluate but for all humankind.

The orientation toward research that I have espoused commits me to views about human nature and social reality that are quite different from those held by most evaluation researchers. The ambiguity and paradoxes in social life, and the tensions between individuals and groups and between groups and the broader society, have positive as well as negative features. I would not impose upon social life an evaluation process that demands uniformity or unidimensionality, although I have recognized that some form of evaluation must and will occur. Ultimately I am more concerned with the consequences of evaluation than with the narrow technical proficiency that has all too frequently dominated efforts in this significant social realm.

## NOTES

1. My intent, as suggested above, is not to rid social research of a standardized set of rules or ideal norms for collecting and analyzing data. My concern is with formulating these so that they can be more useful than those currently espoused. Researchers, especially in conducting evaluation studies, cannot adhere to many of the research procedures that writers of research textbooks or monographs say ought to be followed. The ideal norms should be cast in a more realistic manner. Moreover, many actual norms that are implicitly accepted by researchers should be raised to the level of consciousness and elevated to the realm of ideal norms. I accept the need for a tension between those rules that researchers ought to follow and those that they can or do follow, but the discrepancy between the two should not become so great as to encourage hypocrisy.

2. Countersystem analysis should also prove useful for coping with the "unanticipated consequences" of research programs. Although I cannot pursue the problem herein, I believe that, by thinking in terms of the negation of and logical alternatives to the intended consequences of a program, one might be able to anticipate some of the unanticipated consequences of purposive social action. Unfortunately the unanticipated consequences of purposive action are seldom treated by evaluation researchers, at least in an explicit manner.

Clearly the unanticipated consequences of planned social intervention can be of great significance. For instance, a few years ago I served as a consultant to the Wesley Community Agency's research and social action program (San Antonio, Texas). Buford Farris and Richard Brymer, among others, were seeking to develop an alternative type of organization, one that would serve high-risk families or juveniles. In looking back upon the efforts of this Agency, we see many unanticipated consequences to their program. One of these was the training of persons who later came to head agencies elsewhere and who sought to transfer features of the Wesley model to other settings. A narrow and short-range view of social experiments can lead researchers to overlook the significant implications, both positive and negative, of a social program.

## REFERENCES

Anastasi, A. Psychology, psychologists, and psychological testing. *American Psychologist,* 1967, 22: 297-306.

Bauer, R. A. (ed.) *Social indicators.* Cambridge, Mass.: M.I.T. Press, 1966.

Becker, H. *Outsiders.* New York: Free Press, 1963.

--- . Whose side are we on? *Social Problems,* 1967, 14: 239-247.

Berelson, B., and others. *Family planning and population programs.* Chicago: University of Chicago Press, 1966.

Berman, H. J. Legal reasoning. Pp. 197-204 in *International encyclopedia of the social sciences, IX.* New York: Macmillan, 1968.

Biderman, A. D. Social indicators and goals. In R. A. Bauer (ed.), *Social indicators.* Cambridge, Mass: M.I.T. Press, 1966.

Caro, F. G. (ed.) *Readings in evaluation research.* New York: Russell Sage Foundation, 1971.

Cohen, D. K. Politics and research: evaluation of social action programs in education. *Review of Educational Research,* 1970, 40: 213-238.

Davis, K. Population policy: will current programs succeed? *Science,* November 10, 1967, 158: 734-736.

———. The climax of population growth. *California Medicine,* 1970, 113: 33-39.

Denzin, N. *The research act.* Chicago: Aldine, 1970.

Etzioni, A. and E. W. Lehman. Some dangers in 'valid' social measurement. In B. M. Gross (ed.), *Social intelligence for America's future.* Boston: Allyn Bacon, 1969.

Fanon, F. *The wretched of the earth.* New York: Grove Press, 1965.

Fuchs, V. R. *The service economy.* New York: National Bureau of Economic Research, 1968.

Goffman, E. *The presentation of self in everyday life.* Garden City: Doubleday, Anchor Books, 1959.

Gouldner, A. The sociologist as partisan: sociology and the welfare state. *American Sociologist,* 1968, 3: 103-116.

———. *The coming crisis of Western sociology.* New York: Basic Books, 1970.

Gross, B. M. (ed.) *Social intelligence for America's future.* Boston: Allyn and Bacon, 1969.

Hyman, H. H. and C. R. Wright. Evaluating social action programs. In P. F. Lazarsfeld, H. Sewell, and H. L. Wilensky (eds.), *The uses of sociology.* New York: Basic Books, 1967.

Hyman, H. H., C. R. Wright and T. K. Hopkins. *Applications of methods of evaluation.* Berkeley and Los Angeles: University of California Press, 1962.

Janowitz, M. Foreword. In D. Street, R. D. Vinter, and C. Perrow, *Organization for treatment.* New York: Free Press, 1966.

Jensen, A. R. How much can we boost IQ and scholastic achievement? *Harvard Education Review,* 1969, 39: 1-123.

Koerner, J. D. *The Parsons College bubble.* New York: Basic Books, 1970.

Laing, R. D. *The divided self.* Chicago: Quadrangle Books, 1960.

Lazarsfeld, P. F. and M. Rosenberg (eds.). *The language of social research.* New York: Free Press, 1955.

Lazarsfeld, P. F. and W. Thielens, Jr. *The academic mind.* New York: Free Press, 1958.

McKeachie, W. J. Research on teaching at the college and university level. In N. L. Gage (ed.), *Handbook of research on teaching.* Chicago: Rand McNally, 1963.

———. Student ratings of faculty. *AAUP Bulletin,* 1969, 55: 439-444.

March, J. G. (ed.) *Handbook of organizations.* Chicago: Rand McNally, 1965.

Moynihan, D. P. *Maximum feasible misunderstanding.* New York: Free Press, 1970.

Orne, M. T. On the social psychology of the psychological experiment. *American Psychologist,* 1962, 17: 776-783.

Popper, K. *Conjectures and refutations.* New York: Basic Books, 1962.

Report of the Commission on Testing. *Righting the Balance, I.* New York: College Entrance Examination Board, 1970.

Rossie, P. Practice, method, and theory in evaluating social-action programs. In J. L. Sandquist (ed.), *On fighting poverty.* New York: Basic Books, 1969.

Rosenthal, R. *Experimenter effects in behavioral science.* New York: Appleton-Century-Crofts, 1966.

Scheff, T. J. *Being mentally ill.* Chicago: Aldine, 1966.

Schultze, C. L. The politics and economics of public spending. Washington, D.C.: Brookings Institution, 1968.

Scriven, M. The methodology of evaluation. In S. Tyler, R. M. Gagne, and M. Scriven (eds.), *Perspectives on curriculum education.* Chicago: Rand McNally, 1967.

Sjoberg, G., R. Brymer and B. Farris. Bureaucracy and the lower class. *Sociology and Social Research,* 1966, 50: 325-327.

Sjoberg, G. and L. D. Cain, Jr. Negative values, countersystem models, and the analysis of social systems. In H. Turk and R. L. Simpson (eds.), *Institutions and Social Exchange: The Sociologies of Talcott Parsons and George C. Homans.* Indianapolis: Bobbs-Merrill, 1971.

Sjoberg, G. and R. Nett. *A methodology for social research.* New York: Harper and Row, 1968.

Sjoberg, G. and T. R. Vaughan. The sociology of ethics and the ethics of sociology. In E. Tiryakian (ed.), *The phenomenon of sociology.* New York: Appleton-Century-Crofts, 1971.

Smith, J. O. Social research in a psychiatric setting: the natural history of a research project. Dissertation. Ohio State University, 1969.

Smith, M. S. and J. S. Bissell. Report analysis: the impact of Head Start. *Harvard Educational Review,* 1970, 40: 51-104.

Stinchcombe, A. L. *Constructing social theories.* New York: Harcourt, Brace, and World, 1968.

———. Environment: the cumulation of events. *Harvard Educational Review,* 1969, 39: 511-522.

Suchman, E. *Evaluative research.* New York: Russell Sage Foundation, 1967.

Szasz, T. S. *The myth of mental illness.* New York: Hoeber-Harper, 1961.

Tilly, C., J. R. Feagin and C. Williams. *Rent supplements in Boston.* Cambridge, Mass.: Joint Center for Urban Studies of the Massachusetts Institute of Technology and Harvard University, 1968. Mimeo.

Ward, D. A. Evaluations of correctional treatment: some implications of negative findings. In S. A. Yefsky (ed.), *Law enforcement science and technology.* London: Academic Press, 1967.

Wallace, W. (ed.) *Sociological theory.* Chicago: Aldine, 1969.

Weiss, R. S. and M. Rein. The evaluation of broad-aim programs: a cautionary case and a moral. *The Annals,* 1969, 385: 133-142.

White, O. Jr. and G. Sjoberg. The emerging 'new politics' in America. In M. D. Hancock and G. Sjoberg (eds.), *Politics in the post-welfare state.* New York: Columbia University Press, in press.

Williams, W. and J. W. Evans. The politics of evaluation: the case of Head Start. *The Annals,* 1969, 385: 118-132.

# III

# COST-BENEFIT APPROACH TO EVALUATION

*4*

COST-BENEFIT ANALYSIS:  A METHODOLOGICAL EXPOSITION

JEROME ROTHENBERG

*Massachusetts Institute of Technology*

## 1.  THE STRUCTURE OF SOCIAL EVALUATION

### 1.1  Introduction

Cost-benefit analysis is a technique employed mostly by economists for evalu-ating changes in social situations and the relative desirability of different collective policies. Typical applications would be to ask whether government should enact a certain piece of legislation, or which of a number of different expenditure projects should a particular agency of the government adopt. As a technique it is not a specific set of procedures but a broad general approach. Studies claiming to be cost-benefit analyses have differed in so many small and large ways that an observer might have been led to conclude that they had in common only the claim. Cost benefit *is* a distinctive way of regarding social choice problems, but its concrete applications have considerable variety, some of it the justifiable projection of the differences among the problems and some the result of controversiality in the handling of important components. It is neither unitary nor definitive.

These differences and controversial aspects do not obscure the main emphasis, especially in the wide context of social evaluation in the behavioral sciences. In the present essay I shall attempt to clarify this central emphasis, spending the major part on its general distinguishing features rather than on technical details. I am addressing the essay to social scientists broadly, not solely to economists, and so shall linger over methodological considerations that economists typically take for granted or bear only with impatience. At the end I shall present applications of cost-benefit designed to indicate something of the variety of issues that are encountered.

### 1.2  The Paradigm of Social Choice

Benefit-cost concerns social evaluation, not individual evaluation, but the pre-sumed relationship between the two is one of the two major pillars of the approach.

It must therefore be placed within the perspective of social evaluation. To facilitate this, we briefly examine a paradigm of social evaluation.

First, social evaluation refers to evaluation of social situations from *the point of view of the society*. It can signify a process carried out "by the society," or by an "agent" or "representative" of the society. The sense in which it is most usual to refer to evaluation by the society itself is in choices made by the decision-making institutions of the society. Social choice and social evaluation are here being used nearly interchangeably. A society's relative evaluations of different situations are revealed in its choices among them. Of course, evaluation between some two situations need not be relevant to an actual choice between them, as for example if the situations refer to the past. Evaluations are often carried out without the practical question of selection through public policy being involved. But cost-benefit *is* intimately connected with public policy, hence with choice; the sense in which it delivers evaluation is in the immediate context of social choice. We shall therefore be willing to neglect the distinction between evaluation and choice and use them interchangeably.

The distinction between choices made by the society and by an "agent" on behalf of the society is a deeper one. Here too the context of cost-benefit defines our stance. Integral to cost-benefit is the situation of having to formulate public policy, or to undertake public action in accordance with public policy. Social action is not simply to be observed and understood: it is to be informed, directed. Cost-benefit is an apparatus to be wielded by an agent of the society for the purpose of informing it about desirable directions of action, and perhaps under-taking such action on behalf of the society. The proper context is therefore one of setting out a procedure for judging the relative desirability of different social actions, a procedure that can be used either by agents of the society in preparing its own actions, or by observers who seek to advise or criticize the society on its policies.

Second, the social decision maker is assumed to wish to make rational choices. Rationality here means something quite simple in concept (although not nearly so simple in practice): to choose, under the circumstances, most in accordance with the real aims of the chooser. It does not prejudge the nature of the aim, nor prescribe the actual procedures by which this most fulfilling choice is to be made. It says nothing, for example, about the degree of calculatingness or detachment of the chooser.

Rational choice is assumed to be logically characterized by a distinctive structure of definable elements. Each choosing situation involves alternatives, consequences, values, and criteria. Basic to the existence of a problem of choice is the existence of a set of mutually exclusive alternatives. The problem would be trivial in the absence of more than one alternative. In the present context these alternatives are different public policies or actions. These are to be compared in terms of their relative desirability. But the desirability of the alternatives is derived from the desirability of their consequences. The second element in the situation is the delineation of the consequences of the policy alternatives. These consequences are social states, specified in dimensions relevant to the nature of the policy alternatives. The third element is the comparison of consequences. This can be accomplished only if there is available a criterion in terms of which the relative desirability of different social states can be ordered. The ordering criterion is an essential ingredient of the process. It is not a "natural" construct, implicit in the choosing situation, but an artifact, representing the values or ends or aims of the decision maker. Thus, the overall situation is that of a decision maker with given ends, confronted by a set of mutually exclusive possibilities. He must scrutinize the possibilities with respect to his system of ends, selecting that one which achieves his ends most completely.

This paradigm is broad enough to be consistent with both sides of a fundamental contemporary debate on social choice: totalism vs. incrementalism. The first argues that relevant social evaluation concerns judgments about social states that represent options for radical institutional change. The second argues that social change is highly circumscribed by initial conditions, and that the truly relevant choosing situations involve only marginal changes from the status quo as feasible. The logical structure of the choice situation is unaffected by this opposition. Each position is tantamount to a specializing of the alternatives of choice and the evaluational criterion. The general nature and function of the situational elements, however specialized for these cases, remain unaffected.

Current controversy about the nature of the evaluational criterion may similarly be subsumable within the framework presented, although one form of it does touch on the basic relevance of rational choice. The debate is between a syncretic and a bargaining notion of social ends: between the belief that individual and group divergences in goals are reconcilable into a unitary conception of the public interest, and one that argues that these divergences are not dissoluble, that at best they are conpromised through bargaining. In most versions the argument can be interpreted simply as a difference about the formulation of the evaluational criterion. Whatever the criterion, so long as it is operationally defined, it can be applied in principle to obtain a judgmental ordering of the alternatives of choice.

The version that does raise the question of relevance is that in which the bargaining polarity insists that the criterion is not the ordering of compromises revealed through bargaining, but the process of bargaining itself. The decision-making process itself, and only that, is what is socially valued as an end: the process is the end, the outcomes are simply derivative. Thus, there is no overview evaluation of social alternatives; there is only a process in which individuals and groups follow individual and group advantage with respect to piecemeal public actions. A social policy is simply a resultant of these piecemeal effects, in no part of the system examined or chosen as totalities.

This position does violence to our paradigm and to the cost-benefit approach which depends on it. It significantly narrows the context of social valuation. Social valuation refers only to broad decision-making mechanisms; only individual valuations exist to fill the outcomes of these mechanisms. In this extreme form the position comes close to rejecting relevant social valuation. Within the context of cost-benefit analysis, we must reject it as a valid position within the range of permissible valuational formulations. We do, however, consider a milder variant of it below.

Where does cost-benefit analysis fit into the paradigm of social choice? Its chief issues focus largely, but not exclusively, on the evaluational criterion. Most cost-benefit studies assume that in each choosing situation the relevant set of alternatives is not problematic and is known. Similarly, with the given set of alternatives it is assumed that the consequences are in principle knowable, and can be derived from positive economic analysis. Any practical difficulty in deriving them is not considered a deficiency of the cost-benefit approach but of positive economic analysis. Thus, for each problem the policy alternatives and their consequences are known. The difficulties proper to cost-benefit relate to the specification of the relevant social goals, and to the evaluational criterion which these goals make appropriate.

This delimitation begs a number of important questions. Even conceptually, alternatives and consequences are not so easily disposed of. For some incrementalist and bargaining orientations, the alternatives are critical to social choice situations. Resolution of social conflict is deemed often to depend on the social innovation of devising new alternatives which possess the salutary features of old alternatives while in addition containing some critical compromise component to dissipate a prior impasse. So the significant fewness, the incompleteness, of alternatives, the sequence in which they are formulated, the nontrivial creativity necessary to supplement any such set selectively are central characteristics in the process of social choice.

Similarly, specification of consequence is of great moment to the choosing situation. In the concrete circumstance, not all of even most of the consequences of the various alternatives are known. Existing theory does not suffice to furnish definitive and exhaustive answers. What is more, the degree of detail and even of accuracy obtained depends on the amount of resources deliberately chosen by the decision maker for the purpose. The accuracy obtainable is therefore a policy decision of the same choice situation as that in which the information about consequences is due to be used. At any rate, with information incomplete and inaccurate, it is of the essence of cost-benefit to have to decide which additional pieces of information should be sought and admitted into the analysis.

It is therefore not true that the conceptual problems of cost-benefit are overwhelmingly bound up with goals and evaluative criteria. Nonetheless, these do predominate and are the most distinctive. Hence, we shall be largely concerned with them.

## 2. THE STRUCTURE AND SCOPE OF COST-BENEFIT ANALYSIS: ENDS, MEANS AND SCARCITY

The focus of the cost-benefit approach is the means-ends relationship. This is also the central focus of the discipline of economics. Its centrality stems from the existence of scarcity as the basis of the discipline (as well as of the approach). Under scarcity the productive resources—human and nonhuman—available to the society do not suffice to enable everyone's total wants (needs) to be satisfied. Every possible configuration of use of these resources makes possible a configuration of

CAMROSE LUTHERAN COLLEGE
LIBRARY

partial fulfillments. The target of the economic system is to bring about the best configuration of fulfillments, or at least a configuration not inferior to any other.

A significant characteristic of the means-ends relationship between resource use and want fulfillment is substitutability. This takes a number of forms. On the consumption side, for any one individual, his behavior indicates that when faced with scarcity he is willing to substitute fulfillment of one set of wants for that of a different set. Moreover, for any of these sets of wants fulfillment is attainable by means of more than one set of resource-outcomes: commodities. Thus, wants are substitutable for overall satisfaction; commodities are substitutable for specific satisfactions.

On the production side, a given commodity can be produced alternatively by more than one set of resource inputs. Moreover, for any set of resource inputs the same commodity can be produced by a variety of different techniques: resources and techniques are substitutes in producing any combination of commodities. Finally, with respect to interpersonal distribution, resources can be used alternatively to produce fulfillments of the same and different kinds for different individuals.

With all these forms of substitutability in the presence of scarcity, the target of overall best use of resources involves nontrivial choice: which resources shall be used to produce which commodities, by which techniques, and who shall receive them? An efficient pattern of resource use and commodity distribution represents a compromise between the differential production opportunities which existing resources and the state of technology make possible, and the relative preferences concerning the configuration of commodity production and distribution which the existing population expresses.

Suppose that at the beginning of a period being studied all productive resources are being used in some way or other. Then a change in policy by either a public or private agent means that some resources will be used differently than before (or than otherwise). Then the original resulting configuration of output-distribution will give way to a new configuration. We evaluate the change by comparing the new output-distribution configuration (with its resulting pattern of want-fulfillments) with the old. It has been found convenient to partition the comparison into two categories: benefits and costs. We say that the change is worthwhile if the benefits achieved exceed the costs incurred by making the change. *Both benefits and costs are want-fulfillments:* benefits are the want-fulfillment patterns made possible by the change: costs are the want-fulfillment patterns which were possible with the prior (or the alternative) resource-use configuration but no longer possible with the new one. Benefits are present opportunities, costs are opportunities presently foregone. This is the fundamental meaning. All definitions in terms of commodities or dollars are derivative and ultimately refer back to these notions of real fulfillment opportunities.

Because scarcity and substitutability hold for each economic decision-making, unit as well as for the totality of them, each unit is faced with a basic problem of choice: how to use its limited want-satisfying stock of resources so as to achieve the greatest overall fulfillment in the circumstances facing it. The economist distinguishes two types of tasks for the economic discipline in this context, a positive and a normative: (1) the understanding, explanation, and prediction of how each unit will make this decision, and how these individual choices will interact to produce behavior in the system as a whole; (2) the recommending of prescribing of how each unit *should* (ought to) make its decision so as best to fulfill its wants (ends), and/or how the system as a whole *should* perform to render the best pattern of fulfillments of the constituent wants.

For both of these tasks the economist relies on the notion of rationality as the chief framework. He assumes that the problem consists of a specification of alternatives, cause-effect relationships, and a structure of ends which can order situations in terms of relative degrees of want-satisfaction. Choice, whether being predicted or recommended, involves simply selecting consistently with respect to this preference ordering. Choice is not, and should not be, random, inconsistent, or systematically directed to less want-satisfying alternatives when more want-satisfying alternatives are available.

It must now be clear why every choice by a single economic agent or by "the economic system as a whole" involves a set of alternatives, and therefore the whole logical structure by which we characterized our paradigm of social choice. Every decision about the use of scarce resources precludes all mutually exclusive ways in which these same resources could have been used. Thus, it gives rise to benefits, but to costs as well. It is part of a comparison among options, whether explicit or only implicit. Thus it is either explained or prescribed as an exercise in rationality.

But rationality is interpreted broadly enough to fit the framework of scarcity. Rationality does *not* mean cold-blooded, infinitely scrupulous calculatingness. Decision making is itself an activity that uses up scarce resources (at the very least, time and thought, but usually more). So the costs of an additional gathering of alternatives, elaborating and perfecting of causal relationships, and even ordering of alternative outcomes in terms of want-fulfillments must be considered as an offset to its advantages. A balance must be struck: the decision maker will be rational *not* to be perfectly informed about alternatives and their outcomes or even about his own feelings toward different outcomes, *nor* to be infinitely painstaking about the weighing of his several options. Spontaneity, proximateness, variety, and uncertainty are consistent with rationality.

The same holds for measurability. Rationality does not imply that all outcomes are, or should be, fragmented into a set of profoundly measurable dimensions, which are then reassembled into a single measurable indicator. Measurement is an adjunct to part of the calculation process, useful where possible, but not a necessary condition to rational choice. It is not always true that a rational decision maker will be able either to create or to require an explicit comparability among the several dimensions of the set of outcomes. On the other hand, if he makes decisions among multidimensional outcomes—or outcomes that can be treated multi-dimensionally by an observer—it is sometimes possible for the observer to use the pattern of these decisions to *infer* a set of dependable, consistent, *implicit* comparisons across dimensions. The mensurability and commensurability are observer artifacts *attributed* to the rational decision making.

When the observer is operating prescriptively, he is likely to make explicit use of such a system of mensurable calculation. This is not a falsification of the decision-making process of the agent being advised—or criticized—if the measures on each dimension and the interdimensional comparability adopted are congruent to the *implied* pattern of the agent's own choices. Moreover, since some advisers are hired because they are better informed than the agent, and the agent seeks thereby to become better informed himself, the adviser's explicit mensuration can be an appropriate objectification even in the absence of such congruence if the agent subsequently agrees that the distinctions and measurements made represent an improvement over his prior decision making.

In cost-benefit analysis the analyst attempts to quantify everything and to establish dimensional comparability. This is because he is an adviser, and must make his analysis replicable by other potential advisers (or critics) and by the decision maker whom he is advising. He does not possess the same perceptual capacity or internal evaluational predispositions as his advisee. He must render his study public—interpersonally communicable—and justifiable in terms of his mandate: to accord with the goals of the decision maker he is advising. Thus, our characterization of rationality as having no specific content in terms of the degree or kind of calculatingness attributable to ultimate decision makers is not inconsistent with a cost-benefit technique that claims to be relevant to rational decision making and yet emphasizes extreme, explicit, quantitative calculatingness.

## 3. INDIVIDUAL, GROUP, AND SOCIAL EVALUATION

Cost-benefit analysis is an exercise in *social* evaluation. This social dimension creates very significant problems, and the approach taken toward this dimension is what is most distinctive about this form of analysis. There are issues involving alternatives and criteria.

In the context of individual evaluation or choice, the question of alternatives is not trivial. We have already suggested that the degree of informedness about alternatives is an outcome of the choice process as well as an input into it. Social choice is faced with this complexity as well. But in addition the nature of social alternatives possesses ambiguities absent from the individual context. In both contexts there is uncertainty between the initiation of the "action" and its consequences, arising from inability to control "outside" factors completely. In the social context, however, there is further uncertainty stemming from the fact that under the social action the behavior of the members of the society themselves are not committed but must be predicted. The decision maker is in serious question of what "his" own behavior will be under his "social action." Thus, there is an inability to control critical "inside" factors as well as "outside" factors. Social choice and social behavior are distinct, although they may be linked.

There are at least two upshots. One is that social behavior may occur—and therefore social consequences result—without social choice having taken place.

Social choices set frameworks of rewards and punishments for individual behavior. Within a given framework the pattern of individual actions may change substantially, with large consequent changes in social outcomes. Another upshot is that the social choice may be made with respect to the desirability of the framework, that is, desirability of the social processes within which individual actions are to be channeled, as well as to that of the most probable consequences of any such framework. Given substantial uncertainty between the manner in which individual decisions will be influenced by collective action and the individual *consequences* following upon such influence, collective choices may be decided significantly on the former grounds.

Cost-benefit takes a position on both these problems. While changes in social outcomes need not stem from changes in social choices, cost-benefit analysis is concerned only with situations in which a change in social choice is in question. Moreover it is interested only in one form of social choice: the choice informing *collective* action. The focus is on government policy, so-called public policy. Moreover, the alternatives—mutually exclusive public policies—are evaluated in terms of their most probable consequences (although interval estimates are sometimes resorted to rather than point estimates in making evaluations, to allow for uncertainty of predictions).

The first delimitation represents a perfectly proper specialization of scope carrying no liability. The second does involve a genuine exclusion of possible relevance. Some choices among public policies may well be dominated by valuations placed on the relevant means as well as on the outcomes. Concepts of social fairness or justice, for example, are likely to influence social choice, and these frequently do depend more on the existence of opportunities or types of channels open to individuals than on what the individuals do with their opportunities. It is not in principle impossible to deal with valuation of means, but it would be notably difficult in practice, since most of the technical advance in the field is oriented toward the valuation of consequences.[1]

The issues surrounding criteria for social choice are considerably more formidable, and the devices adopted more seriously deficient and debatable. The fundamental question is: what are the social ends or goals on the basis of which one can derive criteria for making *social* evaluations? To answer this, one must resolve an anterior question: What is the meaning of a *social goal?* Individuals have goals, certain organizations can be spoken of as having goals, but what is the meaning of the goals of society?

To clarify, let us consider four types of decision maker: the individual, the team, the coalition, and the society. The situation of ends for the individual is, although not simple, simplest of the four. The individual is assumed to possess a complete, consistent system of values permitting him to give a complete transitive preference ordering of alternatives. The alternatives can be thought of as single period social states (social outcomes), or many-period sequences of social states; and prospects as well as outcomes can be included, to allow for valuation of means as well as end-states.

The team is somewhat more complicated, and some violence may have to be done to fit concrete real-world organizations into this ideal category. The team is assumed to be a set of individuals who have coordinated their respective roles in such a way that they place the same preference ordering on *all* of the outcomes that are relevant to the functioning of the team. Within this range of outcomes, the team members have truly common interests. Outside this range they need not agree on anything. It is as though the members merge their identities with respect to all matters pertaining to the team's legitimate scope of interaction with the rest of the world. Within this scope we can identify the goals of the team, and these are completely reflective of the goals of the individuals comprising the team.

The same formal properties will be met by any group of individuals who have identical orderings over a specified set of alternatives, whether or not this identicality stems from formal organization of roles or not. The "team" is defined over this set of alternatives and its "goals" are those implied by the common evaluations. It should be noted that it is not similarity of *personal* objectives that constitutes a team, but similarity of attitudes toward the outcomes defined in their full dimensionality, as for example expressing "payoffs" to others as well as to oneself. The first, taken by itself, can lead to the most divergent rather than similar overall evaluations. Thus, while each of twenty dogs chasing the same rabbit may have exactly the same attitude about catching the rabbit, each wants it for himself *as opposed to the others*. The evaluations in the pack are totally diverse. The pack is not a team.

A coalition is considerably more complicated. The several participants modify, or compromise, some of their partly similar, partly divergent outlooks for the purpose of increasing their overall impact on the outer environment. Thus the alliance reflects a partial but not total commonality of goals, even for outcomes that fall within the scope of the group's legitimate interaction with the rest of the world. Alternately, the range of outcomes on which there is perfect agreement is considerably narrower than the range that is relevant to the group's function. The degree of consensus will vary from complete agreement to nearly as much divergence as in the population as a whole, for different subsets of outcomes within the set relevant to the group's function. Moreover, different coalitions will differ with respect to these distributions of consensus. Thus, the degree of commonness involved in different choice situations depends on the particular situation: alternatives and coalition. Thus, the concept of a group criterion must be flexible enough to portray this variable degree or structure of consensuality.

Society can be considered an extremely complicated form of coalition. Surely a consensus of basic values for carrying on relatively orderly group processes is a necessary condition for a going society. The consensus will typically extend to legitimized group decision-making processes: agreements about the *means* by which individual incentives are to be followed. But this degree of agreement is by itself insufficient to generate a social criterion for rating more detailed types of public policy, policies granting different reward structures to individual actions within the same broad framework of mutual interaction. Additional consensus depends partly on the degree of homogeneity in the society and partly on the basic shared norms about the proper scope of cooperative and competitive behavior.

Cost-benefit analysis formulates a social criterion for evaluating detailed public policies by implicitly abstracting what is taken to be the consensual pattern of authoritative decision making, and the distinctive norm about competitive and cooperative behavior, in a mixed market society like that of the United States. Such a criterion is neither correct nor incorrect. It has never been, nor is it ever likely to be, subjected to consensual social evaluation. Rather, to propose it is to propose a value judgment, which will be persuasive to different observers in differing degrees. To this we now turn.

## 4. THE VALUE CONTEXT OF COST-BENEFIT ANALYSIS

The market system is taken as the exemplar of authoritative interpersonal relations. The key characteristics of this system is that it is a congeries of individual exchange transactions. There is no central coordination, no supra-personal direction, of transactions. Decisions are decentralized down to the individual decision maker (which may, however, be a giant composite like General Motors), and "his" exchange decisions are made solely with regard to his own advantage. The system as a whole makes decisions not as a collectivity which supervenes these individualistic transactions but solely as an aggregation of them. Overall well-being in the system is implicitly held to increase as individuals improve their situations competitively, to decrease similarly as they experience worsened situations. Because the unit of interpersonal interaction, the exchange transaction, is voluntary, each such transaction is deemed to reveal an improvement for both partners to the transaction (else one or both would not have entered upon it). Moreover, in the typical case the transaction is assumed not to impinge directly, that is, other than through affecting prices in the market, on other decision makers, so that all mutual adjustments to market conditions are incorporated within the market transactions themselves.

This view leads to two major value emphases: (1) the market valuations which individuals implicitly place on commodities by being willing to trade them on those terms are taken to reflect a common unit of value both as regards the fulfillment of different types of goals for each individual and the fulfillment of goals between one individual and another; (2) overall well-being is a matter of adding together the gains obtained by the totality of market participants. The "general welfare" is a matter of aggregating individual welfares, not of revealing a "collective or corporate will."

Because individual market transactions are the measure of well-being for the group as a whole, the role of government is seen as something very special and circumscribed. The public sector is an instrumentality to enable the people to do for themselves collectively what they cannot do for themselves privately. It must step in where there is a systematic imperfection in a market or markets; or it must act to change an income distribution which is consensually considered undesirable. Market imperfections are structural characteristics such that individual behavior, unexceptionable in itself, may, in their presence, bring about a less desirable overall performance of the system than could have been attained in their absence.

Situations like this calling for public sector aid or direct participation involve market prices that do not reflect the true social opportunities foregone, or involve transactions that do significantly affect third parties directly and so have a welfare impact that is not wholly accounted for by the gains to the transaction's direct participants. Either prices are wrong or the basis for calculating relative advantage is too narrow.

Thus, despite the fact that the approach so far described makes market value a measure of social value, and private calculations of gain and loss the determinants of market values, when public policy is called for—or is at least potentially relevant—the evaluation of each policy option must differ in some respects from a purely private calculation of advantage. The importance and limitations of market prices from the cornerstone of the cost-benefit delineation of an evaluation criterion.

Consider the market system as composed of the n private decision makers plus the public sector as the n + 1 decision maker. Each of the first n chooses among the alternatives facing him (essentially, the different ways that he may use his productive resources, or ownership claims to productive resources) on the basis of what benefits to him each will bring, and what opportunities will be lost to him in return. The alternative chosen is that for which the net advantage—the benefits minus costs—is greatest. The criterion of cost-benefit evaluation is that the addition of the public sector as n + 1 decision maker to this system, with powers of regulation, control, and direct use of productive resources, should increase the total of *private* net advantages to the greatest extent possible. The public sector decision maker should also choose on the basis of which of *its* alternatives gives the greatest spread of its benefits over *its* costs. But "its" benefits and costs are the changes its actions bring about to the situations *of all the other n decision makers*. The public sector has no valuational existence in itself. It operates solely as collective agent for all the others.

We see therefore that this basic value criterion is individualistic, aggregative, interpersonally comparable. Moreover, it derives from a market value analogue and, as we shall see below, uses money values—which thereby creates comparability and tradeoffs with market values—in measuring public policy benefits and costs.

This close linkage with markets and market values must not, however, be misunderstood. One hears often a distinction made between market values and human values as though the two are, at best, different and, more likely, antipathetic. Such an association, if true, would severely flaw cost-benefit analysis.

The association is not, in fact, true. Market values are human values as these values are transmitted through a complicated multi-person decision-making process in which agents with scarce resources are attempting to maximize the power of these resources to fulfill their human wants (not "economic wants": there are no such things). As is typical in the relationship between individual and large group, the norms (prices) the individual must adjust to are a compromise of his and many others' attitudes. But this is typical of the relationship between individual and large group in any society. It does not mean that he is necessarily any more alienated from market values, that they more significantly distort his real priorities and preferences and needs, than other resultants of the individual's interchanges with large heterogeneous social groups.

On the other hand, not all human values are in fact or can be expressed in market values. For our purposes, it is important to make a distinction between the two predicates. Because of the absence of markets in some types of interactions, because of the imperfections in some of the markets that do exist, because of the third-party spillovers resulting from some transactions (what we shall refer to as "externalities"), market values may falsify or omit reference to human values that are relevant. It is the express task of cost-benefit analysis to correct these misrepresentations, to rectify these omissions, that is, to bring human values more accurately and completely to our attention.

## 5. THE MEANING OF BENEFITS AND COSTS

### 5.1 Real Output Change

The benefits and costs accounted for in cost-benefit analysis refer to the changes in well-being of the private agents in the market system. (This restriction of scope means in effect that we are considering the use of cost-benefit analysis in the evaluation only of so-called economic policies—policies involving the use of the scarce productive[2] resources of the society.) Delineation and measurement of these must take into account various complex forms of reverberatory and other interactive impacts in the market system as a whole. Economic theory has developed a framework, general equilibrium analysis, for dealing with problems of this sort. The keynote of the approach is that each change, regardless of where it has its first direct impact, will typically lead to a variety of ramifying indirect impacts whose overall significance may far exceed that of the direct one.

The fundamental criterion is that the benefits of any alternative are the want-gratifications it makes possible anywhere in the system, the costs are the want-gratification opportunities it removes from anywhere in the system. Upon this basis we distinguish among three types of transactions. The first involves a simple transfer of title to existing assets (wealth objects) between the parties to the transaction. Gifts, gambling gains and losses, sales of old art objects and secondhand articles among nondealers are examples. Such transactions do not affect the composition or size of output in the system as a whole. They are called transfers. Unilateral transfers are called transfer payments.

A second type of transaction involves not only a change in the distribution of assets but a change in their composition as well. Through production and trade, a new collection of commodities (in terms of numbers and types) becomes available, but neither the quantities alone nor their aggregate want-gratifying power make it possible to speak of the *size* of output being changed. In effect, composition and distribution of real national income or output is changed but its size is not. We shall call these redistributions.

Finally a third type of transaction is one that involves a change in the size of real national income. Such a change logically need not involve a change in either composition or distribution. Actual changes in size, however, do generally involve both. We call these real output changes. Cost-benefit analysis has historically concentrated on this last category. More recent emphasis on relative income distribution effects for certain types of public policy has brought redistributions to attention as well, although its more important impact has been to draw attention to the redistributional aspects of real output changes.

The chief concern of cost-benefit analysis has been the delineation of real output changes. These have been traced through, and measured by, market values. But market values have a factitious side for this purpose. The issue is contained in the distinction between nominal versus real values. Market values contain two types of information: the terms on which commodities can be traded for money; through this, the terms on which commodities can be traded for one another. Only the second is decisive for the measure of real output changes. The former is not only inessential, it is misleading, for the unit of money can be varied substantially without any change in the want-satisfying power of output. In inflationary periods, nominal market values change appreciably, while the size and composition of output may remain relatively, or actually, constant. An important task of cost-benefit analysis is to attempt to use only the intercommodity tradeoff content of market values. This is accomplished by deflating nominal prices into so-called real prices, that is, to select the set of relative commodity tradeoffs prevailing in a particular period, called the "base period," and then to adjust nominal, observed prices in every other period to this single, unchanged basis by manipulating the index of change from the base prices to the observed prices.

## 5.2  Opportunities Foregone

Real social costs refer to want-gratifying opportunities that are lost to the system as a whole as a result of decisions to use resources in any particular way. The qualification "to the system as a whole" is very important. If agent A loses certain options as a result of a transaction, he has experienced a personal or private cost. It is a social cost if no one else in the system has gained the same options. In a transfer, for example, this would not be so. What A loses B gains. There is no social cost, only private costs. The same can be true of more complicated transactions as well. Suppose specific productive resources are hired to help produce other commodities. If these resources would in fact have been employed to produce those other commodities, then the social cost of this production is such other commodities whose production is now precluded. But if these resources would in fact have been unemployed, no such loss results by employing them here. The social cost is zero.

If all resources are employed at the outset, then any new pattern of use results in original production activities being shut off. Every new pattern of resource use entails social costs, the output lost from curtailed initial uses. But if some resources are unemployed at the outset, then putting those resources to use entails no social costs because no otherwise productive activity is hampered. Of course, even when substantial resources are unemployed, some patterns of new use pull out resources that were or would have been used elsewhere and so entail social costs. This discussion points up the importance of the degree of unemployment of resources to cost-benefit analysis: it is directly relevant to the question of what real production opportunities are lost under any specified pattern of resource use.

## 5.3  Market and Nonmarket Values

To measure the size, composition, and distribution of output, we generally count actual market flows (transactions) for the different economic agents. Specific gains and losses, as well as total productive effort, are typically enumerated this way. But not all policy impacts on want-gratification opportunities occur in the form of direct actual transactions. Public policy may make some individuals better or worse off by affecting the terms on which they carry out a variety of potential transactions. This results either from influencing the market prices facing them, or by changing their overall situation so that they have a new set of relations to the environment including the market. The former effects can be measured in principle by examining the whole complex of transactions entered into by the population, so that transactions far removed from the initial site of impact must be consulted to obtain an accurate picture. But flows of market values do suffice.

The latter effects cannot be completely captured even by the totality of market flows. If the danger of flood is removed from a certain building, or the danger of enemy bombing is added, or a family is required to give up its home because of highway construction, or an individual finds his water flouridated or himself drafted, then well-beings are affected. That some of these effects will have repercussions in market transactions means only that the consequences of the changes in well-being induce changed relations with the market. But these changes will not even in principle correctly measure the initial welfare changes, unlike the first type of effect, since they do not tell us what happened to the "starting positions" from which the participants confront the market as well as the rest of their environment.

Most public policies have both effects: they affect market prices and starting positions. So market transactions will not suffice to measure the total impact. Cost-benefit analysis must supplement such information. It is this supplementation that is often misunderstood. The analyst seeks to accomplish two goals. First, he attempts to find a single-dimensional measure of changes in "starting position" for any decision maker, such that a correspondence can be established between the well-being of the subject under the naturally observable variety of multi-dimensional starting situations and situations where all starting dimensions but one are held constant. The single variable dimension is the dimension of welfare measurement. The dimension conventionally selected to perform this measurement function is market purchasing power. Having established a single dimensional representation of starting positions, the second task is to establish a well-being corresponce between changes in market opportunities (i.e., changes in market prices) and starting positions. By these two procedures, all changes in situation, whether related directly to market transactions or not, are expressed in terms of *hypothetical* market transactions. In effect, "human," "nonmarket" values are translated into market value terms. It is this that is often decried as irrelevancy or dehumanization of values.

In fact, it is neither necessarily irrelevant nor dehumanizing. It is an empirical hypothesis that individuals are willing to substitute different types of gratification for one another in their overall balance of drive and fulfillment. In particular, individuals can feel as well off with greater command over marketable commodities but less of certain nonmarketable gratifications as in the reverse situation. Vulgarly, individuals can be bought off with money.

There *are* moral issues here: one for each individual and one for the observer. Each of the former must decide whether or not additional market power does compensate him for loss of nonmarket commodities like friendship, security, prestige, and power. The observer must decide whether *social* well-being will permit such substitutions, that is, whether there are social value judgments that deny the commensurability.

The cost-benefit analyst takes a distinctive position on both types of issue. He holds that there are no consensual social judgments of the latter sort. In their absence he refuses to impose his own. He therefore accepts whatever judgment each individual makes about his own well-being. Each such judgment will be reflected implicitly in terms of which substitutions the individual reveals himself empirically willing to make to keep his welfare unchanged. Private value judgments enter cost-benefit analysis therefore with respect to the accuracy of the empirical hypothesis about individual substitutability and the operational ability to elicit such implicit tradeoffs from observation.

The procedure just described is possible only under ideal circumstances. In ordinary circumstances nonmarket impacts cannot be brought into dependable correspondence with market values. Either the data on implicit tradeoffs are inadequate, or the tradeoffs observable in fact show undependable, inconsistent correspondences (i.e., the empirical hypothesis about substitutability is suspect). An especially likely situation is that different individuals possess and/or reveal different tradeoffs, so the requirements for a correct measurement of the aggregate of tradeoffs become practically unfeasible. By preventing expression in common units, this state of affairs seriously hampers cost-benefit analysis. The most that can be done is to express the nonmarket impacts in their natural dimensions, as for example morbidity or mortality rates, or number of felonies per 1000 population. Sometimes even the natural dimension cannot be quantified with any fineness, so that differences in impact along this dimension must be largely ignored and only the number of individuals or decision-making units affected can be listed, as for example the number of households displaced from neighborhoods where they have lived for more than, say, two years.

Having expressed outcomes in a variety of natural dimensions as well as, where appropriate, in dollar values, the very difficult task of evaluating what are then multi-dimensional consequences (vectors) must be faced. Most cost-benefit analyses have avoided going this vector outcome route because of a lack of insight as to how to render an evaluative ordering. They typically list only the outcomes that *are* susceptible to monetary expression, aggregate these, and call the reader's attention to the existence of so-called unmeasurable types of impacts that have had to be perforce omitted from the analysis. The more proper procedure is to enumerate and aggregate as many of the nonmonetary dimensions as possible along with the monetary, so that the relevant decision maker can make whatever evaluative tradeoffs he feels proper to his value system.

## 5.4 Internalities and Externalities

The prototype of cost-benefit analysis is the decision making of the individual economic unit, whether household or business firm. Each in effect considers every hypothetical action and asks whether it will gain more than it loses by undertaking the action. Since cost-benefit measures the benefits and costs generated by any action in terms of the effects on each decision-making unit, it would seem that the effect of each action taken by a unit could be measured simply by taking the gains and losses experienced by that unit. This would be so if the only impacts the action had on others operated through changes in the market prices they faced. Whenever the impacts were more direct, in effect, changing their "starting positions"—example, through factory smoke, polluted downstream water, greater knowledge—the primary benefits and costs to the participant would not be the only ones to consider. The spillover or third-part effects would have to be counted separately to ensure completeness. These spillovers are called "externalities," as noted above, and are especially likely to be important in areas where public policies are considered. Indeed, often it is the large-scale presence of externalities that makes collective action justifiable. Hence, in measuring costs and benefits, the analyst must not be satisfied to enumerate solely the outcomes for direct participants. Victims or beneficiaries of externalities must have their net spillover impacts added up as well.

Where externalities are negligible, the social consequences of any prospective action are internalized to the balance of direct participant effects. As a result the private calculations which serve to decide the private desirability of the action are a good reflection of the calculations necessary to establish the social desirability as well. Besides, except for the imperfection of markets, this identification of private and social calculation means that private actions are likely to be appropriate ones. Public correction will be uncalled for in these areas. Where externalities are important, however, the private calculations that serve to determine desirability omit significant outsider effects. Private desirability can diverge substantially from social desirability. So private actions can be seriously improper, and public action becomes a relevant social corrective.

Thus valid social action is intimately connected with situations where private calculations need supplementation from a wider vantage. The need for cost-benefit analysis to go beyond private calculations of advantage, despite the fact that it couches its measurements in market value terms, is therefore integral to the approach. It is of its essence.

This argument can be rephrased. We indicated earlier that cost-benefit analysis defines social costs and benefits as simply a collection of individual costs and benefits. This section establishes a sense in which the individual and social magnitudes can differ. More precisely, the distinction is between individual and social evaluation. Individual evaluation of an action consists in weighing the prospective gains and loses to the initiator of the action. Social evaluation of the same action consists in weighing the prospective gains and losses to everyone affected by the repercussions of the system as a whole. Because of market imputations of these repercussions, the two evaluations are often similar. When they are not, it is not because of any distinctive motivation or character of the private action, or the nature of the private calculations, but because of the structure of the market or of the market bypass nature of the interaction with others' situation. Inappropriate individual actions are not typically meaner or more selfish than appropriate ones.

## 6. INCOME LEVEL AND INCOME DISTRIBUTION

### 6.1 The Level and Distribution of Income

The concepts of the level of income and the distribution of income are the most central of the entire approach. This formulation accounts for what is most distinctive about the actual procedures of cost-benefit. But as it is the core of actual practice it is also its most controversial aspect.

The level of national income (or real national income, or real output) is a measure of the total want-gratifying power of the current flow of goods and services. The distribution of income is a measure of the level of real income of the different members of society, *at each specified level of national income.* The level of national income is assumed to be capable of change without a change in distribution and vice versa. The level of income is at its peak, in each set of circumstances, when it is impossible, for given technology and available resources and consumption preferences of the population to rearrange the overall pattern of resource use so as to increase the total want-gratifying power of output. We say of such a situation that resources are efficiently (or optimally) allocated. If it is possible so to rearrange resource use that the new total exceeds the old, then we say the rearrangement can increase the level of income and hence that the original resource allocation was inefficient (suboptimal).

The use of the cost-benefit criterion has predominantly—although not exclusively, especially in recent work—represented an application of level of income analysis. The conclusion that benefits exceed costs for a given project, or the reverse, has signified that the total level of national income could be, or could not be, respectively, increased by implementing the project. The key to the linkage of cost-benefit with level of income analysis lies in the assumption about interpersonal comparability of welfare changes.

As we indicated above, benefits and costs for any individual are measured, wherever possible, as that amount of purchasing power which, when added to (benefits) or subtracted from (costs) his initial situation, would make him as well off as in the actual situation consequent on whatever project is being evaluated. Because benefits and costs are both expressed in dollars, their difference can signify the *net* impact on that individual. The net effect for other individuals can be similarly expressed. Then—and this represents the critical assumption—a dollar of net impact for one individual has exactly the same social significance as a dollar of net impact for any other. A $50 loss by ten individuals each is exactly offset in aggregate social well-being by a $500 gain by one. Consequently, the aggregate social impact of any given project can be computed simply by taking the algebraic sum of net impacts over the whole population. Any positive sum implies that the level of national income can be increased by the project, that the project will improve the efficiency of resource allocation.

This formulation has an important operational significance. Since the amounts of money which are added together individually represent sums which it would be necessary to add or take away to return each individual to his preproject situation, a positive algebraic sum means that if the project were enacted the resultant distribution of gains and losses would enable those who benefitted on balance to pay enough money to those who lost on balance so that no one was worse off and at least one person better off. Indeed, with enough dividibility in the monetary unit, the pattern of compensating could make everyone better off. Outcomes that have either of these one-way advantages (vector dominance) over another are called "Pareto superior," and a move from an inferior to superior position is called a "Pareto improvement." It constitutes what is probably a highly consensual social value judgment to assume that Pareto improvements increase social welfare.

Thus, the criterion of the algebraic sum of net welfare impacts (also known as "the sum of consumers' and producers' surpluses") establishes whether or not a Pareto improvement could be attained. But its actual attainment almost always requires a set of positive and negative compensatory payments between losers and gainers. Some legislation attempts to compensate some losers for some of their losses, especially when glaring damage is done. However, there probably never has been an explicit attempt in real-world public policy to guarantee that *no one* will end up losing. This means that adopting a certain policy because it will give rise to an outcome which *could be* made Pareto superior to the initial situation is in fact to bring about an outcome which is *not* itself demonstrably better than that initial situation.

If Pareto improvement were the true value criterion, then the logical structure of the evaluation would require that the policy under consideration be the policy as originally formulated *plus* a set of compensatory payments between gainers and losers necessary to convert the unmediated outcome into a Pareto-superior position (relative to the starting point). The absence of the compensation adjunct in cost-benefit applications can be interpreted in at least two ways:

1. The true value criterion is not actual welfare improvement but potential welfare improvement. Public decision making is too complex to require that each agency bear responsibility for overall social welfare. The task can be specialized into two parts: (a) the efficiency with which resources are used, (b) the distribution of the fruits of resource utilization. Specialized responsibility for the former means focusing attention on the maximization of *opportunities* for want-gratification; responsibility for the latter means being concerned with what is actually done with those opportunities. Potential welfare improvement is a statement about opportunities. Compensatory schemes relate to distribution; but the specialization on distribution need not be bound by the social value judgment about distribution implied in Pareto improvement. Other values may be adopted; so the distribution policies adopted need not be the compensatory schemes related to Pareto improvements. In this context, the use of level of income in cost-benefit analysis reflects a

specialization on potential improvement and is therefore only a *partial* indicator. In studies where distributional impacts are estimated as well, the two are coordinate, partial dimensions of social welfare, intended for an integrated use by a more ultimate decision maker (the stage at which the specialized parts are brought together).

2. The true value criterion is actual welfare improvement, and potential improvements are identified with actual improvements. Under this interpretation the interpersonal comparability of net welfare impacts has a deeper meaning than simply bearing upon the possibility of compensation. Dollar impacts across individuals are implicitly deemed to have fully equivalent social welfare significance. Loss of $1000 each by 1000 individuals is assumed to be exactly offset in social value by a gain of $1 million by one individual.

This is a highly suspect procedure. In conventional economic analysis it is assumed that a dollar loss to a poor man involves more welfare loss than a dollar loss by a rich man. Dollars are comparable, but the welfare significances of changed possession of dollars are not obviously comparable and, at the very least, are not well approximated by the assumption of strict equality.

Under this interpretation aggregation alone suffices to produce a complete welfare criterion: actual welfare improvements. Additional information about distribution can, however, be relevant. It can be introduced in the following ways. First, it may be simply added as a separate evaluative dimension. To be relevant, the decision maker must be willing to expand the dimensionality of evaluation. The second method is to separate the net welfare impacts for all of the groups relevant to evaluation and then, on the basis of value judgments concerning the relative social importance of changes for the different groups, to apply relative weights to the several group net impacts. The evaluative criterion becomes a *weighted* sum of group welfare impacts. Here level and distribution considerations are joined in a single dimensional test.

The tradition of economic analysis has made the level of national income the dominant concern of cost-benefit applications. Unlike questions of distribution it appears to be scientifically clean, impartial, tangible. Its single dimensionality makes interpretation of results apparently straightforward. The recent concerns with distribution have not produced attractive, "objective" techniques to counterpart the secure, yet intricate techniques developed to measure level.

Yet some of the strengths of the latter are illusory. In fact, the very appearance of unquestionableness is counterproductive. It discourages closer examination of weaknesses and an appropriate modesty about conclusions. We have already mentioned the incompleteness of the potential welfare criterion and the highly dubious assumption about interpersonal comparisions of welfare change in the version that equates changes in income level with that of actual welfare. A final caution is in order. Deeper welfare analysis discloses that at base income level and distribution cannot really be distinguished. The relative prices that help to define income level are a function of the distribution of purchasing power. Moreover, since the distribution of income that matters is that of gratification levels, this cannot be defined abstracted from concrete commodity distributions (income level) without additional extreme assumptions about interpersonal measurement of gratification. The practical use of the distinction is therefore a very rough and ready matter. It is suggestive and helpful, but not one of the great truths of nature. It must be employed with self-conscious care.

## 6.2  The Individual and the Group:  Situational Relevance of the Distinction

The persuasive impact of the distinction is not self-evident, even to those who are unaware of the subtle vulnerabilities of the approach. Indeed, ironically, it is sometimes appreciated more by those who understand its ambiguous character closely than by those whose knowledge of it is trivial. We recall that a project A can conceivably be declared to raise the level of income higher than project B even if A entails moderate losses relative to B to an absolute majority of the population while concentrating very high gains to a very few. Losers are not likely to favor A even if told that in some sense the community as a whole is better off. The requirements for political action—namely, passage and administration of legislation—are not closely linked to the persuasive thrust of the income level criterion. Information about distribution, on the other hand, furnishes grounds for close predictions about the political patterns of support and opposition to particular programs. Thus, insofar as cost-benefit emphasizes level of income as chief criterion, its relevance as a guide to clients who represent specific constituent groups may be extremely ambiguous. The opposition of losers on particularistic grounds, despite the optimistic assurances of the criterion on a very special brand of universalistic ground, should not be surprising. More explicit attention to distribution may well improve predictability and lead to selection of programs which elicit more widespread approval.

## 7.  PERSPECTIVES

### 7.1  The Relevant Population

An important set of issues concerns specification of the appropriate choosing situation: the right population, the right set of alternatives, and the right form of the criterion. We begin with population.

7a. *The Relevant Population.* The cost-benefit criterion always refers to a particular population: the population for whom changes in well-being are deemed relevant by the appropriate policy maker. The identity of this population is an issue because there is more than one governmental jurisdiction who can make policy, and each has a different population for whose welfare it has designated responsibility. For each governmental decision maker the welfare of anyone outside his jurisdiction need not be considered in his planning. This represents a form of partial view evaluation analogous to that of private sector units relative to the public sector, but is justified by the genuine demarcation of political responsibility into separate units and the prime obligation of each unit to represent its constituencies.

The basic principle here for cost-benefit is that the only population whose well-being must be considered is that for which the policy maker has responsibility. But the whole of this population must be considered, as well as all kinds of effects on this population which might stem directly or indirectly from the policies being considered.

Complexity enters because different governmental units are not independent of one another. In particular, federalism imposes a hierarchy of responsibilities, so that a more local unit carries out its delegated functions in effect *on behalf of* a more encompassing unit. This not only means that there is a dependency relationship between the included and the including units, but also that any two subunits of the same inclusive unit are deemed to be *cooperative* agencies catering to the same overall population. Their mutual exclusiveness is significantly circumscribed.

The problem is further complicated by the fact that the nature of the inter-dependencies may differ from time to time, not solely as a result of specific legislative stipulations, but because the exercise of hierarchical coordination is more active at some times than at others. Exercise of jurisdiction is not cut and dried: it has an important discretionary component to it.

Thus the definition of the relevant population is a matter of perception of the appropriate pattern of political responsibility. As such it is not an invariant of a situation, since it depends on the perceptiveness of the particular individuals who are evaluating policy. In this very human process the role of the cost-benefit analyst is potentially ambiguous. Often he is an outside consultant, asked to perform evaluation for a specific agency of a specific governmental jurisdiction. This agency sees its responsibilities in ways which often differ from the consultant's perception. The latter is likely to see the agency's mission as subsumed within a larger one, larger both with respect to that jurisdiction and to more encompassing jurisdictions. His definition of the relevant population will generally differ from that of his client, with important policy implications. Yet if he acts upon it he is likely to render his advice unacceptable to the client. If he deliberately adopts the vantage of his client, he may do real violence to his conception of the evaluative problem.[3] This last is further complicated by the fact that the analyst often has an audience wider than that of his agency employer, for his work appears in a professional literature. This is especially so where there is no formal employment relationship between analyst and most relevant public agency. The problem of incompatible audiences may then be especially important. This difficulty has no easy resolution. It probably resides in reinvigorating coordinative links among political bodies. Until that occurs, the position of cost-benefit analysis will be essentially ambiguous.

7b. *The Relevant Alternatives.* Everything we have said above about relevant populations applies to relevant alternatives, since what an agency sees as its relevant alternatives stems from its way of regarding its freedom and range of action. This permissible scope depends on the attitudes, the perceptions, and the actions of the electorate and of other government bodies, as well as on the agency's own self-perception. This applies both to a given political jurisdiction as a whole, and to any single agency within that jurisdiction. There is ample ground for expecting divergences in specifying the range of options that may, or must, be considered. Here again the cost-benefit analyst has no invariant rule as to how to adjudicate the divergences.

In addition to this problem there are other issues raised by the question of relevant alternatives. These are very important because they intimately affect the very logical structure of the evaluative procedure.

We can distinguish two types of evaluational situation. In one an explicit menu of different, mutually exclusive policies (e.g., projects) is laid before the policy maker, of which he must select one. In the other the policy maker asks whether or not a specific policy (project) should be enacted. The first type is straightforward, primarily because by definition the difficult problems have all been assumed to be resolved. Rarely is an agency *faced with, or given,* the whole of its relevant menu. The menu must be constructed out of the separate elements that do come to the agency from outside: a set of mission directives, budget allocations, and other constraints bearing on the definition of the policy area and the agency's scope of jurisdiction and freedom of action. Nonetheless, all we need say about this first type is that almost always one of the alternatives in the menu will be the status quo, with status quo defined as no action taken at this time by the agency.

The second situation is more interesting, because it appears to be evaluating a single alternative in a vacuum. This is not so. There is always at least one other alternative implicit in the evaluation. It is a form of status quo position. There are a number of types of status quo, depending on the specifics of the situation. For example, suppose a certain budgetary allocation has been made to an agency. The agency is to decide whether that allocation should go for some project A. One alternative to project A is to return the money to the general fund of the government. Another is to return the money to the private sector. Another is to use it within the same agency but on some as yet unspecified other project. These options represent three different sets of alternatives. The most appropriate one depends on exactly what are the institutional processes that determine the decision-making process in that governmental jurisdiction. If the allocation, once tentatively made, *belongs* to the agency, the third pattern is most relevant. If it does not, and the allocation represents actual revenues or expected proceeds from a tax system which cannot quickly be changed, then rejection of project A sends the money back to the general fund but within the public sector. Finally, if the tax system is quickly adaptable, and project A was the only project being currently considered for public sector expansion, then rejection of A results in cutting the total of tax revenues in the current period, thereby making more resources available in the private sector.

The varieties increase if the initial supposition is changed so that no actual allocation has been made because the resources are not yet under the control of the public sector. That is, sufficient additional tax revenues *will* be levied if project A seems worthwhile, but not otherwise. Here the alternative to project A is the current pattern of resource use in the private sector. It should be noted that this pattern, resulting from *not* taxing additional revenues, is not necessarily the same as that which would result from refunding revenues already collected. The tax instruments involved may differ; but even with variations in the same tax, the private sector behavioral responses differ at different overall revenue levels.

The list of conceivable types of alternatives can be expanded. But the principle is clear: it is of critical importance in a cost-benefit study to specify precisely what are the true alternative options facing the system. This sometimes requires a profound understanding of the decision-making context within which the problem is posed, an extremely difficult task.

Suppose such a specification has been made. What has been specified is either a single alternative or a set of possible alternatives. In both cases the analyst will typically not bring the alternatives explicitly into the evaluation. Rather he will treat these implicitly, as the opportunities foregone by undertaking project A. The net attractiveness of these alternatives is cited as the opportunity costs of project A. This is the gist of our earlier characterization of the real costs of any action as the attractive opportunities foregone. Where the alternative is a single action, real costs are in principle easy to calculate. Where it is a set of possible actions, a further decision has to be made: Which member of this set is to be treated as *the* opportunity foregone? The answer in principle looks easy (it is not in fact so): select that member which would have been chosen in the absence of A. For private sector alternatives this involves predicting the behavioral result of a public policy change: lower taxes, less public borrowing, less public investment, and the like. For public sector alternatives this in effect requires performing an evaluation of all other relevant public projects (the analytic circularity gives way finally to private sector alternatives). In practice this is anything but easy. Actual procedures differ as to whether the released resources are assumed to find their way to the *best* of the available uses or to the average of those available, or whether an empirical attempt is made to predict exactly where the resources would go, which may differ from both of the first. Even under the easier first two approaches—specifying hypothetical as opposed to behaviorally predicted uses—furnishing an estimate is highly demanding.

In the special case where project A involves the use of capital resources whose alternative is private sector use, the conventional way to express the cost of A is either as the rate of return of those resources in their relevant private use (the so-called "cost of capital" or "marginal productivity of capital"), or as the present discounted (capital) value of the net returns in that private use. Under the first, project A benefits are expressed similarly as a rate of return; under the second, as generating a present discounted value of net returns from its public use. In this way benefits and costs are expressed in comparable magnitudes.

7c. *Relevant Evaluation.* We have just noted that to facilitate evaluation, benefits and costs are expressed in the same magnitudes, usually dollar values, but in certain special cases dealing with investment, as rates of return. We have already indicated how benefits and costs are meshed together in the cost-benefit criterion, but it is helpful to draw explicit attention to this criterion again. The reason for doing so is to make a distinction and to dispel a popular notion. The distinction is between benefits minus costs as the criterion and benefits-costs (the benefit-cost ratio) as the criterion. Popularly—especially among governmental agencies—the appropriate criterion is believed to be the benefit-cost ratio. In fact, the correct criterion is the benefit-cost difference, that is, net benefits. We have argued above that this latter always indicates either a potential or actual increase in real income. The benefit-cost ratio does also. The difference is that if all policy alternatives involve the use of the same total amount of resources, adoption of the goal of maximizing either measure will result in the same policy choices being made; but if some of the alternatives involve the use of different total amounts of resources maximization of one will result in a different policy choice than maximization of the other. In the latter case, maximization of net benefits will increase the income level higher than maximization of the benefit-cost ratio.

One last item concerning the structure of comparisons should be sketched here. The comparison situations we have discussed involved alternatives that differed from one another with regard to both benefits and costs. Sometimes, however, there are either natural situations or more frequently situations expressly constructed for the purpose, where an important simplification can be achieved. The several alternatives differ from one another either in the benefit *or* the cost dimension, but not both. The latter of these has been popular especially in the defense establishment and is known as "cost effectiveness" evaluation. Of the two simplifications it is the more important. One of the truly serious difficulties in conducting cost-benefit studies is the lack of bases on which to value the flow of public services: the benefits from public projects. Markets typically do not exist in which these services are sold, certainly not sold to maximize profits. As a partial bypass of the problem of valuing benefits, analysts structure their comparisons by assuming that all the alternatives are fashioned so as to achieve the same output goals. This means that they render the same benefits. They are evaluated in terms of the size of the resource costs necessary to achieve the standardized level of benefits. The least expensive project renders the greatest net benefits and is chosen.

Aside from its more limited reach, the procedure has pitfalls. The choice of alternative may well depend on the level of output selected to standardize the comparison. An alternative that wins at one output level need not win at a different one. The danger is that the cost-effectiveness test will be performed at a level other than what is actually intended in the project, and the results simply projected to the desired level. The choice may then be erroneous. Another difficulty is that in most public functions there are a number of "output dimensions." It is hard to believe that significantly different policy techniques will have the same pattern of consequences in all of the output dimensions. Therefore, fixing a given common level of output for all the alternatives is not likely really to achieve equality in all the output dimensions. Benefits are not really equal for all the alternatives. Hence the cost-effectiveness choice may be misleading. Nonetheless, where valuation of benefits is effectively impossible, it can render important service in helping to abstract a part of the problem that is tractable.

## 8. ISSUES IN THE MEASUREMENT OF BENEFITS AND COSTS

We now touch briefly a few issues involved in the concrete measurement of benefits and costs.

### 8.1 Transaction Gains and Costs

Wherever benefits and costs are reflected in concrete transactions, we take the market values in those transactions as a first approximation of the appropriate measures. There are a number of circumstances under which we wish to modify these, however, for a closer approximation.

(a) Our real target is usually to measure the change in consumers' and/or producers' surpluses, not the mere value of transactions, that is, we wish to measure the value of the new trading *opportunity,* of which the transaction value measures only a portion. Correction typically involves estimating a demand or supply function and measuring areas within them.

(b) Actual market prices may incorrectly reflect the real opportunities foregone. If the relevant market is monopolistic, price systematically distorts the real alternative supply options for the society. Our adjustment must be made that estimates the direction and magnitude of these market distortions. With monopolistic and oligopolistic markets widespread, the whole configuration of distortion is exceedingly complex, and resolution a highly conjectural procedure.

(c) If excise taxes or subsidies appear in the relevant markets, the prices at which transactions occur will reflect these and thus contain a form of static which hides the real production tradeoffs that are possible in the system. Transactions should therefore be valued at factor prices to express production foregone; to express value of benefits, however, market prices are appropriate.

(d) Where transactions give rise to important externalities, these must be explicitly considered. This is not so much a question of modifying the values at which actual transactions occur as separately itemizing the effects. Since they are likely to be nontransactional effects, we speak about them in the next item.

(e) Where output of the public sector is sold to the public, these prices are likely not to bear close relation to opportunity costs, but reflect desired income distribution goals. Adjustment must be made to approximate true social opportunity costs. On the benefit side it is especially important here to try to estimate demand functions so as to express consumer surpluses, since transaction values will typically fall far short of such surpluses.

(f) If the project under consideration would result in a substantial change in either market demand or supply (so-called "lumpiness"), the true impact prices would be different from those currently prevailing. These impact prices should be predicted by estimating supply or demand functions.

## 8.2 Nontransactions Gains and Costs

Most services produced in the public are not sold. There are no market transactions to turn to to measure the value of the benefits generated. (The social opportunity costs are tolerably measured by program costs where properly accounted for.) This is an exceedingly difficult problem. Some outputs are approximated by finding a type of commodity in the private sector which is a close substitute and inferring a value to the public commodity based on the market prices of the private good. This is subject to the errors of imperfect substitutability and a phenomenon akin to the lumpiness problem mentioned above. The assumption is implicitly made that the public and private goods are competing in the same market. The nonsale of the former, however, belies this. If they *were* in market competition the substantially different market supply situation prevailing would cause prices to be different from those observed.

Where no close private substitutes can be found, hypothetical valuations are pieced together from a variety of indirect sources. For example, investigators may attempt to put a social value on human life (e.g., in the context of traffic accidents or health care programs) by observing jury awards for death in court damage suits, or perhaps the cost per decreased accident of constructing a highway improvement designed to increase traffic safety. Such measures are of course conjectural, and some may fail to gain any real consensus among analysts.

As indicated above, to bypass the problem some comparisons are expressly structured as cost effectiveness studies. The problem of benefit measurement is resolved by equating as many outcome dimensions as possible across alternatives.

Another bypass is essentially to give up the attempt to achieve measurement in terms comparable to transaction impacts. Outcomes are rendered in their own natural dimensions, as, for example, number of felonies, patient days of specified illness, deaths. The intent is to present some more ultimate decision maker with a multi-dimensional vector outcome and hope that he will be able to establish the implicit tradeoffs across outcome dimensions necessary to make choices among the several alternative "market baskets" placed before him.

Clearly, the problem of measuring nontransaction impacts, a major part of the domain of cost-benefit, is far from solved.

## 8.3  Opportunity Sets

In view of the difficulties involved in direct measurement of all types of outcomes, certain shortcuts may be used that do not attempt a quantitative, but only a qualitative, evaluation. One such shortcut relates to the presumption that the well-being of an individual is enhanced if he experiences an increase in the opportunities open to him, that is, the addition of some alternatives without the subtraction of any. This can be made more sophisticated by distinguishing between alternatives that might conceivably be chosen in some circumstances and those that would not, being dominated by other alternatives. Then the evaluation would proceed by seeking to discover whether any policy would create a choice-relevant expansion of opportunities relative to any other. If so, such a choice-augmenting policy would be considered superior, regardless of the actual choices made under the different policies. Failure of the test would simply fail to establish any preferences. The procedure clearly can generate only a partial preference ordering among the relevant set of alternatives.

## 8.4  Market Efficiency and Inefficiency

When the kinds of outcome that are generated by alternatives are numerous, as for example where repercussions in various markets must be considered, the cumbersomeness of direct enumeration of all impacts is very great, and its accumulated errors great enough to hide systematic influences, a shortcut procedure can establish whether or not there are likely to be systematic tendencies, and can greatly facilitate measurement by suggesting where one might find already-aggregated, consolidated, netted-out consequences.

The method is to undertake an explicit general equilibrium welfare analysis of the system as a whole under the various alternatives, in other words, to carry out systems analysis before any measurement takes place and even before the nature of appropriate measurement has been decided on. Such an analysis can often suggest what net influences—in both direction and kind—on overall allocational efficiency will occur after all repercussions work themselves out. As such, it helps to identify what types of magnitudes will best capture the flavor of these net influences. Such magnitudes may be far removed from what would suggest itself for direct measurement of enumerated primitive impact. Given the grave difficulties involved in direct measurement of so many types of outcome, the shortcut indirect measurement derived from the general equilibrium analysis certainly seems a promising avenue to explore.

## 9. TIME AND INTEREST RATE

The treatment of time has probably been the most controversial aspect of cost-benefit analysis. It is inherently complex, and no definitive resolution of the issues involved yet exists. We have space only to sketch the overall problem.

Time appears in the analysis in at least three connections, and interest rates are bound up with each of them. We shall mention each: (1) time sequence tradeoffs; (2) time flow comparability; (3) opportunity cost for curable investments.

### 9.1 Time Sequence Tradeoffs

Suppose there are two project alternatives with consequences extending over two years. One has net benefit payoffs of 0,100; the other 100,0. Are there grounds for preferring one over the other? For any consumer faced with these as consumption options, the choice would be decided by his preferences about payoffs sequences. These preferences are referred to as time preferences. It is believed that empirically individuals are present-oriented: because of mortality, impatience, they would prefer the second sequence to the first. This means that at the moment of choosing they rate $1 of consumption in year 2 as worth less than the same $1 consumed in year 1. If asked to give up $1 of this year's consumption in exchange for more of next year's consumption, they would require more than $1 to make them as well off. The rate of tradeoff of consumption in any two (not necessarily adjacent) periods is the marginal rate of time preference.

Consumers are always concretely faced with choices about temporal sequences, since they can borrow or lend (invest) resources, thereby either orienting their consumption toward or away from the present, respectively. They are assumed to make these decisions on the basis of discrepancies between their own tradeoff preferences and those made possible by market transactions. They engage in transactions up to the point where the two tradeoffs are equal. Consumers evaluate consumption streams over time in terms of these preference tradeoffs. But this leads to our second function.

### 9.2 Time Flow Comparability

Suppose we are considering two projects which have a sequence of benefit and cost outcomes over a number of years. In the simplest case let both have constant net benefit flows over time. Then the two can be compared simply by comparing net benefits in any year. Now let them have invariable time streams but with one having annual entries that always exceed the other. Again the comparison is trivial. The problem stops being trivial when the streams cross, so that net benefits in one exceed the other in some years, while the other is greater in other years. The excess in one direction in one year must be compared with the excess in the other direction in another year.

This is accomplished by specifying the preference tradeoff between every pair of years (not necessarily adjacent). This enables, for example, every payoff in year t to be expressed as a payoff with equivalent gratification-potential (or, more simply, as an equally desirable payoff) in year t-1. By such a series of linkages, each payoff in period t can eventually be expressed as an equally satisfactory payoff in the current period, that is, each payoff at any date is discounted back to give a present discounted value. The result is twofold: (1) payoffs in all years are made comparable with one another; (2) by adding together all present discounted values an entire sequence of payoffs can be expressed as a single number, the present discounted value (or really a capitalized value of a benefit stream).

Discounting is a process which can be used with temporal streams of benefits and costs of any type. We have presented it in the context of consumption streams, and so employed as discounting factor the preference tradeoffs derived from marginal rates of time preference. In discussing the third function, we shall show how the same discounting function can be applied to productivity streams emanating from investment activities. The key difference is that the discounting factor must be appropriate to the true choice situation in which each investment activity is embedded. The general principle is that discounting, which expresses only a set of intertemporal tradeoffs, must always express the rates of tradeoff that the particular decision maker would in fact be most willing to make under the specific circumstances.

### 9.3 Opportunity Cost for Durable Investments

A durable investment is a use of resources in which, although the commitment of resources may (or may not) occur within a single time period, the benefits arising from that commitment extend over a nontrivial number of time periods. Investments will differ as to size of the initial commitment, number of years over which the benefits extend, time shapes of these benefits (uniform, rising, falling, etc.), and absolute levels. A technique for rendering different investment prospects comparable is essential. Discounting is such a technique, since it can give the present discounted value of any initial resource commitment, that is it can give both a present discounted value of costs and benefits, thus reducing the entire project to a single dimension: present discounted value of benefits minus costs, or net benefits.

Under certain circumstances a further degree of comparability is useful. To adjust for the fact that different projects may have different sized resource commitments (costs), an internal rate of return (or rate of return over cost) can be calculated for each. This represents the rate of net productivity of the project. It is computed as that discount rate which, when applied uniformly to all benefit elements in the stream, yields a present discounted value equal to that of total costs.

Discounting yields a measure of the capitalized value of net benefits, rate of return calculations yield a measure of the rate of net benefit production. Both can be used to measure either net payoffs to a project under consideration or the opportunity costs of such a project. For the latter the rate of return is more convenient, since alternative investment scale does not have to be specified.

Capitalized net benefits uses a discount factor that reflects market opportunities for temporal tradeoffs. For mutually exclusive alternatives, that with the highest net benefits is chosen. In general, by correctly accounting for opportunity costs, every project with positive net benefits is selected. Rate of return uses an internal discount factor, one that does not reflect either market opportunity or preference temporal tradeoffs. Hence these are introduced by comparing each project with all others, since in terms of temporal sequence it is mutually exclusive with all. In effect the comparison is conducted by asking, for each project, whether its rate of return exceeds that obtainable elsewhere, with market rate of interest often serving as shorthand measure of the set of opportunities available.

Both criteria will render the same verdict on alternatives where a fixed total use of resources is involved; but where variable amounts of resources are involved, maximum capitalized net benefit is the correct criterion while maximum internal rate of return will sometimes diverge.[4]

These three functions of interest rates, essentially comparing different consumption streams, comparing investment streams, and comparing consumption with investment streams, are linked together because transactions engaged in by the respective decision makers form a capital market. In a perfect capital market, prices and volumes of different types of transactions vary until the market interest rates equate the marginal rate of time preference for all consumers and the marginal productivity (internal rates of return) of investment. That is, the rate of return on the marginal project is just equal (2) to that of the next project which is superseded, and (2) to the marginal rate of time preference for all consumers adjusting to their most desired time sequence of consumption. In such an equilibrium each decision maker's choice problem—whether consumer or investor—will permit the same interest rate to be used as a basis for performing the appropriate discounting function: "the" market interest rate.[5]

The real situation is not so simple. First, it is widely held that the capital market possesses a variety of imperfections so that the interest rate on a particular transaction does not reflect the true social opportunity cost in terms of private sector temporal tradeoffs (plus characteristic riskiness). Second, a highly controversial issue has been developed as to whether the discount rate appropriate to a *social* evaluation of temporal tradeoffs is the same as the market rate which reflects predominantly individual private tradeoffs. The notably different time span of private decision makers and government has been adduced as the principal ground for arguing that even a perfect private capital market would yield a rate of discount significantly higher than what is appropriate to public sector attitudes toward the future. The private and social rates of discount differ. Cost-benefit analysis, concerned with public sector decisions, must use the appropriate social discount rate.

The problem for cost-benefit, therefore, is to resolve the question of discrepancies between private and social discount rates arising from both private market imperfections and a different structure of decision making between the two sectors. An appropriate social discount rate must be selected. This must be used on *all* alternative projects, public *and* private, so as to render all public projects comparable with one another, and with the private projects they would supersede.

Unfortunately, no definitive resolution of the problem yet exists. Treatments differ substantially. This is quite important, since differences in discount rate used within the actual range of treatments can radically affect social evaluation in almost every choosing situation. Variations in this factor can effect larger changes in outcome than even substantial errors in most of the other dimensions of the evaluative schema, in situations where the time dimension is important. In the absence of resolution there will continue to be an important source of disagreement about the interpretation of cost-benefit results. One technique that is employed to offset this controversiality is to run the cost-benefit calculations for more than one discount rate—typically a high, middle, and low—and to examine the sensitivity of the results. As suggested above, problems with intersecting, alternative long-term benefit and cost streams are likely to show high sensitivity; but problems with short-term streams and few intersections may be only minimally affected.

## 10. EXAMPLES OF APPLICATIONS

To conclude this essay, we shall very briefly note some of the areas in which applications have been made and indicate the distinctive strategy that has been used in each. No attempt is made to give a detailed appreciation of these treatments. We seek only to suggest how the characteristics of the policy area have influenced the evaluative emphases.

### 10.1 Water Resource Development

This has been one of the oldest of cost-benefit areas, and probably the one receiving most extensive theoretical and applied attention. The programs evaluated have been federal, and have had an area of impact either predominantly or mainly rural or conglomerate—at least not predominantly urban. The benefit area has been wide, and the costs have had a dispersion much wider than the benefit population (chiefly the federal financing of the program). Under these circumstances attention could be focused on level of income effects, with redistributional impacts omitted. The federal jurisdiction also has made questions of relevant population negligible. The chief tasks have therefore resolved around: (1) how to measure the aggregate income-creating effect of an increase in the supply of one input (irrigation water) out of many in a set of production processes (agriculture); (2) how to measure the income effects of an increase in electric power supply, available navigation, flood control, recreation, and the like; (3) how to perform measurements with a production process that produces multiple products, some saleable in ordinary, competitive, commercial markets, some saleable with the special linkages between seller and buyer that characterize a public utility, and some nonappropriable altogether.

Difficult issues are encountered, dealing, among other things, with substitutions among inputs and outputs, with the measurement of diffuse nonmarketable outputs, with allocations of costs in multi-product operations, with the effects on complicated system costs of input-intermediate output configuration changes, with public-private competition in the sale of electricity, and of course with the question of the appropriate social discount rate.

## 10.2 Highways

The highways evaluated have largely involved federal or state projects and have usually been rural or interurban. Recently, there has been a growing interest in intraurban highways, where different problems have been encountered. For the former, here too the diffuseness of adverse effects relative to the beneficiaries, and the presumption that the federal government in particular possessed adequate powers to rectify untoward income distribution effects, if it wished, has led to an omission of distributional considerations. The chief focus has been on income level effects. Three major kinds of impact have been central: the economic significance of the saving of time, both business and consumer; the influence of an improved transportation system on the economic development of a region; and the reflection of benefits to non-highway users in adjacent land prices.

The more recent concerns with urban highways make additional issues relevant. Such highways have a high density use at certain times of the day: they experience rush hour congestion. Moreover, their operation close to and within populous areas results in their having a number of external impingements upon nonusers, such as air pollution, noise, accidents, multi-mode traffice congestion in central business districts, aesthetic affronts, and spatial disruption of urban neighborhoods. Finally, there use is related to the presence and use of certain alternative transport modes, such as rail and bus lines and taxis.

These additional dimensions raise new income level impacts to be measured: congestion effects, the values lost by the various adverse impingements, and the substitution effects on alternative transport modes. In addition, they raise to notable importance the existence and pattern of distribution effects within the city: the portion of the population benefitted, the portions hurt.

The distinction, then, between nonurban and urban highway evaluation is of major importance. The latter raises many of the issues that are raised in evaluating a wide variety of types of projects whose domain is an urban area. We shall see this immediately below.

## 10.3 Urban Renewal

Urban renewal is another example of a type of project whose urban setting raises to importance various repercussions stemming from the highly interdependent character of urban concentrations. Here the central foci are the distribution of land uses within the metropolitan area and the interaction between poverty and the housing market. A variety of subtle, highly indirect income level effects go hand in hand with important redistribution effects. The latter are generally more visible than the former, and the projects appear to many of the relevant population like primarily adversely redistributional programs, where well-to-do established business and residential interests benefit at the expense of the slum (largely ghetto slum) poor. The fact that administration of the program is local accentuates the largely irremediable nature of the distributional impacts. Thus, a spelling out of both income level and distributional effects is essential.

The multi-dimensionality of effects is a special problem, aggravated by the interconnections among types of outcome. Various income level impacts have to be abstracted out of composite relationships like city-suburb competition, poverty-housing-slum causations, land use and efficiency of resource allocation, local government and intra-metropolitan decision making. The last of these opens an extremely important conflict between the relevant population as locus of political responsibility and as the population of project impact. The distribution effects are sizable relative to income level effects and have not been too difficult to delineate, although not at all easy to measure. The income level effects, whose very delineation is critical, given the appearance of distributional dominance, have been controversial. The author's own characterization of these stresses the importance of three kinds of externalities: neighborhood effects on the value of residential location; coherent slum subculture patterning on the self-fulfilling, self-sustaining disabilities of slum living; political jurisdiction interdependencies on the financial and expenditure constraints of central city governments. Measurement of income level effects stemming from these factors is notably difficult. Important categories seem intractable at this time.

## 10.4 Education

Education has recently experienced heavy evaluational attention from a variety of directions, of which cost-benefit is only one. But the perspective of cost-benefit has its distinctive character. The focus has typically been local. While some distributional issues seem important, because competitive advantages are entailed between primary beneficiaries and others, this has been neglected, since the *positive* spillovers of education onto third parties is assumed to be substantial and have usually been omitted (except in specific problems dealing with transmission of new knowledge, but these typically fall under a technical change rubric).

The usual approach in this area is to ask what is the contribution of additional education to national income and then measure this in terms of how additional education enhances the income-earning potential of the primary beneficiaries, those receiving the additional education. Education inputs are usually undifferentiated as to content, and specified only as an additional year at a specified educational level (primary school, high school, college, graduate school). The cost of education is listed as the direct schooling costs (which are intended to cover the real resource costs of providing the schooling, as well as explicit additional expenses facing the students) plus the income opportunities foregone by the students during the extra school year. In earlier studies the whole of the differences in present discounted value[6] of lifetime earnings *associated with* individuals of different schooling was *ascribed to* the effect of schooling. Subsequent studies have attempted to adjust this for differences in ability and family upbringing and connections. The relative displacement effects on job allocations (i.e., education as a rationing device to assign scarce jobs) have sometimes been noted as a further offset but not measured. On the other side, these studies measure only the asserted function of education as building employable skills, that is, as creating human productive capital. They do not deal with the worth of education as a consumption good in itself. This aspect too has generally been mentioned but not measured.

The skill-creating effects of education have been measured with such indirection and paying so little attention to the specific content of the education process that some investigators have seriously doubted their relevance. They have turned instead directly to the schooling process as a process of production and tried to relate specific resource allocations (input combinations) to educational outputs. While measuring the value of various input commitments in terms of money, educational outputs have been measured in "natural" nonmonetary output dimensions (like test scores). Preliminary results suggest that the aggregate, indirect income-enhancing capacities via skill creation may be more problematic than even the later, refined studies have been willing to allow.

## 10.5  Model Cities

This is perhaps the most difficult area of application. It must be pointed out that there is no one version of Model Cities project, nor at this time do there exist projects of any kind well under way. No full-scale cost-benefit study has been undertaken. The present description is therefore meant only as a suggestion of a kind of emphasis that may well be appropriate for some of the local projects that subsequently come into full operation.

Unlike most of the other areas described, many of the projects here may turn out to reflect what seems the major orientation of the national program, namely, a substantial, multi-faceted *redistributional* effort to upgrade the life-chances of poor people living in selected, realtively homogeneous neighborhoods. If this is so, cost-benefit evaluations may focus on the relative *efficiency* with which different resource use configurations succeed in bringing about these redistributions. It is income level effects that may be negligible. Complicated social impacts of project activities on motivations, productive capacity, and decision-making processes may well have to be estimated, as well as more conventional notions of living standards, in order to predict continuing future consequences of present projects. Moreover, in keeping with the emphasis of the program, separable influences may have to be ascribed to the various elements of a single project even though they are expressly called upon to be simultaneously varied, and are understood to have highly interactive effects on the social situation of the target neighborhoods. Social policies operating on social milieux of such high mutual complexity certainly strain the capabilities of cost-benefit analysis. Real ingenuity will be required to fit the instrument to such more and more demanding uses.

## 11.  CONCLUSION

Very little is left for a conclusion. As a broad emphasis on the importance of carefully sifting out the balance of desirable and adverse consequences of an explicitly formulated set of mutually exclusive alternatives, it is unexceptionable.

More narrowly, for providing a detailed framework of such consequences in certain choosing situations, it is an instrument with attractive strengths and probably very poor competition. In other choosing situations, however, where significant distributional consequences are involved, some of its assumptions make it a more controversial instrument, for it is in the area of distributional ethics that its distinctive separation of income level and distribution comes most into question. Even here, although its conclusions must be supplemented and its overall relevance may be ambiguous (especially with regard to its politically perceived legitimacy), it may, from absence of a superior tool, constitute an essential component of social evaluation.

Nonetheless, regardless of its methodological claims, its practical usefulness will be most decisively at the mercy of the availability of data. Very serious inadequacy of relevant data exists in almost every area for which cost-benefit analyses have been undertaken. To some extent this has been, and can be, bypassed by sheer human ingenuity in reformulating problems and reconstructing data. But ingenuity is not a perfect substitute for data availability. Analyses in most fields suffer from crude measures in some categories and total exclusion in others. As more and more intricate social policies require evaluation, the already sorely strained credibility of cost-benefit authoritativeness may dissolve beyond essential communication.

Pessimism may not be called for. Despite data paucity, methodological hangups, and a still-ambiguous political relevance, the technique of cost-benefit has shown remarkable development, both in scope and refinement, over what is still a period of infancy. Having called out so soon after birth for "Drink! Drink!" it is hard to believe that it will not grow fast enough soon to drink us all under the table.

## NOTES

1. We already have dealt above with the extreme version of this emphasis on means: namely, where "social valuation" relates *only* to valuation of very broad alternative decision-making processes in the society. We argued that this probably falls outside the concept of social valuation as a guide to public policy.

2. "Productive" is not meant to carry any pejorative connotation with respect to what is "noneconomic." Use of a different conventional attribution, "tangible," is at least as misleading.

3. Much the same quandry is present with regard to the question of the relevant alternatives, where the client agency is likely to feel that its options are considerably more circumscribed than does its consultant analyst.

4. Use of rate of return is a sequential, incremental manner will make it correct.

5. There are rates on different types of transactions, but differences among them are assumed to reflect differences in riskiness, not intertemporal transfers.

6. Special problems inhere in the appropriate discount rate for this investment in human capital.

# 5

# COST-EFFECTIVENESS ANALYSIS IN EVALUATION RESEARCH

HENRY M. LEVIN

*Stanford University*

## I. INTRODUCTION

### Costs and Public Policy Choices

The purpose of evaluation research is to obtain information that might be used to choose among alternative policies or programs for achieving social objectives. This decision orientation suggests that attempts to ascertain the impacts of the various approaches are not adequate in themselves to make such choices. Associated with any alternative is not only an impact or effect, but also a sacrifice or cost. The lower the cost for obtaining a given result, the greater will be the total impact of the social resources devoted to the problem. The focus of cost-effectiveness analysis in evaluation research is to determine that strategy or combination of strategies that maximizes the desired result for any particular resource or budget constraint.

In order to understand this concern more fully, it is necessary to consider the fact that government agencies and other institutions are faced with finite budgets and other resources for achieving their objectives.[1] Although each agency may have a relatively narrow set of goals, such as reducing crime, improving educational results, curbing pollution, improving nutrition, reducing infant mortality, and so on, there are presumably alternative methods for accomplishing these tasks. Traditionally, evaluation research has occupied itself only with comparing these alternatives with respect to their results. The costs of alternatives have not been considered. Yet, it is obvious that the less the cost of obtaining any particular set of

AUTHOR'S NOTE: This paper was prepared as a chapter for the *Handbook of Evaluation Research* being produced by The Society for the Psychological Study of Social Issues under the editorship of Marcia Guttentag. The author wishes to acknowledge the assistance of Linda Gunzel and Maureen McNulty in the preparation of the manuscript.

results, the greater will be the contribution of the program toward achieving agency goals because the limited resources will provide a greater impact.

In most respects, cost-effectiveness analysis is not a new form of evaluation research so much as it is one that attempts to integrate cost considerations into standard evaluation research designs. Because a major portion of the cost-effectiveness analysis is based upon the comparative effectiveness of the various alternatives, the approach presumes that such information will be provided by experimental or quasi-experimental research. This information on the probable differences in outcomes of particular strategies is then combined with data on the costs of implementing them in order to make cost-effectiveness comparisons. From these comparisons one can make tentative recommendations among alternatives on the basis of which approaches will maximize the desired outcomes for any particular level of resource use.

The vast majority of evaluation research endeavors fail to consider the cost component. This neglect appears to be largely attributable to the fact that much of the methodological basis for evaluation derives from the experimental sciences and particularly their applications in psychology. Because the preoccupation of such studies is with ascertaining whether there are "statistically significant" differences among experimental treatments and between experimental and control populations, this focus has also dominated much evaluation research. Questions of whether statistically significant differences in outcomes are socially significant, and cost analyses of such differences, have not been an important part of the evaluation agenda until quite recently.

Perhaps the willingness to nominate for policy consideration any program that shows statistically significant results in outcomes over alternatives derives from the fact that only too rarely can such differences be found. Under these circumstances, any differences are thought to be important and worthy of being used for policy recommendations by researchers. But such zeal may provide a very misleading answer once costs are taken into account. That is, the alternative that appears to yield better results in terms of comparative effectiveness may have costs that far outweigh its superiority in results.

This natural tendency to ignore costs is reflected by the following example. A study of computer-assisted instruction in mathematics found that children in grades 1-6 who had received such instruction showed greater gains on standardized tests than did students in matched control groups (Suppes and Morningstar, 1969a, 1969b). While this finding is certainly of interest to educational researchers and policy makers, it lacks a comparison of relative costs. Can the same gain in mathematics achievement be obtained for less cost by using a modification of the traditional mode of instruction?

The answer to that question is implied by other data collected for the experiment. It was found that one of the matched "control schools" using conventional instruction showed greater test score gains for grades 4 and 5 than did its computer-assisted counterpart. Further inquiry revealed that the teachers and administrators at the control school had instituted an additional twenty-five minutes per day of classroom instruction and practice in arithmetic for those two grades. The authors concluded tentatively "that twenty-five extra minutes of classroom drill can be more beneficial than five to eight minutes per day of computer-based drill" (Suppes and Morningstar, 1969b: 19).

While precise cost data are not readily available, estimates of comparative costs can be obtained. Because five hours per day of teacher instruction cost the schools in the sample about $350 per child for the year, an additional twenty-five minutes of such instruction had an added cost of about $35 per year. It appeared that the cost of a fully utilized and efficient system of computer-assisted instruction for five to eight minutes of drill and practice a day would be on the order of about $150 per year.[2] Thus, the computer-assisted alternative was about four times as costly as traditional instruction for achieving the same objective. Because the schools were already spending about $700 annually for each pupil, the computer-augmented approach would have required a 20% addition to the school budget in contrast with only a 5% increase for using conventional methods to increase mathematics performance of students.

In the world of public policy, the costs as well as the effects of alternative strategies must be considered in order to maximize the impact of the social resources devoted to the public good. The purpose of this exposition is to provide a framework for integrating costs into the evaluation framework in order to carry out a cost-effectiveness analysis of the various policy choices. Emphasis will be placed on the conceptual framework, methodology, and examples. As in most areas of evaluation, there is no standard set of applied rules that can be mastered to carry out cost-effectiveness comparisons. Rather there is a set of principles and considerations that must be combined with sensitivity, ingenuity, and intuition on the part of the analyst. Much of the focus of this description will be on the principles of their application, with the hope that these have some transferability to other policy evaluations under other circumstances and in other domains.

## Cost-Effectiveness, Cost-Benefit, and Cost-Utility Analysis

Before proceeding with a review of the concepts and their implementations, it is useful to review the history of cost-effectiveness analysis and to compare it with its close relatives, cost-benefit and cost-utility analysis. The father of cost-effectiveness analysis is the more general cost-benefit analysis. The cost-benefit framework allows one to compare the costs and benefits to society of the various policy alternatives confronted. In its most refined form, the technique can be used to take account of such complexities as alternatives characterized by differences in the time allocation of benefits and costs and differences in who receives the benefits and who pays the costs (e.g., rich vs. poor or young vs. old).[4] Moreover, since there is an attempt to compare the monetary value of benefits with the monetary value of costs, the cost-benefit calculus enables the evaluator to use a common yardstick to assess the relative attractiveness of alternatives. Thus, by calculating the costs and benefits of policy alternatives in terms of monetary values, one can compare such dimensions as rates of return on investment, net differences between costs and benefits (net present values), and benefit-to-cost ratios. Of course no alternative would be undertaken whose costs exceeded benefits, and in general the ones that would be selected would be those that maximized the total social benefits relative to costs.

The earliest and perhaps the most imaginative use of cost-benefit analysis for public decision making has been in the evaluation of water resource projects. The Flood Control Act of 1936 required that the Corps of Army Engineers certify a project as feasible unless its total benefits exceeded its total costs. Accordingly, the last three decades have seen extensive development of techniques for measuring the benefits and costs of public investment in activities designed to improve navigation and flood control; to increase the output of hydroelectric power and water usable for agricultural, industrial, and domestic uses; and to expand and enhance the recreational potentiality of water resources (Eckstein, 1958; Krutilla and Eckstein, 1958).

In the application of cost-benefit analyses to water resource projects, most of the costs and benefits can be measured in monetary terms. For example, the costs of dredging and the construction of dams and other facilities, as well as costs of maintenance and operation, can generally be calculated directly from engineering data and cost experiences with similar projects. The monetary values of such benefits as hydroelectric power and water for agricultural, industrial, and domestic purposes can also be estimated by using the market prices of these outputs. The value of flood control can be assessed by deriving estimates of property destruction and loss of life that will be avoided by taming rampant waters. While recreational benefits are harder to determine, several techniques exist for calculating these (Clawson and Knetsch, 1966).

Given these measures of costs and benefits, proposed water resource projects with widely different purposes and in geographically dispersed locations can be ranked according to their net estimated contributions to social welfare (benefits minus costs) and other benefit-cost relationships. This information can be used to allocate the water-resource investment budget to that set of projects which maximize the net value of expected benefits.

A crucial assumption for performing benefit-cost analyses of alternatives is that the benefits or outcomes can be valued by their market prices or those of similar alternatives. Yet, the objectives of many, if not most, social programs often have no market counterpart. If a program is designed to improve the environment, how do we obtain a market price for the reduction of hydrocarbons and visible particles in the air or the reduction of pollution in water? While it is true that some of the benefits of such an action would be reflected in reduced medical costs and the added value of human lives saved, as well as in decreases in pollution-related deterioration of property, it is difficult to quantify the psychic benefits of clean air and water. How do we obtain a price for the aesthetics of open space or of conserving a rare species of bird or animal? What is the market price that will help us assess the benefits of increase in the self-concept, reading level, or music appreciation of a youngster? In each of these instances it is difficult to express outcomes in terms of their market values because a market does not exist for such services.[4]

In such situations the effectiveness of a strategy is expressed in terms of its actual physical or psychological outcome rather than its monetary value. That is, the monetary measures of resource costs are related to the effectiveness of a program in producing a particular impact. When the effectiveness of programs in achieving a particular goal (rather than their monetary values) is linked to costs, the approach is considered to be a cost-effectiveness rather than a cost-benefit analysis. For example, one might examine various alternatives for raising the literacy level of a population, for reducing hydrocarbons in the air, for reducing infant mortality, and so on. In this context, cost-effectiveness analysis enables us to examine the costs of alternative programs for achieving particular types of outcomes, but prevents us from comparing the costs directly with benefits. That is, the cost-effectiveness approach enables us to rank potential program choices according to the magnitudes of their effects relative to their costs, but we cannot ascertain whether a particular program is "worth it" in the sense that benefits exceed costs, because the latter are generally expressed in monetary units while the former are rendered in units of effectiveness for achieving a particular impact.

The cost-effectiveness method was developed primarily by military analysts in their evaluations of weapon systems. Because it is difficult to construct benefit-cost calculations for the horrors of war, the application of the cost-benefit framework to national defense was aimed at achieving particular "objectives" at minimal cost. Such objectives might include the destruction of enemy targets, effectiveness being assessed according to the portion of the specific target likely to be destroyed by various combinations of strategies such as manned bombers versus missiles (Hitch and McKean, 1960). It is probably safe to assert that its application to other social endeavors has not been extensive in part because social evaluators have been less conscious of the importance of costs in decision making than has the Pentagon.[5]

Despite the relatively underdeveloped status of cost-effectiveness analysis as an evaluation tool, it would seem to be a more appropriate approach to many types of evaluations than cost-benefit analysis. In particular, cost-effectiveness comparisons require only that the impacts of alternative strategies along with their respective costs be derived, while the cost-benefit framework requires that we put a monetary value on the impact. Because social experimentation enables us to obtain information on the impacts of alternative treatments or programs, data on effectiveness are easier to provide. That is, the results of policy-oriented experiments or quasi-experiments lend themselves naturally to cost-effectiveness comparisons. To the degree that the effects can also be translated later into monetary values, a cost-benefit framework can be applied at a second stage. Thus, the use of the cost-effectiveness approach does permit one to do a cost-benefit analysis as well, whenever the physical or psychological outcomes can be converted into monetary measures.

For example, a study of alternative population control strategies might evaluate contraceptive techniques and educational programs by their effect on birthrates. The measure of effectiveness for each option would be the reduction in birthrates, as compared with no change or an increase in birthrates among a similar population not participating in the experiment. In this hypothetical experiment, it would be possible to arrive at the levels of effectiveness in reducing birthrates of each combination and type of contraceptive technique and educational approach, and these levels could be compared with the relevant costs. From this information the potential choices could be ranked according to their cost-effectiveness ratios.

While this exercise would enable policy makers to choose among different approaches to reducing population growth, it would not permit them to compare the productivity of using resources for this purpose with that of applying them to improvements in health, education, transportation, or nutrition. Such a comparison would require that the benefits and costs of investing in any particular area be compared with those of other areas. To the degree that reductions in birthrates can be assessed in monetary terms, it is possible to convert cost-effectiveness data into cost-benefit information. Even if the ultimate cost-benefit calculations cannot be made because of inabilities to set a value on the benefits of a program, the cost-effectiveness rankings still represent a valuable basis for choosing among programs that have the same objective. In the presentation that follows, then, the emphasis will be on cost-effectiveness methodology, although it will be stressed that many of the issues are common to both cost-benefit and cost-effectiveness approaches.

Before proceeding to examine more extensively the meaning, methodology, and usefulness of cost-effectiveness analysis, it is useful to define one more related branch of evaluation, cost-utility analysis. While cost-benefit analysis enables a direct comparison of costs and benefits stated in monetary terms and cost-effectiveness analysis represents an attempt to evaluate directly the costs of alternative ways of achieving particular outcomes, cost-utility analysis incorporates the decision maker's subjective views in valuing the outcomes of alternative strategies (Fisher, 1964: 33-48).

In concept, cost-utility analysis relies more heavily upon qualitative factors and subjective judgments than do cost-benefit and cost-effectiveness analysis. As such, it is particularly useful where a complex set of outcomes is associated with each strategy, and they cannot be assessed by market values or other measures common to all of them (Lifson, 1968). Briefly, the decision maker assesses the results of alternative courses of action according to their perceived values of utilities to him. These utilities are then expressed with respect to the costs and the probabilities of obtaining the expected results. The decision maker sets a criterion for making choices, the most common of these being the maximization of expected utility subject to a budget constraint.

## II. THE COST-EFFECTIVENESS TECHNIQUE

The use of cost-effectiveness analysis in evaluation can best be shown by constructing a simple illustration of its use. From this hypothetical example it is possible to grasp the added dimension that the approach provides for social decision making. Following this illustration we will attempt to describe the principles and procedures for considering and measuring costs and effects.

Assume that we are engaged in evaluating programs designed to reduce the rate of recidivism of convicts who are released from the state prison. For purposes of this exercise let us define the rate recidivism as that proportion of former prisoners who are arrested and convicted of criminal acts within five years of being released. The existing program is one that keeps a record of the addresses and employment circumstances of former prisoners, as well as requiring those who are released on parole to report periodically to their parole officers. Beyond these bookkeeping relationships there are no systematic attempts to provide either jobs or psychological counseling and assistance.

To reduce an apparently high rate of recidivism, the State Prison Authority wishes to consider a number of alternative programs for ex-prisoners. These include: (1) a job placement program, (2) a psychological services program, and (3) a program that combines both job placement and psychological services. With the assistance of evaluation experts, a major social experiment is initiated to determine the impacts of the three alternatives on the rate of recidivism. For a period of six months all of the released male prisoners who are returning to the major cities of the state are assigned randomly to one of four groups: (1) job placement, (2) psychological services, (3) combination of job placement and psychological services, or (4) normal existing arrangements for ex-prisoners.

After five and one-half years the experiment ends with the following results. The five-year rates of recidivism were 15% for those in the job placement program; 26% for those in the psychological services program; 12% for those in the combination program; and 37% for those ex-prisoners who received no special treatment. Based upon this appraisal it appears that all programs were more successful than the existing approach, but the combination treatment showed the best results, followed by the job placement program and the psychological services one. Under normal circumstances the evaluation might have ended here with the policy recommendation that the combination program be selected, but we wish to review the costs as well.

Table 5.1 shows a hypothetical cost-effectiveness comparison of the anti-recidivism programs for released prisoners. The three experimental treatments discussed above are compared with the results of the normal program. For simplicity we have assumed that exactly equal numbers—10,000 subjects—were assigned to each group. The five-year recidivism rates are shown, and beneath them in parentheses are noted the rankings of the results (1 is best). Based upon these rates we can calculate the number of persons who were not recidivous, who were not arrested and convicted of criminal acts within five years of their release from state prison.

Hypothetical total costs for each program are shown on the next line. It is assumed that the normal program is least expensive because it is essentially an "auditing" or "accounting" approach for maintaining information on the location and activities of each ex-prisoner. The job placement and psychological services programs are more costly, and the combination of them is the most expensive. It is assumed that some aspects of the combination program are duplicated in the separate ones, so that the cost of the combination approach is somewhat less than the combined total of the two separate components. When these costs are divided among the number of subjects in each group, it is clear that the "normal program" is the least expensive and the combination shows the highest average cost per subject.

But the average cost per subject tells us nothing about the cost for obtaining the

TABLE 5.1  COST-EFFECTIVENESS COMPARISON OF ANTI-RECIDIVISM
PROGRAMS FOR RELEASED PRISONERS

| | Treatment | | | |
|---|---|---|---|---|
| | Job Placement | Psychological Services | Combination of these | Normal Program |
| Experimental population | 10,000 | 10,000 | 10,000 | 10,000 |
| Five-year rate of recidivism | .15 (2) | .26 (3) | .12 (1) | .37 (4) |
| Number of persons not recidivous | 8,500 (2) | 7.400 (3) | 8,800 (1) | 6,300 (4) |
| Total cost | $10,000,000 | $ 9,000,000 | $16,000,000 | $ 5,000,000 |
| Average cost per subject | $1,000 (3) | $ 900 (2) | $1,600 (4) | $ 500 (1) |
| Average cost per nonrecidivous subject | $1,176 (2) | $1,216 (3) | $1,818 (4) | $ 794 (1) |
| Number of persons not recidivous in comparison with normal program | 2,200 (2) | 1,100 (3) | 2,500 (1) | --- |
| Additional cost beyond normal program | $ 5,000,000 (2) | $ 4,000,000 (1) | $11,000,000 (3) | --- |
| Marginal cost per additional non-recidivous subject | $2,273 (1) | $3,636 (2) | $4,400 (3) | --- |

desired criterion, namely the reduction in recidivous subjects. The next line compares the average cost per nonrecidivous subject. According to this comparison, the
"normal" program shows the lowest average cost per nonrecidivous subject,
followed by the job placement program and the psychological services one, while
the combination program seems to have the highest cost. But this comparison is not
completely valid because the programs are being credited for subjects who probably
would not have been recidivous even in the absence of the programs. For example,
the "normal program" is merely a bookkeeping effort. While maintaining regular
contact and information on the activities and whereabouts of released prisoners will
have some effect on the likelihood of their returning to crime, it is likely that even
in the absense of such a program a significant portion of the men would not be
recidivous. Accordingly, using the total number of nonrecidivous subjects as a basis
for calculations understates the cost of each "success", because it counts any
nonrecidivous person as a credit to the program. This bias is most severe for the

"normal program," but it is also evident for the other groups.

These preliminary calculations lead us to the final set of results in Table 5.1. If we assume that the "normal program" is required by law, then we do not have the opportunity to eliminate it. Assuming that each of the other treatments also provides for regular contact with the person and collection of the relevant information, the policy question is what cost (for each *additional* nonrecidivous person) is saved by one of the special treatments. In comparison with the "normal program," the job placement, psychological services, and combination programs enable an additional 2,200, 1,100, and 2,500 persons, respectively (out of 10,000 subjects), to avoid returning to crime and prison. As we noted from the recidivism rates, the combination program seems most successful, followed by job placement and psychological service programs.

But the additional costs beyond the normal program vary from treatment to treatment. While the job placement program cost an additional $5 million, the psychological services cost another $4 million, and the combination program had an added cost of $11 million in comparison with the standard approach. From these data we can calculate the marginal or additional cost for each additional nonrecidivous subject. This varies from $2,273 for the job placement program to $4,400 for the combination approach. In other words, it cost about half as much to reduce recidivism by one person via job placement as via the combination program. The psychological services program was about midway in cost per additional nonrecidivous subject.

In summary, although the experiment demonstrated that the combination program showed the most success in reducing recidivism, its higher cost would not be justified. Rather, job placement would appear to be the most promising approach from the cost-effectiveness vantage point. To illustrate the impact of choice of approach on the budget of the social agency that is administering the program, we can calculate that the cost of "saving" an additional 1,000 released prisoners from returning to prison is about $2.3 million under the job placement program, $3.6 million under the psychological services approach, and $4.4 million under the combination program.

This illustration brings out a number of points. First, often what appears to be the most "effective" program may not be the most *cost-effective*. In this instance the governmental cost for each additional nonrecidivous man would have been twice as high had the most "effective" treatment been used as a basis for program selection. Second, not only may effectiveness rankings differ from cost-effectiveness rankings, but the total social costs of making the wrong choice by not considering program costs may be substantial. Third, different measures of cost may provide different implications, as a comparison of the figures on average cost per subject, average cost per nonrecidivous subject, and marginal cost per additional nonrecidivous subject show. Therefore, it is imperative that the appropriate cost comparison be used in order to obtain appropriate results.

Finally, this particular example lends itself to a subsequent cost-benefit evaluation, since it is possible to assess in monetary terms many of the benefits of attenuating recidivism. The decrease in recidivism is equivalent to a concomitant reduction in crimes against property and people. These can be evaluated, in turn, according to the reduction in social costs associated with these crimes as reflected in decreases in property damage and the medical costs and lost earnings deriving from personal injury and death. Moreover, the increases in earnings and taxes from the employment of each additional nonrecidivous person can be estimated. Finally, the reduction in costs of the legal, penal, and police systems, as well as public assistance for dependents of the prisoner, associated with reduced crime can be calculated. All of these benefits taken together can be compared with the costs of reducing the recidivism rate to determine the value of such programs in comparison with other potential social investments.

While this illustration was used to demonstrate the usefulness of integrating the impacts of various alternatives with their costs, it did not focus on the derivation of cost data and their use, nor did it focus on the nature of the concept of effectiveness. In the next two sections we will address the measurement and application of costs, as well as some issues on measuring effects.

## III. ASSESSING THE COSTS OF ALTERNATIVES

Before proceeding to a discussion of how to measure the costs of alternatives, it is important to set out the conceptual nature of costs. When one normally thinks of costs, he tends to focus on direct expenditures or what are often called accounting costs. That is, the costs of a particular action are commonly viewed as equivalent to the financial outlay associated with that activity. The concept of costs we will use is considerably broader. We define costs as representing that set of social sacrifices associated with any particular choice among social-policy alternatives.

The sacrifice or "opportunity cost" concept is based upon the economic notion of alternative uses of resources. When resources are used for one purpose, they cannot be used for other ends; therefore, the costs to society of choosing an alternative are the sacrifices implied by the "paths not taken." To the degree that these can be measured in monetary terms, we can calculate the costs associated with any alternative. In this sense the term *costs* refers to the monetary value of all the resources associated with any particular action, and their value is determined by their worth in the most productive alternative applications. Thus, the explicit expenditures associated with any particular course of action represent only a partial measure of the total costs.

A few examples of cost assessment are useful for delineating this principle. Using the criterion of costs as a sacrifice of other opportunities (or the value of foregone alternatives), we can examine the cost of a college education. It is obvious that a part of the cost of education is represented by direct expenditure on personnel, materials, and facilities. In addition, more subtle costs are imposed by the fact that individuals who enroll in colleges and universities are foregoing productive employment in the labor force. Not only does this represent a cost to them as individuals in the form of "lost" earnings, but it also represents a cost burden to society in terms of foregone production and tax contributions. Thus, the total cost of a college education includes not only the direct expenditures for education that normally come to mind, but also the implicit costs reflected in the earnings and production foregone by persons enrolling in colleges rather than working in the labor force (Schultz, 1960).

A second example is that of programs that use contributed imputs. For example, some educational and health endeavors draw heavily upon unpaid volunteers who contribute their time and energies. While such inputs will not be reflected in the budgeted costs of the programs, they represent resource costs nevertheless since they could be used for alternative endeavors. Accordingly, we normally impute a value to these contributed inputs in order to be fully aware of their hidden worth if the budget were to reflect the full burden of resource costs.

A final illustration of the divergence between accounting costs and true social costs is the value of client time. Many social endeavors require that the client take a considerable portion of his time to obtain services. The most poignant example probably appears in the health services. Some organizations require greater expenditure of patient time, in queuing and waiting for assistance, than do others. There is clearly a cost to the client or patient in terms of foregone work and other activities. For women the cost may be reflected in monetary outlays for child care, and for both men and women in the workforce there is a potential cost in the form of lost earnings. Even when there are no direct monetary costs due to waiting, there is a sacrifice of other alternatives that would have been undertaken during that time. To the degree that the evaluation of health service alternatives does not account for these costs, it will not reflect accurately the costs of the services.

As we will see below, a group of decision makers may rationally take into account only its own costs when making a choice among alternatives, but this does not mean that costs to other constituencies should be ignored in the overall evaluation. To the contrary, all costs should be reviewed for purposes of uncovering the true social sacrifice of resources associated with a given program and level of effectiveness. Beyond this an assessment can be made of who pays the costs. While the latter is of crucial importance for the decision maker considering a particular program, the former is necessary for overall social evaluations of cost-effectiveness comparisons.

There are two basic steps in determining the costs of particular alternatives. At the first stage it is necessary to determine the specific resources required and to place a monetary value on their use. The second step entails determining which of these costs must be taken into account by any particular decision maker and how he should construct the relevant cost comparison for the application he is concerned with. These phases will be addressed in turn.

## Measuring Costs

The measurement of costs would be a relatively simple task if it were only a matter of scrutinizing accounting statements and selecting the appropriate numbers. Almost never is this the case. To the degree that the cost-effectiveness evaluations are based on social experiments, it is not likely that the collection of cost data was built-in to the evaluation design. When attempts have been made to collect such information, the data tend to be crude and incomplete in comparison with data collected on other aspects of the experiment. Moreover, even if rather precise cost data were derived for an experiment, it is not obvious that the same information could be used as a basis for a full-scale policy implementation. It is often difficult to separate the developmental costs of an experiment from the operating costs of a program; administrative costs of ongoing programs are likely to differ from their experimental counterparts; and the idiosyncracies of the experimental phase may not be duplicated in the routine of application.

In the case that cost-effectiveness comparisons will be based upon evaluations of actual programs rather than experiments, cost information may be easier to derive. Yet, as we noted above, the cost estimates may be incomplete because they are based upon expenditures rather than upon the cost of all resources that enter the program; and the classification of costs may be inappropriate for use in choosing among policy alternatives.

In the long run the best solution to these problems is to construct cost information systems as part of the social experiments and as an integral part of the social programs themselves. This procedure will enable the measurement and monitoring of costs on a continuous and relatively precise basis. It is hoped that an increasing amount of energy will be devoted to integrating cost information into experimental and program designs. Yet, until such information is collected routinely, cost-effectiveness comparisons will have to be made on the basis of ad hoc assessments. Fortunately, the conceptual basis for constructing a picture of costs is similar whether the effort is built into the program being evaluated or is designed as a separate endeavor. Accordingly, one overall approach can be used as a model for cost measurement.

The method of cost estimation advocated here will be denoted the "ingredients approach." The name derives from the focus on listing at the first step the ingredients or inputs required by the program, and assigning costs to them only after all of the ingredients are accounted for. While this priority may seem trivial at first, its importance stems from the attempt at an exhaustive listing of all of the resources utilized by a program. When one focuses immediately on costs, there is a tendency to omit from consideration those inputs that are not obvious or that do not enter budgets explicitly. The ingredients approach requires that the requisite inputs of all types required by a program be recognized for purposes of estimating program costs.

Accordingly, the first order of business is to write a description of the program and its components. From this summary one can attempt to list all of the ingredients that enter the program. Table 5.2 represents a hypothetical worksheet for estimating costs. In the right-hand column all of the program ingredients are listed by major category. These components include personnel, facilities or physical space, materials and equipment, other inputs, and the value of client time. The purpose of the ingredients column is to include exhaustively all of the elements required by the program in as detailed a breakdown as is necessary. Within each category are subcategories. Thus personnel can be divided into administrative personnel and then subdivided again into such specific titles as director, assistant director, secretary, clerical, and so on.

A separate category is set out for the value of client time and other client inputs.

TABLE 5.2  HYPOTHETICAL WORKSHEET FOR ESTIMATING COSTS

| | Total Cost | Cost to Sponsor | Cost to Other Government Levels or Agencies | Contributed Private Inputs | Imposed Private Costs |
|---|---|---|---|---|---|
| Personnel | | | | | |
| | | | | | |
| | | | | | |
| Facilities | | | | | |
| | | | | | |
| | | | | | |
| Material and equipment | | | | | |
| | | | | | |
| | | | | | |
| Others (specify) | | | | | |
| | | | | | |
| | | | | | |
| Value of client time and other client inputs | | | | | |
| Total | | | | | |
| User charges | | -( ) | | | +( ) |
| Other cash subsidies | | -( ) | +( ) | +( ) | |
| Net total | | | | | |

As we asserted above, this resource is often neglected in cost calculations. Such an omission is equivalent to assuming that client time has a value of zero, and under such a presumption policy choices will be insensitive to the burden on the population receiving the services. One should list the number and types of man-days lost by the clients. For example, for an educational project one could provide the number of man-years of work foregone by a particular group of students. Health service programs might show the number of man-days of patient time associated with obtaining treatment, including travel and waiting time. In addition other client inputs should be accounted for in this section, for example, the transportation requirements to obtain services or the required purchase of some complementary ingredient. For example, educational programs often require the private purchase of books and materials, and many social projects have a transportation component.

Cost evaluation must consider these inputs in the total endeavor, whether the costs are borne privately or socially.

Given the list of ingredients, the next step is to estimate their costs. In the present case we will assume a one-year program. Multi-year program comparisons require certain analytical modifications that we will address in a later section. The cost of each ingredient is established either on the basis of cost experiences for that input or some other guideline.[6]

A major rule of cost estimation is to devote attention to any particular category according to the proportion of the total budget reflected by that component. Thus, if a category represents 50% of the total budget, the analyst should allocate around half of his energies to developing cost estimates for that classification. A category that represents only 5% of the total deserves no more than 5% of his attention. The reason for this principle is fairly obvious. Small percentage errors in estimating large categories can amount to large aggregate errors in cost measurement, while even large percentage errors in estimating trivial categories will have little effect on the total cost figure.

Because the personnel category typically accounts for 70 to 80% of the total budget, this component deserves the major share of attention in estimating costs. Fortunately, personnel costs can usually be appraised in a straightforward way from direct cost experience or from programs that use similar personnel capabilities. It is important to include not only salaries and wages, but also fringe benefits and other costs that employers must pay, such as contributions to health, life, and disability insurance plans, to pension plans, and to such payroll taxes as social security. These costs can be as high as one-third of salaries. The value of voluntary personnel is determined by what it would cost if such persons were paid for their services.

The costs of facilities is usually more difficult to estimate. In the simplest case, annual rental payments represent the cost. Where buildings are purchased or where the facilities used are part of a larger endeavor, the assessment of costs is more complicated. The "annual cost" of facilities that have been purchased is obtained by estimating the portion of the facilities used up (depreciated) in an annual period, as well as the opportunity cost of the investment in the sense that the investment could be obtaining social benefits in other uses. The "opportunity cost" aspect can be captured by applying an appropriate rate of interest to the net value of investment. The suitable interest rate depends upon a number of complicated factors, and the issues underlying the choice of rate have been hotly debated (Marglin, 1963; Baumol, 1968). Typically an interest rate of 5 to 10% is imputed.

The cost of depreciation is based conceptually on the fact that facilities have a limited life, so that in principle a portion of them are consumed by each year's use.[7] Thus, if a building has a 30-year life and lacks even salvage value at the end of that period, about one-thirtieth of that building is used up each year (assuming a constant annual depreciation.) In this instance the cost of depreciation would be calculated by taking one-thirtieth of the original cost of the building for each annual period. Added to this would be the opportunity cost of the investment which would be obtained by multiplying the chosen interest rate times the value of the building after present depreciation is accounted for.

To provide a simple example, assume that a project purchases a $900,000 building that has a 30-year life. Using the preceding methods of calculating the annual cost of that building, depreciation would be estimated at about $30,000 a year; and the opportunity cost of the investment would depend upon how much of the investment was depreciated. For example, if the building were 15 years old, we would calculate the opportunity cost for the sixteenth year on only $450,000, or half of the original cost of the building. At an interest rate of 5% that would amount to $22,500. (In the first year the estimated opportunity cost would be about $45,000; in the second year, $43,500; in the third year, $42,000; and so on.) In the sixteenth year, then, the cost of the facility would be $30,000 for depreciation plus $22,500 for the opportunity cost of the investment, with a total annual cost for that year of $52,500.

The measurement of facility costs may require fairly extensive computations if facilities are shared with other programs or are provided by a parent enterprise. In the former case the facilities and other resources may be shared by a number of activities of which only a particular one is the focus of the cost-effectiveness study. In the latter case the facilities may be inseparable in an accounting sense from the larger entity. An illustration of this phenomenon is the determination of the value of high-school facilities devoted to a school dropout program, or the value of the facilities used for an outpatient clinic located in a hospital.

There are several methods of estimating the costs of such facilities. If the total cost of shared facilities can be ascertained from the total rent or by estimating the depreciation and opportunity cost of investment of those that are owned, it is usually possible to prorate these costs among the individual programs. The basis for prorating costs should be some common denominator for all of the programs such as the proportion of the total space used by each program or some other appropriate guideline. This approach can also be used when facilities are provided by a parent enterprise such as a hospital, school, or community center. However, in some cases it is difficult to obtain the information required to prorate costs since this procedure requires data on other projects or on a parent organization that may not be participating in or cooperating with the evaluation. Under such circumstances, it is often preferable to use the alternative method of imputing a rental value equal to the annual rent for comparable facilities. As an illustration, assume that space of a comparable quality can be obtained in a similar location for about $2 per square foot per year. If the program that is being evaluated uses about 1,000 square feet, the imputed cost of facilities would be about $2,000 per annum.

In general, materials and equipment and other inputs can be costed on the basis of expenditures or on the basis of their market values if they have been contributed. The value of client time and other client inputs is based either on direct expenditures of clients where they are evident or on an assessment of the worth of client time. The former category may include client expenditures on books, materials, and other educational inputs in the case of schooling, or the privately borne costs of health programs, such as prescriptions and transportation. The latter category is meant to assess the loss of productive time from other activities, whether in the labor market or in the household. One rule of thumb that is often used to value client time is that of appraising it at its market value with respect to earnings foregone. In order to do this it is necessary to determine the age, racial, and sexual composition of the clientele. From these breakdowns it is possible to use Census data on earnings to determine opportunity cost (Becker, 1964.)

### Treatment of Time in Cost Measurement

Where the program requires more than one year of operation to obtain effects, it is necessary to estimate the costs for each year. There is no problem if the costs do not vary from year to year; however, many multi-year programs required additional allocations in the initial period for training and other start-up costs. Other programs may entail higher costs in the later years. Merely to add annual costs for several years does not provide an appropriate basis for comparing multi-year programs whose costs have different time patterns. Programs that allocate the bulk of their costs in the earlier years are not directly comparable with those that allocate the bulk of their costs in later years because the former entail a higher opportunity cost by sacrificing resources earlier in time; thus those resources are withdrawn from alternative uses for a longer period than when they are used later in the program cycle.

As an illustration, let us consider two alternative programs that show total costs of $500,000 for a five-year period. Assume that program A spends $200,000 for the first year and $75,000 for each of the next four years. Assume that program B spends $50,000 for the first four years and $300,000 for the last year. While both programs expend $500,000 over a five-year period, the social burden is greater for program A.

One way of understanding this concept is to consider the projects as bank accounts with $500,000 in initial deposits. Since account A is drawn upon earlier than B, it will yield less interest, where the interest that is derived represents the productivity of investments of the bank. That is, when the money is spent on the program, it cannot be used for other productive endeavors which the bank would invest in. If we assume that the expenditure transactions that we noted for each year would be consummated on the first day of that year, bank account A (or program A) would accumulate about $43,500 in interest payments at a 5% rate of interest, compounded annually over the five-year period. Bank account B (or program B) would accumulate about $85,500 in interest over the same period.

In short, the expenditure pattern reflected in program A is more costly to society as reflected in foregone interest payments which in turn reflect the productivity of investment in alternative endeavors. (This is one of several places where the economic argument seems to cut corners. The money A spends is back in circulation doing its productive thing at year 1.) The earlier expenditure commitment of program A entails a greater social sacrifice of resources than that of program B even though both spend a total of $500,000 over a five-year period. To make the two comparable with respect to the time allocation, we calculate the present values of their expenditure streams by discounting future costs by a rate of interest that reflects their value in alternative endeavors. The formula for obtaining the present value of a stream of costs is:

$$PVC = \sum_{t=1}^{n} \frac{X_t}{(1 + i)^t}$$

where PVC represents the present value of a stream of costs; $X_t$ denotes the cost for year t; n represents the final year in which costs are incurred; and i represents the appropriate rate of discount or interest. As we noted above, this rate of interest is supposed to reflect the rate of return to society of alternative uses of resources, but the selection of a particular rate depends upon a number of judgments (Baumol, 1968). Most studies utilize a rate of 5 to 10%; however, it is wise to select a number of rates within the appropriate range in order to ascertain the sensitivity of the result to the choice of discount rate.

Table 5.3 applies the present value approach to assessing costs of the two programs presented above. The first and third columns of the table show the allocation of annual costs over the five-year time span for the two alternatives. The second and fourth columns convert each of these annual "future" costs to present values by applying a 5% rate of interest or discount rate to the present value of cost formulation. Thus, the cost for each future year is shown according to its present

TABLE 5.3  CALCULATIONS OF PRESENT VALUE OF COST STREAMS
FOR TWO PROGRAMS

|  | Program A | | Program B | |
|---|---|---|---|---|
|  | (1)<br><br><br>Annual<br>Cost | ((2)<br>Present<br>Value<br>$\frac{X_t}{(1 - i)}t$ | (3)<br><br><br>Annual<br>Cost | (4)<br>Present<br>Value<br>$\frac{X_t}{(1 - i)}t$ |
| Year 1 | $200,000 | $200,000 | $ 50,000 | $ 50,000 |
| Year 2 | 75,000 | 71,429 | 50,000 | 46,619 |
| Year 3 | 75,000 | 68,027 | 50,000 | 45,351 |
| Year 4 | 75,000 | 64,789 | 50,000 | 43,193 |
| Year 5 | 75,000 | 61,703 | 300,000 | 246,812 |
| Total | $500,000 | $465,948 | $500,000 | $432,975 |

value equivalent. Because we assumed that the costs in each year would be incurred on the first day of that year, the present value of the first-year costs is also the annual cost. Each subsequent year, however, is divided by the factor $(1 + i)^t$ where t is set to equal to 1 for the annual cost incurred in the second year, by virtue of the fact that it is allocated on the first day of the second year. When we add the separate present values in columns 2 and 4, we find that the total present value of costs for program A is about $466,000 while for program B it is only $433,000. If the programs showed equal effectiveness, program B would be a preferable policy choice because of its lower costs. In general, any comparison of programs characterized by different time patterns of costs will necessitate the conversion of the annualized costs into present values in order to make them comparable among programs.

## Uncertainty and Cost Measurement

One other general aspect of cost measurement that should be considered is that of uncertainty. In some cases it may be extremely difficult to ascertain the costs of particular program ingredients. This is especially likely to be true in the assessment of programs, constructed on the basis of piecemeal experimental results, which have never been initiated as total programs. To the degree that the uncertainty applies to only a small fraction of the total ingredients (e.g., non-personnel inputs only), the total cost picture might not be affected appreciably by errors in estimating the costs of these inputs.

The usual treatment of uncertainty is to use the most comparable experience available as a basis for cost estimation. Such comparable data can be adjusted for idiosyncracies of the present application. Where the margins of error appear to be extremely large, it is preferable to suggest a reasonable upper boundary and a lower one. Different values can be used within this range to see to what degree the total cost estimates are sensitive to different assumptions. If total costs seem highly sensitive to the assumptions on which the cost estimates for particular components or ingredients are constructed, it is best to use several alternative assessments of costs in the final cost-effectiveness analysis to see if they affect the results. Normally a high and low value are estimated, and the midpoint or some other value within this range is selected as the most likely figure.[8]

### Appropriate Cost Comparisons

As we noted in the illustration on criminal recidivism, cost comparisons are possible. Each is appropriate or inappropriate depending upon the questions one wishes to ask and who is asking the question. It is especially useful to review the allocation of costs among different social entities. From the point of view of society, the total cost of each program must be considered alongside its impact in order to make choices among programs. That is, the most efficient use of the society's resources is made when those programs are selected that show the greatest effects relative to the social sacrifice of resources that they entail. Certainly, an evaluator who is concerned with the largest social perspective will wish to consider the total social costs associated with each alternative.

A public agency may be much less concerned with total social costs than with its own cost burden. That is, a particular governmental unit will be interested primarily in maximizing the impact of its own resources. Its relevant cost comparison will be among the costs it incurs for each alternative, and there will be a tendency of the sponsoring agency to ignore costs borne by other entities.

The worksheet in Table 5.2 is designed to classify the costs among several of these entities including the sponsoring agency, other levels of government and government agencies, and the private sector. For reasons that will be explained, the private sector is divided into contributions and imposed private costs, especially those borne by clients. Because each of these groups may evaluate the "cost-effectiveness" of a program on the basis of its own costs (and benefits), such a classification is rather important for understanding policy choices and political support for particular programs that may appear to be inefficient when total costs and effects are reviewed.

Higher levels of government or other government agencies may contribute to a program by providing particular program ingredients or cash subsidies.[9] For example, some states provide the salaries for reading specialists used by local educational agencies. Another example of a contributed input is the surplus federal properties and equipment given by the federal government to other governmental agencies for public purposes. Cash subsidies are illustrated in public assistance monies used to support housing programs for low-income families. Other examples include the federal subsidies to local governments for acquisition of parks.

Private costs can be divided into contributed inputs and private cash contributions. The former include the value of time of volunteers (especially in hospitals, schools and libraries) and donated facilities, materials, and equipment. In addition, there is that large category of imposed private costs, the direct expenditures required of clients for obtaining the service. These represent a cash subsidy from the client to the sponsoring agency. Examples of user charges include the costs that clients must pay for health services, admissions fees to museums and other public institutions, and tuition and fees at public educational institutions.

To determine the net costs to these entities, both contributed inputs and cash subsidies must be taken into account. The various columns to the right of the Total Cost column enable the costs of ingredients to be allocated among the four classifications. Thus, the totals at the bottom of the columns represent the costs associated with the provisions of the ingredients in the program by each group. But, in addition to these there are cash subsidies to the sponsor from both government and private sources as we described above. Accordingly, at the bottom of the appropriate columns we must add or deduct the value of these cash subsidies to determine the net costs to each constituency.

This adjustment is implemented by adding user charges to the Imposed Private Costs and deducting this subsidy from the Cost to Sponsor. Likewise the case subsidies provided by other governmental levels and agencies and by private contributions should be added to the costs in those columns and should be deducted from the sponsor's costs. These transactions are symbolized by the parentheses with accompanying plus or minus signs. When these accounting transfers are made in the table, the results show the net total costs to each entity. After these adjustments it is obvious that the net cost to the sponsoring agency can be considerably less than the total cost of the program. If a program with relatively high cost-to-effectiveness ratios is more highly subsidized than one with relatively low cost-effectiveness, there is the risk that a sponsoring agency will select the program that is less appropriate from the perspective of the larger society. That is, the cost-effectiveness ratio *to the sponsoring agency* for any program is improved by a larger subsidy. The importance of this point is to illustrate the cause of possible divergence between agency optimization and the maximization of social objectives. Cost-effectiveness evaluation can play an important role in documenting the contradiction.

Other levels of government and private constituencies would opt rationally for programs that minimize the costs to their entity for any given level of program benefits. Thus, it is not difficult to see that each group, comparing its costs to the perceived effectiveness of particular programs, may calculate different priorities. These kinds of conflicts might even be more apparent if we were to analyze the distribution of the tax burden and benefits of particular programs (Gillespie, 1965). The former is generally beyond the scope of a cost-effectiveness analysis, and the latter will be reviewed in the later section on effectiveness.

Cost-effectiveness comparisons are made on the basis of cost compilations that might analyze costs in any one of several ways. The most common of these are: total costs for obtaining a given level of effectiveness, average costs per unit of effectiveness, and marginal costs for additional units of effectiveness.

The comparison of *total program costs* is most appropriate when we are confronted with alternatives of about equal effectiveness. For example, assume that we are confronted with three possible routes for a highway planned between two remote points. Each route has about the same distance, but they differ with respect to the types of construction and the types of property that will have to be condemned enroute. In that case the evaluator might simply wish to calculate the total cost of each alternative and select that choice which minimizes the total project costs.

When programs differ in terms of their effectiveness, it is usually advisable to compare the *average cost* per unit of effectiveness. For example, assume that we evaluate several approaches to decreasing infant mortality, including prenatal educational programs, different approaches to maternal prenatal services, and nutritional supplements. Every woman is assigned randomly to a treatment or to a control group, and the levels of infant mortality are calculated for the groups. The effectiveness of a program can then be stated in terms of the reductions per standard unit (e.g., 1,000 pregnancies) of aborted births and of infant mortality through the first year of life. The programs may show widely varying results and widely varying costs. Accordingly, dividing the reduction in infant mortalities associated with each treatment by the cost of the treatment yields the cost per standard reduction measure.

This average cost per unit of effectiveness has the very desirable quality of permitting cost-effectiveness comparisons among divergent programs with very different characteristics as long as the total costs of the programs are available and the outcomes of the programs are measured in the same effectiveness units. For example, using the concept of average cost per unit of effectiveness, it is possible to compare different remedial-reading programs in terms of the cost per additional point of reading score. Delinquency prevention programs can be evaluated according to their cost for reducing delinquency rates. Health programs can be contrasted on the basis of the cost per standardized reduction in the incidence of diseases.

While the average cost measure is extremely attractive because of its generalizability across widely divergent programs, it is characterized by one major problem. Such a criterion implies that the most efficient ranking of programs at one level of the output scale pertains also to other levels of output. In fact, often programs that show low average cost at modest levels of output will show relative high average costs at greater levels of output and vice-versa. A reason is that technologies vary according to their relative intensity of fixed costs. Fixed costs represent those basic ingredients that must be acquired in order to operate the program. They are invariant with respect to the level of output of the program to the degree that they must be obtained simply to offer *any* level of output, low or high. Accordingly, programs with large components of fixed costs will show relatively high average costs for low levels of output and low average costs for higher outputs.

As an illustration of fixed costs, consider a clinic designed to handle 400 patients per day. The program ingredients include the minimum physical facilities and specialized personnel necessary for operation. Even if only 100 patients a day are serviced, it is difficult to reduce these basic costs; but the average cost per patient will be about four times as high as at full capacity. Variable costs differ according to the number of patients serviced. For example, the number of X-rays, injections, and other patient services will be reduced with lower patient loads, but these costs are likely to be proportionate to patient load. That is, the average variable cost per patient is not strongly affected by scale of operation. If such a clinic were contrasted with a program that simply sent patients to community practitioners, it is possible that, for small numbers of patients, the cost per treatment would be lower for the latter alternative, but, for larger numbers of patients the "economies of scale" reflected in increasing utilization of the fixed overhead of the clinic would likely reduce the average cost of treatment below that for individual practitioners.

Figure 5.1 represents these cost relations. For relatively low numbers of patients it is possible to utilize individual practitioners at a relatively modest cost, but with larger numbers of patients the costs rise gradually because of the need to draw upon the more expensive practitioners in the community and also because the higher demand for practitioner services might stimulate higher prices. In contrast, the cost per patient treatment at the clinic would tend to be very high with few patients, but the cost per patient declines as the number of patients rises. Below about 200 patient treatments per day, the individual practitioner approach shows a lower cost per patient than the clinic, but beyond that level the clinic tends to be more cost-effective.

Comparisons of average cost per unit of effectiveness should be made only at

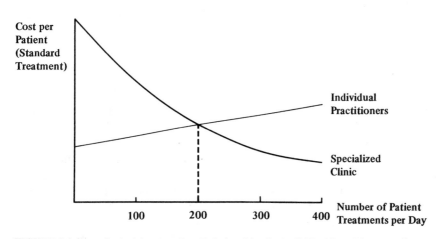

FIGURE 5.1  Hypothetical Average Cost Relationships for Individual Practitioners and a Specialized Clinic

that level of scale that is appropriate to the particular application being considered. Without taking the scale of a program into account, the results may be very misleading. For example, educational television and radio may be much less costly alternatives for teaching reading than their more traditional instructional counter-parts for state and national educational systems with several hundred thousand students. But their high fixed costs make educational television and radio rather costly for teaching reading to student populations of a few thousand.

In some instances it is the additional cost or *marginal cost* per effectiveness unit that is the relevant measure of comparison. This is particularly true where average cost per unit of effectiveness changes according to the scale of program. Assume that the decision maker is faced with the choice of expanding existing programs or initiating another one. In such an event he may be less concerned about the average cost per unit of effectiveness than he is about the additional cost per effectiveness unit entailed in enlarging the existing alternatives or in creating a new program. The measurement of costs would address only those additional ingredients needed to expand the programs from their present levels, and these would be contrasted with the additional units of effectiveness that would result. This marginal-cost approach considers not all the program costs and effects, but only those at the margin. The same criterion can be used for program contraction where the decision maker wishes to choose that combination of programs that will ensure the largest reduction in the budget for a unit decrease in output.

Marginal cost-effectiveness comparisons are also appropriate when decision makers must allocate budget increases or decreases among competing programs (Schultz, 1969; Wildavsky, 1964; Rivlin, 1971). To maximize the impact of an increase, they will wish to allot additional funds to those programs that show the largest gains in output per unit of cost. Conversely, decreases in the budget should be spread among those programs that show the smallest loss of output for a given reduction in support. In these circumstances the analyst must review all potential programs according to how marginal increases or decreases in costs will affect the magnitudes of increases or decreases in output. In this analysis one need not consider all costs and effects, but only marginal costs and effects.

## IV. MEASURING EFFECTIVENESS

Because most evaluation research tends to ignore cost analysis, we have devoted a substantial portion of this effort to the explanation of methods of measuring and analyzing costs. The existing approaches to social evaluation do have much to say about concepts and measures of effectiveness. Before evaluation studies proceed, they must select and operationalize a criterion. This criterion is the outcome or measure of effectiveness that is observed for all the alternative programs or strategies. We will not address the conceptualization and measurement of the criterion to the degree that we have reviewed the cost aspects. Nevertheless, three rather general issues are important to consider: (1) the time pattern of results, (2) measuring multiple outcomes, and (3) distributing effects among different populations.

## The Time Pattern of Results

Just as the time allocation of costs may differ among programs, so may the time pattern of results. Consider two reading programs designed to bring "slow-readers" up to grade level in reading achievement. Program A emphasizes computer-assisted instruction and other technological aids, while Program B concentrates on small-group instruction and tutoring. Students are assigned randomly, and they remain with the program until they reach their grade equivalent in reading, at which time they are transferred to regular reading programs. At the end of five years it is observed that 80% of the children who were enrolled in program A reached this criterion compared with 70% of the children in program B. It is found that similar students who do not receive the special treatments do not obtain grade level reading proficiencies over the same period.

One possible way to carry out a cost-effectiveness comparison is to compare the total costs for the two programs with the total number of children brought up to grade level in reading within five years. This would yield the average cost—properly discounted to obtain its present value—for each program "success." But on further scrutiny we observe that the timing of "successes" varies as shown in Table 5.4. According to this presentation, program B shows relatively earlier successes than program A even though the results for program A surpass those of program B at the end of five years.

The earlier a student is able to read at grade level, the sooner he is able to benefit from regular instruction and to participate in standard reading activities for his age. If society places a premium on bringing students up to that level of proficiency quickly, it is clear that a comparison of the two programs should take the time pattern of impact into account. This adjustment can be made by weighing more heavily in calculations of effects the earlier successes than the later ones.

In the selection on measuring costs we presented a technique for doing this, the application of a discount rate to the stream of annual costs. The same approach can be used for making different time streams of effects more nearly comparable. That is, the additional number of children that are able to achieve at the appropriate reading level can be calculated for each of the five years, and the "present value" of this five-year pattern can be estimated by utilizing an appropriate discount rate much as the present value of costs was determined. The cost-effectiveness comparison of the two programs can then be based on present values of both costs and effects. In this example, the application of "present value" methodology would

TABLE 5.4  PROPORTION OF STUDENT COHORT WHOSE READING ACHIEVEMENT
HAS REACHED THE MEAN ACHIEVEMENT AT THEIR GRADE LEVEL

| By End of Year | Program | |
|---|---|---|
| | A | B |
| 1 | 10 | 30 |
| 2 | 25 | 40 |
| 3 | 40 | 50 |
| 4 | 70 | 60 |
| 5 | 80 | 70 |

improve the relative standing of program B in comparison with using an approach that ignores the time pattern over which program outputs occur. In any endeavor where deferred outcomes are less preferable than present ones, it is wise to ensure that cost-effectiveness comparisons are based upon the appropriate adjustments.

### Effectiveness Measures for Multiple Outcomes

Virtually all of the examples we have used envision the effectiveness of a program as a single output reflected by a single measure, but many social programs are characterized by broad aims that can be reflected in a large number of measurable (and unmeasurable) outcomes.[10] Educational programs that are designed to improve a child's achievement in one subject may also influence his performance in other subjects, as well as his attitudes (Levin, 1970b.) Delinquency prevention programs may not only decrease the amount of juvenile crime, but they may also increase the educational attainments, employability, and welfare of the young adults involved.

The focus on a single criterion measure of effectiveness ignores the other effects of programs. If the other impacts have no value, then there is no harm in omitting them. In all too many cases, however, the other effects are of some importance, and should be considered explicitly. When one considers more than one output, he is faced with the problem of how to integrate them in the cost-effectiveness framework.

Assume, for example, that we are asked to evaluate the effects of two instructional programs on *both* mathematics and reading scores. Table 5.5 shows two sets of hypothetical outcomes. In Case 1, Program A shows greater effectiveness per unit of cost than Program B for both reading and mathematics achievement. Accordingly, the evaluator would recommend the adoption of Program A. But in Case 2, Program A shows a superior effect relative to cost for reading, while Program B is more effective for mathematics. Which program is preferable from the cost-effectiveness vantage? It is obvious that there is no answer a priori. If Program A is chosen we will obtain higher reading scores, but will sacrifice 2 points of mathematics achievement. If Program B is chosen, mathematics scores will be higher, but reading scores will be less than optimal.

TABLE 5.5   HYPOTHETICAL TEST SCORE GAINS PER STUDENT FOR A
GIVEN BUDGET INCREMENT TO EACH OF TWO PROGRAMS

|  | Case 1 | | Case 2 | |
|---|---|---|---|---|
|  | Reading | Mathematics | Reading | Mathematics |
| Program A | 2 | 3 | 2 | 1 |
| Program B | 1 | 2 | 1 | 3 |

The only way we can obtain an unambiguous cost-effectiveness ranking between the two programs is to express the value of the outputs in common units. One of the advantages of cost-benefit analysis is that outputs are converted into monetary values. But it is often difficult to translate changes in attitudes, test scores, and improved health into monetary benefits. The alternative is to assign arbitrary weights to the outputs so that they can be aggregated into an effectiveness index. Because this requires an ethical or normative judgement that may not express the view of everyone concerned, it is best to use several alternative weighting schemes. This approach enables each person to use his own values in scrutinizing the results, and it permits the evaluator to see whether cost-effectiveness rankings of the programs change as output priorities change (Azzi and Cox, 1973; Weisbrod, 1968).

Table 5.6 shows hypothetical effectiveness ratings for the two educational programs represented in Case 2 of Table 5.5. The test score gains for a given budget increment are translated into an effectiveness index by applying weights. When reading scores are assigned a weight of 1 and mathematics scores are assigned a weight of 2, the composite effectiveness score for Program A is 4. The comparable weightings for Program B provide a composite score of 7. Given those weights, Program B is the more effective. If reading gains were valued three times as much as mathematics gains, Program A would show a value of 7 in contrast with a value of 6 for Program B.

To compare program effectiveness the higher rating for any set of weights is underlined and equal ratings are encircled. The display can be summarized by saying that only when the decision maker believes that reading gains are at least three times as important as mathematics gains will he choose Program A. Under other conditions he will either be indifferent to the two programs or choose B. This

TABLE 5.6   EFFECTIVENESS RATINGS OF TWO EDUCATIONAL PROGRAMS
UNDER ALTERNATIVE WEIGHTING SCHEMES

Case 2

Program A
Reading Weights

|                        |   | 1  | 2   | 3    | 4    |
|------------------------|---|----|-----|------|------|
|                        | 1 | 3  | (5) | 7    | 9    |
| Mathematics Weights    | 2 | 4  | 6   | 8    | (10) |
|                        | 3 | 5  | 7   | 9    | 11   |
|                        | 4 | 6  | 8   | 10   | 12   |

Program B
Reading Weights

|                        |   | 1  | 2   | 3    | 4    |
|------------------------|---|----|-----|------|------|
|                        | 1 | 4  | (5) | 6    | 7    |
| Mathematics Weights    | 2 | 7  | 8   | 9    | (10) |
|                        | 3 | 10 | 11  | 12   | 13   |
|                        | 4 | 13 | 14  | 15   | 16   |

approach forces the user to make an explicit ethical decision about the values of the outcomes and enables him to see the cost-effectiveness implications of his value choice. It also permits him to see how sensitive the rankings of the programs are to deviations from his weighting. The usual alternative is to ignore additional outcomes other than the particular one under scrutiny. That method places an implicit value of zero on other effects, and such a value judgment is (by default) not ordinarily obvious to the user of the evaluation findings. Accordingly, the explicit weighting scheme would seem to be a far superior approach for the multiple outcome program comparison.

### Distribution of Effects Among Different Populations

A final aspect of the assessment of effectiveness is to evaluate who receives the benefits of the program. The use of a single effectiveness index for each outcome (e.g., the mean) assumes that the comparable programs have the same distribution of results across the population or that the distributions do not really matter (Azzi and Cox, 1973). The distribution of effects should be evaluated if a movement toward equality of outcomes is desirable. An example is found in education where there is a concern not only with the improvement in achievement test scores associated with a given approach, but also with the distribution of the scores (Block, 1971). In general, a program is considered to be more desirable the greater its ability to produce achievement gains and to reduce the variance in student achievement.

Assume a comparison of two instructional programs with equal average gains in student achievement. On closer scrutiny the first program has increased the test scores of all students by about the same amount, while the second has increased substantially the test scores of the top third of the student population with only modest or insignificant changes among the lower two-thirds. If we were to ignore the distribution of the results, we would rate the two programs equally effective. By attaching any positive value to the distributional consequences of the programs, we would prefer the first program over the second one for the same cost outlay.

Accordingly, when programs with equalization goals are evaluated, some attempt should be made to examine distributional changes as well as the average effect. This can be done in a number of ways (Jamison, et al., 1971). Perhaps the simplest way to measure distributional effect is to compare the change in the variance of the outcome, as well as the change in its level. Other distributional measures may be more appropriate depending upon the desired properties of the indicator (Atkinson, 1970). Given both a measure of change in outcome and its distribution, it is possible to obtain overall indices of effectiveness of programs by weighting the two according to decision priorities. This can be done by treating the measures as multiple outcomes and applying value weights to them in the manner suggested in the previous section. That is, the relative value of changes in the distribution and level of outcome can be assessed by setting out an analysis similar to that in Table 5.6.

Distributional concerns are important also when the production of benefits for one segment of the population is considered to have greater value than equal benefits for other segments. While this judgment is inherently an ethical one (as are all distributional considerations), it can be said that many programs express special concern for poor, aged, and minority populations. For example, consider housing rehabilitation programs that make use of low-cost loans and other subsidies. The effectiveness of such programs might be stated in terms of the number of housing units rehabilitated by such public endeavors. Then the approach that provides the greatest number of rehabilitations for a given cost would appear to be the most cost-effective. But what if the groups who are the primary beneficiaries of each program differ in composition? Under one program it is essentially middle- and upper-class persons who have purchased dilapidated buildings at highly subsidized interest rates; they refurbish the buildings to use as domiciles, or to rent and sell for profit. The other program has helped the poor, minorities, and the aged to form community corporations that systematically renovate the buildings for housing rentals to members of the communities.

If the total number of rehabilitated units were the only criterion of effectiveness, it is likely that the former program would be found to be more effective than the latter. To take the distribution of benefits into account, one can treat each distributional variable as an outcome of the program and weight the variables into the effectiveness index. In this case the proportion of direct recipients or participants who are classified as aged, minority, or poor would be ascertained, along with the number of housing units rehabilitated. These can be valued by alternative rating schemes into overall effectiveness ratings that can be compared with costs.

While the distributional aspects of social programs have been neglected in the past, to ignore them is to make distributional judgments nevertheless. Such an omission represents a tacit acceptance of the existing distribution of benefits of the programs that are being evaluated. Moreover, if the housing example is realistic and representative, a cost-effectiveness analysis that does not consider the distributional aspects of the results may be systematically biased in favor of the middle and upper classes.

## V. ILLUSTRATIONS AND CONCLUSIONS

Now that the rationale and methodology for cost-effectiveness analysis of social programs have been presented, it may be useful to review studies that have utilized this analytical tool. The nuances of the technique are much better reflected in examples than in an abstract description of methods. The fact that cost-effectiveness analysis has not been widely employed for the analysis of social programs handicaps this endeavor; most of the applications have been in the area of military strategies and acquisition of weapon systems (Goldman, 1967; Quade, 1964). Cost-benefit approaches have typically been used for the evaluation of public policy in other areas, perhaps because economists prefer the wider comparability of cost-benefit results. Fortunately, many of the issues raised by cost-benefit techniques are pertinent to cost-effectiveness studies.

In recent years a number of survey articles, bibliographies, and volumes of readings have been published on the subject. The most comprehensive survey articles are those of Prest and Turvey (1965), and Musgrave (1969.) An excellent annotated bibliography is found in Hinrichs and Taylor (1969), and most of the other sources that are cited here offer extensive bibliographies. Among collections of readings on cost-benefit analysis, the most comprehensive are Dorfman (1965), Chase (1968), and Niskanen et al. (1973). These readings cover a wide variety of topics, including recreation, agricultural price supports, transportation, manpower training programs, nutrition, education, health, and methodological issues. Goldman (1967) presents a set of essays on cost-effectiveness analysis in decision making. While some of the issues treated are general, most of the papers concern the application of cost-effectiveness analysis to military decision-making.

### Health Studies

Health programs represent a fertile area for cost-effectiveness and cost-benefit inquiries. Analyses in the health area have been especially varied with respect to subject and methodology. Provocative discussions of the problems in the economic evaluation of health endeavors and suggested directions for their solution are presented in Mushkin (1962) and Weisbrod (1961). The measurement of health is discussed in Hennes (1972).

Among studies of particular health topics, Maidlow and Berman (1972) attempted a benefit-cost analysis of alternative means of treating heroin addicts. A part of their evaluation was based upon the probability that former addicts would return to addiction. Attempts to estimate the costs of particular diseases are presented in Rice (1968) and tied to a general methodology. The costs of mental illness are estimated by Fein (1958), and the costs of syphilis, by Klarman (1965). These two works consider conceptual aspects of measurement.

The economics of preventing infectious kidney diseases is the focus of a study of Menz (1971). This inquiry evaluates the costs and results of a hypothetical program that would be differentiated by several different levels of intervention. Cost-effectiveness of periodic health examination strategies is explored by Forst (1973). The delivery of health services is explored in the work of Smith, Miller, and Golladay (1972), which used a cost-effectiveness framework to determine the optimal roles of paramedical personnel in the production of primary medical care.

### Education and Manpower Training

Numerous cost-effectiveness and cost-benefit studies have been undertaken in the evaluation of educational and manpower training programs. In the area of elementary and secondary education, Corazzini (1968) and Hu, Lee, and Stroms-dorfer (1971) have attempted to compare the costs and benefits of secondary vocational programs with general or comprehensive programs. Each of these explorations reports the conditions under which each of the alternatives might be considered superior. Levin (1970a) carried out a cost-effectiveness analysis of teacher selection where the measure of effectiveness was the increase in verbal acheivement of sixth graders. It was found that the use of more experienced teachers was five to ten times as costly as selecting teachers who showed higher verbal scores on a vocabulary test. Perl (1973) carried out a similar type of analysis for secondary schools. According to his results, the selection of more educated teachers would provide a considerably greater impact on student test scores per dollar of expenditure than reducing the average class size.

A study of the cost and performance of computer-assisted instruction for disadvantaged children (Jamison et al., 1971) deserves special mention. This investigation compared the test gains of children in three programs that utilized computer-assisted instruction (CAI) with those of children who received conventional instruction. Two of the programs focused on mathematics achievement, and the other concentrated on reading skills. In general, the students in the CAI programs outperformed their counterparts in the control groups. The authors also evaluated the distribution of the gains in test scores to see if gains were more (or less) variable in the CAI than in conventional instruction. The CAI students tended to show more nearly uniform gains than did their counterparts. Finally the relative costs of the CAI and conventional instruction were evaluated. The combination of experimental methodology with considerations of the distribution of results and costs makes this study an especially valuable reference.

Studies of dropouts (Weisbrod, 1965), preschool programs (Ribich, 1968: 83-97), and compensatory education expenditures for children from low-income backgrounds (Ribich, 1968: 83-97) have been evaluated with respect to the estimated increase in lifetime income associated with the effects of such programs. It has been found that in general, the costs of such programs exceed the benefits when income production is used as the criterion of success. Broader evaluations of education as a social investment have found relatively high returns in both the United States (Becker, 1964; Hanoch, 1967) and other countries (Psacharopoulos, 1973).

Manpower training programs have been evaluated by cost-benefit and cost-effectiveness techniques; an important and comprehensive review is found in Goldstein (1973). Ribich (1968: 34-50) compared a number of manpower training programs. In general, it appears that the benefits of such programs far exceed their cost. A comparison of particular approaches to "neighborhood youth corps" is presented in Somers and Stromsdorfer (1972). That evaluation included an analysis by race and sex of student of the effects of both in-school and summer youth corps programs with respect to a number of criteria including high-school graduation.

## Other Studies

A wide variety of other subjects has been the focus of cost-effectiveness approaches. Douglas and Tweeten have suggested a method for calculating the cost of controlling crime. Empirical findings on the factors affecting the costs of local police services and fire services in the St. Louis metropolitan area are reviewed in Hirsch (1970: 170-171). A study of the effectiveness of correctional programs is found in Robinson and Smith (1971). Since no correctional program was found to be more effective than any other, it is likely that the least costly one would be preferred; but Robinson and Smith do not present the costs of the alternatives. Empirical analysis of the costs of different service levels of refuse collection at the municipal level is presented in Hirsch (1965).

A substantial number of studies have evaluated the provision of recreational services and facilities. A general review of the issues and methodology is found in Clawson and Knetsch (1966). Specific studies of interest include Mack and Myers (1965) and Krutilla and Cicchetti (1973). Highways and transportation have been the focus of numerous analyses. The evaluation of urban highway programs was undertaken in Mohring (1965) and Kain (1967). Navigation improvements are scrutinized in a cost-benefit framework by Haveman (1973). Cost-benefit studies of urban renewal by Rothenberg (1967) and of infant nutrition by Selowsky (1973) represent exceedingly provocative applications of these analytical tools to those areas.

## Conclusion

The case for carrying out cost-effectiveness analyses of social alternatives is a strong one. Given limited resources to allocate among competing programs, evaluation for social choice must consider both the costs and the results of particular approaches. Yet this branch of inquiry, like most aspects of evaluation, is a relatively young one. The conceptualization and measurement of both costs and outcomes have not and probably cannot be routinized. Accordingly, the judgments of the evaluator in setting out decision rules and guidelines for estimating costs and effects represent a crucial variable in determining the outcome of the evaluation. The omission of particular cost components or program outcomes, the selection of a particularly high or low discount rate for future costs or results, and the method of estimation of costs of program ingredients all represent areas where different judgments may alter appreciably the cost-effectiveness ratings of alternatives (Williams, 1973). The preoccupation with means-ends relations at the expense of considering processes also represents a bias of the approach (Tribe, 1973).

The implications of the foregoing are that the cost-effectiveness analyst and the user of his results should feel obligated professionally to use the tool with wisdom and caution. In particular, the analyst is urged to make his assumptions about cost and output measurement as explicit as possible with a discussion of alternative assumptions and the likely effects that they would have on findings. Where feasible the calculations should by presented on the basis of alternative assumptions so that the reader can choose those that are consistent with his own understanding of the issue. The user should recognize the fact that the conclusions of such studies do not in themselves define a policy action. Rather they serve as useful—and, one would hope, potent—sources of information that must be combined with factors that have not been taken account of in the cost-effectiveness inquiry, in order to make public choices that are sensible, efficient, and equitable. In this context, cost-effectiveness analysis can be a powerful and productive ally.

## NOTES

1. For an overview of public budgeting systems and analysis, see Lee and Johnson (1973.)
2. This estimate was calculated from data provided by Dean Jamison. The actual cost of the program that was used as the basis of the experiment was considerably higher because it was designed for research and development purposes rather than routine application.

3. It is not the purpose of this article to review the enormous theoretical and practical difficulties in deriving allocation decisions that will maximize social welfare. The classical treatment of the subject is found in Pigou (1951), and an excellent critique is Little (1957). Also see the important theoretical dilemma presented by Arrow (1951). The relationship between prices and costs on the one hand and value on the other is a rather complex one. In a capitalist society it is explained primarily by the theory of markets. A fundamental exposition can be found in Samuelson (1970), chaps. 20 and 22-25. The neoclassical treatment is found in Hicks (1946), chaps. 1-5. In recent years the realism of the theory has come under increasing criticism. See for example, Gintis (1972) and Galbraith (1970).

4. While it is possible to attempt to determine how much people would pay for such benefits, it is not clear that they could evaluate accurately the values of services that are highly diffusive and that they might not have experienced. There is also a moral problem in attempting to determine the value of a "social good" whose cost will be apportioned among recipients according to how highly they value it. See Musgrave (1959: 73-89).

5. It is not clear that the political variables that dominate the acquisition of weapons systems have been overcome by the analysts as is evidenced by the typical overruns on costs and underruns on performance of such recent purchases as the F111 and C5A aircraft. In this respect the cost-effectiveness studies of the Pentagon may be primarily academic in value.

6. No attempt is made here to explain basic accounting procedures. There are many readily available sources on this subject, for example, Anthony (1964), Horngren (1967), and Moore and Jaedicke (1967).

7. A discussion of the treatment of depreciation in cost accounting is found in Anthony (1964: 154-172).

8. The underestimation of costs is far more frequent than their overestimation. Certainly a part of this phenomenon is due to the tendency of analysts to be "optimistic" in their cost estimates of projects they favor. For some other reasons see Merewitz (1973).

9. One subsidy we have not mentioned is the set of government services, such as municipal police and fire protection, refuse collection, and so on, provided free of charge to government-sponsored programs. The value of this subsidy might be appropriately estimated from the foregone taxes.

10. The use of experimental techniques for the evaluation of broad-aim programs is beset with difficulties in both conceptualization and application. It has been suggested that a greater emphasis be put on the evaluation of process than end product (Weiss and Rein, 1972; Tribe, 1973).

## REFERENCES

Anthony, R. N. *Management Accounting.* Homewood, Ill.: Irwin, 1964.

Arrow, Kenneth. *Social Choice and Individual Values.* New York: Wiley, 1951.

Atkinson, A. B. On the measurement of inequality. *Journal of Economic Theory,* 1970, 2: 221-224.

Azzi, Corry F. and James C. Cox. Equity and efficiency in program evaluation. *Quarterly Journal of Economics,* 1973, 495-502.

Baumol, W. J. On the social rate of discount. *American Economic Review,* 1968, 58: 788-802.

Becker, G. S. *Human Capital.* Princeton: Princeton University Press, 1964.

Block, J. H. *Mastery Learning.* New York: Holt, Rinehart and Winston, 1971.

Chase, Samuel B., Jr. (ed.) *Problems in Public Expenditure Analysis.* Washington, D.C.: Brookings Institution, 1968.

Chipman, J. S. The nature and meaning of equilibrium in economic theory. Pp. 35-64 in D. Martindale (ed.), *Functionalism in the Social Sciences: The Strength and Limits of Functionalism in Anthropology, Economics, Political Science, and Sociology.* Philadelphia: American Academy of Political and Social Science.

Clawson, Marian and Jack L. Knetsch. *Economics of Outdoor Recreation.* Baltimore: Johns Hopkins Press, 1966.

Corazzini, Arthur. The decision to invest in vocational education. *Journal of Human Resources,* 1968, 3: 82-120.

Dorfman, Robert (ed.) *Measuring Benefits of Government Investments.* Washington, D.C.: Brookings Institution, 1965.

Eckstein, Otto. *Water-Resource Development.* Cambridge: Harvard University Press, 1958.

Fein, Rashi. *Economics of Mental Illness.* New York: Basic Books, 1958.

Fishburn, C. *Decision and Value Theory.* New York: Wiley, 1964.

Fisher, G. H. The role of cost-utility analysis in program budgeting. In David Novick (ed.), *Program Budgeting.* Washington, D.C.: U.S. Government Printing Office, 1964.

Forst, B. E. An analysis of alternative periodic health examination strategies. Pp. 393-409 in Niskanen et al. (1973).

Galbraith, J. K. Economics as a system of belief. *American Economic Review,* 1970, 60: 469-478.

Gillespie, W. I. Effect of public expenditures on the distribution of income. Pp. 122-186 in R. A. Musgrave (ed.), *Essays in Fiscal Federalism.* Washington, D.C.: Brookings Institution, 1965.

Gintis, Herbert. Consumer behavior and the concept of soverignity. *American Economic Review,* 1972, 62: 267-278.

Goldman, T. A. (ed.) *Cost-Effectiveness Analysis.* New York: Praeger, 1967.

Goldstein, J. H. The effectiveness of manpower training programs: a review of research on the impact on the poor. Pp. 338-373 in Niskanen et al. (1973).

Hanoch, G. An economic analysis of earnings and schooling. *Journal of Human Resources,* 1967, 2: 310-329.

Haveman, R. H. The ex-post evaluation of navigation improvements. Pp. 249-276 in Niskanen et al. (1973).

Hennes, J. D. The measurement of health. *Medical Care Review,* 1972, 1268-1288.

Hicks, J. R. *Value and Capital.* 2nd ed. London: Oxford University Press, 1946.

Hinrichs, H. H. and G. M. Taylor. *Program Budgeting and Benefit-Cost Analysis.* Pacific Palisades: Goodyear, 1969.

Hirsch, Werner Z. Cost functions of an urban government service: refuse collection. *Review of Economics and Statistics,* 1965, 47: 87-92.

———. *The Economics of State and Local Government.* New York: McGraw-Hill, 1970.

Hitch, C. J. and R. N. McKean. *The Economics of Defense in the Nuclear Age.* Cambridge: Harvard University Press, 1960.

Horngren, C. T. *Cost Accounting.* Englewood Cliffs, N.J.: Prentice-Hall, 1967.

Hu, Tei-wei, Maw Lin Lee and E. W. Stronsdorfer. Economic returns to vocational and comprehensive high school graduates, *Journal of Human Resources,* 1971, 25-50.

Jamison, Dean, D. Fletcher, Pratrick Suppes and Richard Atkinson. Cost and performance of computer-assisted instruction for education of disadvantaged children. Paper presented at the National Bureau of Economic Research Conference on Education as an Industry, Chicago, June 1971.

Kain, J. F. An analysis of metropolitan transportation systems. Pp. 155-187 in Thomas A. Goldman (ed.), *Cost-Effectiveness Analysis.* New York: Praeger, 1967.

Klarman, Herbert E. Syphilis control programs. Pp. 367-414 in Robert Dorfman (ed.), *Measuring Benefits of Government Investments.* Washington, D.C., 1965.

Krutilla, J. V. and Otto Eckstein. *Multiple Purpose River Development.* Baltimore: Johns Hopkins Press, 1958.

Krutilla, J. V. and C. J. Cicchetti. Evaluating benefits of environmental resources with special application to the Hells Canyon. Pp. 447-475 in Niskanen et al. (1973).

Lee, R. D., Jr., and R. W. Johnson. *Public Budgeting Systems.* Baltimore: University Park Press, 1973.

Levin, H. M. A cost-effectiveness analysis of teacher selection. *Journal of Human Resources,* 1970, 5: 24-33. (a)

———. A new model of school effectiveness. Chap. 3 in *Do Teachers Make a Difference?* Washington, D.C.: U.S. Department of Health, Education, and Welfare, 1970. (b)

Lifson, Melvin W. Value Theory. Pp. 79-112 in J. Morley English (ed.), *Cost-Effectiveness—The Economic Evaluation of Engineered Systems.* New York: Wiley, 1968.

Little, I. M. D. *A Critique of Welfare Economics.* 2nd ed. London: Oxford University Press, 1957.

Mack, Ruth P. and Sumner Myers. Outdoor recreation. Pp. 71-116 in Robert Dorfman (ed.), *Measuring Benefits of Government Investments.* Washington, D.C.: Brookings Institution, 1965.

Maidlow, S. T. and Howard Berman. The economics of heroin treatment. *American Journal of Public Health,* 1972, 1397-1406.

Marglin, S. A. The social rate of discount and the optimal rate of investment. *Quarterly Journal of Economics,* 1963, 77: 95-112.

Menz, F. D. Economics of disease prevention: infectious kidney disease. *Inquiry,* 1971, 3-18.

Merewitz, Leonard. Cost Overruns in Public Works. Pp. 227-295 in Niskanen et al. (1973).

Mohring, Herbert. Urban highway investments. Pp. 231-291 in Robert Dorfman (ed.), *Measuring Benefits of Government Investments.* Washington, D.C.: Brookings Institution, 1965.

Moore, C. L. and R. K. Jaedicke. *Managerial Accounting.* Cincinnati: South-Western Publishing, 1967.

Morris, Douglas, and Luther Tweeten. The cost of controlling crime. *Annals of Regional Science of the Western Regional Science Association,* 1971, 5: 33-49.

Musgrave, R. A. Cost-benefit analysis and the theory of public finance. *Journal of Economic Literature,* 1969, 7: 797-806.

———. *The Theory of Public Finance.* New York: McGraw-Hill, 1959.

Musgrave, Richard A. and Peggy B. Musgrave. *Public Finance in Theory and Practice.* New York: McGraw-Hill, 1973.

Mushkin, Selma J. Health as an investment. *Journal of Political Economy,* 1962, 70: 129-142.

Niskanen, W. A., A. C. Harberger, R. H. Haveman, Ralph Turvey and Richard Seckhauser (eds.) *Benefit-Cost and Policy Analysis 1972.* Chicago: Aldine, 1973.

Perl, Lewis J. Family background, secondary school expenditure, and student ability. *Journal of Human Resources,* 1973, 6: 156-180.

Pigou, A. L. *A Study in Public Finance.* 3rd ed. London: Macmillan, 1951.

Prest, A. R. and R. Turvey. Cost-benefit analysis: a survey. *Economic Journal,* 1965, 75: 683-735.

Psacharopoulos, George. *Returns to Education.* San Francisco: Jossey-Bass, 1973.

Quade, E. S. *Analysis for Military Decisions.* Chicago: Rand McNally, 1964.

Ribich, Thomas. *Education and Poverty.* Washington, D.C.: Brookings Institution, 1968.

Rice, D. P. The Direct and Indirect Cost of Illness. Pp. 469-490 in *Federal Programs for the Development of Human Resources.* A compendium of papers submitted to the Subcommittee on Economic Progress, 1968.

Rivlin, Alice. *Systematic Thinking for Social Action.* Washington, D.C.: Brookings Institution, 1971.

Robinson, James and Gerald Smith. The effectiveness of correctional programs. *Journal of Research in Crime and Delinquency.* 1971, 17: 67-80.

Rothenberg, Jerome. *Economic Evaluation of Urban Renewal.* Washington, D.C.: Brookings Institution, 1967.

Samuelson, Paul A. *Economics.* 8th ed. New York: McGraw-Hill, 1970.

Schultz, Theodore W. Capital formation by education. *Journal of Political Economy,* 1960, 68: 571-583.

Schultze, Charles L. *The Politics and Economics of Public Spending.* Washington, D.C.: Brookings Institution, 1969.

Selowsky, Marcelo. An attempt to estimate rates of return to investment to infant nutrition. Pp. 410-428 in Niskanen et al. (1973).

Smith, K. R., Marianne Miller and F. L. Golladay. An analysis of the optimal of inputs in the production of medical services. *Journal of Human Resources,* 1972, 7: 208-225.

Somers, G. G. and E. W. Stromsdorfer. A cost-effectiveness analysis of in-school and summer neighborhood youth corps: nationwide analysis. *Journal of Human Resources,* 1972, 7: 446-459.

Suppes, Patric, and Mona Morningstar. Computer-assisted instruction. *Science,* 1969, 166: 343-350. (a)

———. Evaluation of three computer-assisted instruction programs. Psychology Series. Stanford, 1969. (b)

Tribe, L. H. Policy science: analysis or ideology? Pp. 3-47 in Niskanen et al. (1973).

Weisbrod, B. A. *Economics of Public Health.* Philadelphia: University of Pennsylvania Press, 1961.

———. Preventing high school dropouts. Pp. 117-148 in Robert Dorfman (ed.) *Measuring Benefits of Government Investments.* Washington, D.C.: Brookings Institution, 1965.

———. Income redistribution effects and benefit-cost analysis. Pp. 177-209 in Samuel B. Chase, Jr. (ed.), *Problems in Public Expenditures Analysis.* Washington, D.C.: Brookings Institution, 1968.

Weiss, R. S. and Martin Rein. The evaluation of broad-aim programs: difficulties in experimental design and an alternative. Pp. 236-249 in Carol H. Weiss (ed.), *Evaluating Action Programs.* Boston: Allyn and Bacon, 1972.

Wildavsky, Aaron. *The Politics of the Budgetary Process.* Boston: Little, Brown, 1964.

Williams, Alan. Cost-benefit analysis: bastard science? and/or insidious poison in the body politick? Pp. 48-74 in Niskanen et al. (1973).

# IV

# EVALUATION OF MENTAL HEALTH PROGRAMS

# 6

# EVALUATION OF COMMUNITY MENTAL HEALTH PROGRAMS

PETER SAINSBURY

*Graylingwell Hospital and*
*Medical Research Council (England)*

The purpose of this chapter is to use concrete examples to illustrate the problems of evaluating mental health programs, with special reference to a comparative evaluation of a community psychiatric service undertaken by Dr. Grad de Alarcon and I. To accomplish this purpose, I will first list the reasons for introducing a new type of psychiatric service in our locality, describe the form that it took, and explain what it was intended to achieve. Then I will outline how the proposal to evaluate certain aspects of it came about and mention some of the difficulties that had to be faced.

Because this was a novel venture, many problems had to be solved in planning the early stages of the research, such as selecting objectives that would not only be feasible but also have practical and scientific value. Similarly, awkward and unfamiliar questions regarding the most appropriate experimental design for such an inquiry had to be answered. For example, is it practicable to obtain a base line or to select a control for a program as diverse as a psychiatric health service?

Other uncertainties arose from the mixture of patients who are referred to a community service, their varied needs, and the wider range of amenities this type of service offers: the requirements of a patient living at home, of the chronically handicapped in the mental hospital, and of the patient attending a day hospital with a short-term illness are very different. We therefore had to determine the grounds on which success in meeting patients' needs would be measured, both in terms of their clinical characteristics and in terms of the facilities provided for them. Other matters on which exacting decisions had to be made were: devising appropriate methods and procedures; selecting variables by which to depict the services; and defining these variables. Choosing the criteria of evaluation, that is, those measures and indices that would reliably describe the operation and effects of this community psychiatric service, was the main priority. Related problems were anticipating the statistical analysis needed to ensure the data would be in the required form and finding the best means of storing and handling a great deal of information on many patients.

Another hazard, though it is one shared by the research worker undertaking any large-scale epidemiological survey or controlled trial, is the efficient administration of the project, the need to ensure that all participants record their observations in the agreed manner, that the requisite data is systematically filed and checked, that no cases are missed, and that the project's timetable is strictly observed.

These problems will be described in the order in which they were encountered when we evaluated the psychiatric services in two administrative districts by comparing a newly introduced community service in Chichester with a hospital-based one in Salisbury. And where it seems appropriate, I will draw on the experiences of my colleagues at the MRC Clinical Psychiatry Unit in assessing other aspects of psychiatric services, including those whose goal is suicide prevention. But each issue will also be considered with the more general aspects of evaluative research into services in view.

## THE NATIONAL HEALTH SERVICE, COMMUNITY SERVICES, AND EVALUATION

Among the salutory consequences of introducing a National Health Service in Britain in 1948 were improved standards for the care of the mentally ill and an extension of the services available to them. Mental hospitals not only began exploring better ways of caring for patients within the hospital but also of bridging the gulf between hospital and community (Sainsbury, 1969b). The reward of these endeavors was the Mental Health Act of 1959. This removed the administrative distinctions between mental and general hospital patients and the remaining barriers between the mental hospital and its community. But it also made the provision of community services mandatory; a progression which has been further advanced by the present policy of the Department of Health and Social Security (DHSS). This policy advocates the winding down and eventual closing of all mental hospitals, with psychiatric units in District General Hospitals being substituted for them. A team of psychiatrists, nurses, and social workers in each district will care for a population of about 25,000, and each unit will be backed up by a comprehensive network of supporting social services, as well as a variety of hostel and other sheltered accommodations. Evaluative research on the needs of a district in beds, places in homes, and staffing, and on many aspects of the feasibility of the proposals has been trifling; and by the same token, the opportunities the introduction of these services offer for such inquiries are enormous.

This official enthusiasm for the extramural care of the mentally ill was preempted by Dr. Carse at Graylingwell Hospital as early as 1956. Moreover, he also anticipated the current, and rather belated, need to assess the practicability, efficiency, and effects of introducing a radical policy of this kind; because, surprisingly, the Health Department had been dilatory in espousing operational and evaluative research into the National Health Services. Recently, publication of the Government's White Paper on research and development (Central Policy Review

Staff, 1971) has spurred such research. But it is not without irony that the act of parliament implementing the White Paper's recommendations transfers funds from the Medical Research Council, the body that attempted the first full-scale evaluation of psychiatric services (one among a number of their projects on services), to the Department of Health which neglected to do so.

## GRAYLINGWELL HOSPITAL AND THE WORTHING EXPERIMENT

This is an appropriate point at which to describe briefly the development of the psychiatric services at Graylingwell Hospital. Graylingwell is responsible for the care of the mentally ill in the county of West Sussex. It is in the northern part of Chichester, the county town, and is on the south coast some 65 miles from London. This county, the catchment area of the hospital, had a population in 1961 of 412,000; and the principle towns for the most part lie along the coast, but Horsham is an important market town 25 miles inland.

The planning of hospital and related services in England is undertaken regionally, so in 1956 it was the South West Metropolitan Hospital Regional Board that approved Dr. Carse's request to set up "an experimental outpatients service in Graylingwell." The proposal was to begin by opening a day hospital and community service center in Worthing, a seaside town well to the east of Chichester with a population of 80,000. The objective was "to discover whether the provision of greatly extended outpatient treatment facilities would reduce the number of patients admitted to Graylingwell and thereby ultimately overcome the overcrowding which was beginning to cause anxiety" (Carse, 1958). Prior to 1956, partly as a manifestation of a national trend and partly as a consequence of Dr. Carse's previous policy of overcoming local misgivings and misconceptions about the lunatic asylum and encouraging informal admissions, admissions to the hospital had increased nearly threefold since the introduction of the NHS; therefore, overcrowding and a shortage of beds, especially for the psychiatric elderly, had become a problem.

To solve it the proposal was to open a day hospital and administrative center, in Worthing in the first instance, and to extend the outpatient service and introduce a scheme of domiciliary treatment. After consultation with the local family practitioners, it was agreed that no patient living in the Worthing district would be admitted to Graylingwell until he had been seen by a psychiatrist and his situation had been fully assessed. At the end of the first year, the immediate goal of this policy had clearly been realized as admissions to Graylingwell had been reduced by 56% (see Figure 6.1).

## THE CHICHESTER AND DISTRICT COMMUNITY SERVICE

The success of the scheme in Worthing led to its introduction in 1958 in the Chichester district, a much less compact area. The population of Chichester at that time was 20,000; the other large town in the district is a seaside resort Bognor Regis (population 28,000), and there is a rural population scattered in villages extending

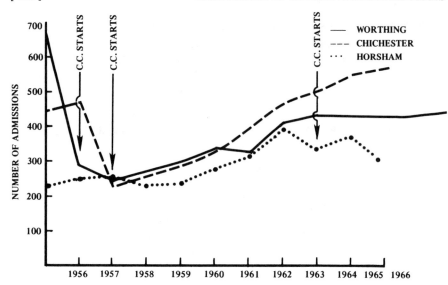

FIGURE 6.1 Admissions to Graylingwell and the Introduction of Community Care in the Three Parts of the Catchment Area

some 20 miles north and 10 miles on either side of Chichester. The purpose of extending the community service to Chichester was to see whether the scheme would be equally successful in a larger area with a more dispersed population, and whether the hospital's psychiatric team could manage without additional staff.

The distinguishing features of the community psychiatric service in Chichester were again that no patient would be admitted without first seeing a psychiatrist either at home, at the day center, or at one of the outpatient clinics in Bognor or Chichester. As it turns out, the initial contact was about equally divided among these three alternatives. The psychiatrist could then treat the patient at home, at the day center, as an outpatient, or by admission to Graylingwell. Collaboration with local general practitioners was close and informal; for example, discussion about patients over the telephone was encouraged. The service was run by the staff of the psychiatric hospital; consequently, its emphasis was on clinical rather than social care. Indeed, at this stage the hospital social worker's role was not at all clearly envisaged, and cooperation with the local social services was not solicited beyond obtaining their agreement to provide transport to and from the day hospital and the clinics. But the extent to which patients were not being treated extramurally is evident from Figure 6.1. The reduction in admissions was from 463 in the year preceding the service to 288 in the year following the start of it, a decrease of over 50%.

## THE MRC CLINICAL PSYCHIATRY RESEARCH UNIT

To complete the setting of the scene requires some mention of research at Graylingwell (Sainsbury, 1971b). Since 1948 the Regional Board had supported a research department in the hospital; but in 1957 it was taken over by the Medical

Research Council, as this national body had the funds needed to expand the department and ensure security of tenure of those employed in it. When the evaluation began in 1959, a psychiatrist, three social workers, and a clerk were available to undertake the research. The psychiatrist, though employed by the Medical Research Council, also had an official appointment as consultant psychiatrist to the hospital. So while the research unit was administratively independent, the clinical scientists nevertheless had a formal status in the hospital and exercised the same privileges as other members of the staff. In this way we obtained the independence essential to such research, particularly in regard to assessing the activities of the hospital; and we jealously maintained it.

## The Independence of the Investigator and Investigated

This relationship between the hospital and the research unit ensured that the investigators would be independent of the service studied, while they were at the same time persona grata with the clinicians and administrators running it.

## A Natural Reluctance to Being Stared At

The fact must be conceded that, by and large, people do not like having their work inspected. Although at the start of the Worthing Experiment the idea of evaluating it was applauded, when the research plans were formulated and presented for discussion, they provoked a quite unanticipated degree of alarm and resistance. Those whose carefully considered policies are being assessed or whose favored ideas appear to be in question or whose expectations seem to be demoted from certainties to possibilities may understandably see the evaluator either as a threat or as superfluous. Consequently, they may use all manner of cajolery to share the planning of the project, and thereby ensure it will become a self-fulfilling prophecy. In this crisis the investigator rapidly assumes the role of a diplomat and conciliator, a part ever so much more easily played when he is not an employee of the originators of the service. Then when calmer times prevail, he can allay misgivings and misunderstandings by pointing out that it is very unlikely that a plan drawn up by experienced administrators will be exposed as unworkable; what will probably emerge are some indications about the groups of patients who will benefit the most from their policy, and how it might be modified to increase its effectiveness with certain other groups. Similarly, he can assert that it is also improbable that one kind of service will be consistently superior to another, and that the evaluation should be seen as attempting to determine with what kinds of patients, in which sorts of amenities, and under what circumstances care is most effective.

Once misconceptions are clarified, the other vital prerequisite—that the research team be independent of the service personnel providing it—will be more readily accepted. Nevertheless, the two need to collaborate harmoniously. So, a third and related consideration is fostering the participation of those providing the services.

## COLLABORATION WITH SERVICE PERSONNEL AND EFFICIENT ORGANIZATION

It follows, therefore, that at the outset thought needs to be given to promoting the interest and willing cooperation of the service personnel in the purposes and the planning of the research. Everyone who will be asked to keep records, notify cases, and so on will need to be carefully briefed. We not only gave our colleagues an outline of the aims and plan of the evaluation, but provided each person with written instructions and explanations of their particular role. Maintaining their active support by regular meetings in which their difficulties could be discussed, their criticisms invited, and their contribution appreciated was well worth the trouble and time it took. The clerk, nurse, or doctor whose normal routine is disturbed or on whose time demands are made will express a genuine wish to be helpful when first approached; but his initial goodwill must be nourished by repeated explanations of the reasons tiresome details are required in the way that they are, at the time that they are, and as often as they are.

Another related but little considered aspect of collaborative research of this kind is the efficient administration of the project in all its details; in our experience it is more likely to founder in this than anything else. Evaluative research entails keeping uniform records, systematically registering patients to ensure no cases are missed, seeing that time schedules are strictly observed (e.g., seeing that patients are examined at the prescribed intervals), and so on. Observing the guidelines for identifying the appropriate patient, arranging appointments with relatives in good time, and planning the follow-up visits were as important to us as the steps followed to obtain cell counts are to a laboratory worker investigating anemia.

Following preliminary discussions with the clinical staff, we decided to evaluate the Chichester rather than the Worthing district. Dr. Morrissey, the clinician in charge of the former, was not only experienced in research and the waywardness of research workers, but had a very genuine interest in our proposals; besides which Chichester is on our doorstep, whereas Worthing is many miles away.

At this point it became necessary to decide on the aims of the evaluation and to specify them precisely, for only then could the next step of planning the detailed strategy be profitably pursued.

## THE GOALS OF A PSYCHIATRIC SERVICE AND EVALUATION RESEARCH

In practice, the immediate purpose of evaluating a service is to determine whether certain objectives are being met; and the investigation of a service is usually prompted by the questions and comments made about it, either by those administering it or by those participating in it. As I have already indicated, the only clearly stated goal of the Worthing Experiment was to reduce admissions to an overcrowded hospital, and then to see whether the same objective could be attained in a more dispersed population, the Chichester district, without increasing the staff of the mental hospital (and hence the cost). Data needed to measure and compare admissions were readily available: records were kept of the number of patients referred from the districts and the proportions admitted before and after the introduction of the service. Indeed our preliminary estimates are described in a preceding paragraph.

But there are other objectives and expected gains, usually more implied than categorically stated, in setting up new services. Policies necessarily tend to be couched in rather general terms. It can be assumed, for instance, that the innovations are intended to reduce morbidity in patients and in the community at large, or that both patients and service personnel will gain in certain other unstated respects, such as better standards of care and an improved efficiency of services. Furthermore, the objectives also tend to differ in emphasis, if not in content, depending on to whom the outline of the new proposals is being addressed, whether to those who will administer them, to those who will operate them, or to those who will make use of them. But if some definite conclusions are to issue from the research, it must be planned so as to answer precisely defined questions. One of the first requirements, therefore, in formulating an evaluative study is to define the aims of the services clearly and exactly; and it will usually devolve on the research worker to do this. Indeed, we found that, while the administrators and service personnel were very ready to discuss their objectives and propose aims of the evaluation, by and large, they expected those who were undertaking the research to take the lead in clarifying issues and selecting priorities.

In addition the evaluator must anticipate some of the consequences of the changes in services which the planners had not taken into account, such as their effects on the morale of the staff whose responsibilities will be affected, or the demands they make on those who will need to assume new roles.

Following discussions with Dr. Morissey, he supplemented the objectives of the Chichester service (besides reducing the admission rate) as follows (Morissey, 1966):

1. To treat the patient in his usual family, occupational, or social environment (where this seemed appropriate), because we expected, other things being equal, this regimen more likely to be successful than routine admission.
2. To reduce institutionalization and recruitment of long stay patients by extending extramural facilities and thereby expediting early discharge from hospital.
3. To select the type of disposition best suited to the needs of the patient and his family. Admission to the mental hospital in the past has often been for custodial reasons or for want of suitable alternatives, rather than on clinical and therapeutic grounds. (We now intend to use social and family considerations to help us decide whether admission, domiciliary, day-hospital, or outpatient care is suitable for a particular patient.)
4. To explore alternatives to admission for the increasing number of geriatric patients (which accompanies the aging of the population in this area) and thus to improve services available to old people.

The aims of community service evaluation were therefore determined by considering:

1. The *stated objectives* of the service. (Those outlined by Dr. Morissey came after the research had started, though we had, in fact, assumed them.)
2. The *unstated but implicit goals* of this particular service in providing new

amenities in the community. We assessed their operation, for example, by describing the number of contacts made with them, the characteristics of patients using them, and whether community patients too readily loose contact with services.

3. *The more general purposes of service evaluation:* meeting previously unmet needs; reducing morbidity (e.g., by seeing patients earlier in their illness); increasing efficiency in terms of the adequacy of the services in relation to their available resources in personnel and money; and satisfying the users of the service.

4. The *unexpected or unconsidered problems* we anticipated a service of this kind might create, such as placing an undue burden on the patients' relatives or household.

5. *Feasibility* in terms of research design and methods.

## THE AIMS OF THE RESEARCH

The aims we eventually chose to give priority to were:

1. To see how the introduction of a community service affects *who gets referred* to the psychiatrist. We proposed to examine the referral rates of the various social and clinical categories of patients as a means of estimating whether needs not previously met were being met; and whether morbidity was prevented by earlier referral when community facilities and collaboration with the family doctor were improved.

2. To see how the community service affects *who gets admitted* and who gets treated extramurally. What considerations, for instance, determine admission when opportunities for treatment at home and in a day hospital are provided. What patients are spared admission altogether, and how does this affect the bed needs, rates of contact with the community facilities, and the need for alternative "places" in the community? Is discharge also facilitated, or is duration of stay in hospital prolonged because patients selected for admission present particularly severe social or clinical problems? And is the number of long-stay, and hence institutionalized, patients diminished?

3. To determine *the effect on the community of treating outside the hospital* patients who would previously have been admitted. As members of the patients' household and his neighbors will be those most closely concerned, how are they affected? What are their welfare and other needs, and is the service meeting them? Because this policy was introducing a novel element in that the burden previously borne by the hospital was being transferred to the patients' relatives, we were also concerned to assess their attitudes to the service. Equally, we were interested to inquire into the attitudes of the general practitioner as he also would be taking a greater responsibility for the sick member of his family than previously.

4. To assess the effects of the new service on *patients' clinical and social outcome*. We wanted to know whether morbidity was reduced because more patients had a better outcome or because they had a shorter duration of

illness, and how this result was achieved in terms of the number and types of contact with the service needed to attain "recovery." In other words, is the service using its man-power more *efficiently* in "containing" morbidity? (Wing and Hailey, 1972)

Many aspects of the service, which might be considered more salient, were omitted: a comparison of the quality of the patients' care and of their daily life inside and outside the hospital, especially the chronically handicapped; staff morale and satisfaction; a full-scale cost-benefit analysis; and a detailed look at the effects on selected groups of patients such as senile dementias, psychopathic personalities, and the schizophrenic who responds poorly to treatment, since these categories present a particular challenge to a community care program.

Once the aims had been precisely stated, the research plan and the criteria of the evaluation could be more readily established; but to determine their feasibility, some pilot inquiries were needed.

## FEASIBILITY AND PILOT STUDIES

The value and practical benefits of evaluative studies to the planners of services, to those providing and those using them are evident enough. But it is less often conceded that original observations of scientific interest can just as easily emerge from applied or strategic research of this kind as from any carefully designed investigation. Thus, in this project, we needed systematically to record defined data on all the mentally ill people in a population; and so our registers, by providing a sampling frame, have prompted a number of useful clinical studies (Thompson, 1970). On the other hand, we also soon realized that some of the questions about services we would have liked to be able to answer were impracticable (q.v.).

Many factors limit the feasibility of evaluating an organization as intricate as a psychiatric service. Planning the research so as to take into account the relevant variables and the methods available for obtaining valid data on them presents formidable problems. We grudgingly came to accept that the evaluator must be realistic about restricting his questions to those for which reliable techniques for obtaining answers exist (or can be devised within a reasonable time), even though this entails relinquishing cherished aims. To compare, for example, the effects on the "quality of life" of the elderly in hospital and at home would entail a lengthy preliminary study to devise methods of reliably estimating this elusive concept. At a more practical level, we had hoped to include a comparative cost-benefit analysis of the community and a control service, but the process of costing the various community facilities, for which no separate accounts were available, and the difficulties of balancing the savings to the Health Service against the increased cost to the social services were beyond our actuarial competence.

Because evaluative research is expensive and time consuming, the temptation is to attempt too much and include too many aims, and this can be self-defeating. Moreover, a research design that is appropriate to settling one question will not necessarily be suited to one of another kind. Thus the matter of priorities in relation to one's resources in research workers and time can be troublesome.

With these uncertainties and vexations in mind, Dr. Morissey and I undertook a pilot study to see if evaluating some aspects of the service, at least, was a practicable proposition (Morissey and Sainsbury, 1959). In particular, we tried to determine whether it was possible: (1) to undertake a retrospective before-and-after study using hospital records; (2) to demonstrate an effect of the community service on the referral and admission rates of various clinical and social categories of patients; and (3) to describe their attributes that related to admission after its introduction. The hospital notes proved to be a reliable source of information only for those items which it is mandatory to record; age, sex, address, marital status, diagnosis, previous admission, dates of admission and discharge, deaths, suicide, and so on. Nevertheless, it was possible to show there had been a significant increase in the rate of referral of patients (+10%), and a decrease in admissions (-51%) during the first year of the service. The decrease in admissions was greater in some groups than others: males, the married, those living near the day hospital, the well-to-do, and patients with affective and neurotic disorders. But more unexpectedly, the duration of stay of admitted patients in 1958 had not appreciably increased when compared with the preceding year.

We concluded that a before-and-after study would only be feasible if it were planned before the start of the new service so that precise and uniform base line information could be obtained and compared with similar data following its introduction; that the operation of a new service during its first year is probably not typical; and that preferably a year or two should be allowed for the organization of the service and the new roles of the personnel to take shape before assessing its efficiency. But more important from the viewpoint of our program, we had shown that the effects of the new service were pronounced and that the effects on patients with differing characteristics could be readily identified. A detailed study would therefore be both worthwhile and possible. We concluded that, in this instance, the preferred design would be a comparison between the Chichester Community Service and another psychiatric service not planned on community lines.

It has been said often, but it bears repeating, that pilot studies to test the limitations of a particular design, the procedural practicability and the reliability of the proposed methods for measuring differences are necessary preliminaries to any large-scale evaluation; it is impossible to anticipate all the obstacles that will be encountered, and only a trial run round the course will reveal those that are insurmountable.

## PLANNING THE EVALUATION

In planning our project, and the same can be said of evaluation studies in general, we used two familiar research strategies: those of an epidemiological survey, and those of the controlled clinical trial in which services instead of drugs are the main independent variables. Nevertheless, each posed very difficult problems of a methodological and organizational kind. To begin with, some questions, notably those posed in the first two aims, can be answered using epidemiological measures, but to do so requires a *comparison* (or control) service. Choosing a service that was suitable, and whose personnel were willing to perform this function, was perhaps the most trying decision we had to make.

Second, to fulfill the epidemiological needs of the research, *every* patient referred to the psychiatrist from two defined populations (the community care and control districts) had to be identified, and uniform information recorded on each of them. Furthermore, selecting and defining the items or variables to describe the patients and the services they received, which were most relevant to the purposes of the research, was another exacting task.

Third, valid criteria had to be devised to measure the effects and effectiveness of the service. Many of our criteria were epidemiological indices, for example, rates of referral, admission rates, duration of stay or contacts with the various facilities, and so on. But few generally accepted standards or norms were available for assessing other aspects of the effectiveness of the service, so we had to devise and test new instruments to measure effects on the family and their needs, and to assess outcome in terms of relief of family burden or social competence.

## THE COMPARISON OR CONTROL SERVICE

The first alternative we considered was a before-and-after design, but for the reasons already discussed, this was impracticable: a study of that kind needs to be planned prospectively. In many situations this would be the requisite approach, for instance, when evaluating the effects of introducing an additional facility to a service or when undertaking an on-going evaluation of changes over long periods of time. Ideally, one would try to obtain reliable base-line data on all those indices in which changes were expected.

The evaluator would like to be able to have the best of both worlds: first to obtain base-line information on the district services and then, at a later date, begin a comparative research in which an untried policy is introduced in one half, while the other perseveres with the previous one. We have recently been fortunate in being able to use such a plan in an evaluation in Southhampton of the DHSS's current policy of basing psychiatric services on units in the District General Hospital (DGH) and providing places in day centers or other accommodation in the community in collaboration with the local social and welfare services. A case register has been set up which will provide the basic statistics needed to describe the current operation of the City's services. Then, in 1975 the City will be divided into two; the services of one half will be provided by the DGH and social services department without recourse to a mental hospital, while the mental health needs of the other half will be met by the local mental hospital and its extramural services.

The final decision to investigate the advantages and disadvantages of the Chichester service was made in 1959, the year after it started, so only retrospective base-line comparisons were possible. But as certain information on patients is required for statutory returns and as this is accurately registered, we were able to report findings on admission trends, discharge, readmission, length of stay, mortality, and suicide by comparing rates before and following the introduction of the service. This before-and-after approach can best be illustrated by reference to suicide.

## Suicide Before and After the Introduction of Community Care

A criterion on which an evaluation of any service fostering extramural care should be assessed is its effects on the incidence of suicide in patients in contact with the service, and on the suicide rate of the population of the service district. Critics of community care often refer to an increased risk of suicide, but a service that claims to reduce morbidity by extending services to more people should be capable of identifying and alleviating the suicidal. The hospital records and those of the coroner are a reliable source of data on suicides as they must be documented.

Dr. Walk (1967) and I examined the incidence of suicide of different populations in Chichester in the five-year period (1952-1956) before the service started and again following its introduction (1959-1963). First we calculated the rate in patients resident in the hospitals. An open-door policy that allows patients freedom to come and go as they wish and the selective admission of the more seriously disturbed and socially disadvantaged patients might have been expected to increase the likelihood of suicide; but we found an identical rate in the two periods. It would seem that the morale in the hospital had not been impaired by diverting staff to work in the community. On the contrary, it appears that when patients have less need to kick against the bricks, suicide is resorted to less often. Another study comparing the national figures for suicide among patients in the era prior to the NHS, after it became established, and following the Mental Health Act shows a significant decrease in patient suicides with increasingly liberal attitudes and less alienation from the community (Sainsbury, 1972).

Second, the suicide rates in the population of the Chichester district were compared in the two periods. When allowance was made for the national trend, there was a small decrease, but this was not greater than chance might have accounted for. Third, the introduction of community care had not been accompanied by an increase in the suicide rate of patients known to the service psychiatrists. (The denominator for the rates was calculated from a census of patients in contact with the service during the two mid-years 1954 and 1961.) We had predicted that, if a community service was successful in preventing suicide, there would be a decrease in the number of suicides of patients known to it. This hypothesis was supported in the case of the elderly patients in whom a significant decrease was found and tended to confirm a conclusion drawn from other findings, namely that the elderly were the members of the community who were benefiting most from the community services.

## A Comparison Between Services

A second possible design open to us was to compare the Chichester service with the more customary hospital-based one in which the only community facilities were the usual outpatient clinics in the local hospitals and consultative domiciliary visits when requested by the general practitioner. The most obvious choice was to compare Chichester with the remaining sector of the Graylingwell catchment area, the Horsham district, where the community program had not yet been introduced. However, the psychiatric team there had already been contaminated by what was happening in the adjoining districts, and they were improvising a modified community program.

The only other alternative was to prevail upon one of the hospitals in an adjoining county to accept the invidious role of being labeled the "traditional," "conservative," or "conventional" service. As it happened, the Medical Superintendent of the Old Manor, Salisbury, was very justifiably proud of the service his hospital gave to the City and its extensive rural hinterland, and had no reason to wish to change it. But he was also satisfied with our attitude toward the evaluation. He recognized that we were not only independent, but also had no preconceived notions that the community service heralded a new era of psychiatry. On the contrary, we had considerable uncertainties as to the likely benefits and banes. Indeed, by this time we had abandoned the simplistic view that an evaluation would label one service as "better" than another; instead, we hoped we might be able to say something about the needs of different types of patients, those whose requirements could best be met by admission to an "asylum" and the skilled management the mental hospital provides, and those who could best be treated at home or in a community facility.

The gratifying consequence was that Dr. Simpson and his staff collaborated unstintingly in the comparative evaluation. The Salisbury service, it should be added, was hospital-based, the majority of patients being directly referred to the hospital by their general practitioners, though the hospital psychiatrist offered domiciliary consultations and held outpatient clinics in Salisbury and the outlying towns. Availability was necessarily the prime consideration in choosing the control service; but it could not have been more apposite: it was tailored to our requirements.

## Similarities and Differences Between the Experimental and Control Services

Salisbury is a near replica of Chichester, geographically and demographically. Both are relatively prosperous county towns surrounded by farmlands on chalk downs. The only obvious demographic difference was the higher proportion of elderly people who had retired to the Sussex coast, not in itself a drawback as the findings were to be expressed as age and sex specific rates. The population of the district was 121,000, about the same as that of Chichester. The material and economic resources of the two services and their quota of beds, personnel, and general practitioners were the same; the only rather paradoxical difference was that the Old Manor hospital had an extra social worker and a more methodically organized psychiatric social work department. Last, in neither area were there any psychiatrists in private practice, we found that general practitioners referred very few patients to psychiatrists in London or elsewhere. Consequently all the mentally ill in both populations needing psychiatric advice were referred exclusively to their respective services. The comparison between the districts and the interpretation of our findings was made more manageable because of these close social similarities, a valuable ingredient of a comparative study such as this.

If a total district service is being evaluated, the ideal procedure of randomly allocating patients to the evaluation group and a comparison group is out of the question; but this procedure is ethical, practicable, and preferable when a new facility has been set up *within* a service to take care of a particular category of patients. Randomly allocated or stratified samples of matched patients are then assessed on the relevant measures under the new and old conditions. It might, for example, be the best way of comparing the quality of care of elderly dements in sheltered accommodation and in the mental hospital. The reason we made no attempt to do this was because manipulations of this kind would have meant tampering with the operation of the service under normal working conditions, the matter we were primarily committed to looking at: a design that would have been the most suitable to investigate one of the service's amenities would have conflicted with that which was appropriate to our other goals.

The final plan of the study, therefore, was first to compare the social and clinical characteristics of all patients referred during at least one year to the community service. As the catchment areas of each service was an administrative district for which a census of the population was available, we could obtain rates of referral, admission, discharge, and so on; and the specific rates of the different demographic and social categories could also be compared. Second, random samples of all referrals to each service were selected and their households circumstances compared in detail by interviewing the responsible relative to elicit the demands made by the patient on the family, and their needs. The samples were then followed through two years to assess their subsequent contacts with the service, their effects on their families, and their clinical outcome.


## COLLECTION OF DATA

The decisions that had to be made were: (1) determining the criteria for including cases in the evaluation; (2) selecting and defining the essential social and clinical information needed on each case in order to realize our aims; (3) ensuring that this data was reliable and uniformly recorded on all the cases in both services. In practice, the last presented the greatest problems because it was dependent upon the willing cooperation of one's colleagues and efficient machinery for checking that all the records were available in the required format.

### 1. Definition of a Case

We aimed to include all new patients referred to the psychiatrists for whatever reason and from whatever source, the principal ones being the family doctor, the social agencies, and the physicians in the general hospital. In defining a "new" patient, we wanted to include as many psychiatric referrals as possible, while at the same time being in a position to compare our data with that available from other workers; but they were confined to studies on first referrals. Consequently, we defined a new case as someone who had not seen a psychiatrist for the preceding six months. In retrospect this was not entirely satisfactory. The better plan would have been first to undertake a census of all patients from the two districts who were in contact with their respective services. The "new" patients could then have been separated out for some analysis, while the effects of the service on patients who had been discharged from the hospital after two or more years, and on the chronically handicapped who were already receiving long-term support as outpatients, could have been more closely studied.

## 2. Selecting and Defining the Variables

The psychiatrists at Graylingwell and the Old Manor agreed to complete the coded clinical information sheet we had prepared (the item sheet) instead of the pages in the hospital case folders they ordinarily used. In this way they were able to record some 80 items of information in a form which would allow most items to be directly transferred to punch cards without adding appreciably to the time needed to take their routine case history. Thus, they recorded duration of illness by ticking one of the categories into which we had divided this item; the composition of the patient's household, his work history, symptoms, and so on were similarly dealt with.

The item sheet included notes defining the categories, explaining procedures for classifying diagnosis (the I.C.D.) and previous history, clarifying ambiguous points, and dealing with omissions or other difficulties. Two clerks trained for the purpose daily registered all admissions, patients referred to clinics and the day hospital, outpatients, and those seen at the general hospital and in their homes. They were also responsible for collecting copies of the item sheets and arranging for omissions to be entered.

The selection of clinical items did not present undue difficulties, though they were limited to basic essentials; in a busy clinic the psychiatrist will not always want to take a full history. However, we did need more social and family background data than customary, and choosing these meant keeping our goals in very clear focus. The problem of selecting them is closely tied up with that of designing this type of inquiry.

Random allocation of cases to the two services was out of the question (q.v.), though it would have controlled many confounding variables. Instead we (the evaluators) needed to have sufficient data on those variables, such as severity of symptoms, social class, or any others, on which the two services might not be balanced and which might be accounting for the differences found between them to enable us to partial out their effects when comparing the services. And predicting those that were most likely to be troublesome is far from easy. They also had to be kept to a minimum, not only because there was a limit to what we could expect the psychiatrist to record, but because the data were already extensive and the analysis was in danger of becoming too unwieldy.

## 3. The Case Register

The systematic recording of uniform information on all referrals meant, in effect, setting up two *case registers,* one for each service, an indispensable tool for collecting the routine descriptive statistics of a service. A case register enables basic identifying, personal, social, and clinical data to be obtained in a standardized form and avoids duplication of cases. Such a procedure is especially valuable where patients are in contact with a variety of facilities: hospitals, hostels, social work services, and domiciliary visits, for example. A case register also allows details of a subsequent event and contacts with the different amenities within the service to be accumulated on each case, or whatever other information might be appropriate to the aims of the evaluation such as his welfare needs, or cost, or failed appointments.

We availed ourselves of many of these advantages. But an additional gain, and one crucial to our plan, is that a case register provides a sampling frame. Accordingly the evaluator can, on the one hand, construct stratified samples of matched patients with specific characteristics, such as he would need if he wanted to compare hospital and domiciliary care of chronic schizophrenics. On the other hand, he may need to draw a random sample of the referrals; and this was true of us. To assess the effects on the family of having a mentally ill member at home, the social needs of the family members, their social circumstances and attitudes toward mental hospital or home care, we decided to visit the homes of an approximately 1-in-3 sample and interview the responsible relative or head of the household. The two cohorts were then followed up for two years: the families' burdens were assessed a second time, the extent to which their needs had been met was scored, and a number of measures of outcome were made. The attitudes of their general practitioners and their families to the respective services were also estimated at this point. The definitions of the criteria for evaluating these effects and the indices used are considered in a later section.

## 4. The Reliability of the Case Register Data

The agreement between psychiatrists on the variables recorded in the coded item sheet was assessed by having two psychiatrists independently examine the first 90 patients. The service psychiatrist saw the patient first, then 48 hours later one or other of two psychiatrists from the research unit also interviewed the patient under the same conditions, that is either at home with relatives or in the outpatient department or in the hospital, allowing the amount of time a busy consultant usually takes. The results showed, for example, that agreement on broad diagnostic categories was 79%; but for organic illness in the elderly, it was 85%; for the functional disorders, 71%; but for neuroses, only 52%. Agreement on a history of previous illness was quite high (68%); on duration of illness, 58%; and on family history of mental illness, 87%. Symptoms of depression and organic disorder also had a high reliability, but symptoms of schizophrenia and neurosis, for example, thought disorder and obsessional ideas, had a low reliability (Kreitman, et al., 1961).

## CRITERIA OF THE EVALUATION: INDICES AND MEASURES

Crucial to any evaluative study of services are the standards by which the new service is to be measured; and what they should be will depend on having clearly defined the objectives of the service and the specific aims of the research. These standards may be set out in terms of the community's needs, the needs of the patients and their households, cost-efficiency, the quality of services, acceptance of and satisfaction with services by users and staff, clinical and social outcome, that is reduction in morbidity (especially by prevention); and so on. Some of the indices and measures we used are discussed next.

## 1. Epidemiological Indices

The first step was to delimit the target population; this, of course, will depend on which objective is under consideration. To realize our first two aims (to see who gets referred and who gets admitted and who gets discharged following the introduction of a community service), the relevant populations were those of the two districts. The national census gives a breakdown by age, sex, class, household composition, and other demographic and social variables, thereby furnishing the denominators for calculating epidemiological indices for specific categories of patients, such as their rates of referral to the services, admission to hospital, discharge, duration of stay, contact with day hospitals, outpatient attendances, and domiciliary visits. The data on the case register provided the numerators for these rates and for further breakdowns by diagnosis, duration of illness, and so on. The registers supplied the denominator for a number of other indices: the proportion of patients with certain social, familial, or clinical characteristics who were admitted; the proportion who were treated in the extramural facilities; and their relative durations of stay and numbers of contacts they made with the extramural services.

Illustrations of the information of this kind that we sought were the number of day hospital attendances made by depressives and schizophrenics, the proportion of people over 65 treated at home and in hospital in the two services, the number of times the psychiatrist visited them in the community service, and the number of contacts the social workers made with various categories of patients in both services.

Combinations of the different measures enabled us to estimate the bed needs per 1,000 population in a service that restricted admissions, that is, the total number of patient/weeks in hospital as a function of the referral rate; the number of beds needed for elderly dementias; the proportion of patients becoming long-stay, and the bed needs for new long-stay patients.

Clearly some criteria are more easily measured than others, and for many no generally accepted standards or norms are available. But whichever aspects are being assessed, the indices or measures used must be precisely defined, relevant to the objectives, and reliable. And this may entail designing and pretesting new instruments to measure the effects of the services.

## 2. Measures of Burden on the Family

The problem can be illustrated by reference to a major aim of our evaluation, namely, to assess the burden on the family of having a mentally ill member at home. Our criteria were the effects on simple, uncontroversial, and objectively definable aspects of family life—those activities that could be reliably rated—such as members having to stay away from work, reduction in family income, and the health of the informant (the responsible relative). Accordingly, a questionnaire was constructed on which these and other pertinent items could be rated as having "no," "some," or a "severe" effect. There are no norms of family burden, but our objective of ascertaining whether family burden was increased in a community service could be achieved by comparing the scores of the families in Chichester and Salisbury at the point when the patient was first referred, when the differences might be expected to be negligible, and again after a decision whether to keep the patient at home or admit him had been taken, when any adverse effects should be measurable. The family burden scores also gave one estimate of the *social cost* to the community of extramural care.

Similarly, the needs of the family and the extent to which these were being met was reckoned by the research social workers marking a checklist of needs at their first visit, then recording social work visits made in each service during two years, and at the end of that time seeing which of the listed needs had been met.

## 3. Outcome Measures

Measuring clinical and social outcome was a particularly intricate matter, and many indices were used. The clinical measures were: (a) mortality rates, (b) the service psychiatrists' ratings of improvement or deterioration at follow up or at the time of discharge, and (c) two of the research psychiatrists' ratings of outcome at the two-year follow-up obtained by comparing their current symptoms with those reported on the item sheet when the patient was first referred. Next, we used combined measures of outcome and consumer satisfaction: (a) a self-rating of improvement made by the patient, (b) an improvement rating by the responsible relative or informant, and lastly, (c) another by the general practitioner.

Measures of improvement that were independent of clinical symptoms were obtained from the change in the effects-on-the-family scores and by the reduction in family problems scores at the end of the two years compared with those at referral; we called these indices *relief of burden.* The idea was that the more disturbed the patient, the greater would be his effects on his family; therefore, a reduction in burden would be a measure of his improvement.

### Outcome and Improvement

We were faced with two problems: one was making the distinction between measuring "outcome" and measuring "improvement" in a before-and-after comparison; the other was how to deal with assessing outcome when we had some ten separate indices of it.

Dr. A. B. Levey, the unit's psychologist, formulated the problems and suggested the following solutions (Levey, 1971). Suppose four patients, A, B, C, and D, had the symptom ratings MI, a low score representing low distress at referral R, and the ratings M2 at follow-up F (see Table 6.1), then the distinction between "improvement" and "outcome" becomes apparent: patient B has improved by 1 scale point while A has not improved at all (see column 3); yet on clinical and theoretical grounds, we would not wish to say that the "unimproved" patient had a poorer "outcome" in terms of either health or response to treatment. A similar argument applies to patients C and D, and again we would not wish to equate the two patients.

TABLE 6.1

| Subject | (1)<br>M1<br>(R) | (2)<br>M2<br>(F) | (3)<br>"Improvement,"<br>i.e.,<br>Difference (D)<br>(D = F - R) | (4)<br>(0)* | (5)<br>Outcome |
|---|---|---|---|---|---|
| A | 1 | 1 | 0 | 2 | second best |
| B | 2 | 1 | -1 | 1 | best |
| C | 1 | 2 | +1 | 5 | worst |
| D | 2 | 2 | 0 | 4 | second worst |

The table shows another anomaly: patients A and D are equal in degree of improvement, but opposite in clinical outcome. Apparently we were not sufficiently precise in defining what we wanted to measure when we chose to evaluate clinical response to community care.

## Measurement of Improvement

Dr. Levey suggested that the term "improvement" can be applied to any satisfactory measure of *change* in status between sessions when either eliminating, ignoring, or equating starting level. And that "outcome" might be appropriately reserved for measures which represent overall *status* on two or more occasions, including the contribution of starting level as part of the score. Four distinct post-treatment (or care) categories can now be recognized: (1) *clinical status,* or how well is the patient after treatment; (2) *improvement* (difference), or how much better is the patient after treatment; (3) *base-free* improvement (ratio or covariance) or how much better is the patient by comparison with others who started at the same level; (4) *outcome,* or how well is the patient before and after treatment.

*Measurement of outcome,* unlike improvement, is a problem that has not previously been formulated as far as I am aware. The problem stems from a situation, often crucial to clinical studies, in which patients at the top (or bottom) of the scale have no room to improve (or worsen). A scale that seems to solve the problem is described mathematically by the following formulas for two occasions and two items:

$$O = M1 + M2 + 2(M2 - M1)$$

where O = outcome,
M1 = score on referral,
M2 = score on follow up.
Application of the scale to the previous example yields the results shown in the last two columns of Table 6.1.

Inspection of the table shows it provides a clinically meaningful ranking of something we call "outcome." The scale also has the properties of expanding the number of scale points and hence the discriminating power of items; outcome is a combined function of starting level and improvement; and in its final form the scale would be additive across several pairs of items and so provide an outcome "score" when several variables are used. And this also contributed to solving our second problem mentioned at the outset of this discussion.

When we correlated a number of the indices of outcome, they appeared to arrange themselves in clusters. The first group comprised the service psychiatrists', the independent psychiatrists', and the patients' ratings. All correlated quite highly with one another, as also did the ratings of the second group, general practitioners and the family; but the correlations between the two groups were much lower. We therefore postulated that dimensions of outcome—perhaps a clinical factor, a family, and social one—might be identified. A cluster analysis was attempted but proved technically unworkable. Our data collecting was not planned with this in mind, nor could the method cope with missing data; not surprisingly, there were many instances of this with ten indices of outcome.

## Indices of Efficiency of the Service

I have already indicated that a full cost-benefit analysis was not practicable, but one measure of efficiency Dr. Grad de Alarcon used was to assess the adequacy of the extramural facilities in meeting their goal of reducing morbidity in terms of manpower and the time the patient spent in contact with services. The number of days in hospital and the number of contacts by patients at the day hospital, as outpatients, and by home visits needed to obtain a rating of much improved or recovered were computed. Using this technique valid comparisons between services were possible for patients in diagnostic categories whose reliability had been found to be high, and who could be matched on severity of illness (Kreitman et al., 1961: 41); the affective disorders and dementias in the elderly met these requirements best.

## Quality and Acceptability of Services

These were not included among the major objectives of the project; nevertheless, some measures of satisfaction with the services were possible. On the one hand, the general practitioners were asked to rate whether each of their patients treated in the community had involved them in more work, and also whether they were satisfied with the service provided. And on the other, the responsible member of the patients' households rated their attitudes (on a scale of 11 items) toward the patient's receiving his treatment at home or being admitted and their satisfaction with the disposal recommended.

## The Reliability and Validity of the Indices

Dr. Grad de Alarcon's assessments of the agreement between the three psychiatric social workers on the interviewing schedule were of interest as at that time few, if any, had attempted to examine the reliability with which social workers record their information (Grad, 1964).

The family interview schedule, from which a number of indices were obtained, contained 72 items, including: the effects on the family (13 items); descriptions of the patient's behavior the family found most worrying (11 items); ratings of attitudes (11 items); ratings of health of the informant, including a short test of neuroticism (2 items); assessments of family circumstances and quality of housing (8 items); list of family needs; and 27 factual items regarding composition of the household, patient's employment, and demographic details (Sainsbury and Grad, 1962). The number of items and hence, the duration of the interview, were deliberately restricted because reliability decreases when too much information is sought.

The relative merits of *an unstructured or structured interview* were also considered. Grad (1964), commenting on family interviewing, has pointed out that, whereas the structured list of questions is more reliable and less subject to interviewer bias, the unstructured interview conducted by an experienced psychiatric social worker is more valid, because the interviewer is given opportunities to judge the situation, establish rapport, and get information as best he can. In this study she combined these two methods by using a partly structured interview which allowed freedom to follow the main topics in a way appropriate to the situation, yet demanded systematic completion of the categorized items. So the responder is guided to each of the main topics (indices) until interviewer has enough information to complete the relevant items.

In the interest of both validity and reliability, we only included items that could be objectively defined. For example, one of the items for assessing the effects on the family was the effect on their income of having the patient at home. This was rated as having "no effect" if the total loss of income had decreased by less than 10%; a decrease of 10% to 50% was rated "some effect"; and a decrease of more than 50% was rated a "severe effect." Where no objective criteria were available, ratings were based on a description of patient's behavior and on concrete examples of its effect on the family. Anchoring examples and definitions for rating were given in an instruction book.

The *reliability* of the schedule was examined by the three psychiatric social workers visiting thirty consecutive families in pairs, the interviews being randomly distributed between the two districts. They were so conducted that one of them interviewed while the other observed, their roles being reversed on the next occasion. Immediately following the visit, each separately made his ratings. As there were three possible pairs, each pair interviewed ten cases together. Their level of agreement was greater than 75% for all 72 items, and above 85% for 63 of them. The causes of disagreement were discussed and found to be due in most instances to inadequate definitions for rating replies; these were then modified.

Ensuring the *validity* of this kind of material is a problem that cannot be wholly solved, but it may be helped by concentrating on "hard" data, by defining items operationally, and by using independent measures of the same item. For example, we categorized "educational status" by both school-leaving age and by type of schooling received; "social status" by income as well as by occupational category; and "social outcome" by amount of employment obtained and by the change in the rating of the burden the illness had caused the family during two years. The correlated scores then provide a measure of the validity of the variable.

We used this technique to assess *severity of illness,* one of the most salient clinical measures, because if the referrals to the two services were clinically comparable, interpretation of the findings would be greatly simplified.

Severity of illness was described in two ways. First we ranked the frequency with which the twenty-eight symptoms on the "item sheet" were recorded in each service. They ranged from such disabling symptoms as delusions and aggression to milder ones such as loss of concentration and insomnia. The high rank correlation (0.88) between the services implied a clinical similarity in the cases referred. Second, severity was measured by the effects the illness had had on the family at the time the patient was referred. This measure seemed as one especially appropriate to an inquiry intended to assess community care; but it also gave us an index of severity independent of the clinical assessments. When a number of effects on the family of a random sample of referrals were added to give a "family problem" score (see Table 6.5), very little difference was again found between the services.

Finally, the patients referred from the two populations were also well matched on nearly all the most relevant demographic, social, and clinical variables. The one respect in which they differed was in the higher proportion of elderly women seen in Chichester. Although this difference does not reach statistical significance, its effects are evident in the slightly higher proportion of widows and retired housewives in the community service, so it has to be allowed for by analyzing our data for the age groups 15 to 64 and 65 and over separately.

Except for a higher proportion than expected of males with neuroses in Salisbury, there were no differences in broad diagnostic categories referred to the two services; and the incidence of previous illnesses was the same. We concluded that although more patients per 1,000 of the population were referred in Chichester, they were clinically very similar to those in Salisbury, and that the higher total rate in the community was not primarily due to more patients in any one category being seen. Such minor differences as were found suggest that the latter was recruiting more elderly patients with organic disorders and fewer neurotics.

In relying on a retrospective analysis of matching, we have been lucky, especially as regards severity of illness; but a comparison of the census characteristics of the two populations and of the medical amenities available to each at the start of the project made it unlikely that the prevalence of mental disorder in the two areas would be different. Nevertheless, our critics find it hard to accept, on the one hand that the community service had a higher overall referral rate than the hospital-based one, and on the other, that the rates for psychoses (functional and organic) were also higher, whereas those for neuroses were the same (Grad and Sainsbury, 1966). They expected, as we did, that extending services would increase the referral rate of minor disorders. Instead, however, the new service appears to be mopping up severe mental illness in old people who were previously overlooked or who were cared for by the general practitioner—only too aware that the hospital would again be unable to find another bed.

### Interviewing in an Evaluative Survey

Drawing on her experience in this project and in another evaluative study of services on the needs of families of the mentally handicapped, Dr. Grad de Alarcon, with Dr. Cocetti ("Interviewing in Psychiatric Field Surveys," in press), has recently given a detailed account of the technique, obstacles, and snares of interviewing informants in their homes. It must suffice here simply to list some attributes of the competent interviewer and the skills she must be able to exercise if she is to complete an assignment and meet acceptable standards of reliability. They are: acquiring familiarity with the questionnaire and interviewing instructions so that it can be used with ease; finding the designated respondent and noting any difficulties in locating the household so that visits by others in the team will be made easier; gaining access to the informant, introducing herself, and gaining cooperation to conduct the interview; explaining the purpose of the interview without biasing the responses; establishing the required setting of the interview, for example, free from interference by other household members; getting the respondent to feel at ease and controlling the interview so that it follows previously determined lines as far as possible; avoiding extraneous topics so as not to waste time while not restricting the information the respondent may have to offer; recording the answers as instructed; checking the questionnaire before leaving to make sure all points have been sufficiently covered, and then editing it as soon as possible; and leaving the respondent in such a frame of mind that any further follow-up interviews will still be acceptable to him. Each of these and other topics are accompanied by useful and commonsense advice about how they may be dealt with.

## ANALYSIS OF THE DATA

### 1. Refusals

Refusals were the first complication. The clinical data provided by the psychiatrists were more often a problem of omission of items rather than one of refusal to give any information, though an occasional patient needed to remain anonymous; however, they were too few to affect our results. Nevertheless, questions of confidentiality could have been irksome. And they can only be circumvented by the mutual trust that comes from a close association with one's colleagues, scrupulousness in filing and safeguarding records, and restricting access to the research team only.

But refusal by the patient's family to be interviewed was a more serious potential source of error. Also social workers or doctors tended more often to be cautious lest the research visit should disturb a delicate situation; understandable attitudes must be anticipated the forestalled by carefully planning the approach to the families, and to one's colleagues, so that they appreciate the research worker's needs and his ability to manage the patients or their relatives skillfully. In this study 1% of families refused.

To deal with the problem of missing data and refusals, we first ensured that all cases were retained in the study and followed up. Second, as a certain amount of basic data was always obtainable from the social workers, doctors, and other sources, the recorded characteristics of the refusals were compared with those who were visited to see if there were differences which were likely to have introduced a bias. Third, in a number of cases with missing data, it was possible to make a "best guess" on the basis of the rest of the data (e.g., May, 1968).

## 2. Analysis

We planned to analyze our data on IBM cards using a counter-sorter, and even though we had not foreseen the complexity of the possible interaction, we came to regret not having adhered to this plan. Not only would we have retained that intimacy with the data which, to me at least, seems to be the way to get the best from it, but would have avoided the endless dislocations which followed transferring to a computer. The Atlas, then a prototype, was the first computer with a sufficient store to accommodate a survey in which many variates were used. Moreover the very first program for social surveys was nearing completion, and it was decided that our data would serve to introduce the computer to a program of this kind; but they never fully came to terms with one another. Only after a very long delay, when the data and revised program were put on a later version of the computer, were we able to obtain the outputs we requested; and then only to a limited extent—a misfortune from which we never wholly recovered, so that many of the interactions originally included on our program have never become available.

## EVALUATION OF SERVICES AND SUICIDE PREVENTION

The effects of services on the incidence of suicide offers an objective, if crude, measure of their effectiveness; but also a pertinent one, as a major aim of services evaluation is to inquire whether they are capable of decreasing morbidity (or mortality) by prevention. Contrary to the arguments of some writers on the subject, suicide is reported with sufficient accuracy to enable us to make valid comparisons between the rates of clinical, social, and demographic groups (Sainsbury, 1973).

A number of observations by Dr. Barraclough and other colleagues at my unit pointed to the likelihood that improvements in the standards of psychiatric and medical services could reduce the incidence of suicide. These studies will be briefly outlined to illustrate various applications of the epidemiological approach to evaluative research.

1. Evidence that improved services may reduce the incidence in suicide were obtained when we undertook a seven-year follow-up of the 558 depressed patients referred to the Chichester and Salisbury services; all but three of them were traced (Thompson, 1970). Ten percent of deaths had been by suicide, a figure well below the 15% found in previous follow-up studies of depressed patients (Sainsbury, 1968). In the period 1961 to 1968, the extended and community oriented services fostered by the Mental Health Act were being implemented, and a possible interpretation of the study could be that this is a factor contributing to the recent fall in our national rate of suicide.

The Salisbury suicide rate was considerably higher than the Chichester Community Service one. The implications both of the observed number of suicides being less than expected (12 as against 20) and of the comparison between the services are that extending services may reduce mortality.

2. Barraclough and Shae (1970) were interested in studying the effectiveness of

a lay service, the Samaritans, in meeting the needs of the suicidal and in preventing suicide. They identified all suicides recorded by the coroner in a number of districts having Samaritan services and sought their names on the Samaritan registers. Four percent of suicides had been known to them, and from this it was possible to estimate the suicide rate of their clients. It was 375/100,000 which, of course, is very high; moreover, 44% of the suicides had died within a month of contact. These figures are very similar to those found by following up depressives known to the psychiatric services—306/100,000 (Thompson, 1970)—and agree with the known tendency for depressives to kill themselves in the months immediately following discharge from hospital.

Incidentally, the best predictors of suicide among the Samaritan clients were a previous history of psychiatric disorders and previous contact with other medical and social agencies. So those with a predisposition to psychiatric illnesses appear to be most at risk, but neither lay nor medical services are adept at recognizing them.

3. This last point was nicely elucidated in another project (Barraclough et al., in press; Barraclough, 1972a), one of the main objectives of which was to assess the suicide's contacts with the medical and other services in the months preceding his death and the standards of care he received. The other aims were to evaluate the suicide's psychiatric and medical status, his social circumstances and life stresses at that time. It was hoped to derive from these data some indications as to whether it was practicable to prevent at least a proportion of suicides by action on the part of the medical and other services.

The design of the evaluation differed in many respects from the comparison between Chichester and Salisbury. In the first place it was retrospective, and in the second it combined both the epidemiological and case-study approaches (Sainsbury, 1972). The homes of 100 consecutive suicides in West Sussex and Portsmouth and a random sample of 150 normal controls, matched on age and sex and drawn from general practitioners' registers (everyone in England registers with a general practitioner), were visited soon after the event. The suicide's relatives, friends, and general practitioner were interviewed; and a questionnaire of categorized items covering the suicide's (and control's) medical and psychiatric history, recent stresses such as bereavement or moving, his social circumstances, especially his ties with his domestic, occupational, and religious group, and the nature and extent of his contacts with services was completed.

The findings pertinent to services and prevention were these: (1) 93% of the suicides had a mental illness independently identified by a panel of psychiatrists, and of these 72% were diagnosed as suffering from a treatable depression (80% if the alcoholics with an affective disorder are included). The salient finding, then, was that the majority of suicides had an easily recognizable illness, and one that responds to modern methods of treatment. (2) Furthermore, a quarter of the suicides had a confirmed history of frequently recurring depression, a form of the illness in which lithium carbonate has been shown to prevent relapses. When Barraclough (1972b) next applied to the suicides the criteria for entry to the trial of lithium reported by Coppen and others (1971), he was able to calculate (using the success rate in preventing relapse obtained in the trial) that 25% of the suicides would have been prevented if those with recurrent depressions had been similarly treated.

The above observations inevitably led us to inquire into the details of what services the depressed and the other suicides had in fact received, and how they were treated by the medical services.

It then emerged that 40% of the suicides had visited their general practitioner in the week (75% in the month) prior to death. These general practitioners recognized their patients' emotional disturbance as 80% were prescribed tranquilizers (63% barbiturates); but only 8 of the 72 uncomplicated depressives were given anti-depressants in inadequate doses (Barraclough et al., 1971). Moreover, over half the suicides had died of poisoning by drugs, 35 depressives taking barbiturates; and of the 17 suicides in whom the act was categorized "impulsive," 15 took barbiturates recently prescribed by their general practitioners.

These findings on contact with medical services and on the suicides' management in terms of diagnosis and treatment strongly imply that, were the medical practitioners better trained in recognizing depressed patients, especially those with an added risk for suicide because of their social circumstances, such as the elderly and bereaved who live alone—some of the characteristics on which suicides differed very markedly from the controls—they could effectively contribute toward the prevention of suicide.

## APPLICATION OF THE RESULTS OF THE EVALUATION

The results of our evaluation clearly had some influence on the later development of the Chichester service, and more particularly on planning services when the Horsham and Crawley district also introduced a community care service in 1963 in the remaining third of Graylingwell's catchment area. No formal meetings were held to discuss the future plans of the services jointly with the research unit; but our close daily contact with the hospital personnel and the responsible senior psychiatrists, and our presence at the monthly meetings of the psychiatric division, through which the psychiatrists' views are conveyed to the administrators of the Hospital Group, were the channels whereby conclusions drawn from the research affected policy.

I will outline the main findings of the comparison between Chichester and Salisbury to illustrate their practical applications. One is the contribution they have made toward planning the objectives of our current evaluative research into the Department of Health and Social Security's new policy of phasing out the mental hospital and making psychiatric units in the district general hospital, in collaboration with the Social Services' Department of the local authority, the pivot of the new psychiatric services. And the other is how the findings bear upon some of the more questionable assumptions of the Department's plans.

The goals of the Chichester psychiatric services were very similar to those now proposed by the Department, namely, to provide for the care of the mentally ill in the local community or in their usual domestic or neighborhood setting as far as possible; and to do so in order to keep admissions to hospital and duration of stay there to a minimum. Indeed, the Department has been more precise in stipulating the beds and places in the community needed to achieve this, a target never defined in Chichester. The guidelines now proposed are: (1) for the adult mentally ill, excluding the dementias of old age, 0.5 beds and 0.65 day places per 1,000 total population; (2) for the elderly patients with severe dementia, but not suffering from other significant physical illness, 2.5 to 3 beds and 2 to 3 places per 1,000 population aged 65 and over; (3) for elderly patients with dementia, whether mild or severe, who are also suffering from physical illness, 10 beds and 2 places per 1,000 population aged 65 and over; (4) a special provision of beds for geriatric assessment, alcoholics, adolescents, and patients needing special protection on a district or regional basis; (5) treatment of all other patients in the community in day centers, hostels, group homes, warden-supervised accommodation, and at home as outpatients; most of these services being furnished by the Social Services in cooperation with the psychiatric team and general practitioners (Grad and Sainsbury, 1966, 1968).

A number of findings have a direct bearing on the policy now being proposed; these will be considered in the context of the four aims of our comparative evaluation.

How did the introduction of a community service affect the referral of patients? (Sainsbury, 1971a) When services are extended, they are more widely used; consequently it is necessary to exercise some caution in predicting future needs from statistics describing current practice. Hence our findings that the referral rates to the community care service were higher for nearly every demographic, social, and clinical category analyzed was not surprising. The referral rates of certain categories, however, were very significantly higher in Chichester than in Salisbury. There were, for example, two referral peaks in both services; one in the age-group 24 to 34 and the other at 65 and over (see Figure 6.2), which probably indicate categories most at risk for mental disorder irrespective of type of service, as they occurred in both of them. But it was just these age groups that also had a *notably* higher referral rate in the community care service. Further analysis showed the peak at 65 and over was due to the high rates of the single and widowed of both sexes, especially those living alone, and the peak at 24 to 34 was accounted for by married women. Moreover the high rates of the former resulted from the referral of more depressive illness and organic dementias in the community service, and in the latter age group from neurotic and depressive disorders (many were housebound, phobic housewives). The high risk of psychiatric illness in young married women was an important observation that has since been confirmed in other surveys.

The data clearly showed first, that the community care policy was preferentially providing a service for the seriously mentally disordered in the community who had previously been neglected, rather than recruiting more people with minor forms of mental illness, and second, that the psycho-geriatric referrals had increased disproportionately. It would therefore appear that the new service was beginning to meet the needs of the elderly whose referral by the general practitioner had previously been discouraged because of the shortage of beds and lack of alternative

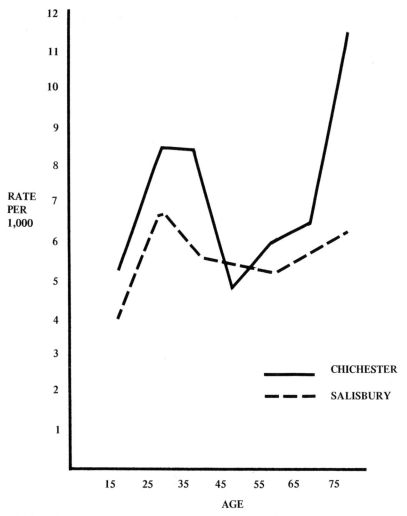

FIGURE 6.2 Total Referral Rates for 1960

provisions. By the same token, in the policy now being proposed, it might be expected not only that the general practitioners, but also the area social work team, will be identifying the aged and other psychiatrically disordered people in the community, and that they will be referring them to the day hospitals and to the other new facilities. Indeed, they will be failing in the role assigned them if they do not. The probability is therefore that demand for care will be substantially higher than the present rate.

On the other hand, when the mean duration of illness at referral of the community and control patients was compared, it was significantly shorter for the former. So the community policy provides better opportunities for early, and perhaps more effective, treatment.

## WHO GETS REFERRED AND WHO TREATED IN THE COMMUNITY

Following the introduction of the Chichester service, the number of admissions was reduced by 50% (Carse et al., 1958); furthermore, when the two services were compared, only 14% of referrals were admitted in the month after referral to the community service as against 52% in the hospital-centered one (the admission rates were 1.0 and 2.8 per 1,000, respectively). And if the referrals aged 65 and over are considered separately, only half as many were admitted in Chichester as in Salisbury (see Table 6.2). This lower admission rate in the community service was maintained throughout the two years (see Table 6.3). The duration of stay in Chichester, however, of patients below the age of 65 was the same as in Salisbury and was longer than the national average; but the length of stay of the elderly was significantly shorter in the community service (29 weeks as compared with 42). It was apparent that rigorously screening patients in the community to determine whether to offer extramural care results in the admission of a selected group of patients: those who are not suitable for treatment at home. Hence, patients who are admitted may also be difficult to discharge and so their length of stay may tend to be longer than present figures indicate.

When the clinical, social, and family factors affecting admission were examined in detail, this supposition was borne out. Social factors were clearly affecting the admission of cases to a greater extent in the community than in the comparison

TABLE 6.2   INITIAL DISPOSAL OF ALL PATIENTS REFERRED TO TWO SERVICES
DURING 1960-1961

|  | Chichester %(N=823) | Salisbury %(N=585) |
|---|---|---|
| Mental hospital | 14 | 52 |
| Other institution | 8 | 5 |
| Admitted | 22 | 57 |
| Day hospital | 15 | — |
| Home care | 16 | 3 |
| Outpatient | 34 | 35 |
| Discharged to GP | 13 | 4 |
| Not admitted | 78 | 43 |

TABLE 6.3   PROPORTION OF PATIENTS ADMITTED TO MENTAL HOSPITAL
AT ANY TIME DURING THE TWO YEARS

|  | Chichester %(N=223) | Salisbury %(N=120) |
|---|---|---|
| Patients aged 15-64 | 34 | 55 |
| Patients aged 65+ | 52 | 79 |
| Mean weeks spent in hospital by admitted patients only | (N=84) | (N=71) |
| Patients aged 15-64 | 20 | 20 |
| Patients aged 65+ | 29 | 42 |

service (Grad and Sainsbury, 1966). Thus the lower socioeconomic groups, elderly patients living with their children, patients whose families had negative attitudes to them, and families with high burden scores were factors determining admission in Chichester, whereas clinical ones were more apparent in Salisbury. The clinical groups most likely to be admitted in the community service were those whose symptoms were socially disruptive or embarrassing, for example, patients showing aggressiveness, embarrassing behavior or suicidal tendencies (the only symptom category in which the proportion admitted in Chichester equalled that in Salisbury); but these symptoms respond to treatment and will not necessarily delay discharge, whereas the socially determined admissions present a more intractable problem whose solution will depend largely on the resourcefulness of the social services team.

Calculations based on the referral and admissions rates of the two services during 1960-1961 and the figures for patient-weeks in hospital obtained from the 1-in-3 sample of patients follow-up for two years shows that bed occupancy in the Chichester service was about that being proposed in the DHSS guidelines.

An estimate of the beds needed in a community service for all adult patients (excluding dementias but including functional disorders in the aged) was 0.58 per 1,000 total population as compared with 0.8 in the hospital-based service in Salisbury, and the DHSS's current estimate of 0.5 beds.

For the group of elderly dements, as defined by the DHSS, the bed needs in the community service for the severe dementias (without physical illness) were 1.8 beds per 1,000 aged 65 and over, which is less than the Department's figures of 2.5 to 3, but in excess of the hospital (Salisbury) services' needs of 2.4. The figures for senile dementias with physical illness were difficult to compare with those now being recommended as they refer to *all* geriatric patients in the districts with physical illness, whether or not they also have a mental disorder.

Another finding which has important implications for the new policy, and an aspect which is causing much concern because many argue that insufficient attention has been given to the problem (Wing and Hailey, 1972), is the build up of *new* long-stay patients, those who remain in hospital for more than one year. We found their bed needs were still considerable. In Chichester, for the elderly with dementias alone, it was 0.5 beds per 1,000 over 65, whereas in Salisbury it was 0.8. These demands would soon block the available beds. Moreover, since 1960, referrals for the Chichester district have increased to such an extent that the *numbers* admitted are now approaching those that lead to the introduction of the service; therefore, in forecasting needs for beds and residential places, allowances should be made not only for a likely increase in referrals, but also for the finding that cases with social problems will be selected for admission.

Other analyses were undertaken to see what categories of patients were treated in which of the community facilities. The one most extensively used in Chichester was domiciliary care, in which the psychiatrist, GP, and social worker treated patients by visiting their homes. This disposal was most often used to care for widowed women with dementias; the day hospital preferentially accepted elderly married depressives (Sainsbury et al., 1967). Nursing homes also admitted many more old people in Chichester than Salisbury; the staff were willing to look after psychogeriatric patients if they knew they could count on psychiatric assistance when it was needed. And this augurs well for the feasibility of the new supervised accommodation in the community.

The social as well as the clinical characteristics of the patients were therefore determining whether they were looked after at home, in the day hospital, or elsewhere; but a community care policy also makes available facilities such as nursing homes, because it is possible to place patients in them if there is easy access to and collaboration with the psychiatric services.

## THE EFFECTS ON THE FAMILY

It has already been suggested that the extramural treatment of patients throws much of the burden previously borne by the mental hospital's trained staff on the community, which, in effect, is the patient's household and family. Using quite conservative measures, we found this to be substantial in terms of effects on the health of the closest relative and on the children, on loss of work and income, physical demands, and disruption of domestic routine and of social and leisure activities. Thus, at the time of referral to both services, the burden on two-thirds of the 410 families was rated as moderate and in 20% as severe (see Table 6.4).

TABLE 6.4   EFFECTS ON FAMILIES WHEN THE PATIENTS WERE FIRST REFERRED

|  | Chichester %(N=271) | Salisbury %(N=139) |
|---|---|---|
| Problem scores |  |  |
| 0 - 1 | 38 | 32 |
| 2 - 3 | 25 | 24 |
| 4 - 5 | 14 | 15 |
| 6+ | 23 | 29 |
| Burden ratings |  |  |
| None | 40 | 29 |
| Some | 42 | 46 |
| Severe | 18 | 25 |

Considering the conservative nature of the measures, our figures reveal the high cost in personal and social hardship that families with a mentally ill member pay. When this cost is examined in light of the fact that, at the point when the patient was referred, 60% of the families had incurred these burdens for more than two years, the importance of a very close look at this aspect of community psychiatry is apparent.

For example, in order to define the families' problems in clinical terms, we recorded which aspects of the patients' behavior had been worrying them. Most troublesome was constant harping on bodily complaints (see Table 6.5). Next were fears that the patient might harm himself, but, unexpectedly, behavior conspicuous

TABLE 6.5  FAMILY PROBLEMS

| Effect on | Families, % | | |
| --- | --- | --- | --- |
| | Some Disturbance | Severe Disturbance | Total Burden |
| Health of closest relatives: | | | |
| Mental | 40 | 20 | 60 |
| Physical | 28 | – | 28 |
| Social and leisure activities of family | 14 | 21 | 35 |
| Children | 24 | 10 | 34 |
| Domestic routine | 13 | 16 | 29 |
| Income of family | 14 | 9 | 23 |
| Employment of others than the patient | 17 | 6 | 23 |

enough to provoke comment from neighbors was the least frequently reported item. Burden also increased with the patient's age; and the demented elderly and psychopathic personality were the two most taxing diagnostic groups.

When the cohorts in each service were followed up for two years and the burden at the beginning, during the period, and at the end compared, all indices showed that the community service left families more heavily burdened. But of particular importance was the finding that the mental health of the closest relative was impaired: over half complained of excessive anxiety due to worrying about the patient; a fifth attributed other neurotic symptoms and a third disturbances in their children's behavior to this cause. This obliges us to consider whether the cost of keeping certain patients at home will be more illness in the community.

However, when the most *severely* affected families were separately considered, their burden was equally relieved in both services, in spite of the community one admitting fewer patients from these families. Similarly, the families with patients over 65 years and those with patients who were never admitted were not significantly more burdened in the community service. So failure to admit is not a sufficient explanation for their having more problems. Further examination of our data then showed that, first, relief of the families' burden in the community service was less satisfactory than in the comparison service when it omitted to provide adequate social support to families. And rather unexpectedly the research social workers' assessments of family needs, and whether these were being met, showed that certain families in Chichester were receiving *less* support than those in Salisbury. The psychiatrist visiting the patient's home does not make an adequate assessment; to do this close partnership with a social worker is essential. Second, there was a group of younger, mainly neurotic patients, who had had at least one admission, but who continued to cause their families problems in the community service, emphasizing the need also to give support to families following a patient's discharge from hospital, especially in a service whose policy is to encourage an early return to his usual social and family setting. A community service is able to ameliorate the burden on a family looking after a patient, who would have been admitted under a more conservative policy, as effectively as does a hospital-centered service, but only when the combined skills of a therapeutic team and GP are available to the family. If the service fails to provide this kind of help, it is likely to add to the community's mental health problems, because the family members, as well as the patient, then fare worse than in a conventional service. Last, outcome in terms of mortality figures was identical in the two services.

How did a community service affect other aspects of the course and outcome of the patient's illness? The psychiatrists' and patients' assessments agreed that, in general, outcome was more favorable in the hospital service; but when improvement was assessed on remission of symptoms, the community service was more effective with the most treatable disorder, depressive illness. In contrast, however, neither relatives nor family doctors, whose appraisal was probably largely based on social behavior, observed a difference in outcome between the services.

When relief of burden on the family was used as an independent measure of outcome, we found that the outcome of patients who caused a *severe* burden was the same in Chichester as in Salisbury. The probable explanation for this is that the psychiatrist was able to recognize, and so take steps to remedy, circumstances in the household likely to have adverse effects on the course of the illness. On the other hand, outcome was consistently less satisfactory in Chichester where family burden had been rated *moderate*; the psychiatrist is not adept at distinguishing less conspicuous hardships and stresses within the family, and fails to take preventative action. So the need for collaboration between psychiatrist and social worker in an extramural mental health program was again very evident.

Consequently, when evaluating the DHSS's new policy, we will need to assess not only the effects on the family when care is given in the day centers, hostels, and district hospital psychiatric units, but also the attitudes of the patient and of his family to them if the new services are to be confirmed as an advance on the present one. In addition it will be important to compare the standards of care and quality of life of those treated in the various community settings with those obtaining in the hospital one.

## DISCUSSION AND CONCLUSIONS

To evaluate the effects of treating patients in the community, all referrals to a service whose policy was to treat patients at home as far as possible was compared with those of a more conservative hospital-centered one, and the burden on the families of a cohort of patients, who were followed up for two years, was assessed. The patients studied covered the whole range of psychiatric referrals from severe psychotics to those seen for an opinion and not diagnosed as ill. Nevertheless, the social cost to their families was found to be high in both services. Even after two years of being in contact with the services, 20% of the families were still burdened.

The social cost of psychiatric care was higher in the community than in the hospital-based service. This was principally due to the greater burden caused by a group of patients who are not usually retained in hospital, even in a service that preferentially admits. The strain on their families was not being recognized because it was not prominent. So our findings emphasize the importance of supplementing the clinical care of a patient treated outside a hospital with a systematic appraisal of the demands being made on the family and then providing them with adequate social support. Without efficiently organized collaboration between the psychiatric and welfare services, both the patient and those in the community closest to him are likely to suffer impairment; and the observation that the effects on the mental health of family members were worse in the community than in the comparison service must sound a note of caution. Nevertheless, since the biggest demand is beds for geriatric patients, and since they presented the most severe problems to their families, the success of the community service in reducing this demand without increasing family burden is noteworthy, as also was the observation that outcome in the Chichester service was able to match the Salisbury one when clinical care was backed by social case work to meet the needs of both the patient and the family. Similarly, the tendency preferentially to admit patients in Chichester whose families' burdens and social problems were marked also indicates that by careful assessment it is possible in a community service to select the most suitable of a number of alternative types of care and determine which one brings most advantage to both the patient and his family. By the same token, better opportunities for discharge can obviate a prolonged stay in hospital, and hence the chronic impairment with which this is associated.

On the credit side too were the findings: first, that the kind of disposal given in the community service was more in keeping with the families' wishes than that given in the hospital-centered one, and our agreed impression also was that many families prefer to care for their sick patients at home even though it entails hardships; and second, that the general practitioners favored the extramural policy even though the cost in their time and extra work was significantly greater (Sainsbury, 1969a).

Finally, the community service was beneficial in other ways: it was more efficient in meeting needs in so far as the rates of referral were increased, especially those of elderly patients, those with serious disorders, the socially disadvantaged (Sainsbury and Grad, 1970), and those known to be most at risk for suicide. People were also seen earlier on in their illness. A community psychiatric service, therefore, has considerable preventive potential for reducing the harmful effects of mental illness and its cost in human suffering.

## REFERENCES

Barraclough, B. M. A medical approach to suicide prevention. *Soc. Sci. and Med.,* 1972, 6: 661. (a)

———. Suicide prevention, recurrent affective disorder and Lithium. *Brit. J. Psychiat.,* 1972, 121: 391. (b)

Barraclough, B. M., J. Bunch, B. Nelson, and P. Sainsbury. A hundred cases of suicide: clinical aspects. *Brit. J. Psychiat.* In press.

———, B. Nelson, J. Bunch, and P. Sainsbury. Suicide and barbiturate poisoning. *J. R. Coll. Gen. Practit.,* 1971, 21: 645.

Barraclough, B. M. and M. Shae. Suicide and Samaritan clients. *Lancet,* 1970, 2: 868.

———. A comparison between Samaritan suicide and living Samaritan clients. *Brit. J. Psychiat.,* 1972, 120: 79.

Carse, J., N. Panton, and A. Watt. A district mental health service: the Worthing Experiment. *Lancet,* 1958, 1: 39.

Central Policy Review Staff. *A Framework for Government Research and Development,* Cmnd. 5046. London: H.M.S.O., 1971.

Coppen, A., R. Noguera, J. Bailey, B. H. Burns, M. S. Swani, E. H. Hare, R. Gardner, and R. Maggs. Prophylactic lithium in affective disorders. *Lancet,* 1971, 2: 275.

Grad, J. Psychiatric social workers and research. *Br. J. Psych. Soc. Wk.,* 1964, 7: 147.

Grad de Alarcon, J., and A. Crocetti. Interviewing in psychiatric field surveys. In P. Sainsbury and N. Kreitman (eds.), *Methods of Psychiatric Research.* London, Oxford University Press. In press.

Grad, J., and P. Sainsbury. Evaluating the community psychiatric service in Chichester: results. *Milbank Meml. Fund Q.,* 1966, 44(1): 246.

Grad, J. C., and P. Sainsbury. The effects that patients have on their families in a community care service: a two year follow-up. *Br. J. Psychiat.,* 1968, 114: 265.

Kreitman, N., P. Sainsbury, J. Morissey, and J. Schrivener. Reliability of psychiatric assessments: an analysis. *J. Ment. Sci.,* 1961, 107: 887.

Levey, A. B. Outcome and improvement, personal communication, 1971.

May, P. R. A. *Treatment of Schizophrenia.* New York: Science House, 1968.

Morissey, J. D. The Chichester and district psychiatric service. *Milbank Meml. Fund Q.,* 1966, 44(1): 28.

Morissey, J. D., and P. Sainsbury. Observations on the Chichester and district mental health service. *Proc. Roy. Med.,* 1959, 52(12): 1061.

Sainsbury, P. Suicide and depression. *Br. J. Psychiat.* 1968, special publications no. 2, vol. 2, A. Coppen and A. Walk (eds.).

———. Community Psychiatric services and the General Practitioner. *J. R. Coll. Gen. Practit.,* 1969, supplement 3, vol. 17. (a)

———. Social and community psychiatry. *Amer. J. Psychiat.,* 1969, 125: 1226. (b)

———. Incidence rates and the evaluation of services. Abstract 289, 5th World Congress of Psychiatry, Mexico City. (a)

———. Medical Research Council Clinical Psychiatry Unit. *Psychol. Med.,* 1971, 1: 429. (b)

———. The social relations of suicide. *Soc. Sci. and Med.,* 1972, 6: 189.

———. Suicide, opinions and facts. *Proc. Roy. Soc. Med.,* 1973, 66: 579.

———, W. R. Costain, and J. C. Grad. The effects of a community service on the referral rates and admission rates of elderly psychiatric patients. *Psychiatric Disorders in the Aged,* p. 23. Proceedings World Psychiatric Association Symposium, London: Geigy, 1967.

———, and J. Grad. Evaluation of treatment and services. In *Burden on the Community, Nuffiels Provincial Hospital Trust,* London: Oxford University Press, 1962.

———, and J. Grad de Alarcon. The effects of community care on the family of the geriatric patient. *J. Geriatric Psychiat.,* 1970, 4: 23.

Thompson, I. G. Suicide and mortality in depression. In R. Fox (ed.), *Proceedings of the 5th International Conference for Suicide Prevention.* Vienna: I.A.S.P., 1970.

Walk, D. Suicide and community care. *Br. J. Psychiat.,* 1967, 113: 1381.

Wing, J. K., and A. M. Hailey. *The Evaluation of a Community Psychiatric Service.* London: Oxford University Press, 1972.

7

# THE EVALUATION CONTRACT: "PARTICIPATIVE
# SYSTEMS ACTUALIZATION RESEARCH"

STEVE PRATT

*formerly*
*Wichita State University*
*Wichita, Kansas*

and

MERLE CANFIELD

*Prairie View Mental Health Center*
*Newton, Kansas*

## I. "CONTRACT-SYSTEMS THEORY":
## CONTEXT FOR THE EVALUATION CONTRACT

Evaluation is not a narrow nor exclusive kind of contract in which only exotic specialists indulge. From birth to death all people are active or passive parties to evaluation contracts which directly or indirectly affect every aspect of their daily lives. Evaluation contracts can be reflexive, within or with ourselves, involving the development and expression of value-object-action preferences and their experiential confirmation or disconfirmation. In the latter sense, all research contracts are a form of evaluation contract, having been designed to evaluate hypotheses, that is, to confirm or disconfirm (to test) hypotheses.

Steve Pratt died during the time that this manuscript was in progress. Steve's wife, Rita, and the second author completed details of Steve's unfinished portion.

Evaluation is not a narrow kind of contract: not only is it involved in, and through, every kind of social-behavioral-systems research, but the evaluation contract, with its research or programatic vehicle, must be conceptualized and carried out within the total relevant field-system of which it is part. "Must" means simply: or run the risk of missing the variance boat. "Total relevant field-system" means to check out potentially relevant contract system fields or social domains, for example, political, economic, other research/program contracts, and so on. For any given evaluation contract, it may not be enough to confine assessment-intervention to one system's inputs or outputs in and of themselves. Input cost-benefit analysis and system outcomes out of context may indicate acceptable efficiency and effectiveness; but the program itself, evaluated within its wider, more meaningful context, may be a complete failure with negative if not catastrophic secondary effects. WIN (OEO Work Incentive Now) Program inputs might show an acceptable cost-benefit ratio against criteria of producing skill-competent graduates; but if no jobs are available for these graduates, resentment and hostility may be the ultimate psychosocial outcome (Goodwin, 1971). Just a few years ago the great white hope for economically disadvantaged Blacks in St. Louis centered on the gigantic Pruitt-Igoe Housing Project. The one positive outcome of that multi-million dollar fiasco has been the development of a new demolition technique.

Evaluation contracts aimed at social-behavioral-system problems invoke the "whole package" willy-nilly, whether the programer-evaluators like it or not. Even the definition of the social problem, as such, has itself been (for better or worse) the outcome of an earlier evaluation process. Selection of a specific "program" to evaluate is arbitrary. Other variables or programs may have an effect on the program being considered. Consequently, the whole package must be considered. If the whole package is operative, whether one likes it or not, it becomes crucial to come up with a theoretical system or conceptual level of accounting sufficient to encompass the systems evaluation process, the social-behavioral contract systems of concern (as subsystems of the human enterprise), and the explicit purpose of evaluation-research intervention. The evaluation contract is directed then at the development, assessment, and use of normative (value-system), descriptive, and interventive taxonomies. As Heilbroner (1970: 209) observed recently, "the formulation of reliable higher-level hypotheses remains the most powerful lever we have for the control of our destinies."

The term "contract," in our conception of the "evaluation contract," is the key to our comprehensive theoretical system which we have called Contract Systems Theory (CST) or Contract Systems Psychology (CSP). As this conceptual frame of reference has been presented elsewhere in considerable detail (Pratt and Tooley, 1967, 1969, 1970a, 1970b), for present purposes we will draw on CSP for constructs germane to human systems evaluation, particularly those most relevant to the evaluation-research-intervention questions: for what? of what? and how? These, of course, are the normative-descriptive-methodological questions that define and/or are defined by the "evaluation contract."

Not only can evaluation-research-intervention (ERI) activities be defined in contractual terms, but all human action systems, between and within all levels of social organization (international to intrapsychic), can be best conceptualized in the "language of contract." Thus the ERI questions are questions about contract systems: ERI for what? is concerned with value systems; of what? is concerned with selective aspects of the social contract systems which comprise structure and dynamics of being and living in the everyday world; and how? is concerned with the development and use of instrumental (methodological) contract systems.

For the two inextricable purposes of understanding the human endeavor (happy or horrendous) and improving the quality of life, the concept of "contract" is proposed as the central or *regnant construct*. As *the* highest-order theoretical construct, *contract systems* defines significant dimensions for all human systems, for all behavioral relationships. The human enterprise in its entirety, or at the individual level, or at any selected "level of integration"—family, organization, institution, neighborhood, community, national, or international—can best be conceptualized in the "language of contract." The *fundamental postulate* asserts that the characterizing essence of human beings consists of and is expressed by (through) the unique capacity to form (enact) contractual relationships.[1] People have the capacity to create and exchange values. Contracts are ends-means *instrumentalities* for the development, expression, and exchange of values. Contracts humanize the earth (both constructively and destructively) and the human-made world operates contractually (Weick, 1969b); both the play and the work of the world are carried out through contractual processes (Pratt, 1972b, 1972c).

Contracts can be explicit or implicit, conscious or unconscious, unilateral or consensual, voluntary or coercive, actualizing or counteractualizing. Contracts are (define or represent) reflexive and reciprocal arrangements, agreements, promises, understandings, expectancies, commitments, covenants—from a New Year's resolution to the United Nations' "Universal Declaration of Human Rights."[2] We make contracts with ourselves and others; others make contracts that affect every aspect of our lives. *Contraho ergo sum* supercedes Descartes' *cogito ergo sum* because it obtains for all human systems—for self, for each ERI contract, for the societal-contract system of a Nation-State.

> Human civilization as it has been known to historical experience is preponderantly a product of *contractual relations*. [von Mises, 1949: 198]
>
> What we call society is a vast network of mutual agreements. . . . Without such agreements *(contract-system networks)* there would be no such thing as society. [Hayakawa, 1967: 213]

Contracts constitute the *integrative function* for all human systems relationships at all social levels of systems organization. Contracts are the glue that holds each person, each organization, and the people-made world together. Contracts make the human world and make the world go 'round. Contract systems can be enacted, kept, carried out, and fulfilled, or broken and violated; they can be authentic or fraudulent (Johnson et al., 1970; Kanfer and Phillips, 1970a); they may be manipulative or exploitive, equitable or inequitable, just or unjust (Adams, 1965; Blau, 1964; Fromm, 1955; Homans, 1958; Shostrum, 1967); in the mathematical language of games theory, they can represent *zero-sum* (win-lose) or *non-zero-sum* games.

As contract systems, having any of the above characteristics, dimensions, or attributes, apply to (are represented by) all forms of social activity, and as evaluation or ERI itself is a form of human endeavor, it can be seen that all CS constructs apply to all systems of evaluation which invariably (explicitly or implicitly) represent ERI *contract* systems. For the social-behavioral sciences, contract-system *conditions* can be treated as ERI conditions, as experimental research conditions (e.g., as predictor or outcome variables), or as system attributes (e.g., correlational variables or factor-analytic matrices, etc.).

## II. SYSTEMATIC PHILOSOPHY AND THE EVALUATION CONTRACT

As a systematic theory, CSP offers its own approach to the Evaluation Contract (EC) called Participative Systems Actualization Research (PSAR). The PSAR:EC is directly concerned with the evaluation-research-intervention (ERI) questions: for what? of what? and how? Thus, the development of normative, descriptive, interventive taxonomies is designed to further human systems actualization.[3]

As we shall see, explication of the three problematic questions (for what, of what, how?) is paradoxically both simple and complex.

Evaluation "of what" introduces further questions about the conceptualization of both *content* and *context.* Broadly, but ultimately crucial to even the most circumscribed ERI problem, what is required is a way of laying out patterns for reality and ways of getting at reality—getting to know it, to understand it, to change it, and to create new realities. The evaluation "of what" requires conceptualization and categorization of "what is" through descriptive or nomological taxonomies; requires productive meanings for "objectivity" that, while necessarily reductionistic, are not inaccurately reductionistic; requires selection of the most relevant CS levels, CS spheres, and specific CS reciprocity networks (CSRN). Here we need to consider how to conceptualize the total reality context, and how to conceptualize the necessary relevant reality within the total context.

For CST, as systematic philosophy, these conceptualizations involve both epistemological and ontological considerations which are crucial for systematic evaluation (ERI).

Epistemology refers to the *process of knowing,* the relationship of the knower to what's to be known, investigated, evaluated; to reflexive study by people, of themselves, others, and their surrounds. As have others (Cantril et al., 1949), we have elsewhere presented a taxonomy of epistemologies which takes the position that all epistemologies can be ordered into one or another of three fundamental types: (1) *auto*-actional epistemologies; (2) *inter*-actional epistemologies; and (3) *trans*-actional epistemologies (Kilpatrick, 1961). The choice among these three epistemological positions is crucial for the PSAR:EC Model, as it is for all ERI action whatever model it reflects. Both the theoretical and the programatic advantage of the transactional approach are being increasingly recognized for the social-behavioral sciences and for science generally (Dewey and Bentley, 1949; Hutcheson and Krause, 1969).

CSP employs a transactional epistemology which it extends into a "*field-theoretical*" approach (Lewin, 1951) in order to provide for an explicit transactional-*field* epistemology. For humans, transactions characteristically represent contract systems, thus for human systems (at all levels of integration) the transactional field becomes the contract systems field (CSF). This conception of Contract-*Systems*-Field (CSF) incorporates the systems and general-systems-theory approach, also social and behavioral exchange theory (Blau, 1964; Homans, 1958; Gergen, 1969), as well as ecological theory through the conceptualization of "social ecology" and "ecological exchange" as essentially contractual (Gladwin, 1967; Barker, 1965; Sells, 1963).

The process of knowing (epistemology) about the conditions of "what is," about "being" including "becoming" (ontology), occurs within the transactional field which obtains in common for, is shared by, and thereby connects epistemology and ontology. Thus, we have an epistemological-ontological transactional field (contractual field for human events).[4]

Within this level of accounting, the PSAR:EC Model is particularly interested in further delineating investigative (heuristic), descriptive (nomological), and prescriptive (normative) conceptual tools. An epistemological-ontological problem central to all ERI work is represented by the need for conceptual tools with which to link *theories* with *empirical events,* conceptual levels of abstraction with empirical levels of system organization (international to intrapsychic).

Feigl and Scriven (1956) introduced the notion of a *nomological net* to encompass the various levels of theoretical constructs in relation to the referential events (at whatever levels of analysis and action). Margenau (1950) elaborated a spacial paradigm for scientific inquiry comprised of blending planes of existence, the inferential or conceptual plane (C-Plane) connecting with the empirical, observable, or protocol plane (P-Plane). Now Northrup's (1974) cogent conception of "epistemic correlation" can be applied to provide for "indices of correspondence" which indicate "degree of correlation" between theoretical constructs (C-Plane) and their empirical grounding (P-Plane).

The PSAR:EC is directed at human systems actualization. This purpose puts major emphasis on value systems. Value theory and action theory are conceptualized as transactionally coupled, through ends-means configurations, and as an inextricable part of the total transactional-field (TF, CSF, or nomological network). Therefore Feigl and Scriven's nomological net is extended to incorporate heirarchical levels of ends-means systems. By thus combining the nomological net with the normative net, we explicitly place the theoretical-empirical components of existence (Margenau) within a heirarchical ends-means context: the nomological net becomes the normative-nomological network (NNN).

Finally, within this multivariate (metataxonomic) field-context, Northrup's invaluable construct of "epistemic correlation," which defines the degree of correspondence between theory and referential empirical events, is enlarged to include value theory, to include the degree of correspondence between a given value theory and its specific empirical referent. There is probably no concept more crucial to all ERI contracts and their outcomes than epistemic correlation in this broadened CSP version. It should be stressed that this *invariably* value-incorporative version is the sense in which epistemic correlation is employed by CSP in relation to its PSAR:EC

Model, and is the evaluative template to be used to check out any current ERI model or program whatever value stance others take, including that of simply ignoring value aspects altogether or of denying that value parameters exist in either the theoretical or empirical components of their intervention. The ultimate conceptual-semantic legerdemain obtains when the quixotic effort is made to exorcise both the value component and the theoretical component of scientific inquiry.

In all evaluative research, achieving a high degree (or a workable degree) of epistemic correspondence is contingent upon "representativeness of design" which requires "representativeness of circumstances," what Brunswik (1946, 1956) as aptly called "ecological validity."

Representatives of circumstances and design can only be achieved when the necessary relevant field of events is made conceptually and empirically accessible by selective focus within the total *heuristic* normative-nomological network (HNNN).

Selective evaluative focus within the encompassing patterning of reality, of "what is" (HNNN), is the work of PSAR:EC–to evaluatively define, articulate, and change (actualize) social-behavioral contract systems (within HNNN) through the development and application of evaluative (normative), descriptive (nomological), and instrumental (methodological) taxonomies. Systems evaluation research, of course, can be designed to reveal the existence of deficiencies or *discrepancies* between negative (counteractualizing) aspects of "what is" or "what could be," and "what should" or "ought to be."

The purpose of the PSAR:EC taxonomies (evaluative-descriptive-instrumental) is to conceptualize, define, assess, and cope with this CS discrepancies. The conjoint roles and significance for systems evaluation of PSAR metataxonomy and discrepancy theory will be discussed below.

### III. PSAR:EC–"LOCUS FOR FOCUS"

International, national, community, family, person–as each of these different systems or system levels can only be understood in "selective relationship" with the others, to study or to change any one of these systems, nothing less than a *"general* systems theory" can be adequate. As we conceptualize the relevant systems as *contract* systems, our approach is a *"general* contract-systems theory," and in this sense a special "general systems theory," special because the human social systems of concern are invariably construed as contract systems.

As we have seen, this special general systems approach is not, nor can it be, limited to consideration of a *class* of systems which are exclusively located at one given social level of integration or level of organization (Novikoff, 1945; Feibleman, 1954). Levels of human systems organization can best be characterized as *interlocking* contract systems (Weick, 1969a, 1969b). To gain purchase on a given target system, at whatever level it obtains, other levels must be systematically considered to formulate the problem appropriately and to check out empirically possible sources of relevant variance.

In explicating contract system *space* as the relevant contract systems *field* (CSF),[5] PSAR is concerned with various taxonomic schema for differentiating and articulating CS spheres and CS levels. Such a schema, for example, might incorporate the following levels (keeping in mind that it should be formulated to best fit the specific problem at hand):

(1) Self-system level. The individual person-as-a-system: the person's self-constituting configuration of contract systems (reflexive and social, present and potential); personality level, for example, intrapsychic or interior CS space, *persona,* and interpersonal or person-group life-space.
(2) Primary-group level, such as family and other face-to-face small-group contract systems (CS).
(3) Organization or institutional CS level.
(4) Interorganizational or coalition CS level.
(5) Community or neighborhood CS level.
(6) State or regional CS level.
(7) National CS level.
(8) International CS level.

Likewise, CS *space* covers CS spheres or domains of human activity such as those usually referred to as the economic sphere and the political, religious, or social spheres—all of which encompass contractually defined relationships, status, position, and roles: family roles (marital, parental) citizenship roles (establishment and counterestablishment), vocational and avocational roles (the arts, recreation) (Pratt, 1972b; Pratt and Tooley, 1970b).

Levels of organization for human systems represent quanitative qualitative *emergents*; thus they cannot be reduced to being considered as nothing more than an aggregate of their parts. The game contract of baseball (including the individual and group behavior of all parties: players, referees, spectators, newscasters, club owners, coaches, et al.) can never be understood, described, predicted, or evaluated by analysis done exclusively at the level of the isolated individual participant (Mandelbaum, 1955).

Or, for example, at the community level, organization contracts can affect each other (as in interorganization collaboration, collusion, or competition), and are also affected by higher-level contract systems on the one hand (e.g., federal or state regulations), and by lower-level small-group and self-system contracts (e.g., Nader versus General Motors) on the other. Organization contracts in turn can transactionally affect both higher societal-level, and lower-level, group or individual contract systems. For any given community social issue or psychosocial problem, it becomes a matter for empirical investigation to determine at which levels the predominant determinants are located. This is the crucial ERI question of "locus for focus" or "levels for leverage." Achieving representativeness of circumstances (of CS *conditions*) and representativeness of design, that it, "ecological validity," is a precondition to positive EC outcomes.

The locus for human actualization, as well as the locus for dehumanization, alienation, or psychosocial disorders, runs through these CS levels and CS spheres of living. One of the most significant and, at the same time, one of the most distorted or neglected problems in the entire field of psychosocial disorders and human actualization is the evaluative analysis of the inextricable relationship between

societal issues (including community-level social problems) and psychosocial disorders at the individual person level: how *social problems* become (are) reflected in
*personal troubles,* in so-called personality disorders, emotional or behavioral disorders, or parataxic interpersonal relationships (Coles, 1967, 1971a, 1971b;
Dabrowski, 1972; Halleck, 1968; Hollingshead and Redlich, 1958; Mills, 1959;
Ruesch and Brodsky, 1968; Sullivan, 1953).

## IV. PSAR:EC–THE DYSTOPIAN-UTOPIAN DISCREPANCY DYNAMIC

The CST approach to evaluation through PSAR (as participative systems *actualization* research) is designed to further human systems *actualization.* Here the value
system is made explicit. Our definition of the concept specifically relates actualization to "*systems* actualization" which, while including the "self-system" (as in
the usual use of the term "self-actualization"), significantly extends the concept to
all human systems *within* and *between* all CS levels and spheres.

This is a crucial extension not only because of the essential inclusion of all
human systems which are thus brought under the purview of explicit value criteria,
but also because this very inclusion is a precondition for operationalizing the
conception of self-actualization. As professionally and popularly employed
(Maslow, 1969, 1971), ignoring a general-systems context, "self-actualization"
invokes an *auto*-actional rather than a *trans*-actional epistemology: self-
actualization *in vacuo* is little more than the myth of Horatio Alger, "up by his own
bootstraps." From the CSP perspective, the term has specific meaning: actualization of the self-as-a-system through a transactional (contractual) process to which
both the individual (self) and other social forces contribute. People, organized and
individually, are both the creatures and creators of their contractual world.

We further differentiate our use of the concept from the way it is used by
others, because our definition of actualization specifically restricts its application to
the creation or fulfillment of potentialities that are positive, which may be neutral
or independent (laisser faire) but in no case can be based on aggrandisement or gain
accruing to one system (organization, group, person) at another's expense. By
definition, this expressly excludes contract systems involving exploitation, sub-
jugation, inequitable or unjust exchange (Adams, 1965; Blau, 1964; Homans, 1958,
1961); system actualization invariably must represent a *non-zero-sum*, never a
*zero-sum,* game contract.

It will be recalled that contract systems are *instrumentalities* for the creation and
exchange of what is valued: "goods," expectancies, behaviors, work remuneration,
obligations-benefits. What is valued, the creation and exchange of whatever is
valued—thus contract systems at all levels—can be actualizing or *counteractualizing.*

## V. PSAR:EC–METATAXONOMY AND
## DYSTOPIAN-UTOPIAN DISCREPANCIES

CSP, as systematic philosophy, has employed the heuristic-normative-nomol-
ogical-network (HNNN) as frame of reference to encompass the epistemological-

ontological "totality of reality." In a generic sense, all human activity and certainly all forms of social inquiry and intervention (including scientific inquiry) are *evaluative*, have evaluative dimensions, represent and are concerned with evaluative contract systems. No choice or decision can be made, nor action taken, without invoking a value system (Boulding, 1966; Smith, 1954).

The PSAR Evaluation-Contract Model (PSAR:EC) is designed to carve out chunks within or slices of the totality of reality (HNNN); to get at a given relevant contract system field (CSF), to get hold of it in order to gain purchase on the particular problem of concern. To engage specific segments of the relevant CSF, PSAR employs it's metataxonomic system. Having the explicit purpose of human systems actualization, the PSAR:EC is designed to find out about "what ought to be" and "what should not be" (*normative*); and how this compares with "what is" or "what could be" (*descriptive*); and how to maximize "what ought to be" (*methodological*).

The task is to delineate "what should be" (actualizing CSs) and "what should not be" (counteractualizing CSs) within present, future, or past CSFs; to assess *discrepancies* between what should be and what should not be, that is, between more utopian (more actualizing) CS conditions and dystopian (underactualized or counteractualizing) CS conditions; and to develop effective methods of intervention designed to reduce, resolve, or eliminate those dystopian-utopian *discrepancies*.[6] This ERI task requires the development of normative, descriptive, and methodological taxonomies.

Taxonomies themselves can of course be taxonomized (analogous to a second-order factor analysis). Thus for evaluative purposes, the PSAR:EC metataxonomy would order any or all extant taxonomies under consideration into one or another of the three basic categories: normative, descriptive, methodological. However, these three types of taxonomies are themselves transactionally interrelated (within HNNN), and the present categorization is to be taken simply as a somewhat arbitrary ordering for logical emphasis—a pragmatic "abstraction of convenience."

It should be noted that some excellent taxonomies of these three types have been reported in recent evaluation research literature, and many such instruments or approaches are accessible for adaptation or for use "as is" within an activist contract systems approach (Buros, 1972; Pratt, 1972b, 1972c; Pratt, et al., 1961; Pratt and Tooley, 1967).

The PSAR:EC *troika* metataxonomy can be used to carry out the CST purpose of human systems actualization, and also to evaluate or check out any other extant taxonomies in terms of their own criteria and also in terms of CST criteria. PSAR:EC operates through the participative development-in-action of these three basic (but inter-related) kinds of taxonomies:

> Type I:   Normative Taxonomies
> Type II:  Descriptive Taxonomies
> Type III: Methodological Taxonomies

In the following brief outline, only some of the more uniquely PSAR:EC characteristics are indicated.

## Type I: Normative Taxonomies

For whatever purpose, anyone could enumerate, classify, or compare any number of extant value systems (past, present, proposed). For a variety of purposes, such value systems could be ordered into intra-related value heirarchies and also could be evaluated in terms of either intrinsic, external, or selected superordinate value criteria.

The PSAR:EC Model can be employed to analyze, compare, and evaluate other current normative taxonomies, as well as for the development-through-action of its own. In checking out other normative systems, the purpose of the first PSAR evaluative template to be applied would be to ascertain whether or not the taxonomy or evaluation contract in question has made its own value system explicit; or whether a concealed value system is exposed by the attempt to deny that values were involved. The latter frequently occurs in conceptual taxonomies that try to take a so-called value-free stance, a posture that, paradoxically, were it possible, would itself constitute a value position (thus non-value-free) but that furthermore represents an epistemologically untenable position. Rather than denying that *any* value system obtains, a value system that in actuality is counter-actualizing may be distorted or denied while a faked positive value system is used in the ERI-contract as a con-game cover. In this case the value system as such is misrepresented, whether unintentionally, through ignorance or misinformation, or intentionally through purposeful distortion as in stereotyping, scapegoating, and blaming the victim. Fraudulent value systems are proffered to conceal machiavellian hidden agendas, monstrous goals are espoused and "sold" as being "good" or "ideal" (the best): the *War* Department, with considerable semantic sensitivity, has been renamed the *Defense* Department with the slogan, "Peace Is Our Profession"; whereas, outcomes in Vietnam indicate ideals of ecocide, genocide, or both.

The second template would check out all normative taxonomies in terms of the PSAR fundamental normative criteria, which requires that the value system not represent zero-sum (win-lose), inequitable, or exploitive contract systems. Where expressed purpose relates to optimal human systems actualization, a higher-level value criteria can be applied which represents the PSAR *ideal* norm: the norm of reciprocal actualization (NORA).

PSAR employs the notion of three aim-value levels as differentiated by Kaplan (1964) in *The Conduct of Inquiry: Methodology for Behavioral Science*. The three aim-value levels are "ideals," "goals," and "objectives": *objectives* are more immediate, more circumscribed, and more readily achievable subtargets; *goals* are intermediate, longer-range, more comprehensive targets; and the *ideal* is the ultimate or perfect (like the Platonic prototype) or what (how) it would be if the conceptualized aim could be exactly and completely achieved or created. For PSAR:EC the formulation and evaluation of ideals, goals, and objectives becomes a participative, empirical, and open-ended process. Type I Taxonomies are directed at the determination of what should be (more utopian) contrasted with what should not be (dystopian), at the evaluative assessment of these discrepancies, and at the evaluation of interventive techniques designed to correct such dystopian-utopian discrepancies (DUD).

As it does for the other two types of Taxonomies (descriptive and method-ological), epistemic correlation provides the crucial measure of the degree of correspondence between theoretical (value-theory) components of the normative taxonomy and their empirical grounding. Assessment of representativeness of circumstances and events (CS conditions) will indicate how adequately this empirical grounding has been incorporated within the normative taxonomic design—in terms of the criteria of ecological validity.

## Type II: Descriptive Taxonomies

As with normative taxonomies (Type I) in general, any number of present, past, or proposed descriptive taxonomic systems (Type II) could be listed, or compared for a variety of reasons. They could likewise be evaluated in terms of intrinsic and related criteria, or in terms of our EC criteria.

That all descriptive taxonomies invariably incorporate value attributes and invoke value theory is epistemologically inescapable. Objects and systems them-selves are invested with and characterized by value attributes; even the initial choice to assign a descriptive label is a value choice having further value implications (frequently disastrous); every descriptive "fact" either reveals or conceals a theory which itself had value dimensions. System value attributes (as well as value theory) are sources of variance, thus an essential aspect of "objectivity."

For PSAR, "objectivity" is defined as the process of getting at the optimal sources of relevant variance (which includes value-system sources). Obviously this more scientific definition of "objectivity" corroborates and complements our broadened reconceptualization of ecological validity in which representativeness of circumstances or events (CS conditions) includes value attributes as essential para-meters. In checking out other, non-PSAR descriptive taxonomies, criteria opera-tionally derived from this extended conception of ecological validity are crucial, whatever the purposes of those taxonomies, whether actualizing or Machiavellian. Particularly in the social-behavioral sciences, professionally popular scientism defines objectivity in a way that paradoxically, "objectivity" precludes objectivity.

The social-behavioral sciences, the humanities, and the arts can be appreciated as complementary ways of characterizing the human condition, the common purpose being to delineate, articulate, and illuminate the world we live in—and to create new realities. Descriptive taxonomies are developed to conceptualize, define, and describe (Gotkin and Goldstein, 1964) the conditions of reality (whether positive or negative).

As we have seen, it is important to develop descriptive schema for the differ-ential characterization and dimensionalization of levels of organization and spheres of endeavor, because the locus for human systems actualization and counter-actualization runs through (within and between) these CS levels and CS spheres.

Type II taxonomies are particularly useful in determining base-line measures necessary to define operationally the *magnitude of discrepancy* between "what is" that "should not be" (qualitative-quantitative) and "what can be" that "should be." This magnitude of discrepancy can be determined as between "what is" (positive or negative) and criteria representing any of the three aim-levels: ideal, goal, objective. In the case in which "what is" is postive, the magnitude of discrepancy could be zero; or it could be zero in terms of criteria for one aim-level (e.g., objective) but not for criteria of another (e.g., goal or ideal); or it could be zero at present but under threat of predicted future counteractualizing CS events (e.g., "We may have to destroy that Vietnamese village in order to save it"; or, "contracts for strip mining will ruin small family-farm communities throughout the state").

Representativeness of circumstances and events (ecological validity) is requisite to determining base-line measures, while the magnitude of discrepancy represents a special normative-descriptive version of epistemic correlation which involves the degree of correspondence (or disparity) between the ideal-goal-objective conceptualization (C Plane) and the empirical conditions-of-the-situation (P Plane). The major PSAR purpose of Type III methodological taxonomies, then, will be to maximize this degree of epistemic correlation at minimum unnecessary cost: the Mini-Max Principle intact except keeping an eye on both the fundamental *non-zero-sum* norm and the *ideal* norm, NORA.

PSAR:EC puts the currently popular "social accounting" approach within its own special general systems (CST) frame of reference which encompasses the CS spheres and levels from international (e.g., magnitude of discrepancy between and within "have" and "have-not" nations) to intrapsychic ("I'm going to take an account of myself and where I'm at"). Thus interest is in social accounting within and between all of these CS levels. Here again the taxonomic development of base-line descriptive measures (as "social indicators") is necessary to operationalize the magnitude of discrepancy.

For the purpose of describing and working with human systems, the "language of contingencies" can be conceptualized as a special case of the "language of contract." The "language of contingencies" can thus be extended to contingency systems within and between all social-behavioral levels. Within this general systems context, whenever we speak of (or work with) contingencies, we are simply using an abbreviation for contractual contingencies or contractual contingency systems (CCS).

Obviously, contractual contingency systems at all levels of social-behavioral organization can be actualizing or counteractualizing; and can be evaluated in terms of the discrepancy between how sets of contingencies "should be" (more utopian) and how they "should not be" (dystopian), in other words, in terms of dystopian-utopian discrepancies (DUD). Descriptive taxonomies in the language of contingencies can be employed to define operationally base-line measures (CCS conditions) in relation to specifiable objectives, goals, and ideals, thus operationalizing measures of the magnitude of discrepancy. Base-line descriptive taxonomies measure present RE conditions and OB capacities (positive and negative). Outcome criteria can be based on measurable objectives involving both RE opportunity structures and behavioral repertoires. Thus the entire armamentarium of behavior theory, including operant conditioning and Contingency management or Contingency Contracting, can be programed within a general systems context, moved into the field, and connected with the newest procedures in the application of social indicators and social accounting at national, community, organization, and individual CS levels (Kanfer and Phillips, 1970a, 1970b; Likert and Bowers, 1969; Pratt, 1972a, 1972b; Pratt and Tooley, 1970a; Tharp, 1972; Tharp and Wetzel, 1969).

## Type III: Methodological Taxonomies

Methodological taxonomies encompass investigative-interventive, innovative, and assessment techniques of all types from a Stanford Binet, factor analysis, and EDP, to the planned use of nonviolence or violence. They are *instrumental* taxonomies that may first of all be directed at "how to" methods for the design of other kinds of taxonomies, normative or descriptive, as well as "how to" develop methodologies designed to affect directly outcomes, methods in research action or social action, strategy, tactics, technology, and procedures—all of which invoke an evaluative context.

It has been indicated that epistemologically, the three types of taxonomies (normative, descriptive, methodological) are inextricably interrelated and that their separation is simply a logical "categorization of convenience." Thus, whether explicitly or implicitly, all methodologies without exception have intrinsic value implications, as does anything that is of human interest, including those methodologies spuriously labeled "objective" meaning "value free." Methodologies are by definition *means,* and means (as well as their effectiveness) can only be defined or evaluated in terms of criteria derived from the *ends* they are designed to enact. Invariably concern is with *ends-means* configurations. Both the development and use of any and all methodological taxonomies unavoidably must occur within the inclusive context of normative and descriptive-nomological taxonomies.

It should go without saying, though social-behavioral scientists seem particularly pollyannish on this point, that Type III taxonomies (as well as Type I or II) can be and are widely put to counteractualizing, exploitative, zero-sum game purposes (Bogart, 1972; Boguslaw, 1965; Denzin, 1970; Horowitz, 1964; Kelman, 1968; Mills, 1959; Sanford, 1969; Sanford and Comstock, 1971). In his cryptic review, James Kelman epitomizes nuclear physicist Kahn's (1972) neomachiavellian text *On Thermoneuclear War* as "a moral tract on mass murder: how to plan it, how to commit it, how to get away with it, how to justify it." Also see *Roots of War: The Men in Institutions that Make Foreign Policy* (Barnett, 1972). And regarding methodology misused by social service professionals in relation to another kind of war read, "The War on Poverty—Political Pornography" (Alinsky, 1965) or *Regulating the Poor: The Functions of Public Relief* (Piven and Cloward, 1971).

Again, the PSAR Metataxonomic Model for Type III taxonomies (as for Types I and II), can be of service to other, non-PSAR, methodological taxonomies. First, if it turns out empirically that a given methodology cannot get the job done, it can be checked out against the more comprehensive model for indications as to why it is missing the variance, particularly in terms of ecological validity and degree of epistemic correspondence. Then, assuming that a given methodology can get the job done, is the job itself, as defined, worth doing: this is the evaluative question of significance as "worthwhileness" (Guttentag, 1971). If the "objective" is found wanting and reformulated to an actualizing or at least to a neutral non-zero-sum objective, will the original methodology (the orginally adequate means) still work?

As others have charged and as ubiquitous billion-dollar programs down the drain so painfully prove, the faulty conceptualization of means-ends methodologies, including how and by whom they are to be conceptualized and carried out (who's included and who's excluded), can guarantee total failure in advance. Programs to be carried out are systems within a broader systems context, and the further problem must be faced of predictable and unpredictable means-end conflicts. Predictable and unpredictable instrumental-consequential (IC) conflicts include the permutations: $I'_{x...n'} \cdot C'_{x...n'}; I'_{x...n'} \cdot I'_{x...n'}; C'_{x...n'} \cdot C'_{x...n'}$.

## VI. PSAR:EC—SOME CONCEPTUAL-METHODOLOGICAL CONSIDERATIONS

### Evaluation Contracts and the PSAR:EC

If the essence of all human endeavor is best characterized as contractual, then all research endeavor, including *evaluation* research, can best be conceptualized as contractual, within a contract systems field (CSF) context.

Furthermore, all of the kinds and aspects of contract systems, operating within the broader CSF, become potentially relevant to all evaluation endeavor (and to all of its SRI components), of whatever kind or purpose. Is the EC (whether stated as such or not) reliable and valid or unreliable and invalid; consensual or coercive; honest or fraudulent; equitable or inequitable; actualizing or counteractualizing; and so on? Have all legitimately concerned parties been adequately represented in conceptualization, negotiation, and implementation of all aspects and conditions of the "whole package" of the SERIC; is negotiation of the contract open-ended and subject to periodic renegotiation? Is the ERIC a reflexive contract in that, with or without outside assistance, a group/organization is involved in the evaluation-development of its own "systems of concern" that is, self-assessment-improvement; or is A evaluating B on behalf of A, or B, or on behalf of a third party, C? Is the stated purpose (or "hidden agenda") of the ERIC to discover and create potentially actualizing systems, or to obstruct and destroy them; to expose and change or eliminate "profitable" counteractualizing systems, or to salvage, strengthen, and reinforce them?

The PSAR:EC Model itself can, of course, be put to several purposes. As has been stressed, its primary purpose is to attempt to further human systems actualization: this includes higher-order reflexive evaluation of progress and failure in such endeavors. Second, this model provides an operational frame of reference with specifiable criteria against which all or any other SRIEC (including its methodology and purpose) can be checked out, then improved or exposed as the case warrants. Other evaluation models, including designs and programs, can be assessed first at the level of their own stated purpose, method, and outcome criteria. But then, after having been evaluated on their own terms, they should also be checked out in terms of the PSAR:EC Model's conceptualization, methodology, and multiple process-outcome criteria, for example, ecological validity and epistemic correspondence, incorporating criteria derived from the two (*basic* and *ideal*) fundamental norms.

Here, we are talking about two levels for checking out the *taxonomization* process-purpose-power of different EC models, first on their own terms, then second, by outside standards (e.g., PSAR:EC Model).

### The PSAR:EC Model—A Brief Recapitulation

Representative characteristics that distinguish this model from others in current use, misuse, or disuse, can be readily recapitulated as follows.[7]

1. At the biological core is "irritability" (capacity to respond or act), which becomes "curiosity" and "concern." Evaluation contracts (SRIEC) are negotiated and carried out to find out what the situation is, what to do about it, how to do it, does it work—for whom, against whom? Irritability, curiosity, concern—but for what, in whose interests, how, at what costs to whom?

2. Evaluation research intervention and the attack on sociopsychological problems are conceptualized and carried out as a "whole package" (SRIEC); thus the methodological myth is countered, the fallacy that research necessarily and invariably precedes practice or application, and that evaluation can only occur *after* the fact, separate from and after research or application.

3. For the PSAR:EC Model, evaluation occurs *through* "research action" (Sanford, 1969, 1970) or "social action research" (action research *as* social action); and conversely, research (all types) and systematic intervention (all types) proceed through evaluation. Evaluation is built-in as an explicit, continuous part of systems development through systems research. Criteria for systems operation and development (e.g., cost-benefit analysis, effectiveness, efficiency) may be employed as assessment indices, but not until they have themselves been evaluated against higher-order criteria including the two fundamental norms.

4. PSAR:EC is a metataxonomic model, as well as a model for taxonomization. It *taxonomizes* taxonomies; it evaluates, classifies, exploits, and copes with extant taxonomies which may be found to be actualizing or incredibly counteractualizing. Taxonomization is its "m.o.": to discover and develop increasingly effective normative, descriptive, and methodological taxonomies (Types I, II, III) directed at human systems actualization, against counteractualizing systems, toward resolution of dystopian-utopian discrepancies.

This model conceptualizes "taxonomization" in the most generic ("whole package") sense possible. Taxonomization becomes the comprehensive process of evaluation, including conceptualization, specification, and operationalization of variables, how to get from here (given set of CS conditions) to there (more desirable set of CS conditions) *and doing it.*[8] Taxonomization gets at relevant sources of variance (*discovery*), and creates new sources (*invention*), and finds out how to put them to work; this is done within and between CS levels and CS spheres of living.

Taxonomization as a method of "successive approximations" will be described below in some detail in the discussion of making progressive "passes" through the PSAR:EC design-model. The number of passes necessary is determined by the number necessary to get the job done: for some evaluation problems, a single pass, empirical or speculative, might suffice; at the other extreme, iterative passes might need to be continued and projected throughout the foreseeable future. Making such evaluative passes is the technique by which taxonomies are developed *through* action—discovered, invented, modified, and improved. By thus maximizing ecological validity and epistemic correspondence, taxonomies can be made increasingly productive.

5. The epistemological orientation is *trans*-actional rather than *auto*-actional or *inter*-actional. For human social systems transactions are essentially contractual, thus we are concerned with contractual-transactions or contract systems, within the relevant CS field (CSF). Ontology and epistemology share this transactional field (TF) or CSF (which can also be stated in the currently popular language of "ecological exchange"); and all evaluation, formal or informal, involves contractual transactions within the relevant CSF.

Within its TF or CSF epistemology-ontology, the PSAR:EC Model investigates the contractual-transactions involving: (1) the evaluators, (2) the evaluating process, (3) those evaluated (person-event-systems), (4) the evaluations, (5) evaluation-derived inferences, and (6) outcome effects. Otherwise stated, in relation to developing new roles in evaluation research (participant-observation-intervention), it is necessary to investigate the transactional-contractual process involving observers, observing process, observed system(s), observations (protocol data), observation-derived inferences, and outcome effects. Again, these are ways of operationalizing the construct of "objectivity" in terms of tracking down, while putting to work, optimal sources of variance.

6. Within this EC Model the current concept of "participant-observer" is extended to include participative-evaluative intervention innovation with emphasis on co-evaluators, co-conceptualizers, co-actualization-agents. In PSAR terms, the EC involves "participative social action research" as "participative systems actualization research."

7. The concept of *reflexive* evaluative intervention is operationalized through criteria for "reflexivity quotients" (RQ), coupled with criteria for systems "actualization quotients" (AQ). Other evaluation research models and programs, in addition to being assessed in terms of their own stated criteria, can also be evaluated in terms of RQ or AQ. A high RQ in and of itself could, of course, be found to be either actualizing (if coupled with a high AQ), or counteractualizing (to whatever extreme) for other systems or even for the group maximizing its own reflexive involvement but with its high RQ coupled with a very low or negative AQ, that is, with a "counteractualizing quotient" (CAQ).

8. In line with its participative, co-evaluation-intervention, reflexive (self-system-agentry) approach, our EC Model (PSAR), advocates evaluation action contracts based on "by" and "with" as preferable to "for" or "to." If unnecessarily introduced or if carried past absolute necessity, "to" mechanizes and dehumanizes; "for" subordinates and fosters dependency; even "with," when continued past common interests or beyond requested resource-person role, may end up in cooptation, preemption, or "professional imperialism." "By," and consensual-interest *coalitions* ("by-with"), frequently identify the most effective (or constructive) evaluation intervention contracts.

9. Within the PSAR:EC frame of reference, "correlational and experimental disciplines" can be combined with research action designs using multivariate methods and high-speed, large-capacity EDP hardware. By synthesizing correlational and experimental designs, both *treatment* and *individual* "error variance" can be taxonomized out (e.g., "partialled out")–or they can be taxonomized in as useful contributory sources of variance. For instance, contrary to customary design, experimentors' and subjects' (as co-evaluation-researchers) own personal stakes-in-outcome and participative subjects' knowledge of hypotheses may both be purposefully maximized within this model, rather than being ignored, suppressed, or controlled as by being "partialled out."

10. All legitimately interested parties to the EC (SRIEC)–evaluation researchers, activists, sponsors, publics–should share full knowledge of purposes, methods, and objectives, and should be equitably represented as active participants (co-systems-actualization agents) in conceptualization, negotiation, and completion of the EC. Ongoing evaluation should assure that role-tasks and benefits are optimal and equitable.

11. This EC Model calls for explicit statement of *aims* taxonomized as (1) *ideal,* idealized prototype of aim; (2) *goals,* major, often long-range, projected outcomes; (3) *objectives,* immediate or short-range, more circumscribed outcomes (Kaplan, 1964). Degree of success or failure in achieving these three levels of aim (Type I taxonomies) is, of course, usually contingent upon the adequacy of descriptive (Type II) and methodological (Type III) taxonomies involved. Again, achievement of these aims can be evaluated in terms of criteria stated or implied by the given program, design, or model in question. Frequently criteria will not be provided or will not have been operationalized; and the three levels, ideal, goals, and objectives (IGO), will not have been adequately included nor differentially specified.

A higher-order evaluation may determine that these given IGO targets themselves, or outcomes representing them, are in reality primarily counteractualizing (even extremely so); or that the public IGO statements serve simply as smokescreen-cover for "hidden agenda" that is counteractualizing. It may also be found that, within and/or between IGO levels, outcomes and/or procedures (ends-means) are either reinforcing or dysjunctive.

For the PSAR:EC Model itself, open-ended IGO level aims would be progressively developed through active participation in their actualization; again, empirically confirmed criteria would stress conceptual pluralism and cultural diversity but would invariably be checked out against the two fundamental norms.

12. Within and between CS spheres or levels, system attributes can be construed as outcomes of antecedent treatments or conditions, selectively chosen, and systematically reintroduced as *inputs.* Thus, sets of system parameters can be treated alternately (successively or simultaneously) as dependent, then as independent variables which can be fed back in through a progressive series of staged inputs-outputs-inputs.

This can be stated simply in ends-means language: PSAR:EC designs provide for the alternating treatment of, or the sequential transformation of, ends into means, with ends (treatment outcomes or chosen attributes) selected at one step in the PSAR:EC progression (or "passes"), fed back in as means in the next (or most appropriate) step, and so forth in spiral iteration.

> What are considered as ends in one set of experiments may be considered as means in another, such means in turn implying another end or set of ends. [Churchman and Ackoff, 1947: 45]

13. By increasing the number of contributary combinatorials through the use of now-available multivariate designs, our EC Model provides for optimal exploitation of *transaction variance* ("interaction variance") from variance sources within and between system levels.

14. Relationships within and between CS spheres and levels can be empirically investigated through change in terms of the contractual process of *ensystematization,* which results from the *inter*-system (e.g., coalition) and/or *intra*-system (e.g., organization contract) representation of relevant (or irrelevant) constituents or parties. The ensystematization process, reflecting actualizing and/or counter-actualizing representation (as sources of variance) within and between levels, can be constructively exploited by PSAR:EC in its attack on problems of human systems actualization and counteractualization. Here again significant social issues should be conceptualized for action in connection with their interrelated "public problems" and "private troubles" (Mills, 1960).

Purpose again is to maximize positive sources of variance and to cope realistically with negative sources. Equitable representation covers creative roles, political-economic-social power-of-agency, conceptual-ethnic-cultural plurality. These are aims (IGO levels) to be achieved through PSAR:EC-type affirmative action, "by whatever means now required," but adhering to the legal principle of the "least drastic (costly) means sufficient to procure necessary results" (Kittrie, 1971; Pratt, 1972a).

15. Without exception, means are treated as components or irreducible ends-means configurations, with the requirement that each means must be systematically evaluated in terms of criteria derived from the end (IGO or subsystems thereof) which it was ostensibly designed to affect. Such ends (or ends-means configurations) must themselves be open to periodic evaluation, not only in relation to program-derived criteria as such, but also in terms of other, or higher-order, criteria, for example, the two fundamental norms.

16. PSAR:EC is a heuristic, open-system model aimed at evaluation through change of "what is" (actualizing and counteractualizing), of what "can be" or "could be" (again positive and/or negative), and of what "ought to be" or "should be," explored through trying to sustain or develop more utopian, less dystopian systems. This includes discovery and invention, as well as critical evaluation (through action) of "happenings" or "system surprises."

17. Designs derived from this model are themselves conceptualized as heuristic guides. Such designs (1---n) can themselves be comparatively evaluated; and those found most effective, empirically, can in turn be modified through passes involving sequential analysis "in which bugs are worked out" and designs further improved

(Asher, 1964; Asher and Post, 1964).

18. System and subsystem effectiveness-efficiency (within relevant CSF) frequently requires periodic, if not continuous, reevaluation to assess full positive-negative range of actualizing/counteractualizing outcome-process variables (Do not overlook secondary as well as primary outcomes, short and long-term outcomes, predicted or surprise system effects—happy or horrendous.); to determine how to cope constructively with such effects in continued design use or redesign.

19. "Principle of specification" is required for all types of taxonomization, whether taken individually or in their inexorable combination: (1) normative (value systems or axiological), (2) descriptive, (3) methodological (interventive, strategy tactics). For instance, inextricable "ends-means" value contexts (Type I) cover IGO levels (explicitly or implicitly) in relation to "what is" (Type II) and how to strengthen or change it (Type III).

20. The PSAR:EC Model is an open system which provides for comparative systematic use (or disuse) of feedback and of fed-back-in or feed-in of outcomes and/or process findings. These findings or outcomes can derive from internal or external sources of variance, individual variables or sets, positive, negative, or mixed. The purpose is *participative* involvement of relevant parties (PSAR:EC) in evaluative gathering of feedback or feed-in data and in its combined line-type and staff-type IGO exploitation. Consider uses in maximizing desired process and outcomes, or in minimizing negative or counteractualizing; relate to policy making, decision and choice, reciprocal role formulation, negotiating, discovering and inventing new actualizing realities, organization contracts (internal) and interorganization coalitions (external), for example, through developmental use of social indicators and social accounting.

21. To the extent that an organization or process represents an essentially closed system, it becomes necessary to conceptually transcend it in order to understand it and, more accurately, reconceptualize it (Godel, 1963); and furthermore, a system can only be thoroughly understood through participatively changing it (Lewin, 1948); thus the business of PSAR:EC is change agentry or more accurately "actualization agentry."

22. The transactional field, as shared by epistemology and ontology, is conceptualized in terms of our *special* general systems theory, that is, "general CSF" which combines systems, levels-of-integration, ecological-exchange, and power-conflict theories.

Ecological validity is maximized (to get the job done through increasing knowledge) through PSAR:EC designs that achieve necessary-to-optimal representation of circumstances (ecological events) within and between CS levels and spheres of living, within the relevant CSF. Epistemic correlation is brought about through open-system designs that achieve as high a degree of correspondence between theoretical-conceptual constructs (C-Plane) and their empirical referents or protocol data (P-Plane) as is practicable. For PSAR:EC this includes interrelationships between the three types of taxonomies (normative, descriptive, methodological), including of course ends-means (or axiological-praxiological) constructs with their "empirical grounding."

23. Through such CST constructs-procedures, the PSAR:EC Model can search out (discover) and create (invent) sources of variance within and between relevant CS levels and spheres of living. Such actualizing variance can be put to work to counter dystopian or counteractualizing systems and to further human enterprise through more utopian actualizing systems.

## VII. PSAR:EC MODEL

In this section a procedure for developing and maintaining the PSAR:EC Model is presented. Figure 7.1 is a methodological map for schematic flow chart of the

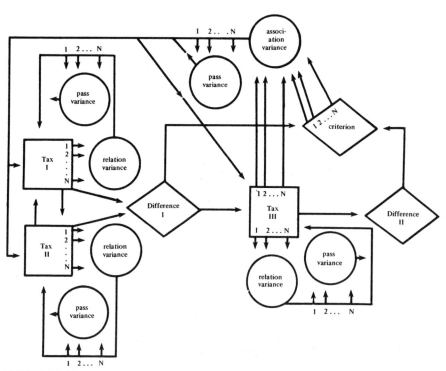

FIGURE 7.1 PSAR:EC Model: Schematic showing components and information-action flow.

operations of the PSAR:EC Model. Four symbols represent components of the model: squares represent taxonomies, circles identify sources of variance, diamonds represent differences between two or more variables, and lines represent the flow of information and the movement of the process to the next step. Four operations make up the PSAR:EC network: within-taxonomy feedback loop processes (Figure 7.2); criterion development processes (Figure 7.5); Type III taxonomy variables/criterion relationships (Figure 7.6); and feedback-to-taxonomy loops. These operations are described in the next four sections.

## A. Within-Taxonomy Feedback Loop Operation

There are three within-taxonomy feedback loops which are presented in Figure 7.2. Each loop represents: the process of taxonomization (squares), assessing relation variance (circles), assessing pass variance (circles), flow of information and movement of the process (lines). Taxonomies have been described in detail above (Section V), but it should be recalled that PSAR:EC Model is an open system with input entering at the taxonomy level.

*Relation variance* is variance due to a change in one or more variables which corresponds to a change in one or more other variables of the taxonomic system. This relation variance may be assessed by a simple empirical observation of the simultaneous change of two variables or by a more complex procedure like factor analysis. Taxonomies generally contain numerous variables, and the use of multi-variate procedures is usually indicated.

*Pass variance* is variance due to a change in repeated measurements of the same or a similar variable or set of variables. Relation variance may or may not be partialled out of the pass variance. Again, as with the relation variance, pass variance may be assessed by simple observation or complex statistics and is usually considered multivariate.

The three path markers (Figure 7.2) from the taxonomy to the relation variance represent one through N variables to be processed by statistical and/or observational procedures. If there is more than one pass, variance due to passes may be assessed. The resulting information is fed back to the taxonomy and is used to facilitate further taxonomization.

Taxonomization is the process of developing, discovering, inventing, and assessing participation, scope, systematic taxonomy relationships, empirical taxonomy relationships, completeness selection, concept description, measurement of concepts, reliability, and validity. The order in which these steps of taxonomization are discussed is not necessarily the order in which they occur in a particular taxonomization process.

1. *Participation.* The crucial question of who participates in an evaluation or research contract has been raised above. The PSAR:EC Model requires that a representative sample of all relevant participants be a part of the ERI (evaluation research intervention) process. If all meaningful variance is to be identified, it is

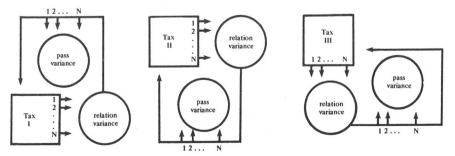

FIGURE 7.2 Within-taxonomy feedback loops for each taxonomy.

usually participants who will be best able to track it down. Professional researchers, full-time evaluators, and other "experts" have a notoriously poor record when it comes to transmitting goals and methodologies most useful to participants into measureable variables. Each time through the feedback loop, participative investigators need to reassess adequacy of participation. Representativeness of participation is essential to "ecological validity," to "representativeness of circumstances," and "representativeness of design" (Brunswick, 1956). Capacity to effect desired outcomes depends upon equitable ensystematized representation, upon optimal participation.

2. *Scope.* The concepts chosen will depend upon the population of concepts, individuals, and systems which the participants wish to represent and to which they wish to generalize their results. If interveners wish to generalize their results to isolated situations, then only those concepts need to be considered in the scope. However, if interveners wish to generalize their results to a situation in which the concepts are embedded in a multiple-concept field, then all relevant concepts of that field system will fall within the scope. Relevant concepts are those which, in whatever way, will have an appreciable affect on specific concepts under consideration.

3. *Systematic Taxonomy Relationships.* Variables of a taxonomy can be organized along two dimensions (and this in spite of whatever other types of organization might be germane to the problem at hand). First, variables could be categorized in terms of areas or CS spheres of living: for example, teaching-learning-doing variables; vocational-avocational variables; social skills like dancing, conversation, cards; personality development-actualization variables; and so on. Second, variables can be taxonomized according to social hierarchy levels: for example, Level I, individual, intrapsychic, personal; Level II, dyads, primary or very small groups; Level III, larger groups or organizations; Level IV, neighborhoods or community segments; Level V, communities, areas, districts; Level VI, interstate, national, or international corporations; and so on. Such a systematic taxonomization (categorization-hierarchization) process was introduced earlier, which stressed that, whatever process-schema is used, the concepts (spheres-levels) must fit both the reality of the situation and the purpose of intervention evaluation.

4. *Empirical Taxonomy Relationships.* Empirical assessment of relationships among the variables of the taxonomy involves two procedures: (1) determining the degree to which variables are interrelated and then categorizing the variables according to such interrelatedness, (2) and determining the degree to which one set of variables is dependent upon the variance of another variable or set of variables and building a hierarchy according to such dependence. The task in this step is to determine which variables are related and then to determine what variables such relationships are dependent upon.

*Interrelatedness* is assessed through the PSAR:EC Model by determining consistency of relationships among variables over passes. Spheres of relationships are categorized by sets of variables which are interrelated but not related to other sets of variables.

*Dependence* is assessed by changing independent or predictor variables over passes and determining variance introduced in dependent variables. Levels of empirical hierarchies are specified by the dependence of one variable on another.

Systematic taxonomy relations (step 3 above) are not necessarily changed as empirical taxonomy relationships become available. It may be useful to retain the systematic taxonomies to generate hypothesis, to select relevant variables, or to determine completeness. For example, intrapsychic variables, feelings, or thoughts might be influenced by, or part dependent upon, group variables (e.g., mores of the group), but such relatedness would not require one to change the systematic taxonomies of intrapsychic and intragroup levels.

5. *Completeness Selection.* The problem of the completeness selection procedure is to select an optimum number of variables which will account for the variance of the taxonomy which participant-investigators consider the scope of the situation to which they wish to generalize results. Consequently, the procedures of scope, systematic taxonomy relations, and empirical taxonomy relations will be used in selecting variables.

The scope of a system is entirely arbitrary from the standpoint of the PSAR:EC Model. Some programs are small, and some are large; some programs are exploratory, while others are comprehensive; the evaluation efforts of a very complex program may be superficial, while the evaluation efforts of a circumscribed program may be quite intensive; some evaluation efforts may emphasize discovery or invention, while others are concerned only with maintaining programs at an optimum level; but all evaluation programs, and consequently the variables selected, are delimited by their scope.

Participant-investigators will rarely, if ever, include all possible relevant variables in their study, and consequently, they must select variables which will account for maximum variance. Scope will determine the spheres and levels chosen from the systematic taxonomy. Investigators can decide on the basis of dependence and interrelatedness of the empirical taxonomy which other variables must be included to encompass the situation to which they wish to generalize. Variables may be eliminated if they are interrelated with other variables or if they are dependent upon higher-order variables. Completeness can be empirically checked by pass variance.

6. *Concept Description.* Once the categories of potential variables are selected, finer descriptions of the concepts need to be made. The task here is to specify the dimensions of the concept(s) in such a way that they can be measured, to define the "real" or "true" variable which the participant-investigator wishes to measure. It will be noted in the next section that there may be a difference between the underlying ("true") concept and the "measured variable." This distinction may be made with each of the three taxonomies and the criterion. These concepts are represented symbolically in the following manner:

$$C_I = \text{Type I taxonomy (Tax I) concepts;}$$
$$C_{II} = \text{Type II taxonomy (Tax II) concepts;}$$

$$C_{III} = \text{Type III taxonomy (Tax III) concepts;}$$
$$C_c = \text{criterion} = (C_{Ip} - C_{IIp}) - (C_{Iq} - C_{IIq})$$

where

$$C_{Ip} - C_{IIp} = \text{Conceptual Difference I;}$$
$$C_{Iq} - C_{IIq} = \text{Conceptual Difference II.}$$

7. *Measurement of Concepts.* In order for concept variables to be placed on continuum, they must be dimensionalized or expressed in measureable terms. The measured taxonomy and measured criterion variables are represented symbolically as follows:

$$M_I = \text{measured Tax I variables;}$$
$$M_{II} = \text{measured Tax II variables;}$$
$$M_{III} = \text{measured Tax III variables;}$$
$$M_c = \text{measured criterion variable} = (M_{Ip} - M_{IIp}) - (M_{Iq} - M_{IIq});$$

where

$$M_{Ip} - M_{IIp} = \text{Measured Difference I;}$$
$$M_{Iq} - M_{IIq} = \text{Measured Difference II.}$$

The measured variable may or may not adequately represent the underlying concept. The difference between the two is the error in measurement and may be stated as:

$$E_I = C_I - M_I = \text{error of measurement of a Tax I variable;}$$
$$E_{II} = C_{II} - M_{II} = \text{error of measurement of a Tax II variable;}$$
$$E_{III} = C_{III} - M_{III} = \text{error of measurement of a Tax III variable;}$$
$$E_c = C_c - M_c = \text{error of measurement of a criterion change variable.}$$

The issues involved here have been developed at length in standard texts on psychometrics (Guilford, 1954).

8. *Reliability.* Reliability can be exemplified as two passes through the within-taxonomy feedback loop. The first pass would be the first test, and the second pass would be the retest. Two or more passes can occur simultaneously, such as two halves of the split-half method of estimating reliability. Because the two variables (tests) should account for the same variance in each pass, any variance identified as variance due to passes would be error variance or variance due to the unreliability of the measuring instrument.[9]

Reliability can be expressed as a variable (test) accounting for the same variance on two passes (Figure 7.3). This can be seen most readily in the test-retest estimate

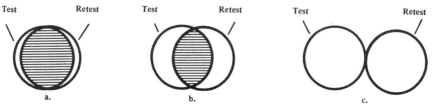

FIGURE 7.3 Venn diagrams representing relative reliability of measurement.

of reliability (major methods of estimating reliability are readily available in the literature). The test-retest estimate of reliability is represented by the hatched areas of the Venn diagrams in Figure 7.3; while inconsistency is seen in the white areas. In figure 7.3a most of the variance is accounted for by the variance of the test scores on a single administration (relation variance), while little of the variance was accounted for by the differences between the two administrations of the test (pass variance). In Figure 7.3b, less of the variance was accounted for by the tests and more by the passes. In Figure 7.3c, all of the variance was accounted for by the passes and none by the tests.

9. *Validity.* Essential components of validity are concept, description, measurement, and reliability. Validity is defined as the degree to which a variable or a combination of variables account for the total variance of the selected scope of the taxonomy. A high validity level can occur only when participation is optimal, the system taxonomy relations are well formulated, empirical taxonomy relations are well established, completeness is optimal, concepts are accurate, and reliability coefficients are high.

When examining the concept by means of the model, there are a number of methods for assessing validity. Our purpose here is not to detail these methods, rather, the attempt is to present a model for using existing methods and to sharpen conceptual tools. Taxonomy development as presented in steps 1 through 8 above is designed to identify and define the relevant variance in any system of variables. Validity as used here (step 9) is the ability to measure that total relevant variance.[10] For each taxonomy, validity is the variance due to variables in the within-taxonomy feedback loop. In Figure 7.4a each of the two variables ($M_{III_1}$ and $M_{III_2}$) accounts for some of the total relevant variance, but they account for almost the same variance. Whereas, in Figure 7.4b, each of the two variables accounts for about the same variance as in Figure 7.4a, but they account for different variance in the total relevant variance, consequently, accounting for more of the total relevant variance than in Figure 7.4a.

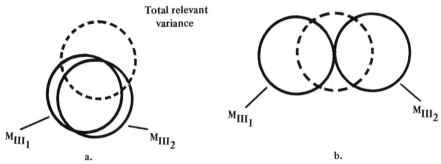

FIGURE 7.4 Venn diagram showing amount of criterion variance accounted for by two Tax III variables.

## B. Criterion Development Operation

The criterion development component has been presented in another context in Sections IV and V. The following discussion seeks to integrate the concepts

presented in these two sections into the schematic model. This criterion development component is represented in Figure 7.5.

The difference (or discrepancy) between "what should be" and "what is not" or
"what should not be" but "what is" before intervention becomes Difference I.
Such differences noted after intervention become Difference II. The difference
between Difference I and Difference II becomes the criterion.

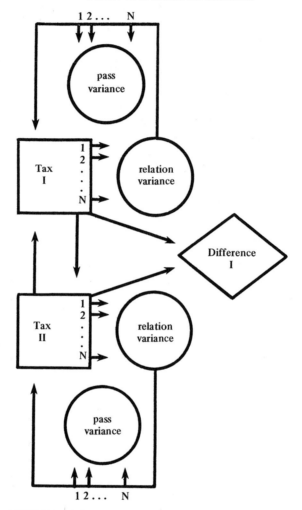

FIGURE 7.5 Criterion development component of PSAR:EC.

## C. Relationship of Tax III Variables and Criterion Variables

This section is divided into two parts: (1) variance due to association among
variables, and (2) variance due to passes. Critics have pointed out pitfalls of the
one-group design and correlational methods as methods to demonstrate that dependent variables are contingent upon independent variables (Campbell, 1969;
Houston, 1972). Throughout the remainder of this chapter, we will refer to the

one-group design and correlational methods as a single-pass method. The problem with the single-pass design is that a set of variables other than the instituted program (independent variables, i.e., Tax III variables) may have caused change which may exist in dependent variables (criterion variables). The issue involved in such an argument is whether or not one can predict outcomes to similar situations. If in the one-pass design there were variables other than the program (Tax III variables) which effected outcomes, then the introduction of the program in the new situation should have no effect. Stated another way, the investigator would have falsely concluded that the program, as such, caused the effect.

It is hypothesized that the degree to which the participant-investigator describes and measures the existence of the target program and simultaneous programs, as well as interactions between the two, is the degree to which he will be able to predict the effectiveness of the program in similar situations of the same scope. Before discussing this approach, three possible ways of estimating degree of control of criterion variables by Tax III variables are outlined.

The orthodox researcher tends to recommend the two-group (two-pass) design. The attempt is made to eliminate or equalize the effect of the variables on the two groups so that the groups are similar in every detail except in terms of the amounts of the independent variable. However, since it is impossible to eliminate all variables, the subjects are randomly assigned to the two groups. This randomization serves to further equalize effects of extraneous variables on the two groups. It is on the basis of such randomization that researchers can predict outcomes in the larger population from which subjects were drawn. That is, if the independent variable affects the criterion with a random group of subjects, one can predict it will affect individuals of the larger population from which they were drawn.

A second possibility is to describe, to measure, and to partial out any variance which may have an effect on the criterion variable. All other variables are assumed to be random. On the basis of partialling out variance which may affect outcomes and randomizing other variables, the investigators assume they can generalize to the population of variables and subjects which were either partialled out or randomized.

A third possibility is to describe, to measure, and to partial "extraneous" variance into the total variance picture rather than to partial it out (whether by randomization, elimination, or statistical control). In this situation all potentially relevant variables which could significantly influence the outcome are included. [11] Relationships within and between sets of variables would be known, and the degree to which these known variables represented the population (of subjects and of variables) to which one wishes to predict could be estimated: that is, by assessing participation, scope, systematic taxonomy relationships, empirical taxonomy relationships, concept description, measurement of concepts, completeness selection, reliability, and validity, the investigators can estimate the degree to which the variables represent the population. This process actually becomes a search for "extraneous" variables rather than a search for a way to eliminate them or their effects. Extraneous variables may become located and purposely designed into the taxonomies in order to increase criterion related variance.

1. *Variance Due to Variables (Association).* The association component (Figure

7.6) assesses the degree of association between the criterion variables and Tax III variables. This component also assesses the variance within each of the two sets of variables. The Venn diagrams in Figure 7.7 represent three possible relationships along a continuum of possible relationships for single or multiple variables of Tax III and criterion variables. In situation a of Figure 7.7, the Tax III variable accounts for a small amount of criterion variable variance (little association); in situation b, there is a considerable amount of variance accounted for; and in situation c, none of the variance is accounted for.

An estimate of the proportion of criterion variance accounted for by the Tax III variance in generalized situations may be made by utilizing the conceptual formula:

$$D_{tot} = A_{tot} \cdot TC_E$$

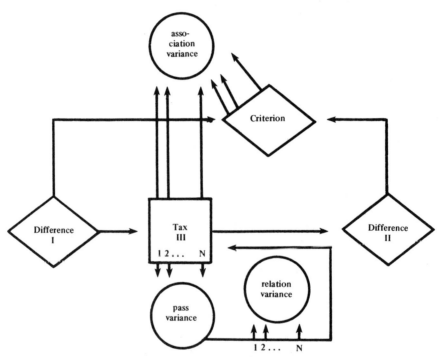

FIGURE 7.6  Association component of the PSAR:EC Model.

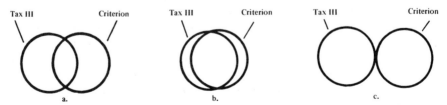

FIGURE 7.7  Three possible relationships along a continuum of relationships.

where

$D_{tot}$ = an estimate of degree of dependence of criterion variables on Tax III. variables;

$A_{tot}$ = total degree of association between criterion variables and Tax III variables;

$TC_E$ = estimated degree of comprehensiveness of the three combined taxonomies.

This formula applies to the total set of criterion and Tax III variables. To estimate the proportion of variance accounted for in a subset of criterion variables by a subset of Tax III variables in generalized situations, the following conceptual formula may be utilized:

$$D_{tot-sub} = (A_{tot} - A_{tot-sub}) \cdot TC_E$$

where

$D_{tot-sub}$ = estimate of degree of dependence of a subset of criterion variables on a subset of Tax III variables in generalized situations;

$A_{tot}$ = Total degree of association between criterion variables and Tax III variables;

$A_{tot-sub}$ = variance due to all variables except those being assessed;

$TC_E$ = estimated degree of comprehensiveness of the three combined taxonomies.

The purpose of this procedure is to determine the degree of control or predictability that a subset of Tax III variables will have on a subset of criterion variables in similar (generalized) situations. The generalized situation may be the "same situation" on a future pass, for example, evaluation to determine which aspects of an existing "mental health" program will be most effective for another "mental health" program across the state.

Each of the indices of the two formulas mentioned above ($D_{tot}$, $D_{tot-sub}$, $A_{tot}$, $A_{tot-sub}$, $TC_E$) is a proportion which assumes a value between zero and one. A value of .35 for the index $A_{tot}$ would indicate some association between the criterion variables and the Tax III variables. Figure 7.8 represents such a relation-

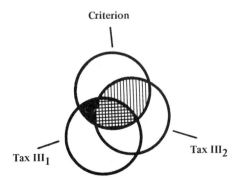

**FIGURE 7.8 Venn diagram illustrating multiple relationship to a criterion.**

ship for two Tax III variables and one criterion variable ($A_{tot}$). The $A_{tot}$ value indicates the portion of total variance of the criterion variables accounted for by all Tax III variables except the variables being assessed. In Figure 7.8, the $A_{tot-sub}$ variance is represented by the hatched *and* cross-hatched areas. This is about 35% of the total criterion variance resulting in the $A_{tot-sub}$ value of .35. The $A_{tot}$ − $A_{tot-sub}$ value indicates the portion of variance of the criterion variables accounted for by a set of variables which is not accounted for by any other variables. The $A_{tot}$ − $A_{tot-sub}$ is represented by the blackened area.

The $TC_E$ value indicates the estimated degree of comprehensive taxonomization for the generalized situation. This index is derived from an assessment of the degree to which taxonomization occurred. The $TC_E$ index is calculated by summing the estimated relevant taxonomization effects and dividing by the number of procedures:

$$TC_E = \frac{P_I + C_I + V_I + P_{II} + C_{II} + V_{II} + P_{III} + C_{III} + V_{III}}{9}$$

where

$TC_E$ = estimated degree of taxonomization;
$P$ = estimated relevant participation (the subscripts I, II, and III indicate the type of taxonomy);
$C$ = estimated completeness;
$V$ = total estimated validity.

Each of the estimates of the formula is a portion of the total inclusion, assuming values between zero and one. It should be noted that scope, systematic taxonomy relationships, and empirical taxonomy relationships are involved in completeness, while concept description, measurement, and reliability are involved in validity. Consequently, all of the procedures of taxonomization make up $TC_E$. Later it will be shown that $TC_E$ can be assessed empirically.

2. *Variance Due to Passes Component.* A pass is completed when a change of variance is noted in the criterion as a result of two sets of Tax III variables being applied in the same or different situations, or when the same set of Tax III variables is applied in different situations. A single pass in one situation may be construed as two passes in another situation. A pass could be a completed project or a change in one or more of the variables. The passes component, like the association component, assesses the estimated degree of dependence of the criterion variables on the Tax III variables for generalized situations. The general formula is stated:

$$D_{tot} = A_{tot} \cdot TC_E.$$

This formula is identical to the one given above. In order to assess dependence of the criterion on a change of Tax III variables, the following formula applies:

$$D_{pass} = (A_{tot} - A_{tot-subp}) \cdot TC_E$$

where

$D_{pass}$ = estimate of degree of dependence of the criterion variables on the Tax III variables;

$A_{tot}$ = total degree of association between the criterion variables and the Tax III variables;

$A_{tot-subp}$ = variance due to all variables except the variables which change over passes

$TC_E$ = estimated degree of comprehensiveness of the three combined taxonomies.

The value $A_{tot}$ represents all of the variance of the criterion accounted for by the Tax III including that due to passes. The value $A_{tot}$ - $A_{tot-subp}$ represents the variance accounted for by passes which is not accounted for by any other Tax III variables or other passes variables not being assessed. Here, again, as with the association component, $TC_E$ is the estimated comprehensiveness of taxonomization.

Traditional researchers recommend that $A_{tot-subp}$ be zero. As indicated above, a zero value is obtained by elimination of all "extraneous" Tax III variables that might be associated with the criterion or by randomizing the subjects between the passes (groups) so that the effects of the "extraneous" variables would not account for criterion variance over passes. Another method is to measure the "extraneous" variance and subtract any of this variance associated with the criterion. The problem with the traditional approach is that the degree to which the "extraneous" Tax III variance which interacts with independent and criterion variance is eliminated or disregarded is the degree to which situations to which one can generalize are curtailed. In controlled experiments, $TC_E$ is high if investigators wish to generalize to other controlled situations. Thus, scope of Tax III covers only circumscribed areas, in which case $TC_E$ is high, but the situations to which the investigator can generalize are limited to those circumscribed areas. That is, when extraneous variables are eliminated, one can generalize only to those situations where such extraneous variables are not present. If the groups are randomized, then the generalized situations are only those where randomization is present.

If investigators wish to predict in lifelike situations, then they must know to what degree the variables are complexly related. If the investigators want only to predict to other like experimental situations, then randomizing and controlling variables increases $TC_E$, but if they want to predict to more complex situations, randomizing and controlling out variables decreases $TC_E$, and $D_{pass}$ becomes less significant.

## D. Feedback to Taxonomy Loops

In the two previous sections feedback to taxonomies, for overall outcomes, was implied but not discussed. In this section a more systematic treatment of feedback to the taxonomy loops is presented.

1. *Feedback to Taxonomy Loops from a Single Pass.* There are three indices of the $D_{tot-sub}$ formula to be considered here: $A_{tot}$, $(A_{tot} - A_{tot-sub})$, and $TC_E$.

If $A_{tot}$ is large, then a significant portion of criterion variance has been accounted for by Tax III variables; if $A_{tot}$ is small, then little criterion variance has been accounted for by Tax III variables; consequently, in this latter case, the within-taxonomy feedback loops need to be reworked. Particular system components to be reconsidered are: systematic taxonomy relations and completeness selection to determine if the choice of variables has been optimal, reliability and validity to determine if the instruments are measuring the desired concepts.

Because $(A_{tot} - A_{tot-sub})$ deals with either individual or subsets of variables, there may be any number of such indices. If the index derived from the individual or set of variables is large, this indicates that the variables should be retained in the taxonomies. If the index is small, then the concept formation, measurement, reliability, and validity components need to be rechecked, or the subset of variables eliminated from the taxonomy.

If no significant values are found in the $A_{tot}$ or $A_{tot-sub}$, then there is no need to determine the value of $TC_E$. If the $TC_E$ value is low, the values in the computation will indicate what areas need to be considered. That is, since $TC_E$ is based on estimates by EC participants, they can readily determine if $TC_E$ is low, and that information can be fed back into the system so that more work can be done with the completeness step in taxonomy development.

In summary, subsets of variables with significant $D_{tot-sub}$ values will be retained in the taxonomies while subsets of variables with small $D_{tot-sub}$ values will need to be reprocessed in the within-taxonomy feedback loops, or be dropped from the system. Although it is not within the scope of this chapter to do so, a cost-benefit for subsets of variables could be ascertained by determining the cost of retaining the subset of variables against the size of $D_{tot-sub}$.

2. *Feedback to Taxonomy Loops from Multiple Passes.* When considering multiple pass issues, it should be recognized that single-pass feedback questions also apply. There are two issues to be concerned with when considering feedback from multiple passes. The first is to observe any change in the value of $D_{pass}$ as a result of a change in the value of one or more variables or of a new set of variables which may have been introduced. Any change in $D_{pass}$ is attributable to a change in the variables. The second issue is to note the value of $D_{pass}$ if no change has been introduced. If $D_{pass}$ is small (that is, no variance due to passes), then more confidence is warranted concerning the understanding of all variables in the system. If, however, $D_{pass}$ is large, then one must suspect $TC_E$ (validity of the system). It has been noted earlier that $TC_E$ on a single pass is estimated by a judgment, but it is at the level of multiple passes that a check on that judgment can be made. The value of $D_{pass}$ without $TC_E$ becomes the new and more objective value:

$$TC_0 = (A_{tot} - A_{tot-subp})$$

where

$TC_0$ = the observed value of taxonomization.

If $TC_0$ is large, then the system is not representative of the generalized situation and more work needs to take place in the within-taxonomy feedback loop. $TC_0$ becomes more reliable with an increase in the number of passes.

### E. Variables, Passes, and Strategies

Some programs are instituted for the stated purpose of attaining certain goals. Such programs have a starting date, a specified budget, and a review date set to see if the program succeeded. Other programs are ongoing, have been in operation for some time, and have no set time at which their success may be determined. These latter programs are assumed to be working effectively (in reality they may or may not be; they may, in fact, be having a counteractualizing effect). Some examples of the former are demonstration and experimental programs such as might be sponsored under a grant from HEW or OEO, while examples of the latter are "mental hospitals" and schools, prisons, service agencies, and nursing homes for aged.

The demonstration program is usually a one-pass affair, although it could involve two groups or methods (two passes). How does an evaluation effort maximize information from such a project? Since there is no variance-due-to-passes component (at least on the overall project level), the variance due to variables must be maximized. The degree to which taxonomization takes place will depend upon available resources, and how important it is to maintain high validities among information ingredients in the system.

Participant-investigators of ongoing programs are in a much better position to use the multiple passes model. In this situation the degree of taxonomization can start at much "lower level" ($TC_E$ can be smaller) and use prior passes to develop both hypotheses and taxonomies. Often in these cases there is a tendency to perceive evaluation as outside the realm of service and sometimes to interfere with service. As presented here evaluation *must* be an integral part of service and service an integral part of evaluation.

## F. Desired Significance of Outcome

Up to this point significance has been used to refer to degree of dependence of the criterion variables by the Tax III without indicating the amount of absolute change of the criterion. There could have been a high degree of dependence without a very large (signficant) change in the criterion variable. Consequently, judgments need to be made about the significance of the change between Difference I and Difference II (size of criterion) when a significant change exists. This judgment can be made a part of the formulas given above thus resulting in an estimate of the worthwhileness of any programs or subset of variables. A formula including worthwhileness for association would be:

$$D_W = (A_{tot} - A_{tot-sub}) \cdot TC_E \cdot W_E$$

where

$D_W$ = the degree of worthwhileness of the subset of variables;
$W_E$ = the proportion of desired criterion obtained;
All other variables have been defined above.

Again, cost-benefit of criterion attainment and cost of applying the subsets of variables could be entered into the formulas.

## G. Comparison of the PSAR:EC Model with Other Models

In comparing the PSAR:EC Model with other models, there are various levels and spheres at which comparisons can be made. The PSAR:EC is a metataxonomic model because it can provide taxonomies for different kinds of models, within which any other models can be classified; and on the other hand it is an evaluation model itself. Comparison with other models will be a matter of fitting the other models into, or checking them out against, the PSAR:EC Model. Users of several other models tend to exclude crucial parts of the PSAR:EC Model as being "unscientific," and it is on the basis of this type of exclusion that significant difference can be noted.

In addition, various aspects of scientific investigation which may not be considered a total model can be fitted into the PSAR:EC Model. At the same time this brief discussion is not intended to be a comprehensive review of research methodology.

Psychometric techniques (Guilford, 1954) have been used primarily to develop some of the Tax II variables to describe individuals and, to some extent, small groups or situations. That is, many psychological tests have been developed to measure psychological attributes (or traits) of individuals. These kinds of techniques have not been used extensively to develop measures for larger systems, such as organizations, neighborhoods, interorganizations, and coalitions. Further, very little has been done with psychometric techniques to develop instruments to measure Tax I (normative) and Tax III (methodological) variables. As discussed in Section II above, social science, in the name of "objectivity," has underproduced and misproduced in relation to value theory or value system sources of variance.

At first glance, it is equally surprising that so little has been done to develop instruments with which to measure qualitative and quantitative methodology variables. In the literature, one infrequently finds a study where investigators have measured differential amounts of given methodologies received: almost always "one group received the treatment" and the "other group did not." It becomes clear that such research design precludes the measurement of the amount of methodology, and it is no longer surprising to find that the psychometric methods have not been used extensively to develop instruments to measure methodology. Studies are designed so that we are blind to what is going on.

Because the area of dependence of criterion variables on Tax III variables (Solomon Four-Groups experimental design) has been given considerable attention in the literature, we will deal with it more extensively here also. It is not considered a more important issue than, say, the introduction of measuring Tax III variables, but these latter issues have been given more attention in other parts of this chapter.

Campbell (1969) has made the clearest statement of the problems of obtaining internal and external validity. Even though he has given much consideration to these issues, he has been most concerned with internal validity. Internal validity is obtained when investigators are sure that the independent variable, and not some other variable, effected the change in the dependent variable. External validity is obtained when subjects and variables of the program represent the situation to which the investigators wish to predict outcomes. The method almost exclusively presented to fulfill internal and external validity is the Solomon Four-Groups design. But as Campbell points out, this only fulfills internal validity requirements *at the cost of external validity.* Quasi-experimental designs have been proposed by Campbell, but recently these have likewise been severely criticized (Houston, 1972).

Central problems with Solomon Four-Groups design are that it does not:

1. Assign top priority to "worthwhileness";
2. Consider external validity;
3. Facilitate observation and measurement techniques, consequently obscuring objectivity;
4. Take into account that it is sometimes impossible or too costly (more lost than gained) to randomize adequately within and/or between real-life social-behavioral systems;
5. Measure variance of independent variables, thus losing the power of "within variance";
6. Include Tax III variables adequately; therefore, the design does not fully represent subjects and variables, and thus it misses potential alternative causes and interaction variance.

The following discussion indicates that, by using the PSAR:EC Model, the investigator can fulfill the requirements of internal validity, as well as meet the requirements of the six points above. The first major difference between the PSAR:EC Model and the Soloman Four-Groups design is keen observation-description-inclusion versus randomization-exclusion. The randomization-exclusion argument goes something like this. Because one cannot know what other variables might be affecting the dependent variable in addition to the independent variable, one should randomize the effects of all possible variables if they cannot be controlled out. The PSAR:EC Model user would want to include variables, describe to what extent they existed in the system situation, and measure their effects. Supporters of the four-groups design might argue that, if two treatment variables exist side-by-side in the same group, one cannot know which variable caused the effect. However, the two independent variables will exist to a greater or lesser extent for each subject in the group and these could (and *should*) be measured so that differential effects can be noted. A four-groups design study typically does not take into account the most likely possibility, that subjects receive differing amounts of the independent variable. It is almost always true that subjects receive differing amounts of the independent variable (or there would be no within variance) and consequently observation and measuring techniques need to be improved.

Second, external validity is much better approximated through PSAR:EC Model and can be tested. It should be kept in mind that the four-groups design makes no claim to external validity. In the taxonomization process, the scope of this generalized situation is defined and the extent to which the generalized situation is observed and measured is estimated by $TC_E$. Further, on subsequent passes $TC_E$ is continually reassessed.

Third, the PSAR:EC Model user goes to as great pains to measure the Tax III variables as it does Tax I and Tax II. Consequently, there is not one group that receives the treatment and another group that does not receive the treatment. Each individual (or ecological exchange unit) receives some amount of the treatment. Consequently, within-group variance is not lost (at least not by design).

Fourth, the PSAR:EC Model user includes rather than excludes potentially relevant variables (or variable sets); consequently, the interaction of variables can be noted. Characteristically, variables tend to change as they are extracted from the real situation in which they are normally embedded. Consequently, in the controlled four-groups design, the variable the investigator identifies, uses, and thinks is like a variable in a noncontrolled situation from which it was derived may, in fact, be quite different. Working within the PSAR:EC Model has the advantage of seeing the variable(s) still embedded in the real-life system, and makes it possible to test its interaction with other variables. The PSAR:EC Model user emphasizes knowing the situation he is investigating, keen observation and measurement, and understanding the complexity of the system under investigation.

## NOTES

1. It is necessary that the "fundamental postulate" and the "regnant construct" of a theoretical system be conceptualized at a "level of analysis" such that "with their corollary constructions" they can track down or be traced through the entire "universe of events" (phenomena) with which the theory is concerned (Kelly, 1955: 44).

2. All "behavioral exchange" (Gergen, 1969) represents *contractual* transactions (Carson, 1969; Jones, 1964; Peterson, 1968). For those with a behavioristic bias, it should be clear that all social behavior as "behavioral exchange" can be defined and described *interchangeably* in the "language of contract" or the "language of contingencies." Invariably, contingencies (OB-RE) involved in all behavioral relationships, both reflexive and between people (individuals, groups, organizations), are contractual contingencies. This applies also to behavior modification, operant conditioning, or "behavior therapy" (Franks, 1969; Krasner and Ullmann, 1965; Ullmann and Krasner, 1965) and has become explicit in current conceptions and programatic applications of "contingency management" or "contingency contracting" (Addision and Homme, 1966; Homme, 1969; Homme and deBaca, 1966; Home and Tosti, 1965; Kanfer and Phillips, 1970b).

3. It should be clear that, while CST has its own special PSAR Model for "actualizing-evaluation" contracts, any and all types of evaluation or ERI contract models can be checked out against this more comprehensive model which subsumes rather than excludes other models. Thus the PSAR:EC Model can be useful to other models if and when they fall short, when they find out that they have missed the variance boat and cannot get the job done.

4. Epistemological-ontological consideration of the total relevant CSF as being *transactional* precludes polar reductionism, whether intrapsychic (as in psychoanalytic) or personalistic reductionism on the one hand, or on the other hand as in absolute cultural relativism or absolute social determinism (the person as putty, *tabula rasa*). A transactional epistemology also assures that ERI designs are not restricted to one-way directionality analyses of cause-effect, but are forced to deal with events as transactions, as two-way or multiple-way, directionality phenomena. "One extreme is to regard all behaviors as being initiated completely from within the organism. The one-sided inadequacy of this view is what so often has called out an equally one-sided opposed view, according to which the organism is wholly passive, and is gradually molded into shape and adapted to living by independent environmental conditions, mechanistically treated. Both of these views, one as much as the other, are alien to us" (Dewey and Bentley, 1949: 143).

5. The construct, *contract systems field* (CSF), provides for the theoretical-empirical synthesis of such key concepts as: field theory, general systems theory, levels of integration, transactional epistemology, exchange theory, social ecology and ecological exchange, commitment and the norm of reciprocity, relative deprivation and cognitive dissonance, games theory, human systems actualization and counteractualization (Pratt, 1967, 1972b, 1972c; Pratt and Tooley, 1969, 1970b).

6. Independently, Sanford (1969: 456) has come to his own version of PSAR applied

within or through an academic setting (the Wright Institute in California). For this evaluative research model, "teaching *is* inquiry, research *is* action: research can release the activism latent in students . . . so a group of students will begin thinking about changing their educational environment in the light of their shared awareness of *discrepancies* between the way things are and the way things might be; and in the climate of today the thought easily becomes father to the deed." In "Whatever Happened to Action Research?" Sanford (1970) reemphasizes the timeliness of the "research-action" approach in evaluation.

7. By necessity sequence is somewhat arbitrary and does not imply relative significance, nor greater degree of connection, as between proximal points, because all are interrelated.

8. Faulty conceptualization of what taxonomization is all about, as expected, produces deficient taxonomies or, at best, limits their power or productivity. Consider taxonomies invariably treated as: closed systems rather than being placed on relatively closed to open systems continuum; linnaeus-type classification of static enumeration rather than as dynamic-dialectic process-event systems; as neo-Aristotelean class-theoretical rather than as post-Newtonian field-theoretical or as a probabilistic events system allowing for indeterminacy, system surprizes or emergents; neo-Baconian simplistic "bundle of bits" empiricism; as a categorization process assumed to be value free; classification systems restricted to "what is" (or was) without projection of what can, could, should, or should not be.

9. While this point is made regarding error variance due to passes, it should be kept in mind that a unique aspect of the PSAR:EC Model is that, whenever practicable and productive, error variance is delimited and then put to work (fed back into the design) to maximize desired outcomes.

10. More programmatically put, the purpose is not so much to measure even the total relevant variance, but to identify the optimal amount of variance necessary to get a given job done.

11. It should be pointed out that the PSAR:EC Model does not exclude the above two-group design but proposes that both the dependent (criterion) and independent (Tax III) variables would be taxonomized in the within-taxonomy feedback loops.

## REFERENCES

Adams, J. S. Inequity in social exchange. Pp. 133-175 in L. Berkowitz (ed.), *Advances in experimental social psychology,* 2. New York: Academic Press, 1965.

Addison, R. M. and L. E. Homme. The reinforcing event (RE) menu. *National Society of Programed Instruction Journal,* 1966, 4(1): 8-9.

Alinsky, S. D. The war on poverty—Political pornography. *Journal of Social Issues,* 1965, 21(1): 41-47.

Asher, J. J. Toward a neo-field theory of behavior. *Journal of Humanistic Psychology,* 1964, 4(2): 85-94.

Asher, J. J. and R. I. Post. The new field theory: An application to postal automation. *Journal of Human Factors Society,* 1964, 517-522.

Barker, R. G. Explorations in ecological psychology. *American Psychologist,* 1965, 20(1): 1-14.

Barnett, R. J. *Roots of war: The men in institutions that make foreign policy.* New York: Atheneum, 1972.

Blau, P. M. *Exchange and power in social life.* New York: Wiley, 1964.

Bogart, L. *Silent politics: Polls and the awareness of public opinion.* New York: Wiley, 1972.

Boguslaw, R. *The new utopians—A study of system design and social change.* Englewood Cliffs, N.J.: Prentice-Hall, 1965.

Boulding, K. E. *The impact of the social sciences.* New Brunswick, N.J.: Rutgers University Press, 1966.

Brunswik, E. *Perception and the representative design of psychological experiments.* Berkeley: University of California Press, 1956.

Brunswik, E. Points of view: Components of psychological theorizing. Pp. 523-534 in P. L. Harriman (ed.), *Encyclopedia of psychology*. New York: Citadel, 1946.

Buros, O. K. *Seventh mental measurement yearbook*. Rutgers, N.J.: Rutgers University Press, 1972.

Campbell, D. T. Reforms as experiments. *American Psychologist*, 1969, 24(4): 409-429.

Cantrell, R. P., M. L. Cantrell, C. M. Huddleston and R. L. Woolridge. Contingency contracting with school problems. *Journal of Applied Behavior Analysis*, 1969, 2(4): 215-220.

Cantril, H., A. Ames, A. Hastorf and W. Ittelson. Psychology and scientific research. Part I: The nature of scientific inquiry. Part II: Scientific inquiry and scientific method. Part III: The transactional view in psychological research. *Science*, 1949, 110: 461-464, 491-497, 517-522.

Carson, R. C. *Interaction concepts of personality*. Chicago: Aldine, 1969.

Churchman, C. W. and R. L. Ackoff. Towards an experimental measure of personality. *Psychological Review*, 1947, 1(54): 41-51.

Coles, R. *Children of crisis: A study of courage and fear*. Boston: Atlantic-Little, Brown, 1967.

–––. *Vol. II of children in crisis: Migrants, sharecroppers, mountaineers*. Boston: Atlantic-Little, Brown, 1971. (a)

–––. *Vol. III of children in crisis: The south goes north*. Boston: Atlantic-Little, Brown, 1971. (b)

Dabrowski, K. Negative adjustment and positive maladjustment. Paper presented at 4th International Congress of Social Psychiatry, Jerusalem, Israel, May 1972.

Denzin, N. K. the use and misuses of social science knowledge. Pp. 127-183 in author's (ed.) *The values of social science*. Chicago: Aldine, 1970.

Dewey, J. and A. F. Bentley. *Knowing and the known*. Boston: Boston Press, 1949.

Feibleman, J. K. Theory of integrative levels. *British Journal of Philosophical Science*, 1954, 5: 59-66.

Feigl, H. and M. Scriven (eds.) *The foundations of science and the concepts of psychology and psychoanalysis*. Minneapolis: University of Minnesota Press, 1956.

Franks, C. M. (ed.) *Behavior therapy: Appraisal and status*. New York: McGraw-Hill, 1969.

Fromm, E. *The sane society*. New York: Holt, Rinehart & Winston, 1955.

Gergen, K. J. *The psychology of behavior exchange*. Reading, Mass.: Addison-Wesley, 1969.

Gladwin, T. Social competence and clinical practice. *Psychiatry*, 1967, 30(1): 30-43.

Godel, K. *Godel's theorem: On formally undecidable propositions*. New York: Basic Books, 1963.

Goodwin, L. On making social research relevant to public policy and national problem solving. *American Psychologist*, 1971, 26(5): 431-442.

Gotkin, L. G., and L. S. Goldstein. *Descriptive statistics: A programed textbook*. New York: Wiley, 1964.

Guilford, J. P. *Psychometric methods*. New York: McGraw-Hill, 1954.

Guttentag, M. Evaluation of social legislation. Pp. 40-46 in F. F. Korten, S. W. Cook, and J. I. Lacey (eds.), *Psychology and the problems of society*. Washington D.C.: American Psychological Association, 1970.

–––. Models and methods in evaluation research. *Journal for Theory of Social Behavior*, 1971, 1(1): 75-95.

Halleck. S. L. Psychiatry and the status quo. *Archives of General Psychiatry*, 1968, 19: 257-265.

Hayakawa, S. I. The language of social control. Pp. 210-217 in E. P. Hollander and R. G. Hunt (eds.), *Current perspectives in social psychology*. 2nd ed. New York: Oxford University Press, 1967.

Heilbroner, R. *Between capitalism and socialism*. New York: Random House, 1970.

Hollingshead, A. B., and F. C. Redlich. *Social class and mental illness*. New York: Wiley, 1958.

Homans, G. C. Social behavior as exchange. *American Journal of Sociology*, 1958, Vol. 63, 597-606.

–––. *Social behavior: Its elementary forms*. New York: Harcourt, Brace & World, 1961.

Homme, L. *How to use contingency contracting in the classroom.* Urbana: University of Illinois Press, 1969.
--—, and P. D. deBaca. Contingency management on the psychiatric ward. Unpublished manuscript. January 1966.
Homme, L., and D. T. Tosti. Contingency management and motivation. *National Society of Programed Instruction Journal*, 1965, 4(7): 1-3.
Horowitz, I. L. *The new sociology.* New York: Oxford University Press, 1964.
Houston, T. R. The behavioral sciences impact-effectiveness model. Pp. 51-65 in P. H. Rossi and W. Williams (eds.), *Evaluating social programs: Theory, practice and politics.* New York: Seminar Press, 1972.
Hutcheson, B. R., and E. A. Krause. Systems analysis and mental health services. *Community Mental Health Journal,* 1969, 5(1): 29-45.
Johnson, R., P. R. Dokecki, and O. H. Mowrer (eds.) *Conscience, contract, and social reality.* New York: Holt, Rinehart & Winston, 1970.
Jones, E. E. *Ingratiation.* New York: Appleton-Century-Crofts, 1964.
Kahn, H., and B. Bruce-Briggs. *Things to come: Thinking about the 70s and 80s.* New York: Macmillan, 1972.
Kanfer. F. H., and J. S. Phillips. Contract psychology: An operational approach to the problem of conscience and self-control. In R. Johnson, P. R. Dokecki, and O. H. Mowrer (eds.), *Conscience, contract, and social reality.* New York: Holt, Rinehart & Winston, 1970. (a)
--—. *The learning foundations of behavior therapy.* New York: Wiley, 1970. (b)
Kaplan, A. *The conduct of inquiry: Methodology for behavioral science.* San Francisco: Chandler, 1964.
Kelly, G. *The psychology of personal constructs.* Vols. I & II. New York: Norton, 1955.
Kelman, H. C. The social consequences of social research. Pp. 32-57 in author's, *A time to speak: On human values and social research.* San Francisco: Jossey-Bass, 1968.
Kilpatrick, F. P. (ed.) *Explorations in transactional psychology.* New York: New York University Press, 1961.
Kittrie, N. N. *The right to be different: Deviance and enforced therapy.* Baltimore: Johns Hopkins Press, 1971.
Krasner, L., and L. P. Ullman (eds.) *Research in behavior modification: New developments and implications.* New York: Holt, Rinehart & Winston, 1965.
Lewin, K. *Field theory in social science.* New York: Harper, 1951.
--—. *Resolving social conflicts: Selected papers on group dynamics.* New York: Harper, 1948.
Likert, R., and D. G. Bowers. Organizational theory and human resource accounting. *American Psychologist.* 1969, 24(6): 585-596.
Mandelbaum, M. Societal facts. *British Journal of Sociology,* 1955, 6(4): 305-317.
Margenau, H. *The nature of physical reality.* New York: McGraw-Hill, 1950.
Maslow, A. H. *The farther reaches of human nature.* New York: Viking, 1971.
--—. Toward a humanistic biology. *American Psychologist,* 1969, 24(8): 724-735.
Mills, C. W. (ed.) *Images of man: The classic tradition in sociological thinking.* New York: George Braziller, 1960.
--—. *The sociological imagination.* New York: Oxford University Press, 1959.
Northrup, F. S. *The logic of the sciences and the humanities.* New York: Macmillan, 1947.
Novikoff, A. B. The concept of integrative levels and biology. *Science,* 1945, 101(2618): 209-215.
Peterson, D. R. *The clinical study of social behavior.* New York: Appleton-Century-Crofts, 1968.
Piven, F. F., and R. A. Cloward. *Regulating the poor: The functions of public relief.* New York: Pantheon, 1971.
Pratt, S. Systematic philosophy and organizational change: The perspective of contract psychology. Paper presented as part of the symposium, The Social-Behavioral Scientist as Mental Hospital Superintendent. American Psychological Association, Washington, D.C., September 1967.

———. Administrative theory and involuntary commitment. Paper presented at symposium, Involuntary Hospitalization–A Service or Disservice for the Hospitalized Patient? American Orthopsychiatric Association, Detroit, Michigan, April 1972. (a)

———. Contract-systems approach to community actualization. Paper presented at 4th International Congress of Social Psychiatry, Jerusalem, Israel, May 1972. (b)

———. Contract therapy: Work and creativity. Paper presented at 4th International Congress of Social Psychiatry, Jerusalem, Israel, May 1972. (c)

———, G. Scott, E. Treesh, J. Khanna, T. Lesher, P. Khanna, G. Gardiner, and W. Wright. The mental hospital and the treatment-field. Monograph No. 8, *Journal of Psychological Studies,* 1960, Vol. 11. Pp. 53-122 in *Research on the psychiatric hospital as a social system.* Third Annual Conference, Social Science Institute, Washington University, St. Louis, March 1961.

Pratt, S., and J. Tooley. Action Psychology. I: Action psychology and social action. II: Some metatheoretical and epistemological considerations. III: Some methodological considerations and the research contract, *Journal of Psychological Studies,* 1967, 15(3), whole-issue monograph.

———. Human systems actualization through "participative organization"–A strategy of contract-systems psychology. Paper presented at Conference on Behavioral Modification as a Function of Social and Interpersonal Factors. Kent (Ohio) State University, April 1969.

———. Mental hospitals as active partners in total community actualization. Paper presented at 7th Annual John W. Umstead Series of Distinguished Lectures, Man, Systems and Mental Health: Complexity, Dynamics and Viability. North Carolina Department of Mental Health, Raleigh, February 1970. (a)

———. Toward a metataxonomy of human systems actualization: The perspective of contract psychology. Pp. 349-379 in A. H. Mahrer (ed.), *New approaches to personality classification.* New York: Columbia University Press, 1970. (b)

Ruesch, J., and C. M. Brodsky. The concept of social disability. *Archives of General Psychiatry,* 1968, 19: 394-403.

Sanford, N. Psychology in action: Research with students as action and education. *American Psychologist,* 1969, 24(5): 544-546.

———. Whatever happened to action research? *The Journal of Social Issues,* 1970, 26(4): 3-23.

———, and C. Comstock. *Sanctions for evil: Sources of social destructiveness.* San Francisco: Jossey-Bass, 1971.

Sells, S. B. An interactionist looks at the environment. *American Psychologist,* 1963, 18: 696-702.

Shostrom, E. L. *Man, the manipulator: The inner journey from manipulation to actualization.* New York: Abingdon Press, 1967.

Smith, M. B. Toward a scientific and professional responsibility. *American Psychologist,* 1954, 9: 513-516.

Sullivan, H. S. *The interpersonal theory of psychiatry.* New York: Norton, 1953.

Tharp, R. Community intervention: A behavioral approach. Symposium presented at American Psychological Association Annual Convention, Honolulu, September 1972.

———, and R. J. Wetzel. *Behavior modification in the natural environment.* New York: Academic Press, 1969.

Ullman, L. P., and L. Krasner (eds.) *Case studies in behavior modification.* New York: Holt, Rinehart & Winston, 1965.

von Mises, L. *Human action: A treatise on economics.* New Haven, Conn.: Yale University Press, 1949.

Weick, K. E. Interlocked behaviors: The elements of organizing. Pp. 43-53 in author's, *The social psychology of organizing.* Reading, Mass.: Addison-Wesley, 1969. (a)

———. The enacted environment. Pp. 63-71 in author's, *The social psychology of organizing.* Reading, Mass.: Addison-Wesley, 1969. (b)

# 8

# ORGANIZATIONAL STUDIES OF MENTAL HOSPITALS

M. POWELL LAWTON

*Norristown State Hospital*

and

JACOB COHEN

*New York University*

The purpose of this article is to review some studies of mental hospitals. The review will cover studies that (a) focus on the organizational functioning of the institution as a total system and (b) contrast the functioning of two or more organizations. A major aim will be to indicate some of the problems involved in defining institutional characteristics, in relating them to member characteristics, and in measuring institutional quality and its predictors. While the mental hospital will be the focus of the review, some methodological references will be made to work in other types of organizations. Some similar studies for institutions for the elderly are reviewed by Lawton (1970a).

## THE INSTITUTION AS A FUNCTIONING SYSTEM

A number of authors have studied single institutions as total functioning systems (Caudill, 1958; Dunham and Weinberg, 1960; Goffman, 1961; Stanton and

AUTHOR'S NOTE: Requests for reprints should be sent to M. Powell Lawton, Philadelphia Geriatric Center, 5301 Old York Road, Philadelphia, Pennsylvania, 19141. Some of the research reported in this chapter was supported by Grant MH-17473, from the National Institute of Mental Health, Mortimer B. Lipton, Principal Investigator.

Schwartz, 1954; Stotland and Kober, 1965; von Mering and King, 1957). These studies have shared the point of view that the behavior of patients and the outcomes of treatment can be understood only within the context of the entire institution. The classical study of a treatment program would attempt to abstract from the total context one aspect of the stimulus environment, a particular therapeutic procedure, and measure its effect upon one class of organizational members, the patients. Some of the studies mentioned have, instead, treated the institution as a more complex system. They have attempted to show, for instance, the intimate association between staff behavior and patient behavior, between treatment ideology of different professions and patient attitudes, or the tension between manifest and latent institutional goals as this affects staff and patient behavior.

This problem is, of course, not a new one. Organizational theorists and researchers (Barton, 1961; Etzioni, 1964; Forehand and Gilmer, 1964; Katz and Kahn, 1966; March, 1964) have proceeded far beyond the case study and single-organizational experimental study. The need to deal with mental hospitals arises partly because they have been inadequately studied as organizations and partly because their content demands new approaches.

Some studies of institutions have focused on organizational functioning and others on the quality of the product, though the latter is, of course, an aspect of the former. We feel that organizational functioning cannot be understood without reference to the quality of product that variations in function may produce; however, many institutional characteristics are not clearly related to quality. Any such characteristics that does not have a clearly evaluative connotation will be referred to as a "process variable," an aspect of the functioning of the institution.

We shall first summarize the research findings that help define functional institutional dimensions. Then, we shall attempt to present in some orderly fashion some of the findings relating institutional process variables to each other or to patient variables. We shall then seek institutional characteristics that are related to output quality criteria and provide a summary of findings in this area.

## THE DIMENSIONS OF TREATMENT INSTITUTIONS

The terms "milieu" and "atmosphere" have been applied to institutions or wards within institutions in a manner remarkable for their lack of definition, or variation in definition. In some studies the major ingredient of the milieu appears to be the attitudes of staff, while in other studies, it is authority and status relationships, and at other times, the characteristics of the patients. Too often milieu has been invested with a somewhat mystical aura, as if there were some secret manufacturing process that combined all the institutional input into a substance which then influenced patient behavior. We shall define an institutional environment whose components are measurable characteristics of people, social structures, and physical environment, and which covary in the functioning of the institution.

This definition implies a multidimensional conception of the institution. Relatively few studies available in the literature have attempted to derive such dimensions. The Veterans Administration Psychiatric Evaluation Project (PEP) studied 12

VA hospitals and 1,274 consecutive newly admitted patients in these hospitals (Cohen, 1964; Davis, 1964; Gurel, 1964). As a part of the project, Davis (1964) reported on a separate factor analytic study of characteristics of the universe of 41 VA neuropsychiatric hospitals, using information that was obtainable from hospital records and reports sent to the central office. These variables included information on size, costs, staffing, hospital programs, and a few characteristics such as architectural style, age of hospital, and setting, as well as application and discharge data. The final three-factor solution resulted in factors identified, first, as Size (including cost and number of lower-level personnel). The second factor reflected the extent to which General Medical and Surgical (as opposed to psychiatric) services were given. The third factor was named nontraditionalism, which contained many items representing a high degree of treatment staff activity and therapeutic aliveness.

Cohen and Struening (1962) addressed themselves to the staff-attitude aspect of milieu with their Opinions on Mental Illness (OMI) Scale. A replicated factor analysis of responses to 70 items by 1,194 employees at two large VA hospitals resulted in five factors: Authoritarianism (belief in relying on coercion to handle patients, according them lower status, antipsychological thinking); Benevolence (unsophisticated kindliness toward patients, belief in the natural moral rightness of humane treatment); Mental Hygiene Ideology (acceptance of modern psychological conceptions of people and of mental illness); Social Restrictiveness (the belief that the protection of society should be the major aim of treatment, and that positive therapy is probably hopeless); Interpersonal Etiology (the ascription of mental illness to problems with significant life figures, childhood deprivation of parental love, or social behavior). On the basis of a demonstration of factorial invariance over three new samples (Struening and Cohen, 1963), a 51-item version of the OMI was utilized to score the five factors. When the scale was administered to 3,148 employees of the 12 PEP hospitals, the hospitals were clearly demonstrated to vary in their scores on the scales, particularly on the Authoritarianism and the Social Restrictiveness scales (Cohen and Struening, 1964). Nineteen occupational groups were also differentiable on the OMI, and 17 of them fell into four clusters according to the pattern of their means on the five factor scale scores (Cohen and Struening, 1963).

Other investigators used item-analysis techniques to scale institutional dimensions. Jackson (1964) assembled a number of statements that verbalized aspects of the treatment environment considered desirable in a therapeutic community, as formulated by Schwartz (1957), such as "Patients are free to select their own activities during the day," or "In general, about 90% of all patients participate in ward activities." The items grouped under each of the six treatment goals were first subjected to a Guttman scale analysis. An item analysis was also done against their ability to discriminate between personnel in a private hospital noted for its therapeutic milieu (N = 11) and those in a state hospital admission ward (N = 18) plus a state geriatric ward (N = 27). Items were discarded that did not either scale according to Guttman criteria or distinguish between the two environmental types, resulting in a 72-item test named Characteristics of the Treatment Environment

(CTE). No data are given on reliability. The CTE was then administered to 840 staff members from diverse occupations employed in four state mental hospitals. Total scores on the CTE were shown, in a series of analyses of variance, to differentiate among the four hospitals, among 26 treatment units in one hospital, and among intensive and continued treatment units over the four hospitals. Employees on intensive treatment units gave a more therapeutic description of the treatment environment than did employees on continued treatment units. Jackson later (1969) subjected the CTE to a component analysis, resulting in factors named Active Treatment ("the degree of staff activity directed toward patient welfare and improvement"); Socioemotional Activity ("the degree to which the environment permits or encourages normal socioemotional relations or activity among patients"); Patient Self-Management ("the degree to which the environment permits or encourages patient responsibility for the management of self or other patients"); Behavior Modification ("the degree to which staff attempts to influence, demand or control specific behaviors of patients"); Instrumental Activity ("the degree to which the environment permits or encourages normal choice or rational problem-solving activity by patients"). The factor analytically derived scales did not systematically correspond to the original six areas of therapeutic atmosphere. Jackson thus provided a scale whose total score's validity was demonstrated in some areas. On the other hand, because of the minimal nature of the original item analysis, there probably remain items that do not contribute to the scale's ability to discriminate among environments. The factors have apparently not yet been used as scales, and the CTE remains a perceived-environment instrument whose relationship to other patient and environmental variables is unknown.

King and Smith (1972) utilized the CTE in a pilot study of employees in six state hospitals. They selected 28 of the items that discriminated best among these hospitals and used them in a later study of 2,737 employees from a purposive sample of 18 state hospitals. A factor analysis of these items resulted in four factors named Staff-Patient Socioemotional Interaction, Patient Autonomy, Staff Involvement in Patient Therapy, and Staff Control of Patient Behavior. The 28-item total scale was named the Treatment Milieu Scale (TMS).

Kellam, Schmelzer, and Berman (1966) sought indices of the atmospheres of psychiatric wards in either directly observable aspects of the ward or in objectively phrased questions asked of nurses about ward rules, staff behavior, and patient behavior. The areas to be covered, how they were combined, and the weighting of the items were determined on an a priori, rather than a factor- or item-analytic basis. Seven indices were constructed and used separately in later analyses: (1) Disturbed Behavior (On a log kept for 30 days, nurses noted all patients who exhibited one or more times any of nine behaviors, such as incontinence, floor-sitting, or assaultiveness.); (2) Adult Status (Nurses were asked about rules, policy, or behavior in 13 areas indicating attempts to treat patients as adults, such as allowing patients in their bedrooms during the day, provision of shower privacy, lack of dehumanization during admission procedures, and so on.); (3) Patient-Staff Ratio; (4) Aloneness (During one week 35 ward surveys were made, counting the number of patients observed to be alone.); (5) Staff-Patient Contacts (The surveys also counted the number of patients interacting with staff.); (6) Cluster Size (The surveys also counted the number of patients observed in each social group.); and (7) Ward Census. Correlational analyses of the relationships among these indices done twice, a year apart, revealed that the three social indices—aloneness, staff-patient contacts, and cluster size—were related to each other; that high staff-patient ratio was associated with a high incidence of disturbed behavior, a large amount of staff-patient contact, and small ward census; and high adult status was associated with small ward census. The indices were used as separate predictors and, as will be noted in the following section, they differed among themselves in important ways in predicting outcome.

Moos and Houts (1968; Moos, 1969) have done extensive work on a schedule designed to evaluate the social atmosphere of psychiatric wards from the point of view of their environmental press on patient and staff. Their Ward Atmosphere Scale (WAS) Form B consists of 130 statements about what behavior typically occurs on the psychiatric ward, as judged by the respondent. There are ten statements presumed to refer to each of 12 press (environmental stimuli tending to evoke particular need-satisfying behaviors—Murray, 1938): Spontaneity, Support, Practicality, Affiliation, Order, Insight, Involvement, Aggression, Variety, Clarity, Submission, and Autonomy. The respondent may be either a staff member or a patient, and the mean scores of either patients or staff may thus be considered a consensual view of the ward ("beta press," as named by Murray). The items were selected from a larger group for their capacity to discriminate individually among 14 widely varying psychiatric wards and their capacity to approximate a 50-50 item split; a balanced number of true and false items are provided to measure each press. Their assignment to any given press category was made on a rational basis. Then extra items were added to estimate halo effect and inconsistency. All the ten-item press scales discriminated among wards for staff responses, and all but one did so for patient responses. The preliminary manual (Moos, 1969) gives norms for 2,444 patients and 1,138 staff, obtained from 116 wards in different geographic areas. The individual press scales have acceptable test-retest reliability over wards, and the ward profiles of mean scale scores remain relatively stable over a year or more. Intercorrelations among subscales were low to moderate over 365 patients. Patients' and staff's perceptions of the ward were similar over 14 wards, as judged by high Pearsonian correlations, but 11 of the 12 differences in absolute level of press as judged by patient and staff were significant. The WAS thus is shown to have a number of positive psychometric characteristics.

A revision has been published (Moos, 1973), utilizing data from over 200 wards. On the basis of psychometric refinements, the scale was reduced to 99 items (Form C). Changes include the dropping of the Variety, Affiliation, and Halo scales, some changed subscale item assignments, and the renaming of a number of scales. The revised manual contains separate norms for Form C based on 160 American wards and 36 British wards.

Ellsworth and his associates (Ellsworth et al., 1971) have derived factored scales representing the perception of the ward milieu by patients ("patient POW") and staff ("staff POW"). The items, assembled from a variety of sources, are statements about administrative practices, patient attitudes and behavior, and staff attitudes and behavior. The responses of 479 psychiatric aides in five Veterans Administration hospitals were used in a principal components analysis, which resulted in four factors: (a) Motivated Professional Staff, the aides' judgment that professional staff are concerned about patients and follow this concern with action in the patient's behalf; (b) Nursing Team as Involved Participants, a feeling that the aide's judgment is valued, accepted, and utilized in the treatment program; (c) Dominant Professional Staff, the aide's judgment that professional staff deliberately assert their higher status in the ward program; (d) Praise for Work. While 70 such items were factored, 30 of the most reliable, most discriminating, and most highly loaded items were utilized to measure these four dimensions.

The factors resulting from a similar analysis (Ellsworth and Maroney, 1972) of 111 patient POW items (N = 1,141 patients in five VA hospitals) were: (a) Inaccessible Staff, the feeling that staff do not communicate well with the patient, and that this lack is translated into a poor ward milieu; (b) Involvement in Ward Management by patients; (c) Satisfaction with Ward; (d) Receptive and Involved Staff, patient's judgment that staff treats patients with human respect; (e) Expectation for Patient Autonomy, staff is seen as supporting the attitude that patients are responsible for their own decisions and the consequences of their behavior. The 49 psychometrically most acceptable items are utilized in scoring these five factors.

Maroney has reported (1969) that the first three staff POW factors discriminated significantly among five hospitals and among the 19 units of these hospitals. Three of the patient POW factors discriminated among the hospitals and all five discriminated among the units. While the factors thus demonstrate good discriminating capacity, the proportion of variance accounted for by interhospital or interunit differences is very small, ranging from .00 to .07. Tentative norms are given, based on 27 wards (Ellsworth, 1969).

The item pools used in deriving the patient POW were, of course, completely different from those used for the nursing staff POW. This difference contrasts with the WAS, where the items for patient and staff are identical. In fact, across the 19 treatment units, only two of the twenty staff-patient POW factor-pair correlations were significant, though others are suggestively high, and, of course, in a larger ward sample, might reach significance (Ellsworth et al., 1971). The observed relationships do call attention to potentially interesting phenomena. The authors observe (Ellsworth et al., 1971: 433) that "the relationships that did occur suggest a kind of reciprocity in the perception of staff and patients." If nursing staff perceived praise for work, patients perceived little Involvement in Ward Management ($r = -.47$). If nursing staff perceived professional staff as Dominant, patients perceived ward staff as Receptive-Involved ($r = .49$). The direction of these two significant correlations suggests that such differences in perception may be worth pursuing.

Maroney (1969) has also reported correlations between the staff POW and WAS press scores for 115 aides, and between the patient POW and WAS scores for 112 patients. In general, there were low but significant correlations between staff perceptions on the two scales (about half of the 52 correlations were significant, the latter ranging from .18 to .44), and even more and higher correlations among the patient POW and WAS scales. Ellsworth and Maroney (1972) also examined the relationships among patient POW and patient WAS scores, finding 39 significant correlations out of the 60 tested.

Spiegel and Younger (1972) used 23 items from the POW scale for both staff and patients in their Ward Climate Inventory (Form G), deriving factors named Personnel Concern for Patients, Patient Concern for Patients, and Ward Morale. There was a strong tendency on all factors and the total inventory score for patients on seven wards to evaluate their wards more negatively than did staff. While the WAS (Form C) scales are not so clearly evaluative as the Ward Climate Inventory Scales, Moos (1973) found a similar tendency for staff's judgments to be more positive on eight of the ten WAS scales. Only Order and Organization showed no staff-patient difference, while staff judged Anger and Aggression to be significantly higher in a sample of 160 wards.

In research still in process, Lawton, Lipton and Cohen (1974) investigated the perception of ward characteristics of 644 patients and 292 staff from 51 wards in 24 treatment units of a large mental hospital. The WAS was used in pilot work, but the language proved so difficult for many patients and some employees that a decision was made to attempt to recruit a more representative proportion of both staff and patients by covering similar content in fewer and more comprehensible items. The Norristown Milieu Scale (NMS) consisted of 60 items factored separately for patients and staff. Staff NMS factors were named Active Patient Initiative, Benevolent Staff, High Structure, Patient Mutuality, Punitive Low Morale, and Chronic versus Active Ward. Patient factors were named Punitive Low Morale, Benevolent Ward, High Structure, and Carefully Planned Program. Another pool of 40 items, the Ward Questionnaire (WQ), was devised to obtain clearly evaluative judgments of the quality of service, administrative practices, and physical environment by staff and patients. A component analysis resulted in five staff factors (Individualized Good Service, Good Housekeeping, Friendly and Concerned Staff, Active Ward, and Physical Comfort), and seven patient factors (Staff Neglect, Comfort I, Institutional Dinginess, Concerned Staff, Institutional Dehumanization, Comfort II, and Environmental Demands). Thus factors were defined uniquely for patients and staff on these two scales. In addition, the responses of both groups can be scored using the factor structure determined either for staff or for patients. While the separate factor structures showed moderate similarity, there was ample basis for using separate dimensions for staff as compared to patients. Finally, another diverse group of 30 items relevant only to patients, the Ward Perception Scale, inquired about patient preferences and behavior in relation to the physical and administrative ward milieu. These items resulted in three factors named Aesthetic Quality, Social Warmth, and Preference for Heterogeneity.

Rice, Klett, Berger, Sewall, and Lemkau (1963) devised a 69-item Ward Evaluation Scale (WES), which asked patients for their evaluations of their ward's physical facilities, patient-staff relations and management, and services given patients. Graham, Allon, Friedman, and Lilly (1971) subjected patients' responses to a component analysis, resulting in five factors that showed little correspondence with the above three rationally grouped sets of items: Staff Interest in Patients,

Cleanliness of Ward, Absence of Disturbing Noise, Staff Permissiveness and Sensitivity, and Patient Comfort. Graham, Lilly, Allon, and Friedman (1971) also factored the responses of a mixed group of 163 psychiatrists, nurses, and aides. A low to moderate congruence of the four staff factors (Considerate Staff, Comfortable Ward, Accessible Staff, and Patient Responsibility) to those found for patients was noted.

## INTERRELATIONSHIPS AMONG PROCESS VARIABLES

Practically every institutional characteristic has been used as a presumptive index of quality, yet the number that have been validated as correlates of directly measured quality (not to mention validated as causative agents of quality) have been few. What we have is a diverse group of process variables that have been variously related to each other, sometimes in multivariate fashion, as in the preceding section, but more frequently in univariate fashion.

The task of organizing the results of studies of process-process relationships is a formidable one. We shall handle it by arbitrarily naming certain variables as independent variables (not always as the investigator did), grouping them on this basis, and considering their correlates, the final dependent variable being, wherever possible, patient behavior. Thus, we shall discuss fixed institutional characteristics, administrative practices, staff behavior, staff attitudes, and patient attitudes and behavior. Occasionally, certain findings may be referred to twice for expendiency in grouping.

### Relatively Fixed Institutional Characteristics

*Size.* Small size was highly associated with high per diem cost in VA mental hospitals (Gurel, 1964; Ullmann, 1967). Ullman's data also showed fewer irregular discharges in small hospitals. On the ward level, large wards were less likely to be accorded adult status in ward policies, but did not differ from small wards in amount of social behavior or incidence of disturbed behavior (Kellam et al., 1966). Among 25 wards, large wards tended to be perceived as low in p Spontaneity and high in Submission by patients; staff perceived the same wards as high in p Submission and p Order, and low in Aggression (Moos, 1969).

In a study of 55 wards in 14 Veterans Administration hospitals, Moos (1972) confirmed the negative relationship between size and Adult Status; but in contrast to the findings of Kellam and associates (1966), he found a positive relationship between size and the incidence of Disturbed Behavior. Moos also found large size to be associated with low WAS (Form C) scores on Spontaneity, Personal Problem Orientation, and Anger and Aggression, and high scores on Staff Control, as perceived by patients. Low Staff WAS scores on Spontaneity, Autonomy, Personal Problem Orientation, and Anger and Aggression occurred more often on large wards. The extent of agreement between staff and patient WAS scores was not related to size of ward. Moos calls attention to the fact that, since size is highly related to both Adult Status and Disturbed Behavior, the correlations among WAS scales and size no doubt reflect input differences in the assignment of patients to the various wards.

*Staff-Patient Ratio.* The PEP study found a greater number of psychologists and social workers in VA hospitals that were recently built, that employed architecture of a specific therapeutic design, and that had higher foster care and employee suggestion activity. This same finding appeared in the factor analysis that defined the community-oriented "nontraditionalism" factor.

Dickey (1964) studied the effectiveness of six treatment teams in geographically determined units of a progressive open hospital. A higher staff-patient ratio was associated with high staff morale, more individual staff time devoted to formal work with patients, and better patient attendance at scheduled activities. In 27 wards studied by Kellam and associates (1966), a high nursing staff-patient ratio was associated with a high degree of staff-patient social contact, and a high degree of disturbed behavior by patients[1] but was not related to patient-patient contact nor to degree of adult status accorded to patients. Patients and staff were in high agreement that wards with high staff-patient ratio were high in p Autonomy and low in p Submission (Moos, 1969).

The following relationships between size and staff-patient ratios were found: Moos (1972, $r = -.15$), Kellam and associates (1966, $r = -.56$), Ullman (1967, $r = -.44$), and Lawton, Lipton, and Cohen (1974, $r = -.29$). While they are all negative, their magnitude varies widely, and is probably a function of the different ward and hospital samples used.

Moos (1972) found only one patient WAS (Form C) scale, Practical Orientation, to be positively associated with a high staff-patient ratio. However, a high ratio was associated with high scores on Involvement, Support, Spontaneity, Practical Orientation, and Order and Organization, and a low score on Staff Control as judged by staff.

*Institutional Type.* Several studies have shown staff attitudes (Gilbert and Levinson, 1957) or consensual ward perceptions (Jackson, 1964; Moos, 1969) to vary among hospitals identified as state hospitals, private hospitals, VA hospitals, or other classifications. However, none of these sampled hospital types systematically enough to be able to offer much information beyond the general idea that therapeutic attitudes may be most prevalent in small, university-affiliated or intensive-treatment hospitals.

## Organizational Rules, Policies, and Procedures

The Adult Status index constructed by Kellam and associates (1966) was not associated with staff-patient ratio, amount of disturbed behavior, or amount of social interaction. Moos (1969) used this same Adult Status index in studying 25 wards, and found that patients perceived high p Spontaneity, high p Support, and low p Submission on wards of high adult status; staff, on the other hand, perceived only high p Affiliation to be associated with high Adult Status, of the 12 press measured by the Ward Atmosphere Scale. He found that the degree of consensus between patient and staff views of ward press was highly related to the amount of adult status accorded the patient; consensus on six of the 12 WAS press was associated with high Adult Status.

By far the most comprehensive study of the social organization and communication patterns in mental institutions was made by Smith (1971), who drew a purposive sample of 18 state hospitals chosen to represent the widest possible diversity in geographic location, size, acute versus chronic patient populations, and resources as reflected in staff and budget. An immense amount of data was collected from interviews and questionnaires completed by administrative, professional, high- and low-echelon nursing staff, and informants for discharged patients, as well as from direct observation and hospital records. The findings of the study defy summarization, being based on several hundred process variables rationally grouped into 32 categories, but all examined in terms of their univariate relationships with six types of criteria, some of which are what are classed in this paper as process variables (e.g., staff morale and staff evaluations). The criteria were adjusted through multiple regression analysis (Cohen, 1968a) to take prior account of hospital size, per-diem cost, staff-patient ratio, and their varying mixes of severely and less severely disturbed patients. In spite of this initial multivariate step, no further attempt was made at data reduction or exploration of the independence or redundancy of the thousands of correlations obtained. The theory and discussion of administrative and organizational relationships are excellent, but a full understanding of the meaning of the findings will have to await the more detailed multivariate analysis now in process by Smith and King.

King and Smith (1972) did deal with the subset of items used in this study to derive the Treatment Milieu Scale described above. They found the total TMS score to be unrelated to staff morale or to staff judgments of the quality of care given by their own hospitals (we see this as a process rather than a quality variable). However, high scores on the Patient Autonomy scale and low scores on the Staff Involvement in Patient Therapy scale were associated with favorable staff evaluations of quality of care. The meaning of the finding that staff who see their hospitals as more actively engaged in direct patient therapy consider their quality of care to be poorer is unclear. It is possible that it requires a higher level of staff sophistication to assume an openly critical attitude toward its own level of care, and that these hospitals are also those that are trying harder to provide more comprehensive care.

## Staff Behavior

A low degree of absenteeism was found by Dickey (1964) among staff teams whose members talked less during therapy (considered a favorable quality indicator), who spent more time in formal patient work, and whose units showed high patient attendance at scheduled activities. Kellam and associates (1966) report significant associations between the amount of observed staff-patient contact and the frequency of patient aloneness and the size of interacting informal groups in 27 wards; however, these correlations are spuriously inflated to an unknown degree since staff-patient contacts were included in cluster size and were mutually exclusive with aloneness. The amount of staff-patient contact was strongly and positively related to the percentage of patients observed once or more in aggressive behavior during one month.

## Staff Attitudes and Perceptions

Gilbert and Levinson (1957) used their Custodial Mental Illness scale in three institutions which, they hypothesized, were ordered in terms of custodialism. In their analysis they combined institution membership and occupational group in such a way as to make analysis of their separate effects impossible, but the institution-by-occupation custodial rank was significantly related to staff members' custodial attitudes.

Dickey's (1964) rationally constructed 80-item Staff Attitudes Survey (SAS) was designed to inquire about employee morale in the areas of leadership, communication, role and status, and team effectiveness. Teams with high morale, as indicated by high SAS scores, were characterized by low absenteeism, less talking in group therapy sessions, more time spent in formal patient work, more time spent in admission evaluations, and better patient attendance at activities.

Jackson's original validation work with the Characteristics of the Treatment Environment scale (1964) revealed that intensive treatment wards were scored higher (more therapeutic) than continued treatment wards. However, when inter-ward comparisons were made in a design including the intensive versus continued treatment dimension, intensive treatment wards were relatively homogeneous in CTE scores; significant interward variation occurred only among continuous treatment wards. He concluded that the intensive treatment wards were run in a fairly uniform way, while the lack of prescribed treatment program on the continuous treatment wards allowed much more diversity to develop.

Staff characterizations of their wards on the Ward Atmosphere Scale (Moos, 1969) did not correlate with the amount of disturbed patient behavior over a 30-day period. Staff's perceptions of their wards showed some low-to-moderate relationships to patients' general satisfaction with the ward, their liking for staff, and their assessment of the extent to which the ward allowed them to test out their own abilities. In a later WAS study (Form C), Moos (1972) found that staff on 55 different wards considered those with much disturbed behavior to be low in Autonomy, Personal Problem Orientation, Anger and Aggression, and Staff Control. One can assume that the low level of aggressiveness and control perceived in high-disturbance wards may reflect the tendency of older and more chronic patients to show behavioral disturbances of a kind not representing intense management problems. Moos also found that wards which accorded a high level of Adult Status to patients were viewed by staff as high in Spontaneity, Autonomy, Personal Problem Orientation, and Anger and Aggression.

Houts and Moos (1969) also developed a Ward Initiative Scale, where patients could indicate the extent to which they took initiative in seven areas: Affiliation with patients, Revealing the self to others, Involvement with the ward, Aggression, Seeking Variety, Submission to staff, and Autonomy toward staff. Five press scores from the WAS discriminated staff perceptions of 23 wards; these five staff perceptions were associated with a number of patient perceptions on the Ward Initiative Scale. The p Affiliation staff score, for example, was positively associated with patient initiatives in the Self-Revelation, Involvement, and Aggression areas, and negatively associated with Submission. Moos (1969) explored further the similarities and differences between staff and patient perceptions of 14 wards, and found that, for 6 of the 12 WAS press, there was a moderately high inverse relationship between extent of patient-staff discrepancy and the amount of Adult Status granted patients.

Sidman and Moos (1973) developed a pool of descriptions of helping behavior between patients and staff or among patients, and obtained ratings from 226 patients of the frequency with which these kinds of help were experienced on nine state hospital wards. Ward means for the larger categories of types of help were correlated with WAS scores (Form C). They found a modest level of congruity between the wards' characteristic level of helping behavior and "favorable" perceptions of the ward atmosphere.

Ellsworth and associates (1971) found covariation between staff POW scores and patient characteristics over 19 wards. Nursing staff perceived professional staff as more highly motivated and themselves as receiving more praise for word on wards with older patients. They saw professional staff as more dominant on wards with high proportions of schizophrenia, and less dominant in wards with more married patients. A low nursing-staff-to-patient ratio was found in wards whose nursing staff considered professional staff highly motivated and who saw themselves as receiving high praise for work and strongly involved as participants in ward procedures.

## Patient Attitudes and Perceptions

Surprisingly little research has explored patients' attitudes toward mental illness, their staff, and their environment, particularly in a way that would allow treatment units to be compared. The original Ward Evaluation Scale of Rice, Klett, Berger, Sewall, and Lemkau (1963) showed that patients evaluated wards in a new hospital more highly than wards in an old or a moderately old hospital. The WES did not discriminate among four wards contrasting in acute versus continuous treatment within the new hospital. It did show higher evaluations of a "good" continuous treatment ward in the old hospital, as compared to a "poor" continuous treatment ward.

Moos (1969) found a large number of significant associations among five patient-rated ward scores on the WAS and three patient evaluations of their wards, and between patient WAS scores and most of the patient Ward Initiative Scale scores. These correlations seem to indicate that Spontaneity, Affiliation, Insight, and Autonomy are highly valued by patients, and that there is a definite link between the perceived press of the ward and the patient's translation of the press into opportunities for himself.

The patient POW (Ellsworth et al., 1971) showed that patients on wards with high proportions of schizophrenics saw staff as more Receptive-Involved; patients on wards with longer average periods of hospitalization were more satisfied with ward life; and wards with high proportions of married patients and higher professional-staff-to-patient ratios were more likely to have patients considering themselves to be highly involved in ward life. Ellsworth and Maroney (1972) found that wards with higher mean patient age and longer mean time in hospital had higher POW Satisfaction with Ward scores and lower Involvement in Ward Management scores.

This section on interrelationships among process variables should demonstrate clearly that one could go on forever trying to interrelate these kinds of variables without adding a great deal to the knowledge about the relationships among patient input, institutional programs, and output quality. Many of these same process variables take on clearer meaning when they are related to quality criteria, as indicated in the next section.

### Institutional Quality

The quality of output of treatment institutions has been investigated at some length in single-institution studies, where two or more treatments are contrasted. The problems are greatly magnified when comparisons are made among institutions. Possible types of quality criteria are: (a) direct output measures (discharge rate, length of admission, rehospitalization rate, or time out of hospital); (b) longitudinal measures (measurement of criterion behaviors or states at two or more points in time); (c) judged quality measured cross-sectionally (attitudes toward the institution, evaluations of it, or morale measures of its patients are presumed to represent a net balance of the effect of the institution on patients).

The direct output measure has been most frequently used, though the longitudinal measurement has been increasingly utilized in recent years. Before reviewing the studies of correlates of quality, it is necessary to call attention to the variety of direct-output measures used by different investigators. Their relationship to one another varies, and studies must be compared taking into account the fact that they sometimes measure quite different outcomes.

*Turnover Rate.* Turnover rate is the simplest and most frequently reported measure (Ellsworth, Dickman, and Maroney, 1972; Moos and Schwartz, 1972; Moos, Shelton, and Perry, 1973; Spiegel and Younger, 1972). This is simply the ratio of the number of discharges during a given period to the total census. The denominator of this term is given greater precision by calculating, as the VA does in its statistical reporting, the average daily patient load (ADPL) over the entire period.

Other investigators have examined specific kinds of turnover with the idea that some are more meaningful than others. Cohen (1964) took account of the fact that many discharges or leaves were brief, and used as the numerator of the turnover measure the number of *first significant releases* (FSR), that is, a discharge followed by at least 90 days of continuous residence in the community. Ullmann (1967) added to this concept the element of length of hospitalization prior to the FSR in his *early first significant release* criterion. An early FSR required not only the 90-day community tenure, but a period of hospitalization prior to release not to exceed 274 days.

*Readmission Rate* (number of readmissions divided by ADPL) is another measure of effectiveness of community tenure. A related measure was used by Moos and Schwartz (1972). They reasoned that the most severe test of ability to live in the community is among unmarried schizophrenics; thus they used the number of days these patients remained in the community as their index of effectiveness. Cohen (1964) used the same index in more general form, number of *in-community days* for all released patients, calculated at different follow-up intervals after release.

For other purposes, hospital effectiveness may be measured in terms of its release rate for chronic patients, *reduction in long-term population.* Ullman (1967) and Ellsworth, Dickman, and Maroney (1972) calculated turnover rate using as the numerator only releases of patients who had been continuously hospitalized for two years or more.

Finally, special types of separations may be seen as negative indicators of quality, such as leaving against medical advice or surreptitiously ("elopement"). These types of irregular releases have been used to calculate *dropout rate* (Moos and Schwartz, 1972; Moos, Shelton, and Perry, 1973; Spiegel and Younger, 1972).

The relationship of process variables to direct-output and longitudinal criteria will next be reviewed, followed by a section on process correlates of judged quality.

*Size of Treatment Unit.* Recent therapeutic philosophy, most notably the report of the Joint Commission on Mental Illness and Health (Joint Commission, 1961), has strongly favored small hospitals and small wards. Two studies have supported this suggestion. The PEP Project (Cohen, 1964; Davis, 1964; Gurel, 1964) utilized as its major direct output criterion the number of in-community days (ICD) between the day of the patient's admission and the end of several different follow-up periods (six months, one, two, three, and four years). They also used as a criterion the number of days between admission and the first significant release (FSR). In order to relate hospital characteristics to patient output criteria, patient input variance was removed by using 64 different social and psychiatric patient characteristics as predictors in a multiple regression analysis, leaving as residual variance that which, presumably, was attributable to differences among institutions. Size was measured by the average daily patient load. Small size was very significantly associated with the ICD criterion at all followup periods, and FSR through the first year following admission. Size, of course, was not independent of other institutional characteristics. For example the factorially derived "nontraditionalism" variable was correlated .5 with size.

Ullmann (1967) extended the PEP study to 30 VA hospitals and 7,212 patients, utilizing data that could be gained from standard patient and hospital reporting forms in place of periodic evaluations of individual patients. His output criteria were early FSR and turnover. Early FSR may be characterized as "quick effectiveness" and turnover as "extended effectiveness," or effectiveness associated with low long-term chronicity. Size correlated -.37 with early FSR, and the correlation remained at -.34 when staff-patient ratio was partialed out. High turnover was significantly related to small size, but when the effect of staff-patient ratio was partialed out, the relationship of size to turnover fell below nominal statistical significance (.24, .23, and .30, for the three turnover criteria).

In contrast to these studies, Kellam and associates (1967) used the ward as their unit of study in a multihospital drug research project. Twelve wards in four hospitals were studied; their analysis is solely by ward, and does not deal with interhospital differences. Evaluations of 202 newly admitted patients were done prior to treatment and six weeks following treatment with one of four drugs. In their study, longitudinal outcome measures were used: changes in three global illness ratings by personnel, and before-and-after scores in 14 Inpatient Multi-dimensional Psychiatric Scale factors (IMPS—Lorr, Klett, McNair, and Lasky, 1963), and seven Ward Behavior Rating Scale factors (Burdock, Hakerem, Hardesty, and Zubin, 1960). Size was one of eight ward atmosphere characteristics used as independent variables. Three-factorial (drugs x sex x size) analyses of covariance for each of the 24 criterion scores, using pretreatment score as the covariate, were performed. Omitting all effects involving only drugs and/or sex, each criterion score could be examined for the effect of size alone and in interaction with drugs and/or sex. Low ward census was significantly associated with a lack of improvement in seven of the 96 possible main and interaction effects involving size and the 24 psychiatric criteria. Two other indices of ward atmosphere that are, like size, to some extent determined by hospital policy decisions (high staff-patient ratio and high Adult Status) also showed an unexpected association with lack of improvement.

The fact that no criterion showed an improvement associated with small size, and that there appeared to be a pattern whereby opposite-direction effects appeared consistently in other areas reflecting hospital policy led the authors to give considerable weight to this only marginally significant set of relationships involving ward size. However, they are grossly in error when they state, "Out of 192 possible relationships between the 24 symptom measures and the eight dimen-sions of ward atmosphere there were 80 significant ones" (Kellam et al., 1967: 152). Actually, there were 192 main effects tested, but the 80 significant relation-ships included, in addition to main effects, first- and second-order interactions; there were a total of 768 main and interactive effects tested. Kellam and associates point out that disturbed patients tended to be assigned to smaller wards; even though input status is equalized on the particular criterion variables, the probably intrinsic confounding of poor prognosis and small size is an insurmountable defect in the design of the study. Thus, for two reasons their conclusions must be much more tenuously accepted than their discussion indicates: the confounding of patient prognosis and ward size, and the fact that the incidence of significant relationships was not impressively greater than chance expectation.

Linn (1970) studied the discharge rates in one year (proportion of discharges, leaves, deaths, and transfers to total number of beds) of 12 geographically scattered state hospitals. His results are all presented as bare rank-difference correlations between discharge rate and single variables, with no attempt to explore their interrelationships. Within this limitation, he found small size to be associated with high discharge rate.

Ellsworth, Dickman, and Maroney (1972) studied the effectiveness of 36 VA hospitals that had instituted unit systems as of 1969. Small size was significantly associated with an increase in turnover rate as compared to turnover six years previously. After choosing the 10 most productive (in terms of turnover and reduction in long-term chronic population) and the 10 least productive unitized hospitals, they found that mean number of patients per unit was 141 in the most productive and 266 in the least productive.

The weight of evidence from the VA studies thus clearly favors the suggestion that small size is associated with patient improvement. On the other hand, the findings of Kellam and associates do suggest that there is further need for investigation of the conditions under which size is associated with outcome. Ullmann's study demonstrates the complexity of the size effect in showing the interaction of size and staffing level with quality criteria.

*Staff-Patient Ratio (per diem cost).* Most of the thrust of mental health planners has gone in the direction of increasing the staff-patient ratio. Yet, in single hospitals the demonstrable effects of doing so have not always been positive (e.g., Bay and Feldman, 1962). Since both the PEP study and the Ullmann replication found that staff-patient ratio was almost perfectly correlated with per diem cost, the two will be considered simultaneously. In the PEP study (Gurel, 1964), high staff-patient ratio was associated with both the ICD and FSR criteria in the same temporal pattern as size (that is, a decreasing relationship over time), but the magnitude of the relationship was lower than for size. Ullmann (1967) found staffing, either taken alone or with size partialed out, to be unrelated to his early FSR output criterion. On the other hand the turnover criteria correlated .66, .48, and -.73 with staffing, the correlations remaining significant after size was partialed out (.57, .37, and -.65). Thus, while low chronicity occurred in VA hospitals which were well staffed, early release occurred in any of the staff sizes represented in the universe of these VA psychiatric hospitals. Linn (1970) also found attendant-to-patient ratio to be positively correlated with discharge rate.

Patient-staff ratio was also related to patient change by Kellam and associates (1967). As was true of ward size, seven of the possible 96 main effects and interactions involving staffing were significant in the direction opposite to that predicted (e.g., a decrement in functioning was associated with being on a well-staffed ward); one effect was in the predicted direction.

Using each state's aggregate reports on its mental hospital system to the National Institute of Mental Health, Lasky and Dowling (1971) found consistently significant rank-difference correlations between patient-staff ratio and turnover (net release rate). The size of this relationship steadily increased from .29 in 1963 to .65 in 1967, suggesting a trend toward either the more effective utilization of extra staff in increasing turnover or a demonstration of the fact that high turnover required more staff.

Patient-staff ratio in six treatment teams assigned to the six units of an open hospital was related to patient change criteria and length of hospitalization by Dickey (1964). The longitudinal criterion was algebraic total change scores in the MACC Behavioral Adjustment Scale Form II (Ellsworth, 1962), filled out at pre-post intervals ranging from one week to 12 months, on all patients who were resident in the hospital during a four-month period. Length of hospitalization was calculated separately for patients discharged during the four-month period and for those still hospitalized in the last day of the period. For the discharged patient, greater length of hospitalization was considered a success since it would indicate that he stayed in treatment. For the nondischarged patient, a shorter length of hospitalization was considered a positive indicator, since he would be less "chronic" than the patient who had been hospitalized a longer time. There was a clear tendency for higher staff-patient ratio to be associated with shorter periods of hospitalization for the nondischarged patients; there was a marginal association between higher staff proportion and more positive MACC change scores; staffing was not related to length of hospitalization of the discharged patients. These results suffer from failure to control patient input, and from the somewhat idiosyncratic definitions of what constitutes a favorable length of hospitalization. However, in general, they are consistent with the findings of the PEP and Ullmann studies.

*Distribution of Cost/Staffing.* The number of almost any type of personnel employed by hospitals correlated with the total per diem cost of the hospitals. Among the 12 PEP hospitals Gurel (1964) looked at the temporal trends of relationships between staff-patient ratios for various occupations and ICD and FSR. He found that significant relationships to the criteria remained at longer follow-up times for physical medicine and rehabilitation, social work, and psychology staff-patient ratios than for ratios of some other occupational groups. Ullmann (1967) found that, when size of hospital, proportion of psychiatric beds, and the correlations among size and staffing in different professions were controlled, the only professional groups whose relative size showed significant correlations with effectiveness were physicians and social workers, positively, and physical medicine and rehabilitation workers, negatively. It seems likely that these relationships may all be understood in terms of staffing policies geared primarily either to short-term or chronic care.

Both studies analyzed further the allocation of total costs. The PEP study (Gurel, 1964) showed high positive relationships between the percentage of all expenditures for general administration and for patient care, on the one hand, and both the ICD and FSR criteria, on the other. The percentages devoted to housekeeping and to engineering (maintenance) were just as highly and negatively related to the criteria. However, no analysis of these distributions is presented so as to define the covariation effects of total cost or size on these relationships. There is at least some reason to believe that these are incidental effects of size and total staff-patient ratio. Ullmann did show that as size increased, the percentage of cost devoted to food and shelter increased. After controlling for size and proportion of psychiatric beds, there still was a significant positive association between percentage devoted to general administration and the early FSR criterion, and a negative association between percentage devoted to food and shelter and early FSR. Utilizing the turnover criterion, high food and shelter expense proportion was associated with low turnover; a high proportion of expense devoted to nonnursing patient care was associated with high turnover.

Ullmann traced further the aspect of administrative costs that might account for the association with output criteria. Dividing administrative costs into percentages spent for supply, personnel office, fiscal office, registrar, and manager, he found that the larger the proportion devoted to the registrar's office, the more FSR and higher the turnover, holding constant size and psychiatric emphasis. The functions of the registrar seem to relate particularly to the facilitation of the transmission of information regarding patients. They handle patient records, do the clerical chores relevant to patient treatment, handle benefits of various types, and work with extra-hospital communications about patients. One might wonder whether, in our present impoverished state of treatment knowledge, these information-processing and communication tasks may be more critical to disposition than treatment procedures themselves.

*Staff and Patient Attitudes and Perceptions.* Cohen's and Struening's OMI (1962) was given to 3,148 staff members in the 12 Veterans Administration Hospitals of the PEP study, representing half of the total number employed in each of the eight major occupational groups at each hospital. Utilizing the profile of mean scores on the five OMI scales for each of the 12 hospitals to define its "treatment atmosphere," a clustering technique yielded two clusters containing seven and three hospitals, respectively, with two hospitals remaining unclustered. The subscales responsible for the major differences between the two major clusters were Authoritarianism and Social Restrictiveness. Using the patient input-adjusted ICD scores for the hospitals (derived for the PEP study) as criteria, the two clusters did not differ significantly. However, when the N was increased by considering the two unclustered hospitals as not authoritarian-restrictive (i.e., seven authoritarian-restrictive hospitals were compared to five nonauthoritarian-nonrestrictive hospitals), use of several different statistical tests resulted in high effectiveness scores being marginally related to low authoritarian-restrictiveness. The tenuousness of the findings makes the acceptance of results necessarily tentative, but the difficulty of dealing with a small N is a major extenuating circumstance.

A high morale score on Dickey's (1964) Staff Attitude Survey was significantly related to patients' improvement on MACC scores, and to the length of hospitalization for the nondischarged patients, done across the six units.

Early versions of the POW were used by Ellsworth (1965) in a study of the therapeutic outcome of patients assigned to wards utilizing three contrasting treatment programs; assignment was made so as to equalize the three wards in five patient input characteristics. The treatments were: (a) a doctor-centered traditional ward; (b) a team-centered ward; and (c) a patient-centered, peer-group oriented ward. As judged by several criteria involving both discharge from hospital and postdischarge community adjustment, the doctor-centered program was least effective. Scores on several staff and patient POW scores were associated with the type of treatment program. No data relating the POW scores of individual patients to their individual therapeutic outcomes are presented, but the association between POW scores and treatment types, plus the differential outcomes of the three treatment types, is taken as evidence of successful outcome being related to POW scores. On these early POW versions, staff factors named Ineffective Problem Solving and Distrust of Administration were higher in the doctor-centered (least effective) program; Reciprocal and Open Communication and Satisfaction with Immediate Supervisor were lowest in this same program. Two of the eight patient POW factors were highest in the patient-centered (most effective) approach: The Patient as Active Participant and Patient Concern for Each Other. These conclusions were not borne out by later work. Ellsworth has commented that "the problem in drawing conclusions from a sample of one ward is that it might not be representative of other authoritarian wards" (Ellsworth, personal communication, June 28, 1974). Clearly, greater elucidation is necessary to disentangle the three factors of ward perception, treatment type, and outcome from each other.

The more recent POW versions were used in a cooperative study of the effectiveness of 19 psychiatric units (Ellsworth et al., 1971) on (a) 929 admissions who had been in the community 90 days or more prior to a hospital admission occurring during the project period (the "admission" patients) and (b) 1,826 patients resident on the wards as of the project beginning date (the "resident" patients). One outcome criterion was release rate, the second, length of community tenure, that is, discharge from the hospital within six months and maintenance of community status for a minimum of 90 days. A high release rate was taken as evidence of "efficiency," and a high community tenure rate as evidence of "effectiveness."

Wards where aides saw themselves as participants in the treatment process and as recipients of praise, and professional staff as highly motivated, had lower efficiency (low release rates) but greater effectiveness (high community tenure rates). Wards where aides saw professional staff as dominant were characterized by low community tenure rate (low effectiveness). No patient POW score was significantly related to any of the criteria. Stepwise multiple regression analyses were run to predict outcome from the best combination of one staff and one patient POW score. A significantly predicting R for admission patients for the efficiency dimension was obtained; low staff-perceived Praise for Work and low patient-perceived Expectation for Patient Autonomy were associated with high release rate. On the other hand, greater effectiveness among resident patients was associated with nursing-staff-perceived highly motivated professional staff and high patient Involvement in Ward Management (as perceived by patients).

Thus, this study seems somewhat related to findings from the PEP study, showing that "success" in intensive treatment wards may be different from that in chronic wards. In the present case effective units seem to be characterized by a high degree of involvement of both patients and aides, plus an underplaying of involvement by higher-level staff. On the other hand, the efficient ward is likely to be one with a dominant professional staff and relatively uninvolved patients and aides.

Ellsworth and Maroney (1972) used the POW as a predictor of changes in adjustment following discharge from three different wards. A number of indices of adjustment were rated by 352 patients' family members with respect to prehospitalization status, and again four weeks after discharge. The patients completed the POW immediately prior to discharge. Small but significant associations were found between good community adjustment (controlled for prehospitalization status) and a low score on the POW Inaccessible-Staff factor and a high score on Receptive and Involved Staff. They also found that two of these wards contrasted markedly in the extent to which they could be characterized by features consistent with scores on these two factors. They reasoned that the effect of these contrasting milieux would be different, depending on whether a patient's characteristics were consonant or dissonant with his milieu. Thus, they made predictions that better posthospital adjustment would result when patients showing seven different characteristics had been treated in Ward A, which had both more accessible and more receptive staff. The two wards did not differ in measured community adjustment scores of their discharged patients, but the patients with high prehospital "anger" ratings and those with some college education did better, as predicted, when they had been treated in Ward A than when treated in Ward B.

Spiegel and Younger (1972) found that patient scores on their WCI did not differ across seven wards. Higher staff-rated scores on Personnel Concern for Patients and on Ward Morale were associated with low elopement rate. Staff WCI scores were not significantly related to the other two criteria, release rate and length of community stay of unmarried schizophrenic discharges. They also examined the discrepancies between patient and staff WCI scores, and found that large discrepancies on Personnel Concern for Patients (staff viewing the ward more favorably than patients) were associated with high release rate, long community tenure, and low elopement rate. A similar excess of favorable staff ratings on Ward Morale was associated with low elopement rate.

Moos and Schwartz (1972) used the WAS with patients and staff in seven large wards at one VA hospital to predict dropout rate, discharge rate, and the in-community days among unmarried schizophrenics criterion. There were scattered relationships between patient WAS scores and the three criteria. Four staff-perceived scores were associated with low dropout rate: high Involvement, high Support, high Program Clarity, and low Anger and Aggression. Wards which both patients and staff characterized as being high in Staff Control had good records on the community tenure criterion. Using the individual WAS statements in item analyses against each of the three criteria, Moos, Shelton, and Perry (1973) constructed a "dropout scale," a "release-rate scale," and a "community tenure scale" with a larger sample of patients and wards than was used in the previous study. The content of the items suggest that a practical, well-ordered, and clearly goal-oriented milieu characterized program success by all three criteria. In addition, a supportive staff-involved environment characterized low-dropout wards. High discharge rate was associated with low expressiveness of feeling, while long community tenure occurred more often among dischargees from wards that encouraged free expression of anger.

King and Smith (1972) related their TMS factors to turnover rate, "net release rate" (a measure of trend over time in excess of discharges or admissions), and two sets of ratings of in-community adjustment of patients discharged from 11 hospitals. A high level of Staff-Patient Socioemotional Interaction was associated with high turnover rate and high Patient Autonomy with high net release rate. Patient Autonomy was negatively related to one of the community adjustments indices, however. Also, in contrast to the tendency noted above for high Staff Involvement in Patient Therapy to be associated with staff ratings of poor quality of care in their hospitals, this factor was positively related to both of the community adjustment criteria. While the meaning of their sometimes conflicting findings is not clear, they are consistent with the evidence of Ellsworth and associates (1968) that the criteria for intra-hospital adjustment as judged by staff are not the same as those making for a favorable community adjustment.

*Staff Behavior.* Dickey (1964) calculated absenteeism for all employees in her six units over a three-month period and used the percentage having zero absences as a predictor of output quality. Low absenteeism was related to MACC improvement scores and to the length of hospitalization of discharged patients.

She also related the distribution of staff time spent in four roles or tasks to the outcome criteria: (a) the mean percentages of staff members in each unit participating in group therapy sessions, (b) amount of time staff spent in formal work with patients, (c) amount of time spent in informal work with patients, and (d) amount of time spent in admission evaluations. Nine of the twelve relationships between staff time and MACC improvement or length of hospitalization (discharged and nondischarged patients) were significant and in the predicted direction: less group therapy participation, more time spent in formal patient work, and more time spent in informal patient work were associated with only one of the criteria, longer time in hospital for discharged patients. Linn (1970) found that a large amount of physician time spent on the ward, a large number of staff-patient meetings, and a high rate of staff-patient interaction were associated with high discharge rate.

In the Ellsworth, Dickman, and Maroney (1972) study of unitization, an index of "ideal unitization" was constructed from four processes: the admission of patients by rotation alone (i.e., few selective admissions to particular units); judgments by staff that different units were, in fact, composed of similar patient mixes; feedback to staff on the results of treatment; and the presence of competition among units. High unitization thus measured was highly related to turnover rate among the eight hospitals with small units, but not among those with larger (more than 112) units, nor was this score related to community tenure. The best-predictive type of staff behavior was the percentage of patients discharged to special community facilities (halfway houses, domicilaries, etc.), which was positively related to both criteria.

*Patient Behavior.* Surprisingly, there have been few attempts to relate the occurrence of elective patient behaviors to outcomes across institutions. Dickey (1964) examined the mean percentages of each of the six treatment unit patient populations attending scheduled therapeutic activities over a two-week period. There were no significant relationships between attendance and the direct outcome criteria.

Kellam and associates (1967) provide data relating patient outcomes to modal patient characteristics of the environment in which the target patients live, the "suprapersonal environment" (Lawton, 1970b). Three of these suprapersonal variables—disturbed behavior, aloneness, and low cluster size, either as main effects or in interaction with sex or type of drug—were associated with lack of improvement in the various rating scales used as output criteria; the other, staff-patient contact, showed only a chance number of criterion correlations. Thus, Kellam and associates conclude that the type of patient that surrounds him is a critical element in the course of the target patient's illness. As mentioned earlier, it is difficult to come to such a conclusion when the suprapersonal environment itself determines which patients are to be assigned to the ward. Only the combination of random assignment of patients to the different wards or, more practically, application of covariance or multiple regression analysis using relevant patient input covariates, might disentangle the confounding of input and prognosis.

On the other hand, Linn (1970) found no relationship between the discharge rates of 12 hospitals and the modal age, self-care, or psychotic-symptom rate of the hospitals. He did find, however, that rate of patient participation in therapy, rate of patient-to-patient interaction, and amount of patient activity were related to discharge rate.

*Other Institutional Variables.* While institutional characteristics are, we feel, best understood as they occur in clusters, rather than individually, some that have been studied individually will be briefly mentioned here. The PEP study (Gurel, 1964) found that hospitals built in a type of *architecture* that featured small treatment units (influenced by the psychiatrist Paul Haun) were likely to have early success, but this gain was not maintained over follow-up times longer than six months. This variable is confounded with date of construction, staffing pattern, and type of treatment program. The amount of individual therapy given to the PEP patient Ss was negatively related to the ICD and FSR criteria, while the group therapy rate for the entire hospital, as well as for PEP patients alone, was positively related to the criteria at early, but not later, follow-up periods. The electroshock rate, percentage of open wards, and percentage of privileges showed little or no relationship to the criteria. The presence of foster home care programs, but not a patient-employee program, was associated with high ICD and early FSR at later follow-up times. The number of volunteer hours was negatively related to both criteria.

Two indices of the quality and number of personalized facilities and furnishing were unrelated to discharge rate in Linn's 12 hospitals.

Ullmann (1967) corroborated the PEP finding that the number being treated in a family care program was positively related to high turnover in its minimization of long stays, but was not related to early FSR. Pressure of applications (expressed as number of applications divided by average census) was very significantly associated with early FSR turnover.

In the study by Kellam and associates (1967), 11 of 76 possible main and interactive effects involving Adult Status and symptom improvement were significant in a direction counter to expectation, that is, higher Adult Status was granted on wards where patients improved the least. The authors offer as an explanation the suggestion that the high Adult Status wards may have had a therapeutic philosophy that was too tolerant of illness and thus allowed the patients to wallow in their sickness rather than conform to social expectation.

This section allows for several general comments about the direct measurement of output quality and the search for correlates of quality. First, there are a variety of deficiencies in the criteria themselves. Both ICD and FSR, as well as other possible indices concerned with in- and out-of-hospital time, are extremely gross indices of output quality. They are subject to wide variation among institutions as a result of differing standards of admission and discharge. Furthermore, standards for discharge decisions change with new knowledge or fashion in psychiatry. Thus, it is difficult to compare two discharge rates done at different times. These limitations, which appear to be intrinsic to the use of hospitalization versus discharged status as a criterion, must be balanced against the unquestioned advantage that these criteria have very high objectivity. The direct measurement of change in patient symptoms or behavior, on the other hand, is theoretically capable of on-target measurement of those patient attributes that the treatment institution is meant to change, and is thus potentially more relevant to quality measurement than discharge data. However, it is obvious that objectivity and cross-institution reliability of measurement are more difficult to attain with the usual measures of intra-individual change. One need not restate the many problems of scaling, reliability, and validity that such measurement requires. We have a Hobson's choice between partly relevant but objective criteria, and partly objective but relevant criteria. Work by Ellsworth, Foster, Childers, Arthur, and Krocker (1968) suggests that assessment of the patient's level of adjustment in the community through perceptions of patients themselves, hospital staff, and relatives offer another important type of quality criterion.

A second observation is that the scope of work in this area is extremely limited, much of our information depending on work done at VA hospitals. This means that, despite the interhospital differences demonstrated, the total range of variation of the qualities studied is far less than if the same number of institutions under a variety of auspices could have been studied. Plainly, the field would benefit greatly from the mere replication of the PEP or Ullmann studies on other aggregates of institutions.

Third, the high intercorrelation of the PEP study's major independent variables, Ullmann's work with partial correlations, and the results from multivariate analysis of institutional characteristics indicate the difficulties involved in the attempt to assess the effects of individual institutional qualities as independent variables. The field is just beginning to try to determine which qualities vary simultaneously and which are relatively autonomous in their effects. If there is danger in assuming too readily that institutional variables are independent, there may be just as great a danger in assuming that the reduction of a correlation by removing the influence of a third variable necessarily means that the first two variables have no intrinsic causal relationship.

Fourth, input control is essential when using patient outcome as a quality criterion. It seems self-evident that sets of institutions and certainly sets of wards within an institution as they exist in nature do not contain random samples of patients upon admission; on the contrary, selective factors, sometimes of a crucial, criterion-relevant nature, determine whether a patient goes here or there. Obviously, the fact that hospitals have higher mortality rates than private homes does not suggest that sick people should refuse hospitalization. No more does the finding that wards using restraints have lower discharge rates necessarily mean that the former causes the latter. The ideal and traditional solution to such problems of ambiguous causal direction is the experiment—random assignment to controlled treatment conditions—and such a research strategy is to be used whenever possible. When not possible, one is thrown back upon other means of achieving interpretability of outcomes by assuring the comparability of patient input across conditions. One must resort to procedures of statistical control in which criterion-relevant patient attributes (e.g., age, marital status, length of prior hospitalization) are used as covariates. The analysis of covariance with multiple covariates may be found awkward. Recent methodological advances in the use of incremental multiple regression analysis (Cohen, 1968a, 1968b) provide a flexible device for incorporating any variables, however scaled, as covariates. These methods also include provisions for curvilinearity, interactions, and missing data, problems that frequently loom large in the study of institutions.

Fifth, while inter-institution and intra-institution studies, and combinations of the two, have been reviewed, there have been few attempts to compare indices of quality, or to determine the process correlates of quality in a way to allow one to determine the relative contributions of within- and among-institution effects.

The sixth and seventh issues are methodological problems widely shared across the spectrum of behavioral science, but are nevertheless critically important in the study of institutions. Insufficient attention is paid to issues of the *size* of effects, recourse being generally taken to significance tests as arbiters of what deserves emphasis. The use of directly meaningful outcome criteria and the conversion of significance test results to proportions of variance accounted for are strongly recommended. (See Cohen, 1965: 101-106; Friedman, 1968; and Vaughan and Corballis, 1969). A related problem is the neglect of issues of statistical power, the probability of detecting effects. Institutional studies must seek to generalize from typically *few* hospitals or wards, necessitating that statistical error of *both* the first and second kind (commission and omission) be kept in some useful balance. This problem is extensively treated in Cohen (1969).

Finally, it should be obvious right away that everything thus far presented is correlational and allows very little room for attributing causation. While we shall later speculate on which relationships may be causal, it is plain that firm conclusions may be drawn only from controlled experiments in this macrosystem.

## PROCESS CORRELATES OF JUDGED QUALITY

Intelligence testing began by determining empirically which tasks distinguished among those judged bright and those judged dull by teachers. Much of our knowledge about personality testing has also been gained through this method. It is, therefore, somewhat surprising to find relatively little done in comparing institutions or wards within institutions in this manner, through global judgments of quality by "experts," followed by an empirical determination of the correlates of judged quality. For better or for worse, accrediting bodies generally make a priori judgments about which process qualities are desirable, and obtain a final judgment of an institution's quality on the basis of summed ratings of these process qualities. One difficulty is that, aside from accrediting bodies, few people have access to enough institutions to make comparable judgments. In any case, it would seem desirable to attempt to determine what some of the institutional characteristics are that occasionally make consensus possible that "institution A is good," but "institution B is bad."

Most of the few such studies that could be found involved the investigator's ordering or categorizing treatment units in terms of overall quality, or some related dimension, and determining which institutional qualities were associated with his criterion. Klett, Berger, Sewall, and Rice (1963) had 190 patients on eight chronic wards of a state hospital complete the Ward Evaluation Scale. Two wards were judged by the authors to be model exit wards, four were considered average, and two were distinctly older and less adequate than the others. Patients showed significant tendencies to rate the "better" ward more highly in total evaluation as well as in the subareas of facilities, management, and services.

Moos (1969) found that when patients on 23 wards rated their general satisfaction with their wards, six of the seven WAS press scales completed by patients for this study showed very high correlations with quality. When staff rated the same 23 wards, the Affiliation and Autonomy scales of the WAS were marginally correlated with patient ratings of satisfaction. Thus, while patients and staff do differ significantly in their descriptions of ward atmosphere, there is some degree of consensuality in relating these atmospheres to patient satisfaction.

The current research by Lawton, Lipton, and Cohen (1974) sought quality criteria in 20 ratings by six research workers and a different set of rankings on four qualities by 20 administrative and professional personnel, all of whom were relatively familiar with all of the 24 treatment units but not assigned to any unit. A component analysis of these consensual scores resulted in three indices of quality: Institutionalism, Quality of Administrative and Therapeutic Staff, and Quality of Nursing Staff. A variety of process variables were related to these criteria through hierarchical multiple regression analysis, utilizing patient input variables and other characteristics as covariates.

Large size of ward was associated with high Institutionalism and low Administrative-Therapeutic Staff Quality independently of both patient input characteristics and of patient scores on the Norristown Milieu Scale, the Ward Questionnaire, and the Ward Perception Scale.

High staff-patient ratio was associated with both high-quality Administrative-Therapeutic staff and Nursing Staff, with patient input and size of ward controlled.

Patient input, size of ward, and staff-patient ratio were controlled prior to consideration of staff attitudes and quality. High criterion ratings of Institutionalism were characteristic of wards whose staffs were low in Morale, considered their wards as Highly Structured, low in Patient Mutuality, Good Service (sic), and Inactive Ward. Finally, poor Nursing Staff Quality was associated with staff attitudes indicating low Structure, low Benevolence, and Active Ward.

The associations of patient attitude factors with the quality criteria were trivial, once their background characteristics, behavioral status, diagnosis, and ward size and staffing patterns were controlled for.

A set of organizational variables was created. First, Staff Morale was the sum of ratings on 8 items inquiring about job satisfaction. Second, 41 items relating to relatively objective ward practices and conditions as rated by the charge nurse or attendant were factored, resulting in factors named Patient Autonomy, Benign Neglect, and Laissez-faire Atmosphere. Third, aggregate unit data on accidents, compliance with patient-care and record-keeping routines, absenteeism, and turnover (all from standard hospital records) were factored, resulting in factors labeled Conscientious Record Keeping, Behavioral Morale, and Active Treatment. Finally, staff judgments of the adequacy of 39 physical facilities on their wards, when factored, yielded satisfaction scores on Ward Spaces, Solitary Facilities, Enriching Facilities, and Instrumental Facilities. Exercising prior control on patient input, size, staff-patient ratio, and staff attitudes, an independent contribution of low Patient Autonomy to the Institutionalism, poor Administrative-Therapeutic Staff Quality, and poor Nursing Staff Quality criteria was found. Conscientious Record Keeping was also associated with good staff quality of both types. The other organizational variables had relationships with quality that were either low in magnitude or statistically insignificant.

Finally a set of measures dealt with the presence or objective quality of a variety of physical characteristics of the ward or unit. Eighteen items representing the quality of daily maintenance observed on repeated tours through each ward yielded average ward scores on factors named Ward Cleanliness, Well-supplied Ward, and Neat Bedrooms. Thirty relatively fixed physical features of the ward and its furnishings were noted or rated by observation. When factored, these gave scales named Large Institutional Structure, Effort to Individualize, and Homelike versus Institutional Furnishings. The presence of another overlapping set of 39 fixed features was determined by inquiry, and yielded factors named Enriched Environment and Well-equipped Institutional Environment versus Sparce Individualized Environment. A last set of factors was derived from square-footage measurements of nine types of spaces, yielding factors labeled Enrichment Space, Basic Ward Space, and Non-Living Space.

These physical factors were examined as they successively accounted for incremental variance in quality criteria, controlling for patient input, size, and staff-patient ratio. Poorly Supplied Ward, Neat Bedrooms, and Highly Institutionalized Furnishings were associated with high scores on Institutionalism. The Effort to Individualize, presence of Homelike Furnishings, and large amount of Enrichment Space factors were associated with good quality of Administrative-Therapeutic Staff. Finally, Ward Cleanliness, Enriched Environment, and Sparse Individualized Environment scores were associated with good Quality of Nursing Staff.

At this point it would seem to be worthwhile to attempt to study samples of institutions, utilizing consensual criterion judgments of experts who did not know which institutional variables might be under study. Accrediting bodies, in particular, should use their unusual opportunity of gaining experts' evaluations of institutions to further our knowledge about the components of quality.

## DISCUSSION

### What Are the Functional Dimensions of Treatment Institutions?

The attempt to define dimensions of the treatment milieu is still in its infancy. Dimensions derived thus far are primarily a function of the selection of variables put into the analyses. Thus, the factor analysis in the PEP project was rich in objectively measurable institutional variables, but very sparse in direct behavioral or attitudinal variables. The latter formed the universe for the Cohen and Struening OMI studies (1962; 1963; 1964). The OMI items express employees' generalized attitudes toward mental illness, mental patients, and treatment of patients. Other attitudinal definitions of milieu, such as those gained from the Jackson CTE (1964) are made up from employees' characterizations of their own behavior, their perceptions of the administrative practices of themselves, their peers, their superiors, and their subordinates, and their perceptions of the total milieu. Moos's WAS scale (1969) asks patients and staff to abstract typical aspects of the ward from specific behavior of both staff and patients. The Ellsworth patient POW (1965; Ellsworth et al., 1971) is composed of items reflecting staff behavior, administrative practices, and higher-order characterizations of the milieu. The staff POW, on the other hand, is exclusively composed of items relating to nursing staff's attitudes toward and perceptions of the professional staff. The items in the WES of Rice and associates (1963) relate to physical characteristics of the ward, services provided, and administrative practices. The diverse instruments used by Smith (1971) and Lawton, Lipton, and Cohen (1974) utilized the broadest number of domains.

Naturally, with such diverse raw material for the extraction of milieu dimensions, to say nothing of differences between institutional contexts, the similarities among different investigators' findings might well be expected to be minimal. Perusal of the item-content of the factors defined by the many investigators does allow some rough grouping into milieu-characteristic domains that seem to recur across studies. Table 8.1 shows the authors' categorization of factors from studies whose factor compositions were available and whose content dealt with patient or staff cognitions of specific ward environments. Factor names shown in parentheses are assigned to more than one column of Table 8.1, since their content overlapped with two of the present authors' categories. In other cases, two factors from the same study, while being statistically differentiated and given different names by the investigator, appeared to be similar in meaning and are designated as (a) or (b). There does seem to be enough replicability across studies to encourage a continued search for measures with general application to a variety of situations. Inspection of Table 8.1 suggests that Ward Morale, Order and Organization, and Activity Level recur slightly less frequently than the other milieu characteristics.

### Relationships Among Process Variables

While much may be learned by studying the relationships among process variables, the interrelatedness of many of them makes for a confusing lack of structure. Multivariate analysis has the greatest advantage of reducing the number of separate variables to be comprehended. Functional dimensions of institutions as defined by factor analytic techniques are probably the most useful higher-order process variables. However, a beginning on a carefully conceived conceptual basis such as Moos

TABLE 8.1 MILIEU CHARACTERISTICS BASED ON PATIENT AND STAFF ATTITUDES AS NAMED BY VARIOUS INVESTIGATORS, GROUPED IN TERMS OF FACE SIMILARITY

| Investigator(s) Suggested Name | Staff Involvement | Patient Autonomy | Staff Control | Patient Mutuality | Ward Morale | Order and Organization | Activity Level |
|---|---|---|---|---|---|---|---|
| Jackson (1969) CTE | Socioemotional activity | (a) Patient self-management (b) Instrumental activity | Behavior modification | | | | Active treatment |
| Ellsworth et al. (1971) POW (Patient) | Receptive and involved staff | (a) Patient involvement in ward management (b) Expectation for patient autonomy | | | Inaccessible staff | | Satisfaction with ward |
| King and Smith (1972) TMS | Staff-patient Socioemotional interaction | Patient autonomy | Staff control | | | | |
| Spiegel and Younger (1972) WCI | Personnel concern for patients | | | Patient concern for patients | Ward morale | | |
| Moos (1973) WAS | (Support) | Autonomy | Staff control | (a) (Support) (b) (Personal problem orientation) | | (a) Order and organization (b) Program clarity | Involvement |
| Lawton, Lipton, and Cohen (1974) NMS (patient factors) | (Benevolent ward) | | (a) (Punitive low morale) (b) High structure | (Benevolent ward) | (Punitive low morale) | Carefully planned program | |
| Lawton, Lipton, and Cohen (1974) NMS (staff factors) | Benevolent staff | Active patient initiative | (Punitive low morale) | Patient mutuality | (Punitive low morale) | High structure | Active ward |

Factors in parentheses have content related to two milieu characteristics.
Factors designated as (a) and (b) are factors from a single investigation that appear to represent the same milieu characteristic.

used for the WAS (1973), followed by extensive exploration of its concurrent and predictive validities, plainly has much to be said for it in terms of the clarity of the concepts involved.

The difficulty of any summary statement regarding relationships among process variables derives partly from the fact that all such data are correlational in nature and that no process variable can be considered an indicator of quality simply by assertion. Our eventual understanding of institutions will be helped most by research which manipulates institutional variables experimentally and measures their impact in terms of validated quality criteria.

## Process Correlates of Institutional Quality

The studies that have been reviewed offer support for the following process correlates of output quality among institutions or among treatment units: small size, high staff-patient ratio, high cost per patient day, low authoritarian staff attitudes, high general administrative cost allocation (registrar especially), low proportion of food and shelter cost allocation, high staff morale, pressure of many applications, and the existence of strong family care programs. Process correlates of quality appearing only once, or with less clear significance, are: low staff absenteeism, allocation of staff time to patient care, nonpathological social milieu of the ward, unitization within a small-ward setting, good staff record-keeping practices, a number of staff housekeeping practices and physical-environmental ward characteristics, high percentage of staff who are physicians, psychologists, or social workers, and high group therapy rate. The necessity for further work is indicated by a few dissonant findings, such as a set of negative relationships between quality of care and institutional variables like small size, high staff-patient ratio, percentage of rehabilitation workers, number of volunteers, good housekeeping and incidence of individual therapy.

It is more difficult to integrate the findings that have related ward and hospital characteristics as perceived by staff and patients to quality criteria. Table 8.2 lists the relationships between the three major types of outcome measures and the six domains of milieu characteristics shown in Table 8.1. Many of the relationships between these process and criterion variables have proved to be statistically insignificant; Table 8.2 lists only those that were significant, that were categorizable, and that appeared most acceptable from an experimental-design point of view.

It is immediately clear that staff perceptions are much more likely to be associated with outcome than are patient perceptions. One can advance a number of hypotheses for future research that might account for this situation. Most obviously, fewer investigators have worked with patient attitudes. Also, it is usually staff who make the decisions about discharge and readmission, and who make the expert ratings. They thus are likely to use the same values in characterizing their milieu as they do in their decision making. Further, there is probably more intrinsic test-taking error in patients' responses. It may also be that patients discern the relevant institutional dimensions less clearly than staff.

The only category with impressive performance in prediction is Staff Involvement. Patient Autonomy and Ward Morale were related to favorable outcome to a somewhat lesser extent.

TABLE 8.2   PROCESS CORRELATES OF QUALITY:  STAFF AND PATIENT
PERCEPTIONS AND BEHAVIOR

| Process Characteristic | Quality Criterion | | |
|---|---|---|---|
| | Patient Movement | Symptom or Behavior Improvement | Experts' Evaluation |
| **Staff Perceptions and Behavior** | | | |
| Staff Involvement | Ellsworth et al. (1971) King and Smith (1972) Moos and Schwartz (1972) Spiegel and Younger (1972) | | Lawton et al. (1974) |
| Patient Autonomy | King and Smith (1972) | King and Smith (1972) (inverse relationship) | Lawton et al. (1974) |
| Staff Control | Cohen and Struening (1962) (inverse relationship) Moos and Schwartz (1972) | | |
| Patient Mutuality | | | Lawton et al. (1974) |
| Ward Morale | Ellsworth (1965) Spiegel and Younger (1972) | Dickey (1964) | Lawton et al. (1974) |
| Order and Organization | Moos and Schwartz (1972) | | Lawton et al. (1974) (a direct and an inverse relationship to 2 different criteria) |
| Activity Level | Moos and Schwartz (1972) | | Lawton et al. (1974) (a direct and an inverse relationship to 2 different criteria) |
| **Patient Perceptions and Behavior** | | | |
| Staff Involvement | | Ellsworth and Maroney (1972) | |
| Patient Autonomy | Ellsworth (1965) | Ellsworth (1965) | |
| Staff Control | Moos and Schwartz (1972) | | |
| Patient Mutuality | Ellsworth (1965) | Ellsworth (1965) | |
| Ward Morale | | Ellsworth and Maroney (1972) | |
| Order and Organization | | | |
| Activity Level | | | |

Except when otherwise noted, the relationship between the process characteristic named and a favorable criterion score was direct.

Whether any of these process characteristics are themselves worthy of being used as quality criteria is another question. The correlational nature of the data, strictly speaking, would prohibit it. One can very easily trace, in the history of the VA hospital, how a changing philosophy of treatment produced many postwar hospitals with a cluster of characteristics: small size, proximity to university, active consultant program, high cost per patient day, high staff-patient ratio, and a policy emphasizing quick turnover. If these hospitals have no room for chronic patients, the chronic patient must go to the older hospitals, which are large, less centrally located, and have a tradition of relatively low staff-patient ratios. While size thus may have a high negative relationship to turnover, it is less than certain that the small size is responsible for the good record on turnover. Even authoritarianism may be an attitude developed in response to the necessity of treating chronic patients, rather than a cause of low turnover. Thus, until evidence becomes available from experimental studies, and the correlational aspects are studied over a wider variety of institutions, it seems premature to use any of these process correlates of quality as criteria themselves.

On the other hand, much may still be learned from investigating further the characteristics of "good" and "bad" institutions. It would also improve our conceptions of institutional quality to know the relationship between quality as judged by experts and quality as judged by patients, as reflected on patient or staff morale, as measured by patient change, and as measured in objective output indices such as early release and turnover.

## DIRECTIONS FOR FUTURE RESEARCH

The call for better criteria of mental health has been made so frequently that it is trite to belabor the issue. However, achieving this goal is central to the problem of defining institutional quality. How else can we know a "good" from a "bad" institution other than by applying the test of whether the product of one tends to be superior to another in mental health, by some definable standard? It nevertheless seems that we are far distant from the time when such criteria will be at hand and must therefore look ahead to doing the best we can, given the realistic, unsatisfactory bag of criteria that we now possess.

Some basic components of potentially rewarding future research are a planful sampling of institutions, the adequate representation of institutional domains and characteristics within domains, the assessment of quality from a variety of points of view (including the judgments of "experts"), the coupling of longitudinal design to the multivariate study, and direct intervention across institutions.

### 1. Institutional Sampling

Institutions and wards vary as individuals do, and wherever possible, should be sampled or studied as universes. The VA studies have given a good picture of variation among this type of hospital, but it is rare to find such a range of other mental hospitals represented. An ideal study might draw a random sample of institutions or a sample stratified by sponsorship, size, or location, and survey the universe of treatment units within each institution. For example, the growing importance of statewide mental health planning might make possible a study of the natural variation in milieu among all the hospitals in a state system. Where drawing a sample is beyond the means of study, the next best alternative would be to choose representative institutions that vary maximally in some of the more important dimensions, as Smith (1971) did.

## 2. Representation of Relevant Institutional Domains and Characteristics

The research reviewed above sometimes deals with variables from a single domain (e.g., the OMI items are limited to the domain of staff ideology), but more typically with variables from an assortment of the domains. The application of factor analytic techniques to such an assortment of items yields factors that reflect the functional relationships among the items. If the item pool contains only one or two items representing a particular domain, these items may load with a larger number of items from another domain with which they have a functional, but not a conceptual, relationship.

Understanding of the two domains may be retarded by the combination of inadequate item sampling of each domain, and the inclusion of both domains in exploratory factor analyses. Thus, it may be preferable to separate domains on a rational basis, and to factor separately the items representing each domain. The relationships among domains can then be explored by utilizing the measures of factors in each domain. As an example, the WES (Rice et al., 1963) contains items representing physical characteristics, services, and administrative practices. Ideally, a literature search should produce a universe of items representing each of these three domains. A sample of items should be drawn from each, and factored separately. The resulting factors could be augmented with new items, and the derivation process continued until stable and replicable factors representing the physical environments, services, and administrative practices emerged. What one would learn from this study of the internal structure of each of these domains would be quite useful in its own right. Then, this knowledge could be augmented by entering stable, internally consistent measures of the factors from all domains into a single factor analysis and/or a series of multiple regression analyses. The former would clarify the concepts within each domain, while the latter would advance understanding of the entire system.

The study should represent each of the major process variable domains:

(1) Physical characteristics of the ward, building, or institution, and its proximate physical setting, including characteristics determined by physical structure and/or administrative decisions (cost, staffing, size, distribution of personnel).

(2) Administrative practices (from the largest social systems, such as federal and state levels, down to board of directors, administrative chiefs, and lowest-level ward administration).

(3) Services, programs, activities offered.

(4) Patient variables
   (a) Input characteristics (attributes of patients admitted, or as of time of initiating study).
   (b) Suprapersonal environment (modal characteristics of all patients living in one physically defined area).

     (c)  Attitudes and ideology regarding self, mental illness, and treatment unit.

     (d)  Patient's evaluation of any institutional variable (e.g., physical plant, other patients, staff).

     (e)  Perception of any institutional variable.

     (f)  Behavior, such as amount, type, complexity of behavior, psychopathology, and so on.

  (5)  Staff variables

     (a)  Personal characteristics

     (b)  Attitudes, ideology, role conception.

     (c)  Staff's evaluation of institutional variables (including morale, job satisfaction, treatment program evaluation).

     (d)  Perception of any institutional variable.

     (e)  Communication, flow of information.

     (f)  Behavior, such as amount and type of interaction with patient, type of behavior control exercised, and so on.

  (6)  Suprapersonal environmental characteristics

From the point of view of a subject (patient or staff member), an extremely relevant aspect of the milieu is the characteristics of the people in his environment. Lawton (1970b: 41) has described the suprapersonal environment as

> . . . a group of spatially clustered individuals. The modal characteristics of the spatially clustered group are the units of the suprapersonal environment. The more homogeneous the group is with respect to the modal characteristic, the greater is its effect on the individual . . . such suprapersonal environmental characteristics are directly perceivable, cognitively comprehensible, and potentially behaviorally activating.

The more the individual deviates from a given suprapersonal environmental characteristic, the more salient a stimulus to his behavior this modal characteristic of the people in his environment becomes for him. A black living in a suburban town of whites would experience this type of social stimulus very acutely. Kellam and others (1967) have utilized this concept in attributing a significant portion of behavior change in a patient to the amount of disturbed behavior recorded on that patient's ward. In another mental hospital setting, Kahana and Kahana (1970) demonstrated improvement in the affective and cognitive status of elderly patients admitted to an age-integrated, as compared to an age-segregated, ward. In any multiward or multihospital longitudinal research where the individual patient is the subject of study, suprapersonal characteristics should be thoroughly considered. Such factors as the age, sex, social class, predominant diagnosis, and so on, of the modal patient in a unit may be significant determinants of outcome.

  (7)  Contextual variables of neighborhood, community, or larger region.

     (a)  Economic status of the geographic region.

     (b)  Social characteristics of the region.

     (c)  Political characteristics of the region.

(d) Climate of attitude toward mental health of the population of the region.

(e) Topography, climate, physical structures of the region.

The above characteristics, properly augmented and detailed, represent the treatment system components of the type of institution with which we are concerned. In outline form, the transactional, interrelated nature of the components is not fully conveyed. For example, the number of square feet of common space on a ward is one usable component of a system to characterize a treatment unit, as is its ward census. However, the number of patients and staff observed in the common space of a ward is a function of several system components and cannot properly be uniquely assigned to the physical plant, the administrative practices, the patient, or the staff domain. Thus, rather than arbitrarily making a priori designations of the domain to which a characteristic belong, one might, alternatively, let this decision be made empirically by subjecting the large number of heterogeneous variables to a factor analysis, and working with higher-order factors toward a parsimonious choice of dimensions that describe the milieu.

Multiple data sources should be used wherever possible. Thus, staff and patients may both rate the same feature of the institution. The application of multimethod factor analysis (Lorr and Hamlin, 1971) would attempt to index a single dimension in several ways: by an objective archival index, a rating done on its perceived presence, and by direct observation of behavior, for example.

Wherever possible, the multiple data sources should have some parallel elements. The WAS has identical elements responded to by patients and staff, while the staff and patient POW are totally incommensurate. Having differing elements does have the advantage of tailoring content specifically to the target subject group. It would be possible to devise staff and patient forms with a subset of items that are common to both, and scorable with the same norms, and a subset unique to one or the other group. The latter could be combined with items from the common subset to provide measures of qualities unique to the group in question.

## 3. The Varieties of Quality

We have discussed the surprising scarcity of data that attempt a consensual definition of institutional quality. Within a state there should be a number of people with knowledge of more than one treatment institution who could profer evaluative judgments of the goodness of care offered. The status of the judge (patient, staff member, relative, citizen, accrediting body member, bureaucrat) would afford a basis for exploration of the meaning of quality. Inquiry into reasons for the judgments could yield information on the dimensions of perceived quality, which could then be related to process variables.

## 4. Longitudinal Multi-Institutional Studies

The PEP study is apparently still in process, measuring the change over time in patient symptoms and relating these to the milieu characteristics of the institution. A natural sequel would be the addition of a longitudinal component to the multi-institution study suggested in this section, where systematic sampling of all domains is done, and where the change in both patients and institution over time is mapped. Thus, the dependent variable of patient well-being as of some follow-up interval would be investigated as a function of the original status of the patient, the original institutional characteristics, and the *change* in institutional characteristics over the same time period.

## 5. Intervention Research

The most difficult task of all would be to introduce innovative programs into a number of institutions in such a way as to result in an experimental and a control group of institutions. However, the tendency toward centralized organization of mental health services may make such a task possible. Where one is concerned with effects at a ward, rather than institutional, level, the mechanics of intervention would be less difficult. As in working with individuals, account would have to be taken of the initial status of the institution as it might potentially affect the mean change of the patient within it, that is, the interaction of treatment and institutional characteristic.

In conclusion, it seems that the potential knowledge to be gained from multi-institution and multi-ward research is great. A formidable obstacle to the conduct of such research is the expense of studying large numbers of people and institutional units. The model of cooperative effort provided by the VA Program Evaluation staff, which conducted the PEP study, might well be followed by national organizations and funding bodies in the separate areas of the mental hospital, the community mental health center, the geriatric institution, housing for the elderly, the institution for the mental retarded, or childrens' residential treatment centers.

### NOTE

1. This relationship may, of course, be a result of the fact that wards for more acutely disturbed patients have more staff assigned to them.

### REFERENCES

Barton, A. *Organizational measurement.* Research Monograph No. 2. Princeton, N.J.: College Entrance Examination Board, 1961.

Bay, A. P. and P. E. Feldman. *Aide staffing pattern: Its effects on hospital program.* American Psychiatric Association Mental Hospital Service Supplementary Mailing No. 155, October 1962.

Burdock, E. I., G. Hakerem, A. S. Hardesty and J. Zubin. A ward behavior rating scale for mental patients. *Journal of Clinical Psychology,* 1960, 16: 246-247.

Caudill, W. *The mental hospital as a small society.* Cambridge: Harvard University Press, 1958.

Cohen, J. A rationale and method for psychiatric hospital assessment. Intramural Report 64-5, Psychiatric Evaluation Project, Veterans Administration Hospital, Washington, D.C., 1964. Pp. 1-17.

———. Some statistical issues in psychological research. In B. B. Wolman (ed.), *Handbook of clinical psychology.* New York: McGraw-Hill, 1965.

———. Multiple regression analysis as a general data-analytic system. *Psychological Bulletin,* 1968, 70: 426-443. (a)

———. Prognostic factors in functional psychosis: A study in multivariate methodology. *Transactions of the New York Academy of Science,* 1968, 30: 833-840. (b)

———. *Statistical power analysis for the behavioral sciences.* New York: Academic Press, 1969.

Cohen, J. and E. L. Struening. Opinions about mental illness in the personnel of two large mental hospitals. *Journal of Abnormal and Social Psychology,* 1962, 64: 349-360.

———. Opinions about mental illness: Mental hospital occupational profile clusters. *Psychological Reports,* 1963, 12: 111-124.

———. Opinions about mental illness: Hospital social atmosphere and patient time in the hospital. *Journal of Consulting Psychology,* 1964, 28: 291-198.

Davis, J. E. Empirical dimensions of psychiatric hospital organization. Intramural Report 64-5, Psychiatric Evaluation Project, Veterans Administration Hospital, Washington, D.C., 1964. Pp. 19-35.

Dickey, B. A. Intra-staff conflict, morale, and treatment effectiveness in a therapeutic community setting. Paper presented at the annual meeting of the American Psychological Association, September 1964.

Dunham, H. W. and S. K. Weinberg. *The culture of the state mental hospital.* Detroit: Wayne State University Press, 1960.

Ellsworth, R. B. *The MACC Behavioral Adjustment Scale, Form II.* Beverly Hills, Calif.: Western Psychological Services, 1962.

———. Patient and staff perceptions of relatively effective and ineffective psychiatric treatment programs. Paper presented at tenth annual conference, Veterans Administration Cooperative Studies in Psychiatry, New Orleans, March 1965.

———. Instructions for scoring patient Perception of Ward (POW) Scale. Roseburg, Ore.: Veterans Administration Hospital, 1969. Ditto report.

———, H. R. Dickman, and R. J. Maroney. Characteristics of productive and unproductive unit systems in VA psychiatric hospitals. *Hospital and Community Psychiatry,* 1972, 23: 261-268.

Ellsworth, R. B., L. Foster, B. Childers, G. Arthur, and D. Kroeker. Hospital and community adjustment as perceived by psychiatric patients, their families, and staff. *Journal of Consulting and Clinical Psychology Monograph,* 1968, 32 (Part II): 1-41.

Ellsworth, R. B. and R. J. Maroney. Characteristics of psychiatric programs and their effects on patients' adjustment. *Journal of Consulting and Clinical Psychology,* 1972, 39: 436-447.

Ellsworth, R. B., R. Maroney, W. Klett, H. Gordon and R. Gunn. Milieu characteristics of successful psychiatric treatment programs. *American Journal of Orthopsychiatry,* 1971, 41: 427-441.

Etzioni, A. *Modern organizations.* Englewood Cliffs, N.J.: Prentice-Hall, 1964.

Forehand, G. A., and B. H. Gilmer. Environmental variation in studies of organizational behavior. *Psychological Bulletin,* 1964, 62: 361-382.

Friedman, H. Magnitude of experimental effect and a table for its rapid estimation. *Psychological Bulletin,* 1968, 70: 245-251.

Gilbert, D. C. and D. M. Levinson. Role performance, ideology and personality in mental hospital aides. Pp. 197-208 in M. Greenblatt, D. J. Levinson, and R. H. Williams (eds.), *The patient and the mental hospital.* New York: The Free Press, 1957.

Goffman, E. *Asylums.* Garden City, N.Y.: Doubleday, 1961.

Graham, J. R., R. Allon, I. Friedman and R. S. Lilly. The Ward Evaluation Scale: A factor analytic study. *Journal of Clinical Psychology,* 1971, 27: 118-122.

Graham, J. R., R. S. Lilly, R. Allon and I. Friedman. Comparison of the factor structures of staff and patient responses on the Ward Evaluation Scale. *Journal of Clinical Psychology,* 1971, 27: 123-128.

Gurel, L. Correlates of psychiatric hospital effectiveness. Intramural Report 64-5, Psychiatric Evaluation Project, Veterans Administration Hospital, Washington, D.C., 1964. Pp. 37-66.

Houts, P., and R. Moos. The development of a Ward Initiative Scale for patients. *Journal of Clinical Psychology,* 1969, 25: 319-322.

Jackson, J. Toward the comparative study of mental hospitals: Characteristics of the treatment environment. Pp. 35-87 in A. F. Wessen (ed.), *The psychiatric hospital as a social system.* Springfield, Ill.: Charles C. Thomas, 1964.

Jackson, J. Factors of the treatment enviornment. *Archives of General Psychiatry,* 1969, 21: 39-45.

Joint Commission on Mental Illness and Health. *Action for mental health.* New York: Basic Books, 1961.

Kahana, B. and E. Kahana. Changes in mental status of elderly patients in age-integrated and age-segregated hospital milieus. *Journal of Abnormal Psychology*, 1970, 75: 177-181.

Katz, D. and R. Kahn. *The social psychology of organizations.* New York: Wiley, 1966.

Kellam, S. G., S. C. Goldberg, N. R. Schooler, A. Berman and J. L. Schmelzer. Ward atmosphere and outcome of treatment of acute schizophrenia. *Journal of Psychiatric Research*, 1967, 5: 145-163.

Kellam, S. G., J. L. Shmelzer and A. Berman. Variation in the atmospheres of psychiatric wards. *Archives of General Psychiatry*, 1966, 14: 551-570.

King, J. A. and C. G. Smith. The treatment milieu and prediction of mental hospital effectiveness. *Journal of Health and Social Behavior*, 1972, 13: 180-194.

Klett, S. L., D. G. Berger, L. G. Sewall and C. E. Rice. Patient evaluation of the psychiatric ward. *Journal of Clinical Psychology*, 1963, 19: 347-351.

Lasky, D. I., and M. Dowling. The release rates of state mental hospitals as related to maintenance costs and patient-staff ratio. *Journal of Clinical Psychology*, 1971, 27: 272-277.

Lawton, M. P. Institutions for the elderly: Theory, content, and methods for research. *The Gerontologist,* 1970, 10: 305-312. (a)

———. Ecology and aging. Pp. 40-67 in L. Pastalan and D. H. Carson (eds.), *Spatial-behavioral relationships in the aged.* Ann Arbor: University of Michigan Press, 1970. (b)

———, M. B. Lipton, and J. Cohen. Criteria for the evaluation of mental health programs. National Institute of Mental Health Grant, MH-17473. Norristown State Hospital, Norristown, Pa., 1974.

Linn, L. S. State hospital environment and rates of patient discharge. *Archives of General Psychiatry,* 1970, 23: 346-351.

Lorr, M. and R. M. Hamlin. A multimethod factor analysis of behavioral and objective measures of psychopathology. *Journal of Consulting and Clinical Psychology,* 1971, 36: 136-141.

Lorr, M., C. J. Klett, D. M. McNair and J. J. Lasky. *Inpatient Multidimensional Psychiatric Scale.* Palo Alto, Calif.: Consulting Psychologist Press, 1963.

March, J. G. (ed.) *Handbook of organizations.* Chicago: Rand McNally, 1964.

Maroney, R. J. Program milieu and treatment effectiveness. Paper presented at the annual meeting of the American Psychological Association, Washington, D.C., September 1969.

Moos, R. *Ward Atmosphere Scale: Preliminary Manual.* Stanford, Calif.: Stanford University Medical Center, 1969.

———. Size, staffing, and the psychiatric ward treatment environment. *Archives of General Psychiatry,* 1972, 26: 414-418.

———. *Ward Atmosphere Scale Manual.* Stanford, Calif.: Department of Psychiatry, Stanford University, 1973.

———, and P. Houts. The assessment of the social atmosphere of psychiatric wards. *Journal of Abnormal Psychology,* 1968, 73: 595-604.

Moos, R. and J. Schwartz. Treatment environment and treatment outcome. *Journal of Nervous and Mental Diseases,* 1972, 154: 264-275.

Moos, R., R. Shelton and C. Perry Perceived ward climate and treatment outcome. *Journal of Abnormal Psychology*, 1973, 82 291-298.

Murray, H. A. *Explorations in personality.* New York: Oxford University Press, 1938.

Rice, C. E., S. L. Klett, D. G. Berger, L. G. Sewall and P. V. Lemkau. The Ward Evaluation Scale. *Journal of Clinical Psychology*, 1963, 14: 251-258.

Schwartz, M. What is a therapeutic milieu? Pp. 130-144 in M. Greenblatt, D. G. Levinson, and R. H Williams (eds.), *The patient and the mental hospital.* New York: The Free Press, 1957.

Sidman, J. and R. Moos. The relationship between psychiatric ward atmosphere and helping behavior. *Journal of Clinical Psychology*, 1973, 29: 74-77.

Smith, C. G. Mental hospitals: a study in organizational effectiveness. Notre Dame, Ind.: Department of Sociology and Anthropology, University of Notre Dame, 1971. Mimeo report.

Spiegel, D. and J. Younger. Ward climate and community stay of psychiatric patients. *Journal of Consulting and Clinical Psychology*, 1972, 39: 62-69.

Stanton, A. H. and M. S. Schwartz. *The mental hospital*. New York: Basic Books, 1954.

Stotland, E. and A. L. Kobler. *The life and death of a mental hospital*. Seattle: University of Washington Press, 1965.

Struening, E. L. and J. Cohen. Factorial invariance and other psychometric characteristics of five opinions about mental illness factors. *Education and Psychological Measurement*, 1963, 23: 289-198.

Ullmann, I. *Institution and outcome: A comparative study of mental hospitals*. New York: Pergamon, 1967.

Vaughan, G. M. and M. C. Corballis. Beyond tests of significance: Estimating strength of effects in selected anova designs. *Psychological Bulletin*, 1969, 62: 204-213.

Von Mering, O. and S. H. King. *Remotivating the mental patient*. New York: Russell Sage Foundation, 1957.

9

# CONSUMER FEEDBACK IN MEASURING THE EFFECTIVENESS
# OF MENTAL HEALTH PROGRAMS

## ROBERT B. ELLSWORTH

*VA Hospital, Salem, Va.*

While millions of tax dollars are spent each year on the delivery of mental health services, almost no accurate information is available regarding the costs and effectiveness of different programs. Accurate data on program costs are difficult to establish, for they should include not only the direct costs of services to the client, but also the indirect costs attributable to lost productivity, dysfunction of other family members, additional costs of support services by other agencies, and so on. Data on direct costs are comparatively easy to obtain while indirect costs are more difficult to assess. Most difficult but at least equally important, however, is the assessment of treatment effectiveness. At one time, legislators generally accepted the testimony of mental health professionals in establishing funding priorities for mental health services. Such testimony is now generally recognized as inadequate for evaluating program effectiveness. Unless significant progress is made in measuring program effectiveness, the mental health professions will find that decisions about programs priorities will be made in terms of direct cost factors along. Programs that cost the least per client will be implemented, and the mental health professional, by default, will have lost much of the opportunity to identify and introduce the most effective treatment approaches for his clients.

Often assumed as the primary reason for poor evaluation is the lack of adequate funding. Even when the evaluation part of demonstration programs has been adequately funded, the quality of the evaluation has typically been disappointing. In most grant proposals, the section on evaluation is typically little more than a ritualistic statement of intent (Cottrell, 1967). For so long have our intentions been good in this regard that many feel we are already at the point of continuing or discontinuing programs on the basis of evaluation research (Campbell, 1969).

Nothing could be further from the truth, for only in a few treasured instances is there a well-considered and realistic plan for program evaluation. In their review of the federal government's Evaluation Policy, Wholey and associates (1970: 15) conclude that adequate evaluation of social programs has been almost nonexistent. Even when evaluation studies have been adequately funded, they typically have been poorly conceived, or carried out with such lack of uniformity that the results from one study cannot be compared with those of other studies. The result is that programs that cost the public millions or even billions of dollars have not been adequately evaluated. Adequate funding for evaluation, then, does not typically produce the kind of results that allows one to conclude that one approach is more effective than another.

One major problem in program evaluation is that of deciding what data to collect in evaluating outcome. The groups most directly affected by the results of mental health services are the patients receiving therapy, and the significant others who are affected by the patients' adjustment. In addition, the reactions of the staff who provide services and the sponsors whose material support provides the opportunity for treatment should also be considered (Krause, 1969). But there is little agreement between patients, families, and therapists as to treatment effectiveness and results (Carr and Whittenbaugh, 1969; Storrow, 1960). Data from one source, then, do not provide an adequate index of effectiveness as viewed by those most directly involved in and affected by treatment.

Each data source has its own strengths and weaknesses. Patients are the best source for measuring felt distress, self-confidence, and the like, but their reports of behavioral adjustment have not been particularly reliable or valid (Paul, 1966). Trained observers have been used in some well-funded research studies, but this approach is prohibitively expensive for routine program evaluation. Tradition compels us to regard significant others (usually patients' relatives) as too biased to be used as objective raters. Data from this source, however, have been found to be quite reliable and valid (Bentinick et al., 1969; Ellsworth et al., 1968; Katz and Lyerly, 1963, Michaux et al., 1969; and Pasaminick et al., 1967). Staff reaction is also important, for their support often determines whether or not a particular approach is implemented or continued (Lamb et al., 1969). And finally, the agency must operate programs that do not result in excessive costs or complaints to legislators and agency heads who allocate funds.

The approach to program evaluation focused on in this paper is consistent with Paul's (1967) conclusion that the most promising criteria are those behavioral changes that occur outside the treatment setting. It matters little if the client learns to adjust well to the hospital setting or in relating to his clinic therapist if his behavior at work or his relationship to family members is not satisfactory. A basic assumption made by many mental health professionals has been that a client's adjustment and behavior in the treatment setting is highly related to his adjustment in other settings. This assumption is not correct, for patients often behave quite differently in treatment settings than they do in community settings (Buss et al., 1962; Ellsworth et al., 1968; Katz et al., 1967; Sinnet et al., 1965; Wood et al., 1962). The measures of program effectiveness that deserve most attention, then, are measures of clients' behavior in the community setting. This is not to say that clients' self-reports and staff observations are not useful, for ideally all are needed to provide an overall picture of program effectiveness. But these measures have typically been used in evaluation studies, while ratings of clients' community adjustment, probably the most meaningful measure of treatment outcome, have received scant attention.

Adequate program evaluation requires a great deal more than choosing the best measures of treatment outcome. Resistance to evaluation from both clinical staff and program administrators has accounted for much of the poor or nonexistent program evaluation. Part One of this paper discusses some of these problems and suggests some approaches to handling this resistance. Part Two represents the reliability and validity of the scales that were developed for use by significant others to rate clients' community adjustment. Part Three discusses some of the technical problems in program evaluation, such as those created by data loss, nonspecific effects common to most treatment approaches, and so on. Many of the experiences and conclusions presented in this paper are based on the observations of the author in attempting to evaluate the outcomes of psychiatric hospital and community clinic treatment.

## PART ONE.　RESISTANCE TO EVALUATION

### Resistance from Clinical Staff

Resistance from clinical staff appears to stem primarily from the fear that their efforts may not be measurably effective. As Goltz and associates (unpublished) point out, clinicians are not likely to cooperate in a process that might demonstrate their ineffectiveness. In our own work with clinic directors, for example, the fear was openly expressed that program evaluation may indicate their services had no measurable impact on clients' adjustment. In working with hospital treatment teams, the fear that the data would show their program to be less effective than other programs was evident. When the treatment outcomes were above average for their patients, the staff usually had no difficulty in concluding that the data accurately reflected the effectiveness of their program. When the data suggested less-than-average effectiveness, staff complained about the inaccuracy of relatives' ratings, assignment of sicker patients to their program, and researcher bias affecting the presentation of data regarding their program. Sometimes after the researcher left the meeting, the staff would explore, in private, the possibility that the data indicated a decrease in program effectiveness (Ellsworth, 1973).

A frequently heard complaint from clinical staff is that people cannot be reduced to numbers, and that each person's difficulty is unique. While recognizing that each person is unique, those familiar with measurement problems have found, also, that there are domains of adjustment behaviors common to most people, and that an individual's improvement can be reasonably estimated from ratings on these adjustment factors. Behavior therapists who focus on the treatment of specific symptoms, for example, often report generalized improvement in personal comfort and social relationships. In their review of behavior therapy studies in psychiatry,

Meyer and Chesser (1970: 113) reported that improvement in target behavior appeared to be accompanied by more widespread beneficial effects.

Some attempts have been made to construct individualized rating scales to measure the extent to which each patient attains the treatment goals specified as most relevant for him (Kiresuk and Sherman, 1968). Early experience indicates, however, that goal attainment scaling is not particularly useful for program evaluation. Cline and associates (1973) evaluated a program in which patients tended to fall short of the goals set with them. This could mean either that the program was relatively ineffective, or that the goal attainment scalers were overly optimistic. They suggest that some external criteria are needed for program evaluation since the initial setting and scaling of goals vary among different interviewers. Goal attainment scaling, however, does appear to be an excellent method for identifying what problems need attention, and for establishing, with the client, a realistic treatment contract. But it is difficult to see how such a method could be used to measure accurately the comparative effectiveness of different treatment approaches and programs.

An anti-empirical attitude among many clinicians is evidenced by their reluctance to utilize the findings of treatment evaluation studies, and slowness in changing their practice in light of these findings. Debated over the years was whether the efficacy of psychotherapy has been demonstrated. In 1959, Stevenson pointed out that personal conviction and tradition rather than evidence sustained the practice of psychotherapy. He concluded that the expenditure of millions of dollars per year on a practice with undemonstrated value was a "major scandal of our profession" (Stevenson, 1959: 120). In 1964, Cross reviewed the few studies evaluating the effectiveness of psychotherapy and concluded that its efficacy had not been established, a conclusion again reached by Bergin (1966) in his review two years later. Well designed experimental studies have shown that patients treated with both psychotherapy and drugs show no more improvement than those treated with drugs alone, a finding consistent for both outpatients (Brill et al., 1964) and hospitalized schizophrenics (May, 1969). While brief, time-limited psychotherapy may be helpful to many patients and families (Shlien, 1957; Lorr et al., 1966), particularly at a time of crisis (Levy, 1966), it must be concluded that the value of prolonged psychotherapy remains undemonstrated.

Despite this body of evidence questioning the efficacy of prolonged psychotherapy, this approach remains the treatment of choice in many mental health settings. It does not seem particularly well suited to clinic practice, however, for clients are generally seen less than five times (Lamb et al., 1969). Most of these abbreviated contacts appear to result from unilateral decisions on the part of the patient rather than an intended strategy of time-limited therapy. When the alternative of planned time-limited psychotherapy was proposed, a great deal of resistance to this approach arose from the outpatient staff, who preferred traditional, time-unlimited, psychodynamically oriented therapy (Lamb et al., 1969: 217-238). The director of that center identified the most difficult and major problem (unanticipated) as one of resistance among professionals to change (ibid.: 15). In most settings, decisions regarding approaches to treatment are arrived at through debate and the exercise of professional prerogatives. Little if any attempt has been made to resolve these questions through systematic evaluation of alternative approaches, or to systematically analyze results from other studies in planning treatment strategies.

Some important questions regarding the value of differing patterns in mental health care have arisen from conflicting results of treatment outcome studies. Preliminary evidence suggests, for example, that the primary function of the psychiatric hospital is that of rapid symptom reduction and early release (Deiter et al., 1965; Mendel, 1966), but there is some evidence favoring prolonged treatment (Gralnick, 1969). Controversy has also arisen regarding the value of differing patterns of aftercare. There are some who regard aftercare as perpetuating dependency and patienthood. One study suggests that people who sever contact with mental health professionals after release are rehospitalized less often than those who maintain contact (Michaux et al., 1969). Other studies suggest the contrary (Kliewer, 1970; Zolik, 1967). What probably occurs is that short-term treatment and aftercare may be helpful for some patients, but harmful for others. Needing careful evaluation, then, are comparisons of treatment effectiveness of outpatient, day care, and short-term inpatient programs, and perhaps most important, which patients profit most from what approaches.

Fewer still have been evaluation studies examining alternative programs in terms of their costs and benefits. One exception is a study by May (1969), in which he compares the cost and effectiveness of drugs, individual therapy, ECT, and supportive milieu for hospitalized schizophrenics. For these patients, the most effective treatment (drugs) would have cost the state of California $10 million a year less than the less effective approaches of psychotherapy and supportive milieu (May, 1969). Among VA psychiatric hospitals, the cost per patient treated was two and one-half times as much in the least efficient low turnover hospital than in the most efficient hospitals ($3,700 versus $1,500 per patient). And cost per patient released was over four times greater in the least efficient hospitals, $7,800 versus $1,800 (VA report to Congress, 1969). Differences in direct costs between alternative programs, then, are often very great. But data on treatment effectiveness are also required in order to make intelligent decisions regarding the best utilization of scarce and expensive mental health manpower. It is amazing that the expenditure of billions for services has not already stimulated a demand for adequate cost-benefit data.

## Resistance from Administration

Resistance from administration also accounts for the dearth of good program evaluation. It is a characteristic of public officials to win confidence by advocating programs and reforms as though they were certain to be successful (Campbell, 1969). If public officials or administrators have committed themselves in advance to the efficacy of their program, they are not in a good position to risk learning of failure. Under these circumstances, lack of concrete evidence increases their feeling of security.

To many administrators, also, the prerogative of exercising control over programs that are implemented may be more important than the discovery of which approach works best. This investigator has experienced, on more than one occasion, an administrator's displeasure over the findings of a particular program evaluation. The community adjustment outcomes of those receiving ECT, for example, were compared with those of patients not receiving ECT. Both groups were matched on initial community adjustment. The finding of "no greater improvement" for those selected for ECT was quite upsetting to the service chief who advocated ECT, and in turn to the hospital director who did not like to have his chief upset. No public attention was paid to the results, and no change in the frequency of ECT use was noted.

On another occasion, it was discovered by this author that alcoholic patients chosen for a special program had initially better outcomes, but that the differences between those assigned to the special alcohol and those assigned to regular ward programs were not apparent six months after release. The hospital administrator in this instance complained that such data made it difficult for him to request additional funds for the expensive-to-operate special program. Some staff on the regular wards urged that patients be assigned randomly to the special and regular ward programs to see if treatment results were comparable. This was resisted by the staff assigned to the special program, as well as those administratively responsible who had decided in advance that the special program would be better for alcoholic patients. The fact that patients were sent to the hospital specifically for the special program was cited as a primary reason patients could not be assigned randomly. That the more expensive program may not have been better for patients was not regarded as important enough to be explored.

This writer has reached the conclusion that concern about treatment effectiveness is not necessarily the primary goal in many psychiatric hospitals. The maintenance of traditional prerogatives and role status is at least as important as concern about treatment effectiveness, particularly when data from studies of treatment effectiveness challenge the assumptions of key staff in the institution. During another research study, one psychiatric ward team altered the role of their psychiatric aides in an attempt to increase treatment effectiveness. This team, who had been given feedback about their patients' posthospital adjustment, discovered that those patients who adjusted best following discharge had been those who had had most contact with staff. The team increased the likelihood of meaningful staff-patient interaction by developing a more active treatment role for their psychiatric aides. Subsequent to this role change, that program became unusually effective in that their patients functioned better upon returning to the community than patients from other programs (Ellsworth, 1973). As this program reached its peak in treatment effectiveness, however, a series of administrative actions took place that affected some of the key personnel in that program (Ellsworth and Ellsworth, 1970). Following these actions, the exit interviews with patients revealed that the aides played a less active role in treatment, and the improvement in the posthospital adjustment of that program's patients fell below that of patients from other programs.

Shortly following the administrative actions that disrupted that program's treatment effectiveness, this researcher was notified by the hospital director that his research was not relevant, and that his activities within the hospital were themselves disruptive. Regarding the relevance of the research, a subsequent independent investigation concluded: "In short, the problem seems to have been that the research was relevant, and that the director didn't like the results" (Rorer, 1970: 9-10). With respect to the researcher's disruptiveness, the reported concluded:

> His research was designed to challenge established procedures, by imposing deliberately designed changes on those procedures, and by its very nature, research of this kind is bound to be disruptive. The feedback of data showing wards to differ in their effectiveness, the increase in treatment responsibility and the results showing that aides and assistants can be as effective as, if not more effective than, the personnel in the "superior" professions, all must have created discontent and questioning, and must have seemed disruptive to those who found security in an established system. [ibid.: 10]

## Summary and Suggestions

One of the major problems in utilizing program evaluation results is that program research does require that decisions no longer remain the exclusive prerogative of either the professional or the program administrator. At first glance, it would seem that the quality of services to the public should be more important than the maintenance of the traditional prerogatives of any group. If mental health professionals do not become seriously concerned with the problems of comparing the treatment effectiveness of different approaches, then program decisions will continue to be made on the basis of administrative fiat and the traditional prerogatives of staff.

This is not to say that administrators and clinicians should accept and act on the results of any evaluation study. Poorly designed studies are unfortunately the rule rather than the exception, and one must carefully evaluate the design and results of evaluation studies. Organizations, however, do resist change. Evaluation, which implies change, is threatening and therefore resisted. And the researcher does not help matters any by conducting poorly designed studies, or studies that measure irrelevant variables.

The researcher must recognize that one of the traditional prerogatives of the professionally oriented person has been that he has had the unquestioned right to determine the best treatment for his client. The professional's fear that the administrator or researcher is "going to tell me what to do" accounts for much of the resistance to program evaluation. It has proven helpful to emphasize that feedback from research can be used by the professional to assist him in making better treatment decisions. And staff accept feedback best when it is emphasized that it is the program concept or treatment philosophy that is being evaluated, not personal dedication or staff efforts. But the challenge from research of the professional's unquestioned prerogative to determine the treatment for each client is real, and should be faced openly.

In the final analysis, the key to whether evaluation research is accepted and utilized by any agency depends largely on the attitude of the administrator. An excellent recommendation that would be extremely helpful to administrators has been proposed by Campbell (1969). He suggests that administrators stop advocating in advance that a particular approach will solve the problem, and focus instead on identifying the seriousness of the problem and the importance of finding adequate solutions. Within this framework, the administrator, agency head, or legislator would propose that different approaches to the problem be tried and evaluated, and that the most effective be adopted.

The acceptance of evaluation studies also depends on the skills of the researcher. He must be able to help the staff identify their treatment objectives, and to devise methods that measure them. He must reduce the personal threat to staff by stressing that it is the program or treatment concept that is being evaluated, not the personal competence of staff members themselves. And evaluation must be well designed and relevant. Although serious technical problems face the evaluation researcher, good assessment is within the design capability of a knowledgeable researcher. Some solutions to the technical problems of program evaluation are discussed in the following sections of this paper.

## PART TWO.  MEASURING PROGRAM EFFECTIVENESS

This paper is concerned primarily with measuring treatment effectiveness, or the benefit part of the cost-benefit concept. Differences in direct program costs vary widely and are extremely important in program evaluation; but good measures of program effectiveness are also needed. While treatment effectiveness will not always ensure program survival (as just seen in the preceding section), the most often stated purpose of mental health agencies is to provide effective services to clients.

The two groups most directly affected by the effectiveness of mental health services are patients and their significant others. Most evaluation studies include self-report data from patients, either from interviews or through psychological tests. Rarely are attempts made to obtain systematic reports from significant others in evaluating treatment outcome. This part of the paper explores an approach to program evaluation that focuses on the observations of those who are most familiar with client behavior, namely, significant others. This approach to program evaluation has an added advantage over most others; namely, it does not require great expenditures of funds or professional staff time.

### The Criterion Problem

Perhaps, the most important consideration in selecting from among different measures of program effectiveness is their comparative validity as indices of clients' adjustment. Although patients are in the best position to describe their feelings of felt distress, troublesome symptoms, and so on, their reports of change are not particularly reliable or valid (Paul, 1967). Amount of change scored from the ratings of significant others has demonstrable validity, as will be seen later in this section. An earlier finding was that ratings by significant others were better predictors of length of hospital stay and rehospitalization than patients' ratings (Ellsworth et al., 1968: 9). If one accepts Horst's (1966) conclusions that the best index of a measure's validity is its relationship to socially significant behavior, then relatives' ratings have a great deal of relevance.

Tradition compels us to regard patients' relatives as too biased to be used as objective raters, but others have found that data from this source was quite reliable and valid (Bentinck et al., 1969; Katz and Lyerly, 1963; Michaux et al., 1969). One recent study (Pasamanick et al., 1967) compared the treatment outcomes of schizophrenics assigned to one of three groups: regular hospital treatment, immediate return to the community on placebos with nurse visits, and return to the community on drugs with nurse visits. These researchers found that identical conclusions about the comparative treatment effects of the three approaches on the community adjustment of individual patients were arrived at from the ratings of psychiatrists, nurses, and relatives (ibid.: 118).

It should be emphasized again that ratings completed in the treatment setting are not good indices of patients' adjustment in other settings such as the community (Buss et al., 1962; Ellsworth et al., 1968; Katz et al., 1967; Sinnett et al., 1965; Wood et al., 1962). A patient rated as anxious prior to admission, for example, is not necessarily anxious on the admission ward. A somewhat angry patient at release may be rated as friendly or not friendly three weeks later in the community.

Some recently collected data at the Roseburg VA hospital (unpublished) again confirm the low relationship between ratings of hospital and community adjustment. At the time of a patient's release, ward staff ratings were obtained regarding (a) patient's cooperation and motivation, (b) prediction of patient's community adjustment three weeks after release, and (c) probability of his return within six months. Ratings from all staff were pooled. The scores for each of the three areas correlated .24, .25, and .28 ($p < .01$ for 121 patients) with relatives' ratings of community adjustment three weeks after the patients' release. Patients also rated their own cooperation and motivation, and their predictions of posthospital adjustment and probability of return. Their ratings correlated only .08, .19, and .12 with relative-rated posthospital adjustment, and were not statistically significant ($N = 94$). A moderate amount of agreement was found between staff and patients' ratings just prior to release, with correlations between .30 and .43. But neither staff nor patient ratings at exit showed much relationship to posthospital community adjustment.

Most hospital program research has focused on in-hospital changes, based on the assumption that people behave fairly consistently in different settings, an assumption increasingly challenged by research findings (Mischel, 1968). Since hospital-based ratings do not indicate that the patient who shows better adjustment or more improvement in the hospital will also be better adjusted or more improved in the community, ratings of patients' community adjustment are regarded as a better estimate of program effectiveness.

## Developing a Measure of Community Adjustment

Over the past seven years, three forms of a Personal Adjustment and Role Skill Scale have been developed for use by significant others. The first PARS Scale was used to evaluate the community adjustment of male hospitalized veterans with a diagnosis of schizophrenia. The second PARS Scale was an expanded version of the first and was used for measuring the treatment outcome of all psychiatric veterans including alcoholics. The third version was again expanded to include relevant behaviors for nonhospitalized community clinic clients. At this time, also, a female form of the PARS Scale was developed. It was discovered that items reflecting improvement were not necessarily the same for male as for female clients.

*PARS-I Scale.* The PARS-I Scale is a 39-item 4-point rating scale developed for use by the relatives of hospitalized veterans with a diagnosis of schizophrenia (Ellsworth et al., 1968). A factor analysis of these items revealed that some factors needed expansion.

The original scale, however, did demonstrate that the ratings of patients' community adjustment by significant others were quite reliable and reasonably valid, as compared with the ratings of professionally trained staff (Ellsworth et al., 1968: 15-23). Three reliability estimates were made, namely split-half, inter-rater, and test-retest. Reliability estimates for scores derived from relatives' ratings were found to be as high as those from staff ratings, generally in the .70 to .90 range. In terms of comparative validity, we examined how well adjustment scores from each data source predicted (1) length of hospital stay, (2) return to the hospital, and (3) the patients' ratings of their own adjustment. The validity coefficients (multiple R's) for both staff and relatives averaged around .40. We concluded, then, that ratings by patients' relatives were as reliable and valid as those of professional staff.

Also discovered from this research was that the ratings of both patients' relatives and follow-up staff reflected significant improvement in the community adjustment of hospitalized veterans. Comparing pre and post treatment ratings by significant others, patients improved significantly in such Personal Adjustment areas as Confusion and Agitation Depression, but not in the Role Skill areas of Employment and Social Involvement. These data indicated that relatives' ratings reflected improvement of hospital treated patients, but that treatment apparently improved patients' personal adjustment but not their instrumental performance, a finding reported by others (McPartland and Richart, 1966).

*PARS-II Scale.* The PARS-II Scale was expanded to 89 items, 39 of which came from the original scale. Some of the additional items were based on the work of Berger and associates (1964), Katz and Lyerly (1963), and Roen and Burnes (1966). The patient sample was composed of psychiatric admissions (veterans) who were not hospitalized more than two weeks elsewhere in the month prior to admission, and who named a significant other able to provide prehospital adjustment ratings. About 25% could not be rated because they had been hospitalized elsewhere recently, 16% had no known informants, and 14% named uncooperative or unknowledgeable informants. Thus, ratings were collected on 45% of all admissions. The average age of the veteran admission sample was 42 years. Forty-three percent were currently married, 28% were once married, and 19% were single. One-third were diagnosed psychotic, one-third nonpsychotic, and one-third alcoholic. One-half had completed high school. Thirty-three percent had not been hospitalized within the last five years, while 35% had been hospitalized within the last year.

All 89 items of the PARS-II were evaluated on test-retest reliability (one week interval) and ability to discriminate between pre and post hospital adjustment. The

79 items with the highest reliability and discriminant validity were factor analyzed using a principal components analysis with verimax rotation. Seven factors emerged on the second form of the PARS Scale (Ellsworth, 1968), four Personal Adjustment factors identified as Interpersonal Involvement, Confusion, Anxious Depression, Angry Agitated, an Alcohol Abuse factor, and two Role Skill factors identified as Outside Social Involvement and Employment.

*PARS-III Scale.* The PARS-III Scale was developed to work with Oregon's community clinics. The PARS-II Scale did not include items regarding adjustment behaviors felt by clinic staff to be significant in marriage and parent-child relationships, and it was not entirely appropriate for female clients. It was also important to determine whether or not the factor structure of PARS-II items would be similar to that of PARS-III items with a sample of outpatient clients rather than hospitalized veterans. Two forms were constructed, one for clinic males (118 items) and one for clinic females (120 items). About half of the items came from previous scales measuring the community adjustment of veterans, while the remainder were added by a committee of clinic staff. Each of the 118 (male) and 120 (female) items used in the PARS-III Scale was tested for ability to differentiate between pre and post treatment groups of clinic clients. The items that best differentiated between pre and post treatment groups (90 items for males and 82 items for females) were than factor analyzed using a principal components procedure with a verimax rotation. As will be seen shortly, the factor analysis of PARS-III items for the male clinic clients yielded the same seven adjustment dimensions as those found with hospitalized males, although somewhat different items and client populations were used.

All of the community clinic PARS-III sample was composed of currently married people since the ratings were collected from husband and wife pairs. The pre and post treatment male groups averaged 38 years of age, while female groups averaged 33½ and 34½, respectively. With regard to education, both male and female pre and post treatment groups were nearly identical, averaging between 11.7 years (posttreatment female group) to 12.3 years (posttreatment male group). Posttreatment males, however, received direct services somewhat less often than females, with 65% of the males and 86% of the females having been seen more than three times at the clinic. On family income, somewhat more of the posttreatment families earned over $10,000 per year (25% versus 16%), while more of the pretreatment group earned less than $7,000 (48% versus 38%). Since previous evidence suggests that treatment does not increase earnings (Ellsworth et al., 1968), the greater incidence of higher income in the posttreatment group may mean either that high income families more often remained in treatment for at least three sessions, or that low income families were less likely to provide follow-up information.

*Adjustment Dimensions for Males.* PARS-III ratings of 65 pretreatment and 64 posttreatment males were collected by 22 of Oregon's community clinics. These ratings by significant others (usually the wife) were factor analyzed, using a principal components analysis and verimax rotation.

Seven factors, very similar to those found on the Veterans PARS-II Scale, were readily interpretable. Four Personal Adjustment areas, an Alcohol/Drug Abuse factor, and two Role Skill dimensions were identified, differing somewhat in content from the Veterans' PARS-II factors because new items had been added. The PARS-III factors for males included: (A) *Interpersonal Involvement*—shows consideration for and interest in the significant others (rater), listens and talks about things including important matters and angry feelings. (B) *Confusion*—loses track of time, has forgotten important things, seems in a daze, sits and stares, needs supervision, has difficulty making decisions and going ahead and doing things. (C) *Anxiety*—has difficulty eating and sleeping, feels nervous, restless, tense, and guilty. (D) *Agitation-Depression*—says people don't care, are unfair and push him around; feels upset, complains, has damaged things; says something terrible will happen, that life isn't worth living, and that things look hopeless. (E) *Alcohol/Drug Abuse*—drinks or takes drugs to excess, becomes drunk or high, lets drinking or drugs interfere with family and job, and spends money unwisely. (F) *Employment*— is employed, earns adequately, looks forward to work and is satisfied with job and fellow workers. (G) *Outside Social*—attends and participates in activities and recrea- tion outside the home. One additional area of Parenthood Skills can be scored separately when children are in the home, although these items were found to be part of Factor A, Interpersonal Involvement.

*Adjustment Dimensions for Females.* Ratings were collected on 69 pretreatment and 63 posttreatment females, using the best 82 items on the female PARS Scale. The factor analysis yielded six clearly interpretable factors measuring three Personal Adjustment factors, an Alcohol/Drug Abuse area, and two Role Skill dimensions. The PARS-III factors for females were: (A) *Interpersonal Involvement*—shows affection toward, interest in, consideration of, and concern about significant others (rater), and communicates openly and clearly, including her angry feelings. (B) *Confusion*—forgets to do important things, has to be reminded of things, seems dazed and preoccupied, loses track of time, and needs supervision. (C) *Agitation*— acts upset, suspicious, restless and nervous; talks of being afraid, and says that things look hopeless. (D) *Alcohol/Drug Abuse*—includes drinking or taking drugs to excess, becomes drunk or high; and lets drinking or drugs interfere with family relationships. (E) *Household Management*—shops, prepares dinner, cleans, does the laundry, and other chores. (F) *Outside Social*—attends and participates in activities outside the home, and has visitors. Two optional areas of adjustment can be rated on the female form of the PARS Scale, Employment and Parenthood Skills. Employment emerges as a separate factor on the male form of the PARS, but could not be included in the factor analysis for females since less than half of the female sample was employed. For females normally expected to work, however, the Employment area is rated. Parenthood Skills can also be rated when there are children in the home, although it did not emerge as a separate factor.

### Reliability and Intercorrelations of Community Adjustment Dimensions

As seen in Table 9.1, the test-retest and internal consistency (alpha) of the PARS Scale dimensions were generally satisfactory. The reliability of the Outside Social scale for adult females, as rated by their husbands, was somewhat low.

The intercorrelations of pretreatment PARS-II scores are presented in Table 9.2.

TABLE 9.1   RELIABILITY OF PARS RATINGS BY SIGNIFICANT OTHERS

| | Personal Adjustment | | | | | Role Skills | |
|---|---|---|---|---|---|---|---|
| | Interpersonal Involvement | (non) Confusion | Anxiety | Agitation/ Depression | Alcohol/ Drug | Employment or Household Management | Outside Social |
| Test-retest, admission ratings, one week interval | | | | | | | |
| (a) 31 veterans, PARS II | .93 | .91 | .87 | .91 | .96 | .98 | .85 |
| (b) 27 veterans, PARS III | .80 | .87 | .90 | .87 | .92 | .95 | .82 |
| Internal consistency pretreatment ratings, 65 clinic males, PARS III | .93 | .87 | .79 | .89 | .86 | .89 | .79 |
| Internal consistency pretreatment ratings, 69 clinic females, PARS III | .89 | .80 | | .90 | .92 | .82 | .65 |

TABLE 9.2   INTERCORRELATIONS BETWEEN PARS FACTOR SCORES*

| | Personal Adjustment | | | | | Role Skills | |
|---|---|---|---|---|---|---|---|
| | Interpersonal Involvement | (non) Confused | (non) Anxious | (non) Agitated/ Depressed | Alcohol/ Drug | Employment | Outside Social |
| A. Interpersonal Involvement | | .56 | .40 | .48 | .13 | .14 | .51 |
| B. (non) Confused | .58 | | .35 | .44 | .15 | .12 | .31 |
| C. (non) Anxious | .34 | .42 | | .53 | .24 | -.11 | .37 |
| D. (non) Agitated-Depressed | .49 | .67 | .48 | | .34 | -.06 | .29 |
| E. Alcohol/Drugs | .44 | .43 | .38 | .52 | | -.05 | .13 |
| F. Employment | .16 | .24 | .28 | .43 | .22 | | .03 |
| G. Socially Active | .43 | .18 | .29 | .17 | .20 | .27 | |

* Intercorrelations above diagonals are for prehospital PARS II scores, 225 veterans. Intercorrelations below diagonals are for pretreatment PARS III scores, 65 clinic males. All adjustment areas were scored so that a high score reflected good adjustment.

As can be seen, the PARS-II scores for veterans were moderately interrelated with correlations between .35 and .56. (All adjustment areas were scored so that a high score reflected good adjustment.) Although not presented here, it should be noted that the intercorrelation of posttreatment scores for veterans were typically .10 to .20 points higher than those presented in Table 9.2, indicating less independence among adjustment areas following treatment. This suggests that posttreatment improvement (or lack of it) generalizes across adjustment areas.

For pretreatment clinic males, the PARS-III intercorrelations (below diagonal) were generally similar to those for veterans, with one major exception. The outpatient male who drinks to excess was typically less well adjusted in the four Personal Adjustment areas (r's .38 to .52) than one who does not. For hospitalized veterans, excessive drinking was only minimally related to the prehospital Personal Adjustment areas (r's .13 to .34).

The PARS-III intercorrelations for clinic females are not presented, in part because the PARS factors have not as yet been replicated. The intercorrelations presented in Table 9.2 showing moderate relationships among the Personal Adjustment factors were also found for females. With females, however, Household Management was moderately correlated (r's .42 to .48) with the three Personal Adjustment areas. Employment scores for males, as already noted, were only minimally related to Personal Adjustment.

### Discriminant Validity of Community Adjustment Dimensions

A scale that is most useful for measuring adjustment in clients receiving mental health services is one that best reflects the status of these clients, and is sensitive to the kinds of changes that occur in their behavioral adjustment before and after treatment. Goff and associates (1971) reported that the PARS Scale significantly differentiated clinic clients from nonclients. Adults who came for counseling were rated by a significant other, and contrasted with ratings of nonclient adults (parents of child guidance cases, etc.). Female clinic clients had significantly lower scores than their nonclient counterparts in the areas of Interpersonal Involvement and Household Management, and significantly higher scores in Agitation and Confusion. There were no significant group differences in Outside Social, Employment, and Parenthood Skills. In general, then, female clients were more poorly adjusted before treatment than nonclients, especially in the Personal Adjustment areas.

For males, the pretreatment behavior of clients also reflected a poorer adjustment than that of nonclients in all Personal Adjustment areas. Clients were significantly lower in Interpersonal Involvement and higher in Agitation-Depression, Confusion, and Anxiety. In the Role Skill areas, clients had significantly lower scores in Outside Social, but not in Employment or Parenthood Skills. Alcohol/Drug Abuse was also higher in clients than nonclients. As with females, then, the Personal Adjustment areas most clearly differentiated the behavior of male clients from that of nonclients.

McPartland and Richart (1966) have reported that mental health services often result in a significant reduction of distressing symptoms but less change in work and social activities. A scale purporting to measure adjustment that is relevant to clients receiving treatment, then, should reflect improvement in distressing symptoms but not necessarily in areas of instrumental performance. PARS III data were examined to see if Personal Adjustment scores changed more than Role Skills in clients rated before and following treatment, and whether or not hospitalized patients differed from clinic clients.

Pre and post treatment PARS III ratings from significant others were analyzed for both hospitalized and clinic male and female clients. Data were collected by community clinics in Oregon and Minnesota, and state hospitals in Oregon, Washington, and California. Clinic clients must have been seen at least three times to be included in the sample, and posttreatment ratings were requested from the same respondent 90 days after the time of the first treatment session. This 90-day interval was necessary in order to avoid the confusion as to when a case was "closed." Posttreatment ratings for hospitalized patients were obtained one month after their release.

*Adjustment Differences for Females.* Pre and post treatment ratings on females were obtained from the same respondent on 141 clinics and 133 hospitalized clients. About two-thirds of the clinic clients (98) and one-half of the hospitalized patients (69) had children in the home and were rated on Parenthood Skills. Between 25% (37) of female clinic clients, and 30% (41) of the hospitalized female patients had been employed and were rated on this area as well. The statistical significance of pre and post treatment differences was estimated using a t test for correlated means.

As can be seen in Table 9.3, the largest changes in pre and post treatment adjustment occurred in the Personal Adjustment areas for both clinic and hospital female patients. For both female samples, the changes in Confusion and Agitation were the most significant. In the Role Skill areas, the changes in Household Management and Outside Social were most significant, while Employment scores changed least.

The pretreatment adjustment of clinic females was also found to be better than that of hospitalized patients in many areas. In order of the significance of differ-

TABLE 9.3  PRETREATMENT AND POSTTREATMENT ADJUSTMENT MEANS FOR HOSPITALIZED AND CLINIC FEMALES

| | Clinic Females (N=141) | | | Hospitalized Females (N=133) | | |
|---|---|---|---|---|---|---|
| | Pre | Post | t value | Pre | Post | t value |
| Interpersonal Involvement | 33.14 | 35.57 | 4.87** | 31.01 | 36.36 | 6.45** |
| Confusion | 22.38 | 19.35 | 7.56** | 27.31 | 19.87 | 12.11** |
| Agitation | 28.77 | 24.45 | 7.95** | 31.44 | 22.62 | 12.61** |
| Alcohol/Drug | 4.32 | 4.03 | 2.20* | 4.61 | 3.67 | 5.50** |
| Household Management | 31.60 | 32.96 | 3.07** | 28.47 | 31.71 | 6.04** |
| Outside Social | 14.05 | 15.11 | 3.24** | 11.70 | 13.29 | 3.96** |
| Parenthood Skills | 21.19 | 22.23 | 1.85 | 20.80 | 22.90 | 3.95** |
| Employment | 19.16 | 19.51 | .54 | 17.22 | 18.44 | 1.06 |

* p < .05 for appropriate df.
**p < .01 for appropriate df.

ences, pretreatment clinic patients were better adjusted than their hospitalized counterparts in the areas of Confusion (t = 7.16), Outside Social (t = 4.60), Household Management (t = 3.68), Agitation (t = 3.29), and Interpersonal Involvement (t = 2.40). There were no significant differences in the pretreatment adjustment of clinic and hospitalized females in the areas of Alcohol/Drug Abuse, Employment, or Parenthood Skills.

Differences in the posttreatment adjustment of clinic and hospital females were negligible. Except for the areas of Outside Social (t = 3.40) and Agitation (t = 2.18), the posttreatment adjustment of hospital-treated patients was as good as that of clinic-treated females. While females admitted to hospitals were initially sicker than clinic females, they generally showed more change in adjustment and were, therefore, about as well adjusted following release as females treated in community clinics.

*Adjustment Differences for Males.* The same clinics and state hospitals also obtained pre and post treatment ratings on male clients from the same respondent. Initial and follow-up ratings were obtained on 92 clinic males and 81 hospitalized patients. Two-thirds of clinic males (60) and almost half (35) of the hospital patients were rated on Parenthood Skills.

As with females, the largest posttreatment differences for males occurred in the Personal Adjustment areas. As seen in Table 9.4, the areas of Confusion, Anxiety, and Agitation-Depression showed significant posttreatment improvement for both clinic and hospitalized males. Interpersonal Involvement did not change significantly, an unexpected finding. Improvement in the Role Skill areas did not occur with the exception of a significant decrease in Alcohol/Drug Abuse by hospitalized patients.

The male clinic clients were also better adjusted than their hospitalized counterparts in the pretreatment areas of Anxiety (t = 6.63), Agitation-Depression (t = 5.35), Employment (t = 5.56), Confusion (t = 3.11), Alcohol/Drug Abuse (t = 2.65), and Outside Social (t = 2.43). Following treatment, however, those who had been hospitalized were more poorly adjusted only in the areas of Employment

TABLE 9.4   PRETREATMENT AND POSTTREATMENT ADJUSTMENT MEANS FOR CLINIC AND HOSPITALIZED MALES

|  | Clinic Males (N=92) | | | Hospitalized Males (N=81) | | |
|---|---|---|---|---|---|---|
|  | Pre | Post | t value | Pre | Post | t value |
| 1. Interpersonal Involvement | 32.67 | 33.68 | 1.45 | 33.87 | 35.17 | 1.65 |
| 2. Confusion | 24.65 | 22.94 | 3.10** | 27.65 | 23.57 | 5.26** |
| 3. Anxiety | 13.10 | 11.04 | 4.88** | 16.82 | 12.55 | 8.37** |
| 4. Agitation/Depression | 22.00 | 19.24 | 3.57** | 28.02 | 19.99 | 9.57** |
| 5. Alcohol/Drug | 10.96 | 10.51 | 1.16 | 13.24 | 10.52 | 4.60** |
| 6. Employment | 21.94 | 22.47 | .78 | 15.31 | 15.94 | .66 |
| 7. Outside Social | 9.42 | 9.80 | 1.09 | 8.00 | 8.93 | 1.89 |
| 8. Parenthood Skills | 19.52 | 20.20 | 1.30 | 19.26 | 20.95 | 1.68 |

**p < .01 for appropriate df.

($t = 5.48$) and Anxiety ($t = 2.65$). In the other areas of adjustment, however, the posttreatment adjustment of hospital patients was as good as that of clinic clients. Thus, patients who were hospitalized were rated by their significant others as more poorly adjusted initially than clinic males. Both groups improved significantly in most Personal Adjustment areas, with hospitalized patients showing somewhat more improvement. Following treatment, hospitalized patients were as well adjusted as their clinic counterparts except in the areas of Employment and Anxiety.

## Summary and Conclusions

Probably the most useful measure of treatment impact is the client's adjustment in the community. Since patient behavior in the treatment setting was found to be largely unrelated to his adjustment in other settings, staff ratings of symptoms or behavior are not a particularly relevant measure of treatment outcome.

With scales specially constructed for use by significant others, factor analyses revealed that the adjustment dimensions for male clinic clients and hospitalized patients were similar. The adjustment dimensions for adult outpatient females were also quite similar to those for males.

Ratings by significant others were found to be reliable and valid estimates of community adjustment for both clinic clients and hospitalized patients. The traditional assumption that relatives are too biased or untrained to provide valid data is not supported by our findings. The ratings of significant others were also consistent with two expectations: (1) that clients in treatment would show more change in Personal Adjustment than in Role Skill areas, and (2) that clinic clients would be better adjusted than hospitalized psychiatric patients. The latter expectation was confirmed in the pretreatment adjustment differences of clients and patients, but the posttreatment adjustment of patients released from hospitals was generally as good as that of clients who had been treated by clinics.

Revised scales[1] have been constructed for both males and females, based on both clinic and hospital populations. The revised scales are shorter, consisting of 34 items for females and 37 items for males. Items measuring Household Management have been added in male form. Items for the revised PARS Scales were selected using the criteria of: (1) highest factor loadings, (2) best retest and alpha reliability, (3) highest F ratio differentiating among clinic, hospital, and nonclient persons, and (4) t values differentiating the pre and post treatment adjustment of hospital and clinic samples. The revised scales also permit an individualized scoring for each person. The initial rater is asked to indicate those areas that are most and least relevant to that person's adjustment. Pre-post score changes in those areas judged most relevant are given extra weight in computing overall adjustment changes.

PARS Scale data, then, can be used to assess treatment outcome, and to compare the effectiveness of one program with that of another. This approach has the distinct advantage of being far less costly than direct interview approaches. It also assesses treatment outcome from the viewpoint of significant others, a group directly affected by mental health services but rarely used to help evaluate them. This is not to say that data from patients and staff are unimportant, for complete program assessment requires their use also. But data from relatives has been largely ignored, and should be used to assess program effectiveness. Certain technical problems arise in the use of data from significant others, however, and are examined in the next section.

## PART THREE. TECHNICAL PROBLEMS IN PROGRAM EVALUATION

One primary reason so little program evaluation has been done is that the traditionally trained researcher has been taught methods that are largely inappropriate in the clinical setting. In the traditional experimental study, the researcher seeks control over the treatment condition (independent variable) and applies a variety of design and methodological strategies aimed at holding all other variables constant (Evenson, 1970). In experimental studies, one usually assigns subjects to treatment groups in random fashion, and complete data on all subjects are standard. With this kind of controlled study, the researcher can be relatively confident that differences in the subsequent behavior of the experimental group are a function of their exposure to the treatment variable. In reality, however, one is rarely able to find traditionally designed experimental studies that have been successfully completed in the mental health field (Schulbert et al., 1969: 13).

One modification of the traditional experimental design used in mental health research is that used in many drug studies. The researcher assigns subjects to experimental (drug) and control groups, but has no control over the hundreds of events that affect the behavior of the patients during the course of the drug study. In these studies, it is assumed that the uncontrolled events will affect each group equally. If control and experimental patients are treated in the same ward by the same staff, who do not know which patients are receiving the experimental drug, this assumption is probably correct. Under these circumstances, the differences in the behavior of the experimental and control groups are probably a function of the drug effects.

When the researcher is faced with comparing the effects of Program A in one setting with those of Program B in another setting, additional problems develop. A major problem is that if the researcher finds that patients in Program A have better treatment outcomes than those of Program B, he is never certain just what in Program A produced the results. Also, unless he has been able to assign patients randomly, he is not even certain that the outcome of Program A was due to program effects rather than to differences in patients treated by Programs A and B.

In many program evaluation studies, one is not only unable to control all the relevant treatment variables and to assign patients in random fashion, but one faces such problems as data loss. This is especially troublesome when follow-up data are collected after the patient has left the treatment setting. In order to avoid this, most program evaluators collect data while the patient remains in the treatment setting. But as already seen, these data are not adequate if one wishes to know something about the program's effect on the patient's behavior in other settings. Faced with these kinds of problems, program evaluation is more like that of introducing a sophisticated information system rather than implementing an experimental study. And program evaluation becomes increasingly scientific as one designs his study so as to minimize the possibility that outcome differences are a function of such uncontrolled factors as population differences, differential data loss, and the like.

Although experimental designs are preferred, good approaches to program evaluation have been worked out when true experiments are not possible. Campbell (1969) has listed the common sources that can produce differences between groups when in fact no real differences occurred, or conversely, can obscure true differences. There are nine threats to internal validity (ibid.: 411), including selection (differential recruitment of comparison groups), regression artifacts (pseudo shifts occurring when repeated measures are taken on an initially extreme group), and the differential loss of respondents from comparison groups. In reaching conclusions about the results of his study, the researcher must consider carefully rival hypotheses such as these in interpreting his results. Having done so, it then is not sufficient for the experimental perfectionist to simply point out other possible alternatives; rather he should also demonstrate their plausibility.

This section of the paper considers the threats most likely to affect internal validity when using the ratings of significant others in reaching conclusions about program effectiveness. By taking these problems into account, it is possible to reach valid conclusions about the comparative effectiveness of different programs. The final part of this section will present a proposed strategy for such evaluation.

### Threats to the Validity of Outcome Results

*Regression Effects.* Regression effects, according to Campbell (1969: 414) are probably the most recurrent form of self-deception in the experimental social reform literature. Regression effects are most likely to occur when persons are selected or programs implemented on the basis of extreme scores. A highway safety program, for example, tends to be implemented when traffic fatalities are extremely high. From regression effects alone, one would predict that the next measurement of highway fatalities would show a drop toward the mean. When a drop toward the mean is observed, however, it has been the practice to attribute the change to program effects.

Patients in crises who seek mental health services often deviate markedly from the mean in their initial adjustment scores. Even if no improvement occurs, the next rating of their adjustment most often will reflect change toward the mean. This is especially true in self-rated discomfort where patients rate themselves as significantly improved following their acceptance for treatment. Often, no further improvement is shown over the course of treatment (Strupp and Bloxom, 1973). Another problem with regression effects is that they are most likely the greatest when the instrument is least reliable because chance fluctuations in scores are larger under these circumstances (Lord, 1962). Thus, the reliability of scales used to evaluate treatment effects becomes an extremely important consideration.

The amount of score change attributable to regression effects can be estimated for the PARS Scale, using repeated ratings by the same raters within the first week of hospitalization. Although it is important to estimate the amount of this score change attributable to regression effects, it should be remembered that if comparison groups are similar on initial adjustment ratings, the relative effects of Programs A and B can be estimated from posttreatment ratings. To estimate the amount of score change due to regression effects, the relatives of 27 hospitalized veterans rated the patient a second time within a week of his admission. This interval was short enough so that they could remember the patient's preadmission behavior, but not long enough for him to return to the community. All scores were standardized to facilitate comparisons, using a mean of 50 and a standard deviation of 10. Also, the standard scores in the negative areas (confusion, etc.) were reversed so that a high score always indicated good adjustment. Equal numbers of pre and post treatment scores were used in order to provide an adequate sample of rated adjustment.

The first rating by significant others had a standard score average for the four Personal Adjustment areas of 47.48. The second rating, one week later, averaged 48.58, a gain of 1.10 standard score points. Thus, for patients whose adjustment deviated sufficiently to warrant psychiatric hospitalization, there was some regression toward the mean in the second rating. The amount of pre-post treatment change typically found for hospitalized veterans averaged 5.50, from 47.25 to 52.75. Of this 5.50 average score change, then, 1.10 points (20%) could be attributed to regression effects.

Two interesting things occurred in this regression effect data. First, the second scores did not necessarily indicate better adjustment in all areas. For the positively scored area of Interpersonal Involvement, the second scores were lower than the first. This indicated a poor adjustment, and the standard scores dropped. In the negative areas, such as Confusion, the second scores were also lower. This indicated improvement, and the standard scores increased. In other words, all raw scores dropped on the second rating as one would expect from the regression effect. But the drop in raw scores in Interpersonal Involvement suggested poorer adjustment (and standard scores dropped) while the raw score drop in Confusion suggested improvement (and standard scores rose). This suggests that one can minimize the regression effect by having a balance of positively worded behavior items, where a high score indicates good adjustment, and negatively worded items, where a high score indicates poor adjustment.

The second interesting thing in regression effect data was that those patients who had the most extreme scores initially, showed the biggest drop in raw scores one week later. This would also be an expected regression effect. It illustrates, however, that if one compares the treatment outcomes of a more extreme group with that of a more average group, the more extreme group will show more raw score change. Whether or not this score change suggests good or poor adjustment depends, of course, on the content of the items and whether a high score indicates good or poor adjustment. But it does confirm the pseudo shifts that were pointed out by Campbell (1969: 411) that occur more often in the scores of extreme groups.

*Data Loss.* Data loss is also one of the serious threats to the validity of one's conclusions regarding program effectiveness. Data loss is a serious problem when significant others are asked to provide ratings of patients' pre and post treatment community behavior. Loss of data collected in the treatment setting is minimal, but staff ratings and patient self-reports have little relationship to community behavior, as already discussed. The cost of sending observers into the field, on the other hand, is usually prohibitive. Researchers using ratings from significant others must be prepared to deal with the data loss problem.

During four years of evaluating three psychiatric programs in a Veterans Administration hospital, data loss was a major concern in reaching valid conclusions regarding program effectiveness. During this time, 2,698 patients were admitted to this hospital. Of these, 1,102 (41%) were ineligible for evaluation by the PARS Scale. Of these ineligibles, 665 had been hospitalized over two weeks elsewhere prior to their transfer to our hospital. These patients could not have been rated on their community adjustment preceding admission because they had not been in the community. Another 437 were drifters with no known informants.

With 59% (1,596/2,698) of the admission sample eligible for PARS evaluation, a common and legitimate criticism from clinical staff was: "How can you evaluate the effectiveness of our program when you have data on only some of the patients treated? Perhaps those on whom you don't have data did better." It must be acknowledged that data loss does not permit one to conclude that he has a representative sample of the population. But this is more a problem of external validity (Campbell, 1969: 411); namely, the problem of to what extent one can generalize from his data. Obviously, one cannot say with confidence that Program A had the same effect on all patients admitted to it when change scores were computed on only a portion of the patients treated in Program A. But gathering data on certain patient groups would not invalidate drawing conclusions about those patient groups on whom data were gathered, and generalizing to similar patient groups. Also, data gathered on similar groups of patients in different programs would allow one to draw valid conclusions about the comparative effectiveness of different programs.

The kind of data loss that may invalidate the conclusions that one draws from treatment outcome data is that which occurs during and after treatment. Even failure to obtain initial data on 386 (24%) of the eligible patients should not reflect the quality of treatment outcome simply because the treatment effects have not yet occurred. The failure of the patient to stay at least two weeks (Table 9.5, 2A), on the other hand, might suggest poor response to and dissatisfaction with treatment. Also, if relatives refused to provide follow-up ratings on 20% of Program A patients, but only 5% of Program B patients, then one would seriously have to consider that Program A was less effective than Program B. Data loss that occurs during or after treatment at a different rate for one program than another may invalidate the conclusions one can draw from his data regarding the comparative effectiveness of programs.

Our experience with differential rates of data loss during treatment indicates that this type of data loss usually supports rather than negates the conclusions one draws from the outcome averages of different programs. In one program that became most effective, as measured by outcome scores, the amount of data loss from patients' leaving early (within two weeks after admission) was less than those leaving early from programs with lower outcome scores. No attempt was made to obtain outcome ratings on patients who left early because it seemed unlikely that much of a treatment effect could have occurred. But in the most effective program,

TABLE 9.5   DATA LOSS IN INFORMATION SYSTEM USING PARS RATINGS
BY SIGNIFICANT OTHERS

| | Data loss of total sample | | Data loss possibly reflecting response to treatment | |
|---|---|---|---|---|
| | Number | Percent | Number | Percent |
| 1. 1967-68 Project cohort | 1,596 | | | |
| A. Usable questionnaire not returned | 386 | 24% | | |
| B. Initial ratings obtained | 1,210 | 76% | | |
| 2. Program evaluation cohort | 1,210 | | 1,210 | |
| A. Left before 2 weeks | | | 109 | 9% |
| B. Enters special inpatient program (alcohol, industrial, geriatric, etc.) | | | 123 | 10% |
| C. Enters special outpatient program (Foster home, domiciliary) | | | 63 | 5% |
| D. No rater response to follow-up request | | | 107 | 9% |
| E. Initial rater has not seen patient since release | | | 173 | 14% |
| 3. (Follow-up completed) | | | (635) | (52%) |

Note: Complete pre- and post-hospital data on 40% (635/1,596) of the initially eligible cohort, and 52% (635/1,210) of cohort used for program evaluation.

only 6% left early while 12% left early from the less effective program. Subsequently, the first program became less effective, and the rate of patients' leaving early rose to 18% (Ellsworth, 1973).

Data loss from follow-up may also reflect poor outcomes for those patients whose raters provided initial but not posttreatment ratings. Kish and Hermann (1971) found that with alcoholic patients, 60% of those who did not respond to a follow-up questionnaire were doing poorly. But uncooperativeness on the part of the relative also may reflect the fact that the patient is functioning normally and that the relative does not want to be bothered (Pasamanick et al., 1967: 44). In our own research (Ellsworth, 1973), there was no difference in the rate of follow-up data loss as programs became more or less effective, as measured by outcome scores. If one has a differential loss of follow-up data from one program, he must consider seriously that the program may be less effective. If data loss after treatment is similar for different programs, then one can usually feel confident that outcome ratings reflect the comparative effectiveness of different programs.

Data loss could be cut drastically by obtaining only posttreatment ratings of judged improvement from respondents. As will be seen, this decreases the efficiency with which one can test for the statistical significance of program differences. But where data loss is a serious problem, this alternative should be considered.

*Differential Recruitment.* Differential recruitment of subjects for comparison groups also threatens the validity of one's conclusions about treatment outcome. It is best to assign subjects randomly. Lacking this, it is important that one gather careful data on the characteristics of his populations to see if they are similar. It is also helpful if one goes a step further and determines which of the population characteristics are related to treatment outcome. In our previous work cited above, we discovered that education was somewhat related to outcome scores. It became especially important to determine whether or not our comparison groups differed on education. Even random assignment does not always ensure populations with similar background characteristics, and it is well to evaluate the similarity of comparison groups, especially on those characteristics related to treatment outcome.

Other threats to internal validity are not as serious a problem with PARS data as those already discussed. In designing evaluation studies, however, one should consider Campbell's (1969) list of common threats to validity, and the possible alternative rival explanations that may account for the results obtained.

## Problems in Measuring Change

The amount of pre-post treatment score change, and the posttreatment outcome score itself, are both highly related to initial adjustment scores, but in opposite directions. Patients who are initially poorly adjusted (extreme scores) typically show more score change than those who were initially better adjusted (Luborsky, 1962; Zlotowski and Cohen, 1965). But the poorly adjusted pretreatment patient also is likely to remain more poorly adjusted following treatment than his initially better adjusted counterpart. If uncorrected change scores are used to measure the effects of different treatments, then the observed change scores could result in a built-in bias if one treatment approach was assigned to an initially poorly adjusted group (who would show more pre-post gain). If uncorrected outcome scores are used, on the other hand, they would be biased in favor of an initially better adjusted group who would also be better adjusted following treatment.

Methods for calculating posttreatment scores have been suggested by several investigators (Cronbach and Furby, 1970; DuBois, 1957; Lord, 1962). The most frequently used approach is to remove that portion of the change or outcome score that is a function of the initial level of adjustment. These corrected or residual change scores are "base free" in that they are not correlated with initial adjustment differences. As such, residual scores[2] are more likely to reflect treatment effects rather than initial score differences among patients. Residual scores are helpful not only when groups receiving different treatments had different levels of initial adjustment, but also in studies attempting to identify variables associated with improvement. The use of base-free residual scores ensures that variables correlated with the amount of improvement are not found simply because they were also correlated with initial adjustment differences. One final advantage is that residual scores should minimize the differences in rating style among raters. As long as the same rater is used for pre and post treatment ratings, residual scores should not be affected by consistent rater bias, as discussed elsewhere (Ellsworth et al., 1968).

As seen in Table 9.6, residual scores are indeed "base free" in that they are uncorrelated with initial adjustment (row A-3, Table 9.6). Uncorrected outcome scores (row A-1) and gain scores (row A-2) are significantly correlated with initial adjustment. Patients who are better adjusted initially tend also to have higher outcome scores (r's .49 to .55) than those more poorly adjusted (row A-1). But patients who were initially better adjusted also show less gain (row A-2) than those

TABLE 9.6  SOME CHARACTERISTICS OF VARIOUS ADJUSTMENT SCORE MEASURES*
(PARS II, N=419 MALE VETERANS)

| | Personal Adjustment | | | | | Role Skills | |
| | Interpersonal Involvement | Confusion | Anxiety | Angry/Agitated | Alcohol/Drugs | Employment | Outside Social |
|---|---|---|---|---|---|---|---|
| A. Correlations between prehospital adjustment and | | | | | | | |
| 1. Uncorrected outcome scores | .50 | .44 | .40 | .49 | .51 | .55 | .55 |
| 2. Uncorrected gain scores | -.53 | -.48 | -.53 | -.49 | -.74 | -.49 | -.44 |
| 3. Residual change scores | .00 | .00 | .00 | .00 | .00 | .00 | .00 |
| B. Correlations between residual change outcome scores and | | | | | | | |
| 1. Uncorrected outcome scores | .87 | .90 | .92 | .87 | .86 | .84 | .84 |
| 2. Uncorrected gain outcome scores | .85 | .83 | .85 | .87 | .67 | .87 | .90 |

* Scored so that a high score indicated good adjustment.

who were initially worse (r's -.44 to -.74). Thus, initial adjustment is related to both outcome and gain scores. This illustrates the earlier discussion that different conclusions about treatment effectiveness can be reached from uncorrected gain and outcome scores. If treatment A and treatment B are equally effective, but initially poorer adjusted patients are assigned to treatment A, gain scores will favor treatment A. If outcome scores are used, they will favor treatment B. Residual scores, however, are not related to pretreatment score differences. In comparing the effects of treatments A and B, residual scores would reflect treatment differences rather than group differences in initial adjustment scores.

Besides being uncorrelated with initial adjustment scores, residual scores have the added advantage of being highly correlated with both outcome scores and gain scores. As seen on the bottom part of Table 9.6, residual scores correlated between .84 and .92 with uncorrected outcome scores, and between .67 and .90 with uncorrected gain scores. As such, residual scores are measures of both posttreatment functioning as well as improvement.

Once again it is important to emphasize that residual scores were computed only when the same rater evaluated both pre and post treatment adjustment. When different raters were used, the correlation between pre and post treatment scores dropped to around .20 (except for Employment, which remained high). Thus, the residual scores developed for "same" raters cannot be applied to "different" raters. The pre-post correlations were so low in the latter group that residual scores would not have controlled for much of the effects of initial score differences.

Another important consideration in using residual scores is to make certain that the correlations between pre and post treatment scores for group A are similar to those of group B. If they are not, then one should probably use outcome scores only and some type of block design approach to the analysis.

Despite the apparant advantages of residual scores for measuring improvement, Cronbach and Furby (1970) do not recommend their use in most instances. They recommend that random assignment to treatment groups be adhered to, and analysis of covariance be used if initial differences among groups occur. They point out that when groups are not randomly assigned, other uncontrolled variables may affect outcome scores. For example, patients with chronic disorders may be hospitalized while those having more recent difficulty may be referred to a mental health center. Controlling only for the effects of initial adjustment differences on outcome would not be sufficient, for there may also be a differential reaction of chronic-patients-to-hospitals versus acute-patients-to-clinics.

Another disadvantage of residual change scores is that they are somewhat more susceptible to errors of measurement since they are computed from two sources (pre and post), each of which has some measurement error (Lord, 1962: 32). This problem becomes increasingly serious as the reliability of the instrument decreases.

## Comparative Validity and Utility of Different Scoring Methods

The decision to use or not use residual change scores should not be made on theoretical grounds alone. Comparisons of the utility and validity of change scores, outcome scores, and residual scores should also be made.

For a sample of 419 hospitalized veterans, various adjustment scores were computed from PARS Scale community adjustment ratings. The adjustment scores considered were: (1) initial pretreatment ratings, (2) uncorrected outcome scores, (3) uncorrected gain scores, and (4) residual scores. In addition, Cronbach and Furby (1970) suggest that residual scores be corrected for both pretreatment and demographic variables. With the sample of 419 veterans, for example, respondents' ratings of patients' "recency of adequate functioning" and "suddenness of onset" correlated around .20 with the residual scores corrected only for initial adjustment. Although this is substantially lower than the correlations between initial and outcome adjustment ratings, the residual scores are not "base-free" from time-one background characteristics and should be corrected for their effects as well.

A second set of residual scores (b) was computed by correcting for the effects of both initial adjustment and background. As already seen in Table 9.6, the correlations between initial adjustment and outcome averaged around .50. Adding background data to initial scores resulted in multiple R's averaging around .53, accounting for an increase of only about three percent of the outcome score variance. Once the influence of initial adjustment on outcome had been accounted for, the added effect of other variables was small. Nevertheless, the validity of residual (b) scores is evaluated as well.

In choosing between the different methods of scoring outcome, the validity of initial scores, three-week gain scores, three-week uncorrected outcome scores, and three-week residual scores (a) and (b) was estimated. Used to estimate the predictive validity of these different scores was the respondent's judgment of overall improvement at six months after release, and rehospitalization within that time. In judging improvement, significant others were asked to evaluate the veteran's overall improvement using a 6-point scale ranging from "much worse now than he was" to "very much better." The validity of these scores was also estimated from their predictive relationship to rehospitalization within six months after release. At the time of the three-week postrelease rating, the significant other may know whether or not the veteran is likely to be returning to the hospital. While this may contaminate the relationship between three-week posthospital ratings and rehospitalization to some extent, rehospitalization serves as a useful index in estimating posthospital adjustment.

As seen in Table 9.7, initial adjustment ratings are not a particularly valid predictor of adjustment within the six months following treatment, as one might expect. Gain scores correlated somewhat higher with judged improvement and community stay. The most valid measures of posttreatment adjustment, however, were outcome and residual scores. Residual (b) scores corrected for both initial adjustment and demographic differences appear slightly less predictive than residual scores corrected only for initial adjustment. Since residual (a) scores are much simpler to evaluate than residual (b) scores (which require a multiple regression program), residual (a) scores are recommended.

Another finding evident in Table 9.7 is that the Personal Adjustment scores at three weeks are more predictive of posttreatment adjustment than are the Alcohol/ Drug or Role Skill scores. The judged improvement and rehospitalization are more

TABLE 9.7 COMPARATIVE VALIDITY OF DIFFERENT PARS II ADJUSTMENT SCORE MEASURES

| | | Personal Adjustment | | | | | Role Skills | |
| --- | --- | --- | --- | --- | --- | --- | --- | --- |
| Correlations with | | Interpersonal Involvement | (non) Confusion | (non) Anxiety | (non) Angry Agitated | Alcohol/ Drug Abuse | Employment | Outside Social |
| 1. Relative's judgment | Initial | .11 | .20* | .11 | .16 | .12 | .07 | .09 |
| of improvement at | Gain | .21* | .20* | .22* | .18 | .03 | .00 | .12 |
| 6 months (N=285) | Outcome | .34* | .39* | .38* | .35* | .22* | .07 | .21* |
| | Residual (a) | .33* | .34* | .36* | .31* | .19 | .04 | .19 |
| | Residual (b) | .28* | .28* | .29* | .24* | .12 | -.01 | .13 |
| 2. Stay in community | Initial | -.01 | .04 | .10 | .10 | .10 | .00 | .01 |
| (N=134 rehospital- | Gain | .22* | .14 | .19* | .18 | .01 | .06 | .10 |
| ized and 285 non- | Outcome | .21* | .18 | .30* | .28* | .15 | .06 | .10 |
| rehospitalized | Residual (a) | .25* | .18 | .29* | .26* | .12 | .07 | .11 |
| veterans) | Residual (b) | .25* | .18 | .28* | .24* | .10 | .06 | .11 |

* Low but definite relationship, r .20 – .39

highly correlated with the Personal Adjustment scores of Interpersonal Involvement, Confusion, Anxiety, and Anger than with the Role Skill scores of Employment, Outside Social Involvement, or Alcohol/Drug Use. As already seen in Tables
9.3 and 9.4, the Personal Adjustment areas are also significantly and positively
affected by both hospital and clinic treatment, while the Role Skill areas are less
affected. The Personal Adjustment factors, then, are more clearly measures of
"adjustment" while the Role Skills can perhaps be regarded as behaviors related to
life-style.

In testing for differences in program treatment effectiveness, residual scores have
certain advantages over unadjusted outcome scores. Since initial ratings correlate
between .40 and .55 with outcome ratings (Table 9.4), a significant amount of the
variance in outcome ratings is accounted for by individual differences in pretreatment adjustment. When testing for the effects of different programs on posttreatment adjustment, one is primarily interested in the variance accounted for by
program differences. If the variance in outcome scores attributable to initial
adjustment can be controlled, then a more efficient test of program effects is
possible. In this respect, then, residual scores that are unrelated to initial adjustment differences should be superior to uncorrected outcome scores in statistical
tests of program effects.

The following study illustrates the advantage of testing for program effects with
residual rather than uncorrected outcome scores (Ellsworth, 1973). Male psychiatric veterans were assigned randomly to one of three treatment teams in a
psychiatric hospital. During part of the experiment, one psychiatric team received
feedback regarding the posthospital adjustment of their patients. The other two
teams received no follow-up ratings. From preliminary data, the feedback team
discovered that patients who had contacts with several staff had a better posthospital adjustment than patients who had contacts with only a few staff. This
team expanded the number of potentially therapeutic staff by giving primary
responsibility for group work to psychiatric aides and actively involving them in
decision making. During an eight-month period, the frequency with which the
patient named (on exit interview) the aide as most helpful to him increased
significantly over the other wards, indicating that the aide was playing a more
significant treatment role.

The treatment outcome for the feedback and nonfeedback wards was evaluated
from respondent's ratings of community adjustment. The significance of differences
in program effects was tested using both residual and uncorrected outcome scores.
There were no significant differences between programs on the posthospital adjustment of patients in the Role Skills areas of Employment and Outside Social
activities, or Alcohol/Drug use. Residual score differences, however, indicated that
the feedback ward patients were significantly better adjusted in the Personal
Adjustment areas than their non-feedback ward counterparts. The difference
reached .the .01 level of significance for the areas of Confusion ($t = 2.81$, $p < .01$
for 166 df) and Agitation-Depression ($t = 2.71$); and the .05 level for Interpersonal
Involvement ($t = 2.40$) and Anxiety ($t = 2.17$). Using uncorrected outcome scores,
none of the differences were significant at the .01 level. Differences in favor of the
feedback ward reached significance at the .05 level for three areas, namely,

Interpersonal Involvement ($t = 2.19$), Confusion ($t = 2.22$), and Agitation-Depression ($t = 2.23$).

As can be seen from the example above, using residual scores to compute the significance of differences between treatment groups resulted in a gain in efficiency when testing for the statistical significance of differences between groups. When the four Personal Adjustment areas were combined into a total score, the t value for program uncorrected outcome score differences rose from 2.36 ($p < .05$) to 2.92 ($p < .01$) when residual scores were used, a gain of 24%. As noted earlier, increased efficiency occurs when one removes from the outcome score variance that proportion of variance attributable to initial differences.

Norms for residual scores have been established across a wide variety of treatment settings so that the clinician can determine for his clients whether or not they changed more or less than clients elsewhere with similar pretreatment ratings. Analysis of covariance would also control for the effect of initial ratings on outcome when testing for the statistical significance of treatment group outcomes. But analysis of covariance would be less useful to the clinician than residual scores in determining for a particular client whether or not he improved as much as similar clients treated previously.

### Nonspecific Effects

In treatment program evaluation, it must be recognized that change in patients also occurs for reasons other than the specific effects of the treatment approach itself. People at a time of crisis often make changes on their own without professional help. In his review of research in psychotherapy, Bergin (1966) reports that control patients, who sometimes get help from such sources as friends and clergymen, improve about as much as patients seen in formal therapy. This finding of similar outcome for therapy and control subjects has recently been supported by Schorer, Lowinger, Sullivan, and Hartlaub (1968). In this study, 41 outpatients were placed on a waiting list but obtained treatment elsewhere, while 55 remained untreated by professionally trained therapists. While 78% of the treated group were rated as improved, almost as many (65%) of the untreated group were seen as improved. Among those rated as improved, the amount of symptom relief was somewhat greater in the improved control group than in the improved therapy group.

Much of the improvement seen in any helping relationship is the clients' response to nonspecific or placebo effects. The placebo effect, first identified in drug studies, accounts for between 26 and 50% of the therapeutic response (Lowinger and Dobie, 1969). In psychotherapy, the nonspecific factors affecting outcome include the patient's belief in the efficacy of treatment and the skill of the therapist, and his own expectations for improvement. That these nonspecific or placebo factors account for much of the response to psychotherapy has been well documented (Goldstein, 1962), and need not be considered in detail here.

Another study by Mendel (1966) illustrated the importance of patient expectation in treatment outcome. Patients assigned randomly of 7-day, 30-day, and 90-day treatment wards had similar outcomes in terms of release and posthospital adjustment. When patients on the 7-day ward were held for 10 days, however, they expressed disappointment because this meant they had not improved sufficiently to warrant release. When patients were discharged earlier than 30 or 90 days, they too expressed disappointment for not receiving all the treatment they believed was coming to them (Mendel, 1965).

Therapy outcome, then, is a function of both treatment specific and treatment nonspecific factors. In general, it would appear that such specific effects as the type of treatment account for less of the client's improvement than such nonspecific factors as the client's commitment to change at the time of crisis, and his engaging in a relationship that supports expectation for change. This is not to say that there are no differences in the effectiveness of treatment approach A and B. What should be concluded is that the common nonspecific features in all helping relationships account for most of their effectiveness (Frank, 1969). In evaluating a particular treatment approach, then, the clinician cannot make any claims regarding the efficacy of an approach just by demonstrating that clients improve. What he must also demonstrate is that his approach helps people improve more than can be attributed to the nonspecific effects found in most helping relationships.

Treatment effectiveness for the three ward programs in the study cited previously (Ellsworth, 1973) was estimated by combining the residual gain scores for all patients released during each three-month period. Fourteen of these three-month averages were computed for each ward, or a total of 42 outcome scores for all three wards. These gain scores, based on an average N of 18 patients, were relatively stable across time.[3] These residual gain scores for wards averaged 7.7, with a standard deviation of ± 1.7, indicating that the differences between programs and the variations in them over time did not fluctuate widely.

Recall from the previous section on regression effects that a change of 1.10 standard score points toward the mean occurred between the first rating and the second rating one week later. This accounted for 20% of the change in the pretreatment-posttreatment average standard scores. Thus, it seems reasonable to conclude that about 20% of the 7.7 average residual score gain shown by ward programs was attributable to this regression effect. Changes beyond this can be attributed to both nonspecific and specific effects of treatment. It is difficult to decide how much score change is a result of such nonspecific effects as the patients' and relatives' expectation that hospitalization would be helpful, and the like, and how much gain is added by a specific and effective treatment approach. The score gain observed for the most effective program was about two residual score points greater than the average residual gain shown for all wards. This suggests that the score gain attributable to nonspecific effects is larger than that shown when a ward introduces a specifically effective treatment approach.

In order to partial out the relative effects of various nonspecific factors, a series of experimental studies would be required. Patients could be assigned randomly to different groups, controlling for the effects of no pills, placebos, and active drugs; clearly communicated expectations that patients could resolve their problems without help versus with help; inpatients versus outpatient treatment; time-limited versus unlimited psychotherapy; support from professionally trained versus non-professionals or friends, and so forth. Since studies have already shown that nonspecific and placebo effects contribute significantly to improvement, it seems clear that the treatment rituals themselves affect outcome to a much greater extent than most mental health staffs realize.

## OVERVIEW AND RECOMMENDATIONS FOR EVALUATING PROGRAMS

One of the first important problems the researcher must face is resistance to evaluation from mental health administrators and professionals alike. As discussed in Part One, the attitude of the administrator toward program evaluation is a key factor in whether or not adequate evaluation occurs and survives. The sources of resistance to evaluation are many, including the threat to the professional's established prerogative of deciding which treatment is best for his clients, and the administrator's traditional role of advocating in advance that his approach is the best one to deal with a particular problem. Neither the professional nor the administrator who exercises these prerogatives will welcome the potential threat posed by program evaluation. Resistance to evaluation has been increased also by the inability of many researchers to design and carry out relevant studies.

In approaching the problem of evaluating treatment programs, recall that clients' behavior in the treatment setting is often unrelated to their adjustment in their living and work settings. For this reason, staff ratings of client behavior in treatment are not as relevant as measures of community adjustment. Ratings of client behavior by significant others were found to be as valid and reliable as staff ratings of community adjustment. Data from this source also has the important advantage of being much more economical than staff ratings, and captures the viewpoint of a group directly affected by mental health services but rarely used to help evaluate them.

The technical problems in program evaluation are complex but do not necessarily jeopardize the validity of conclusions reached about program effectiveness. Program evaluation rarely meets the criteria set forth for traditional laboratory experiments. But evaluation becomes increasingly scientific as one designs his study so as to minimize the threats to validity of conclusions reached from evaluation studies. Common threats to valid conclusions include data loss, regression effects typically found in repeated measures, and assignment of nonsimilar subjects to treatment groups.

One of the weaknesses of data from significant others is the problem of data loss, especially that which occurs after subjects are assigned to treatment groups. The investigator who uses the approach of obtaining pre and post treatment ratings from the same rater has the greatest problem with data loss. This design allows one to increase the efficiency of testing for the statistical significance of differences between programs by using residual scores or analysis of covariance, but the researcher must make certain that one program does not have a higher percentage or type of data loss than other programs.

### A Proposed Strategy for Program Evaluation

As must now be obvious, a program advocate must do more than demonstrate that his clients improve. Some change in the ratings of clients' behavior occurs just from rating them a second time, for extreme scores show some regression toward the mean on rerating. In addition, a great deal of change occurs from nonspecific treatment effects. When a client in stress comes to a source he expects will help him, change in adjustment usually occure. Most of the improvement shown in treatment, then, appears to be in response to the nonspecific factors found in most treatment approaches.

The added effects of a specific approach are not easy to measure. In this investigator's experience, when they do occur, they are considerably less than those attributable to the nonspecific factors common to most programs. The three hospital treatment programs referred to in this study were, on the surface at least, very different from one another in terms of treatment philosophy and approach to patients. One ward was rather authoritarian and doctor-centered, one was more benevolent in staff attitudes, and a third was a patient-managed level system staffed by those who rejected traditional benevolent and authoritarian attitudes toward mental illness (for program descriptions and attitude differences, see Childers, 1967; Ellsworth, 1965 and 1970; Mabel, 1971). But only during one eight-month period was one program significantly more effective than the others. At other times, the treatment outcomes for a three-month period were significantly higher (or lower) for one ward than for another, but these differences were not consistent over time. Thus, the specific effects of staff attitudes and program philosophy apparently were not major determinants of treatment effectiveness.

One way to estimate the specific effects of a particular program would be to establish base rates of response to programs in general. These base rates of change would reflect primarily the client's response to the nonspecific factors common to various approaches. If a program exceeded the base rate response, one could consider seriously the possibility that response to treatment was enhanced by that specific program. Conclusions drawn from such data are more reasonable when one also has knowledge of those client characteristics that are related to treatment outcome, and can compare the base rate population and the special program population on these treatment-related background characteristics. If these treatment-related characteristics are similar for both groups, then outcome differences are more likely to be a reflection of differences in program effectiveness. For years, the California Youth Authority has used this approach to identify effective approaches (Gottfredson, 1969). Using biographical data known to be related to parole violation, a prediction is made for each offender. If offenders assigned to a given treatment succeed significantly more often than predicted, then that difference is considered to be an indication of program effectiveness. Promising programs are identified, and their effectiveness can be established using an experimental design with random assignment to treatment conditions.

An approach similar to that described above is hereby proposed in the search for effective programs in mental health. As already seen, the pretreatment PARS adjustment scores are highly predictive of outcome scores when the same rater is used. This allows one to calculate residual scores by removing from the outcome scores that proportion of variance related to initial adjustment. Base rate residual scores have now been established for a wide range of clients treated in various inpatient and outpatient settings. Using these data, posttreatment improvement can be predicted from initial scores for clients assigned to different treatment conditions. If the clients of one treatment approach typically exceed that amount of improvement predicted for them (positive residual scores), then that approach can be regarded as more effective than most. Stated another way, the added effects specific to a particular treatment approach can be estimated by the extent to which clients' score gains exceed the score changes of base rate clients.

The major problem with this base rate comparison occurs when a client population treated by a particular approach differs in important ways from the base rate population. When this occurs, the validity of one's conclusions about treatment effectiveness becomes increasingly uncertain. This problem is of concern especially when a treatment population differs from the base rate population on background characteristics related to outcome ratings. But as already seen, when outcome scores are corrected for initial adjustment, background characteristics add little to the relationship between initial characteristics and outcome adjustment ratings. Recall that initial adjustment ratings account for most of the variance in outcome ratings, especially when the same rater is used. Another problem occurs when large differences exist in the pretreatment adjustment of one group as compared with the base rate group. In this case, the use of residual scores to correct statistically for the effect if initial differences on outcome does not guarantee that the proper allowances have been made (Lord, 1962).

Except for the situations described above, using this residual score or deviation-from-base-rate approach to program evaluation allows clinic and hospital staff to search for the most efficient and least expensive procedures that produce the best results. Equally important, one can also begin to identify the characteristics of those who respond well and poorly to different approaches, provided that adequate background and patient characteristics data are kept. Hypotheses derived from this approach to program evaluation can then be confirmed by randomly assigning patients to treatment groups using a more experimental research design. The deviation-from-base-rate approach, using PARS Scale ratings by significant others, however, should result in fairly valid comparisons of program effectiveness. The validity of conclusions about program effectiveness is enhanced if one seriously considers and explores various alternatives, such as differential data loss, that may have accounted for outcome differences between groups. As the various alternative explanations are ruled out after careful exploration, the investigator can become increasingly confident that obtained outcome differences are related to program effects rather than to uncontrolled population differences.

## NOTES

1. Available from: Institute for Program Evaluation, Box 4654, Roanoke, Va. 24015.

2. A simple formula for obtaining residual scores is presented by Hayes and Peprusic (1963). The residual score is the outcome standard score, minus the initial standard score multiplied by the correlation between initial and outcome scores.

3. The estimate of program effectiveness based on averaged gain scores becomes more stable

as the sample size increases. Averaged gain scores based on N of between 10 and 16 patients had a standard error of the mean of about 1.95. An N of 17 to 20 resulted in a standard error of about 1.55. When the sample size was between 21 and 31, the mean standard error was about 1.34. A sample size of at least 17, and preferably 21 or greater, is recommended in order for the estimate of program effectiveness to be reliable.

# REFERENCES

Ackner, B., A. Harris and A. J. Oldham. Insulin treatment of schizophrenia: A controlled study. *Lancet*, 1957, 272: 607-611.

Ackner, B. and A. Oldham. Insulin treatment of schizophrenia: A three-year follow-up of a control study. *Lancet*, 1962, 281: 504-506.

Anderson, Mary Lou, P. R. Polak, D. Grace and Aldora Lee. Treatment goals for patients from patients, their families and staff. *Journal of the Fort Logan Mental Center*, 1965, 3: 101-115.

Bentinck, Catherine A., B. A. Miller and A. D. Pokorny. Relatives as informants in mental health research. *Mental Hygiene*, 1969, 53: 446-450.

Bergin, A. E. Some implications of psychotherapy research for therapeutic practice. *Journal of Abnormal and Social Psychology*, 1966, 71: 235-246.

Berger, D. G., C. E. Rice, L. G. Sewall and P. V. Lemkau. Posthospital evaluation of psychiatric patients: The social adjustment inventory method. *Psychiatric Studies and Projects*, 1964, 2(15).

Brill, N. Q., R. R. Koegler, L. J. Epstein and E. W. Forgy. Control study of psychiatric outpatient treatment. *Archives of General Psychiatry*, 1964, 10: 581-595.

Buss, A. H., H. Fischer and A. J. Simmons. Aggression and hostility in psychiatric patients. *Journal of Consulting Psychology*, 1962, 26: 84-89.

Campbell, D. T. Reforms as experiments. *American Psychologist*, 1969, 24: 409-429.

Carr, J. E. and J. Whittenbaugh. Sources of disagreement in the perception of psychotherapy outcomes. *Journal of Clinical Psychology*, 1969, 25(1): 16-21.

Childers, B. A ward program based on graduated activities and group effort. *Hospital and Community Psychiatry*, 1967, 18: 289-295.

Cline, D. W., D. L. Rouzer and D. Bransford. Goal attainment scaling as a method for evaluating mental health programs. *American Journal of Psychiatry*, 1973, 130: 105-108.

Cottrell, L. S. Forward in *Evaluative Research* by E. A. Suchman. New York: Russell Sage Foundation, 1967.

Cronbach, L. J. and Lita Furby. How we should measure change—or should we? *Psychological Bulletin*, 1970, 74: 68-80.

Cross, H. J. The outcome of psychotherapy: A selective analysis of research findings. *Journal of Consulting Psychology*, 1964, 28: 413-417.

Deiter, J. B., D. B. Hanford, R. T. Hummel and J. E. Lubach. Brief inpatient treatment—a pilot study. *Mental Hospitals*, 1965, 16: 95-98.

DuBois, P. H. *Multivariate correlational analysis*. New York: Harper, 1957.

Ellsworth, R. B. A behavioral study of staff attitudes toward mental illness. *Journal of Abnormal Psychology*, 1965, 70: 194-200.

———. Measuring personal adjustment and role skills (the PARS Scale for veterans). *Newsletter for Research in Psychology*. VA Center, Hampton, Va. 1968, 10: 9-12.

———. Upgrading treatment effectiveness through measurement and feedback of clinical outcomes. *Hospital and Community Psychiatry*, 1970, 21: 115-117.

———. Feedback: Asset or liability in improving treatment effectiveness? *Journal of Consulting and Clinical Psychology*, 1973, 40: 383-393.

———, Leslie Foster, B. Childers, G. Arthur and D. Kroeker. Hospital and community adjustment as perceived by psychiatric patients, their families, and staff. *Journal of Consulting and Clinical Psychology*, 1968, 32(5), Part 2. Monograph supplement.

Ellsworth, R. B. and Joan R. Ellsworth. The psychiatric aide: Therapeutic agent or lost potential? *Journal of Psychiatric Nursing*, 1970, 8: 7-13.

Evenson, R. C. A systematic and comprehensive approach to practical program evaluation within the department of mental health. Elgin, Ill.: Elgin State Hospital, 1970. Unpublished paper.

Frank, J. D. Common features account for effectiveness. *International Journal of Psychiatry*, 1969, 7: 122-127.

Goff, C., G. Osborne, K. Campbell and M. Fletcher. Preliminary report on the use of the PARS Scale by Oregon's community mental health clinics, 1971. Unpublished.

Goldstein, A. P. *Therapist-patient expectancies in psychotherapy*. New York: Pergamon Press (MacMillan), 1962.

Goltz, B., R. A. Sternbach and T. N. Rusk. A built-in evaluation system in a new community mental health center. Unpublished.

Gottfredson, D. M. Research—who needs it? *Research Report*, 1969, 2: 11-17. Department of Institutions, State of Washington.

Gralnick, A. The psychiatric hospital as a therapeutic instrument. New York: Brunner/Mazel, 1969.

Hayes, W. L. and W. Peprusic. Statistics for Psychologists. New York: Holt, Rinehart & Winston, 1963.

Horst, P. *Psychological measurement and prediction*. Belmont, Calif. Wadsworth, 1966.

Katz, M. M. and S. B. Lyerly. Methods for measuring adjustment and social behavior in the community: 1. rationale, description, discriminative validity, and scale development. *Psychological Reports*, 1963, 13. Monograph supplement 4-V13.

Katz, M. M., H. A. Lowery and J. O. Cole. Behavior patterns of schizophrenics in the community. Pp. 209-230 in M. Lorr (ed.), *Explorations in Typing Psychotics*. New York: Pergamon Press, 1967.

Kiresuk, T. J. and R. E. Sherman. Goal attainment scaling: A general method for evaluating comprehensive community mental health programs. *Community Mental Health Journal*, 1968, 4: 443-453.

Kish, G. B. and H. T. Hermann. The Fort Meade alcoholism treatment program, a follow-up study. *Quarterly Journal of Studies on Alcohol*, 1971, 32: 628-635.

Kliewer, D. From aftercare to community care. Final report, Mid-Kansas Rural Aftercare Demonstration. Prairie View Mental Health Center, Newton, Kansas, 1970.

Krause, M. S. Construct validity for the evaluation of therapy outcomes. *Journal of Abnormal Psychology*, 1969, 74: 524-530.

Lamb, H. R., D. Heath and J. J. Downing (eds.) *Handbook of community mental health practice*. San Francisco: Jossey-Bass, 1969.

Levy, R. A. Six-session outpatient therapy. *Hospital and Community Psychiatry*, 1966, 17: 340-343.

Lord, F. M. Elementary models for measuring change. In C. W. Harris (ed.), *Problems in measuring change*. Madison: University of Wisconsin Press, 1962.

Lorr, M., D. M. McNair and A. P. Goldstein. A comparison of time limited and time unlimited psychotherapy. Cited in Goldstein et al. *Psychotherapy and the psychology of behavior change*. New York: Wiley, 1966.

Lowinger, P. and Shirley Dobie. What makes the placebo work? *Archives of General Psychiatry*, 1969, 20: 84-88.

Luborsky, L. Clinician's judgments of mental health. *Archives of General Psychiatry*, 1962, 7: 407-417.

Mabel, S. Outcome of patients taking over a "critical" staff function. *Hospital and Community Psychiatry*, 1971, 22: 25-28.

May, P. R. A. *Treatment of schizophrenia*. New York: Science, 1969.

McPartland, T. S. and R. H. Richart. Social and clinical outcomes of psychiatric treatment. *Archives of General Psychiatry*, 1966, 14: 179-184.

Mendel, W. Concepts of effective intensive short-stay treatment programs. Paper presented at

VA-NIMH conference on communalities in innovative mental health programs. Denver, December 15-17, 1965.

———. Effects of length of hospitalization on rate and quality of remission from acute psychotic episodes. *Journal of Nervous and Mental Disease,* 1966, 143: 226-233.

Meyer, V. and E. S. Chesser. *Behavior therapy in clinical psychiatry.* Baltimore: Penguin Books, 1970.

Michaux, W. W., M. M. Katx, A. A. Kurland and Kathleen H. Gansereit. *The first year out.* Baltimore: John Hopkins Press, 1969.

Mischel, W. *Personality and assessment.* New York: Wiley, 1968.

Pasamanick, B., F. R. Scarpitti and S. Dinitz. *Schizophrenics in the community.* New York: Appleton-Century-Crofts, 1967.

Paul, G. L. *Insight vs. desensitization in psychotherapy: An experiment in anxiety reduction.* Stanford: Stanford University Press, 1966.

———. Strategy of outcome research in psychotherapy. *Journal of Consulting Psychology,* 1967, 31(2): 109-117.

Roen, S. R., and A. J. Burnes. *The community adaptation schedule.* New York: Behavioral Publications, 1966.

Rorer, L. Summary of the Ellsworth affair. *Oregon Psychological Association Newsletter,* December 1970, 17(2): 9-18.

Saenger, G. Patterns of change among treated and untreated patients seen in psychiatric community mental health clinics. *Journal of Nervous and Mental Disease,* 1970, 150: 37-50.

Schorer, C. E., P. Lowinger, T. Sullivan and G. H. Hartlaub. Improvement without treatment. *Diseases of the Nervous System,* 1968, 29: 100-104.

Schulberg, H. C., A. Sheldon and F. Baker. *Program evaluation in the mental health fields.* New York: Behavioral Publications, 1969.

Shlien, J. M. Time-limited psychotherapy: An experimental investigation of practical values and theoretical implications. *Journal of Consulting Psychology,* 1957, 4: 318-322.

Sinnett, E. R., W. E. Stimpert and E. A. Straight. Five-year follow-up of psychiatric patients. *American Journal of Orthospychiatry,* 1965, 35: 573-580.

Stevenson, I. The challenge of results in psychotherapy. *American Journal of Psychiatry,* 1959, 116: 120-123.

Storrow, H. A. The measurement of outcome in psychotherapy. *Archives of General Psychiatry,* 1960, 2: 142-146.

Strupp, H. H. and A. L. Bloxom. Preparing lower-class patients for group psychotherapy: Development and evaluation of a role-induction film. *Journal of Consulting and Clinical Psychology,* 1973, 41: 373-384.

Suchman, E. A. *Evaluative Research.* New York: Russell Sage Foundation, 1967.

VA Report to the House of Representatives Committee on Veterans Affairs. Washington, D.C., 1969.

Wholey, J. S., J. W. Scanlon, H. G. Duffy, J. S. Fukumoto and L. M. Vogt. *Federal evaluation policy.* Washington, D. C.: The Urban Institute, 1970.

Wood, E. C., J. M. Rakusin, E. Morse and R. Singer. Interpersonal aspects of psychiatric hospitalization. *Archives of General Psychiatry,* 1962, 6: 46-55.

Zlotowski, M. and D. Cohen. Effects of change in hospital organizations upon the behavior of psychiatric patients. Paper presented at the meeting of Eastern Psychological Association. Atlantic City, April 1965.

Zolik, E. S., Edna M. Lantz, and R. Sommers. Hospital return rates and pre release referrals. Paper presented at the 75th Annual Convention, American Psychological Association, Washington, D.C., 1967.

# 10

# EVALUATING RESIDENTIAL TREATMENT PROGRAMS FOR DISTURBED CHILDREN

RODERICK P. DURKIN

*Manhattan Childrens' Treatment Center*

and

ANNE BOTSFORD DURKIN

*Adelphi University*

Each night some 150,000 children and adolescents go to bed in approximately 2,500 child care institutions, of which only about 200 provide treatment. (Pappenfort et al., 1968: 450, 451). Of these 150,000 children, about 110,000 were judged to be disturbed; of these, only 14,000 or about 13% were receiving treatment. The predominant service modality for those who do receive treatment is inpatient care which is lengthy and costly, with treatment ranging from $500 to $1,500 monthly in private institutions (Redick, 1969). In the recent epidemiological studies of Langner and associates (1969), large numbers of children showing marked psychiatric impairment were found in the community, with disproportionate numbers coming from families living on welfare and from low income groups. Where these children find their way into the network of caregivers, they are likely to be disproportionately placed as delinquents in training or reform schools, in homes for the retarded, or in adult wards of state hospitals.

While estimates such as the above are necessarily crude at best, it is obvious that there is a critical demand for services in child mental health. In addition to the cost of residential treatment, its capacity to reach only a small percentage of the population, the shortage of trained personnel, and overloaded facilities, there is growing criticism of the theory and practice of residential treatment itself (Maluc-

AUTHORS' NOTE: This research was supported by the U.S. Office of Child Development Grant #OCD CB 319. The authors wish to express their appreciation to Jerome Beker for his patient and thorough reading of earlier manuscripts, and to Jim Thomas for his contribution to the review of the literature.

cio and Marlow, 1972; Rubin and Simson, 1960). One of the alternatives that has gathered momentum is the replacing of large, total institutions isolated from natural families and communities with a variety of smaller, more community-oriented and open programs with a spectrum of conjoint treatment services. However, large numbers of disturbed children will continue to require residential treatment. To upgrade the effectiveness of such programs, to assess their adequacy, and to delineate the processes of residential treatment, it is important that we know how to describe, analyze, and evaluate programs that attempt to both "raise" and "treat" children.

Program evaluation is considered an obligation by most treatment programs, and such studies are important because they reflect a variety of strategies of evaluation and illustrate many of the difficulties endemic to evaluative research. This chapter is a critical review of some significant studies of institutions providing residential treatment for disturbed children and adolescents and seeks to examine the different approaches to evaluation in terms of their strengths and limitations. For the purpose of this review, the term "evaluation" is expanded to include not only (1) goal attainment studies, including outcome and follow-up studies, of the extent to which a program achieves its goals, but also (2) process evaluations, and (3) systems analyses, including some comparative and descriptive studies. Studies are discussed in terms of these categories, which, since they are necessarily somewhat arbitrary, are based upon the main emphasis of each study.

The comparative and descriptive studies we have included in the category of systems evaluations focus on the recurring problems and inherent dilemmas of social systems which seek to both "raise" and "treat" children, that is, they deal with roles of child care workers or the integration of the "raising" (enculturation) and treatment spheres of residential treatment. Although the distinction between description and analysis of social systems is a fine one, the distinction has been made here according to the extent to which the description relates to the "efficiency" of the residential treatment program's functioning as a social system, its subsystems, and its linkages with suprasystems such as the community, family, and network of caregivers. The more narrowly descriptive works excluded from the scope of this paper, such as that of Bettleheim (1950), Redl and Wineman (1951), and others, have been adequately reviewed by Maluccio and Marlow (1972).

As will become evident in the course of this review, our own contention is that systems analyses which evaluate residential treatment programs qua institution or social system are potentially of greater practical and theoretical significance for these programs than the outcome, follow-up, or process evaluation. Following a review of the three categories of evaluative studies, a generalizable, evaluative model using an open systems perspective for analyzing the ways in which residential programs are organized to achieve their various goals is presented. Because of the limitations of goal-attainment research and because of the practical and methodological problems of assessing small residential programs, the proposed model attempts to provide a framework for evaluating programs as social systems while not necessarily precluding more long range outcome studies. The model is evaluative in that: (1) it provides a comprehensive conceptualization of residential treatment programs which is prerequisite to experimentation and evaluations, as well as to dealing with the program's relationships with other institutions and systems, and (2) it examines programs holistically and makes explicit the functioning and relative contributions of their subsystems. The value of this approach, given the difficulties inherent to evaluative research, will become more obvious as other approaches to evaluation are reviewed.

Considering the already broad scope of this chapter, a variety of topics have necessarily been excluded. For example, it goes without saying that many disturbed children are placed in correctional facilities rather than treatment facilities, since delinquency can be regarded as a criminal offense or as a character or behavior disorder. Selection for the category of delinquent, retarded, or disturbed is most likely affected by such variables as income level, resources, ethnicity, and the like. However, this chapter deals with studies of programs for delinquents, retarded, and adult patients only where they are relevant to either the substantive or the methodological considerations of the main focus of this chapter, the evaluation of residential treatment programs for disturbed children. In one instance, *Organization for Treatment* (Street, Vinter, and Perrow, 1966), a study of the effectiveness of different types of organizations for delinquents is considered as an example of a comparative evaluation.[1]

Similarly, the general methodological and practical problems of evaluative research will not be considered in this context except where relevant to a specific study. These more general issues and problems in evaluative research have been discussed in a variety of sources, a very few of which have been included among the references.[2]

It should be noted that other authors have reviewed the literature on evaluative research in this area, for example, Shyne (1973), Gershenson (1956), Simon (1956), and Dinnage and Pringle (1967). Generally these reviews do not focus on the problems of program evaluation, but where they do review evaluative studies, these will be discussed in the course of this review.

Finally, numerous readings on residential treatment have been published, most recently those by Whittaker and Trieschman (1972) and Weber and Haberlein (1972). Where relevant to evaluation, these, too, are cited, but in general it can be said that these readings suffer from failure to be integrated around developing models of treatment, evaluating the effect of residential programs, or confronting the inherent problems of such programs. A publication of papers celebrating Bellefaire's anniversary, *Healing Through Living* by Mayer and Blum (1971), does deal with some of these problems, such as role conflicts experienced by child care workers, teachers, and therapists in a residential setting and problems that arise in coordinating the group living, education, and therapy spheres of residential programs. As a problem-oriented book on residential treatment, it is recommended.

## GOAL ATTAINMENT EVALUATIONS

In their follow-up study, Lander and Schulman (1960) express the view that the evaluation of the effectiveness of a milieu, and by extension of a program as well, is more difficult than the evaluation of the effectiveness of individual treatment because of the greater number of variables in the milieu, less adequate theory about their therapeutic significance, less knowledge of group dynamics and similar institutional influences upon the individual, and the like. Perhaps for this reason, most evaluations of residential treatment programs have been descriptive and impressionistic, which, as Gershenson (1956) points out, are prerequisite to hypotheses and to subsequent experiments.

Studies that have attempted to evaluate programs are most often goal-attainment studies, which have generally been of two sorts. Some have developed specific measures of outcome, such as work records, police arrests, or changes in attitudes or personality traits.[3] The other, perhaps more common, strategy is the follow-up study which seeks to measure a program's success or effectiveness by looking at the postprogram adjustment of the patients as measured by recidivism or success.[4]

**Outcome Evaluation**

Goldenberg's study, *Build Me A Mountain: Youth, Poverty and the Creation of New Settings* (1971), is primarily a goal-attainment study in which changes in attitude, work performance, arrests, and records of experimental and control groups were compared. As an evaluative study it is one of the more complete and rigorous in that it uses an experimental and control group, has pre and post measures of both attitudes and behavior, and demonstrates a relationship between attitudes and behavior.

The Residential Youth Center, as described in the book, was in large part an outgrowth of discontent and dissatisfaction with the Job Corps Program during the most recent war on poverty. In their contacts with New Haven youth involved in the Job Corps, the author and his colleagues and founders of the center realized that the program had serious limitations, including isolating individuals from their homes and communities, and its inability, in part due to size, to meet the needs of many of the youths. As a result, many of the boys had dropped out of the Job Corps and returned disillusioned to their home communities.

Taking a different tack, the center sought to keep the boys in their home communities and to maintain their ties there. The center housed 20 adolescent boys who lived at the center and who participated in group and individual therapy and in counseling sessions while working in the Neighborhood Youth Corps or in other community jobs. The program is of particular interest in that it has implications for the urban poor whose critical need of services and assistance has been documented in the studies of Langner and associates (1969).

In a discussion of the research problems, Goldenberg (1971: 334) states:

> Given the frame of reference of its critics, one would be hard pressed to try to justify the existence of action research on the basis of the criteria (i.e., objectivity, control and replication) usually associated with the process of scientific inquiry. . . . All too often, those involved in the area of action research have been placed in the position of first apologizing for and then defending what has come to be labelled parochially as an "inferior" (rather than a "different") approach to the problems of assessing highly volatile and complex settings.

By way of background, an account of one staff member's response to the research during a meeting is given by Goldenberg (1971: 338) as follows:

> *Butch:* I've been sitting here and listening to you guys talk about research for about a half-hour now, and frankly the more I hear the more pissed-off I'm getting about all this research bullshit! Right now I don't give a good god-damn if I never hear another word about research or statistics for the rest of my life. Now, you guys can call this a sensitivity issue or any thing you want, but all I know is that I've had it up to here with this research crap. . . . I am sick and tired of sitting here and being told that now, after being in the Center for about five months, my kid is going to work 38 percent more of the time than before he came into the RYC. Big fucking deal! What the hell does that tell me? And what's more, what the hell does that tell people who don't know about the RYC, about the guts of this operation? Nothing. Nothing at all. Its a lot of bullshit.
>
> *Kelly:* Butch, I think you're going overboard on this.
>
> *Butch:* The hell I am. I put my blood and guts into working with Ev and his crazy mother and all I come away with is that Ev is going to work 38 percent more of the time. Big god-damn deal. Where's Ev in all this? Where am I? Where's there anything that tells about what goes on between us day in and day out?
>
> *Scotty:* I think I know what's bugging you, Butch, but you know as well as I do that whether or not we get refunded depends a helluva lot on what these statistics show after a year.
>
> *Butch:* Look Scotty, you don't have to remind me about that. I know all about it. Washington wants statistics: CPI wants statistics; the whole world wants statistics. I know all that shit and I know its important. All I'm saying is that, whether or not we're refunded, if the research doesn't tell it like it really is—you know, what it feels like to work in a place like this, what its like to pour your whole self into a kid—then from my point of view it isn't worth a shit.

This attitude is often typical of those involved in programs and of their attitudes about research and its value.

The evaluative section of the book accordingly begins with a detailed description of one day in the life of a counselor. This detailed description provides a sense of what life is like at the center and is also evaluative in the sense that it is a detailed observation of a program similar to Barker's *One Boy's Day* (1951).

Following this richly descriptive chapter is the more traditional evaluation. For political reasons the participants in the program could not be randomly assigned. The local poverty agency insisted that the program take the 25 most troubled boys in the community. This list of names was submitted from the various agencies in New Haven; the most difficult 25 were taken into the program as an experimental group; the next most difficult 25 were used as a control group. Obviously the further one departs from truly randomized experimental and controls, the less rigorously the data can be interpreted, and the more open to interpretations are the findings.

Goldenberg (1971: 400) states that boys coming into the program were given a structured interview:

... designed to tap the following dimensions: self concept, social expectations, social causality, attitudes toward parents, attitudes toward authority, personal time orientation (past, present, future), alienation, hostility, reality functioning and impulse control, need for achievement, need for affiliation, task versus people orientation, dependence-independence and social responsibilities.

These interviews were tape recorded and used throughout the program.

In addition, the evaluation sought to assess changes in both attitudes and behavior. In the realm of attitudes, questionnaires revised to be appropriate in terms of vocabulary and degree of difficulty were used in a pre and post test designed to test the experimental and control group.

Differences in a pre-post design between the experimental and control groups revealed that the experimental group became less alienated (with the differences significant at the .01 level), less authoritarian (significant at the .05 level), more trusting (significant at the .10 level) and more positive in views about the world (significant at the .05 level). Differences between the control and the experimental group prior to entering the Residential Youth Center were nonsignificant on all of these scales.

In addition to and perhaps more important than changes in attitudes as measured by paper and pencil tests, comparisons were made between the control group and the Residential Youth Center (RYC) group on work attendance at the Neighborhood Youth Corps jobs before, during, and after the program. These data were available from unobtrusive, nonreactive measures (Webb et al., 1966), namely, work attendance records at the Neighborhood Youth Corps office. Prior to the beginning of the program, the control group was attending work 86.4% of the time, while the RYC-bound group showed up 66.1% of the time, with a difference of 20.3%. At the point of entering the program, the trends had reversed, with the RYC group attending 85.1% and the control group 55.4%. The trend continued 36 weeks after entry into the RYC program with the RYC group attending work 97.5% of the time and the control group, 56.1%. The differences between these percentages are significant at the .001 level.

Wages showed a similar relationship. The experimental group had an income of $25 a week as compared to $29 a week for the control group. Nine months later, the RYC group was earning $45.11, an increase of 80.4% as compared to the control group's salary of $20.72, a decrease of 28.6%.

Another behavioral measure used in the evaluation of the program was the comparison of the number of days spent in jail before and after the program. In the nine months prior to opening the residential youth center, the boys in RYC spent 153 days in jail, as compared with the control group's 140 days. In the nine months after the opening of the youth center, the RYC group spent 70 days in jail, a decrease of 54%, and the control spent 258 days, an increase of 85%.

These findings can be interpreted in several ways. For example, those in the youth center had better legal resources and support and consequently, were jailed less often. Similarly, a Hawthorne effect could be argued for the initial effect of entering the program, that is, the enthusiasm and excitement of the program influenced the boys to attend work more often, which they did at the opening of the center. The fact that the control group was not randomly assigned raises further problems, in that a regression-from-the-mean phenomenon may be taking place, namely, the boys on the top of the New Haven "most troublesome boys" list could only improve, while the next 25 most troublesome could still get "worse."

Of interest is the author's attempt to relate attitudinal measures to behavioral ones, wherein lies the meaningfulness of the outcome study. The lack of congruence between attitude and behavior, from Machiavellianism on down, makes this an important part of the evaluation, both as a research finding and in terms of rounding out the evaluative strategy. Work attendance was positively correlated with Machiavellianism, with the probability smaller than .07, and with alienation at the .01 level. Both Machiavellianism and alienation were significantly correlated at the .01 level with promotion on the job (Goldenberg, 1971: 413, Table 9.4).

Unfortunately, a long-term follow-up study of the boys involved in the program has not been reported, although it would undoubtedly illuminate the question of how enduring the program-induced changes were. As Goldenberg points out, it is difficult to extrapolate from such small samples in terms of program evaluation. Considering the difficulties inherent in outcome studies, however, this evaluation is remarkable, both in the extent to which it meets experimental rigor and in the significance of the outcome.

Perhaps more interesting than the outcome study evaluation is the analysis of the creation of the program, which is readily translatable into a systems analysis and is included in this section for the sake of continuity. The chapter on the creation of new settings makes explicit some of the choices faced in the course of developing an organization. A variety of assumptions regarding organizations, the poor, and psychotherapy are discussed in terms of their implications for program organization. Another set of assumptions discussed is that which prevents institutions from developing means of assessing themselves. For example, the author Goldenberg (1971: 99) says:

> By far the most important consequence of the assumption that the institution need not overly concern itself with its own mental health, is that the institution rarely attempts to develop or build itself any viable mechanism for preventing or dealing with its own problems. By viable mechanism, we mean any processes that would enable the institution systematically and regularly to take a long hard look at its functioning, its growth and its conflicts. The fact that few institutions or institution builders ever developed such vehicles for self-scrutiny should not be taken as evidence of bad faith, poor judgment or questionable motives. It is the ineffable result of the situation in which an organization does not view itself, its staff and its problems as legitimate, important, or of concern.
>
> ... the tendency of an institution to avoid looking at itself and to refrain from the often agonizing search to develop internal mechanisms for dealing with its own problems does not bring with it any guarantee that certain various problems will not occur. All it does is guarantee that when such problems arise, they will be dealt with haphazardly, instinctively and reflexively. In short, they will be dealt with in precisely the kinds of ways that the

institution would never condone or allow to happen where it is dealing with a problem of any of its clients.

The founders of the Residential Youth Center made some explicit decisions to avoid the problems of the pyramidal organization, to develop mechanisms of self-scrutiny, and to provide ongoing feedback about the effectiveness and functioning of the program. For example, one reason for choosing sensitivity training for staff was to provide participants with a continual supply of data and information that they could use to evaluate the effectiveness of individuals and of the organization itself. Much of the descriptive material included in the book is derived from logs of these daily sensitivity training sessions. Goldenberg (1971: 162) says that the meetings allowed staff to:

> ... look at ourselves, who we were, how we were changing and to judge whether or not these changes—either in ourselves or in the setting—were of an enhancing or self-defeating variety.

In the case of the center, a mechanism for ongoing self-evaluation was formalized and built into the organization. The potential of such ongoing mechanisms will be discussed further after a review of some other evaluative strategies.

## Follow-up Evaluation

As of 1947 the Rhyther Child Center was one of the few institutions to have conducted a systematic follow-up study of its services for disturbed children (Johnson and Reid, 1947). Ambiguous criteria for successful treatment and lack of a control group make the results subject to interpretation, but considering the few systematic follow-ups of discharged children, the study remains of historical interest.

Harold Silver's "Residential Treatment of Emotionally Disturbed Children: An Evaluation of 15 Years' Experience" (1961) is a follow-up study of children placed at either Bellefaire or the Hawthorne Cedar Knolls residential treatment centers. While sparse in detail and specifics, this study has obvious methodological problems with regard to the reliability of the judgments about improvement and the measures of durability of treatment and awareness of need for it on the part of both parents and child.

The study seems to show that it is easier to treat less difficult children and that outcomes appear to be positive no matter how poorly measured. However, it represents an attempt to do a more methodologically sound study than, for example, Levy's (1969) study of 100 former patients hospitalized between 1945 and 1960 at the Menninger Clinic; in this study judgments about outcome were arrived at by letters and telephone calls and were not based on empirical measures of adjustment, much less on direct interviews of the patients.

Benjamin Garber's book, *Follow-up Study of Hospitalized Adolescents* (1972), is a follow-up study of adolescent boys and girls who were hospitalized between 1958 and 1968 at the Psychiatric and Psychosomatic Institute of the Michael Reese Hospital in Chicago. The objectives of the study were:

1) to determine the adolescent population and its hospital course, 2) to determine what has happened to former adolescent patients and their status of current functioning, 3) to get some idea of their reaction to and their utilization of the hospital and the adolescent program and 4) to extract variables from the hospital stay that would relate to current functioning. [Garber, 1972: xi]

In the introductory chapter the author reviews a variety of follow-up studies and concludes:

The early follow-up studies, although covering large populations, were not uniform in treatment methods. They were also quite vague in their delinea-tion of criteria for improvement. They seemed to have different foci such as diagnosis, description of population, disposition, and current functioning. The therapeutic modalities employed in the hospital stay came as an after-thought. [Garber, 1972: 13]

Discussing the methodological considerations in his study, Garber suggests that there are four types of follow-up studies, namely, those dealing with (1) the informational level, (2) systematic data gathering, (3) systematic comparisons, and (4) control studies. The author describes his study as including 1 and 2, that is, using clinical interviews and gathering information and providing systematic data analysis. He contrasts clinical and empirical research and develops a justification for combining the two approaches. By precluding outcome studies and systematic comparisons with a control study, however, he clearly limits the experimental rigor of his design.

Four developmental tasks, derived from a basically psychoanalytic theory of adolescence, were used to develop systematic ratings of the posthospital adjustment of the adolescents. In this statement the rationale for using a task-oriented assess-ment of the completion of developmental tasks is made explicit. In describing why he chose to assess posthospital functioning in terms of these developmental tasks rather than symtomatology, Garber (1972: 46, 47) says:

There is a rather striking agreement in psychoanalytic literature about the clinical dilemma of adolescence. The ego structure in adolescence is in a state of marked flux and weakness owing to the growth process. This condition of flux causes psychiatric symptoms when present, to be vague and ill defined and to be unstable, with patients shifting from one category of disorder to another. Often only follow-up of later developments in the patient's life can determine whether a given symptom picture represented psychopathology or merely an intensification of the difficulties of adolescence. Psychiatric symptoms are common and transient in most adolescents.

Hospital records, including nursing notes, of 164 adolescents were reviewed for basic data, and all were systematically abstracted with the aid of 43 on-line, precoded questions.[5] Data were obtained on 120 patients. The author and another psychiatrist then sought to interview patients, and 71 of these were interviewed in a face-to-face situation. Most interviews were conducted at the hospital in a clinical manner during a 45 to 60 minute structured interview designed to cover various areas of current functioning. The remaining patients were interviewed by phone, with a questionnaire designed to cover similar material, or information was gathered from other sources such as parents, other patients, and former therapists.

The interviews and various data were coded, and patients were rated on a 5 point rating scale to assess their level of current functioning with regard to employment, social activities, interpersonal relations, scholastic activities, family relations, drugs, rehospitalization, and the like. Patients were divided into a high functioning group, which included 45 former patients; a moderately functioning group of 46 former patients; and a low functioning group, which consisted of 24 former patients.

In general it appears that people did improve after hospitalization. Members of the high functioning group tended to be seen more in the interviews, were employed or attending school, and were less inclined to be rehospitalized. These people usually went home after discharge. None were diagnosed as psychotic at follow-up, and no association was found between the various interpersonal aspects of the hospital milieu, that is, those that said that they were satisfied with or liked therapists, nursing staff, and so on.

The low functioning group was described as a drifting or nonfunctioning group. This group of patients was seen as isolated and spending most of their time at home or in and out of hospitals. The group that was not followed up, including 44 of the patients, did not appear to differ significantly on the basis of their hospital experience, namely, involvement in the program with the group and staff and having the interest of staff. They also appear to have been significantly less self-destructive, were given less medication, ran away less often, and appeared less significantly improved at discharge.

The author attempts to assess patients' feelings about the hospital. Generally very few felt that interpersonal relationships were negative. The most positive relationships were felt to be with the nursing staff, and the most negative reactions were to the school program. Suggestions for improving the program included more structure: tighter controls were suggested by more disturbed patients, while less structure and more freedom were requested by healthier patients.

In a final stage of the research, two-by-two chi square analysis attempted to sort out the relationship of the hospital experiences with current functioning. Unfortunately, the total percent of significant relationships is not given, and it is difficult to assess the meaning of the significance level which was set at 10%. Improved functioning at the 10% level was related to length of stay in the hospital, being a private patient, discharge diagnosis, condition on discharge, optimism of staff, involvement with adolescent group, involvement and interest of the staff, and a lack of medication in the hospital. The two best predictors of current functioning were medication in the hospital and involvement with and interest in staff. Those patients who did not receive medication and who were well regarded by and involved with staff seemed to have done better. Since medication was used rarely, it appears that use of medication is highly related to prognosis. In short, it appears that healthier patients did better at follow-up, a not too remarkable conclusion.

In summarizing the findings about the high functioning group, Garber (1972: 156) says:

> The high functioning group was making it in all areas, while the moderate functioning group showed certain isolated areas of poor functioning. But overall one can say that 91 out of 115 former patients were making it in the community.

There are, of course, other possible explanations, such as that the group that was contacted was preselected and healthier.

Of interest is Garber's (1972: 157) conclusion:

> The extraction of eight variables from the hospital course that correlated with current functioning is the so called "goal" of our research project. These variables can serve as useful guidelines for future adolescent inpatients and can be used as predictors of outcome. The clinical value and significance of these findings need to be tested and replicated by clinicians and researchers alike. If these and other variables of hospital course can be isolated, the specific matching and tailoring of the therapeutic milieu to particular patients can prove a useful and valuable clinical tool. Although the number of possible predictors is great, the painstaking transformation of clinical data into operationally useful and measurable factors is the major task of research of the therapeutic process.

In comparison with other clinical, nonsystematic follow-up studies, this study rates well. The author sought to develop systematic data to establish reliabilities between ratings and to relate hospital variables to outcome. It clearly appears, despite the obvious limitations of bias introduced by those conducting the interviews with patients they knew and the problems resulting from the lack of the control group, that outcome was related to prognosis: healthier people, healthier at intake and healthier during the course of their hospital stay, did better at discharge. While the study represents a major step, compared to previous outcome studies, in specifying the measures of functioning and hospital experience, its conclusions are limited by the lack of a control group. The true significance of the relationships is unclear because of the lenient 10% level of significance, expecially since a large but unspecified number of chi square tests was conducted. The author, however, did not opt for such a rigorous research project; and given his limited goals, he appears to have achieved them, namely, to have combined a clinical study with systematic data collection. His procedures are described, instruments are presented in appendices, and the study could be replicated, which represents considerable advance over other outcome studies. The extent to which it is an evaluative study is questionable; some efforts were made to relate outcome to patients' perception of the hospital. The study is primarily a study of the outcome of adolescent disturbance rather than an evaluative study of a psychiatric hospital.

Allerhand, Weber, and Haug's book, *Adaptation and Adaptability: The Bellefaire Follow-up Study* (1966), is a follow-up study of 50 boys who had been institutionalized at Bellefaire, a residential treatment center for about 150 disturbed children and adolescents, mainly male, Jewish, and middle class from midwestern urban areas. The children lived in cottages of about a dozen, went to school at the center (although some went to school or work in the community), and for the most part, were receiving individual treatment in casework. The sample comprised all but three boys who had been discharged during a three and one-half year period (1958-1961) and who had been at Bellefaire at least 6 months. The follow-up took place over two years after discharge when they were, on the average, about 18 years old.

The primary object of the study was to "describe their fate" at the time of follow-up, including the "circumstances within the living situation that might aid in establishing and articulating more effective aftercare plans" (Allerhand et al., 1966: 21). The design involved collecting data on each child at four points in time: (1) at three points during institutional stay, namely, three months after admission, fifteen months after admission, and at discharge; and (2) at the follow-up point one to two years later. Raw data for the residential period came from the institution's past records, for example, treatment plans, staff evaluations, and caseworker, unit worker, or teacher reports. For the follow-up, the raw data consisted of transcripts of approximately one to one and one-half hour interviews with the boy, his parents, and his therapist. The data were rated independently by a dozen trained judges (two judges independently rating each record) using scales developed by the research team.

The theoretical orientation was that "man's functioning must be viewed as an interaction between the self and the setting, simultaneously reckoning with developing structural factors" (Allerhand et al., 1966: 2). In this orientation, the concept of adaptability is seen as central because

> a particular level of adaptability is the current integration of the individual's structural development with the resultant interaction between him and all the factors so far included in his life space. [Allerhand et al., 1966: 3]

"Adaptability" is defined as a "state of readiness to meet demands on a selective basis" (Allerhand et al., 1966: 3) and is assumed to increase as the normal child grows. The second major concept, "adaptation," is defined as "behavior resulting from an individual's application of his available adaptability to circumstances in the perceived environment with which he desires continuity" (ibid.: 3), that is, the individual uses his capacity.

Adaptation was operationalized in terms of role fulfillment. For the three residential time points, ratings of role fulfillment that were assumed to reflect consistent, age-related norms appropriate to individual life in three areas (adults, peers, tasks) and in two settings (school and cottage) were made using case records. In the follow-up interview, transcripts were rated for interpersonal (family, peers) and cultural (school, work, leisure, economic) role fulfillment according to community norms.

To measure adaptability during residence (at three months only), an index was derived from IQ, Rorschach protocols, and ratings of casework accessibility, with its subareas of verbal accessibility, motivation to change, self-awareness, and global trust. The follow-up adaptability measure, called Intrapsychic Balance Index, was derived from ratings on 24 scales in the areas of self-attitudes, conduct, energy, growth, and identity. Very little explanation is offered to justify the choice of these components or their relation to "adaptability."

A third variable concerned influences on the child. Essentially these were rated as constant at Bellefaire, but the follow-up situation was rated in terms of stress or support. Some additional measures included staff assessments, for example, treatment plan, discharge evaluation, and caseworker's aims.

Most of the numerous ratings on seven-point scales were ultimately combined into 5 indices: (1) adaptability during and after treatment, (2) role fulfillment during and after, and (3) situational stress after treatment. On each index, scores were simply dichotomized, for example, "minimally adequate" or "inadequate" in role fulfillment. These scores permitted only nominal statistics, for example, percent adequate and chi square tests. No psychometric data are provided about these scales and indices, that is, their reliability or internal consistency. We are only told that interjudge correlations ranged from .50 to .77, and coefficients of agreement (same or adjacent score on 7 point scales), from 79% to 93%.

In examining the data, the main focus of the study was adaptation and adaptability in the community at follow-up and the relationship of these to concurrent situational factors or to prior institutional measures, that is, both research indices and staff evaluations. In addition, changes during the residential period were examined, along with the predictive value of measures earlier in treatment, with regard to role fulfillment by discharge time.

The findings from this institutional period can be noted first in passing. Overall role fulfillment ("adaptation") improved somewhat between admission and discharge, with the "minimally adequate" boys increasing from 56% to 73%. This trend conceals great variability with individual children regressing or improving. The younger ones (under 13) improved more, but they started at a lower level and never caught up with the older ones. (The authors assume the younger children to be more maladjusted to warrant separation from home in the first place; however, it could be that the norms applied in judgment were not adequately related to age.) Peer relationships were not as good as adult ones, reflecting perhaps the problem that the peers were also maladjusted and could not provide good models. Cottage behavior was found more adequate than school behavior.

In casework, which was evidently a major aspect of treatment, the workers tended to raise their goals over time, and the children did, to some extent, become more involved. Responsiveness to casework—for example, at 15 months—was related to overall role fulfillment at the time of discharge. Similarly related to adaptation at discharge were the adaptability measures after admission and some staff evaluations earlier in treatment. If improved functioning at Bellefaire was the criterion, one might say the institution was having some success and that certain measures earlier in treatment had some predictive value for who would do well.

However the criterion is functioning in the community afterward, and Allerhand and associates (1966: 140) state:

Perhaps the most striking finding of the study is that none of the measurements of within-Bellefaire performance at discharge, either in casework or in cottage and school roles, were useful in predicting postdischarge adaptability and adaptation.

Adaptability at admission was the only research index that related significantly to follow-up measures, specifically to follow-up adaptability (intrapsychic balance) and to cultural role fulfillment four or five years later. Regular staff evaluations on particular items, such as whether a child would profit from casework, could go out to school or work in the local community, or had improved in treatment, were, in general, better predictors of follow-up adequacy than the research measures. The authors discuss this stronger association, not in terms of inadequate research instruments, but as representing in part a self-fulfilling prophecy: children who were seen as more hopeful in fact got better treatment.

At follow-up, 71% of the boys were judged to be at least adequate in their overall adaptation, and 57% in their adaptability. When the milieu of the boys was rated, 68% were judged to be in situations that were at least partly supportive. Adequacy of follow-up adaptation and adaptability was found to be significantly related to whether the postdischarge situation was supportive or stressful. Turning again to the Bellefaire measures, the authors say that, only when the situation to which the child returned was taken into account, were performances at Bellefaire related to postdischarge adequacies.

In fact, they do not directly test for this. It would entail holding the situation constant and, in separate analyses for the stressed and supported boys, comparing adequacy at Bellefaire with adequacy on three dependent measures, that is, follow-up adaptability and adaptation in both interpersonal and cultural areas. If they had done this, they would have noted that the discharge role-fulfillment measures still failed to relate to follow-up measures in any consistent way; and although admission adaptability differentiated better, certain staff evaluations remained the best. Nor do they note that current situation by itself relates more strongly to the dependent measures than do the Bellefaire measures alone; for example, on 12 out of 15 comparisons (5 Bellefaire and 3 follow-up measures), the "adequate at Bellefaire but stressful situation now" cases do more poorly than "inadequate at Bellefaire but supportive situation." Instead they are concerned to show how situation interacts differentially with status on various Bellefaire measures. They argue that, for those high on admission adaptability, situational stress does not differentiate on the follow-up measures: these boys do fairly well anyway, while for those low in earlier adaptability, the current situation makes a significant difference. Conversely, for those adequate in discharge role fulfillment (or in response to casework), situational conditions have a crucial influence, while for the inadequate, they make little difference and such boys tend to do poorly anyway. These inferences go beyond the data, for whether or not certain comparisons reach conventional significance levels has as much to do with different subsample sizes as with differences on the dependent measures.

The study cannot evaluate the success of Bellefaire's program, since there is no control group. It cannot say whether the boys had improved in community functioning *because* they went to Bellefaire, or even *that* they had improved after admission, since no measure was applied both at admission and at follow-up; the two adaptability measures were quite different from each other.

The primary purpose of the study by Taylor and Alpert, *Continuity and Support Following Residential Treatment* (1973), was to examine the postdischarge adaptation of children after residential treatment at Children's Village, sponsored by Child and Family Services of Connecticut. The objects of the study were specifically: (1) to assess how children were adapting after treatment; (2) to examine discharge plans for children for the degree to which they were specified; (3) to assess the degree to which postdischarge environments were supportive and stressful; (4) to attempt to understand the relationship between postdischarge environments and treatment; and finally (5) to explore the reasons some children did not respond to postdischarge services. In a sense the study is a logical extension of the study by Allerhand and associates (1966) and is also related to the suggested findings of Ellsworth and associates (1968), Kane and Chambers (1961), Mora et al. (1969), and others that behavior and adjustment may be functions of situations more than of personality characteristics.

The 186 children selected for the study had been in the Children's Village treatment program for 6 months or longer. Of the 186 children selected for the study, only 75 were found who agreed, or whose guardians agreed, to participate in the study.

A version of the Roen-Burns' Community Adaptation Scale was used, and adaptation and admissions were measured by broad diagnostic categories. Children designated psychotic, borderline, or character disorders on the basis of case records were independently rated. Degree of change during residential treatment was rated on the basis of a sense of self-worth and improved behavior. Supports in the community after discharge were measured by the child's perception of the availability of help from such people as parents, relatives, friends, neighbors, and staff at Children's Village. Continuity was defined by the degree to which a child lived continuously with his own or adopted parents following discharge. The discharge plans were taken directly from plans made in the case records.

Four hypotheses (Roen and Burns, 1968: 50, 51) were tested:

1) The greater the degree of continuity in postdischarge environment, the greater the degree of the child's adaptation to the environment.

2) The greater the degree of support in the postdischarge environment, the greater the degree of the child's adaptation to the environment.

3) The greater the degree of pre-admission adaptation, the greater the degree of post-discharge adaptation.

4) The greater the degree of adaptation gained in the institution, the greater the degree of post-discharge adaptation.

Hypothesis 2 and, to some extent, hypothesis 1 were supported by the data, which found that the child's perception of family and/or other support, early detection of the child's problem, professional help prior to admission, and parental visiting and involvement during treatment were also associated with the degree of continuity and perceived support in the environment. Little relationship was found between preadmission and postdischarge adaptation. Such factors as problems which were not long standing, age, a stable family situation, and family's knowledge of the availability of help were significantly related to postdischarge adaptation.

Hypothesis 4 was rejected. Adaptation achieved while in treatment was found to be essentially unrelated to postdischarge adaptation, with the exception of parent-child contacts during placement and staff contacts during placement, that is, variables that are more likely related to family adjustment rather than to in-treatment adjustment. In terms of practical implications, the authors suggest the need for continuous family involvement prior to and during treatment and during aftercare.

Kane and Chambers (1961) who view "improvement as a qualitative change in a patient's ability to cope with his environment, irrespective of original diagnosis or extent of illness," followed up 24 children seven years after they had been discharged from a residential center. They theorize that

> since functional illness is a social phenomenon, improvement is also socially determined. And it is this network of complex interactions that makes it next to impossible to quantify improvement in any way that will yield a true picture. . . . Outcome is related not only to original diagnosis but also to a complex of attitudinal and social factors. In many cases one is left to conclude that the critical elements in improvement can never be isolated. Or sometimes, improvement, like beauty, lies in the eyes of the beholder [Kane and Chambers, 1961: 1026]

Their study focuses on such factors as parental attitudes toward the child and satisfaction with posttreatment arrangements, expectations for the child by both parents and people involved in his or her treatment, and the dynamics of family relationships, that is, environmental influences and their effect upon outcome. They conclude that "improvement is determined by the environment and not by clinically established norms" (ibid.).

Davids and associates (1968), recognizing the need for studies of such factors affecting the long-term outcomes of residential treatment, found in their follow-up study that evaluations of adjustment following treatment were unrelated to such treatment variables as IQ, drug therapy, psychotherapy, prognosis, school experiences, or hospital adjustment, but were related to presenting symptoms at the onset of treatment. In his review of the follow-up studies of Brown (1960), Eaton and Menalascino (1967), Rutter (1965), and Eisenberg (1956; 1957), Davids call attention to:

> the generality of the finding that treatment variables (especially conventional psychotherapy) seem to bear little relationship to subsequent adjustment, as indicated in these independent studies, involving children diagnosed as autistic, atypical, schizophrenic or passive-aggressive. Moreover, in several of these follow-up investigations, it has been found that the best predictors of later adjustment were the child's complaints and presenting symptoms at the onset of treatment. These findings suggest that the main factors determining outcome of psychiatric treatment may not be the specific therapies employed but the kinds of symptoms and behaviors the patients bring with them to the treatment setting. [Davids et al., 1968: 474, 475]

Davids quotes Eisenberg as stating, "Our follow-up study fails to reveal any correlation between formal psychiatric treatment and clinical outcome" (ibid.: 473).

These follow-up studies raise fundamental issues about the relation of in-house adjustment to postprogram adjustment and about the extent to which the apparent success of treatment may be due to removal of the child from stressful situations. The studies of Allerhand and associates (1966), Kane and Chambers (1961), and others all indicate that extensive aftercare is essential to marshalling family and community support for sustaining and augmenting gains in treatment. From their findings, it is evident that the effects of residential treatment can be undone or supported and augmented, depending upon the nature and extent of aftercare services. The conditions before and after treatment may, in effect, be more important than the fact that the child was in treatment. Since maturational and situational influences may confound measures of posttreatment outcomes, attempts to measure the outcome of treatment can probably be best measured at discharge with the recognition that long-term adjustment may be a different question. However, to the extent that treatment is extended to take into account these other environmental and maturational variables, by such means as family therapy and aftercare services, the outcome of treatment and the outcome of subsequent adjustment tend to merge, that is, the concept of treatment becomes more salient to the concept of subsequent adjustment and adaptation. Consequently, program evaluation depends to some extent on how narrowly defined the program's goals and responsibilities are.

For example, Benjamin and Weatherly (1947), whose study followed up children after posthospital periods of 1, 2, and 3 years, found that such variables as psychophysical maturation, the interruption of the child-parent neurotic cycle, the decreasing dependency upon parents that came with maturation, and a widening social radius were important in explaining improvement in adjustment. These variables are not treatment ones in the narrow sense, but recognition of their therapeutic significance within a treatment program may make it possible to make treatment perspective more realistic and treatment outcome more durable in its impact on the patient and his or her environment.

The findings of these studies have important program implications. As a result of such a follow-up study, described in a paper by Mora and associates (1969), the Astor Home for Children redirected its focus on in-house residential treatment to a more community-oriented model with preadmission planning with families, intensive aftercare with families or group homes, attempts to mobilize community resources for the children, and the like. The need for such a redirection "became apparent after the children began to be discharged" and "at the end of a five year pilot project. The need for a continuation and expansion of services was obvious even on the basis of the limited data available."[6] In this instance, relatively on-going feedback from limited data was used to broaden the treatment perspectives and expand program goals and activities to include support for posthospital adjustment.

The limitation of such follow-up studies is that they are usually not completed for a long time after the child has been in treatment and thus are unlikely to provide the ongoing feedback necessary for midcourse program corrections. They often, though not necessarily, fail to assess the relative contributions of the different aspects of treatment, that is, psychotherapy, education, group living, separation from family pathology, and so on. Where the findings are not clear-cut or are negative, the results are difficult to interpret. They may indicate that the program was effective, but the child's improvement was undone by return to the community or the situation from which he had been removed.

Paul Lerman (1968), in a provocative interpretation of recidivism as an outcome measure, argues that, if programs claim success when patients do not recidivate after returning to the community, they must likewise hold themselves responsible for those who do recidivate. Why? Because presumably the successes are as much functions of the postinstitutional experience—that is, the result of factors independent of the program—as the failures. In reanalyzing data from a variety of follow-up studies and analyzing the comparability of control groups, Lerman concludes that the criteria of relative failure may be a more accurate and truthful means of evaluating programs than that of relative success.

For example, in reanalyzing data from California's experimental community treatment project (Warren et al., 1966). Lerman points out that the differences between the randomly assigned control and experimental group revocations may have been due to the fact that, although the rates of parole violations were similar, the experimental group was less likely to have their parole revoked than the control group. Consequently, the experimental and control groups appear to differ not in their own behavior but in the behavior of the parole officers with respect to revocation of parole.

In reviewing studies which claim success, he reanalyzes data to include delinquents not counted in final outcome measures because they were dropped from programs before completing the program; these delinquents he describes as "internal failures." Adding these internal failures to the number of delinquents who recidivate, Lerman concludes that private programs have about the same rate of relative failure as public programs, and that in both cases:

> It is not sufficient merely to assume that assessing success is the relevant evaluative problem. One must be willing to face the possibility that the program is associated with high rates of failure. Instead of the success of a program, it might be more relevant to evaluate its failure.
>
> . . . Regardless of the type of program investigated, residential institutions for delinquents . . . are characterized by high rates of potential failure. . . . researchers interested in evaluating new programs should focus on the problem of whether or not (and how) failure rates have been reduced—not whether an institution can claim success. [Lerman, 1968: 56]

Finally, Lerman proposes that successful treatment and humanitarianism are independent issues. In the case of the California Treatment Program experiment for example, he says:

> If lighter sentences do not increase the risk of failure, then why not be more humane and equitable? Keeping boys in the community is undoubtedly a lighter sentence than sending them away. But California has found that this probably does not increase the risk of failure.

. . . If it is decided to advocate humanitarianism in its own right, the social policy issue becomes much clearer. [Lerman, 1968: 64, 63]

In summary, his reinterpretation of the data and the inclusion of "internal failures" bolsters his criticisms of recidivism as a measure by which programs can be evaluated and of the way in which these measures are used to justify a program's funding, philosophy, and treatment of delinquents. His analysis of the concepts of humanitarianism and treatment outcome should help to clarify these issues in program evaluation.

In summarizing the provacative implications of this paper, Lerman (1968: 64) says:

> Social welfare institutions are too heavily subsidized, indirectly and directly, for social workers not to take the responsiblity for knowing what has happened to the people served. A good start can be made by keeping track of all the people not completing treatment, discontinuing service, dropping out of programs, and running away. Rigorous and non-deceptive social book-keeping may yield discomforting facts about agencies' success and reputation. It is hoped that we will be aware of defensive reactions and remind ourselves that we entered social work to serve people in trouble—not established agencies, ideologies and methods.

Problems with outcome criteria, as discussed by Alt (1964), Lerman (1968), and Simon and Gershenson (1956) are but one limitation of outcome studies, whether these be goal-attainment of follow-up studies. Outcome studies have been criticized by Baker (1969), Etzioni (1960), Schulberg and Baker (1968), and others for a variety of reasons, including:

1. The delay in providing relevant feedback about effectiveness to the program.
2. The relative disregard (again, unless designed differently) of the intramural functioning of the program, and hence of the institution as a social system.
3. The inability (unless designed otherwise) to delineate the relative contribution of the various components of the program to the outcome; in other words, emphasis on the net effectiveness of the program.
4. The difficulty in differentiating formal goals from informal and unrecognized goals.

In addition to and aside from such practical considerations as cost, the relative lack of ongoing and useful feedback, and the fact that outcome studies rely heavily on such measures as recidivism, changes in mental health, and interpersonal functioning, outcome studies may be of little value statistically because of inadequate sample size and control groups. There is a trend in the residential treatment of children toward small, decentralized treatment programs, halfway houses, and group homes. Cohen (1969) has delineated the relationship of sample size to statistical power, and it is likely that most studies of residential treatment programs with fewer than ten children would preclude the finding of meaningful significant differences. The lack of adequate sample size is often aggravated by the lack of a randomly assigned control group and the ever-present problems of unreliable and invalid measures of outcome. Where such measures are employed, they are often used in multivariate analysis and thus require relatively large samples which are again precluded by small decentralized programs.

## PROCESS EVALUATION

One strategy for overcoming these limitations of outcome studies is to look at changes in the course of treatment. Majorie Monkman's book, *A Milieu Therapy Program for Behaviorally Disturbed Children* (1972), is an example of process evaluation, which attempts to assess change in individuals as a result of their participation in a treatment program.

The first major goal of the research project was to conceptualize the ongoing service program in such a manner that the significant therapeutic variables could be identified, taught, replicated, and evaluated. Other goals of this research project included: developing useful techniques of child care staff in their interactions with children, developing a training curriculum for staff, establishing clinical criteria for the children's progress and instruments to measure change, and finally "to develop and operate an effective program that produced significant and lasting changes of its residents, in the direction of better social adaptation" (Monkman, 1972: 6).

The study reports in detail many aspects of the program and its development, including staff training and roles, and this would constitute useful reading for anyone operating a behavioral modification program. Although the program faced all the difficulties of conceptualizing complex social behavior and its meaning within a behavioristic framework, the thoroughgoing application of behaviorist principles to so many facets of the program, while at the same time tailoring it to each individual child, is impressive.

However, the study purports to be a process evaluation of efforts to conceptualize the major variables in the milieu, and it must be judged according to its success in this respect. If the crucial variables have successfully been identified and conceptualized, then manipulation of these variables would have a significant impact on the children's behavior.

Four basic instruments were used. One of these was a daily behavior checklist where staff simply checked whether the child had, for example, brushed teeth, reached school on time, made bed, and so on. Scores during orientation provided baselines for choosing any target behaviors for improvement and for measuring subsequent change. Second, each child carried around a daily mark sheet, which listed appropriate social behavior and provided spaces for staff to deduct or assign marks and to indicate how many marks were spent later that day. Although central to the whole reinforcement system, this could not be used for measuring behavior, since reinforcement was inevitably variable and intermittent. Third, a punishment form recorded each sequence of punished behavior in detail and the penalty. Fourth, independent observers filled out ranking sheets of nine samples of each child's behavior.

Basically three types of data are reported which would assess behavioral impact:

1. The self-contained punishment study assigned each child randomly to a time out or loss of marks schedule after the orientation period. After some weeks, each child switched to the other schedules. Findings of this study were that punishable behaviors dropped markedly from the orientation baseline after the schedule was initiated and that they dropped lower on the time out than on the loss of marks system. The difference, however, was not great, and the order in which the schedules were introduced appeared unimportant.
2. Only three children were discussed in detail. On the basis of these, the relation between the treatment plans and, for example, independent observers' ratings were, while suggestive, based on too few cases to say if the behavior was responding to modification.
3. A pilot follow-up study was planned but not reported in detail.

Monkman has attempted to deal with the difficulties of process evaluations, such as delineating the relationship between treatment variables and target behaviors with a sufficiently large sample size. However, the study is still faced with the limitations of a process evaluation vis-à-vis the long-term outcome. As discussed by Allerhand, Weber, and Haug (1966) and Lerman (1968), such process evaluations are limited, since program adjustment is not necessarily related to postdischarge adjustment. Conversely one can legitimately question the effectiveness of a program which demonstrates improved in-house adjustment by means of a process evaluation on the basis of its therapeutic relevance for the patient's adjustment in the community, since presumably, one goal of residential treatment is to improve lifelong adjustment.

A working solution to the dilemma posed by these two different evaluative strategies is suggested by Nelson, Singer and Johnsen (1973). In their work at the Adler Center where Monkman's study was conducted earlier, they suggest a four step model of evaluation. This model of evaluation is of particular interest in that it suggests the need for viewing behavior in a variety of contexts, that is, different stages, and thus addresses itself to the problem discussed previously, that what is often regarded as pathological behavior may be more situations-specific than has been recognized. Knowing the lack of relationship between in-house behavior and pre and post placement behavior, the authors emphasize the importance of evaluating the success of treatment in terms of changing behavior and for different points in time.

1. As a first step in evaluation, they suggest that baseline data be collected prior to admission. It is important at preadmission that unacceptable behavior be specifically delineated and that specific goals be set for the individual which will help the individual to function better in the systems of school, family, and community after discharge from the program.
2. The second step is residential baseline data regarding deviant behavior. Of the relationship between behavior in a residential setting and behavior in a community setting, the authors say:

Because we assume that behavior is situationally determined, it becomes relevant to ask when the deviant behaviors observed in the community (and for which the child had been admitted to a treatment facility) can be elicited in the residential setting. If they do not occur when the child is removed from the community setting, they are inaccessible to modification outside of that setting (at least to those relying on behavioral methods of treatment). If behaviors do occur in the residence, it cannot be assumed they will occur with the same intensity and frequency as they did in the community, and the residential facility will need to determine its own baseline from which to measure progress within the facility. [Nelson et al., 1973: 951]

Some might argue that, although deviant behavior may be different in a residential facility and in the community, it springs from the same underlying pathology or illness, and consequently, treatment will modify the symptoms which occur in the different situations; the authors clearly do not accept this view.

3. The third step in evaluation is behavior at the time of discharge at which point comparisons can be made between behavior at admission and at discharge.

4. The fourth step is community follow-up. It is behavior upon return to the community which is important in the evaluation of a program. In this regard, the authors state:

Most evaluations are limited to steps 2 and 3. However, when viewing behavior from the transactional system model advocated here, steps 1 and 4 become crucial. In fact, evaluations concerning effectiveness of treatment at every level must focus upon and show an appreciation of the network of systems from which the individual developed his particular style of life and behavior patterns. Viewing behavior from an ecological and transactional viewpoint has provided us with a prospective for approaching the criterion problem. We are thus now in a position to answer the question, "how well is the child able to make it back into the community situation?"—which is perhaps the only true criterion for the evaluation of a residential treatment. [Nelson et al., 1973: 952]

What most programs seeking evaluation desire is relatively immediate, concrete, and practical feedback on how to reorganize their activities to achieve their goals. The potential utility of the four step model for small institutions, constrained by time and resources, can be illustrated. One of the authors wrote all of the 171 residential treatment programs listed as Child Welfare League of America members and requested copies of any evaluative studies that had been conducted in order to survey the types of evaluations the programs had undertaken and/or considered worthwhile. Nine studies that could be considered evaluative in a broad sense were returned.

On the basis of this survey, it appears that the programs conducted some low-cost, in-house, informal inquiries into the postdischarge experiences of patients. By and large these studies were essentially descriptive, lacked a control group, and provided some very limited feedback in terms of the effectiveness of the program. However, these inquiries varied in the degree to which they were systematized or comparable, and they contained obvious problems, such as sample size and unclear definitions of success criteria.

If programs conduct their own evaluations, it would be best if they did it in a standardized, systematic way which could be incorporated into the record-keeping system throughout the program's involvement from preadmission to follow-up and aftercare. It would be useful for such programs to develop measures, as is suggested in the four step model of Nelson and associates (1973), of functioning at the different points in time and to build these into the record-keeping system so that they could be compared at different points in time. While the results might be limited for want of control groups, a by-product of research would be to focus attention on what appears to have been previously neglected: both preadmission contacts with children and their families and aftercare services. On-going evaluation could thus be conducted as part of service.

## SYSTEMS EVALUATIONS

### The Supra System

The four step model logically leads to an examination of the residential center within the context of the larger social system, that is, the network of caregivers, the family, and the community. Studies of the epidemiology of "mental illness" among children are relevant to the evaluation of networks of treatment facilities in assessing how well they meet the needs of the children in the population. Presumably in a rational, system-wide allocation of resources, priorities should be assigned and children referred to the most appropriate facilities. The recent work of Langner and associates (1969) and Pappenfort and associates (1968), referred to in the introduction, and that of Sattler and Leppla (1969) are relevant here. The problems of assessing treated, untreated, true prevalence of, and incidence of psychiatric disorders among adults is problematic. The use of diagnostic categories with children and adolescents is more so. Childhood disorders are difficult to diagnose reliably and are likely to be confounded with age-specific disorders (Murphy, 1963), transitory stress reactions, developmental lags, and the like. These problems in assessing the nature and seriousness of psychiatric impairment which are so troublesome for epidemiological studies are equally troublesome for studies which attempt to assess treatment programs by measuring changes in individuals' psychiatric status as a result of treatment.

Maluccio's study, *Residential Treatment of Disturbed Children: A Study of Service Delivery,* examines the delivery of service throughout an entire system rather than within one specific program. It is significant for evaluation in that it documents the extent to which the participation of a residential program in a system of caregivers has vital implications for its success or failure. The study clearly indicates first, that whatever success may have occurred in residential treatment was intimately related to the entire system of services for the child and his family and second, that evaluation of a specific program must consequently consider the larger system of services provided for the child prior to and after discharge from residential treatment.

The study seeks to examine the experiences of 215 children placed in residential treatment under the auspices of the Rhode Island Beneficiary Program between 1964 and 1970. Data for the study were collected from case records and included information about the children, their families, demographic characteristics, contact with agencies and reports from the treatment institutions describing preplacement services, referral, placement, treatment, outcome of treatment and aftercare services. Treatment institutions were also asked to fill out questionnaires regarding treatment because the records were uneven; the use of case records constitutes the limitation of the studies.

In general the children were characterized by a variety of physical and emotional health problems and tended to come from families living at a marginal level with an average income level of about $7,000 per year. Referral for treatment was typically initiated by school or social agency, and in two-thirds of the cases, occurred three or more years after the individual problems were first recognized by a community agency or professional person outside the family. It is significant that residential treatment was often a desperate decision made after the child had had some contact with and exposure to services with his family. Whether these services were adequate to prevent eventual placement or not was not answered, but in general the services tended to be fragmented, uncoordinated, and generally inadequate, which raises the question of how many children might have avoided residential placement had better services been provided.

At the time of the study, 125 children had been discharged. The treatment programs were asked to evaluate the children at time of discharge with the criteria left to the discretion of the institution. About 37% were considered substantially improved; 11%, moderately improved; 22%, minimally improved; and 30%, unimproved. Considering the severity of the children's difficulties, family situation, and conditions prior to placement, such a success rate may be considered satisfactory, although the definitions of success are elusive, and as Alt has pointed out, criteria for measuring success are difficult to agree upon.

Several questions are raised by this finding: (1) Presumably some of the youngsters might have gotten worse and decompensated as a result of placement, yet no category was made for these cases. (2) What is the relationship of success at time of discharge to overall success? Functioning within the context of a sheltered residential program may be very different from functioning in a more stressful life in the community with one's family.

Two-thirds of the children were placed in settings outside Rhode Island which obviously limited the extent to which parents could be involved in treatment programs. The research of Allerhand and associates (1966) and Taylor and Alpert (1973) indicates that such continuity and parental support is crucial to a successful outcome following residential treatment.

Data on postdischarge functioning was fragmentary, and the institutions had no procedures for gathering such information. This raises the issues of the criteria of success: Should evaluation be made at the time of discharge, or should it take into account later adjustment, that is, is it the responsibility of a residential treatment program in defining its success to be responsible for returning an individual to a hazardous, pathogenic environment? The data collected indicated that the treatment institutions did make specific recommendations for aftercare services but that they did little follow-up. Aftercare for the child and his family has been demonstrated to be important in the continuing functioning of the child, and the need was obviously there in these cases.

Maluccio (in press: 15) summarized his study as follows:

> The limitations suggested by this study are not unique; essentially they represent criticisms of the system of residential treatment that have been repeatedly noted in research undertakings, clinical writings, and practice experiences throughout the country. The most serious limitation has to do with the seeming inability of existing community agencies to deal systematically with the needs of the child and his family even after there has been a recognition of emotional disturbance. In case after case, there is evidence of fragmentation of services, insufficient inter-agency collaboration and the poor use of personnel, professional and community resources.

These criticisms are directed at the use of resources both prior to and after placement.

Maluccio's study was employed by a task force examining the beneficiary program of the state of Rhode Island. Recommendations made on the basis of the study included: (1) that the state resources be centralized, and (2) that the responsibility for disturbed children be placed with a single agency in order to provide a focal point for planning and management, to promote a more effective relationship between private agencies and public agencies, and to stimulate a comprehensive program to meet the needs of the children through a closer coordination of services.

Networks of services, such as mental health services, can be studied from the vantage point of either particular agencies within a system of agencies or the flow of patients through the system. In "Network Analysis as a Method for the Evaluation of Service Delivery Systems," Burgess, Nelson, and Wallhaus approach the problem of evaluating entire systems of caregivers by means of a network analysis.

One may argue that a relatively effective program may appear ineffective because of the disorganization of the community or the lack of support services following discharge. Clearly the effectiveness of any individual institution is, to a large extent, related to the parameters and constraints of the whole network of services. As residential treatment programs develop a more open, community orientation, it will be necessary for program evaluation to consider the constraints imposed on particular agencies by the network of services of which they are an integral part. The proposal to apply network analysis is significant for program evaluation in that it provides a conceptual framework for viewing the institution in the context of the larger system.

The authors develop measures for defining the effectiveness of the system by looking at the amount of time a person spends in an agency and his progress through the network. They also develop measures of "cycling" or repetitions of contacts with an agency, which suggest that services failed to meet their stated goals. The authors suggest that a variety of problems in services delivery (e.g., reasons for cycling, comparative effectiveness of outpatient and inpatient services, etc.) can be approached using a network analysis approach.

Thomas, in "Community-Oriented Care in Children's Institutions" (1972), gives a preliminary report of an attempt to evaluate and experiment with a statewide network of child care services. In the first year of the project, the researchers developed a survey designed to assess the extent to which the child care institutions in Georgia were community versus non-community-oriented, and to provide base-line data for assessing the impact of programs introduced to change existing institutions toward greater community orientations. Three different strategies of change were then utilized in a quasi-experimental manner to assess techniques for changing the institutions. The assessment of these different strategies for change was a goal of the second year of the project.

Thomas describes the rationale for these experiments:

> Two basic criticisms are leveled against children's institutions. First, they are charged with adjusting children to institutions rather than preparing them for a return to community living. Secondly, they are viewed as refusing to serve or otherwise not serving those children most in need of residential care. . . . Our experiment must seek to reverse these conditions, in as many ways as possible. We aim to reduce the focus on institutional adjustment and foster preparation for community living. We also aim at moving institutions toward accepting more and more difficult and other types of children such as sibling groups—in need of residential care but not now getting it.
>
> In part, these goals can be approached only in so far as we move institutions away from acceptance of their dumping ground role and toward an aggressive innovative stance in providing services to children in need. They must become increasingly agressive, also in demanding responsible and continuing involve-ment from parents, agencies and others in the lives of children in residence. Finally, they must be moved toward a conscious awareness of and prevention of the process of institutional adjustment. [Memorandum of the Regional Institute of Social Welfare, School of Social Work, University of Georgia, p. 1]

Five instruments were developed for obtaining data on the children and their families. Nearly all of the resident children (1,800) had been tested throughout the system and these data had been used to examine the effects of staff-child inter-action on treatment and to assess the effects of the structure of programs on children. Another group of instruments was collected to assess the staffs' orienta-tion toward their jobs, their receptivity to community-oriented care, and their philosophy about child-rearing practices.

The institutions selected for the study varied in terms of their current baseline of community orientedness. While it was clearly impossible to assign institutions randomly to different conditions, reasonably experimental conditions were im-posed in that they were matched on the basis of previously known baseline information, the agendas for change were similar, and the roles of staff as change agents were comparable. Each approach differed in the way it sought to use participants in the discussions to stimulate social pressure and to provide informa-tion relevant to family-oriented care.

The content or focus for the three different approaches to bringing about change was identical and had essentially two dimensions. The first dimension emphasized responding to community need with subparts defining service needs, processing of services needs, and adaptation to new ones. The second dimension emphasized preparing residents for return to the community through institutional program experiences, through decision-making involvement, and through preparation in placement planning and follow-up services.

One of the preliminary findings reported by the principal investigator at a conference was the effect of decentralizing decision-making in institutions. The principal investigator suggested that, in decentralized institutions, the staff have more impact on the behavior of children than staff in institutions where decision making takes place at higher levels. He suggested that, if you have good staff in an institution, decentralize it and they may be more effective in working with children. If you have poor staff, "keep them under your thumb" and prevent them from doing harm. These findings were based on data derived from questionnaires and collected from the staff and children in various institutions. These tentative findings and many others which should be forthcoming in final reports and publications will no doubt be of great value in understanding the processes of residential treatment and exploring strategies for changing both individual institutions and systems of institutions toward improved, community-oriented care.

In terms of research such a program is of great significance in that, systems-wise, it deals with the entire state system of child care services, develops baseline measures, and experiments with different strategies for increasing community orientation. The extent to which a technique is successful can be assessed in comparison to baseline data and to institutions which used other techniques. In short, the research is remarkable for its scope and its attempt to utilize, in so far as is possible, relatively rigorous experimental procedures. It promises to shed much light on the relative effectiveness of various techniques in orienting child care institutions to community needs and to preparing children for return to the community rather than for life in institutions.

Lewis (1968) reports results of a preliminary evaluation of the Re-Ed project, which has been described elsewhere (Hobbs 1964; 1966). The data gathered in the evaluation of the program reflect the program's emphasis upon the ecological context of the child's behavioral difficulties and, by implication, the program's and the evaluation's recognition of the fact that the effect of any institution is determined largely by its place within the larger social system. For example, Lewis (1968: 17) says:

> Because of the ecological bias in appraising children's problems, in establishing goals and developing programs of re-education, the data gathered to help evaluate the effectiveness of the Re-Ed schools lean heavily on the perceptions of the child by those who are his natural evaluators: his parents, teachers, and peers. They are asked to describe him during the application process—before he is enrolled in the Re-Ed school—on check lists, rating scales, open ended questions and sociometric questionnaires. They describe his behavior again after he has returned from the Re-Ed school and still again after he has been home for more than a year. These periodic assessments are

aimed at plotting changes in valence of the child for those who know him
best and whose judgments about the adequacy of his performance are most
potent. This emphasis in evaluation is based on the assumption that a more
positive appraisal of the child's performance is essential to reinstatement of
mutually rewarding relationships that in the past have been blocked during
the time he was seen "as emotionally disturbed."

Data were collected a few weeks prior to admission, 5 to 6 months after
discharge, and 18 to 20 months after discharge. At these points, the following
instruments were used:

1. The child's mother, the worker from the referring agency, and the liason
   teacher assessed the child's behavior on a five point scale ranging from
   "worse" to "greatly improved."
2. On a symptom check list of 36 behaviors "ascribed for emotionally disturbed
   children," the parents were asked to indicate the frequency of each behavior
   in the preceding two weeks.
3. A Social Maturity Scale adapted from the Vineland Social Maturity Scale was
   filled out by the parents.
4. A semantic differential scale measured the discrepancy between what the
   child was like in comparison to what the parents wanted the child to be like,
   with 19 items, such as happy, sad, adventurous, and timid.
5. On a scale developed to assess student role behavior, 27 questions were
   presented, such as "Does he usually listen well enough to understand directions?" and "Is he careless or lazy about his work?" These items were
   designed to reflect teachers' expectations of the child.
6. Tapping another facet of the child's adjustment, sociometric data were
   collected by the child's peers, such as "Who would you invite to your
   birthday party?" of "Who would you not invite to your birthday party?"

In general the three separate observers—parents, teachers, and peers (i.e., his or
her natural evaluators)—who know the child in different contexts, found that about
three-fourths of the children seemed to have improved on a variety of dimensions.
In discussing the results Hobbs (1964: 24) states:

> We are faced with the very real question of how much an emotionally
> disturbed child's behavior may be expected to change simply by getting a
> year or two older and having additional experiences and opportunities that
> had not been available before. The social maturity scale is the most extreme
> example of this source of uncertainty. One would be surprised if the child,
> even one who could be called emotionally disturbed, did not have signifi-
> cantly higher social maturity ratings after a lapse of two years. Our concern is
> evaluating a program of treatment is the extent to which one may attribute
> the change to treatment rather than to maturation alone.

The author is obviously aware of the problems of conducting evaluative studies in
the absence of an appropriate control group, and so on. It goes without saying that
one would expect an improvement in social maturity in the course of almost two
years between the pre and post observations.

However, the study is of interest as an evaluative study in that the instruments are tailored to assess the goals of the program, namely, to achieve a greater harmony between the child and his or her family, community, and school. This is related to the goal of the Re-Ed program, not to treat a disturbed child with a specific psychopathology but instead to change a disturbed ecological unit, that is, to make the child more acceptable and his environment more accepting.

A study by Bower and associates (1969) of the Re-Ed project, while not a systems approach, illustrates another strategy of evaluation: observation by a panel of experts knowledgeable in the field of residential child care. The evaluators made relatively independent observations of the program over a period of years and in the process, shared and discussed them. Given their experience and knowledge of the field, and considering the problems of evaluative research, such an approach to evaluation may prove useful and inexpensive. Concerning the issues of evaluation and of sustaining support for the program on the basis of such an evaluation, Hobbs, says in the introduction (to Bower et al., 1969: 2):

> The idea of asking four men to watch closely the development of a project and to assert finally their appraisal of it is a simple one. Statistical results however favorable seldom determine the fate of social institutions. What is most important in assessing a new idea is the evaluation of informed, competent, professional observers whose judgement is respected by their professional colleagues and by the decision makers in society.

We will return to this idea, of observation by a professional as a means of evaluation, at a later point.

### The Residential Center as a Social System

Another type of systems evaluation is the analysis of the residential center as a social system. Systems analyses are evaluative in the sense that they examine the functional and dysfunctional aspects of programs and the extent to which programs meet the requirements or prerequisites of social systems. A systems-type evaluation may examine a program in terms of the efficiency of its allocation of resources. Intramural program evaluation in a systems perspective, in contrast to evaluations of the supra systems of which the residential program is but a part, addresses itself simultaneously to the overall, net efficiency of the total program and to the relative contribution of each system or component of the program, such as therapy, education, and child care.

One such study is *The Dynamics of Residential Treatment* (1968) by Polsky and Claster in collaboration with Goldberg in which the analysis of social systems is utilized to conceptualize the dynamics of residential treatment. They discuss the goals of this research and its implications for residential treatment and the role of child care workers as follows:

> We probe beneath the label "residential worker" to examine the actual demands and responsibilities placed upon this pivotal position. If we can uncover the interplay of functional activities in the role, we can begin to develop the appropriate training program for persons in charge of this

complex system. A valid portrayal of the diverse functions within the overall
role may enable us to develop a more effective treatment approach to cottage
and institutional life. [Polsky and Claster, 1968: 11]

The authors relate Parson's (1951) functional imperatives to four major aspects of
the child care worker's role: (1) nurturer and comforter; (2) counselor, guide, and
teacher; (3) mediator, integrator, and custodian; and (4) monitor and supervisor.
Using these functional roles, the authors analyze the role of the cottage worker
within the social system of the cottage and the larger institution.

The research model for the study was based on cottage comparison. Modes of
staff functioning in each of the three cottages were compared. Individual counselors' methods were contrasted, differences among cottage peer groups were
assessed, and finally, these different levels of comparisons were interrelated. Data
were collected in the course of systematic observations which were carried on in
three senior cottage units and represented systematic and comprehensive observations of cottage life. Schedules were established for making observations, and
observers were trained in the demarcation and coding of events. The final observation schedule consisted of 31 items and an instruction manual which specified
guidelines for coding events and pinpointing the criteria for coding distinctions.

Reliabilities of the observations consisted of two aspects:

1) The first is selection of the event and the reliability in coding the content
   of the event. In selecting events, reliabilities were established by having
   two observers select events and rate them over a three week period prior to
   the period of the study. Reliabilities for coding 218 dually observed events
   ranged between 57% and 98% with a median of 69%.
2) Items involved in the coding of items concerning monitoring, guidance,
   support and integration were coded less reliably due to the greater amount
   of inference required. They were coded with 50% agreement for the boy's
   behavior and 59% for the staff behavior and were judged to reflect
   difficulties inherent in such complex judgement. [Polsky and Claster,
   1968: 34]

For one such item on the observation scale, item 20, there was 50% agreement on
the function emphasized by staff in the initial period. It increased to 75% during
the middle phase and fell off to 56% in the final phase. The authors say of their
levels of reliability:

On the basis of this experience we would emphasize the need for greater
sustained attention to the reliability of the observations than was maintained
in this study. [Polsky and Claster, 1968: 34]

The comment speaks for itself and for the study which is based on these data and
their coding.

Observations about staff functioning in relation to the boys in each of three
different cottages were compared. In addition, staff variability within the three
cottages was examined by analyzing the content of staff-child interaction in terms
of variations in and contrasts of the different functional imperatives that staff

emphasized. Breakdowns of the emphasis of functions by boys and counselors were made on the basis of individual cottage, staff, and boy.

In discussing the findings, the authors state:

> We take the position that there is no fixed pattern of counselor emphasis that is best for all situations, but that each group must be diagnosed and a plan formulated in relation to this diagnosis. At this point, let us simply state some working principles that should be taken into account in developing such a group treatment plan.
>
> 1) Autonomy—The resident group should learn to run itself.
> 2) The ultimate primacy of the consummatory functions—for a resident group to function autonomously it must not get bogged down in the instrumental activities of custodial and individual gratification; it must eventually see instrumental functions as the means to achieve the ultimate gratifications of goal attainment in integration.
> 3) Time sequence of functions—staff should not move too quickly toward consummatory functions. There is a natural sequence of group development, as there is in individual child development. In the case of the residential cottages, a foundation of adaptation and individual gratification must be achieved first. The success of the goal attainment in the integration effort is built on this foundation.
> 4) Identification—If the group respects a counselor they may begin an activity to win his approval even though they don't see it as meeting their needs at the time.
> 5) Internalization—An activity at first carried out to gain adult approval can come to be satisfying in itself as it becomes part of the residents' value structure. [Polsky and Claster, 1968: 60]

Such a group treatment plan, while tentative, takes into account the nature of the group, how the various functions are met, the variations within the group and among different individual and group roles, and it represents an attempt at a more precise prescription for creating and using a therapeutic milieu. The degree to which the "treatment plan" is carried out can be assessed quantitatively and its effect determined. In short, such a system analysis of the group provides the theoretical basis for developing and assessing treatment plans.

The authors use the concept of role to examine the nature of peer group structures and describe emergent roles in the peer group, that is, the responsibilities that exist before anyone steps in to meet them. For example, there may be a battle between two boys for leadership of cottage peers. The leadership position for which they are struggling is a role and the struggle itself is evidence that there is something meaningful for which they are competing. The degree of peer group structure was measured by determining the extent to which there was a consensus on who the incumbents of given roles were. The cottages were found to differ not so much in the roles per se as in the degree of respect afforded different roles.

The relationship between peer group structure and cottage management is subsequently explored. In general, it is suggested that, while personality characteristics may explain some of the qualities of the peer group, the peer group also responds to the staff, staff's enacting of roles, and their selective emphasis on functional imperatives. The authors suggest that, as a result of the stronger emphasis on integration found in one cottage, the cottage had developed more positive peer roles than the other cottages.

Going beyond the relation of peer group structure, values, and role emphasis to look at the cottage staff, the authors related data to the larger institution:

> Based upon the data that we have gathered, we can make several interpretations about the worker's role in the cottage and the institution. The unanticipated consequences of the custodial emphasis is the imposition of minimumly accepted standards upon the residents in the cottage. The minimum standard performance tends to become a common pattern for most residents and thus become maximum standards for them. Minimum performance by workers and residence leads to a discrepancy in the organizational goals held by the administrators and the way of life that is generated in the cottages. Pressures are then placed upon supervisors to check more closely upon cottage workers. This increases the visability of the actual relationship between workers and residents in the cottage, leads to increasing tensions, and disturbs the equilibrium of the system. [Polsky and Claster, 1968: 49]

Some of the more significant achievements of the authors are their development and application of a social systems perspective, their analysis and description of the program, and their attempt to provide or to develop empirical measures to describe and evaluate the program. The authors state:

> In advancing a concept of residential care which includes description, evaluation and planning for a cottage social system, we are indicating an ideal. It does not, of course, come about all at once. But in time and with proper training we suggest a team of cottage workers can learn to develop rather comprehensive plans for cottages and periodically reassess and reformulate them within this social system theory of child care. [Polasky and Claster, 1968: 149-150]

It is in this regard that Polsky and Claster make the most important contribution to the evaluation of residential treatment programs, namely, analyzing and describing them within the theoretical framework of a social systems analysis. Whatever the limitations, specifically the reliability of their observations and the usefulness of the functional imperatives, their emphasis on the residential treatment program as a social system will go a long way toward achieving their goal of formulating the empirical work on a sufficiently broad theoretical base so as to render it applicable with minimum variation to small group systems in diverse other settings as well. The significance of their application of a systems approach is expressed succinctly by Leonard S. Cottrell of the Russell Sage Foundation which sponsored the study:

> . . . a sophisticated analysis of the social and cultural processes in a given institution is a basic requirement for any intelligent planning for the development of a therapeutic milieu. This is no job for amateurs. The level of technical knowledge and skill required is fully comparable to that required for the understanding of intrapsychic processes.

... the mere juxtaposition of a social science based restructuring of the institutional milieux and a clinical procedure based on one or another of the variants psychodynamic theory will not be sufficient for an adequate program. Clinical analysis and treatment directed toward the individual must be conducted with a clear knowledge and understanding of what is taking place in the social context; and the strategy of milieu structuring must take fully into account the clinical analyses of the person involved. [Polsky and Claster, 1968: 7, 8]

Another contribution is their sensitivity to the many conflicts inherent in the custodial and therapeutic responsibilities of the resident care workers. For example, they conclude that overbearing concern with the custodial functions is incompatible with therapeutic goals. They suggest that the solution is to upgrade the child care worker's job by implementing

1) a new concept of child care work that transcends the custodial emphasis but does not deny its crucial importance,
2) a training program in which workers can develop practical group and community skills and a deeper theoretical understanding of working with residents so as to constantly increase their decision making and autonomy; and
3) recruitment of more competent workers who can be trained to assume these new tasks in child care. [Polsky and Claster, 1968: 177]

Objective descriptions and theoretical understandings of residential treatment programs, such as provided by *The Dynamics of Residential Treatment,* are essential to the development of more effective, objective, and transmittable ways of organizing and maintaining residential treatment programs for children.

In an earlier study, Polsky and Kohn (1959) adapted Bales's Interaction Process Analysis (1950) to produce individual and group curves and to pin down pathological group processes in order to study groups before, during, and after therapeutic intervention. The study is significant for showing how strategic areas for intervention into the cottage culture could be identified, which helped to bring the cottage culture into line with larger therapeutic goals and values, that is, to allow more efficient use of the cottage and the group as a therapeutic tool.

*Cottage Six: The Social System of Delinquent Boys in Residential Treatment* (1962) by Polsky, is a study of the often-neglected impact of peer group cultures on residential treatment. It was a participant observation study of a cottage, which was generally regarded as the toughest in a large residential treatment program. The book is significant in that it emphasizes the need for understanding both intrapsychic phenomena and the subculture or peer group influence on therapeutic endeavors.

In analyzing the delinquent subculture in *Cottage Six,* Polsky delineates the norms, activities, internal organization, and the personalities of the members involved in the delinquent subculture. In a section on deviant processes, he suggests that there are five different styles of interaction and corresponding peer group roles which members learn to conform to and which reaffirm group norms.

The boys in fact spent the majority of their time with peers, while the professional staff, who are in many ways closest to individual boys, are paradoxically the farthest removed from the cottage sub-culture.

... The staff are not only isolated from the boys in the functioning of the institution; they are also remote from the boys in terms of their cultural backgrounds and values [Polsky, 1962: 150]

Summarizing his analysis of the delinquent subculture and its relationship to the longer organization and therapeutic goals, Polsky (1962: 170) says:

While the professional staff are preoccupied with changing individual boys' values and personality structures, the cottage social organization subverts their efforts. A stable pattern of accommodation emerges between cottage staff and boys, on one hand and, on the other, between the professional and non-professional child care staff. These systems cooperate implicitly to sustain the boys' organization in the cottage. The tough aggressive peer leader in the community covertly receives recognition not only from the cottage staff but from the removed professional group as well.

Polsky's study is a systems evaluation in that it analyzes the delinquent subgroup within the context of therapeutic goals and the organization of the residential treatment facility. It is also an example of the usefulness of participant observation, and the data clearly demonstrate the way in which the organizational goals were subverted by the delinquent subculture.

Finally, a book of readings by Polsky and associates, *Social System Perspectives in Residential Treatment* (1970), seeks to "present, within a coehesive theoretical framework, an accumulating base of theory and treatment in residential institutions" (Polsky et al., 1970: 3). The book examines, within a general theory of social action framework, the way residential treatment institutions maintain themselves, adapt to external and internal changes, and most important, the way many unintended consequences of residential institutions affect the achievement of therapeutic goals.

In general the book is valuable in that it represents a much needed attempt to "demonstrate that contemporary social science does have an over-arching theory that is useful to practitioners" (Polsky et al., 1970: 3). In terms of the attempt to conceptualize residential treatment from a social systems perspective and in terms of the content of the articles, the book makes a significant and useful contribution.

Although most of the articles are not specifically relevant to the analysis, and in that sense, to evaluation of residential treatment programs for disturbed children, some articles do deal with the organizational dilemmas inherent in residential treatment. For example, Piliavin's article, "Conflict between Cottage Parents and Caseworkers" (1963), describes a study of the attitudes of cottage parents and caseworkers toward each other as expressed in interviews. In both custodial and treatment-oriented programs, including one that sought to meliorate the commonly recognized mutual antagonisms, he found that the caseworkers were critical of cottage parents because of their emphasis on control, their intrusion into casework, and their inability to carry out treatment plans. Conversely, cottage parents tended to regard caseworkers as unrealistic in regard to their relations with children and their expectations about "treatment." Concurrent with these mutually negative attitudes was the fact that caseworkers and cottage parents had little formal or even informal contact. The author questions whether more contact between them might exacerbate the conflict. In conclusion, the author suggests a major restructuring of the roles, such as locating caseworkers in the cottage or having one professional assigned both casework and cottage parent responsibilities.

In "Changing Delinquent Subcultures: A Social Psychological Approach" (1970), Polsky discusses methods for evaluating change in the group's structure and interaction. Rather than trying to assess changes in individual personality traits and attitudes, he says:

> Any evaluative program for gauging change in a group natural setting offers tremendous problems for those who are sticklers for reliability and validity. The fact is, we have little systematic knowledge of successful intervention in a delinquent group as an ongoing social system. Although there have been more than seventy years of experimentation with these strategies, little work has been done to date to validate their therapeutic influence. Empirical experiments are sorely lacking in the field.

> The measurement of change from a delinquent social structure to a less delinquent one involves focusing upon the boys' interactions, the group norms and roles, and the extent of involvement in nondeviant activities. Each one of these realms of group processes can be defined in operational terms. In our studies, we have focused primarily on peer group interactional processes as a basic criterion of change. [Polsky, 1970: 696]

These and other articles are of both substantive and theoretical value. Although the diversity of the articles and their theoretical framework precludes a tighter integration into a theory of social action, the book provides a much needed social systems perspective, viewing treatment endeavors in a social context and viewing that context holistically and in terms of the interrelations of the various components.

Henry, in an article entitled "Types of Institutional Structures" (1957), also employs a systems approach to contrast two types of social structures characteristic of residential treatment centers. The author describes four types of structures and contrasts the structure characteristic of the Sonia Shankman Orthogenic School with that of a more traditional and psychiatric hospital.

The Orthogenic School is regarded as a structure with simple, undifferentiated subordination: there is one director with a staff responsible for all phases of the operation. The staff are responsible for the child care and individual psychotherapy and have an intense involvement in all phases of the child's life. Contrasted with this is a system with multiple, differentiated subordination. In such a system the therapeutic tasks of a psychiatric hospital are typically broken down into nursing care, individual psychotherapy, child care, educational programs, occupational therapy, and the like. Staff, such as nurses, are subject to multiple supervision, from physicians, from charge nurses, from the department head, and so on.

This paper is extremely important as an attempt to analyze the types of social structures utilized in various organizations and to trace out the impact these social systems have on the values, roles, and relationships of staff, the systems of authority, and the role of the director. In mental health settings particularly many organizational problems are understood in terms of psychological explanations, such as personality conflicts.[7] The relative lack of awareness of how programs are organized in relation to their goals in startling when contrasted with the level of psychological awareness, which, while valuable, is not necessarily applicable and often reflects relative naivete about organizational analysis, social structure, and the analysis of social structures vis-à-vis their implications for therapy.

Approaching these problems from a systems perspective, this paper explicates the ways in which particular structures affect the endeavors of the actors in the systems; such as analysis, of how the program is organized to achieve its goals, is essential as the first step of evaluation.

In a table contrasting the two different organizations with regard to their physical plants, task performances, worker personalities, and directors, Henry (1957: 59) summarizes the differences in terms of the actors' expectations which are logically related to the way the programs are organized:

> The differences presented in this table are paralleled by differences in value orientation. A review of the analysis of the structures and their properties shows that the differences between them are identifiable, specific and systematic, and thus leaves no doubt that the identified properties are inseparately related to the structure types. From this it flows that, when certain properties, such as autonomy and attachment, are desired, a specific type of structure must be devised to produce them as a necessary consequences; and that when certain properties appear within the system, their origins must be sought first in the structure of the system.

In summary, Henry's article illuminates a much neglected area of residential treatment, the organization of programs vis-à-vis their goals and the far-reaching consequences of specific organizations for the actors. It is an excellent example of a systems analysis.

## Comparison of System Efficiency

Where program evaluation is concerned, comparative evaluations may be difficult because, as Henry's article illustrates, each program may present a unique configuration or organization of its activities. A difficulty for comparative evaluations arises in that there may not be systematic points of comparison between programs. Evaluation must consequently take into account the concepts of equicausality and equifinality. In brief equicausality means that you can arrive at different ends with the same initial factors and, conversely, equifinality means that you can arrive at the same end by different routes. In short, residential treatment can be provided in a variety of ways and there are many different configurations of the basic elements for caring for and treating children. Given the problem of defining clearly what successful treatment is, much less defining clear, reliable, and valid operational measures, the possibilities for comparative outcome studies with instruments which are relevant across programs are severely limited.

In fact, however, people choose between programs, and comparative evaluations are of practical value, however limited they may be theoretically. It is unlikely that new programs will be created but more likely that custodially-oriented programs will be upgraded in the direction of a treatment orientation. Presumably comparative evaluation of some sort will play a role in these choices.

An excellent example of a comparative evaluation of the effectiveness of different types of institutions is *Organization for Treatment* (Street et al., 1966). It is of particular interest to a systems evaluation in that, while it seeks to assess outcomes in the different institutions, it avoids the difficulties and lack of applicability of outcome studies because it deals with the issue of how effectively institutions are organized to achieve their goals. The study is also unique in that it provided relatively ongoing feedback to the institutions which allowed them to make "midcourse" corrections; this relatively immediate use of data is often impossible with outcome studies.

It is also of interest in that it portrays a variety of resources for the treatment of delinquents. In this country, 50% of the delinquents are treated in what would roughly be considered custodial orientation, while the remaining delinquent population is divided equally among the treatment and reeducational-developmental institutions. The data on inmate and staff attitudes in these institutions have important implications for our ideas about the treatment of delinquents.

Its strategy of evaluation is to compare the different institutions chosen on the basis of their different philosophies of treatment and organizational structures and to relate these differences to measures relevant to evaluation, namely, attitudes of staff toward inmates and of inmates toward staff, the program, themselves, and peers. A comparative evaluation of different organizations and of their impact on inmates at one point in time has the advantage of avoiding a follow-up study and the methodological and practical problems involved with it. As criteria for success it uses positive attitudes about staff, institution, and peers instead of measures of recidivism and the like. The assumption is made that positive evaluations of the institution and personnel can be equated with success and thus are the criteria for evaluations of comparative success.

The authors describe their research as:

> . . . comparative, inclusive and to some extent longitudinal. We studied a non-random sample of 6 institutions, selected to maximize differences in goals but including both public and private, and large and small organizations. The study was inclusive in embracing all major levels of organizational activity along with relevant groups external to the institutions. It was longitudinal not only in that we attempted to reconstruct the histories of these organizations but also in that we collected the major bodies of our data at two points in time, although only one year apart. [Street et al., 1966: 22-23]

Six institutions were chosen which emphasized one of these goals: (1) obedience and conformity, (2) re-education and development, and (3) treatment. The researchers had hoped to find an institution reflecting mixed goals, but did not. Data were collected by making observations of all aspects of the program. Interviews, both structured and unstructured, of all segments of the staff, including administrators, educators, and inmates, were conducted; anonymous questionnaires were administered to both staff and inmates. A search of the records and written material describing the program was made in order to provide demographic and other information about staff and inmates. Two surveys were taken approximately a year apart to provide data on the impact of more recent treatment orientations in the institutions. Between the first and second wave of questionnaires, executive seminars were set up so that data derived from the first study could be fed back to the organization, both to facilitate change and to make the evaluative data more readily available to the institutions.

One of the important hypotheses tested was whether institutions' goals would have an effect on the organization and on the behavior of staff and inmates, that is, whether the treatment ideology affected the organization and roles of those within the organization. Briefly, the results of the study indicate that the goals of the institutions were reflected to a large extent in organizational behavior and attitudes, including staff perceptions of the institution, their beliefs about the inmates, and their techniques for handling inmates. Executive strategies in dealing with the external environment, defining staff roles and tasks, and the internal organization were similarly found to be related to goals. It was found that staff-inmate authority relations, rewards and sanctions, and the characteristic types of control were generally related to the type of organization and to staff perception of the inmates. The more treatment- or educationally oriented programs had more positive responses in terms of inmate attitudes than the obedience-conformity institutions.

Some of the other interpretations of the findings raise questions about Goffman's stereotype of the total institution (1961). The study indicated that the six institutions varied considerably with regard to their internal structure and orientation to patients, and that the stereotype of the total institution was just that—a stereotype—often inexact in particular cases. Other findings were that executives were relatively ignorant of many aspects of their organization, including the backgrounds of staff and the daily activities of individuals. In all institutions the executives were concerned about staff not relating properly to the inmates. Depending upon the type of institution, the executives felt that staff were either overly involved (in the treatment setting) or not strict enough (in the custodial setting). The authors suggest that there is a need for executives to have ongoing and current information about the functioning of their institution and staff.

In these comparative evaluations, significant data were the responses of the inmates about the value of the institution, their perceptions of relationships with staff, their self-concepts, and their attitudes about peers and the inmate culture. Some of the variation in these attitudes could be explained by background information, such as number of arrests and convictions and socioeconomic background, which was related to the selective recruitment of inmates. Despite this factor, inmate attitudes about the institutions and themselves were related to the nature of the institution. Thus, while some of the variance could be accounted for by the characteristics of the inmate population, the effects of the organization, its goals, and its relationships were pronounced.

Delinquent subculture and peer group resistance to institutional change have been the concerns of both correctional and treatment programs. The study found that the leaders and followers were more antagonistic to institutions with a custodial orientation and consequently sought to subvert it. Their subversion often entailed playing it cool and appearing to conform while subverting the system. In the same institutions, staff held negative and antagonistic views of peer groups and, as a result, were likely to set in motion a self-fulfilling prophecy, which further antagonized and exacerbated the conflict.

In conclusions drawn from this study, the authors suggest that the success of the re-education and developmental type programs was close to that of the far more costly treatment-oriented ones, as measured by inmates' perception of the institution, self-concept, and so on. They caution, however, that the differences may have been the result of the fact that the re-education programs were smaller, the fact that they were relatively open institutions, and consequently, that their inmates were involved in the community. Should these institutions have developed their own schools and become closed, they might have been found to "backslide" to the level of the more custodial programs. This finding is suggestive and provides some empirical data for the introduction of treatment concepts into correctional facilities. However, differences in the institutions could theoretically be explained in terms of other variables such as size, unique history, staff commitment, and the like, and it is difficult to extrapolate because of the uncontrolled variables.

The authors were concerned with the introduction of a treatment orientation into custodial institutions. They did not find a bifurcation between treatment-oriented and custodial staff, but they did suggest that the success of making such a transition was, to a large extent, dependent upon the way in which the treatment orientation was introduced into the program and the degree of support and flexibility staff had in implementing programs. There are many ramifications associated with the introduction of a treatment orientation based on the model of two person therapy into an institution, and enthusiastic support and leadership are necessary ingredients in integrating the treatment orientation with a basically custodial one.

## Descriptive Studies

Much of the research to date has been descriptions of individual treatment programs written by people involved in these programs, and frequently the descriptive accounts are mixed with efforts to explicate and justify a particular program's approach and rationale. These descriptions are perhaps the first level of evaluative research, and some of these are included here, either because of their historical importance or because they deal with systems at a more descriptive level.

Relatively few residential treatment programs have been created de novo. More typically they have evolved from orphanages and shelters on the one hand, or from hospitals seeking to minimize the hospital culture because of its inappropriateness for socializing children, on the other. Alt's book, *Residential Treatment for the Disturbed Child* (1960), provides an engaging account of the evolution of a residential treatment program from its early days as a state training school, when the neighbors were notified by a blast on the powerhouse whistle that a boy had run away and that anyone returning him would receive a reward. The book is of particular value as a record, documented with personal observations and memoranda of the transition. This transition is of particular relevance because it is unlikely that many new treatment programs will be built to provide treatment for the many disturbed; more likely, existing institutions will change in the direction of becoming more treatment-oriented. Other literature which discusses such transitions and traces out the repercussions on staff, patients, and communication of changes in administrative or formal systems can be found in Berman (1961), Konopka and others (1961), and the previously cited preliminary study of Thomas (1972).

Descriptive studies of residential treatment programs for children which are historically important include Reid and Hagen's *Residential Treatment of Emotionally Disturbed Children: A Descriptive Study* (1952), Loughmiller's book *Wilderness Road* (1965), the Child Welfare League of America's publication *From Chaos to Order: A Collective View of Residential Treatment of Children* (1972), and Martin Gula's *Agency Operated Group Homes: A Casebook* (1965).

While not evaluative in nature, Reid and Hagan's study developed comparative descriptions which provide baseline information about 12 different residential treatment programs. With regard to determining the comparative efficacy of the treatment programs, the authors (1952: viii) state:

> Determination of the comparative efficacy of treatment procedures used must await a much greater refinement of research method than is available at the present. Longitudinal, clinical studies may be necessary to resolve these questions. However, at this stage of knowledge these different approaches to the treatment of children are a positive manifestation. For, were only one method followed, discovery of new techniques in this area would be seriously jeopardised.

This statement continues to be applicable to the determination of the comparative efficacies of treatment procedures and of residential treatment itself.

A similar casebook, edited by Gula, describes 15 group homes and is significant in that the use of group homes in the treatment of disturbed children is increasing. While descriptive in a nuts-and-bolts fashion, *Agency Operated Group Homes: A Casebook* (Gula, 1965) does provide some basic data on how a variety of group homes is sponsored, organized, and used for treatment. This approach is relevant given the trend away from large total institutions and the attempt to develop community-based facilities to avoid the problems of prolonged institutionalization, as well as to prepare children for community living.

*From Chaos to Order: A Collective View of Residential Treatment of Children* (1972), written by a variety of task forces drawn from members of the American Association of Children's Residential Centers, provides an overview of problems in residential treatment. Among other topics, it deals with the administrative problems of interrelating residential treatment and individual psychotherapy in the residential setting, the elements and structure of a therapeutic milieu, and the roles of child care workers and teachers in the residential setting. In the introduction, the current state of affairs in residential treatment is described as follows:

> Residential treatment is today trembling on the brink of becoming a science. Until recently, it was about at the same level of sophistication as say,

motherhood; it was humane, intimate, complicated and important, but rather undescribable and unqualifiable—some people did it well, some poorly and it was hard to tell anyone "how to".

In the hands of many current practitioners it has gradually come to assume the dimensions of a skill and a practice; in the hands of a few it is becoming almost a science. We might say that we are in the alchemist stage of development; we have many questions and many methods, but we are not always sure that our answers are the right ones, or that our methods will bring us answers to them. [Child Welfare League of America, 1972: 1]

In a section on organization, communication, and structure, the authors summarize the book by saying that the recurrent organizational problems in residential treatment, some of which are characteristic of all organizations, must be given attention if the organizational and professional goals of residential treatment are to be efficiently integrated. While it would be difficult to build a case against developing organizations that fit the various characteristics that are subsequently described (i.e., clear definition of organizational goals and individual roles, control and mediation of structural conflicts, maximally efficient programs, etc.), the specific means for achieving a correct and efficient integration of the various components of the organization are not spelled out. Nonetheless, the authors do attempt to delineate problem areas and to specify criteria for effectivè organization, communication, and structure.

In contrast to other books reviewed, Loughmiller's book *Wilderness Road* (1965) describes a radical alternative social system for the residential treatment of disturbed children, raises questions about the use of the school or hospital as the model for residential treatment programs, and makes a compelling case for the therapeutic potential of a flexible, open-ended, child-oriented, year-round camping program.[8] The author builds a strong argument for removing children from the pressure cooker of school, work, and family, the institutions in which they have experienced failures, and from programs, such as residential treatment programs, which tend to reflect the assumptions and expectations of these institutions. Camping is generally less threatening, is generally accepted as a positive experience, and may allow the creation of a milieu more tailored to the needs, interests, and abilities of each camper. While the evaluation of the program is too sketchy, the book raises some provocative questions about residential treatment models.

## Subsystems: Conflicts and Working Solutions

Residential treatment programs have often been examined in terms of their three major spheres of activity, namely, therapy, education, and child care. For historical and other reasons, programs have integrated, emphasized, and designed these spheres in different ways and have arrived at unique solutions geared to their own resources, orientations, and philosophies. The fact that programs have different routes to a variety of types of treatment makes it difficult to develop a comprehensive and coherent body of knowledge and theory about residential treatment. Commenting on this, Whittaker (Whittaker and Trieschman, 1972: 105,106) has said:

From its beginning, residential treatment has been operating on a patchwork of theoretical remnants borrowed from child guidance practice, traditional psychotherapy, social group work and special education. The actual practices and standards of evaluation for residential treatment have had more to do with the needs and requirements of the mental health professionals than with the needs of the children such settings were designed to serve. Most so-called therapeutic milieus (and who would admit to having anything else?), pay lip service to the value of life space therapy, while still placing primary responsibility for treatment in the 50 minute hour. It would seem time that those professionals interested and involved in residential treatment begin to develop models of intervention that would eventuate in a unified theory base for residential therapy . . .

Given the diversity of philosophies and programs, the concept of equifinality, introduced earlier, is important because it takes into account the fact that programs can have different organizations, rationales, and strategies for providing residential treatment. It follows, then, that one may have to look at each program in terms of its own world view, organizational strategies, and unique configurations of resources, personalities, and so on. Given that organizing programs in different ways does not preclude goal achievement and as there is yet to be demonstrated a "correct" way of providing treatment, it follows that one approach to evaluation is to assess the efficiency of each organization, irrespective of its outcome and comparisons to other programs.

Cutting across the issue of unique configurations of subsystems is the issue of how programs attempt to both "raise" and treat in the same setting. The potential incompatibility of the socializing and treatment goals of these institutions is a structural dilemma reflected throughout the literature. Redl and Robinson (1956), for example, distinguish between the needs of the children as children whose development must be stimulated, as contrasted with their needs as patients, whose pathology must be taken into account in ward design and control. Bettleheim and Sylvester (1948) make the same point in discussing "psychological institutionalism," an emotional syndrome developed by children institutionalized in nontherapeutic institutions.

When an adult comes into a residential facility, his or her "illness" is presumably the focus of attention. The work of Goffman (1961) and others highlights the dangers of prolonged institutionalization and has raised the question of the extent to which the chronic schizophrenic syndrome may be an iatrogenic illness or an adaptation to the culture of the hospital. Since children normally undergo enculturation in the years in which they are also being treated, the risks of their being inadvertently socialized to the patient role are greater. While theoretically the goals and means of treating children and "raising" them are separable, the distinctions are easily blurred in the day-to-day routines, activities, and the nature of the relationships between staff and children.

In the early development of residential treatment, the emphasis was on therapy, while child care and education assumed less importance.[9] The purpose of the residential aspect of the center was often to contain the children in the interim when they were not in therapy. The therapy was often analytic in nature and, in many ways, incompatible with involvement in the child's living situation. In the psychoanalytic frame of reference, the therapist seeks minimal reality-oriented involvement with the patient and uses his neutrality to highlight the patient's transference. For example, a psychiatrist was on a hospital ward when one of his patients grabbed the keys and ran off with them. He turned to the nurse, whose role is to carry out doctor's orders, and told her to retrieve the keys. She protested, saying that he should do it since he was bigger. His reply was, "I can't do that, he's my patient."

In one program the author is familiar with, the therapist had administrative control over the children. It was the therapist's role to decide when a child was ready to go home, to decide on foster placement, approve weekend passes, and the like. Such administrative responsibilities may conflict with therapeutic goals. In this setting, child care workers were expected not to deal with unconscious material but to refer it back to the therapist who would handle it in the context of the therapy session. This left staff dealing with acting-out behavior but with no means of treating it as such. It also appeared that children were reluctant to get involved in heated negative transference with their therapist because they were aware that the therapist also made the decisions about their going home and so on. As a result, they may have shied away from such therapeutic involvement.

The issue of confidentiality in residential treatment has also been a vexing problem in the past. To what extent can a therapist discuss what has gone on in the therapy sessions with child care workers when, in the narrow psychoanalytic sense, this is confidential? A similar conflict arises in group therapy. In many group therapy situations, individuals have relatively little contact with one another outside the therapy session, and they discuss their problems, anxieties, and difficulties with people they are not involved with in everyday situations. Group therapy with individuals who live in the same setting, such as the cottage, has the potential of transforming the personal problems discussed into ammunition to be used in the living situation. The more psychoanalytically oriented therapies particularly accentuate this conflict, and the literature reflects the difficulty of coordinating the child-caring and therapeutic responsibilities of the residential treatment center, which permeate every aspect of residential treatment.

The almost ubiquitous split and chronic misunderstandings between child care staff and therapists are evidence of the disparity between the goals of treating and raising children. As discussed by Pilivian (1963), caseworkers typically resent child care staff's apparent disregard for treatment plans and therapeutic considerations and their preoccupation with control and order. Conversely, child care staff typically resent the unrealistic expectations of therapists and their lack of understanding of the difficulties of living with and controlling disruptive children. Irrespective of the amount of communication between these two, the different nature of their responsibilities, functions, perspectives, and relationships with the children leads to conflicts which originate in the conflict between the goals of child rearing and therapy. Perhaps only a major restructuring and reconceptualizing of these roles to synthesize and integrate the functions of therapy, child care, and education will eliminate these conflicts.

Some of the working solutions to this dilemma have been reallocations of the therapeutic responsibilities which, depending on the nature of therapy, were formerly restricted to a therapist's conducting play therapy, behavior modification, reality therapy, or interpretations of resistance and transference. Child care worker, educator, and therapist roles are currently undergoing redefinition in this regard. What Bettleheim (1950) refers to as a marginal interview, what Fraiberg (1956) calls residential casework, and what Redl (1959) calls life space interviewing reflect this redefining.

Bettelheim (1950: 35) describes the marginal interview as:

> . . . a conversation between the participant observer and one or more of the participants. It is interpretive in character but does not need to interfere with the momentary activity of the group or individual. The purpose may be to clear up an anxiety that interferes with enjoyment or participation in an activity, or it may be to warn the child of an unavoidable outcome of his behavior that he does not seem to foresee. The talk may simply help him to understand the reasons for his actions, or explain a piece of behavior in another individual that he seems to have misunderstood, etc. One characteristic of this type of marginal conversation is that while it may change the course of events, or the child's view of them, it does not replace the action; the emphasis is rather on their continuing without unnecessary interference. It should rather clear the blocked channels of solitary activity or social interaction, but never take their place.
>
> In this sense it is ego supporting, because it bolsters the ego in continuing the now more reality-correct activity. It does service for the child as in a better integrated child his own ego would serve him.

Redl's (1959) and Wineman's (1959) articles on the life space interview present it as a means of breaking down the division of staff roles into those who do therapy and those who put the children through daily routines. The life space interview, the goals of which have been described by Redl as "emotional first aid on the spot" and "clinical exploitation of life events," may provide the missing link between analytic therapy in the 50-minute session and milieu therapy, where everything, including the physical plant, may be considered in terms of its therapeutic value. The use of the life space interview by child care workers requires training in the technique, awareness of indications and counterindications, the long- and short-range goals of it, and the like, and necessitates as well communication between therapists and child care workers. Most important of all, the inclusion of the life space interview among the techniques of the child care worker redefines the worker's role and has far-reaching implications for the role structure of the residential treatment center (Dittman and Kitchener, 1959).

The number of labels there are for residential staff—child care workers, cottage parents, counselors, house staff, and so on—reflects the different conceptions of the role and different attitudes toward it. Alt (1953) has stressed the lack of agreement about treatment philosophies and methods and the ramifications of these disagreements for other related issues in residential treatment, such as the qualifications and functions of the staff. There is a corresponding wide range of conceptions of what constitutes adequate preparation and appropriate training for this role. In-service training, and various efforts to utilize conferences to integrate the treatment and management aspects of training to the role, that is, training the staff while integrating them with and encouraging communication with other staff, are described by Matsushima (1964) and Weber (1957).

Bettleheim, on the other hand, stresses, not preparation for performance of specific tasks, but psychological and social development of staff in the hopes that both staff and patients will benefit from the staff's deeper awareness of their own emotions, which are aroused by work with disturbed children (Bettleheim and Wright, 1955). Similarly, Schrager (1954) focuses on role conflicts of staff and sees supervision as role clarification, as freeing the worker to act by helping to increase awareness of self as well as of the differing individual needs of the children. All of these labels, training approaches, role definitions, and the like reflect the need for each institution to develop working solutions to the dilemma of raising and treating children.

Another working solution to the dilemma of combining the child care and treatment functions of the residential center has been to try to combine therapy and child care under the aegis of a broadened concept of education similar to the European Educateur model, which Bissonnier (1963: 636) describes as follows:

> The three basic tasks of the Educateur are that of serving as a capable overseer of a group of maladjusted children and insuring good order while at the same time executing his essential life tasks; playing the role of older brother or sister or parent when the family is not able to fulfill its social and educative obligation toward their children. At a higher level, the Educateur is coordinator of the daily life activities insuring a cohesive unity in the child's or adolescent's life and also of bringing about a kind of de-conditioning of the disturbed behavior in a milieu that is less frustrating for the child.

In a comprehensive and thorough paper, Linton (1971) presents a rationale for an American Educateur approach to child care and contrasts the European use of the Educateur with the use of child care in the United States. He argues convincingly for its appropriateness and feasibility in residential treatment. Rieger and Devries, in their paper "The Child Mental Health Specialist: A New Profession" (1974), also advocate the use in residential programs of child mental health professionals trained in child care, education, and clinical management. They discuss the development of such a role and the training program for such specialists at the Camarillo Children's Treatment Center in California.

In his paper "An American Application of the European Educateur Concept" (1973), Barnes emphasizes the conceptual clarity, body of knowledge, and skills (i.e., the professional identity) provided by the educateur model, in contrast to the confusion and ambiguity of the surrogate parent role, as variously labeled cottage parent, house staff, and child care worker.

The attempt to synthesize the goals of "raising and treating" children under one aegis is the core of the Educateur model. All residential treatment programs must grapple with the tension between these goals, and the working solutions they develop have far-reaching implications for the social system of the program—its roles, intramural organization, systems maintenance, and so on. As a result, the organization of programs provides a basis for program analysis and cross-program comparisons.

## PROPOSED MODEL FOR EVALUATING RESIDENTIAL TREATMENT PROGRAMS FOR DISTURBED CHILDREN

The problems with outcome studies, including (1) the lack of reliable and valid outcome measures, (2) inadequate control groups and sample size, and (3) their failure to provide relatively immediate and useful information for residential treatment programs, have been discussed above. Given the limitations of the above models of evaluation and the profound difficulties of assessing changes in individuals, perhaps we should attempt to evaluate programs qua organizations instead of trying to assess them in terms of their impact on people.

The model proposed here is intended to provide an appropriate framework for evaluating residential treatment programs for disturbed children in terms of their efficiency as institutions while not necessarily precluding more long-range outcome studies. The model proposes a systems type evaluation of the treatment program qua social system in terms of the way it is organized and allocates its resources to achieve its goals. This type of evaluative research entails two perspectives. It seeks to assess: (1) the extent to which a program achieves its goals, and (2) the efficiency of its intramural functioning vis-a-vis these goals. Fallding (1962) describes evaluative research as follows:

> We imply objective evaluation of two kinds, in fact, whenever we give a function. Basically, we are making a judgment as to whether the expenditure that goes into the creation and maintenance of the arrangement is worthwhile; but we determined this worthwhileness by both a backward and a forward look, as it were. The backward look tries to sum up the efficiency of the arrangement in producing its effects. To the extent that it is inefficient, wasteful, it is dysfunctional in a way. The forward look examines whether the effects themselves are valuable in terms of some schedule of needs which we postulate for the life of man in society. [Polsky, 1970: 16]

It is more the exception than the rule for institutions to take the backward and forward look, to examine systematically their goals and the particularized means for achieving them and to develop a coherent and rational allocation of resources. The experience of many researchers has been that, in the process of seeking to formulate appropriate, answerable hypotheses, they assist, or in many cases force, a program to clarify its goals and the means of achieving them.

For example, Rashkis (1960) asks the rhetorical question, "How can a hospital, a ward or an institution or community be best organized so that they will have maximum efficiency?" He answers: "Do research!" He notes the tendency of patients to improve more in settings where research is being conducted and suggests that the activities of research require that the goals and structure of the organization be explicitly defined. Staff consequently have a greater degree of clarity about the structure, roles, allocation of authority, and the like, and are more organized and effective. By imposing a degree of organization, research also tends to organize the hospital experiences for the patients.[10] In any event, the process of defining and analyzing the goals of the organization may in and of itself increase the efficiency of the organization.

More typically, this clarification has been downgraded to the status of a by-product or fringe benefit of the evaluative study. This model specifically seeks to promote the clarification of the functioning of the program as a primary goal of research, that is, to enhance the program's self-awareness so that it can monitor its own functioning. The contribution of evaluative research may de facto be to help a program recognize the relationship between what it wants to do and what it is actually doing. Even more basic, it may help a program decide what it wants to do. Such a delineation is a prerequisite to evaluating a program in terms of the efficiency of its functioning, the feasibility of its goals, structural incompatibilities in the program, wasteful allocation of resources, or dysfunctional relationships of subsystems. The resulting delineation of the program's intramural functioning may provide the greatest benefit to the program, particularly in comparison to the cost and benefits of a long-range outcome study.[11]

It would be premature to suggest that the analysis proposed in this model can, at this point, develop reliable and valid measures of the "efficiency of the organization." This is made more difficult in that measures of the efficiency of an organization which are appropriate for cross-program comparisons are yet to be developed. The measures of efficiency are perhaps at this point equally as crude as outcome measures. The type of evaluation provided by this model is a logical analysis of programs; that is, programs are analyzed in terms of their logical consistency.[12]

This model will delineate the various components or subsystems of residential treatment programs and the interrelationships of these subsystems. It will address itself to the goals of the system and the means of achieving them. It will examine the roles within the system and other specific prerequisite processes, all vis-à-vis the functioning of the total system. Some concepts of open system theory, as described by Miller (1971) and Bertalanffy (1968), are employed, as are some of the structural-functional concepts of Parsons (1951) and Merton (1957).[13] One of the advantages of an open systems perspective is that it facilitates generalizations and comparisons to other types of systems, ranging from the biologic cell and personalities to nation-states (Ackoff, 1960). The advantages of this generalizability and its emphasis on communalities of systems qua systems, however, is accompanied by the limitation of not being tailored to some of the unique characteristics of residential treatment programs for children. Thus, open systems theory terms have been modified and supplemented to take into account the specifics of residential treatment programs, and the model could be described as a modified open systems model.

One reason that an open systems perspective was deemed appropriate is the fact that residential treatment programs are becoming increasingly involved in their communities, making necessary a conceptual framework that can deal with the interrelationships or linkages of the program with other institutions, communities, and families. Still another reason for choosing this perspective is its emphasis on the individual's interaction with the environment.[14] Probably more is known about changing environments and their behavioral correlates than is known about changing "core personality," which argues for an environmental or milieux approach for therapy programs. An open systems perspective was utilized because of its ability to address itself to this relationship between personality and milieu, which is of obvious importance in milieux therapy residential programs which specifically seek to create and maintain a therapeutic milieu.[15] Finally, this perspective is appropriate for evaluating the treatment of children who are also undergoing a process of enculturation, which is, by definition, internalization and assimilation of roles, values, attitudes, and the like.

The following are some of the terms and concepts employed by the open systems model:

1. *Inputs* are the ideas, beliefs, personalities, material, personnel, and moneys that enter the program. The model proposes that a census of the allocation of these resources be made to help delineate the functioning of the system and its priorities.

2. *Goals.* Social systems may be characterized in terms of their formal and informal goals. An evaluation of a program assesses goal achievement and the allocation of resources pursuant to goal achievement.

Etzioni (1960) has commented on the disparity between formally stated goals and what people actually do on a day-to-day basis. Informal and de facto goals, such as maintaining job security, and a variety of systems-maintenance goals, such as maintaining staff morale, need to be considered in program evaluation, particularly as they effect the primary goals. Throughout this model, the achievement of these de facto goals and of the primary goals of rehabilitation, custodial care, and socialization for adulthood will be emphasized, particularly as they relate to other aspects of the model such as roles, social processes, or functional prerequisites. It is important that proximal goals be defined. The elusiveness and lack of clarity involved in describing long-term or distal goals, such as improved functioning, curing illness, successful treatment, and low recidivism, are confounded with the problems of developing operational measures to determine the extent to which these distal or long-term goals are achieved. Each program working within its own rationale can describe a series of proximal goals which are presumably coordinated into a theoretical and practical approach to providing residential treatment. While not addressing the issue of whether a particular model of treatment is effective or not in terms of whether it achieves long-term or distal goals such as rehabilitation, it is possible to determine whether a program is achieving its proximal goals.

For example, proximal goals might include providing comfortable housing with adequate, nonpunitive staff. Proximal goals might also include training staff in life space interviewing techniques, holding children to commitments in terms of reality therapy techniques, or conducting behavior modifications. To conduct behavior modification, individuals presumably need to know baseline data about the patient, the contingencies of the behavior, and in what way it is positively or negatively reinforced. In short, proximal goals tend to be specific and concrete and are consequently more accessible to evaluation. The degree to which a program achieves its proximal goals can be assessed through a variety of techniques such as participant observation and interviewing.

Goals to be considered in program evaluation include the following:

a. *Treatment.* Presumably the primary goal of residential treatment programs for disturbed children is to rehabilitate them psychologically. Outcome studies have tended to emphasize this goal and have sought to assess its achievement with measures of changes in mental health, interpersonal relations, attitudes, or recidivism.

b. *Socialization or enculturation.* Residential treatment programs must provide both treatment and socialization experiences necessary to prepare children for adulthood by developing their job, academic, and interpersonal skills, and their personality. An assessment of the adequacy of this socialization, independently and in combination with the extent to which all goals are achieved (i.e., a goal attainment type evaluation), is necessary to assess the net success of a program.

c. *Custodial care of children.* How well children are cared for in terms of their health, food, shelter, and living conditions.

d. *In-service training,* developing models for similar programs, conducting research, may also need to be considered as goals in evaluating the net success of a program.

e. *Isolating disruptive individuals* to protect society until they are ready to return to it.

3. *Roles.* The model suggests that all statuses within the program be specified and that the roles of administrator, teacher, cottage parent, psychotherapist, cook, and janitor be delineated with regard to their behavior proscriptions and prescriptions. These roles should then be related to the primary and secondary goals of the institution. In other words, each set of role-related activities must be related to the specific means of achieving the program's variety of goals.

4. *Subsystems or Components of the Program.* Subsystems include educational programs, vocational training programs, psychotherapy, residential care, recreation, and so on. The model requires that these subsystems or components of the program be analyzed in terms of their relationships and relative contributions to each of the goals of the program. These components and their goal-specific activities must be related to each of the goals.

5. *Supra-Systems.* The linkages and the nature of the contact between various supra-systems, such as the community, family, and network of service agencies, and the program should be delineated.

6. *Intramural Processes.* A list of functional prerequisites for residential treatment is proposed which is similar to the functional prerequisites of society as described by Aberle and associates (1950) in their paper, "The Functional Prerequisites of Society." In most instances these prerequisites are readily translatable into systems terms. For the purposes of this model some processes are differentiated in order to focus on and emphasize process-speicifc behaviors which are important to the common to residential treatment programs.

The following is a list of proposed functional prerequisites, or more simply, processes that occur in the course of residential treatment. The degree to which these processes are positively related to the program's goals is, of course, relevant to the evaluation of residential treatment programs.

    a. *Communication.* All of the participants in the social system must exchange information with one another about areas of the system relevant to them. An analysis of such communication can determine who says what, to whom, and where, relevant to achieving goals, enacting roles, utilizing inputs, and so on. For example, where, how, and by whom are treatment plans for specific children developed? Are they developed at staff meetings, over coffee? With whom does the administrator communicate directly and about what? In short, the researcher should delineate the nature and content of the communication network.

    b. *Accountability.* The ways in which individuals are held accountable for their behavior is part of the larger problem of social control. All roles have prescribed and proscribed behaviors, for the performance of which individuals are held accountable and one can analyze the techniques, rewards, and sanctions used to hold people accountable. For example, does voluntary compliance prevail, or are punishment, intimidation, and withholding privileges used? By whom and in regard to what behaviors? An inventory of the techniques of social control could be part of the analysis of the process of accountability.

    c. *Decision Making.* How are decisions made, with regard to what, and by whom? What, by whom, and how is relevant information gathered, and what are the priorities in terms of the values that prevail in making decisions? Who makes what types of decisions within the social system, pursuant to what goals and roles, and how is compliance obtained? These questions would be asked in a study of decision making.

    d. *Monitoring.* Who collects information about the ongoing functioning of the program and its "efficiency"? How is such information collected, processed, and used? The effectiveness of this monitoring of the program is vital for "making midcourse corrections," that is, for ongoing self-evaluations. It is the purpose of this model to sensitize individuals to the ongoing functioning of the system and to help them develop the means for monitoring the system objectively and comprehensively. The ability to do this would be most relevant to administrators and could be built into their sphere of activities.

    e. *Coordination of Activities.* Closely related to monitoring is the coordination of the various activities, subsystems, and individuals pursuant to the program's various goals. Such things as who is responsible for the overall coordination of the program, how is it coordinated, and on the basis of what information need to be delineated.

    f. *Staff Support.* The success or failure of "people changing institutions" is most dependent on staff's effectiveness, cooperation, and ability. In the pressure cooker of residential treatment programs, their effectiveness is directly related to the support they receive. Exhausted, demoralized, and overwhelmed staff preclude the achievement of many goals. The nature and extent of the network of staff support should be delineated by analyzing the ways in which staff are supported financially, emotionally, and by their supervision.

These then are the terms and concepts of the model. A program or system would be delineated with regard to its inputs, roles, goals, and its related supra-systems and subsystems. Finally, the functional prerequisites or processes would be examined vis-a-vis the other aspects of the model. For example, a specific role can be analyzed in terms of its goal-oriented behavior, its allocation of inputs, and its participation in a variety of the intramural processes, such as communication and decision making.

This model is intended to delineate both the communalities of residential treatment programs and the unique configurations of specific programs. It is hoped that such a model can clarify what is actually occurring in a program in comparison to what a treatment model, similarly delineated, requires in terms of roles, goals, processes, and so on. For example, in a program utilizing behavior modification, one could identify the type of behavior that is meant to be reinforced and compare it with behavior that is in fact being reinforced; how this relates to the goals of the program and such processes as social control would be the next logical question to ask. Other types of treatment plans could similarly be described in terms of their implications and demands on the entire social system. Once a model has been delineated, a variety of research techniques can be used to determine the degree to which the required model is what people are actually promoting. Research techniques such as self-report questionnaires, random time sample observations, "provoked incidents," and interviews can be used.

One can comment also on the efficiency of the functioning system. Weiss (1972: 30) criticizes Schulberg and Baker (1968) when they suggest that the researcher should help an institution determine the optimal allocation of its resources and argues that this would require the researcher to know more than the institution itself knows, a situation she feels rarely occurs. However, the precision of such an estimate of an optimal allocation does not require the exactitude of a least squares fit, but is more on the order of a commonsense, rough estimate of the allocation of resources. For example, if more time is spent in paper work than with patients, then clearly given the primary goal of treatment, it is a poor allocation of time. One can, in terms of the proposed model, conduct a census of all the resources or inputs of the system and determine how effectively and efficiently time, money, staff, facilities, and energies are being invested.

## Application of the Model

Given the number of new, small residential programs and the lack of clarity about understanding how milieu therapy works—if it works—it is likely that this very simple conceptualization of programs will require much work before more precise types of evaluation can be conducted. In terms of developing a model for treatment, a census may be taken of its inputs (i.e., time, energy, moneys, personalities, resources, material, etc.) vis-a-vis the various components of the program, with attention to which roles and which processes receive what share of these resources. Conducting such a census would help to delineate a model of programs, therapeutic strategies, and tactics.

In tracing inputs and outputs, one can also determine the interrelatedness and nature of the various components of the program. For example, outputs will include discharged patients with possibly improved mental health functioning, changed interpersonal skills, patients participating in the community, and reports. Some of these outputs will return to the system as feedback, some of which (e.g., measures of recidivism and rehabilitation) can be used to ascertain goal attainment, as in an outcome study. In such a study, data might be collected on recidivism, improved functioning, changes in personality traits or attitudes, and so on. Given the emphasis in the proposed model on the functioning of the system (i.e., the study of the organization qua social system), these outcome variables can be related to process variables, such as degree of selective participation in the program, adjustment within the program, and a variety of variables that both characterize and are salient to the program, including size and ethnic background of staff and size of program. To enhance the usefulness of the evaluation, outcome variables can be related to institutional characteristics and processes which are amenable to change, such as size of residential unit and composition of staff, rather than the highly personal and ideosyncratic, such as the nature of the neuroses of one house staff.

To incorporate a systems analysis in an outcome study, hopefully with a randomly assigned control group, would be to follow the four step process of data collection proposed by Nelson, Singer, and Johnsen (1973) which was discussed earlier. Such data collection would become part of the ongoing record-keeping system of the institution. Irrespective of the program's position on the nature of the therapeutic endeavor, baseline measures of symptomatology could be objectively assessed with behavior ratings, descriptions, and case history material prior to admission to the program; these same measures could be made at discharge from the program and at appropriate periods of follow-up. In this way, in addition to a randomly assigned control group, each person could act as his own control; otherwise, such a control group is confounded by the natural processes of maturation. Such measures, in combination with outcome measures comparing experimental and control groups, would be useful.

While in residence, the daily behavior ratings as described by Gleuck and his associates (1967) would be useful. This would provide a process type evaluation (i.e., Are symptoms reduced in the course of treatment?), as well as some measures of the effectiveness of the institution. Recognizing the relative uselessness of standard nursing notes in a psychiatric hospital, Gleuck and his associates sought to make the data collected in nursing notes more accessible and more easily collected. They developed a system of daily behavior ratings to comprise factor analytically derived scales of relevant behavior, such as aggression, withdrawal, and somatatizing symptoms.

On a daily basis, nursing and ward staff fill out optically scanned behavior ratings which can be completed within a few minutes. These ratings are fed into an optical scanner and a computer where they are then available for instant retrieval.

Staff can go to an online data station and, by punching up a patient's number, obtain the individual's cumulative 9-day ratings on a variety of scales. These ratings are drawn in comparison to the mean for the group on the respective behavior rating scales. In this way it is possible to "keep one's finger" on the pulse or mood of the group and on individual patients, both individually and in relationship to the group.[16] The monitoring of the group would help make possible the midcourse corrections necessary for improving residential care. In addition, the automated nursing system provides the data base for process evaluations of the individual.[17]

While the use of optical scanners, online computers, and other such equipment may be beyond the means of many small residential treatment and group home programs, the idea of daily behavior ratings holds great promise. A pool of items could be developed for domains of behavior relevant to the residential treatment program. The individual items should be concrete and specific, and minimize the need for inferences about behavior. Items such as "hallucinated," and "resisted routine," require relatively little inference and may be keys to the current psychological state of the individuals and the group. It is important that such items have a middle range of reliability; in other words, they should measure neither the unchanging and enduring characteristics of the individual nor the characteristics which change in a capricious way. They should instead be objective measures of ongoing behavior which are likely to fluctuate from day to day and yet are indicators of behavior relevant to residential treatment. Such items could be built into behavior rating scales and scale scores kept on a cumulative daily basis. Without the online computer backup, such information could not be used as readily in an ongoing way, but with small patient populations; such records could be kept on a daily basis and, with some clerical help, would provide an ongoing monitoring of the group and patient behavior.

A by-product of such research, which in and of itself might justify the use of such a note system, is that it requires each staff member to have some contact with the patient during the day and to think about the various behavior domains tapped by the items. With some modification this appears to be one of the most useful possibilities for ongoing individual and program evaluation in the small residential treatment programs where other types of research are precluded.

In addition to such process measures and measures prior to admission and at discharge, ratings of behavior—presumably paper-and-pencil tests of attitudes, personality traits, and so on—might be useful. Here it is important to realize that, to some extent, one must develop a workable compromise between tests designed to assess specific aspects of unique programs and those that assess overall changes in personality. Wherever possible communality of outcome measures—that is, using the same instruments—would facilitate cross-program comparison and evaluation. In any event, measures that are both reliable and valid, to the extent that paper-and-pencil measures can be, and ones that are also appropriate to the specific goals of the program, such as changing impulse-ridden youngsters and alienation, must be utilized.

Given the tendency of paper-and-pencil measures not to correlate with behavior measures, behavior measures should be recorded. Unobtrusive measures similar to those used by Goldenberg (1971)—work attendance, salaries, number of arrests rehospitalization—need to be considered. However, many behavioral measures, such as recidivism, are not necessarily a reflection of the extent of one's improvement but of other factors such as socioeconomic class.

As discussed in the various papers on the Re-Ed program (Hobbs, 1964, 1966) which view residential treatment as in interlude in the client's life, evaluative research should examine changes in the ecological unit; that is, changes in the acceptability of children and in the perceptions of family, teachers, and the like. Preplacement planning and maintaining contact with the family during and after treatment are clearly indicated as essential elements for sustaining gains made in residential treatment.

An evaluation of any treatment center must take into account the relationship of the center and residential treatment to the supra-systems. As was indicated in the research of Maluccio (1974), many individuals eventually placed in residential treatment were known to agencies on an average of three years before, at which time a cheaper and more effective alternative to residential treatment would have been preventive programs. The residential treatment program needs to be seen in the larger context of the network of social services available to children. Here the work of Thomas (1972) and his experiments in making residential treatment programs more community-oriented are instructive and suggest that residential treatment be viewed within the larger social context. These, then, are the types of expanded evaluations that might be available.

Where such a social systems analysis is combined with an outcome study, some obvious methodological problems arise. Clearly the further one departs from randomly assigned control groups toward comparison groups or no control groups, or even in the direction of utilizing the quasi-experimental design and comparison groups as suggested by Campbell and Stanley (1966), the less meaningful are the results. Certainly political, practical, and ethical considerations may limit the use of such control groups; but until comparisons are made as close to randomly assigned control groups as possible, evaluative research assessing the impact of programs on people will be severely limited. The tighter the experimental design, the use of randomly assigned control groups, and so on, the more useful are the results both in terms of evaluating the effectiveness of programs and in terms of developing a theory of residential treatment.

### Self-Evaluation

Perhaps the quickest and most efficient type of evaluation for small programs lacking adequate sample size, control groups, and willingness to wait for results of a long-term outcome study would be the participant observations of persons familiar with residential treatment (e.g., the study of the Re-Ed program by Bower et al., 1969). Larger programs that could afford a permanent participant observer could develop such a role, as described by Caudill in *The Psychiatric Hospital as a Small Community* (1958).

His participant observation study of psychiatric hospital as a small society is evaluative in the broad sense: while not an outcome study of "success in treatment," it is a study of the hospital's functioning as a social system, and his detection of the collective disturbance has obvious implications for the hospital's effectiveness as a system.[18] In the concluding chapters of his book, he suggests the possibility of developing a clinical anthropology. Discussing the role of a clinical anthropologist, Caudill (1958: 345) says:

> Perhaps the most important clinical job that such a person could do, . . . would be to keep track of the entire system of the hospital over time and to communicate his observations and suggestions concerning the state of the system at appropriate regular staff meetings and conferences. In general the term "clinical anthropology" that is introduced here denotes both a practical undertaking of serious responsibilities in the work of the hospital or other medical study and an approach to research through observation and inter- viewing in which emphasis is on a day-to-day contact with people in meaning- ful situations.

Given the need of hospitals to have relatively immediate feedback about their functioning, which is generally not produced in long-term outcome studies of discharged patients, this type of evaluation might prove to be the most practical and useful evaluation a program could undertake.[19]

Monitoring the ongoing functioning of a program is most often included among the responsibilities of administrators, and among administrators there is a folklore and variety of cues used to assess the functioning of the institution. In a large institution it would be feasible for someone to assume the sole responsibility for such monitoring and providing feedback. In a smaller institution, this function might be officially incorporated as one aspect of the administrative role. Following an analysis of the program in terms of some theoretical model, such as the proposed open systems model, the clinical anthropologist could check the program for the degree to which it is accomplishing what it has set as proximal goals. Logically derived suggestions could be made for improving the efficiency of the program on a daily basis.

Organizations tend to have, at least informally, built-in mechanisms for self- evaluation and self-correction. Such evaluation occurs regularly in most residential treatment programs: staff members pair off with fellow staff they prefer to work with; they hold almost unending discussions over coffee or in the neighborhood bar about other staff members, or about administrative and organizational problems; children seek out children and staff they prefer. Staff frequently make suggestions to one another about how to work with children or other staff. It has been said, too, that children "vote with their feet," that is, make known their preferences and responses to the institution by seeking out particular staff, running away, or avoiding particular aspects of the program.

Such informal evaluations as staffs' criticisms of one another and staff and children's sociometric choices could be formalized, as were the staff T groups, described previously in Goldenberg's study (1971), which served to provide feed- back for ongoing evaluations of one another and the institution's functioning. In addition, sociometric choices could be solicited from staff and children either by a relatively neutral member of the staff or by an outsider whose role it is to monitor the program. The sociometric data would provide an evaluation of which people work together and their different styles of relating. Where such data are employed to allow staff and the children some freedom of choice in terms of friendships, roommates, work hours, and so on (within the constraints imposed by the therapeutic considerations), soliciting sociometric choices would be useful in at least three ways. First, it would serve to provide systematic information for evaluating the program. Second, it would allow the recipients of treatment a more active role in the governing of their own affairs. Third, if such data were incorporated into the collection of ongoing records, they would have a great deal of relevance for the assessment of the progress of individual patients.

For the purposes of an ongoing evaluation, it would be important to collect such data so as to represent all members of the institution. As in the kula ring study of Malinowski (1922), which traced the ritual exchange of bracelets and necklaces over hundreds of miles of open water, the individual participant had little understanding of the workings and significance of the overall kula ring. It was Malinowski, with an outside and holistic perception of the kula ring, who was able to understand its functioning. Of the individual participants Malinowski (1922: 23) said:

> . . . . [they] have no knowledge of the total outline of any of their social structure. They know their own motives, know the purpose of individual actions and rules which apply to them; but how, out of these the whole collective institution shapes, this is beyond their mental range. Not even the most intelligent native has any clear idea of the Kula as a big, organized social construction, still less of its sociological functions and implications. If you were to ask him what the Kula is, he would answer by giving a few details, most likely by giving his personal experiences and subjective views on the Kula, but nothing approaching the definition just given here. Not even a partial coherent account could be obtained. For the integral picture does not exist in his mind; he is in it, and cannot see the whole from the outside.

A comprehensive overview of the system is what is required and in fact is most useful in program evaluation.

## SUMMARY

This chapter has reviewed some of the evaluative literature on residential treatment programs for disturbed children. Evaluative studies were categorized according to whether their approach was predominantly goal attainment or process; studies that examined programs as social systems or within the context of larger systems were categorized as systems type evaluations. Selected studies were discussed in terms of their relative merits and limitations, many of which were characteristic of and inherent to the type of evaluation (e.g., follow-up studies) in which the study was categorized.

Studies that attempted to evaluate programs by assessing their impact on people were found, in the course of the review, to be beset with a variety of methodological problems. A different strategy was proposed, namely, to describe and analyze—to evaluate—programs qua social systems in terms of the "efficiency" of their organization in relation to their various goals. A generalizable model using an open systems perspective was proposed to describe and analyze residential treatment programs for children. While not purporting to be a panacea to the problems of program evaluation, the model seeks to provide a more immediate and useful type of feedback. This model does not preclude a goal attainment type of evaluation, given the necessary experimental and control groups, reliable and valid outcome measures, and the like. Finally, some specific recommendations for program evaluation were made, such as incorporating data relevant to evaluation into case records and formalizing and improving the existing mechanisms for monitoring the ongoing function of programs.

No matter what evaluative strategy one employs, there is not at this time a litmus paper for testing how good or how inadequate programs are. The old proverb, "When you see a bear dance, you don't ask how well," might summarize the current state of evaluative research in this area. Perhaps more modest expectations of evaluative research are in order. For example, just as the Re-Ed program has given up the goal of effecting "cures" in favor of the more modest one of helping children to become more acceptable and their families, teachers, and communities, more accepting, so might evaluative research adjust its sights toward providing useful feedback to programs to help improve their functioning.

In an important book, *Successful Group Care: Explorations in the Powerful Environment,* Wolins (1974) and others examine the group care provided by such programs as the Austrian Kinderdorf, the Soviet boarding schools, and the Israeli Kibbutz, with respect to their potential usefulness. In his preface, Wolins asks the rhetorical question, "Can group care be constructive?" and replies:

> Mention an institution, a group care program, and the image evoked is negative. Erving Goffman's *Asylum,* the horror stories of *Snake Pit,* the pitiful behavior of normal human beings under the stress of prison life—all these and many other carefully documented, regrettable consequences of group life always stand before us. This kind of human community has great power, and it is seen generally as the power to coerce, to deprive the individual or initiative and direction, to install in him a sense of slavery and mechanical obedience.
>
> Are there no successful socializing experience—the positive outcomes of such group environments where the power of a small community is turned to the promotion of a capacity to "love and work"? The present volume attempts to assemble descriptions of such settings, to provide a positive answer to the very crucial question: Can group care be constructive? Obviously it can— sometimes beyond expectations. Some of the conceptions, practices, evidence and conclusions are here. Hopefully they will provide some balance to what has been such a one-sided view. [Wolins, 1974: ix]

In "Group Care: Friend or Foe," Wolins discusses six conditions that seem to lead to positive group care, and he explores reasons these conditions are difficult for Americans to accept:

> If these are the requirements of a powerful environment conducive to change, where does the American child-care practitioner stand on them? It seems that

for reasons of faith, history, and political propriety he may have difficulty with every one of the six conditions that seem to lead to the results seen in the most successful group care settings. Adherence to traditional interpretations of Freudian theory predisposes him toward familial rather than group substitutes. This also precludes clear separation and social integration of institutional children. He is cautious about peer influences, believing that in adolescence they are directed away from or against adult values. Historically he has had an abhorrence of child labor, since it evokes in him images of English spinning mills and American sweatshops. He fears strong ideology because in a pluralistic environment it leads to disagreement, which our society, operating under the "unity-in-diversity" motto, has yet to harness successfully to productive purposes. Yet these seem to be the ingredients of good group care for some children. [Wolins, 1974: 289]

Residential institutions are clearly highly influential, and even with the move toward a greater community orientation, there will continue to be a need for programs that both raise and treat children. Given this, it will be a responsibility of the evaluative researcher, working within severe methodological constraints, to help improve the quality of such programs by assessing their impact and/or by providing them with useful feedback about their efficiency in marshalling powerful social forces for raising and treating children.

## NOTES

1. Evaluative research on residential programs for juvenile delinquents has not been included in this review, except for Street et al. (1966), which is duscussed as an example of a comparative evaluation, and Lerman's (1968) discussion of the California Community Treatment Project Study (Warren et al., 1966) and his evaluation of the Highfields Experiment (Weeks, 1968). For research in this area, the reader is referred to Beker and Herman's (1972) detailed appraisal of the California Differential Treatment Typology and to the thoughtful case study of the Massachusetts reform of its juvenile correctional system by Ohlin and associates (1974). More general reviews of delinquency research are provided by Hirschi and Hanon (1967) and Shyne (1973).

2. For the purposes of this chapter, the practical and methodological problems of evaluative research are not examined. Other chapters in this volume deal with these problems, as do Schulberg and Baker (1968), Schulberg et al. (1969), Suchman (1968), Tripodi et al. (1969), and Weiss (1972).

With regard to some of the methodological issues, such as participant observation, see Baker (1969), Beller (1959), Weick (1968), and Wright (1960). Interviewing is discussed by Cannell and Kahn (1968). Cohen discusses statistical power, experimental design, and sample size (1969), and the use of multiple regression (1968). Cronbach and Meehl (1955) discuss reliability and validity of measures. Campbell and Stanley (1966) present a variety of experimental and quasi-experimental designs particularly relevant to evaluative research. McGuire (1968) has written extensively on attitudes and attitude change which is relevant for program evaluation. Finally, Webb and associates (1966) discuss the use of unobtrusive measures which may prove helpful for field and evaluative research. Beyond these selected references, the reader is referred to other chapters in these volumes and to the relevant literature.

3. For an excellent case study of an evaluation of a residential program, see Hyman et al. (1962) and Riecken (1952).

4. Alt (1964) discusses the concept of success and the various definitions relevant to residential treatment of children. For a discussion of some of the outcome criteria problems in follow-up evaluations, see Pollack et al. (1968).

5. Instruments used in this study were included in appendices and may be found there.

6. For details of this study, see Astor Home for Children (1963) and Mora et al. (1969).

7. Durkin (1967) analyzes some of the social functions of psychological interpretations in a residential treatment program for children.

8. Loughmiller (1965) briefly cites a follow-up study of boys who participated in the program over a 12 year period and reports that 70.8% were in the upper two categories of adjustment; i.e., "fairly good" and "excellent." He (1965: 31) comments, "We have good reason to believe that the present results are as good as or better than the former as we are not better staffed and have had more experience." No details of the study were provided in this book.

9. For a thorough and practical discussion of the therapeutic potential of "nontherapy" time, see Trieschman et al., *The Other 23 Hours* (1969).

10. An alternative explanation is that the more organized hospitals are more likely to undertake research.

11. For a discussion of some of the limitations of outcome studies, see Ellsworth et al. (1968) and Schulberg and Baker (1968). Levine (1968) has discussed the relevance of cost-benefit analysis as an approach to program evaluation.

12. Durkin (1974) has utilized the model to describe and analyze a summer camp and follow-up program for poverty and/or disturbed adolescents. The program is analyzed in terms of its logical consistency with theories of social influence and group dynamics.

13. It is beyond the scope of this chapter to discuss in detail the rationale for an open systems perspective or to review relevant literature on organizational theory. The reader is referred to Silverman (1971), Rice (1963), and Katz and Kahn (1966).

14. For an analysis of personality as an open system, see Allport (1960). Durkin (1972), using a theory of social influence, discusses the relationship of personality and milieu.

15. Essential to an understanding of milieu therapy is an understanding of the process of internalization vis-a-vis the "raising," i.e., enculturation, and treating of children. Internalization may occur through identification, developing a reinforcement history, gaining insight, learning roles, etc. The means by which attitudes, values, motivation, and behavior become internalized is central to any theory of milieu therapy.

16. Caudill (1958) and Stanton and Schwartz (1954) have pointed out the relationship of group mood and symptomatology.

17. Rosenberg et al. (1967) discuss the monitoring of individual behavior with online computers in terms of its relevance in making clinical decisions.

18. Kobler and Stotland's (1964) autopsy of a hospital that was closed as a result of a loss of hope and consequent wave of suicides among staff and patients is a dramatic example of the system-wide effect of hospital mood.

19. Caudill (1958) and Stanton and Schwartz (1954) have discussed the importance of monitoring the ongoing functioning of hospitals. Feeney (1973), in discussing the limitations of outcome type evaluations, proposes ways of providing ongoing feedback to improve the operation of residential treatment settings. While he does not regard this as evaluative per se, it is evaluation as the term is defined in this chapter.

## REFERENCES

Aberle, D.; A. Cohen; A. Davis; M. Levy; and F. Sutton. "The Functional Prerequisites of a Society." *Ethics,* 1950, 60: 100-111.

Ackoff, R. L. "Systems, Organizations and Interdisciplinary Research." *General Systems Yearbook,* 1960, 5: 1-8.

Allerhand, Melvin E.; Ruth E. Weber; and Marie Haug. *Adaptation and Adaptability: The Bellefaire Follow-Up Study.* New York: Child Welfare League of America, 1966.

Allport, G. "The Open System in Personality Theory." *Journal of Abnormal and Social Psychology,* 1960, 61 (3): 301-310.

Alt, Herschel. "Responsibilities and Qualifications of the Child Care Worker." *American Journal of Orthopsychiatry,* 1953, 23: 670.

———, *Residential Treatment for the Disturbed Child.* New York: International Universities Press, 1960.

———. "The Concept of Success in Residential Treatment - An Administrator's View." *Child Welfare,* 1964, 43 (8): 423.

Astor Home for Children. *What We Have Learned: A Report on the First 10 Years of the Astor Home, a Residential Treatment Center for Emotionally Disturbed Children.* New York: Astor Home for Children, 1963.

Baker, Frank. "An Open Systems Approach to the Study of Mental Hospitals in Transition." *Community Mental Health Journal,* 1969 5 (5).

Bales, Robert F. *Interaction Process Analysis.* Cambridge, Mass.: Addison-Wesley, 1950.

Barker, Roger. *One Boy's Day.* New York: Harper, 1951.

Barnes, F. Herbert. "An American Application of the European Educateur Concept." Paper presented at the Association of Psychiatric Services for Children, Chicago, November 16, 1973.

Beker, Jerome and Doris S. Herman. "A Critical Appraisal of the California Differential Treatment Typology of Adolescent Offenders." *Criminology,* May 1972.

Beller, E. K. "Direct and Inferential Observations in the Study of Children." *American Journal of Orthopsychiatry,* 1959, 29: 560-573.

Benjamin, Anne and Howard E. Weatherly. "Hospital Ward Treatment of Emotionally Disturbed Children." *American Journal of Orthopsychiatry,* 1947, 17 (4).

Berman, Samuel P. "Some Lessons Learned in Developing a Residential Treatment Center." (Edgewood Children's Center, Webster Groves, Mo.). *Child Welfare,* 1961, 40 (4).

Bertalanffy, Ludwig von. *General Systems Theory: Foundations, Development, Applications.* New York: G. Braziller, 1968.

Bertalanffy, L. "General Systems Theory and Psychiatry." *American Handbook of Psychiatry,* 1969.

Bettelheim, Bruno. *Love is Not Enough.* Glencoe, Ill.: Free Press, 1950. P. 386.

——— and Emmy Sylvester. "Therapeutic Milieu: For Emotional Disorders Due to Institutional Living." *American Journal of Ortho-Psychiatry,* 1948, 18 (2): 191.

Bettelheim, Bruno and Benjamin Wright. "Staff Development in a Treatment Institution." *American Journal of Ortho-psychiatry,* 1955, 35 (4).

Bissonnier H. La Profession d'educateur specialise et son evolution. Separata de "A Crianco Portugesa" Lisbon Portugal. In T. Linton, "The European Educateur Model: An Alternative and Effective Approach to the Mental Health of Children," *The Journal of Special Education,* 1963, 3 (4): 325.

Bower, E.; R. Laurie; C. Struther; and R. Fetherland. "Project Re-Ed: New Concepts for Helping Emotionally Disturbed Children: Evaluation by a Panel of Visitors." Nashville, Tenn.: John F. Kennedy Center for Research on Education and Human Development, George Peabody College for Teachers, 1969.

Brown, J. "Prognosis from Presenting Symptoms of Preschool Children with Atypical Development." *American Journal of Orthopsychiatry,* 1960, 30: 382-390.

Burgess, John; Ronald H. Nelson; and Robert Wallhaus. "Network Analysis as a Method for the Evaluation of Service Delivery Systems." *Community Mental Health Journal,* 1974. In press.

Campbell, D. and J. Stanley. *Experimental and Quasi-Experimental Designs for Research.* Chicago, Ill.: Rand McNally, 1966.

Cannell, C. and R. Kahn. "Interviewing," In G. Lindsey and E. Aronson (eds.), *The Handbook of Social Psychology.* Reading, Mass.: Addison Wesley, 1968.

Caudill, W. *The Psychiatric Hospital as a Small Society.* Cambridge, Mass.: Harvard University Press, 1958.

Child Welfare League of America. *From Chaos to Order: A Collective View of the Residential Treatment of Children.* Compiled by members of the American Association for Children's Residential Centers. New York: Child Welfare League of America, 1972.

Cohen, J. "Multiple Regression Analysis as a General Data-Analytic System." *Psychological Bulletin,* 1968, 70: 426-443.

——— *Statistical Power Analysis for the Behavioral Sciences.* New York: Academic Press, 1969.

Cronebach, L. and P. Meehl. "Construct Validity in Psychological Tests." *Psychological Bulletin,* 1955: 281-302.

Davids, Anthony; Richard Ryan; and Peter Salvatore. "Effectiveness of Residential Treatment." *American Journal of Orthopsychiatry,* 1968, 38: 469-475.

Dinnage, Rosemary and M. L. Kellmer Pringle. *Residential Child Care—Facts and Fallacies.* New York: Humanities Press, 1967.

Dittman, A. T. and H. L. Kitchener. "Life Space Interviewing and Individual Play Therapy—a Comparison of Techniques." *American Journal of Orthopsychiatry,* 1959, 29: 19-26.

Durkin, R. "Social Function of Psychological Interpretations" *American Journal of Orthopsychiatry,* 1967, 37: 956-962.

———. "Personality and Milieu: A Theory of Social Influence." 1972. Unpublished manuscript.

———. "A Model for a Summer Camp and Follow-Up Program for Poverty and/or Disturbed Teenagers." 1974. Unpublished manuscript.

Eaton, L. and F. Menalascino. "Psychotic Reactions of Childhood: A Follow-Up Study." *American Journal of Orthopsychiatry,* 1967, 37: 521-529.

Eisenberg, L. "The Austistic Child in Adolescence." *American Journal of Psychiatry,* 1956, 112: 607-612.

———. "The Course of Childhood Schizophrenia." *Archives of Neurology and Psychiatry,* 1957, 78: 69-83.

Ellsworth, R. B.; Leslie Foster; B. Childers; G. Arthur; and D. Kroeker. "Hospital and Community Adjustment as Perceived by Psychiatric Patients, Their Families and Staff." *Journal of Consulting and Clinical Psychology,* 1968, 32 (5), Part 2. Monograph supplement.

Etzioni, A. "Two Approaches to Organizational Analysis: A Critique and a Suggestion." *Administrative Science Quarterly,* 1960, 5: 257-278.

Fallding, H. (1962) "Functional Analysis in Sociology." In H. Polsky, D. Claster and C. Goldberg (eds.), *Social Systems Perspectives in Residential Institutions.* East Lansing: Michigan State University Press, 1970.

Fanshel, David. "Child Welfare." Pp. 85-143 in Henry S. Mass (ed.), *Five Fields of Social Service: Reviews of Research.* New York: National Association of Social Workers, 1966.

Feeney, George M. "The Use of Feedback to Improve the Operation of Residential Treatment Settings." *International Journal of Mental Health,* 1973, 2 (2): 81-93.

Fraiberg, Selma. "Some Aspects of Residential Casework with Children." *Social Casework,* April 1956, 37 (4): 159.

Garber, B. *Follow-Up Study of Hospitalized Adolescents.* New York: Brunner/Mazel, 1972.

Gershenson, Charles P. "Residential Treatment of Children: Research Problems and Possibilities." *Social Service Review,* 1956, 30 (3): 268-275.

Glueck, E. and S. Glueck. *Unravelling Juvenile Delinquency,* Cambridge, Mass.: Harvard University Press, 1968.

Gleuck, B.; M. Rosenberg; and C. Stroebel. "The Computer and the Clinical Decision Process." *American Journal of Psychiatry,* 1967, 124:5.

Goffman, E. *Asylums.* Garden City, N. Y.: Doubleday Anchor Books, 1961.

Goldenberg, I., *Build Me a Mountain: Youth, Poverty and the Creation of New Settings.* Cambridge: MIT Press, 1971.

Gray, William; Frederick Duhl; and Nicholas Rizzo. *General Systems Theory and Psychiatry.* Boston: Little Brown, 1969.

Gula, M. *Agency Operated Group Homes: A Casebook.* Washington, D. C.: Children's Bureau, 1965.

Henry, J. "Types of Institutional Structures." *Psychiatry,* 1957, 20: 47-60.

Hirschi, T. and S. Hanon. *Delinquency Research.* Glencoe, Ill.: Free Press, 1967.

Hobbs, Nicholas. "The Process of Reeducation." Paper delivered at the first Annual workshop for the Staff of Project Re-Ed., in Gatlinburg, Tenn., September 1, 1963 (1964).

———. "Helping Disturbed Children: Psychological and Ecological Strategies. *American Psychologist,* 1966, 21: 1105-1115.

Hyman, H.; C. Wright; and T. Hopkins. *Applications of Methods of Evaluation.* Berkeley: University of California Press, 1962.

Johnson, Lillian and Joseph Reid. *An Evaluation of Ten Years Work with Emotionally Disturbed Children.* Seattle: Ryther Child Center, 1947.

Kane, Ruth Powell and Guinevere S. Chambers. "Seven Year Follow-Up of Children Hospitalized and Discharged from a Residential Setting." *American Journal of Psychiatry,* 1961, 117: 1023.

Katz, Daniel and Robert Kahn. *The Social Psychology of Organization.* New York: Wiley, 1966.

Kobler, A. and E. Stotland. *The End of Hope: The Life and Death of a Hospital.* New York: Free Press, 1964.

Konopka, Gisela; F. Kamps; J. Wollinga; and P. Hovda. "Implications of a Changing Residential Treatment Program." *American Journal of Orthopsychiatry,* 1961, 31 (1): 17-39.

Lander, Joseph and Rena Schulman. "The Impact of the Therapeutic Milieu on the Disturbed Personality." (Hawthorne Cedar Knolls School, Hawthorne, N.Y.) *Social Casework,* 1960, 41 (5).

Langner, T.; E. Greene; J. Herson; J. Demson; J. Goff; and E. McCarthy. "Psychiatric Impairment in Welfare and Non-welfare City Children." Paper presented at the American Psychological Association Convention, September 1969.

Lerman, Paul. "Evaluating Studies in Institutions for Delinquents: Implications for Research and Social Policies." *Social Work,* 1968, 3: 55-64.

Levine, Abraham S. "Cost Benefit Analysis and Social Welfare Program Evaluation." *Social Service Review,* 1968, 42 (2): 173-183.

Levy, E. "Long Term Follow-Up of Former In-patients at Children's Hospital of the Menniger Clinic." *American Journal of Psychiatry,* 1969, 125: 1633-1639.

Lewis, Wilbert W. "Project Re-Ed: The Program and a Preliminary Evaluation." Prepared as a chapter in C. Rickard (ed.), *Unique Programs in Behavior Re-Adjustment,* 1968.

Lindzey, G. and E. Aronson. (eds.) *The Handbook of Social Psychology.* Reading, Mass.: Addison Wesley, 1968.

Linton, T. "The Educateur Model: A Theoretical Monograph." *The Journal of Special Education,* 1971, 5 (2): 155-190.

Loughmiller, C. *Wilderness Road.* Austin, Texas: Hogg Foundation for Mental Health, University of Texas, 1965.

McGuire, W. "The Nature of Attitudes and Attitude Change." Pp. 136-314 in G. Lindzey and E. Aronson (eds.), *The Handbook of Social Psychology.* Reading, Mass: Addison-Wesley, 1968.

Malinowski, B. *Argonauts of the Western Pacific,* New York: Dutton, 1922.

Maluccio, Anthony N. "Residential Treatment of Disturbed Children: A Study of Service Delivery." *Child Welfare,* 1974. In press.

——— and Wilma D. Marlow. "Residential Treatment of Emotionally Disturbed Children: A Review of the Literature." *The Social Service Review,* 1972, 46 (2): 230-250.

Matsushima, John. "Communication and Cottage Parent Supervision in a Residential Treatment Center." *Child Welfare,* 1964, 43 (10), 529-534.

Mayer, M. and A Blum (eds.) *Healing Through Living.* Springfield, Ill.: Charles C. Thomas, 1971.

Merton, R. *Social Theory and Social Structure.* Glencoe, Ill.: Free Press, 1957.

Miller, E. G. and A. K. Rice. "Systems of Organization." Tavistock pamphlet number 3. London, Eng., 1967.

Miller, James. "The Nature of Living Systems." *Behavioral Science,* 1971, 16 (4).

Miller, James G. "Living Systems; Basic Comments Concepts." *Behavioral Science,* 1965, 10: 193-237.

Monkman, M. *A Milieu Therapy Program for Behaviorally Disturbed Children.* Springfield, Ill.: Charles C. Thomas, 1972.

Mora, George et al. "A Residential Treatment Center Moves Toward the Community Mental Health Model." *Child Welfare,* 1969, 48 (10) 585-590.

Murphy, Lois B. "Problems in Recognizing Emotional Disturbance in Children." *Child Welfare,* 1963: 473-487.

Nelson, Ronald H.; Mark J. Singer; and Lawrence O. Johnsen. "Community Considerations in the Evaluation of a Children's Residential Treatment Center." Proceedings, 81st Annual Convention, APA, 1973. Pp. 951-952.

———. "The Application of a Residential Treatment Evaluation Model." 1974. Unpublished paper.

Ohlin, L.; R. Coates; A. Miller. "Radical Correctional Reform: A Case Study of the Massachusetts Youth Correctional System." *Harvard Educational Review,* 1974, 44: 74-111.

Pappenfort, Donnell M.; Adelaide Dinwoodie; and Dee Morgan Kilpatrick. *Population of Children's Residential Institutions in the United States.* Chicago: Center for Urban Studies, University of Chicago, 1968.

Pappenfort, Donnell M.; Dee Morgan Kilpatrick; Robert W. Roberts (eds.). *Child Caring: Social Policy and The Institution.* Chicago: Aldine, 1973.

Parsons, T. *The Social System.* Glencoe, Ill.: Free Press, 1951.

Piliavin, Irving. "Conflict between Cottage Parents and Caseworkers." *Social Service Review,* 1963, 37: 17-25.

Pollack, M.; S. Levenstein; and D. Klein. "A Three Year Posthospital Follow-up of Adolescent and Adult Schizophrenics." *American Journal of Orthopsychiatry,* 1968, 38: 94-109.

Polsky, Howard. *Cottage Six: The Social Systems of Delinquent Boys in Residential Treatment.* New York: Russell Sage Foundation, 1962.

———. "Changing Delinquent Subcultures: A Social Psychological Approach." Pp. 683-699 in Howard W. Polsky, Daniel S. Claster and Carl Goldgerg (eds.) in *Social System Perspectives in Residential Institutions.* East Lansing: Michigan State University Press, 1970.

——— and Daniel S. Claster, in collaboration with C. Goldberg. *The Dynamics of Residential Treatment: A Social System Analysis.* Chapel Hill: University of North Carolina Press, 1968.

Polsky, Howard W.; Daniel S. Claster; and Carl Goldberg, (eds.) *Social Systems Perspectives in Residential Institutions.* East Lansing: Michigan State University Press, 1970.

Polsky, Howard and M. Kohn. "Participant Observation in a Delinquent Subculture." *American Journal of Orthopsychiatry,* 1959, 29: 737.

Rashkis, H. A. "Cognitive Restructuring: Why Research is Therapy." *AMA Archives of General Psychiatry,* 1960, 2: 34-612.

Redick, Richard. "Residential Treatment Centers for Emotionally Disturbed Children—1968." Statistical Note 11. NIMH, OPPE, November 1969.

Redl, Fritz. "Strategy and Techniques of the Life Space Interview." *American Journal of Orthopsychiatry,* 1959, 29: 1-18.

——— and G. W. Robinson. "Child Psychiatry: Hospital Aspects." *Mental Hospitals,* 1956, 7: 38-41.

Redl, F. and D. Wineman. *Children who Hate: The Disorganization and Breakdown of Behavior Controls.* Glencoe, Ill.: Free Press, 1951.

Reid, Joseph H. and Helen R. Hagan. *Residential Treatment of Emotionally Disturbed Children: A Descriptive Study.* New York: Child Welfare League of America, 1952.

Rice, A. K. *The Enterprise and Its Environment: A Systems Theory of Management Organization.* London, England: Travistock, 1963.

Rieger, N. and A. Devries. "The Child Mental Health Specialist: A New Profession." *American Journal of Orthopsychiatry,* 1974, 44: 150-158.

Riecken, H. W. *The Volunteer Work Camp: A Psychological Evaluation*, Cambridge, Mass.: Addison-Wesley, 1952.

Roen, S. R. and Alan J. Burns. *Community Adaptation Schedule*. New York: Behavioral Publications, 1968.

Rosenberg, Mervin; Bernard G. Gleuck, Jr.; and Charles F. Stroebel. "The Computer and the Clinical Decision Process." *American Psychiatric Association, 1967*.

Rubin, Eli Z. and Clyde B. Simson. "A Special Class Program for the Emotional Disturbed Child in School: A Proposal." *American Journal of Orthopsychiatry*, 1960, 30 (1): 144-153.

Rutter, N. "The Influence of Organic and Emotional Factors on the Origins, Nature and Outcome of Childhood Psychosis." *Developmental Medicine and Child Neurology*, 1965, 7: 518-528.

Sattler, Jerome M. and Bruce W. Leppla. "A Survey of the Need for Children's Mental Health Facilities." *Mental Hygiene*, 1969, 53 (4): 643-645.

Schrager, Jules. "A Focus for Supervision of Residential Staff in a Treatment Institution." *Bulletin of the Menninger Clinic*, 1954, 18: 64.

Schulberg, Herbert C. and Frank Baker. "Program Evaluation Models and the Implementation of Research Findings." *American Journal of Public Health*, 1968, 58 (7).

Schulberg, H.; A. Sheldon; and F. Baker. *Program Evaluation in the Health Fields*. New York: Behavioral Publications, 1969.

Sheldon, A. and F. Baker. *Systems of Medical Care*. Cambridge, Mass.: MIT Press, 1970.

Shyne, Ann W. "Research on Child-Caring Institutions," Pp. 107-1414 in Donnell M. Pappenfort, Dee Morgan Kilpatrick and Robert W. Roberts (eds.), *Child Caring: Social Policy and the Institution*. Chicago: Aldine, 1973.

Silver, Harold. "The Residential Treatment of Emotionally Disturbed Children: An Evaluation of 15 years' Experience." (Hawthorne Cedar Knolls, Hawthorne, N.Y., and Bellefaire, Cleveland, Ohio.) *Journal of Jewish Communal Service*, 1961, 38 (2).

Silverman, D. *The Theory of Organizations*. New York: Basic Books, 1971.

Simon, Abraham J. "Residential Treatment of Children: Unanswered Questions." *Social Service Review*, 1956, 30: 26.

Simon, Abraham J. and Charles P. Gershenson. "Residential Treatment of Children." *Social Service Review*, September 1956.

Stanton, F. and S. Schwartz. *The Mental Hospital*. New York: Basic Books, 1954.

Street, David; Robert D. Vinter; and Charles Perrow. *Organization for Treatment: A Comparative Study of Institutions for Delinquents*. New York: Free Press, 1966.

Suchman, E. *Evaluative Research: Principles and Practice in Public Service and Social Action Programs*. New York: Russell Sage, 1968.

Taylor, Delores and Stuart Alpert. *Continuity and Support Following Residential Treatment*. New York: Child Welfare League of America, 1973.

Thomas, George. "Community-Oriented Care in Children's Institutions." Second Year Interim Report on project funded by Office of Child Development, Grant #OCD-CB-106, conducted by Regional Institute of Social Welfare Research, University of Georgia, 1260 So. Lumpkin Street, Athens, Georgia 30601. 1972.

Trieschman, Albert E.; James K. Whittaker; and Larry K. Brendtro. *The Other 23 Hours*. Chicago: Aldine, 1969.

Tripodi, Tony; Erwin Epstein; and Carrol MacMurray. "Dilemmas in Evaluation Implications for Administrators of Social Action Programs." 1969.

Vinter, R. and M. Janowitz. "Effective Institutions for Juvenile Delinquents: A Research Statement." *Social Service Review*, 1959, 33: 118.

Warren, M.; T. Neto; B. Palmer; and K. Turner. *Community Treatment Project—Fifth Program Report: An Evaluation of the Community Treatment for Delinquents*. Sacramento: California Youth Authority, 1966.

Webb, E.; D. Campbell; R. Schwartz; and L. Sechrest. *Unobstrusive Measures: Nonreactive Research in the Social Sciences*. Chicago, Ill.: Rand McNally, 1966.

Weber, G. H. "The Use of the Conference Method in the In-Service Training of Cottage Parents." *International Journal of Social Psychiatry,* 1957, 3: 49.

Weber, G. and B. Haberlein. *Residential Treatment of Emotionally Disturbed Children.* New York: Behavioral Publications, 1972.

Weeks, A. *Youthful Offenders at Highfields: An Evaluation of the Short-Term Treatment of Delinquent Boys.* Ann Arbor: University of Michigan Press, 1968.

Weick, K. "Systematic Observational Methods." P. 357 in G. Lindzey and E. Aronson, (eds.), *The Handbook of Social Psychology.* Reading, Mass: Addison-Wesley, 1968.

Weiss, C. *Evaluation Research.* Englewood Cliffs, N.J.: Prentice Hall, 1972.

Whittaker, James K. and Alfred E. Trieschman (eds.) *Children Away from Home:* A Source *Book of Residential Treatment.* Chicago: Aldine-Atherton, 1972.

Wineman, David. "The Life-Space Interview." *Social Work,* January 1959.

Wolins, Martin (ed.) *Successful Group Care: Explorations in the Powerful Environment.* Chicago: Aldine, 1974.

Wright, F. "Observational Child Study." Pp. 71-139 in P. Mussen (ed.), *Handbook of Research Methods in Child Development.* New York: Wiley, 1960.

*11*

# DIFFERENTIAL USE OF MENTAL HEALTH SERVICES: SOCIAL PATHOLOGY OR CLASS VICTIMIZATION?

RICHARD N. BRANDON

*U.S. Senate Budget Committee*

## I. INTRODUCTION

This study will explore the use of social area analysis as one means of evaluating the impact of the CMHC program in New York. The federal act of 1963 which created the program embodied several major goals of the dominant portion of the psychiatric profession: provide alternatives to care in large, distant state hospitals; provide care in community of residence (defined as a "catchment area" of 75,000 to 200,000 population) in small facilities; provide a comprehensive set of alternatives to hospitalization—clinic, partial hospitalization, rehabilitation, consultation and education services; provide continuity of care among these components. To these was added in 1965 a major concept of the Great Society social programs: orient service to communities rather than individuals, including community participation in decisions. The breadth of these goals requires us to examine the entire service system, rather than just the demonstration projects receiving federal funding.

Previous studies (notably Hollingshead and Redlich, 1958) have extensively explored the impacts of individual level characteristics upon how many people receive what service with what result. A different approach is necessary, however, to measure effects at the community level. We must first test what "localization" of service to a catchment area means within a large city. We will accomplish this by

ACKNOWLEDGMENTS: Mr. Brandon finds his list of indebtedness to be almost as long as his study. Dr. Oliver P. Williams, Chairman of the Political Science Department at the University of Pennsylvania, first introduced him to social area analysis and has been of continued aid; Dr. Edwind T. Haefele has provided critical focus and encouragement as dissertation advisor. Mr. Abbott Weinstein, Director of Clinical and Statistical Information Systems, New York State Department of Mental Hygiene, developed the extensive information system from which most measuring the relationship between the utilization rate for each type of service and the provision of service in or near the area of residence. We must then test what characteristics of communities are relevant to utilization, exploring measures of socioeconomic status, housing conditions, and family and social (dis)organization, with the effect of geographic accessibility (facility coverage) held constant.

The analyses of social area characteristics and service accessibility as predictors of utilization set the scene for the program evaluation by describing the pattern of interaction in the total mental health service system. Most evaluations of program impact focus on inputs: organizational characteristics or the change in amounts of service provided at a given facility over time (before and after the program started). While we cannot yet measure the ultimate outcome on psychosocial functioning of clients and other community members (see a good attempt in Myers and Bean, 1968), we will focus on the intermediate step: the type and amount of service received by area residents. Since the CMHC Act attempted to change directly the mix of service received by area residents, and only indirectly the quality of service obtained, the measurement of utilization rates addresses the major expected output of the program. We will relate input to output by measuring the effect of providing various types and amounts of service within residential areas.

Throughout the analysis we will be particularly concerned with the underlying question of whether to consider the high rates of utilization of MH services observed for lower socioeconomic groups to be evidence of a high incidence of pathology due to the stress engendered by their circumstances, of subcultural deviations from middle-class norms of behavior, or of the workings of social control mechanisms forced upon disadvantaged groups and manifested in social programs and service facilities. To deal with this question, we will introduce comparable area-based rates of reported juvenile delinquency.[1] While the causes of delinquency are much in dispute, there is general agreement in characterizing it as deviance and applying various forms of social control to reduce it. We will also find that analysis of nonlinear and stratified relationships in the mental health service utilization data is particularly helpful in clarifying the relationships of socioeconomic characteristics, institutions, and deviant behavior. Nonlinear and stratified analysis will add many unexpected effects and greatly enrich the findings.

This framework obviously takes a broad view of the federal MH program as a strategy to impact the total set of services provided to residents of a community,

of the data are drawn and has provided a fund of good advice, personal encouragement, and—through the agency of Albert Maiwald, Robert Poulin, and Fred Winsor—good raw data. Vital support for the study and much wisdom about mental health services was provided by Dr. June J. Christmas, Commissioner of Mental Health Services, New York City. Earlier support and encouragement was provided by Barbara B. Blum, Deputy Commissioner. Thanks are also due to friends and colleagues who engaged in the pilot planning project task force for the Bedford-Stuyvesant CMHC. Above all, the work would not have been completed without the advice, data, support, and personal encouragement of Dr. Elmer L. Struening and his colleagues at the New York State Department of Mental Hygiene/Columbia University School of Public Health: Gregory Muhlin, Dr. Patricia Cohen, Barry Milcarek, Gerhard Raabe, and Mattie L. Jones.

rather than just a means of providing one high quality service at a facility labeled CMHC. The breadth of federal intent becomes clear when one examines the report of the Joint Commission on Mental Illness and Health (JCMIH, *Action for Mental Health,* 1961) created by the Mental Health Study Act of 1955, the relevant congressional hearings, or the debates over the Act which emerged (see Connery, 1968). While one may argue whether the implementation of the Act was reasonably related to these goals (I have argued that it was not, at least as applied to large urban areas), it is in terms of its impact on the total system of care that the program should be evaluated. This becomes even clearer when one recognizes that the federal CMHC Act of 1963 served to codify as national policy an approach that was already accepted by the vanguard of the mental health profession. The states of New York, California, New Jersey, Minnesota, Connecticut, Maine, Indiana, Vermont, and Wisconsin all had community MH services acts prior to 1960 (Hearings, 1963: 83). To obtain a measure of the independent effect of CMHCs, therefore, we will have to model the interaction of utilization rates, social area characteristics, and facility coverage for all types of facility and all areas of the city. For example, three CMHCs in NYC are operated by voluntary (nonprofit, private) hospitals, three by municipal hospitals. To measure the impact of CMHCs in these communities, we will therefore require independent estimates of the impact of voluntary and municipal hospital coverage in areas of specified social characteristics. Only then may the effects of CMHC programs be distinguished from the effects of expanding the hospitals which received the grants to operate them. Fortunately, stepwise multiple regression techniques are perfectly suited to making such distinctions.

In conclusion, we will see that, while facility coverage in general and CMHC coverage in particular have a great deal of impact on overall service utilization, these effects are almost entirely a product of the social characteristics of areas in which facilities are located. The CMHC programs will be shown to have virtually no effect on the relative utilization rates of outpatient versus inpatient service alternatives.

## II. THE CMHC PROGRAM:
## OPERATIONALIZING THE GOALS OF THE FEDERAL LEGISLATION

The program whose impact we are evaluating here exists at two levels. At the broadest level, "Community Mental Health" refers to an amalgam of clinical orientations, social ideologies, and state, local, and national programs. At a narrower level, the program may be defined as the attempts of the U.S. government to crystallize these trends into a set of strategies, operating principles, and funding regulations for the Community Mental Health Centers Act of 1963. For strategic purposes, we will draw our formal propositions for analysis from the crystallization represented by the Act. However, in recognition of the fact that the Act is an attempt to interject federal policy into an ongoing system of state, county, municipal, and private activities, we will use a set of testing techniques which compare service utilization in areas covered by federally funded CMHCs with all other areas of New York City.

A good summary of the development of the program can be found in Connery (1968); other helpful discussions are presented by Mechanic (1969) and Kahn

(1969). For the present analysis, we will focus on certain major provisions of the Act and the underlying assumptions about the nature of the service system and how it operates. The major provisions of the Act refer to:

1. Provision of services to a defined geographic area, of relatively small size (the localization hypothesis);
2. Provision of a "comprehensive" set of services of graded intensity in varying structures (the comprehensiveness hypothesis);
3. The shift of predominance from long-term, custodial services to short-term, nonhospital services (the prevention hypothesis).

We will first discuss the overall strategy of the CMHC Act in order to derive appropriate measures of impact for our study. We will then formulate the provisions and goals of the Act into a set of testable propositions of the operation of the MH service system into which the federal program was thrust.

## A. Federal Intervention Strategy: Input Versus Output Measures

The goals of the federal program on involvement in community mental health are, as for most social programs, multiple and diffuse. However, analytical hindsight allows us to make a basic distinction among possible strategies and characterize certain goals logically implicit in the actions taken. While we may thus *not* be evaluating *decisions* of individual or organizational actors in terms of their motivations, goals, values, and so on, we *are* evaluating the *impact of the implicit decisions of the aggregate political system.*

The most basic level of decision was whether to focus on the *ultimate goals* of improving the effect of service upon individual clients, or to focus on the *proximate goals* of instigating change in the input system by which other actors effect change in ultimate goals. For example, dissatisfaction with the type of care then provided to mental patients by states and localities could have produced a decision to supplement or supplant that care with directly provided federal care, on the model of Public Health Service hospitals or Veterans Administration services, each of which is a limited method of circumventing the normal federalized relationships. The decision actually made, however, was to develop a two-part grant system to modify inputs of other actors: the first part was a construction program to house facilities in community settings as a replacement to isolated state hospitals; the second was a set of incentive grants to expand local services to become comprehensive, with comprehensiveness defined not as some aspect of the client-therapist relationship, but as the range of input services provided. Indeed, the nature of expansion was to change the structure under which services were provided, rather than to change the nature of the services themselves.

An evaluation of the impact of the federal program, therefore, must answer two questions: (1) Did the grant incentive program actually produce a change in the input structure of service provided? and (2) Did the new input structure produce any different results in the treatment of clients? If the answer to (1) is "No," then question (2) becomes moot. While a humane and logically consistent evaluation effort should focus on ultimate, client-oriented goals, I would argue that in the present context, it is strategically preferable to focus on the changes in the input structure (i.e., upon service system supply). The most critical basis for this contention is the history of legislative action.

The basic rationale presented by the Kennedy Administration to the congressional committees considering the bill was as follows:

1. The bulk of services provided at state hospitals were custodial, not therapeutic; moreover, conditions were so bad as to constitute a national disgrace;
2. Recent advances in drug therapy (mostly tranquilizers) and experimental community programs indicated that patients could be treated with better effect, at lower long-term cost, in community facilities;
3. Professional and community opinion had advanced far enough to allow an end to the extrusion of individuals whose behavior might annoy others, but who were not really dangerous;
4. State hospital admissions could be reduced by 50%, if the federal government provided sufficient funds to construct alternative facilities and provided staffing grants as an inducement to convert staff assignments (HR Report # 694, 1963; Testimony of Boisfuillet Jones before Senate Committee on Labor and Public Welfare, 1963).

The deplorable conditions of large institutions had been documented many times and the negative effects of institutionalization carefully studied (Goffman, 1961; Stanton and Schwartz, 1954). The first contention is, therefore, considered a sociological truism at this point.

The second contention, when examined closely, seems to have been widely supported in theoretical writings in professional journals between 1950 and 1960, and held by a group of leading psychiatrists who had influence at NIMH and the APA. However, an examination of the research literature, particularly the experimental projects cited in the congressional hearings (Greenblatt, et al., 1963; Zwerling and Wilder, 1961), shows that the demonstrations cited were few in number, involved small numbers of patients (100+), and produced results open to a variety of interpretations. Moreover, the studies focused mostly upon what could be done to avoid hospitalization for individual clients, rather than upon what would affect hospitalization rates for a community.

The level of public opinion seems to have been inferred rather optimistically from a study funded under the Mental Health Study Act of 1955 (Gurin et al., 1960). However, the report of the Joint Commission on Mental Illness and Health (JCMIH), created by the 1955 Act, gave a more realistic appraisal of the level of rejection of persons with a psychological disorder, and its recommendations stressed public education campaigns to make service changes feasible (JCMIH, 1961).

*Action for Mental Health,* the report of the Joint Commission which helped precipitate the 1963 legislation, did provide·an optimistic reading of the effects of drugs and programs to prevent hospitalization. We may thus conclude that, although the empirical basis was tenuous, the finding that different program input arrangements produced desired impacts at the client level had been made to the satisfaction of the psychiatric community (at least the dominant elements thereof) and the executive and legislative branches of government. However, there is quite a distance from the acceptance of research indicating that, under certain conditions, certain persons can be maintained in the community, to a program intended to shift the focus of treatment from the hospital to alternative programs. The Joint Commission's recommendations regarding hospitalization were far more moderate, calling for improved hospital facilities and increased training of hospital staff, as well as alternative programs (JCMIH, 1961: xvii):

> The objective of modern treatment of persons with major mental illness is to enable the patient to maintain himself in the community in a normal manner. To do so, it is necessary (1) to save the patient from the debilitating effects of institutionalization as much as possible, (2) if the patient requires hospitalization, to return him to home and community life as soon as possible, and (3) thereafter to maintain him in the community as long as possible.

This view of hospitalization was probably close to center. Advocates of community mental health tend to see prolonged hospitalization as required by society rather than the patient. More traditional psychiatrists consider patients to be ill and see the knowledge of cure at a minimal stage; hospitalization can be minimized by drugs which alleviate symptoms of depression or violent behavior, but is still necessary for treating the causes of illness which are intrapsychic, biochemical, or some mixture of the two. The orientations of the NIMH leaders who molded the final CMHC Act were far in advance of the center of the profession. However, the need for federal legislation to incorporate conflicting views and allow sufficient leeway in professional orientation to be implemented nationwide produced a package that included hospitalization and its alternatives as part of the five required "basic services," and did not dictate the therapeutic orientation to be practiced within the required program structures.

At this point it is interesting to remark upon Moynihan's argument that the Kennedy-Johnson social programs represented a "professionalization of reform" (Moynihan, 1965). By this he means that the initiative for programs came not from the demands of the clients who would benefit or from a broad intellectual support for reform as was found in the New Deal. Rather, programs were generated by professional administrators, social scientists, and therapists who were able to analyze governmental statistics, research findings, and generalize their perceptions of individuals' needs into large-scale programs. In the CMHC program, we see the impetus for reform coming from the professional groups represented by the Joint Commission and NIMH. Moreover, with national program design based upon a professional ideology, rather than upon a demand of clients and communities, we see the development of a program more advanced than many professionals or communities were willing to implement. To maintain disturbed persons in the community requires a willingness of families, landlords, and neighbors to accept unusual speech or behavior patterns. An illustration of this gap is found in the fact that in 1974—ten years after the CMHC Act and twenty years after the New York State Community Mental Health Services Act—there is a major controversy in the urban areas of New York over a state policy of not institutionalizing persons with a marginal level of social competence (see series of *New York Times* articles, 1974). The salience of the issue is demonstrated by the fact that it has produced special state budget appropriations and that both gubernatorial candidates raised it as a campaign issue and the Commissioner was replaced after the election.

The significance of the professionalization of reform embodied in the CMHC Act is that it implies, as a logical and political requirement, an indirect strategy of implementation. States, localities, and professionals must first agree to provide services under a different set of program structures (a different physical setting, a different administrative structure linking multiple forms of service, a different number of hours per day). The minimal goals of structural change are defensive; the CMHC's prime goals of "continuity" and "comprehensiveness" of care refer not to direct treatment goals, but to assuring clients that they will not "fall between the cracks" and that the service alternative to which they are admitted will be appropriate. This aspect of defense is clearly stated in the Joint Commission Report (JCMIH, 1961: 25). After noting a 15% rate of spontaneous remission, or recovery without any treatment, it is stated:

> How much more [than the 15%] depends in part, as we know from the studies of Stanton and Schwartz (1954) and others, on what is done in the routine management of the patient to aggravate his condition, "set him back," and thereafter fix his disorder in a treatment-resistant form. In short, it is as important to guard a patient against the *wrong* treatment as it is to institute active therapy likely to produce favorable results.

The leaders of the profession thus saw the bulk of the nation's services to be so poor as to preclude any positive effects of therapy. The first order of business was thus to create a tolerable set of institutions, then to increase the effectiveness of therapy provided. Given this perception, well documented by statistics on overcrowding, staff-patient ratios, and expenditure levels, the overall thrust of the Act must be seen as inducing organizational change, and this is the intended direct result. Ultimate provision of therapeutic intervention is the intended indirect result. Client effects are the result of the interaction of such direct intervention relationship with the program context and setting. One would, of course, like to know whether there has been any consistent relationship between innovation in therapeutic methods and program structure (as a result of orientations of clinicians to change, of local government pressure, or funding incentives). While such innovations may or may not have been intended, such a finding would be an intervening variable explaining the relationship of the findings between the first (program structure change) and second (impact on clients) questions raised above. We must still address the logically prior question, "Did the federal program meet its proximate goals of changing program input structure?" before addressing the ultimate question of whether such changes, in the actual form and context in which they were made, produced changes (intended or unintended) in individual clients or communities.

## Conceptual Orientation

Etzioni's concepts of organizational "scope" (1961: 161) and "pervasiveness" (1961: 163) are helpful in understanding the structural goals of the community mental health centers program:

Organizations whose participants share many activities are *broad* in scope.... *Narrow* organizations are those in which participants share few activities. These may be instrumental activities, as in business unions, or expressive activities, as in social clubs.

The range of pervasiveness is determined by the number of activities in or outside the organization for which the organization sets norms. Pervasiveness is small when such norms cover only activities directly controlled by the organizational elites; it is larger when it extends to other activities carried out in social groups composed of organizational participants; . . .

Referring specifically to mental hospitals, Etzioni (1961: 165) notes:

Typical coercive organizations are broad in scope but low in pervasiveness. If emphasis on coercion declines, as when rehabilitation becomes more pronounced in prison, or therapy in mental hospitals, scope tends to decline and pervasiveness to increase. . . . The organization strives now not merely to control public behavior in the compounds of the coercive organization, but also to affect internalized values, and thus to change private behavior as well as future behavior outside the organization.

Etzioni was referring to changes of orientation within mental hospitals. The CMHC program involved generalizing those changes to an entire range of activities conducted outside the hospital. Thus, by treating clients at outpatient clinics, with partial hospitalization, and in rehabilitation (often called resocialization) programs, it was intended to reduce the scope of organizational infringement upon the clients' lives. With the decline in scope was to come an increase in pervasiveness. These new programs involved working with not only the individual client, but also his family, school, and place of employment; his capacity to function in these activities was to be increased by therapeutic intervention in this expanded number of living activities (social functions), not just intervention in his verbal or physical expressions concerning his activities. Etzioni further notes that such a shift also entails a shift from a coercive to normative mode of compliance. How was such a shift to be effected, if popular norms would not accept persons exhibiting bizarre or threatening behavior in public? The answer was the required component of a "consultation and education" program, to make community residents aware of the different type of services to be offered and prepare the ground for a new program orientation.

What is critical, however, is that the federal program does not mandate these shifts that are internal to program operations. Rather, it mandates different structures, assuming that the tendencies described by Etzioni will indeed produce different outcomes. *That is, noting the inverse correlation between scope and pervasiveness, the Act mandated a change in scope, assuming a change in pervasiveness would occur.* It might have been equally reasonable to mandate a change in pervasiveness by promulgating program operation criteria independent of program structure, assuming that either programs would consequently narrow their scope, or that only narrow-scope programs would apply and be approved for funding. Had the latter strategy been adopted, evaluation of the program would require us to test the level of pervasiveness achieved by the programs "to affect internalized values, and thus to change private behavior as well as future behavior outside the organization." A structural scope strategy was adopted, and the program must be evaluated accordingly, since we are evaluating the hypotheses of the program, not Etzioni's hypotheses concerning the relation between scope and pervasiveness. (It should be noted that Etzioni refers to a correlational tendency, not to a causal impact in either direction.)

The initial problem one must confront is how to develop operational measures of the goals of mental health services. One possibility is the use of attitude survey questionnaires (see Rabkin, 1972, for a review of the literature on such scales). The difficulty here, as in any values research, is how to relate expressed values to values operative in actual behavior. The basis of such attitude scales is that there is a fairly well-developed and consistent "mental health ideology," which is embodied in federal and New York State legislation for one and two decades, meaning that it is the official position of those controlling funding for such services. Within such a restricted area as New York City, where there is much professional interaction and a general welfare orientation supportive of the mental health ideology has been dominant for forty or fifty years, one could predict rather invarient response across institutions (with variation occurring among ranks, confirming Etzioni's differentiation of "peer cohesion" from "hierarchical cohesion"). One might therefore reject the expressed values approach in favor of operationalizing Etzioni's concepts of scope and pervasiveness of organizational influence upon participants' behavior; scope is defined as "the number of activities in which their participants are jointly involved"; pervasiveness "is determined by the number of activities in or outside the organization for which the organization sets norms" (Etzioni, 1961: 160, 163). As Etzioni points out, while reduction in scope of control implies less coercion and more emphasis on normative control, effective use of normative control requires increased pervasiveness into multiple aspects of participants' social life. While pervasiveness is nearly impossible to measure on a large scale (because, like "the impact of MH therapy," it operates over a long period of time and actual behavior is subject to a vast number of external influences), scope is rather conveniently operationalized by the breakdown of five basic MH services used by NIMH and throughout the professional literature. These five—emergency room 24-hour hospitalization, partial hospitalization, outpatient care, consultation and education—fit onto a reasonably consistent ordinal scale of decreasing scope (with somewhat variant positions for rehabilitation), involving both hours out of the day in which the client is participating and the degree to which other persons are involved (an aspect of pervasiveness, which fits the negative relationship with scope hypothesized by Etzioni). By measuring the differential use of these services by different socio-spatial groups, and relating them to access patterns, we can therefore infer which of several alternative explanations for facility location and orientation is operative. It will be noted that the above analysis has been drawn from reference to participants in an ongoing structure, without reference to the individual's path of entry as a participant.

Two other classes of explanation would focus at the individual level. The first is the client demand level, popular in the medical literature, which conceives of a service provided as a benefit to a population which needs it ("population at risk") and desires it ("demand" as measured by utilization rates of facilities and waiting lists). More incisive analysts note that medical services in general and mental health services in particular tend to generate their own demand; most of the economic assumptions about availability of alternative services and consumer information levels from which economic demand models derive are not met in the provision of public health or mental health services. The extreme contradictions to such a model are, of course, the still numerous instances of involuntary commitment and the constrained "choice" of psychiatric service to avoid criminal prosecution or incarceration for acts ranging from drug use to murder.

This hypothesis leads to a second class of explanations, which would emphasize social values of deviance control by classing mental health facilities with prisons. (There is a strong basis in sociological theory and American history to support this equivalence. Cf. Goffman, *Asylums,* 1961; Rothman, 1971; Etzioni, 1961; Shaw and McKay, 1969.) Rather than focusing on social control, however, one could begin to deal with the behavior of participants not by concepts of incentive (which Etzioni employs, following Simon; cf. March and Simon, 1958), but by concepts of *defenses against control.* In such a formulation, admission rate to mental health facilities would be labeled not utilization (demand model), but induction or capture rate. Our emphasis would not be just on the overall rate of induction, but the differential induction into services with varying levels of scope of control. Thus, a high SES area might have a low overall induction rate; moreover, it would have a lower rate of induction into facilities with a high scope of control. Both of these rates would be dependent upon availability of resources to avoid being controlled.

When one considers such a "defensive resources" model and how it might work, one is struck by the closeness of the relevant personal resources and the social criteria psychiatrists usually add to clinical criteria when deciding whether to admit a person to a hospital: able to hold a job, travel to work or therapy; have an intact family; stable living arrangement (housing); good physical health. Failure to meet these criteria indicates to the psychiatrist that the person is unlikely to maintain himself, take medication, show up for outpatient therapy. However, meeting these criteria also implies an independence from psychiatric control, since all of these factors will make a client able to avoid transferring his relevant world from community to hospital. In brief, these resources represent connections to persons or social structures, which expect the individual to maintain interaction and which can come to retrieve him if he is absent for long. Conversations with many hospital psychiatrists indicate that the desire of a family to hospitalize a client or keep him at home is often the strongest factor in the doctor's decision whether to admit. The unfortunate result may be that unconnected individuals are forced to accept the hospital as a substitute family. (We will explore family structure as a predictor in more detail in a later section.)

Hollingshead and Redlich (1958: 210-212) provide an interesting illustration of this by breaking down the social class relationship to prevalence (total treated cases) into: incidence (new cases), reentries, and persons under continuous treatment (see Table 11.1).

*It is evident that the powerful relationship they observed between social class*

TABLE 11.1  PREVALENCE VERSUS INCIDENCE AS A FUNCTION OF SOCIAL CLASS*
(Rates/$10^5$)

| Class | Prevalence (All cases) | Incidence (New cases) | Reentries | Continuous Treatment |
|-------|----------|----------|-----------|-----------|
| I-II | 553 | 97 | 88 | 368 |
| III | 528 | 114 | 68 | 346 |
| IV | 665 | 89 | 59 | 516 |
| V | 1,668 | 139 | 123 | 1,406 |
| Total | 808 | 104 | 76 | 638 |

* From Hollingshead and Redlich (1958 210-211).

*and prevalence is really an artifact of the rate at which patients accumulate, or fail to be discharged.* The incidence rate is nonlinear with class, and the differences between the lowest class (V) and the others is a fraction of the difference in continuously treated cases.

In terms of "defensive resources," then, this suggests that the most deprived persons simply have the least capacity to free themselves from hospital control once inducted.

We shall explore this possibility in our New York City data later in the paper by comparing the predictors of admissions with no prior service to those for total admissions. If the observed correlations between social class and utilization are in fact reflective of the personal or environmental situation of affected individuals, then our model should predict better for new entrants into the system. However, if the relationship is an artifact of the selective effect of public institutions in admitting and holding lower class persons, then the model should predict better for total admissions.

To set the CMHC program in perspective relative to the whole mental health service system into which it was thrust, two comparisons are particularly relevant. First, what is the size (budget, personnel, patients) of the CMHC program relative to the whole system. Second, what is the size of the CMHC program relative to other federal inputs in the mental health system.

For New York City, the breakdown of costs for local municipal and voluntary services is estimated in Table 11.2 (Hearings, 1973: Christmas). We thus see that, of total mental health service costs of $560 million for New York City residents, there is a federal contribution of $170 million (30%), but that only $8 million (1.4% of the total) is through the CMHC program. The total CMHC program accounts for only 3.6% of the total service system. Of the federal share, 58% of contributions to local services and 95% of total contribution are going to support the in-hospital services CMHCs were designed to replace.

Since the Medicaid legislation which causes this anomaly was not passed until 1965, it is clearly not a factor that should have been anticipated in the 1963 Act. However, it will help to moderate our expectations about the impact of the program.

TABLE 11.2   SOURCES OF FUNDING FOR PUBLICLY MENTAL HEALTH/MENTAL
RETARDATION SERVICES TO NEW YORK CITY RESIDENTS*

a.  1972-73 Budgeted Expenditures, in $ Millions

| | | |
|---|---|---|
| Local Services | | |
| (N.Y.C. budget) | Total Public Expenditure | 170 |
| | City and state share | 144 |
| | Federal share | 26 |
| State Operated Services | | |
| (hospitals, schools for | Total Expenditure | 390 |
| MR, aftercare clinics) | State share | 246 |
| | Federal share | 144 |
| Total, Local and State | | |
| Services | Total Public Expenditure | 560 |
| | City and state share | 390 |
| | Federal share | 170 |

b.  Breakdown of Federal Contribution to Local Services

| | |
|---|---|
| Total Federal Contribution | 26 |
| Federal contribution to CMHC grants | 8 |
| Federal share of medicaid/medicare | 18 |
| Breakdonw of medicaid/medicare | |
| Inpatient service | 15 |
| Outpatient service | 3 |

* Local services costs derived from 1972-73 budget of New York City Department of Mental
Health and Mental Retardation Services; state costs estimated by projecting 1970 cost
estimates supplied by NYSDMH.

By employing a multiple regression model and applying it to areas covered by all types of facilities, we will be able to differentiate the effect of the CMHC program from other federal resources, and derive some inferences about the relative effects of program versus fee for service strategies.

## C.  Statement of Goals as Hypotheses:
## The Use of Social Area Analysis to
## Test Various Aspects of Community Mental Health
## Ideology in New York City

### I. Introduction

The federal CMHCs Act was predicated upon certain concerns and beliefs about the ways in which people used the mental health service system and how it treated them. Due to interaction of these beliefs with simultaneous trends in social psychology and in urban politics, the program that emerged placed an emphasis upon "aggregate phenomena:"—areas, communities, groups, organizations—rather than upon individuals. However, the original clinical basis of community psychiatry was derived from data about how individuals acted and responded to the service system. A social area analysis of use of the mental health service system will allow us to test how well the findings and beliefs about individuals carried them to aggregates.

## II. Various Concerns and Tenets of Community Mental Health Movement Expressed as Hypotheses

### A. PREVENTION HYPOTHESES

#### 1. PRIMARY PREVENTION (STRESS HYPOTHESIS)

"Primary prevention" in medical jargon refers to the prevention of a disorder by alleviating the conditions likely to cause it. In the area of physical health, there is a well-accepted body of knowledge demonstrating the ability to prevent disease through efforts at sanitation and nutrition. In mental health, this knowledge has been analogized into a body of literature usually called "stress theory," a set of propositions regarding the ways in which social-environmental stress can either cause a "mental illness" or reduce an individual's or family's capacity to cope with normal stresses of life.[2] In this study, we will draw on past findings and test the ways in social-environmental factors relate to patterns of utilization of mental health services.

Test: Multiple $R^2$ of regression, utilization rate = f(social area characteristics)

#### 2. SECONDARY PREVENTION

This refers to the hypothesis, also drawn from analogy to physical disease, that intervention early in the course of a disorder will prevent the need for more intensive treatment of a disorder discovered at a later stage. In service-system terms, this translates to the hypothesis that individuals treated early at outpatient or day/night programs will not require hospitalization. While it has been demonstrated at the individual level that hospitalization can be avoided by providing other supports, it has yet to be demonstrated that, for a given population, provision of alternatives to hospitalization will decrease hospital utilization rates (see JCMIH, 1961; Weinstein and Patten, 1969). Social area analysis will allow us to test directly whether use of one type of service enhances or prevents use of other services, when socioeconomic factors are controlled.

Tests:  a) Partial correlation coefficient between outpatient and inpatient utilization rates should be significantly negative, when social area characteristics (SACs) and facility coverage are controlled, if there is a tradeoff between services at community level of analysis.

  b) The ratio of inpatient to outpatient utilization rates is more a function of service system coverage than social area characteristics.

#### 3. TERTIARY PREVENTION

The hypothesis that a greater level of psychosocial functioning can be obtained, and further service (need for) reduced if treatment is provided in a certain type of facility (CMHC model).

Test: $UR_{Readmissions} = -f(facility\ coverage)$, when SACs controlled

That is, as facility coverage increases, particularly CMHC facilities, the rate of readmissions should decrease.

*B. COMPREHENSIVENESS HYPOTHESIS*

This is closely related to the secondary prevention hypothesis, maintaining that if services are rendered in a setting that offers a full range of alternatives to deal with all aspects and stages of an individual's disorder, there will be more appropriate placement, resulting in not only reduced hospitalization, but also in lower dropout rate (due to less dissatisfaction), and an enhanced capacity of family and community support systems to maintain the individual within the community.

This is a critical hypothesis for testing the impact of the CMHC in large urban areas, since it implies that there will be different results if a client is treated in a setting providing at least five basic services, from those found in a hospital which provides both hospitalization and OP clinic service.

Test: When SACs are controlled,

the inpatient/outpatient ratio ⎫
the total utilization rate         ⎬   will be significantly different
the withdrawal rate                ⎭

in areas covered by the following facility types:

1. Federally funded CMHC
2. Non-federally funded CMHC
3. Voluntary or municipal hospital, without CMHC
4. Control: all other areas

*C. LOCALIZATION HYPOTHESIS*

*1. SPACE FRICTION HYPOTHESIS*

Persons will only travel certain distances (times) to receive service. This intervenes in the secondary prevention hypothesis, since it implies not only that more people will use a close-by service, but also that they will select the closer of two services, even if it is less appropriate.

Tests: $UR_T = f(SD_T)$, where $SD_T$ is standard distance from area of residence to service type T

$UR = f(\text{facility coverage})$

That is, the rate of utilization should decrease as distance traveled increases; conversely, increased facility coverage should reduce distance traveled and thus increase utilization rate.

*D. EXTRUSION HYPOTHESIS*

This is largely contradictory to most of the above hypotheses. It posits that rates of mental health service utilization, particularly hospitalization, are less a function of either the environment (primary prevention hypothesis) or the service system (secondary prevention, comprehensiveness, and localization hypotheses), than of the unwillingness of family or others to tolerate certain behaviors. Unfortunately, this hypothesis could be supported by similar findings to the stress hypothesis, with simply a different interpretation of the meaning of the SACs. However, there are some tests that will allow us to differentiate this component.

Tests:  a) How mental health service utilization rates (URs) correlate with other extrusion measures: delinquency, criminal arrest.
   b) What SACs factors do hospital and nonhospital utilization rates correlate with—same or different
       —family support versus environmental conditions
       —economic resources for alternative treatment
   c) Do same SACs predict total admissions rate ($UR_{TOT}$) and rate of admissions with no prior service ($UR_{NPS}$)?

## III. The Model and the Variables Measured

### A. THE MODEL IN PATH FORM

We may describe the overall model within which we will test the program hypotheses by the following simplified "path diagram" (cf. Duncan, 1966). Each path is mediated by complex structures, which will be discussed in the body of the paper.

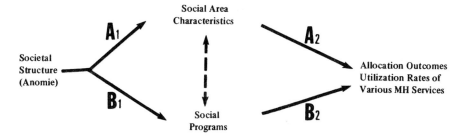

The social structure path (A) is mediated by such factors as social integration, community disorganization, family disorganization, personal frustration, and alienation. The social program path (B) is mediated by distribution over social space, size of facility or budget, and auspice (public or private). We can thus specify the following set of variables:

### 1. UNIT OF ANALYSIS = "health area" (n = 333)

A geographic area having a mean population of approximately 24,000, composed of even aggregations of census tracts, and used for reporting and planning purposes by health and mental health agencies.

### 2. DEPENDENT VARIABLES

   a. Utilization rate (UR) = estimated annual admissions to service/population
      Note: rates are age-adjusted; separate rates are calculated for each type of service.
   b. Juvenile delinquency rate (JD rate) = Number reported juvenile offenses/population age 7-20

Note: this second dependent variable is added as a control, for the purpose of general discussion of social deviance, since it is recorded by an independent governmental system.

### 3. INDEPENDENT VARIABLE SETS

    a. Social Area Characteristics: area rates for income; racial/ethnic attributes; age, structure, community environment (housing); family structure and composition. Variables are grouped theoretically, not empirically.[3]

    b. Facility Coverage: location of various facilities within the same health area (average population of approximately 24,000) or same catchment area (average population of approximately 200,000) as the area for which UR is observed.

To test the hypothesized causal paths of the model, we will employ the multiple regression techniques suggested by Blalock (1961), Duncan (1966), and Cohen (1968). This approach offers us the advantage of being able to sort out and summarize the effects of a large number of interrelated variables. While the regression model will be the overall framework in which data are analyzed, some of the most interesting results will be obtained by exploring the ways in which the linear regression model must be modified to incorporate relationships which do not meet the requirements of being linear, additive, and continuous.

By testing the impact of CMHCs on utilization rates within this broad model, we will be able to distinguish the effects of the program from the effects of the social characteristics of areas in which the program has been implemented and the rest of the service system into which the CMHC was introduced.

### B. CHOICE OF VARIABLES TO TEST THE MODEL

#### 1. DEPENDENT VARIABLES: UTILIZATION RATE AS A MEASURE OF PATHOLOGY, SERVICE LEVEL OR CLASS INTERACTION

The model introduced in the first section of this paper depends upon the predominance of social area characteristics in predicting mental health service utilization rates. We must, therefore, examine closely the theoretical nature of the relationships among social variables, facility location, and utilization before proceeding to the empirical relationships.

Our contention that these relationships ultimately depend upon societal values about subcultural behavior patterns stems from the definitional ambiguity and empirical unreliability of what mental health services are supposed to do.

Cumming (1968: 113) provides us with a striking demonstration of the failure to develop clear operational criteria in the entire realm of personal social service:

In 1922, Mary Richmond defined "differential casework" as "those processes which develop personality through adjustments consciously effected, individual by individual, between men and their social environment." . . . Later, psychiatric theory affected casework practice, but, as Perlman's (1957) definition showed, the goal remained utopian, the method vague: "Casework is a process used by certain human welfare agencies to help individuals cope more effectively with their problems in social functioning."

It is certainly not novel to point out that where goals are utopian and methods vague, there is a great freedom to manipulate lives and act upon personal value biases in the name of social welfare. What is important for our study is that the definitional ambiguity extends beyond the theory of casework to public expectations of who is to be served, by whom—the basis for the questions of program structure with which we are concerned. Schon has described such problems in detail for services to the blind, and stated the inability to quantify the relevant target population as a basic principle of social services (Schon, 1971: 207). While we contend that careful demand modeling allows one to make useful quantifications of service level without an ultimate counting of need, the problem of conflicting expectations remains critical. Ryan (1969: 52) has pointed out that there is a dual connotation to the term "mental health services," as both:

a. "all professional services directed to the emotionally disturbed that are intended to ease their distress"

b. "services that require psychiatric training or training in closely allied fields."

In the first part of this paper, we discussed the ideology of the community mental health movement in terms of Etzioni's distinction between "scope" and "pervasiveness" of an organization's relationship to individuals. The distinction is again relevant. It is the goal of reducing scope of activities but increasing the pervasiveness into many aspects of an individual's life that is entailed in Ryan's first connotation. In the name of comprehensiveness and continuity of care, we run a great risk of invading privacy and fostering dependence. Moreover, extension into many aspects of life increases the probability of imposing the values of government or its agents upon recipients of service.

Different expectations about mental health services as a function of social class have been documented in numerous small sample studies (Hollingshead and Redlich, 1958; Redlich, Hollingshead, and Bellis, 1955; Overall and Aronson, 1963). Dohrenwend has added to this data about comparative tolerance of deviance among psychiatrists, community leaders, and an ethnic group cross-section: While in his study psychiatrists ranked as more seriously ill the description of withdrawn schizophrenics, the combined community leader and ethnic group sample "were most likely to see as serious those cases that threaten others: the paranoid, the alcoholic, and the juvenile character disorder" (Dohrenwend, 1967: 424). However, in Myers and Bean's (1968) followup of former patients, reports of symptoms actually observed by other family members placed much less emphasis on alcoholism (12% response) and violence (8%), and more on apparent nervousness (60%), worrying and complaining (40%), and generalized unhappiness and perceived hopelessness (29%). We thus see a misattribution of threatening behavior by community leaders and followers.

The most critical comparison for our study is that between client and therapist. In a highly controlled study of family background and child behavior problems,

Langner (1973) administered a direct psychiatric interview to 271 of the 1,034 sampled children upon whom he received a detailed behavioral questionnaire. From information obtained in the interviews he developed a Total Impairment Rating (T.I.R.) to reflect psychiatric judgment. The correlation coefficients between the specific behavioral factors and the psychiatric judgment (T.I.R.) ranged from -.06 to +.54 (Pearson's r). This indicates an extremely low level of consonance. Moreover, Langer also found that only about 50% of seriously impaired children had been referred for service. Commenting upon the results, Langner (1973: 23) states:

> In fact, we know from previous studies that psychiatric impairment is only a partial factor, and race, religion, socioeconomic status, age, sex, type of treatment available, cultural attitudes toward the behavior involved, etc., may be just as important or possibly more important in the determination.

Since we are concerned with rates of admitted patients, all of whom meet professional criteria for impairment, we wish particularly to emphasize the dominant cultural values in psychiatric judgment. In Table 11.3 we have sorted the 18 Child Behavior factors reported by Langner by the level of correlation with psychiatric judgment of T.I.R. (see Langner, 1973: 29, Table 7). While we cannot make definitive judgments on such a resorting (with no controls for characteristics of the psychiatrists), and the overall range of correlations is low, it seems clear that the behavior patterns most affecting psychiatric judgments (r = .3-.5) relate to conflict and aggression; that except for Mentation ("mixes up words, has trouble remembering things), training and development occupy a middle range (r = .2 - .3); that items referring to extreme passivity and dependence produced no correlation (r $\leq$ .19) with psychiatric judgment. To the extent that lower socioeconomic groups tend to exhibit more aggressive/conflictive behavior as a norm, we would expect members of such groups to be disproportionately admitted to psychiatric service as a function of psychiatrists' values about such behavior, rather than of clients' level of distress.

TABLE 11.3

| Behavior Factor | Correlation of TIR | Behavior Factor | Correlation of TIR |
|---|---|---|---|
| Mentation Problems | .54 | Repetitive Motor Behavior | .26 |
| Fighting | .50 | Training Difficulties | .25 |
| Conflict with Parents | .49 | Late Development | .24 |
| Regressive Anxiety | .46 | Sex Curiosity | .11 |
| Isolation | .41 | Weak Group Membership | .10 |
| Delinquency | .36 | Unanxious/Mildly Antisocial | -.06 |
| Self-destructive Tendencies | .29 | Competition with Others | .03 |
| Delusions/Hallucinations | .28 | Undemandingness | -.02 |
| Conflict with Siblings | .27 | Dependence/Unassertiveness | .01 |

* Derived from Langner (1973), Table 7.

An interesting example of such a tendency is reported by Wiltse (1963: 809) in reference to a groups of families in San Francisco who received Aid to Dependent Children funds:

> Our initial reading of case records left us with just such an impression—that we were dealing with a very sick group of people for whom the potentialities for quick improvement in personal and social functioning were limited. I hasten to point out that this initial impression was not substantiated; they were not as ill as they first seemed, and improvement as a result of our efforts was greater than expected.

Wiltse characterizes the relevant syndrome as "pseudo-depression"—symptoms of immobilization, isolation, poor appetite and health, poor appearance—similar to symptoms of psychological depression, but "pseudo" because they are based upon actual situations rather than psychologically distorted perceptions.

The tendency to substitute professional judgments for those of either society or client goes under the rubrics of "diagnosis" or "clinical evaluation." The willingness to engage in such substitution may be inherent in the need to develop personality theory, but it leads even proponents of cultural relativity into areas dangerous for social policy. Thus, discussing the cultural context in which deviance is defined, Seward (1972: 15) writes:

> Clinical evaluation of deviance or conformity always depends on the dynamics motivating the behavior. Insofar as it represents personal choice rather than social compulsion, it may be healthy; insofar as it expresses hostile acting out, however rationalized, it signifies pathology.

Once the therapist sets himself as judge of motivations for behavior, he has assumed a major function of social policy. If hostility, however rationalized, signifies pathology, then the client's right to perceive and appraise the reality of his circumstances is withdrawn. The ultimate dependence of definitions of mental health or pathology upon one person's opinion of another's motivations speaks against any possibility of a truly objective, operational definition.

Given this background of ambiguity and unreliability in professional judgments, and the consistency with which such judgments are related to various aspects of poverty and victimized racial and ethnic groups, we must approach our analysis in constant awareness of several alternatives, not just of explanation, but of definition:

1. There is a higher rate of "social pathology" among the victimized classes; since residential areas are highly segregated, the members of victimized classes live together in areas which consequently exhibit high rates of "social pathology." Social pathology is a *condition of the individual* affected by his relationships with other individuals and groups.
(or) 2. There is something about the physical and social environment of the areas of the city into which the victimized classes are segregated that *causes* "pathology." One of these aspects may be the awareness of victimization and segregation.

(or)  3. The individual (1) and environmental (2) causes may be mutually reinforcing over time, causing a growing rate of spatial segregation of both classes and behavior patterns.

(or)  4. Recorded measures of the above relationships may simply reflect the attitudes of majorities toward victimized minorities. In direct form, this would be the tendency to characterize as pathological certain subcultural styles (more physical expression, less verbal articulateness, greater hostility and alienation, different family roles and child-reading practices). This would produce value-biased results on population surveys of symptoms or behavior patterns, showing minorities or victimized classes to be indeed "pathological."

The indirect form of this bias is even more interesting, because it represents a political "double bind." The logic goes something like this:

a. The well-meaning middle and upper classes consider lower-class attitudes, behaviors, and values "pathological" (i.e., disagreeable, morally wrong, and/or dangerous);

b. To "help" the classes suffering the pathology (and protect themselves from its consequences at either the individual level or personal violence or the aggregate level of political discontent), the middle and upper classes mount social programs to modify these behavior patterns; of course, such programs will be conducted in the areas where the target populations reside;

c. The areas where the programs are conducted will thereby show, on officially recorded statistics, much higher rates of "incidence of pathology" or "admissions to service" or "referrals to service." Moreover, the correlation between income/race-ethnic classes and such rates will increase over time, as programs grow, create constituencies (of professionals as much as communities), and generate their own demand. The generation of demand may be as much the product of society defining social programs as the appropriate solution to lower-class problems as it is of successful operation of the programs meeting clients' goals.

There is a peculiar irony here. Psychological approaches to lower-class deviance from middle-class norms have largely evolved as an alternative to punitive approaches: reform schools and prisons have been replaced by counseling and hospitalization to bring lower-class deviants under control by providing them the same insights into the causes of their problems as are engendered in upper and upper-middle class socialization. However, concepts of norms and deviance have difficulties in crossing class boundaries.

Lower-class groups may have such high levels of certain behaviors that they become the norm, or a second norm. For example, the average illegitimacy rate is 34.6% of live births for areas with a median family income (MFI) of less than $9,000; it is 7.4% for areas with MFI above $9,000. Similarly, the mean child dependency ratio is 0.78 for low-income areas, 0.46 for middle-income areas. (Plotting these two distributions yields a clearly bimodal situation, with from one to three standard deviations between the means.) When we have bimodal distributions, deviance has three possible reference points:

1. Variance from the overall mean, which is a point between the two modes which very few cases approximate;
2. Variance from the mean of the group that is politically or culturally dominant;
3. Variance of a case from the mean of the appropriate half of the distribution.

Each of these definitions would have problems. The overall mean is a statistical artifact, rather than a representation of either social values or common behavior. Use of the dominant group's mean for other groups has several difficulties. First, it involves transferring a value out of the context in which it has meaning. Socialization to a norm requires indulgence or deprivation of related values, which may be lacking. Second, the concept of socialization to a norm is based upon a set of processes stemming from the presumption that most persons and structures hold a certain value or practice a certain behavior, so that the unsocialized individual will be confronted continually with the appropriate model. Substitution of political dominance for widespread behavior, and therapeutic programs for continual confronation with referent groups and behavior models, may provoke hostility more than compliance, or may simply be doomed to ineffectiveness through the obvious discrepancy between norms as stated and norms as observed. While imposition of dominant group norms may be oppressive or ineffective, recognition of multiple norms may be equally so, as when reduced teachers' expectations for black students produces lowered achievement.

If many members of a minority group are striving to achieve dominant group norms, they may consider programs based upon their present behavior patterns or social conditions to be efforts at "keeping them in their place." Rainwater and Yancey (1967) demonstrate this problem in chronicling reactions to the Moynihan Report on "The Negro Family: The Case for National Action." Moreover, the problems causing distress to individuals may derive specifically from their frustration in trying to achieve dominant group norms, as demonstrated by Parker and Kleiner. They found that within an all Negro sample in Philadelphia, the group treated for emotional problems had greater discrepancy between aspiration and achievement than the nontreated community sample (Parker and Kleiner, 1966: 90). However, the differences appear not in income and occupational discrepancies, but in "striving scale," in which the respondent defines for himself the "best possible life" and "worst possible life" and places himself between them. Throughout the various components of the study, this scale consistently distinguishes the treated or high symptom populations better than income, occupation, and educational goals. Parker and Kleiner attribute this to the "self-anchoring" nature of the scale, inferring that the relevant goal-striving stress is derived from aspirations different from those of middle class society. However, it is also possible to interpret the "striving scale" as a generalized expression of unhappiness, in which case its relationship to treated emotional problems becomes tautological. To seek psychiatric help, one must be unhappy with the way one's life is going; those persons accepted for treatment are reinforced by professionals in their perception that they are failing to fulfill role expectations or achieve some attainable goals.

The topic of juvenile delinquency has produced a considerable literature including both ecological analysis of rates for geographic areas and local social structures and personality factors. We will not deal with this topic at length here (see a good review of the literature, concepts and the history of their development by Short in Shaw and McKay, 1969). It is helpful, however, to refer to Shaw and McKay's (1969: 316) succinct summary of the implications of multiple norms for understanding "deviant" behavior:

> In cases of group delinquency it may be said, therefore, that from the point of view of the delinquent's immediate social world, he is not necessarily disorganized, maladjusted, or antisocial. Within the limits of his social world and in terms of its norms and expectations, he may be a highly organized and well-adjusted person.

"Group delinquency" of course refers to gang phenomena, where the evidence of continuous subgroup socialization is clear. However, when one leaves the framework of individual psychodynamics and begins to discuss *rates* of mental health for social groupings, the conceptualization becomes unclear. If there is a subcultural norm of certain behaviors which are divergent from and repugnant to the majority or dominant group culture, then the norm/deviance concept is no longer strictly applicable. Rather, one is talking about a divergence of values. When socialization of norms becomes entrenched in public policy and institutions, as in mental health services, one must deal with the question of who is socializing whom, into whose norms.

The relationship of localization and prevention hypotheses in the CMHC program then becomes clearer. If hospitalization reflects a decision to extrude an individual whose behavior is repugnant to the community, and if a CMHC program is successful in adapting to local community norms, then the rate of hospitalization should decrease as individual behavior is judged by the most appropriate standards.

The "double bind" becomes evident when one tries to imagine an argument over the interpretation of the data as evidence of class victimization versus social pathology.

For instance, data from the present study show a strong positive correlation between mental health facility admission rates and juvenile delinquency rates. Further, both rates correlate with similar socioeconomic characteristics. Social program proponents would argue that, since the victimized classes show all forms of social pathology, both rates should be high, and the positive correlation indicates that public programs are serving the people who need them most. If one argues next that one goal of mental health programs is to produce lower juvenile delinquency rates, the response is that such solutions take many years, more resources than are currently provided, and techniques of intervention are still at a relatively primitive level. If one points out that the correlation between "pathology" rates and SES are increasing over time, despite the activity of programs, it can be responded that social stratification and residential segregation are also increasing over time. Increased social stratification would produce a higher level of either absolute or perceived deprivation (Rainwater and Yancey, 1967), while a constant level of deprivation with an increased level of residential segregation would also produce a higher correlation between social deprivation and incidence rates (of pathology) at the aggregate or community level of analysis.

At this broad level of debate there is a logical stalemate. It is therefore necessary to explore further evidence as stated above. Before doing so, it will be helpful to explicate the major theoretical concepts underlying the relationships between social variables and mental health, and to review the way these concepts have been used in the major literature of the field.

## 2. INDEPENDENT VARIABLES: SOCIAL AREA CHARACTERISTICS

### a. Definition of Concepts

When one reviews the literature on race, class, mental health, and social policy, the pervasiveness of the concept of *anomie* is striking. Of course, many scholars date modern sociology from Durkheim's studies. However, the concept has undergone marked efflorescence from its original formulation as the lack of regulated relations among organs and classes (Durkheim, 1933/1964: 368) to more limited concepts of personal alienation and frustration community or family disorganization and social integration. We may clarify the issue by arranging the concepts into a series of system levels.

1. *Anomie.* This is a *societal level* concept, applying to whole nations or multinational cultures. The concept refers to an entire range of values and behaviors, including both norms and deviations from norms. There is then an emphasis upon formal (juridicial) and informal (moral) mechanisms for imposing social order and limiting the magnitude of deviance relative to the norms. In Durkheim's formulation, *anomie* will occur when the division of labor in society does not produce social solidarity inspired by regularized roles and interactions (1933/1964: 368) or when there is a forced division of labor based upon the failure of social inequalities to "exactly express natural inequalities;" that is, when there is class oppression (1933/1964: 373).

2. *Social Integration.* This is also a societal level concept. However, it tends to be formulated only in terms of the informal mechanisms, and thus lends itself to application at lower levels of the system, such as subcultures or communities. While the concept of anomie emphasizes mechanisms for maintaining order, social integration is usually conceptualized as the degree to which deviation from norms actually appears. That is, it is the behavioral manifestation of order ("solidarity") or anomie. (We are not here referring to the level of interaction or transaction, which is hypothesized by Karl Deutsch to produce integration. In Durkheim, level of transaction is the basis of "organic solidarity," is a function of the division of labor, and may produce either solidarity or anomie.)

Durkheim has argued that to be effective, norms must be universally respected; but for crime to exist, norms must be not quite universal. To paraphrase, they must be universal in concept, but only nearly universal in practice (1933/1964: 103). Social disintegration, then, refers to the degree in which norms depart from universality in practice. One way in which we can assess social area characteristics and predict their impact upon deviant behavior is the degree to which they are distributed about a single mean (norm) or form a bimodal distribution between upper and lower classes. If our argument in the previous section about the likely occurrence of class oppression through definitions of deviance is true, then we should expect that the best predictors will be those with a bimodal distribution. If the argument does not hold, then the best predictor variables should be those which exhibit a wide range of continuous variance, since they will reflect behavioral patterns which cut across social class. In sum, working within Durkheim's social inequality formulation of anomie, we shall take as our operational definition of the social disintegration the existence of multiple norms of behavior. Since we are dealing at the aggregate level of areas, with considerable heterogeneity built into each observation, demonstration of multiple norms (bimodal distributions of area means) will be that much more powerful.

3. *Community Disorganization or Disintegration.* This is an application of the social integration concept to groups or areas much smaller than nations or societies. Usually these are small municipalities or neighborhoods within large municipalities. Since the legal, economic, and moral forces are assumed to exist at a broader system level, the emphasis here is again upon the behavioral manifestations of local responses to external forces. However, it is usually unclear whether such local behaviors represent a group phenomenon caused by the immediate social environment, or an aggregation of similar individual responses to external forces. Physical features of the local environment are often treated as indicators or causes of social factors.

4. *Family Disorganization.* This is perhaps the most abused concept in the set. In some cases, broken families are treated as a *measure of anomie,* on the supposition that families are a microcosm of the larger social order. In other instances, broken families are considered the *result of anomie,* as when economic discrimination is said to have destroyed the role of father in the American Negro family (Frazier, Moynihan). Finally, the breakdown of complete consanguine families is often treated as a cause of personal alienation and thereby a *cause of anomie,* due to the failure to socialize individuals into stable roles. Our analysis will test the relationship between family structure and variables at other levels.

5. *Personal Alienation or Frustration.* While this is clearly a concept referring to individual level responses to social forces, it is often generalized into a group phenomenon. Thus, if a large number of individuals experience alienation from their work or group affiliations (a manifestation of anomie), then a widespread "state of alienation" or "alienation of a group" is often said to exist. We will insist, however, upon the distinction of alienation from anomie, so as to preserve a purely individual level of explanation within our analysis.

*b. Conceptual Levels and Policy Implications*

When arrayed in this manner, it becomes clear that social integration, community disorganization, and family organization have developed as intermediate concepts linking societal structures to individual behavior. Such interpolations are necessary not just to explain complex behavior patterns, but also to allow the application of sociological theory within politically relevant contexts. For example, sociological theory may place the causes of juvenile delinquency in structures to which the concept of anomie is appropriate: national or international trends in income distribution, job markets, racial discrimination, legal mechanisms, socialization patterns, moral philosophy. In the United States, however, the federal system places responsibility for dealing with delinquency (deviant behavior) at the state and local level. We thus have a need to link theories of causes to direct explanations of effect, so that reasonable policies can be developed to deal with (help or punish) persons or groups in whom the effects of anomie are displayed. Intermediate level explanations are thus required, in the form:

Societal level (structural) patterns (A),

Produce alternative individual (behavioral) patterns (B1) or (B2),

In the presence of intermediate level (community or family) patterns (C1) or (C2).

That is, $(A) + (C1) \rightarrow (B1); (A) + (C2) \rightarrow (B2)$. By acting upon the relevant conditions at the intermediate level, desired individual behavior may be produced prior to or despite inability to produce changes in the societal level structures. If such policies are adopted, it is necessary to justify them in terms of theories linking all levels, for two reasons. First, societal level causes may be so powerful as to eliminate any intermediate level differentiations among their effect. Second, changes in societal level patterns may change the types of differentiation produced by intermediate conditions. For example, a societal level pattern of inequality of wealth may translate to individual deviance by way of forcing poor persons in urban areas to live in conditions of extreme overcrowding, leading to a high level of personal frustration. A community level program to either provide more housing space to poor persons, or to aid poor persons to develop mechanisms to cope with the frustrations of living in overcrowded conditions would therefore reduce the level of deviance. If in the first case, the societal level impact of inequality were so strong as to act multiply through overcrowded housing, unemployment, consumption capacity (e.g., regressive taxes), educational discrimination, availability of recreation, and transportation facilities, then local action in one area would simply increase the impact of the others as intermediate causes. In the second case, even if overcrowded housing were the single intermediate cause, changes in societal policies affecting the distribution of housing would modify the capacity of local housing programs to reduce deviance.

The literature on social policy and strategies for change is replete with demonstrations and arguments about the relative impacts of structural and intermediate level variables, and about the capacity to produce change in either or both of them. The present study is concerned with

1. Keeping the appropriate levels and distinctions clear.
2. Testing the relevance of certain individual level patterns at the community level (the program hypotheses presented in the first part of the paper).

3. Demonstrating the importance of the way individual level observations are fed back in conditioning policies at both the intermediate (family, community) and structural (nation, society) levels.

4. Seeking to measure the degree of local institutional bias in observing distributions of individual behavior. If the type or level of reporting the incidence of certain individual behaviors is systematically biased by either structural or intermediate factors, then structural level policies are likely to be biased in favor of perpetuating or expanding those institutions.

To the degree that structural and intermediate variables act independently, we may choose between them as alternative sources of explanation. To the degree that they interact, we may consider the intermediate variables as conditioning factors which differentiate the observed behaviors which result from structural causes.

### C. Conceptual Levels and Geographic Areas

It is now necessary to relate our discussion of levels of analysis to the use of geographic areas as units of observation. We have arranged our series of major concepts into levels based upon two criteria:

(1) *conceptual criteria* ranking "ultimate" causes at the highest level, "proximate" or "instrumental" causes at the intermediate level, and direct observations of individual manifestations of behavior at the lowest level;

(2) *aggregative criteria,* by which phenomena observed or inferred from largest groupings are placed at the highest level, individual or smallest groupings at the lowest. While at first glance these aggregative groupings may imply a consistent parallel ranking of larger to smaller geographic areas, the situation is actually more complex. Use of area rates allows us to relate individual, group, and environmental phenomena in a single analytic scheme. The conceptual criteria, however, allow us to distinguish between appropriate conceptual levels for different rates observed for the same geographic unit.

*Income and race* are two variables whose effects are clearly determined by societal level structures. However, we can observe their impact at the local level by observing that persons carrying similar racial and income attributes are clearly segregated into specialized areas of New York City. When we measure the concentration or mean level of the attributes (percent black; median family income) for a geographic area, we are accounting for structural level impacts. Other measures are clearly related to the *local (residential) environment:* persons per room, substandard housing, vacant units, number of dwelling units per structure. Accounting for the impact of these variables tells us something about the nature of the community in which persons live, which is important in two ways.

First, it tells us about certain stimuli which people will be presented with on a daily basis. Stress theory suggests that individual behavior will be conditioned in part by such stimuli. Second, housing and neighborhood conditions largely reflect local political decisions toward social groups. In this respect, we may consider community environment a translation or conditioning of social structure variables at a more direct level.

An intermediate set of variables relates directly to the *stability of expectations about the environment in which one lives;* rate of immigration, percent moved in last two or five years. While these have structural causes and are aggregations of individual or family behavior, as rates they have a clear environmental meaning. Less clear in meaning are *aged and child dependency ratios.* Environmentally, these relate to the population turnover or stability described above. However, they also relate to economic and family structure variables at a lower level of analysis. We will, therefore, treat them as separate entities.

Other rates tell us not about community disorganization, but *family organization:* illegitimacy, fertility, husband-wife headed households, mothers in the labor force. A community composed of many disorganized families could, in conceptual terms, develop highly organized structures for survival. Child and Aged Dependency ratios are reflections of the family organization patterns (empirically as well as conceptually).

Measures of *personal alienation or frustration*—school dropouts, juvenile delinquency, mental health admissions—are the dependent variables which we expect to be manifestations of the various group level differentiations. They are thus not equated with disorganization, but are the hypothesized outcome of disorganization, as disorganization is evidenced by variables at the levels described above.

A final group of variables is of particular interest. These variables tell us not about the residents of an area or the conditions in which they live, but about the *political reaction of societal decision makers to their perceptions of areas.* This is the manifestation of feedback of behavior into structural theories which we mentioned above. Thus, if we find a consistent pattern in the number and type of mental health facilities located in areas of similar characteristics, we may infer that decision makers have consistent perceptions about those areas. If mental health facilities, gang workers, and police forces are highly concentrated in high percent black or Puerto Rican areas, we may infer that decision makers expect high rates of deviant behavior to occur in these areas. Finally, if reported rates of occurrence are biased by this concentration of reporting agencies, then the perception will be reinforced by the information fed back into the system. A major effort in further studies will therefore consist of describing the pattern of facility location in terms of social space, of relating that pattern to measures of individual deviance, and of comparing "need/demand," "societal decision," and "economic forces" models of explaining these relationships.

Because nonlinear analysis will be critical for analyzing the role of the facility location variables, it will be helpful to explain now how we will utilize nonlinear relationships to help untangle individual from group phenomena.

Spatial segregation of persons of like individual attributes (income, race, ethnic background) eases the manipulation of data, but complicates interpretation of results. If we observe different rates of reported deviance for areas that are 50, 75, and 100% black, it is difficult to determine whether the results we observe are due to simply increasing the probability that a black person will be encountered, or whether the proportional racial composition has an "emergent" effect as a social environment acting upon individuals. To the extent that we can measure the impact of such variables as family composition and family structure, which are believed to reflect such environmental phenomena, we can distinguish the two. To the extent that income, race, or ethnicity exert an independent effect after intermediate variables are controlled, we are left with confusion between individual and aggregate level explanations. If the effect of race were strictly at the individual level, then the relationship between deviance and percent population of a given race would be perfectly linear. If the effects were individual, but were compounded over time or magnified by a "contagion effect," then the distribution would be a logarithmic function. If there were environmental effects caused by or correlated with a specific proportional balance of race/ethnic composition, then we could expect curvilinear functions of a higher order. Actually, such functions could reflect a series of discrete groupings or classes, rather than a continuous set of points with related attributes. That is, if similar rates of deviance were found in areas that were 45% and 55% black, then there might be a single category of the range 40-60% black that has relatively homogeneous characteristics as compared to say, ranges 60-80% and 15-40% black. However, we would have to demonstrate homogeneity not just on the dependent variable, but upon all interacting independent variables, to justify use of such discrete categories.

In brief, a linear relationship leaves us no way of distinguishing individual from environmental effects; certain nonlinear relationships can imply such distinctions. Since we have found nonlinearities, we will explore the question at some length in a later section.

### D. Illustrations of Conceptual Levels From Major Findings in the Literature

In reviewing the literature on social class and mental health, we have found similar phenomena measured in different ways, leading to explanations drawn from various levels of conceptualization. To clarify the confusion, we will briefly discuss some of the major findings in light of the distinctions made in the previous section. We stress that we are not simply discussing the "ecological fallacy" in the interpretation of data. Rather, we are discussing alternative formulations of the theoretical contexts to which these data are applied. The total chain whose links we will be discussing is schematically described in Figure 11.1. It should be borne in mind that we are dealing at the aggregate level. Therefore, we are not implying that tax laws make a particular worker poor, but that tax laws tend to make workers as a group poorer. Similarly, we are not implying that juvenile courts or mental hospitals make a particular black a juvenile delinquent or psychiatric patient, but rather that the mode of operation of these institutions tends to induct and label blacks who live in predominantly black areas. The systematic bias in the way institutions deal with individuals combines with the structural forces which society exerts upon those individuals to produce observed patterns of behavior. We thus pose for sake of argument that an anomic society could act directly through its agencies to produce reported cases of deviance, as well as through fostering social disintegration.

Leighton's various studies (Kaplan, 1971) are based upon a formulation of *social disintegration* as a cause of mental ill-health, due to interference with individual level "strivings" for physical and emotional goals.

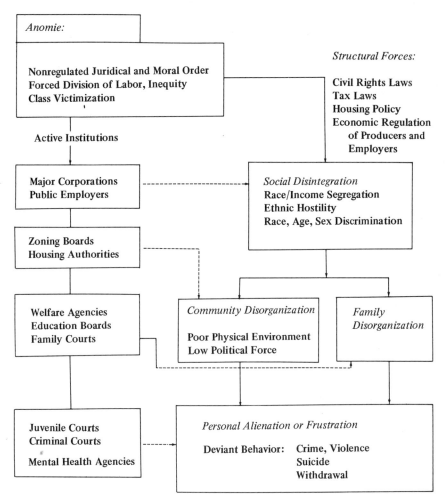

FIGURE 11.1 The Transmission of Anomie Through Active Institutions and Structural Forces
         of Society

Examples of disintegration are evident in societies that have been disrupted by forced migration, wars, economic disaster, industrial revolution, and extremely rapid acculturation. As a result, defects appear in the patterns of communication, leadership, followership, and cooperation; and failures occur in the functions concerned with the provisions of food, shelter, and clothing, the protection of health, the maintenance of law and order, defense against enemies, the care of children, the satisfaction of emotional needs, and other functions essential for the survival and welfare of the society. [Leighton, in Kaplan, 1971: 60]

This characterization closely parallels Durkheim's concept of "organic solidarity," a set of related functions by which organized collective action enhances and protects the quality of life, while making demands for authority and control. However, the emphasis on functions (similar to Parsons's integrative patterns), leaves out Durkheim's factor of "mechanical solidarity," the collective conscience that operates to bind individuals to society. We thus see the difference between *anomie* and social disintegration as the difference between a consciously regulated (or perversely regulated) set of relationships supporting a moral order in the former, as opposed to disintegration of an unconscious set of functional patterns which derive from efficiency of interaction (division of labor), but which are not bound to a moral conscience. The element of class victimization which underlies Durkheim's *anomie* or Marx's conception of alienation is thus lacking.

Social disintegration is a complex condition without a cause, whereas anomie and alienation are a syndrome with multiple causes located in the values of individuals and classes.

Hollingshead and Redlich (1958) were more attuned to evidence of victimization as an explanation of the nonlinear relationship they found between treated mental illness and social class. Biases in diagnosis and dispositions of similar deviant behaviors were clearly evidenced. They thus explained the observed differences among social classes by the action of certain institutions—psychiatrists, hospitals, clinics—as well as social norms in classifying emotional stress as illness or deviance. While their research was carried out within the context of a single community and a particular history of social differentiations, their conclusions are clearly at the level of *anomie* since they incorporate both systematic forces and conscious interaction among subgroups. What we are really discussing is alternative explanations of the chain of phenomena linking societal to individual level behavior. Compounding the complexity is the fact that, except for formal legislation or compacts, societal level behavior cannot be observed:[4] it can only be inferred from aggregations of individual level behavior. The passage from Leighton quoted above actually describes several clusters of aggregate phenomena which are postulated to have an effect upon individuals beyond that which they experience directly. That is, a society that does not provide adequately for "care of children" is postulated to have effects upon all individuals in society, not just the children who are inadequately cared for.

Further down the chain between societal and individual behaviors are *community phenomena*. The rationale for including these in the explanation is elegantly stated by Faris and Dunham (1939: 158):

> Successful transmission of the essential standardized view of the world, and therefore successful production in the person of a sufficiently normal mental organization, requires a normal family life, normal community life, reasonable stability and consistency in the influences and surroundings of the person, all supported on a continuous stream of intimate social communication. In the disorganized areas of the large industrial city many of these necessary conditions are lacking.

It is thus proclaimed that a host of intermediate structures carry the societal message to the individual, causing him to be integrated into or alienated from "the essential standardized view of the world."

When we examine Faris and Dunham's measures of these intermediate structures, however, we find that they are of two types: physical environment (industrial or commercial land-use, substandard housing) and aggregations of individual characteristics (type of dwelling unit owned or rented, percent nonwhite, percent foreign born, education, occupation, etc.). Because the two are highly related, it is difficult to tell which level we are talking about. A prime example is the high rate of alcoholic psychoses among residents of the rooming house area: are we talking about an environmental effect or describing the distribution of individuals over spaces where they can obtain housing? While the authors are explicitly aware of the difference, and use various controls to help answer it, we note a divergence between alternative intermediaries between societal structure and individual behavior. The relations of slum housing and industrial sites to concentration of certain social classes can be taken as a societal decision reflecting lack of moral concern for lower-class welfare by upper classes. That is, we could infer anomie from the predominance of environmental over individual factors.

We find a definite confusion among levels of explanation in Lander's (1954) discussion of his findings in terms of anomie, where anomie is measured by differential juvenile delinquency rates among subareas of a city. While juvenile delinquency has something to do with lawlessness, and lawlessness has to do with anomie, the construct of anomie as a set of legal and moral relationships within and among classes does not have direct meaning at this level of analysis. Lander's main argument is that, since juvenile delinquency peaks in 50% black areas, and is lowest in all white and all black areas, that anomie is a function of transition and culture conflict, as opposed to stable communities. His findings that the best predictors of differential juvenile delinquency rates were percent black and percent home ownership clearly places his analysis at either the community or individual level. Explanations in terms of anomie would have to deal with the overall level of delinquency as a function of economic and cultural changes. By way of contrast, we note the finding of the Burstein report (1972) that the overall rate of juvenile offenses in New York City increased from 52.5 per 1,000 youths in 1965 to 70.1 in 1970, and that the rate of increase was higher in nonpoverty than poverty areas. While these rates are not reported as part of a detailed study, they are suggestive of the kinds of findings for which concepts at the level of anomie might well be applied.

Also at the community level, it is interesting to note the findings of Galle, Gove, and McPherson (1972) in a study of 1960 rates of juvenile delinquency and mental hospital admissions for Chicago. Applying multiple regression techniques, they found that, while population density measured as persons per acre had little independent effect, density measured as persons per room or units per building were important predictors. This implies a predominance of individual living situation over community environment as an explanation. Moreover, their analysis indicates that the density factor is an intervening variable for social class (occupational status, education, income) and ethnicity (percent Negro, percent Puerto Rican, percent foreign born). These variables account for most of the explained variance in both juvenile delinquency rate and mental hospitalization rate.

From the above studies we obtain the impression that the best predictors of deviance are attributes of the individuals segregated into various communities, rather than some characteristics of the communities themselves. However, a force-ful argument for the spatial ecology approach—which characterizes the function of specialized neighborhoods within a diverse city—comes from Shaw and McKay (1969: 315) who have analyzed time series data on rates of juvenile delinquency in Chicago from 1920 to 1962:

> It is recognized that the data included in this volume may be interpreted from many different points of view. However, the high degree of consistency in the association between delinquency and other characteristics of the community not only sustains the conclusion that delinquent behavior is related dynam-ically to the community but also appears to establish that all community characteristics, including delinquency, are products of the operation of general processes more or less common to American cities. *Moreover, the fact that in Chicago the rates of delinquents for many years have remained relatively constant in the areas adjacent to centers of commerce and heavy industry, despite successive changes in the nativity and nationality composi-tion of the population, supports emphatically the conclusion that the delinquency-producing factors are inherent in the community* [italics added].

Shaw and McKay do not attribute causality to the physical environment of industrial areas. Rather, they describe a process by which certain areas of the city serve as the receptacles for whichever group—European immigrants, blacks, Puerto Ricans—has the lowest socioeconomic status at a given time. This low status in turn leads to a low level of socialization in dominant norms, which leads to deviate behavior. They note in particular that six areas deviated from the tendency for JD rates to remain stable from 1935 to 1960. Three were areas of consistently high black population from 1935 onward, which declined in JD rate; three were areas of major black influx, which increased in JD rate. At this point one may easily jump to major structural variables and conclude that whatever areas have the lowest income *and* most recent social upheaval will have the highest rates of deviance, that it is the interaction of these factors rather than sociocultural behavior patterns which produce deviant behavior.

How then are we to account for our finding in New York that for the highest percent black, geographically stable areas, the JD rate turns upward rather than down (see Figure 11.2)? One may suspect that it is an *artifact of denominators*. The actual frequency of juvenile offenses declines in the 90-100% black areas, but the youth population declines even more, producing an increased rate. We could then speculate that, as a result of historical artifacts (gang membership, police surveil-lance), there is a certain threshold of number of cases reported, which is indepen-dent of the population-based probability of occurrences. That is, if an area has a gang membership of 500 youths out of a youth population of 5,000, a decline in youth population to 4,500 may not affect the number of gang members or the number of reported offenses, but would increase the rate of occurrence.

A second alternative explanation may lie in *density of interaction*. We are not here referring to population density per acre, which Galle, Gove, and McPherson (1972) have shown to be a poor predictor. Rather, we are referring to the *density*

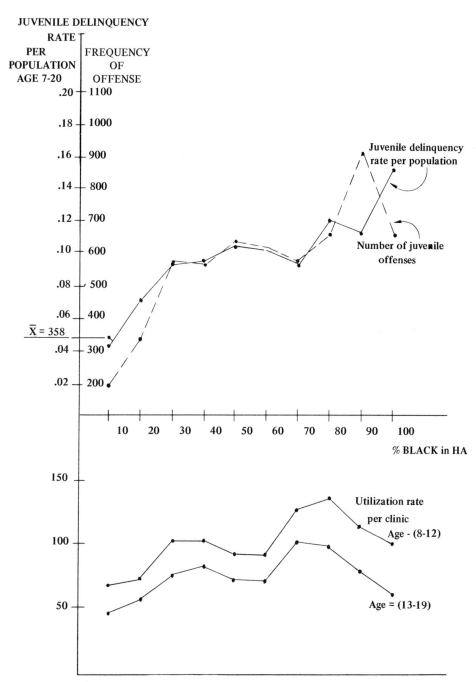

FIGURE 11.2  Juvenile Delinquency Rate as a Function of Percent Black Population

*of interactions with agencies or institutions which convert a private act or emotion into a public artifact* (reported offense or mental health facility admission). Shaw and McKay's finding that most areas retain a stable delinquency rate despite population changes, and that high delinquency areas are in the commercial center of New York City suggest that this may be true. Similarly, Lipsky (1969) has written of the mutual interdependence of police and offenders in maintaining a certain pattern of behavior. For MH admissions, the presence of mental health facilities acting as "street level bureaucrats" may also perform the *function of converting private acts to public artifacts in the areas near them,* and of maintaining a stable level of such interaction over time. Thus, if mental health facilities are located in commercial areas, we would expect two mutually reinforcing tendencies. First, behaviors performed by residents of those areas would tend to be "publicized," subjected to continual scrutiny and reacted to because they impinge upon other persons. Second, the public recognition of certain behavior could easily be converted to a reported artifact, due to the presence of a "street-level bureaucrat" seeking to have the causes of that behavior defined within the province of his authority.

Thus, in seeking to explain the nonlinearities we have observed for MH utilization rates as a function of race and income, we will have to explain whether the peaks occur in areas where public social interaction is relatively dense.

Perhaps the most controversial set of social indicators are those which relate to family structure. As we mentioned above, family variables are treated in various ways. Since our society considers maintaining a marriage a basic social function, a high rate of divorce or separation is taken as an indication that a large number of adults are failing in their social roles, with the causes determined by social or economic stresses. Of course, if one is discussing children rather than adults, a high rate of broken marriages is taken to be a stressor, which is then a causal factor in the child's behavior (as opposed to a result in the adult analysis).

Thus, it is commonly reported (at the individual level) that divorced or separated persons have higher mental hospitalization rates than married persons (see Redick and Johnson, 1974, for 1970 U.S. figure). However, persons who live alone also have a higher rate than married persons. While these data support the interpretation of marital status as role fulfillment, it cannot be said whether failure to marry represents a role failure or simply deprives a person of support. Thus, Levy and Rowitz (1973) report that in Chicago, never-married persons have the highest hospitalization rate, then widowed, divorced, or separated, then married. They conclude (1973: 36): "Thus, marriage appears to give some protection to the individual as regards extrusion from the community into a mental hospital." The fact that widowed persons rank with divorced or separated supports this interpretation of the protective grouping over the social or psychological failure of the individual. Fried (1969: 156), however, reports that lower-class families have a lower tolerance of "disordered behavior" and "more readily seek hospitalization for malfunctioning family or community members. Protection thus may be replaced by extrusion as a function of class.

The protective factor also seems important for children, since Redick and

Johnson (1974) also report the following clinic admission rates for persons under 14 years of age:

|                          | Rate Per 100,000 |
|--------------------------|------------------|
| Living with both parents | 250              |
| Living with mother only  | 665              |
| Living with no parents   | 873              |

Similar patterns are found for white and nonwhite, but income and other factors are not controlled. Different child-rearing practices can modify the effects of parental presence. For example, Keller (1963) found, among a small sample (n=46) of urban white and black poor families, that only one-half regularly ate one meal a day with one or more parents and were thus deprived of organized conversation and socialization. These children may suffer the ill-effects of nonprotection, despite family structure. On the other hand, in a large-scale, well controlled study, Langner and his associates (1973) found that higher income, better educated mothers were more likely to recognize psychological problems and seek help for their children. Langner and associates further found that parental "coldness" was an important predictor of psychological distress symptoms. While the available report of Langner's study does not present most of the specific relationships between familial and societal factors and psychological symptoms, he does present an interesting differentiation between various societal and familial factors and "superfactors" of symptom clusters (Langner, 1973, Table is):

> The behavior rubric labelled Anxious-Fighting-Depressed was influenced mainly by family characteristics (parent and parent-child factors). The Organic-Developmental rubric (which involved isolation, delusion, school problems, memory loss, concentration difficulty, speech problems, etc.) was influenced mainly by physical illness in the child, and secondarily by social background factors. Delinquency (including early independence, peer group membership, etc.) showed no relationship to physical illness, very little to family variables, but a moderate amount to demographic (class and race) variables.

When we approach the social environment from the perspective of the child, then, we observe that environmental factors are important for different behaviors. In Langner's discussion, however, it is impossible to tell whether family "disruption" is a measure of the stress to which a child is subjected, or is a factor which weakens the child's capacity to deal with other stresses. In the first instance, family disruption would be a cause of anomie; in the second, it would be a result.

A third interpretation of family disorganization is that it is a measure or a cause of social disintegration. For adults, a high rate of abandonment of the socially expected family role is taken to indicate a weakening of the norms which reinforce that role. For children, lack of an intact family is taken to mean a lack of adequate role models necessary for psychosocial development, as well as a weakened capacity to socialize the child into normal role expectations. Such failures of development and socialization are often taken as causes of juvenile delinquency in individuals.

This formulation brings us closer to the heart of the problem of using family structure variables in the form of rates for geographic areas. A high rate of disorganization may tell us nothing about the psychology or behavior of individuals who live in that area. Moreover, we know that family structure variation is closely related to variations in class, ethnic, and age variables. In addition to interpreting family structure as a mediator between social structure and individual behavior, we must also separate two classes of meaning for geographic rates of family variables.

1. *Descriptions of behavior patterns of socioeconomic groups.* We know that particular ethnic groups (e.g., Italians) place a strong value on traditional family patterns, while among others these patterns are frequently broken (e.g., urban blacks). Given these relationships, the family structure rates may simply be intensified in the sense that they indicate those members of the ethnic group who act in a way particularly differentiated from members of other ethnic groups. If this is so, then we would expect the correlations between family variables and deviant behavior to approach zero when race, ethnic, and income variables are controlled.

2. *Functions of specialized residential areas.* We know that, in addition to racial, ethnic, and income specialization, there are certain areas of New York City which perform special residential functions. For example, large areas of Queens are the desired quasi-suburban areas for raising children. Thus, the age structure is lower there, and percent of intact families is higher. Queens has the highest average income of any borough, reflecting the youth of its population, the competition for its open space, and the discrimination against black and Puerto Rican families. Midtown Manhattan, while having as many or more high-income households as Queens, is specialized as a residential area for young professionals who are not yet married, older professionals who have a less traditional orientation to family life, and persons who prefer small families and apartment living. Finally, large parts of Bronx and Brooklyn contain the aging population from earlier migration to the City; these are areas succeeding generations have fled to avoid the stigma of ethnic identification. To some extent, these family functions of areas cut across class and ethnic boundaries, producing some heterogeneity. The exception are black and Puerto Rican ghettos, whose specialty is only to contain those persons excluded from the other areas. However, there is some functional differentiation between the core and the fringes of ghettos. In sum, then, we have two alternative ways of describing the spatial specialization of the City: by social class dimensions and by family structure dimensions. By use of multiple regression analysis, we will be able to measure the relative impact of each upon the spatial distribution of deviant behavior.

If the first class of interpretations holds, then we will be led to see family structure rates as a true reflection or result of anomie: in those areas affected by a "forced division of labor" (racial oppression), there will be a weakening of the norms of family life and an increase in deviant behavior. If the correlations between family structure and deviance approach zero when race/ethnic/income (structural) variables are controlled, then family structure will be merely an indicator, rather than a result of structural anomie.

If the second class of interpretations is favored, that family structure predicts deviance, regardless of race/ethnic/income structure, then we may conclude that family factors exert a mediating or independent effect upon deviance.

*IV.  Data:  Definitions, Sources, and Quality*

*A.  DEPENDENT VARIABLES = Utilization Rates (UR)*

Definition:  Admission counts by area of residence per 1970 census population, age adjusted.

Abbreviations:  subscripts refer to (1) *type of service* (e.g., $UR_{OP}$ is outpatient utilization rate); or

(2) to *subsample of persons admitted,* where

$UR_{TOT}$ = all admissions

$UR_{NPS}$ = admissions with no prior service (new entrants to service system)

$UR_{READ}$ = readmissions or admissions reporting prior service at another facility.

(3) A ratio has been calculated of inpatient admissions to (inpatient + outpatient admissions). Where this is calculated from total admissions, the acronym URIPCL is used; where calculated from new entrants (no prior service) only, the acronym IPCLNP is used as a variable name.

Source and Quality of Admissions Counts: Admission counts are derived from a reporting system developed by the New York State Department of Mental Hygiene ("Multi-State Information System," Local Services Module) and required of all facilities licensed or funded by the state to provide mental health or mental retardation services. The system includes a one-page admission form (mix of hand-coded and machine-readable optical marking) required to be submitted for any person seen at least once in an outpatient facility or a hospital (3% of hospital admission forms report termination the same day, indicating that virtually all spend at least one night in the hospital). Forms are completed by the facility and mailed to Albany for final coding, editing, and entry to file. There is probably some variation across facilities—particularly outpatient facilities—as to what level of inquiry and discussion constitutes an initial visit and thus generates a form. The formal definitions are completely inclusive, and most agencies seem to want to maximize their official admission statistics, but acceptance of medical responsibility for casual inquiries and time cost of completing forms may limit reporting at many agencies.

The admission report includes basic demographic information (age, sex, race-ethnic group, religion, marital status, education, income), service history, and a diagnosis and appraisal of symptoms presented. (Because we shall not be using most of the information collected, we refer the reader to the Local Services Reporting Manual, New York State Department of Mental Hygiene, Office of Clinical and Statistical Information Systems, for detailed definitions and instructions.) While much of the information is unreported, the basic age and sex characteristics and area of residence are reported for virtually all clients. There is probably some systematic underreporting due to failure to submit forms, but this does not seem to affect the bulk of facilities. Place of residence is coded as a "health area,"—an aggregation of census tracts averaging about 24,000 population, which has a long history of official use in New York City. Codes are obtained from an address manual published by the New York City Office of City Planning. Data for the present study were extracted[5] by the State Department from its edited master file to include all transactions involving New York City residents for the three month period, January 1 to March 31, 1972. Counts of admissions for each health area of residence, by age, sex, race-ethnic group, prior service, and type of care were prepared by the New York City Health Services Administration. All further editing of the counts, conversion to age-adjusted rates, and analytic tasks were programmed by the author using the facilities of the Harvard University Computer Center. While a full year's data might have been preferable, this particular sample was chosen because of special efforts that all facilities be included (a major municipal hospital did not report prior to this sample period). Admission rates are mostly quite stable across quarters, with the exception of a decrease in outpatient admissions during the summer. The large size of the file—33,085 admissions in the sampled quarter, after editing and purging—means that, while there are probably many undetected miscodings and missing forms, as long as they are randomly distributed they will not affect the major results of the regression analysis.

Our sample systematically excludes any persons treated out of New York State. Less than 3% are treated out of the City but in the State. Since there is a particularly high concentration of psychological resources within New York City, we do not think this is a serious source of bias.

Finally, while our sample includes private clinics and hospitals, it does not include private practitioners outside these facilities. There is, therefore, probably serious underreporting at the upper end of the income scale, which may account for the sharp drop in utilization rate among families with a median income between $15,000 and $25,000 (See figures 11.5, 11.6, and 11.7). However, the smooth curve observed to this point and the analysis presented below of areas with medium income above $9,000 indicate that this exclusion of private practitioners probably does not bias our results significantly in the $9,000 to $15,000 per year range.

*B. INDEPENDENT VARIABLES*

*1. SOCIAL AREA CHARACTERISTICS*

Social Area Characteristics (abbreviated SACs) data were all provided by the Epidemiology of Mental Disorders Research Unit of the New York State Department of Mental Hygiene. These variables are derived from two sources. The bulk of the variables used are transformations of U.S. Census data for 1970, with appropriate denominators for rates developed by the Epidemiology Group. An additional group of variables were developed by the Epidemiology Group from the New York City Department of Health's Birth Registry Tapes. The only variables in our final set derived from this source are Age-adjusted Fertility Rate (VAR089). and Percent of Live Births Out of Wedlock (Illegitimate) (VAR090). The denominator for VAR089 is the appropriate number of women resident in the area; the denominator for VAR090 is the total number of live births recorded. Follow-up studies of this

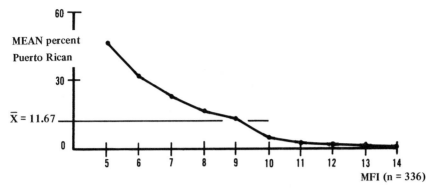

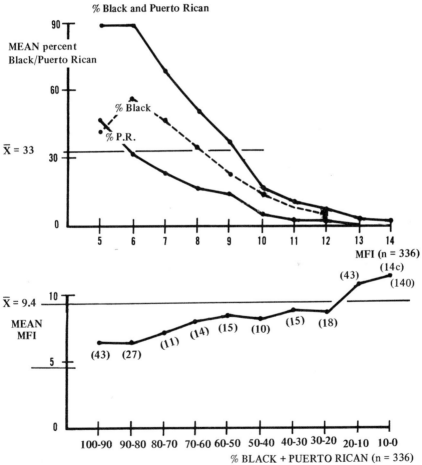

FIGURE 11.5  Percent Black and/or Puerto Rican Population Related to MEDIAN FAMILY
            INCOME (MFI)
            (Unit = Health are of residence)

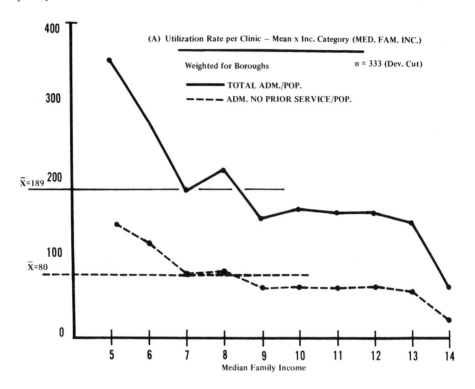

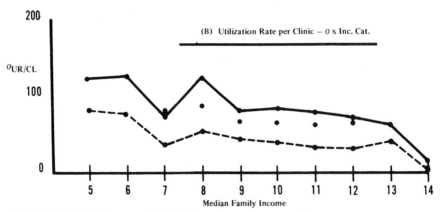

FIGURE 11.6 (C): Frequency Distribution of MEDIAN FAMILY INCOME
(in number of areas, not adjusted for population)

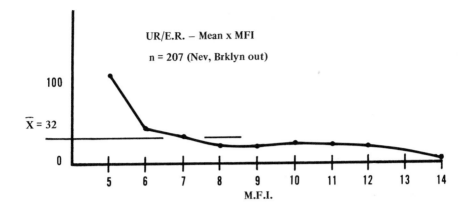

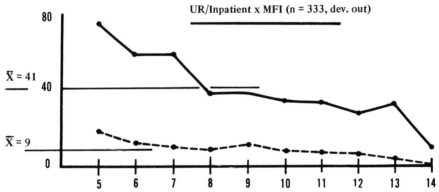

FIGURE 11.7  Mental Health Utilization Rate As a function of MEDIAN FAMILY INCOME (MFI)

Note for Figures 11.5, 11.6, and 11.7:
Definition of Categories for Median Family Income (U.S. Census)

|  | Category | Income |
|---|---|---|
|  |  | $ |
|  | 1 | < 1,000 |
|  | 2 | 1,000 - 1,999 |
|  | 3 | 2,000 - 2,999 |
|  | 4 | 3,000 - 3,999 |
|  | 5 | 4,000 - 4,999 |
|  | 6 | 5,000 - 5,999 |
|  | 7 | 6,000 - 6,999 |
|  | 8 | 7,000 - 7,999 |
| MFI = LOW | 9 | 8,000 - 8,999 |
| MFI = HIGH | 10 | 9,000 - 9,999 |
|  | 11 | 10,000 - 11,999 |

| 12 | 12,000 - 14,999 |
| 13 | 15,000 - 24,999 |
| 14 | 25,000 - 49,999 |
| 15 | $\geqslant 50,000$ |

registry have shown it to be quite complete and accurately coded. The census variables used, by conceptual dimension, are listed on the following page. At this point we are listing only the original variables. As the analyses progressed we made two types of transformations. In several cases we found curvilinear relationships between SACs variables and UR, as tested by both scattergrams and regressions with linear and squared terms.

Several of the social area variables which we had expected to be highly correlated to utilization rate produced linear bivariate correlations near zero. Examination of scattergrams suggested that we had a second-order, paraboloid functions—that is, U-shaped curves. Such a curve produces a zero-order correlation coefficient if it is symmetrical; a low correlation if it is asymmetrical. (As an aside, our findings suggest that one should be suspicious of any argument based upon finding a near-zero linear correlation, if scattergrams or mathematical tests for curvilinearity are not presented. Such spurious negative findings seem to be common.) To test for such a quadratic relationship, we ran a separate regression for each variable, entering first the linear term $(X_i)$, then the quadratic term $(X_i)^2$. When the addition of the quadratic term produced an increase in explained variance of at least 5%, we considered the relationship to be truly curvilinear. In most cases, explained variance increased in the range 5 to 10%, which corresponds to an increase in the simple correlation coefficient of .22 to .32. Because we are concerned to obtain a single Beta and estimate of explained variance for each variable, we transformed the variable into a "Q-variable" calculated as

$$Q - x_i = B_1 x_i + B_2 (x_i)^2$$

where $B_1$ and $B_2$ were obtained from the regression of utilization rate (Y) on $x_i$ and $(x_i)^2$. Each variable was regressed independently and separately for outpatient and inpatient rates. Regression constants were ignored, since our analysis is only concerned with Beta's and percent explained variance, both of which are independent of scale.

In a few cases, the spurious zero correlation was found to be due to an interaction with income: that is, the same variable takes on different meanings at different levels of income. Creating an "I-variable" equal to the product of variable $(x_i)$ and (median family income)$_i$ thus creates an expanded scale reflecting the interacting variation of income and the base variable.

Table 11.4 show the results of the tests for curvilinearity. We can see that, in many instances, adding a quadratic term greatly increases the percent variance explained, by as much as 14% for UR Clinic (Aged Dependency Ratio and Percent of Mothers in Labor force) and 24% for UR Inpatient (Percent of Population that is Male). In several cases, transformation to a quadratic term converts a variable of negligible importance to one that is significant: 092, 116, 112 for UR Clinic; 092, 116 for UR Inpatient.

TABLE 11.4   TEST OF CURVILINEAR (QUADRATIC) RELATIONSHIPS, UR=f (SACs)

| | Variable | Simple r | Linear R-squared | Additional R Sq, Quadratic Term $(X^2)$ | Total $R^2$ (Quadratic Pair) |
|---|---|---|---|---|---|
| | **UR Clinic** | | | | |
| 080 | Median family income | -.46 | .22 | .07 | .29 |
| 091 | Child dependency ratio | .49 | .24 | .10 | .34 |
| 092 | Aged dependency ratio | -.27 | .07 | .14 | .21 |
| 116 | Percent of population that is male | -.31 | .10 | .10 | .20 |
| 124 | H&W family, age 14-44, + child | .22 | .05 | .01 | .06 |
| 087 | Percent of persons living alone | -.01 | .00 | .03 | .03 |
| 112 | Percent of mothers in labor force | -.23 | .05 | .14 | .19 |
| | **UR Inpatient** | | | | |
| 080 | Median family income | -.44 | .19 | .01 | .20 |
| 091 | Child dependency ratio | .28 | .08 | .05 | .13 |
| 092 | Aged dependency ratio | -.20 | .04 | .06 | .10 |
| 116 | Percent of population that is male | -.07 | .00 | .01 | .01 |
| 124 | H&W family, age 14-44, + child | .02 | .00 | .01 | .01 |
| 087 | Percent of persons living alone | .15 | .02 | .00 | .02 |
| 112 | Percent of mothers in labor force | -.06 | .00 | .02 | .02 |

Table 11.5 defines all of the variables included in the final Social Area Characteristic set (SACs) and indicates which were transformed for curvilinearity (Q) and which for income interaction (I).

*2. FACILITY COVERAGE*

The author coded each health area's Facility Coverage from a compilation of facility locations prepared under his direction by the Systems Analysis Unit, New York City Department of Mental Health and Mental Retardation Services, for the same year as the admissions sample. Three sets of scores were used:

1. Dummy coding (0/1) = (absent/present) on a set of variable reflecting all types of *facilities located in the same health area;* a health area can have more than one type of facility, since each is scored on a different variable.
2. Dummy coding (0/1) of all types of *facilities located within the same catchment area* (population approx.=200,000) as health area.
3. Interval scale coding of a set of variables reflecting number of clinics dollar amount of annual clinic budget and number of hospital beds located within health area and catchment area.

All variables scored on a health area basis were adjusted for population size, so that they are of the form "Number of clinics per population." For variables coded (0/1)

TABLE 11.5   CENSUS VARIABLES USED IN FINAL SACs SET,
BY CONCEPTUAL DIMENSION

Community Environment/Housing

| Var094 (I)* | Median persons per room in dwelling unit |
| Var078 (I) | Percent of persons living in overcrowded units |
| Var088 | Percent of units in area that are vacant |
| Var084 | Percent of units lacking standard plumbing |

Family Structure

| Var112 (Q)** | Percent of mothers in labor force |
| Var087 | Percent of persons who live alone |
| Var124 (I) | Percent of families headed by husband and wife, age 14-44 with child less than age 18. |
| Var089 | Age-adjusted fertility rate |
| Var090 | Percent of live births out of wedlock |
| Var113 | Percent of adult persons divorced |
| Var128 | Percent who drive to work |
| Var136 | Percent of children, age 3-4, in school |
| Var111 | Percent of households with female head |

(Age)

| Var091 (Q) | Child dependency ratio |
| Var092 (Q) | Aged dependency ratio |

Sex

| Var116 (Q) | Percent of population that is male |

Mobility

| Var096 | Mobility Index—weighted by distance of move from previous residence |
| Var122 | Percent of households moved since 1968 (2 years to census) |

Female Education and Occupation

| Var132 | Mean education, females, age 15-44 |
| Var134 | Percent of females, age ≥ 25, education < 8th grade |
| Var117 | Percent of female sales and clerical workers |

Race/Ethnic

| Var115 | Percent of Black |
| Var110 | Percent of Puerto Rican |
| Var083 | Percent of parochial school (correlates with percent of Irish and Italian) |

Income/Employment

| Var118 | Percent of males in labor force work < 40 weeks per year |
| Var085 (Q) | Male unemployment, age 16-21 |
| Var080 (Q) | Median family income (MFI) |

*   (I) Refers to a variable that is transformed to reflect interaction with median family income.
**  (Q) Refers to a variable that is transformed to reflect a quadratic relationship with utilization.

a scalar of 0.5 was added to differentiate the low probability of a clinic being located in a small area from the higher probability of its being in a large area. Most facility coverage variables were highly correlated with each other, so a set of five was selected to reflect differences between municipal and voluntary auspice, and the assumed (and tested) relevance of the smaller size area to clinics and the larger area to hospitals.

*Clinic Coverage Variables*

    1. BUDGET        Total Annual Budget ($1000s) of all clinics located in same catchment area

    2. P162            Number of adult clinics–municipal (H.H.C.)[6] located in health area, per population.

    3. P167            Number of adult clinics–voluntary,[7] located in health area, per population

*Hospital Coverage Variables*

    1. Var106        Number of Voluntary hospital beds (psychiatric) located in catchment area

    2. Var107 (Q)   Number of municipal (H.H.C.) psychiatric hospital beds located in catchment area

It was originally hypothesized that the actual distance traveled from residence to facility would be an important predictor of Utilization Rates. A special set of programs was developed by the New York City Health Services administration to calculate such distances from (x,y) coordinates of facility locations and geographic centroids of residential areas. A final program was then written to calculate a Standard Distance measure for each age group and type of care. Unfortunately, the original distance calculation program misattributed ages in many cases, so, we had to rewrite the final program to give a single distance traveled measure spanning all age groups for outpatient and inpatient facilities. As expected, high and low income groups react differently to spatial location of facilities, so our final distance traveled variables are modified to reflect interaction with income. The variables are:

Clinic

    I458            Standard distance traveled, residence to clinic/median family income

Hospital

    I470            Standard distance traveled, residence to hospital/median family income

Since the bivariate analysis showed that the distance measured without the income interaction produced near-zero correlations with Utilization Rate, only the interaction term was included in the final regressions. However, the income variable is included, so the interaction term is not merely reflecting variance in the denominator.

*V. Results of the Regression Analysis*

The multiple regression findings presented below are the conclusion of several months of data analysis, building from much lower levels of analysis such as examination of bivariate correlations and scattergrams. We will be asking the reader to follow a lengthy discussion of complex relationships involving many variables. It therefore seems desirable to present a summary of overall findings which make the analytic structure clear, rather than go step by step through all the analytic tasks performed. In later papers we shall explore the various component relationships. Exploration of individual (bivariate) relationships preceded the multiple regression and the regression includes transformations to reflect the curvilinearity and inter-actions revealed at lower levels of analysis. Since at this stage our aim is to measure the relative impact of different variables upon utilization rate, we have simply run the model with appropriate transformations substituted for raw data. Thus, for a term which relates in the curvilinear form $[UR = \beta_1 X_1 + \beta_2 X_1{}^2 + C]$ to Utilization Rate, we have substituted the term $[QX_1 = b_2 X_1 + b_2 X_1{}^2]$ into the regression. This will give us the best estimate of '$\beta$' and 'F' scores for variable $X_1$ in a situation of multiple controls. In a later section we will discuss the implications of the particular curvilinear functions observed.

## A. PREVENTION HYPOTHESES

### 1. PRIMARY PREVENTION/STRESS HYPOTHESIS

This hypothesis underlies the most critical disputes in the field of mental health. As treatment modalities have drawn upon metaphors from physical medicine, so the language of cause and prevention has drawn upon physical concepts of public health. The body of literature commonly referred to as "stress theory" incorporates three classes of propositions. The first holds that the stress of poor living conditions—either physical or social environments—directly causes emotional strain leading to emotional disorder in persons experiencing those conditions. The second holds that environmental stress is additive to the normal stresses of life and inhibits an individual or family from adequately coping with normal stresses of job, home, school, and so on. The third proposition almost posits a contagion of mental illess: if other family members are afflicted, and an individual (particularly a child) must interact with abnormal persons, the stresses or peculiar patterns of child rearing will cause an emotional disturbance. The proposed analogies to public sanitation and epidemic control lead proponents to argue that the largest scale promotion of mental health can be achieved by eliminating the environmental stresses, rather than just helping an individual cope with them through adjustment of his psycho-logical reactions.

It should be noted that the stress hypothesis is quite different from the "population at risk" concept. The latter infers that certain subgroups of the population are more likely to experience mental disorder, due to either genetic or personal psychological causes. Thus, each poor man has fewer resources, including usually education and job gratification as well as money, to cope with the vicissi-tudes of the world around him. Such poor men as a group form a population at risk. It is only due to the fact that society segregates such persons into certain parts of the city that one discovers a higher "incidence" of distress in poor areas, not due to any environmental cause of poor living conditions or social interaction. The importance of the distinction is that the "population at risk" concept implies that neither preventive nor remedial efforts at the community (environmental) level will be fruitful. Rather, only changes in the fundamental societal structures which oppress the poor and race-ethnic minorities can prevent disorders. In the mean time, remedial work can help alleviate distress for the affected individual.

Since the large cities of our nation are so highly segregated spatially, it is practically impossible to separate the fact of being poor from the fact of living in a poor area, of being black from living in an area where black people live. However, by examining the content of the rates of social characteristics which describe such areas, it is possible to infer alternative models which seem to favor factors closer to societal structures or factors closer to individual relationships and living conditions. Using the Simon-Blalock method, one can then test models as to their consonance to the statistical implications of a causal or developmental sequence, and reject some models. For the reasons discussed above, we have proposed the following working models:

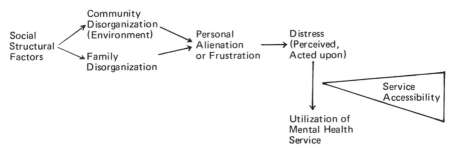

If the partial correlations between service Utilization Rate (UR) and the Structural variables (income, race-ethnic) approach zero as Community and Family variables are entered, then the model is not rejected. If these partials are significantly reduced, but remain significantly greater than zero, then a direct effect of structural variables plus the indirect effects hypothesized would be suggested.

We will discuss the relationships among the various Social Area Characteristics (SACs) in a later section. For this initial summary we are concerned with testing the most basic relationships necessary to support the primary prevention hypothesis.

First, is there a systematic relationship between Social Area Characteristics (SACs) and mental health service Utilization Rate (UR)? Columns (A) and (D) of Row A in Table 11.6 show that there clearly is. Entering our full set of SACs, we explain 54% of the variance in total outpatient admission rates (UR/TOTAL) and 44% for inpatient. These figures correspond to multiple correlation coefficients (R) of 0.73(F=13.18, df=305) and 0.66(F=8.84, df=305), which indicate a strong association.

Even at this most basic level we have two competing hypotheses which must be tested. First, there is the "drift hypothesis," which has been posited in terms of both downward social mobility for mental patients at the individual level and settlement in areas accessible to service at the ecological level. *If our observed relationship between total utilization rate and social characteristics were purely a matter of geographic "drift," then we would expect it to disappear for new admissions with no prior service, and to be intensified for readmission.*

TABLE 11.6  PERCENT OF VARIANCE IN UTILIZATION RATES EXPLAINED BY A SET OF
SOCIAL AREA CHARACTERISTICS (SACs, 27 VARIABLES) AND A SET OF FACILITY
COVERAGE VARIABLES (FACs, 8), BY ORDER OF ENTRY INTO REGRESSION EQUATION

| Row | | Outpatient Utilization | | | Inpatient Utilization | | |
|---|---|---|---|---|---|---|---|
| | | TOTAL ADMISSIONS | ADMISSIONS, NO PRIOR SERVICE | READMIS-SIONS | TOTAL ADMISSIONS | ADMISSIONS, NO PRIOR SERVICE | READMIS-SIONS |
| A | SACs | .54 | .49 | .53 | .44 | .38 | .44 |
| B | FACs | .04 | .04 | .03 | .05 | .01 | .05 |
| | and CMHC | .03 | .03 | .02 | .01 | .01 | .01 |
| C | Other service | .004 | .02 | .003 | .005 | .03 | .006 |
| D | Total $R^2$ | .61 | .57 | .58 | .50 | .43 | .51 |
| E | CMHC | .11 | .12 | .08 | .01 | .03 | .01 |
| F | Clinic Coverage | .14 | .10 | .14 | .22 | .06 | .23 |
| G | Hosp Coverage | .06 | .03 | .08 | .02 | .04 | .02 |
| H | $\Sigma$ FACs | .32 | .24 | .30 | .25 | .13 | .22 |
| I | SACs | .29 | .31 | .28 | .26 | .28 | .28 |
| J | Other Service | .00 | .02 | .00 | .00 | .03 | .00 |
| | Total $R^2$ | .61 | .57 | .58 | .53 | .43 | .52 |
| F | | 12.5 | 10.7 | 11.3 | 8.9 | 7.5 | 8.7 |
| df | | 37/295 | 37/295 | 37/295 | 37/295 | 37/295 | 37/295 |

Examining the remaining columns of Row A, we see that, while the relationship with SACs is stronger for readmissions than for new entrants, for both inpatient and outpatient rates, the difference is small. While not rejecting the geographic drift hypothesis, we can estimate its impact at about 4 to 7% of total variance, that is, as the increment in explained variance obtained by adding readmissions to new entrants (who have no prior service).

The second competing hypothesis is that the observed relationship is strictly an artifact of the location of public mental health facilities in relatively deprived areas; the areas with high Utilization Rates, then, would be those with a high level of service accessibility. To test this alternative, we compare the top (Rows A-D) and bottom (Rows E-R) parts of Table 11.6. These report stepwise regressions of the same variables with reversed order.

For example, in the first run, we first enter Social Area Characteristics (SACs) and explain 54% of the variance in total outpatient admission rates; entering Facility Coverage variables (FACs) then adds 7%, for total $R^2$ of 61%. In the second run, we entered the facility variables first and accounted for 32% of variance; entering SACs second added 29% overlaps with the facility location effect, while 29% is independent of Facility Coverage. Similarly, for total inpatient rates, of 44% explained by SACs, up to 18% overlaps with Facility Coverage and 26% is independent.

Conversely, only 7% of outpatient rate variance and 6% of inpatient are explained by Facility Coverage independent of social characteristics.

Thus, we cannot completely reject this alternative to the primary prevention hypothesis. However, the relative amounts of variance explained indicate that SACs are more important in predicting utilization than is Facility Coverage.

In sum, we may conclude that, while areas of specified social composition will display high or low Utilization Rates regardless of the accessibility of facilities, these differences will be modified by the actual facility location pattern. The relative impact of SACs and FACs seems to be about the same for both new entrants and readmissions, with Facility Coverage being somewhat stronger for readmissions. We thus have fairly consistent support at this basic level for the primary prevention or stress hypothesis.

A third test is also available at this level: we may compare the regression results across age groups. If the relationship between UR and SACs is due merely to the use of public facilities by poor people, or to a broad social policy of acting upon minorities, then we should expect the results to be relatively invariant across age (unless we have different social policies for different age groups of poor or minority persons). Conversely, if SACs describe environmental "stressors," then we should expect different stressors to impact upon the behavior of children and adults.

Because the preponderance of inpatient admissions are adults, we will confine our analysis to outpatient services. Table 11.7 presents the Beta scores and percent of explained variance for two regressions. Our argument here rests not on the strength of the relationship between UR and SACs, but upon a different pattern of relationships. We must therefore present the individual scores for each variable. For sake of brevity we show only two age groupings: 13 to 19 and 20 to 59. Our analyses have indicated that these breaks and the large adult grouping will not distort relationships observed for a finer set of categories.

While there are some noticeable differences in the Child and Adult regressions, the results are remarkably similar. The major social characteristics predicting in both cases are Family Structure variables, particularly Percent of Illegitimate Births, Percent of Mothers in the Labor Force, Percent of Complete Families with Child Fertility Rate, and Age Structure. Race-Ethnic variables (percent black) and Income are also important for both. Facility Coverage is equally important, but the child rate seems to be more influenced by clinic coverage, while the adult rate is more responsive to CMHC and hospital coverage.

Noteable differences in the SACs are the impact of Percent Attending Parochial School (close to percent Irish and Italian) on child admissions (negative) but not adult. Adult admissions are related to Percent Vacant Units (negative) but child admissions are not. We will defer discussion of possible interpretations of these differences until a later section.

For the present discussion, it seems reasonable to say that it is difficult to discern different sets of role or environmental stress producing child and adult admissions; however; the meaning of the similarity is unclear. If family roles involve shared expectations and reciprocal behavior, then stresses may act similarly upon children and adults. If family disorganization is a result of racial and income factors, which are seen to be important, then the same factors could produce the

TABLE 11.7  BETA SCORES OF MULTIPLE REGRESSIONS OF OUTPATIENT UTILIZATION RATES, BY AGE

| Variable | Code | Description | UR/Total Age=13-19 | | UR/Total Age=20-59 | UR/Total All Ages (WTD) |
|---|---|---|---|---|---|---|
| FACs: | CMHC | | .09 | (.03) | .17* | .20* |
| Clinic: | I458 | Dist to clinic/median family income | .06 | | -.13 | -.08 |
| | Budget | Clinic $ in CA | .04 | | .05 | .12 |
| | P162 | #HHC-Adult -Clinics/Population | -.01 | | .01 | .02 |
| | P167 | #V02-Adult -Clinics/Population | .14* | (.13) | .01 | .08 |
| Hospital: | I470 | Dist to I.P./median family income | -.00 | | .12* | .08 |
| | V106 | # Vol Beds in CA | .09 | | .15* | .11* |
| | V107 | #HHC Beds in CA | -.08 | (.02) | -.14 | -.14* |
| SACs: | (R² - FACs) | | | (.18) | (.19) | (.32) |
| Community: | I094 | Income x median number of persons/room | .04 | | .01 | .00 |
| | I078 | Percent of persons in overcrowded units | .04 | | .02 | .06 |
| | V088 | Percent of units vacant | .01 | | -.23* | -.11 |
| | V084 | Percent of units lacking plumbing | -.04 | (.06) | .19 | .13 |
| Family: | Q112 | Percent of mothers in labor force | .21 | | .30* | .26* |
| | V087 | Percent of persons who live alone | -.25 | | .08 | -.12 |
| | I124 | Income x husband and wife with child | -.10 | | -.27* | -.22 |
| | V089 | Fertility rate (age-adjusted) | .25 | | .24 | .21 |
| | V090 | Percent of illegitimate births | .32 | | .91* | .82* |
| | V113 | Percent of divorced persons | .22 | | .28* | .21* |
| | V128 | Percent who drive to work | .13 | | .07 | .16 |
| | V136 | Percent of children, age 3-4, in school | .23* | (.11) | .10 | .10 |
| Age: | Q091 | Child dependency ratio | .11 | | .16 | .38* |
| | Q092 | Aged dependency ratio | -.12 | (.01) | .29* | -.03 |
| Sex: (Family) | Q116 | Percent of male population | .12 | | -.11 | .05 |
| | V111 | Percent of female heads of household | .28 | | -.33 | -.21 |
| Mobility: | V096 | Mobility index | .00 | | .15 | .07 |
| | V122 | Percent moved > 1968 | -.08 | | -.02 | -.08 |
| Female Education and Occupation: | V132 | Mean education, females, 15-44 | -.08 | | .27 | .18 |
| | V134 | Percent female, 25+, educ. < 8th Grade | -.08 | | .19 | .15 |
| | V117 | Percent female sales and clerical workers | .21 | | .23 | .21 |
| Race/Ethnic: | V110 | Percent Puerto Rican | .21 | | -.17 | .04 |
| | V115 | Percent Black | -.22 | | -.41 | -.33 |
| | V083 | Percent parochial school | -.33 | | -.06 | -.17 |
| Income/ Employment: | V118 | Percent males work < 40 wks | .11 | | -.05 | -.05 |
| | V085 | Male unemployment, 16-21 age | -.02 | | .05 | .02 |
| | V080 | Median family income | -.57 | | -.27 | -.34 |
| | (R² - Total) | | | (.44) | (.50) | (.60) |
| | F | | | 6.7 | 8.4 | 13.0 |
| | df | | | 35/297 | 35/297 | 35/295 |

* F ≥ 5.0

same family stress leading to similar Utilization Rates for different age groups. Indeed, family structure may be so closely linked to socioeconomic and racial factors as to eliminate the observation of age differences. However, the fact that Family variables remain significant even when race and income are entered suggest that this latter possibility is not occurring.

Finally, the similarity of social characteristic-UR relationships across age may reflect a consistent set of social policies toward certain groups, rather than a consistent stress. The fact that Family variables are similar, even after differing effects of Facility Coverage (an important aspect of social policy) are controlled, lessens the likelihood of this explanation.

In summary, we have found consistent evidence of a strong relationship between Social Area Characteristics and mental health service Utilization Rate, and this relationship remains significant after controls for age and Facility Coverage. We therefore find considerable support for the operation of something like the stress hypothesis (primary prevention) and little evidence yet to contradict it. The subject will be pursued in greater depth later in the study.

## 2. SECONDARY PREVENTION/AVOIDANCE OF HOSPITALIZATION

This is one of the most interesting hypotheses, because it allows us to test directly whether an individual-level research finding is applicable at the community level. Various studies have shown that, under various conditions, patients can be maintained in the community if they are given the support of outpatient, day-care, or rehabilitation programs. Moreover, it is analogized from the disease model that intervention at an early stage of distress in a less intense setting (outpatient clinic) can ameliorate the disease and prevent its progress to an advanced stage requiring hospitalization. These two factors have led to a widespread belief, embodied in the CMHC program, that such a tradeoff exists at an aggregate level. That is, if sufficient outpatient resources are provided to treat a large proporation of cases early on, then the overall rate of hospitalization will go down.

Testing this proposition with cross-sectional data, we would expect to find a spurious zero-order correlation between inpatient and outpatient rates, due to the high utilization by socioeconomically deprived groups and use of alternative resources (private practitioners) by high income groups. We might also expect the presence of hospitals with both large outpatient and inpatient services to mask a negative correlation. We must therefore test the proposition by observing the partial correlation coefficient between $UR_{CLINIC}$ and $UR_{IP}$ as Social Area Characteristics (SACs) and Facility Coverage (FACs) are controlled.[8]

A second test is performed by calculating a ratio of (inpatient) to (inpatient + outpatient) services. Such a ratio should be more a function of service system coverage than Social Area Characteristics if the hypothesis is not to be rejected. Table 11.8 summarizes the results.

It is clear that, contrary to the hypothesis, the positive correlation between outpatient and inpatient rates remains positive, even when variables accounting for the majority of variance are controlled. Moreover, the observed correlation is due more to the common influence of social characteristics in predicting both rates than to the presence or absence of any type of facility. In particular, coverage by a CMHC has virtually no effect on this positive correlation.[9]

Perhaps most interesting is the difference between new entrants and admissions with prior service. For the latter, the observed correlation is almost entirely a function of SACs. While SACs cause a significant decrease (+0.41 to +0.25) for new entrants, the partial is still significant. Persons with no prior service enter both inpatient and outpatient services at a high or low rate that is only partly dependent upon social variables and hardly dependent upon facility location. The partial of 0.227 thus suggests that about 5% of the variance in either inpatient or outpatient rates is due to a residual propensity to use service. Areas with high rates of returning clients have them for both types of service if they exhibit certain social characteristics, and have low rates if they exhibit opposite characteristics. One cannot say definitely whether controlling for SACs leaves a random relationship

TABLE 11.8a  PARTIAL CORRELATIONS OF UR/OP WITH UR/IP, ALL AGES*

|  |  | Total Admissions | No Prior Service | Readmissions |
|---|---|---|---|---|
|  | Zero-order, r | +.383 | +.412 | +.366 |
| (Reg=17,19) | SACs controlled | +.104 | +.253 | +.078 |
| (Reg=24) | FACs controlled | +.253 | +.350 | +.247 |
| (Reg=24) | SACs and FACs controlled | +.090 | +.227 | +.089 |
| (Reg=24) | FACs detailed: |  |  |  |
|  | CMHC | .367 | .384 | .360 |
|  | +Clinic coverage variables | .237 | .350 | .221 |
|  | ++Hospital coverage variables | .253 | .350 | .247 |

\* F > 2.0 for all partial correlations reported.

TABLE 11.8b  PARTIAL CORRELATIONS OF UR/OP x UR/IP, TOTAL ADMISSIONS

|  |  | Adolescent (Age=13-19) | Adult (Age=20-59) |
|---|---|---|---|
|  | Zero-order, r | +.199 | +.301 |
|  | SACs controlled |  |  |
|  | FACs controlled | +.145 | +.226 |
| (Reg=24) | SACs and FACs controlled | +.119 | +.076 |
|  | FACs detailed: |  |  |
|  | CMHC | .200 | .285 |
|  | +Clinic coverage variables | .128 | .214 |
|  | ++Hospital coverage variables | .145 | .226 |

between inpatient and outpatient rates or simply eliminates sufficient variance to reduce the correlation toward zero. Since the zero-order correlation was 0.37 and the multiple $R^2$ with just SACs was 0.53, the partial correlation was based upon increasing explained variance from 14% $(0.37^2)$ to 53%. While this is a substantial reduction in unexplained variance, it is not so large as to necessitate the partial approaching zero. We may therefore infer that, beyond the mutual effect of SACs, some areas exhibit a selection of one or the other service, while others utilize them equally.

*The findings with regard to areas covered by CMHCs are clear. There is no evidence of an influence on relative rates: both rates are higher in CMHC-covered areas.* Since this holds for new entrants, the failure to observe a negative partial cannot be due to a buildup of chronic cases not amenable to preventive activities.

Since clinic coverage does seem to have some impact for readmissions, we may infer that it is interposed in the referral process in the manner described by the path diagrams in Figures 11.3 and 11.4. We have taken the conservative method of representing path values by the percent of variance explained (jointly and independently) rather than the partial correlation coefficients or Beta weights suggested by Duncan (1966). We have done this because at this summary level, the factors represented are *uncombined sets of variables*. Representing their effects by $R^2$, calculated both jointly with and independently of other variables (See Table 11.6) allows us to meet the requirement of a linear, additive set of variables. The dotted

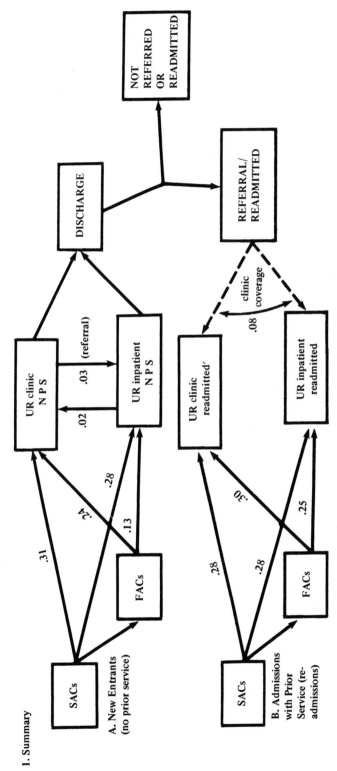

FIGURE 11.3 Relative Effects on Utilization Rate of Social Area Characteristics (SACs) and Facility Coverage Variables (FACs)
(Path entries are percent of variance explained)

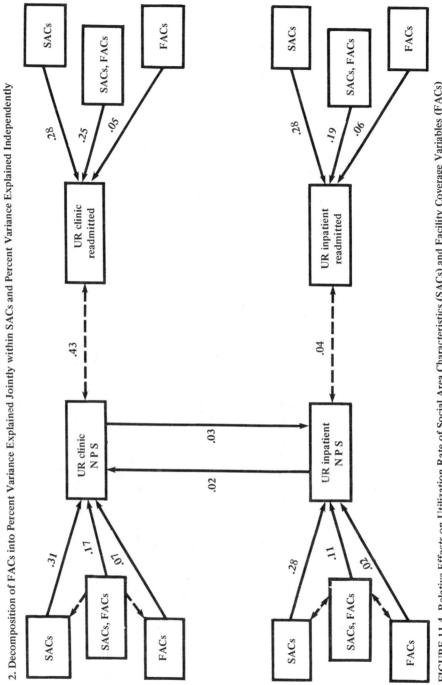

2. Decomposition of FACs into Percent Variance Explained Jointly within SACs and Percent Variance Explained Independently

FIGURE 11.4   Relative Effects on Utilization Rate of Social Area Characteristics (SACs) and Facility Coverage Variables (FACs)

lines show the linkage between new entrants and readmissions. The second diagram decomposed the FACs path into the parts acting jointly and independently of SACs variables.

Before moving to the next test, it will be prudent to check the partial correlations between inpatient and outpatient rates separately for children and adults. It is possible that the positive partial we have observed is due to a tradeoff between age groups (e.g., high adult/low child inpatient; high child/low adult outpatient) producing a consistent age-adjusted rate. We have age-specific calculations available only for total admissions at this time. These are presented in Table 11.8b.

Again, we find that controlling facility coverage does not reduce the correlation near zero, far less make it negative. We do find that adult Utilization Rates are more responsive to the effect of social area variables, and are also more highly intercorrelated at the zero-order level. Controlling for age, therefore, strengthens our inference that there is no service tradeoff or substitution at the area level. Rather, rates of utilization of both services are due to the effect of social area characteristics.

Our next test of the secondary prevention hypothesis (avoidance of hospitalization) is based upon a similar multiple regression, using the ratio URIPCL = $(UR_{IP})/(UR_{IP} + UR_{OP})$ as dependent variable. (Curvilinear terms were included for the sake of consistency, even though they are not as important as for the separate inpatient and outpatient rates.) Entering SACs first, we find they account for 20% of the variance in the ratio; entering the FACs variables, we find they account for an additional 7%. Reversing the steps, if we enter the FACs first, they account for 8% of variance, without CMHC, which adds 0.3% (F insignificant = 1.3); adding the

TABLE 11.9 PERCENT OF VARIANCE IN INPATIENT/OUTPATIENT RATIO EXPLAINED BY SACs AND FAC

| | Y = INPATIENT (INPATIENT + OUTPATIENT) | | | |
|---|---|---|---|---|
| | Total Admissions | | Admissions No Prior Service | |
| 1st SACs | .20 | | | |
| FACs | .07 | | | |
| Inpatient rate | | | | |
| Outpatient rate | | | | |
| Total $R^2$ | | | | |
| FACs | | | | |
| CMHC | .00 | | .00 | |
| Clinic coverage | .02 | | .04 | |
| Hospital coverage | .06 | | .05 | |
| $\Sigma$ FACs | | .08 | | .08 |
| $\Sigma$ SACs | | .15 | | .14 |
| Inpatient rate | | | | |
| Outpatient rate | .17 | | .08 | |
| Manhattan location | .02 | | .07 | |
| Total $R^2$ | | .39 | | .37 |
| F | 2.7 | | 3.3 | |
| df | 36/296 | | 36/296 | |

full set of SACs then adds 15% of variance, bringing the total $R^2$ to 0.23 (F = 2.5) (see Table 11.9). When we calculate the rate separately for admissions with no prior service, we find similar results. Of course, the amount of facility coverage is critical to the argument. It is possible that there is a relatively high utilization rate of clinics, but it is insufficient to prevent a high rate of hospitalization. If there is any service tradeoff, then we should at least expect clinic coverage to have a negative Beta with $UR_{IP}$, when all other variables are controlled. In particular, CMHC coverage should affect the IP/OP ratio.

Some minor support for the hypothesis is found in the strong Betas for number of municipal hospital beds (VAR 107): -.14 with $UR_{OP}$, +.25 with $UR_{IP}$ and +.32 with the inpatient/outpatient ratio. Judging by F-scores, this is the most important facility variable for predicting inpatient rates. Clinic budget in the catchment area yields moderately positive Betas for $UR_{OP}$. However, its correlations with inpatient rates are seen to be an artifact of social area characteristics, since the Betas tend toward zero when SACs are added to the equation (see Table 11.10).

The Beta scores for CMHC coverage are quite interesting. They are significantly positive for $UR_{OP}$ and also for $UR_{IP}$, but insignificant for the ratio. The impact of

TABLE 11.10 EFFECT UPON BETA WEIGHTS OF FACILITY COVERAGE VARIABLES WHEN SACs ARE ADDED IN A STEPWISE MULTIPLE REGRESSION*

| | Outpatient | | | | | |
|---|---|---|---|---|---|---|
| | $UR_{OP}$-TOT Just FACs | $UR_{OP}$-TOT SACs Controlled | No Prior $UR_{OP}$-Service Just FACs | No Prior $UR_{OP}$-Service SACs | $UR_{OP}$ FACs | Readmission |
| CMHC | .28 | .20 | .26 | .20 | .21 | .17 |
| Clinic Variable | | | | | | |
| Distance traveled | .23 | -.08 | .09 | -.10 | .20 | -.07 |
| | .32 | .12 | .13 | .08 | .41 | .16 |
| Municipal clinic | .01 | .02 | .04 | .05 | -.01 | -.01 |
| Voluntary clinic | .09 | .08 | .08 | .08 | .04 | .05 |
| Hospital Coverage | | | | | | |
| Distance traveled | .19 | .07 | .08 | .05 | .19 | .08 |
| Voluntary beds | -.00 | .11 | .02 | .08 | .02 | .09 |
| Municipal beds | -.26 | -.14 | -.14 | -.07 | -.32 | -.21 |
| Partial Correlation with Inpatient Rate | (.25) | (.09) | (.29) | (.23) | (.25) | (.08) |

| | Inpatient | | | | | |
|---|---|---|---|---|---|---|
| | $UR_{IP}$ Just FACs | TOTAL ADM SACs | $UR_{IP}$ Just FACs | No Prior Service SACs | $UR_{IP}$ FACs | Readmission SACs |
| CMHC | .09 | .11 | .18 | .13 | .04 | .08 |
| Clinic Variable | | | | | | |
| Distance traveled | .31 | .03 | .19 | .05 | .28 | .02 |
| | .19 | -.01 | -.04 | .09 | .23 | -.04 |
| Municipal clinic | -.08 | -.06 | -.06 | -.03 | -.07 | -.05 |
| Voluntary clinic | .02 | .01 | -.01 | .02 | .03 | -.02 |
| Hospital Coverage | | | | | | |
| Distance traveled | .12 | .05 | .09 | .05 | .10 | .04 |
| Voluntary beds | -.02 | -.01 | -.20 | -.03 | .05 | -.00 |
| Municipal beds | .14 | .25 | .08 | .01 | .13 | .28 |
| Partial Correlation with Outpatient Rate | (.26) | (.10) | (.35) | (.22) | (.25) | (.10) |

| | Inpatient/ (Inpatient + Outpatient) | | | |
|---|---|---|---|---|
| | Total Admissions | | Admissions, No Prior Service | |
| | Just FACs | SACs $E^{QN}$ | Just FACs | SACs in $E^{QN}$ |
| CMHC | -.07 | -.02 | .02 | .01 |
| Clinic | .12 | .08 | -.02 | .06 |
| | -.08 | -.08 | -.23 | -.04 |
| | .01 | .02 | .01 | .03 |
| | -.06 | -.08 | -.05 | -.01 |
| Hospital | -.05 | -.04 | .00 | .02 |
| | -.10 | -.13 | -.20 | -.12 |
| | .31 | .32 | .22 | .11 |
| Partial Correlation with Outpatient Rate | (-.40) | (-.43) | (-.24) | (-.28) |
| Total $R^2$ | (.08) | (.23) | (.08) | (.22) |

* See Table 11.6 for F-test scores. All are significant.

CMHC coverage seems to be to strongly increase the clinic utilization rate (B = .20; F = 21.6), moderately increase the hospitalization rate (B = .11; F = 5.5), but not to affect the ratio between the two.

In terms of secondary prevention, these findings imply that, while providing a predominance of clinic or hospital service nearby will shift the relative utilization rates slightly, providing a comprehensive set of services at the same location will not necessarily reduce the rate of hospitalization.

*B. COMPREHENSIVENESS HYPOTHESIS*

This hypothesis predicts that a different pattern of utilization will occur not just due to proximity to one or another service, but due to the effect of providing a set of at least five services (clinic,.emergency, inpatient, partial hospital, consultation and education) coordinated or operated by a single center. In the previous sections we analyzed the impact of CMHC coverage as one of many variables affecting the sample of all areas. We will now attempt to focus more narrowly on the relationship of CMHC coverage to other types of facilities in the system, and to measure differences within the subsample of areas covered by CMHCs.

In Table 11.6 we saw that CMHCs have a considerable relationship with outpatient rates, accounting for 8 to 11% of variance when entered first; however, they accounted for only 1 to 3% of inpatient rate variance. Moreover, when we controlled the effect of Social Area Characteristics and other types of facilities, and entered CMHCs in the equation last, the percent of variance explained was reduced to 2 to 3% for outpatient and 1% or less for inpatient rates. Our initial conclusion is, therefore, that the effects of CMHCs on utilization rates are almost entirely accounted for by other aspects of the service system.

However, when we enter borough (county) of residence into the equation—which corresponds to some major differences among CMHCs—the amount of unique variance explained increases to 7% for outpatient and 3% for inpatient. This suggests that we will have to introduce a second level of controls and break CMHC coverage down into its components (municipal and voluntary auspices) which happen to be differentiated by boroughs (two voluntary CMHCs are in Brooklyn one is in Richmond; two municipal are in Bronx, one in Manhattan; both non-federal voluntary CMHCs are in Manhattan; Queens had no CMHCs at the time of this sample).

Table 11.11 summarizes the percent variance explained by CMHC coverage with various controls. Table 11.12 describes the unique variance explained by each variable with all other controlled (semipartial correlation, squared). It is clear that, while social area characteristics explain far more variance than facility coverage, this is partly an artifact of (or overlapping with) borough differences. When borough variables are added to the equation, the unique contribution of SACs is halved from 17 to 18% to 9% (columns 2,5 versus 3,6 in Table 11.12). A corresponding increase in explained variance for outpatient rates is evidenced for CMHC variables, bringing them far above other facility variables and close to SACs in importance.

Observing this intervening "masking" effect of borough of location suggests to us that the minimal effect of CMHC coverage in terms of explained variance may be

TABLE 11.11  PERCENT OF VARIANCE IN UTILIZATION RATES EXPLAINED BY CMHC VARIABLE, UNDER DIFFERENT CONTROLS (DIFFERENT ORDER OF ENTRY INTO EQUATION)

|  | UR/Outpatient | | UR/Inpatient | |
|---|---|---|---|---|
|  | Total | No Prior Service | Total | No Prior Service |
| No controls, borough weighted | .11 | .12 | .01 | .03 |
| No controls, borough not weighted | .15 | .17 | .06 | .12 |
| CMHC - voluntary | .13 | .16 | .03 | .11 |
| CMHC - municipal | .01 | .01 | .00 | .00 |
| CMHC - nonfederal | .01 | .00 | .03 | .01 |
| SACs only controlled | .05 | .05 | .03 | .02 |
| SACs + borough controlled | .08 | .08 | .03 | .04 |
| Boroughs only controlled | .11 | .12 | .01 | .06 |
| SACs and hospital clinic coverage controlled | .03 | .03 | .01 | .01 |
| Percent of Unique Variance ($sr2$) | | | | |
| A. No Borough control | | | | |
| CMHC - voluntary | .031 | .035 | .015 | .017 |
| CMHC - municipal | .008 | .005 | .000 | .000 |
| CMHC - nonfederal | .005 | .001 | .001 | .002 |
| Number of voluntary hospital beds | .002 | .001 | .000 | .000 |
| Number of municipal hospital beds | .005 | .004 | .019 | .000 |
| B. Boroughs in equation | | | | |
| CMHC - voluntary | .052 | .056 | .013 | .025 |
| CMHC - municipal | .015 | .000 | .008 | .008 |
| CMHC - nonfederal | .005 | .001 | .002 | .001 |
| Number of voluntary hospital beds | .002 | .001 | .000 | .000 |
| Number of municipal hospital beds | .009 | .008 | .014 | .000 |

TABLE 11.12  PERCENT UNIQUE VARIANCE EXPLAINED (sr2)

| | Outpatient--No Prior Service | | | Inpatient  No Prior Service | | |
|---|---|---|---|---|---|---|
| | Borough Weights | No Borough Control | Boroughs in Equation | Borough Weights | No Borough Control | Boroughs in Equation |
| A. CMHC | .031 | .041 | .067 | .013 | .019 | .034 |
| B. Clinic | .013 | .015 | .018 | .005 | .004 | .005 |
| C. Hospital | .007 | .007 | .011 | .002 | .002 | .003 |
| [ΣFACs] | [.05] | [.06] | [.10] | [.02] | [.03] | [.04] |
| D. Community Environment | .020 | .018 | .019 | .013 | .012 | .005 |
| E. Family Structure | .056 | .040 | .017 | .033 | .062 | .013 |
| F. Age Ratio | .057 | .083 | .038 | .032 | .050 | .010 |
| G. Sex Ratio | .001 | .000 | .000 | .000 | .001 | .000 |
| H. Mobility | .010 | .002 | .001 | .020 | .020 | .011 |
| I. Female Education | .011 | .013 | .009 | .011 | .005 | .003 |
| J. Race/Ethnic | .003 | .005 | .002 | .010 | .019 | .009 |
| K. Income/Employment | .006 | .008 | .003 | .005 | .011 | .001 |
| L. Σ Unique Contribution | .215 | .233 | .185 | .144 | .205 | .094 |
| M. Joint Contribution [n-1] | .334 | .349 | .458 | .259 | .238 | .482 |
| N. Total $R^2$ | .549 | .582 | .643 | .403 | .443 | .576 |
| O. Σ Unique SACs Only [L-(A+B+C)] | .164 | .170 | .089 | .124 | .180 | .090 |

due to major differences among the facilities. To explore these differences, we will present three additional analyses:

1. Divide CMHC coverage into voluntary, municipal, and nonfederal auspice;
2. Examine results for the lower income areas only;
3. Examine regression results for areas covered by CMHCs only.

1. Looking at the lower half of Table 11.11, we see that, while the borough "masking effect" is general, it is strongest for outpatient rates. Most interesting is the fact that the impact of CMHCs is mostly due to voluntary-hospital-based facilities. Further, the voluntary hospitals in Manhattan which are offering a comprehensive set of localized services (nonfederal CMHCs) do not affect utilization rates. We know this is not because of their location in the Manhattan institutional center, since introduction of borough controls leaves their contribution unchanged. To further explore the difference between municipal and voluntary auspice, we have calculated the unique contribution of the number of municipal and voluntary hospital beds in the areas (variables 107,106). We see that the CMHC (voluntary) effects upon outpatient rates are independent of the effect of hospital coverage. For inpatient, municipal hospital coverage is equal to voluntary CMHC for total admissions, but not for new entrants (no prior service). Moreover, the voluntary hospital effect is negligible. We may therefore conclude that CMHCs have a small but independent impact upon utilization rates only where the CMHCs are based upon voluntary hospitals and operated under the federal program (i.e., 13 health areas in Brooklyn and Richmond).

2. Examining Table 11.13, we see that reducing the sample to low-income areas

TABLE 11.13 PERCENT VARIANCE EXPLAINED – STEPWISE, BY INCOME

| | Outpatient | | Inpatient | |
|---|---|---|---|---|
| | $UR_{TOT}$ | $UR_{NPS}$ | $UR_{TOT}$ | $UR_{NPS}$ |
| MFI – Low | | | | |
| SACs | .52 | .53 | .62 | .54 |
| CMHC | .14 | .14 | .06 | .07 |
| Clinic | .03 | .03 | .05 | .02 |
| Hospital | .01 | .02 | .01 | .01 |
| Boroughs | .07 | .02 | .07 | .09 |
| Total $R^2$ | .72 | .74 | .82 | .72 |
| MFI – High | | | | |
| SACs | .47 | | .76 | |
| Clinic | .04 | | .01 | |
| Hospital | .03 | | .01 | |
| CMHC | .02 | | .02 | |
| Voluntary | (.01) | | (.00) | |
| Municipal | (.00) | | (.00) | |
| Nonfederal | (.01) | | (.02) | |
| Boroughs | .11 | | .01 | |
| Other Service | .01 | | .00 | |
| Total $R^2$ | .68 | | .81 | |

TABLE 11.14  PERCENT VARIANCE EXPLAINED BY CMHC VARIABLE
FOR SUBSAMPLES BY MEDIAN FAMILY INCOME; BOROUGH, SACs CONTROLLED

|  | Outpatient Utilization Rate | Inpatient Utilization Rate |
|---|---|---|
| MFI* = all | .07 | .03 |
| MFI = low | .14 | .06 |
| MFI = high | .02 | .02 |

* MFI = Median family income: low ≤ 9,000; high > 9,000.

doubles the percent of variance explained by CMHCs to 14% for outpatient, 6 to 7% for inpatient. This is consistent with the hypothesis that low-income areas are more affected by facility location and that CMHCs will offer easier entry to these groups. However, the major impact is still seen to be in outpatient admission, rather than in hospitalization rate.

Since most areas covered by CMHCs are lower income, we do not expect the CMHC variable to have much effect in the higher income subsample. This is confirmed by the data on the lower half of Table 11.13. Extract Table 11.14 summarizes the results of the income division. The fact that CMHC coverage affects outpatient rates more than inpatient rates even for low-income areas reinforces our contention that the CMHC program has tended to add additional clinic services without affecting the underlying process by which poor persons are institutionalized.

3. The previous sections have measured the impact of CMHC coverage relative to all areas, thus controlling for a full range of social area characteristics and facility types. Within that broad context, where our model explains 60 to 80% of variance in utilization rates, CMHC coverage explained only 1 to 7%, and 14% for low-income areas. In general, we have observed that social characteristics are the best predictors of UR, even when Facility Coverage is considered.

While we consider the above approach to be the most valid for reasons presented in the opening section of the paper, it may be instructive to apply the model to just those 54 (of the 333 total) health areas which are covered by CMHCs. If we still find that SACs are an important predictor of utilization among areas covered by CMHCs, then we may continue to infer that introduction of a CMHC has not produced a major change in the dynamics of the system.

Reduction of our sample to 54 cases means that we cannot continue to use the full battery of 38 variables by which we have described the system. As noted above, we have used this large number of variables in order to test various hypotheses about social structure and demonstrate that certain variables do not have a significant effect. For stability, we have chosen several variables from each conceptual dimension. We can therefore reduce our total number of variables by selecting one or two from each dimension and our total $R^2$ should not be drastically reduced.

Table 11.15 summarizes the results. It is clear that the model still predicts differences within the CMHC sample quite well, and that social area characteristics explain well over half the variance within the sample. We do note, however, that the differentiation between voluntary and municipal auspices continues to be impor-

TABLE 11.15   PERCENT VARIANCE EXPLAINED AREAS COVERED BY CMHC

| | Outpatient | Inpatient | |
|---|---|---|---|
| SACs (10 variables) | .62 | .55 | |
| FACs | .20 | .11 | |
| Clinic coverage | .02 | .03 | |
| Hospital coverage | .03 | .01 | |
| CMHC | | | |
|   Voluntary | .14 | .04 | |
|   Municipal | .01 | .02 | |
|   Nonfederal | .00 | .00 | |
|   Boroughs | .03 | .09 | |
|     Total $R^2$ | .86 | .74 | |
| (f, df) | (9.76;20/33) | (5.17;15/38) | Inpatient/ (Inpatient + Outpatient) |
| | Outpatient | Inpatient | |
| FACs–TOT | .36 | .22 | .08 |
| CMHC | | | |
|   Voluntary | .24 | .01 | .00 |
|   Municipal | .00 | .14 | .01 |
| Clinic | .02 | .01 | .05 |
| Hospital (14%) | .10 | .06 | .01 |
| SACs | | | |
|   Structure | .37 | .40 | .27 |
|   Race/Ethnic | .08 | .02 | .12 |
|   Income/Employment | .00 | .00 | .00 |
| | [.45] | [.42] | [.39] |
| Boroughs | .05 | .11 | .04 |
|     Total $R^2$ | .86 | .76 | .51 |
| (F; df) | (11.57;18/35) | (6.66;17/36) | (2.24;17/36) |

tant for outpatient (14% of variance after SACs controlled), and borough differentiations are important (9%) for inpatient. Two more questions are thus in order: how much variance will SACs explain if we first control for facility auspice; how does the pattern of unique contributions among the various SACs dimensions compare to the pattern observed for all areas (see Table 11.22). To make this comparison directly, we have run new regressions (with the reduced variable sets) for subsamples of areas covered by CMHCs and not covered by CMHCs.

Table 11.15 shows that, as in the total sample, initial control of facility coverage significantly reduces the level of impact of SACs within the CMHC sample, but that the contribution of SACs to explained variance is still quite large. Table 11.16 shows that this holds for both inpatient and outpatient utilization rates, and holds whether one examines variance explained by SACs as a percent of total variance or as a percent of variance explained by the model. In all instances, restriction of the sample to CMHC areas increases the contribution of SACs.

We may therefore draw a strong inference that, while CMHC coverage has increased the overall level of utilization, it has not eliminated social differentiation.

TABLE 11.16   PERCENT OF VARIANCE EXPLAINED BY SACs,
WITH ALL FACs CONTROLLED

|  | Outpatient | Inpatient | IP/IP+OP |
|---|---|---|---|
| A. Percent of Total Variance (100%) | | | |
| 1. Total sample | .28 | .26 | |
| 2. CMHC areas | .45 | .43 | .39 |
| B. Percent of Explained Variance ($R^2$) | | | |
| 1. Total sample | .42 | .37 | |
| 2. CMHC areas | .56 | .66 | .83 |

If Social Area Characteristics can explain 45% of total variance among areas covered by CMHCs, after voluntary-municipal auspice differences are controlled, then we strongly suspect that the CMHCs have not changed the underlying social dynamics of the system.

However, to make such a strong statement, we must consider not only the percent variance explained by SACs variables, but also the Beta weights of particular variables. A statement such as "the underlying social dynamics of the system remain unchanged" would require that the same SACs variables predict UR in the same way, whether one considered the areas covered by CMHCs or other areas.

Unfortunately, our analysis is complicated here by the fact that reduction of the sample size (through stratification) required reduction of the large number of variables, included in the original set. We have already found that there are complex interactions among social variables and that our multiple Betas are often of opposite sign from the bivariate correlation coefficients. By eliminating particular members of the variable set, we may change the role played by each variable (see Table 11.17).

For example, let us consider our underlying structural variables: racial-ethnic group and income-employment factors. Comparing columns (A) and (B) of Table 11.18, we see that, for UR $_{Outpatient}$ , the bivariate correlations are almost identical in the two subsamples, suggesting similar social dynamics. When we examine the Betas, which change signs in several cases, we see that percent black becomes more important in CMHC areas and low income more important in non-CMHC areas. For inpatient rates, the income Beta actually has opposite signs for CMHC (-.34) and non-CMHC (+.17) areas; however, it is necessary to decide whether this is due to the impact of different facility operations, or to different relationships among the social variables in the two subsample. Table 11.17 shows that the bivariate correlations among are mostly similar, except those involving the variable Percent of Units Lacking Plumbing.

Examining Table 11.20, which lists the Beta scores for all SACs variables on CMHC and non-CMHC subsamples, we see again that, while the directions are consistent, the magnitudes are often quite different. For example, Percent Female Head of Household is much more important for the non-CMHC areas for outpatient, but more important for the CMHC areas for inpatient. Community/ environment (housing) variables seem more important for differentiating within the CMHC subsample than outside it.

One clue as to whether the differences are due to facility operation or to interaction among social characteristics peculiar to the CMHC subsample is to compare the means (t-test) of the two groups. We have done so in Table 11.21.

The CMHC areas are clearly different regarding age structure (younger), racial-ethnic composition (fewer blacks, more Puerto Ricans, Irish, and Italians); more· substandard housing, greater mobility (in-migration), and fewer drive to work (less middle-class familism).

We are led to believe that, since the bivariate correlations between SACs variables and Utilization Rates are similar for CMHC and non-CMHC areas, but the social composition of the areas is different, multivariate relationships (Betas) observed are due to interactions among social area characteristics. We may therefore state tentatively that, in areas covered by CMHCs, there seems to be a modification in the dynamics by which they are related. In CMHC areas, low income seems to be less of an impediment to obtaining outpatient services. The avoidance of service by traditional Catholic groups is, if anything, heightened, and blacks seem to avoid or be refused service relative to other groups. It is quite interesting that the inpatient/outpatient ratio (URIPCL) which is poorly predicted by the model overall is well predicted ($R^2= 0.51$) for areas covered by CMHCs. Examining the Betas, we observe tendencies for black areas to utilize more inpatient service, and higher income groups to utilize more outpatient service.

In summary, then, the changes in Beta scores may weaken our contention that CMHCs have left the underlying social dynamics of mental health services unchanged, but the specific changes observed suggest a continuation of socio-economic discrimination under the program. However, more detailed analysis will be required before this observation can be considered more than tentative.

## C. EXTRUSION HYPOTHESIS

As discussed above, this hypothesis interprets the phenomenon of service utilization as an indication of the degree to which individuals are rejected by family, friends, and community. Unfortunately, we could pose this rejection in two forms which would yield opposite results in the same test. First, we could posit extrusion as a phenomenon related to immediate family and living circumstances. If so, we would expect family and community variables to be the major predictors of utilization, or to predict hospitalization more highly than outpatient admission. On the other hand, if one posits that extrusion occurs at the level of major class interaction, then we would expect structural (income, race/ethnic) variables to account for admission better than family variables. We must therefore consider extrusion to be an alternative explanation to the stress hypothesis for the same observations.

The fact that facility coverage explains more variance for outpatient than inpatient rates is compatible with either the stress hypothesis (persons admitted to inpatient feel greater distress, will travel farther) or with the extrusion hypothesis (families wishing to extrude a member will travel farther to place him in a hospital than to gain admission to a clinic).

TABLE 11.17  BIVARIATE CORRELATIONS AMONG SACs,
BY CMHC VERSUS NON-CMHC SUBSAMPLES

|  | 080 | 078 | 128 | 196 | 132 | 184 | 115 | 110 | 183 | 111 | % Males 16-21 Unemployed Q/P 085 |  |
|---|---|---|---|---|---|---|---|---|---|---|---|---|
| Child dependency ratio | .79 | .84 | -.13 | -.07 | -.61 | -.27 | .85 | .50 | -.68 | .80 | .39 |  |
| MFI |  | .92 | -.35 | .00 | -.80 | -.20 | .76 | .82 | -.77 | .93 | .47 |  |
| Percent of persons in overcrowded units |  |  | -.25 | -.13 | -.86 | -.18 | .84 | .76 | -.84 | .90 | .50 |  |
| Percent who drive to work |  |  |  | -.46 | -.03 | +.48 | -.14 | -.33 | .09 | -.42 | -.20 |  |
| Mobility |  |  |  |  | .43 | .34 | .04 | -.11 | .04 | .11 | -.13 |  |
| Mean female education |  |  |  |  |  | .29 | -.62 | -.76 | .78 | -.69 | -.46 |  |
| Units lack plumbing |  |  |  |  |  |  | -.27 | -.17 | .11 | -.11 | .19 |  |
| Percent Black |  |  |  |  |  |  |  | .51 | -.80 | .84 | .43 |  |
| Percent Puerto Rican |  |  |  |  |  |  |  |  | -.72 | .75 | .47 |  |
| Percent who attend parochial school |  |  |  |  |  |  |  |  |  | -.79 | -.56 |  |
| Percent of female heads of household |  |  |  |  |  |  |  |  |  |  | .46 |  |
|  |  |  |  |  |  |  |  |  |  |  |  | NOP/091 |
| $UR_{OP}$-TOT | .52 | .53 | -.23 | -.11 | -.51 | -.07 | .48 | .30 | -.49 | .51 | .36 | .59 |
| $UR_{IN}$-TOT | .10 | .13 | -.35 | .13 | .03 | .49 | .19 | -.05 | -.19 | .25 | .20 | .10 |

|  | 080 | 078 | 128 | 196 | 132 | 184 | 115 | 110 | 183 | 111 | 085 |  |
|---|---|---|---|---|---|---|---|---|---|---|---|---|
| Child dependency | .73 | .76 | -.28 | +.15 | -.59 | +.01 | .42 | .71 | -.50 | .65 | .42 |  |
| MFI |  | .87 | -.58 | .14 | -.77 | +.34 | .64 | .77 | -.68 | .90 | .58 |  |
| Percent of persons in overcrowded units |  |  | -.58 | .19 | -.84 | .24 | .61 | .78 | -.67 | .83 | .60 |  |
| Percent who drive to work |  |  |  | -.38 | .37 | -.43 | -.38 | -.48 | .32 | -.64 | -.37 |  |
| Mobility |  |  |  |  | .11 | .08 | .02 | .25 | -.11 | .16 | .04 |  |
| Mean female education |  |  |  |  |  | -.14 | -.48 | -.71 | .57 | -.67 | -.50 |  |
| Units lack plumbing |  |  |  |  |  |  | .40 | .06 | -.26 | .40 | .24 |  |
| Percent Black |  |  |  |  |  |  |  | .23 | -.71 | .84 | .54 |  |
| Percent Puerto Rican |  |  |  |  |  |  |  |  | -.49 | .61 | .46 |  |
| Percent who attend parochial school |  |  |  |  |  |  |  |  |  | -.72 | -.55 |  |
| Percent of female heads of household |  |  |  |  |  |  |  |  |  |  | .60 |  |
| Males 16-21, Unemployed |  |  |  |  |  |  |  |  |  |  |  |  |
|  |  |  |  |  |  |  |  |  |  |  |  | NOP/091 |
| $UR_{OP}$-TOT | .43 | .47 | -.22 | .04 | -.37 | .15 | .35 | .41 | -.49 | .45 | .33 | .48 |
| $UR_{IP}$-TOT | .31 | .28 | -.41 | .22 | -.13 | .52 | .25 | .15 | -.25 | .31 | .20 | .11 |

TABLE 11.18

|  | $UR_{Outpatient}$ | | $UR_{Inpatient}$ | | $UR_{IPCL}$ | |
|---|---|---|---|---|---|---|
|  | CMHC | Other | CMHC | Other | CMHC | Other |
| A. Simple 'r (bivariate correlation) |  |  |  |  |  |  |
| Percent Black | .48 | .35 | .19 | .25 | -.03 | .05 |
| Percent Puerto Rican | .30 | .41 | -.05 | .15 | -.26 | .05 |
| Percent who attend parochial school | -.49 | -.49 | -.19 | -.25 | .12 | .02 |
| Median family income | .52 | .43 | .12 | .32 | -.20 | .13 |
| Male unemployment | .36 | .33 | — | — | — | — |
| B. Beta weight, boroughs controlled (multiple regression coef.) |  |  |  |  |  |  |
| Percent Black | -.71 | -.15 | -.08 | -.05 | .45 | .04 |
| Percent Puerto Rican | .32 | .18 | .09 | .01 | -.85 | -.16 |
| Percent who attend parochial school | -.42 | -.28 | -.40 | -.02 | -.20 | .28 |
| Median family income | -.23 | -.45 | -.34 | .17 | -.23 | .32 |
| Male Unemployment | .03 | .08 | — | — | — | — |

TABLE 11.19  MEAN H.A. SCORES, BY SUBSAMPLE

| | CMHC | Non-CMHC | Total Sample | $* > p \leq 0.01$ $\dfrac{x - u}{t \cdot s/\sqrt{n-1}}$ |
|---|---|---|---|---|
| Child dependency ratio | -12.56 | -14.95 | -14.55 | * 9.48 |
| Aged dependency ratio | .19 | .21 | .21 | * 5.0 |
| Median family income | -37.06 | -37.58 | -37.49 | |
| Percent of persons in overcrowded units | .23 | .21 | .22 | |
| Percent who drive to work | 19.25 | 24.51 | 23.73 | * 6.05 |
| Mobility index | .74 | .64 | .66 | * 6.67 |
| Mean female education | 1.65 | 1.60 | 1.61 | |
| Percent of units that lack plumbing | .04 | .03 | .03 | * 4.5 |
| Percent Black | .19 | .23 | .23 | * 2.5 |
| Percent Puerto Rican | .18 | .11 | .12 | *10.0 |
| Percent who attend parochial school | .23 | .21 | .21 | * 2.86 |
| Percent of female heads of household | .20 | .19 | .19 | |
| UR$_{OP}$-TOTAL | 72.09 | 39.51 | 43.10 | |
| UR$_{IP}$-TOTAL | 24.89 | 15.51 | 16.58 | |
| Male unemployment, 16-21 | 59.12 | 56.29 | | |

TABLE 11.20   BETA'S BY CMHC/NON-CMHC SUBSAMPLES

| | | UR/Outpatient | |
| | | CMHC | Other |
|---|---|---|---|
| Community | Percent of persons in overcrowded units | -.32 | -.14 |
| Family | Percent of female heads of household | .12 | .62 |
| | Percent who drive to work | -.51 | .04 |
| Age | Child dependency ratio | .58 | .23 |
| Mobility | Mobility index | -.12 | .00 |
| Race/Ethnic | Percent Black | -.71 | -.15 |
| | Percent Puerto Rican | .32 | .18 |
| | Percent who attend parochial school | -.41 | -.29 |
| Income/ | MFI | -.23 | -.45 |
| Employment | Male unemployment | .03 | .08 |
| $R^2$ | | .86 | .45 |
| F | | 11.6 | 12.1 |

| | | UR/Inpatient | |
|---|---|---|---|
| Community | Percent of units that lack plumbing | .66 | .37 |
| Family | Percent of female heads of household | .71 | .10 |
| Age | Child dependency head | -.02 | .02 |
| | Aged dependency ratio | .36 | .01 |
| Mobility | Mobility index | -.16 | .09 |
| Female Education | Mean education, 15-44 | .31 | .03 |
| Race/Ethnic | Percent Black | -.08 | -.05 |
| | Percent Puerto Rican | .09 | .01 |
| | Percent who attend parochial school | -.40 | -.02 |
| Income | Median family income | -.34 | .17 |
| $R^2$ | | .76 | .57 |
| F | | 6.7 | 20.3 |
| df | | 17/36 | 18/264 |

One partial test might be the relation of inpatient and outpatient rates. Hospitalization constitutes a greater degree of extrusion—removal from the community—than does outpatient treatment. We would therefore expect that after facility variables are controlled, SACs would predict more highly for inpatient than outpatient care. In Table 11.6 we see that this does not occur. When facility coverage is controlled, SACs account for 31% of variance in UR for new entrants to outpatient care and 28% for readmissions; SACs account for 28% of variance in either new or return admissions to inpatient service (local hospitals). However, let us assume that unexplained variance is due to sampling error and other random factors, and that the model produces a larger $R^2$ for outpatient rates because they exhibit greater variance than inpatient rates. It is then better to express the relative amount of variance, rather than as a percent of 100. Calculated in this fashion, SACs account for 54% and 48% of explained variance for outpatient, but 65% and 55% of explained variance for inpatient admissions. Given the closeness of percent variance explained, it may be helpful to examine in more detail the effect of the various sets of social characteristics employed. First, let us examine the percent of variance explained by the various sets, after facility coverage is controlled. In Table 11.22, percent of uniquely explained variance is calculated from the semipartial correlation coefficients for a set of variables, at a step prior to the introduction of structural (race/ethnic, income) variables, rather than from the stepwise regression techniques used for Table 11.6.

The overall model is supported by observing that the partial correlation coefficients for the structural variables approach zero, and that they only add 1% to explained variance, after facility, community, and family variables are controlled. We therefore examine the independent relations between the intervening variables and utilization.

It is clear (from comparing Rows A-G, Table 11.22 that the highest independent contributions are from family structure and facility coverage for outpatient rates.[10] A similar pattern appears for inpatients with no prior service. However, the pattern shifts considerably when we compare new entrants with readmissions, for inpatient utilization, family structure, and geographic mobility are majority determinants for new entrants. For readmissions, however, these variables are less important, and community (living conditions[11]) and facility coverage become most important. This suggests extrusion at the extreme: after discharge, expatients gravitate or are pushed to the rooming house and hotel areas near the hospitals. They live in isolated conditions and are frequently rehospitalized. The predominance of family structure and mobility for new entry rates could be interpreted as extrusion of those who lack families and stable community ties; however, it could also mean that populations with the least stable family and community linkages undergo the greatest stress with the least protective resources, and thus exhibit high admission to psychiatric hospitals.

The new entrant/readmission comparison for outpatient rates is more complex. Again we find that facility coverage is more important for readmissions than new entrants. However, the relative importance of community and family variables changes differently. For outpatients, family factors and education are more important for readmission than first admission; community conditions and age structure (child dependency ratio) are more important for first admissions. This suggests that family and environmental conditions exert stressing forces which produce new entry; level of intact families and education then indicate persistence at obtaining outpatient treatment and avoiding hospitalization. Such an inference would be more strongly supported if these variables are also important in predicting inpatient/outpatient ratio.

When we examine the bottom half of Table 11.22, an interesting pattern emerges. The joint contribution to variance among all social area characteristics (Row I) is mostly the same for all rates. The major difference in $R^2$ between inpatient and outpatient seems to be due to the lower *independent* contribution of

TABLE 11.21   PERCENT VARIANCE UNIQUELY EXPLAINED (SEMIPARTIAL $r^2$) BY VARIABLE GROUP STRUCTURAL VARIABLES (RACE, ETHNICITY, INCOME) EXCLUDED

| Row | | Outpatient | | | Inpatient | | |
|---|---|---|---|---|---|---|---|
| | | UR/Total | UR/NPS | UR/READM | UR/Total | UR/NPS | UR/READM |
| A. | Facility Coverage | .076 | .055 | .081 | .038 | .020 | .037 |
| B. | Community/Environment | .011 | .025 | .011 | .033 | .018 | .037 |
| C. | Family Structure | .088 | .075 | .093 | .044 | .044 | .035 |
| D. | Age Ratios | .027 | .056 | .008 | .002 | .019 | .000 |
| E. | Sex Ratio | .000 | .002 | .002 | .017 | .002 | .016 |
| F. | Mobility | .003 | .014 | .001 | .002 | .026 | .005 |
| G. | Female Education and Employment | .025 | .005 | .024 | .007 | .012 | .009 |
| H. | Σ Unique Contribution | .230 | .232 | .220 | .143 | .141 | .139 |
| I. | Joint Contribution | .357 | .306 | .328 | .331 | .221 | .335 |
| J. | Total $R^2$ | .587 | .538 | .548 | .474 | .362 | .474 |
| K. | Σ Unique Contribution, SACs only | .154 | .177 | .139 | .107 | .121 | .102 |
| L. | Joint Contribution, SACs only (=Row I, Table 11.6 Row K) | .136 | .133 | .141 | .145 | .161 | .134 |
| M. | Total Contributions, SACs only (K + L) FACs Controlled | .29 | .31 | .28 | .25 | .27 | .27 |
| | N | 333 | 333 | 333 | 333 | 333 | 333 |
| | df | 29/303 | 29/303 | 29/303 | 29/303 | 29/303 | 29/303 |
| | F | 14.85 | 12.16 | 12.67 | 10.32 | 6.01 | 10.08 |

TABLE 11.22   TOTAL VARIANCE ($R^2$) EXPLAINED BY MODEL

| | Outpatient | | | Inpatient | | | Inpatient/Outpatient | |
|---|---|---|---|---|---|---|---|---|
| | UR/Total | UR/NPS | UR/Readmissions | UR/Total | UR/NPS | UR/Readmissions | Total Admissions | NPS |
| (   ) MFI=All | .61 | .57 | .58 | .51 | .43 | .51 | .25 | .29 |
| (142) MFI=Low | .68 | .65 | .66 | .58 | .57 | .59 | .41 | .47 |
| (191) MFI=High | .63 | .60 | .60 | .58 | .36 | .63 | .37 | .35 |

both facility coverage and social area variables for inpatient. In general, there is a strikingly consistent progression in amount of variance explained by facility location: $UR_{IP\text{-}NPS} < UR_{IP\text{-}READM} < UR_{OP\text{-}NPS} < OP_{READM}$. The joint and total contributions of SACs variables are much more equal across the various rates, without a consistent ordering.

In summary, then, we may say that inpatient rates are less influenced by nearby location of a facility, which is consistent with the extrusion hypothesis, but not conclusive. While social area characteristics seem equally important for inpatient and outpatient rates, the differences in particular relationships also support, but inconclusively, the extrusion hypothesis. Finally, we are less able to distinguish unique effects of social area and facility location variables for inpatient than for outpatient admissions. This suggests either a social policy of locating hospitals in particular areas, an effect of hospital location on social composition of surrounding neighborhood, or, most strongly, for the geographic drift hypothesis. The drift hypothesis, in turn, is closely related to the extrusion hypothesis, but emphasizes extrusion occurring after hospitalization as a cause of rehospitalization, rather than prior extrusion as a cause of initial hospitalization. Thus, our findings are supportive of the extrusion hypothesis, but not conclusive; we will therefore make further references and tests as we examine the relationships among social variables in more detail.

Conceiving of extrusion as occurring at the highest level of the system— privileged groups defining the behavior of underprivileged groups as pathological— allows us another inferential test. There is a high degree of correspondence between income level and white/nonwhite rates in residential areas of New York City. Moreover, there is a clearly bimodal distribution of areas by income level (see Figures 11.5, 11.6, and 11.7). If the negative correlation between socioeconomic status and mental health service utilization rates is simply due to such class bias, then we should find that, by dividing the sample into upper and lower income groups (at median family income <$9,000), we eliminate much of the explanatory power of the model. If, on the other hand, similar social area characteristics still predict variance within both halves, then we have strong support for social stress as opposed to class victimization. Finally, we may find that the explanatory power of the model does not decrease, but that different relationships among the variables are observed. In that case we might conclude, depending upon the particular variables, that victimization is a more appropriate explanation for the lower half, and stress is more appropriate for the upper half. Table 11.23 summarizes the results in terms of percent of variance explained.

We see immediately (in the figures extracted below) that splitting the sample by income increases the predictiveness of the model for both inpatient and outpatient admissions, with the sole exception of inpatient admissions with no prior service in high areas. We must therefore reject the simple possibility that mental health facility utilization is entirely a lower-class phenonenon. (Our data are drawn only from public facilities, not private doctors or profit-making private hospital). However, we have considerable mean utilization, considerable variation in utiliza-

## TABLE 11.23  PERCENT VARIANCE EXPLAINED (STEPWISE)* BY SACs, FACS, BY MFI=HIGH/LOW

### A. MFI=Low

| | Outpatient | | | Inpatient | | |
|---|---|---|---|---|---|---|
| | UR/Total | UR/NPS | UR/Readmission | UR/Total | UR/NPS | UR/Readmission |
| SACs | .53 | .30 | .19 | .51 | .09 | .00 |
| FACs | .10 | .03 | .05 | .06 | .04 | .14 |
| CMHC | .04 | .02 | .08 | .00 | .05 | .05 |
| Other Service | .00 | | | .00 | | |
| Total R² | .68 | .35 | .33 | .58 | .18 | .24 |
| CMHC | .29 | | | .03 | | |
| Clinic Coverage | .06 | | | .15 | | |
| Hospital Coverage | .05 | | | .04 | | |
| Σ FACs | .38 | | | .22 | | |
| SACs | .29 | .30 | .34 | .36 | .38 | .35 |
| Other Service | .00 | .01 | .00 | .01 | .01 | .00 |
| Total R² | .68 | .65 | .66 | .58 | .57 | .59 |

### B. MFI=High

| | Outpatient | | | Inpatient | | |
|---|---|---|---|---|---|---|
| | UR/Total | UR/NPS | UR/Readmission | UR/Total | UR/NPS | UR/Readmission |
| SACs | .55 | .00 | .00 | .52 | .01 | .00 |
| FACs | .07 | .06 | .17 | .05 | .03 | .14 |
| CMHC | .00 | .02 | .06 | .00 | .04 | .02 |
| Other Service | .01 | | | .01 | | |
| Total R² | .63 | .08 | .23 | .58 | .08 | .16 |
| CMHC | .00 | | | .00 | | |
| Clinic Coverage | .15 | | | .10 | | |
| Hospital Coverage | .05 | | | .03 | | |
| Σ FACs | .20 | | | .13 | | |
| SACs | .42 | .51 | .36 | .44 | .26 | .46 |
| Other Service | .01 | .01 | .01 | .01 | .02 | .01 |
| Total R² | .63 | .60 | .60 | .58 | .36 | .63 |

### C. Percent Variance Explained, Inpatient/Outpatient Ratio, by MFI=Low/High

| | MFI=Low | | MFI=High | | MFI=All | |
|---|---|---|---|---|---|---|
| | Total Admissions | Admissions NPS | Total Admissions | Admissions NPS | Total Admissions | Admissions NPS |
| CMHC | .04 | .00 | .00 | .00 | .00 | .00 |
| Clinic Coverage | .06 | .02 | .02 | .10 | .02 | .04 |
| Hospital Coverage | .04 | .06 | .07 | .05 | .05 | .05 |
| Σ FACs | .13 | .08 | .09 | .15 | .08 | .08 |
| SACs | .28 | .31 | .26 | .18 | .15 | .14 |
| Manhattan | .01 | .08 | .02 | .03 | .02 | .06 |
| Total R² | .41 | .47 | .37 | .35 | .25 | .29 |

* See Table 11.25 for F, df.

tion rate (see Figure 11.6b), and a consistent set of relationships ($R^2 \approx 0.6$) in the upper income group. Moreover, we know that this is not due to our cut-point being set too low because, while income remains an important variable differentiating hospitalization rate for areas below \$9,000, it has no impact for areas above \$9,000.

Table 11.24 breaks the total variance explained into the independent contributions of social area characteristics (SACs) and facility coverage (FACs). Here we find that, for all outpatient and inpatient rates (except inpatient-no prior service), social area characteristics actually explain more variance for higher income areas. Facility coverage explains a higher percentage of variance for the lower income group. We could infer either that lower income persons are drawn into service by the placement of facilities near them, or that they will travel less distance to obtain service than will higher income persons, and thus are more susceptible to facility coverage effects.

We can explore the details of these relationships by consulting Table 11.25, which lists the Betas observed for each variable by income group. Table 11.26 lists the percent of variance explained by each group of variables.

Looking first at the facility coverage variables, we note that CMHC coverage is only important for lower income areas, since virtually no upper income areas are covered by a CMHC. However, the failure to obtain a negative relationship (Beta) between CMHC coverage and hospitalization remains, despite the income split. For low income groups, presence of a municipal hospital clinic (P162) or a large amount of total clinic budget in the area is a positive predictor of utilization. For upper income groups, however, presence of a voluntary clinic (P167) is the important predictor. This is a significant indication of two sets of service for the two classes. Moreover, presence of a large municipal hospital (V107) actually decreases the rate of outpatient utilization while increasing the inpatient rate, suggesting that these institutions tend to induct persons living near them and not keep them in the community. We thus have evidence for the extrusion hypothesis as a function of societal decisions about locating facilities.

The social variables present a far more complex picture. For both types of service, we obtain quite different Betas. In fact, we observe four instances of change of sign for outpatient rates and ten instances for inpatient, not counting those cases where a significant Beta approaches zero. What this says to us is that *some variables take on different meanings at different levels of income.* While such a finding can be compatible with a stress hypothesis, it greatly complicates such an interpretation. Let us focus on the family structure variables, since these tend to be the strongest predictors and also to exhibit curvilinear relationships which we will be discussing later (these curvilinearities are *not* just due to interaction with income, except for VAR 124 = husband and wife families, age 14-44, with child). We observe changes of sign* or significance in the following family variables:

|  | Outpatient | | | Inpatient | | |
|---|---|---|---|---|---|---|
|  | Low | High | All | Low | High | All |
| Percent of Mothers in Labor force | + | 0 | + | 0 | 0 | 0 |
| Percent of persons who live alone | + | − | − | 0 | + | 0 |
| H&W, 14-44, +child | + | − | − | + | − | − |
| Percent live births out of wedlock | + | + | + | − | + | + |
| Percent divorced | 0 | + | + | 0 | 0 | 0 |
| Percent of households with female head | − | 0 | − | − | + | 0 |
| Child dependency ratio | 0 | + | + | 0 | 0 | + |

* (−) = Beta negative; (3) = Beta Positive; (0) = Beta not significant

The relationship between municipal facility location and inpatient versus out-patient utilization for low-income areas is so important that we have extracted the particular figures to clarify and emphasize the results. Note that these Betas reflect the simultaneous control of all other variables in the model. We thus have evidence

### Extract from Table 11.25. Beta scores, MFI = low

|  | UR/Outpatient | UR/Inpatient |
|---|---|---|
| Number of municipal hospital clinics in health area/population | +.12 | −.13 |
| Number of municipal hospital beds in catchment area/population | −.28 | +.12 |

for the extrusion hypothesis as a function of societal decisions in locating municipal facilities. Where municipal outpatient clinics are available to poor people, inpatient hospitalization rate goes down. On the other hand, we seem to observe the inverse of a prevention effect: where large municipal hospitals are in poor areas, the inpatient rate goes up *and* the outpatient rate goes down. Poor people thus receive neither a continuum of service nor an offering of what is appropriate; rather, they get what is placed near them.

The social variables present a far more complex picture. We have already noted that splitting the sample by income increases the impact of facility variables for the lower group and the impact of social variables for the upper group. It will be interesting to see whether the large independent effect of SACs in explaining differential utilization in the upper half is due to graduations of race-ethnic and income status within the broad classes, or whether it is due to family and community factors. Table 11.26 shows the percent of variance uniquely explained ($sr^2$) for each variable group.

Structural factors of race, ethnicity, and income are clearly minor for all groups as predicted by the overall model. The greatest independent effect observed for structural variables is the explanation of 3% of variance in inpatient rates by income-employment for lower income areas only. However, a clear differentiation in relationships between upper and lower income samples is evident. For outpatient

TABLE 11.24.   BETA SCORES OF MULTIPLE REGRESSION, INPATIENT AND OUTPATIENT UTILIZATION
RATES (TOTAL ADMISSION) BY MEDIAN FAMILY INCOME (MFI)=LOW (≤$9,000/YEAR) OR HIGH (≤$9,000/YEAR)

| | Utilization Rate | | | | | |
| --- | --- | --- | --- | --- | --- | --- |
| | Outpatient | | | Inpatient | | |
| Variable | MFI=All | MFI=Low (Reg=25) | MFI=High (Reg=26) | MFI=All | MFI=Low (Reg=25) | MFI=High (Reg=26) |
| **FACs** | | | | | | |
| CMHC | .20 | .31 | .06 | .11 | .12 | .07 |
| Clinic: | | | | | | |
| Distance to clinic | -.08 | -.09 | -.02 | .03 | .01 | -.09 |
| Clinic dollars in catchment area | .12 | .26 | .04 | -.01 | .01 | -.08 |
| Number of adult clinics/population | | | | | | |
| Municipal | .02 | .12 | -.08 | -.06 | -.13 | -.02 |
| Voluntary | .08 | .03 | .19 | -.01 | -.02 | .02 |
| **Hospital** | | | | | | |
| Dist/Inc | .07 | .05 | .13 | .05 | .04 | -.02 |
| Number of voluntary beds in catchment area | .11 | .24 | .04 | -.01 | .11 | -.15 |
| Number of municipal beds in catchment area | -.14 | -.28 | -.22 | .25 | .12 | .24 |
| **SACs** | | | | | | |
| [R², FACs] | [.32] | [.38] | [.20] | [.25] | [.22] | [.13] |
| **Community** | | | | | | |
| Inc x Med Per/Room | .00 | .14 | .03 | -.08 | -.06 | -.04 |
| Percent of persons in overcrowded units | .06 | -.03 | .03 | .27 | .12 | .07 |
| Percent of units that are vacant | -.11 | -.10 | -.17 | -.10 | .45(1) | -.46 |
| Percent of units that lack plumbing | .13 | .05 | .18 | .29 | -.28(1) | .76 |
| **Family** | | | | | | |
| Percent of mothers in labor force | .26 | .22 | .09 | -.05 | .00 | .10 |
| Percent of persons who live alone | -.12 | .20 | -1.30 | .07 | .09 | .47 |
| Inc x H&W (14-44) with child | -.22 | .24 | -.74 | -.16 | .17 | -.34 |
| Age-adjusted fertility rate | .21 | .16 | .36 | .29 | .29 | .24 |
| Percent of live births out of wedlock | .82 | .46 | .39 | .32 | -.22 | .19 |
| Percent of adult persons divorced | .21 | .10 | 1.18 | .06 | -.06 | .05 |
| Percent who drive to work | .16 | -.06 | .28 | .30 | -.07 | .54 |

| | | | | | | |
|---|---|---|---|---|---|---|
| **Family (continued)** | | | | | | |
| Percent of Children, age 3-4, in school | .10 | .04 | .21 | -.21 | -.18 | -.06 |
| Percent of households with feamle head | -.21 | -.18 | .05 | .04 | -.18 | .19 |
| Child dependency ratios | +.38 | .05 | .31 | .10 | -.05 | -.08 |
| **Age** | | | | | | |
| Aged dependency ratios | -.03 | -.06 | +.09 | .04 | -.09 | .19 |
| **Sex** | | | | | | |
| Percent of population that is male | .05 | .15 | -.16 | .18 | .32 | -.07 |
| **Mobility** | | | | | | |
| Mobility index (distance) | .07 | -.16 | .05 | .03 | -.17 | .17 |
| Percent of households moved since 1968 | -.08 | .14 | -.10 | .03 | .19 | -.00 |
| **Female Education and Occupation** | | | | | | |
| Mean education, females 15-44 | .18 | -.18 | -.05 | .25 | .53 | -.22 |
| Percent of females age 25+, education <8th grade | .15 | .06 | -.14 | .00 | -.02 | .00 |
| Percent female sales and clerical workers | .21 | .16 | .11 | .08 | -.07 | -.17 |
| **Race-Ethnic** | | | | | | |
| Percent Puerto Rican | .04 | -.15 | -.15 | -.02 | .28 | -.05 |
| Percent black | -.33 | -.23 | -.15 | -.22 | .31 | -.39 |
| Percent who attend parochial school | -.17 | -.23 | .01 | -.03 | -.10 | -.05 |
| **Income/ Employment** | | | | | | |
| Percent of males in labor force who work <40 weeks | -.05 | -.09 | .20 | .14 | .20 | -.15 |
| Male unemployment, age 16-21 | .02 | .01 | .06 | -.02 | -.19 | .12 |
| Median family income | -.34 | .01 | -.08 | -.06 | .29 | .02 |
| $R^2$ - Total | [.60] | [.67] | [.62] | [.51] | [.58] | [.57] |
| F | 13.0 | 6.2 | 7.2 | 8.7 | 4.1 | 5.9 |
| df | 35/297 | 35/106 | 35/155 | 35/297 | 35/106 | 35/155 |

TABLE 11.25.   PERCENT UNIQUE VARIANCE (sr$^2$) EXPLAINED BY VARIABLE GROUPS, MEDIAN FAMILY INCOME = HIGH/LOW

| | Utilization Rate | | | | | |
| | Outpatient | | | Inpatient | | |
| | MFI=All | MFI=Low | MFI=High | MFI=All | MFI=Low | MFI=High |
|---|---|---|---|---|---|---|
| CMHC | .03 | .04 | .00 | .01 | .01 | .00 |
| Clinic coverage | .01 | .02 | .03 | .00 | .01 | .01 |
| Hospital coverage | .02 | .02 | .03 | .03 | .00 | .04 |
| Σ 1-3 | [.06] | [.08] | [.06] | [.03] | [.02] | [.05] |
| Community/environment | .01 | .01 | .01 | .03 | .04 | .15 |
| Family structure | .10 | .04 | .19 | .04 | .04 | .07 |
| Aged population | .00 | .00 | .00 | .00 | .00 | .01 |
| Sex ratio | .00 | .00 | .01 | .02 | .03 | .00 |
| Mobility | .00 | .01 | .00 | .00 | .01 | .00 |
| Female education and employment | .01 | .01 | .00 | .00 | .02 | .01 |
| Σ 4-9 | [.12] | [.07] | [.22] | [.09] | [.13] | [.24] |
| Race/ethnic | .01 | .01 | .01 | .00 | .01 | .02 |
| Income/male employment | .01 | .00 | .01 | .01 | .03 | .01 |
| Σ 10-11 | [.02] | [.02] | [.02] | [.01] | [.04] | [.03] |
| [R$^2$] | .60 | .67 | .62 | .51 | .58 | .57 |
| N | 333 | 142 | 191 | 333 | 142 | 191 |
| df (regression/residual) | 35/297 | 35/106 | 35/155 | 35/297 | 35/106 | 35/155 |
| F | 12.98 | 6.24 | 7.22 | 8.70 | 4.10 | 5.88 |

utilization, family structure variables are extremely important (19% of variance uniquely explained) for the upper income areas, but much less so for lower. A similar effect of less degree is observed for inpatient rates. In addition, a strong impact in explaining inpatient rates is observed for environmental (housing) variables for the upper income areas, but is much weaker for lower income areas.

These differences are consistent with the overall model, but suggest an important elaboration. Structural variables of race-ethnicity and income are major determinants of mental health utilization rates and operate through mediating variables of family and community disorganization and facility location. However, structural variables are only operative for areas with median family income below $9,000 per year (1970 census), probably due to the segregation of residential areas by race and income. It might be argued that since race and income are not effective for middle class areas and other social variables come into play, that race and income variables are spurious and not necessary to the model at all. However, in the following discussion we will show that not only are different social variables effective for upper and lower income areas, but also that they operate in such dramatically different fashion as to preclude considering them to be prime causal agents in the model. It seems that having an intact family is important for predicting utilization among both lower and upper income areas. However, the consistent pattern of intact family with children correlating positively with utilization only seems to apply to lower income groups. Divorce has a higher mean but lower variance for lower income areas and only relates to utilization for the upper income group. Living alone, female heads of households, and working mothers seem to have different meanings according to income.

A most interesting pattern is observed for the percent black population variable. When all income groups are combined, percent black has a negative Beta with both inpatient and outpatient utilization rates. That is, when income, facility coverage, and all other variables are controlled, black areas get less service. When we split the sample by income, however, an important difference appears: the Beta for inpatient rate turns positive. Among the poorer groups, using the public rather than private facilities, black areas have a disproportionately high rate of admission to inpatient and relatively low rate of admission to outpatient facilities.

We may therefore draw a tentative conclusion that similar social behaviors are treated differently for members of different classes and races. Thus, it is not family or environmental conditions that define stress, but the interaction of a person's social status with varying norms of behavior. To the extent that there are two or more norms for a particular behavior[13], and the members of one subgroup are subjected to the norms of another, we may infer that extrusion is operating at the broadest level of the social structure.

## VI. Conclusion: Major Findings, Implications for Policy and Further Research

In this paper we have discussed the major goals of the CMHC program and presented summary evidence regarding the level of achievement of these goals. This initial summary indicates that, while facility coverage and program structure have a small independent effect on MH service utilization, the greatest effect is due to social area characteristics (SACs) and to the joint action of social characteristics and facility location. This joint action is suggestive of a situation where the actual operation of the system is affected more by implicit than explicit political decisions. That is, an explicit decision would entail promulgation and implementation of a certain type of service program dedicated to announced goals and related to the particular characteristics, needs, or desires of the population to be serviced. An implicit decision may be inferred when, with no such promulgation, we find a consistent relationship between the social characteristics of areas and the type of facilities located in or near those areas. Our finding of prediction of differential utilization rates by the joint action of SACs and facility coverage indicates that such implicit decisions are indeed the major force in mental health services. Thus, when we observe that CMHC coverage independently explains only 3% of variance in outpatient admissions, 1% for inpatient and 0% for the inpatient/outpatient ratio (see Table 11.6), we must look elsewhere for explanation. Because the other variables in our model account for about 60% of variance in utilization, we are on safe grounds in concluding that the major factor in utilization is the distribution of social groups and non-CMHC services. In terms of evaluating a particular explicit social program, this finding is also critical. It suggests that *when there is a large ongoing system of service (state, municipal, and voluntary hospitals), a program strategy based upon awarding grants for creation of alternative projects will not produce any significant change in the pre-existing system.*

This finding is consistent with our initial discussion of the need to evaluate the CMHC program with explicit reference to the ongoing service system.

## A. SUMMARY OF FINDINGS

While many of the particular relationships we have found among variables are interesting, the major findings with strong policy implications seem to fit into five groups:

1. Social area characteristics seem to be the major causal factor for mental health service utilization rates.
2. There is considerable overlap in the effects of social area characteristics and facility coverage; that is, they appear to be mutually reinforcing.
3. The independent effects (Betas) for percent black or Puerto Rican population, for the low income areas, relate to increased hospitalization and decreased outpatient service.
4. We observe no prevention effect at the community level of analysis; this holds true whether we consider CMHCs, clinics, hospitals, or the total array of municipal and voluntary facility coverage.
5. The entire system is stratified by income level, with different sets of relationships observed for low and middle income groups.

We shall now proceed to discuss the implications of these findings.

1. *Social area characteristics seem to be the major causal factor determining*

*mental health service utilization rates.* When any type of facility coverage is controlled in a stepwise multiple regression, social area characteristics (SACs) independently predict a large proportion of variance in utilization rates. This appears to hold equally whether one examines inpatient rates or outpatient, new entrants to service, readmissions, or total admissions (see Table 11.6). This finding may be interpreted to suggest that either the stress hypothesis, social pathology hypothesis, or class victimization hypothesis may be true. We will attempt to differentiate among when analyzing our other findings. The implication for policy is that in planning services, one may expect that persons living in areas with certain social characteristics will travel to utilize service, regardless of where it is provided; others will ignore service even if it is close by. However, since many of the family structure variables exhibit curvilinear relationships to utilization rate, prediction of high or low utilization must be based upon a cluster of several factors; simple linear assumptions do not hold true when multiple factors are analyzed.

The finding that the effects of social area characteristics are largely independent of facility location has important implications for planning services in a context of shifting populations. We have three possibilities. The first is that propensity to utilize service inheres in the subculture of particular social groups; as they move, the pattern of demand for service moves with them. The second possibility is that population shifts represent changes in the social status of certain groups: acculturation, increased education and income, changing age structure. If so, then as groups move, their demand for mental health services will change due to underlying changes in their social position (if our model is correct). Finally, a social group may remain geographically stable, as in ethnic ghettos, but experience changes in social status.

While complete answers to these problems can be only provided by observing the relationships over time, our differentiations of social structural factors (income, race-ethnicity) from family and community factors allows us to shed some light on the situation. We have observed (Table 11.26) that, as predicted by our overall model, the correlations between structural variables and utilization approach zero as intervening variables are introduced, particularly family structure and community (housing) variables. Thus, if a change in social status by certain groups was not accompanied by cultural changes affecting family organization, one would expect their utilization rates to remain relatively stable. Conversely, if a change in social status were accompanied by an adoption of middle-class norms concerning family structure, then one would anticipate a change in utilization rates. The situation is of course complicated by the fact that we have observed not only divergent social norms for income classes, but also different relationships between these factors and mental health service utilization at different income levels. Thus, it is conceivable that, if subcultural patterns of family organization remain stable during changes in social status, changes in utilization will occur as a function of income level. However, since the income stratification in our sample relates so highly to the segregation of blacks and Puerto Ricans, it is not possible to draw any firm inferences from our cross-sectional data. That is, if the middle income stratum came to include larger numbers of blacks and Puerto Ricans, the patterns observed at each income level might become less different. Given this variety of possibilities, public policy should avoid large capital investments that are likely to rigidify the pattern of service locations when demand for service may be shifting.

2. *Overlapping effects of social area characteristics and facility coverage variables.* We find that both sets of variables act in a mutually reinforcing pattern to produce relatively high utilization of all services by areas of low income; high black or Puerto Rican population; high fertility, illegitimacy, divorce, or working mothers, but also a high rate of intact young families with children; and poor community living conditions. Because this overlap represents between one-half and one-third of the variance explained, there seems to be a clear political decision to deal with the social problems of these areas by the provision of mental health services. While the overall effect of this policy seems to be a location of services near the groups that want or need them the most, the different relationships of municipal and voluntary service coverage are disturbing. Specifically, the finding that, *for low income areas, proximity to a municipal inpatient facility decreases outpatient utilization,* while, for middle income areas, *proximity to a voluntary hospital increases outpatient utilization,* suggests that the overall impact of facility location policy tend to institutionalize low income persons at a disproportionate rate. Questions of equity in distribution of services should therefore be reexamined in terms of freedom from institutionalization. Allocations of service to the most vulnerable groups (poor, black, Puerto Rican) should therefore be balanced to avoid large hospitalization services in favor of outpatient facilities. Moreover, specific operational mechanisms should be developed to prevent inappropriate hospitalization, since we have seen that this effect is largely independent of facility location.

3. *The independant effects (Betas) for percent black or Puerto Rican population, for the low income areas, relate to increased hospitalization and decreased outpatient service.* The simple correlations between percent black or percent Puerto Rican and either outpatient or inpatient utilization rates are all strongly positive (+.32 to +.53). However, when we account for the multiple relationships and examine the low income areas separately, we find a different pattern. The Beta for outpatient services turns negative (as it does for the total sample of all incomes), while the Beta for inpatient services is positive (it is negative for the total sample of all income). Thus, when we examine all income levels, the independent effect is that black and Puerto Rican areas are relatively under-served with both outpatient and inpatient services. When we examine low income areas separately, and control all other factors, *blacks and Puerto Ricans tend to be under-provided with outpatient services and over-provided with hospitalization services.* It should be noted that, because of the way people travel or are taken to services, this discriminatory effect could not be observed simple from the correlation of race-ethnicity with facility location. Rather, it could only be observed by calculating the total utilization rate for areas, regardless of where they were served.

The policy implications here are consistent with those stated above. Since the discriminatory effects of the system only emerge when examining multiple inter-relations, the solution seems to lie not in simple questions of facility location, but in operational questions relating to policies and procedures for intake, diagnosis, and disposition.

4. *We observe no prevention effect at the community level of analysis; this holds true whether we consider CMHCs, clinics, hospitals, or the total array of municipal and voluntary facility coverage.* By tracing the simple and partial correlations between inpatient and outpatient utilization rates, we have tested the proposition that provision of service alternatives will produce differential utilization of services. What we have found is that areas that make heavy use of one type of service make heavy use of all others. This seems to be mostly a function of social area characteristics, since controlling for these variables significantly reduces the partial correlation. (See Table 11.8; note however that the partial remains positive when outpatient rates are correlated with state inpatient admissions instead of local inpatient admissions. This is a special test performed on similar 1970 data.) No facility coverage variable—CMHC, clinic coverage, or hospital bed coverage—or the combination of all of them has any significant effect upon the positive partial correlation between inpatient and outpatient rates. We therefore conclude that, if prevention is to occur at the community level, it must come not from the mere provision of service alternatives, but from the manner in which these services are run. At least in the foreseeable future of high demand, hospitals will be able to fill their beds, even if individual patients are diverted to outpatient alternatives. One must therefore expect an increase in any type of service to generate a corresponding increase in others, due to increased case-finding and referral, as well as a tendency to hold clients in the system once inducted.

This latter tendency is supported by our findings comparing the use of the model for new entrants into the mental health service system (admissions with no prior service) and readmissions. We observe (see Table 11.6) that, while the impact of social area characteristics is about the same for new entrants and readmissions, the impact of facility coverage is quite different. When facility coverage is entered first, it explains 6% more variance in outpatient utilization for readmissions, and 9% more variance in inpatient rates (Row H). However, when SACs are first controlled (Row B), the variance explained by FACs becomes about equal for outpatient rates, but is still much higher for inpatient readmissions ($\Delta R^2=0.05$) than for new entrants ($\Delta R^2=0.01$). We may thus tentatively conclude that proximity to a service facility is less important in determining the first entry to service than to the tendency to return for more service. Further, the tendency for increased readmissions in areas with high service availability is greater for inpatient than outpatient service. The predominance of a 5% independent effect of facility location upon inpatient readmission rates may be taken as a measure of the "drift effect," in the form of an accumulation of chronic inpatients relocating to hotel and rooming house districts near the Manhattan hospitals.

In summary, the observed positive correlation between inpatient and outpatient utilization rates is independent of difference in facility coverage and relates highly to social characteristics, as well as to a tendency to hold clients in the service system once admitted.

5. *The entire system is stratified by income level, with different sets of relationships observed for low and middle income groups.* The entire conceptualization for linking social characteristics to mental health service utilization must be elaborated in light of our finding that many of the most critical social variables are highly related to income level, and income is distributed bimodally within New York City. Thus, when the low and middle income areas have entirely different ranges for certain social variables, we must talk not of a societal norm but of two or more class-related norms. Because we have demonstrated that many of these social variables relate to mental health service utilization in opposite directions for low and middle income groups, and facility coverage variables also relate differently, it becomes reasonable to talk of a stratified system or dual system of service. Moreover, since the income stratification closely corresponds to the segregation of black and Puerto Rican groups from others, it becomes cogent to consider class interaction in explaining the dual systems. Thus, if low and middle income groups have different norms for certain critical social behaviors (e.g., percent of illegitimate births), then it is not reasonable to talk of deviation from an overall societal norm as explaining the differences in mental health service utilization rates. Rather, the failure of low income groups to adopt middle class norms may cause the middle class to impose mental health services as a mechanism of social control. This type of explanation becomes even more applicable when the social behavior in question relates to mental health service utilization in opposite direction for different income levels. For example, one might expect that rates of living alone or living in an intact family (husband and wife plus child) would differ in higher and lower income areas. One might also expect these conditions to operate in similar fashions to engender stress or protect individuals from the effects of other stressors. We observe, however, that having a high proportion of young families with children related to a high level of mental health service utilization in low income areas and that the reverse is true for middle income areas. One might therefore suspect that adhering to a condition valued for stability in the middle class produces a stress for the lower class. Alternatively, leaving aside the language of stress, one could argue that middle-class professionals label as mentally deviant those persons who fail to meet their behavioral norm, when actually the deviant persons are those who violate their own norm to simulate middle class norms. Thus, as we have argued, the ultimate question is what referent group will set the values that are to be "norms" versus those that are to be "deviance." Certainly the impact of income parameters in the fashion described makes it more reasonable to speak of social areas characteristics as class-determined values rather than as "social pathology." It then follows that imposition of mental health services across class boundaries can be as much victimization as service.

Finally, it should be noted that, in several instances, (percent of mothers in the labor force; aged and child dependency ratios; sex ratio) we have observed U-shaped relationships that are independent of income level. In these cases, we may infer that deviance from the overall norm *in either direction* is symptomatic of conditions leading to increased utilization of mental health services.

In general, our critical implication here is that expectations concerning the nature of family and community disorganization variables must take account of the income stratum being considered. Clearly one cannot transfer middle class values of family structure to the lower class—not just because of a different frequency of occurrence, but because of different social meanings attached to each arrangement.

## B. IMPLICATIONS FOR FURTHER RESEARCH

Throughout the study we have argued the case for evaluating programs within a full range of interacting social and institutional forces, and shown that failure to do so may produce spurious results. Similarly, we have shown that failure to test for complex, nonlinear relationships may also produce spurious results, particularly in the case of finding no correlation between two variables. We have made a case for conducting analysis at the aggregate or community level and shown the feasibility of doing so; it need hardly be said that this is only part of the picture and that we have not even attempted to address issues occurring at the individual level of anlysis. The reader should be sensitive, however, to certain basic limitations in the data which led to restrictions in the research design; further studies could well build upon this base and seek data that will overcome these limitations.

1. *Generality of results.* While New York City has a tremendous diversity of populations and services, as a whole it has a greater density of mental health professionals than any other part of the country. New York State has the greatest tendency to hospitalize patients (on a per population basis) and maintains the largest state hospital system of any state in the nation. The impacts of social characteristics and facility coverage may have different form when the range of variables is extended or where populations are spread over greater distances.

2. *Time Series Analysis.* The primary data from this analysis are cross-sectional. Inferences about causal relationships are thus quite risky. Moreover, while most of the CMHC programs in question had been in effect about 5 years at the time of data collection, a 10 or 25 year latency might be required for changes at the aggregate level, particularly for preventive effects. Moreover, as racial and ethnic groups experience changes in social status, the relative impact of specific social area characteristics may well change. It is therefore necessary both to replicate the same findings at different time periods, and to introduce change variables where causal interpretations are sought. Thus, examining the change in population characteristics such as racial composition or age structure in the period prior to measuring utilization may tell us more about utilization rates than does the absolute level of those variables. Finally, we have observed a large overlap in the placement of facilities and certain critical social characteristics. To complete the analysis it would therefore be desirable to trace the development of the service system over time and relate growth and placement of services to changing population characteristics.

3. *Related Services.* The line drawn around the mental health service system has been based upon formal licensing and funding criteria. A functional definition

might well expand the system to related or alternative services, such as VA hospitals, family and youth counseling centers, general medical facilities, clergy, and individual mental health practitioners not related to agencies.

4. *System Pathways.* The strong finding of positive partial correlations among utilization rates for multiple types of service suggests a revolving door. To fully understand this process, it will be necessary to track individuals as they move among various facilities. Because we have found evidence of a structure that discriminates in service dispositions among clients of different income and race-ethnic background, point-of-entry and rejected applicant data should be collected. To relate these behaviors to the questions of underlying norms which we have raised, it would then be necessary to compare client expectations about the types of service to be received with staff perceptions. Where a few such studies have been done, they have been conducted for single facilities. As such they are simply not applicable at the community level of analysis and may, as we have shown for prevention of hospitalization, actually produce misleading results.

## NOTES

1. Limitations of space have prevented us from reporting results of this comparison in the present paper.

2. For reviews of the stress literature, see Dohrenwend and Dohrenwend (1969).

3. It will be helpful to note at the outset why we have not employed a factor analysis to aggregate the social area characteristics into a few summary factors, despite the fact that various analyses have shown this to be workable (Tryon, 1955). First, the nonlinearity of some of the relationships contradicts assumptions of factor analysis. Second, the size of the geographic units employed (NYC Health Areas, mean population $\approx 24,000$) introduces a considerable amount of heterogeneity of areas on most measures. We would thus observe a concomitance of variables (i.e., a loading on same factors) drawn from different conceptual dimensions, such as high vacancy rates in the waterfront areas which are included in high income districts of Manhattan's West Side. By keeping individual variables separate, we can measure those aspects of a heterogeneous area which are most relevant to our dependent variables. Finally, our most important reason for not employing factor analysis is a conceptual argument. Proponents of factor analysis (or cluster analysis) maintain that a conceptual dimension (e.g., family disorganization) is valid only if the various measures of it are intercorrelated at whatever level or analysis is employed. If, however, the dimensions we are testing are treated theoretically as levels in a causal or developmental sequence, then two measures may reflect alternatives responses at the same level. For example, high income produces both high rent apartment districts in Manhattan and high cost single-family dwellings in Queens. Similarly, high divorce rates and high rates of female-headed households are conceptually similar as measures of family disorganization, but they appear in different areas of the City, dependent upon structural features of income, age structure, and race/ethnic composition. They would thus appear as correlated to different factors or as correlated in opposite directions to the same factor. We have, therefore, decided to incorporate a relatively large number of variables, choosing several to represent different aspects of four conceptual levels:

1. Societal Structure: income and race/ethnic segregation
2. Community Disorganization/Residential Environment: persons per room; overcrowded units; vacant units; substandard units; mobility index; percent who have moved since 1968.
3. Family Disorganization
4. Personal Alienation or Frustration: mental health service Utilization Rate; JD rate.

4. Durkheim argued, in *Suicide,* that a per-population rate such as suicide was indeed an observation of societal behavior, since it can be related to other societal level phenomena and

observed across societies to follow regular patterns. However he did not directly address the problem of relating the aggregate to the individual level.

5. Abstract file includes codes for type of facility and type of client. Admissions for "Mental Retardation," as opposed to "Mental Health" problems were edited out, slight ($\approx 5\%$) reducing the file.

6. Municipal facilities are operated by the quasi-independent Health and Hospitals Corporation (H.H.C.), successor to the New York City Department of Hospitals.

7. Voluntary facilities are operated by private, nonprofit corporations and derive their funding from a mixture of public and private sources.

8. See Blalock (1961) on this method.

9. We have replicated these results using 1970 data for Local Outpatient, Local Inpatient and State Inpatient admissions data. The positive partials follow similar patterns for State hospital Inpatient admission rates, but are even higher than those reported here.

10. It should be noted that, while the figures appear quite low when expressed as unique percent of variance, an entry of 0.075 corresponds to a partial order correlation of 0.27, which at the 29th order is quite significant; moreover, these figures are truly additive.

11. The unique contribution for community/living conditions increases from 0.037 to 0.064 if we include the one extremely high $UR_{IP}$ case in lower Manhattan which is excluded.

12. Beta is positive; (-)=Beta is negative; (0)=Beta is not significant.

13. As noted above, quality of norms was tested by comparing mean values of social characteristics for lower and middle income areas.

## REFERENCES

Alford, Robert R. (1971). "The Political Economy of the American Health System." Madison: Department of Sociology, University of Wisconsin. Mineo—Monograph in works.

Anderson, James G. (1972). "Effects of Social and Cultural Processes on Health." *Socio-Economic Planning Science* 8 (1): 9-22.

Bardach, Eugene. (1972). *The Skill Factor in Politics: Repealing the Mental Commitment Laws in California.* University of California Press, 1972.

Bellak, K., Leopold and Bertram Black, (1960). "The Rehabilitation of Psychotics in the Community." *American Journal of Orthopsychiatry* 30: 346.

Bendix, R. and S. M. Lipset, [eds.] (1953) *Class, Status and Power.* New York: Free Press of Glencoe.

Blalock, H. M. (1961) *Causal Inferences in Nonexperimental Research.* Chapel Hill: University of North Carolina Press.

Bloom, Bernard L. (1968) "An Ecological Analysis of Psychiatric Hospitalizations." *Multivariate Behavioral Research,* October.

Brenner, M. Harvey. (1973) *Mental Illness and the Economy.* Cambridge: Harvard University Press.

Bullough, Bonnie. (1974) "The Source of Ambulatory Health Services as it relates to Preventive Care." *AJPH* 64 (6).

– – –. (1972a) *Poverty, Ethnic Identity and Health Care* New York: Appleton-Century-Crofts.

– – –. (1972b) "Poverty Ethnic Identity and Preventive Health Care." *Journal of Health and Social Behavior.* 13: 349-359.

Burstein, Abraham C. (1972) *New York Community Corporation Areas* (The Burstein Report). Report of New York City Human Resources Administration, March 1972.

Campbell, Donald T. (1969) "Reforms as Experiments." *American Psychologist* 24: 409-429.

Campbell, D. T. and J. Stanley, (1963) *Experimental and Quasi-Experimental Designs for Research.* Chicago: Rand McNally.

Caro, Francis G. [ed.] (1971) *Readings in Evaluation Research.* New York: Russell Sage Foundation.

Clausen, John (1971) "Mental Disorders." In R. K. Merton and R. Nisbet, *Contemporary Social Problems.* 3rd ed. New York: Harcourt, Brace, Jovanovich.

Cohen, A. K. and J. F. Short, Jr. (1971) "Crime and Juvenile Delinquency." In R. K. Merton and R. Nisbet, *Contemporary Social Problems.* 3rd ed. New York: Harcourt, Brace, Jovanovich.

Cohen, Jacob (1968) "Multiple Regression as a General Data-Analytic System." *Psychological Bulletin* 70 (6): 426-443.

Connery, Robert H. et al. (1968) *The Politics of Mental Health.* New York: Columbia University Press.

Coser, Lewis A. (1956) *The Functions of Social Conflict.* New York: Free Press of Glencoe.

Cox, Kevin R. (1973) *Conflict, Power and Politics in the City: A Geographic View.* New York: McGraw-Hill.

Cumming, Elaine (1968) *Systems of Social Regulation.* New York: Atherton Press.

Dohrenwend, B. P. and Dohrenwend, B. S. (1969) *Social Status and Psychological Disorder: A Causal Inquiry.* New York: Wiley Interscience.

Dohrenwend, Bruce P. and Chin-Shong, Edwin. (1967) "Social Status and Attitudes Toward Psychological Disorders: The Problem of Tolerance of Deviance." *A.S.R.* 32: 417-432.

Duhl, Leonard J. (1963) *The Urban Condition: People and Policy in the Metropolis.* New York: Basic Books.

Duhl, Leonard J. and R. L. Leopold, [eds.] (1968) *Mental Health and Social Policy.* San Francisco: Jossey-Bass.

Duncan, O. D. (1966) "Path Analysis: Sociological Examples." *American Journal of Sociology* 72: 1-16.

Durkheim, Emile (1933/1964), *The Division of Labor in Society.* Glencoe, Ill.: Free Press. Paperback in 1964.

Earickson, Robert (1970) *The Spatial Behavior of Hospital Patients: A Behavioral Approach to Spatial Interaction in Metropolitan Chicago.* Research paper No. 124. Department of Geography, University of Chicago.

Ehrenreich, Barbara and John Ehrenreich. (1971) *The American Health Empire: Power, Profits and Politics.* New York: Vintage Books.

Etzioni, Amitai (1961) *A Comparative Analysis of Complex Organizations: On Power, Involvement and Their Correlates.* New York: Free Press of Glencoe.

Fairweather, George K. (1968) *Methods for Experimental Social Innovation.* New York: Wiley.

Faris, R. E. Z. and H. W. Dunham, (1939) *Mental Disorders in Urban Areas.* Chicago: University of Chicago Press.

Feldman, Arnold S. and Charles Tilly (1960) "The Interaction of Social and Physical Space." *A.S.R.* 25: 877-884.

Felix, Robert H. (1963) "Community Mental Health." *American Journal of Orthopsychiatry.* 33: 788.

Foucault, Michel (1965) *Madness and Civilization.* New York: Random House (Vintage Books, 1973).

Fried, Marc (1964) "Effects of Social Change on Mental Health." *American Journal of Orthopsychiatry.* 34.

Fried, March (1969) "Social Differences in Mental Health." In J. Rosa, A. Antonovsky, and I. K. Zola, *Poverty and Health: A Sociological Analysis.* Cambridge: Harvard University Press.

Galle, O. R.; W. R. Gove; and J. M. McPherson, (1972) "Population Density and Pathology: What Are the Relations for Man?" *Science* 176 (April 7).

Gannon, Collin A. (1972) "Consumer Demand, Conjectural Interdependence, and Location Equilibrium in Simple Spatial Duopoly." *Papers of the R.S.A.* 28.

Gasscote, Raymond M.; J. N. Sossex; E. Cumming; and L. H. Smith, (1969) *The Community Mental Health Center: An Interim Appraisal.* Washingtonton, D.C.: Joint Information Service of APA.

Gerth, H. H. and C. Wright Mills, [eds.] (1946) *From Max Weber.* New York: Oxford University Press.

Goffman, Erving (1961) *Asylums.* Garden City, N.Y.: Anchor Books.

Greenblatt, M.; R. Moore; R. Albert; and M. Solomon, (1963) *The Prevention of Hospitalization.* New York: Grune and Stratton.

Griffith, John R. (1972) *Quantitative Techniques for Hospital Planning and Control.* Lexington, Mass.: Lexington Books, D.C. Heath.

Gurin, G., J. Veroff, and S. Feld, (1960) *Americans View Their Mental Health.* New York: Basic Books.

Hearings (Serial No. 93-39) Before the Subcommittee on Public Health and Environment and the Committee on Interstate and Foreign Commerce. House of Representatives, 93rd Congress, May 9 and June 15, 1973, "Oversight Over the Administration of the Community Mental Health Centers."

Hearings on a Bill to Provide for Assistance in the Construction and Initial Operation of Community Mental Health Centers, Before the Subcommittee on Public Health and Welfare of the Commission on Interstate and Foreign Commerce, March 26, 27, 28, 1963.

Hinkle, Lawrence E. (1961) "Ecological Observations of the Relation of Physical Illness, Mental Illness, and the Social Environment." *Psychosomatic Medicine* 23 (4): 289.

Hollingshead, A. B. and F. C. Redlich, (1958) *Social Class and Mental Illness.* New York: Wiley.

Hunter, Albert. "The Ecology of Chicago: Persistence and Change, 1930-1960." *American Journal of Sociology* 77 (3): 425-444.

Isard, Walter, et al. (1960) *Methods of Regional Analysis: An Introduction to Regional Science.* Cambridge: MIT Press.

Jacob, Philip E. and James F. Jacob, (1962) "Values and Their Function in Decision Making." *American Behavioral Scientist Supplement,* May.

Joint Commission on Mental Illness and Health (1961) *Action for Mental Health.* Final Report of the Joint Commission on Mental Illness and Health, 1961. New York: Basic Books.

Kahn, Alfred J. (1969) *Studies in Social Policy and Planning.* New York: Russell Sage Foundation.

Kantor, Mildred B. [ed.] (1965) *Mobility and Mental Health.* Springfield, Ill.: Charles C. Thomas.

Kaplan, Berton, H. [ed.] (1971) *Psychiatric Disorder and the Urban Environment.* New York: Behavioral Publications.

Kaplan, Seymour R. and Roman Melvin, (1973) *The Organization and Delivery of Mental Health Services in the Ghetto: The Lincoln Hospital Experience.* New York: Praeger.

Keller, Suzanne (1963) "The Social World of the Urban Slum Child." *American Journal of Orthopsychiatry.* 33: 823.

Klein, Donald C. *Community Dynamics and Mental Health.* New York: Wiley.

Kluckhohn, Clyde et al. (1951) "Values and Value Orientations in the Theory of Action." In Parsons and Shils (eds.), *Toward a General Theory of Action.* Cambridge: Harvard University Press.

Lander, Bernard. (1954) *Towards an Understanding of Juvenile Delinquency.* New York: Columbia University Press.

Langner, T. S.; J. C. Gersten; J. Eisenberg; E. L. Greene; and J. H. Herson (1973) *Children Under Stress: Family and Social Factors in the Behavior of Urban Children and Adolescents,* New York: Columbia University Press.

Lee, E. S. (1964) "Socio-Economic and Migration Differentials in Mental Disease." *Milbank Memorial Fund Quarterly* 41: 249-268.

Lemert, Edwin L. (1964) "Social Structure, Social Control and Deviation." In M. Clinard (ed.), *Anomie and Deviant Behavior.* New York: Free Press of Glencoe.

Lemkau, Paul (1955) *Mental Hygiene in Public Health.* New York: McGraw Hill.

Lemkau, Paul (1957) "Planning Mental Health Programs for New York City." In Milbank Memorial Fund, *Programs for Community Mental Health.* New York.

Levy, L. and L. Rowitz (1973) The Ecology of Mental Disorder. New York: Behavioral Publications.

Lipsky, Michael (1969) "Towards a Theory of Street-level Bureaucracy." Paper prepared for presentation at 1969 Annual Meeting of the American Political Science Association.

Lubove, Roy (1965) *The Professional Altruist.* New York: Atheneum (paperback edition, 1973).

March, James G. and Herbert A. Simon (1958) *Organizations*, New York: Wiley.

Marmor, Theodore R. (1970) *The Politics of Medicare*. London: Routledge and Kegan Paul.

Marris, Peter and Martin Rein, (1967) *Dilemmas of Social Reform*. London: Routledge.

Marshall, A. W. and H. Goldhamer, (1955) "An Application of Markov Processes to the Study of the Epidemiology of Mental Disease." *American Statistical Association Journal,* March.

Mechanic, David (1969) *Mental Health and Social Policy*. Englewood Cliffs, N.J.: Prentice Hall.

Milbank Memorial Fund (1962) *Decentralization of Psychiatric Services and Continuity of Care*. New York: Milbank Memorial Fund.

Moynihan, D. P. (1965) "The Professionalization of Reform." *The Public Interest*, no. 1, Fall.

Myers, Jerome R. and Lee L. Bean, (1968) *A Decade Later: A Follow-up of Social Class and Mental Illness*. New York: Wiley.

New York State Temporary Commission to Revise the Social Service Law. (1972) *Report on the Preliminary Recommendations on Social Services and Income Maintenance of the Temporary State Commission to Revise the Social Services Law*. Albany, December.

Overall, B. and H. Aronson, (1964) "Expectations of Psychotherapy in Patients of Lower Socioeconomic Class." *American Journal of Orthopsychiatry*, 33: 421.

Parker, S. and R. J. Kleiner, (1966) *Mental Illness in the Urban Negro Community*. New York: Free Press.

Pressman, Jeffrey, L. and Aaron Wildavsky, (1973) *Implementation*. Berkeley: University of California Press.

Rabkin, Judith G. (1972) "Opinions about Mental Illness: A Review of the Literature." *Psychological Bulletin* 77 (3).

Rainwater, Lee and William L. Yancey, (1967) *The Moynihan Report and the Politics of Controversy*. Cambridge: MIT Press.

Redick and Johnson (1974) NIMH Statistical Note #100. U. S. Department of Health, Education and Welfare.

Redlich, F.; A. Hollingshead and E. Bellis, (1955) "Social Class Differences in Attitudes Toward Psychiatry." *American Journal of Orthopsychiatry* 16: 60.

Rosenthal, Gerald D. (1964) *The Demand for General Hospital Facilities*. Hospital Monograph Series No. 14. Chicago: American Hospital Association.

Rothman, David J. (1971) *The Discovery of the Asylum*. Boston: Little Brown.

Ryan, W. (1969) *Distress in the City*. Cleveland: Case Western Reserve University Press.

Schneider, Jerry B. (1967) *The Spatial Structure of the Medical Care Process*. RSRI Discussion Paper Series, No. 14. Philadelphia: RSRI.

Schon, Donald A. (1971) *Beyond the Stable State*. New York: Norton.

Seward, Georgene H. (1972) *Psychotherapy and Culture Conflict in Community Mental Health*. New York: Ronald Press.

Shaw, Clifford R. and Henry D. McKay, (1969) *Juvenile Delinquency in Urban Areas*. 2nd ed. rev. Chicago: University of Chicago Press.

Shubik, Martin [ed.] (1964) *Game Theory and Related Approaches to Social Behavior,* New York: Wiley.

Simon, Herbert A. (1947) *Administrative Behavior*. New York: Free Press.

Smith, D. M. (1966) "A Theoretical Framework for Geographical Studies of Industrial Location." *Economic Geography*, April.

Spitzer, Robert L. and Jean Endicott, (1974) "Psychiatric Ratings Scales in the Evaluation of Psychiatric Treatment." In Reedman and Kaplan, *Comprehensive Textbook of Psychiatry.*

Stanton, F. and S. Schwartz, (1954) The Mental Hospital. New York: Basic Books.

Sullivan, Harry Stack (1964) *The Fusion of Psychiatry and Social Science*. New York:

Szasz, Thomas (1970) *Ideology and Insanity*. Garden City, N.Y.: Anchor Books.

Tryon, Robert C. (1955) *Identification of Social Areas by Cluster Analysis*. Publications in Psychology, vol. 8, no. 1, pp. 1-100. Berkeley: University of California Press.

Turner, R. and M. Wagenfeld, (1967) "Occupational Mobility and Schizophrenia: An Assessment of the Social Causation and Social Selection Hypotheses." *American Social Review* 32: 104-113.

Van Arsdol, Maurice, Jr.; S. Carmiler, and C. Schim, (1958) "The Generality of Urban Social Area Indexes." *American Sociological Review* 23: 277-284.

Wachs, Martin and Gordan T. Kumagai, (1973) "Physical Accessibility as a Social Indicator." *Socio-Economic Planning Science* 7 (October): 437-456.

Weinberg, S. Kirson [ed.] (1967) *The Sociology of Mental Disorders* Chicago: Aldine.

Weinstein, Abbott S. and Robert E. Patton, (1969) "Trends in Chronicity in the New York State Mental Hospitals." Paper presented at APHA meeting, Philadelphia, Pa., November 10. Mimeo.

Wilder, J. F.; G. Leven, and I. Zwerling. "A Two Year Follow-up Evaluation of Acute Psychotic Patients Treated in a Day Hospital." *American Journal Of Psychiatry* 122: 1095.

Wilder, J. F. (1971) Discussion of M. Herz et al., "Day Care versus Inpatient Hospitalization: A controlled Study." *American Journal of Psychiatry* 127 (April): 1381.

Wilson, Robert A. (1971) "Anomie in the Ghetto: A Study of Type Race and Anomie." *American Journal of Sociology* 77 (1).

Williams, Oliver P. (1971) *Metropolitan Political Analysis.* New York: Free Press.

Wiltse, Kermit T. (1963) "Orthopsychiatric Programs for Socially Deprived Groups." *American Journal of Orthopsychiatry* 33: 806.

Zwerling, I. and J. F. Wilder. (1961) "An Evaluation of the Applicability of the Day Hospital in Treatment of Acutely Disturbed Patients." *The Israel Annals of Psychiatry and Related Disciplines* 2: 162-185.

*12*

# THE ROLE OF ATTITUDES TOWARD MENTAL ILLNESS IN EVALUATION OF MENTAL HEALTH PROGRAMS

JUDITH G. RABKIN

*New York State Department of Mental Hygiene*

## INTRODUCTION

### Attitudes and Evaluation

The attitudes of others toward mental illness constitute a major component of the experience of being labeled mentally ill. Once it becomes public knowledge that a person has spent time in a mental hospital, or even that he has in the past or is presently receiving psychiatric treatment, the attitudes of most of the people with whom he is involved are almost always affected, for the most part negatively. In the pursuit of friends, a job, a place to live, schooling, or even the maintenance of family relationships, the present or former mental patient generally finds that his psychiatric difficulties have created for him a master status, to borrow a sociological term, which takes precedence over, or at least influences, nearly everything else that people know about him. It is almost inevitably true that this status of mental patient leads to a diminution of sympathy, respect, and friendliness on the part of most other people, which exacerbates whatever social difficulties culminated in the assignment of a psychiatric diagnosis to begin with. Since low self-esteem is characteristically associated with so many psychiatric disorders, mental patients are peculiarly vulnerable to the opinions and appraisals of other people, and this sensitivity renders the stigma of being labelled mentally ill even harder to bear.

Mental health workers have attitudes toward mental illness just as others do. While professionals in the field are generally better informed than the public at large about matters such as etiology and outcome of various disorders, there remain extreme divergences of belief and opinion even among the most highly trained. Mental health workers with positions of less prestige, such as hospital aides, often have attitudes indistinguishable from those prevailing in their home communities, and they are not necessarily better informed or more enlightened about mental illness than are their blue-collar neighbors.

If mental patients are sensitive to the opinions of other people encountered in the course of their daily living, they are particularly influenced by those of the mental health workers involved in their treatment and rehabilitative programs. Such workers, who are assigned by society an authoritative position vis-a-vis the patients in their care, often control the very destinies of such patients. Staff members' attitudes toward mental illness in general, their expectations regarding the patients they work with, and the extent to which their personal attitudes coincide with the prevailing treatment philosophy of their place of work inevitably play integral roles in the success of therapeutic efforts. Their evaluation offers one form of approach to the broader task of assessing the efficacy of mental health programs.

Attitudes of mental health workers are directly relevant to patients' experience in treatment and custodial programs. Public attitudes toward mental illness are also appropriate areas of study in understanding the relative successes of various treatment programs, especially those located within communities. These are becoming increasingly common in conjunction with the emergence of social psychiatry as an ideological and strategic base for psychiatric undertakings. Knowledge of public attitudes is of direct significance to those whose task it is to operate and evaluate primary prevention, early intervention, and community treatment programs for psychiatric patients. Whether or not the local community around a treatment center is rejecting, disinterested, or angry about its presence will influence not only the willingness of residents to seek treatment before it becomes an action of last resort, but also the extent to which patients will be rebuffed by their neighbors when their patient status becomes known.

Attitude measurement is also a needed tool in evaluating the effects of programs of public education regarding mental health and illness, which have been conducted for many years on local, state, and national levels. Periodic surveys of public opinions about mental illness provide feedback regarding the impact of ongoing educational campaigns, the nature of the message that is reaching the public, and areas about which people need additional information or clarification. The efficacy of different methods of presentation can readily be compared, as can the relative responsiveness of people to different kinds of messages, and of different groups within the population to a given message.

In short, it is becoming increasingly recognized that psychiatric patients and those who deal with them exist in the larger framework of society, and that it is imperative in planning, carrying out, and evaluating treatment programs to be aware of the attitudes toward psychiatric disorders and their treatment that prevail in this larger framework.

Until now, applications of attitude measurement to program evaluation have seldom been undertaken; they are cited primarily as guidelines for future studies. The work that has been done regarding attitudes toward mental illness is extensive but in general has not yet been systematically related to behavior of staff, of patients, or of program outcomes. Since the late 1940s when the first studies were designed, there has emerged a substantial body of research concerning the delineation of attitudes held by the public and by mental health professionals, characteristics of disturbed behavior found to influence such attitudes, characteristics of respondents and of communities that are themselves associated with variations in attitudes, and the relationship between attitudes and behavior. The following review of this literature is in chronological format, describing early studies, subsequent trends, and the present status of the field. It is hoped that such an overview will offer researchers in program evaluation a solid basis for the future application of attitude measurement to their studies of mental health programs.

## Definitions and Populations

Some prefatory remarks regarding definitions of mental illness and the distribution in the population of those labeled mentally ill may clarify the scope of the problem under consideration. Although, in general, mental health professionals are reluctant to specify precisely what is meant by "mental illness," in the realm of attitude studies the term characteristically is used to refer to those whom professionals would describe as severely disturbed. Members of the general public use the terms mental illness and mental patients in relation to psychiatric hospitalization. As Johannsen (1969) observed, "The lay public seems to adhere to a single operational definition of the mental patient. To the average man, a person becomes a mental patient only when he enters a psychiatric hospital." This label applies for an indefinite period after hospital discharge, but is not in general used for psychiatric patients seen only in private consultation or in clinics. In attitude research, investigators generally endorse this interpretation of the term "mental illness." Most attitude scales in wide use, such as the Opinions about Mental Illness Scale of Cohen and Struening (1962), state in the instructions to respondents that use of the term "mental patient" refers to hospitalized patients only. While there is unquestionably some extension to either extramural patients seen in clinics or privately, or to those simply regarded as eccentric in the mind of the individual respondent, it is reasonably accurate to conclude that, in studies of attitudes toward mental illness, the term is meant to refer to those who are presently hospitalized or have been so in the past.

The number of patients who have been in psychiatric hospitals is higher than most people would guess, since they tend to be concentrated within particular demographic groups and therefore are not often visible to the majority of middle-class Americans. Annual prevalence counts of mental hospital patients provide an estimate of this population which, in former time of prolonged hospitalization, may have been adequate but presently are misleadingly low. After a century of growth, the number and length of stay of mental hospital populations began to decline in 1956 and, with the exception of the pediatric group for whom there had been no facilities earlier, has continued to decline with the rate of decrease accelerating since 1960. In recent years, admission rates have increased while hospital stays have been shortened radically for the vast majority, so that the turnover is great even though the number of patients hospitalized at any one time is relatively low. For example, a census of patients in private hospitals in 1969 reported the presence of 9,725 patients, but over 93,000 patients had been in and out of these same hospitals during the year.

The actual number of Americans who have been in mental hospitals is high. It is estimated that one of every two hospital beds in the country is occupied by a mental patient (Rogow, 1970). In 1966, after ten years of declining hospital censuses, there were still 450,000 patients in public hospitals. In 1971, a total of nearly 1.8 million people spent some time in mental hospitals during the course of the year, of which 42% were in public mental hospitals (Ozarin and Taube, 1974). These figures encompass long-term patients as well as new admissions, and include readmissions. The median length of stay in 1971 in public mental hospitals was 41 days, and less than that in private and general hospitals, indicating a substantial turnover. These figures make it clear that a considerable proportion of the population has spent time in mental hospitals, or knows others who have. Accordingly, the problem of attitudes toward the mentally ill can be recognized as a significant public health issue.

Mental patients are not randomly distributed in the general population but tend to be concentrated within definable groups and geographical areas. According to recent congressional testimony, commitment rates in different parts of the country vary more than 800%. For over 30 years it has been observed in many large cities that poor people living in socially disorganized and physically deteriorated neighborhoods contribute disproportionately to the ranks of state hospital inmates, as do minority group members, young men who display socially objectionable behavior, recent immigrants, the elderly, and the unmarried.

## Overview of Chapter

It may be helpful to offer a brief outline of this chapter to indicate its scope and organization. There are seven major sections of unequal length. The first reviews historical trends in mental illness, and is followed by a survey of measures and research designs commonly employed in this area of study. The third section is a broadly selective review of studies of public attitudes toward mental illness. After the early major work in this field is described in some detail, more recent studies conducted since 1960 are grouped in terms of the orientation and general findings of their investigators.

The fourth, fifth, and sixth sections of this review concern characteristics of patients, of respondents, and of communities that have been found to influence degree of public acceptance of mental illness. Many of these studies have been presented in detail elsewhere in the literature by the author and by others, and therefore few are described individually here. Instead, major replicated findings are summarized with references to representative studies in each area.

The seventh section is entitled "Attitudes and Behavior." The author considers first the general state of the art of attitude research, the relation of attitudes to observed behavior, and factors contributing to the characteristically notable discrepancies reported between them. After these general findings are noted, studies are presented which concern the relationship between attitudes toward mental illness and behavior toward the mentally ill, or between attitudes toward mental patients and patients' behavior. A general summary and suggestions for future areas of investigation conclude the presentation.

## HISTORICAL TRENDS IN ATTITUDES ABOUT MENTAL ILLNESS

Definitions of deviant behavior and the assignment of labels to such behavior strongly influence attitudes toward those regarded as deviant. The label seems to activate pre-existing beliefs and value systems, usually to the detriment of the individuals so labeled. A brief historical overview of such definitions and concomitant attitudes reflects the extent of their interaction.

By referring to behavioral deviance as mental *illness* as we do today, we imply that such a condition is a burden, a handicap caused by the invasion of a foreign agent analogous to a germ or a virus which attacks an innocent host and lingers interminably. This construction underlines the undesirable nature of the condition, which most people would like to avoid having themselves or witnessing in others. The problem that currently concerns so many in the mental health professions is not this negative evaluation of mental illness, but the accompanying rejecting attitudes manifested toward the mentally ill and formerly ill, together with other implications inherent in the medical model regarding etiological theory, therapeutic stance and the feasibility of preventative strategies.

In a very real sense, mental patients have taken the place of lepers as targets of public disgust, dislike, and rejection. As Foucault (1965) has so eloquently described, insanity was defined as "unreason" and typically considered a part of everyday life from the time of the Greeks through the Middle Ages, when those who behaved peculiarly were labeled madmen or fools. Not until the seventeenth century were such people regarded as a public threat and confined to special institutions, many of which had served as leprosariums until that disease disappeared from the Western world. The constitution of madness as a mental *illness,* the introduction of the medical model to psychiatric formulations occurred at the end of the eighteenth century and led to the rise of the "scientific psychiatry" of the nineteenth century.

With less drama but more specific documentation, Bockhoven (1963) and Caplan (1969) have traced the history of American psychiatry from the eighteenth century, with its emphasis on moral (i.e., psychological) treatment, to the medicalization of emotional disturbances in the nineteenth and early twentieth centuries. Moral treatment consisted of temporarily sending the disturbed individual to a "retreat" where "he was made comfortable, his interest aroused, his friendship invited, and discussion of his troubles encouraged" (Bockhoven, 1963: 12). This approach was based on the assumptions that disturbed behavior was caused either by ignorance or by incorrect understanding—that is, a cognitive deficit—and that it could be modified by manipulation of social and psychological variables.

In the mid-nineteenth century, both of these assumptions were abandoned, as was moral treatment itself. Instead, it became generally believed that disturbed behavior was the result of a physical disease of unknown etiology, existing like an ulcer within the patient, caused genetically or by a harmful external agent. Gaylin (1973) has noted that, since the leading cause of psychosis in the nineteenth century was advanced syphilis, this conceptualization did have some validity, though it was inappropriately extended to account for all varieties of psychiatric disorder. Based on this formulation of mental illness as the product of physical disease, it was believed that treatment must consist of chemical or physical methods. Since such means were then unknown, patients seldom received more than custodial care.

In the absence of clearcut medical reasons for these changes in policy and treatment, it is likely that dimensions of the prevailing social climate played a significant role. Bockhoven noted several contributing factors: lack of inspired leadership after the innovators of moral treatment died; failure to plan ahead for adequate facilities so that the existing ones became terribly overcrowded, and the rather abrupt appearance after the Civil War of large numbers of "foreign insane paupers" of low social and economic status who largely replaced the middle-class Yankee patients who had formerly constituted the majority among patient populations. As the mental hospitals changed from homelike havens to huge custodial warehouses, discharge rates declined steadily.

After the turn of the century in the United States, the first signs of renewed interest appeared regarding the methods and underlying philosophy of moral treatment, and in the ensuing years there has evolved a point of view in the mental health professions that is quite independent of the biological conceptions of the 1800s. It has become increasingly acknowledged by many professionals in the mental health field that mental illness can be understood as an exaggeration of particular behaviors common to all men. Allowing for possible genetic predispositions, such exaggerations are presumably brought about by stressful life conditions and result in impairment of the ability to cope with prevailing social expectations and standards. According to this viewpoint, psychopathology is not seen as a subdermal phenomenon but as the product of transactions between the individual and his social and physical environment. This necessarily entails a shift away from the traditional medical model of disease toward essentially psychosocial conceptions of problems in living. Whereas psychiatric symptoms used to be interpreted as signs of physical illness and then, in the psychoanalytic frame of reference, seen as defenses against the individual's internal processes, it is now becoming more common to define a symptom as a way of dealing with external events or other people (cf Haley, 1963).

Although so many mental health workers are finding these revised notions about psychological disorder helpful in their thinking and their work, it is possible to find exaggerations or distortions in their applications. For example, Seidenberg (1971) has observed that drug companies, in their communications with physicians, are trying to increase the indications for drug use by relabeling as pathological ordinary conditions of living ranging from the tedium of housekeeping to changes associated with aging. Others regard Szasz's continued attacks on the "myth" of mental illness as a doubtful contribution to thinking about the nature of disorders, though his motivation, unlike that of the drug companies, is not questioned. Another potential difficulty concerns the tendency of community-minded mental health professionals to become what some consider excessively involved in social action campaigns such as rent strikes or protest marches, instead of remaining within more traditional roles for which they have presumably been trained. These problems remain minor in comparison to the benefits derived from development of this psychosocial model of behavior.

Replacement of the medical model by a psychosocial or transactional or public health model in the mental health field represents a fairly recent change in view among a particular segment of the more highly trained professionals—primarily among those with postgraduate training—and is not as often found among lower-ranking personnel in psychiatric institutions or the general public. As the following review of the literature indicates, it has often been observed that psychiatrists, psychologists, and social workers differ from nurses, aides, and even nonpsychiatric physicians in their opinions about mental illness, and this seems inextricably related to their modified conceptions of the nature of mental illness itself.

## MEASURES AND DESIGNS

Before reviewing specific studies, it may be helpful to describe in some detail the measures and designs most commonly used. Aside from public opinion surveys, studies of public attitudes toward mental illness, described in the following section below, rely almost exclusively on two kinds of measures, the Star vignettes and social distance scales, with the occasional addition of fairly direct questions regarding beliefs about the mentally ill. Studies presented below which delineate characteristics of patients and of respondents that influence attitudes toward the mentally ill, generally use formal multi-item scales; Gilbert and Levenson's Custodial Mental Illness Ideology Scale (CMI) and Cohen and Struening's Opinions about Mental Illness Scale (OMI) have been most widely used. While other attitude questionnaires have been developed in this area, such as Wright's (1966) Mental Illness Questionnaire, Froemel's ATMI, and Reznikoff's (1963) Multiple Choice Attitudes Questionnaire, these instruments have been used primarily or exclusively by their authors, and their usefulness has not yet been clearly established.

The Star vignettes consist of six case history descriptions, each presenting in nontechnical language a different pattern of disturbed behavior. The cases include a neurotic depressive, a paranoid schizophrenic and a simple schizophrenic, an alcoholic, juvenile conduct disorder, and a phobic-complusive neurotic. In many studies, the juvenile conduct disorder is omitted, and is sometimes replaced by a description of a normal person. Respondents are usually asked whether each of the characterizations seems to be mentally ill. They may also be asked to rank them in terms of perceived pathology, social distance, or other parameters. Individuals or groups of respondents can then be compared in terms of their notions of what constitutes abnormal behavior.

Social distance scales consist of six to eight ordered statements which vary along a continuum of social interaction. The respondent is asked to indicate for each item whether he will accept that level of interaction with a hypothetical person. The overall format of social distance scales was developed by Bogardus (1933), who originally studied the social positions of various ethnic and racial groups. Whatley

(1958) used the concepts of Bogardus and adapted them to study the extent to which social interactions are acceptable with the formerly hospitalized, those with "mental problems," and "people who see a psychiatrist." Whatley's modification has served as a model for subsequent studies of social distance and the mentally ill, though his name is not often associated with it. As noted with respect to the Star vignettes, respondents' answers to social distance scales usually are tabulated, by group, as percent willing to accept each level of interaction.

As these measures and analyses suggest, many of the studies of public attitudes toward mental illness are extremely unsophisticated, both in method and in underlying assumptions about behavior. A single item is often presumed to evaluate adequately an attitude or point of view, and attitudes are typically regarded as one-dimensional. None of these studies of public attitudes identifies behavioral correlates of the attitudes or beliefs being measured.

In contrast to the simple instruments used in most studies of public attitudes, the major tools used to investigate attitudes toward mental illness among mental health personnel, students, and other selected groups are, in general, carefully constructed to conform to complex models of behavior. Gilbert and Levenson and their associates defined and studied the nature of the ideological positions of humanism versus custodialism, and constructed the Custodial Mental Illness Ideology Scale (CMI) to elicit these positions. The CMI consists of 20 Likert-type statements of opinion on basic questions concerning mental illness and patient care, and was designed to place respondents along a single continuum of attitudes ranging from custodialism to humanism. The extreme custodial point of view holds that mental patients cannot ever be really cured, that they are potentially dangerous and need external controls; in general, it is associated with authoritarianism and is highly correlated with the California F Scale. Its converse, humanism, is related to a generally egalitarian orientation. While the CMI's authors assume that attitudes about mental illness fall within a single dimension, related studies have shown that the polar extremes can be further subdivided. Thus Sharaf and Levinson focused on psychotherapeutic versus sociotherapeutic orientations, both conceptualized as variations of the "humanistic" ideology. The concept of custodialism, aligned as it is with authoritarianism, similarly lends itself to further refinement.

The CMI was the first carefully designed, psychometrically adequate instrument developed to assess attitudes toward mental illness. However, workers in this field became increasingly unhappy with its underlying assumption, that such attitudes fall within a single descriptive dimension. When Cohen and Struening (1962) developed a multidimensional scale, Opinions about Mental Illness (OMI), most investigators adopted it rather than the CMI to assess such attitudes.

The OMI was developed from a pool of 70 Likert-type opinion items which were written by the authors or adapted from Nunnally's questionnaire, the California F Scale, and the CMI. They were administered to two large samples of VA hospital personnel. The responses of each sample were factor-analyzed, and five independent factors were identified. Scales were then developed from the original 70 items to measure each of these factors, so that the final 51-item OMI questionnaire provides five separate scores for each respondent. The five factors are:

*Factor A: Authoritarianism.* This is clearly identified with the California F Scale and includes its authoritarian submission and anti-intraception combined with a view of the mentally ill as an inferior class requiring coercive handling.

*Factor B: Benevolence.* A kindly, paternalistic view toward patients whose origins derive from religion and humanism rather than science.

*Factor C: Mental Hygiene Ideology.* This orientation maintains that "mental illness is an illness like any other." A medical model is adapted to psychiatric problems, focusing on individual maladaptation.

*Factor D: Social Restrictiveness.* Its central belief is that the mental patient is a threat to society, particularly the family, and must therefore be restricted in his functioning both during and after hospitalization.

*Factor E: Interpersonal Etiology.* The positive pole of this factor reflects the belief that mental illness arises from interpersonal experience, especially deprivation of parental love during childhood.

In a later study Cohen and Struening (1963) demonstrated the factorial stability of these opinions across three samples of mental hospital personnel identical in occupational-professional composition, but greatly varied in religious preference and regional background. The results of the three factor analyses of the 1963 study provide the basis for the current scoring of the 51 items into the measures of the five factors described above. Psychometric properties of the five factor scales are also included.

The four scales described thus far were designed to assess attitudes about mental illness and mental patients. A related but slightly different approach was followed by Souelem, who developed two forms of a 36-item scale with dichotomous agree-disagree format, meant to elicit patients' attitudes toward mental hospitals. The scale has also been used to assess attitudes of various professional groups who deal with mental patients. Kahn and his associates developed a 100-item scale meant to cover 12 areas measuring patients' attitudes toward psychiatrists, mental illness, and hospitalization in an attempt to improve upon the Souelem scale, which they regarded as too generalized. The scale was given to 54 patients, and the 45 most reliable items were subjected to factor analysis. Seventeen factors emerged, of which the first five account for half the total variance. The authors had expected factor analysis to reduce in number the original 12 dimensions they had concep-tualized, but the opposite occurred. They later felt these results were meaningful in describing the complexity of attitudes involved. They believed that earlier work oversimplified these attitudes. For example, the variable of control, typically regarded as unidimensional, was found to include several subdimensions including accepted restriction and resented restriction. Each of these, in turn, was influenced by other variables such as dependency or psychological-mindedness. In short, the study suggests that the attitudes involved in mental illness are far more complex and interrelated than is generally acknowledged.

In addition to the more widely used questionnaires, it seems worthwhile to note Baker and Schulberg's Community Mental Health Ideology Scale (CMHI), which covers a point of view largely omitted in questionnaires constructed before this dimension became popular. The CMHI is designed to measure an individual's degree of adherence to community mental health ideology. Originally consisting of 88 Likert-type items representing five conceptual categories, its final form contains 38 items representing three concepts which were found to characterize this ideological orientation. These concepts include focus on the total population rather than just those actively seeking psychiatric help, involvement of a variety of community resources in working with patients, and preventive efforts via environmental intervention. The validity and reliability of the scale are good, and it has been used effectively to differentiate professional groups in terms of the extent of their endorsement of this attitude dimension.

At present the most widely used instrument for the measurement of attitudes toward mental illness continues to be the OMI. Although it has been variously criticized as too complex (cf. Lawton, 1964) or incomplete, it seems to be the most comprehensive, reliable, and valid instrument now available for the measurement of attitudes toward mental illness, and is accordingly most popular among investigators in this field.

Studies using the OMI usually administer it before and after a planned intervention, such as academic training or exposure to mental patients, and changes in scores are sought. Although a handful of studies falling in this general format have tried to define behavioral correlates of attitude changes, the large majority have been content to point to changes in attitude scale scores as evidence of successful training.

Studies of public attitudes measure the extent of stigma and social rejection associated with mental patients. In contrast, studies of mental health personnel and students characteristically focus on their ideological positions, beliefs about the origins, nature, and outcomes of mental illness, and an estimate of the respondents' positions on an authoritarian-nonauthoritarian personality continuum. As a result, findings from studies of these different populations are often difficult to equate and compare.

## PUBLIC ATTITUDES TOWARD MENTAL ILLNESS

The stigma of the label "mental illness," has been widely documented since the early 1950s. It has become generally acknowledged that, within a psychiatric hospital where most patients have been sent against their will, inmates seldom share the rights, liberties, and satisfactions that civilians enjoy. Mental patients have for years been regarded with more distaste and less sympathy than virtually any other disabled group in our society, and in fact their handicaps are partly attributable to public attitudes of rejection and avoidance.

When the major studies in this field were conducted in the 1950s, mental health professionals were deeply troubled by public inability to identify mental illness as an illness like any other, and by the lack of public endorsement of the mental health ideology including use of the medical mode of illness that prevailed among American professionals after World War II. At that time, a great effort was launched to educate the public to accept these beliefs about mental illness by means of public education campaigns in the popular media, academic instruction in college psychology courses, and political efforts at local, state, and national levels.

In the 1960s, studies of public attitudes toward mental illness seemed to fall into two categories: those that led investigators to feel optimistic about the improved movement's concepts of mental illness, and those whose investigators did not share this optimism or conceptual orientation. Psychiatrically oriented workers generally favored the mental health movement's efforts to publicize the medical model of mental illness, while those adhering to a pychosocial or sociological orientation tended to view these efforts as a "moral crusade," and an objectionable one at that. Since these two groups sought different goals with respect to public opinion, it is not surprising that they have differed in their evaluation of the present state of public attitudes and the directions to be taken in future efforts at public education. After describing the basic studies, conducted largely in the 1950s, which clearly established the quality and degree of public rejection of the mentally ill, the work of the "optimists" and the "pessimists" or psychiatrically oriented and socio‑logically oriented investigators of the 1960s will be considered in turn, followed by a general analysis of where things stand in the 1970s.

## Early Major Studies

A classic experimental study of opinions about mental illness was conducted by Cumming and Cumming (1957) in a small, rural, agricultural Canadian town in the province of Saskatchewan during 1951. The investigators planned to evaluate attitudes toward mental illness and their mutability by testing residents before and after a 6-month educational campaign designed to promote more accepting atti‑tudes toward mental illness. They stressed three propositions in their educational films and group discussions: first, that the range of normal behavior is wider than often believed; second, that deviant behavior is not random but has a cause and thus can be understood and modified; and third, that normal and abnormal behavior fall within a single continuum and are not qualitatively distinct. The townspeople readily accepted the first two propositions, and in fact went beyond psychiatrists in the range of behavior regarded as normal. But the third proposition was so unpalatable that the community eventually rejected the entire educational program.

As summarized by Susser and Watson (1962), these results were taken to indicate that the sample feared mental illness and tried to ignore its manifestations as far as possible: thus the first proposition was compatible with their outlook. When an individual's behavior became too deviant to overlook, the community wanted him to be segregated through hospitalization; to some extent, acceptance of the second proposition provided justification for such action, since hospitalization could be regarded as the treatment of choice in the interest of the patient as well as the community. The third proposition dealt with causes. It was disturbing because it suggested that anyone could become insane under certain circumstances; this idea conflicted with the predominant values of the people of this community, and was rejected to protect these values. In short, the Cummings' study demonstrated the initially negative attitudes toward labeled mental illness of a middle-class com‑

munity, their relationship to a more extensive system of values, and the unfeasibility of modifying a specific attitude at variance with this system.

Most investigations of public attitudes toward mental illness have been based on a survey rather than experimental model. An early and simple survey was carried out in 1947 by Ramsey and Seipp (1948 a,b). A stratified sample of 345 adults in Trenton, New Jersey, were asked six questions meant to elicit their notions about the etiology and treatment of mental illness. The questions reflected a rather Victorian conception of psychopathology, including items such as, "Do you believe that insanity is God's punishment for some sin or wrongdoing?" and queries regarding its inheritability and contagion.

Because of the restricted concepts of etiology reflected in these questions, together with the brevity of the interviews and absence of statistical analysis, the findings were limited. The authors reported that respondents with higher educational and occupational levels were less apt to view mental illness as punishment for sin or the outcome of poor living conditions, were less inclined to believe in the deleterious effects of associating with the mentally ill, and were less pessimistic about chance for recovery. The study remains significant today both because it was one of the first efforts to investigate systematically public attitudes toward mental illness, and because of the elaborate care taken with sample selection. The sample that was interviewed was broadly representative of the total population of Trenton in terms of sex, age, race, education, nativity, religion, and occupational class, with findings considered in terms of all these variables. Perhaps it is partly due to the rigorous standards of this early study that sampling typically has been handled competently in this research domain.

Far more sophisticated and extensive was a six-year survey conducted during the 1950s by Nunnally (1961), to see what the public knows and feels about mental illness and treatment. A sample of 400 respondents was designed to be nationally representative in terms of sex, age, education, income, and religion. Public knowledge was determined by means of 180 opinion statements to which respondents answered on a 7-step rating scale of agree-disagree.[1] Public attitudes, apart from knowledge, were then assessed by means of semantic differential scales, free association tests, including items referring to psychiatrists and mental patients, and paired comparison items.

Summarizing overall public attitudes, Nunnally reported that, "as is commonly suspected, the mentally ill are regarded with fear, distrust and dislike by the general public" (1961: 46). The stigma associated with mental illness was found to be very general, both across social groups and across attitude indicators, with little relation to demographic variables such as age and education. "Old people and young people, highly educated people and people with little formal training—all tend to regard mentally ill as relatively dangerous, dirty, unpredictable and worthless" (ibid.: 51). A strong negative halo surrounds the mentally ill: "they are considered, unselectively, as being all things bad" (ibid.: 233). However, these "bad" attitudes were not held because of existing information or even misinformation about mental illness by the public, but rather because of *lack* of information. While marked differences were found as a function of age and education regarding kinds of information held, differences in attitudes were small. The younger, better educated held slightly less derogatory attitudes, but their attitudes were still markedly negative.

Despite her lack of publications, Shirley Star has had enormous influence on investigations of public attitudes toward mental illness. Her contributions are both methodological and substantive. She wanted to know whether people could identify various kinds of behavior as manifestations of mental disturbance, and with this goal in mind she formulated the six case history descriptions often referred to as the Star vignettes described above.

In the early 1950s, Star asked 3,500 respondents whether each of these cases was mentally ill. In her unpublished but often cited monograph, "The Dilemmas of Mental Illness," she found that only the most extremely disturbed behavior was recognized as such by the majority of her respondents, that they tended to resist calling anyone "mentally ill" and did so only as a last resort (Joint Commission on Mental Illness and Health, 1961: 75). Star contributed the method of case history descriptions that has been used in most subsequent studies of public attitudes, and established a baseline of public resistance to the perception or labeling of mental illness that has served as a standard for measuring attitude changes since that time.

In a study entitled, "Social Attitudes Toward Discharged Mental Patients," Whatley (1958) investigated the social consequences of psychiatric hospitalization. He successfully demonstrated that people tend to keep a distance between themselves and former patients, creating for the latter a type of social isolation which enhances their problem of social readjustment after being away.

During 1956, Whatley administered his social distance scale to a stratified sample of 2,001 Louisiana residents. The scale initially consisted of eight statements, to which respondents agreed or disagreed, regarding willingness to associate with ex-patients, ranging from minimal to intimate social involvement. The most neutral item stated that, "It is best not to associate with people who have been in mental hospitals"; over 80% of the respondents disagreed. The most intimate item stated, "If I needed a baby-sitter, I would be willing to hire a woman who had been going to see a psychiatrist." (Despite the power of this item, it has been omitted along with one other, in most subsequent studies of social distance.) Only 15% of Whatley's respondents would hire her, though 36% would not oppose their daughter's marriage to "a man who had been to see a psychiatrist about mental problems," or so they said. In general, Whatley found that tendencies to shun or restrict social interaction with ex-patients were most likely to arise in situations of closeness, while attitudes of social acceptance were greatest in relatively impersonal situations. The significance of this study is in both method and content; by bringing up the issue of social intimacy versus distance, and providing a strong measure, Whatley introduced a major dimension in the analysis of public attitudes toward the mentally ill.

In the course of their massive study of social class and mental illness in New Haven, Hollingshead and Redlich (1958) investigated attitudes toward psychiatry and treated illness expressed by families of patients and a stratified sample of the general public. Higher social status was associated with more knowledge about psychiatrists and psychiatric treatment, greater willingness to seek such help, and greater competence in arranging for it. Lower social status was found related to lack of information, resistance, and sometimes open antagonism to psychiatric intervention. Members of the lowest social class almost never actively sought psychiatric help for themselves or relatives; those in treatment were usually "dumped into the laps of psychiatrists by authorities in the community" (1958: 340). The lower the class, the more likely that mental illness was seen as a frightening somatic disease.

In short, by 1960 it was unambiguously established that mental patients were dimly regarded in the public view. The label was feared; people tended to overlook behavior that professionals regarded as pathological, evidently as a mechanism of denial rather than because of greater tolerance of deviance. When the label was authoritatively assigned, the person so labeled was stigmatized and shunned. People did not subscribe to the medical model of mental illness as often as mental health professionals would have liked, and furthermore were generally outspoken about the discomfort and anxiety evoked in them by the subject of mental illness and the presence of a person so labeled.

### Recent Studies: Research Since 1960

Based on studies conducted during the 1960s, a more optimistic appraisal has been expressed by some researchers, most of whom conceptualized mental illness in the traditional psychiatric framework of a medical model, including the assumption that psychopathology exists within the patient in one form or another. These investigators are encouraged by their findings that an increasing proportion of the public believes that mental illness is an illness like any other, that more and more respondents identify case history descriptions as being mentally ill, and that the desire to keep a social distance from ex-patients seems to be declining. Nevertheless, there continue to be strong feelings among other investigators that the public still is fearful and ignorant of mental illness, and that the stigma remains. Spokesmen of this position generally subscribe to a psychosocial or social deviance model of mental illness, where mental patients are regarded as those who engage in certain types of deviant behavior. They would not regard as notably fruitful a greater public acceptance of the medical model, even if such acceptance were demonstrated to their satisfaction, which is not always the case. These investigators characteristically are associated with the thinking of the community mental health movement where primary prevention and early treatment in the community are emphasized, and hospitalization is regarded as a choice of last resort. These divergent evaluations of current public attitudes seem at least partly due to differences in underlying ideologies and research strategies which lead to differences in expectation regarding amount and direction of attitude change regarded as necessary or desirable.

### Optimistic Findings

Crocetti, Lemkau, and their colleagues represent the more optimistic view of public attitude change. They have conducted a series of studies, starting with a 1960 Baltimore sample stratified for age, education, and income (Lemkau and

Crocetti, 1962; Crocetti and Lemkau, 1963). In most of their work, measures include three Star vignettes which portray a paranoid schizophrenic, simple schizophrenic, and an alcoholic. A social distance scale using six of Whatley's eight items was also used, and in some studies additional questions were asked. The 1937 Baltimore adults comprising their sample were rather poor, uneducated, and of low social rank. Forty percent were black and, as the authors point out, almost all belonged to that segment of the population described in other studies as most likely to have rejecting attitudes toward mental illness. The authors obtained results which they feel refute such findings, however. In the 1960 Baltimore study, half of the sample identified all three case histories as being mentally ill, and a large majority thought that each of the persons described should see a doctor. Responses to a questionnaire were interpreted as displaying an "enlightened" attitude by the sample as a whole.

Another large study was conducted ten years later in Baltimore by the same research group (Crocetti, Spiro, and Siassi, 1971). A probability sample of 973 was drawn from a population of 8,000 United Automobile Workers Union members and their wives, most of whom were white and middle-aged. Respondents were asked two questions and given a set of social distance scales. To the question, "Do you think people who are mentally ill require a doctor's care as much as people who have any other sort of illness?" over 99% answered "yes." Eighty-nine percent agreed that "most people who are mentally ill can be cured with proper treatment." The authors concluded that the blue-collar workers surveyed were optimistic about treatment and were not extremely rejecting, and that these results do not support the general view that psychiatric patients are stigmatized. On methodological grounds one may wonder about the validity of the conclusions in terms of the structure of the questions used: the 99% affirmation of the first question may merely be a testimony to its effectiveness in influencing respondents; the questions bear within them multiple assumptions and qualifications which seem to render the interpretation of their responses somewhat uncertain.

Meyer (1964) replicated Lemkau and Crocetti's 1960 Baltimore study in another Maryland community of 6,000, using the same measures plus 10 items about information and opinions held, such as "almost all patients who have a mental illness are dangerous." His results were similar to those of the Baltimore study, and he too concluded that the public displayed greater tolerance in verbally expressed attitudes toward mental illness than was earlier found by the Cummings in their landmark study.

Rootman and Lafave (1969) wondered whether the changes in attitude reported by Lemkau and Crocetti were due to disparities in sampling between studies since the Cummings had dealt with a rural agricultural population in Canada and they had studied an urban American sample. Rootman and Lafave, therefore, selected another rural Canadian town and compared the attitudes of its residents with those reported by the Cummings in 1951. They reported that their respondents seemed to have more information about mental illness and to place less social distance between themselves and the mentally ill than did those in Cummings' sample, and they concluded that, in the province of Saskatchewan, rural attitudes toward mental illness have become more accepting over the past twenty years. Unlike most other investigators, they took the precaution of specifying that the changes reported refer only to expressed attitudes, and may or may not reflect changes in actual behavior.

Bentz and Edgerton (1971) conducted a comparable study using 1,400 respondents in predominantly rural areas of North Carolina and Virginia, most of whom were low-income, poorly educated Baptists, both black and white, who were largely semiskilled or unskilled. They wanted to verify a finding reported by Phillips (1967) that people who identified someone as a mental patient would prefer to maintain greater social distance from the mentally ill than those who did not make such an identification. Using the same design, they reported no difference between respondents who identified the case histories as mentally ill and those who did not, with respect to the social distance they wished to maintain from the mentally ill. While these results do not corroborate those of Phillips, neither do they support the conclusions of Lemkau and Crocetti, who believed that better labeling led to greater public tolerance. Indeed, labeling skill or knowledge seems, in this study at least, unrelated in either direction to the issue of public willingness to associate with disturbed people.

Another study by Bentz and Edgerton (1970) compared attitudes of these 1,400 "general public" respondents with the attitudes of 418 community leaders in the same geographical areas, using a 157-item questionnaire. They found similarly favorable attitudes in both groups, including nearly unanimous agreement that "a lot can be done to prevent mental illness" and that mental patients can be helped. Over half believed that mental patients are better off in the community than in a mental hospital. The authors concluded that their respondents have more realistic and more favorable attitudes than had been shown by earlier studies. Ring and Schein (1970), interviewing nearly 400 upwardly mobile, lower middle income black adults in Philadelphia, found a generally "enlightened" climate of opinion about mental illness, including widespread adoption of the medical model.

Gove and Fain (1973), wondering about stigma caused by psychiatric hospitalization, interviewed 429 patients one year after their admission to a Washington state hospital. At that time, 83% were in the community. They were asked about changes that may have occurred since the time before hospitalization with respect to employment, household functions, income, family relationships, and activities outside the home. As a group, patients tended to report that their hospitalization was beneficial and that resulting stigma was not a major problem to them. Most patients reported no change in the areas surveyed; changes that did occur tended to be favorable. The authors concluded that, despite the negative public stereotype of the mentally ill, people do not discriminate against a former patient when actually confronted by him; they say they will act in an inhumane way, but really do not. Unfortunately, while the study's general design was well conceived, the results were presented in percentages only, with no statistical consideration of probabilities or interactions and no analyses of response in relation to other characteristics or the patients and their families. The authors' conclusions are consequently less persuasive than they might have been had more care been devoted to data analysis.

In short, a variety of studies using similar designs and measures but different samples have been conducted since 1960, whose results lead their authors and their readers to feel that notable progress has been made in improving public attitudes toward mental illness. As Crocetti and associates (1972) have summarized their position, they feel that the public *has* learned to identify mental illness as such, feels medical care for mental illness *is* warranted, and does *not* place a sizable social distance between selves and the mentally ill.

As a group, these studies have selected respondents and questionnaire items with great care, but their data analyses have been characteristically unsophisticated. Findings are presented descriptively, usually in the form of percent of sample agreeing with each item, without providing a framework within which the reader can evaluate the significance of the results, or the size of observed effects.

There is a certain lack of clarity in the labeling used by many investigators, since the terms "mental illness," "unwanted behavior," "People who bear the label 'mentally ill,' " and "ex-mental patients" are used more or less interchangeably. As Sarbin and Mancuso (1972) point out, it is not necessarily valid to assume, without investigating the point, that public attitudes are the same toward presently ill or formerly ill (but presumably cured) individuals.

Nevertheless, the cumulative impact of these studies demonstrates an increase during the 1960s in public acceptance of the medical model of mental illness and less extreme overt rejection of those labeled mentally ill, at least in terms of pencil and paper measures.

## Pessimistic Findings

Another series of studies also conducted during the 1960s provides less grounds for optimism regarding public tolerance and enlightenment regarding mental illness. Their results suggest that the mentally ill are still heavily stigmatized (Tringo, 1970; Blizard, 1970), that educational programs have had only minor effect on public ignorance about mental illness (Sarbin and Mancuso, 1972), and that, when people encounter any form of mental illness that is labeled as such, they respond with the same dislike, fear, and aversion that traditionally has been manifested toward mental patients in American society. On the basis of these findings, if they are accepted as their authors present them, it would seem that the problems of social rejection of mental patients has actually become more serious and widespread in recent years as the extramural treatment emphasis of the prevailing community psychiatry movement has led to the presence of increasing numbers of acutely disturbed as well as ex-hospitalized people in the community.

In 1961, the Final Report of the Joint Commission on Mental Illness and Health cited society's rejection of the mentally ill, and noted "a major lack of recognition of mental illness as illness and a predominant tendency toward rejection for both the mental patient and those who treat them" (*Action for Mental Health,* 1961). Perhaps the most prolific and persuasive adherent to this view is the sociologist D. L. Phillips, who has, during the last decade, published a series of studies employing case history descriptions and social distance measures to document his conviction that deviant behavior that is labeled mental illness continues to be avoided and rejected by the great majority of people. His earlier studies (1963, 1964) concerned the influence of choice of help source consulted, visibility of the disturbed behavior, and gender of the disturbed person on the degree of rejection expressed by respondents. Using sophisticated methodology and statistical analysis, he found a significant relationship between help source sought out and extent of rejection (1963). An individual was increasingly rejected as he is described as consulting a clergyman, physician, psychiatrist, or having been in a mental hospital. This correspondence between amount of rejection and selection of help source follows the findings of the Joint Commission on Mental Illness and Health noted above.

Schroder and Ehrlich (1968) replicated this study using psychiatric nurses of varying levels of experience instead of untrained women as Phillips did. Bord (1971) also repeated and extended this design using 350 college students enrolled in introductory sociology classes. Bord presented quite persuasively alternative interpretations for the levels of rejection and responses to help source found in all three studies. His rationale is based on the issues of amount of information available to respondents in the task of evaluating the seriousness of the cases presented, and the extent to which the described behavior seems unpredictable and dangerous to the respondent. He argued that the increasing rejection Phillips observed successively associated with clergyman, physician, and psychiatrist does not actually represent added stigma emanating from these help sources as Phillips suggested. Rather, the psychiatrically naive respondents in Phillips's sample used the named help source as an additional source of information regarding the seriousness, and thus offensiveness, of the described behavior. The psychiatric nurses in Schroder and Ehrlich's sample did not need this information because they could evaluate and classify the described cases from the behavior alone, so in this study the variable of help source was less significant in its effect. In short, Bord declared, the help-source variable does not have an important effect on psychiatrically aware respondents who can evaluate more salient sources of information.

Just as help source associated with behavior descriptions is capable of influencing attitudes, the choice of labels used in conjunction with such descriptions has long been recognized as a determinant of public attitudes. Years ago Nunnally (1961) searched in vain for relatively neutral labels, finding that those in common public use all bear negative connotations. He demonstrated differences in the degree of their aversiveness: "insane man" is more apt to arouse negative reactions than "mental patient" or "emotionally disturbed man." Husek and Bobren (1964) reported the same results, concluding that labels are indeed important attitudinal determinants. Sieveking and Doctor (1969) found that the college students they studied made large distinctions in personal desirability and potential to do harm between people with minor (nervousness, underachievement, neurosis, marital problems) and major (mental illness, psychosis, addictions) psychological problems, regarding the latter with considerably less trust and comfort. As Bord noted with respect to the help source associated with behaviors, it seems likely that labels are most influential for audiences who are rather unfamiliar with the behaviors they refer to, and who rely on the labels as additional information regarding the seriousness of the conditions presented.

Phillips (1966) designed an ingenious study to portray the negative impact on public attitudes of a history of psychiatric hospitalization. His subjects, white married women, were each given five case history paragraphs using four of Star's disturbed behaviors in addition to one of a normal man. The individuals described in these paragraphs were said either to have never sought professional help, or, alternatively, were said to have been formerly mental hospital patients. Without the label of mental illness, the normal case was overwhelmingly perceived as such: over 98% of the respondents who were told he had never sought professional help would let their daughters marry such a man, and all would rent him a room, work with him, have him in a club or as a neighbor. In striking contrast, when this same case history was followed by the information that he was an ex-mental patient, only 17% of the respondents would consider him as a son-in-law, and less than half would rent him a room. Since his current behavior, by itself, was consistently identified as normal, his rejection by subjects who were told he had been hospitalized seems entirely due to the stigmatizing effect of a history of mental hospitalization. This seems an excellent demonstration of negative public attitudes to a past history of mental illness, suggesting that the public does not really believe that mental illness is a transient condition.

In his next study, Phillips (1967) sought to define the relationship between people's capacity to identify mental illness as such and their attitudes toward those so labeled. Phillips was responding to the findings of Lemkau and Crocetti (1962) described earlier that the public was getting better at labeling behavior mental illness which they regarded as a worthwhile change. It was Phillips's contention that the improved ability of the public to assign the label of mental illness to deviant behavior was associated with rejection of the people so labeled, and accordingly was no improvement at all. In this paper he presented a small study of 86 subjects who were given three of the Star descriptions of disturbed behavior, each description being followed by social distance questions regarding the person just presented. Afterward, the respondent was asked whether the person described was mentally ill. He expected and found that subjects who identified the cases as mentally ill wanted to maintain a greater social distance than those not making such a judgment. Whether these differences were statistically significant is not reported, but the author concluded firmly that the ability to correctly identify behavior as mental illness is associated with rejection.

While Phillips's work during the 1960s was the most sustained program to counter the encouraging conclusions of the psychiatric investigators, other sociologically oriented studies lent support to his observations. Tringo (1970) sought to establish a hierarchy of preferences in the public view among various categories of the disabled, ill and stigmatized. He adapted from Bogardus (1925) a social distance scale with a 9-point response range, the extreme responses to which were "would marry" and "would put to death." Nearly 500 young respondents were asked to rate 21 disability groups. They gave first preference to the physically disabled, followed next by sensory disorders, and last by brain and social disorders. The four disabilities that were consistently ranked lowest by all respondents were ex-convict, mental retardation, alcoholism, and mental illness in last place of all. While demographic characteristics were found to influence the extent of social distance expressed toward various disability groups, they did not affect the relative position of groups in the hierarchy.

Approaching the problem of stigma from another viewpoint, Farina (1971) has considered the effect of a past psychiatric history on employability and on judgments of competence and likeability. In an experimental setting he found that the experimenter was seen as less adequate and was liked less by those subjects who had been led to believe that he had been in a mental hospital. In a more complicated design, using previously unacquainted pairs of male college students in a laboratory setting, he showed that merely believing that the other person had been told he was a mental patient led the first person to act in a manner that did alienate his partner. In fact, the partner had not been so informed. In a third design, Farina demonstrated that those who bore the label of mental patient, even when they were really normal, felt less comfortable, performed more poorly on a simple manual task, and were seen by others as more anxious than subjects not so labeled.

### Equivocal Findings

In the foregoing discussion, studies have been broadly grouped in terms of the amount of progress noted and degree of acceptance currently seen in public attitudes toward mental illness. Before evaluating the relative merits of these positions, two additional collections of findings, which are less clearcut in their outcome, will be considered. The first of these is the elaborate public survey conducted in New York City in 1963 by the Columbia School of Public Health and the New York City Community Mental Health Board, whose findings were reported by Elinson and associates in 1967, and the second concerns the recent political career of Thomas Eagleton.

The format and scope of the Columbia study is more comparable to the work of Nunnally (1961) than to the other studies described. Elinson and associates concluded that their findings "showed clearly that there are chinks in the traditional public armor of rejection of the mentally ill." Selecting from their extensive data, they found that the view is now quite prevalent that "mental illness is an illness like any other," and optimism prevails that it is treatable. Yet at the same time, over three-quarters of the respondents agreed with the statement that "unlike physical illness, which makes most people sympathetic, mental illness tends to repel most people." Only 16% admitted to being repelled by mental illness themselves, however, so that, at the least, one can say that candid rejection of mental illness seems to be less socially acceptable to confess than it used to be.

Three-quarters of the respondents in the Elison survey considered patients in mental hospitals "in many ways like children," and less than half would have as a baby-sitter a woman who had been in a mental hospital or even one who had gone to a mental health clinic. The majority also believed that outpatient treatment is less stigmatizing than hospitalization. No public concensus was elicited on the subject of the chronicity of mental illness: 49% agreed that "most mental patients continue to show signs of their illness long after they leave the hospital." In brief summary, the data from this large-scale survey in the early 1960s suggest that the medical model of mental illness is becoming commonly known and accepted: respondents are less willing to openly voice negative feelings about mental patients, but they are still regarded as undesirable companions—unreliable, immature, not really trustworthy, with a more or less chronic loss of status.

On first consideration, the spectacular rise and fall of Thomas Eagleton during the 1972 presidential compaign hardly seems to offer evidence of greater public tolerance of mental illness in the 1970s. Once his multiple psychiatric hospital-ization and electroshock treatments for depression were made public, he became to McGovern a political liability and was compelled to depart from the national scene. This would seem a straightforward response of rejection in reaction to revelation of a prior history of mental hospitalization, as Phillips (1967) neatly demonstrated.

At least two additional factors complicate the situation, however. The first is that Eagleton's failure to inform McGovern of this history at the time of his selection was seen as a cognitive or moral failing quite apart from the matter of his current psychiatric fitness for office. The other complicating consideration in the Eagleton affair is the likelihood of divergence of opinions among the public at large, the press, and the politicians. According to interviews and surveys conducted by national magazines, the public seems to have been far less dismayed about Eagle-ton's psychiatric history than columnists and politicians were and presumed the public to be.

Respondents seemed relatively unmoved by disclosures about Eagleton in polls conducted at the time. In a *Time* magazine (August 7, 1972: 12) poll of a national sample of 1,015 eligible voters, only 5.2% of the respondents indicated that they would change their vote to support Nixon, while 3.8% said they were more inclined to vote for McGovern, in reaction to the disclosures about Eagleton's past hospital-izations. *Newsweek* also conducted a poll about Eagleton with broadly similar results (August 7, 1972: 12). These measures of public response certainly suggest a fair amount of public tolerance for, or at least indifference to, a record of past mental illness in a candidate for national office. Both *Time* and *Newsweek* con-cluded that the public seemed more sympathetic to Eagleton than did the press, the politicians, labor leaders, and big contributors.

In a commentary written at the time, *Science News* (August 5, 1972) ran a story entitled, "The Eagleton Affair: Stigma of a Mental Disorder," whose title ade-quately summarizes the content. It may be, however, that the stigma in this incident was more a matter of political apprehensions and anticipations than actually expressed public attitudes. As Gaylin (1973) noted in an essay about Eagleton in the *New York Times* Magazine Section, the mere fact that there was extended debate about Eagleton's fitness for office reflects an unquestionable change in public attitude, since 50 or even 25 years ago it would have been an utterly untenable option.

On the other hand, the experience of Gerald Ford, seeking congressional con-firmation of his nomination for the vice-presidency eighteen months later, attests to the persistence of stigma emanating from a purported history of psychiatric treatment. On the first day of Senate committee hearings on his nomination, he was obliged to deny any history of psychiatric consultation. As Hutschnecker (1973) noted subsequently, it is still an unforgivable sin, a "kiss of death," for a national politician to seek psychiatric help of any form.

## Comment

In reviewing the findings of the last 20 years to evaluate how much public opinion has changed and where it stands today, several major points seem to emerge from the prevailing controversies. First, regardless of one's ideological point of view, it seems evident that people are better informed about mental illness now. It would be unlikely for an investigator today writing a questionnaire to inquire, as Ramsey and Seipp did in 1947, whether "insanity is God's punishment for some sin." The concept of mental illness as retribution seems to be fading from middle-class discourse about mental illness, though moral issues remain, and both social and medical considerations have become more significant.

A second point is that the message, "mental illness is an illness like any other," has been widely disseminated; people seem to accept it as the "correct" thing to believe. In this sense Crocetti and his colleagues are accurately reporting the propagation of the medical model. But the public, as Sarbin and Mancuso (1972) vigorously point out, seems ultimately unconvinced of the explanatory value, or at least the implications of this conceptual framework. Ex-mental patients are simply not perceived with the same trust, good will, and restoration of the former "normal" status that is assigned to ex-medical patients. In the context of Eagleton's candidacy, *Time* observed that "there was some feeling that . . . criticism [of Eagleton] was unfair, that mental illness should be regarded like any other illness and not held against a man once he is cured" (August 7, 1972: 12). But these sentiments did not prevail; even if the public believed that Eagleton's was an illness like any other, he was not, in the final analysis, regarded as cured. This continued differentiation between mental and physical illness is reflected in the question of the Columbia survey (Elinson, 1967) to which 77% of their respondents agreed: "Unlike physical illness which makes most people sympathetic, mental illness tends to repel most people," while only 16% of these respondents themselves confessed to being repelled by mental illness. It seems, then, that people know they should regard mental illness as an illness like any other, but their feelings are not regularly shaped by this cognitive awareness.

Contributing factors to the problem of defining the capacity of the public to identify mental illness as such, and the issue of public tolerance of the mentally ill are methodological ones regarding size and significance of effect. To state that the public can recognize case descriptions of mental illness, what proportion of the sample must so label the cases, and how many cases must they label? To declare that the public rejects the mentally ill on a social distance scale, what amount of social distance constitutes rejection and what proportion of a sample must choose the social distance that is established as rejecting? The percents and proportions in themselves are inscrutable: what does it mean if,for example, 62% of a sample calls a case description of alcoholism a manifestation of mental illness, and 40% so labels a compulsive-neurotic case? Is this public recognition or not? The significance of such figures becomes apparent, if at all, only through comparisons with other findings in studies using the same format, measures, and presumably comparable samples. Since precise replication was never a strong point in the behavioral sciences, these criteria are rarely met. Still, trends over time do emerge, and sample variations become less important when enough studies show similar trends. In terms of percent of population appying thy label of mental illness to case descriptions of deviant behavior, it seems unarguable that the public's ability to label mental illness in this manner has steadily increased over the last 20 years.

More difficult questions concern the amount of social distance the public likes to maintain from those labeled mentally ill, and whether the amount measured on social distance scales in fact constitutes public rejection of the mentally ill. If, for example, 55% of a sample disagrees that "most women who have gone to mental health centers could be trusted as baby-sitters" (Elinson et al.: 20), is there public rejection? Is there even public consensus? If 62% of another sample disagrees with the statement, "every mental hospital should be surrounded by a high fence and guards," is this a display of public acceptance?

In a letter to Phillips challenging his citation of their findings, Crocetti and Lemkau (1965) offer one way of interpreting data of this nature: they refer to social distance studies regarding entirely separate groups in the population to be used as a frame of reference. In an effort to support their favorable interpretation of the finding that 51% of their sample would consider marriage to a former mental patient, they cite the early work of Bogardus (1925, 1928), who studied the prejudices of native Americans toward various racial and ethnic groups, such as Negroes and Jews. In the course of his studies he found that 54% of his sample would be willing to accept kinship by marriage to Germans; in other words, 46% would not consider such a relationship with an ethnic group that was not commonly regarded as discriminated against or held in low public esteem in the 1920s. Crocetti and Lemkau make the entirely reasonable point that their finding of 51% acceptance of kinship by marriage to ex-mental patients is comparable to Bogardus's finding of 54% acceptance of German ethnics: if the latter were not considered social rejects, then there would be no justification to so regard mental patients, at least in terms of a social distance measure. This kind of comparative statement does seem to bear more influence than the simple declaration that a certain percent of sample response on a certain item does or does not constitute social rejection. Results would be far more meaningful in the context of a much broader network of indices of social distance.

As a general overview of the status of public attitudes toward mental illness in the early 1970s, it seems reasonable to endorse Halpert's (1969) conclusion that people are distinctly better informed and disposed toward mental patients than they have been, but a major portion of the population continues to be frightened and repelled by the notion of mental illness. Today, as in times past, when people encounter the description or presence of someone who has been labeled mentally ill, they are not pleased to meet him.

## CHARACTERISTICS OF PATIENTS AND TREATMENT SITUATIONS THAT INFLUENCE DEGREE OF PUBLIC ACCEPTANCE

### Characteristics of Patients

Over the last several years it has become increasingly apparent that the public makes a variety of distinctions in their responses to disturbed behavior. Attitudes are determined to some extent by degree of unpredictability and loss of accountability, by personal characteristics of the persons manifesting the behavior, the particular symptoms and diagnostic category involved, the visibility of the disturbed behavior, and the extent to which violence is an issue.

As noted above, the public apparently is willing to regard as normal a much broader range of behavior than experts would thus define, as long as the behavior is not labeled a manifestation of mental illness. It is presumably not deviance or eccentricity per se that is troubling as much as certain characteristics which seem exclusively attributed to mental patients. Chief among these are the characteristics of unpredictability and lack of accountability (Nunnally, 1961; Cumming and Cumming, 1965; Johannsen, 1969; Bord, 1971). As Nunnally observed, lack of predictability seems to be a cornerstone of public attitudes toward the seriously disturbed. "Because unpredictable behavior is frightening and disruptive, much societal machinery is devoted to making the behavior of individuals predictable to others." Gross unpredictability is virtually always intolerable and culminates in rejection and avoidance. Johannsen suggests that society views the mental patient as representative of all its unpredictable elements and uses institutionalization as a way of labeling these elements for easy identification in the future.

Accountability refers to the attribution of responsibility for behavior. If an individual is regarded as accountable for his actions and he behaves in a deviant fashion, he is typically regarded as immoral or bad, not sick. If the acts are not seen as intentionally perpetrated, the person is seen as sick (See, 1968). In an apparent exception to this generalization, Fletcher (1969) found that, in the case where aggression was a major feature of disturbed behavior and the individual was regarded as accountable, psychiatric referrals nevertheless continued to be recommended by the respondents in his study. Still, it seems that in general, when deviant behavior appears unpredictable and the individual is seen as not accountable for his actions, people tend to employ a psychiatric framework, label the person mentally ill, and thenceforth keep out of his way.

Personal characteristics of the person described in a case presentation have been shown to influence the likelihood and extent of their social rejection. Males, for example, are more heavily stigmatized for deviant behavior than are females (Phillips, 1964; Linsky, 1970). Social class has long been seen as a determinant of public tolerance for deviance: the lower the social status of the deviant person, the more likely is their rejection and exclusion from the community (Linsky, 1970; Goffman, 1961; Bord, 1971). An extremely sharp increase in hospitalization rates has often been reported for those in the lowest social class position (Class 5 in Hollingshead and Redlich's scheme), but there is also a linear negative correlation between social rank and hospitalization rate throughout the range. Even mental health professionals have more positive attitudes toward upper-class patients than those of low status (Myers and Schaffer, 1954; Belknap, 1956). Linsky found that members of low status ethnic and racial groups and those who lack social ties in the community are also more apt to be excluded for acting deviantly than are others. It is perhaps relevant to observe in passing that these are the groups that are heavily overrepresented among state mental hospital admissions.

With the exception of the gender distinction noted above, which probably stems from differential normative expectations regarding the relative stamina of men and women, these findings are concordant with the extensive work in interpersonal attraction which is one of the branches of attitude research. Positive relationships between attraction felt for a person and the similarity of his beliefs, attitudes, values, personality characteristics, and interest to those of the respondent who is judging his attractiveness have been found so consistently in the literature that analysts of the field conclude that further demonstrations of such relationships are quite unnecessary (Fishbein and Ajzen, 1972).

People respond differently to various kinds of symptoms. Physical symptoms like migraine headaches, neurodermatitis, and so forth seem more respectable than behavioral ones like phobias and tics. When deviant behavior includes violence as a major component, this symptom pattern is, understandably, quickly rejected apart from any question of seriousness of the psychopathology. The amount of mystification involved in symptoms also seems to matter: in *Life* magazine there is a description in the amount of change in audience reaction on the Dick Cavett Show to Eagleton's detailed explanation of what he really felt like and did when he was "depressed," how hard it was to get out of bed, how he endlessly postponed tasks he knew had to be done, avoided seeing friends, and so forth (*Life*, August 11, 1972: 31). Once his illness was de-mystified and people understood what "depression" meant, they responded with enormous sympathy and understanding instead of the rather icy calm that had greeted his appearance initially. So it is that seemingly incomprehensible behavior, such as hearing voices, is more repellant than behavior which seems within normal understanding only too extreme, such as manic phases.

The public tends to reject disturbed behavior that is socially visible, even if it is not severe in terms of its incapacitating effects on the patients. In our culture it is less socially acceptable to behave in a disruptive, bizarre, or troublesome fashion than to act withdrawn, detached, or depressed. Thus a paranoid schizophrenic is more often identified as mentally ill than a simple schizophrenic, an acting-out child more often than a withdrawn one (Lemkau and Crocetti, 1962; Phillips, 1964; Yamamoto and Dizney, 1967). The more socially threatening the behavior, the greater the social rejection (Blizard, 1970). Manis and associates (1965) found that, contrary to their predictions, psychiatrists as well as the general public were more influenced by the social visibility than the severity of symptoms in deciding whom to label mentally ill, based on a set of twenty descriptive paragraphs. The authors suggested that the cultural content of these descriptions, regarding degree of social conformity, served as the primary determinant among the samples they studied.

### Characteristics of the Treatment Situation

Characteristics of the treatment that psychiatric patients receive have also been associated with the amount of stigma generated by the patient role. As Hirsch and Borowitz (1973) have noted, the treatment site, method, frequency, and therapist type are all relevant factors. Hospitalization, especially when involuntary and in public facilities, arouses the most strongly negative feelings. Next in order are the private mental hospital, the psychiatric service in general hospitals, hospitals with integrated psychiatric and medical beds, and then rest homes and spas. This ordering of treatment site is usually justified on the basis that it is related to severity in the mind of the public, but traditionally the major correlate has been the socioeconomic status of the patient (Klee et al., 1967). Only the wealthy patronize rest homes and spas; only the powerful are put on neurological wards rather than psychiatric ones in prestigious hospitals to maintain the pretense of medical rather than psychiatric disorder, and only the poor and powerless (with rare exceptions) are committed to state mental hospitals.

At the present time, there is a definite trend away from the use of state mental hospitals. The state of California has gone so far at to plan their abolition within five years, and rely instead on hospital and clinic facilities within local communities. Because third-party payments (Blue Cross, private insurance plans, Medicare) have begun to cover short-term psychiatric hospitalizations, many general hospitals have established psychiatric units. Today, the majority of psychiatric inpatients go to general hospitals in their communities rather than the more stigmatizing psychiatric hospitals (Gordon, 1973). It is noteworthy that this far-reaching change in treatment locale, together with the present prevailing emphasis on outpatient community services, has been brought about by economic rather than therapeutic considerations.

Treatment methods also are presumed to imply different degrees of severity, and consequently of stigma, in the public view. Paradoxically, though somatic symptoms are more socially acceptable than purely psychiatric ones, somatic therapies are thought to imply greater severity than verbal ones, and so are viewed more negatively (c.f. the Eagleton affair). Hirsch and Borowitz list verbal treatment methods in order of perceived decreasing severity; individual psychotherapy; marital and family therapy, group therapy; encounter, T-group, and marathons.

Treatment frequency is another parameter associated with public estimates of psychiatric disorders. In the view of the general public, less frequent visits are taken to suggest less serious psychopathology, but within the mental health professions, the converse is assumed. That is, psychoanalytic patients who see their therapists three to five times weekly are believed less seriously disturbed by professionals than patients who have weekly or biweekly appointments, who presumably receive supportive rather than psychodynamic forms of psychotherapy. These notions are themselves being reevaluated as traditional psychoanalytic treatment becomes less and less common, again partly for economic reasons but also because other treatment methods associated with less frequent visits are becoming increasingly popular and widespread.

Finally, the type and training of the therapist who is consulted has some bearing on the presumed severity of the patient's disorder, as Phillips (1963) and others have noted. It is generally assumed that visits to nonpsychiatric personnel suggest conditions of lesser severity. Least stigmatizing would be consultations with pharmacists, clergymen, or perhaps marriage counselors; most stigmatizing are visits to psychiatrists. In fact, the training of mental health specialists is associated with the fees they charge, and is also associated with the probability of their actually seeing patients in low-cost clinics. Accordingly, regular consultation with psychiatrists is a luxury only upper-middle class patients can afford. Even when third-party payments modify this form of financial segregation, the majority of more highly trained professionals, who generally have a surfeit of patient referrals, prefer to see middle- and upper-class patients who are characteristically more articulate, better educated, more introspective, and generally more amenable to talking therapy than are lower-class patients. Actually, psychiatrists and Ph.D. psychologists in private practice typically see the least disturbed segment of the psychiatric population in their consultation rooms, public opinion notwithstanding.

In short, the amount of public rejection or acceptance of deviance is partly determined by personal attributes of the person described as deviant and also by his treatment situation. If investigators wished to maximize public aversion to a case description, the person would be described as male, lower-class, probably black, violent, hearing voices, showing bizarre behavior, and lacking social ties within the community. Variations between studies in degree of public rejection elicited may indeed be related to the particular characteristics assigned to the case histories presented to the respondents.

## CHARACTERISTICS OF RESPONDENTS THAT INFLUENCE DEGREE OF PUBLIC ACCEPTANCE[2]

### Demographic Characteristics

Different people have different attitudes about nearly everything, including mental illness. Respondents can be differentiated on the basis of their age, education, occupation, race, ethnicity, social class, and actual experience with mental patients; each of these variables has been related to attitudes manifested toward the mentally ill.

Perhaps the most extensive work regarding attitudes toward mental patients has focused on those engaged in the mental health field, since the impact of these attitudes is increasingly regarded as integral to the experiences and careers of the patients who are exposed to them.

Most studies of the attitudes held by mental health workers have considered employee subgroups separately. Investigators have typically reported that personnel with lower status are more authoritarian and restrictive in their attitudes toward mental patients, while those with advanced professional training—psychiatrists, psychologists, and social workers—show more awareness of the strengths patients possess, are more liberal and tolerant in their attitudes, and are more optimistic about their prospects for recovery. (Cohen and Struening, 1962, 1963, 1965; Appleby et al., 1961; Reznikoff, 1963; Reznikoff et al., 1964; Wright and Klein, 1966; Williams and Williams, 1961; and Vernallis and St. Pierre, 1964). These investigators used a variety of attitudinal measures, including the Opinions about Mental Illness Scale (OMI), the Custodial Mental Illness Ideology Scale (CMI), and specially constructed questionnaires. While attitudes were fairly distinct as a function of occupational category within the mental health field, several studies suggested that these attitudes seem largely shaped by age, education, and social class, just as choice of occupation is often largely dictated by these variables.

While mental health workers with advanced professional training are more liberal and tolerant in their attitudes toward mental patients than workers of lower occupational rank, widely divergent ideological positions are to be found, even within the same profession. Baker and Schulberg's CMHI Scale, a single-factor measure of community mental health beliefs, was used to rank selected professional groups in terms of their adherence to this attitude dimension. The psychologists included in this study (postdoctoral students in community mental health and members of the American Psychological Association's Division 12, Clinical psychology) obtained the highest scores. Occupational therapists came next, followed by a random sample of members of the American Psychiatric Association. The lowest scores, indicating least acceptance of community mental health beliefs, were those of a random sample of the American Psychoanalytic Association. The authors found several correlates to this attitude dimension, such as age and occupation. Those who scored high were apt to be younger and have received their training more recently. They spent more of their time in administration, teaching, and community consultation and were relatively less involved in direct patient treatment. They tended to work in universities, community clinics, hospitals, and schools rather than in private practice.

Ehrlich and Sabshin differentiated three rather independent ideological orientations among psychiatrists: psychotherapeutic, somatotherapeutic, and sociotherapeutic. The psychotherapeutic position espouses the principles of the mental hygiene movement, accepts the medical model of mental illness, and is endorsed by more psychoanalytic and dynamically oriented psychiatrists. The somatotherapeutic point of view is comparable to that of the directive-organic, advocating chemical and physiological etiological explanations and therapeutic strategies. The sociotherapeutic position is largely concerned with the network of people, places, and things constituting the ecology in which patients live; its adherents devote their therapeutic efforts to family and environment rather than to the inner mental mechanisms analyzed by advocates of the psychotherapeutic position. It is probably endorsed by the same people who would obtain high scores on Baker and Schulberg's CMHI Scale. The instrument used to identify these three ideologies was a 28-page questionnaire of opinion statements in Likert format, covering the areas of etiology, nature of the therapeutic process, appropriateness of different therapeutic procedures for different diagnostic groups, and beliefs about the therapeutic competencies of various mental health specialists. Embedded in this questionnaire were three scales specifically designed to measure commitment to each of the three postulated orientations. As Sabshin points out, this questionnaire dealt predominantly with issues related to psychiatric hospitalization because it was written in the late 1950s when there was great interest in milieu therapy. A follow-up study now under way includes items regarding activities in a community context, which hardly existed fifteen years ago.

One of the most consistent findings throughout this research area is the strong relationship observed between the age and education of respondents, their degree of prejudice in general, and rejection of the mentally ill in particular (Middleton, 1953; Lawton, 1964, 1965; Clark and Binks, 1966; Ramsey and Seipp, 1948; Freeman, 1961; Bates, 1968; Bordeleau et al., 1970). The older the individual, the more unsympathetic, intolerant, rejecting, and distant are his attitudes about the mentally ill. Overall findings suggest that mental patients' attitudes are like those of nonpatients of comparable age, education, and social class, and that the condition of patienthood does not significantly alter their beliefs and judgments (Giovanni and Ullman, 1963; Manis et al., 1963; Bentinck, 1967). Although the two variables of age and education are characteristically correlated in that older groups tend to have received less education than younger groups, each variable has predictive value when the other is controlled for. As Freeman (1961) has observed, it would seem that other socialization agents apart from the formal educational system have had differential effects on the young and old with respect to attitudes about mental illness.

Those of high and low social status view the mentally ill somewhat differently. Hollingshead and Redlich (1958) noted that, as a rule, among relatives of mental patients, the lower the class, the greater the feelings of fear and resentment; the higher the class the greater the feelings of shame and guilt. Negative feelings in general are more pronounced among lower class groups. Dohrenwend and Chin-Shong (1967) similarly found attitudinal differences as a function of social class. Higher-status groups, having in the course of their formal education been exposed to the psychiatric point of view, are more apt to regard deviant behavior as a manifestation of mental illness than are lower-class groups, who tend to overlook disturbed behavior or regard it as bad and serious but not mentally ill. But once lower-class groups decide that an individual is indeed mentally ill, they are more rejecting than higher-status groups. As these authors noted, they regard what they define as mental illness with the same intolerance they feel toward any behavior, custom, or appearances that deviate from their norm. "Lower-status groups are predisposed to greater intolerance of the kinds of deviance that both they and higher-status groups define as serious mental illness. Their definition of serious mental illness is narrower than that of higher-status groups, giving the appearance of greater tolerance of deviance *from the vantage point of the higher-status groups, including the mental health professions*" (Dohrenwend and Chin-Shong, 1967: 432).

While leading educational seminars for union stewards, Dworkin (1969) observed that working class members typically conceived mental illness as a dichotomous condition, an all-or-none affair with no intermediary stages between being crazy and being normal. Mental patients were thought to be irrational and incompetent in all areas of functioning. Consequently, it was very difficult for these people to admit having any sort of personal problem, to say nothing of seeking professional help, since this would be regarded as an admission of being "crazy." Dworkin concluded that, for many prospective patients from working class backgrounds, a "corrective educational experience" about the nature and treatment of mental illness would have to precede the "corrective emotional experience" of psychotherapy if they are ever to seek help voluntarily.

Freeman (1961), studying attitudes toward mental illness among relatives of ex-mental patients, found that, as expected, age and education were associated with attitudes. He observed no relationship, however, between these attitudes and social class independent of education and a measure of verbal ability. He felt that the strong relationship obtained by Hollingshead and Redlich (1958) can be accounted for by the inclusion of education in their social class index, and suggested that "enlightened attitudes toward mental illness can be more parsimoniously accounted for on the basis of differential verbal ability than on the basis of differences in 'style of life' " (Freeman, 1961: 65). Bord (1971) also made the point that the traditional unsympathetic attitudes toward mental illness are acquired during early socialization, and the psychiatric perspective is encountered only later as one moves through the formal education system. If the educational process is attenuated, as it is for lower-class members, there is little opportunity to become acquainted with "enlightened" mental health ideology. In any case, it has been empirically demonstrated that measures of either education or social class do serve to differentiate respondents regarding their degree of tolerance for the mentally ill.

Because the variable of racial membership is so closely related to conditions of status, class, income, and education, it is truly difficult to isolate attitudes toward mental illness specifically attributable to race. There is some evidence to suggest that blacks tend to be more traditional and less sympathetic toward those labeled mentally ill. Fournet (1967) studied several Louisiana communities using biographical information, the OMI Scale and three case history vignettes, and reported that black respondents were more authoritarian and restrictive in their attitudes toward the mentally ill than were the white respondents, and were also more reluctant to seek professional help. Similarly, Crocetti and Lemkau (1963) reported that, at each educational level except the lowest, fewer blacks than whites expressed very favorable attitudes toward psychiatric home care instead of hospitalization. In both of these studies the overriding influence of class and education cannot be ruled out. In Fournet's southern sample it is likely that blacks occupied the lowest social position of any group studied, and Crocetti and Lemkau found no attitudinal differences among very poorly educated black and white respondents. The greater observed rejection associated with blacks may simply be a function of minimal education and very low status. Blacks who share middle-class values and behavioral standards have not been found to be more rejecting than their white counterparts (Ring and Schein, 1970), which supports the general conclusion that race, by itself, does not substantially influence attitudes toward mental illness.

Variations in attitudes toward mental illness due to ethnic membership have also been considered. In general, observed differences due to ethnicity alone have been small. Karno and Edgerton (1969) were interested in seeing why Mexican-Americans were so strikingly underrepresented as psychiatric patients in Southwestern hospitals and clinics, and conducted systematic household interviews of Mexican-Americans and native Americans of comparably low socioeconomic status. They found very few differences between groups regarding their perceptions and definitions of mental illness. Subsequent analysis (Edgerton and Karno, 1971) revealed a division within the Mexican-American group in terms of primary culture allegiance. The more acculturated Mexican-Americans, who preferred to be interviewed in English, were indistinguishable from other Americans in their attitudes toward mental illness; those still involved in their Mexican heritage, who chose to be interviewed in Spanish, held more conservative, "old-fashioned" views of mental illness.

Guttmacher and Elinson (1971), studying over 2,000 respondents belonging to eight ethnoreligious groups in New York City, reported comparable results regarding the impact of acculturation. In their study, only the newest arrivals, the Puerto Ricans, differed substantially from the rest in less often ascribing deviant behavior to mental illness. The authors also noted that this response pattern is associated with low occupational rank, and since Puerto Ricans as a group occupied the lowest occupational rank, their perceptions of behavior could be attributed at least partly to social factors. In short, ethnic membership by itself has not proved as relevant as recency of acculturation in determining acquaintance with behavioral norms and conceptions of deviance that prevail among the majority in America.

## Experience and Instruction:  Attitude Change

It has been generally assumed that actual contact with mental patients will have a beneficial effect on peoples' attitudes toward mental illness, and efforts are made to induce the public to visit institutions, help out in volunteer programs, and otherwise associate with patients. A great many studies have been conducted to evaluate the impact on attitudes of such contact; most studies have concerned college students participating in volunteer programs and nursing students after their psychiatric affiliation programs. The general design of such studies is to give a standard attitude questionnaire, most commonly the OMI, before and after contact with mental patients, often using control groups of students who had no exposure to them. It is assumed that favorable results always consist of lowering scores on the factors of Authoritarianism and Social Restrictiveness, and raising scores on the factors of Benevolence, Mental Hygiene Ideology, and Interpersonal Etiology.

Such changes in questionnaire scores have been observed with remarkable regularity (Canter and Shoemaker, 1960; Gelfand and Ullman, 1961; Holtzberg and Gewirtz, 1963; Johannsen et al., 1964; Lewis and Cleveland, 1966; Ralph, 1968; Kolmer and Kern, 1968; Kulik et al., 1969; Smith, 1969; Chinsky and Rappaport, 1970; Beckman, 1972; this is a representative rather than exhaustive listing of such studies). Their results seem straightforward enough, though not always replicated. There does, however, seem to be an undeniable quality of indoctrination in the nature of the students' experiences. It would be unlikely if they had not gotten the message, implicitly or explicitly, that they were supposed to adopt more humanistic views toward mental patients.

In addition to these studies of attitude changes among mental health workers as a result of practical experience, several investigators have considered the impact of psychology courses on the attitudes of undergraduates (Costin and Kerr, 1962; Dixon, 1967; Gulo and Fraser, 1967; Graham, 1968). Although some positive results have been reported, the overall findings suggest that changes in attitudes about mental illness after taking psychology courses, when they occur, are probably not related to the academic content of the courses, but to such factors as the teacher's attitude, or to the nature of the students' abilities or ongoing belief systems. Thus, variables' "in" the teacher or "in" the student rather than in the course material seem to account for most of the attitude changes reported after enrollment in psychology classes.

Slightly more complex in design is a study by Pryer, Distefano, and Marr (1969) examining the separate effects of OMI scores of experience as psychiatric attendants and of intensive formal training. One group of newly hired attendants were given the OMI, then were trained eight hours a day for five weeks and retested. Another group, whose members had worked from four to seven months were given the OMI, then participated in a half-time training program (4 hours daily for ten weeks) and were retested. The authors found no effect of experience alone on attitudes. Formal training did influence the separate factor scores of Mental Hygiene Ideology and Interpersonal Etiology, but the other three factor scores were not altered by either experience or training.

While studies of college and nursing students' attitudes toward mental illness before and after instruction or training continue to be published in quantity and are a popular subject for graduate student papers, they do not really add substantially to knowledge in the field. One study reports a decline in Social Restrictiveness scores after training, another shows higher Interpersonal Etiology scores, a third finds no change, and cumulatively they do not add up to much. Furthermore, these authors typically imply that it is "good" to have higher Benevolence scores, for example, and "bad" to have high Social Restrictiveness scores, without any consideration of the complex interplay between attitudes of the individual worker, the prevailing atmosphere of the treatment establishment, or the nature of the patient population. Certainly no empirical work has been done relating these individual factor scores to behavioral criteria such as hospital discharge rates or social rehabilitation in the community. When one considers in addition that the instruments commonly used were not designed to yield change scores in the first place, and that no demonstration has yet been offered regarding the correspondence between changes in scores derived from pencil-and-paper questionnaires and actual changes in staff-patient transactions, the fruitfulness of carrying out additional studies utilizing this general approach appears to be questionable indeed.

In contrast to the foregoing studies of students and employees, Holmes[3] investigated changes in attitudes of staff and members of community recreational centers after exposure to psychiatric patients; they were not particularly motivated to become more understanding of patients as students may be. The mental patients in this study were brought from nearby hospitals to participate in some of the social recreational activities of the centers. Using OMI and behavioral measures (e.g., attendance records, complaints about the patients), he compared attitudes of staff and members before and after the introduction of this kind of program within a given center, and also compared attitudes at centers with and without such a program. Despite an excellent design and statistical elegance seldom encountered in this area, no consistent attitude changes were observed either within or between centers. Exposure to psychiatric patients had negligible effects on measures of attitudes or behavior change regarding mental illness.

Volunteer work with psychiatric patients by college students had no observable lasting effects on those who volunteered, according to a follow-up study conducted by Kish and Stage (1973). Alone among those who have studied changes in questionnaire responses in college volunteers, Kish and Stage sought observable attitudinal and behavioral consequences ten years after volunteer experiences at a local Veterans Administration hospital. Comparing questionnaire responses of volunteers with a matching stratified sample of nonvolunteer classmates, they found no significant differences between groups in terms of attitudes toward mental illness, later volunteer work with psychiatric patients, or involvement in legislative efforts promoting mental health goals. The authors concluded that their data provided no evidence to support the hypothesis that "a voluntary experience in a psychiatric hospital effectively liberalizes a person's opinions about mental illness."

It would seem, then, that contact with patients by itself is not a sufficient condition for attitude change, in the absence of motivation on the part of those who are exposed to the presence of patients. Johannsen (1969) suggests that the critical factor may be the introduction of the mental patient into a role that can be perceived as representing "normal" behavior. Tours of institutions, like tours of zoos, may arouse feelings of pity or revulsion, but almost never stimulate a sense of respect and empathy regarding the inmates; it is only when roles are transformed and patients are given "normal" role assignments that they seem human like you or me. That is why events like camping trips with patients, recently described enthusiastically in the psychiatric literature, seem far more conducive to attitude change on the part of those who join the patients than visits to look at them in their forlorn and not-quite-human conditions of hospitalization. In short, personal contact by itself is no guarantee of attitude change; but if people are predisposed or motivated to improve their opinions of the mentally ill, as volunteers, students, or newly hired aides are apt to be, then personal experience does consistently result in more favorable expressed attitudes.

## CHARACTERISTICS OF THE SOCIAL CONTEXT
## THAT INFLUENCE DEGREE OF PUBLIC ACCEPTANCE

As noted in the introductory section of this paper, most people define mental illness and mental patients in terms of whether treatment, usually including hospitalization, is involved. Since the likelihood of psychiatric hospitalization is related to such contingencies as the proximity and size of such facilities, the prospective patient's eligibility and financial status, and since government allocation of funds influences the availability of hospital beds, the number of people in a given area who can be hospitalized or otherwise treated is subject to considerable variation.

Consequently, different communities have different levels of familiarity with mental health professionals and services, different experiences regarding ease of access to treatment, and different conceptions regarding how common or unusual it is to be a psychiatric patient.

The ready availability of psychiatric services in a community influences local norms regarding the social acceptability of psychiatric treatment, and also encourages the formulation of various problems within a psychiatric framework. As Gaylin (1973) observed, the mere presence of psychiatric services "permits the people who are enduring certain problems to think in terms of psychiatric solutions." The presence of clinics and private therapists invariably creates a market for their services so that treatment becomes more common where it is more readily accessible. Gaylin declared, "If we double the number of psychiatrists in this country, we are guaranteed to double the number of the mentally ill, if this is tabulated as the number who are treated for psychiatric illness." This phenomenon is not the exclusive property of psychiatry, but applies equally well to the availability and community use of services as diverse as surgery and piano lessons.

It seems possible that in areas enjoying a proliferation of treatment modalities such as day hospitals, night hospitals, halfway houses, emergency walk-in clinics, and crisis centers, less stigma will be attached to mental patients than in areas where treatment consists of sojourns, often prolonged, in distant hospitals. As noted earlier, acceptance of the mental patient is facilitated by seeing him in a role that can be regarded as "normal." If a man can function adequately in a job during the day while returning to the more sheltered environment of a night hospital or halfway house after working hours, he appears less different than if he vanishes from the community altogether. Because the public at large does regard time spent in a general hospital as less stigmatizing than time in a mental hospital, as Elinson et al. (1967) reported, it follows that part-time hospitalization in one of the new kinds of facility casts even less of a "black mark" against a person.

While outpatient treatment instead of hospitalization or rehospitalization might encourage greater public acceptance of the mentally ill, problems may arise when a community is faced with increasing numbers of chronically disturbed people in its midst. Their presence may actually have negative impact on public attitudes, perhaps offsetting the gains accruing from changing norms associated with more common use of psychiatric facilities. While various writers suggest different probable effects on community attitudes stemming from the current de-emphasis of psychiatric hospitalization, wide-ranging empirical studies have only begun to be conducted in this area.

Reports from California provide preliminary evidence that massive state hospital discharges can provoke intense community objections and alarm. In 1967, when Reagan took office, there were 15 state hospitals with a population of 21,000 mental patients in California. His administration announced plans to phase out all mental hospitals in the state by 1982, and to prohibit indefinite involuntary commitment. By 1973, with only 6,800 mental patients remaining hospitalized, public dissatisfaction had reached such proportions that legislative hearings were instituted to consider possible consequences of the discharge program. At the hearings, individuals and community representatives complained of the burden thus transferred to patients' families and neighborhoods (*Psychiatric News,* November 1973). The issue became a political one during the 1973 elections when Democratic gubernatorial contenders accused Reagan of "dumping" patients into communities unprepared to care for them. In response, the Reagan administration decided to suspend indefinitely its phasing-out program of state hospitals, and to continue operation of the 11 state hospitals still open (*Psychiatric News,* December 1973). In this instance, negative public attitudes toward community maintenance of formerly hospitalized mental patients were articulated with sufficient force to influence state laws and procedures regarding treatment options for the mentally ill.

The long-term hospitalized patient often no longer has a family to return to; therefore, arrangements must be made for housing as well as follow-up rehabilitative efforts. It has been observed in California that chronic patients who are discharged do not actually become integrated into the community but typically are placed in boarding homes or family-care homes structured very much like hospital wards. The caretakers who operate such homes place primary emphasis on docility and decorum, encourage ex-patients to remain passive and isolated from the community so as not to arouse neighbors' antagonism, and often favor excessive medication to achieve these ends (Lamb and Goertzel, 1971; Aviram and Segal, 1973). Accordingly, these chronic ex-patients still maintain their patient role and identity, are segregated and stigmatized, are expected to remain indefinitely dependent and regressed, and are not really in the community at all. In Aviram and Segal's words, they have been shifted from "back wards" to "back alleys," and the dynamics of exclusion continue to operate (1973: 131).

Comparable reactions have developed in response to New York State's current discharge policy, in response to which the inpatient census of state hospitals dropped from 78,000 to 43,000 in five years. At least in California, special housing arrangements are prepared for newly discharged long-term hospitalized patients. In New York, ex-patients usually must resort to the welfare system for care. Typically they end up in single room occupancy hotels which are concentrated in decaying portions of New York City, and live alongside addicts, prostitutes, ex-convicts, and other social outcasts. As in California, communities are organizing their objections to the presence of ex-patients, who often appear in considerable numbers, and the elected representatives of such areas are beginning to make their complaints heard. There is a growing demand for state legislation to change the present system, which is claimed to hurt the patients and menace the communities. The Queens District Attorney has undertaken an investigation into the aftereffects of the state's discharge program (*New York Times,* January 23, 1974), and the New York City Deputy Mayor has initiated meetings to discuss possible legislative revisions.

In New York, where special housing provisions are not available to ex-patients as they are in California, the ex-patients seem to be more visible and visibly objectionable to their new neighbors. In general, many long-term hospitalized patients returning to communities as a result of state policies display a variety of socially disabling handicaps which are indeed difficult to overlook. After years of incarceration, many have discarded the most basic social amenities, and offend sensibilities by such behavior as "wandering helplessly in the streets, urinating and defecating in public, exposing themselves before women and children, terrifying apartment-house dwellers by riding up and down in automatic elevators, cursing pedestrians, collapsing from intoxication" (*New York Times,* January 21, 1974: 31). It is not surprising that community resentment to their presence is widespread and vocal, especially since no individual or governmental agency seems responsible for their behavior and its consequences.

It is to be hoped that these are transitional and temporary problems occurring while the whole system of care for the mentally ill is being reshaped; careful monitoring of the destinies of ex-patients and community reactions to them is certainly indicated. This whole research area is of particular significance since the changes in admission and discharge procedures pioneered by California and New York are being adopted across the country. As the community mental health movement stresses local outpatient care for almost all patients, and as legislators continue to be impressed with the fiscal savings incurred by such changes in treatment policies, there will be an increasing number of both acutely and chronically disturbed people in communities. As seen in California and New York, severe problems in community relations are apt to emerge. If public attitudes and reactions are neglected, the eventual outcome may be a retreat to exile and custodial care for those mentally ill people who depend on public treatment and care. The consequences of the new discharge programs require systematic examination, both for their effects on ex-patients and with regard to public beliefs, attitudes, and behavioral responses.

## ATTITUDES AND BEHAVIOR

### Attitude Theory and Research[4]

Among investigators of attitudes toward mental illness it is commonly suggested or implied that attitudes are precursors or determinants of overt behavior. Studies are often designed so that attitudes are measured initially, some intervention such as practical training is introduced, and then changes in attitudes are sought on the assumption that attitudes correspond to behavior and that changes in professed attitudes will be accompanied by changed actions. Such studies seem to be based on a very simple model of human behavior in terms of which a unitary attitude will, if properly assessed, correspond to a single action. The complexities of personal, situational and normative influence are usually excluded from consideration, and the compound natures of both attitude and act are characteristically overlooked.

Such assumptions regarding the association between attitudes and acts, words and deeds, are not generally supported by empirical observations. In most studies, little relationship has been observed, and the two behavioral domains—verbal statements of attitude and behavioral deeds—have remained largely uncorrelated. Wicker (1969) carefully reviewed studies comparing measures of both categories of information and found that attitudes are typically unrelated or only slightly related to actions, that correlations between attitudes and overt behavior are rarely above .30 and often near zero, and that only seldom can as much as 10% of the variance in overt behavioral measures be accounted for by attitudinal data.

Even more dramatic are the reports by Wicker and others (Ebbesen, 1971; Deutscher, 1966) that, in many studies, substantial proportions of subjects show striking discrepancies between their words and actions. In LaPiere's (1934) classic investigation of prejudicial attitudes and acts, he drove ten thousand miles with a Chinese couple, visiting hotels and restaurants around the country in the early 1930s. Of the 251 establishments they visited together, only one refused to accommodate them. Six months after LaPiere and the Chinese couple had been served by a hotel or restaurant, LaPiere sent a questionnaire asking whether Chinese guests would be accepted; responses were almost uniformly negative.

For many years, these and comparable results have been cited as evidence that attitudes do not influence behavior significantly. However, it is becoming recognized that possible flaws can pass unnoticed for a long time, or that the facts can be misused by both the original investigator and subsequent workers in the field when basic assumptions are not examined. For example, LaPierre's study has recently been reviewed by Dillehay (1973), who concluded that the measure of attitude was probably obtained from a different person than the one furnishing the measure of behavior; that is, hotel clerks and waiters served the Chinese guests and LaPiere, but the owner or manager probably answered the questionnaire. Further, performance of duties, expressed as service, constitutes a different kind of role behavior than official statement of policies. Dillehay's point is that the evidence from LaPiere's study, and that of the other classic studies cited regarding attitude and behavior, do not actually address the issue and should be considered irrelevant in this context.

Even when discrepancies between attitudes and behavior of the same individual are observed, it is possible that lack of any inherent relationship between the two may not be the major factor involved. In view of the enormous numbers of attitudes each of us harbors about various issues, the well-recognized difficulties in correlating behaviors of the same person in different situations, the array of situational factors inevitably present in any setting which influence our reactions, together with the usual methodological difficulties in selecting and measuring salient attitudinal dimensions and behaviors, the lack of success in linking a particular attitude with a particular action is not remarkable. In fact, the question itself begins to seem ill-advised: instead of asking *whether* there is a relation between attitude and behavior, we should investigate *when* such relationships occur.

Fishbein and Ajzen (1972), in a thorough survey of the recent literature on attitudes and opinions, make it quite clear that traditional measures of attitudes are only appropriate as independent variables when one is concerned with a *variety* of behaviors as the dependent variable. When the investigator seeks to predict a specific act, he is far more likely to succeed if he uses a measure of the subject's attitudes toward his engaging in such an act than if he measures the subject's attitude toward the object in general. Because this distinction between a single act and a multiple act criterion is so often overlooked, and because attitude measures are often selected inappropriately, efforts to relate attitudes and behavior are usually unproductive. Fishbein and Ajzen conclude that studies of predictors of specific acts should focus on behavioral intentions to perform such an act, or attitudes toward that act, and that traditional attitude measures should be reserved for designs with a multiple act criterion.

Even when attitude measures are used appropriately, they are seldom the major determinants of behavior. It is generally accepted that factors other than attitudes have great impact on actions. These may be broadly classified as personal and situational. Personal factors include other attitudes, values and beliefs, competing motives, and social and cognitive characteristics of the respondent. Situational factors encompass the influence of other people, social norms and expectations, and the number of alternative behaviors possible in a given setting. These variables are seldom present singly, and their interactions often account for more of the variances than their separate effects (Fishbein and Ajzen, 1972).

Situational and personal factors can detract from the strength of the relationship between a particular attitude and a particular behavioral response in a variety of ways, as Kiesler and associates (1969) have pointed out. In general, there will not be a high correlation between attitude and behavior if situational pressures contribute substantially to the observed behavior, as they almost always do. For example, a prospective employer who considers the application of an ex-mental patient is far more apt to be influenced by the number of other applicants available at the moment than by his general attitudes toward mental illness.

If competing attitudes are ignored, the investigator may be accurately measuring a relatively unimportant determinant of behavior. For example, willingness of a Southern restaurateur to serve black patrons may be related to his attitudes regarding acceptable public behavior, his desire to earn a living, his concerns about obeying the law, and his feelings about black people. He is also likely to be influenced by the appearance and apparent status of the prospective patrons, the number of people observing the incident, and even the time of day with respect to how busy he is. Given this array of interacting variables, one could scarcely hope to find a powerful relationship between a questionnaire score on prejudice and the behavioral response of the restaurateur in a particular instance.

Another source of discrepancy concerns the problem of equating "item difficulty" from questionnaire to behavioral measures. It is certainly easier to express prejudice or any other negative feeling in response to a mailed questionnaire than it is to act in a prejudicial manner to people standing politely in front of you. Such a vast discrepancy in item difficulty has been cited by Kiesler and associates (1969) as a major criticism of the LaPiere study, for instance. On the other hand, if one objects to mental patients, this face-to-face situation would encourage the respondent to emphasize his good will, as Bord (1971) has observed, even if he would oppose appropriations for a local mental health center in the anonymity of a voting booth.

Although other behavioral determinants have been noted, a final example will illustrate the problems of finding direct correspondence between an attitude and an action. Most questionnaires refer to representative or typical cases, such as "the typical Negro" or "mental patients in general," which tend to evoke some culturally defined stereotype. In contrast, in behavioral measures the respondent is faced with a particular individual who seldom resembles the stereotype image and who may seem more or less attractive and acceptable than the stereotype suggests. Furthermore, the researcher does not always know what stereotype is conjured up by the questionnaire respondent: for example, the term "politician" may bring to mind a corrupt ward heeler or a distinguished elder statesman.

In short, behavior in any given instance is multiply determined. Every attitude and every act has several components and is subject to a variety of influences. Using a complex model of behavior, as it seems essential to do, we are led to study relationships among an array of attitudes and an array of behaviors. Analysis of conditions which promote such relationships and which describe when they prevail may then contribute substantially to our understanding of both attitudes and behavior.

## Research Relating Attitudes and Behavior Toward Mental Illness

Few studies have been designed to explore specifically the behavioral correlates of attitudes toward mental illness. Clinical observations of Rossman and Miller (1973) and studies by Cohen and Struening and by Ellsworth suggest that both the behavior of those whose attitudes are measured and the behavior of patients faced with such attitudes are valid topics of investigation. Their work together provides the most positive evidence now available of a link between attitudes and behavior regarding mental illness. Studies by Fischer (1971) and Cassel and associates (1970) illustrate the feasibility of more modest research designs in this area, while exemplifying methodological pitfalls which may contribute to inconclusive results. After reviewing competing observations drawn from epidemiological data, some overall conclusions are offered regarding the present status of findings relating attitudes and behaviors concerning mental illness.

Before reviewing these studies, it seems prudent to note again that, while attitudes may significantly contribute to treatment outcome, they are characteristically less potent predictors than other variables such as the personal characteristics of the patients and staff being studied. Further, for hospitalized patients, treatment outcome is not a unitary variable but consists of at least two major components: length of hospitalization before discharge, and duration of stay in the community following discharge. Ellsworth and associates (1971) refer to the former as a measure of treatment efficiency which is directly related to program costs, and the latter as a measure of effectiveness, representing program benefits. They caution against disregarding either criterion of treatment outcome, and believe that cost-benefit ratios will come to receive increasing consideration in evaluation of mental health programs. This, however, reaches toward complexities not yet approached by empirical studies of attitudes toward mental illness and behaviors, which presently must focus on the more basic issue of demonstrating a simple link between them.

Clinical observation has contributed evidence linking prevailing public attitudes toward mental illness and patients' behavior. A recent report concerns the reactions of hospitalized adolescents to the withdrawal of Senator Eagleton as vice-presidential candidate in 1972. Rossman and Miller (1973) described a sudden outbreak of disruptive group interactions among male teenage inpatients that coincided with the social furor erupting in the newspapers when Eagleton's psychiatric history was revealed. The authors speculated that the adolescents, "feeling angry and helpless over their projected role as second-class citizens (a vision confirmed by the Eagleton affair), dealt with their anxiety by 'identification with the aggressor.' " Such behavior suggests that, even in closed hospital wards, patients may be susceptible to prevailing social attitudes.

Another investigator who dealt with the Eagleton affair was Tolor (1973), who studied college students' attitudes toward mental illness as measured by the Opinions about Mental Illness Scale (OMI) and reactions to Eagleton. He divided respondents into high scorers (scores above the median) and low scorers (below the median) on each of the five OMI factors and then compared their responses to seven yes-no items concerning Eagleton and one question about party affiliation. Of 40 comparisons (highs and lows on each of the five factors, for eight questions), 17 showed significant differences using chi square analyses. Despite methodological problems, a reasonably consistent pattern emerged: respondents who scored above the median on the factors of Authoritarianism, Benevolence, and Social Restrictiveness, and those who scored low on the factor of Interpersonal Etiology, tended to be Republicans, showed a greater interest in preserving the status quo, believed that a history of emotional disturbance should disqualify candidates from serving in high office, and generally approved of Eagleton's departure from the Democratic slate. These results demonstrate a logical consistency between expressed political and mental health views, and serve to further validate the interpretations assigned to the OMI factors.

As part of the large and elaborate Psychiatric Evaluation Program conducted within the Veterans Administration hospital system in the early 1960s with an almost exclusively schizophrenic population, a series of studies was undertaken by Cohen and Struening (1964, 1965) regarding the effects of hospital atmosphere on length of patient stay. The staff members of 12 neuropsychiatric hospitals were given the OMI. Responses were analyzed for each occupation group, across hospitals, and also for each hospital's total staff.

Cohen and Struening found that, while occupational groups differed significantly from each other in their attitudes, the climate in any given hospital was largely determined by the attitudes of aides and nurses because they comprised the large majority of the staff. Hospitals differed clearly in their overall attitudinal climate regarding attitudes toward mental illness. Patients in hospitals with a strong Authoritarian-Restrictive atmosphere spent fewer days in the community in the six months after date of admission than did patients in other hospitals, when other variables such as symptom pattern at admission were controlled for. In short, these authors found a relationship between prevailing attitudes held by mental hospital personnel and the discharge timing of the mental patients they worked with. From these studies it is not clear whether patients remained longer in hospitals with Authoritarian-Restrictive climates because the staffs maintained a more rigorous criteria for discharge or because staff attitudes impeded patient rehabilitation; but, whether staff attitudes affected their own behavior or the patients' behavior, a link between attitude and actions is nevertheless demonstrated.

Ellsworth (1965) approached the task of reconciling attitudes and behavior from a different viewpoint. He gave attitude scales including the OMI to 65 aides and nurses of a Veterans Administration hospital, and then studied the correspondence of their professed attitudes to ratings of their actual behavior made by mental patients on their wards. Patients' ratings were scored and then averaged by ward, so that group data rather than individual evaluations were related to staff members' attitude scores. Ellsworth found that some attitude factors were correlated with behavior he regarded as congruent, some factors were related to seemingly incongruent behaviors, and still others had no significant behavior correlates. The greatest success is establishing a behavioral link was for the factor of Restrictive Control: a staff member who strongly endorsed this attitude was seen by patients as an impatient, rigid, domineering, inconsiderate person who did not trust, relate to, understand, or respond to patients. These results are consonant with those of Cohen and Struening regarding the relative ineffectiveness of hospitals with an Authoritarian-Restrictive attitude climate in returning patients to the community. The two studies both indicate that the attitude of restrictiveness does make a difference in staff behavior and seems to influence effectiveness in patient rehabilitation. Other attitudinal dimensions have not yet been reliably linked to behavioral correlates, and their effects on patients remain to be seen.

The foregoing studies were elaborate, elegant, and expensive. A small and more readily repeated design by Fischer (1971) dealt with relationships, among incoming college students, between attitudes toward mental illness and intentions to work as a volunteer with mental patients. Before classes started, students were invited to participate in a companion program at a nearby mental hospital. Then they were given scales assessing social desirability, altruism, and attitudes about mental illness. A correlation of .36 was obtained between scores on altruism and intention to participate in the companion program, but beliefs about mental illness had little bearing on either altruism measures or intention to serve in the companion program. Failure to find such links is not remarkable since the author evidently did not take into account competing needs, attitudes, or situational variables, such as the number of courses students were taking, the amount of free time available for extracurricular activities, financial need, or academic standing. On the other hand, a positive relationship was obtained for the measure of altruism so that these were evidently not critical oversights. Following the suggestions of Fishbein and Ajzen (1972), it seems quite likely that, if attitudes toward the act of volunteering to work with mental patients were measured, instead of the far broader category of attitudes toward mental illness, the sought-after relationships might be found.

Another simple study was conducted by Cassell, Carlton, and Rothe (1970), who investigated the hypothesis that more effective psychiatric hospital workers would have better attitudes about mental illness. They looked for a relationship between supervisors' job effectiveness ratings of practical nurses and attendants, and their OMI scores, but found no significant correlations. This failure to relate attitude measures and behavioral ratings may be due to either one or both of two reasons. The assumption that certain OMI responses are intrinsically "better" than others may be erroneous, or else more salient factors than the general one of attitudes toward mental illness may shape the job performance of the observed staff members, a point discussed above. Regarding the first consideration, there is certainly a set of values at least implicit to middle-class researchers in the OMI factor labels. It sounds bad to be authoritarian or socially restrictive, and good to accept propositions regarding the interpersonal etiology of mental illness. What such interpretations overlook is the class-bound nature of opinions about mental illness, the findings that working class members characteristically get higher scores on measures of authoritarianism, are generally more restrictive and critical of behavior they regard as deviant, and finally, that most patients in state and federal mental hospitals where studies are usually conducted share the outlook and prejudices of others of their class, not those of the professionals who study or treat them (cf. Bentinck, 1967).

Kish and associates (1971) apply similar considerations to evaluations of attendants' work and emphasize that the extent to which attitudes of staff members are related to the effectiveness of their job performance depends quite directly on the situational demands of the particular ward milieu to which they are assigned. Ellsworth (1965) extends this point one step further to suggest that different attitudes also probably have various effects on different kinds of patients. It has long been recognized among clinicians, for example, that a manner of distant reserve is far more effective in dealing with paranoid patients than an effusive warmth. While empirical findings in this area are notably lacking, it seems plausible to assume that congruence of attitudes toward mental illness between the individual worker and his colleagues, and perhaps the patients he deals with, is important in evaluating his job effectiveness, rather than searching for abstractly defined "better" attitudes to identify the more competent staff members.

A different approach to estimating the association between attitudes toward mental illness and behavior is to consider public attitudes in relation to the public's help-seeking behavior for emotional problems. Halpert (1969) has noted that studies made at intervals during the past twenty years reflect little change in the public's recalcitrance in seeking psychiatric care. Now, as earlier, he found, people turn to their clergymen, family doctor, relatives, or friends before resorting to psychiatric consultation. Under the auspices of the Joint Commission on Mental Illness and Health in the late 1950s, a national survey found that many of those who said they could have used help but did not seek it were deterred by either shame or ignorance about how to obtain psychiatric help. Similar results regarding who is first consulted were found more recently in the New York City survey conducted by Elinson and associates (1967). From these observations, Halpert concludes that, whatever progress has been made in eliciting from the public more positive attitude statements about mental illness, it has not been matched by a more "enlightened approach" in seeking help for one's own emotional problems.

Halpert's view of these findings is not the only possible interpretation. It could be argued, for instance, that people first turn to their family, friends, and regular doctor when they are troubled because it is these people who are most apt to be helpful; only if the magnitude of the problem renders their participation insufficient does it become appropriate to seek specifically psychiatric intervention. It is also likely, as Goffman (1961) pointed out some time ago with respect to psychiatric hospitalization, that contingencies such as ready access to treatment resources, ability to pay for them, family social status, and other personal and situational variables are the major determinants of help-seeking behavior, apart from attitudes toward mental illness.

The impact of contingencies on help-seeking behavior has been illustrated by findings of the Boston Mental Health Survey conducted between 1960 and 1962 and published by Ryan in 1969. In briefest summary, the survey found that, for every thousand people in the general population, 150 are identified as emotionally disturbed. Only 10 of these 150 ever get help from mental health professionals: 5 go to mental hospitals, 4 go to outpatient clinics (of these, only 2 become engaged in treatment), and 1 sees a psychiatrist privately. Of the 140, about 40% (56 people) are taken care of by nonpsychiatric physicians, and social agencies like settlement houses see about 10. Overall, about two-thirds get some sort of help; one third get nothing at all. Of course, some may not seek help; but in any case, as Ryan put it, "there is no place, there are no people, there is no time available to them" (1969: 12). These dramatic findings of failure of the mental health professions to provide services for those already identified as emotionally disturbed in a city as richly endowed with psychiatric facilities as Boston leads one to wonder whether Halpert is correct in attributing failure to receive treatment to individual motivation. It seems more likely that the basic issue concerns adequate delivery of health care services to the public at large, and particularly to the working and nonworking poor.

## Comment

While work in the area of attitudes toward mental illness is vulnerable to criticism regarding lack of clearcut behavioral correlates, as are attitude studies in most other domains, there are encouraging indications apart from the research findings reported above. General social conditions tend to validate the positive overall attitude changes that have been widely observed. Community facilities for extramural treatment of psychiatric patients have increased enormously in the last 15 years, while state and federal laws regarding the rights of mental patients have become significantly more sympathetic than they used to be. Day and night hospitals, local crisis clinics, and outpatient treatment centers are becoming increasingly available throughout the country, and public acceptance is obviously essential to their continued existence and governmental funding. It has also been suggested that public attitudes toward mental illness are a legitimate subject of analysis apart from the degree of their relationship to actual behavior since they constitute an aura or climate of opinion which the mental patient encounters in his everyday living and which therefore affect him in their own right.

One may conclude that, even if improved attitudes are not strongly or consistently associated with more civilized and more pleasant behavior with regard to mental patients, these attitudes are associated with the legal and economic conditions which determine the therapeutic options available to patients, and as such seem to be valid subjects for investigation. It would indeed be reassuring, however, if the nature and extent of the relationships between attitudes and behavior were further clarified in this field, as in others.

## SUMMARY AND RECOMMENDATIONS

### Summary

Public attitudes toward mental illness have been systematically evaluated during the past 25 years, and their historical antecedents have been traced back considerably further. By 1960 it was clearly established that mental illness was feared, and those labeled as mental patients were disliked and avoided by most people. The public was not as quick as mental health professionals to label odd or deviant behavior as mental illness, but once the label was assigned, either by the community or by professionals, the response was characteristically negative and rejecting. It was widely felt that the mentally ill were rather hopelessly troubled people who probably could not be rescued but who were not terribly worthwhile to begin with. The label of mental illness usually led to irreversibly diminished standing in the eyes of the community, which of course exacerbated whatever problems of adjustment were initially present.

Even before 1960, the stigma of mental illness was sufficiently established so that broadly based educational and ideological compaigns were undertaken to promote to the public the concepts of psychopathology then prevailing among mental health professionals. These were developed within a medical model of illness, and included the beliefs that mental illness is an illness like any other, that it can strike anyone, that its victims are entitled to physicians' care, and that the illness can be conquered.

These educational efforts undeniably have had an impact on American thinking about mental illness. Studies of the 1960s have convincingly demonstrated growing public awareness of these tenets. However, many would agree that there seems to be a discrepancy between these mental health programs of public education and contemporary psychiatric thinking, since the public continues to be taught about the medical model of mental illness at the same time that an increasing number of professionals are extending their conceptualizations of mental illness to include, and give major emphasis to, a transactional or psychosocial model of health and disturbance.

The gross inhumanity of involuntary psychiatric hospitalization, its immense financial cost, the emergence of psychotropic drugs, and the development of alternative styles of treatment have together impressed many mental health professionals and legislators with the undesirability of inpatient care for mental illness, and with the consequent need for identification of populations at risk in the community to facilitate early intervention and treatment. Once such an epidemiological framework is adopted in the search for precipitating factors, attention becomes addressed to stressful aspects of everyday living such as poverty, overcrowding, unemployment, and social isolation. At this point it no longer seems helpful to regard mental illness as an illness like any other which can strike anyone at any time, as a germ or a virus might do. Alternative formulations of a psychosocial nature are more appropriate to public health considerations, including studies of distributions of disorder, the planning of prevention efforts, and evaluation of rehabilitation programs intended to return or maintain the patient in his community.

## Recommendations

Future evaluations research regarding attitudes toward mental illness and programs to modify these attitudes will be facilitated if the following matters are considered. To begin with, it is quite clear by now that attitudes toward mental illness include several components, some of which are a function of relatively enduring personality traits such as authoritarianism, while others are related to more accessible dimensions such as educational exposure. Mental health campaigns are apt to influence only those attitudinal components associated with information level, such as beliefs about psychiatric etiologies, and have little effect on those associated with underlying personality characteristics. Furthermore, some attitudinal components are more directly associated with propensities for action than are others, and if one is concerned with predicting or shaping behavior, the appropriate attitudinal component must be selected for study. In view of these considerations, attitude components and their measuring instruments must be selected to coincide with the objectives of the particular investigation to be undertaken.

Much of the work in this field has been strikingly unsophisticated in terms of design, instrument selection, and statistical analysis. Investigators of public opinions such as Crocetti have generally taken care that their samples accurately represent the populations to which the results are meant to apply. In contrast, the majority of studies regarding attitude change have used the most convenient subjects—usually college and nursing students—whose subordinate status virtually defines their willingness to show that their professors or supervisors have influenced their attitudes. At the least, one may legitimately wonder about the permanence or significance of reported attitude changes among students; indeed, the few studies of attitude change among people who have no reason to please their investigators suggest that enduring attitude modification is difficult to bring about.

Another major problem that applies particularly to studies of attitude change but affects most work in the area has to do with measuring change. None of the instruments commonly used, such as the OMI or CMI, were designed to measure change. Assuming that the instruments are highly reliable over time (and we have to make this assumption since no empirical evidence has been gathered to prove the point), how much change is needed to be regarded as a meaningful alteration of attitude, either for individuals or groups? How much difference between groups must there be in order to conclude that they are basically similar or different in their attitudes? These issues concern not only statistical but also practical significance.

Even if the attitudinal measures are able to portray changes or differences adequately, none presently in wide use offers a comprehensive assessment of possible alternatives. Those employed in studies of public opinions generally concern peoples' ability to label mental illness as such, and their willingness to become personally involved with ex-patients (or those not hospitalized). Studies of students or mental health professionals usually use more elaborate questionnaires such as the CMI and OMI. While the OMI is presently the most comprehensive instrument available in terms of its factorial composition, it largely omits references to the ideas and attitudes associated with social psychiatry and community psychology which have become increasingly popular and widespread since the OMI was published. Either the OMI must be revised and updated to include this dimension, or supplementary measures should be included in current assessment efforts.

Finally, as noted earlier, statistical analyses have been remarkably unsophisticated in most work regarding attitudes toward mental illness. Because attitudes and behavioral influences are multidimensional, their investigation is facilitated by the use of multivariate research designs. Not only is it apparent that several factors usually operate simultaneously, but their interactions are often as powerful as their separate effects. Simple calculations of percent agree and disagree to various attitude measures hardly do justice to the task at hand, and in fact may produce misleading and dubious results.

Apart from these methodological improvements, studies in this field must be altered in their overall focus to include and give greater emphasis to the behavioral correlates of attitudes toward mental illness. In such undertakings it probably would be wise to heed the recommendations of Fishbein and Ajzen concerning the use of a multiple act rather than a single act criterion in the search for relationships with attitude measures. In addition to small-scale classroom or laboratory studies of such relationships, an epidemiological approach might lend itself to the identification of behavioral correlates of measured attitudes in everyday living. For example, selected geographical communities might be compared regarding such matters as provisions made for mental patients, commitment patterns, and use of psychiatric treatment facilities. If more accepting attitudes are manifested by residents in areas with greater availability and use of various psychiatric facilities, as might be anticipated, it must then be determined whether the association is causal, and if so in what direction. Alternatively, attitudes of local residents may be unrelated to the nature, number, and utilization of community psychiatric facilities, particularly if policies regarding hospitalization and treatment are made at the state level, as in California, or nationally, as in the case of third-party insurance payments like Medicare. Studies of public reactions to the ongoing major changes in the legal rights of and treatment strategies for psychiatric patients are sorely needed. The preliminary work of Aviram and Segal (1973) in this context offers fruitful guidelines for controlled studies of patients' fate and community reactions to new legislative and administrative programs for the care of those labeled mentally ill.

Another important but neglected area of research concerns the correspondence of expressed attitudes to treatment outcome. While the work of Ellsberg and of Cohen and Struening provides imaginative leads, little basic information has been gathered to document the impact of various attitudes on different kinds of patients. One formulation might be expressed thus: In what kinds of social-attitudinal structures do patients most effectively develop the social competence and adaptive skills which will help them lead more productive lives? Another approach to the general area might be to inquire in what kinds of treatment climate will a given mental health worker with specified attitudes about mental illness be able to function most effectively. A related topic would be the investigation of different types of patients and the treatment philosophies and attitudes most suitable to their prompt recovery. We also need to know how major differences in attitudes toward the causes and treatment of mental disorders among treatment team members, administrators and clinicians influence the effectiveness of mental health programs. In general, studies of interactions between patient, staff, and program attitudes and assumptions represent a more complex level of understanding, and depend on the prior delineation of direct relationships between attitudes and behaviors.

The foregoing questions are not intended to exhaustively categorize the work yet to be done, but rather to indicate several important areas presently receiving little attention in the literature.

## NOTES

1. It is most important to emphasize that, in any extensive survey such as this, excerpts of results can be selectively interpreted to support either positive or negative conclusions. The various items cannot be formally combined to produce a single definitive conclusion: questions are often designed to be inconsistent with each other so that respondents may agree that "some people are born with the kind of nervous system that makes it easy for them to become emotionally disturbed," and also agree that "most people who have nervous breakdowns have had more real problems than normal people." It is not unusual for commentators, other investigators, and even the authors themselves to emphasize or selectively cite the former result to support a position that the public conceives of mental illness in genetic terms, or the latter result to endorse a transactional view of mental illness in the public mind. At best, the most objective commentator tries to delineate overall trends and avoids underreporting of results that detract from the overall picture while at the same time reaching some meaningful, unambiguous conclusion.

2. Many studies have been done in this area and are described in detail elsewhere (e.g., Rabkin, 1972). In the interest of brevity, only their major results are summarized in this review.

3. D. Holmes, "Changes in Attitudes about Mental Illness" (mimeographed: New York: Center for Community Research, 1968).

4. The following discussion is in no way intended to review comprehensively the complex and extensive work done in the general areas of attitude research and theory. Rather, selected issues are considered which seem particularly relevant to the presentation of public and professional attitudes toward mental illness and their implications for evaluation research.

## REFERENCES

Appleby, L., N. C. Ellis, G. W. Rogers, and W. A. Zimmerman. A psychological contribution to the study of hospital structure. *Clinical Psychology,* 1961, 17: 390-393.

Aviram, U. and S. Segal. Exclusion of the mentally ill: Reflection of an old problem in a new context. *Archives of General Psychiatry,* 1973, 29: 126-131.

Bates, J. Attitudes toward mental illness. *Mental Hygiene,* 1968, 52: 250-253.

Beckman, L. Locus of Control and attitudes toward mental illness among mental health volunteers. *Journal of Consulting and Clinical Psychology,* 1972, 38: 84-89.

Belknap, I. *Human problems of a state mental hospital.* New York: McGraw-Hill, 1956.

Bentinck, C. Opinions about mental illness held by patients and relatives. *Family Process,* 1967, 6: 193-207.

Bentz, W. K., and J. W. Edgerton. Concensus on attitudes toward mental illness. *Archives of General Psychiatry,* 1970, 22: 468-473.
Bentz, W. K., and J. W. Edgerton. The consequences of labeling a person mentally ill. *Social Psychiatry,* 1971, 6: 29-33.
Blizard, P. The social rejection of the alcoholic and the mentally ill in New Zealand. *Social Science and Medicine,* 1970, 4: 513-526.
Bockhoven, J. S. *Moral treatment in American psychiatry.* New York: Springer, 1963.
Bogardus, E. S. Measuring social distances. *Journal of Applied Sociology,* 1925, 9: 299-308.
Bogardus, E. S. *Migration and Race Attitudes.* Boston: Heath, 1928.
———. A social distance scale. *Sociology and Social Research,* 1933, 17: 265-271.
Bord, R. Rejection of the mentally ill: Continuities and further developments. *Social Problems,* 1971, 18: 496-509.
Bordeleau, J., P. Pelletier, L. Panacci, and L. Tetreault. Authoritarian-Humanitarian index in a large mental hospital. *Diseases of the Nervous System,* 1970, 31 (II, suppl.): 166-174.
Canter, F. M., and R. Shoemaker. The relationship between authoritarian attitudes and attitudes toward mental patients. *Nursing Research,* 1960, 9: 39-41.
Caplan, R. *Psychiatry and the community in nineteenth-century America.* New York: Basic Books, 1969.
Cassel, R., M. Carlton, and M. Rothe. Comparing opinions about mental illness for hospital attendants and practical nursing students. *Nursing Research,* 1970, 19: 268-272.
Chinsky, J., and J. Rappaport. Attitude change in college students and chronic patients: A dual perspective. *Journal of Consulting and Clinical Psychology,* 1970, 35: 388-394.
Clark, A. W., and N. M. Binks. Relation of age and education to attitudes toward mental illness. *Psychological Reports,* 1966, 19: 649-650.
Cohen, J., and E. L. Struening. Opinions about mental illness in the personnel of two large mental hospitals. *Journal of Abnormal Social Psychology,* 1962, 64: 349-360.
———. Opinions about mental illness: Mental hospital occupational profiles and profile clusters. *Psychological Reports,* 1963, 12: 111-124.
———. Opinions about mental illness: Hospital social atmosphere profiles and their relevance to effectiveness. *Journal of Consulting Psychology,* 1964, 28: 291-298.
———. Opinions about mental illness: Hospital differences in attitude for eight occupational groups. *Psychological Reports,* 1965, 17: 25-26.
Costin, F., and W. D. Kerr. The effects of an abnormal psychology course on students' attitudes toward mental illness. *Journal of Educational Psychology,* 1962, 53: 214-218.
Crocetti, G., and P. Lemkau. Public opinion of psychiatric home care in an urban area. *American Journal of Public Health,* 1963, 53: 409-417.
———. On rejection of the mentally ill. *American Sociological Review,* 1965, 30: 577-578.
Crocetti, G., H. Spiro, and I. Siassi. Are the ranks closed? Attitudinal social distance and mental illness. *American Journal of Psychiatry,* 1971, 127: 1121-1127.
Crocetti, G., H. Spiro, P. Lemkau, and I. Siassi. Multiple models and mental illnesses: A rejoinder to failure of a moral enterprise: Attitudes of the public toward mental illness, by T. R. Sarbin and J. C. Mancuso. *Journal of Consulting and Clincial Psychology,* 1972, 39: 1-5.
Crow, C. M., R. Mowbray, and S. Bloch. Attitudes of medical students to mental illness. *Journal of Medical Education,* 1970, 45: 594-599.
Cumming, E., and J. Cumming. *Closed ranks: An experiment in mental health.* Cambridge, Mass.: Harvard University Press, 1957.
Cumming, J., and E. Cumming. On the stigma of mental illness. *Community Mental Health Journal,* 1965, 1: 135-143.
Deutscher, I. Words and deeds: Social science and social policy. *Social Problems,* 1966, 13: 235-254.
Dillehay, R. On the irrelevance of the classical negative evidence concerning the effect of attitudes on behavior. *American Psychologist,* 1973, 28: 887-891.
Dixon, C. R. Courses on psychology and students' attitudes toward mental illness. *Psycho-

*logical Reports,* 1967, 20: 50.

Dohrenwend, B. P., and E. Chin-Shong. Social status and attitudes toward psychological disorder: The problem of tolerance of deviance. *American Sociological Review,* 1967, 32: 417-433.

Dworkin, G. Teaching the boys in the back rooms: A program for blue-collar workers. *Mental Hygiene,* 1969, 53: 258-262.

Ebbesen, E. Attitudes toward attitude change. *Contemporary Psychology,* 1971, 16: 36-37.

Edgerton, R. B., and M. Karno. Mexican-American bilingualism and the perception of mental illness. *Archives of General Psychiatry,* 1971, 24: 286-290.

Elinson, J., E. Padella, and M. Perkins. *Public image of mental health services.* New York: Mental Health Materials Center, 1967.

Ellsworth, R. B. A behavioral study of staff attitudes toward mental illness. *Journal of Abnormal Psychology,* 1965, 70: 194-200.

Ellsworth, R., R. Maroney, W. Klett, H. Gordon, and R. Gunn. Milieu characteristics of successful psychiatric treatment programs. *American Journal of Orthopsychiatry,* 1971, 41: 427-441.

Farina, A. Mental illness and the impact of believing others know about it. *Journal of Abnormal Psychology,* 1971, 77: 1-5.

Fishbein, M., and I. Ajzen. Attitudes and opinions. *Annual Review of Psychology,* 1972, 23: 487-544.

Fischer, E. Altruistic attitudes, beliefs about psychiatric patients, and volunteering for companionship with mental hospital patients. *Proceedings, Annual Convention of American Psychological Association,* 1971, 6: 343-344.

Fletcher, C. R. Measuring community mental health attitudes by means of hypothetical case descriptions. *Social Psychiatry,* 1969, 4: 152-156.

Foucault, M. *Madness and Civilization: A history of insanity in the age of reason.* (Trans. by R. Howard) New York: Pantheon, 1965.

Fournet, G. Cultural correlates with attitudes, perception, knowledge and reported incidence of mental disorders. *Dissertation Abstracts,* 1967, 28(1B): 339. See pp. 74, 78.

Freeman, H. E. Attitudes toward mental illness among relatives of former patients. *American Sociological Review,* 1961, 26: 59-66.

Gaylin, W. What's normal? *New York Times Magazine Section,* Sunday, April 1, 1973, pp. 14, 54, 56, 58, 59.

Gelfand S., and L. P. Ullman. Change in attitudes about mental illness associated with psychiatric clerkship training. *International Journal of Social Psychiatry,* 1961, 7: 292-298.

Gilbert, D. C., and D. J. Levinson. "Custodialism" and "humanism" in staff ideology. Pp. 20-35 in D. J. Levinson and R. H. Williams (eds.), *The patient and the mental hospital.* Glencoe, Ill: Free Press, 1957.

Giovannoni, J. M., and L. P. Ullman. Conceptions of mental health held by psychiatric patients. *Journal of Clinical Psychology,* 1963, 19: 398-400.

Goffman, E. *Asylums.* New York: Doubleday Anchor, 1961.

Gordon, A. Mental Health: A time of change. *Physician's World,* 1973, 1: 41-44.

Gove, W., and T. Fain. The stigma of mental hospitalization. *Archives of General Psychiatry,* 1973, 28: 494-500.

Graham, G., Jr. Effects of introductory and abnormal psychology courses on students' attitudes toward mental illness. *Psychological Reports,* 1968, 22: 448.

Gulo, E. V., and W. Fraser. Student attitudes toward mental illness. *College Student Survey,* 1967, 3: 61-63.

Guttmacher, S., and J. Elinson. Ethno-religious variations in perceptions of illness. *Social Science and Medicine,* 1971, 5: 117-125.

Haley, J. *Strategies of psychotherapy.* New York: Grune and Stratton, 1963.

Halpert, H. P. Public acceptance of the mentally ill. *Public Health Reports,* 1969, 84: 59-64.

Hirsch, J., and G. Borowitz. The tyranny of treatment. Paper read at American Psychiatric Association Convention, Hawaii, May 8, 1973.

Hollingshead, A. B., and F. C. Redlich. *Social Class and Mental Illness.* New York: Wiley, 1958.

Holtzberg, J. D., and H. Gewirtz. A method of altering attitudes toward mental illness. *Psychiatric Quarterly Supplement,* 1963, 37(1): 56-61.

Husek, T. R. Persuasive impacts of early, late, or no mention of a negative source. *Journal of Personality and Social Psychology,* 1965, 2: 125-128.

Husek, T. R., and H. Bobren. The relative importance of labels and behavior descriptions in determining attitudes toward labeled behavior. *Psychological Record,* 1964, 14: 319-325.

Hutschnecker, A. The stigma of seeing a psychiatrist. *New York Times,* November 20, 1973, p. 39.

Iguchi, M. T., and R. C. Johnson. Attitudes of students associated with participation in a mental hospital volunteer program. *Journal of Social Psychology,* 1966, 68: 107-111.

Johannsen, W. J. Attitudes toward mental patients: A review of empirical research. *Mental Hygiene,* 1969, 53: 218-228.

Johannsen, W. J., M. C. Redel, and R. G. Engel. Personality and attitudinal changes during psychiatric nursing affiliation. *Nursing Research,* 1964, 13(4): 343-345.

Joint Commission on Mental Illness and Health (eds.) *Action for Mental Health.* New York: Basic Books, 1961.

Karno, M., and R. Edgerton. Perception of mental illness in a Mexican-American community. *Archives of General Psychiatry,* 1969, 20: 233-238.

Kiesler, C. A., B. E. Collins, and N. Miller. *Attitude change: A critical analysis of theoretical approaches,* New York: Wiley, 1969.

Kish, G., K. Solberg, and A. Uecker. The relation of staff opinions about mental illness to ward atmosphere and perceived staff roles. *Journal of Clinical Psychology,* 1971, 27: 284-287.

Kish, G. B., and T. Stage. College student mental hospital volunteers: Any benefits to the student or to society? *Journal of Community Psychology,* 1973, 1: 13-15.

Klee, G., E. Spiro, A. Bahn, and K. Gorwitz. An ecological analysis of diagnosed mental illness in Baltimore. Pp. 107-148 in R. Monroe, G. Klee, and E. Brody (eds.), *Psychiatric epidemiology and mental health planning.* Psychiatric Research Report 22, American Psychiatric Association, 1967.

Kolmer, M., and H. Kern. The resident in community psychiatry: An assessment of changes in knowledge and attitudes. *American Journal of Psychiatry,* 1968, 125: 698-702.

Kulik, J., R. Martin, and K. Scheibe. Effects of mental hospital volunteer work on students' conceptions of mental illness. *Journal of Clinical Psychology,* 1969, 25: 326-329.

Lamb, H. R., and V. Goertzel. Discharged mental patients—Are they really in the community? *Archives of General Psychiatry,* 1971, 24: 29-34.

LaPiere, R. T. Attitudes vs. Actions. *Social Forces,* 1934, 13: 230-237.

Lawton, M. P. Correlates of the opinion about mental illness scale. *Journal of Consulting Psychology,* 1964, 28(1): 94.

———. Personality and attitudinal correlates of psychiatric-aid performance. *Journal of Social Psychology,* 1965, 66: 215-226.

Lemkau, P., and G. Crocetti. An urban population's opinion and knowledge about mental illness. *American Journal of Psychiatry,* 1962, 118: 692-700.

Lewis, I. L., and S. E. Cleveland. Nursing students' attitudinal changes following a psychiatric affiliation. *Journal of Psychiatric Nursing,* 1966, 4: 223-231.

*Life,* August 11, 1972, p. 31.

Linsky, A. Who shall be excluded: The influence of personal attributes in community reaction to the mentally ill. *Social Psychiatry,* 1970, 5: 166-171.

Manis, J. G., C. L. Hunt, M. J. Brawer, and L. C. Kercher. Public and psychiatric conceptions of mental illness. *Journal of Health and Human Behavior,* 1965, 6: 48-55.

Manis, M., P. S. Houts, and J. B. Blake. Beliefs about mental illness as a function of psychiatric status and psychiatric hospitalization. *Journal of Abnormal and Social Psychology,* 1963, 67: 226-233.

Meyer, J. Attitudes toward mental illness in a Maryland community. *Public Health Reports,* 1964, 79: 769-772.

Middleton, J. The prejudices and opinions of mental hospital employees regarding mental illness. *American Journal of Psychiatry*, 1953, 110: 133-138.

Myers, J. K., and L. Schaffer. Social stratification and psychiatric practice: A study of an out-patient clinic. *American Sociological Review*, 1954, 19: 307-310.

*Newsweek*, August 7, 1972, pp. 12-16.

Nunnally, J. *Popular conceptions of mental health: Their development and change.* New York: Holt, Rinehart and Winston, 1961.

Ozarin, L., and C. Taube. Psychiatric inpatients: Who, where and future. *American Journal of Psychiatry*, 1974, 131: 98-101.

Phillips, D. L. Rejection: A possible consequence of seeking help for mental disorders. *American Sociological Review*, 1963, 28: 963-972.

———. Rejection of the mentally ill: The influence of behavior and sex. *American Sociological Review*, 1964, 29: 679-687.

———. Public identification and acceptance of the mentally ill. *American Journal of Public Health*, 1966, 56: 755-763.

———. Identification of mental illness: Its consequences for rejection. *Community Mental Health Journal*, 1967, 3: 262-266.

Pryer, M., M. Distefano, and L. Marr. Attitude changes in psychiatric attendants following experience and training. *Mental Hygiene*, 1969, 53: 253-257.

*Psychiatric News*, Patients' families protest liberal laws on commitment. July 18, 1973, p. 19.

*Psychiatric News*. California shelves plans for abolishing hospitals. December 19, 1973, p. 1.

Rabkin, J. G. Opinions about mental illness: A review of the literature. *Psychological Bulletin*, 1972, 77: 153-171.

Ralph, D. E. Attitudes toward mental illness among two groups of college students in a neuropsychiatric hospital setting. *Journal of Consulting Psychology*, 1968, 32: 98.

Ramsey, G. V., and M. Seipp. Attitudes and opinions concerning mental illness. *Psychiatric Quarterly*, 1948, 22: 428-444. (a)

———. Public opinions and information concerning mental health. *Journal of Clinical Psychology*, 1948, 4: 397-406. (b)

Reznikoff, M. Attitudes of psychiatric nurses and aides toward psychiatric treatment and hospitals. *Mental Hygiene*, 1963, 47: 354-360.

Reznikoff, M., M. D. Gynther, L. C. Toomey, and M. Fishman. Attitudes toward the psychiatric milieu: An inter-hospital comparison of nursing personnel attitudes. *Nursing Research*, 1964, 13: 71-72.

Ring, S., and L. Schein. Attitudes toward mental illness and the use of caretakers in a black community. *American Journal of Orthopsychiatry*, 1970, 40: 710-716.

Rogow, A. The *Psychiatrists*. New York: Putnam's Sons, 1970.

Rootman, I., and H. Lafave. Are popular attitudes toward the mentally ill changing? *American Journal of Psychiatry*, 1969, 126: 261-265.

Rossman, P., and D. Miller. The effect of social prejudice on hospitalized adolescents. *American Journal of Psychiatry*. 1973, 130: 1029-1030.

Ryan, W. (ed.) *Distress in the city*. Cleveland: Press of Case Western Reserve, 1969.

Sarbin, T. R., and J. C. Mancuso. Failure of a moral enterprise: Attitudes of the public toward mental illness. *Journal of Consulting and Clinical Psychology*, 1970, 35: 159-173.

Sarbin, T. R., and J. C. Mancuso. Paradigms and moral judgements: Improper conduct is not disease. *Journal of Consulting and Clinical Psychology*, 1972, 39: 6-8.

Schroder, D., and D. Ehrlich. Rejection by mental health professionals: A possible consequence of not seeking appropriate help for emotional disorders. *Journal of Health and Social Behavior*, 1968, 9: 222-232.

Schumach, M. Halfway houses for former mental patients create serious problems for city's residential communities. *New York Times*, January 21, 1974, p. 31.

———. D.A. checking Creedmoor and its release of patients. *New York Times*, January 23, 1974, p. 37.

*Science News*. The Eagleton Affair: Stigma of mental disorder. August 5, 1972, p. 85.

See, P. The labeling and allocation of deviance in a southern state: A sociological theory, *Dissertations Abstracts*, 1968, 29(2A): 687-688.

Seidenberg, R. Drug advertising and perception of mental illness. *Mental Hygiene*, 1971, 55: 21-31.

Sieveking, N., and R. Doctor. Student attitudes toward physical, psychological and social problems. *Proceedings of the 77th Annual Convention, American Psychological Association*, 1969, 4: 855-856.

Smith, J. J. Psychiatric hospital experience and attitudes toward 'mental illness'. *Journal of Consulting and Clinical Psychology*, 1969, 33: 302-306.

Susser, M. W., and W. Watson. *Sociology in Medicine.* London: Oxford University Press, 1962.

Szasz, T. *Law, liberty and psychiatry.* New York: MacMillan, 1963.

Tolor, A. Opinions about mental illness and political ideology. *American Journal of Psychiatry*, 1973, 130: 1269-1272.

Tringo, J. L. The hierarchy of preference toward disability groups. *The Journal of Special Education*, 1970, 4: 295-306.

Vernallis. F. F., and R. G. St. Pierre. Volunteer workers' opinions about mental illness. *Journal of Clinical Psychology*, 1964, 20: 140-143.

Whatley, C. Social attitudes toward discharged mental patients. *Social Problems*, 1958-1959, 6: 313-320.

Wicker, A. Attitudes versus actions: The relationship of verbal and overt behavioral responses to attitude objects. *Journal of Social Issues*, 1969, 25: 41-78.

Williams, J., and H. M. Williams. Attitudes toward mental illness, anomia and authoritarianism among state hospital nursing students and attendants. *Mental Hygiene*, 1961, 45: 418-424.

Wright, F. H., and R. A. Klein. Attitudes of hospital personnel and the community regarding mental illness. *Journal of Counseling Psychology*, 1966, 13: 106-107.

Yamamoto, K., and H. F. Dizney. Rejection of the mentally ill: A study of attitudes of student teachers. *Journal of Counseling Psychology*, 1967, 14: 264-268.

*13*

# THE FAMILY AS REACTOR TO THE MENTAL ILLNESS OF A RELATIVE

DOLORES E. KREISMAN

and

VIRGINIA D. JOY

*New York State Department of Mental Hygiene*

One of the few persistent statistics to crop up in the mental health literature is that 30% of those discharged from mental hospitals return to the hospital during the first year following discharge. Over a longer period of time, the statistics are even bleaker. In New York State, for instance, more than 60% of all admissions to state hospitals are readmissions; and for many patients, rehospitalization has occurred more than once and has become a way of life. It has been customary to refer to this series of hospitalizations as the "career" of the mental patient.

The contemporary, widespread policy of short-term, multiple hospitalizations which has fostered this pattern means that the chronic patient continuously hospitalized for many years is becoming a thing of the past. No longer does a psychiatric hospitalization inaugurate a process by which the patient is increasingly removed from family view and contact and, ultimately, from family concern. On the contrary. For while foster care or halfway houses may figure prominently in the literature on rehabilitation of mental patients and may even be strongly recom-

AUTHORS' NOTE: The preparation of this article was supported in part by the National Institute of Mental Health Grant 1 RO MH 2157-02. Portions of this paper appeared in *Schizophrenia Bulletin*, NIMH, Fall 1974.

mended for specific patients, in reality the scarcity of these facilities most often results in the return of the patient to a family setting. This is particularly so in the early stages of the patient's career when it is tacitly assumed by both family and state that, should the family be available, it will replace the state as society's agent in the further care and control of the patient. This assumption probably holds whether the patient actually does return to the family, moves to his own quarters, or is a resident of a sheltered communal environment.

As a result of current hospital policy and the assumption of family responsibility, the family is more than ever involved in long-term interaction with the "former" patient. In light of these circumstances, it is puzzling that programs designed to maximize the probability of a patient's successful return to the community have not been more interested in the impact upon the family of that return. Perhaps this omission results from the fact that we remain tied to the traditional sociopsychological approach to the family which has been unidirectional and concerned mainly with the family as an etiological factor in the origin or outcome of the disorder. Consequently, family models of psychopathology based on the symptomatology of the parents, the specific types of interactions between parent and child, or the idea of a disorganized family social system have been widely used with varying degrees of success to explain the family's role in contributing to or maintaining the state in which the disordered person finds himself.

Yet, while the case for family etiology is still uncertain (Frank, 1965; Mosher and Gunderson, 1973), we do know that family members who have a psychiatric disorder can and frequently do have profound effects on other family members. The ambiguous nature of psychiatric illness (at least in its early stages) and the episodic eruptions of deviant behavior which cannot easily be interpreted within the conventional framework of normative behavior and which may be perceived as a threat to stable family relationships (Clausen, 1959) are stressors which are only partly alleviated with the definition of the problem as "mental illness". As often as not, both emotional and economic roles must shift as the family reorganizes itself to take on the responsibilities of a poorly functioning member. The patient may come to be considered a burden, not only because he cannot pull his own weight, but because the restrictions of living with a mentally ill person may disrupt the entire web of social relationships of other family members. For instance, if families feel more tied to the house when the patient returns home, they may find themselves unable to maintain satisfactory social relationships with other people and may become increasingly insulated and resentful.

With hospitalization or diagnosis, an individual is marked as mentally ill; and for some families, stigma with its consequences of shame and concealment becomes an important factor in their response to this stressful situation. In other families guilt may dominate, for unless they subscribe to a theory of etiology invoking gods, demons, or accidents of nature, they are confronted by the prevailing professional opinion that the family is in the main responsible for the condition of the patient. In still other families, the knowledge that someone close to them is sick may evoke enormous anxiety over their own vulnerability, with anger and rejection of the patient a possible outcome. In this connection, Bettelheim (1974) has suggested that the reason for the expressed attitude that the mentally ill are dangerous stems not so much from our feeling endangered by them as from a fear that we, too, might become this way.

It would be unwise, however, to consider this gloomy account of the possible reactions to the behavior or deficiencies of a sick member and the chronic strain entailed as the full picture. Some families, for at this point unspecified reasons, do have the psychological resources to cope with such a continuing and unsettling event. In fact, the family may be more empathic towards the deviant. That very sense of vulnerability which provokes anxiety may also result in a keener understanding of the patient's pain and his lack of responsibility for his present condition. For some families, the stress will result in a heightening of family solidarity and a fuller appreciation of the patient's meaning to them. The literature does offer some support for these views. As we shall see, the negative attitudes commonly found in the general public cannot be so easily attributed to family members. Stigma, for instance, is not reported by family members as often as might be expected. This is not untenable if one considers that a history of affectional ties to a person is likely to result in a definition of him which encompasses a great deal more than his deviance, thus mitigating the sense of stigma.

Given such a wide variety of possible reactions, each of which could be implicated in the success or failure of the posthospital career of the patient, it is indeed difficult to understand why the career of the family has been so sadly neglected. Only recently have investigators turned their attention to an investigation of the family as a reactor to the mental illness of a member. The results of such investigators are of critical importance to those concerned with rehabilitation, recidivism, and theories of family etiology.

For one thing, such a change of focus permits the specification of the kind of adaptation which occurs when a functioning family interacts over time with a deviant member for whom the family feels or is considered responsible. For another, it permits a fuller description of the system in which the patient operates, one to which he may return, and one which will, in all likelihood, be of great significance in determining his prognosis. In addition, research on the family as reactor (although the literature has rarely been used to this end) may help clarify issues of causality by isolating the part the family's reaction to deviance plays in the family's current interaction patterns. The frequently held assumptions in family etiology research that (1) the family's behavior instigates the patient's behavior, (2) the family we observe now has remained unchanged through time, and (3) any inferences of the past based on observations in the present are valid if they "make sense" have been legimately questioned by Fontana (1966) as being unnecessarily simple. They are clearly in need of correction and the inclusion of the family as a response rather than stimulus in the description of the patient's family system will immeasurably broaden its conception and permit an important first step to be taken toward the development of an interaction approach to the problems of etiology and rehabilitation.

The introduction of the family as a subject of study in the attempt to understand the response to mental illness occurred in the early 1950s when a theoretical interest in deviance and social control (Parsons, 1951, Schachter, 1951; and Festinger et al., 1952) and in social perception (Bruner and Tagiuri, 1954) provided a conceptual framework for social scientists who had become concerned with the mentally disordered patient and his family (Parsons and Fox, 1952; Yarrow, Schwartz, Murphy, and Deasy, 1955). Not too much later, the practical needs of hospital psychiatry to assess the effects of the then innovative programs of community care for mental patients turned the attentions of psychiatric researchers to the families of patients as agents of rehabilitation and bearers of burden (Brown, et al., 1958).

The convergence of these two lines of interest, practical and theoretical, led Clausen and Yarrow (1955) to undertake the pioneering research which dealt specifically with the problems and attitudes of the families of mental patients. They had little relevant research to guide them as their legitimately sparse bibliography made amply clear. Even as late as 1959, four years after the appearance of their report, a review of the literature by Spiegel and Bell for the *American Handbook of Psychiatry* cited Clausen and Yarrow as the major source for the section of the paper dealing with the impact of mental illness on the family.

The findings of the Clausen and Yarrow investigation reflected the natural history of the wife's reaction to her husband's deviant behavior. In ordering the literature to be reviewed in this article, we too will be employing a loosely defined natural history approach, one that derives somewhat from the presentation of Clausen and Yarrow and their associates but has the changes and extensions necessary to allow for the incorporation of new materials and different points of view. In this way we shall cover the evolution by the family of the mental illness hypothesis and the family's consequent attitudes and behavior in response to the labeling and hospitalization of the relative. In the final section we will be concerned with the relationship family attitudes, particularly tolerance of deviant behavior, have to outcome after discharge. Throughout, our intention has been to direct our colleagues' attention to an existent literature which, while scattered and not as coherent as might be desired, may still assist them in their conceptualization of the family-patient interaction and in evaluating the effect it may have on the patient's successful return to the community.

## THE FAMILY'S DEFINITION OF THE PROBLEM

Research on non-psychiatrically involved samples indicates that the public labels very few behaviors as indicating mental illness. There appears also to be a general consensus that the public's attitudes toward the mentally ill in affective, cognitive, and conative terms is largely negative (see Rabkin, 1972, and Chapter 12 in this volume for a review of opinions of mental illness). Given a definition of mental which is narrower than that used by professionals, and a setting in which attitudes are largely negative, how do families explain and react to the behavior of a relative who will later be labeled "mentally ill"?

The family's attempt to understand the meaning of the behaviors they observe is thought to follow a predictable course showing both acceptance and denial, certainty and uncertainty. It is not unlike Lederer's description (1952) of the reaction of patients to physical illness. He noted three definite, established stages of response. The first of these, the transition period from health to illness, was characterized by an awareness of symptoms, some anxiety over their presence, denial or minimization of symptoms, and some residual anger or passivity. If symptoms persisted and the interruption of everyday routines continued, then diagnosis and therapy resulted and the patient was encouraged to accept the "sick role". This marked the second stage. The third was concerned with convalescence and return to the functioning adult role again. For part of his formulation of this sequence, Lederer drew upon Roger Barker's (1948) earlier discussion of the physically disabled.

Lederer's analysis of the sick role was the product of his own observations and dealt primarily with the *patient's* changing perceptions. Yarrow, Schwartz, Murphy, and Deasy (1955) described a very similar process governing the *family's* coming to terms with the symptoms of mental illness. The wives of 33 patients hospitalized for mental disorder were interviewed a number of times from soon after the hospitalization of the husband until six months after the patient returned home or until one year after hospitalization. The investigators described the phases the wife went through in defining her husband's behavior: the shifting interpretations, the occasional outright denial, and the stable conclusion, once a threshold for tolerance had been reached, that the problem was psychiatric or, at least, one that could not be dealt with by the family alone. The family's naivete about psychiatric symptoms, the deviant's fluctuating behavior, and the observed presence of lesser forms of the symptoms in "normal" people—all acted as factors operating against a swift recognition of mental illness. Yarrow, Schwartz, Murphy, and Deasy (1955: 23) concluded, "The findings on the perceptions of mental illness by the wives of patients are in line with the general findings in studies of perception. Behavior which is unfamiliar and incongruent and unlikely in terms of current expectations and needs will not be readily recognized, and stressful or threatening stimuli will tend to be misperceived or perceived with difficulty or delay."

Psychological explanations of deviant behavior were rarely invoked by the family during the early stages of mental illness (decompensation). The most frequently given explanations tended to be those attributing the behavior to character weakness, physical ailments, or situational factors. For instance, only 24% of the mainly middle-class wives in Yarrow, Schwartz, Murphy, and Deasy's study (1955) saw something seriously wrong or mentally wrong when their husbands first displayed overt symptoms. When such interpretations were made, anger was occasionally used as a means of social control in an attempt to bring the husband's behavior into line. By the time successive redefinitions had taken place and hospitalization was imminent, slightly less than one-third of the total sample of the wives of neurotics and psychotics and 20% of the wives of the psychotic patients still denied that their husbands were mentally ill.

Similarly, 18% of Lewis and Zeichner's (1960) sample of the families of 109 first admissions at three Connecticut state hospitals denied the patient's mental illness when they were first interviewed approximately three weeks after a family member's hospitalization. In 40% of the cases the illness was first recognized by a physician or someone outside the family. Mayo, Havelock, and Simpson (1971) reported that 19 nonpsychotic men in a mental hospital and their wives tended to accept a physical view of the husband's illness and that this general disbelief in the psychological determinants of the patients' state was at variance with the staff's view of the nature of the illness.

Some attempts at identifying the correlates of a psychological versus nonpsychological point of view were made in the works of Hollingshead and Redlich (1958), Freeman (1961), and Linn (1966). In the first two studies, social class or education was the moderating variable; in the last, family relationship. In Hollingshead and Redlich's sample of New Haven residents, the families of the three lowest class patients (Classes III, IV and V) showed a marked tendency to rely on somatic theories, heredity, or the "evil eye" to explain the aberrant behavior. Classes I and II, on the other hand, had more rational and detailed information about their relative's illness and explained the deviance on the basis of nerve strain, fatigue, or overwork. In contrast to Hollingshead and Redlich, Freeman (1961) found that education, but not other indicators of social class, and age were factors in the attitudes of relatives of discharged patients in the Boston area. He studied the relationship between the attitudes relatives held regarding the etiology of mental illness, attitudes toward mental hospitals, the normality of former patients and the imputed responsibility of patients for their condition. A psychogenic view was related to feeling that the patient could recover and was not to blame for his illness. On the whole, better educated and younger relatives had more positive attitudes to the patient.

Linn (1966) interviewed either the wives or mothers of 34 recently hospitalized schizophrenic men and found that mothers more often than wives had a psychological explanation of cause, while wives tended to impute physical and environmental causes to the behavior of their husbands. Linn reasoned that, because wives more than mothers were concerned with role performance, they were more likely to see the illness in terms of negligence in fulfilling role obligations, that is to say, as a function of character weakness (e.g., idleness) or as a result of environmental problems.

The view that motivation and values could affect the perception of other people, so much a part of the *zeitgeist* of the 1950s, generated an interest in the psychological impediments to a mental illness explanation of deviant behavior. Generally, it was assumed that the closer the relationship to the deviant, the greater the perceived threat and anxiety resulting from a psychological definition of the deviance, with the consequence that, all other things being equal, closeness results in delay or outright denial. Schwartz (1957) was the first to observe and report the occurrence of this phenomenon in her investigation of the family's response to the mental illness of a member. Shortly after, Rose's (1959) study of the families of hospitalized patients in Massachusetts and Mills's (1962) impressions of English families in a similar situation both offered corroboration that the closer the tie of the relative, the less ready was the family to perceive mental illness.

Still further confirmation came from Sakamoto (1969) who concluded on the basis of his experiences as a family therapist in Japan that, for mental illness, *distance* appears to facilitate a diagnosis of psychological disturbance. He conjectured that it was a particular type of closeness, the symbiotic tie between parent and child, which functioned to impede the parents' early recognition of their sons' schizophrenia. Sakamoto did not believe that this relationship was culturally determined and found support for his conclusion in the observation of the same phenomenon in families of American patients (Wynne et al., 1958).

This line of research has not gone unchallenged, and the simple hypothesis that closeness is associated with delayed recognition has not stood the test of time. Both the type of symptom and aspects of the patient-family relationship have been shown to be related to the recognition of mental illness.

Using a focused interview technique, Clausen (1959) interviewed the spouses of 23 male and female schizophrenics and concluded that, where symptomatic behavior was directed against the spouse, there was more likelihood that a deviance framework would be used to interpret the behavior. Safilios-Rothschild (1968) replicated Clausen's study in Greece and confirmed his findings. In fact, Safilios-Rothschild disputed Schwartz's original hypothesis because she found that spouses who were maritally satisfied, and therefore assumedly close, did not arrive at a deviance explanation later than dissatisfied spouses. Both Clausen and Safilios-Rothschild observed that the definition of the behavior as deviant actually resulted in feelings of relief for the spouse since the marriage was no longer perceived of as threatened.

In another study (Sampson et al., 1962), two types of marital accommodations were isolated which were so high in their tolerance of deviance that either the patient or the community were responsible for first labeling the behavior as deviance and then arranging for hospitalization. Yet neither of these accommodations could conventionally be called close, and in both cases it was the withdrawal from the deviant early in the marital relationship which permitted bizarre behavior either to go unnoticed or to be explained in normal terms. Sampson and his associates intensively interviewed 17 schizophrenic women and their husbands during and after the wife's first hospitalization and found that some marriages were characterized by mutual withdrawal, others by the wife's continued intense relationship to her mother. In both situations it was not until the conventional accommodation was threatened and new role behaviors required that the deviant behavior become troublesome and, consequently, noticed.

Perhaps the hypothesis that emotional closeness delays labeling has attracted more attention than other problems in family labeling because it was clearly stated and could be derived from a popular theoretical position (perceptual defense theory). As a consequence, research on this hypothesis has done more than demonstrate the existence of an imperfect relationship between closeness and delay. More complex interactions invoking such variables as quality of the relationship between patient and family and whether symptoms are directed against a family member have resulted in alterations in the original formulation.

It is puzzling that symptoms, the observable manifestation of mental illness, have not been more widely examined with regard to labeling. The manner of onset, the nature of symptomatic behavior, and the family's ability to tolerate those symptoms being displayed are likely to have some effect on the rapidity with which the problem is defined. For instance, when onset is gradual and symptoms not too bizarre, as is frequently the case in the undifferentiated chronic schizophrenic, deviance may come to be expected of the individual, interpreted as "normal" for him, and may not be perceived as especially different or upsetting. Similarly, a high tolerance of deviance, resulting from the interaction of personal history and cultural expectations, may also serve to retard a psychological explanation of the deviant behavior.

Three articles in the literature deal with typologies or classifications of the family's response to the mental illness of a member. Because these typologies have not been tested on samples other than the original and do not appear to have generated further research, neither their utility nor their heuristic power has been demonstrated. It is possible that they have not been used because it is expected that they will suffer, as do most typologies, from a lack of generalizability to new samples, an incomplete description of the data, or the inability of researchers other than the originator to use them satisfactorily. In any event, the absence of any follow-up study of these systems of classification makes it difficult to ascertain their value or deficiencies.

Korkes's (1959) interview study of the parents of 100 schizophrenic children yielded four basic "ideal" types: (1) The Dissociative-Organic Type—parents falling into this category disavowed responsibility for the child's condition and generally offered a biological explanation for it; (2) The Affiliative Type—this type of family acknowledged its own interpersonal influences as etiological factors; (3) The Dissociative-Social Type—the parents disavowed any responsibility and offered an extrafamilial explanation for the disorder; (4) A residual category composed of parents who were highly and continually uncertain about etiology and the role they themselves played in their child's illness. Korkes's data supported her expectation that parents who accepted personal responsibility were more liekly to undergo profound changes in personal values, marital relationships, and child-rearing behavior. These parents perceived the patient as a human being with comprehensible responses who could be included in family life.

Two aspects of family response to deviance interact in an effort by Spitzer, Morgan, and Swanson (1971) to develop a typology describing the family's role in the evolution of the psychiatric patient's career. The family's level of expected performance and its propensity to label the deviance in conjunction with the family's appraisal of deviance, its decision to utilize psychiatric help, and its implementation of psychiatric care yielded eight family subtypes. The subtypes bear such engaging names as stoics, poltroons, happenchancers, and do nothings. Yet the substantive description of each subtype does not seem to be precisely derivable from the component variables in the system. The authors, however, were able to classify 76 of the 79 families of first admission patients in the above typology.

A concern with the sociocultural determinants of definitions of mental illness led Schwartz (1957) to order three commonly occurring definitions of deviance (characterological, somatic, and psychological) along four variables (partial-global extent, alterability, recent-remote occurrence, and situational-somatogenicpsychogenic cause). Eighty percent of her sample of wives of recently admitted patients were found to give psychological explanations ("not completely crazy" or "out of his mind") of their husband's illness. A patient who was defined as "out of his mind" was thought to have a global, unalterable, and recently occurring illness. In contrast, being "not completely crazy" was alterable, of recent origin, and only partially disabling. None of these definitions could be differentiated by cause.

Whatever the value of these particular typologies, it is clear in reviewing the research on family labeling that families attempting to define the problem posed by psychologically deviant behavior acted as do most people when confronted with ambiguous or stressful stimuli. They generally engaged in a process of redefinition in which they were slow, first, to view their sick member as deviant, and second, to view him as a deviant because of psychological aberrations. As expected, education and social class, which are associated with greater psychological sophistication and therefore reduce ambiguity, were related to the type of explanation utilized. Intimacy or psychological closeness acted as an impediment to labeling the behavior as deviant only if symptoms were not directed against a significant other. In certain cases, withdrawal, not intimacy, in an ostensibly close relationship explained the delay in defining the behavior appropriately. These findings have led to a revision of the original closeness-delay hypothesis.

## THE FAMILY'S ATTITUDES TOWARD THEIR DEVIANT MEMBER

By the time hospitalization occurs, most families have come to believe that their deviant member is mentally ill. The possible consequences of such a belief can be theoretically represented by a wide range of affective and behavioral responses. On the one hand, families could show increased support and tolerance for their ill member and, because of their concern, be more aware of affectionate ties. Such positive affect would be a reaction similar to that frequently shown the physically ill. On the other hand, quite different responses may occur. When symptoms are unpredictable or bizarre, the family may become fearful. Anger may occur because of the patient's disruptiveness, or because of family resentment due to increased strain. In cases where the appearance of mental illness arouses guilt, or if the illness is evaluated in moral terms, attitudes of shame and rejection might be expected. In reality, it is likely that a complex amalgam of all of these best represents the family's evaluation with variables such as length and number of hospitalizations, type of symptoms, prehospitalization family interaction, prognosis, and socio-cultural status, to cite a few, determining the intensity with which such attitudes are held. A neutral affective dimension of family attitudes appears unlikely since hospitalization cannot help but be a significant event in the family's experience.

Despite the wide range of possible responses to deviance in the family, professional interest seems to have concentrated on the negative response to the patient and particularly on the issue of stigma, with the consequence that shame or stigma and social rejection have been among the most studied aspects of family attitudes and behavior. Such a limited focus is probably the result of two factors: (1) a generalization to the family of the negative opinions the general public holds (see

Rabkin, 1972), and (2) the commonly held assumption shared by many mental health professionals that mental illness is indeed shameful.

In his essays on stigma, Goffman (1963) has not only summarized and elaborated on the professional consensus about the public's reaction to deviance but has provided some insights into the mitigating role which intimacy can play in that reaction. As a rule, when interaction is minimal and affective regard is low, the stigmatized person is assigned a nonhuman quality. The assignment of this quality to the deviant permits the environment to discriminate against him and encourages those who interact with him to behave as if the stigma were the essence of the person. The inevitable outcome of this process is generally believed to be rejection of the deviant.

However, the more intimate the relationship between the stigmatized and the other, the less the stigma defines the person so that closeness permits one to see qualities other than the flaw. But to be associated with a stigmatized person brings with it its own dilemma. Since a close relationship results in being "tainted" oneself, a relative can choose either to embrace the fate of the stigmatized person and identify with him, or to reject sharing the discredit of the stigmatized person by avoiding or terminating the relationship.

Goffman presents a persuasive and tenable case the occurrence of stigma and rejection in response to mental illness, but research on this point, as we shall see, is far from conclusive. People who have had close contact with mental patients do not appear to be as prejudiced against them as those who have not, but there is little evidence that they accept the fate of the stigmatized person for themselves. At the same time, when rejection does occur it is not clear that its antecedents are to be found mainly in the family's sense of its own stigmatization.

Yet even within the limitations which a stigma-social rejection framework imposes, certain gaps in research interest are apparent. The literature on the family's affective response to the patient is unquestionably scant and simplistic, and research on the beliefs families of the mentally ill have about patients generally, and about their patient in particular, is virtually nonexistent. A study such as that carried out by Nunnally (1961) on the structural coherence of the affective and cognitive components of the public's attitudes toward the mentally ill has yet to be done with the family as its subject.

Social rejection studies reflecting the anticipated or actual behavioral outcome of interaction with a deviant are, as expected, more numerous. They are technically more sophisticated, but they are not especially complex in their conceptualization of the possible antecedents of rejection.

## Studies of the Family's Affective Response

The family's affective response is generally assessed either through direct questioning or by use of a semi-structured interview which maximizes the probability of the occurrence of affective responses. Occasionally affect is inferred from behavioral measures, as in the case of shame where withdrawal from friends or the concealment of the patient's illness is considered sufficient to justify the inference.

One of the earliest studies (Yarrow, Clausen, and Robbins, 1955) examining family attitudes did so in the context of Lewin's (1948) social psychological theory of minority group belonging. Families in that sample behaved as if they were minority group members and characteristically showed feelings of underprivilege, marginality, extreme sensitivity, and self-hatred. Fear of the patient was reported by Waters and Northover (1965), who interviewed the wives of long-term schizophrenic patients two to five years after discharge. Wives were often found to be frightened of their husbands and experienced long periods of tension in the home. Schwartz (1956) and Clausen (1959) reported a considerable amount of anger and resentment on the part of husbands and wives toward their mentally disordered spouses prior to hospitalization.

Some studies have gone beyond the descriptive level. Hollingshead and Redlich (1958) examined social class differences in the family response to mental illness and found that, while resentment and fear were prevalent reactions in lower class families, shame and guilt were more pronounced in the upper classes. However, a more intensive interview of a schizophrenic subsample (N = 25) in that study (Myers and Roberts, 1959) indicated that shame at having an "insane person" in the family was a common reaction in Class V, the lowest social class. As a result of this shame and a general reluctance to involve themselves with authorities, Class V patients were most often hospitalized by people outside the family. In contrast, Class III families sought a physician's help once decompensation occurred and seemed to be more concerned with the patient's recovery than with feelings of shame and futility.

The general trend, however, despite the expectations of social scientists or the anticipations of common sense, is for families to report little fear, shame, anger, or guilt. For example, about 50% of Lewis and Zeichner's (1960) sample expressed a sympathetic understanding of the patient, only 17% expressed hostility or fear, and the remainder were either ambivalent or puzzled at their relatives' illness. In Rose's study (1959) relatively little stigma and shame were evident in the feelings of family members.

The most positive response to the mentally ill occurred in a sample of Cape Coloured families in South Africa. The families of a group of never hospitalized chronic schizophrenics appeared to have great warmth and love for the sick person (Gillis and Keet, 1965). Even those families in the comparison group who had hospitalized a relative continued to express great sympathy for him and maintained regular contact with him.

Theoretically, feelings of shame and stigma should be particularly aroused in situations where a public display of deviance makes the label obvious to onlookers, when, as Goffman would say, the "descredit" is clearly observable. When unusual behavior is not evident, then it is less likely that shame would be a salient aspect of the attitude toward the patient. For instance, when families worry little about embarrassing behaviors or behaviors that cause trouble to the neighbors, as occurred in Grad and Sainsbury's study (1963b), one might deduce that symptoms are neither bizarre nor easily noticeable. In that case, little shame would be expected. This relationship was somewhat confirmed in a two year study of home care for schizophrenic patients by Pasamanick, Scarpetti, and Dinitz (1967). The main study group consisted of potential patients who were returned to the home at the point when admission to the hospital was sought. Potential patients were given drugs or placebo, visited regularly by a nurse, and seen occasionally by a psychiatrist. The same treatment was given a second group of "ambulatory schizophrenics" (cases referred to the study by clinics or physicians in the area) who were living at home and had never sought admission to the state hospital. In both the main group and the ambulatory group, a comparison of family response at intake and six months after revealed that an already low level of shame and fear (approximately 15%) lessened even more over time for both the drug and placebo groups. At the six month interview, drug condition made no difference in family reports for the ambulatory group; however, for the main group, only 2% of the families in the drug sample reported being ashamed or afraid, while 7% of the families in the placebo sample were ashamed and 13% were afraid. Because patient behavior was, in part, related to experimental condition, and because shame and fear decreased after contact with the hospital, it appears that, where shame and fear do occur, they are as likely to be the consequences of unrestrained behavior as of the formal labeling of the patient.

The relationship of secrecy, concealment, and withdrawal from friends to feelings of shame and the perception of stigma seems obvious, and Yarrow, Clausen, and Robbins (1955) and Goffman (1963) have been concerned with this problem. Goffman, whose formulations are similar to Lewin's (1948), distinguished between the discredited person who is obviously marked, and the discreditable person whose stigma is not so noticeable. For the discreditable person and his close associates, concealment is possible, and the problem for them then becomes one of information management if secrecy is desired. How then do families deal with the question of information sharing about the sick person?

No studies have examined the issue of noticeability of symptoms and the ease with which they can be defined as signs of psychological aberration and related these variables to secrecy. Thus the test of the connection between secrecy and discreditability has not yet been made. There are indications, however, that, at least for some families, efforts at concealment do occur.

One-third of the wives in Yarrow, Clausen, and Robbins's (1955) study demonstrated a pattern of aggressive concealment. Friends were dropped or avoided, and occasionally respondents moved to a different part of town. Another third of the wives had a few favored people to whom they talked, people who would understand the problem or who had been in a similar plight. The family who shared the "taint" was almost always told, particularly if they were living close by, and sometimes blamed. The remaining third could be described as communicating extensively, and expressed fewest fears of dire social consequences. While two-thirds of the sample had deliberately concealed the information about their husbands' illness to a greater or lesser degree, everyone had told at least one person outside the family, usually a personal friend.

Rose's (1959) sample did not report such seclusive behavior. He interviewed the principal or next-of-kin visitor of a sample of 100 currently hospitalized patients in a Veterans Administration Hospital in Massachusetts. The median hospital stay for the patients was nine years. The majority of the relatives spoken with claimed that they felt no stigma and that they had discussed the illness with other people. In 1961, Freeman and Simmons reported the results of a five-item index of stigma developed for use in their long-term study of the families of recently discharged mental patients. The items dealt primarily with the respondent's behavior with regard to secrecy and social withdrawal. Only 10% of the sample indicated agreement with two or more of the items, and only 12% agreed with the most popular stigma item, "not telling fellow workers about the patient." Six percent reported avoiding friends. Agreement with at least one of the stigma items was positively related to severity of symptoms (a finding similar to that of Pasamanick, Scarpetti, and Dinitz, 1967), social class, and a perception that "others" were unfriendly to them.

Unlike the results in Yarrow, Clausen, and Robbins's study, a very few of the people in Rose's and Freeman and Simmons's samples reported avoiding friends. This contradiction may be due to the different types of respondents sampled. Yarrow, Clausen, and Robbins's sample consisted of the wives of first admission patients. Rose's sample included the relatives of long-term patients, and Freeman and Simmons's sample was mixed in terms of number of hospitalizations. It is likely that experience with mental illness plays a role in the eventual reaction of the family to the patient. If this is so, a person faced with the first hospitalization of a relative may feel shame and anger and try to conceal the hospitalization but still not reject the patient, while those people whose relatives have been hospitalized a number of times, or for prolonged periods, may have accommodated themselves to the situation and no longer keenly feel and report shame. Lengthy or multiple hospitalizations may make impossible any attempts at concealment and may erode much of the willingness of the family to tolerate once again the patient's disruptive presence. So few studies have reported an analysis of their data in terms of number or length or hospitalizations that the process of accommodation to recurrent or prolonged disturbance in family life is virtually uncharted.

Social class was related to the openness with which the patient's illness was discussed in the Hollingshead and Redlich study (1958). There was a marked tendency for most relatives in all classes to be secretive about the mental illness; however, the ostensible reasons for secretiveness differed in each class. Class I showed the least overt concern. Classes II and III worried about how public knowledge would affect the families chances of getting ahead. Class IV reported the classic shame associated with stigma, and Class V was secretive because of a wish to prevent snooping and interference with the family. Similar results were found by Myers and Bean (1968) in their 10 year follow-up of part of the Hollingshead and Redlich sample.

On the whole, the pattern of results with behavioral indicators of stigma (reports of concealment) confirms that of attitudinal studies of affect. Shame, fear, and anger are present in some cases, but do not appear to occupy as central a position as might be expected. It is difficult to draw any clear conclusions about the response of family members from these studies, but it would be unwarranted to underestimate the presence of negative affect even where data is reported to the contrary.

As in other areas of attitude measurement on sensitive issues, negative affect is generally underreported, and the absence of any controls for social desirability or acquiescence makes it almost impossible to judge the extent to which the respondents' statements truly reflect their evaluations. It is possible, of course, that further research utilizing better measurement devices and exploring interactions rather than main effects will result in a sharper and more accurate picture of the family's feelings about a patient member. However, it seems equally important to expand the conceptual and theoretical notions which have determined the variables chosen for research if a fuller, more complex picture is to emerge.

While contemporary usage generally regards the affective dimension as the major defining dimension for attitudes, this does not mean that nonevaluative beliefs or behavioral predispositions are unimportant. A conceptualization of attitudes which involves affective, cognitive, and behavioral components allows one to speak meaningfully of the psychological structure of an attitude, to investigate the relationship among these components, to assess and predict the effect of change in one on the other, and to relate these data to behavior.

Much of the research on attitudes, particularly in the mental health field, attempts to measure action tendencies and is ultimately concerned with the prediction of overt behavior. This is certainly a most difficult task, requiring as it does knowledge of the actor's feelings, beliefs, and postulated action tendencies along with knowledge of the situational and cultural demands impinging on him. Situations of any complexity are likely to render a number of attitude systems relevant at the same time, and attempts at predicting outcome from a single variable are likely to meet with failure. To give just one example, a family may be thought to provide a proper setting for the rehabilitation of a patient because they express affection and warmth toward the patient and want him home. Yet the family's beliefs about the impossibility of their ability to care for him or their fear of his bizarre behavior may show themselves in stringent attempts to monitor his activities upon his return, and this in turn may effectively sabotage the patient's attempts at rehabilitation.

### Studies of Social Rejection

Studies of the behavioral component of attitudes toward the mentally ill can most easily be grouped under the heading of social rejection since they measure a projected tendency to accept or reject a person or class of people.

Much of the research on this subject has drawn heavily on work done in the social psychology of ethnic prejudice, and, in fact, the principle measuring tool used in studies of rejection of the mentally ill (the social distance scale) was developed by Bogardus in 1925 to ascertain the degree of intimacy permitted by one group of people to another. The social distance scale consists of a number of ordered statements which vary the degree of intimacy of social interaction. The respondent is asked to indicate for each item whether he will accept a particular type of interaction with a *hypothetical* person; for example, whether he would permit a mentally ill person to work with him or to dine at his home or to marry his daughter. A person's attitude is inferred from the highest level of interaction he will accept with the target person.

The remaining studies in this section have focused on the family's attitude or actual behavior toward their hospitalized member and the willingness of the family to reaccept the patient into the home once discharge is a possibility.

*Social Distance.* To determine the avoidance reactions of the general public to former mental patients, Whatley (1959) administered an eight-item social distance scale to 2,001 persons in Louisiana. The eight items ranged from those involving "minimal ego involvement" (associating with a former mental patient) to those with "maximal ego involvement" (permitting a person who has been in psychiatric treatment to babysit with your child). The results generally indicated that the younger and more educated the respondent, the more likely he was to be willing to admit a former mental patient into a close relationship with him. Whatley additionally asked questions about whether the respondent had ever visited a mental hospital or, more crucial for our purposes, knew of any reported cases of mental illness in the family. Neither visiting a mental hospital nor having a mentally ill person in the family had any effect on attitudes toward the mentally ill.

Bizon, Godorowski, Henisz, and Razniewski (no date) studied a quota sample of Warsaw's residents and found that the closer the previous contact with the mentally ill, the greater was the expressed willingness to accompany former mental patients to the theater, to invite them to a birthday party, and to befriend them on a lonely trip.

The results of Chin-Shong's study (1968) of attitudes toward the mentally ill in an extremely heterogeneous, urban American sample (N=151) appear less than clear-cut. Using a social distance scale similar to Whatley's, Chin-Shong examined the effects of degree of closeness to a particular mental patient on social distance from mental patients generally. Analysis of the data showed that there was a significant decrease in attitudinal distance to the hypothetical patient if the respondent had a close tie with an actual mental patient; however, the results were not linear. There was more acceptance if the patient known was a close friend than if he was a family member. It appears that having a patient in the family was sufficiently threatening to mitigate some of the effects of intimacy. While the effect of family ties in this study were not strong, they were not absent as in Whatley's original study.

Chin-Shong's data further suggested that knowing many patients casually was less effective in decreasing rejection than being closely related to a patient. People with close ties to mental patients, unlike those without them, did not reject the hypothetical patient more when they perceived him to be dangerous and accepted him more when they judged their patient-relatives to have improved. Chin-Shong interpreted this as supporting Goffman's contention that intimacy forces an awareness of the other personal characteristics of the stigmatized person. Age and education continued to be correlated in the expected direction with attitudes toward mental patients.

The question of the impact of hospitalization and its consequences for labeling was the focus of Phillips's work (1963). Phillips, like Scheff (1963), believes that the symptoms of mental illness are not easily identifiable by the lay public and that other cues are therefore necessary to define the behavior as mental illness. One such cue is the source of help that is sought to deal with the problem. Phillips studied the relationship of the type of help source to the evaluation of five people described in Star's (1955) vignettes of psychiatric syndromes in a sample of 300 married white women living in a suburb in northeastern United States. The description of a psychiatrically symptomatic person and the help source were varied in a Graeco-Latin square design. After each vignette the respondent was asked a series of social distance questions. For each form of sickness described, the rejection score was less when no help source was mentioned and highest when the mental hospital was mentioned as the help source. This basic association was maintained within age groups, religious groups, and social class groups. However, if the respondent had known either a family member or friend who had actually sought help for emotional problems, the rejection scores changed. If a *respondent's* relative had sought help, then, in the hypothetical cases, rejection was highest if either *no help was sought* or *if the help source was a hospital,* and rejection was lowest for those whose help source was a physician. Overall, respondents with family members who had been mentally ill were less rejecting than those having a friend or knowing no one with emotional problems.

Swanson and Spitzer (1970) wanted to test three hypotheses derived from Goffman's formulations. Specifically, they were interested in: (1) how people who are mentally ill stigmatize others who are similarly afflicted; (2) how relatives of the mentally ill stigmatize the mentally ill; and (3) how the propensity of the patient and his family to stigmatize changes as the patient moves through the prepatient, inpatient, and postpatient phases. Six hundred and seventy patients and their families were interviewed at different points in the patients' career using Whatley's social distance scale. The results on family attitudes indicated that the significant others were less rejecting of the mentally ill than the patients themselves and were considerably more stable in attitude from phase to phase. This tolerance was unaffected by age, sex, social class, or diagnosis of the patient. Swanson and Spitzer see this as evidence of a general solution of the dilemma of the tainted person. Because the attitudes of the significant others were more accepting than those of the patients, they concluded that the family had embraced the patient's fate rather than the alternative of avoiding or terminating the existing relationship.

All in all, there is a slight trend for people who have had close contact with the mentally ill to be less rejecting in terms of the degree of social interaction they say they will accept. This conclusion can only be made very warily, however, since the paucity of studies on this topic limits the generalizability of the results.

*Visiting.* Visiting seemed on the whole to be an excellent indicator of the family's attachment to the patient. While abandonment was occasionally reported, it was generally related to chronicity (Rose, 1959; Sommer, 1959; Rawnsley et al., 1962), class (Myers and Roberts, 1959; Myers and Bean, 1968), or age (Rose, 1959).

The study that most completely described visiting behavior was carried out by Rawnsley, Loudon, and Miles (1962) in Wales. The records of 230 public and private patients were searched to determine whether the patients were visited, how often they were visited, and by whom. Although 67% of the patients in the study had spent more than two continuous years in the hospital, 72% of the total sample were visited at least once during the year. Twenty percent of the patients had absolutely no visible contact (visits, parcels or letters) with anyone outside the hospital. For all age groups, visiting was inversely correlated with length of hospital stay. Visiting was more frequent for married patients than for single patients, but after ten years of hospitalization, single men and married women were the two least visited groups.

The patient's "deculturation" as a result of prolonged hospitalization was the subject of Sommer's studies of letter writing (1958) and visiting (1959). Approximately 12% of the 1,600 patients in a mental hospital in Saskatchewan had been visited at least once during the three-week study period, and 10% had either sent or received a letter during a later two-week period. When these patients were compared to a random sample of the hospital's patient population, it was found that contact was related to sex and length of stay in the hospital. Women sent and received more letters and were visited more often. Patients who had been hospitalized longer had fewer visitors and less letter-writing contact. Interestingly enough, distance between hospital and home residence was not related to visiting behavior.

An informal analysis of interviews with 100 patients' relatives revealed that younger patients and those with fewer years of hospitalization had more family contact (Rose, 1959). This finding is similar to those of Rawnsley and associates and Sommer. The principal visitor was more likely to be the mother (a reflection of the fact that most of the sample of patients was unmarried); but when wives were the principal visitors, patients were visited less often than when parents were the principal visitors.

In contrast to Rose's study Yarrow, Clausen, and Robbins (1955) found that wives and children of patients visited regularly, but that parents and in-laws, who would visit in the early weeks of hospitalization, were unlikely to return after one or two visits. The patient's mother was sometimes an exception to this pattern. Schwartz (1956), reporting on the same data, lists four reasons for the drop in visiting. All have an underlying anxiety dimension and deal mainly with the patient's unpredictability of behavior and his nonperformance of role functions.

It appears in one study that, when the patient is visited, he is visited often; but that when he is not visited, he is completely abandoned. Evans, Bullard, and Solomon (1961) found that 20% of their sample had not been visited at all during the previous year. However, 75% of those who were visited were seen at least once a month. This is a considerable degree of contact, especially in view of the fact that all of these patients had been hospitalized for at least five years, and 50% of the family sample was pessimistic about outcomes for their patient-relatives.

Gillis and Keet (1965) interviewed a sample of 16 hospitalized and 16 nonhospitalized chronic schizophrenics and their relatives. Both samples consisted of South African Cape Coloureds, and were fairly well matched in demographic characteristics. The average duration of illness in both groups was eight years. Where the patients were hospitalized, the relatives were not uninterested in the welfare of the patient. Their families visited and brought gifts; they simply did not want the patient home. By placing the patient in the hospital, they had absolved themselves of all responsibility for the patient's condition and now saw the doctor as the main figure in the care of the patient.

A relationship between social class and visiting patterns was observed by Myers and Roberts (1959) and Myers and Bean (1968). These studies indicated that less visiting, gift giving, and correspondence occurred in Class V than in any other class.

The Gillis and Keet study is particularly interesting because it sets into juxta-position two measures of social rejection: visiting and reaccepting the patient. Under most circumstances visiting is less likely than reaccepting the patient to be burdensome and/or disorganizing to the family, even when the hospital is a considerable distance from the home. One person may be delegated or take on the responsibility of providing support for the patient and acting as the intermediary with the hospital, thus relieving the other members of the family of the need to concern themselves with the patient. (This may account for the dropping away of most of the family reported in Yarrow, Clausen, and Robbins, 1955; and in Schwartz, 1956). Not visiting can consequently be considered the strongest measure of rejection. While visiting and rejection of the patient's presence in the household seemed to be strongly related in some studies (Alivisatos and Lyketsos, 1964; Myers and Bean, 1968), they were apparently independent in others (Gillis and Keet, 1965; Rose, 1959). The relationship between visiting and the propensity to accept the patient on discharge would appear to yield a useful index of attachment to, or rejection of, the patient.

*Reaccepting the Patient.* Cumming and Cumming (1957) have recounted an instance where a woman, who had openly complained of being subjected to "sex rays" for many years, was shunned by her sister only after she had been hos-pitalized briefly. The sister, unwilling to take the patient home where she had been living continuously until her hospitalization, declared that, now that her sister was sick, there was no telling what she might do. The Cummings commented somewhat ironically, "Mental illness, it seems, is a condition which afflicts people who must go to a mental institution, but up until they go almost anything they do is fairly normal" (1957: 101). While this may be something of an exaggeration, there is evidence that expectations about cure and homecoming are more pessimistic among family members than among the public at large.

In one of the rare studies comparing *beliefs* about mental patients in relatives and nonrelatives, Swingle (1965) asked guests at an "Open House" at a Veterans Administration hospital to judge how many mental patients out of a hundred behaved in certain specified ways. He found that relatives expected approximately 50% of all mental patients to be incapable of returning home after treatment. Nonrelatives (guests with no relatives or acquaintances in the hospital) expected fewer patients (40%) to be unable to return home. Swingle also reported trends for relatives to believe that more patients would always remain patients and to perceive fewer patients as being able to conduct themselves properly in town on a one-day pass. However, relatives and nonrelatives did not differ in their perception of the friendliness or violence of mental patients.

This pessimism about recovery has its behavioral counterparts in studies dealing expressly with family response to a patient-relative's discharge. Rose (1959) observed that, while most families were verbally agreeable to the idea of discharge, they became resistant once the likelihood of discharge was a reality. Reluctance to take the patient home increased with the number of years the patient had spent in the hospital (see also Rawnsley, Loudon, and Miles, 1962).

Hollingshead and Redlich (1958) noticed a similar reluctance to have the patient return in some of the families they studied and offered a social class explanation for this behavior. Since Classes IV and V (the two lowest social classes) tended least often to have a psychological explanation for the deviant behavior they were exposed to, the authors had assumed that more deviance was generally tolerated in these two classes. However, on closer examination, they discovered that many patients in Class V were not discharged because nobody wanted to take them home. This last finding was confirmed and elaborated on by Myers and Bean (1968), who interviewed 387 of the 1,563 relatives of patients who were originally in Hollingshead and Redlich's sample. They found that, with each successive hospitalization, more lower class families cut ties with the patient. The harsh reaction to the label of mental illness, as well as the alleviation of a sense of burden in the families, operated to reduce contact with the patient and interest in him. As a result, discharges in the lower classes decreased more over time than in any other class.

Perhaps the harshest judgment of patients recorded was made by the families of 300 chronic hospitalized schizophrenics in Greece. Alivisatos and Lyketsos (1964) had hypothesized that, in a traditional society where the moral obligations of the family were still strong and there were few special agencies to treat the mentally ill, patients or former patients would be readily reaccepted into the family. Instead, the investigators found that many families ceased to consider the ill person as a family member and felt no obligation for his care at all. Families who originally had been, on the whole, quick to hospitalize (70% sought help within a year after they suspected a problem) were slow to accept the patient home again (88% of the total sample wanted the patient to remain in the hospital). In almost 50% of the sample, the family required total cure as a condition for reaccepting the patient.

Another form of social rejection, the desire to separate from the patient and, more important, an actual separation or divorce from the patient, is a measure of the response to patients by people who have an acquired, terminable relationship to them. Rogler and Hollingshead (1965) did a multiple interview study of 20 married lower-class Puerto Rican couples in which at least one of the spouses was schizophrenic and compared their responses with those of 20 neighboring couples with no known history of psychiatric disorder. When asked whether they would marry the same person, a different person, or not marry at all if they had the decision to make today, fewer of the spouses of schizophrenics would marry the same person than would spouses of normals.

Where divorce rates for patients are compared to rates in the general public, they are generally higher. Adler (1955) reported an increased divorce rate for her patient population, and former patients in an English sample had a divorce and separation rate three times the national average (Brown, Bone, Dalison, and Wing, 1966). Seven of the eleven married chronic schizophrenic patients who had been selected for special treatment by Evans and associates (1961) had either been divorced or were separated.

Not all studies indicated such bleak rejection on the part of the family. Some studies reported more favorable attitudes to discharge, and it appeared that the patient's return was welcome. Evans, Bullard, and Solomon (1961) interviewed the families of chronic hospitalized schizophrenics who were in a special program preparing them for discharge. Almost 50% of the families favored the release of patients who had been hospitalized for five years or more. Most of these families had a hopeful but realistic view of the patient's future behavior.

Freeman and Simmons (1963) found that 95% of their informants and other family members wanted the patient to live in the household. Similar figures were reported by Brown, Bone, Dalison, and Wing (1966) in a study of 251 English families who were seen five years after the discharge of a schizophrenic relative. Seventy-five percent of the families welcomed the patient home, 15% accepted him, and only 12% wished him to live elsewhere. This was true despite the fact that, during the six months prior to the interview, severe or moderate distress was reported by 30% of the families of first admission patients and 59% of the families of multiple admission patients. In an earlier study by some members of the same group, Wing, Monck, Brown, and Carstairs (1964) reported that, of the 99 relatives of English male patients, 40% indicated that they would welcome him home, 25% said they would accept the patient, 21% were doubtful about how they felt, and 13% were actively opposed to the return of the patient. No family, however, refused to take the patient back when he was discharged. The willingness of English families to care for their mentally disordered relatives and to delay sending them to the hospital is further supported by Mills (1962). Most recently, Barrett, Kuriansky, and Gurland (1972) found that 60% of the 85 families interviewed four weeks after patients were discharged expressed pleasure at the sudden return of a patient due to an unexpected hospital strike in New York State.

The question of who is willing to receive mental patients and why is a complicated one. Both acceptance and rejection have been reported in the literature. Overall impressions seem to differ depending on the values and experiences of the observer. Lidz, Hotchkiss, and Greenblatt (1957), on the basis of their collective clinical experience, have spoken of stigma and withdrawal from the patient starting at the time of hospitalization. Lemkau (1968: 353), on the other hand, cited the "well-known clinical experience that families often resist the hospitalization of persons and that they often remove family members from the hospital against medical advice, facts not easily made consonant with a rejecting attitude toward mental patients."

Certainly, the absence of systematic empirical studies which take into account such reality factors as economic and social pressures on the family, optimism about outcome, the role the patient plays in the household, and life-cycle variables permits just this sort of individual speculation based on personal experience.

While social rejection derives logically from a consideration of stigma, the relationship is not as clear-cut in the families of patients as in the general population. It may be that, in these families, rejection is more closely attuned to the practical realities of life to which we have alluded. For instance, in Grad and Sainsbury's study (1963b), 81% of the rejecting and negative relatives had reality problems while only 62% of the "accepting" group were rated as having such problems. In any case, when the family ceases to interact with the patient because it believes that the patient's condition is irreversible (Cumming and Cumming, 1965), a not untenable notion in view of current recidivism rates, or if discharge plans are met with theoretical approval but actual reluctance, then one must introduce the issue of the cost to the family of maintaining ties with the mentally disordered.

Elaine Cumming (1968) has forcefully brought our attention to the fact that we pay only lip service to the patient's own community, the family and friends who must live with him when he returns after hospitalization. In the United States, she argues, we have ignored the aggravation placed on the community by the zeal for sending patients home. British psychiatric researchers have been more concerned with the family. They were the first to raise the issue of family burden in their research. The picture that emerges from their studies is that of a family willing to receive the mentally ill member back into the home, at least after the initial hospitalizations, but nonetheless hard pressed by the strain and demands of living with a former patient. The family is shouldering a burden because one of them is mentally ill. With the increasing shift in hospital policy toward early release of the patient and home care, the degree to which the family is able or desires to take on and live with this burden is extremely important.

The first study in this area was done in England in the early 1960s (Grad and Sainsbury, 1963a and b). The authors were interested in seeing whether the trend toward caring for the patient in the community really meant putting additional burden on the family. Families of patients referred to two different types of hospitals were interviewed at one month and at two years after referral. One hospital had a traditional policy of removing the patient from the community; the other stressed community care. The interviewing was done by a psychiatric social worker who estimated the burden on the family by rating the effect the patient had on the family's income, social activities, domestic and school routines, the strain on other family members, and problems with neighbors. The authors hypothesized that burden would be greater when the hospital had a community care approach. This was confirmed. However, they believed it was not because of the greater care required by the patient in the community care program, but because burden was significantly lightened in families in the traditional hospital condition due to the regular visits to the home by the social work staff.

Somewhat later, Hoenig and Hamilton (1969), also in England, studied family burden in two communities where home care was the preferred method of treatment. The sample consisted of 179 families who had lived continuously with a former patient for the four years prior to being interviewed. The investigators differentiated between *objective* burden and *subjective* burden by asking the family a single question on perceived burden and comparing that to a social worker's rating of the family's objective burden. Fifty-six percent of the families were rated as operating under an objective burden, with the parental home seemingly less burdened than the conjugal home. Fourteen percent of the families reported severe subjective burden, 40% reported moderate burden, and 46% reported no burden at all. None of the families who were rated as having no objective burden reported any subjective burden. If the patient was older, from a conjugal home, rated as sicker, or had spent more time in the hospital during the study period, then more subjective burden was experienced. The authors concluded that there was a great deal of *subjective tolerance* in view of the high objective burden.

While 90% of the families in this study were rated as sympathetic to the patient, 56% experienced great relief when inpatient admission was resorted to. Sixty-three percent of the latter group had complained of at least "some" burden. Overall, the families reported a remarkably high degree of satisfaction with the hospital and the treatment of the patient there. It was not reported whether this was truly satisfaction, a rationalization of their decision to hospitalize or an acquiescent or socially desirable response.

One of the British studies uncovered very little objective burden in the families of schizophrenic patients (Mandelbrote and Folkard, 1961). Only 4 out of 171 families were judged to be suffering any distress of patient burden. Brown, Bone, Dalison, and Wing (1966) questioned this underreporting of burden and referred to the high percentage of unemployed men (40%) in the sample as reason enough to be skeptical of the findings. However, the unusually high proportion of first admissions (59%) in the sample may account for the low rate of observed burden.

The reduction of burden and the sense of relief that was experienced by some families as a result of hospitalization of the patient (Myers and Bean, 1968; Grad and Sainsbury, 1963b; Hoenig and Hamilton, 1969) may be reason enough to explain their rejecting behavior. Kelman (1964), in discussing the implications of labeling and hospitalization for the families of brain-damaged children, states that lower class deviance is recognized but that it is not assigned the same priority of familial concern and resources as other, more pressing problems. In this context, hospitalization and abandonment may be viewed as the removal of one more draining problem (see Myers and Roberts, 1959, and Myers and Bean, 1968, on this point). As demonstrated by Barrett, Kuriansky, and Gurland (1972), when the patient contributed to the household rather than taxed its limited resources, there was significantly greater likelihood that the patient would remain out of the hospital. In such cases, the imputation of "felt" stigma as a cause for rejection of patients in high problem groups may hardly be relevant to the issues determining behavior in these families.

## THE PATIENT RETURNS HOME

Since the outcome of interactions between individuals is so often highly influenced by the relevant attitudes of each individual, it has been generally assumed that the impact of those attitudes would strongly affect the experiences and posthospital adjustment of the patient. Indirect support for this assumption is available from studies showing that successful outcome was associated with the family settings to which patients returned (Davis, Freeman, and Simmons, 1957; Carstairs, 1959; Freeman and Simmons, 1963; Wing, Monck, Brown, and Carstairs, 1964; Michaux, Katz, Kurland, and Gansereit, 1969). It is not unlikely that differing attitudes and expectations held by siblings, spouses, or parents are at least partly responsible for such findings.

Studies in which family attitudes appear as independent variables which influence community adjustment have generally concerned themselves with: (1) positive or negative attitudes toward the patient, (2) attitudes about mental illness and mental hospitals, and (3) attitudes regarding tolerance of deviance. Usually investigators have assessed relatives' attitudes through an intensive, generally semi-structured, interview or series of interviews. Measurement techniques have varied considerably in sophistication. Both direct and indirect measures have been used; and response categories have ranged from a yes-no to a Likert format. In some cases overall ratings were made by trained interviewers. The most commonly used indicators of outcome have been community stay versus rehospitalization, and community adjustment as shown by rating of symptomatology and role performance.

## Outcome and Family Attitudes Toward the Patient

A direct test of the hypothesis that the positive or negative attitudes of a relative were related to outcome was conducted by Kelley (1964) working with the Psychiatric Evaluation Project of the Veterans Administration in Massachusetts. Family acceptance, whether the patient was wanted at home, the degree of understanding of the patient, attitudes toward the hospital, and attitudes toward deviant behavior were not found to be significantly related to patient outcome as measured by exacerbation of symptoms in a group of 65 discharged schizophrenics. A replication of the study (reported by Kelley in the same article) confirmed these findings.

Significant results, however, were reported by Carstairs (1959), who found that success in remaining in the community was associated with greater welcome, whether there was a "key person" (a woman willing to involve herself with the patient), positive attitudes, and a perception that the patient was not dangerous. Similarly Barrett and associates (1972) reported a significant relationship of family attitude to outcome. If the caretaker family recalled that its initial reaction was "very pleased," patients tended to remain out. Fifty-seven percent of the relatives of patients who remained out of the hospital were initially "very pleased" at the patient's release; only 7% of the relatives of those who returned responded in this way. If the attitude of the family was negative, neutral, or simply "pleased," patients tended to return. In the same interview, when families were asked how they felt about the patient's discharge after the patient had been home awhile, this same relationship was present to an even greater degree. Standard of living was also significantly related to community stay; patients with poorer caretaker families showed a greater tendency to remain out of the hospital.

While on the surface it appears reasonable to assume that family acceptance of the patient indicates a beneficial atmosphere for the former patient and would be positively correlated to outcome, the matter is not so simple. Brown, Carstairs, and Topping (1958) found that former patients living with mothers or wives had higher readmission rates than those living with siblings, distant kin, or in lodgings. They concluded that it was not always wise to send a schizophrenic back to close parental or marital homes, even if the ties were affectionate. In an attempt to explicate this finding, Brown, Monck, Carstairs, and Wing (1962) interviewed 128 recently discharged patients and their female relatives and maintained contact with them throughout the first year after discharge. Utilizing the notion of an optimal level of emotional arousal, the authors hypothesized that a mental patient's behavior would deteriorate if he returned to a home where there was strongly expressed emotion of any sort. They further reasoned that, in those families where emotions ran high, rehospitalization could be avoided if family contact was minimal. Emotionality was measured by rating the interaction of the patient and his key relative on content of speech, tone of voice, and gestures. Their main hypothesis was confirmed. Patients had deteriorated in 75% of the "emotional" homes and in only 33% of the "nonemotional" homes. Extent of family contact was important, however, only for those moderately or severely disturbed at discharge. When past history, home situation, and condition at discharge were taken into account, the relationship between emotionality and deterioration was weakened, although not wholly destroyed.

In order to extend and refine this relationship, Brown, Birley, and Wing (1972) interviewed 101 schizophrenic patients and their families both before and after discharge. As in the previous study, the interaction of patient and relative in a joint interview was rated. An emotional expression score was derived using the number of comments denoting criticism, hostility, dissatisfaction, warmth, and emotional overinvolvement. Again a significant association between high expressed emotion and relapse was found. The most significant component of this score was number of critical comments. Warmth could not be used in the overall index because it showed a curvilinear relationship with relapse. Patients in homes showing moderate warmth had the lowest relapse rate. Low warmth relatives tended to be critical and high warmth relatives were overinvolved. Their data indicated that it was the emotional expression, not previous work or behavior impairment, that was associated with relapse. Symptoms were also related to relapse, but independently of emotion.

This line of research is as important for its general theoretical and methodological implications as for its substantive findings. It clearly points to the need to examine more complex relationships. It is not enough to relate family attitudes to outcome. Patient attitudes, their consequences for family attitudes, and patient behavior are equally important, and have too often been ignored. In the few studies attending to both patient and family attitudes, they were rarely analyzed in conjunction with one another. Yet the interaction between these sets of attitudes, their fit with one another and with various behaviors, will have to become the focus of new research if we believe that the forces which influence relapse are embedded within a social matrix context. The use of an interactionist strategy would not only be consonant with the ecological approach utilized by many within the field of psychology today but would inevitably lead to the much needed use of increasingly sophisticated methodological techniques.

## Outcome and Family Attitudes Toward Mental Illness and Mental Hospitals

Among early studies relating attitudes regarding mental illness or mental hospitals to outcome, one by Davis, Freeman, and Simmons (1957) found that patients with high performance levels were most likely to have relatives with an environ-mental view of mental illness, favorable attitudes to mental hospitals, and the belief that mental illness does not basically change a person. In a long-term study conducted by two of these authors, Freeman and Simmons (1963), similar attitudes were again measured. Relatives of successful patients tended to see them as normal and somewhat blameless, and had positive attitudes toward the hospital. The more educated the respondent, the less the likelihood of blaming the patient. Attitudes on the etiology of mental illness were unrelated to any measure of rehabilitation, but the authors felt this to be a function of poor scale construction. They did find that the family's perception of management problems and the patient's sympto-matic behavior were associated with return to the hospital (see also Myers and Bean, 1968).

Lorei (1964) administered the Opinions about Mental Illness (OMI) scale (Cohen and Struening, 1962) to the relatives of 104 released patients and correlated these scores with success or failure in remaining in the community for nine months. Only three of the five OMI factors related significantly to outcome. Low scores on Authoritarianism and Restrictiveness and a high score on Benevolence were associ-ated with the patient's remaining in the community. Scores on Interpersonal Etiology and Mental Hygiene Ideology were unrelated to community stay. These findings are in line with those previously noted (Davis, Freeman, and Simmons, 1957). The family's perception of the patients as not unlike normals and not responsible for their condition was related to success in the community but not to recidivism.

In another study using the OMI, Bentinck (1967) gathered data from 50 male schizophrenics and their relatives and 50 male medical patients and their families nine months after discharge from the hospital. Families of mental patients differed from families of medical patients only in that the latter endorsed items of Mental Health Ideology more than the former. Contact with a mental patient appeared to be associated with less acceptance of the medical model of mental illness. While Bentinck did not relate scores to outcome, but simply compared the four groups, her study did indicate a potential source of conflict for the mental patient both in the hospital and after his return. The relatives of mental patients, who generally came from the same social background as blue-collar hospital workers, were found to have attitudes more like those of the blue-collar hospital personnel than those of mental health professionals. They were generally more pessimistic about treatment outcome, more restrictive, and more authoritarian than mental health professionals. Thus, in both the hospital and the home setting, patients must deal with people who have ideologies unlike their professional therapists.

## Outcome and Family's Tolerance of Deviance

Since the behavior demonstrated by a former patient is occasionally disruptive and may be considered deviant by the family, a prominent subject for investigation has been the relatives' attitudes regarding deviant behavior. For instance, Deykin (1961) interviewed either the patient or family in a follow-up of 13 chronic cases and judged the patient's community adjustment by examining personal appearance, psychiatric and social functioning, and quality of interpersonal relationships. While the families in her sample were receiving intensive casework help, which may have influenced both tolerance and outcome, she concluded that family and community tolerance for the ex-mental patient was one of the central factors relating to successful discharge, even for those patients who showed poor community adjustment. Deykin hypothesized that the family's deep love and guilt about the patient's illness were responsible for the low recidivism rate.

Generally, however, it has been hypothesized that tolerance of deviant behavior as shown by low expectations regarding work and social participation is a key factor affecting outcome. Lower class patients and/or those returning to parental homes (each were considered to be returning to settings with lower expectations regarding performance) were expected to have fewer relapses, or at least fewer rehospitalizations. An early study by Freeman and Simmons (1958, 1959) provided support for these derivations. Poorly performing patients who managed to remain in the community tended to be lower class, had other males in the family to take over their roles, and were living in parental rather than conjugal homes.

Mothers, in fact, were found to be more tolerant of deviant behavior in studies by Brown, Carstairs, and Topping (1958), Brown, Bone, Dalison, and Wing (1966), and Linn (1966). On the other hand, Michaux, Katz, Kurland, and Gansereit (1969) reported a greater relapse rate for those returning to parental homes, and the relationship of social class and expectations to performance did not hold up for acute female mental patients returning to conjugal homes (Lefton, Angrist, Dinitz, and Pasamanick, 1962). Posthospital performance in the latter study was best predicted by illness rather than by class or expectations. The authors speculated that Freeman and Simmons's results may be true only for chronic male patients.

In order to obtain longitudinal data and to refine and extend their ideas, Freeman and Simmons (1963) conducted their classic year long study of the posthospital experience of 649 men and women. In this study, the culmination of earlier investigations with the Massachusetts-based Community Health Project, Freeman and Simmons interviewed a key relative twice after the patient returned home. The informant (usually spouse or mother) was seen at about six weeks and one year after discharge. The interview tapped relatives' expectations regarding work, social participation, and symptomatology, and the perceived performance in these areas. With respect to tolerance of deviance, they found, somewhat surprisingly, that relatives' expectations regarding work and social participation were high. In fact, former patients were expected to perform like anyone else. There was little change in expectations throughout the posthospital year. Tolerance of deviance was directly related to performance—the higher the expectation, the higher the performance—but unrelated to successful community tenure. Unlike the results of their earlier study, and in partial confirmation of Lefton and associates (1962), social class was unrelated to either expectations or successful community tenure. Social class was, however, related to performance.

Tolerance of deviance, defined as the extent to which a family will keep a symptomatic former patient at home, was the subject of two reports by Angrist, Lefton, Dinitz, and Pasamanick (1961, 1968). Drawing heavily on Freeman and Simmons's conceptual and methodological model, they focused their attention on the posthospital experience of women only. In the earlier article (1961) they described the results of a follow-up study of a sample of 264 women consecutively discharged from Columbus Psychiatric Institute in Ohio. This hospital is a short-term intensive therapy facility where 90% of all admissions are voluntary and 75% are first admissions. Thus, the patient sample was from a higher socioeconomic class, and had fewer psychotics and multiple admission patients than is usual in samples drawn from state hospital populations. A significant other, generally a husband, was interviewed six months after discharge by a social worker using a structured interview. Low tolerance of deviance was significantly related to higher social class and to good posthospital performance, even when severity of illness was controlled.

The final, more extensive analyses of these same data and data from a control sample of the former patients' female neighbors and their significant others were reported in Angrist and associates (1968). A smaller sample of schizophrenics was also interviewed at one year after discharge, and comparisons between and within the research groups were then made. The major hypothesis that tolerance of deviance (symptom tolerance) and role expectations would predict rehospitalization was not confirmed. Similarly, social class did not have a marked relationship to rehospitalization. As in Freeman and Simmons's study (1963), tolerance of deviance and expectations were related to performance with high level performers having significant others low in tolerance and high in role expectations. Social class played no part in the posthospital performance of married women, at least directly. It did influence performance indirectly via class related role expectations. The most significant predictor of failure and rehospitalization in this study was the reappearance of symptoms.

Relatives of normals and former patients differed on tolerance of deviance on only three items. When relatives of patients having organic problems were removed (these relatives were a special group low in expectations and high in tolerance), there were no differences between relatives of normals and the relatives of former patients except, obviously, in their perception of psychological difficulties.

A recent study by Michaux and associates (1969) also examined the family's expectations of the patient and the patient's social role performance although the investigators did not specifically focus on tolerance of deviance. Monthly interviews were conducted with patients, and in most cases, a selected family member. Among other measures, information on the level of satisfaction with the patient's free time activities, the family's satisfaction with the patient's performance, and the occurrence of symptoms were collected. The patient's poor social role performance and the families' dissatisfaction derived from their high but unmet expectations for the patient were significant but not powerful predictors of rehospitalization. These findings were at variance with those of Freeman and Simmons (1963) and Angrist and associates (1968). In common with the above studies, an increase in general psychopathology was noted by the family prior to hospitalization.

In summary, we find conflicting results regarding the influence of positive familial attitudes on outcome. Emotional expressiveness and differential attitudes about mental illness were significantly related to outcome. Tolerance of deviance, whether defined by low expectations regarding work and social participation or the extent to which families will keep a symptomatic patient at home, has been only slightly related to relapse. Returning to a family low in tolerance of deviance was likely to result in higher role performance, but did not prevent rehospitalization. Similarly, returning to a family which displays understanding and noncritical attitudes may increase the chances for success, but this does not reduce rehospitalization rates when the strains become too great. Mills (1962) noted that, even though families were willing to care for their symptomatic relatives, once the stress of living with the sick member became too great, the hospital was more often seen as attractive and as a place for cure. If cure did not take place, a deterioration of the relationship between patient and family ensued. This process has also been discussed by Pitt (1969), who saw the patient using up the "reservoir of good will" held by the family.

On the whole, we are confronted with a scarcity of significant results relating family attitudinal variables to successful outcome. The only finding that appears and reappears consistently in the literature is that failure in the community and subsequent return to the hospital is accompanied by the reappearance of symptoms (Freeman, 1961; Freeman and Simmons, 1963; Angrist et al., 1968; Pasamanick et al., 1967; Michaux et al., 1969; and Brown et al., 1972).

## CONCLUSIONS

The studies of the family's early reaction to the mental illness of a relative provide a first step in understanding the initial perception of deviant behavior, attempts at explanation, and the response to the deviant. While these studies have been enlightening and heuristic, they have suffered from the shortcomings frequently found in the initial exploration of a complex phenomenon. With a few exceptions, much of this research has been impressionistic in nature, inconsistent, descriptive rather than explanatory, limited in scope and techniques, and has failed to incorporate the type of controls which would permit clear conclusions to be drawn. Further difficulties in interpretation have resulted from the use of small samples and the lack of rigorous sampling procedures.

The affective components of the attitude to the deviant and the sense of burden which the family feels have still been inadequately treated. Anger, anxiety, fear for one's own sanity, and guilt over the role the family may have played in the etiology of the condition have been virtually ignored in the attempt to further elaborate more general attitudes of acceptance or rejection. Also relatively untouched has been the family's beliefs about its patient-relative. Some studies have inferred the family's cognitions of the patient from the responses to items about a hypothetically mentally ill person, but items directly examining their beliefs about their own deviant family member have rarely been included as part of the research design. Finally, the interactions of the various aspects of attitude (affective, conative, and cognitive) and their relationships to behavior still remain a subject for systematic study.

Contradictory data abound on almost every subject which has been discussed in this paper. It is entirely possible that these contradictions reflect true differences in the real world. Yet scant effort has been made to explain the differences or to resolve them. Perhaps this is due to a scatter-shot approach by researchers who, with a few exceptions, have failed to follow through on promising leads in their own data. The lack of sustained interest has left us with fundamental pieces of information missing, and the promise in the early and thoughtful work reported by Clausen and Yarrow has hardly been actualized.

Research on the relationship of family attitudes to outcome has more often been conceptually sophisticated and programmatic. Yet here again results are inconsistent. This may be because few studies have focused on complex interrelated variables. For example, little effort has been directed at the measurement and analysis of patient and family variables in conjunction with one another. In addition, investigators have mainly studied families containing a sick member and have failed to establish any comparative baselines of attitudes for families with a member exhibiting a different type of deviance or for families without any sick member at all.

The perennial question of directionality is also a problem. Much of the research has viewed the patient in the role of reactor to the attitudes and behavior of the family. Researchers have assumed that family attitudes to deviance strongly influence the behavior of the former patient, particularly with regard to community tenure. Such a unilateral perspective has led them to neglect research aimed at distinguishing the extent to which attitudes of relatives are a function of the condition of the patients with whom they reside. Both Freeman and Simmons (1963) and Angrist and associates (1968) initiated their research with the hypothesis that family attitudes determined patient functioning. They concluded, however, that tolerance and expectations *reflected* patient functioning.

Evidence to support this conclusion comes from a dissertation that examined the effect of multiple hospitalizations on the role the patient plays within the family (Dunigan, 1969). This study of 66 husbands of patient-wives with varying numbers of hospitalizations indicated that there is a critical point at which expectations and tolerances change. Husbands seemed able to cope with one or two hospitalizations and to make temporary role adaptations to the deviant behavior of the wife-mother. With three or more hospitalizations, husbands were seen to withdraw from the wife, lower their role expectations, and make other more permanent arrangements for the continued functioning of the household. These, in turn, served to strain marital ties and to isolate the wife within the family setting. Dunigan concluded that families eventually exhaust their resources to expand and contract in ways that keep the wife-mother a contributing member of the family system.

This promising move toward studying the ongoing process of patient-family relationships would be furthered still more by the use of nonretrospective longitudinal research which would follow the family through the various phases of its reciprocal role in the mental patient's career. Such a process approach enhances the likelihood of identifying critical points at which special intervention procedures could be made available to patients and/or families.

It is interesting to note that most investigators have concentrated on women's perceptions and expectations as they relate to male patients. While this is understandable in terms of the supportive role females in our society are expected to play regarding the sick, we are left with meager knowledge regarding the perceptions and expectations of males and the differential effect on the family of the illness of men or women. One study which did present comparative data on this point (Rogler and Hollingshead, 1965) reported striking differences in the response of the family and the effects on it of having a wife or a husband as the ill member. When husbands were ill, the wife frequently added his work role to her own nurturant one, and the family was maintained as a functioning unit. Illness on the part of the wife had a pervasive and destructive influence on the family organization, since the husbands were unable or unwilling to take on parts of the female role. While this study was done in a traditional society (Puerto Rico) where male and female roles were more clearly elaborated, it does alert us to the various modes of adaptation to a stressful situation which may occur in our society as a result of sex role and life-cycle differences.

In general, it seems apparent that rather than dealing with main effects, we are dealing with an intricate set of interacting variables. What appears necessary is truly multivariate research which evaluates the family's response to its patient-relative along a number of dimensions such as the personalities of its members, its socio-cultural position, prior and contemporaneous experience with the patient, its attitudes and expectations, and the stresses acting upon it at any particular time, to name a few.

Such investigations are rarely likely to uncover out-and-out acceptance or rejection by the family. Nor will they permit unqualified positive or negative assessments of the appropriateness of returning the patient to the family setting. The more common picture will be one of a family holding ambivalent feelings and exhibiting a complex and, at times, contradictory pattern of responses on the various dimensions measured. At this point the basic research which would allow us to identify and establish the relative weights of predictors of successful outcome for both patient and family remains to be done. Only then will we be able to predict with some degree of certainty whether a particular family will be able to support efforts at rehabilitation or will, no matter how unwittingly, sabotage those efforts. It would appear obvious, however, that optimal conditions for posthospital adjustment will vary with each patient and his family. In some cases, the cost to the patient of placement with his family may be too great. Similarly, there will be families for whom the strain may be so debilitating that we are, in effect, destroying the family in the effort to care for the patient. In other cases, the patient's return to the family may be feasible only with some support to the family, whether it be the relief afforded by the use of family maintenance counseling, an occasional homemaker, or the placement of the patient in a day facility.

In every case consideration must be given to the effect of any decision or program on all parts of the system in which the patient exists. This means that the patient, the family, the community, and those social agencies that are implicated in the care of the mental patient must all be examined and evaluated before the success of a program can be judged adequately. To consider one to the exclusion of the others is to imperil those goals which may be most desired.

## REFERENCES

Adler, L. Patients of a State Mental Hospital: The Outcome of Their Hospitalization. Pp. 501-523 in A. Rose (ed.), *Mental Health and Mental Disorder*. New York: Norton, 1955.

*Alivisatos, G. and G. Lyketsos. A Preliminary Report of a Research Concerning the Attitude of the Families of Hospitalized Mental Patients. *International Journal of Social Psychiatry*, 1964, 10: 37-44.

Angrist, S.; M. Lefton; S. Dinitz; and B. Pasamanick. Tolerance of Deviant Behavior, Posthospital Performance Levels and Rehospitalization. *Proceedings of the Third World Congress of Psychiatry*. Vol. I. Toronto: University of Toronto Press, 1961. Pp. 237-241.

———. *Women After Treatment: A Study of Former Mental Patients and their Normal Neighbors*. New York: Appleton-Century-Crofts, 1968.

Barker, R. The Social Psychology of Physical Disability. *Journal of Social Issues*, 1948, 4: 28-34.

Barrett, J., Jr.; J. Kuriansky; and B. Gurland. Community Tenure Following Emergency Discharge. *American Journal of Psychiatry*, 1972, 128: 958-964.

Bentinck, C. Opinions About Mental Illness Held by Patients and Relatives. *Family Process*, 1967, 6: 193-207.

Bettelheim, B. *A Home For the Heart*. New York: Knopf, 1974.

Bizon, Z.; K. Godorowski; J. Henisz; and A. Razniewski. The Attitudes of Warsaw Inhabitants Toward Mental Illness. Warsaw, Poland: Laboratory of Social Psychiatry, Department of Psychiatry, Medical School. N.D. Mimeographed.

Bogardus, E. Measuring Social Distance. *Journal of Applied Sociology*, 1925, 9: 299-308.

Brown, G.; J. Birley; and J. Wing. Influence of Family Life in the Course of Schizophrenic Disorders: A Replication. *British Journal of Psychiatry*, 1972, 121: 241-258.

Brown, G.; M. Bone; B. Dalison; and J. Wing. *Schizophrenia and Social Care*. London: Oxford University Press, 1966.

Brown, G.; G. M. Carstairs; and G. Topping. Posthospital Adjustment of Chronic Mental Patients. *Lancet*, 1958, 2: 685-689.

Brown, G.; E. Monck; G. M. Carstairs; and J. Wing. Influence of Family Life in the Course of Schizophrenic Illness. *British Journal of Preventive and Social Medicine*, 1962, 16: 55-68.

Bruner, J. and R. Tagiuri. The Perception of People. Pp. 634-654 in G. Lindzey (ed.), *Handbook of Social Psychology*. Cambridge: Addison-Wesley, 1954.

Carstairs, G. M. The Social Limits of Eccentricity: An English Study. Pp. 373-389 in M. K. Opler (ed.), *Culture and Mental Health: Cross Cultural Studies*. New York: Macmillan Company, 1959.

Chin-Shong, E. Rejection of the Mentally Ill: A Comparison with the Findings on Ethnic Prejudice. Unpublished Doctoral Dissertation. New York: Columbia University, 1968.

Clausen, J. The Marital Relationship Antecedent to Hospitalization of a Spouse for Mental Illness. Annual Meeting of American Sociological Association, Chicago, September, 1959.

Clausen, J. and M. R. Yarrow (eds.) The Impact of Mental Illness on the Family. *Journal of Social Issues*, 1955, 11 (4).

Cohen, J. and E. Struening. Opinions About Mental Illness in the Personnel of Two Large Mental Hospitals. *Journal of Abnormal and Social Psychology*, 1962, 64: 349-360.

Cumming, E. Community Psychiatry in a Divided Labor. Pp. 100-113 in J. Zubin and F. Freyhan (eds.), *Social Psychiatry*. New York: Grune and Stratton, 1968.

Cumming, E. and J. Cumming. *Closed Ranks: An Experiment in Mental Health Education*. Cambridge, Mass.: Harvard University Press, 1957.

Cumming, J. and E. Cumming. On the Stigma of Mental Illness. *Community Mental Health Journal*, 1965, 1: 135-143.

Davis, J.; H. Freeman; and O. Simmons. Rehospitalization and Performance Levels of Former Mental Patients. *Social Problems*, 1957, 5: 37-44.

Deykin, E. The Reintegration of the Chronic Schizophrenic Patient Discharged to His Family and Community as Perceived by the Family. *Mental Hygiene*, 1961, 45: 235-246.

Dunigan, J. Mental Hospital Career and Family Expectations. Laboratory of Psychosocial Research, Cleveland Psychiatric Institute, Cleveland, Ohio, 1969. Mimeographed.

Evans, A.; D. Bullard, Jr.; and M. Solomon. The Family as a Potential Resource in the Rehabilitation of the Chronic Schizophrenic Patient: A Study of 60 Patients and their Families. *American Journal of Psychiatry*, 1961, 117: 1075-1083.

Festinger, L.; H. B. Gerard; H. Hymovitch; H. Kelley; and B. Rosen. The Influence Process in the Presence of Extreme Deviates. *Human Relations*, 1952, 5: 327-346.

Fontana, A. Familial Etiology of Schizophrenia: Is Scientific Method Possible? *Psychological Bulletin*, 1966, 66: 214-227.

Frank, G. H. The Role of the Family in the Development of Psychopathology. *Psychological Bulletin*, 1965, 64: 191-205.

Freeman, H. Attitudes Toward Mental Illness Among Relatives of Former Patients. *American Sociological Review*, 1961, 26: 59-66.

*Freeman, H. and O. Simmons. Mental Patients in the Community: Family Settings and Performance Levels. *American Sociological Review*, 1958, 23: 147-154.

―――. Social Class and Posthospital Performance Levels. *American Sociological Review*, 1959, 24: 345-351.

―――. Feelings of Stigma Among Relatives of Former Mental Patients. *Social Problems*, 1961, 8: 312-321.

―――. *The Mental Patient Comes Home*. New York: Wiley, 1963.

Gillis, L. and M. Keet. Factors Underlying the Retention in the Community of Chronic Unhospitalized Schizophrenics. *British Journal of Psychiatry*, 1965, 111: 1057-1067.

Goffman, E. *Stigma: Notes on the Management of a Spoiled Identity*. Englewood Cliffs, N.J.: Prentice Hall, 1963.

Grad, J. and P. Sainsbury. Evaluating a Community Care Service. Pp. 303-317 in H. Freeman and J. Farndale (eds.), *Trends in the Mental Health Services*. New York: Macmillan, 1963. (a).

―――. Mental Illness and the Family. *Lancet*, 1963, 1: 544-547. (b).

Hoenig, J. and M. Hamilton. *The Desegregation of the Mentally Ill*. London: Routledge and Kegan Paul, 1969.

Hollingshead, A. and F. Redlich. *Social Class and Mental Illness*. New York: Wiley, 1958.

Kelley, F. Relatives' Attitude and Outcome in Schizophrenia. *Archives of General Psychiatry*, 1964, 10: 389-394.

Kelman, H. The Effect of a Brain Damaged Child on the Family. Pp. 77-98 in H. G. Birch (ed.), *Brain Damage in Children*. Baltimore, Md.: The Williams & Wilkins Co., 1964.

Korkes, L. The Impact of Mentally Ill Children Upon their Parents. Unpublished Doctoral Dissertation. *Dissertation Abstracts*, p. 3392, June 1959.

Lederer, H. How the Sick View Their World. *Journal of Social Issues*, 1952, 8: 4-15.

Lefton, M.; S. Angrist; S. Dinitz; and B. Pasamanick. Social Class, Expectations and Performance of Mental Patients. *American Journal of Sociology*, 1962, 68: 79-87.

Lemkau, P. Evaluation of the Effect of Changes in Environmental Factors, with Special Attention to Public Attitudes Toward Mental Health and Mental Illness. Pp. 349-362 in J. Zubin and F. Freyhan (eds.), *Social Psychiatry*. New York: Grune & Stratton, 1968.

Lewin, K. Self Hatred among Jews. Pp. 186-200 in G. Lewin (ed.), *Resolving Social Conflicts*. New York: Harpers, 1948.

Lewis, V. and A. Zeichner. Impact of Admission to a Mental Hospital on the Patient's Family. *Mental Hygiene*, 1960, 44: 503-509.

Lidz, T.; G. Hotchkiss; and M. Greenblatt. Patient-Family-Hospital Interrelationships: Some General Considerations. Pp. 535-543 in M. Greenblatt, D. Levinson and R. Williams (eds.), *The Patient and the Mental Hospital*. Glencoe, Ill.: Free Press, 1957.

Linn, M. Of Wedding Bells and Apron Strings: A Study of Relatives' Attitudes. *Family Process*, 1966, 50: 100-103.

Lorei, T. Prediction of Length of Stay Out of the Hospital for Released Psychiatric Patients. *Journal of Consulting Psychology*, 1964, 28: 358-363.

Mandelbrote, B. and S. Folkard. Some Factors Related to Outcome and Social Adjustment in Schizophrenia. *Acta Psychiatrica Scandinavica*, 1961, 37: 223-235.

Mayo, C.; R. Havelock; and D. Simpson. Attitudes Towards Mental Illness Among Psychiatric Patients and Their Wives. *Journal of Clinical Psychology*, 1971, 27: 128-132.

Michaux, W.; M. Katz; A. Kurland; and K. Gansereit. *The First Year Out: Mental Patients After Hospitalization.* Baltimore: Johns Hopkins Press, 1969.

Mills, E. *Living with Mental Illness: A Study in East London.* London: Routledge and Kegan Paul, 1962.

Mosher, L. and J. Gunderson. Special Report on Schizophrenia: 1972. *Schizophrenia Bulletin,* NIMH, Issue 7, Winter, 1973.

Myers, J. and L. Bean. *A Decade Later: A Follow-up of Social Class and Mental Illness.* New York: Wiley, 1968.

Myers, J. and B. Roberts. *Family and Class Dynamics in Mental Illness.* New York: Wiley, 1959.

Nunnally, J. *Popular Conceptions of Mental Health: Their Development and Change.* New York: Holt, Rinehart and Winston, 1961.

Parsons, T. *The Social System.* Glencoe, Ill.: Free Press, 1951.

Parsons, T. and R. Fox. Illness, Therapy and the Modern Urban American Family. *Journal of Social Issues,* 1952, 8: 31-44.

Pasamanick, B.; F. Scarpetti; and S. Kinitz. *Schizophrenics in the Community: An Experimental Study in the Prevention of Rehospitalization.* New York: Appleton-Century-Crofts, 1967.

*Phillips, D. Rejection: A Possible Consequence of Seeking Help for Mental Disorders. *American Sociological Review,* 1963, 28: 963-972.

Pitt, R. The Concept of Family Burden. Unpublished paper presented at the Annual Meetings of the American Psychiatric Association, 1969.

Rabkin, J. Opinions About Mental Illness: A Review of the Literature. *Psychological Bulletin,* 1972, 77: 153-171.

Rawnsley K.; J. B. Loudon; and H. L. Miles. Attitudes of Relatives to Patients in Mental Hospitals. *British Journal of Preventive and Social Medicine,* 1962, 16: 1-15.

Rogler, L. and A. Hollingshead. *Trapped: Families and Schizophrenia.* New York: Wiley, 1965.

Rose, C. Relatives' Attitudes and Mental Hospitalization. *Mental Hygiene,* 1959, 43: 194-203.

Safilios-Rothschild, C. Deviance and Mental Illness in the Greek Family. *Family Process,* 1968, 7: 100-117.

Sakamoto, Y. A Study of the Attitude of Japanese Families of Schizophrenics Toward their Ill Members. *Psychotherapy and Psychosomatics,* 1969, 17: 365-374.

*Sampson, H.; S. Messinger; and R. Towne. Family Processes and Becoming a Mental Patient. *American Journal of Sociology,* 1962, 68: 88-96.

Schachter, S. Deviation, Rejection and Communication. *Journal of Abnormal and Social Psychology,* 1951, 46: 190-207.

*Scheff, T. The Role of the Mentally Ill and the Dynamics of Mental Disorder: A Research Framework. *Sociometry,* 1963, 26: 436-453.

Schwartz, C. The Stigma of Mental Illness. *Journal of Rehabilitation,* 1956, 21: 7.

———. Perspectives on Deviance: Wives' Definitions of their Husbands' Mental Illness. *Psychiatry,* 1957, 20: 275-291.

Sommer, R. Letter-Writing in a Mental Hospital. *American Journal of Psychiatry,* 1958, 115: 514-517.

———. Visitors to Mental Hospitals: A Fertile Field for Research. *Mental Hygiene,* 1959, 43: 8-15.

Spiegel, J. and N. Bell. The Family of the Psychiatric Patient. Pp. 114-149 in S. Arieti (ed.), *The American Handbook of Psychiatry.* New York: Basic Books, 1959.

Spitzer, S.; P. Morgan; and R. Swanson. Determinants of the Psychiatric Patient Career: Family Reaction Patterns and Social Work Intervention. *Social Service Review,* 1971, 45: 74-85.

Star, S. The Public's Ideas about Mental Illness. National Opinion Research Center. Chicago: University of Chicago, 1955. Mimeographed.

Swanson, R. and S. Spitzer. Stigma and the Psychiatric Patient Career. *Journal of Health and Social Behavior,* 1970, 11: 44-51.

Swingle, P. Relatives' Concepts of Mental Patients. *Mental Hygiene,* 1965, 49: 461-465.

Waters, M. and J. Northover. Rehabilitated Long Stay Schizophrenics in the Community. *British Journal of Psychiatry,* 1965, 111: 258-267.

*Whatley, C. Social Attitudes Toward Discharged Mental Patients. *Social Problems,* 1959, 6: 313-320.

Wing, J.; E. Monck; G. Brown; and G. M. Carstairs. Morbidity in the Community of Schizophrenic Patients Discharged from London Mental Hospitals in 1959. *British Journal of Psychiatry,* 1964, 110: 10-21.

Wynne, L.; I. Ryckoff; J. Day; and S. Hirsch. Pseudomutuality in the Family Relations of Schizophrenics. *Psychiatry,* 1958, 21: 205-220.

Yarrow, M.; J. Clausen; and P. Robbins. The Social Meaning of Mental Illness. *Journal of Social Issues,* 1955, 11: 33-48.

Yarrow, M.; C. Schwartz; H. Murphy; and L. Deasy. The Psychological Meaning of Mental Illness in the Family. *Journal of Social Issues,* 1955, 11: 12-24.


*These articles are also to be found in S. Spitzer and N. Denzin (eds.) *The Mental Patient: Studies in the Sociology of Deviance.* New York: McGraw Hill, 1968.

# V

# SELECTED CONTENT AREAS IN EVALUATION RESEARCH

*14*

# IS EARLY INTERVENTION EFFECTIVE?

## URIE BRONFENBRENNER

*Cornell University*

## I. THE PROBLEM

It is now a decade since early intervention began to be applied as a strategy for counteracting the destructive effects of poverty on human development. This approach had its roots in an emergent body of theory (Hebb, 1949) and research in the 1950s pointing to the beneficial effects of early stimulation both in animals and humans.[1] The implications of this work for education in early childhood were developed in a highly influential book by Hunt (1961). Additional support for Hunt's thesis came from Bloom's widely quoted but questionable conclusion, based on an analysis of the impressive predictive power of IQ scores obtained by five years of age, that "about 50 percent of intellectual development takes place between conception and age 4" (Bloom, 1965: 88).

It was in this context that the first well-designed experimental programs of preschool intervention were instituted by Kirk (1958), Gray (Gray and Klaus, 1965), and Weikart (Weikart, Kamii, and Radin, 1964), and produced dramatic initial gains of up to 15 or more IQ points in the space of a few months. Primarily for reasons of social policy rather than demonstrated scientific validity, these experiments were followed almost immediately by the widespread adoption of programs at the state and federal level, most notably Head Start. As a result, the

AUTHOR'S NOTE: To an extraordinary degree, the author has been indebted to his colleagues in the preparation of this analysis. All of the original research reported here was done by others. In addition to printed material, Drs. Phyllis Levenstein, Earl Schaefer, Susan Gray, and E. Kuno Beller generously provided as yet unpublished follow-up data from their projects. Dr. Levenstein also carried out a number of supplementary analyses to clarify points in question. Especial appreciation is expressed to Dr. Lois-Ellen Datta of the Office of Child Development, who critical question of the long-range effect of early intervention was by-passed, at least temporarily.

In the meantime, researchers continued their work. They not only replicated their initial results with new groups of children, but also began to gather information on the performance of "graduates" of the program after they had entered school. Such follow-up data have recently become available from more than a half dozen preschool projects. The results can shed some light on five questions of considerable scientific and social import:

1. Do children in experimental programs continue to gain in intellectual development so long as intervention continues, or at least do they maintain the higher level achieved in the initial phase?
2. Do children continue to improve, or at least to hold their own, after termination of the program, or do they regress to lower levels of function once the program is discontinued?
3. Is development enhanced by beginning intervention at earlier ages, including the first years of life?
4. In terms of long-range impact, what kinds of programs are most effective?
5. Which children from what circumstances are most likely to benefit in the long run from early intervention?

## II. THE NATURE AND LIMITATIONS OF THE DATA

Follow-up data are available from two types of early intervention projects. The first and more familiar approach centers on a preschool program conducted in a group setting outside the home. A second strategy, used both independently and as supplementary to the first, involves a regularly scheduled home visit by a trained person who works both with the child and with his parents, usually the mother.

### Criteria for the Selection of Projects

In selecting studies of either type for inclusion in the primary analysis, we have employed three criteria: (1) systematic follow-up data must be available for at least two years after termination of intervention; (2) similar information is provided for a control group matched on relevant personal characteristics (e.g., age, ability) and background variables (e.g., social class, race); and (3) the data must be comparable from one project to another. The rationale for each of these criteria is self-evident. Two years was regarded as a minimum for gauging long-range aftereffects of the program. A control group is necessary to determine whether observed changes are specifically attributable to the intervention program as such, rather than to external circumstances or events. As we shall see, the necessity of a control group is confirmed by evidence from the studies to be examined of changes in IQ, both in

brought to my attention important studies published only as reports to sponsoring agencies and gave me the benefit of her unparalleled knowledge of research in the area and her balanced judgment on issues both of science and of social policy. Thanks are also due to Dr. Joan Bissell, Dr. Boyd McCandless, and Carmela Mondelli for invaluable assistance.

experimental and control groups, as a function of conditions independent of the intervention procedures themselves. Finally, the comparability of data across projects is essential for assessing the relative effectiveness of different intervention strategies.

## Limitations of the Data

These three criteria, necessary as they are, unavoidably have the effect of restricting the number of projects that can provide a basis for analysis, and, what it even more regrettable, the kind of data that can be examined. Information available across the board is limited to the cognitive area only and consists of IQ scores on the Stanford-Binet (with a few exceptions as noted), and, once the children have entered school, measures of academic achievement on standardized tests. Because different tests were used for this purpose in the various projects, the raw scores on subtests were converted into grade equivalents and averaged, yielding a single score that permitted some comparability from one project to the next.

The restriction of available data to measures of this type sets important limitations to the conclusions that can be drawn. First, there are many important aspects of the development of the human being besides the intellectual, especially the particular kinds of cognitive skills measured by standardized tests. In terms of the child's fulfillment as a person, such factors as emotional security, self-esteem, and the realization of special talents may be no less important than intellectual performance. As for the social realm, especially in our times, such qualities as generosity, cooperativeness, responsibility, and compassion may be of greater moment both to self and society than the ability to perform the restricted kinds of cognitive tasks called for in objective tests. These tasks are especially circumscribed in tests designed for children at the preschool and primary levels (to which our data are limited) in which the emphasis is much greater than it is at older age levels on items requiring recognition of and information about particular objects, pictures, and words with which the child is presumed to have prior familiarity. Thus at these earlier age levels, even the Stanford-Binet reflects substantial components of acquired knowledge, skill, and simple rote learning. The last factor is even more pronounced in the tests of academic achievement currently available for kindergarten and primary levels. Furthermore, since the kinds of objects and facts with which the children are expected to be familiar are far more common in middle class than in less favored environments, the obtained results may often underestimate the potential of children from disadvantaged families. There is also the question of whether the forms of preschool intervention which are most successful in raising the child's performance on objective tests may do so at the price of inhibiting the development of other desirable human qualities, including even such intellectual functions as critical analysis, curiosity, and creative thought. We shall consider some evidence bearing on this issue later in the report.

In the light of all these considerations, *it is of the utmost importance to recognize that the failure of one or another form of preschool intervention to increase or maintain the levels of performance in objective tests of intelligence or achievement must not be interpreted as evidence that such programs are not contributing in important ways to the development and welfare of the child, and for that matter, of his family, community, and even the society as a whole.* All these programs have important objectives outside the purely cognitive sphere, and even within that area, these objectives are broader, deeper, and more humane than the restricted aspect of the child's performance measured by standardized tests, especially the kinds of tests used at younger age levels.[2]

Nevertheless, bearing all these caveats in mind, the available data are not without considerable scientific and social significance. There are few scientists or citizens who would dismiss as inconsequential the demonstration that a particular form of early intervention can enable children to solve problems of the type presented on tests of intelligence at a level of competence comparable to that of the average child of the same age. Whereas performance below the norm on tests of this kind cannot be taken as firm evidence that the child lacks mental capacity, attainment of the norm year after year does mean that the child both possesses intellectual ability and can use it. As we have pointed out, it would be necessary to ensure that the method of intervention employed did not have adverse effects on other aspects of development. But given this assurance, the discovery of such a method would be a significant achievement. It is from this perspective that the present analysis was undertaken.

*Description of Programs.* There are seven projects which meet the criteria we have set. Five involve intervention primarily in preschool settings; two are home-based. A summary of each program is provided in Table 14.1. The first entry supplies basic identifying information, including the name of the project, the locale, the principal investigator, and the sources from which basic data were obtained. The remaining sections described the sample, the nature of the intervention, and the selection and character of the experimental and control groups. Included in the description of the sample are the criteria employed for admission to the program, as well as any available information on the extent of attrition both in terms of self-selection prior to the beginning of the intervention and dropout rate over the course of the program.

*Supplementary Sources.* Especially in view of the small number of projects that conformed to the specified conditions, we shall also draw on the results of other intervention studies which failed to fulfill one or another of our three requirements but provided evidence that could be used to challenge, confirm, or clarify conclusions drawn from the primary investigations. There are twenty such additional researches which fall into three general categories. The seven studies in the first group are evaluations of experimental preschool programs. Deutsch and his colleagues (1971) have reported results from a five-year intervention effort, beginning at age three and ending when the children were in the third grade. Unfortunately, no funds were available either to continue the program or conduct a follow-up. Karnes (1969) and her colleagues (Karnes et al., 1972) have conducted an admirable comparative study of the effectiveness of different preschool curricula. There are follow-up data for three years after termination, but no untreated control group was included in the experimental design. Sprigle's (1972) and Van De Riet's (1972) "Learning to Learn" program is still under way so that follow-up data are available for one year only. Caldwell and her colleagues (Caldwell and Smith, 1970; Brown and Caldwell, in press) have reported gains in IQ achieved by 30 preschoolers after one or more years of participation in a developmental day care setting, but no follow-up data are provided. Di Lorenzo (1969) has carried out a comparative study of preschool programs in eight New York State communities, but the two-year follow-up focused only on academic achievement with no data on intelligence. Finally, two large-scale investigations have been conducted comparing different education strategies employed in two nationwide intervention programs, Head Start (Bissell, 1971) and Follow Through (Stanford Research Institute, 1971a, 1971b; Soar, 1972).

A second group of studies analyzed effects on parent intervention, particularly as this strategy related to preschool programs. A series of four investigations by Karnes and her colleagues (Karnes, 1969; Kirk, 1969; Karnes et al., 1968; Karnes and Badger, 1969; Karnes et al., 1969a, 1969b, 1970), an experiment carried out by Gilmer and associates (1970), a longitudinal study by Gordon (1971, 1972, 1973), and two studies by Radin (1969, 1972) provide important evidence on the interaction between parent intervention and group programs at the preschool and kindergarten levels, and Smith (1968) documents the only research we have been able to find on the effects of parent intervention in elementary school through sixth grade. Although only one (Gilmer et al., 1970) of these studies involves any follow-up after termination of the program, all have been included because their careful experimental design permits clarification of the independent and joint contributions of different intervention strategies.

A third group of studies (Heber, et al., 1971; Skeels, 1966; Skodak and Skeels, 1949), understandably small in number, describe more radical intervention strategies in which primary responsibility for the care and upbringing of the child was entrusted to someone other than his own parents. A description of each of the foregoing intervention programs will be provided when the results are presented.

Finally, in order to understand the processes underlying particular intervention strategies and their relative effectiveness, this analysis draws heavily on basic research in child development, particularly investigations of socialization processes as they affect cognitive growth in early childhood.

### III. SOME METHODOLOGICAL PROBLEMS

Certain features of the data presented in Table 14.1 merit special attention because they point to problems of experimental design that have important bearing on the interpretation of results. We shall first describe these features and then examine their methodological implications.

1. *IQ as a Criterion of Selection.* In two of the studies (Weikart and Hodges), only those children were included in the sample who fell within an IQ range of 50 to 85. None of the other studies imposed this kind of requirement.

TABLE 14.1.  PRESCHOOL INTERVENTION PROGRAMS

| Identifying Data | Sample | Nature of Intervention | Experimental and Control Groups |
|---|---|---|---|
| Howard University Preschool Program Washington, D.C. Elizabeth Herzog (Herzog Newcomb, and Cisin, 1973, 1972a, 1972b; Kraft Fuschillo, and Herzog, 1968) | Black children in generally good health from families selected at random from four census tracts in Washington inner-city neighborhoods. All parents had to agree in advance to have their children attend the preschool program if selected. No other requirements. Approximately 68% of families below poverty line; 18% on welfare, median income about $3,500 but extending up to $10,000. About 25% of parents graduated from high school, 90% unskilled labor, remainder skilled and semiprofessional. 28% of the mothers worked, and apparently all of the fathers when present. No father in 40% of the homes. Median number of children in the family 4. The "no-show" rate was over 30% during the recruitment phase, but attrition was very low thereafter. | "A well-run middle class nursery school, with no specific 'enrichment' features." Children attended full day for 5 days a week. Each group of twelve had its own teacher and two or three teachers' aides. Weekly parent meetings were held at the university plus individual contacts with families, usually unscheduled. "In the hope of consolidating any benefits . . . a series of special school situations was arranged for the 30 experimental children during the three years immediately following nursery school." These included being in the same class in kindergarten, extra teachers and aides, in enriched curriculum, special trips, and assignment of a social worker to the children's families. | 30 children from one census tract were designated as the experimental group and 69 from the other three tracts as the control group. The experimental group ended up with a higher percentage of intact families (66% versus 16%), and slightly smaller families. |
| Perry Preschool Project, Ypsilanti, Michigan David P. Weikart (Weikart et al., 1970; Weikart, 1967) | Black children from disadvantaged homes residing in a city of 50,000 on the fringe of metropolitan Detroit. To qualify all children had to have IQs between 50 and 85 with no discernible organic involvement. In addition, families had to fall below a low cutting point on a cultural de- | Half-day classes, five days a week, from mid-October through May for two years. Curriculum derived mainly from Piagetian theory and focused on cognitive objectives. Four teachers for each group of 24 children with emphasis on individual and small group activities. Teachers made week- | Children from the total sample were divided at random into experimental and control groups with some matching on social class, IQ, boy/girl ratio, and percent of working mothers. The groups appear to be well matched on other variables as well. Although there |

| | | |
|---|---|---|
| privation scale based primarily on parents' education and occupation, and also number of persons per room in the home. Parents' education averaged below tenth grade; occupations over 70% unskilled; half the families are on welfare; no information on income; 14% of fathers unemployed. Average number of children in the family 4.8: 48% of the children have no father in the home; about 28% working mothers. There appears to have been little self-selection of families in the sample, and attrition during the course of the project has been low. | ly 90-minute home visit "to individualize instruction through a tutorial relationship with the student and to make parents knowledgeable about the educative process ... mothers are encouraged to observe and participate in as many teaching activities as possible during the home visits." | were 5 waves of experimental and control groups initiated over a period of years, the waves have been pooled in reporting follow-up data. |
| Early Training Project<br>Nashville, Tennessee<br>Susan W. Gray (Gray and Klaus, 1970; Klaus and Gray, 1968)<br><br>Black children from families "considerably below" the poverty line. Selected on the basis of parents' occupation (unskilled or semiskilled), education (average below eighth grade), income (average $1,500), and poor housing conditions. No data on welfare status or percent of parents unemployed; one-third of the homes with no father; median number of children per family 5. Both self-selection of families at entry and attrition over the course of the study appear to have been minimal. | In summer, daily morning classes emphasized the development of achievement motivation, perceptual and cognitive activities, and language. Each group of 19 had a Black head teacher and three or four teaching assistants divided equally as to race and sex. In dealing with the children, staff emphasized positive reinforcement of desired behavior. The weekly home visit stressed the involvement of the parent in the project and in activities with the child. Home visits lasted through the year. | Sixty-one children from the same large city were divided at random into two experimental groups (E1 and E2) and one control group (C1). The remaining control group (C2) consisted of 27 children from like backgrounds residing in a similar city 65 miles away. Group E1 attended the ten-week intervention program for three summers plus three years of weekly meetings with a trained home visitor when preschool was not in session. Group E2 began the program a year later with only two years of exposure. |

TABLE 14.1. *(continued)*

| Identifying Data | Sample | Nature of Intervention | Experimental and Control Groups |
|---|---|---|---|
| Philadelphia Project Temple University E. Kuno Beller (1972) | Children from urban slum areas of North Philadelphia, 90% Black. Families in target mainly employed in unskilled or semiskilled labor with median income of $3,400. Children admitted to the nursery group were selected from families responding to a written invitation, who also met the following criteria: "dependency of family on public services, mothers working, and broken homes." Kindergarten group consisted of children from the same classroom attended by nursery children, but without prior nursery experience. First grade group was composed of children entering the same classrooms but without prior nursery or kindergarten experience. Attrition was 10% by the time the original groups reached fourth grade. | Nursery groups composed of 15 children with one head and one assistant teacher for four half days a week, with a fifth day devoted to staff meetings, teacher training, and parent conferences. "The program was a traditional one" emphasizing "curiousity for discovery . . . creativity . . . warm, personalized handling of the child . . . balance of self-initiated instructed activities." Kindergarten and first grade classes consisted of 25 to 30 children, meeting five half days a week, with one head teacher and an aide or assistant teacher. Work with parents and home visits were conducted by a home-school coordinator. | A major purpose of the research was to examine the effect of age at entry into school by examining intellectual development of three comparison groups starting in nursery, kindergarten, and first grade, respectively. Groups were matched on age, sex, and ethnic background. No data are available on comparability of the three groups in terms of education, socioeconomic status, or family structure. Comparison at time of entry into school, on three different tests of intelligence and on other psychological measures, however, revealed no significant differences. The children from all three groups attended the same classrooms through Grade II, but by Grade III children were dispersed over many schools. |
| Indiana Project Indiana University Bloomington, Indiana Walter L. Hodges (Hodges et al., 1967) | Five-year-old children in good health predominantly White, from Bloomington and small semirural Indiana communities, selected on the basis of low-rated "psychosocial deprivation," and Binet intelligence score between 50 and 85. Average length of schooling for parents just below tenth grade. No information on welfare status or income. Fathers' | Group E1 was exposed to a special "diagnostically based curriculum" designed to remedy specific deficits of individual children through "an intensive, structured, cognitively-oriented" program. The children met daily for morning sessions. To increase the likelihood of adoption of the program by the public schools, "the teacher to child ratio was smaller in | One experimental group (E1) and control group (C2) were constituted by random assignment. Group E1 attended one year of the specially designed kindergarten program in Bloomington. C2 was composed of at-home controls from the same city. Children in Group C1 attended regular kindergartens newly established in several semirural Indiana |

| | | | | |
|---|---|---|---|---|
| | occupation approximately 70% unskilled and 8% semiskilled; 12% unemployed; one-third of the mothers work; 20% of the homes have no father present; average number of children in the family 5; no information is available on the degree of self-selection among sample families. There was only one slight attrition over the course of the study. | the present study than that reported in the other preschool projects. . . . For the same reason, no work was done with the families of the subjects." | towns. This was a "traditional kindergarten," providing facilities and equipment similar to those for C2, but without the special "diagnostically evolved" curriculum. Group C3 consisted of at-home controls in these same localities. In general, the families in the experimental group were rated by investigators as more disadvantaged than those in the control group, but this difference is not reflected in indices of socioeconomic status, family size, parents' education, or occupation. | Chosen from different neighborhoods to avoid contamination. "Comparisons between the groups revealed only small differences, many of which favored the control group, on the family variables that might be expected to influence the child's intellectual development." |
| Infant Education Research Project Washington, D.C. Earl S. Schaefer (Schaefer, 1972a, 1968; Schaefer and Aaronson, 1972; *Infant Education Research Project,* 1972) | Fifteen-month-old Black male infants selected from door-to-door surveys of families in two low socioeconomic inner-city neighborhoods in Washington. To be accepted, families had to meet four criteria: (1) income under $5,000; (2) mother's education under twelve years; (3) occupation either unskilled or semiskilled; and (4) willingness to have infant participate in either the experimental or control group. In addition, "an attempt was made to choose participants from relatively stable homes, not so noisy or overcrowded as to interfere with the home tutoring sessions." No other background information available. Of the 64 subjects in the original sample, 48 (equally divided between experimental and control group) were available for the final follow-up. | Trained tutors worked with each child in the home for one hour a day, five days per week, from the time the child was 15 months old until three years of age. The main emphasis was on development of verbal and conceptual abilities through the use of pictures, games, reading, and puzzles. "Participation of the mother and of other family members in the education of the infant was encouraged but not required." | | |

**TABLE 14.1.** *(continued)*

| Identifying Data | Sample | Nature of Intervention | Experimental and Control Groups |
|---|---|---|---|
| Verbal Interaction Project Mineola, New York Phyllis Levenstein (1972a, 1970) | Infants 2 to 3 years of age, 90% Black, from disadvantaged families in three Long Island suburbs. To qualify mothers had to be eligible for low income housing with an education not higher than high school graduation. About 25% of the families were on welfare. Average education of parents was eleventh grade; fathers apparently all employed; about 65% unskilled or semiskilled. About 35% of the fathers work; 30% of the fathers absent. Average number of children per family, 3-4. Self-selection involved in willingness of mothers in experimental group to participate. Attrition especially high in untreated control groups. Average IQ of mothers of children in the experimental groups was 83; in the control group, 88. | Semiweekly half-hour visits in the home for seven months each year by trained worker who stimulated interaction between mother and child with the aid of a kit of toys and books referred to as VISM (Visual Interaction Stimulus Materials). | Randomized by housing project. The several experimental and control groups differ on age of entry into the program (2 versus 3, see Table 11.3), length and intensity of intervention, and prior experience. Groups E1 and E2 had one year of the regular program at two years of age followed by a much abbreviated program in the second year as follows. Group E1 received seven visits in which the focus of attention was on the kit of materials with no involvement of the mother in interaction with the child. Group E2 was given the regular program but with half as many visits as in the first year. Group E3 received the full program for two years beginning at two years of age. Groups E4 and E5 were both given one year of the regular program at age three, but Group E had served the previous year as a "placebo" control group which had received the semiweekly visits but without exposure to the special kit of materials or encouragement of mother child interaction. The visitor simply brought a gift and played records for the child. Seven of the eight groups are generally comparable on major background variables, but one control group (C2) was far out of line with better educated mothers, smaller families, higher occupational status, no absent fathers, etc. |

2. *Ensuring Parental Motivation.* A number of the programs accepted for admission only families who had agreed in advance to enter their children in the intervention program if they were chosen for the experimental group (Herzog, Schaefer, Levenstein). Other projects did not exact such prior commitment.

3. *The Factor of Age.* In the majority of the programs, intervention began when the child was 3 years old, but there was some variation both across and within projects. Schaefer's subjects were 15 months old, three of Levenstein's experimental groups began with two-year-olds, Beller's youngest comparison group entered preschool at age 4 as did one of Gray's groups (E2), and the Hodges project began at the kindergarten level. This means that, at the end of follow-up, Schaefer's and Levenstein's subjects were only entering school, whereas the children in the Weikart, Beller, and Gray studies were already in third and fourth grade.

4. *Differences in Degree of Deprivation.* Although the children in every study came from disadvantaged homes, there was still some variation in the degree of deprivation and related characteristics from one sample to the next. Specifically:

　　a. Gray's program appears to have reached the least favored families. The sample is described as "considerably below the poverty line," with no mothers receiving more than an eighth grade education (as compared with an average of tenth grade or higher in the other projects).

　　b. Next in line were the Hodges, Weikart, and Beller[3] programs, where the families were somewhat better off but still limited in educational and occupational level.

　　c. In the two Washington projects (Herzog and Schaefer), there is evidence of less stringent circumstances as well as selectivity on motivational grounds. Both studies required willingness to have the child participate in the intervention program regardless of whether he ended up in the experimental or control group. In Herzog's sample, though the families came from inner-city neighborhoods, only 18% were on welfare (in comparison to 50% for the Weikart project) and some had incomes as high as $7,000 to $10,000. Schaefer's families, while not exceeding a $5,000 income, were restricted to "relatively stable homes" in which tutoring could be successfully conducted. There is also the probability of some self-selection in terms of allowing a tutor to come into the home.

　　d. At the upper end of the continuum is Levenstein's sample, with parents' education averaging eleven years, small families, and considerable self-selection in terms of mother's willingness to participate in the at-home sessions. Nevertheless, there is no doubt that the families represented a disadvantaged group, since the average IQ of the mothers was about 85.

5. *Forming Experimental and Control Groups.* The latter were of four different types.

　　a. *Randomized local control groups.* These were created by randomly

assigning children to a treated or untreated group from a relatively
homogeneous parent sample of families living in a particular neighborhood.

   b. *Nonrandom local control groups.* In the Beller study, control groups
   consisted of children in the same classes who had not had preschool
   experience.

   c. *Geographically randomized control groups.* In the Herzog, Schaefer,
   and Levenstein studies, experimental or control status was randomly
   assigned to groups living in different but comparable neighborhoods in
   the same or different communities.

   d. *Nonrandomized distal control groups.* Gray and Hodges each set up one
   control group in another but similar community. No random selection
   was involved.

We now turn to a consideration of the relevance of each of these factors for the
interpretation of results, beginning with one that introduces an artifact into the
data.

### The Effect of Initial IQ Level

If only those cases are included in the sample who fall below a specified IQ
score, the increase obtained at the next test period is likely to be spuriously high.
The artifact comes about in the following fashion. Children falling below the
cutting point on the first screening test are likely to include some who obtained a
low score for fortuitous reasons (for example, fatigue, distraction, or emotional
disturbance). At the time of the second test, these children tend to do better, and
thus raise the mean score of the entire group by some amount over and above any
impact of intervention. This phenomenon, commonly known as *regression to the
mean,* introduces a spurious element into all studies in which IQ is used as a basis
both for the selection of subjects and the evaluation of their progress. Because the
cut-off point is applied to the entire sample, the operation of the artifact is
manifested by the presence not only of a marked gain for children exposed to
intervention, but an appreciable though smaller increase for the control group as
well. Since one can never rule out the possibility that both the experimental and
control groups are being influenced, as in this instance, by some common factor,
the appropriate measure of the impact of intervention over time is not simply the
gain achieved in the course of the program but the difference between this gain and
any corresponding change in the control group over the same period.[4]

The phenomenon of regression to the mean explains the finding commonly
reported in intervention studies that the children in the program who show the
largest IQ gains are those with the lowest initial IQ scores. For example, in a study
by Karnes (1969), children from disadvantaged backgrounds entering five different
preschool intervention programs were stratified on the basis of their intelligence
quotients into three groups: IQ scores of 100 or above, 90 through 99, and 70
through 89. At the end of the first year, the average gain, across all five programs,
for the lowest ability group was approximately twice that for children with
beginning IQs of 100 or above. The same ratio of 2 to 1 still obtained in comparing

overall gains two years after completion of the program. A similar effect was found in the Herzog project included in our primary analysis (Herzog et al., 1972a, 1972b). The investigators divided the sample at the median in terms of initial IQ scores. Over the two years of preschool intervention, the children in the low ability group (IQ below 80) showed a gain of 21 points compared to 9 for those having IQs of 80 or over. Results of this kind suggest the optimistic conclusion that, among disadvantaged children, it is those with the lowest IQs who can benefit most from early intervention. As we have already seen, however, such a conclusion is warranted only if there has been adequate control for spurious gains produced by regression to the mean. In addition, it is desirable to reduce error variance by selecting samples on the basis of multiple criteria rather than of a single test score. To this writer's knowledge, the only research approaching these requirements is the Herzog study. In Table 2 of their reports (Herzog et al., 1972a, 1972b), the investigators present results for both experimental and control subjects of low and high ability. At the end of intervention, the difference in gain between experimentals and controls was higher by 6 points for the children of lower IQ, but the effect was not tested for statistical significance and washed out by the time the children were in second grade. Thus the available evidence does not yet justify the conclusion that disadvantaged children with the lowest IQs benefit most from early intervention.

## The Role of Age

As a number of investigators have pointed out (Bloom, 1965; Coleman, 1966; Deutsch, 1960; Di Lorenzo, 1969; Hayes and Grether, 1969; Schaefer, 1972b), the effects of deprivation become progressively greater as the child gets older. In fact, as we shall see in Schaefer's study, before the age of two, children from disadvantaged families tend to obtain normal scores on tests of mental development. Thereafter, the level drops rather suddenly and may continue to decline in environments that are especially impoverished. Moreover, as the disadvantaged child gets older and enters school, he tends to get further and further behind his classmates. With respect to intervention research, this means that, for samples from very deprived environments, not only the control group but even the experimental subjects in the program may decline in IQ, especially at older age levels. Indeed, programs initiated at older age levels may not produce gains as large or enduring those produced by programs begun when the child is only two or three years old.

## The Effect of Variations in Degree of Deprivation

The foregoing discussion suggests that intervention may be less effective with children who come from the most disadvantaged homes. Data in support of this conclusion are provided by Herzog and her colleagues (1972a, 1972b), who sought to determine how the child's response to intervention was influenced by the degree of deprivation in his environment. Because all of the children in the program came from disadvantaged families, it was necessary to identify variables that would differentiate levels of deprivation within this relatively homogeneous group. To accomplish this purpose, Herzog and her colleagues utilized a combined index based on two factors: the number of years of education of the child's mother, and the ratio of persons per room in the home. When the sample was divided into a low and high group on the basis of this index, the analysis revealed that children in the relatively less deprived group gained more from the program and retained a larger proportion of their gains. In fact, two years after completion of intervention, only the more favored group showed a statistically significant difference between experimental and control children. The bitter impact of this set of findings is epitomized in the title of the most recent report published by the Herzog group: "Double Deprivation: The Less They Have, The Less They Learn" (Herzog et al., 1972b). This harsh dictum conveys a note of fatalism which is not entirely justified, since, as we shall see, the data permit other, more encouraging interpretations. But, for the moment, we are concerned with the methodological implication of Herzog's findings: they indicate that projects involving children from relatively less deprived homes are likely to get more favorable results, in terms of both immediate and long-term outcomes.

## The Effect of Requiring Prior Commitment

A similar result appears likely when all families are required in advance to agree to continue in the study regardless of whether they are subsequently assigned to the experimental or control group. Although such a procedure ensures greater comparability in motivation of the two groups, it may also have the effect of selecting from the disadvantaged population those parents who have the highest interest and motivation in furthering the development of their children. As a result, children enrolled in programs employing such a criterion may show greater gains. Indeed, the high level of motivation in such samples may result in increases not only for experimental subjects but for the control group as well, particularly if both are located in the same community so that control families can become informed about the program.

## Problems of Comparability Between Experimental and Control Groups

The most comprehensive and effective strategy for minimizing any initial differences between experimental and control groups involves random assignment of individual children to one or the other group from a relatively homogeneous sample. This was the procedure followed by Weikart, Gray (C1 group only) and Hodges (C2 group only). Elegant as this method is, it entails some problems. First, randomness does not guarantee equality on all relevant variables. To correct for chance discrepancies, the composition of each group can be adjusted, as Weikart did, to ensure comparability in such critical factors as initial IQ and socioeconomic level. Even without such adjustment, however, a reasonably satisfactory match is usually achieved as evidenced by comparative data on the social backgrounds of experimental and control groups cited by Weikart (1970), and Hodges (1967).

Even though comparability is achieved initially, it may gradually be lost through selective and differential dropout rates from the experimental versus the control group over time. Fortunately, as indicated in Table 14.1, this did not occur in any of the randomly created experimental and control groups employed in the studies under investigation.

But the most serious limitation of the strategy of randomization derives from its social consequences. Since the families from a relatively homogeneous sample usually live in the same community, or even neighborhood, and since they show an interest, or at least a willingness, to enroll their children in an intervention program, the members of the experimental and control group are likely to be in communication with each other, and the latter to be influenced by the program indirectly through contagion. In other words, the control group too may show some gains. When this occurs, differences between groups are reduced and the true impact of intervention is underestimated. This phenomenon has been referred to by Gray as "horizontal diffusion" (Gray and Klaus, 1970).

One technique for counteracting this effect is to establish control groups that are, at least to some extent, geographically separated. This method was employed by Schaefer, Herzog, Levenstein, Gray (C2 group), and Hodges (C3 group). The procedure followed by Gray and Hodges of setting up a control group in another city or town increases the risk of a major source of confounding neatly avoided in the method of random assignment. Clearly all parents in the experimental group must be willing to enroll their children in the intervention program. If families in a control group located elsewhere are not presented with the same real possibility and then matched on their readiness to take advantage of it, marked differences may result in favor of what becomes a more highly motivated, self-selected experimental group.

In neither the Gray nor the Hodges study is any indication given of how children were recruited for the distal control group. The manner of selection is described, however, in a third instance of nonrandomized assignment, this one occurring within the confines of a single community. In the Beller project, the nursery group was drawn from disadvantaged families who had responded positively to a written invitation to enroll their children in a preschool intervention program for three-year-olds. The invitation was sent to all parents of children attending four schools in a slum area of Philadelphia. The second comparison group was not formed until the nursery group entered kindergarten, and consisted of children entering the same classes who had not had prior preschool experience. Presumably this group included some families who had received the invitation in the previous year, and others who had not. No information is provided on this score. The third comparison group was not created until both the preceding groups had reached the first grade, and included only those children who were entering school for the first time. The three groups were matched on age, sex, and ethnic background, but not on parents' education or occupation, or willingness to enroll a child in an early intervention program. The groups did not differ significantly on three tests of intelligence and other psychological measures administered after each group entered school, a fact which Beller (1973) feels demonstrates the absence of sampling bias. In this reviewer's judgment, however, one cannot dismiss the possibility that the parents differed in their aspirations for the child, interest in education, and other social factors usually associated with these motivational variables. Unfortunately, the study provides no comparative data on the background characteristics of the three samples. The author states: "We did not attempt to find out why some children entered school earlier and others later" (Beller, 1972: 40). In view of these circumstances, it is impossible to determine to what extent the emerging differences in IQ score were due to program or to sample variation.

The bias introduced by failure to control for motivational differences between the experimental and control group may be avoided through the technique employed by Schaefer, Herzog, and Levenstein of requiring all participants in the study to indicate their prior willingness to enroll their children in an intervention program and then assigning experimental or control status at random from different housing projects or neighborhoods. When the principle of random assignment is applied to groups rather than individuals, there is, of course, a greater likelihood that the treated and untreated groups may differ by chance on important confounding variables. A dramatic example is provided by the C2 grouping in Levenstein's study, which turned out to be the least disadvantaged of any experimental or control sample included in the analysis.

## Some Methodological Hypotheses

In the light of several confounding factors outlined above, it is apparent that certain of the studies presented in Table 14.1 are likely to yield more gratifying results than others simply by virtue of the character of the sample and the method employed for setting up experimental and control groups. It is instructive to anticipate how these sources of variation may be reflected in particular projects and their respective experimental and control groups. We do so in the form of a series of methodological hypotheses focused on the major issues we have raised.

1. *Regression to the Mean.* Greatest gains in IQ, at least initially, are likely to be shown by the two projects (Weikart and Hodges) that used IQ as a criterion for admission. Similar but smaller increases are also to be expected in the corresponding control groups.

2. *The Effect of Differences in Motivation.* With other factors held constant, emerging differences between treated and untreated groups can be expected to be greater when the control group has been selected without regard to the family's motivation to enter their child in the experimental intervention program. An opportunity for checking this expectation arises in the two projects (Gray and Hodges) that have employed both a randomly assigned local control group and a distal one established on an ad hoc basis.

3. *Variations with Age.* If other factors are held constant, experimental gains and differences between treated and untreated groups should be greater and more enduring for programs involving the youngest children (Schaefer and Levenstein). Decline in IQ, among members of experimental and control groups, should be especially marked among older children from the most deprived groups (Gray).

4. *Differences in Degree of Deprivation.* If other factors are held constant, experimental gains and differences should be greater and more enduring in the projects utilizing samples that are most selective in terms of social backgrounds and motivation. Conversely, the effects should be smaller and lost more quickly in the more deprived samples. Also, to the extent that control groups exhibit systematic changes over time, they should parallel the

above trends in reduced degree. In light of the evaluation of relative deprivation made in the preceding section, IQ gains and differences should be
greatest for the Levenstein project with the Schaefer, Herzog, Hodges,
Weikart, Beller, and Gray programs following in that order.

It should be noted that some of the foregoing methodological hypotheses
predict contradictory results, whereas others offer alternative grounds for expecting
the same finding. In the latter case, we can, of course, expect no resolution of the
issue. Moreover, even when a methodological effect is present, it may be overridden
by genuine differences in program effectiveness. We are faced, therefore, with a
difficult and hazardous task of analysis. With but seven studies typically including
no more than one experimental and one control group, any inferences are subject
to substantial sampling errors, not to mention errors of judgment. But, on the
premise that some imperfect knowledge carefully considered is better than none,
the task appears worth undertaking. What do the data say?

## IV.  SOME EFFECTS OF PRESCHOOL INTERVENTION IN GROUP SETTINGS

What the data say with respect to the results of group intervention is shown in
Table 14.2. For each study, the table records the number of subjects, IQs achieved
in successive years by experimental and control groups, and the differences between
them. The scores given first are those obtained by both groups before the program
began. A double line indicates the point at which intervention was terminated. At
the bottom, major changes over time are summarized in terms of initial gain
(before-after difference in the first year of treatment), gain two years after all
intervention was terminated (shown because it permits a comparison of all seven
studies), and overall gain (difference between initial IQ and last follow-up score
three to four years after the children left the program). Also shown are differences
between these gains for the experimental, control, and comparison groups. Finally,
the bottom row records the average grade equivalent attained on a test of academic
achievement administered in the final year of follow-up. Unless otherwise noted,
significant differences between experimental and control groups for each year are
designated by asterisks, one for the 5% level and two for the 1%. The absence of
asterisks indicates that the difference was not reliable. Ordinarily no significance
tests are available for gain scores, but these are shown in the few instances when
they were computed by the original investigator.

### General Trends

The results themselves exhibit two striking and consistent patterns; one of them
is heartening, the other not so. First, it is clearly evident from every project that
preschool intervention is effective in producing substantial gains in IQ that are
generally maintained so long as the program lasts. And therein lies the more
sobering message. By and large, the experimental groups do not continue to make
gains when intervention is continued beyond one year, and even more regrettably
the increases achieved in the initial phase, even the largest ones, tend to "wash
out." In general, one year after intervention is terminated, the IQ of the "grad-

TABLE 14.2. EFFECTS ON LATER INTELLECTUAL DEVELOPMENT OF INTERVENTION PROGRAMS IN PRESCHOOL SETTINGS
(DOUBLE LINE DESIGNATES POINT AT WHICH INTERVENTION WAS TERMINATED.)

| | Herzog | | | Weikart | | | Gray | | | | | Beller | | | Hodges | | | | |
|---|---|---|---|---|---|---|---|---|---|---|---|---|---|---|---|---|---|---|---|
| | 1 | 2 | 3 | 4 | 5 | 6 | 7 | 8 | 9 | 10 | 11 | 12 | 13 | 14 | 15 | 16 | 17 | 18 | 19 |
| | E | C | E-C | E | C | E-C | E1 | E2 | C1 | C2 | E-C1[b] | C1 | C2 | C3 | E | C1 | C2 | C3 | E-C2 |
| N | 30 | 66-62 | | 58-13[a] | 65-15[a] | | 19 | 19 | 18 | 23 | | 57-50 | 53-46 | 57-53 | 11 | 11 | 13 | 13 | |
| Age 3 Before | 81 | 85 | -4 | 79.7 | 79.1 | .6 | 87.6 | 92.5[c] | 85.4 | 86.7 | -1.4[c] | | | | | | | | |
| Age 3 After | 91 | 85 | 6 | 95.8 | 83.4 | 12.4** | 102.0 | 92.3[c] | 88.2 | 87.4 | 11.8*[c] | | | | | | | | |
| Age 4 Before | 96 | 88 | 8** | 94.7 | 82.7 | 12.0** | 96.4 | 94.8 | 89.6 | 86.7 | 6.0 | 92.1 | | | | | | | |
| Age 4 After | 97 | 90 | 7 | 90.5 | 85.4 | 5.1* | 97.1 | 97.5 | 87.6 | 84.7 | 9.7* | | | | | | | | |
| Kindergarten Before | | | | | | | 95.8 | 96.6 | 82.9 | 80.2 | 13.3*[g] | 98.6 | 91.2 | | 74.5 | 75.0 | 74.5 | 72.5 | 0 |
| Kindergarten After | | | | | | | | | | | | | | | 93.8 | 87.5 | 80.9 | 81.3 | 12.9* |
| Grade 1 | 95 | 89 | 6 | 91.2 | 83.3 | 7.9** | 98.1 | 99.7 | 91.4 | 89.0 | 7.5* | 98.4 | 94.4 | 89.9 | 97.4 | 83.2 | 91.7 | 84.8 | 5.4 |
| Grade 2 | 92 | 87 | 5 | 88.8 | 86.5 | 2.3 | 91.2 | 96.0 | 87.9 | 84.6 | 5.7* | 97.8 | 92.8 | 88.6 | 94.9 | 85.5 | 89.2 | 86.5 | 5.7 |
| Grade 3 | 87 | 87 | 0 | 89.6 | 88.1 | 1.5 | — | — | — | — | | 97.6 | 93.1 | 89.3 | | | | | |
| Grade 4 | | | | | | | 86.7 | 90.2 | 84.9 | 77.7 | 3.5*[e] | 98.4 | 91.7 | 88.6 | | | | | |
| Initial Gain | 10 | 0 | 10 | 16.1 | 4.3 | 11.8 | 14.4 | 5.0 | 2.8 | .7 | 6.9 | 6.5* | 3.2 | -1.3 | 19.3 | 12.5 | 6.4 | 8.8 | 12.9 |
| Gain 2 Years After | 14 | 4 | 10 | 11.5 | 4.2 | 7.3 | 3.6 | 3.5 | 2.5 | -2.1 | 1.1 | 6.3 | 1.6 | -.6 | 20.4 | 10.5 | 14.7 | 12.0 | 5.7 |
| Overall Gain | 6 | 2 | 4 | 9.9 | 9.0 | .9 | -.9 | -2.3 | -.5 | -9.0 | 1.3 | 6.3 | .5 | -1.3 | 2.1 | 2.0 | 1.8 | 1.5 | .4 |
| Achievement Level | No difference | | | 2.1 | .6 | 1.5*[f] | 3.7 | 4.0 | 3.8 | 3.4 | .2 | — | — | — | | | | | |

a. N's decrease because only earlier waves reached grade school (see Table 14.1).
b. Published significance level includes C2.
c. Intervention began one year later in E2; hence C1 includes E2 for this age group only.
d. Significance of difference not tested.
e. Difference significant for the distal control group (C2) only.
f. Difference significant for girls only.
g. A reduced parent intervention program was continued through grade one.

uates" begins to drop, the difference between the experimental and control groups gradually decreases, the once impressive gains are reduced to a few points, and, what is most crucial, the average IQ of the experimental group often falls back into the problem range of the lower 90s and below.

The regressive trend is most apparent in the three projects that have followed their subjects the longest after school entry, up to four years after completion of the program. In the Herzog and Weikart studies, which involved two years of intervention beginning at age 3 with gains of 15 points while the program was in operation, the experimental and control group showed practically no difference by the time the children were in the third grade.[5] Although the Gray study still shows a statistically significant difference between experimentals and controls in the fourth year of follow-up, the results are even more disappointing, for, if IQ score is taken as a criterion, both of the experimental groups end up no better off than they were when they started seven years earlier. The first experimental group, which had entered a three-year intervention program with an average IQ of 88, rose to a high of 102 within the first year, but began to fall while the children were still in the program and by fourth grade had dropped back to its original level. The second experimental group, entering a year later, started a higher point[6] but showed a similar parabolic pattern.

## Some Deviant Cases

There do appear to be some exceptions to the generally downward trend, but on closer inspection these turn out to be faulted by the methodological artifacts which we anticipated.

*Regression to the Mean.* For example, inspection of the gains recorded in the last three rows of the table reveals dramatic increases that appear to endure in the case of two experimental groups. The highest initial gain of 19 IQ points achieved in the Hodges program was still holding its own two years after intervention had been terminated. The next highest initial leap of 16 points, attained in the Weikart program, dropped to 10 points four years after intervention when the children were in the third grade, but it was then the highest achieved in any of the five projects. The spurious nature of these high increases becomes obvious when we recall that these are the only two studies that used initial IQ as a basis for selection of subjects. In short, the gains are inflated by regression to the mean. The extent of the artifact is indicated by the increase recorded for the same period by the corresponding control groups, an initial gain of 4 points in the Weikart project and from 6 to 9 points in the Hodges study. (The C1 control group is excluded because these children were exposed to a regular kindergarten program.) An unbiased estimate of the accomplishment of the two experimental groups is provided by the difference score in the last column for each project. At the end of second grade, the difference between randomized treated and untreated groups was 5.7 IQ points in the Hodges program, 2.3 points in the Weikart study, both insignificant differences.

*Motivational Effects.* From the viewpoint of stability and durability of experimental effects, the Beller program might seem to be the most effective. There is no problem with regression to the mean; the differences between comparison groups are consistently significant and actually increase somewhat four years after intervention was terminated. The difficulty, of course, is the possibility of motivational bias in favor of the nursery families who were self-selected through their positive response to a written invitation sent out by the schools, and against the children in the third comparison group, whose parents did not enter them in school until the first grade.

To complete the roster of exceptions, the Gray program still shows a significant difference four years after termination between both experimental groups and the distal control group. Unfortunately, this promising finding is confounded by failure to control for differences in motivation to enroll the child in an early intervention program. This effect may be checked by comparing the scores of the randomly selected local versus the ad hoc distal control groups in the Gray (C1 versus C2) and Hodges (C2 versus C3) projects. A comparison of the relevant series of means in Table 14.2 reveals that, in almost every instance, the former are higher than the latter. The trend is evident not only in IQ scores but also in achievement test results. Although the IQ differences in any one year are not significant, it seems probable that the overall discrepancy would turn out to be reliable had it been tested. Moreover, over the full range of seven years encompassed by the Gray project, the difference becomes progressively larger.

All of these facts are in accord with the expectation that failure to control for parents' motivation produces a bias in favor of the experimental group. Although the magnitude of this bias is qualified by the possibility of horizontal diffusion in the local setting,[7] it is unlikely that effects of contagion are powerful enough to explain all of the difference.

In the light of the foregoing analysis accounting for apparent exceptions to the general trend, our original conclusion still stands; namely, *the substantial gains achieved in the first year of group intervention programs tend to wash out once the program is discontinued.*

### Relevant Evidence from Other Studies

Additional support for this conclusion comes from four other longitudinal studies which, on one or another ground, failed to meet our criteria for inclusion in the primary comparison group.

*Sprigle's "Learning to Learn" Program.* Sprigle's "Learning to Learn" Program, enrolling children from low income Black families in Jacksonville, Florida, is still under way (Sprigle, 1972; Van De Riet, 1972, Resnick and Van De Riet, 1973). One experimental group, which gained 17 points during two years of intervention, has now been followed for one year in the public schools. The IQ achieved at this point shows a slight drop, which, taken by itself, justifies no conclusion.

*The Di Lorenzo Research.* A second study, however, permits extension to the next grade level. In an evaluation of the effects of preschool programs introduced in eight New York State communities, Di Lorenzo (1969) still found significant differences between randomized experimental and control groups through the first grade on tests of academic achievement. (No intelligence tests were included in the follow-up battery.) But in the one community in which follow-up was continued for an additional year because of "notable success . . . the significant results achieved by this program, which were sustained through the first grade, were no longer visible at the end of second grade" (Di Lorenzo, 1969: VII-15).

In addition to providing confirmatory evidence, Di Lorenzo reports data not available from the other studies covered in this analysis, which, at first glance, appear to contradict a conclusion reached earlier. In addition to a randomized control group, this investigation included two samples of nondisadvantaged children who were randomly assigned either to the control group or to the experimental classes. In contrast to their disadvantaged classmates, these children were mostly White, and came from middle class families living in residential sections of two suburban communities. The mean family income for this sample was about $12,000, and the average education of parents was two years of college. Under the circumstances, it seems more appropriate, and less cumbersome, to refer to this group as "advantaged children" rather than merely "nondisadvantaged" as Di Lorenzo does.

In the course of the one-year preschool intervention program, both the advantaged and disadvantaged children showed statistically significant increases in comparison to their respective controls, but in general, the disadvantaged gained more than the advantaged.

Upon first consideration, this finding appears to run counter to Herzog's results and her disheartening conclusion that "the less they have, the less they learn." Here it was those who had more who learned less. The critical factor, of course, is the fact that Herzog's sample was drawn entirely from inner-city neighborhoods with a median income of $3,500 and only 25% high school graduates. Much of what these children, along with the disadvantaged children in the New York State study, gained from preschool intervention was already present in the homes of the advantaged children in the Di Lorenzo sample. The latter were starting from a much higher base, an average IQ of 105 compared to 91 for their disadvantaged classmates.

Additional light is shed on this issue by the results of tests of language development administered in the New York State project. Whereas the disadvantaged children in the program showed significant gains in language level compared to their controls, the advantaged children did not. In Di Lorenzo's view,

> This finding seems to confirm the assertion that the home environment of the disadvantaged preschool child is lacking in the opportunity for language development. The language programs offered added nothing to these levels to the non-disadvantaged child's environment that was not present in his home. [Di Lorenzo, 1969: V-25]

Finally, the Di Lorenzo study presents our first clear evidence on the comparative effectiveness of different types of preschool programs. The curricula employed in the eight communities ranged from the traditional nursery school approach emphasizing free play to kindergarten programs focusing on explicit learning goals. On the basis of a careful analysis, the eight projects were classified along this continuum into three groups, highly structured, moderate, and unstructured, and then compared on measures of intelligence and language development. Most of the significant differences between experimental and control groups were found in the more academic, cognitively oriented programs. This contrast was even more pronounced in the analysis of carry-over effects of the program into kindergarten and first grade. So long as significant differences could be detected, they were "attributable to the cognitive rather than the nursery programs" (Di Lorenzo, 1969: VIII-15).

*Karnes's Curriculum Comparison.* Remarkably similar but more differentiated conclusions were reached by Karnes (1969) in her comprehensive follow-up study comparing the effectiveness of three preschool curricula for groups of disadvantaged children. The first was a traditional nursery school emphasizing informal learning. The second employed the Bereiter-Engelmann (1966) approach designed to teach basic rules and logical structures involved in language usage, arithmetic, and reading. The third was a special curriculum developed by Karnes emphasizing verbal interaction as a means to foster understanding of mathematical concepts, language, reading, science, and social studies. For the first two years of the study, two other programs were included: a Montessori preschool focused on sensory-motor development, and a community nursery school similar to the one described above but including both advantaged and disadvantaged children. At the end of the first year of intervention, the results in terms of IQ and other cognitive measures showed clear superiority for Karnes's Direct Verbal program and the Bereiter-Engelmann curriculum, with the other three trailing behind. Karnes explains the relative inferiority of the two nursery groups on the grounds of insufficient cognitive structure. The poor performance of the Montessori group is analyzed in the following terms:

> The failure of the Montessori children to demonstrate appreciable progress seems to invalidate the notion that the level of structure relates to the progress made by the disadvantaged child. The Montessori program provided a high degree of structure in terms of careful planning for the kinds of motor-sensory activity appropriate to development. . . . The Montessori teacher provided a "prepared environment" but did not systematically engage the child in verbalizations or require such verbalizations as part of the definition of productive involvement. This failure of the Montessori program resulted, at least during the intervention period, in somewhat regressive language behavior. Structured emphasis on motor-sensory development without similar concern for verbal development programmatically moves in the wrong direction for the disadvantaged child. [Karnes, 1969: 13]

In the second year of the program, all five groups attended regular kindergarten in the morning. In the afternoon the children in the Karnes and Bereiter-Engelmann treatments continued to receive special training whereas the other groups did not. This differences was reflected in continuing IQ gains for the latter groups and by a decline for the other three. When the children entered first grade, the follow-up was continued for the Karnes, Bereiter-Engelmann, and traditional nursery groups. By the end of the year, the descending IQ curves for all three groups began to converge toward the bottom of the now-familiar parabola, and the differences among them became nonsignificant. Unfortunately, the absence of an untreated control group precludes comparison with the other studies in our analysis. Karnes's own conclusion is similar to our own.

> The deterioration in language and intellectual functioning which occurred at the termination of intensive programming demonstrates the need for continued intervention. [Karnes, 1969: 22]

*Deutsch's Five Year Intervention Program.* The results of continued intervention with an even more deprived group than Karnes's subjects, who lived in depressed neighborhoods of Champaign-Urbana in central Illinois, are reported in a study by Deutsch (1971) carried out with disadvantaged youngsters from urban slums in New York City, including Harlem.

> In general, the families involved in this program live in conditions of economic deprivation; in crowded and unsafe housing; in an area characterized by high drug addiction rates, high crime rates, low-employment rates, and inadequate health facilities. [Deutsch, Taleporos, and Victor, 1972]

The intervention program began when the children were three years of age and continued into the schools until the end of the third grade. Because there was no follow-up after completion of intervention, the study did not permit evaluation of long-term effects and was excluded for that reason. Both initial gains and differences between the randomized experimental and control groups were quite small (7 points), and the means for the experimental group showed the characteristic hairpin turn while the children were still in the program. At the final testing, after the children had been exposed to five years of intervention, the IQ difference between the experimental and randomized control group was a nonsignificant 4 points (97 versus 93).

## The Issue of Program Length

Deutsch's results raises an important question. Does the length of program bear any positive relation to outcome? Hopefully, a child who has had the benefit of an intervention program for two or three years would gain more and retain the gain longer than one who has participated for one year only. The data of Table 14.2 are hardly reassuring on this score, at least so far as preschool programs in group setting are concerned. There are four experimental groups who were exposed to intervention for more than a year beginning at three years of age. If one takes into account that Herzog's subjects continued to receive special treatment for three years after nursery school, including extra teachers and an enriched curriculum, then two of the programs involved at least three years of intervention (Herzog and Gray's E1) and another two (Weikart and Gray's E2) had two years. Of these four, only one shows some rise after the initial gain (Herzog), two show essentially no change (Weikart and Gray's E2) and the third (Gray's E1), like Deutsch's experimental group, actually declines. It is significant, in the light of our expectations regarding the impact of degree of deprivation on response to intervention, that the Gray and Deutsch samples are the most economically depressed of any included in this analysis.

The hope that longer programs may ensure more enduring gains is also disappointed. If one takes as a criterion the difference in gain between experiment and control groups two years after completion, then the 6 point IQ difference produced by one year of intervention in the Hodges study holds its own against the corresponding 7 point discrepancy achieved in two years by Weikart's project and clearly surpasses the 1 point residual remaining after three years (to be sure, mainly during summers) of Gray's program. It is disheartening that the differences are so small when the years are so long!

Is it possible that the absence of any cumulative effect of intervention programs in these studies is a function of their failure to employ the kind of structured curriculum emphasizing verbal interaction that Di Lorenzo, Karnes, and others have shown to be optimal for disadvantaged children? It is significant in this regard that the two projects in this analysis which produced the smallest initial experimental effects (Herzog and Beller) were the only two to follow a traditional nursery school approach with emphasis on free play and informal activities. In contrast, the Weikart and Gray, and Hodges projects, which, in an evaluation by Bissell (1970), were classified as "structured cognitive programs," were the most effective at the beginning. The fact that they, too, ultimately showed a declining curve (in Gray's project, while intervention was still in progress) suggests that even the best curriculum cannot immunize a disadvantaged child against developmental decline once he is cast back into his old environment.

*Group Intervention: Early versus Late.* In Table 14.2, all of the groups exposed to more than one year of intervention entered the program at three years of age. The questions therefore arises whether greater gains might not have been achieved had intervention begun earlier, in the first or second year of life. Data bearing on this issue have been reported from a project directed by Caldwell (Brown and Caldwell, 1972) in which thirty disadvantaged preschoolers who had entered the program at different ages, beginning with six months, achieved gains in IQ. To test for the influence of age at entry, the total sample was divided into two groups, those who had been admitted before the age of three (N = 19) and those enrolled after (N = 11). Average IQs for the two groups at the time of admission were 101 and 102, respectively; the scores following intervention were identical, 119, for a gain of 17 and 16 points, respectively. Thus Caldwell's results lend further support to the conclusion that neither longer or earlier exposure to group intervention produces greater effects.

*The Effect of School Entry.* An increase in IQ following the initial gain did occur, however, in almost every group, treated or untreated. It took place not while intervention was going on but afterward and was more pronounced in the control than in the experimental groups. We refer to the consistent rise in score after the children first entered school. On the fifteen treated and untreated groups in Table 14.2 twelve exhibited this effect. Of the remaining three, one was the experimental group in the Weikart project, which had been exposed to a highly cognitively oriented, Piaget-type curriculum producing the highest genuine initial gain observed in any group program; the C2 control group of the Hodges program had already been in a regular kindergarten for a year; and the C2 sample in the Beller study was a negatively selected group composed of children from families who, for one reason or another, did not enter their children in school until first grade, even though public kindergartens existed in the community.

The explanation for this highly consistent phenomenon, as well as for the exceptions to the rule, seems almot self-evident. When the disadvantaged child receives additional cognitive stimulation, as he typically does upon entry into school, his capacity to perform on tests of cognitive function is enhanced. This is particularly true for a youngster who is exposed to an educational program for the first time, which is what happens in a control group. The reaction was less pronounced in the experimental groups since they had already had such a broadening experience at the beginning of intervention. The slight drop exhibited by what was probably the most cognitively stimulated of these groups, that in Weikart's program, approximates the reaction of a middle class child, who, like the advantaged children in Di Lorenzo's sample, has already experienced much of what ordinary school has to offer.

But why does this opening up of new horizons for the disadvantaged child fail to have enduring effect? The answer again may lie not within the preschool experience but in the home and its environment, an issue we shall examine when we consider the effectiveness of home-based intervention programs.

## The Effectiveness of School-Age Intervention

A second and more consequential issue is also raised by Deutsch's results. If extended into the schools, can experimental programs achieve and maintain the impressive gains produced by intervention at younger age? At least for kindergarten and first grade, the prospect is a hopeful one. In Table 14.2, the two projects (Gray and Hodges) operative at the kindergarten level show differences between experimental and control groups which compare favorably with those with younger children both in the same and other programs. Corroborative data come from the Sprigle project which reports high gains and experimental differences in IQ through the first grade. Finally, and most significantly, preliminary results are being reported for the first two years (kindergarten and first grade) of the nationwide, federally sponsored Follow-Through program which extends the basic philosophy of Head Start into the primary grades. The program is being carried out at centers scattered over the nation and employing a variety of educational approaches. An evaluation of the relative effectiveness of these different strategies, as well as the overall impact of the program, is being carried out with a national sample of over 3,900 children enrolled in Follow-Through classes and a comparison group of over 2,000 entering school in kindergarten or first grade.

*Some Early Findings from Follow-Through Programs.* No data from intelligence tests are available, but preliminary analysis of performance on academic achievement tests (Stanford Research Institute, 1971a, 1971b) indicates that Follow-Through children made significantly larger fall-to-spring gains in achievement than did children in the comparison sample. In addition, the analysis examined which children made the most gains and identified three trends, two of them corroborating conclusions already found in other studies. First, since Follow-Through classes included some students above the poverty line, it was possible to compare program efficiency for advantaged versus disadvantaged children; consistent with Di Lorenzo's findings, larger achievement gains were made by Follow-Through participants in both kindergarten and first grade who were below the OEO poverty line. Second, the children who made the most gains tended to come from programs with more highly structured curricula. Finally, higher gains were made by children who had participated in Head Start prior to enrolling in the Follow-Through program.

Encouraging as these findings are, they must be viewed with some caution. To consider the points in reverse order, the conclusion that children who had been Head Start did better than those who had not was apparently based on a simple comparison of the two groups without control for possible differences in family background factors such as education, or interest in furthering the child's development. It is possible, therefore, that the obtained result reflects differences in sample rather than effectiveness or prior intervention. Assuming that the finding will be confirmed in a more refined analysis, one may ask why the effects of group intervention should be cumulative in this instance when they were not in the other studies we have examined. One possible consideration lies in the comprehensive character of both the Head Start and Follow-Through programs; that is, they are concerned not only with providing an educational program, but also with meeting the needs of the child and his family in the areas of health and social service. We shall return to a consideration of this point in later discussion.

*Which Curriculum Is Best?* With respect to the differential impact of various curricula, there can be little doubt that more structured programs are more effective for disadvantaged children at the preschool and primary level. This conclusion has been elegantly confirmed by a recent observational study conducted by Soar (1972) in 151 Follow-Through classrooms for which achievement data were made available from the national study. His principal finding was that "greater amounts of teacher control, structure, focus, and convergence, or lesser amounts of pupil freedom, exploration of ideas, or experimental teaching led to increased pupil cognitive growth, especially in the skill measures" (Soar, 1972: 147).

Having established the superiority of cognitively oriented approaches, we must now take cognizance of some of their limitations. First, the criterion of cognitive growth in all the other studies we have examined is performance on objective tests designed for the primary grades. We remind the reader of the stated limitations of such instruments and the functions they measure. Second, there is evidence that highly structured curricula may have some less commendable side effects outside the sphere of academic achievement. Thus Bissell (1971), in an analysis of results from a national research program evaluating different approaches in Head Start, found that children enrolled in more structured programs were more likely to give passive responses on the Hertzig-Birch (Hertzig et al., 1968) measures of coping style. According to Bissell, the results "suggest that the children have learned what a question is and what an appropriate answer is." Such an orientation may be far more adaptive to the kinds of tasks required of the child in the primary grades than to the expectations of intellectual initiative in defining and solving problems encountered in the upper grades.

In the same vein, preliminary results of the Follow-Through analysis indicate that changes in attitude toward school and learning were more likely to occur in the so-called Discovery approaches rather than the Structured Academic, although it was children enrolled in the latter programs who made particularly large gains. Moreover, in the Discovery groups, there was a strong association between positive shifts in attitudes toward school and gains in achievement. No such relation obtained in the Structured Academic approaches. Finally, the Soars have demonstrated that greater amounts of academic growth over the summer were associated with an unstructured individual teaching style during the preceding school year rather than with a structured, direct style (Soar, 1966; Soar and Soar, 1969). Given these facts, it no longer follows that the latter orientation should be the chosen strategy in group intervention programs at the preschool or school-age level. Rather one looks to some optimal mix that begins with firm structure but invites discovery in gradually increasing measure.

*The Effectiveness and Long-Range Potential of Follow-Through.* Finally, on the basic issue of the effectiveness of Follow-Through programs, a serious question is introduced by the failure in the analysis to control for differences in background characteristics of families in the Follow-Through and comparison groups. The available information indicates that the median level of education for the former was in the high school range, but, for the latter, close to eighth grade. Even if the observed difference remains after appropriate statistical corrections for this bias, there is the possibility of important motivational difference between the two groups, the effect of which we have yet to examine.

But the all-important question is whether the difference will continue to obtain for children enrolled in the Follow-Through program in subsequent grades. It is significant in this regard that, in Table 14.2, the most substantial drops in IQ of both experimental and control groups occur past the first grade in the Gray project, which we identified as serving the most environmentally deprived families. Similarly, Deutsch's experimental subjects, who appear to have come from a severely depressed and socially disorganized slum, showed a drop in IQ between the first and fourth grade even though the intervention program was still in operation. It has been fashionable to blame the schools for the erosion of competence in disadvantaged children after six years of age. The decline of IQ in Deutsch's experimental subjects, who were enrolled in an innovative and enriched educational program, suggests that the fault lies in substantial degree beyond the doors of the school.

*Growth and Decline In and Out of School.* The source of the problem, and its potential solution, are suggested by a series of studies in which familiar data are analyzed in a new, simple, and revealing fashion (Hayes and Grether, 1969; Soar, 1966; Soar and Soar, 1969). Whereas ordinarily investigators assess academic gains by examining changes from fall to spring, these researchers also looked at the remaining inverval from spring to fall. In other words, what happens over the summer?

A typical answer appears in Hayes and Grethers's analysis of results on reading achievement tests from several hundred thousand students enrolled in grades 2 through 6 of the New York City school system. Although pupils from various social and ethnic groups start at markedly different levels in the fall and gain at somewhat different rates during the year, the main difference occurs over the summer. Over the vacation, White pupils from advantaged families continue to gain at about the same rate, whereas those from disadvantaged and Black families not only progress more slowly but actually reverse direction and lose ground, so that by the time they return to school they are considerably further behind their classmates from more favored circumstances. The authors estimate that "the differential progress made during the four summer months accounts for upwards of 80 percent of differences between the economically advantaged all White schools and the all Black or Puerto Rican ghetto schools" (Hayes and Grether, 1969: 7).

The authors conclude that "half or more of the differentials in reading and word knowledge are associated with non-school periods" (ibid.: 10). It would be a mistake, however, to attribute this 50% entirely to extracurricular factors. For example, we have already noted that greater amounts of academic growth over the summer were associated with an unstructured, rather than direct, individual teaching style during the preceding school year (Soar, 1966; Soar and Soar, 1969). Nevertheless, Hayes and Grether are probably justified in their conclusion that the substantial difference in academic achievement across social class and race found by the end of the sixth grade is not "attributable to what goes on *in* school, most of it comes from what goes on *out* of school" (ibid.: 6). Consistent with this conclusion, Coleman (1966) found that very little of the variation in school performance was accounted for by differences associated with the school: the most powerful predictors were background characteristics of the child's family.

The implications of this state of affairs for the design of intervention programs have been eloquently stated by Hayes and Grether (1969: 10):

> If our conclusion is correct, our whole approach to equalizing educational opportunities and achievements may be misdirected. Enormous amounts of money and energy are being given to changing the school and its curriculum, retraining its teachers, and tinkering with its administrative structure—local, city, and state. We may be pouring money and energy into the one place which our results say is not primarily responsible for the . . . differentials that have been measured.

The conclusion serves as an appropriate transition to our examination of the effects of home-based intervention programs. Before doing so, it may be well to forestall what to the reader may now appear as a foregone conclusion; namely, that group intervention programs in preschool or school settings are, as Hayes and Grether have proposed, misdirected efforts. Our analysis will not lead to such a verdict; rather, it will point to strategies that combine elements from both home and preschool programs, conduct operations in each context, introduce into each context activities and above all human beings from the other half of the child's world so that he can benefit from the potentially great contribution of both hemispheres.

## V. SOME EFFECTS OF HOME-BASED INTERVENTION

The form of Table 14.3 is the same as that of Table 14.2, but the substance is somewhat different. In contrast to group intervention projects, most experimental

TABLE 14.3.  EFFECTS ON LATER INTELLECTUAL DEVELOPMENT OF HOME-BASED INTERVENTION PROGRAMS
(DOUBLE LINE DESIGNATES POINT AT WHICH INTERVENTION WAS TERMINATED; SINGLE BROKEN LINE DESIGNATES POINT OF ENTRY INTO SCHOOL.)

| | Schaefer[a] | | | Levenstein I[c] | | | | | Levenstein II | | | | |
|---|---|---|---|---|---|---|---|---|---|---|---|---|---|
| | 1 | 2 | 3 | 4 | 5 | 6 | 7 | 8 | 9 | 10 | 11 | 12 | 13 |
| | E | C | E-C | E1 | E2 | E3 | C1 | E-C1[d] | E4 | E5 | E6 C3 | C3 | E-C |
| N | 24 | 24 | | 6 | 7 | 21 | 8 | | 8 | 15 | 7 | 10 | |
| Age 1 Before | 105.9 | 109.2 | -3.3[b] | | | | | | | | | | |
| Age 1 After | 95.3 | 89.4 | 5.9 | | | | | | | | | | |
| Age 2 Before | 99.6 | 90.2 | 9.4 | 82.8 | 82.6 | 90.1 | 91.4 | -8.7 | | | | | |
| Age 2 After | | | | 101.8 | 101.1 | 101.8 | 89.8 | 11.6* | | | | | |
| Age 3 Before | 105.6 | 89.4 | 16.2 | 102.6 | 105.0 | | | | 91.1 | 87.6 | 91.3 | 91.0 | -3.5 |
| Age 3 After | | | | | | 108.6 | | | 101.3 | 102.4 | 95.8 | – | 6.4 |
| Age 4 Before | 99.1 | 90.1 | 9.0 | 98.5 | | | | | 106.6 | | | | |
| Age 4 After | | | | 103.6 | 103.6 | 108.2 | 85.0 | 16.0[b] | | | | | |
| Kindergarten Before | 97.8 | 92.8 | 5.0 | – | | | | | | | | | |
| Kindergarten After | 100.6 | 96.9 | 3.7 | | | 107.2 | | | | 103.8 | 101.1 | | |
| Grade 1 | | | | 98.8 | 100.6 | 105.4 | 88.8 | 10.9[b] | 104.5 | 94.4 | 104.3 | 96.3 | 0 |
| Grade 2 | | | | 95.6 | 100.3 | | 86.6 | | 108.5 | 95.0 | 110.7 | 97.0 | |
| Initial Gain | -10.6 | -19.8 | 9.2 | 19.0* | 18.5* | 11.7* | -1.6 | 20.4* | 10.2 | 14.8* | 4.5 | | 8.7[b] |
| Gain 2 Years After | -8.1 | -16.4 | 8.3 | 15.7* | 21.0* | 17.1* | -6.4 | 24.8[b] | | 16.2* | 9.8[b] | – | 5.3 |
| Overall Gain | -5.3 | -12.3 | 7.0 | 16.0* | 18.0* | | -2.6 | 19.6 | 13.4[b] | 6.8[b] | 12.9 | 5.3 | 2.2 |
| Achievement Level | .7 | .7 | 0 | 1.2 | 1.4 | | 1.2 | .1 | 2.1 | 1.5 | 1.6 | | .2 |

a. Bayley Infant Scale was used for first three testing periods; thereafter, Binet was used.
b. No significant tests available for this value and rest of column.
c. Cattell Test used at age 2.
d. E = ½(E1 + E2).

groups in these home-based programs not only improve on their initial gains but hold up rather well three to four years after intervention has been discontinued. The differences between experimental and control groups do decrease after the program is ended, but the decline is due less to a drop in mean for the treatment group than to a rise in the controls. In fact, the phenomenon of what might be called "the climbing control group" is universal for the home-based studies of Table 14.3. Moreover, the effect is much more pronounced than in the single instance in which we have encountered it previously in the Herzog project. Because, in all three cases, we are dealing with untreated subjects, the explanation must be sought not in the nature of intervention but in the characteristics of the sample. What all three projects have in common in this respect is the admission requirement that parents be interested and willing to enroll their child in the program even at risk that he might end up in the control group. Moreover, in the two home-based projects, they had to go a step further and allow a stranger to enter the door. Finally, the most demanding condition was exacted in the Levenstein study, which required the mother to participate in intervention activities both during and in between visits.[8] Appropriately enough, it is this project which exhibits the steepest climbs on the part of untreated subjects.

It seems reasonable to conclude that the climbing control group resulted from the self-selection of families in terms of their motivation to provide educational experience for the child. The more motivation was required, the more selective the sample of parents, and the more likely their children were to make a gain in IQ even if not admitted to the intervention program.

Finally, there is evidence that the self-selection took place in terms not only of attitudes and interests but of social characteristics as well. The Levenstein sample has been identified as the least disadvantaged of the seven included in this analysis. For example, the average education of the parents was the highest for any project—eleventh grade, just below the cutting point for admission. This process of psychological and sociological self-selection apparently reached its high point in the C2 control group, which, as indicated in Table 14.1, turns out to be exceptional even for Levenstein's families. All of the mothers had finished high school, there were no absent fathers, none of the families was on welfare, the size of the family was the smallest, and the weight of the child at birth the highest found in any of the seven subsamples of the study. The rocket-like ascent of 13 points in IQ[9] exhibited by the children of these self-selected low-income families randomly assigned to a control group contrasts dramatically with the 10 point decline shown by the negatively selected distal controls in the Gray study. When one adds to this comparison the performance of the respective experimental groups in the two projects, the total picture presents striking evidence of the influence of the degree of social (and thereby motivational) deprivation on response to intervention. In this respect, Herzog's verdict appears correct: "The less they have, the less they learn."

But motivational and social characteristics are not the primary factors that differentiate the home-based programs of Table 14.3 from the group intervention projects of Table 14.2. First, and most obviously, the former began working with the child at an earlier age. Second, whereas all the center-based programs involved placing the child for several hours daily in group settings outside the home, the Schaefer and Levenstein projects consisted solely of home visits of an hour or less and emphasized interaction on a one-to-one basis between child and adult. A more detailed analysis of the data and methods of these early intervention studies sheds further light on the specific nature of the critical factors involved.

## Schaefer's Infant Education Research Project

The one and one-half year olds entering Schaefer's program, although they were children from disadvantaged families, differ from all other, older entering groups in two respects. First, their initial test scores equal or exceed the norms for the population, as well as the beginning score for all the older age groups. Second, in contrast to the results of all the other intervention programs, Schaefer's experimental group actually shows a drop after the initial intervention period (when the children were almost two years old).As Schaefer points out, this pattern is in fact typical for very young children from disadvantaged families and reflects the manner in which an inadequate environment, unless counteracted by intervention, begins to impair the child's development by the second year of life.

> Several studies have found that low socioeconomic groups do not show low mental tests scores prior to 18 months of age . . . The somewhat below average scores for the experimental group at 21 months and the increasing scores while the child remained in the program . . . suggest that . . . experience prior to 15 months might have adversely influenced mental development but the home tutoring program then stimulated a more rapid rate. [Schaefer, 1968: 2]

As a result, Schaefer recommends that early intervention programs "should begin before 14 months of age, a conclusion that was supported by the tutors' reports that some of the infants showed signs of early deprivation at the time tutoring began" (Schaefer and Aaronson, 1972).

At the same time, the fact remains that the average IQ of the tutored children, as well as the difference between experimental and control groups, dropped after termination of the program; and, as shown in the last line of Table 14.2, the treated and untreated subjects were exactly equal in their performance on the Stanford Achievement Test administered at the end of the first grade. Indeed, the groups were virtually identical even on each of the four subtests. This erosion of initial effects has prompted Schaefer to further analysis of his data and reevaluation of the basic strategy to be employed in early intervention.

Before turning to a consideration of this important reappraisal, we call attention to another research confirming Schaefer's negative result and conclusion. Utilizing an ingenious experimental design, Kirk (1969) sought to determine whether a tutoring program carried out with very young children could produce greater gains than those typically achieved with preschool children at later ages. In his study, fifteen infants between one and two years old were exposed to one year of home-based daily tutoring emphasizing eight areas of cognitive development. In comparison with a randomly selected control group, the experimental infants showed a significant increase in IQ of 5 points. At the conclusion of tutoring, the experimental group was enrolled for one year in a Karnes-type preschool program for three year olds and gained an additional 11 points. As we have seen, and as Kirk points out, an initial rise of only 5 points in IQ is quite small in comparison with the gain typically achieved in group intervention projects. It is even more usual for intervention to achieve a greater gain in the second year than in the first. On these grounds, Kirk concluded that a tutoring program before the age of two was not as effective as group intervention in the later preschool years. At the same time he emphasized that

> . . . This experiment does not exclude the possibility of obtaining marked improvement in children when intervention is initiated at home at the age of one or two, if the intervention consists of a program in the home that includes more than one hour of tutoring plus a program of parent training and parent interaction. [Kirk, 1969: 248]

It is precisely in this same direction that Schaefer was led by the disappointing results of his own program. Having noted that tutoring affected not only the behavior of the child but also of the mother, and that mothers in the experimental group differed appreciably in their reactions both to the child and to the program (Schaefer, 1968), Schaefer undertook an analysis of the relation between patterns of mother-child interaction during the tutoring session and the IQ obtained by the child at the end of intervention (Schaefer and Aaronson, 1972). The results revealed a cluster of variables that was negatively correlated with mental test achievement at the end of the program (i.e., at three years of age), as well as with ratings of the child's task-oriented behavior. The components in the cluster included such factors as Withdrawal of Relationship, Hostile Detachment, Low Interest in the Child's Education, Low Verbal Expressiveness, and Low Involvement with the child. On the basis of this analysis, the authors concluded:

> Data from this project have provided additional evidence that maternal positive involvement, interest in the child's education, and verbal expressiveness with the child are related to his early intellectual development. . . . the relationship between a mother's acceptance of the child and her educational efforts is paralleled by the relationship between the child's competence and his adjustment. [Schaefer and Aaronson, 1972]

This conclusion, in turn, has led Schaefer to question prevailing strategies of early intervention for limited periods in group settings. He called instead for "early and continuing education" which should be "family-centered rather than child-centered."

> Evidence that mean IQ scores increase during intensive intellectual stimulation and decrease after such stimulation is terminated [is] cited as supporting family-centered programs designed to increase adequacy of family education throughout the period of child development. [Schaefer, 1970: 78]

With respect to the content of such a program during the early years, Schaefer and Aaronson (1972) offer a specific recommendation: "The experience of this project would not support an emphasis upon promoting early sensory-motor development but would support the development of early relationships, interests, and language."

No data bearing directly on the effectiveness of Schaefer's recommendations are available from his own tutoring program, which, as he regretfully points out, was focused on the child rather than the family. Levenstein, however, apparently quite independently, followed precisely the strategy advocated by Schaefer. We shall shortly look to the results of the Levenstein program for evidence on the scientific validity and practical effectiveness of Schaefer's recommendations.

But before doing so, we would warn against premature dismissal of Kirk's and Schaefer's tutoring approach. For reasons that are already apparent, programs modeled on this prototype may be able to reach families that are not accessible to strategies of direct parent involvement of the type developed so successfully by Levenstein, even though such strategies may be more effective once the family has agreed to cooperate. Indeed, the use of a tutor may be most appropriate as a transition phase to programs focused on enhancing parent-child interaction of the type we next examine.

### Levenstein's Verbal Interaction Project

By and large Levenstein's results lend support to Schaefer's predictions, both negative and positive. On the one hand, the impact of an oppressive environment, not yet evident in Schaefer's younger entrants, is already apparent in Levenstein's two and three year olds. Although the suburban environment from which her subjects came was less deprived than that of Schaefer's infants from the Washington slums, her cases obtained initial IQs in the 80s and low 90s, comparable to the scores obtained by their mothers, and well below the national norm. Moreover, Levenstein's five experimental groups not only attained this norm following initial intervention but generally maintained a 15-point or greater superiority over controls (and over their own mothers) three to four years after termination of the program. Moreover, the differential performance of the five experimental groups exhibits a consistent pattern. The three groups (E1–E3) that began the program at two years of age showed greater initial and overall gains, but their "head start" was confounded with longer and somewhat more intensive treatment. As indicated in Table 14.1, each of these groups, after completing the regular program in the first year, also received some kind of intervention during a second year, Group E3 getting the full treatment; Group E2, an abbreviated version; and Group E1, exposure to toys only. Final IQ levels attained by each of these groups vary directly with the intensity of the program received.

Confirmatory evidence that even the weakest of these treatments, exposure to toys alone, has a significant effect is available from the results of a special control group which was employed for one year only and hence not included in Table 14.2. This group received the special kit of toys, was visited regularly, but no demonstrations or encouragement were given for mother-child interaction. These children showed a statistically significant rise of 5 points, compared to the typical initial gain of 12 to 19 points recorded in Table 14.2. Thus the sheer availability of educational materials designed to foster mother-child interaction contributed to a rise in IQ in the first year, but this increase was not so great as that obtained by demonstrating and encouraging use of the materials in the course of mother-child interaction. Finally, the control group, which received biweekly visits but without exposure either to the special kit of materials or encouragement of mother-child interaction, showed comparatively little change.

We turn next to the two groups who entered the program at three years of age. Both groups gained significantly.[10] One of these, E4, still maintained an impressive IQ level three years after intervention, but the other showed an appreciable loss of 8.6 points over the same period. Reference to Table 14.1 reveals an important difference in the prior experience of the two groups, E4 having served as a "placebo" control in the previous year; that is, the family received biweekly visits for seven months, although without demonstration and encouragement of mother-child interaction focused around educational materials. It would appear that the provision even of such attenuated support of the mother-child system was not without some cumulative effect.

Viewed as a whole, the results from Levenstein's five differentially treated experimental groups suggest that the earlier and more intensely mother and child were stimulated to engage in communication around a common activity, the greater and more enduring the gain in IQ achieved by the child. Given the encouraging results of Levenstein's program, both in terms of immediate and longer range effects, it is important to examine more closely the activities that actually took place during the intervention sessions. Who was the home visitor and what did she do?

At the beginning, Levenstein employed trained social case workers in the role of what she called the Toy Demonstrator, but for later experimental groups, the task was carried out by nonprofessionals, many of them mothers from low income neighborhoods. That the latter turned out to be no less effective than the former is indicated by the performance of the two experimental groups (E3 and E4). As can be seen from the series of means for these groups in Table 14.3, the gains were as large and enduring as any achieved in the course of the program to date.

After the initial experiment (Levenstein, 1970), Toy Demonstrators for subsequent groups were trained in a one month eight-session training workshop led by the former Toy Demonstrators (Levenstein and Levenstein, 1971). The training continued, after they had begun their assignment, through weekly conferences in which their work was supervised and orientation was given for the particular techniques to be used in each family session.

The nature of the sessions themselves is described by Levenstein and Sunley (1968: 118) as follows:

Each time [the Toy Demonstrator] brought with him, as gifts for the child, one or two new Verbal Interaction Stimulus Materials (VISM) to "demonstrate" to the child and mother together. The VISM were commercially available toys and books carefully chosen for their verbal, perceptual, conceptual, and motor stimulus properties and were of increasing complexity. The length of each VISM Session was flexible, with a range from 20 to 55 minutes but averaging 32 minutes. During the session the social worker encouraged the mother to exploit the stimulus properties of the materials for verbal interaction. He used principles of positive reinforcement in building a sense of of competence in both mother and child and served as a model to the mother in interacting with the child. The VISM were then left with the dyad for daily use of the mother and child together. At each visit the social worker "reviewed" VISM previously assigned and emphasized the importance of mother-child play interaction with verbalization between visits. By the end . . . each experimental child had received 23 VISM [toys and books] . . . the same for each child in approximately the same order.

It is obvious that the home visitor did much more than is conveyed by the title of Toy Demonstrator. The reason the visitor was identified by this modest label becomes apparent from the following instructions:

Treat the mother as a colleague in a joint endeavor in behalf of the child. Share your verbal stimulation techniques with her by demonstrating them in play with her child; then draw her into the play, and take a secondary role as soon as you can while she repeats and elaborates what she has seen you do. Encourage her to play and read with the child between Home Sessions. Keep constantly in mind that the child's primary and continuing educational relationship is with his mother; do all you can to enhance that relationship. . . . [Levenstein, 1970: 429]

In the light of the above description, and the systematically varying results obtained with the several experimental and control groups, it should be apparent that Levenstein's approach cannot be equated with the more general types of parent involvement typically employed as a supplement to group intervention programs (see Table 14.1). The strategy involves a particular kind of experience that is focused in its purpose, sustained, sequential, and highly structured in cognitive, social, and motivational terms. It is instructive to examine each of these aspects in turn.

On the cognitive side, Levenstein's strategy clearly incorporates many of the same elements that were present in the structured curricula of the initially most effective group intervention projects such as those of Weikart, Gray, Karnes, and others. The situation is not one of free play but guided involvement in activities adapted to the development of language and thought.

But it is in the social sphere that Levenstein's method is most distinctive. There are two critical aspects in which it differs from the two other approaches we have examined thus far: intervention in group settings, and tutoring in the home. First, Levenstein's strategy has as its target not the child as an individual, but the *mother-child dyad as an interactive system*. Second, the principal and direct agent of intervention becomes not the teacher nor the tutor, but the mother. As a result, intervention is not restricted to the period while the child is at the center or the tutor is in the home. Nor does it terminate at the end of the program, but continues so long as the patterns of joint activity and interaction between mother and child endure.

The above defining properties of the Levenstein approach bear a striking resemblance to the conditions identified, from an examination of an extensive body of research, as most conducive to development in early childhood. Bronfenbrenner (1968a) analyzed data from over 150 studies on the effects of early environmental deprivation and stimulation in animals and humans. The researches included investigations both in natural settings and in laboratory experiments. Two subsequent analyses (Bronfenbrenner 1968b, 1973) focused on the implications of the findings for human development. The principal conclusion, indicated by convergent evidence from different sources, was:

> In the early years of life, the psychological development of the child is enhanced through his development in progressively more complex enduring patterns of reciprocal continent interaction with persons with whom he has established a mutual and enduring emotional attachment. [Bronfenbrenner, 1973]

The fact that these same elements played a significant role in Levenstein's program is indicated by the analysis she carried out of observational data collected during home visits. The results revealed that the aspect of maternal behavior most strongly related to the child's gain in IQ was a "verbal interaction cluster" involving "responsiveness to the child, clarity of explanation, expressed approval, and the use of reason" (Levenstein, 1972c).

Additional evidence on this issue comes from a recent report by Gordon (1973). Observations of mothers and infants from disadvantaged families revealed some patterns of interaction that related positively to mental development and others that related negatively.

> The positive pattern was the ping-pong pattern. . . . The pattern is back and forth. I do something, you do something, I do something, you do something. . . . On the other hand, sustained adult behavior, talking away at the child, without allowing him to respond or necessarily paying any attention to his responses . . . has a negative correlation to Bayley scores. [Gordon, 1973: 33]

As the foregoing conclusions and findings imply, reciprocal interaction between mother and child involves both cognitive and emotional components which reinforce each other. The special significance of this interplay has been spelled out by Bronfenbrenner in the following three propositions derived from his analysis of the available research evidence.

> *Proposition 1.* Psychological development of particular behavioral capacities in the infant is brought about through the infant's participation in progressively more complex patterns of contingent, reciprocal interaction with the mother (or substitute caretaker).
> *Proposition 2.* The infant's participation in progressively more complex patterns of interaction with the mother also has the effect of strengthening his dependency drive toward the mother.
> *Proposition 3.* The strengthening of the dependency drive in turn accelerates the infant's psychological development by motivating him to be attentive and responsive to those aspects of the mother's behavior which signal probable satisfaction or frustration of his dependency drive.

> [Bronfenbrenner, 1968b: 252]

In other words, when the pattern of reciprocal interaction takes place in an interpersonal relationship that endures over time (as occurs between mother and child), it leads to the development of a strong emotional attachment which, in turn, increases the motivation of the young child to attend to and learn from the mother. Moreover, Bronfenbrenner's (1968a) survey of the research evidence indicated that the infant's dependency on the mother develops gradually over the first year of life, reaches a maximum in the second year, and then decreases as the young child forms new attachments and interests. This finding implies that a mother-infant intervention program begun before three years of age would be more effective than one initiated later. Levenstein's results are consistent with this expectation, but, in view of the small number of cases in the older experimental groups (8 and 16), replication is highly desirable.

The type of mother-infant interaction developed in Levenstein's program has yet another consequence for the development of the young child. A follow-up analysis by Bronfenbrenner (1972) of studies published after 1968 highlighted the fact that reciprocal interaction involved not only a two-way process, but also a two-way effect. Particularly during the first two years of life, the mother not only influenced the development of the infant, but the infant influenced the mother, first by attracting her attention and then, over time, by shaping her behavior through the selective reinforcement of quieting, smiling, vocalization, and manipulative behavior (Bell, 1968; Rheingold, 1969; Moss, 1967). For example, the infant not only imitates the mother beginning as early as six months of age (Gardner and Gardner, 1970), but the mother also imitates the behavior of the child, particularly when he begins to vocalize, and this in turn facilitates his development (Bee et al., 1969; Gordon, 1973; Hess, Shipman, Brophy, and Bear, 1968, 1969; Jones and Moss, 1971; Kagan, 1968, 1971; Moss, 1967; Tulkin and Cohler, in press; Tulkin and Kagan, 1970). In other words, *the mother not only trains the child, but the child also trains the mother.* Furthermore, as revealed in the Bee, Gordon, Hess, Kagan, and Tulkin studies, it was precisely in the sphere of responsiveness to the child's acts and verbal interaction with him that mothers from disadvantaged families differed from their middle class counterparts.

These findings illuminate the process through which the Levenstein approach achieves its substantial and persisting increase in the intelligence quotients of children from low income families. The strategy addresses processes not in the child but in the two-person system which sustains and fosters his development. Moreover, since it is the product of mutual adapation and learning, the system exhibits a distinctive hand-in-glove quality, and thereby an efficiency, that would be difficult to achieve in nonenduring relationships. Finally, since the participants remain together after intervention ceases, the momentum of the system ensures some degree of continuity for the future. As a result, the gains achieved through this kind of intervention strategy are more likely to persist than those attained in group preschool programs, which, after they are over, leave no social structure with familiar figures who can continue to reciprocate and reinforce the specific adaptive patterns which the child has learned.

Finally, Levenstein's approach involves motivational factors at still another level. The first of these levels lies, in a sense, beyond the control of the program itself, but nevertheless plays a significant part in its effectiveness. This is the fact, already noted, that the disadvantaged families who participate are preselected in terms of their interest, willingness, and ability to take an active part in the intervention process. But there is also a second motivational set, which is a product of the way in which the program is designed. It is reflected in the Toy Demonstrator's title, in the auxiliary role in which he presents himself and ultimately functions, and in the primary and even exclusive focus of attention on the mother-child dyad. In most early intervention programs, parent involvement is an adjunct to a group program in a preschool setting. In Levenstein's project, parent involvement stands alone, and it takes place in the home, where, from the point of view of the child, the parent reigns.

In view of the promise of Levenstein's approach, the question arises whether the same results can be obtained by other workers especially with families from more deprived backgrounds than those found in poverty pockets of Long Island suburbs. Reassuring evidence on this score comes from eighteen replications of her work conducted with a wide variety of low income populations in eight states from New Mexico to Massachusetts (Levenstein, 1972). Of these, eight have completed one year of the program, and four have gone through a second year. In general, the children appear to come from more disadvantaged families than those included in Levenstein's original groups. For example, they include rural White families with an average education of eight to nine years, Black children from foster homes in New York City, and an American Indian tribe in extreme poverty and isolation on a New Mexico Indian reservation. Consistent with these more deprived backgrounds, the gains are not as great as those achieved by Levenstein's own sample, but they are still substantial. For example, the four projects that have completed the second year show an overall increase of 15 points in IQ. Regrettably, there are no control groups, and, of course, no follow-up data are as yet available. It therefore remains to be seen whether the gains endure once intervention is terminated, particularly after the children enter school.

A second issue concerns the specific factors that operate to produce the observed changes in cognitive development. Although the pattern of results of the five experimental groups shown in Table 14.3 sheds some light on this question, the size of each group was typically very small, often only 8 to 10 cases. Hence there is a need for cross-validation of these findings. In addition, Levenstein's results suggest an alternative strategy not tested in her own project. Through appropriate experimental variation, she demonstrated that neither a friendly visit nor the provision of instructional materials was sufficient by itself to produce the major effect; the critical element involved inducing interaction between mother and child around a common activity. Additional support for this conclusion comes from Schaefer's project. There the home visitor worked only with the child. Even though the tutor spent five times as many hours per week in the home as Levenstein's Toy Demonstrator, and did so for a much longer period (15 months versus 7), the results were hardly comparable either in magnitude or durability. Presumably the difference was due to the fact that in the latter program, the mother herself took over the intervention function.

But to achieve this end, is it necessary always to involve both mother and child? Perhaps the same result can be obtained by working mainly with the mother? And if this could be done at the center, with mothers being instructed as a group, the program would be much more economical both in money and time.

Although no follow-up data are as yet available, a series of studies directed by Karnes at the University of Illinois contributes important information bearing on the foregoing issues.

*Karnes's Experimental Programs for Disadvantaged Mothers.* The studies employ a strategy of intervention very similar to Levenstein's so far as home visits are concerned, but involves new elements that provide an instructive contrast. The series of experiments was initiated following the tutoring project discussed previously (Kirk, 1969) in order to determine whether substituting the mother for the tutor would produce more satisfactory results. The first study we shall examine dealt with infants one to two years of age. A sample of families living in an economically depressed neighborhood was drawn from the rolls of the Public Health Department and Office for Aid to Dependent Children. In addition, "acutely disadvantaged neighborhoods" were canvassed to locate families in need unknown to the referring agencies. From this group, fifteen mothers with infants in the stated age bracket were invited to attend a two-hour class each week in which they would be instructed in teaching techniques to be used with the infant at home. In order to provide for a baby-sitter, the mothers were paid a $1.50 an hour to attend these meetings and transportation was furnished.

> In general, the weekly meetings were divided between child- and mother-centered activities. The first category included the presentation of educational toys and materials with an appropriate teaching model.... The mother-centered activities involved group discussion directed toward child rearing problems in today's society but was intended to foster a sense of responsibility in the mothers for themselves, their families, and the community in which they live. [Karnes and Badger, 1969: 251]

Eleven educational toys, designed to create opportunities for verbal development, were demonstrated to the mothers, and books were suggested to encourage language interaction between mother and child. In addition, staff members made at least monthly visits to the home in order "to reinforce the teaching principles introduced at the meetings and to help each mother establish a working relationship with her baby" (Karnes and Badger, 1969: 251). In sum, the approach was very similar to that of Levenstein, but differed in three respects: most of the instruction was carried out with mothers at group meetings, home visits occurred once—or occasionally twice—a month instead of semiweekly, and the program lasted fifteen months instead of seven.

The original plan called for a comparable control group and follow-up until at least three years of age, but because of termination of funding, these intentions could not be realized. In lieu of a randomized control group, the authors established a comparison group of 15 selected from among over 50 disadvantaged children on whom test results were available. The controls were pair-matched on age, sex, educational level of the mother, welfare status, and a variety of other variables. At the end of the program, the experimental group obtained a mean of IQ of 106, 16 points higher than the comparison group.

The authors acknowledge that, despite the careful effort to ensure comparability, "a conspicuous variable remains uncontrolled . . . the mothers of the experimental children demonstrated a concern for the educational development of their child" (Karnes et al., 1970: 927).

To check on this possible bias, the researchers compared the IQs of six experimental subjects to scores obtained by their older siblings when they had been of the same age, which, of course, was prior to the mother's participation in the intervention program. A 28 IQ point difference in favor of the experimental subjects was obtained. Even though the N in the second comparison is small, taken together the two results present impressive evidence for program effectiveness.

In this same study, Marnes and her colleagues also sought to discover whether. any factors in the background of the child influenced his capacity to profit from this form of intervention. Although the number of cases was small, one contrast was so pronounced as to merit serious consideration. In the experimental group, there were six mothers who worked full time. Both in terms of mental test scores and measures of performance in program activities, their children "uniformly fell below . . . the children of mothers who were not employed on a full-time basis outside the home" (Karnes et al., 1970: 260). Correspondingly, differences were evident in the behavior of the two groups of mothers. Not only did the full-time working mothers show "markedly poorer" attendance at the weekly group meetings, but they also received the lowest ratings on quality of mother-child interaction observed during home visits.[11]

Taking into account the consistently inferior pattern of response exhibited by both mother and child among families with working mothers, Karnes and her colleagues (1970: 260-261) state:

> It seems fair to conclude that, in spite of verbal support of the program, the six mothers who were fully employed did not have the time or energy to implement program goals . . .

> In general, mothers employed on a full-time basis outside the home cannot effectively participate, and their children may be better served through day-care placement.

Several caveats appear to be in order with respect to this conclusion. First, it is based on a small number of cases. Second, in comparison with a sample such as Levenstein's, the families come from more depressed neighborhoods, and have a higher proportion of absent fathers (about 83%). In a less disadvantaged group, like Levenstein's, the disruptive effect of full-time work may not be as great. Unfortunately, Levenstein's data are not broken down by full-time versus part-time employment, a distinction which would appear to be critical in terms of the mother's availability to the child. Finally, the results were restricted only to the immediate effects of intervention; it is conceivable that a follow-up study would reveal residual benefits even for children of mothers who work full time. Nevertheless, the findings set serious qualifications on the effectiveness of this form of intervention with infants under two years of age when the mother is employed on a full-time basis.

Another study by Karnes and her colleagues (1968, 1969b) demonstrates that the same strategy is effective with four-year-old children, although in reduced degree. As before, mothers living in economicially depressed neighborhoods attended weekly two-hour instructional meetings, and in addition, the teachers visited the home at two-week intervals to demonstrate teaching techniques. The program lasted twelve weeks and produced a significant mean gain of 7 points compared to no difference for a carefully matched control group drawn from the same sample of families.

Karnes and her colleagues (1968: 182-183) identify four factors as contributing to the positive results of the program:

First, mothers were paid for attending the meetings and were fully recognized as important members of the intellectual team. Second, as opposed to a lecture approach, the mothers were actively involved in developing materials to be used during the week with their children. The training situation was not threatening and provided opportunity for a positive relationship with school authority figures. Third, the teachers visited in homes. . . . Fourth, because the mothers had made many of the instructional materials and understood their use, they could approach the teaching of their children with confidence. They could readily observe the progress of their children and were immediately rewarded for their maternal efforts.

These four factors once again underscore the importance of enabling the parent to function as the primary agent of intervention and to receive recognition in that role.

At the same time, the 7-point increase attained by these four-year-olds is considerably lower than the typical gain achieved with younger children both by Levenstein and Karnes. The poorer performance is probably accounted for both by the fact that the program was shorter—only seven weeks—and by the fact that the children were two to three years older.

Since Karnes's mother-intervention program contains all of the elements of Levenstein's approach, it represents an independent development confirming the effectiveness of the general strategy, in this instance for families somewhat more disadvantaged than the samples with whom Levenstein worked. In addition the Illinois studies demonstrate that similar effects can be obtained, at least initially, with less frequent home visits. This does not mean, however, that fewer home visits can accomplish the same result, for the Karnes experiment involved several compensating features. First, the experimental difference of 16 points in IQ in Karnes's infant studies was obtained after fifteen months of intervention, compared with the seven months typical for the youngest age group in Levenstein's program. Second, Karnes introduced an additional motivational factor by having the mothers meet in a group which could provide mutual reinforcement and a source of security. Indeed, it is possible that the prospect of going out to such a group for instruction was less forbidding than being taught by a stranger alone in one's own home, and this factor could have contributed to the acceptability of the program to a more deprived group than that reached by Levenstein.

An additional experiment by the Karnes group (1969b), however, indicates that motivational factors at the group level operate in an even more complex way than that envisioned in the foregoing paragraph. Encouraged by the results of the mother-intervention program, the researchers sought to get the best of both worlds by combining it with a preschool program for the children themselves. For this purpose, the mothers' program was added for a group of disadvantaged four-year-olds entering the Karnes preschool at age four. The mother-involvement segment was conducted along the lines previously described. The three teachers who conducted the meetings for mothers also taught their children, and "made a major effort to coordinate the teaching efforts at home with those at school" (Karnes et al., 1969b: 205).

IQ gains achieved over a two-year period were compared with those obtained in other similarly selected preschool classes whose mothers did not participate in a special program. Given the positive results attained previously with children of the same age by a program of mother-intervention only, the results of the combined strategy came as a disappointing surprise. The 14 point gain in IQ made by the control group of children in preschool only was actually larger than the 12 point rise achieved by the experimental group, but the difference was nonsignificant. The control group did score reliably higher in tests of language development.

Why did the mother-intervention program fail to make any added contribution? In the judgment of the original investigators, the explanation lies in a constellation of factors connected with the amalgamation of the mother-child program with that of the preschool. The crucial change was a marked reduction in the number of at-home visits. The authors' account of this change and its motivational consequences is illuminating:

> The mother-involvement program necessarily required expansion from twelve weeks to seven months and specific accommodations since the children now received instruction at school as well as at home. In retrospect, accommodations which seemed appropriate at the time may have inhibited the performance of this group. In the earlier, short-term program the teachers delivered materials to mothers who had been absent and also made home visits at two-week intervals to evaluate the appropriateness of the activities by observing mother and child at work, to demonstrate teaching techniques, and to assess the extent to which mothers were working with their children. When the program was extended, these visits were abandoned. Teachers continued to deliver materials each week to mothers who had been absent and made the three home visits required of all teachers during the seven-month Ameliorative preschool. The weekly checklist used by each mother in the short-term study to record the time spent daily working with her child on the various teaching assignments (reading aloud, finger plays, games, counting, etc.) was also discontinued in the longer study. Since the preschool and the mother-involvement program were conducted by the same staff members, it was assumed that these teachers without the weekly checklist and the biweekly home visit would be able to evaluate the appropriateness of the activities used in at-home instruction and the effectiveness and regularity of the instruction

by mothers through monitoring the child's performance at school, especially since the activities designed for at-home use closely correlated with the classroom program.

These changes, which seemed relatively minor at the time coupled with the child's preschool attendance may have significantly altered the mother's perception of her role in this program. In the short-term study, the mother was aware that she was the only active agent for change in her child, and as she became convinced of the merit of the program, she increasingly felt this responsibility. The fact that project staff placed a similar value on her role was demonstrated to the mother by the weekly checklist and the biweekly home visits to evaluate her work. In the longer study, mothers appreciated the value of the activities for their children but may have over-emphasized the role of the preschool in achieving the goals of the program. Teachers through their actions rather than direct statement, may have unwittingly reinforced this devaluation of mother-child interaction by making the purpose of home visits the delivery of materials to absentee mothers. The emphasis of home visits had changed from concern over mother-child interaction to concern over the presence of materials, and it was not unreasonable for some mothers to feel that the materials themselves were the essential ingredient in effecting change. Through the weekly checklist the *mother* had reported what she taught *at home,* but during the three visits made in conjunction with the operation of the preschool, the *teacher* reported on the progress of the child *at school.*

Mothers in the short-term study saw the major intent of the program to be the benefits which fell to their children. In the longer study, since the children also received the benefits of a preschool experience, the mothers tended to use the mother-involvement program to meet personal needs. Instead of a mother's program *for children,* the program may have been seen as a mother's program *for mothers.* Evaluations of the longer program, both verbal and written from teachers and mothers, support this view. Mothers frequently commented on their enjoyment of the social aspects of the program and on the genuine pleasure they experienced in making educational materials for their children, but a disturbing number of mothers also indicated at the end of the year that the primary use of these materials at home was by the child alone or under the direction of older siblings. Apparently mothers felt that they had fulfilled their responsibility to the program when they sent their children to school, attended a weekly meeting, and made educational materials, and, indeed, this level of involvement represented a major commitment. To some extent, mothers may have substituted these experiences for direct mother-child interaction, a consequence counter to the intent of the study, and that substitution may have been detrimental to the development of verbal expressive abilities. The solitary involvement of the child with the materials or their use with a sibling not trained to encourage verbal responses is consistent with such a performance. [Karnes et al., 1969b: 211-212]

Additional evidence consistent with the authors' interpretation comes from the attendance record of mothers at the weekly meetings. Although, as before, the child's admission into the program was contingent upon the mother's willingness to participate in the meetings, in the joint treatment group only half the mothers were present at any one meeting and "one-fourth essentially did not participate in the program."

The results of Karnes's "combined strategy" experiment provide further support for the central principle that emerged from Bronfenbrenner's analysis of research studies and characterized the most successful experimental groups in the Levenstein and Karnes mother-intervention projects: to repeat, *the psychological development of the young child is enhanced through his involvement in progressively more complex, enduring patterns of reciprocal, contingent interaction with persons with whom he has established a mutual and enduring emotional attachment.* Ordinarily such persons are the child's parents or other members of his immediate family. The research results suggest further that *any force or circumstance which interferes with the formation, maintenance, status, or continuing development of the parent-child system in turn jeopardizes the development of the child.* Such destructive forces may be of two kinds. The first and most damaging are externally imposed constraints, such as inadequate health care, poor housing, lack of education, low income, and, under certain circumstances, necessity for full-time work, which prevent the mother from doing what she might be quite willing to do given the opportunity and the knowledge. Second, there are social forces and educational arrangements that diminish the status and motivation of parents (both mothers and fathers) as the most powerful potential agents for the development of their child. By communicating to the parent that someone else can do it better, that he or she is only an assistant to the expert who is not only more competent but actually does the job, some social agencies, schools, and even intervention programs undermine the principal system that not only stimulates the child's development but can sustain it through the period of childhood and adolescence. Where this system has been crippled by external circumstances, as occurs for millions of families in our nation, there is no adequate support for such learning as the child achieves in school with the result that he loses ground, especially over the summer.

Indeed, given the circumstances, it is somewhat astounding that the minimal change in the environment represented by a home visitor working with mother and child together once or twice a week is enough to bring the mother-child system to an effective level of function that endures beyond the period of intervention. As we shall see, however, parent intervention programs are not, by themselves, sufficient to provide for the child's development, especially as he grows older. Other approaches, including group programs, turn out to play an important role.

### Parent Involvement in Group Intervention Studies

Even when the home visitor meets weekly with mother and child together, the gratifying results achieved by Levenstein and Karnes are not likely to occur without the explicit and sustained focus on the development of verbal interaction around cognitively challenging task found in these two projects.

Evidence for this negative conclusion has already been before us in the data of Tables 14.1 and 14.2. Reference to the former reveals that two of the group intervention projects, Weikart's and Gray's, included weekly home visits (of 45 and 90 minutes duration, respectively) as an integral part of the experimental program.

As with Levenstein and Karnes, the main purpose of the home visit was education to demonstrate instructional materials and approaches and to encourage the mother to adopt these materials and modes of response in working with her child. Yet, as we have seen, neither of these programs achieved the immediate or, especially, the longer range experimental effects produced in Levenstein's project. To be sure, in both the Gray and Weikart studies, the home visits were an adjunct to a preschool program which was clearly viewed as the principal vehicle of intervention. From this point of view, the erosion of initial gains in the two programs provides corroborative evidence for Karnes's conclusion that combining the two strategies, especially where it shifts attention, responsibility, and status away from the parent as the primary agent of intervention, can undermine the potential effectiveness of the parent phase of the program. The result, if our analysis is correct, is to impair the capacity of the program to create lasting effects. The diminution of parental status and responsibility may have been somewhat greater in the Weikart project, since apparently there the home visitor's role was explicitly structured as that of expert and tutor, although the parents' contribution was also recognized.

> Home visits are conducted with two objectives: To individualize instruction through a tutorial relationship with the student and to make parents knowledgeable about the educative process so that, as part of their everyday life, they will foster their children's cognitive growth. To achieve this end, mothers are encouraged to observe and participate in as many teaching activities as possible during the home visits. [Weikart, 1967: 106] [12]

The role of tutor to the child was neither explicit nor even particularly salient in the Gray project. Principal emphasis appears to have been placed on maintaining

> an active liaison between home and school. . . . In addition to explaining the school activities to the parents, the home visitor also suggested some things the parent might do in response to the children's communications about activities in school. . . . The home visitor emphasized to the parents the importance of making an interested, encouraging, and reinforcing response to the reports and materials the children brought from school. [Klaus and Gray, 1968: 20]

It is clear from the foregoing accounts that, in addition to being secondary to the preschool program, the at-home parent involvement components of the Weikart and Gray projects did not incorporate the strong emphasis on the importance of the mother and her sustained verbal interaction with her child in relation to a challenging common task. Under these circumstances, it is not surprising that the home-based components in these programs did not ensure the larger and longer-lasting gains achieved in Levenstein's project.

*The Independent Contribution of Parent Involvement.* Confirmation for the foregoing conclusions comes from a study conducted by Gilmer et al. (1970) The objective was to assess the effectiveness of mother intervention conducted both jointly with and separately from the regular preschool curriculum in Gray's program. The research involved three different experimental treatments. In the so-called Maximum Impact Group, both the mother and the target child in the family came to the center for training sessions. The child received the regular preschool curriculum of the Gray program five days a week. The mother came once a week to participate in

> a sequential process of skill development and movement from directed observations to actual classroom participation in a teaching role. At a later point in the program a home-visiting teacher called at the home to stimulate use of the mother's newly learned skills in the training program. Continual reinforcement was provided in small group meetings, where the mothers shared successes with their peers. [Gilmer, 1970: 6-7]

In the second treatment, the target child of the family attended the same preschool, but no program was provided for the mother. These children were designated the Curriculum Group. A third experimental group had no direct contact with the center but were visited weekly in the home by a staff member "who worked directly with the mothers and used the child to demonstrate the techniques and procedures consistent with the classroom programs" (Gilmer et al., 1970: 7).

The families in the study were drawn from a Black population living in a large housing project. Since the project was one of the better ones in the city, "its inhabitants would only be considered moderately disadvantaged" (ibid.: 5). The average IQ of the mother was 82. For reasons to be indicated, all families had to have at least two children of preschool age, with the younger sibling being at least 18 months of age. "A further restriction was the availability and willingness of the mother to spend one-half day a week working in the project. Because of these restructions there was some difficulty in constituting groups" (ibid.: 5).

The older of the two siblings was designated as the target child, and these children were assigned at random to the three experimental treatments with 15 to 19 subjects in each. The investigators report that "some non-random choices were necessary, however, because of differences in the availability of mothers" (ibid.: 7). In this writer's judgment, the nature of the bias thus introduced is reflected in two distinguishing characteristics of the Home Visitor sample. This group ended up with children one year older than those attending preschool; that is, they were five years old compared to three or four. In addition, their mean IQ at the beginning of the study was 6 points lower than for the other two experimental groups (84 versus 90). Both of these differences are relevant to the interpretation of results.

The two comparison groups for the target sample (with 13 subjects in each) were children from the same housing project enrolled in local preschool programs. A determined effort was made to match groups on demographic characteristics but no data are provided to indicate the success of the attempt.

Intervention was carried out for a two-year period for the two groups enrolled in preschool, and one year for the Home Visitor Group, with a one year follow-up for the former and two for the latter. The results reveal a 16 point initial gain for the Curriculum Group, 11 points for the Maximum Impact, and only 4 points for the Home Visitor Group. Each increase was statistically significant, with the first two being reliably larger than the third. All three groups showed a decline after the first year of intervention, but the loss is a nonsignificant 3 to 4 points for the two groups exposed to parent involvement as compared to a reliable 10 point decrease for the Curriculum Group, most of the drop occurring in the year following termination of the program.

These results are in accord with several generalizations that have emerged from our analysis. Thus the failure of the Maximum Impact Treatment to surpass the Curriculum Group constitutes a replication of Karnes's finding that parent intervention, when combined with and made secondary to a preschool program for the child, is not likely to produce large gains.

The poor performance of the Home Visitor Group in comparison with the other two, or with the results of programs for mothers conducted by Levenstein and Karnes, appears to be a function of three factors which are confounded in the present instance, but one of which can be assessed independently on the basis of results from the second phase of the Gilmer study to be discussed below. First, the intervention lasted for only one year, as compared with two years for both of the groups attending preschool. Second, the low gains could have resulted, in part, from negative selection of the sample in terms of IQ and related characteristics. Third, the poor performance is also consistent with the inverse relation previously observed between the age of the child and the effectiveness of parent intervention. The highest and most enduring gains were obtained with two-year-olds (Levenstein and Karnes). Then in ascending order of age but decreasing experimental effect came three-year-old children (Levenstein), four-year-olds (Karnes), and now youngsters at five, for whom the impact was almost negligible. It is important to recognize that the inverse relation applies to the age of the child at which parent intervention is not merely being conducted but is being initiated for the first time. Finally, the failure of the children in the Home Visitor Group to make substantial gains could be a function in part of the less concentrated parent intervention program, which clearly did not match the intensity of Levenstein's or Karnes's effort to induce verbal interaction between mother and child around a challenging task, or their emphasis on the importance of the parent as the primary agent of intervention.

At the same time, the failure in Gilmer's project of parent intervention to contribute substantially to initial gains should not becloud its significance impact on the "staying power" of the positive changes that were achieved. The Curriculum Group, though it achieved the highest initial gains of 16 points in IQ, lost 10 of these points over the next two years, including one year while the program was still in operation. In sharp contrast, both of the experimental groups exposed to parental involvement decreased only 3 to 4 points over the same period. Moreover, contrary to both the other groups, the Home Visitor sample was not receiving any intervention during the second year when it showed its 4 point drop, and actually made up 3 of these points in the following year. *In other words, although parent intervention does not achieve as high gains in the later preschool period, it appears to retain its power to sustain increases attained by whatever means, including group programs in preschool settings.* To use a chemical analogy, parent intervention functions as a kind of *fixative,* which stabilizes effects produced by other processes. From a psychological perspective, the phenomenon adds weight to our conclusion that *a home-based program is effective to the extent that the target of intervention is neither the child nor the parent, but the parent-child system.* From the point of view of human development generally and early intervention in particular, this system is especially important in two respects. First, particularly during the first three years of life, it is the major source of the forces affecting both the rate and stability of the child's development. Second, at least through the preschool years, the system retains its power to sustain and give momentum to whatever development the child achieves within or outside the family setting. It is as if the child himself had no way of internalizing the processes which foster his growth, whereas the parent-child system does possess this capacity. If so, this fact has obvious and important implications for the design of intervention programs, at least for children in the first five years of life. It remains to be seen whether the family continues to exhibit this sustaining power after the child enters school. But first we must take note of the primary contribution of the research by Gilmer and her colleagues.

*The Impact of Vertical Diffusion.* In addition to supporting and extending generalizations previously reached, the Gilmer study adds some new information on an important fringe benefit of parent intervention. In their longitudinal study, Klaus and Gray (1968) had reported significant differences in the third through fifth year favoring not only the experimental subjects, but also their younger siblings as compared with the younger siblings of both control groups. Most of this variance was being carried by the younger siblings closer in age to the target-age children. Gray referred to this effect as "vertical diffusion." The Gilmer study sought to analyze the phenomenon systematically and it was for this reason that the sample was restricted to families consisting of at least two children of preschool age. The investigators analyzed the progression of IQ scores not only for the target subjects but also for their younger siblings in each of the experimental groups as well as in the control group.

Consistent with the authors' hypothesis, the younger siblings whose mothers had participated in the intervention program, whether in the Maximum Impact or Home Visitor Group, obtained higher IQs both during and after the program than the younger brothers and sisters of children either in the Curriculum or Control group. Scores in the latter two groups were virtually identical. Although further replication is needed, these results not only provide clear evidence of vertical diffusion within the family but point to still another advantage of parent intervention programs as against those focused primarily on children in group settings: in the former the benefits extend to the younger siblings; in the latter such effects appear to be negligible.

One additional feature of the results merits attention since it resolves one of the ambiguities noted in discussion of the initial phase of the Gilmer study. The younger siblings in the Maximum Impact Group understandably did not obtain as high scores as their older brothers and sisters who were the actual targets of intervention. But, in the Home Visitor Group, the relationship was actually reversed: although the home intervention was directed at the older child, it was the younger child who made the higher score—a difference of 8 points (no significance test is given). The gap widened even further when, in the second year of the study, the target children of the Home Visitor program, who were then six years old, entered school, and the focus of the home intervention was shifted to the younger child. By the end of the year, the average IQ for the younger sibs was 11 points higher than that achieved by their older brothers and sisters also after one year of exposure to the same program—99 compared to 88.

Why should one group of children fail to profit from home-based intervention while their younger brothers and sisters, brought up in the same family, showed gains not only during the program but even before it began, as a function of vertical diffusion?

The resolution of the paradox is found in a simple fact: the younger siblings were of course younger than their older brothers and sisters who served as the original Home Visitor Group. This latter group, it will be remembered, were five years old when the program began. Their siblings, at the start of intervention, were one to three years younger. With family background and mode of intervention held constant, 11-point difference in IQ testifies to the importance of initiating parent intervention in the first three years of life while the dependency drive is at its height and the mother has not yet developed firmly-established patterns of response, or lack thereof, in relation to the child in question. From this point of view, the earlier parent intervention is begun, the greater the benefit to the child.

### The Strengths and Limitations of Family-Centered Intervention

We are now in a position to weigh the pro's and con's of an intervention strategy for mother and child built on the Levenstein-Karnes model. The strengths of the approach are clearly impressive in terms of productiveness, performance, and practicality. On the first count, this form of family-centered intervention, when applied in the first three years of life, produces initial gains that are as great as or greater than those obtained either through group programs in preschool settings or tutoring conducted in the home. More significant, even when parent intervention is introduced after three years of age, the gains are substantially more resistant to erosion after formal intervention is discontinued. This indicates that at least some of the forces enhancing and sustaining the child's development have been incorporated into his enduring environment in the home.

Again in contrast to group programs for children, the family-centered approach benefits not only the target child, but also his younger siblings, although how far down the age line vertical diffusion penetrates beyond the next youngest child remains to be investigated. There is also the possibility that, if influence extends to other children in the family, it may affect other adults as well. *Indeed, the power of this strategy, and its practical utility may be considerably enhanced by involving in the training sessions not only the mother but also the father and other adult members of the family.*[13] It is a reflection of the narrow view our society holds of the nature and status of the paternal role, particularly in relation to young children, that the father has not been considered as an important target of intervention efforts, although his actual and potential effect on the development of the child may be as great or greater than the mother's (Bronfenbrenner, 1961, 1973).

But parents not only serve as the agents of intervention in this approach; they are themselves affected, even in spheres of activity lying outside the parental role.

For example, there is evidence that participation in the program for the sake of her child brings important fringe benefits for the development of the mother. Witness the following account by the Karnes group of by-products of their mother-child intervention program for young infants.

> The confidence and capabilities demonstrated by the mothers within the program were reflected in increased community involvement. Four mothers assumed responsibility in the summer recruitment of Head Start children, and one was hired as an assistant teacher and promoted later to the position of head teacher. Two mothers spoke of their experiences in the mother training program at a Head Start parent meeting. Finally, total group involvement was demonstrated at a local Economic Opportunity Council meeting called to discuss the possibility of establishing a parent-child center in the community. Twelve of the 15 mothers attended this meeting and were, in fact, the only persons indigenous to the neighborhood in attendance. [Karnes et al., 1970: 931-932]

A similar effect is reported by Gilmer and her co-workers.

> Not reported in the results section is a careful study that was made of the changes in life style of the mothers in the treatment groups. . . . To the extent that one may attribute the life style changes to the involvement of the mothers in the program, we have here some of the most interesting results of the study. These findings, however, should certainly be interpreted with caution because, over a period of two and one half years in the late 1960s, many social changes were taking place.

> Still we find that many of the mothers went on to finish their high school education and enrolled in training courses to upgrade vocational skills. Several have taken positions in preschool and day care centers. Five of the mothers at one time were functioning as home visiting teachers themselves.

> Interest and participation in community affairs broadened. Social contacts with other members of the community increased markedly. There were cooperative outings, a rotating book library, and the establishment of a bowling league which included fathers. One somewhat ironic effect of the program, from the standpoint of maintaining statistical control, was the wish of many of the parents to move out of the housing project to more improved housing. There were increases in the number of checking and savings accounts, which almost none of the parents had before the study began.

> These changes in life style would seem to be the result of the development of environmental mastery, which may be expected to have a supporting effect on the children's continued development. [Gilmer et al., 1970: 47-48]

Finally, the parent intervention approach has practical advantages as well. It is clearly more economical, both of time and money, than daily tutoring of the type carried out in the Schaefer and Kirk projects. As for group preschool programs, Gilmer and her co-workers (1970: 17-18) estimated that weekly visits in their home-based treatment cost "only about one-fifth that [for] the Maximum Impact Group." Even when one takes into account the fact that the latter program also involved bringing mothers weekly to the center plus periodic home visits, and that

Levenstein's program required two home visits per week, the advantages in terms of cost-effectiveness are substantial. Moreover, it appears likely that Karnes's practice of conducting group meetings for mothers can reduce the number of home visits necessary to maintain the level of growth achieved in Levenstein's project. What the optimal ratio between home and center visits may be remains to be investigated.

In sum, the psychological and practical adventures of the family-centered approach to early intervention clearly offer great promise for the future. But effective as this strategy is, it cannot work miracles. Nor is it the sole, sufficient, or even feasible solution for many disadvantaged families whose children could profit from early intervention. In many homes, the conditions of life are so inhumane that, so long as they persist, the parent has neither the will nor the capacity to participate in educational activities with the child. Under these circumstances, any realistic strategy of intervention must begin by meeting the family's basic needs for survival. We shall address this fundamental problem in due course. But first we must take account of shortcomings inherent in the parent intervention method itself. Even when the parent is willing and able to cooperate, the strategy is limited in what it can achieve. For example, although the erosion of IQ gains after Levenstein's program ended was much less than in other projects, it was nevertheless present. Indeed, in terms of reading achievement at the end of first grade (see bottom line of Table 14.3), the difference between experimental and control groups was both nonsignificant and considerably smaller than the corresponding values for group intervention programs. It is clear that the substantial gains and differences in IQ produced by the Levenstein program were not reflected in the children's performance in first grade as measured by a standardized test of reading proficiency.[14]

And even the marked differences in IQ obtained in the Levenstein program are subject to important qualification. Although the infants were followed for two to four years after completion of intervention, they were still very young at the time of the last testing, two to three years younger than the children assessed in Grades 3 and 4 of the Weikart and Gray studies. In other words, Levenstein's subjects have not yet reached the ages at which the effects of what Deutsch and his colleagues (1971) have called cumulative deficit becomes most apparent. Once they do so, it seems quite likely that, as with the graduates of group programs, IQ levels will begin to drop, albeit more slowly, and the differences between experimental and control groups will gradually disappear.

But are not such losses readily avoided simply by continuing the parent intervention program? After all, it was only after the home visits were terminated that the typically 15 point IQ gain achieved in Levenstein's project began to erode. Had the visits been continued until the children entered school, would not all have been well? Perhaps so. We cannot know for sure until we try it, but there are some ominous signs. One is the failure of achievement test results to parallel the substantial differences in IQ still evident for Levenstein's subjects when they entered first grade. The disparity suggests that parent intervention alone may not be sufficient to enable the disadvantaged child to hold his own in school. But what if home visits are continued through the preschool years and are accompanied by a group intervention program to prepare the child for learning in a classroom setting?

This is what was done, of course, in both the Gray and Weikart projects, and, after only one year in school, the scores of the experimental group began to descend, and the experimental effects to dwindle. To be sure, the parent intervention program was not as focused or sustained as that employed by Levenstein or Karnes. Perhaps more important, as indicated by the work of both Karnes and Gilmer, the potential of the program to enhance the child's development was attenuated by combining parent intervention with a children's preschool.

We thus find ourselves on the horns of a dilemma. On the one hand, parent intervention alone, with all its benefits, may have limited capacity to prepare the child for learning skills and subject matter in a school setting. On the other hand, preschool intervention alone, with all its benefits, appears to have limited capacity to sustain gains once intervention is discontinued either permanently, or temporarily during vacations or over the summer. Conversely, each strategy possesses the advantages that the other lacks. Parent intervention can sustain developmental gains; preschool programs produce larger increments in the years just preceding school entry and can provide a cognitively structured curriculum more closely attuned to the child's future educational experience. Yet the obvious answer of combining the two approaches apparently entails a risk of reducing the power of parent intervention to enhance the child's cognitive development, at least as measured by IQ.

## VI. A SEQUENTIAL STRATEGY FOR EARLY INTERVENTION

Once the dilemma is defined, it points to its own resolution. When Karnes and Gilmer found that attaching a parent intervention component to a children's preschool undermined the effectiveness of the former, they were working with four-year-olds who were entering both programs for the first time. It is an open question, therefore, whether this debilitating effect of combining parent intervention with preschool would have occurred had these same four-year-olds been involved in a family intervention program since early infancy, two to three years prior to entering preschool. Moreover, we also know that, unlike group intervention, parent-centered efforts are more effective the earlier they are begun. Taken together, these facts point to *a phased sequence* in which family-centered intervention is begun when the child is one or two years old and continues to be the primary focus of activity during the early years. Preschool components are not introduced until later, are offered at first only on a reduced basis, but are gradually extended as the child approaches school age. Throughout however, in keeping with the principal lesson emerging from our analysis, the family is clearly identified and encouraged to function as the primary agent of intervention for the child.

### The Gordon Project

A program involving such a phased sequence is currently being conducted by Gordon (1971, 1972, 1973) with indigent families from twelve Florida counties. A weekly home visit is being conducted for the first two years of life, with a small group setting being added in the third year. About 175 children were randomly distributed into eight groups, systematically varied with respect to age at entry and length of exposure to the program, with one group receiving no treatment whatsoever.

Although no measures of intellectual level were obtained at the beginning of the program, Gordon (1973) has recently reported Binet IQs for each group five years after intervention was started; that is, from two to four years after "graduation." Of the seven experimental groups, the only three that still differed from controls by more than 5 IQ points (with means from 95 to 97 in the last year of follow-up) were those that had received parent intervention in the first year of life and continued in the program for either one or two consecutive years. Groups which started parent intervention later, whose participation was interrupted for a year, or who were exposed to parent and group intervention only simultaneously, did not do as well. Moreover, the addition of group intervention in the third year did not result in a higher IQ for those groups that had this experience. Indeed, in both instances in which parent intervention in the second year was followed by the addition of preschool in the third, the mean scores showed a drop over the two year follow-up period. In contrast, the two groups for whom parent intervention was continued for a second year without the addition of a group program either held their own or gained during the follow-up period, despite the fact that they were tested three rather than only two years after intervention had ended.

Looking at the results in greater detail, of the four groups tested two years after leaving the program, the only one showing significantly greater superiority over the controls (8 points) had had two years of parent intervention beginning in the first year of life, with group intervention added in the third. Next in line were the children entering at two years of age who had received one year of home visits with a group program added in the second year. Although this group had showed a reliable superiority over the control group one year after completion of intervention, by the second year of follow-up their mean score had dropped several points so that the difference was no longer reliable. The lowest mean IQ scores were obtained by the two samples who had attended the group program in the third year with no parent intervention in the preceeding year.

Of the two groups tested three years following termination, the one that had received only parent intervention for the first two years of life still differed significantly from the controls. The second group, which had experienced only one year of parent visits at age 2, did not show a reliable difference. Finally, the one group that had been exposed to parent intervention only during the first year of life was still a significant 9 points higher in IQ four years after leaving the program. Moreover this group was the only one to show a rise in IQ between the end of intervention and the most recent testing four years later.

Taken as a whole, Gordon's results lend support to the following conclusions:

(1) The generalization that parent intervention has more lasting effects the earlier it is begun can now be extended into the first year of life.

(2) When parent intervention precedes group intervention, there are enduring effects after completion of the program, at least throughout the preschool years.

(3) The addition of a group program after parent intervention has been carried

out for a one- or two-year period clearly does not result in additional gains, and may even produce a loss, at least when the group intervention is introduced as early as the third year of life.

But, what if the preschool component is not added until the children are four or five years old? Data bearing on the questions are available from two experiments reported by Radin (1969, 1972).

## The SKIP Experiment

To provide a meaningful follow-up experience in school for children completing preschool programs, Kingston and his co-workers established the Supplementary Kindergarten Intervention Program, known by the acronym SKIP (Radin, 1969). The program involved two components. One was a special class supplementing the regular kindergarten session with a Piagetian curriculum emphasizing cognitive development. The second component is described as entailing "intense parent involvement in the educative process." This phase of the program was implemented by a "home counselor" who, in a series of visits, planned activities with the mother which paralleled those being carried out by the child at school. Since the latter spent the full day attending either regular or SKIP kindergarten, he was not present during the home visit. The activities suggested by the counselor for the mother to carry out with her child were specifically designed to meet the child's developmental needs as diagnosed by his kindergarten teacher. There was a strong cognitive element:

> Some activities focused on classification on one criterion, then according to another. Others emphasized ordering objects in a single dimension (seriating). Still others centered on "if-then" relationships. [Radin, 1969: 258]

At the same time, care was taken to cast the mother in an active role.

> At all times, effort was made to have the mother see herself as a resource person capable of helping her child to learn. Few materials were taken into the home. Rather, items typically found in the kitchen or living room, such as toss pillows and dishes, were used as instructional material. It was felt that only in this way would the mother lose her awe of the teaching process and gain confidence in her own abilities. [Radin, 1969: 253]

Because the issue of stabilization of initial gains was regarded as most critical for disadvantaged children of high ability, the SKIP program selected for admission disadvantaged children who had IQs in the upper 40% of those who had just "graduated" from local preschools and were about to enter kindergarten. These 36 youngsters were divided into three groups of 12, matched on sex, race, and Binet IQ. They were also found to be roughly comparable in number of children in the family (between 4 and 5) and age of mother (early thirties). Group I received the full program. They attended a supplementary SKIP class four half-days per week when the regular kindergarten was not in session; in addition, their mothers received biweekly visits from a counselor. Group II attended supplementary SKIP classes, but their mothers were not visited. Group III, the control sample, was offered no program beyond their regular half-day kindergarten class.

Over the course of the academic year, Group I made a gain of 14 points in IQ, significantly larger than that for the other two, whose 6 and 7 point increases were not reliably different. Similar results were obtained on the Metropolitan Reading Readiness Test. The mothers' responses to a questionnaire measuring stimulation taking place in the home before and after the program showed significant improvement for Group I only.

The critical analysis, however, turned out to be the comparison between children who had attended a preschool program involving an intensive parent-intervention program and those who had not. Two of the preschools had contained this element; in the third (ironically a Head Start class), this feature was absent. Although the N's were small, the trend was unmistakable. The largest gain in IQ of 16 points was made by the children in Group I who had been involved in a parent-intervention program during their preschool years. This increase was significantly greater than that obtained by all the rest of the sample (averaging 6 points). Next in line were the children in Groups II and III who had also attended this kind of preschool, with gains of 11 and 10 points, respectively. All the children who had not previously participated in a parent intervention program during preschool showed smaller increases than those who had had this experience. Moreover, whereas the children in Groups I and III showed reliable increases of 6 and 7 points, respectively, those from Group II actually showed a loss of 6 points.

The full significance of this pattern of results becomes evident when we take note of the following facts.

(1) All of the children whose preschool experience had included a parent intervention component made significantly higher gains than those who had attended preschools without this element.[15] (The mean increases for the two samples were 13.7 and 2.5 points, respectively.) This trend was apparent even for those children not enrolled in the SKIP curriculum.

(2) Among children whose preschool experience *had* included parent intervention, exposure to a supplementary Piaget-type curriculum did not result in any extra gain in IQ *unless their mothers were also receiving home counseling.* The children in the SKIP program whose mothers were not visited essentially made no higher gains than those enrolled in regular kindergarten.

(3) Among children whose preschool experience had *not* included parent intervention, half-day regular kindergarten supplemented by another half-day of a specially-designed Piaget-type curriculum did not produce additional IQ gain.

(4) Children who experienced no parent-intervention, either in preschool or school, but who spent the full day first in a regular and then in a special kindergarten program fell 6 points in IQ during the kindergarten year.

(5) No such drop was shown by children who either:

(a) attended the regular but not the special kindergarten and hence were home half the day with their mothers

(b) attended both the regular and special kindergartens for the full day, but whose mothers participated in the biweekly home intervention program.

Although taken by itself this pattern of results might be seen as a chance phenomenon in view of the small number of cases involved, its remarkable consistency with the principal conclusions derived from a large number of studies examined in this analysis suggests that the findings are valid. Specifically, Radin's results, viewed in the context of the studies reviewed earlier, point to the following conclusions:

(1) Although parent involvement in the later preschool years does not by itself produce large gains in mental development, it increases the impact of any subsequent group intervention carried out in school, particularly if a program which enlists the parent in support of the child's learning activities is continued into the primary grades.

(2) In contrast, the absence of parent involvement in the preschool period, or the failure to carry over this component into the early grades, reduces the impact of any classroom intervention program, particularly if the latter, by keeping the child for the full day, reduces the time that he might otherwise spend with his parents.[16]

Radin (1972) has just replicated her findings in a second study designed to provide a direct test of the hypothesis that prior exposure to parent intervention enhances the impact of subsequent group programs. Three matched groups of 21 to 28 four-year-olds from lower class homes were exposed to a preschool program supplemented with biweekly home visits. In one group, the visitor worked directly with the child, the mother not being present. In a second group, the visitor employed the same activities as a basis for encouraging mother-child interaction. In the third group, mother-child intervention was supplemented by a weekly group meeting led by a social worker and focusing on child-rearing practices conducive to the child's development. At the end of the first year, all three groups made significant gains in IQ but did not differ reliably from each other. In addition, the mothers in the two treatments involving parent intervention showed changes in attitude interpreted as more conducive to the child's development, with the greatest shift observed in the group receiving home visits supplemented by weekly meetings.

During the following year, when the children were attending regular kindergarten (with no parent intervention program), the children who had been tutored directly in the preceding year made no additional gains in IQ, whereas the two groups exposed to prior intervention achieved further increases of 10 to 15 points. Radin (1972: 363) concludes:

In general the findings of this study suggest that a parent education component is important if the child is to continue to benefit academically from a compensatory preschool program, although there may be no immediate effect on the youngsters. . . . A parent program does appear, however, to enhance the mothers' perception of themselves as educators of their children and of their children as individuals capable of independent thought. Thus, perhaps, new maternal behaviors are fostered which are conducive to the child's intellectual functioning.

It is to be emphasized that Radin's parent program, like all the other effective parent strategies we have examined, focuses attention on interaction between parent and child around a common activity. This approach is to be distinguished from the widespread traditional forms of parent education involving courses, dissemination of information and counseling addressed only to the parent. There is no evidence for the effectiveness of such approaches (Amidon and Brim, 1972).

In terms of implications for program development, Radin's results warn against the complete continuation of parent-involvement strategies once the disadvantaged child enters school. To do so is to risk the fate of "washed out" gains characteristic, to a greater or lesser degree, of every preschool project we have examined. But the same proviso carries a constructive implication. As we have seen, there are grounds for believing that, if a strong parent intervention program is continued into the early grades, initial gains can be sustained and perhaps even extended.

In summary, Radin's results call attention to still another fringe benefit of parent intervention. To expand our earlier chemical analogy, this approach not only provides a *fixative* that conserves effects achieved through intervention; it also serves as a *catalyst* which enhances the impact of other programs which may accompany or follow the parent intervention phase.

### Early Intervention, How Late?

How long does parent involvement continue to exercise such benign powers? Radin's data indicate that the beneficial influence is substantial if parental intervention is introduced before the child enters school, but the effect is reduced if home visits are not begun until the kindergarten year.

But what if the child is six, or eight, or older? Is it then too late for parent intervention to exercise its conserving and catalytic power.

Unfortunately, there is little research on the question, primarily because in American society the school undertakes to educate the child without family interference. The causes and consequences of this development have been summarized by this writer elsewhere (Bronfenbrenner, 1972). In recent years, however, primarily as an outgrowth and extension of family-oriented preschool intervention programs, there have been attempts to break with tradition, and to evaluate the consequences. The results not only call the tradition into question but offer promise for the future.

*Parental Involvement in Project Follow-Through.* The most important and widespread development of this kind is, of course, Follow-Through, which includes as one of its defining features the involvement of parents both in major decision making and in the day-to-day operations of the program. We have already reviewed the results of preliminary analyses suggesting that this national effort is producing cognitive gains through the first grade, especially on the part of children who had the prior benefit of Head Start. It is now appropriate to report from these same preliminary analyses findings on the attitudes and activities of the parents (Stanford Research Institute 1971a, 1971b). The results indicate that, in comparison with the control group, Follow-Through parents were more aware of their children's school programs, more likely to visit school and work in classrooms as paid volunteers, more likely to talk to teachers and other school staff, and more convinced of their ability to influence school programs. As before, these findings are subject to qualification because of failure to control for differences in parental education and other background factors between the Follow-Through and control samples. It remains to be seen whether more refined analysis will confirm the results and whether the gains continue to be maintained, and perhaps enhanced, as the children in the program proceed through elementary school. And even if the results continue to be encouraging, the design of the national study does not permit evaluation of the independent contribution of the home-bases versus classroom components of the program.

*The "School and Home" Project.* There is at least one study, however, that overcomes some of these shortcomings. It evaluates the impact of a parent-involvement program from kindergarten through sixth grade in the context of an appropriate experimental design (Smith, 1968). Although the research is cross-sectional rather than longitudinal, this limitation speaks more directly to our interests since it permits assessing the effectiveness of parent involvement when it is introduced at later stages of the child's development. The project, carried out in Flint, Michigan, involved approximately 1,000 children from low-income families, most of them Black, attending two public elementary schools. Children of similar socioeconomic background in another elementary school were selected as a control group. In the experimental schools, the regular curriculum was supplemented by a program requiring parents and teachers to work together in furthering the child's educational progress. The effort involved parents in activities both at home and in the school.

On the home front, parents, including fathers, were requested to read aloud to their children, listen to their children read, read regularly themselves in the presence of their children, show interest by looking at the child's work, and give encouragement and praise as needed and deserved. In addition, parents were asked to provide a quiet period in the home for reading and study. During this time the television or radio was to be turned off and telephone callers were to be asked to phone back later. Parents were requested to occupy the attention of younger children. The parents were not asked to help the child with homework; instead, they were informed that the teacher would be checking on whether the child did his work rather than how well the task was done. "Every child could therefore be successful, provided that his parents were giving the needed support at home" (Smith, 1968: 97).

The parents were also encouraged to get the child to bed regularly each night, and get him up each morning "with adequate time for a good breakfast" (Smith, 1968: 94). A children's dictionary was also made available to each family with a child in grades 4 through 6. Families were asked to write their names in the dictionary and encourage its use. Many other innovations were introduced to provide support in the home for the child's activities at school.

The program also brought the parents into the school. This was accomplished by a group of 30 volunteer mothers who assigned themselves specific blocks in the school district and made a personal call on every family inviting the parents to a program "to learn what they could do to help their children achieve better in school" (Smith, 1968: 95). Parents who did not attend a meeting were visited by a parent who had, and brought up to date. In addition, parents and other residents of the neighborhood who held skilled jobs were asked to visit classrooms to explain their work and to indicate how "elementary school subjects had been important to them in their lives" (Smith, 1968: 102).

Parents reactions to the program were solicited in a questionnaire which resulted in a 90% return. Particularly favorable attitudes were expressed toward the home study program and reading experiences. Ninety-nine percent of the respondents wished the program to continue.

Unfortunately, systematic data on the children are limited to gain scores on tests of reading achievement administered in Grades 2 and 5. Since the two tests were administered in November and May, the normal increase would be expected to be five months. In the second grade, this gain was in fact achieved both in vocabulary and comprehension measures. The grade equivalent of the combined gain score for one experimental school was 6.4, the other 5.1; the corresponding rise in the control group was 3.9, a difference that is significant both statistically and psychologically. At the fifth grade level, the two experimental groups exceeded both the norms and the control group in the test of vocabulary, but only one of the groups "fulfilled its quota" on measures of reading comprehension. This pattern is reflected in the grade equivalents of the combined gain scores, which were 6.0, 3.7, and 1.7, respectively.

Since in both the second and fifth grade, parent involvement was being introduced for the first time, the results indicate that parent intervention is effective even with children who are initially exposed to this experience at ages 11 or 12. What would have happened had parent involvement taken place continuously from kindergarten on? If the results of studies at earlier ages (Levenstein, Radin, Follow-Through) can be taken as a valid indication, the effects would have been cumulative both in magnitude and in staying power, but this expectation needs to be confirmed in actual practice.

One other feature of the Smith project is especially noteworthy, for the school-age child-parent involvement took a different form from that in the preschool years. Instead of being directly involved in the teaching of the child, the parent was asked to take a supportive role, to reinforce educational activities instead of participating in them. Indeed the instructions to the teachers stipulated that the assigned home activities "should require no teaching by the parent" (Smith, 1968: 96). This meant that every parent could do his part without having to be in command of school subject matter. And the research results indicate that the supportive function had a significant effect on the child's learning. Once again the family emerges as the system which sustains and facilitates development spurred by educational experience outside the home.

*When Is Intervention Most Effective?* The findings of Smith's study, however, should not be taken to mean that children for whom parent intervention is introduced at later ages will benefit as much as those for whom it is begun earlier, especially in the preschool years. We know that this strategy is optimally effective in the first three years of life and there is some evidence that the effects are cumulative, at least during the preschool years, as revealed in results obtained by Levenstein (at ages two and three), Radin (ages four and five), and the Follow-Through program. (Children who had been in Head Start did better than those who had not, although this result needs to be checked with a more refined analysis controlling for parents' education.)

In summary, intervention programs which place major emphasis on involving the parent *directly* in activities fostering the child's development are likely to have constructive impact at any age, but the earlier such activities are begun, and the longer they are continued, the greater the benefit to the child. The optimal period for such intervention is during the first three years of life.

It is important to recognize that the above conclusion applies to a particular form of early intervention and not to any and all intervention strategies. There is no evidence from this analysis, for example, that preschool programs in group settings produce greater, more enduring, or cumulative gains if children are entered earlier and remain longer under treatment. The specificity of the critical period to parent intervention reflects the fact that the focus of attention in this strategy is not the child but the parent-child system which, once activated at a constructive level, can both foster and sustain the child's development as a function of educational experience both within and outside the family.

But one major problem still remains. Given that the optimal period for parent intervention is in the first three years of life, or at least before the child enters school, implementation of this strategy still requires the cooperation of the family. And, as we have already noted, many disadvantaged families live under such circumstances that they may be neither willing nor able to participate in the activities required by a parent intervention program. Does this mean that the best opportunity for the child must be foregone? Is there any alternative course? In our last section we turn to an examination of the problem and some possible solutions.

## VII. THE ECOLOGY OF EARLY INTERVENTION

If we are to find an appropriate strategy of intervention for the child of a family living in the depths of poverty, we must first understand the nature of the problems the parents face in seeking to bring up their children. Some indication of these problems appears in the reports of the two projects which attempted to institute some form of parent program with families from relatively more deprived environments. These were the Gray and Weikart studies. We have already considered several reasons why the fairly substantial home-visit components in these two programs did not produce the gratifying results achieved by Levenstein. But what if a combination of Levenstein's semiweekly intensive home visits and Karnes's group meetings for mothers had been employed with Gray's or Weikart's samples? For that matter, given the clearly stated recognition by both of the latter investigators of the importance of fostering mother-child interaction around a common task, why did they not give greater emphasis to such activities in their home-based programs? A somewhat sobering answer to both these questions is found in the careful reports of both researchers. Witness the following account from Gray's program:

> A first objective of the home visitor was to involve the parent as an active participant in the project. This was no easy task, because most of the parents were experiencing the helplessness that so frequently characterizes deprived populations. Many of the homes had no father present; consequently, the mother had to work at low-paying jobs for long hours. In addition, she had the responsibility for the care of a large family, without many of the conveniences of middle-class homes. As a result, most of the mothers carried responsibilities that sapped their energies, both physical and emotional. Thus, any requests that demanded additional time and energies would seem over-whelming. [Klaus and Gray, 1968: p. 21]

In the Weikart project some of these same problems are documented in quantitative terms. For example, over 30% of the home visits could not be completed because no one was at home. From the point of view of demonstrating and teaching, one of the major problems was inadequate illumination; lighting was rated in the lowest step of a four-point scale in 50% of the homes. The mother's participation, rated on a three-point scale, was described as no more than "slight" in 20 to 25% of the visits. On the average, three children were present during the training visit, and the rise in IQ score was inversely related to the number of children in the room at the time of the visit. A second factor associated with lower IQ gain was residence in public housing. On this score, Radin and Weikart (1967: 189) had the following to say:

> One hypothesis is that the dense concentration of lower-lower-class families, typical of public housing, results in a scarcity of children and parents who are school-oriented and can serve as models. The second hypothesis relates to the characteristics of those who seek and secure public housing. Perhaps in this decade, residence in a governmental project carries the stigma of poverty and is avoided by those who are upwardly mobile. The home environment of individuals with higher aspirations may not be sufficiently stimulating to permit full intellectual development in young children, yet it may be capable of establishing the foundation for future growth. Thus, children raised in this milieu may be better able to respond to a highly enriched nursery school program.

The presence of other children is seen by the authors as interfering with the mother's responsiveness and as a source of distraction for the target child. In the investigator's view, this finding points to the "necessity for privacy" if the training session is to be effective.

What these data and observations indicate is that the situation under which the more severely deprived families have to live often does not permit the kind of sustained effort in a one-to-one relationship with the child that is required in Levenstein's approach.

But thus far we are still dealing with families who are prepared to admit a stranger into their home and to participate with him in creating an educational experience for their child. This already implies a degree of motivation and organization that is not likely to be found among families living in the most oppressive and impoverished circumstances.

## The Scope of Deprivation

How many families are there whose conditions of life are such that it becomes difficult to meet the basic psychological needs of their children? The following statistics provide some indication.

> Among families living in poverty, 45 per cent of all children under six were living in female-headed households; in non-poverty families the figure was only 3.5 per cent. In two-parent families where the husband earned less than $7,000, 35 per cent of the mothers worked. These women work because they have to.

> There are nearly six million preschool children whose mothers are in the labor force. Of these, one million live in families below the poverty line (e.g. income below the $4,000 for a family of four). An additional one million children of working mothers live in near poverty (income between $4,000 and $7,000 for a family of four). All of these children would have to be on welfare if the mother did not work. Finally, there are about 2.5 million children under six whose mothers do not work, but where family income is below the poverty level without counting the many thousands of children in families above the poverty line who are in need of child care services, this makes a total of about 4.5 million children under six whose families need some help if normal family life is to be sustained. [Bronfenbrenner and Bruner, 1972: 41]

## Breaking the Ecological Barrier

What kind of program can reach the children of these families and set them on the course of normal development?

*The Milwaukee Project.* There is a radical answer to this question, and it is being tried. It involves essentially removing the child from his home for most of his waking hours, placing him in an environment conducive to his growth, and entrusting primary responsibility for his development to persons specifically trained for the job. This is the strategy being employed in an unusual experiment conducted by Heber and associates (1971). The sample consisted of Black mothers of newborns who were living in an economically depressed area of Milwaukee and had IQs of 75 or less. Case studies included in the Progress Report leave no doubt of the severely deprived status of the homes. Forty mothers and their babies were assigned at random to an experimental or control group. In the experimental group, separate intervention programs were established for mother and child. Recognizing that deprivation begins to exert its destructive impact early in life, Heber initiated intervention for the children when they were three months of age. At this point each child was assigned a highly trained teacher who

> was responsible for his total care, including: feeding and bathing, cuddling and soothing, reporting and recording general health, as well as organizing his learning environment and implementing the education program. . . . During a brief period of 2 to 8 weeks . . . the teacher worked with her child in the home until the mother expressed enough confidence in the teacher to allow the child to go to the center. [Heber, 1971: 51-52]

The teachers were paraprofessionals selected from the same neighborhood in which the children lived, "thus sharing a similar cultural milieu" (ibid.: 49). Persons selected were those who, in the judgment of the staff, were "language facile, affectionate people who had had some experience with infants or young children" (ibid.: 49).

The center was a 14-room duplex house with many "nooks and crannies where teachers could work with children on a very intimate one-to-one basis" (ibid.: 57). The children stayed at the center from 8:45 in the morning until 4:00 in the afternoon. Each child remained with his primary teacher until he reached 12 to 15 months of age. At that time he was paired with other teachers and children so that, by about 18 months, he was grouped with two other children and came into contact with three different teachers. From 18 months each teacher was given responsibility for approximately ten children whom she saw in groups of 2 to 4 depending on age. The teacher was required to familiarize herself with one of the three academic areas (mathematics, language, reading). The three teachers in each classroom shared responsibility for other areas, such as art and music.

At the beginning of the project there were 20 teachers for the 20 infants. As the children grew older, the program took on more of the features of preschool, some younger children were added, and the center was moved to a building containing six classrooms. At the time of the most recent progress report, there were 25 children between the ages of 2 and 5 being cared for by 9 teachers, approximately a 3 to 1 ratio.

The educational program is characterized by the authors as "having a cognitive-language orientation implemented through a structured environment by prescriptive teaching techniques" (ibid.: 57). An examination of the curriculum suggests that it belongs in Bissell's (1970) "structured-cognitive" category, and hence can be expected to be quite effective.

Before turning to the results of intervention with the children, it is important to take note of the parallel program conducted for their mothers. This involved two phases. The first was a job training program to raise their employment potential. The work for which they were trained was that of nurse's aide in a private nursing home. The mothers were first taught some basic skills in reading, writing, and arithmetic and then given on-the-job training in two nursing homes.

The second phase of the program involved training in homemaking and child-rearing skills. The status and degree of success of these two training programs is summarized by Heber (1971: 71-72) as follows:

While the occupational rehabilitation component of the maternal program appears to have been quite successful to date, major problems with respect to adequacy of homemaking skills and care and treatment of children remain to be resolved with a number of experimental families. With many of the mothers now successfully employed, the maternal program is shifting to an increased emphasis on training in general care of family and home, budgeting, nutrition and food preparation, family hygiene and the mother's role in child growth and development.

No such qualification is in order with respect to results of the program for the children. At the time of the latest report, the original infants were about four years of age. On a variety of measures, the experimental and control groups began at the same point and then diverged, the differences between them increasing over the years. The IQ data present a typical picture. At one year of age, both groups scored a mean just under 115, not unusual on infant tests. By two years of age, the experimental group had risen to 120, the controls had dropped to about 95. At three, the experimentals had risen slightly and the controls fell a comparable amount. At four, both groups decreased somewhat but maintained their 28 point difference.

These results raise a number of important questions of science, of practicality, and of ethics. At the moment, our concern is with the first two categories. With respect to cognitive development, there can be little question that the program has been astoundingly successful and will probably continue to be so as long as intervention lasts. The success is entirely to be expected since the program fulfills every requirement we have stipulated as essential or desirable for fostering the development of the young child. It began by creating an enduring one-to-one relationship involving reciprocal interaction around activities challenging to the young child. With the teacher still remaining the primary agent of intervention, group experiences were gradually introduced emphasizing language and structured cognitive activities. The entire operation is being carried out by a group of people sharing and reinforcing a common commitment to young children and their development. In short, all the requirements of the sequential strategy are being met and the child is developing accordingly. The first problem will arise if and when intervention is discontinued. What will happen then is an open question. If the children remain with their mothers and enter the schools in their deprived neighborhoods, it is unlikely that they will maintain their superior levels of mental development.[17] Even though the mothers' jobs and skills have been upgraded, it seems doubtful that they, or other members of the family, will be able to sustain the children's development, an activity for which the family has received no special preparation and in which they have played only a secondary part since the child was three months old. If the children obtain sources of stimulation and support outside the home and neighborhood, their cognitive development may continue to flourish. But whatever happens to them intellectually, serious questions arise about their development in other spheres, especially in terms of identity formation in their relation to their family or to other children in the neighborhood from whom they are partially isolated so long as they continue in the program.

Until the data come in, the answers to these questions must remain speculative. But in one future domain the facts seem clear. The program is, and will continue to be, as expensive as it is effective, perhaps more so. And in terms of large-scale applicability, the costs are prohibitive.

Is there another approach? Is there some other way to reach the child in the severely deprived home and ensure his development without separating him from his family for most of the day and, at great cost, delegating primary responsibility for his development to highly trained personnel working in a specially designed setting in ways that are alien to his own family and background?

*The Skeels Experiment.* There is an affirmative answer to these questions, and it is backed up by factual evidence, indeed by an IQ gain exactly as great and demonstrably far more enduring than that presently achieved in the Milwaukee project. The evidence comes from Skeels's (1966) remarkable follow-up study of two groups of mentally retarded, institutionalized children, who constituted the experimental and control groups in an experiment he had initiated thirty years earlier. (Skeels, Updegraff, Wellman, and Williams, 1938; Skeels and Dye, 1939) The average IQ of the children and of their mothers was under 70. When the children were about two years of age, thirteen of them were placed in the care of female inmates of a state institution for the mentally retarded with each child being assigned to a different ward. The control group was allowed to remain in the original–also institutional–environment, a children's orphanage. During the formal experimental period, which averaged a year and a half, the experimental group showed a mean rise in IQ of 28 points, from 64 to 92, whereas the control group dropped 26 points. Upon completion of the experiment, it became possible to place eleven of the experimental children in legal adoption. After 2½ years with their adoptive parents, this group showed a further 9-point rise to a mean of 101. Thirty years later, all of the original thirteen children, now adults, in the experimental group were found to be self-supporting, all but two had completed high school, with four having one or more years of college. In the control group, all were either dead or still institutionalized. Skeels concludes his report with some dollar figures on the amount of taxpayers' money expended to sustain the institutionalized group, in contrast to the productive income brought in by those who had been raised initially by mentally deficient women in a state institution.

The Skeels experiment is instructive on two counts. First, if Heber demonstrated that disadvantaged children of mothers with IQs under 75 could, with appropriate intervention, rise 28 points in IQ to well above the norm, Skeels showed that retarded mothers themselves can achieve the same gains for children under their care at substantially less expense. How was this accomplished? The answer is found in Skeels's (1966: 17) observations and analysis of what occurred in the wards:

> ... it must be pointed out that in the case of almost every child, some one adult (older girl or attendant) became particularly attached to him and figuratively "adopted" him. As a consequence, an intense one-to-one adult-child relationship developed, which was supplemented by the less intense but frequent interactions with the other adults in the environment. Each child had some one person with whom he was identified and who was particularly

interested in him and his achievements. This highly stimulating emotional impact was observed to be the unique characteristic and one of the main contributions of the experimental setting.

But the interpersonal relationship was not the only feature that contributed to the children's development. There were at least two other significant elements:

> . . . the attendants and the older girls became very fond of the children placed on their wards and took great pride in them. In fact, there was considerable competition among wards to see which one would have its "baby" walking or talking first. Not only the girls, but the attendants spent a great deal of time with "their children" playing, talking and training them in every way. The children received constant attention and were the recipients of gifts; they were taken on excursions and were exposed to special opportunities of all kinds. [Skeels, 1966: 16-17]

> The spacious living rooms of the wards furnished ample space for indoor play activity. Whenever weather permitted, the children spent some time each day on the playground under the supervision of one or more older girls. Here they were able to interact with other children of similar ages. Outdoor play equipment included tricycles, swings, slides, sand boxes, etc. The children also began to attend the school kindergarten as soon as they could walk. Toddlers remained for only half the morning and 4- or 5-year olds, the entire morning. Activities carried on in the kindergarten resembled preschool rather than the more formal type of kindergarten. [Skeels, 1966: 17]

Taken together, these three features constitute three essential components of the sequential strategy we previously identified from other research as optimal for the development of the young child: the initial establishment of an enduring relationship involving intensive interaction with the child; priority, status, and support for the "mother-child" system; the introduction, at a later stage, of a preschool program, but with the child returning "home" for half the day to a highly available mother substitute. The only element that is missing is the systematic involvement of the child in progressively more complex activities, first in the context of the mother-child relationship and later, in the curriculum of the preschool program. Had these elements of cognitively challenging experience been present, it is conceivable that the children would have shown even more dramatic gains in IQ, approaching the levels achieved by Heber's experimental group.

*Ecological Intervention as a Strategy.* Both the Heber and Skeels experiments also include a new element not present, at least in significant form, in the other intervention programs we have examined. This element is in fact the most critical, for it gives rise to all the other conditions essential for intervention to be effective. This "enabling act" took the form in both instances, of a major transformation of the environment for the child and the persons principally responsible for his care and development. In the Heber project the restructuring was accomplished by delegating primary responsibility for the child's development to specially trained personnel in a setting specifically designed for the purpose. In Skeels's experiment, the transformation of the environment involved removing the children from the orphanage, and placing them, one to a ward, in the institution for mentally retarded female adults. We shall refer to this kind of reorganization as *ecological intervention* since it requires a major change in the environment in which both mother and child are living. The essence of the strategy is a primary focus neither on the child nor his parent nor even the dyad or the family as a system. Rather, the aim is to effect changes in the *context* in which the family lives; these changes in turn enable the mother, the parents, and the family as a whole to exercise the functions necessary for the child's development. Our purest case of ecological intervention, therefore, is found in Skeels's experiment. There entire new patterns of behavior were produced by placing the child and his mentally retarded de facto foster mother in an environment in which the basic needs for life were already met and the care of the child became a major activity receiving the social support of the entire community. There was no training program for either mother or child; the situation simply provided *opportunity and status for parenthood,* and the participants in the situation took it from there.

The presence of such an opportunity, of course, does not guarantee that normal development will take place. There is little question, for example, that Skeels's children would not have maintained their impressive IQ gains had they remained in the institution in later childhood instead of being adopted. In fact, the two cases who stayed longest began to show a drop before they left. But if the presence of the opportunity for a parent to fulfill the role has no certain consequences, its absence is unequivocal in terms of the effect on the child; so long as the situation does not permit parental functions to occur, the child's development is impaired. This conclusion is clearly indicated in the results of Bronfenbrenner's analyses (Bronfenbrenner, 1968a, 1968b; Bronfenbrenner and Bruner, 1972) of published research on effects of early deprivation and stimulation. These analyses led to the formulation of two general principles. The first, which we have already cited, defined the properties of the reciprocal system necessary to foster and sustain the development of the young child. The second stipulated the conditions which this system, in turn, required for its creation and survival

> The extent to which such a reciprocal system can be developed and maintained depends on the degree to which other encompassing and accompanying social structures provide the place, time, example, and reinforcement to the system and its participants. [Bronfenbrenner, 1973: 10]

The need for ecological intervention arises when the foregoing prerequisites are not met by the environment in which the child and his family live. This is precisely the situation which obtains for many, if not most, disadvantaged families. The conditions of life are such that the family cannot perform its child-rearing functions even though it may wish to do so. Under these circumstances no direct form of intervention aimed at enhancing the child's development or his parents' child-rearing skills is likely to have much impact. Conversely, once the environmental prerequisites are met, the direct forms of intervention may no longer seem as necessary. After all, middle class families, who are well fed, well housed, well cared for medically, and well educated, do not need special intervention programs either for parents or for children to ensure that the latter can learn in school. These families seek such programs, however, to enable the child to realize his full potential, and are probably well advised to do so.

The implication of the foregoing discussion is obvious. *Ecological intervention must be the first step in any sequential strategy of the type we have proposed.* It may well be that the most powerful technique for achieving substantial and enduring growth in IQ, and in other more significant spheres of development, for children living in the most deprived circumstances *is to provide the family with adequate health care, nutrition, housing and employment.*

Unfortunately, researchers have not given consideration to so simple-minded a hypothesis so that there is little direct evidence to support or challenge its validity. Data consistent with such an expectation, however, abound in the results of this analysis. Repeatedly we have observed that the effectiveness and, indeed, the feasibility of intervention varied inversely with the degree of deprivation. The children from the least disadvantaged families were those who profited most from early intervention, or, for that matter, were even enrolled in the programs in the first place. The neediest families were not even reached.

But if ecological intervention is the answer, what is keeping us from carrying it out? The answer to this question is found in what is virtually a defining characteristic of the strategy: *ecological intervention almost invariably requires institutional change.* Where families are living in difficult but still viable circumstances, the institutional change may involve no more than the formation of a group committed to a common activity, as with Karnes's mothers. But where basic needs for survival and growth are unfulfilled, the necessary institutional changes are more far-reaching and difficult to achieve. But unless such changes are effected, more direct forms of intervention, be they home visits, preschool programs, or both, can have little impact on the most deprived families, whose children stand in greatest need of help.

*Opportunity and Status for Parental Activity.* But even when the basic needs for survival are met, the conditions of life may be such as to prevent the family from functioning effectively in its child-rearing role. As we have seen, an essential prerequisite for the child's development is an environment which provides *substantial opportunity and support for parental activity.* If, to provide an adequate income, both parents have to work full time, it becomes extremely difficult for either of them to carry on the kind of sustained patterns of interaction we have found to be essential for the development of the young child. It will be recalled that, in Karnes's parent intervention project for one- and two-year-olds (Karnes et al., 1970), the disadvantaged mothers who were employed full time showed the poorest quality of mother-child interaction, and this inferiority was reflected in the development of their children. Although the finding needs to be replicated in larger samples, it seems highly likely that it reflects a serious obstacle to effective parent intervention in the early years.

The results of Heber's project, and even more than those of Skeels's, suggest that, in the last analysis, it is the absence versus the presence of adequate opportunity and status for parental activity that is the most crucial factor affecting the early development of the disadvantaged child. Once children from severely deprived backgrounds were placed in a situation where such opportunity and status prevailed, even though in the wards of an institution at the hands of its mentally retarded inmates, the interactive processes so necessary to the children's development were set in motion and the children prospered. As we have already noted, it is the presence of these interactive patterns that primarily distinguished the early child-rearing practices of middle class families from those living in poverty (Bee, et al., 1969; Hess, Shipman, Brophy, and Bear, 1968; Kagan, 1968, 1971; Tulkin and Cohler, in press; Tulkin and Kagan, 1970).

*The Skodak and Skeels Study.* The significance of this difference is dramatized in an important investigation by Skodak and Skeels (1949) of the effects of adoption on the development of 100 children whose true parents were both socioeconomically disadvantaged and mentally retarded. The children were separated from their true mothers before six months of age and placed in foster families who "were above the average of their communities in economic security and educational and cultural status" (Skodak and Skeels, 1949: 88). The average IQ of the children's true mothers was 86; by the age of 13, the mean IQ of their children placed in foster homes was 106. In an attempt to identify the critical factors producing this difference, Skodak and Skeels compared the characteristics of those foster homes in which children had shown significant gains in IQ over a ten-year period (N = 7), and those in which the children had remained stable or shown some loss (N = 11). At the time of the first testing, when the children were 2½ years old and had been with the foster family for most of the period, the mean IQs for both groups were already above average, 117 and 114, respectively. By age 13½ there was a difference of 25 points in IQ between them (104 versus 129). In view of the homogeneous social and cultural backgrounds of the foster parents, neither education nor occupational level discriminated between the two sets of homes. The decisive factors which emerged are the same as those previously identified in other studies.

> There is considerable evidence for the position that as a group these children received maximal stimulation in infancy with optimum security and affection following placement at an average of three months of age. The quality and amount of this stimulation during early childhood seemed to have little relation to the foster family's educational and cultural status. [Skodak and Skeels, 1949: 111]

The three highly successful examples of ecological intervention we have described have scientific and social significance that extends beyond the children and families directly affected. This significance is threefold.

1. The results demonstrate that *severely disadvantaged children of mothers with IQs well below average (under 75 in Heber's project, below 70 in Skeels' follow-up study, and averaging 85 in the adoption research) are not doomed to inferiority by unalterable constraints either genetic or environmental.*
2. The findings show that substantial changes in the environment of the child and his principal caretakers can produce positive developmental changes considerably greater and more enduring than those achieved by the most effective intervention techniques when the home environment is left essen-

tially unaltered. Thus the largest differences between experimental and control groups in group intervention programs ranged between 8 and 13 points in IQ for parent intervention programs between 14 and 16 points, whereas for ecological intervention, the differences were 25 to 28 points.

3. The processes and effects produced through ecological intervention substantiate the critical role in early development played by an enduring one-to-one relationship involving the child in verbal interaction with an adult around cognitively stimulating activities.

At the same time, all three examples of ecological intervention we have cited involved the radical change of transferring the child from his original oppressive environment into a more favorable one in which primary responsibility for his care was entrusted in persons other than his own parents. This is clearly a strategy of choice, both psychologically and morally, when the true parents have no claim on the child, as occurred in both of the situations studied by Skeels and his colleagues. As we have already noted, however, such a course is problematic, both on scientific and ethical grounds, when the child still remains a member of his family. Under such circumstances, can anything be done for the seriously disadvantaged families whose basic needs for survival are being met but whose lives are so burdened as to preclude opportunity for effective fulfillment of the parental role?

*Family Support Systems.* No answers are available to this question from our analysis of the research literature, for, as we have indicated, ecological intervention is as yet a largely untried endeavor both in our science and in our society. The available research does, however, identify some of the major ecological barriers to the effective operation of the family in its child-rearing functions. Recognition of these barriers suggests measures that might make a difference, and therefore ought to be examined and perhaps tried on an experimental basis. We proceed with a series of such untested but promising strategies of ecological intervention. As we have anticipated, most of these measures require substantial changes in the major institutions of our society, not only those having direct impact on children and families—such as housing, health and welfare services, schools, churches, and recreation programs—but also other organizations and enterprises whose impact on family life is often unrecognized but nonetheless profound. These include primarily business and industry, but also urban planning, transportation, shopping facilities, and a host of other conditions determining when and how a family can spend time with its children.

The proposals which follow make no attempt to be comprehensive. They address what appear to this writer to be the most urgent needs, and represent examples of the kinds of possibilities that might be explored. All of these proposals have as their objective *providing support systems for families.* The proposals fall into four major areas: A. The family and the world of work; B. The family and the school; C. The family and the neighborhood; and D. The family and the home.

### A. *The Family and the World of Work.*

1. *Provision and encouragement of part-time jobs for parents of young children.* No single parent of young children should be forced to work full

time or more to provide an income at or below the poverty line. The statement applies with equal force to families in which both parents are compelled to work full time or longer to maintain a minimum subsistence level. Under such circumstances, a parent wishing to do so should be enabled to remain at home for part of the day. The following measures could help achieve this objective:

     a. Welfare legislation should be amended so as to encourage rather than penalize disadvantaged parents, especially single parents, who wish to work part-time in order to be able themselves to care for their own children.

     b. To free parents in poverty from full-time employment so that one of them can care for the children, federal and state programs should provide funds for parental child care at home in lieu of wages.

     c. Employers should be encouraged by persuasion, union pressure, or state and federal tax benefits, to create more part-time positions with priority in employment given to parents of young children.

     d. Federal or state legislatures should pass Fair Part-Time Employment Practices Acts prohibiting discrimination in job opportunity, rate of pay, seniority, fringe benefits and status for parents who seek or are engaged in part-time employment.

2. *Flexibility of work schedules.* Employers should be encouraged through persuasion, union pressures, tax benefits, or other means to modify work schedules so as to enable parents to be home when their children return from preschool or school, thus decreasing the need for baby-sitters during the child's working hours or for "latchkey" arrangements for older children.

B. *The Family and the School.*

3. *Parent apprentice programs in the schools.* Although many severely deprived families are not accessible to parent intervention programs, all future parents can be reached while they are still in school. Programs should be instituted as early as elementary school in which students of both sexes are given extended opportunities, under supervision, to participate in work with young children, including their own brothers and sisters. Such experience could be facilitated by locating day care centers, preschools, and Head Start programs in or near schools, so that they could be utilized as an integral part of the curriculum. The older children would be working with the younger ones on a regular basis. In addition, they would escort the little ones to and from school or center, and spend some time with them out of school. Visiting the younger children in their own homes and observing and helping parents in their activities with the child would not only contribute to training for parenthood but also give recognition to the parent as a person of status and expertise. Parent intervention, of the kind developed in the Levenstein and Karnes projects, should be carried out for students and the youngsters under their charge.

4. *Breaking down the wall between family and school.* Further experimenta-

tion is needed along the lines of Smith's "Home and School" program to enlist parents in support of the child's activity in school through specific practices which they carry out in the home and to introduce parents as active participants in school programs by having them tell about their jobs, take groups of children to visit their place of work, and be identified to the children by teachers and administrators as important partners in the educational process. In particular, parents should play a leading role in the Parent Apprentice Program outlined above.

C.  *The Family and the Neighborhood.*

   5. *"Parent-Child Support Systems" in the neighborhood.* In every low-income housing project or disadvantaged neighborhood there should be organized a *parent-child support system* on a cooperative basis. All parents with young children (as well as those expecting a first arrival) would automatically become members of the *support system* and any other residents in the neighborhood could join. The support system could be called upon, especially in times of emergency, for mutual assistance or advice in the care of children. It would also be the focal point for organizing parent intervention programs.

   6. *Family neighborhood centers.* Essential to the operation of the family support system is a *family neighborhood center* where parents and others concerned with the care of the young can meet to see demonstrations, hear talks, share ideas, and discuss common problems. Students enrolled in Parent Apprentice Programs (see above) would also participate in the activities of the center.

D.  *The Family in the Home.*

   7. *Pre-child parent intervention.* The optimal time to begin parent intervention is well before the child is born or even conceived. The first step in such intervention would be to ensure the mother adequate medical care and nutrition prior to, during, and after the pregnancy. Provision should also be made at this time for adequate housing, and stable employment for the husband, if possible. At the very least the mother should be assured an adequate income during pregnancy and the early years of the child's life. Along with meeting these basic needs, a program of parent intervention could be instituted on the Levenstein-Karnes model including both group meetings and home visits. It would be essential for the expectant parents to work directly with a young child. Such opportunities could be created through the Parent-Child Support System in the neighborhood. Such a practice would also enhance a sense of common purpose, mutual assistance, and importance of the parental role among the members of the community.

   8. *Homemaker service.* Many disadvantaged parents are unable to spend time in activities with their young children because of other demands in the home, such as care of old or sick relatives, meeting the needs of a large family, housekeeping under difficult conditions, and the like. Local residents trained as homemakers, or high school students in the Parent

Apprentice Program could take over some of these responsibilities during regular visits so that the parent could be free to engage in activities with the younger child.

9. *"Family Emergency Insurance."* Many families in poverty live on the edge of disaster. They are barely able to get along. If a child becomes ill, the parent cannot afford to stay home from work. If the car or the home heater breaks down, there is no money for repairs. And if the parent himself becomes ill, even when the medical bills are paid for, there may be no one to take care of the children. In middle class families these are temporary emergencies that can be handled by dipping into the reserve. In poor families, the temporary emergency can precipitate enduring family breakdown. A federally sponsored "Family Emergency Insurance" at low premium rates that would pay for itself but could be drawn upon quickly when misfortune struck could help forestall family disruption and thus sustain the development of the child.

10. *Parent Intervention through Television.* Most American families consist of two parents, one or more children, and a television set. The segregation by age which characterizes American society at large (Bronfenbrenner 1970, 1972) is reflected in television by separate programming for parents and children. The power of television to facilitate the child's cognitive development has been demonstrated by the evaluation of the effects of "Sesame Street" (Bogatz and Ball, 1971).[18] If the findings of our analysis can be generalized, then the educational effects of children's television programs could be considerably enhanced by involving parents in activities with the children both on the screen, and, especially, in the home. Indeed, coordination of television programming with home visits and group meetings with parents could do a great deal to reinforce both parent and child in establishing developmentally advantageous patterns of interaction and activity. Finally, television programming could also enhance the status of parenthood in American culture. At the present time, the picture of the family presented on the television screen is either a fairy tale or a farce, with father and mother cast in highly stereotyped roles. There is little to suggest the challenge, complexity, and reward of being a parent, especially to fathers. Programs focused on these themes, addressed to both children and adults, would contribute to making parenthood a more attractive and respected activity in the eyes of children, parents, and the society at large.

## VIII. FACTS AND PRINCIPLES OF EARLY INTERVENTION: A SUMMARY

The conclusions of this analysis are presented in the form of a summary of the research findings and a set of generalizations to which they give rise.

### A. Summary of Research Results

1. *Preschool Intervention in Group Settings.* The results are based on twelve studies involving children ranging in age from one to six. Eight of these researches

included comparisons between randomly constituted experimental and control groups. Conclusions regarding program effectiveness are cited only if supported by results from such comparisons.

a. Almost without exception, children showed substantial gains in IQ and other cognitive measures during the first year of the program, attaining or even exceeding the average for their age.

b. Cognitively structured curricula produced greater gains than play-oriented nursery programs.

c. Neither earlier entry into the program (from age one) nor a longer period of enrollment (up to five years) resulted in greater or more enduring cognitive gains.

d. By the first or second year after completion of the program, sometimes while it was still in operation, the children began to show a progresssive decline, and by the third or fourth year of follow-up had fallen back into the problem range of the lower 90s and below. Apparent exceptions to this general trend turned out to be faulted by methodological artifacts (e.g., self-selection of families in the experimental group).

e. The period of sharpest decline occurred after the child's entry into regular school. Preliminary data from the Follow-Through program suggest that this decline may be offset by the continuation of intervention programs, including strong parent involvement, into the early grades.

f. The children who profited least from the program, and who showed the earliest and most rapid decline, were those who came from the most deprived social and economic backgrounds. Especially relevant in this regard were such variables as the number of children in the family, the employment status of the head of the household, the level of parents' education, and the presence of only one parent in the family.

g. Results from a number of studies pointed to factors in and around the home as critical to the child's capacity to profit from group programs both in preschool and in the elementary grades. For example, several researches revealed that the greatest loss in cognitive performance of disadvantaged children took place not while they were in school, but over the summer months. During this same period, disadvantaged children living in favorable economic circumstances not only maintained their status but showed significant gains.

2. *Home-based Tutoring Programs.* The results of the two studies in this area were similar to those for preschool programs in group settings. Children showed dramatic gains in IQ while the project was in operation but began to decline once the home visits were discontinued.

3. *Parent-Child Intervention.* A total of nine studies, involving children from the first year of life through elementary school, focused simultaneously on parent and child (almost exclusively the mother) as the targets of intervention. In seven of these researches, the principle of random assignment (either of individuals or groups) was employed in the designation of experimental and control subjects. Again conclusions regarding program effectiveness are cited only when supported

by results from comparisons of randomly constituted experimental and control groups.

a. Parent-child intervention resulted in substantial gains in IQ which were still evident three to four years after termination of the program (Gordon, 1972, 1973; Levenstein, 1972a). In none of the follow-up studies, however, had the children yet gone beyond the first grade.

b. The effects were cumulative from year to year, both during intervention (Levenstein 1972a) and, in some instances, after the program had ended (Gordon, 1973; Levenstein 1972a).

c. The magnitude of IQ gain was inversely related to the age at which the child entered the program, the greatest gain being made by children enrolled as one- and two-year-olds (Gilmer et al., 1070; Gordon, 1972, 1973; Karnes et al., 1968, 1969a, 1969b, 1970; Levenstein, 1972a; Radin, 1969, 1972; Stanford Research Institute, 1971a, 1971b).

d. Parent intervention was of benefit not only for the target child but also for his younger siblings (Gilmer et al., 1970; Klaus and Gray, 1968, 1970).

e. Gains from parent intervention during the preschool years were reduced to the extent that primary responsibility for the child's development was assumed by the staff member rather than left with the parent, particularly when the child was simultaneously enrolled in a group intervention program (Gilmer et al., 1970; Karnes et al., 1969b).

f. By the time the child was five years old, parent intervention appeared to have little effect so far as gains in intellectual development are concerned. *But children who were involved in an intensive program of parent intervention during, and, especially, prior to their enrollment in preschool or school, achieved greater and more enduring gains in the group program* (Gilmer et al., 1970; Gordon, 1972, 1973; Radin, 1969, 1972; Stanford Research Institute, 1971a, 1971b; Smith, 1968). This effect on group programs did not appear until children were at least three years of age, but was still strongly in evidence in the one project in which parent intervention was continued through the sixth grade (Smith, 1968). Thus, from the third year onward, parent intervention seemed to serve as a catalyst for sustaining and enhancing the effects of group intervention.

g. Parent intervention influenced the attitudes and behavior of the mother not only toward the child but in relation to herself as a competent person capable of improving her own situation (Gilmer et al., 1970; Gordon, 1973; Karnes et al., 1970).

h. Families willing to become involved in parent intervention programs tended to come from the upper levels of the disadvantaged population. Research findings indicate that, at the most deprived levels, families are so overburdened with the task of survival that they have neither the energy nor the psychological resources necessary to participate in an intervention program involving the regular visit of a stranger to the home (Klaus and Gray, 1968; Radin and Weikart, 1967).

i. The complexity of findings on the effects of parent intervention prompted a more detailed analysis of the role of parent-child interaction in fostering the child's psychological development. An examination of the research literature (Bronfenbrenner, 1968a, 1968b, 1972) indicated that, in the early years of life, the key element was the involvement of parent and child in verbal interaction around a cognitively challenging task. A second critical feature was the fact that the mother not only trained the child but the child also trained the mother. A third factor was the existence of a mutual and enduring emotional attachment between the child and adult. It is by capitalizing on all these elements, by taking as its focus neither the child nor the parent but the parent-child system, that parent intervention apparently achieves its effectiveness and staying power. It is as if the child himself had no way of internalizing the processes which foster his growth, whereas the parent-child system does possess this capability.

   j. Along with advantages, parent intervention appears to have serious limitations in terms of its applicability and effectiveness with families at the lowest extreme of the socioeconomic distribution.

   4. *Ecological Intervention.* The research results indicate that, for the children from the most deprived groups, no strategy of intervention is likely to be effective that focuses attention solely on the child or on the parent-child relationship. The critical forces of destruction lie neither within the child nor within his family but in the desperate circumstances in which the family is forced to live. What is called for is intervention at the *ecological level,* measures that will effect radical changes in the immediate environment of the family and the child. Only three studies of this kind were found in the research literature (Heber et al., 1971; Skeels, 1966; Skodak and Skeels, 1949). The major findings were as follows:

   a. *Severely disadvantaged children of mothers with IQs well below average (i.e., below 70 or 80) are not doomed to inferiority by unalterable constraints either genetic or environmental.*
   b. Substantial changes in the environment of the child and his principal caretakers can produce positive developmental changes considerably greater (gains of 25 to 28 IQ points) and more enduring than those achieved by the most effective intervention techniques when the home environment is left essentially unaltered.
   c. The processes and effects produced through ecological intervention substantiate the critical role in early development played by an enduring one-to-one relationship involving the child in verbal interaction with an adult around cognitively stimulating activities.

## B. Some Principles of Early Intervention

   The principles are stated in the form of propositions specifying the elements that appear essential for early intervention programs to be effective. Although derived from results of a substantial number of studies by different researchers, these generalizations should still be regarded as tentative. Even where the supportive findings have been replicated, they are susceptible to alternative interpretations, and the crucial experiments are yet to be done.

To indicate the extent to which each of the following generalizations are supported by research results, we shall label each one by a symbol. The superscript "i" denotes that the conclusion is *inferred* from the evidence; the superscript "r" means that the generalization is supported by *replicated results* obtained in two or more well-designed studies described in the main body of this analysis, but that there is need for further research designed specifically to test and refine the proposition in question.

1. *General Principles*[20]

   a. *Family Centered Intervention.*

   The evidence indicates that the family is the most effective and economical system for fostering and sustaining the development of the child.[r] The evidence indicates further that the involvement of the child's family as an active participant is critical to the success of any intervention program.[r] Without such family involvement, any effects of intervention, at least in the cognitive sphere, appear to erode fairly rapidly once the program ends.[r] In contrast, the involvement of the parents as partners in the enterprise provides an ongoing system which can reinforce the effects of the program while it is in operation, and help to sustain them after the program ends.[r]

   b. *Ecological Intervention.*

   The first and most essential requirement is to provide those conditions which are necessary for life and for the family to function as a child rearing system.[r] These include adequate health care, nutrition, housing, employment, and opportunity and status for parenthood.[i] These are also precisely the conditions that are absent for millions of disadvantaged families in our country.[r]

   To provide the conditions necessary for a family to function will require major changes in the institutions of the society and the invention of new institutional forms.[i] The results of this analysis offer no guidance on the development of new systems for providing adequate health care, nutrition, housing, or income, but they do suggest strategies for increasing opportunity and social reward for the functions of parenthood. These include extending the number and status of part-time jobs available to disadvantaged parents of young children,[i] establishing more flexible work schedules,[i] introducing Parent Apprentice Programs in the schools to engage older children in supervised care of the young,[i] involving parents in the work of the school,[r] creating patterns of mutual assistance among disadvantaged families living in the same neighborhood,[i] meeting the basic needs of young families, (including supervised experience in child care) before they begin to raise children,[i] providing homemaker services,[i] making available insurance to meet family emergencies,[i] and using television an an adjunct to parent-child intervention.[21]

   c. *A Sequential Strategy of Intervention.*

   A long-range intervention program may be viewed in terms of five stages. Although the program may be begun with benefit to the child at any age,[r] initiating appropriate intervention at earlier stages can be expected to yield cumulative gains.[r] Ideally intervention should not be interrupted (for then the gains achieved are gradually eroded[r]), and there should be continuity from one phase to the next.[i] During every stage the first requirement is to meet the family's basic needs as outlined above.[i] Thereafter, intervention is differentiated to accommodate the developmental level of both family and child as indicated below.

2. *Stages of Intervention.*

*Stage I. Preparation for Parenthood.*

Ideally, intervention begins before the family is formed when the future parents are still in school. This initial phase involves providing school children of both sexes practicum experiences in the care of the young.[i] In addition, attention is given to the health requirements of the future mother in terms of nutrition and preventive medical care.[i]

*Stage II. Before Children Come.*

The next critical point for intervention is after the family is formed but before any children are born. Here the initial emphasis is to ensure adequate housing, health care, nutrition, and economic security before, during, and after pregnancy.[i] This is also the optimal period for introducing a parent intervention program with some experience with young children provided before the family's own offspring arrive on the scene.[i]

*Stage III. The First Three Years of Life.*

During this period the primary objective is the establishment of an enduring emotional relationship between parent and infant involving frequent reciprocal interaction[r] around activities which are challenging to the child.[r] The effect of such interaction is to strengthen the bond between parent and child,[r] enhance motivation,[r] increase the frequency and power of contingent responses,[r] produce mutual adaptation in behavior,[r] and thereby improve the parent's effectiveness as a teacher for the child,[i] further the latter's learning,[r] and, in due course, establish a stable interpersonal system capable of fostering and sustaining the child's development in the future.[r] The development of such an enduring pattern of attachment and interaction can be facilitated through a parent intervention program involving the following elements.

(1) The program includes frequent home visits in which parent and child are encouraged, by example and with the aid of appropriate materials, to engage in sustained patterns of verbal interaction around tasks which gradually increase in cognitive complexity as a function of the child's development.[r]

(2) The parent devotes considerable periods of time to activities with the child, specifically those introduced during the home visit.[r]

(3) The role of the parent as the primary agent of intervention is given priority, status, and support from the surrounding environment.[r] Intervention programs which cast the parent in a subordinate role or have the effect of discouraging or decreasing his participation in activities with the child are likely to be counterproductive.[r]

(4) The effectiveness and efficiency of parent intervention can be increased by extending activities so as to involve all members of the family.[i] In this way

the effects of vertical diffusion to younger siblings can be maximized[r] while older family members, including father, relatives, and older brothers and sisters, can participate as agents of intervention.[i] Such expansion, however, should not be allowed to impair the formation and uninterrupted activity of enduring one-to-one relationships so essential to the development of the young child.[i]

(5) The effectiveness and efficiency of parent intervention can be enhanced through group meetings designed to provide information, to demonstrate materials and procedures, and to create situations in which the confidence and motivation of parents (and other family members) is reinforced through mutual support and a sense of common purpose.[r] Such meetings, however, must not be allowed to take precedence over home visits or the periods which the parent devotes to playing and working with the child.[r]

*Stage IV. Ages Four through Six.*
During this period, exposure to a cognitively oriented preschool curriculum becomes a potent force for accelerating the child's cognitive development,[r] but a strong parent intervention program is necessary to enhance and sustain the effects of the group experience.[r] This combined strategy involves the following features.

(1) The effectiveness of preschool experience in a group setting is enhanced if it is *preceded* by a strong parent intervention program involving regular home visits.[r]

(2) After preschool begins, the parent program must not be relegated to secondary status if it is to realize its potential in conserving and facilitating the effects of group intervention.[r] Both phases of the combined strategy should reinforce the parents' status as central in fostering the development of the child.[i] A program which places the parent in a subordinate role dependent on the expert is not likely to be effective in the long run.[r]

*Stage V. Ages Six through Twelve.*
Of special importance for sustaining the child's learning in school is the involvement of parents in supporting at home the activities engaged in by the child at school and their participation in activities at school directly affecting their child.[i] The parent, however, need no longer be the child's principal teacher as at earlier stages. Rather he acts as a supporter of the child's learning both in and out of school, but continues to function, and to be identified by school personnel, as the primary figure responsible for the child's development as a person.[i]

Taken as a whole, the foregoing principles imply a major reorientation in the design of intervention programs and in the training of personnel to work in this area. In the past, such programs were primarily child-centered, age-segregated, time-bound, self-centered, and focused on the trained professional as the powerful and direct agent of intervention with the child. The results of this analysis point to approaches that are family-centered rather than child-centered, that cut across contexts rather than being confined to a single setting, that have continuity through time, and that utilize as the primary agents of socialization the child's own parents, other family members, adults and other children from the neighborhood in which he lives, school personnel, and other persons who are part of the child's enduring environment. It is beyond the scope of this paper to attempt to spell out the implication of this reorientation for the organization of services, delivery systems, and training. Many developments in the desired direction are already taking place. It is hoped that this analysis may accelerate the process of social change in the major institutions of our nation directly affecting the lives of young children and their families.

In concluding this analysis, we reemphasize the tentative nature of the conclusions and the narrowness of IQ and related measures as aspects of the total development of the child. We also wish to reaffirm a deep indebtedness to those who conducted the programs and researches on which this work is based, and a profound faith in the capacity of parents, of whatever background, to enable their children to develop into effective and happy human beings, *once our society is willing to make conditions of life viable and humane for all its families.*

## NOTES

1. For an analysis of these studies, see Bronfenbrenner 1968a.

2. The development in recent years of reliable observation techniques for assessing the cognitive, emotional, and social behavior of young children in natural settings (e.g., Schoggen and Schoggen, 1971) gives promise that in the near future we shall have valid evidence regarding the effects of early intervention on other important aspects of the child's development beyond those measured by conventional tests of intelligence and achievement.

3. In the absence of specific background data on parents' education and other background characteristics, especially for the self-selected experimental group, it is difficult to assess the degree of deprivation for this project. The median income is considerably higher than that for Gray's project ($3,400 versus $1,500), but the sample is drawn from an urban slum area, where the cost of living would be appreciably higher. At the same time, in contrast to the two Washington projects, all the families were not preselected for willingness to have their children participate in an intervention program.

4. This procedure also takes into account the tendency of both experimental and control groups to show some gain because of practice effect.

5. In the Weikart project, there was some evidence of a residual, experimental effect in academic achievement, but this was limited to girls.

6. Probably because of somewhat more favorable family circumstances as reflected in a higher average income and half as many families with absent fathers (Klaus and Gray, 1968: 5-7).

7. Indirect evidence in support of this possibility is cited by Klaus and Gray (1968: 55-59).

8. It is significant that the attrition in this program was high, but limited to the control group. It seems plausible that these "dropouts" had volunteered in the hope of participating in the program and left when this hope could not be realized.

9. The gain cannot be attributed to diffusion from an experimental group, since treated and untreated families were located in different communities.

10. The failure of the three-year-old group to show appreciable differences between

experimentals and controls is a function of sample bias in the C2 control, which, as we have seen, is not comparable to the other groups in the study.

11. Lower attendance, motivation, and teacher effectiveness were also observed among the mothers of the younger infants under 18 months. No corresponding difference was perceptible, however, in the mental development of their children, who obtained the highest post-Binet scores of any subgroup in the sample. It is possible that the inferior response of the mothers was a function of weaker feedback from the younger infant in terms of what are ordinarily looked for as signs of maturity in a young child (e.g., talking). If so, this phenomenon could be taken into account by alerting the mothers to the signs of development in very young children.

12. A more recent publication (Weikart et al., 1971) reflects the evolution of a greater emphasis on the role of the mother: "During the course of the Ypsilanti Project, two general purposes evolved for the home teaching: 1) to involve the mother in the teaching process in order to give her a background on knowledge concerning the educational needs of her child so that she could provide educational support at home, and 2) to implement the curriculum on a one-to-one basis with the child in the house. In order to prevent home teaching from becoming merely a tutorial session between teacher and child, it is important that the teachers make a concentrated effort to deal with any problems that may arise while the mother is learning to become an active participant in the educational process" (Weikart et al., 1971: 79).

13. On the question of whether other adults from depressed neighborhoods, would be willing to participate, the following observation by Karnes et al., is *a propos:* "As a matter of fact, teachers reported that parents, relatives, sibling and even neighbors sometimes assembled for the teachers' visits." (1968, p. 182)

14. That early parent intervention did have some later impact in the school setting, however, is indicated by two other types of data collected by Levenstein. Of all children in experimental groups, only two—or fewer than 5%—were not promoted to the next grade level; among the controls, the rate was three times as high (16%). Also, children in the program were rated more favorably by their teachers than were the controls. One cannot rule out the possibility, however, that the teachers were influenced by knowledge, acquired from the mothers of the children themselves, that the family had participated in the intervention program.

15. Because the children had not been assigned on a random basis to preschools with and without a parent involvement component, it is conceivable, but unlikely, that some other correlated factor accounts for the observed difference.

16. It may be significant in this regard that, of the longitudinal group intervention projects described in Tables 14.1 and 14.2, the two that produced the smallest initial experimental effects (Herzog and Beller) were the only ones to have full-day programs. The issue is confounded, however, by the fact that they both also employed a traditional nursery school approach with emphasis on free play rather than structured cognitive experience.

17. In a recent interview, Caroline Hoffman, director of the preschool program of the Milwaukee project, stated that the children are about to enter first grade in the regular Milwaukee schools. "We won't know until then whether they can maintain their high standings, or whether, cut loose from our special training and away from this special environment, they will begin to slip back" (*New York Times,* July 17, 1972).

18. For example, children who viewed the program over a two-year period showed 9 to 15 point gains on the Peabody Picture Vocabulary Test. These children and their families of course represent a self-selected group, especially in terms of motivation, so that it is difficult to know how much of the effect is attributable to the program itself.

20. The propositions are stated in terms of parent rather than mother alone in the belief that subsequent research will indicate that they apply as well to the father, or any other older member of the household who is prepared to assume a major and continuing responsibility for the care of the child.

21. A more extended discussion of the rationale and nature of the foregoing proposals appears in Bronfenbrenner and Bruner, 1972.

# REFERENCES

Amidon, A. and O. G. Brim. What do children have to gain from parent education? Paper prepared for the Advisory Committee on Child Development, National Research Council, National Academy of Science, 1972.

Bee, H. L., L. F. Van Egeren, A. P. Streissguth, B. A. Nyman and M. S. Leckie. Social class differences in maternal teaching strategies and speech patterns. *Developmental Psychology,* 1969, 1: 726-734.

Bell, R. Q. A reinterpretation of the direction of effects in studies of socialization. *Psychological Review,* 1968, 75: 81-95.

Beller, E. K. Impact of early education on disadvantaged children. In S. Ryan (ed.), *A Report on Longitudinal Evaluations of Preschool Programs.* Washington, D.C.: Office of Child Development, 1972.

Beller, E. K. Personal communication, 1973.

Bereiter, C. and S. Engelmann. *Teaching Disadvantaged Children in the Preschool.* Englewood Cliffs, N.J.: Prentice-Hall, 1966.

Bissell, J. S. *The Cognitive Effects of Preschool Programs for Disadvantaged Children.* Washington, D.C.: National Institute of Child Health and Human Development, 1970.

———. *Implementation of Planned Variation in Head Start: First Year Report.* Washington, D.C.: National Institute of Child Health and Human Development, 1971.

Bloom, B. S. *Compensatory Education for Cultural Deprivation.* New York: Holt, Rinehart and Winston, 1965.

Bogartz, G. A. and S. Ball. *The Second Year of Sesame Street: A Continuing Evaluation.* Vol. 1 and 2. Princeton, N.J.: Educational Testing Service, 1971.

Bronfenbrenner, U. The changing American child: A speculative analysis. *Merrill-Palmer Quarterly,* 1961, 7: 78-84.

———. Early deprivation: A cross-species analysis. Pp. 627-764 in S. Levine and G. Newron (eds.), *Early Experience in Behavior.* Springfield, Ill.: Charles C. Thomas, 1968. (a)

———. When is infant stimulation effective? Pp. 251-257 in D. C. Glass (ed.), *Environmental Influences.* New York: Rockefeller University Press, 1968. (b)

———. *Two Worlds of Childhood: U.S. and U.S.S.R.* New York: Russell Sage Foundation, 1970.

———. The Roots of Alienation. Pp. 658-677 in U. Bronfenbrenner (ed.), *Influences on Human Development.* Hinsdale, Ill.: Dryden Press, 1972.

———. Developmental research and public policy. In J. M. Romanshyn (ed.), *Social Science and Social Welfare.* New York: Council on Social Work Education, 1973.

——— and J. Bruner. The President and the children. *New York Times,* January 31, 1972.

Brown, S. J. and B. M. Caldwell. Social adjustment of children in day care who enrolled prior to or after the age of three. *American Journal of Orthopsychiatry.* In press.

Caldwell, B. M. and L. E. Smith. Day care for the very young—prime opportunity for primary prevention. *American Journal of Public Health,* 1970, 60: 690-697.

Coleman, J. S. *Equality of Educational Opportunity.* Washington, D.C.: U.S. Office of Education, 1966.

Deutsch, M. Minority groups and class status as related to social and personality factors in scholastic achievement. Society for Applied Anthropology, Monograph No. 2. Ithaca, N.Y.: New York State School of Industrial and Labor Relations, Cornell University, 1960.

Deutsch, M., et al. *Regional research and resource center in early childhood: Final report.* Washington, D.C.: U.S. Office of Economic Opportunity, 1971.

Deutsch, M., E. Taleporos and J. Victor. A brief synopsis of an initial enrichment program in early childhood. In S. R. Ryan (ed.), *A Report on Longitudinal Evaluations of Preschool Programs.* Washington, D.C.: Office of Child Development, 1972.

Di Lorenzo, L. T. *Pre-kindergarten Programs for Educationally Disadvantaged Children: Final Report.* Washington, D.C.: U.S. Office of Education, 1969.

Gardner, J. and H. Gardner. A note on selective imitation by a six-week-old infant. *Child Development,* 1970, 41: 1209-1213.

Gilmer, B., J. O. Miller and S. W. Gray. *Intervention with Mothers and Young Children: Study of Intra-Family Effects.* Nashville, Tenn.: DARCEE Demonstration and Research Center for Early Education, 1970.

Gordon, I. J. *A Home Learning Center Approach to Early Stimulation.* Gainesville: University of Florida, Institute for Development of Human Resources, 1971.

———. *A Home Learning Center Approach to Early Stimulation.* Gainesville: University of Florida, Institute for Development of Human Resources, 1972.

———. *An Early Intervention Project: A Longitudinal Look.* Gainsville: University of Florida, Institute for Development of Human Resources, College of Education, 1973.

Gray, S. W. and R. A. Klaus. Experimental preschool program for culturally-deprived children. *Child Development,* 1965, 36: 887-898.

———. The early training project: The seventh-year report. *Child Development,* 1970, 41: 909-924.

Hayes, D. and L. Grether. The school year and vacation: When do students learn? Paper presented at the Eastern Sociological Convention, New York, New York, 1969.

Hebb, D. O. *The Organization of Behavior.* New York: Wiley, 1949.

Heber, R., H. Garber, S. Harrington and C. Hoffman. *Rehabilitation of Families at Risk for Mental Retardation.* Madison: Rehabilitation Research and Training Center in Mental Retardation, University of Wisconsin, October 1971.

Hertzig, M. E., H. G. Birch, A. Thomas and O. A. Mendez. Class and ethnic differences in responsiveness of preschool children to cognitive demands. *Monograph of the Society for Research in Child Development,* 1968, 33: (1).

Herzog, E., C. H. Newcomb and I. H. Cisin. Double deprivation: The less they have the less they learn. In S. Ryan (ed.), *A Report on Longitudinal Evaluations of Preschool Programs.* Washington, D.C.: Office of Child Development, 1972. (a)

———. But some are poorer than others: SES differences in a preschool program. *American Journal of Orthopsychiatry,* 1972, 42: 4-22. (b)

———. *Preschool and Postscript: An Evaluation of the Inner-City Program.* Washington, D.C.: Social Research Group, George Washington University, 1973.

Hess, R. D., V. C. Shipman, J. E. Brophy and R. M. Bear. *The Cognitive Environments of Urban Preschool Children.* Chicago: University of Chicago Graduate School of Education, 1968.

———. *The Cognitive Environments of Urban Preschool Children: Follow-up Phase.* Chicago: University of Chicago Graduate School of Education, 1969.

Hodges, W. L., B. R. McCandless and H. H. Spicker. *The Development and Evaluation of a Diagnostically Based Curriculum for Preschool Psychosocially Deprived Children.* Washington, D.C.: U.S. Office of Education, 1967.

Hunt, J. McV. *Intelligence and Experience.* New York: Ronald Press, 1961.

*Infant Education Research Project.* Washington, D.C.: U.S. Office of Education Booklet #OE-37033.

Jones, S. J. and H. A. Moss. Age, state, and maternal behavior associated with infant vocalizations. *Child Development,* 1971, 42: 1039.

Kagan, J. On cultural deprivation. Pp. 211-250 in D. C. Glass (ed.), *Environmental Influences.* New York: Rockefeller University Press, 1968.

Kagan, J. *Change and Continuity in Infancy.* New York: Wiley, 1971.

Karnes, M. B., W. M. Studley, W. R. Wright and A. S. Hodgins. An approach to working with mothers of disadvantaged preschool children. *Merrill-Palmer Quarterly,* 1968, 14: 174-184.

Karnes, M. B. *Research and Development Program on Preschool Disadvantaged Children: Final Report.* Washington, D.C.: U.S. Office of Education, 1969.

Karnes, M. B. and E. E. Badger. Training mothers to instruct their infants at home. Pp. 249-263 in M. B. Karnes, *Research and Development Program on Preschool Disadvantaged Children: Final Report.* Washington, D.C.: U.S. Office of Education, 1969.

Karnes, M. B., A. S. Hodgins and J. A. Teska. The effects of short-term instruction at home by mothers of children not enrolled in a preschool. Pp. 197-203 in M. B. Karnes, *Research and Development Program on Preschool Disadvantaged Children: Final Report.* Washington, D.C.: U.S. Office of Education, 1969. (a)

Karnes, M. B., A. S. Hodgins and J. A. Teska. The impact of at-home instruction by mothers on performance in the ameliorative preschool. Pp. 205-212 in M. B. Karnes, *Research and Development Program on Preschool Disadvantaged Children: Final Report.* Washington, D.C.: U.S. Office of Education. (b)

Karnes, M. B., J. A. Teska, A. S. Hodgins and E. D. Badger. Educational intervention at home by mothers of disadvantaged infants. *Child Development,* 1970, 41: 925-935.

Karnes, M. B., R. R. Zehrbach and J. A. Teska. An ameliorative approach in the development of curriculum. Pp. 353-381 in R. K. Parker (ed.), *The Preschool in Action.* Boston: Allyn and Bacon, 1972.

Kirk, S. A. *Early Education of the Mentally Retarded.* Urbana: University of Illinois Press, 1958.

———. The effects of early education with disadvantaged infants. In M. B. Karnes, *Research and Development Program on Preschool Disadvantaged Children: Final Report.* Washington, D.C.: U.S. Office of Education, 1969.

Klaus, R. A. and S. W. Gray. The early training project for disadvantaged children: A report after five years. *Monographs of the Society for Research in Child Development,* 1968, 33 (4, Serial #120).

Kraft, I., J. Fushillo and E. Herzog. Prelude to school: An evaluation of an inner-city school program. *Children's Bureau Research Report Number 3.* Washington, D.C.: Children's Bureau, 1968.

Levenstein, P. Cognitive growth in preschoolers through verbal interaction with mothers. *American Journal of Orthopsychiatry,* 1970, 40, 426-432.

———. *Verbal Interaction Project.* Mineola, N.Y.: Family Service Association of Nassau County, 1972. (a)

———. But does it work in homes away from home? *Theory Into Practice,* 1972, 11: 157-162. (b)

———. Personal communication, 1972. (c)

——— and S. Levenstein. Fostering learning potential in preschoolers. *Social Casework,* 1971, 52: 74-78.

Levenstein, P. and R. Sunley. Stimulation of verbal interaction between disadvantaged mothers and children. *American Journal of Orthopsychiatry,* 1968, 38: 116-121.

Moss, H. A. Sex, age, and state as determinants of mother-infant interaction. *Merrill-Palmer Quarterly,* 1967, 13: 19-36.

Radin, N. The impact of a kindergarten home counseling program. *Exceptional Children,* 1969, 36: 251-256.

———. Three degrees of maternal involvement in a preschool program: Impact on mothers and children. *Child Development,* 1972, 43: 1355-1364.

——— and D. Weikart. A home teaching program for disadvantaged preschool children. *Journal of Special Education,* Winter 1967, 1: 183-190.

Resnick, M. B. and V. Van De Riet. Summary evaluation of the Learning to Learn program. Gainsville: University of Florida, Department of Clinical Psychology, 1973.

Rheingold, H. S. The social and socializing infant. Pp. 779-790 in D. A. Goslin, *Handbook of Socialization Theory and Research.* Chicago: Rand McNally, 1969.

Schaefer, E. S. *Progress Report: Intellectual Stimulation of Culturally-Deprived Parents.* National Institute of Mental Health, 1968.

———. Need for early and continuing education. Pp. 61-82 in V. H. Denenberg (ed.), *Education of the Infant and Young Child.* New York: Academic Press, 1970.

———. Personal communication, 1972. (a)

———. Parents as educators: Evidence from cross-sectional longitudinal and intervention research. *Young Children,* 1972, 27: 227-239. (b)

——— and M. Aaronson. Infant education research project: Implementation and implications of the home-tutoring program. Pp. 410-436 in R. K. Parker (ed.), *The Preschool in Action.* Boston: Allyn and Bacon, 1972.

Schoggen, M. and P. Schoggen. *Environmental forces in home lives of three-year-old children in three population sub-groups.* Nashville, Tenn.: George Peabody College for Teachers, DARCEE Papers and Reports, vol. 5, no. 2, 1971.

Skeels, H. M. Adult status of children from contrasting early life experiences. *Monographs of the Society for Research in Child Development,* 1966, 31 (Serial #105).

———. and H. B. Dye. A study of the effects of differential stimulation on mentally retarded children. *Proceedings and Addresses of the American Association on Mental Deficiency,* 1939, 44: 114-136.

Skeels, H. M.; Updegraff, B. L. Wellman and H. M. Williams. A study of environmental stimulation: An orphanage preschool project. *University of Iowa Studies on Child Welfare,* 1938, 15 (4).

Skodak, M. and H. M. Skeels. A final follow-up study of 100 adopted children. *Journal of Genetic Psychology,* 1949, 75: 85-125.

Smith, M. B. School and home: Focus on achievement. Pp. 89-107 in A. H. Passow. (ed.), *Developing Programs for the Educationally Disadvantaged.* New York: Teachers College Press, 1968.

Soar, R. S. An integrative approach to classroom learning. NIMH Project Number 5-R11MH01096 to the University of South Carolina and 7-R11MH02045 to Temple University, 1966.

———. *Follow-Through Classroom Process Measurement and Pupil Growth (1970-71).* Gainesville: College of Education, University of Florida, 1972.

———. and R. M. Soar. Pupil subject matter growth during the summer vacation. *Educational Leadership Research Supplement,* 1969, 2: 577-587.

Sprigle, H. Learning to learn program. In S. Ryan (ed.), *A Report of Longitudinal Evaluations of Preschool Programs.* Washington, D.C.: Office of Child Development, 1972.

Stanford Research Institute. *Implementation of Planned Variation in Head Start: Preliminary Evaluation of Planned Variation in Head Start According to Follow-Through Approaches (1969-1970).* Washington, D.C.: Office of Child Development, U.S. Department of Health, Education and Welfare, 1971 (a)

Stanford Research Institute. *Longitudinal Evaluation of Selected Features of the National Follow-Through Program.* Washington, D.C.: Office of Education, U.S. Department of Health, Education and Welfare, 1971. (b)

Tulkin, S. R. and B.J. Cohler. Child rearing attitudes on mother-child interaction among middle and working class families. Paper presented at the 1971 meeting of the Society for Research in Child Development.

Tulkin, S. R. and J. Kagan. Mother-child interaction: Social class differences in the first year of life. *Proceedings of the 78th Annual Convention of the American Psychological Association,* 1970, 261-262.

Van De Riet, V. A sequential approach to early childhood and elementary education. Gainesville, Florida: Department of Clinical Psychology, University of Florida, 1971.

Weikart, D. P. *Preschool Intervention: A Preliminary Report of the Perry Preschool Project.* Ann Arbor, Mich.: Campus Publishers, 1967.

———. A comparative study of three preschool curricula. A paper presented at the biannual meeting of the Society for Research in Child Development, Santa Monica, California, March 1969.

——— et al. *Longitudinal Results of the Ypsilanti Perry Preschool Project.* Ypsilanti, Mich.: High/Scope Educational Research Foundation, 1970.

Weikart, D. P., C. K. Kamii and M. Radin. *Perry Preschool Progress Report.* Ypsilanti, Mich.: Ypsilanti Public Schools, 1964.

Weikart, D. P., L. Rogers, C. Adcock and D. McClelland. *The Cognitively Oriented Curriculum.* Washington, D.C.: National Association for the Education of Young Children, 1971.

# 15

# EVALUATION OF PUBLIC HEALTH PROGRAMS

THOMAS W. BICE

*Washington University (St. Louis)*

and

ROBERT L. EICHHORN

with the assistance of

DENISE A. KLEIN

*Purdue University*

Evaluation in public health encompasses a broad range of activities and programs generally aimed at protecting, preserving, or promoting the health of populations. These include traditional environmental control programs and mass immunization campaigns, and medical care programs, as well as, more recently, efforts intended to increase individuals' access to personal health services. As in other realms of social intervention, programs designed to improve or maintain health may be evaluated from several perspectives and at different levels, ranging from studies of the medical efficacy of specific treatments, investigations of costs of alternative treatments, evaluations of organizational mechanisms through which treatments are delivered, and so on. As one proceeds along this continuum from evaluations of medical efficacy of specific treatments to studies of the effectiveness and efficiency of health services systems, the scope and complexity of relevant factors increase, and, in consequence, classical methods of evaluation become correspondingly less applicable.

This chapter deals with issues in and methods of evaluating intervention

AUTHORS' NOTE: In part, the ideas set forth here grew out of the authors' examination of the Experimental Health Services Delivery Systems Program. The work was supported by Bureau of Health Services Research Grant No. 3 R18 HS-01145 and Contract No. HSM 110-HSRD-151.

strategies quite distant from the point at which providers and consumers of care meet, namely, those aimed at improving health through planning, management, and regulation of health delivery systems. In particular, we focus on the voluntaristic approach in which community decision organizations[1] are the principal "experimental treatments." We contend that this class of interventions, as typically structured, confronts the evaluator with rather unique and relatively complex problems that render classical evaluation methods unfeasible, if not irrelevant. In such circumstances, evaluators will necessarily find themselves drawing more upon the art rather than the science of evaluation,[2] where breadth of concern and insight rather than experimental design will be the basis of proof.

## COMMUNITY HEALTH DECISION ORGANIZATIONS

Warren defines community decision organizations as corporate bodies that "constitute the means through which the community attempts to concert certain decisions and activities"[3] and notes that their rationale presumes "a higher aggregate utility is attainable through joint decision-making and action ... than if decisions within each field of concern were left to what Banfield[4] calls 'social choice.' "[5] Such organizations typically do not deliver social or medical services directly to clients, and neither do they usually have administrative control over provider organizations' resources; rather, community decision organizations are characteristically *voluntary* groups whose powers over their environments derive from the aggregate influence of their membership and the usually limited authorities provided them by their sponsors.

The rise of such corporate bodies in the health sector is correlated with beliefs about causes behind socially undesirable characteristics of health services, as well as with prevailing political philosophies. It is a logical consequence of the view that attributes problems (e.g., rising costs, inequitable allocation, etc.) to social disorganization within the health sector rather than to solely market imperfections and is in keeping with traditional values that prefer local autonomy over centralized federal control.

By the late 1960s, the social disorganization diagnosis of the nation's health services ills had found favor among individuals, groups, and organizations of widely different political hues. The problems attributed to the nation's health "nonsystem" were, of course, neither newly created nor previously unknown to observers of American medical care.[6] Rather, the inescapable press of events following the massive and rapid introduction of federal programs during the Johnson Administration had chastened policy makers who earlier had responded to health care problems with market-oriented initiatives, that is, by increasing demand or supply or both. The social disorganization explanation thus became toward the close of the decade the official definition of the situation, as evidenced by the Nixon Administration's proposed solutions:

> ... with few exceptions, the [Administration's health] strategy seeks to modify the entire *system* of health care. It became abundantly.clear, in the process of defining precisely the nature of "health care crisis," that the most

basic and widespread problems were in fact systemic, and that further categorical and piecemeal efforts would very likely exacerbate rather than ameliorate the problems.[7]

The dilemma faced by those who supported greater federal responsibility for health care, specifically a national health insurance scheme, was how to incorporate fiscal and quality controls into a plan to assure that federal monies would be effectively and equitably allocated, while preserving local autonomy and control. It would be difficult to imagine a presidential philosophy more congenial than the Nixon Administration's to John Stuart Mill's cautioning that "it is but a small portion of the public business of a country which can be well done, or safely attempted, by the central authorities." Such views were, however, increasingly being adopted by the political left as well, for the "bureaucracy problem"[8] provided ample evidence of disorganization at the federal level that mirrored the chaos at the local level.[9]

With a nearly universally accepted position at the outset of the 1970s that more responsibilities for planning and management of health services should be delegated to states and localities,[10] attention focused naturally on what was known from experiences of previous efforts to encourage collective rationality in the health sector. At that time, the federal government was supporting two programs enacted in the mid-1960s, the Regional Medical Programs (RMP) and Comprehensive Health Planning (CHP), and a demonstration project, Experimental Health Services Delivery Systems (EHSDS), which presumably could yield important lessons upon which to base policy. One seeks in vain, however, for findings from evaluation studies that offer clear-cut directions to policy makers. Although aspects of each program have been studied by various investigators, none can estimate unequivocally their impacts on the health of populations, isolate their unique contributions to the organization and delivery of health services, or even describe coherently and concisely what local organizations do and have done. This state of affairs, we suggest, is due to several conceptual and methodological issues that have not been satisfactorily resolved by social scientists concerned with the study of organizations and political processes, as well as to fundamental ambiguities built into such programs.

## HEALTH PLANNING AND MANAGEMENT ORGANIZATIONS

Until the mid-1960s, the federal government did little to influence the private practice of medicine in the United States. Before the enactment of the Sheppard-Towner Act in 1921, which provided funds for maternal and child health services, federal involvement in health was limited primarily to public health.[11] Passage of the Social Security Act in 1935 established an administrative vehicle for a federal role in social welfare and, ultimately, health care; but successive efforts to extend health care benefits, beginning in the late 1930s and continuing throughout the following decade, were thwarted. A limited attempt to provide assistance for the impoverished through the Kerr-Mills Act was adopted in 1960. As of the mid-1960s, however, little had been proposed or initiated at the federal level to meet the health care needs of the disadvantaged. Yet the inexorable march of health care costs, fed by advancing technology and specialization, continued. The crisis of inequitable access to medical services, long a feature of American health care, was clearly visible in the nation's central cities and rural areas.

The long awaited federal response was unleashed in a flurry of legislative activity during the Johnson Administration.[12] Under the umbrella of the War on Poverty, federally funded health care centers for the poor were established following enactment of Partnership for Health legislation. The direct service strategy, later to be eschewed by the Nixon Administration, gave rise to neighborhood health centers, migrant health centers, maternal and infant care centers, mental health centers, and Model Cities clinics—all supported with federal funds administered by newly created or expanded federal bureaucracies.

The mid-1960s also witnessed a major victory in the struggle for national health insurance, as the Social Security Act was amended to provide federal funds for health care services of the aged and the poor. Title XVIII (Medicare) entitled Social Security beneficiaries to participate in federally funded insurance programs; Title XIX (Medicaid) provided federal matching monies to states for the care of welfare recipients and the medically indigent.

While direct service and social insurance programs were, no doubt, providing benefits to underserved segments of the American population, it soon became apparent that they were not unalloyed successes. Purchasing power was enhanced, thus stimulating demand; but supply did not respond, which created inevitable inflationary pressures. More than fifty pieces of health legislation enacted during one presidential administration were being administered by at least twenty-three agencies of government operating under four hundred discrete authorities. The federal government had moved with unprecedented scope and speed to alleviate longstanding problems, but had done so with no overarching policy. The formulation and implementation of local and regional policy were left to RMP, CHP[13] and, later, EHSDS.[14]

CHP and EHSDS differed fundamentally from the strictly categorical programs of the 1960s. Each was designed to bring into existence a system of health services delivery where duplications of effort and gaps in performance were thought to exist. (RMP was established with a similar intent for the treatment of heart disease, cancer, and stroke.) The categorical programs, on the other hand, provided services to those with presumed or demonstrated needs without basically altering existing organizational arrangements.

### Regional Medical Programs

Among the many weaknesses of the American medical system has been its inability to translate advanced medical science and technology from research and training centers into the body of skills and knowledge applied by practitioners in the community. RMP legislation was intended to remedy this situation by encouraging and assisting in "the establishment of regional cooperative arrangements among medical schools, research institutions, and hospitals, for research training (including continuing education) and related demonstrations of patient care."[15]

The report of the President's Commission on Heart Disease, Cancer and Stroke, which called for the Regional Medical Program, envisioned that advanced technology would be channeled to communities from research and training institutions through regional centers, where services would be delivered and continuing education for local practitioners implemented. As enacted, however, the program was stripped of its services capabilities and transformed into primarily a granting agency. Powerful interest groups—particularly the American Medical Association—opposed the federal government's sponsoring centers which would compete in the practice of medicine with local practitioners.

To accomplish the purposes of the act, Regional Advisory Groups were constituted in 56 regions. Comprised of representatives of medical schools, teaching hospitals, state and local health departments, private practitioners, and the general public, advisory groups were charged with devising plans and authorizing expenditures of federal grant monies for innovative programs. Thus, RMP was to enhance coordination and integration of health services via a voluntary, pluralistic mechanism that decentralized decision-making.

## Comprehensive Health Planning

Although the federal government had attempted to stimulate planning and coordination of health services through Hill-Burton and RMP, it had done so following a categorical approach. Hill-Burton dealt with construction and planning for facilities; RMP ostensibly concentrated on particular disease entities. No single agency had responsibility for total, comprehensive health planning. Only one year after enactment of RMP legislation, Congress moved to fill this void. The instrument was to be a network of voluntary comprehensive health planning agencies charged with mandates to develop long-range, statewide, and local plans for environmental as well as personal health services.

As with RMP, CHP was preceded by a report of a federal commission that called for more sweeping powers and responsibilities than were ultimately adopted in authorizing legislation. [16] In particular, the commission recommended that there be created in regions throughout the United States health planning councils "responsible for general health services and facilities within the context of the region's total spectrum of health services." [17] "Planning" was defined as an "action process" in which councils would not only devise blueprints, but would take steps to implement recommendations. Based on careful and extensive study of health care needs, councils, through exercise of their pluralistic influence, were to effect major permanent changes in health services delivery.

Legislation authorizing CHP, like RMP legislation before it, specified, however, that comprehensive health planning was to be accomplished without interference in prevailing patterns of medical practice. Thus, CHP was, in effect, given the charge to develop plans but prevented from implementing them.

CHP was organized in two layers. Each participating state established a statewide (CHP[a]) agency to oversee planning throughout the state. At the local level, areawide (CHP[b]) agencies were to be responsible for planning within designated regions. Plans developed by these so-called "b" agencies were to be reviewed by the umbrella statewide agency.

As voluntary organizations, CHP agencies were mandated to include on their councils consumers as well as representatives of provider institutions and associations, with at least 51% of their membership drawn from consumer groups. Additionally, to preserve local autonomy, CHP agencies were funded by formula grants in which federal monies were to be matched by state and local contributions.

## Experimental Health Services Delivery Systems

In the spring of 1971, the Health Services and Mental Health Administration (HSMHA) launched a program intended to be a major social experiment in the management of community-wide health services systems. Architects of the EHSDS project proposed to test, in several types of geopolitical regions, whether improvements in personal health services could be gained through greater exercise of collective rationality and coordination of federal grants-in-aid programs. At the local level, voluntary corporations comprised of all relevant interest groups were, over several years, to assess their health care delivery systems and plan and execute needed changes. The necessary authority and control over local providers of health services were initially to be provided by the federal government, as theretofore discrete, categorical sources of support were to be conjoined and delivered en bloc to EHSDS corporations, which would, in turn, disperse them in accordance with locally determined priorities. As the corporations matured, they were to extend their management roles to include responsibility for allocation of all funds for personal health care, public and private, to the ends of developing health care systems that would ensure equitable access to all citizens, lower costs, and improve quality.

Nearly three years after its inception, EHSDS remains an official federally funded demonstration program. In nineteen communities throughout the United States, ranging from entire states to small isolated rural areas, EHSDS "management" corporations meet, deliberate, conduct studies, assist other organizations, advise governmental agencies, plan, and carry out a range of other activities generally related to health and health care. None, however, manages its community's total health care system nor any significant part of it, including those services supported by federal aid.

At this moment, RMP, CHP and EHSDS have not been adequately assessed as instruments for effecting change in the delivery of health care, for reasons we will discuss.

## ORGANIZATIONAL EFFECTIVENESS

The criteria one uses when evaluating an organization's effectiveness will be largely determined by the way in which he conceptualizes an "organization." As formal organizations have stimulated theory and research among sociologists, social psychologists, economists, and other social scientists, there is no consensus about how the concept should be defined and operationalized. Each discipline is attracted by different aspects of formally organized collectivities. Within sociology, one finds three prominent perspectives, each having a characteristic way of defining organizations and evaluating their effectiveness: (1) the *goal-oriented* approach,[18] (2) the *system-resource* approach,[19] and (3) the *incentive system* approach.[20] As it would be impossible to provide a full exposition of these perspectives in this chapter, we will characterize only their major differences and implications for evaluative research.

The goal-oriented approach relies for its definition of an organization on the existence or attribution of corporate objectives or purposes. An organization is conceived of as a purposive body as if it were an organic whole. As organizations exist to accomplish their objectives, it follows that the goal-oriented approach leads the evaluator to ask, "Are they doing what they were established to do?" The system-resource approach gives primacy to the dynamic influence of an organization's environment and the organization's ability to adapt. Rather than positing immutable goals, adherents of this perspective conceive of organizations as rather opportunistic collectivites that seek to marshal resources from their surroundings. Hence, survival is the ultimate criterion of success. Finally, the incentive system framework views organizations as formally constituted marketplaces within and through which members attempt to maximize their individual utilities. An organization is merely an arena in which atomized interests variously compete, coalesce, and conflict. [21] From this viewpoint, retention of members is of critical importance: the evaluator asks, "Is the organization able to motivate participation by members?"

None of these frameworks embodies in an internally consistent manner all relevant criteria for evaluating organizations. Taken together, however, they direct attention to several dimensions, all of which deserve consideration when assessing the effectiveness of community decision organizations dedicated to planning and/or management of health care systems. The three perspectives should be viewed, not as competing paradigms, but rather as different levels of analysis, proceeding from social atoms (incentive systems) to organic wholes (goal-oriented, system-resource).

Thompson's [22] eclectic approach to assessment of organizations provides a general scheme that integrates the parts and the whole. He identifies two essential "variables of assessment" whose intersection defines evaluation situtations calling for different evaluation strategies. Evaluation situations arise out of variations in the degree of agreement among organizations' members on *standards of desirability* and in the degree of *understanding about causal relationships.* Taking only extreme values of these variables, Thompson defines four types of assessment situations (Table 15.1) and three assessment techniques. In Cell I, where cause-effect relationships are reasonably well understood and an organization's members agree on what

TABLE 15.1. THOMPSON'S ASSESSMENT SITUATIONS

|  |  | Understanding of Cause-Effect Relationships | |
| --- | --- | --- | --- |
|  |  | Complete | Incomplete |
| Standards of Desirability | Crystallized | I | II |
|  | Ambiguous | III | IV |

they hope to accomplish, an evaluation of *efficiency* is called for. The question here is not "what will work," for that is known. Rather, the evaluator's task is to determine whether the agreed upon objectives can be achieved with less cost by some other means. In Cell II, members agree on ends but are not certain how to achieve them. Hence, their activities are subjected to an *instrumental,* or *impact,* evaluation, ained at determining whether (or the extent to which) they lead to desired ends. In Cell III, the organization's problem stems from its inability to determine what it wants to accomplish; effective technologies are in hand to achieve alternative goals. Finally, in Cell IV the evaluator is confronted with the worst of all possible situations, where an organization cannot agree on what to do, and, were it able to arrive at an objective, would be ill-equipped with knowledge about how to proceed. In both situations where objectives are problematic, Thompson suggests that the evaluator employ a *reference group* strategy, which relies on comparisons between similar organizations to determine which is "better" in some respect.

The bulk of literature on evaluation strategies and techniques assumes situations described by Cells I and II, that is, circumstances in which desired outcomes are known and commonly endorsed by interested actors. The typical experience of community decision organizations in the health sector, however, is otherwise. Comprised of representatives of interest groups, charged by their sponsors with vague, utopian objectives, and inadequately equipped with imperfect technologies, RMPs, CHPs, EHSDSs, and similar corporate bodies find themselves uncomfortably but undeniably in Cell IV.

## CHARACTERISTICS OF COMMUNITY HEALTH
## DECISION ORGANIZATIONS

Community health decision organizations created to date share several common features and circumstances that cause them to suffer similar fates and greatly complicate the evaluator's task. RMP, CHP, and EHSDS were created to plan, to supplant social choice decision-making in the health sector with collective rationality, and to do so through voluntary corporate bodies. According to Dahl and Lindblom,[23] success in such endeavors requires that organizations have the ability to calculate rationally and have control over events to which their plans are addressed. As they take as given consensus on goals, rational calculation subsumes both of Thompson's variables of decision. Since goals and objectives cannot be assumed to exist a priori, we would add a third necessary condition for successful planning: the ability of an organization to arrive at collective decisions regarding desirable outcomes, priorities, and means. Thus, to be an effective planning body, community health decision organizations must accomplish (in this order) consensus formation, rational calculation, and control. In turn, these constitute relevant, albeit sometimes elusive, criteria for evaluation.

## CONSENSUS FORMATION

Legislation establishing RMP and CHP and administrative guidelines mandating EHSDS's objectives and structures left each with nearly insurmountable impediments to consensus formation. As is characteristic of much social reform legislation, official goals of these programs are couched in lofty platitudes quite distant from existing reality. CHP, through its planning, was to promote and assure "the highest level of health attainable for every person, in an environment which contributes positively to healthful individual and family living."[24] EHSDS was to be an experiment in management of total health services systems aimed at improving access to care, containing costs, and maintaining or improving quality. At these levels of formulation, only the malevolent would oppose in principle the objectives of community health decision organizations. Improving access, attaining the highest level of health for everyone, controlling costs, and so on, however, create internal contradictions requiring choices among priorities.[25] Further, such objectives ultimately translate into changes in life-styles of people and institutions, their autonomy, income, opportunities, or other cherished values. Legislation and guidelines offer program directors little assistance in determining which of many conceivable routes organizations should travel to reach their utopias.

It could be argued (as indeed it is) that such direction from federal laws and agencies is antagonistic to traditional values underlying federal-state relationships. Local determination and control, a keystone of the American republican political system, dictated that RMP, CHP, and EHSDS bodies establish their own "operative" goals.[26] In this sense, therefore, the federal programs were effectively devoid of evaluatable objectives.[27]

Given that RMP, CHP, and EHSDS were constituted as essentially empty vessels to be filled by local voluntary corporations, the structures and compositions mandated for them diminished probabilities of consensus formation. Local corporations' memberships were to include the greatest possible range of interests, as providers, consumers, representatives of government agencies, and other actors were to join in efforts to further the public interest. Democratic values, combined with notions about the superior quality of decisions fashioned from diverse experience, dictated such structures. But diversity of experience spawns diversity of interests, and community health decision organizations inherited the latter from the former.

As decision-making is a precondition for action, evaluation of community health decision organizations may begin with assessment of collective decisions, the process as well as their content. Establishing criteria for such assessments, however, presents difficulties. What, for instance, is the correct or a desirable collective decision-making process? Apart from technical aspects, such as the degree to which valid information is considered, types of formal and informal decision rules employed, and so on, collective decision-making is essentially a political process in which interest groups attempt to maximize their gains. It is not even clear that an organization should be given low marks in an evaluation for being unable to arrive at collective decisions. As we have noted, the probabilities of a collective's achieving consensus on particular issues are partly determined by the mix of interests among its members. Hence, few agreements will be reached by multi-interest groups in which values are polarized and intensely held. Labeling such groups as ineffective in terms of consensus formation is akin to saying that it is undesirable for people to express and act in accordance with their beliefs.

Evaluating the content of collective decisions presents similar sorts of problems.

An evaluator would like to know, given the state of objective reality, whether organizations arrive at "correct" decisions, or do they elect to act on irrelevant and trivial matters. Such an assessment presumes that the investigator himself can know the nature of objective reality, which would be feasible in only limited instances. As RMP, CHP, and EHSDS were to accomplish changes in the performance of entire health services systems, however, the evaluator must also devise the "correct" or "most desirable" ordering of alternative priorities. This would require that he apply a set of value judgments about what is most important, most needed, and so on in a community. The source and specification of these values are obviously problematic. Whose preferences should be used—the evaluator's, the mayor's, the majority of residents? Clearly, results of an evaluation of the content of decisions will depend on whose utility schedule is applied as the criterion. Who is to say that the desires and values of a community health decision organization are not appropriate or optimal?

## RATIONAL CALCULATION

Planning is, by definition, a rational process. Once desired ends are known, rationality dictates that choices among alternative means be based on empirical observation. Thus, architects of CHP and EHSDS, and to a lesser extent, RMP, gave data collection important roles. Again, however, the ethereal quality of program objectives mitigated against rational calculation, a situation further complicated by the rather primitive states-of-the-art in health services research and its base disciplines. CHP's intent to improve health and EHSDS's effort to increase access have no agreed-upon operational counterparts. There simply are no standard definitions and yardsticks for measuring these and other such elusive concepts. [28] In consequence, planners have relied on rather crude proxy measures or, more typically, on process variables. Attention focuses, not on health as an outcome, but rather on use of medical services, consumption of drugs, and the like, variables that can reasonably be considered inputs in the production of health. As the relative contributions of these factors to ultimate outcomes are unknown, [29] planners must be content with limited forms of rationality.

Even were relationships among process and outcome measures strong, planners' abilities to predict future world states are seriously impaired by incomplete knowledge of how parts of health services systems interact, by the rapidly changing and largely unpredictable nature of medical needs and technologies, and by the openness of the systems for which they plan. A current issue, for instance, centers on how to develop mechanisms to assure quality of care. Various alternatives are proposed that will, no doubt, have different implications for costs of care, use of services, manpower requirements, and so on. Knowledge necessary for predicting in advance direct and indirect effects of alternatives is fragmentary and incomplete. The same could be said for health maintenance organizations, national health insurance, and other innovations currently under consideration. Of course, all the evidence is never in: uncertainty is inevitable in planning. In health care, however, fundamental uncertainty is compounded by the pace of change in medical science, geographic mobility of providers and consumers, and exogenous disturbances from a community's economic and political sectors. All combine to make forecasting into the near future difficult and into the distant future a largely meaningless exercise.

Finally, community health decision organizations lack the power to coerce compliance with their requests for information. Most practitioners and hospitals, being in the private sector of the economy and in competition among themselves, are reluctant to release data to voluntary planning organizations. Further, were providers to agree to comply voluntarily with requests for information, it is unlikely that data from different institutions and practices could be readily aggregated. Providers and third party intermediaries have historically gone their separate ways in data accumulation.[30]

Evaluation of planning in terms of organizations' approaches to rational calculation confronts the investigator with some of the same intractable conundra raised by assessment of rational calculation. In this realm, however, there are at least a few relatively well codified standards of desirability. Specifically, there exist criteria for evaluating technical qualities of data collection, processing, analysis, and interpretation. In the EHSDS program, for instance, each corporate body was required to mount household surveys (as well as other data collection efforts) to measure its community's use of services and needs for care. To assist corporations in completing this task and to assess the quality of the data, DHEW contracted with a university-based group. Using several evaluative dimensions, such as the adequacy of sampling techniques, interviewer training and supervision, and the like, the group was able to identify sites where the technical adequacy of the data collection process was deficient. Such judgments were feasible, for the folklore of survey research and research on survey methods point to techniques and procedures which are known to be related to the technical quality of the data, that is, reliability and concurrent validity.

Aside from technical evaluations of the quality of data, however, are issues of substance. That is, are the data collected by an organization relevent to the problems it wishes to attack; are the data being organized in a consistent and suitable framework; and are they being used by decision makers? The first of these questions—are the data relevant?—is amenable to limited assessment; the latter two are less so. Relevance of information may be judged against standards derived from the state-of-the-art of health planning. Regional planning for hospitals, for instance, requires as a minimum information about current supplies and occupancy rates and projections of population compositions. More elaborate projections might also incorporate data on case mixes, likely changes in the organization of primary care, and so on. The universe of variables considered in such plans is amenable to assessment in terms of completeness, at least according to expert judgment.

The framework within which these data are organized is less easily evaluated, for standards of desirability are not well codified. This is a consequence of the state-of-the-art in knowledge about the health sector's dynamics and its unstable character. Health services researchers have not yet devised a general model of the system that would serve as a criterion set for this form of evaluation. Current models would discriminate primarily among only the extremes. In consequence, planners, when they can afford to do so, probably overcollect, a strategy that results in "data flooding" and ultimately militates against organizing information in meaningful and useful contexts while raising the costs of information gathering.[31]

Use of data by decision-makers is an elusive dimension for evaluation, for it rests on value judgments and political considerations as well as purely technical interpretations. Data are bloodless and objective; decisions and actions are vital and subjective. As health services information is rarely compelling in terms of either technical and conceptual criteria or the clarity and persuasiveness of suggested actions, it is easily (and often) relegated to minor roles in community decision-making. Decisions are data strained through values; evaluators again face the dilemma of selecting someone's values when attempting to determine whether information is used appropriately.

## CONTROL

The third ingredient of successful planning and management of health care systems is control, the ability to implement plans and changes. Without it, planning is essentially an academic exercise, and management, by definition,[32] is non-existent. Typically, initial formulations of planning and management programs (in the form of recommendations to the federal government by advisory commissions) incorporate strong means for achieving control or at least imply that they are necessary; however, in the crucible of compromise where legislation and guidelines are formulated, they are softened and diluted. RMP was to be a program in which new medical technology was to be applied through regional medical centers.[33] CHP, in its original formulation by the National Commission on Community Health Services, was to engage in "action planning."[34] EHSDS corporations were to manage the allocation of federal funds "conjoined" from several federal sources.[35] RMP, however, was not allowed to support centers that would compete with private practitioners; CHP was constrained from interfering with patterns of medical practice;[36] and EHSDS corporations never received their promised "conjoint" funds. Thus, as established, community health decisions organizations were provided with limited powers over their environments.

Unable to coerce compliance and cooperation, community health decision organizations rely on appeals to rationality and the public interest as techniques of control or (more accurately) influence. These are the strategies of the politician, not of the systems engineer: the technique for success probably is to be found in a hybrid of the ideas of Norman Vincent Peale and Machiavelli. In consequence, they tend to be situationally unique, fashioned from formal and informal interconnections among people and institutions,[37] which are never fully visible to the observer, nor readily analyzable from a strictly rational perspective.

In such circumstances, evaluation is once again thwarted by the essential political and value-laden nature of the process to be assessed. Should an organization suffer in an evaluation because its executive director and the mayor each would prefer that the other leave town? Likewise, is a dynamic organization that achieves consensus on sweeping innovations and erects detailed and technically sound plans for their implementation to be considered a poor one if recalcitrant institutions remain unmoved and unmovable in defense of the status quo? This is the stuff of revolutions, and reasonable people disagree about how much of a "good thing" ought to be force-fed to people.[38]

## CONCLUSIONS

Our purpose in this chapter has been to point up and illustrate features of community health decision organizations that complicate their evaluation. Our concluding comments will suggest ways to deal with the complexity. In sum, we have attempted to show that assessment of these bodies is akin to evaluating government (albeit governments that lack powers of coercion) where technologies for rational calculation are highly important. As such circumstances are quite distant from assessment situations in which tests of efficiency or impact are feasible, they call for evaluation strategies that relax assumptions of the classical experimental design.

Instances of federal health planning and management programs attempted to date in the United States are not only "broad-aim" programs,[39] but, because of their roots in a political philisophy of local determination and democracy, they are also variable-aim programs. Each corporate body is charged with dealing with the totality of health care in its community (i.e., broad-aim), but to do so on the basis of what it finds most pressing and feasible. Because communities differ, both in terms of what is "objectively needed" and what is subjectively wanted, federal programs will be collections of highly differentiated local programs (i.e., variable-aim).

The implications of broad and variable-aim projects for program evaluation are as certain as they are frustrating to the evaluator. He will not have available crisply stated goals agreed to by all individual projects; experimental stimuli (i.e., structures, compositions, and resources of corporate bodies) will vary from site to site; and, variations in environmental factors will be confounded with (indeed nearly indistinguishable from) experimental treatments. Control groups will not exist for programs with national coverage (e.g., CHP) and will be largely irrelevant for these placed in "test communities" (e.g., EHSDS). So much is missing of what is minimally required by "strong" evaluation strategies that even reasonable approximations of efficiency and impact assessments are hardly possible.

It should be noted that the evaluator does not escape these problems through simple semantic devaluation from "impact evaluation" to "process evaluation." Indeed, substitution of assessment of process for evaluation of impact is feasible and desirable only when program objectives and knowledge of how to achieve them are in advanced stages. Where both are lacking or are primitively formulated, process evaluation is analogous to recording the wanderings of a drunken man, a fundamentally nonrational process. If one is uncertain about where he is headed, doesn't know how to get there, or will be unable to recognize that he has arrived, the documentation of the process by which he traverses a space can scarcely be transformed into efficiency or impact language.

This is not to say, however, that documentations of process are irrelevant or ought not to be done. To the contrary, they are currently the most satisfactory means for acquiring understandings of how these programs are constituted and what they do. To eschew them because they do not conform to some ideal is to accept the nihilistic position that, since nothing of use can be learned, no learning will be attempted, a logic that encourages repetition of mistakes and accounts for a vacuum of knowledge about community health decision organizations.

Weiss and Rein have suggested an approach to this type of documentary analysis, which they variously label "process-oriented qualitative research," "historical research," or "case study or comparative research." [40] It relies essentially on collection of qualitative information [41] over time from a relatively small number of cases. Applied to community health decision organizations, attention would naturally focus on matters such as how communities organize corporations and recruit and motivate members, where they derive resources (monetary, political, as well as others), how they arrive at collective decisions and on what basis, the means employed to implement innovations, and how various actors in communities view their contributions. Within this documentation, impact evaluations of particular innovations and activities might be feasible, using "stronger" techniques described elsewhere in this volume.

It is not desirable, however, to conceive of a project's overall worth in terms of a batting average, in which the number of discrete program accomplishments is taken as the sole criterion of success. Rather, in the assessment of community health decision organizations, we must cautiously attempt to distinguish values from science while avoiding the trap of distinguishing means from ends. Voluntary planning and management of community health systems is both an end and a means: the process itself embodies values worthy of defense and doubly so when it leads to achievement of community objectives, however defined. That the process is imperfect on scientific and technical grounds is unavoidable, for democracy is a sometimes costly, cumbersome, and inefficient route to collective rationality. The evaluator's task is to point it toward "better" ways, while understanding that his notion of "better" may have overlooked subtle but important values.

## NOTES

1. R. L. Warren, "The Interorganizational Field as a Focus for Investigation," *Administrative Science Quarterly*, 1967, 12 (December): 396-419.

2. C. H. Weiss, "Where Politics and Evaluation Research Meet," *Evaluation*, 1973, 1 (3): 37-45.

3. Warren, op. cit., 400.

4. E. C. Banfield, *Political Influence* (New York: Free Press, 1961).

5. Warren, *op. cit.,* 400.

6. R. R. Alford, "The Political Economy of Health Care: Dynamics Without Change" *Politics and Society*, 1972, 4 (Winter): 127-164.

7. E. L. Richardson, Address before the Institute of Medicine, Washington, D.C., May 10, 1972 (mimeographed).

8. J. Q. Wilson, "The Bureaucracy Problem," *The Public Interest*, 1967, 6: 3-9.

9. United States Congress, Senate, Committee on Government Operations, Subcommittee on Executive Reorganization and Government Research, *Federal Role in Health: Report Pursuant to Senate Resolution 390,* 91st Congress, 30 April 1970, Senate Report 91-801.

10. See, for instance, Committee for Economic Development, Research Policy Committee, *Building a National Health-Care System* (New York: CED, 1973).

11. E. M. Burns, *Health Services for Tomorrow* (New York: Dunellen Publishing Company, 1973); J. J. May, *Health Planning: Its Past and Potential,* Health Administrative Perspectives No. A5 (Chicago: Center for Health Administration Studies, 1967).

12. J. L. Sundquist and D. W. Davis, *Making Federalism Work* (Washington, D.C.: The Brookings Institution, 1969).

13. The Hospital Survey and Construction Act (the Hill-Burton program, P.L. 79-725), enacted in 1946, also provided for areawide planning for health care facilities. Within each participating state, Hill-Burton provisions have been implemented by voluntary Hospital Planning Councils, typically comprised of hospital administrators, voluntary associations, and state and local government agencies. These councils serve as intermediaries, carrying out reviews of applications for grants and loans and making recommendations to the federal government. The basis for deciding whether new facilities or improvements are needed has been a major problem in coordinating hospital care under Hill-Burton, for few states have developed clear-cut plans and guidelines for making such demonstrations. Thus, while Hill-Burton has been successful in stimulating construction, it has been less successful in implementing areawide coordination among hospitals. See H. E. Hilleboe and A. Barkhuus, "Health Planning in the United States: Some Categorical and General Approaches," *International Journal of Health Services,* 1971, 1 (2): 134-148.

14. Originally, EHSDS was called the Experimental Health Services Planning and Delivery Systems Program. "Planning" was subsequently deleted from the program's title. See P. J. Sanazaro, "Federal Health Services R & D under the Auspices of the National Center for Health Services Research and Development," in E. E. Flook and P. J. Sanazaro, eds., *Health Services Research and R & D in Perspective* (Ann Arbor: University of Michigan, Health Administration Press, 1973).

15. Heart Disease, Cancer and Stroke Amendments of 1965, P.L. 89-239. For a description of RMP, see W. A. Glaser, "Experiences in Health Planning in the United States," prepared for a Conference on Health Planning in the United States, Columbia University, June 4-6, 1973 (mimeographed); Hilleboe and Barkhuus, *op. cit.*

16. Commission on Community Health Services, *Health is a Community Affair* (Cambridge: Harvard University Press, 1967).

17. *Ibid.,* 131.

18. As the goal-oriented approach dominates sociological theory and research on organizations, most standard texts are based on this approach. See, for example A. Etzioni, *A Comparative Analysis of Complex Organizations* (New York: Free Press, 1961). For a critical review, see P. Georgiou, "The Goal Paradigm and Notes Towards a Counter Paradigm," *Administrative Science Quarterly,* 1973, 18 (September): 291.

19. E. Yuchtman and S. Seashore, "A System Resource Approach to Organizational Effectiveness," *American Sociological Review* 1967, 32 (December): 891-903.

20. Georgiou, *op. cit.*; D. Katz and R. L. Kahn, *The Social Psychology of Organizations* (New York: Wiley, 1966).

21. For an early statement of this perspective, see C. I. Barnard, *The Functions of the Executive* (Cambridge: Harvard University Press, 1948). Economists and others concerned with collective decisions are particularly fond of this conceptualization. See J. N. Buchanan and G. Tullock, *The Calculus of Consent: Logical Foundations of Constitutional Democracy* (Ann Arbor: University of Michigan Press, 1969); J. S. Coleman, "Loss of Power," *American Sociological Review,* 1973, 38 (February): 1-17.

22. J. D. Thompson, *Organization in Action* (New York: McGraw-Hill, 1967).

23. R. A. Dahl and C. E. Lindblom, *Politics, Economics, and Welfare* (New York: Harper and Row, 1953).

24. P.L. 89-749, *Comprehensive Health Planning and Public Health Service Amendments of 1966* (Washington, D.C.: Government Printing Office, 1966).

25. For instance, assuming that a community has a relatively fixed resource base for health services, attempts to maximize equity of access and quality (conceived of as the "best" medical care available) simultaneously will meet with certain failure. On this point, see: U. E. Reinhart, "Proposed Changes in the Organization of Health-Care Delivery: An Overview and Critique," in "Health and Society," *Milbank Memorial Fund Quarterly,* 1973, 51 (Spring): 169-222.

26. Perrow distinguishes "operative" goals from "official" goals, the former being operationally defined. An organization may elect to reduce the number of hospital beds in its region (a real goal) in order to control costs of medical care (an ultimate goal). See C. Perrow, "The Analysis of Goals in Complex Organizations," *American Sociological Review,* 1961, 26 (December): 854-866.

27. For this reason, evaluation of RMP, CHP and EHSDS usually focuses on "process criteria," which, as we will show later, are inadequate substitutes for impact criteria in goal-oriented evaluations.

28. For a review of health status indicators, see S. Fanshel and J. W. Bush, "A Health Status Index and Its Application to Health-Services Outcomes," *Operations Research,* 1970, 18 (November-December): 1021-1066.

29. Nuffield Provincial Hospitals Trust, *Medical History and Medical Care* (London: Oxford University Press, 1971).

30. J. H. Murnaghan (ed.), "Ambulatory Medical Care Data: Report of the Conference on Ambulatory Medical Care Records," *Medical Care,* 1973, 11 (March-April): supplement.

31. A. Etzioni, *The Active Society* (New York: Free Press, 1968), 144-145.

32. B. M. Gross, *The Managing of Organizations: The Administrative Struggle* (London: Free Press of Glencoe, 1964).

33. R. M. Battistella, "The Course of Regional Health Planning: Review and Assessment of Recent Federal Legislation," *Medical Care,* 1967, 5 (May-June): 149-161.

34. Commission on Community Health Services, *op. cit.,* 167-183.

35. Sanazaro, *op. cit.*

36. Battistella, *op. cit.*

37. See Banfield, *op. cit.*

38. CHP has been given quasi-regulatory functions under several state "certificate-of-need" statutes and under the Section 1122 amendments to the Social Security Act. To date, there is little evidence on how these have affected either the organizations themselves or the communities they serve. See C. C. Havighurst, "Regulation of Health Facilities and Services by 'Certificate of Need,' " *Virginia Law Review,* 1973, 59 (October): 1143-1232.

39. R. S. Weiss and M. Rein, "The Evaluation of Broad-Aim Programs: A Cautionary Case and a Moral," *Annals of the Academy of Political and Social Science,* 1969, 385: 118-132.

40. Ibid., 243.

41. Quantitative data are not excluded where they exist.

*16*

# EVALUATION OF NEW CAREERS PROGRAMS

JOAN GRANT

and

J. DOUGLAS GRANT

*Social Action Research Center*
*Oakland, California*

"I have a lot of concerns about this phony program called new careers. It
has nothing to do with what I had in mind when I wrote a book, which really
talked about changing the nature and quality of life. It had nothing to do
with conning some poor people into doing some lousy jobs" (Pearl, 1969; 7).

The term *new careers* came into being when Arthur Pearl and Frank Riessman
collaborated on a book, *New Careers for the Poor: The Nonprofessional in Human
Service* (1965). The book described a way of providing permanent, socially useful
jobs with career potential for unskilled, uneducated, and unemployed people. In
the five years since its publication, new careers has been the focus of numerous
pieces of federal legislation, has acquired the status of a separate office within the
Department of Health, Education, and Welfare, and has developed into a minor
social movement. But its accomplishments fall far short of what was envisioned in
the book.

New careers is a concept embracing radical and long-term change in the provision
of human services—education, health, and other aspects of human welfare. Its
premises are that change is needed in the structure and functioning of the agencies
which provide these services and in the educational institutions which train and
accredit the people who work in them.

New careers offers an alternate way to develop human service manpower from the presently used training-before-employment model. It proposes new entry positions into human service agencies, the positions to provide training as a part of the entry job, the training to be linked with formal education which is appropriately modified to meet the needs of these new kinds of workers. It provides for upward job mobility by spelling out a career ladder that allows promotions on the basis of combined experience on the job and concurrent education.

New careers is not an add-on procedure. To be effective it requires changes in organizations—in civil service systems, in social agencies, and in educational institutions. It requires changes in professional staff roles, functions, attitudes, and training. It is expected to lead to new, more appropriate, and more effective forms of service.

New careers is not to be confused with the use of nonprofessionals in human service work. The armed forces have long used paraprofessionals in medical, education, and training functions. Self-help organizations use lay people to work with persons whose problems are ordinarily seen as requiring professional service. Nonprofessionals have been used extensively as aides in education, welfare, and corrections programs to relieve professional shortages or in the absence of money to hire professionals. More recently they have been employed in specific efforts to establish better communication between agency and clients. There have been a number of attempts to use clients as workers in delinquency prevention programs. The Economic Opportunity Act of 1964 gave impetus to the expansion of nonprofessional employment. The hiring of nonprofessionals had not been envisioned under the Act but developed as a way of obtaining the participation of residents in community planning and action programs that the Act required.

Several demonstration projects about this time became identified with the new careers idea. In New York, Mobilization for Youth was involved with the hiring and training of low-income people from the community for work in a variety of new community action roles as well as for work with agencies serving the community (Pearl and Riessman, 1965; Riessman, Oct. 1963, Nov. 1963). Although this project was not at that stage concerned with careers, Riessman's experience there in training nonprofessionals and training trainers contributed heavily to the development of the new careers concept. The Center for Youth and Community Studies (later the Institute for Youth Studies) at Howard University in Washington, D.C., began a series of career development projects with youth. The first of these, the Community Apprentice Program (President's Committee, 1965), was both shaped by and contributed to Pearl's development of the new careers idea. In California the New Careers Development Project (Grant, 1968; Grant and Grant, 1967, 1970) began training men confined in state prisons for what was originally hoped would be careers in administration of justice agencies but which turned into broader program development roles in antipoverty programs. At Lincoln Hospital in the Bronx the Neighborhood Service Center Program (Hallowitz and Riessman, 1967; Riessman, 1966), with Riessman as co-director, trained residents from the community as mental health workers in storefront service centers.

In 1966 Congressman Scheuer of New York introduced an amendment to the Economic Opportunity Act that gave new careers a legislative and funding base. The amendment, Section 205(e) of the Economic Opportunity Act of 1967, was passed in October of 1966. Some 20,000 people have been through programs authorized by this legislation. There are now 109 such programs operating over the country with a current enrollment of about 9,000 people. New careers programs funded under the Scheuer amendment are currently administered through the Department of Labor, some through the Concentrated Employment Program (CEP), some as independent entities. As this is written there are moves to merge new careers programming with other manpower programs where, new careers proponents fear, it will be effectively scuttled. The outcome of this is still in doubt.

There are a number of other federally financed programs whose funding is authorized under legislation containing new careers language and which can be considered as potential new careers programs. They can be found under education, vocational rehabilitation, health manpower, housing, delinquency, corrections, law enforcement, and social security auspices. Few such programs operate without federal funds but at least two have been undertaken by local government agencies.

The concept of new careers is a complex one which has never been actually realized in practice. New careers is based upon a full employment plus economy. The programs funded today under the EOA and others, variously funded, which call themselves new careers are at best steps in development toward the new careers idea and at worst euphemisms for putting poor people to work in dead-end jobs on temporary soft-money federal funding.

The evaluator of a new careers program must look simultaneously at several factors. What is the impact of the program on the new careerist participants? On the professionals with whom they work? On the participating agencies and educational institutions? On the agency clients and the community at large? Granted a program attempts to meet new careers requirements, it may advance in some areas but not in others, or may advance in different areas at different rates of speed. A program may be successful at creating a large number of new entry jobs, filling these with people who show a high degree of stability in the program, and providing opportunities for individuals to advance from the point of entry, but it may do so while having little or no impact on the agencies in which the new careerists work nor on the functions performed by the agency professionals. Another program may fail to provide career ladders for its supposed new careerists and have a high dropout rate, but the program may start an agency on the road to examining the appropriateness and effectiveness of its entire service delivery system. Which of the two is the more effective?

The evaluator has four places to look in his efforts to assess program impact: the program's organization and staff, the new careerists, the participating organizations, and the community. The four areas are discussed separately below, with some of the evaluation problems each entails. Issues in setting up an overall evaluation design are discussed in a later section.

## PROGRAM ORGANIZATION AND STAFF

Anyone attempting to move into the new careers evaluation field would do well to get some historical perspective and current information through past and current issues of the *New Careers Newsletter,* published by the New Careers Development

Center, School of Education, at New York University. The Center gained its original support largely from a Ford Foundation grant. The *Newsletter* deals with developments in legislation, programs, and social action relating to new careers. It reports shifts in thinking about new careers and its implementation, developments in the organization and ideology of new careerists, details of new programs, modifications in civil service and other accrediting agencies, developments in education that help foster new careers, and evaluation studies. It also contains a list of relevant publications available through the Center and through other auspices. The *Newsletter* is the best overall source of information on the new careers field.

Another important resource is the *New Careers Program Assistance Bulletin* published by the National Institute for New Careers of the University Research Corporation, a private organization in Washington, D.C., which has been under contract to the Department of Labor for the past three years to provide technical assistance to the new careers projects under its jurisdiction. The *Bulletin* offers information on new careers programs throughout the country and on related developments in federal agencies, discussions of problem areas, summaries of research reports, and a section on publications.

Two early publications offering an overview of the problems and issues in implementing new careers programs are available from the Center for the Study of Unemployed Youth at New York University (New York University, 1966; Schmais, 1967).

## Organization

The funding and legislative background of a given program set the initial organizational constraints under which it must operate. A new careers program is generally funded through a larger entity, often a community action agency, sometimes a unit of local government. There is, usually, some core staff which may or may not be responsible for the various program components. These components include the following, though not all may appear in any one program.

a. Job development (finding agency placements for the new careerists)
b. Recruitment of a pool of potential new careerists
c. Selection of new careerist trainees
d. Orientation (to the program, to the job, and/or to the "world of work" which usually means how to dress, how to show up on time, and how to fill out forms)
e. Training (core training which is sometimes part of orientation and which may prepare new careerists for human service work generally training for specific jobs, and/or inservice training)
f. Education (remedial, and/or continuing education, usually linked to job upgrading)
g. Supportive services (financial counseling and aid, child care, transportation, legal services, personal counseling)
h. Supervision on the job
i. Technical assistance to employing agencies
j. Evaluation

Typically the central or core staff of a program is small. The program components may be assigned or contracted out, singly or in combination, to other groups or organizations. Responsibilities may overlap. The work of the contributing organizations may or may not overlap in time. Core staff may exert some control or direction over their activities or they may operate completely independently and bypass the core staff. Administration and direct operational responsibility may be separated. Communication among the various components may be informal, may be channeled through the core staff into regular meetings or seminars, or may be absent.

To take an example, hypothetical but not untypical: a new careers program director is hired by a community action agency to run the new careers component of CEP. He has an assistant and a secretary. He reports to CEP staff and his disbursement of funds is controlled by them; they in turn are subject to local community and state political pressures. Recruitment and selection are contracted out to the state employment service which also finds clients for the other manpower components of CEP. The director has the task of developing agency job placements. A university-based group provides an initial training program, independent of the agencies in which the new careerists will be placed. Remedial education is offered through the secondary school system. The director tries to work out some arrangement with the local community college for admitting the program participants and setting up special courses, but his job development task leaves him little time and this is not his field of expertise. His assistant is expected to provide continuing consultation to the agencies on the utilization of the new careerists and on job upgrading but finds his time taken up in dealing with the resistances and misconceptions of the line staff who directly supervise the new careerists and who have received little or no orientation to the program. Placements are so scattered among agencies that communication between agency line staff, policy-making staff, and new careerists is a major obstacle. Some monies are available through CEP for transportation and child care for the new careerists and a voluntary university student group offers personal counseling, but financial and other situational crises occur repeatedly. Because of federal budget uncertainties continued funding of the program is in doubt. New careerist paychecks are sometimes late. Evaluation is undertaken while the program is moving into its second year by a university graduate student working on a dissertation.

Such a program hardly offers the optimal climate for the development of a new careers strategy. Pearl has said that there are no new careers programs, only new careers development programs, that is, programs developing toward the new careers model. The assessment of how far toward this model is part of the evaluator's problem.

## Staff

The evaluator's next concern is with the persons in charge of the total program and of its major components. There are two questions: what are their articulated goals for the program, their strategies for reaching them, and the assumptions on which the strategies are based? and what is their commitment to the stated goals? The specification of goals and strategies and the assumptions underlying them is important both to assess the extent to which the program approximates the new careers model and also to determine points of conflict within the program between key staff people. Different interpretations of what the program is about, based on differing and often unarticulated goals and assumptions about how to reach them, appear to be major sources of intra-program conflicts.

Program goals may focus on solving an agency's manpower problems, on making service more responsive to community needs, on providing jobs for poor people, or on developing career opportunities. What is expected of new careerists and attitudes toward them and their work will differ in each case. Differences may also occur in the assumptions made about what is necessary to qualify new careerists for employment: the development of skills, including the education that will permit advancement in a career ladder, or attitude change and rehabilitation. Further, staff may define their task as helping new careerists fit into existing systems, or as turning new careerists loose to help change systems. Where staff know little about new careers, as is often the case, it is important to know what technical assistance is available and how it is utilized; and the willingness of staff to learn.

The question of staff commitment or integrity may be one of the factors leading to high staff turnover, a problem that plagues many of the programs to date. Appointments to program positions have sometimes been offered as political patronage and staff may spend most of their time in political games. In other cases there may be extraordinary staff expenditures of time, effort, and inventiveness.

Almost all program reports, whether or not intended as evaluation studies, touch on some of these organization and staff issues. A report that does so explicitly and systematically is an evaluation of eleven new careers programs (Ballard and Alley, 1968) commissioned by the Department of Labor and conducted by the Economic Systems Corporation. In this study evaluators—persons with some direct knowledge of new careers programs who shared a common frame of reference—made on-site observations for periods of two or three days at three points in the program's operation. The evaluators met with program directors, with staff responsible for such major program components as training and education, with staff from the employing agencies, and with small groups of new careerists. Each of the eleven separate evaluation reports deals at length with the program's table of organization, its implications for program operation, staff understanding of the new careers model, internal staff problems, and staff integrity in conducting the program. A report of the school community worker component of the Richmond, California, new careers program (Conway, 1967) offers excellent documentation of the issues arising from the differing goals and expectations of core staff, agency staff, and the community, their impact on the attitudes and functioning of the new careerists, and the shaping of the program over a two-year period by individual persons and by events in the larger community. Also in California, an early report of the new careers parole aide program in the Department of Corrections (Fagerstrom, 1968) discusses in some detail the differences in staff attitudes toward and perceptions of the new careerists in different parts of the agency and the effect these have on new careerist roles and performance. In another evaluation study funded by the Department of Labor (Larson et al., 1968) the structure of the nine agencies involved in the Minneapolis new careers program is examined as well as the hierarchy of authority to deal with new careers, the machinery in each agency for upward mobility, staff attitudes, and the atmosphere in which the new careers program operates.

A look at the new careers setting forms an important base from which to assess the effectiveness of the program itself. If training is ineffective or irrelevant the fault may lie neither with the design or execution of the training program but stem rather from the fact that training staff and job development staff are working from two different sets of premises and toward two different goals. If, as is the case with almost all new careers programs, there is limited job mobility for the new careerists this may come about not because of the recalcitrance of the agencies involved but rather because the sponsoring entity or core staff directing the program have no real commitment to the development of careers and have given it only the token support necessary to qualify for federal funding.

## THE NEW CAREERISTS

A new careers program can be looked at from the point of view of how the individual participants perform and develop or how the participating organizations modify and change their functioning. This distinction is somewhat artificial and made for ease of presentation. But it is also intended to point up the fact that most evaluators look at a program in terms of its impact on individuals and pay little attention to the more important but touchier issues of organization change.

### Were They Successful?

Early in the development of the new careers concept the question was raised whether it would in fact be possible to train millions of poor people for jobs in the human service field, to place them in human service agencies, and to have them remain for a period of time without having the system blow up. The question has long since been answered in the affirmative. A year ago there were estimated (Gartner, June 1969) to be some 400,000 nonprofessionals (paraprofessionals, subprofessionals—none of these terms is completely satisfactory) working in education, health, welfare, recreation, corrections, law enforcement, and community action agencies in entry level, aide-type (no necessarily new careers) positions. On the whole these agencies have continued to function, with a few notable exceptions—for example, the 1968 strike by psychiatric aides in Topeka, Kansas, state hospitals, who staged a work-in to demonstrate against inadequate patient care and lack of upgrading (Efthim, 1968; New Careers Newsletter, 1968, No. 2); the 1969 shutdown by nonprofessionals and professionals of the Lincoln Hospital Mental Health Services in the South Bronx, largely over the issue of community control (New Careers Newsletter, 1969, no. 2)—though these disturbances may be viewed as transient phases in programs undergoing positive development.

Most new careers program reports are content to give the per cent of entrants who stay with the program as a measure of success. At the very least, such statements should include a comparable time base for the new careerists. For example, a survey of 53 new careers programs across the country (Wilson et al., 1969) reported that 85% of the nearly 10,000 participants had stayed with the program, citing the high retention rate as one measure of program achievement, but the figure was arrived at apparently without regard for the time the program had begun and the length of time the individual new careerist had been with it (these ranged apparently from one month to two years). In any case, job stability is not necessarily a sign of new careerist success since stability, particularly in an entry level job, may mean merely that the new careerist has nowhere else to go.

Job mobility (e.g., moving from trainee status to civil service status) and increases in earning have also been used as measures of success. These hold more promise since it is then possible to assess the extent to which the new careerist has in fact moved out of poverty or has begun movement on a career ladder. Mobility and earnings, however, may be more a function of what is happening with organizational, funding, and government structures than of anything the new careerist himself is doing. In a study of 26 new careerists who had been placed in a variety of public and private New York City social agencies (National Committee on Employment of Youth, 1970) an attempt was made to assess performance on the basis of movement from entry class to higher ones and of the amount of salary paid after a two year period. It was concluded that both job status and salary differentials were a function chiefly of agency differences and not of differences among the new careerists.

A more relevant but more difficult approach to new careerist success in the area of performance evaluation. Assessment has been tried using ratings by staff (training, supervisory, and professional co-worker), by new careerists, and by outside consultants. A study of aides in several differently funded programs in Los Angeles schools (Los Angeles Unified School District, 1969) used questionnaires to obtain ratings and evaluative comments from aides, teachers with whom they worked, principals, other staff members and (for one program) a sampling of parents. Questionnaire returns tended to be low for the aides (generally about two-thirds) and for parents (less than half). The data were used to identify areas of effective aide support to the schools and to assess the extent to which aides were able to improve communication between the school and the home. Frequency tabulations and excerpts from questionnaire responses are presented.

Staff ratings are limited by the amount and kind of contact between staff and new careerists and may in any event tell more about staff attitudes toward new careerists or toward rating scales than about how the new careerist actually performs. They are probably most useful when they refer to the performance of specific tasks rather than to general job behavior. For example, in a project to train home health aides (Hoff et al., 1968) ratings of work performance were obtained 15 weeks after the completion of training from the supervisors of all aides who obtained employment. The ratings, made on a 3-point scale, covered 30 items of specific job behavior. The items were later grouped into those referring to technical skills, attitudes and interpersonal relationships, and professional conduct and work habits. There was little spread among the ratings given (the lowest rating was seldom used), though the attitude cluster showed a wider variation of scores than the other two. This may mean that the ratings did not adequately differentiate aide performance; but in view of the specificity of the items rated (e.g., "able to dress and undress paralyzed patient"), it is more likely that they indicated satisfactory performance by all aides.

The ultimate test of course is the new careerist's performance as it affects clients. Some kinds of roles lend themselves to performance evaluation more readily than others. For example, if the new careerist's function is an outreach service, the number of people he is able to bring in for agency service compared with the number brought in during comparable time periods by professionals provides a ready way of assessing his usefulness for this particular function. Contra Costa County, California, reported (*New Careers Newsletter,* 1968, no. 6) that health aides were able to reopen 26 or 30 cases the Health Department had had to close because professional staff could make no further contact with the families. These are relatively simple success measures, though they do not answer the question of why the aides were successful. Other roles are more difficult to evaluate. Studies of the performance of school children before and after an aide program was introduced have suffered from problems of collecting complete data, the adequacy of tests to measure change, and difficulties in interpreting what changes actually mean: does a child gain in score on a reading or arithmetic test because of the presence of the aide, because of the altered performance of the teacher, because of related shifts in school climate, or because of factors unrelated to the aide program.

A carefully designed study of teacher aides (Minneapolis Public Schools, 1967) looked at gains in children's scores on the Metropolitan Readiness Test for nine second-semester kindergarten classes, three with no aides, three with one aide each, and three with five aides per class. Using analysis of covariance to adjust for differences in pretest scores, a significant group effect was found. Mean gains were significantly higher for the one aide than the no aide condition; gains were also higher for the five aide than the no aide groups but did not reach significance. With the small number of classes involved there was no way of controlling or studying teacher effects (the same three teachers worked in the no aide and five aide conditions, another three worked in the one aide condition). Such analysis may be possible in a study currently underway in Oregon (Conant, 1970) which involves sizable numbers of classrooms and in one proposed for the Los Angeles City Schools (Husek-Rosen, 1970). The latter calls for looking at the effects of high and low saturation of aides within and between eight schools on pupil achievement, pupil attitudes toward school, and the instructional process.

The evaluation of the School Community Worker Program (Conway, 1967) has attempted the most comprehensive analysis of new careerist impact on clients. The five new careerists were used as liaison with parents and the community and as staff in a "cooling off room" to which troublemakers were sent. It was hypothesized that use of the new careerists would reduce class management problems, resulting in more time available for instruction and an improved climate for learning. Behavior in the classroom was studied through direct observation of pupil teacher relations in the two target schools and in a control school using such items as classification of the role taken by the teacher (instructor versus disciplinarian), interactions rated was warm on the part of the teacher, and interactions rated as warm, compliant, resistant, calm, or emotional on the part of the students. The study report, which apparently gives only a small proportion of the data gathered, infers the impact of the new careerists by noting shifts in percentages within each school from the fall to the spring of the first year of the program. No significance tests are reported.

Other measures of school behavior used were frequency of tardiness and numbers of unexcused absences (no data is given), truancy rates, and suspension rates. The use of the latter was made difficult by the inadequate records kept at most schools. The author also notes the confounding effect of the then new state law which limited suspensions per year to ten days per pupil, thus causing most pupils to be suspended for short periods early in the year, receiving the balance of their ten day "share" in May or June.

An attempt was also made to assess the program's impact on pupil academic achievement, although none of the new careerists had any instructional role. This assessment was part of a larger evaluation study which included assessment of the counseling program at other schools in the district. Analysis of variance was used to evaluate differences in the reading score gains of students receiving service from the new careers program and from the counseling program, by sex and by grade level, with differences in I.Q. adjusted by analysis of covariance. As is often true with school-wide testing programs, tests were not administered in all classes and absences were not made up. Only one comparison is reported in this study, a report of pre and post mean reading scores for one of the new careers schools and two control schools for fifth grade Negro boys. No differences were found. The author suggests the instruments were not sensitive enough and also points out that the poorest students academically received the most service from the new careerists.

A third approach to evaluation was a measure of pupil perceptions of the new careerists and of pupil attitudes toward their opportunities and chances in life. A fourth was made through a survey of parental reactions to the program. Parents in the target schools who had had some contact with the new careerists were compared with those who had not on their attitudes to the school and to the teachers (the parents were matched on the sex, race, grade, and achievement test scores of their children). In both cases the data suffer from the lack of significance tests and from interpretations that sometimes reach to make a case for the effectiveness of the new careerists. The problem of confounding variables is raised but not explored. Nonetheless these efforts are notable as rare attempts to seek information directly from the consumer of the service product.

A companion study in the Richmond new careers program (Smith, 1967) looked at the impact of five police-community relations aides (PCRAs) assigned to the juvenile section of the Richmond Police Department on delinquency rates. An experimental-control design, intended to compare recorded delinquency in the target area with delinquency in an adjacent control area, broke down early in the project when it was found that the PCRAs were servicing juveniles throughout the city. Evaluation was then limited to the target area and to boys in grades 7 through 10 in 1965, the beginning of the project. The sample of 851, nearly half of the population, was divided into three groups on the basis of amount of service received from the PCRAs during the project period. It was found that those receiving extensive service were more likely to have a record of delinquent behavior prior to the onset of the project than those receiving slight service or no service at all and that they also scored lower on academic achievement tests. However, when rates of juvenile offenses for the two years of the project were compared with those for the year prior to the project the group given extensive service showed a decline while the group receiving slight service or none showed an increase.

A good overall statement on performance evaluation is a survey report from the New Careers Development Center (Gartner, June 1969). The report summarizes evidence on the effect of paraprofessionals on an agency's service product (most of them nonprofessional rather than new careers programs), citing studies in health, mental health, education, social service, law, research, and work with senior citizens. The studies are reported in no detail and many were not intended as evaluations, but they give a broad survey of the range and diversity of nonprofessional skills and the variety of approaches to measuring their effectiveness. These include ratings or statements by teachers and administrators, reports of shifts in professional performance, time saved by the professional through paraprofessional help, numbers of people served by paraprofessional staff and, similarly, numbers brought into service who had not formerly been reached, shifts in delinquency rates, academic achievement or other performance measures on children, kinds and levels of jobs held by paraprofessionals trained several years before, and cost-benefits.

## Who Was Successful?

The question of whether poor people can perform effectively in new human service roles is better rephrased as: who can do what tasks with what degree of effectiveness? As far as we know, no one has approached this in a systematic way. Some attention has been given to the selection process and some studies have been done of persons who have entered then dropped out of the program.

*Selection.* There are two approaches to selecting new careerists. One is represented by the Howard University Community Apprentice Program (President's Committee, 1965): the participants had to be out of school, out of work, without pending arrest, sentence, or communicable disease, and able to read at a fifth grade level; they also had to show up for an interview. Most programs set far more stringent standards. In a report on New York's Public Service Careers Program (National Committee on Employment of Youth, 1969) the authors state that it is important to screen carefully for interest and capacity. Many others talk of the importance of motivational factors. A study of welfare aides (Cudaback, 1969) used not only a vocational achievement level but two specially designed questionnaires, one on community and life experiences and one in which the welfare aide applicant was asked to describe her actions in potential job situations. The problem with such approaches is not only that they are screening out devices, but that they preclude collecting systematic information on who can and cannot function in a given paraprofessional role. Pressures for having no failures or at least no boat-rocking are understandable but, as in other areas, hinder the growth of knowledge and freeze existing programs by the assumption that the program is right and if the new careerist can't get with it, the selection process is at fault. Levine and Pearl

(1965) have argued for minimal entry standards, then sorting out for relevant differences the dropouts and poor performers using demographic variables, measures of language skills and cognitive functioning, and such personal data as alienation, self-concept or identity, personal-social functioning, and coping skills. Exclusion criteria are usually set up to handle anxieties of staff rather than as a rational application of knowledge about nonprofessionals. It is interesting to note that the California new careers study (Fagerstrom, 1969) reports some evidence that staff attitudes toward exclusion variables (in this case, an arrest record) may be modified by face-to-face experience with new careerists.

Two studies have made attempts to introduce systematic variation into the selection process. In the Community Apprentice Program (President's Committee, 1965) all candidates were classified as high, medium, and low risks on the basis of a "socioeconomic profile." They were then paired on the basis of risk level, age, and sex and one member of each pair selected on a chance basis for training, those remaining forming a control group. In a program to train counseling interns to work with groups of human service aides (Klein et al., undated) selection was deliberately made for variation in academic achievement, experience with youth, and facility in working with youth. Selection staff observed the candidates in small discussion groups, rated them on ten items assumed to denote good group leadership, then used the ratings to divide those finally selected into high and low risk groups. The ratings were kept from the training staff but the two risk groups were readily identified by them. Because of this and because the selection staff had high total but low item reliability the authors suggest that what was actually measured was some kind of social desirability. The study was further complicated when some of the trainees were assigned to work in one-to-one relationships instead of with groups, thus making the selection criteria irrelevant. In any event, as in the prior study, risk category did not predict performance.

There are a number of selection problems still awaiting study. New careers programs have been charged with creaming from the available pool, although we have no evidence yet as to the significant dimensions for creaming. What happens as one dips deeper into the pool? Most new careers slots are filled by women. Is it possible to masculinize the human services so that appropriate roles will be sought by and filled effectively by men? Is it better to draw from persons indigenous to the neighborhood in which they will work or from those outside of the neighborhood?

Finally, what is the best way to go about selecting people? There are some interesting leads here. In the Howard University study referred to above the young people were given initial training that exposed them to work in child care, recreation, and research. Their final work assignments were made by peer and self selection. To the dismay of staff some of the tougher boys went into the day care program, arguing that placement in recreation centers would place them in ambiguous positions with their peers; they did in fact do very well in day care. A study of new careerists in a family planning program (Gartner, June 1969) used a panel of professional and nonprofessional judges to predict success in performance; they found that professionals predicted success better for some functions, but nonprofessionals were better predictors for other functions. Role playing situations similar to those for which the person is being trained were used in the group leader training program (Klein et al., undated) and in the California offender new careers project (Grant and Grant, 1967), but no efforts were made to test the success of this method compared to others. Since in many programs selection is out of the hands of either program or evaluation staff—for example, when referrals are made by the state employment service—the evaluator may be limited to learning the basis on which it has been made.

*Dropouts.* Studying program dropouts has also been used as a guide to determining who can be effective. In a study of the Minneapolis new careers program (Larson et al., 1969), a comparison was made of 105 dropouts and 155 persons who remained in the program using a series of demographic variations, a questionnaire on work interests, and a self-concept inventory. All dropouts who could be contacted were also interviewed on their program experiences and reasons for leaving. The original intent of the study was to predict who would be likely to drop out and to make recommendations for further recruitment. The authors found no single factor that could be linked to dropping out. They made an effort to look for interaction effects by partitioning their sample on sex, race, and prior occupation, found a few significant differences (e.g., older white women were more likely to stay with the program than any other group), but nothing that they felt could be described as a consistent pattern. This approach assumed that dropouts are a function of new careerist inadequacy rather than program inadequacy. There are undoubtedly persons who cannot perform on the job, for whatever reason, but there are also dropouts because of external events unrelated to the program (e.g., illness), because of failure of program components (e.g., misrepresenting or not explaining the program adequately during recruitment or orientation), and— perhaps most important—because the population on which new careers programs draw is economically marginal and many persons, especially men who are heads of families, literally cannot afford to remain as participants. The authors appear to recognize this, for their recommendations as a result of the study have to do with changes in the operation of the program rather than with restrictions on the kind of persons selected.

A smaller study of the California Department of Corrections new careers program (Fagerstrom, 1969) compared 13 dropouts with 27 stayins on a number of demographic variables but again found no systematic differences. It was noted that there were differences between the official (recorded) reasons for termination and the reasons reported in interviews. It was suggested that some of the aides may have been dropped because of failure to conform attitudinally rather than because of failure to perform on the job. This study, unlike the Minneapolis one, reported time in the program before dropping out.

**What Makes for Success?**

Each new careerist passes through a variety of processings during the course of his participation in the program. The question of success can be extended as follows: who can do what tasks with what degree of effectiveness given what kind of training, education, supportive services, and supervision on the job?

*Training.* Each new careers program has its own unique variation of what constitutes the training experience. For some there is a pre-placement orientation, followed by a mixture of part-time work experience and part-time training. For some training is accompanied by exposure to job settings without real work responsibilities. For others training begins with job placement. Training can be specifically job-related or can be labelled core or generic training which denotes usually that it is concerned with broad subject areas like "personality development" or with functions that might be applicable to a variety of human service jobs. In some cases the ongoing training constitutes a kind of forum in which the new careerists can air grievances, share experiences, and exert pressure for changes within the program.

A problem in many programs is that training staff are functionally and usually administratively separate from the staff of the agencies in which the new careerists are placed. For most new careerist positions there are no clearly defined and tested roles for which training can be developed and the separation between agency and training staff increases the difficulty of designing training that is job-relevant.

There are two steps in evaluating training programs: how is the new careerist changed as a result of his training experience; and what effect does this have on his job performance. Most training evaluations have concentrated on the former. The approaches used include counts of the number completing the training sequence, ratings by new careerists and their trainers of the adequacy and effectiveness of training, and measurements of the learning that has occurred during training. There are problems with each. Completion of training does not necessarily reflect either learning or capacity to perform on the job unless it is tied to clearly demonstrated ability to perform tasks known to be job-relevant. Assessments of training made by new careerists after training is completed may be hard to separate from current feelings about their employment situation. A more sophisticated approach used in the Counselor Intern Training Program (Klein et al., undated) asked trainees to rate their own capabilities in a number of job-related tasks both before and after training, but the authors note that it is difficult to separate behavior changes from shifts in self-perception. In this case the trainees showed little change in their ratings: was this because training had no impact or because they initially had an inflated perception of their capabilities? Their trainers rated the trainees lower prior to training than did the trainees themselves; their post-training ratings were similar to those made by the trainees. Were the trainers showing an initial bias reflecting low expectations of the trainees or were their first ratings more realistic than those made by the trainees? (Initial expectations that new careerists can do almost anything might had led to a decrease in post-training ratings.) The same study also noted that ratings given on global (poorly defined) characteristics such as creativity and initiative tended to be higher than those given on specific skills and behavior. Where ratings are used it is thus important to have very clear role definitions in order to separate shifts in trainee behavior from shifts in rater perceptions.

Measures of learning of the content presented in training avoid some of the pitfalls of ratings but are not free of problems. In the Home Health Aide Project (Hoff et al., 1968) plans for pre and post training measurement were curtailed when it was found that the aides were too frightened by test-taking to obtain accurate pre-training measures. The authors also point out that such tests do not measure ability to transfer learning to a work situation. Levine and Pearl (1965), summarizing training evaluations done at Howard University's Center for Youth and Community Studies, point out that both information tests and measures of problem-solving techniques have presented methodological problems, the former because they are often too gross to measure change, the latter chiefly because of lack of opportunity to validate against actual job performance. They discuss efforts to gather data about the learning process, in particular the role of the trainer and his interaction with the group, the nature of group interaction, the group's ability to focus on issues and make and implement decisions about group behavior, and the trainee's utilization of his training. A novel feature of these efforts was the use of trainees to collect data on training, with spot checks by evaluation staff to verify the accuracy of the trainee reports and evaluations. Their paper contains a model of a training evaluation design, including input, process, and outcome variables.

A major study of 15 new careers type programs in schools (Bowman and Klopf, 1967) attempted to evaluate the learning of training content through a pre and post training instrument which asked training staff and trainees to rate on scales of frequency and helpfulness a variety of activities in which teacher aides might be engaged. Success of training was to be measured by increased similarity of scores between the two groups following training. The approach failed in large part because the two groups showed little differentiation on the pre-test. The approach also failed to deal with the relevance of the instrument to job performance.

The Counselor Intern Training Program (Klein et al., undated) developed a questionnaire to measure learning of principles and techniques as opposed to straight information. The trainees were asked a series of questions about a leader's role with youth using an actual protocol of a meeting of a boys' group. Differences between pre and post scores on this and also on an information test were not significant by a sign test. The authors state, however, that an examination of individual score changes and pre and post test responses showed that most of the trainees showed evidence of learning; that content areas well covered in training were the most adequately learned; and that intensity of coverage appeared to be more important than the method of presentation, despite the fact that the trainees preferred other methods than the straight lecture.

Evaluations of training are of limited utility if the training is treated as an end in itself rather than as a means toward effective job performance, increased feelings of competence, or some other desired outcome. No one has yet tried to systematically vary training input then observe the impact on job performance. The California offender study referred to above (Grant and Grant, 1970) found no differences in job performance when training was carried out by professional staff, by a mixture of staff and trainees, or largely by trainees, but since these were informal observations made on a small group they offer only interesting leads for further study.

Ratings by job supervisors offer one way to validate training against job performance. In the Counselor Intern Training Program (Klein et al., undated) the 14 trainees were evaluated biweekly on their grasp of the operational context within which they functioned, their skill in performing specific tasks, their strengths and weaknesses, and changes in their performance over time. Eleven of the group showed improvement in ratings, though there is no indication of the length of time between the two sets of ratings reported. The ratings moreover were for performance in concurrent field work assignments rather than in the jobs for which they were being trained, and some of the supervisors were also instructors in the training program. A more independent evaluation was made in the Home Health Aide Project (Hoff et al., 1968) discussed earlier. Here job supervisors were asked to rate the graduates of the training program on their performance on 30 clearly and specifically defined items of job behavior. Evaluation of training related to a more restricted goal was reported by the welfare aide study cited above (Cudaback, 1968). Training of the aides included frequent tests of training content similar to tests used by civil service. The aides passed the actual civil service test at the end of training "significantly ahead" of others taking the examination.

If orientation or training experience can be found to be positively related to job performance, some argument can be made for its utility. If such relationship is not demonstrated, it remains to be shown whether the new careerist failed the training program (by not understanding or attending to it), or whether the training program failed the new careerist (by teaching skills or information never used on the job).

*Education.* Two types of formal education are offered, not necessarily in the same program. Remedial education gives help in elementary or high school level reading and arithmetic with the goal of helping the new careerist acquire the high school equivalency without which he will not be eligible for a post-training job or for advancement from his entry level position. The proportion of people who acquire a certificate of equivalency is usually used as the measure of success. Achievement tests have also been used to measure the effectiveness of remedial education, though these may pose several problems. These included in one study (Hoff et al., 1968) lack of instruments brief enough to be nonthreatening yet precise enough to measure improvement, contamination of initial scores by cheating, and difficulty in determining the proportion of test gains attributable to increase in knowledge, decrease in nervousness, and improvement in test-taking skill.

A detailed report on the education component of the New York Public Service Careers Program (National Committee on Employment of Youth, 1969) presents mean test gains over four months on the California Achievement Test and some data relating initial achievement score to the months needed in basic education to reach readiness to take the GED examination. This study also reports new careerist reactions to the basic education program through questionnaire responses and a detailed evaluation of the instructors and their teaching techniques by an outside consultant who observed a number of classes. A similar report is given on the English as a Second Language component of the program which involved full-time language training for Spanish-speaking potential new careerists. Here movement from the remedial program into job training and basic education was the goal and measure of achievement. The outside consultant in this case observed classes, interviewed staff, and administered a questionnaire in Spanish to small groups of students, following this with a group discussion of the program. Achievement test gains over ten months are also given though interpretation is hindered because different tests were used at the two points in time.

Participation in remedial programming is seldom optional where it is offered as a program component. Participation in higher education sometimes is. It has been pointed to as an indicator of new careerist motivation and thus as a measure of success. In point of fact, programs differ in the ease of access to higher education and the extent to which it is encouraged by the employing agency. In some programs it is an integral part of the work-training experience. In others it is encouraged and released time with pay, with or without assistance in meeting the expenses of fees and transporation, is offered. In others it is left up to the individual new careerist to pursue with the assumption that he will find ways to manage both the time and the expense. Further, programs differ in the extent to which participation is seen as job-relevant. Where there are clearcut career ladders and higher education is one way to move up them participation means something different to the new careerist than it does in programs where education is only vaguely seen as a means of self-improvement.

When higher education is built into a new careers program, a host of interesting but mostly untested questions are raised. Three approaches and sets of assumptions have been used in the college level teaching of new careerists: develop special classes for them since they are too unfamiliar or uncomfortable with formal education or too culturally different to respond to ordinary methods of teaching; develop special classes for them because most college courses are too irrelevant to their needs, with or without opening these to the college population at large; let them participate in regular college work, with or without providing associated tutoring and counseling services. Mixtures of all three are sometimes used. Which approach is best, or more properly, which approach is best for which new careerists and which goals? Do new careerists require special, more action-oriented teaching styles or in fact do all students do better with such an approach, the new careerist being only a special example? Do new careerists perform best when learning with other new careerists or when they are mixed with other college students? What kinds of teaching staff work best with what kinds of new careerists? What should be the role of the agency in helping design the content of the teaching curriculum? What makes course work "relevant"?

The Minneapolis new careers program has done the most with these questions. University of Minnesota staff have been intimately involved with new careers training and education for several years. It has been shown that new careerists, most of whom are assigned to the General College in the University though they do not meet the entrance requirements, perform comparably to students as a whole and that they can acquire academic credentials. Attention has also been given to differences among new careerists as students and to their varying needs for educational support (Knop et al., 1969; Wattenberg, 1968). A number of new courses have been designed for the new careerists and there have been some efforts to systematically vary teaching approaches, for example, contrasting one section of a course attended only by new careerists with one attended by both new careerists and regular students and one attended by both new careerists and regular students and one attended by regular students only (Wattenberg, 1970). Whether new careerists participating in given kinds of education programs actually perform better on the job has yet to be determined. It has also yet to be determined for their professional co-workers.

*Supportive Services.* There have been no systematic studies of the need for or effectiveness of supportive services. Program observers generally note gaps in service, such as inadequate transportation or lack of means to help new careerists cope with sudden financial crises. Similar information has been obtained when new careerists have been interviewed about program participation. Financial problems loom largest in most programs. It has been noted for example that having a regular paycheck makes a new careerist more accessible to his creditors and that new careerists often have difficulty in budgeting a monthly instead of a weekly check.

The only evaluation of supportive services as such was made in New York's Public Service Careers Program (National Committee on Employment of Youth, 1969) in which an outside consultant, using interviews with staff and new careerists and the results of a new careerist questionnaire, reported on the effectiveness of the program's counseling staff and the problems created by varying staff roles and staff attitudes toward their own work.

The kind and quality of services needed depend both upon the life situations of the new careerists and the special demands placed upon them by their jobs. In addition to the question of determining needs, there is the further question of the ways in which needs can best be met: by referral to outside agencies, by program personnel, by the new careerists themselves, or by other specially trained non-professionals. The latter have been shown to be very effective in reducing turnover in a manpower training program for youth (*New Careers Newsletter,* Aug. 1967).

*Job Supervision and Relations With Professionals.* Evaluations of job supervision have been based sometimes on the observations of program staff or outside consultants, sometimes on the feedback obtained by interview or questionnaire from new careerists and their supervisors. Some evaluations focus on the new careerists, some on the professionals with whom they work.

The School Community Worker Program evaluation (Conway, 1967) considers the problems raised for the new careerists by conflicts among professional staff, by dual supervision (core program versus agency staff) and by the differing perceptions of the new careerists' roles and expectations for their loyalty. The National Committee on Employment of Youth's career mobility study (1970) found that the trainee's perception of his future mobility was related to his attitude toward his supervisor, most strongly so when the supervisor represented an extreme position of a continuum of new vs. old approaches to supervision.

The welfare aide study (Cudaback, 1968) reports briefly on the results of intensive interviews with a random sample of 21 staff who were asked their opinions of aide skills and problems of aide-professional teamwork and on a poll of a sample of 159 staff who were asked about their attitudes toward the aide program. The parole aide study (Fagerstrom, 1968, 1969) also concentrates on the impact of the program on the staff. The reports note the problems created by race and class bias, by staff concern that the new careerists might be a threat to their jobs (would they take over? would they show up the professionals by being more effective?), and by resentment that the new careerists were handed things (e.g., an education) for which they had had to work. Shifts in attitude over time are noted, for both aides and staff, as reflected in changes in vocabulary and dress. Differences among the "unit subcultures" of the agency are also discussed, particularly differences in the value systems and conceptions of program goals of the staff working in each unit. The parole study, among others, points up the problems of collecting data on new careerists and the program through the employing agencies. Even though in this case evaluation was done by the agency itself, research staff were asked not to approach those staff units which were most resistant to the new careers program. Some formal interviews were conducted, but a good deal of the data was obtained through casual contacts and observations and through attendance at aide meetings.

Many questions remain for systematic study. Can professionals work successfully as communicators and supervisors with nonprofessionals? what kinds of skill and skill training are needed? what kinds of professional attitudes and stance and what kinds of relationships contribute most to effective performance in a given situation (for example, it has been noted that both hostility and uncritical enthusiasm have been detrimental to new careerist functioning)?

## IS THE NEW CAREERIST A CHANGED PERSON?

Personal and social role changes in new careerists are often described. There are many case study type of references in program reports to increased feelings of competence and self-worth as a result of program participation, particularly as participants have shifted from welfare status to earning money. Attention is also often given to more external manifestations of role changes—shifts in dress, speech, work habits, and attitudes. These have not been systematically studied, nor the kinds of experiences on the job that lead to them, nor their relation to actual job performance. We do not yet know what changes, beyond the job opportunity and perhaps the acquisition of specific job skills, are necessary for the new careerist to function in his new work role, or more precisely, what changes are necessary for specified kinds of new careerists to function in specified kinds of work roles.

Two major issues have been raised in this area. One stems from the statements on delinquency and opportunity structure by Cloward and Ohlin (1961): Is access to a job all that is needed to move the poor out of poverty and into the economic mainstream, or is something more required—some attention to problems within the person that hinder making use of the opportunity or some additional kinds of learning to which he needs to be exposed? As a result of their experiences with offender new careerists the Grants proposed a study (National Council on Crime and Delinquency, 1967) in this area. The original study differed from many programs in that there was rapid advancement and assumption of responsibility by the new careerists following training although there was no formal career ladder. It was noted that some of the trainees seized opportunities quickly and effectively while others, specifically those from whom most might have been expected, were in constant difficulty and needed continual support. A follow-up study of these and other new careerists was planned in which small groups of new careerists and significant others in their lives would be brought together with staff from their employing agencies to study the relationships between personal and job functioning and development. The study has not yet been funded but a pilot study of Mexican-American new careerists (Grant and Rodriguez, 1970) has been conducted.

The other issue has been phrased in several ways. Is it necessary to middle-classize the nonprofessional so he can negotiate his career or is it possible for him to retain his basic values and orientation, shifting only enough in his job-related behavior to function in the work setting? Is some conflict with professionals necessary to maintain a ghetto identification? If the professionals with whom he works are accepting and genuinely respect the new careerist, does the need to defend a ghetto identification disappear and become replaced by a desire for assimilation? If his role is that of linker between agency and clients and he assimilates, does he lose his effectiveness? Does being respected by professionals mean selling out? Does participation in a new careers program coopt the potential for social action? This issue has become tied to points of view about social change: does one work within the system and thus strive to become a part of it, or does one fight efforts at assimilation, use the new career placement as a way of mobilizing community involvement, and force system change from without? The value aspects of these questions have become so loaded they are difficult to study. The only relevant investigation is reported by the Minneapolis new careers program (University of Minnesota, June 1969) which concludes that "professionalization" is a process of adding on new role skills and does not require giving up roles acquired earlier.

### Does New Careers Pay Off?

From the standpoint of the funding source, is putting a person in a new careers program any improvement over alternative uses of funds and manpower? Several studies have compared training costs with monies saved on welfare support and/or with new monies generated by the employed new careerist. In a study of aides in a county welfare department (Cudaback, 1968) the potential welfare costs to the county of the 14 women, all prior AFDC recipients who are now employed as aides and living independently of welfare funds, is reported. The estimate takes into account the number and ages of the children involved, though the data is not fully presented. A study of home health aides (Hoff et al., 1968) computed the annual return of tax dollars to the public (federal income plus state sales taxes) and compared it with training costs to obtain an annual return on money invested in training. The estimate assumes the aides are all employed full-time and, apparently, that they had supplied no tax dollars prior to training. The study also computed returns on the training investment for those aides who had formerly been on welfare, combining tax dollar returns with savings in AFDC support. A study of costs and benefits in the Minneapolis new careers program (Brandt, 1968) also uses savings in welfare costs as one measure of benefits, using projections over a 20 year period and making some assumptions about the employment status of the program participants over this time. Welfare savings are combined with estimates of tax returns on the additional earnings made possible by education over the same period for a projection of future benefits which are then compared with project costs for a two-year period. A different measure is proposed in a paper on public service jobs for urban ghetto residents (Harrison, 1969), the present value of the extra GNP contributed over a six year period by a newly trained worker in a public service job. The GNP projections are made using three alternative discount rates and three sets of assumptions about the magnitude of the contribution per new worker. They are then compared with two estimates of training costs.

These studies are restricted to the benefits obtained by having new careerists employed rather than unemployed or underemployed. Less attention has been given to the benefits obtained by having new careerists employed effectively. The School Community Worker Program report (Conway, 1967) suggests that the new careerists can save the schools money by improving attendance (thus making them eligible for increased funds from the state) and by decreasing vandalism. Some figures in support of the latter are given. It is also suggested that the new careerists can expand services to clients beyond those previously provided by making home visits and by in-school counseling contacts. Numbers of visits and counseling contacts are reported, but these are not related to client effects.

Only one cost-benefit study that we know of has approached the issue of service to the client. This research in progress is being conducted by Eaton Conant of the Industrial Relations Institute of the University of Oregon under an Office of Education grant. The study is notable for its focus on the service product, both efforts to assign costs to the direct observation of work activity and to apply cost-effectiveness analysis to learning achievement under various staffing patterns. The study is described (Conant, 1970) as follows:

Costs and benefits of conventional, single teacher classroom staffing patterns are being compared to the costs and benefits associated with staffing patterns that assign teaching aides to teachers.

The principal cost categories that are being compared for the two staffing patterns include costs of recruitment, costs of current classroom operations, and instructional labor costs. Recruiting and current operations costs are being determined from budgets, expenditure records, and review of program operations. Details concerning differences in instructional labor costs for the nonaide and teacher-with-aide situations are being obtained by performing activity observation studies of teachers and aides in class situations. The objective of the observation studies, which are carried out in classes, is to identify changes that may occur in teacher teaching and nonteaching activities when aides are introduced as teaching assistants. When activity changes are identified, the study is assigning costs to the relative activity changes observed by assigning appropriate hourly labor cost figures to the task data.

Relative benefits of the teaching aide programs in the district are under investigation in the following ways. First, benefits are being assessed in terms of potential cost savings nonprofessional program arrangements may obtain in comparison to costs of conventional staffing arrangements. One model being tested for cost savings analysis assumes that districts may employ aides as a substitute for expanding the certified teaching staff in districts. The model then examines the possibilities that program quality can be maintained when lower salaried aides are recruited and substituted for teachers who might otherwise be employed.

The prinicipal effort to identify aide program benefits involves attempts to identify and compare learning achievement gains of children who are instructed under alternative staffing arrangements. Thus in ghetto schools in a northwest city reading achievement scores have been obtained for children who are being instructed by single teachers, teachers who have aides assigned for reading remedial instruction, and by remedial reading aides.

The observation studies, mentioned above, indicate that in this school district aides are instructing children during the school day for slightly more net teaching time daily than either teacher with or teacher-without-aides assigned to them. Correlation analysis is being used to determine if the children who are instructed by both teachers and aides in the teacher-with-aide situation are making greater achievement gains than children in the conventional single teacher setting. The cost-effectiveness analysis will then relate the relative costs of the staffing alternatives (labor costs principally) with relative achievement gains experienced in the different staffing patterns to obtain cost-effectiveness ratios.

Finally, the study is experimenting with more abstract models of aides staffing arrangements to explore cost-effectiveness implications of alternative aide assignment possibilities. For example, the real observation data about teacher and aide labor inputs are being used to project alternative labor input and cost patterns where it is assumed that limited changes are made in actual staffing schedules that have been observed.

## THE PARTICIPATING ORGANIZATIONS

A study that limited itself to the questions discussed above, no matter how well thought through and thorough the evaluation, would miss the whole point of new careers. New careers envisions changes in systems—in the organizations that provide delivery of human services, the colleges and universities that provide manpower for them, and the civil service entities that test and certify that manpower.

### Employing Agencies

If a new careers program is working as intended, changes can be expected in the structure of the agency, in staff roles and functions, in the agency's service product, and in the agency's relationship with the community.

First, what moves has the agency made to accommodate nonprofessionals within its table of organization? Are aide or trainee positions introduced into the agency as token appendages to the existing system without in fact modifying it at all (which is likely to happen when the nonprofessional task is a minor part of what the professional is already doing) or does the use of nonprofessionals entail some reorganization in the agency's personnel structure (which is more likely to happen when the nonprofessional job has been developed as a result of a task analysis of the agency's functions)? What strategies have been worked out to assume the full costs of the new careerists after federal funding ceases and to make their positions permanent?

Almost all new careers programs report the lack of viable career ladders (or lattices) as the major program weakness. Even among persons dedicated to careers it is sometimes assumed that the presence of new careerists within an agency will in itself create pressures for change and force the development of career ladders. There is little evidence that this has happened, at least in established agencies in which new careerists represent a small addition to the work force. What has been done about the question of upward mobility is crucial in transforming a nonprofessional job into a new career. For example, do the entry positions include opportunities for experiences that will lead to job upgrading or is the entry position such that no upward movement can logically develop (as with a teacher aide whose job is limited to cleaning erasers and running errands and a ditto machine)? Have career ladders been spelled out for the entry positions? Are links built into existing promotional ladders, or are new ladders created parallel to the existing ones (both models have been used in new careers programs)? What opportunities are there for horizontal mobility, allowing increases in salary within a given grade for those who do not choose to move to different functions? For diagonal mobility, allowing movement from one agency to another? Most important, what is the relation between what's on paper and what really happens to new careerists in the system? When there is disparity, can this be traced to failure of commitment on the part of top agency staff, or to problems external to the agency?

It is expected that the functions and roles of professional staff will change as a result of new careerist participation. When new careerists take on a piece of existing functions, either as junior professionals or by assuming a part of the professional's job that is really nonprofessional in character, it is expected that professionals will be freed to exercise their truly professional skills. What in fact does the professional do with his freed time? When new careerists perform new functions that professionals have neither the time nor the skill to handle it is expected that the professional's performance will be enhanced. How is the professional's role changed and in what ways is his effectiveness altered? What new skills does he develop? In many cases new careerists are expected to help the professional better understand his clients. How does the professional's perception of his clients change? Does he become more tolerant or more sensitive to their needs? Does the work of new careerists lead professionals or their administrators to a questioning of professional practices? Does it force greater accountability for the effectiveness of professional service? When professionals function as supervisors to new careerists they often report less time available to work with clients. What are the demands of supervision and how well are professionals prepared to meet them? What staff training and development are offered by the agency for both professional and nonprofessional to facilitate communication between the two and to improve the quality of their work?

It is expected that the use of new careerists will improve the agency's service product, both through services performed by the new careerists and through improved professional performance. What changes take place in service delivery as a consequence of nonprofessional participation? Does service improve in any demonstrable way—in its quantity, its quality, its accessibility?

Finally, what happens to the agency vis-à-vis the community? Is there more sharing within the agency itself between administrators and staff, and between staff and clients? Do new careerists facilitate feedback from clients to the agency and does this in any way affect agency practice? Are there shifts in community attitudes toward the agency and toward the adequacy of services it provides? Is there increased input from the community to the agency as a result of the new careerists' work or are new careerists used solely to interpret the agency to the community and to diminish the pressures it places on the agency for change?

Several studies have dealt at length with the agencies employing new careerists, the shaping of the program by the agency and the program's impact on the agency, and the problems of institutionalizing new careers positions (see especially Ballard and Alley, 1968; Fagerstrom, 1969; Larson et al., 1968; National Committee on Employment of Youth, 1967, 1970; and Gartner, April 1969 for a summary of these issues). There have been three attempts to develop models for nonprofessional utilization and to use them to understand the development of new careers within the agency.

The evaluators of the Minneapolis new careers program, in a study of the nine participating agencies (Larson et al., 1968), developed a "function-model" of nonprofessional tasks as a way of classifying aide jobs. The model consists of nine sets of job duties, grouped into three major functions: influencing (orienting clients, bridging between agency and clients), service (expediter, outreach, developer), and therapeutic (role model, supportive role, helping role, intervention role). There is no hierarchy among these functions, either of complexity or desirability. Rather the model is intended as a way of describing what aides do and making comparisons across agencies. It was found that some agencies have aides performing a variety of functions while others limit aides to one function at a time. The authors suggest that some functions may offer a better basis for developing careers than others, that inservice training is essential to give direction to whatever functions are performed, and that jobs with a variety of functions may be more meaningful than those with only one.

Fagerstrom (1969) discusses the implications of two organizational models utilized in the California Department of Corrections new careers program. The first deals with the assignment pattern of the parole aides: assignment to a regular parole unit (assignment of the aide to one parole agent on a permanent or on a rotating basis, or assignment of the aide as a resource to all agents in a unit) versus assignment to a special parole unit. The second model, which cuts across the first, concerns the aide's major function: line functions (the aide doing low level agent tasks or providing new services on an individual case basis, the career goal being a parole agent job) versus staff functions (the aide providing increased client services through his knowledge of the community, the career goal being a newly created career staff position). These models emerged as part of the agency's efforts to implement the new careers program in various parts of the state. The effect of these models on the attitudes of agents and of aides is considered, as well as their relation to staff perception of program goals and their implications for training.

The career mobility study (National Committee on Employment of Youth, 1970) developed what is described as an approximation to a functional task analysis of the jobs performed by the 26 new careerists in the study through a checklist of job tasks filled out by each new careerist and by his supervisor. The 25 tasks were clustered into five main categories: outreach; information and communication (verbal); information and communication (written); administration, organization, and supervision; and testing and teaching. It was found that most of.the new careerists held generalized jobs requiring the performance of a large number of tasks; that the same tasks tended to be performed in all agencies, despite differences in agency service goals and the nonprofessional job titles used; and that the same tasks tended to be performed by young college graduates in entry level jobs in these same agencies. The task analysis was used to verify agency reports of broadening of services to clients and increasing involvement with the community.

The most sophisticated effort to look at what new careerists do is described as part of an approach to job and career development (Fine, 1967; Wiley, 1969). A set of scales of worker functions related to data, people, and things has been developed which can be used to describe job tasks in an ordering of increased complexity and which provides a standardized vocabulary that can be applied across job fields and to professionals and nonprofessionals alike. To use these scales it is necessary that the agency first specify clearly the tasks that need to be performed. Defining tasks in terms of functions then offers a base for reorganizing tasks into jobs and for developing career ladders based on a rational utilization of worker training, education, and experience.

## Education

Movement up career ladders is still strongly tied to academic credits and degrees. A new careers program is not expected to work unless it is linked with an appropriately modified educational system. This includes modifications in entrance requirements, in course content, and in credentialling procedures. No one has yet set up such a system, but movement toward this goal can be documented.

First, is there access to secondary and higher education for the new careerists? Are admission procedures modified when necessary to allow new careerists to qualify as students who would otherwise not do so? Courses offering college credit are sometimes set up for trainees in a new careers program, but this is often done through an extension division or through some other special arrangement that does not permit the credits earned to be applied toward a degree. Is the new careerist, once admitted, in the same status as a regularly admitted student, and if not, what moves have to be made before he can be so admitted?

Education is expected to provide the new careerist with the theoretical knowledge he needs to perform on the job. Education in a new careers program should not only parallel but be integrated with concurrent work experience. Changes can thus be expected in the content of what is taught and in its methods of presentation. What efforts have been made to link course content to the work in which the new careerist is engaged? How have agency staff been brought into the planning and carrying out of the educational program? One would expect more learning through doing and more active participation by the new careerist than is the case with regular course work. Are the new careerists able to feed their work experience into their ongoing education, and are they able to translate what is learned back into their work activities?

Education is also expected to help the new careerist acquire the credentials necessary for upward job mobility. Various modifications in accrediting procedures have been reported, for example, allowing academic credit for work experience by on-site teaching or by appointing agency staff to teaching positions, or by setting up special degree programs short of the B.A. Such credits are of little use, however, unless they can be applied toward degrees in four-year colleges and/or accepted as part of the necessary credentials by civil service and by employing agencies. What efforts have been made to link education to career mobility?

The University of Minnesota has made a number of changes as a result of its participation in the Minneapolis new careers program (Minneapolis New Careers Program, 1969; University of Minnesota, February 1969; Wattenberg, 1968). For example, part of the core curriculum developed for new careerists through General Extension is now being made a part of the standard curriculum for General College students. Twelve new careerists have been hired part-time as Cultural Education Specialists to serve as resources to faculty in courses related to social problems, poverty, and race. They have assisted in courses in education, social work, sociology, social studies, and dentistry. Moves toward a credentialling system have been made by developing a 45 credit certificate, though this has yet to be accepted by civil service and by employers.

The only effort we know of actually to alter the total educational experience and tie it in with work experience is a demonstration currently under way in the administration of justice field (Frankel et al., 1969). The goal of the demonstration is the development of a model of education from the third year of high school through the four years of college that will integrate education with preparation for and participation in work activity. Participants in the demonstration include staff and new careerists from potential employing agencies (probation and parole) and teachers and students from a high school, a community college, and a four-year college. Sample courses are being developed as well as procedures for using student contracts with the educational institution to fulfill educational goals. Small scale implementations of the model are planned for the coming year.

## Civil Service

The policies of civil service systems often represent a major obstacle both in making entry positions permanent and in developing career ladders. Entry requirements may be waived for new careerists but it is apparently far harder to break the traditional link between education and advancement beyond the entry level, despite the fact that there is little evidence that the possession of a B.A. in itself has any discernible relationship to job performance. However, many civil service systems have made moves to modify both testing procedures (e.g., eliminating written examinations) and job requirements (e.g., giving credit for life experience or for training given on the job in lieu of education), and in some cases they have shown greater readiness to move than the agencies they serve. What moves have been made by program staff to work with civil service (and with professional organizations and unions where necessary) to change requirements for jobs or to redesign jobs for both professionals and nonprofessionals? What has been done to establish links between entry jobs and existing career ladders or to develop new career ladders? What efforts have been made to look at the tasks performed by the agency, to relate these to agency goals, and to restructure jobs at both professional and nonprofessional levels?

These issues are discussed at some length in the career mobility study referred to above (National Committee on Employment of Youth, 1970). It was found that even agencies not under civil.service set up barriers to career advancement very much like those found in agencies under civil service regulation. Great confusion was found within and between agencies on the designation of jobs considered professional and those considered nonprofessional and in at least one both kinds of workers were performing identical tasks. Unions were found to have had a positive effect in the agencies studied on wages and job benefits but little impact so far on opportunities for career advancement. Potential conflicts with unions over the issue of job restructuring were noted, the pressures to advance new careerists through reclassifying jobs conflicting with the job security of existing union members. In other areas, however, unions are reported to be playing a major role in developing opportunities for job upgrading (Gartner, April 1969).

## THE COMMUNITY

New careers programs have had a number of unanticipated spinoffs. One of the most important is the movement of new careerists into community and political action roles. New Careerists are reported to have become involved in community organizations, often around job-related activities, as a result of their participation in the program. There are a number of local as well as national new careerist associations. New careerists have organized to bring pressures for change on the agencies in which they work and on professional organizations. They have been involved in political campaigns. New careerists have testified before congressional committees and have been responsible for helping draft both state and federal legislation.

The interests of new careerists have in many instances merged with community demands for improved services and for control over agencies serving the community (Gartner, April 1969; National Committee on Employment of Youth, 1970). New careers programs have also become the ground for power struggles between agencies and the community and among factions within the community. In many large cities new careers programs have included mainly blacks. In some, chicano groups have begun to challenge this apparent domination, and the issue of community control has turned into the issue of whose community is being represented. As in other reform efforts there is the question of how much energy is being drained off into jurisdictional disputes. This provides some evidence against the argument that new careers coopts the potential for social action. But all new careerists do not necessarily move in this direction. What conditions within the new careerist participants, within the program, and within the larger community make for commitments to social action? What effect does action by new careerists have on the effectiveness and viability of the new careers program?

## ISSUES IN OVERALL EVALUATION DESIGNS

The evaluation efforts reviewed thus far have varied from unsystematically obtained impressions of program staff to comparisons between questionably adequate experimental and control groups. There are available, however, three models for longitudinal evaluation of total new careers programs. The National Committee on Employment of Youth developed such a model as part of its evaluation of the New York Public Service Careers Program (1969). Operations research presented another (1968) in its approved proposal to the Office of Economic Opportunity for a three year cross-program evaluation of five federal manpower training programs, one of which is new careers. The third was developed as a part of the Economic Systems Corporation new careers evaluation report (Ballard and Alley, 1968).

Among the three arise issues concerning (1) the use of control groups and the question of matching, (2) the use of multiple regression and/or equivalents which do not make the assumption of linearity, (3) the appropriate kinds of outcomes to use for cost/benefit analyses, and (4) the use of program development and organization change as outcomes.

### Control Groups and Matching

Objections to random selection of persons for training or other service programs are usually made on the grounds that some persons would be harmed by a given treatment or, alternatively, that it would be wrong to deny a given treatment to a person assumed to benefit from it. Operations Research handles this issue for its five program evaluation through what it calls an idealized sample design. The design calls for obtaining a probability sample of the target population, then determining the eligibility of each person in the sample for each available program. Persons found eligible for only one program are divided randomly into a control group and a group for which attempts are made to recruit them into the program. Persons eligible for more than one program are divided randomly into four groups, one to be used as a control. For the other three, attempts are made to recruit into programs for which they are eligible, one group being allowed to choose the program they will enter, one group being assigned by an expert to the program considered best, and one group being assigned to programs on a random basis. The proposal refers to two studies in which this design was successfully employed, one on the potential impact of medical rehabilitation services carried out in Baltimore by the Commission on Chronic Illness, the other in Kansas City by Community Studies, Inc. and the University.

Another approach to this problem is offered by Wilkins (1969; see Figure 16.1). His model was developed for confined offenders who had no choice over treatment assignment, but it is applicable to the same problem posed by the Operations Research evaluation.

Possible alternatives to random assignment designs are discussed in the Operations Research proposal. Here they are in the field of quasi-experimental designs and nonequivalent control groups discussed by Campbell and Stanley (1963). These alternatives break down to two basic categories. One is the use of natural groups,

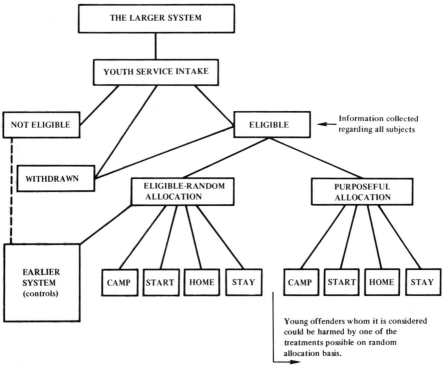

**FIGURE 16.1** Evaluation of Penal Measures

such as other classes of students in evaluating the effect of variation in classroom instruction. This can be viewed as a representative design issue (Brunswik, 1947) where statistical control can be used over the natural variance occurring across kinds of programs and kinds of inputs in kinds of situations. Multiple regression with its alternatives (see discussion below) can be used to test the impact or a given intervention as a variable in the multiple regression equation. This is an extension of statistical control through the use of covariance designs.

The second is the creation of a control population by some system of matching. As opposed to the sophistication of the Operations Research model, that proposed by the National Committee on Employment of Youth uncritically advocates the use of a group of matched controls. They argue, "Given the probability that it will not be feasible to place serious reliance on a highly experimental approach within the context of the proposed evaluation, it is important to identify and define a *control* group of individuals with characteristics similar to that of the experimental group. This group will *not* participate in the New Careers program, but they will be included as part of the follow-up study to provide comparative data as to differences in terminal (end of study) job satisfactions, career advancement, and economic upgrading, if any. . . . Careful matching of controls with those receiving training is very important precisely because randomization is not used in assignment of treatments to subjects." There is no discussion of the impossibility of defining a comparable control group, nor of the variables on which matching is supposed to take place, nor of the pitfalls in analyzing and interpreting data derived from such a matching procedure. In addition to Campbell and Stanley's (1963) cautions about creating controls through matching, there is a discussion of matching in Wilkins' book *Social Deviance* (1965). Both are must readings for anyone approaching evaluation designs for new careers.

There are three essential arguments against matching rather than applying statistical techniques for control. First is the problem of unknown correlates of the variables used for matching with the dependent variable and other variables assumed to define the population. For example, one of the more obvious population contaminations through matching on measured intelligence is its impact on the ethnic mix of the groups so matched. A second problem is the regression effect which occurs when the control group selected by matching has a different mean and distribution than the population from which it was drawn. The third is the inappropriateness of estimates of error variance where there is not base of randomization.

These quasi-experimental-control designs are not to be confused with stratified designs where random assignment to experimental and control groups within a stratification with a known relationship to the dependent variable is used. When we reach this level of sophistication in new careers research we can improve upon (reduce the N's needed for a given level of significance) by introducing stratification into random assignment designs. This is a completely different game than artificially matched groups without randomization.

At least until we have learned much more about the parameters in the natural variance of existing program models, we should concentrate on determining the nature of variation among what is, rather than getting hung up on measuring differences between what is and what is not, that is, an artificial control. The question becomes what is the relevant information over a representative set of programs which will help us predict—contribute to the accountable variance—of identified outcomes. From this information concerning what makes a difference we can construct new models to put into the field of competitive programs for further clarification of the significant patterning of variables for increased efficiency— improved outcomes through approximations. This calls for continued system building and system testing through the use of multivariate prediction techniques.

## Multiple Regression

The Operations Research model depends upon a multiple regression analysis over kinds of programs to determine what new careers program variables over what input variables contribute how much to identifiable outcomes.

The proposal raises the issue of the excessive amount of information conceivably useful in the prediction equation and poses two procedures for deciding what information to use. The first is analysis of variance to determine which variables have first order correlations with the dependent variable and to test hypothesized specific interaction effects. One would then include in the multiple regression analyses those variables and hypothesized interactions which were found to independently related to the outcome criterion. The multiple regression would allow a weighting of each variable, including the interactions, as to the magnitude of the contribution to the accountable variance.

The second proposed solution to the variable selection problem is the Automatic Interaction Detector (AID) program developed by the University of Michigan (Sonquist and Morgan, 1964). The advantage of AID is that it provides an efficient means for detecting all interaction effects between a prespecified set of variables. Regarding one of a set of thirty-seven variables as a dependent variable, "the analysis employs a nonsymmetrical branching process, based on variance analysis techniques, to subdivide the sample into a series of subgroups which maximize one's ability to predict values of the dependent variable. Linearity and additivity assumptions inherent in conventional multiple regression techniques are not required."

Other solutions are available (MacNaughton-Smith, 1963) and have been shown to improve the prediction obtained by multiple regression alone (Gottfredson and Ballard, 1966). The optimal form of multivariate analysis in prediction techniques will be a continuing problem. For the present one should use alternative solutions with cross-validation groups to empirically test which solution is most effective with which sets of data.

The problem cannot be avoided by simply testing differences between experimental and pseudo-control groups as proposed in the National Committee on Employment of Youth model. Statistical control must be employed and provision must be made for the limitations imposed by multiple regression additive and linearity assumptions.

## Kinds of Outcomes for Cost/Benefit Analyses

In addition to benefits accruable through changes in the new careerists themselves, it is plausible that benefits will be obtained through increased effectiveness of service to clients. Children will learn more, welfare recipients will be healthier, probationers will be less delinquent. The Operations Research proposal nicely states the possible benefits to be analyzed concerning the development of the new careerist, but they do not consider the benefits for improved client output which follows from analysis such as that described above (Conant, 1970) where students have more time in a learning situation when new careerists are used as instructors than when teachers do the instructing alone. These findings take on particular benefits significance when improved learning scores accompany the improved classroom situation.

Further, we should look for benefits from increased organizational efficiency. The staff participation introduced through new careers could bring better communication, better attendance, and more effective performance among all persons working in an agency. In spite of some reported initial resistance to new careers by agency staff, there are also reports of a contagion effect (Grant and Grant, in press) which would result in improved morale and functioning for the entire staff. Recent work with the Oakland, California, Police Department (Toch, 1969) suggests the power of a general participation staff and program development strategy for increasing organizational efficiency.

| Phases | Strategies | | | | | |
|---|---|---|---|---|---|---|
| | $S_1$ | $S_2$ | ... | $S_j$ | ... | $S_k$ |
| $P_1$ | $P_{11}$ $I_{11}$ $O_{11}$ $F_{11}$ | $P_{12}$ $I_{12}$ $O_{12}$ $F_{12}$ | ... | $P_{1j}$ $I_{1j}$ $O_{1j}$ $F_{1j}$ | ... | $P_{1k}$ $I_{1k}$ $O_{1k}$ $F_{1k}$ |
| $P_r$ | $P_{r1}$ $I_{r1}$ $O_{r1}$ $F_{r1}$ | $P_{r2}$ $I_{r2}$ $O_{r2}$ $F_{r2}$ | ... | $P_{rj}$ $I_{rj}$ $O_{rj}$ $F_{rj}$ | ... | $P_{rk}$ $I_{rk}$ $O_{rk}$ $F_{rk}$ |

Goal ("Ideal") for Interface

$P_{rj}$ is expecteds given Strategy j and Phase r for planning.
$I_{rj}$ is expecteds given Strategy j and Phase r for implementation.
$O_{rh}$
$O_{rj}$ is expecteds given Strategy j and Phase r for operations.
$F_{rj}$ is expecteds given Strategy j and Phase r for feedback.

FIGURE 16.2 Interface for Developmental Model for Evaluating Social Science Programs

## Program Development and Organization Change As Outcomes

The Economic Systems Corporation model is concerned with organization change within agencies as an outcome for evaluation. Program development is described as movement toward a goal over a set of interfaces where an interface is defined as a potential interchange between the new careerist and a facet of the program. Subgoals to the total program development goal can be stated for each interface. Movement can be broken down into phases, and alternative strategies identified for movement toward both total goal and subgoals within each phase. From the strategies it is possible to identify what would be expected to happen if the movement necessary for the appropriate change in development to occur were taking place. Evaluation observations can also be identified to allow determination of the extent to which the expected is actually occurring. These expecteds can be stated for planning, staffing, implementing, operating, follow-up, and feedback for each phase of the developmental process. Figure 16.2, taken from the Economic Systems Corporation report, presents the model schematically for four program areas.

New careers represents an attempt to bring about institutional change. Many of the issues raised in this review have implications beyond the evaluation of specific new careers programs, to the development of a strategy for studying change itself.

## REFERENCES

Ballard, K. B. and S. R. Alley. Pilot evaluation of selected new careers projects. Unpublished manuscript, AVCO Economic Systems Corporation, Washington, D.C., 1968.

Bowman, G. W. and G. J. Klopf. New careers and roles in the American school: A study of auxiliary personnel in education. Unpublished manuscript, Bank Street College of Education, New York, 1967.

Brandt, R. S. Extracts from: Costs and benefits of the Minneapolis new careers program. Unpublished manuscript, New Careers Research, General College and Minnesota Center for Sociological Research, University of Minnesota, 1968.

Brunswik, E. Systematic and representative design of psychological experiments. University of California Syllabus Series, No. 304, 1947.

Campbell, D. T. and J. C. Stanley. Experimental and quasi-experimental designs for research. Chicago: Rand McNally, 1963.

Cloward, R. A. and L. E. Ohlin. Delinquency and opportunity. Glencoe: Free Press, 1961.

Conant, E. Personal communication, Feb. 1970.

Conway, L. The school community worker program. Unpublished manuscript, Survey Research Center, University of California at Berkeley, 1967.

Cudaback, D. Summary report on Welfare Service Aide Project. Unpublished manuscript, School of Social Welfare, University of California at Berkeley, 1968.

Efthim, A. We care in Kansas: The non-professional revolt. The Nation, Aug. 5, 1968.

Fagerstrom, M. N. A preliminary evaluation of the new careers program in the California Department of Corrections, June 1967-June 1968. Unpublished manuscript, Bay Area Research Unit, California Department of Corrections, 1968.

———. New careers program, California Department of Corrections, December 1967-December 1969. Unpublished manuscript, Bay Area Research Unit, California Department of Corrections, 1969.

Fine, S. Guidelines for the design of new careers. Kalamazoo, Mich. W. E. Upjohn Institute for Employment Research, 1967.

Frankel, H., J. D. Grant, J. Milligan, and M. James. Technical report: developing new career ladders, with appropriate educational components, in the administration of justice. Unpublished manuscript, Social Action Research Center, Oakland, California, 1969.

Gartner, A. The use of the paraprofessional and new directions for the social service agency. Public Welfare, 1969, 117-125.

———. Do paraprofessionals improve human services: A first critical apppraisal of the data. New York: New Careers Development Center, New York University, 1969.

Gottfredson, D. M. and K. B. Ballard. Offender classification and parole prediction. Unpublished manuscript, Institute for the Study of Crime and Delinquency, Vacaville, California, 1966.

Grant, J. D. The offender as a correctional manpower resource. In F. Riessman and H. I. Popper (eds.), Up from poverty. New York: Harper and Row, 1968.

———. Delinquency prevention through participation in social change (new careers in the administration of justice). Paper prepared for Delinquency Prevention Strategy Conference sponsored by the Juvenile Delinquency Task Force of the California Council on Criminal Justice, Santa Barbara, February 1970.

——— and J. Grant. New Careers Development Project: final report. Unpublished manuscript, Institute for the Study of Crime and Delinquency, Sacramento, California, 1967.

Grant, J. and J. D. Grant. Client participation and community change. Pp. 262-277. In D. Adelson and B. L. Kalis (eds.), Community psychology perspectives in mental health. Scranton: Chandler Publishing, 1970.

Grant, J. D. and J. Grant. Contagion as a principle in behavior change. In H. C. Rickard (ed.), *Unique programs in behavior readjustment.* Elmsford, N.Y.: Pergamon Publishing, in press.

Grant, J. D. and M. Rodriguez. Final report: beyond the opportunity structure. Unpublished manuscript, Social Action Research Center, Oakland, California, 1970.

Hallowitz, E. and F. Riessman. The role of the indigenous nonprofessional in a community mental health neighborhood service center program. *American Journal of Orthopsychiatry,* 1967, 37: 766-778.

Harrison, B. Public service jobs for urban ghetto residents. *Good Government,* 1969, 1-20.

Hoff, W. P. Stewart, S. B. Gross and J. C. Malcolm. Home Health Aide Pilot Training Project: final evaluation report. Unpublished manuscript, Alameda County Health Department, Oakland, California, 1968.

Husek-Rosen and Associates. Evaluation design for the education aides program of the Los Angeles city school districts. Unpublished manuscript, Los Angeles, 1970.

Klein, W., M. Levine, B. MacLennan, W. Walker and J. R. Fishman. Leadership training for new careers: The non-professional counselor, supervisor and trainer. Unpublished manuscript, Institute for Youth Studies, Howard University, undated. Reprinted by Information Clearinghouse, New Careers Development Program, University Research Corporation, Washington, D.C.

Knop, E., M. Thompson and R. F. Falk. Education and job success in a new careers program. Unpublished manuscript, New Careers Research, General College and Minnesota Center for Sociological Research, University of Minnesota, 1969.

Larson, P., N. Beldin and R. F. Falk. A critique of agencies in the Minneapolis new careers program. Unpublished manuscript, New Careers Research, General College and Minnesota Center for Sociological Research, University of Minnesota, 1968.

Larson, P., M. Bible and R. F. Falk. Down the up staircase: A study of new careers dropouts. Unpublished manuscript, New Careers Research, General College and Minnesota Center for Sociological Research, University of Minnesota, 1969.

Levine, M. S. and A. Pearl. Designs for the evaluation of training programs: Training report C. S. No. 13. Unpublished manuscript, Center for Youth and Community Studies, Howard University, 1965.

Los Angeles Unified School District. Evaluation reports: Economic Opportunity Act programs 1968-1969. Unpublished manuscript, Los Angeles, 1969.

MacNaughton-Smith, P. The classification of individuals by the possession of attributes associated with a criterion. *Biometrics,* June 1963.

Minneapolis New Careers Program. University component: A summary of the program and its second year's objectives. Unpublished manuscript, Minneapolis, 1969.

Minneapolis Public Schools. Teacher aide program—a research report. Unpublished manuscript, Special School District #1, Minneapolis, 1967. Reprinted by New Careers Information Clearinghouse, New Careers Institute, University Research Corporation, Washington, D.C.

National Committee on Employment of Youth. Models of subprofessional employment. I. The community action program model. Unpublished manuscript, New York, 1967.

———. An evaluation of the Public Service Careers Program for the Manpower Career Development Agency. Unpublished manuscript, New York, 1969.

———. Where do they go from here? A study of the roads and roadblocks to career mobility for paraprofessionals working in human service agencies. Unpublished manuscript, New York, 1970.

National Council on Crime and Delinquency. Beyond the opportunity structure. Proposal submitted to National Institute of Mental Health, MH 14345-01, 1967.

*New Careers Newsletter.* Job coaches reduce turnover. New Careers Development Center, New York University, August 1967, p. 8.

*New Careers Newsletter.* Kansas psychiatric aides move for better service and new careers. New Careers Development Center, New York University, 1968, 2 (2): 1.

*New Careers Newsletter.* Evaluation. New Careers Development Center, New York University, 1968, 2 (6): 6.

*New Careers Newsletter.* The politics of mental health. New Careers Development Center, New York University, 1969, 3 (2): 1.

New York University, Graduate School of Social Work, Center for the Study of Unemployed Youth. Summary of proceedings: Workshop on nonprofessional careers for disadvantaged youth. New York, December 1966.

Operations Research Incorporated. Manpower evaluation study. Proposal prepared for Office of Economic Opportunity in response to RFP No. RPP/E-69-20, November 1968.

Pearl, A. Quoted in New careerists probe their para-professions, Reports on higher education. Western Interstate Commission for Higher Education, November 1969, p. 7.

——— and F. Riessman. *New careers for the poor: The nonprofessional in human service.* New York: Free Press, 1965.

President's Committee on Juvenile Delinquency and Youth Crime. *Training for new careers: The Community Apprentice Program.* Washington, D.D.: U.S. Government Printing Office, 1965.

Riessman, F. The revolution in social service: The new nonprofessional. Unpublished manuscript, Mobilization for Youth, New York, November 1963.

———. Strategies and suggestions for training nonprofessionals. Unpublished manuscript, Albert Einstein College of Medicine, New York, 1966.

Schmais, A. *Implementing nonprofessional programs in human services.* Center for the Study of Unemployed Youth, Graduate School of Social Work, New York University, 1967.

Smith, W. R. Police-community relations aides in Richmond, California. Unpublished manuscript, Survey Research Center, University of California at Berkeley, 1967.

Sonquist, J. A. and J. N. Morgan. The detection of interaction effects: A report on a computer program for the selection of optimal combinations of explanatory variables. Unpublished manuscript, University of Michigan, 1964.

Toch, H. Change through participation (and vice versa). Unpublished manuscript, School of Criminal Justice, State University of New York at Albany, 1969.

University of Minnesota. Cultural education specialists. Unpublished manuscript, Office of New Careers, February 1969.

University of Minnesota. Up the up staircase: Impressions of the new careerist as student. Unpublished manuscript, Office of New Careers, June 1969.

Wattenberg, E. Progress report on education, first fiscal year ending June 30, 1968. Unpublished manuscript, Minneapolis New Careers Program, University of Minnesota, 1968.

———. Special curriculum for university new careers program in the General College. Unpublished manuscript, Office of New Careers, University of Minnesota, 1970. Reprinted by New Careers Information Clearinghouse, University Research Corporation, Washington, D.C.

Wiley, W. W. Six steps to new careers. In *Methods for manpower analysis,* No. 3: A systems approach to new careers. Kalamazoo, Mich.: W. E. Upjohn Institute for Employment Research, 1969. Reprinted by National Institute for New Careers, University Research Corporation, Washington, D.C. as Comprehensive health services—career development issues, 1970, No. 1.

Wilkins, L. T. *Social deviance: Social policy, action, and research.* Englewood Cliffs, N.J.: Prentice-Hall, 1965.

———. *Evaluation of penal measures.* New York: Random House, 1969.

Wilson, J. C., J. R. Fishman and L. E. Mitchell. An assessment of technical assistance and training needs in new careers projects being sponsored by the United States Training and Employment Service, Manpower Administration, U.S. Department of Labor. Unpublished manuscript, National Institute for New Careers, University Research Corporation, Washington, D.C., 1969.

# CUMULATIVE BIBLIOGRAPHY

## A

Aberle, D., Cohen, A., Davis, A., Levy, M., & Sutton, F. "The functional prerequisites of a society." Ethics, 1950, 60: 100-111.

Ackner, B., Harris, A., & Oldham, A. J. "Insulin treatment of schizophrenia: A controlled study." Lancet, 1957, 272: 607-611.

Ackner, B. & Oldham, A. "Insulin treatment of schizophrenia: A three-year follow-up of a control study." Lancet, 1962, 281: 504-505.

Ackoff, R. L. "Systems, organizations and interdisciplinary research." General Systems Yearbook, 1960, 5: 1-8.

Adams, J. S. Inequity in social exchange. In L. Berkowitz (ed.) *Advances in experimental social psychology*. New York: Academic Press, 1965.

Addison, R. M. & Homme, L. E. "The reinforcing event (RE) menu." National Society of Programed Instruction Journal, 1966, 4(1): 8-9.

Ader, R. & Hahn, E. W. "Effects of social environment on mortality to whole body-x-irradiation in the rat." Psychological Reports, 1963, 13: 24-215.

Ader, R., Kreutner, A., & Jacobs, H. L. "Social environment, emotionality and Alloxan diabetes in the rat." Psychosomatic Medicine, 1963, 25: 60-68.

Adler, L. Patients of a state mental hospital: The outcome of their hospitalization. In A. Rose (ed.), *Mental health and mental disorder*. New York: W. W. Norton, 1955.

Albee, G. W. "The short unhappy life of clinical psychology." Psychology Today, 1970, 4(4): 42-43, 74.

Alford, R. R. "The political economy of health care: Dynamics without change." Politics and Society, Winter 1972, 4: 127-164.

Alford, R. R. "The political economy of the American health system." Unpublished monograph, Department of Sociology, University of Wisconsin, Madison, 1971.

Alihan, M. A. *Social ecology*. New York: Columbia University Press, 1938.

Alinsky, S. D. "The war on poverty—political pornography." Journal of Social Issues, 1965, 21(1): 41-47.

Alivisatos, G. & Lyketsos, G. "A preliminary report of a research concerning the attitude of the families of hospitalized mental patients." International Journal of Social Psychiatry, 1964, 10: 37-44.

Alksne, H. "Interviewing the narcotic addict." Paper presented at the meeting of the American Association for Public Opinion Research, 1960, summarized, Public Opinion Quarterly, 1960, 24(3): 473-474.

Allerhand, M. E., Weber, R. E., & Haug, M. *Adaptation and adaptability: The Bellefaire follow-up study*. New York: Child Welfare League of America, 1966.

Allport, G. "The open system in personality theory." Journal of Abnormal and Social Psychology, 1960, 61(3): 301-310.

Alt, H. "Responsibilities and qualifications of the child care worker." American Journal of Orthopsychiatry, 1953, 23: 670.

Alt, H. *Residential treatment for the disturbed child*. New York: International Universities Press, 1960.

Alt, H. "The concept of success in residential treatment—An administrator's view." Child Welfare, October 1964, 43(8): 423.

Amidon, A. & Brim, O. G. "What do children have to gain from parent education?" Paper prepared for the Advisory Committee on Child Development, National Research Council, National Academy of Science, 1972.

Amos, W. H. "Teeming life as a pond." National Geographic, 1970, 138: 274-278.

Anastasi, A. "Psychology, psychologists, and psychological testing." American Psychologist, 1967, 22: 297-306.

Anderson, J. G. "Effects of social and cultural processes on health." Unpublished manuscript.

Anderson, M. L., Polak, P. R., Grace, D., & Lee, A. "Treatment goals for patients from patients, their families and staff." Journal of the Fort Logan Mental Center, 1965, 3: 101-115.

Anderson, R. L. & Bancroft, T. A. Statistical theory in research. New York: McGraw-Hill, 1952.

Andervont, H. B. "Influence of environment on mammary cancer in mice." Journal of the National Cancer Institute, 1944, 4: 579-581.

Angrist, S., Lefton, M., Dinitz, S., & Pasamanick, B. Tolerance of deviant behavior, posthospital performance levels and rehospitalization. In Proceedings of the Third World Congress of Psychiatry (Vol. 1). Toronto: University of Toronto Press, 1961.

Angrist, S., Lefton, M., Dinitz, S., & Pasamanick, B. Women after treatment: A study of former mental patients and their normal neighbors. New York: Appleton-Century-Crofts, 1968.

Anonymous. "California shelves plans for abolishing hospitals." Psychiatric News, December 19, 1973: 1.

Anthony, R. N. Management accounting. Homewood, Ill.: Richard D. Irwin, 1964.

Appleby, L., Ellis, N. C., Rogers, G. W., & Zimmerman, W. A. "A psychological contribution to the study of hospital structure." Clinical Psychology, 1961, 17: 390-393.

Argyris, C. "Diagnosing defenses against the outsider." Journal of Social Issues, 1952, 8: 24-34.

Aronson, S. H. & Sherwood, C. "Researcher versus practitioner: Problems in social action research." Social Work, 1967, 12(4): 89-96.

Arrow, K. Social choice and individual values. New York: John Wiley, 1951.

Asher, J. J. "Toward a neo-field theory of behavior." Journal of Humanistic Psychology, 1964, 4(2): 85-94.

Asher, J. J. & Post, R. I. "The new field theory: An application to postal automation." Journal of Human Factors Society, 1964. 517-522.

Assael, H. & Eastlack, J. O., Jr. "Better telephone surveys through centralized interviewing." Journal of Advertising Research, 1966, 6: 2-7.

Astor Home for Children. What we have learned: A report on the first 10 years of the Astor Home, a residential treatment center for emotionally disturbed children. New York: Astor Home for Children, 1963.

Athey, K. R., Coleman, J. E., Reitman, A. P., & Tang, J. "Two experiments showing the effect of the interviewer's racial background on responses to questionnaires concerning racial issues." Journal of Applied Psychiatry, 1960, 44(4): 244-246.

Atkinson, A. B. "On the measurement of inequality." Journal of Economic Theory, 1970, 2: 221-224.

Attkisson, C. C. et. al. "A working model for mental health program evaluation." Unpublished manuscript, November 1973.

Aubert, V. "Chance in social affairs." Inquiry, 1959, 2: 1-24.

Aviram, U. & Segal, S. "Exclusion of the mentally ill: Reflection on an old problem in a new context." Archives of General Psychiatry, 1973, 29: 126-131.

Azzi, C. F. & Cox, J. C. "Equity and efficiency in program evaluation." Quarterly Journal of Economics, 1973, 87: 495-502.

# B

Babigian, H. M. The role of psychiatric case registers in the longitudinal study of psychopathology. In M. Roff & D. Ricks (eds.) Life history research in psychopathology. Minneapolis: University of Minnesota Press, 1970.

Bahn, A. K., Gardner, E. A., Alltop, L., Knatterud, G., & Solomon, M. "Admission and prevalence rates for psychiatric facilities in four register areas." American Journal of Public Health, 1966, 56(12).

Baker, F. "An open systems approach to the study of mental hospitals in transition." Community Mental Health Journal, 1969, 5(5).

Bales, R. F. *Interaction process analysis.* Reading, Mass.: Addison-Wesley, 1950.

Ballard, K. B. & Alley, S. R. "Pilot evaluation of selected new careers projects." Unpublished manuscript, AVCO Economic Systems Corporation, Washington, D.C., 1968.

Ballard, R. G. & Mudd, E. H. "Some theoretical and practical problems in evaluating effectiveness of counseling." Social Casework, 1957, 38: 534.

Banfield, E. C. *Political influence.* New York: Free Press, 1961.

Banks, J. A. "The group discussion as an interview technique." Sociological Review, 1957, 5: 75-84.

Bardach, E. *The skill factor in politics: Repealing the mental commitment laws in California.* Berkeley: University of California Press, 1972.

Barker, R. "The social psychology of physical disability." Journal of Social Issues, 1948, 4: 28-34.

Barker, R. *One boy's day.* New York: Harper & Co., 1951.

Barker, R. G. "Explorations in ecological psychology." American Psychologist, 1965, 20(1): 1-14.

Barker, R. G. *Ecological psychology.* Stanford: Stanford University Press, 1968.

Barnard, C. I. *The functions of the executive.* Cambridge, Mass.: Harvard University Press, 1948.

Barnes, F. H. "An American application of the European educateur concept." Paper presented at the Association of Psychiatric Services for Children, Chicago, November 16, 1973.

Barnett, R. J. *Roots of war: The men in institutions that make foreign policy.* New York: Atheneum, 1972.

Barraclough, B. M., Bunch, J., Nelson, B., & Sainsbury, P. "A hundred cases of suicide: Clinical aspects." British Journal of Psychiatry, in press.

Barraclough, B. M. & Shae, M. "Suicide and Samaritan clients." Lancet, 1970, 2: 868.

Barraclough, B. M., Nelson, B., Bunch, J., & Sainsbury, P. "Suicide and barbituate poisoning." Journal of the Royal College of General Practitioners, 1971, 21: 645.

Barraclough, B. M. "A medical approach to suicide prevention." Social Science and Medicine, 1972, 6: 661.

Barraclough, B. M. "Suicide prevention, recurrent affection disorder and Lithium." British Journal of Psychiatry, 1972, 121: 391.

Barraclough, B. M. & Shae, M. "A comparison between Samaritan suicide and living Samaritan clients." British Journal of Psychiatry, 1972, 120: 79.

Barrett, J., Jr., Kuriansky, J., & Gurland, B. "Community tenure following emergency discharge." American Journal of Psychiatry, 1972, 128: 958-964.

Bartko, J., Strauss, J., & Carpenter, W. "An evaluation of taxometric techniques for psychiatric data." Classification Society Bulletin, 1971, 2: 2-28.

Barton, A. H. & Anderson, B. Change in an organizational system: Formalization of a qualitative study. In A. Etzioni (ed.), *A sociological reader on complex organizations.* New York: Holt, Rinehart & Winston, 1969.

Barton, A. *Organizational measurement* (Research Monograph No. 2). Princeton, New Jersey: College Entrance Examination Board, 1961.

Bass, R. D. *A method for measuring continuity of care in a community mental health center.* DHEW Publication No. (HSM) 72-9109, 1972.

Bates, J. "Attitudes towards mental illness." *Mental Hygiene,* 1968, 52: 250-253.

Battistella, R. M. "The course of regional health planning: Review and assessment of recent federal legislation." Medical Care, 1967, 5: 149-161.

Bauer, R. M., ed. *Social indicators.* Cambridge, Mass.: MIT Press, 1966.

Baumol, W. J. "On the social rate of discount." American Economic Review, 1968, 58: 788-802.

Bay, A. P. & Feldman, P. E. *Aide staffing pattern: Its effects on hospital program.* American

Psychiatric Association Mental Hospital Service Supplementary Mailing, No. 155, October, 1962.

Becker, G. S. *Human capital.* Princeton: Princeton University Press, 1964.

Becker, H. S. "Interviewing medical students." American Journal of Sociology, 1956, 62(2): 199-201.

Becker, H. S. & Geer, B. "Participant observation and interviewing: A comparison." Human Organization, 1957, 16(3): 28-32.

Becker, H. S. *Outsiders.* New York: Free Press, 1963.

Becker, H. S. "Whose side are we on?" Social Problems, 1967, 14: 239-247.

Becker, M. H. "Factors affecting diffusion of innovations among health professionals." American Journal of Public Health, 1970, 60(2): 294-304.

Beckman, L. "Locus of control and attitudes toward mental illness among mental health volunteers." Journal of Consulting and Clinical Psychology, 1972, 38: 84-89.

Bee, H. L., Van Egeren, L. F., Streissguth, A. P., Nyman, B. A., & Leckie, M. S. "Social class differences in maternal teaching strategies and speech patterns." Developmental Psychology, 1969, 1: 726-734.

Beigel, A. Evaluation on a shoestring. In Wm. A. Hargreaves et al. (eds.), *Resource materials for community mental health program evaluation.* San Francisco: NIMH, 1974.

Beker, J. & Herman, D. S. "A critical appraisal of the California differential treatment typology of adolescent offenders." Criminology, May 1972.

Bell, R. Q. "A reinterpretation of the direction of effects in studies of socialization." Psychological Review, 1968, 75: 81-95.

Bell, W. Urban neighborhoods and individual behavior. In M. Sherif & C. W. Sherif (eds.), *Problems of youth: Transition to adulthood in a changing world.* Chicago: Aldine, 1967.

Bellar, L. & Black, B. "The rehabilitation of psychotics in the community." American Journal of Orthopsychiatry, 1960, 30: 346.

Beller, E. K. Impact of early education on disadvantaged children. In S. Ryan (ed.), *A report on longitudinal evaluations of preschool programs.* Washington, D.C.: Office of Child Development, 1972.

Beller, E. K. "Direct and inferential observations in the study of children." American Journal of Orthopsychiatry, 1959, 29: 560-573.

Beller, E. K. Personal communication, 1973.

Belnap, I. *Human problems of a state mental hospital.* New York: McGraw-Hill, 1956.

Belson, W. A. "Tape recording: Its effect on accuracy of response in survey interviews." Journal of Marketing Research, 1967, 4: 253-260.

Bendix, R. & Lipset, S. M., eds. *Class, status and power.* New York: Free Press of Glencoe, 1953.

Benjamin, A. & Weatherly, H. E. "Hospital ward treatment of emotionally disturbed children." American Journal of Orthopsychiatry, October, 1947, 17(4).

Benny, M., Riesman, D., & Star, S. "Age and sex in the interview." American Journal of Sociology, 1956, 62(2): 143-152.

Bentinck, C. "Opinions about mental illness held by patients and relatives." Family Process, 1967, 6: 193-207.

Bentinck, C. A., Miller, B. A., & Pokorny, A. D. "Relatives as informants in mental health research." Mental Hygiene, 1969, 53: 446-450.

Bentz, W. K. & Edgerton, J. W. "Consensus on attitudes toward mental illness." Archives of General Psychiatry, 1970, 22: 468-473.

Bentz, W. K. & Edgerton, J. W. "The consequences of labeling a person mentally ill." Social Psychiatry, 1971, 6: 29-33.

Bereiter, C. & Engelmann, S. *Teaching disadvantaged children in the preschool.* Englewood Cliffs, N.J.: Prentice-Hall, 1966.

Berelson, B. et al. *Family planning & population programs.* Chicago: University of Chicago Press, 1966.

Berger, D. G., Rice, C. E., Sewall, L. G., & Lemkau, P. V. "Posthospital evaluation of

Cumulative Bibliography

psychiatric patients: The social adjustment inventory method." Psychiatric Studies and Projects, 1964, 2(15).

Bergin, A. E. "Some implications of psychotherapy research for therapeutic practice." Journal of Abnormal and Social Psychology, 1966, 71: 235-246.

Berkson, J. "Tests of significance considered as evidence." Journal of the American Statistical Association, 1942, 37: 325-335.

Berman, H. J. Legal reasoning. In D. Sills (ed.), *International encyclopedia of the social sciences* (Vol. 9). New York: Macmillan and Free Press, 1968.

Berman, S. P. "Some lessons learned in developing a residential treatment center (Edgewood Children's Center, Webster Groves, Mo.)." Child Welfare, April 1961, 40(4).

Bernstein, B. Social class, speech systems and psycho-therapy. In L. Riessman, B. Cohen, & M. Pearl (eds.), *Mental health of the poor.* New York: Free Press, 1964.

Bertalanffy, L. V. "General systems theory: A critical review." General Systems, 1962, 7: 1-20.

Bertalanffy, L. V. General system theory and psychiatry. In S. Arich (ed.), *American handbook of psychiatry.* New York: Basic Books, 1966.

Bertalanffy, L. V. *General system theory: Foundations, development, applications.* New York: G. Braziller, 1968.

Bettelheim, B. & Sylvester, E. "Therapeutic milieu: For emotional disorders due to institutional living." American Journal of Orthopsychiatry, April, 1948, 18(2): 191.

Bettelheim, B. *Love is not enough.* Glencoe, Ill.: Free Press, 1950.

Bettelheim, B. & Wright, B. "Staff development in a treatment institution." American Journal of Orthopsychiatry, October, 1955, 35(4).

Bettelheim, B. *A home for the heart.* New York: Alfred A. Knopf, 1974.

Biderman, A. D. Social indicators & goals. In R. A. Bauer (ed.), *Social indicators.* Cambridge, Mass.: MIT Press, 1966.

Binet, A. & Simon, T. "Méthodes nouvelles pour le diagnostic du niveau intellectuel des anormaux." Année Psychologie, 1905, 11: 191-244.

Bissell, J. S. *The cognitive effects of preschool programs for disadvantaged children.* Washington, D.C.: National Institute of Child Health and Human Development, 1970.

Bissell, J. S. *Implementation of planned variation in Head Start: First year report.* Washington, D.C.: National Institute of Child Health and Human Development, 1971.

Bissonnier, H. La profession d'educateur specialise et son evolution. Separata de "A Crianco Portugesa" Lisbon, Portugal. In T. Linton, "The European educateur model: An alternative and effective approach to the mental health of children." Journal of Special Education, 3(4): 325.

Bizon, Z., Godorowski, K., Henisz, J., & Razniewski, A. "The attitudes of Warsaw inhabitants toward mental illness." Warsaw, Poland: Laboratory of Social Psychiatry, Department of Psychiatry, Medical School. N.D. (Mimeographed).

Blalock, H. M. *Causal inferences in nonexperimental research.* Chapel Hill, N.C.: University of North Carolina Press, 1961.

Blau, P. M. *Exchange and power in social life.* New York: John Wiley, 1964.

Blayney, J. R. & Hill, I. N. "Fluorine and dental caries." Journal of the American Dental Association (Special Issue), 1967, 74: 233-302.

Blizard, P. "The social rejection of the alcoholic and the mentally ill in New Zealand." Social Science and Medicine, 1970, 4: 513-526.

Block, J. H. *Mastery learning.* New York: Holt, Rinehart & Winston, 1971.

Bloom, B. L. "An ecological analysis of psychiatric hospitalizations." Multivariate Behavioral Research, October, 1968, 3(4): 423-464.

Bloom, B. L. "Human accountability in a community mental health center: Report of an automated system." Community Mental Health Journal, 1972, 8(4): 251-259.

Bloom, B. S. *Compensatory education for cultural deprivation.* New York: Holt, Rinehart & Winston, 1965.

Blum, R. H. & Downing, J. J. "Staff response to innovation in a mental health service." American Journal of Public Health, 1964, 54: 1230-1240.

Blythe, R. H. "The economics of sample-size applied to the scaling of sawlogs." Biometrics Bulletin, 1945, 1: 67-70.

Bockhoven, J. S. *Moral treatment in American psychiatry.* New York: Springer, 1963.

Boek, W. E. & Lade, J. H. "A test of the usefulness of the postcard technique in a mail questionnaire study." Public Opinion Quarterly, 1963, 27(2): 303-306.

Bogardus, E. A. "Measuring social distances." Journal of Applied Sociology, 1925, 9: 299-308.

Bogardus, E. S. *Migration and race attitudes.* Boston: D. C. Heath, 1928.

Bogardus, E. S. "A social distance scale." Sociology and Social Research, 1933, 17: 265-271.

Bogart, L. *Silent politics: Polls and the awareness of public opinion.* New York: John Wiley, 1972.

Bogatz, G. A. & Ball, S. *The second year of Sesame Street: A continuing evaluation* (Vol. 1 & 2). Princeton, N.J.: Educational Testing Service, 1972.

Boguslaw, R. *The new utopians—A study of system design and social change.* Englewood Cliffs, N.J.: Prentice-Hall, 1965.

Bord, R. "Rejection of the mentally ill: Continuities and further developments." Social Problems, 1971, 18: 496-509.

Bordeleau, J., Pelletier, P., Panacci, L., & Tetreault, L. "Authoritarian-humanitarian index in a large mental hospital." Diseases of the Nervous System, 1970, 31 (II, Suppl.): 166-174.

Borgatta, E. F. "Research problems in evaluation of health service demonstrations." Milbank Memorial Fund Quarterly, April, 1966, 44(2).

Boruch, R. F. "Problems in research utilization: Use of social experiments, experimental results and auxiliary data in experiments." Annals of the New York Academy of Sciences: Critical Human Behavioral Research Issues in Social Intervention Programs, June 22, 1973, 218: 56-77.

Bottenberg, R. A. & Ward, J. H., Jr. *Applied multiple linear regression* (PRL-TDR-63-6). Lackland Air Force Base, Texas, 1963.

Boulding, K. E. *The impact of the social sciences.* New Brunswick, N.J.: Rutgers University Press, 1966.

Bovard, E. W. "The balance between negative and positive brain system activity." Perspectives in Biology and Medicine, 1962, 6: 116-127.

Bovard, E. W. "The effects of social stimuli on the response to stress." Psychological Review, 1959, 66: 267-277.

Bower, E., Laurie, R., Struther, C., & Fetherland, R. *Project Re-Ed: New concepts for helping emotionally disturbed children: Evaluation by a panel of visitors.* John F. Kennedy Center for Research on Education and Human Development, George Peabody College for Teachers, Nashville, Tenn., 1969.

Bowman, G. W. & Klopf, G. J. "New careers and roles in the American school: A study of auxiliary personnel in education." Unpublished manuscript, Bank Street College of Education, New York, 1967.

Box, G. E. P. & Tiao, G. C. "A change in level of a non-stationary time series." Biometrika, 1965, 52: 181-192.

Branch, T. "Courage without esteem: Profiles in whistle-blowing." Washington Monthly, 1971, 3(3): 123-140.

Brandt, R. S. Extracts from: "Costs and benefits of the Minneapolis new careers program." Unpublished manuscript, New Careers Research, General College and Minnesota Center for Sociological Research, University of Minnesota, 1968.

Brenner, M. H. *Mental illness and the economy.* Cambridge, Mass.: Harvard University Press, 1973.

Brill, N. Q., Koegler, R. R., Epstein, L. J., & Forgy, E. W. "Control study of psychiatric outpatient treatment." Archives of General Psychiatry, 1964, 10: 581-595.

Bronfenbrenner, U. "The changing American child: A speculative analysis." Merrill-Palmer Quarterly, 1961, 7: 73-84.

Bronfenbrenner, U. When is infant stimulation effective? In D. C. Glass (ed.), *Environmental influences.* New York: Rockefeller University Press, 1968.

Bronfenbrenner, U. Early deprivation: A cross-species analysis. In S. Levine & G. Newton (eds.), *Early experience in behavior.* Springfield, Ill.: Charles C. Thomas, 1968.

Bronfenbrenner, U. *Two worlds of childhood: U.S. and U.S.S.R.* New York: Russell Sage Foundation, 1970.

Bronfenbrenner, U. & Bruner, J. "The President and the children." New York Times, January 31, 1972.

Bronfenbrenner, U. The roots of alienation. In U. Bronfenbrenner (ed.), *Influences on human development.* Hinsdale, Ill.: Dryden Press, 1972.

Bronfenbrenner, U. Developmental research and public policy. In J. M. Romanshyn (ed.), *Social science and social welfare.* New York: Council on Social Work Education, 1973.

Brooks, M. P. "The community action program as a setting for applied research." Journal of Social Issues, 1965, 21(1): 29-40.

Brosin, H. W. et al. "Computers in psychiatry." American Journal of Psychiatry, January 1969 (Supplement), 125(7).

Brown, G., Carstairs, G. M., & Topping, G. "Posthospital adjustment of chronic mental patients." Lancet, 1958, 2: 685-689.

Brown, G., Bone, M., Dalison, B., & Wing, J. *Schizophrenia and social care.* London: Oxford University Press, 1966.

Brown, G., Monck, E., Carstairs, G. M., & Wing, J. "Influence of family life in the course of schizophrenic illness." British Journal of Preventive and Social Medicine, 1962, 16: 55-68.

Brown, G., Birley, J., & Wing, J. "Influence of family life in the course of schizophrenic disorders: A replication." British Journal of Psychiatry, 1972, 121: 241-258.

Brown, J. "Prognosis from presenting symptoms of preschool children with atypical development." American Journal of Orthopsychiatry, 1960, 30: 382-390.

Brown, J. D. *The human nature of organizations.* New York: Amacon, 1973.

Brown, S. J. & Caldwell, B. M. "Social adjustment of children in day care who enrolled prior to or after the age of three." American Journal of Orthopsychiatry, in press.

Bruner, J. & Tagiuri, R. The perception of people. In G. Lindsay (ed.), *Handbook of social psychology.* Reading, Mass.: Addison-Wesley, 1954.

Brunswik, E. Points of view: Components of psychological theorizing. In P. L. Harriman (ed.), *Encyclopedia of psychology.* New York: Citadel, 1946.

Brunswik, E. *Systematic and representative design of psychological experiments.* University of California Syllabus Series (No. 304), 1947.

Brunswik, E. *Perception and the representative design of psychological experiments.* Berkeley: University of California Press, 1956.

Bryant, E. C., Gardner, I., Jr., & Goldman, M. "Responses on racial attitudes as affected by interviewers of different ethnic groups." Journal of Social Psychology, 1966, 70(1): 95-100.

Buchanan, G. & Wholey, J. "Federal level evaluation." Evaluation, 1972, 1(1): 17-22.

Buchanan, J. N. & Tullock, G. *The calculus of consent: Logical foundations of constitutional democracy.* Ann Arbor: University of Michigan Press, 1969.

Bucher, R., Fritz, C., & Quarantelli, E. L. "Tape recorded interviews in social research." American Sociological Review, 1956, 21: 359-364.

Bucher, R., Fritz, C., & Quarantelli, E. L. "Tape recorded research: Some field and data processing problems." Public Opinion Quarterly, 1956, 20(2): 427-439.

Buckley, W. Society as a complex adaptive system. In W. Buckley (ed.), *Modern systems research for the behavioral scientist.* Chicago: Aldine, 1968.

Bullough, B. *Poverty, ethnic identity and health care.* New York: Appleton-Century-Crofts, 1972.

Bullough, B. "Poverty, ethnic identity and preventive health care." Journal of Health and Social Behavior, 1972, 13: 349-359.

Bullough, B. "The source of ambulatory health services as it relates to preventive care." American Journal of Public Health, June, 1974, 64(6).

Burdock, E. I., Hakerem, G., Hardesty, A. S., & Zubin, J. "A ward behavior rating scale for mental patients." Journal of Clinical Psychology, 1960, 16: 246-247.

Burgess, J., Nelson, R. H., & Wallhaus, R. "Network analysis as a method for the evaluation of service delivery systems." Community Mental Health Journal, in press.

Burns, E. M. *Health services for tomorrow.* New York: Dunellen, 1973.

Buros, O. K. *Tests in print.* Highland Park, N.J.: Gryphon Press, 1961.

Buros, O. K. *Seventh mental measurements yearbook.* Highland Park, N.J.: Gryphon Press, 1972.

Buros, O. K. *Seventh mental measurements yearbook.* Rutgers, N.J.: Rutgers University Press, 1972.

Burstein, A. C. *New York Community Corporation Areas* (The Burstein Report). Report of N.Y.C. Human Resources Administration, March 1972.

Buss, A. H., Fischer, H., & Simmons, A. J. "Aggression and hostility in psychiatric patients." Journal of Consulting Psychology, 1962 26: 84-89.

Butkus, D., Powell, J., Souders, C., & Boroskin, A. *Individualized data base, manual of reports* (IDP Pub. Series-No. 5). Pomona, California: Neuropsychiatric Institute, Pacific State Hospital, January, 1974.

## C

Cahalan, D., Tamulomis, V., & Verner, H. W. "Interviewer bias involved in certain types of attitude questions." International Journal of Opinion and Attitude Research, 1947, 1(1): 63-77.

Caldwell, B. M., & Smith, L. E. "Day care for the very young—Prime opportunity for primary prevention." American Journal of Public Health, 1970, 60: 690-697.

Calhoun, J. B. "Population density and social pathology." Scientific American, 1962, 206(32): 139-146.

Campbell, A. & Converse, P. E. *The human meaning of social change.* New York: Russell Sage Foundation, 1972.

Campbell, D. T. "Factors relevant to the validity of experiments in social settings." Psychological Bulletin, 1957, 54: 297-312.

Campbell, D. T. & Clayton, K. N. "Avoiding regression effects in panel studies of communication impact." Studies in public communication. Department of Sociology, University of Chicago, 1961, No. 3, 99-118 (Bobbs-Merrill Reprint No. S-353).

Campbell, D. T. & Fiske, D. W. "Convergent and discriminant validation by the multitrait-multimethod matrix." Psychological Bulletin, 1959, 56: 81-105.

Campbell, D. T. & Stanley, J. C. *Experimental and quasi-experimental designs for research.* Chicago: Rand McNally, 1963.

Campbell, D. T. From description to experimentaion: Interpreting trends as quasi-experiments. In C. W. Harris (ed.), *Problems in measuring change.* Madison: University of Wisconsin Press, 1963.

Campbell, D. T. & Stanely, J. C. Experimental and quasi-experimental designs for research on teaching. In N. L. Gage (ed.), *Handbook of research on teaching.* Chicago: Rand McNally, 1963. (Reprinted as *Experimental and quasi-experimental design for research.* Chicago: Rand McNally, 1966.)

Campbell, D. T. "Invited therapy in an archival or institutional-records setting: With comments on the problem of turndowns." Northwestern University, August, 1965. (Mimeographed).

Campbell, D. T. Administrative experimentaion, institutional records, and nonreactive measures. In J. C. Stanley (ed.), *Improving experimental design and statistical analysis.* Chicago: Rand McNally, 1967.

Campbell, D. T. & Stanley, J. C. Experimental and quasi-experimental designs for research on teaching. In N. L. Gage (ed.), *Handbook of research on research and teaching.* Chicago: Rand McNally, 1963. (Reprinted as *Experimental and quasi-experimental design for research.* Chicago: Rand McNally, 1966.)

Campbell, D. T. & Ross, H. L. "The Connecticut crackdown on speeding: Time-series data in quasi-experimental analysis." Law and Society Review, 1968, 3(1): 33-53.

Campbell, D. T. Quasi-experimental design. In D. L. Sills (ed.), *International encyclopedia of the social sciences* (Vol. 5). New York: Macmillan and Free Press, 1968.

Campbell, D. T. & Stanley, J. C. *Experimental and quasi-experimental designs for research.* Chicago: Rand McNally, 1968.

Campbell, D. T. "Reforms as experiments." American Psychologist, 1969, 24: 409-429.

Campbell, D. T. "Treatment-effect correlations and temporal attenuation of relationships in longitudinal studies." Northwestern University, December, 1969. (Mimeographed).

Campbell, D. T. & Erlebacher, A. How regression artifacts in quasi-experimental evaluations can mistakenly make compensatory education look harmful. In J. Hellmuth (ed.), *Compensatory education: A national debate* (Vol. 3). New York: Brunner/Mazel, 1970.

Campbell, D. T. & Ross, H. L. The Connecticut crackdown on speeding: Time-series data in quasi-experimental analysis. In E. R. Tufte (ed.), *The quantitative analysis of social problems.* Reading, Mass.: Addison-Wesley, 1970.

Campbell, D. T. "Time-series of annual same-grade testings in the evaluation of compensatory educational experiments." Northwestern University, April, 1970. (Mimeographed).

Campbell, D. T. "Experimentation revisited." Evaluation, 1973, 1(3): 7-13.

Campbell, D. T. Making the case for randomized assignment to treatments by considering the alternatives: Six ways in which quasi-experimental evaluations in compensatory education tend to underestimate effects. In C. A. Bennett & A. Lumsdaine (eds.), *Experiments and evaluations.* New York: Academic Press, in press.

Campbell, D. T. "Assessing the impact of planned social change." Lecture at Conference on Social Psychology, Budapest, Hungary, May, 1974.

Cannell, C. F. & Kahn, R. L. Interviewing. In G. Lindzey & E. Aronson (eds.), *The handbook of social psychology* (Vol. 2). Reading, Mass.: Addison-Wesley, 1968.

Cannon, W. B. "Stresses and strains of homeostasis." American Journal of Medical Science, 1935, 1: 189.

Canter, F. M. & Shoemaker, R. "The relationship between authoritarian attitudes and attitudes toward mental patients." Nursing Research, 1960, 9: 39-41.

Cantrell, R. P., Cantrell, M. L., Huddleston, C. M., & Woolridge, R. L. "Contingency contracting with school problems." Journal of Applied Behavior Analysis, 1969, 2(4): 215-220.

Cantril, H. *Gauging public opinion.* Princeton: Princeton University Press, 1944.

Cantril, H., Ames, A., Hastorf, A., & Ittelson, W. "Psychology and scientific research. Part I: The nature of scientific inquiry. Part II: Scientific inquiry and scientific method. Part III: The transactional view in psychological research." Science, 1949, 110: 461-464; 491-497; 517-522.

Caplan, N. & Nelson, S. D. "On being useful: The nature and consequences of psychological research on social problems." American Psychologist, 1973, 28(3): 199-211.

Caplan, R. *Psychiatry and the community in nineteenth-century America.* New York: Basic Books, 1969.

Caro, F. G., ed. *Readings in evaluation research.* New York: Russell Sage Foundation, 1971.

Carr, J. E. & Whittenbaugh, J. "Sources of disagreement in the perception of Psychotherapy outcomes." Journal of Clinical Psychology, 1969, 25(1): 16-21.

Carse, J., Panton, N., & Watt. A. "A district mental health service: The Worthing experiment." Lancet, 1958, 1: 39.

Carson, R. C. *Interaction concepts of personality.* Chicago: Aldine, 1969.

Carstairs, G. M. The social limits of eccentricity: An English study. In M. K. Opler (ed.), *Culture and mental health: Cross-cultural studies.* New York: Macmillan, 1969.

Cartwright, D. C. & Howard, K. "Multivariate analysis of gang delinquency: I ecological influences." Multivariate Behavioral Research, 1966, 1: 321-371.

Cartwright, D. S. Ecological variables. In E. F. Borgatta (ed.), *Sociological methodology.* San Francisco: Jossey-Bass, 1969.

Cassel, J. & Tyroler, H. A. "Epidemiological studies of culture change I: Health status and recency of industrialization." Archives of Environmental Health, 1961, 3: 25.

Cassel, J. "The relation of the urban environment to health." Mt. Sinai Medical Journal, in press.

Cassel, J. Health consequences of population density and crowding. In *Rapid population growth*. Baltimore: National Academy of Sciences, Johns Hopkins Press, 1971.

Cassel, R., Carlton, M., & Rothe, M. "Comparing opinions about mental illness for hospital attendants and practical nursing students." Nursing Research, 1970, 19: 268-272.

Cattell, R. B. *The scientific analysis of personality.* Baltimore: Penquin, 1965.

Cattell, R. B. Psychological theory and scientific method. In R. B. Cattell (ed.), *Handbook of multivariate experimental psychology.* Chicago: Rand McNally, 1966.

Cattell, R. B., ed. *Handbook of multivariate experimental psychology.* Chicago: Rand McNally, 1966.

Caudill, W. *The mental hospital as a small society.* Cambridge, Mass.: Harvard University Press, 1958.

Caudill, W. *The psychiatric hospital as a small society.* Cambridge, Mass.: Harvard University Press, 1958.

Central Policy Review Staff. *A framework for government research and development.* Cmnd. 5046, London: H.M.S.O., 1971.

Chadwick, E. *Report on the sanitary condition of the labouring population of Great Britain.* Edinburgh: Edinburgh University Press, 1965. (Originally published, 1842.)

Chandler, M. "An evaluation of the group interview." Human Organization, 1954, 13(2): 26-29.

Chapin, F. S. *Experimental design in sociological research.* New York: Harper, 1947.

Chapin, F. S. *Experimental designs in sociological research* (rev. ed.). New York: Harper, 1955.

Chase, S. B., Jr., ed. *Problems in public expenditure analysis.* Washington, D.C.: Brookings Institution, 1968.

Chein, I. *Some epidemiological vectors of delinquency and its control: Outline of a project.* New York: Research Center for Human Relations, New York University, 1963. (Mimeographed).

Cheng, T. H. "Schistosomiasis in mainland China: A review of research and control programs since 1949." American Journal of Tropical Medicine and Hygiene, 1971, 20: 26-53.

Child Welfare League of America, Inc. *From chaos to order: A collective view of the residential treatment of children.* New York: Child Welfare League of America, Inc., 1972.

Childers, B. "A ward program based on graduated activities and group effort." Hospital and Community Psychiatry, 1967, 18: 289-295.

Chin, R. The utility of systems models and developmental models for practitioners. In W. G. Bennis, K. D. Benne, & R. Chin (eds.), *The planning of change* (second ed.). New York: Holt, Rinehart & Winston, 1961.

Chin-Shong, E. *Rejection of the mentally ill: A comparison with the findings on ethnic prejudice.* Unpublished doctoral dissertation, Columbia University, 1968.

Chinsky, J. & Rappaport, J. "Attitude change in college students and chronic patients: A dual perspective." Journal of Consulting and Clinical Psychology, 1970, 35: 388-394.

Chipman, J. S. The nature and meaning of equilibrium in economic theory. In D. Martindale (ed.), *Functionalism in the social sciences: The strength and limits of functionalism in anthropology, economics, political science, and sociology.* Philadelphia: American Academy of Political and Social Science, 1965.

Christenson, W. N. & Hinkle, L. E. "Differences in illness and prognostic signs in two groups of young men." Journal of the American Medical Association, 1961, 177: 247-253.

Christian, J. J. & Williamson, H. O. "Effect of crowding on experimental gramuloma formation in mice." Proceedings of the Society of Experimental and Biological Medicine, 1958, 99: 385-387.

Churchman, C. W. & Ackoff, R. L. "Towards an experimental measure of personality." Psychological Review, 1947, 1(54): 41-51.

Ciarlo, J. Personal communication , August, 1974.

Cicirelli, V. et al. *The impact of Head Start: An evaluation of the effects of Head Start on children's cognitive and affective development.* Report presented to the Office of Economic Opportunity pursuant to Contract B89-4536, June, 1969, Westinghouse Learning Corporation, Ohio University. Distributed by Clearinghouse for Federal Scientific and technical Information, U.S. Department of Commerce, National Bureau of Standards, Institute for Applied Technology (PB 184 328).

Clark, A. W. & Binks, N. M. "Relation of age and education to attitudes toward mental illness." Psychological Reports, 1966, 19: 649-650.

Clausen, J. & Yarrow, M. R., eds. "The impact of mental illness on the family." Journal of Social Issues, 1955, 11(4).

Clausen, J. *The marital relationship antecedent to hospitalization of a spouse for mental illness.* Annual Meeting of American Sociological Association, Chicago, September, 1959.

Clausen, J. Mental disorders. In R. K. Merton & R. Nisbet (eds.), *Contemporary social problems.* New York: Harcourt Brace Jovanovich, 1971.

Clawson, M. *Methods of measuring the demand for and value of outdoor recreation* (Reprint No. 10). Washington, D.C.: Resources for the Future, Inc., 1959.

Clawson, M. & Knetsch, J. L. *Economics of outdoor recreation.* Baltimore: Johns Hopkins Press, 1966.

Cline, D. W., Rouzer, D. L., & Bransford, D. "Goal attainment scaling as a method for evaluating mental health programs." American Journal of Psychiatry, 1973, 130: 105-108.

Cloward, R. A. & Ohlin, L. E. *Delinquency and opportunity.* Glencoe: Free Press, 1961.

Cobb, S., King, S., & Chen, E. "Differences between respondents and non-respondents in a morbidity survey involving clinical examinations." Journal of Chronic Diseases, 1957, 6: 95-108.

Cohen, A. K. & Short, J. F., Jr. Crime and juvenile delinquency. In R. K. Merton & R. Nisbet (eds.), *Contemporary social problems.* New York: Harcourt Brace Jovanovich, 1971.

Cohen, D. K. "Politics & research: Evaluation of social action programs in education." Review of Educational Research, 1970, 40: 213-238.

Cohen, J. "Factors of resistance to the resources of the behavioral sciences." Journal of Legal Education, 1959, 12: 67-70.

Cohen, J. & Struening, E. L. "Opinions about mental illness in the personnel of two large mental hospitals." Journal of Abnormal and Social Psychology, 1962, 64: 349-360.

Cohen, J. & Struening, E. L. "Opinions about mental illness: Mental hospital occupational profile clusters." Psychological Reports, 1963, 12: 111-124.

Cohen, J. *A rationale and method for psychiatric hospital assessment* (Intramural Report 64-5). Psychiatric Evaluation Project, Veterans Administration Hospital, Washington, D.C., 1964.

Cohen, J. & Struening, E. L. "Opinions about mental illness: Hospital social atmosphere and patient time in the hospital." Journal of Consulting Psychology, 1964, 28: 291-298.

Cohen, J. & Struening, E. L. "Opinions about mental illness: Hospital social atmosphere profiles and their relevance to effectiveness." Journal of Consulting Psychology, 1964, 28: 291-298.

Cohen, J. Some statistical issues in psychological research. In B. B. Wolman (ed.), *Handbook of clinical psychology.* New York: McGraw-Hill, 1965.

Cohen, J. & Struening, E. L. "Opinions about mental illness: Hospital differences in attitude for eight occupational groups." Psychological Reports, 1965, 17: 25-26.

Cohen, J. "Multiple regression analysis as a general data-analytic system." Psychological Bulletin, 1968, 70: 426-443.

Cohen, J. "Prognostic factors in functional psychosis: A study in multivariate methodology." Transactions of the New York Academy of Science, 1968, 30: 833-840.

Cohen, J. *Statistical power analysis for the behavioral sciences.* New York: Academic Press, 1969.

Cohen, J. "Eta-squared and partial eta-squared in fixed factor ANOVA designs." Educational and Psychological Measurement, 1973, 33: 107-112.

Cohen, J. & Cohen, P. "A method for handling missing data in multiple regression/correlation." Paper presented at the Annual Meeting of the Society of Multivariate Experimental Psychology, November 1973.

Coleman, J. S. et al. *Equality of educational opportunity.* Washington, D.C.: Government Printing Office, 1966.

Coleman, J. S., Katz, E., & Mensel, H. *Medical innovation: A diffusion study.* New York: Bobbs-Merrill, 1966.

Coleman, J. S. "Loss of power." American Sociological Review, 1973, 38: 1-17.

Coles, R. *Children of crisis: A study of courage and fear* (Vol. I). Boston: Atlantic-Little, Brown, 1967.

Coles, R. *Children of crisis: Migrants, sharecroppers, mountaineers* (Vol. II). Boston: Atlantic-Little, Brown, 1971.

Colombotos, J., Elinson, J., & Loewenstein, R. "Effect of interviewer's sex on interview responses." Public Health Reports, 1968, 83(8): 685-690.

Colombotos, J. "Personal versus telephone interviews." Public Health Reports, 1969, 84(9): 773-782.

Commission on Community Health Services. *Health is a community affair.* Cambridge, Mass.: Harvard University Press, 1967.

Comrey, A. L. *A first course in factor analysis.* New York: Academic Press, 1973.

Conant, E. Personal communication, February 1970.

Conger, J. J., Sawrey, W., & Turrell, E. S. "The role of social experience in the production of gastric ulcers in hooded rats placed in a conflict situation." Journal of Abnormal and Social Psychology, 1958, 57: 216.

Connery, R. H. et al. *The politics of mental health.* New York: Columbia University Press, 1968.

Conway, L. "The school community worker program." Unpublished manuscript, Survey Research Center, University of California at Berkeley, 1967.

Cooley, W. W. & Lohnes, P. R. *Multivariate procedures for the behavioral sciences.* New York: John Wiley, 1962. (New edition published 1971.)

Coombs, L. & Freedman, R. "Use of telephone interviews in a longitudinal fertility study." Public Opinion Quarterly, 1964, 28: 112-117.

Cooper, E. M. *Guidelines for a minimum statistical and accounting system for community mental health centers.* DHEW Publication No. (ADM) 74-14, 1973.

Coppen, A., Noguera, R., Bailey, J., Burns, B. H., Swani, M. S., Hare, E. H., Gardner, R., & Maggs, R. "Prophylactic lithium in affective disorders." Lancet, 1971, 2: 275.

Corrazzini, A. "The decision of invest in vocational education." Journal of Human Resources, 1968, 3: 82-120.

Coser, L. A. *The functions of social conflict.* Glencoe: Free Press, 1964.

Coston, R. & Kerr, W. D. "The effects of an abnormal psychology course on students' attitudes towards mental illness." Journal of Educational Psychology, 1962, 53: 214-218.

Cottrell, L. S. Foreword. In E. A. Suchman, *Evaluative research.* New York: Russell Sage Foundation, 1967.

Couch, A. & Kenniston, K. "Yeasayers and naysayers: Agreeing response set as a personality variable." Journal of Abnormal and Social Psychology, 1960, 60: 151-174.

Cox, D. R. *Planning of experiments.* New York: John Wiley, 1958.

Cox, K. R. *Conflict, power and politics in the city: A geographic view.* New York: McGraw-Hill, 1973.

Crano, W. D. & Brewer, M. B. *Principles of research in social psychology.* New York: McGraw-Hill, 1973.

Crocetti, G. & Lemkau, P. "Public opinion of psychiatric home care in an urban area." American Journal of Public Health, 1963, 53: 409-417.

Crocetti, G. & Lemkau, P. "On rejection of the mentally ill." American Sociological Review, 1965, 30: 577-578.

Crocetti, G., Spiro, H., & Siassi, I. "Are the ranks closed? Attitudinal social distance and mental illness." American Journal of Psychiatry, 1971, 127: 1121-1127.

Crocetti, G., Spiro, H., Lemkau, P., & Siassi, I. "Multiple models and mental illnesses: A rejoinder to failure of a moral enterprise: Attitudes of the public toward mental illness, by T. R. Sarbin and J. C. Mancuso." Journal of Consulting and Clinical Psychology, 1972, 39: 1-5.

Cronbach, L. J. *Essentials of psychological testing* (rev. ed.). New York: Harper & Row, 1960.

Cronbach, L. J. & Azuma, H. "Internal-consistency reliability formulas applied to randomly sampled single-factor tests: An empirical comparison." Educational & Psychological Measurement, 1962, 22: 645-666.

Cronbach, L. J. & Furby, L. "How we should measure "change"–Or should we?" Psychological Bulletin, 1970, 74: 68-80.

Cronbach, L. J. & Meehl, P. "Construct validity in psychological tests." Psychological Bulletin, 1955, 52: 281-302.

Cross, H. J. "The outcome of psychotherapy: A selective analysis of research findings." Journal of Consulting Psychology, 1964, 28: 413-417.

Crow, C. M., Mowbray, R., & Bloch, S. "Attitudes of medical students to mental illness." Journal of Medical Education, 1970, 45: 594-599.

Croxton, F. E., Cowden, D. J., & Klein, S. *Applied general statistics* (third ed.). Englewood Cliffs, N.J.: Prentice-Hall, 1967.

Cudaback, D. "Summary report on Welfare Service Aide Project." Unpublished manuscript, School of Social Welfare, University of California at Berkeley, 1968.

Cumming, E. & Cumming, J. *Closed ranks: An experiment in mental health education.* Cambridge, Mass.: Harvard University Press, 1957.

Cumming, E. *Systems of social regulation.* New York: Atherton Press, 1968.

Cumming, E. Community psychiatry in a divided labor. In J. Zubin & F. Freyhan (eds.), *Social psychiatry.* New York: Grune & Stratton, 1968.

Cumming, J. & Cumming, E. "On the stigma of mental illness." Community Mental Health Journal, 1965, 1: 135-143.

Curran, W., Laska, E., Kaplan, H., & Bank, R. "Protection of privacy and confidentiality." Science, November 1973, 182: 797-802.

Curston, E. E. "On correlation coefficients." Psychometrika, 1966, 31: 605-607.

# D

Dabrowski, K. "Negative adjustment and positive maladjustment." Paper presented at the Fourth International Congress of Social Psychiatry, Jerusalem, Israel, May 1972.

Dahl, R. A. & Lindblom, C. E. *Politics, economics, and welfare.* New York: Harper & Row, 1953.

Dahling, R. L. Shannon's information theory: the spread of an idea. In *Studies of innovation and of communication to the public studies in the utilization of behavioral science* (Vol. 2). Stanford, Calif.: Institute for Communication Research, Stanford University, 1962.

Dasgupta, P., Sen, M., & Marglin, S. A. *Guidelines for project evaluation.* New York: United Nations, 1972.

David, M. "The validity of income reported by a sample of families who received welfare assistance during 1959." Journal of the American Statistical Association, 1962, 57(321): 680-685.

Davids, A., Ryan, R., & Salvatore, P. "Effectiveness of residential treatment." American Journal of Orthopsychiatry, April 1968, 38: 469-475.

Davis, D. E. & Read, C. P. "Effect of behaviour on development of resistance in trichinosis." Proceedings of the Society of Experimental and Biological Medicine, 1958, 99: 269-272.

Davis, H. Innovation and change. In S. Feldman (ed.), *Administration in mental health.* Springfield, Ill.: Charles C. Thomas, 1973.

Davis, J., Freeman, H., & Simmons, O. "Rehospitalization and performance levels of former mental patients." Social Problems, 1957, 5: 37-44.

Davis, J. E. *Empirical dimensions of psychiatric hospital organization* (Intramural Report No. 64-5). Psychiatric Evaluation Project, Veterans Administration Hospital, Washington, D.C.

Davis, K. "Population policy: Will current programs succeed?" Science, November 10, 1967, 158: 734-736.

Davis, K. "The climax of population growth." California Medicine, 1970, 113: 33-39.

Dawes, R. M. & Corrigan, B. "Linear models in decision making." Psychological Bulletin, 1974, 81: 97-106.

Dean, L. R. Interaction, reported and observed: The case of one local union. *Human Organization,* 1958, 17(3): 36-44.

Deiter, J. B., Hanford, D. B., Hummel, R. T., & Lubach, J. E. "Brief inpatient treatment—A pilot study." Mental Hospitals, 1965, 16: 95-98.

Deming, W. E. *Some theory of sampling.* New York: John Wiley, 1950.

Deming, W. E. Boundaries of statistical inference. In N. L. Johnson & H. Smith (eds.), *New developments in survey sampling.* New York: John Wiley, 1969.

Denzin, N. K. *The research act.* Chicago: Aldine, 1970.

Denzin, N. K. The uses and misuses of social science knowledge. In N. K. Denzin (ed.), *The values of social science.* Chicago: Aldine, 1970.

DeSainz, D. "The public health nurse as research interviewer." Nursing Outlook, 1962, 10: 514-516.

Deutsch, M. et al. *Regional research and resource center in early childhood: Final report.* Washington, D.C.: U.S. Office of Economic Opportunity, 1971.

Deutsch, M. "Minority group and class status as related to social and personality factors in scholastic achievement." Society for Applied Anthropology Monograph No. 2. Ithaca, N.Y.: New York State School of Industrial and Labor Relations, Cornell University, 1960.

Deutsch, M., Taleporos, E., & Victor, J. A brief synopsis of an initial enrichment program in early childhood. In S. R. Ryan (ed.), *A report on longitudinal evaluations of preschool programs.* Washington, D.C.: Office of Child Development, 1972.

Deutscher, I. "Words and deeds: Social science and social policy." Social Problems, 1966, 13: 235-254.

Dewey, J. & Bentley, A. F. *Knowing and the known.* Boston: Boston Press, 1949.

Dexter, L. A. "Role relationships and conceptions of neutrality in interviewing." American Journal of Sociology, 1956, 62: 153-157.

Deykin, E. "The reintegration of the chronic schizophrenic patient discharged to his family and community as perceived by the family." Mental Hygiene, 1961, 45: 235-246.

Diamond, S. *Information and error.* New York: Basic Books, 1959.

Dickey, B. A. "Intra-staff conflict, morale, and treatment effectiveness in a therapeutic community setting." Paper presented at the annual meeting of the American Psychological Association, September 1964.

Dillehay, R. "On the irrelevance of the calssical negative evidence concerning the effect of attitudes on behavior." American Psychologist, 1973, 28: 887-891.

DiLorenzo, L. T. *Pre-kindergarten programs for educationally disadvantaged children: Final report.* Washington, D.C.: U.S. Office of Education, 1969.

Dinnage, R., Pringle, M., & Kellmer, M. L. *Residential child care—Facts and fallacies.* New York: Humanities Press, 1967.

Dittman, A. T. & Kitchener, H. L. "Life space interviewing and individual play therapy—A comparison of techniques." American Journal of Orthopsychiatry, 1959, 29: 19-26.

Dixon, C. R. "Courses on psychology and students' attitudes toward mental illness." Psychological Reports, 1967, 20: 50.

Dohrenwend, B. & Snell, B. "Some effects of open and closed questions on respondent answers." Human Organization, 1965, 24(2): 175-184.

Dohrenwend, B. "Social status and psychological disorder: An issue of substance and an issue of method." American Sociological Review, 1966, 31: 14-34.

Dohrenwend, B. & Chin-Shong, E. "Social status and attitudes toward psychological disorders: The problem of tolerance of deviance." American Sociological Review, 1967, 32: 417-432.

Dohrenwend, B., Snell, B., Colombotos, J., & Dohrenwend, B. P. "Social distance interviewer effects." Public Opinion Quarterly, 1968, 32(3): 410-422.

Dohrenwend, B. P. & Dohrenwend, B. *Social status and psychological disorder: A causal inquiry.* New York: Wiley Interscience, 1969.

Dohrenwend, B. P. "Psychiatric disorder in general populations: Problem of the untreated case." American Journal of Public Health, June 1970, 60: 1052-1064.

Dohrenwend, B. P., Egri, G., & Mendelsohn, F. "Psychiatric disorder in general populations: A study of the problem of clinical judgment." American Journal of Psychiatry, April 1971, 127(10): 1304-1312.

Dorfman, R., ed. *Measuring benefits of government investments.* Washington, D.C.: Brookings Institution, 1965.

Dotson, F. "Intensive interviewing in community research." Journal of Educational Sociology, 1954, 27: 225-230.

DuBois, P. H. *Multivariate correlational analysis.* New York: Harper, 1957.

DuBos, R. *Man adapting.* New Haven: Yale University Press, 1965.

DuBos, R. "The human environment in technological societies." Rockefeller Review, July-August 1968.

Duhl, L. J. *The urban condition: People and policy in the metropolis.* New York: Basic Books, 1963.

Duhl, L. J. & Leopold, R. L., eds. *Mental health and social policy.* San Francisco: Jossey-Bass, 1968.

Duncan, O. D. "Path analysis: Sociological examples." American Journal of Sociology, 1966, 72: 1-16.

Dunham, H. W. & Weinberg, S. K. *The culture of the state mental hospital.* Detroit: Wayne State University Press, 1960.

Dunham, H. W. "Social structure and mental disorders: Complete hypotheses of explanation." Milbank Memorial Fund Quarterly, 1961, 39: 259-310.

Dunigan, J. *Mental hospital career and family expectations.* Cleveland, Ohio: Laboratory of Psychosocial Research, Cleveland Psychiatric Institute. (Mimeograph).

Durkheim, E. *[The division of labor in society]* (G. Simpson, trans.). New York: Free Press of Glencoe, 1964. (Originally published, 1933).

Durkheim, E. *[Suicide]* (J. Spaulding & G. Simpson, eds. and trans.). Glencoe: Free Press, 1951.

Durkin, R. "Social function of psychological interpretations." American Journal of Orthopsychiatry, 1967, 37: 956-962.

Durkin, R. "Personality and milieu: A theory of social influence." Unpublished manuscript, 1972.

Durkin, R. "A model for a summer camp and follow-up program for poverty and/or disturbed teenagers." Unpublished manuscript, 1974.

Dworkin, G. "Teaching the boys in the back rooms: A program for blue-collar workers." Mental Hygiene, 1969, 53: 258-262.

**E**

"The Eagleton affair: Stigma of mental disorder." Science News, August 5, 1972, 102: 85.

Earhardt, C. "Statistics, a trap for the unwary." Obstetrics and Gynecology, 1959, 14: 549-554.

Earickson, R. "The spatial behavior of hospital patients: a behavioral approach to spatial interaction in metropolitan Chicago." University of Chicago, Department of Geography, Research paper No. 124, 1970.

Eaton, L. & Menalascino, F. "Psychotic reactions of childhood: A follow-up study." American Journal of Orthopsychiatry, 1967, 37: 521-529.

Ebbeson, E. "Attitudes toward attitude change." Contemporary Psychology, 1971, 16: 36-37.

Eber, H. W. "Multivariate analysis of a vocational rehabilitation system." Multivariate Behavioral Research Monograph (No. 66-1). Fort Worth, Texas: TCU Press, 1966.

Eber, H. W. "Multivariate analysis of a rehabilitation system: cross validation and extension." Multivariate Behavioral Research, 1967, 2(4): 477-484.

Eckland, B. K. "Retrieving mobile cases in longitudinal surveys." Public Opinion Quarterly, 1968, 32: 51-64.

Eckstein, O. *Water-resource development.* Cambridge, Mass.: Harvard University Press, 1958.

Eckstein, O. A survey of the theory of public expenditure criteria. In J. M. Buchanan (ed.), *Public finances: needs, sources, and utilization.* Princeton: Princeton University Press, 1961.

Edgerton, R. B. & Karno, M. "Mexican-American bilingualism and the perception of mental illness." Archives of General Psychiatry, 1971, 24: 286-290.

Edwards, A. E. *Experimental design in psychological research* (rev. ed.). New York: Rinehart, 1960.

Edwards, A. L. *Techniques of attitude scale construction.* New York: Appleton-Century-Crofts, 1957.

Edwards, A. L. "Social desirability or acquiescence in the MMPI: a case study with the SD scale." Journal of Abnormal and Social Psychology, 1961, 63: 351-359.

Edwards, J. H. Familial predisposition in man. In C. E. Ford and H. Harris (eds.), *New aspects of human genetics* (Vol. 25). London: British Medical Bulletin, 1969.

Edwards, W. "Tactical note on the relation between scientific and statistical hypotheses." Psychological Bulletin, June 1965, 63(6): 400-402.

Edwards, W. "Social utilities." The Engineering Economist, Summer Symposium Series, VI, 1971.

Edwards, W., Lindman, H. & Savage, L. J. "Bayesian statistical inference for psychological research." Psychological Review, 1963, 70: 193-242.

Edwards, W., Phillips, L. D., Hays, W. L., & Goodman, B. C. "Probabilistic information processing systems: design and evaluation." IEEE *Transaction on Systems Science and Cybernetics,* 1968, SSC-4: 248-265.

Efthim, A. "We care in Kansas: the non-professional's revolt." Nation, August 5, 1968: 70-72.

Ehrenreich, B. & Ehrenreich, J. *The American health empire: power, profits, and politics.* New York: Vintage Books, 1971.

Ehrlich, J. S. & Riesman, D. "Age and authority in the interview." Public Opinion Quarterly, 1961, 25(1): 39-56.

Eiduson, B. T. "Replacing traditional records by event reports." Hospital and Community Psychiatry, March 1966, 17(3).

Eisenberg, L. "The autistic child in adolescence." American Journal of Psychiatry, 1956, 112: 607-612.

Eisenberg, L. "The course of childhood schizophrenia." Archives of Neurology and Psychiatry, 1957, 78: 69-83.

Elinson, J., Padella, E., & Perkins, M. *Public image of mental health services.* New York: Mental Health Materials Center, 1967.

Elliott, L. L. "Effects of item construction and respondent aptitude on response acquiescence." Educational and Psychological Measurement, 1961, 21: 405-415.

Ellison, D. L., Hessler, R. M., Hitchcock, J., & Wolford, J. "Problems in developing a community-based research component for a mental health center." Mental Hygiene, 1971, 55(3): 312-318.

Ellsworth, R. B. *The MACC behavioral adjustment scale, form II.* Beverly Hills, Calif.: Western Psychological Services, 1962.

Ellsworth, R. B. "A behavioral study of staff attitudes toward mental illness." Journal of Abnormal Psychology, 1965, 70: 194-200.

Ellsworth, R. B. "Patient and staff perceptions of relatively effective and ineffective psychiatric treatment programs." Paper presented at 10th annual conference, Veterans Administration Cooperative Studies in Psychiatry, New Orleans, March 1965.

Ellsworth, R. B. "Measuring personal adjustment and role skills (the PARS Scale for veterans)." Newsletter for Research in Psychology, 1968, 10: 9-12.

Ellsworth, R. B. "Instructions for scoring patient Perception of Ward (POW) Scale." Roseburg, Oregon: Veterans Administration Hospital, 1969. (Mimeographed).

Ellsworth, R. B. "Upgrading treatment effectiveness through measurement and feedback of clinical outcomes." Hospital and Community Psychiatry, 1970, 21: 115-117.

Ellsworth, R. B. "Feedback: asset or liability in improving treatment effectiveness?" Journal of Consulting and Clinical Psychology, 1970, 40: 383-393.

Ellsworth, R. B., Dickman, H. R., & Maroney, R. J. "Characteristics of productive and unproductive unit systems in VA psychiatric hospitals." Hospital and Community Psychiatry, 1972, 23: 261-268.

Ellsworth, R. B. & Ellsworth, J. R. "The psychiatric aide: Therapuetic agent or lost potential?" Journal of Psychiatric Nursing, 1970, 8: 7-13.

Ellsworth, R. B., Foster, L., Childers, B., Arthur, G., & Kroeker, D. "Hospital and community adjustment as perceived by psychiatric patients, their families and staff." Journal of Consulting and Clinical Psychology, 1968, 32(5, Part 2, Monograph supplement): 1-41.

Ellsworth, R. B., Maroney, R., Klett, W., Gordon, H., & Gunn, R. "Milieu characteristics of successful psychiatric treatment programs." American Journal of Orthopsychiatry, 1971, 41: 427-441.

Ellsworth, R. B. & Maroney, R. J. "Characteristics of psychiatric programs and their effects on patients' adjustment." Journal of Consulting and Clinical Psychology, 1972, 39: 436-447.

Elpers, J. R. The practical development and implementation of management information systems for community mental health programs. Santa Ana, Calif.: Orange County Department of Mental Health.

Elster, R. S. & Dunnette, T. D. "The robustness of Tilton's measure of overlap." Educational and Psychological Measurement, 1971, 31: 685-698.

Etzioni, A. "Two approaches to organizational analysis: a critique and a suggestion." Administrative Science Quarterly, 1960, 5: 257-278.

Etzioni, A. A comparative analysis of complex organizations: On Power, involvement and their correlates. New York: Free Press of Glencoe, 1961.

Etzioni, A. Modern organizations. Englewood Cliffs, N.J.: Prentice-Hall, 1964.

Etzioni, A. The active society. New York: Free Press, 1968.

Etzioni, A. " 'Shortcuts' to social change?" Public Interest, 1968, 12: 40-51.

Etzioni, A. & Lehman, E. W. Some dangers in "valid" social measurement. In B. M. Gross (ed.), Social intelligence for America's future. Boston: Allyn & Bacon, 1969.

Evans, A., Bullard, D., Jr., & Solomon, M. "The family as a potential resource in the rehabilitation of the chronic schizophrenic patient: A study of 60 patients and their families." American Journal of Psychiatry, 1961, 117: 1075-1083.

Evans, S. H. & Anastasio, E. J. "Misuse of analysis of covariance when treatment effect and covariate are confounded." Psychological Bulletin, 1968, 69: 225-234.

Evenson, R. C. "A systematic and comprehensive approach to practical program evaluation within the department of mental health." Unpublished paper, Elgin State Hospital, Elgin, Illinois, 1970.

F

Fagerstrom, M. N. "A preliminary evaluation of the new careers program in the California Department of Corrections, June 1967-June 1968." Unpublished manuscript, Bay Area Research Unit, California Department of Corrections, 1968.

Fagerstrom, M. N. "New careers program, California Department of Corrections, December 1967-December 1969." Unpublished manuscript, Bay Area Research Unit, California Department of Corrections, 1969.

Fairweather, G. Methods for experimental social innovation. New York: John Wiley, 1967.

Fairweather, G. Experimental innovation defined. In H. H. Hornstein et al. (eds.), Social intervention: A behavioral science approach. New York: Free Press, 1971.

Fairweather, G. "Innovation: A necessary but cosufficient condition for change." Innovations, 1973, 1: 25-27.

Fairweather, G., Sanders, D. H., & Tournatzky, L. G. *Creating change in mental health organizations.* New York: Pergamon, 1974.

Fallding, H. Functional analysis in sociology. In H. Polsky, D. Claster, & C. Goldberg (eds.), *Social systems perspectives in residential institutions.* East Lansing: Michigan State University Press, 1970.

Fanon, F. *The wretched of the earth.* New York: Grove Press, 1965.

Fanshel, D. Child welfare. In H. S. Mass (ed.), *Five fields of social service: Reviews of research.* New York: National Association of Social Workers, 1966.

Fanshel, S. & Bush, J. W. "A health status index and its application to health-services outcomes." Operations Research, 1970, 18 (November-December): 1021-1066.

Farina, A. "Mental illness and the impact of believing others know about it." Journal of Abnormal Psychology, 1971, 77: 1-5.

Faris, R. E. L. & Dunham, W. H. *Mental disorder in urban areas.* New York: John Wiley, 1963.

Farr, W. *Report on the mortality of cholera in England in 1848-49.* London: H. M.S.O., 1852.

Fay, H. J. & Norman, A. "Modifying the problem-oriented record for an inpatient program for children." Hospital and Community Psychiatry, January 1974, 25(1): 28-30.

Feeney, G. M. "The use of feedback to improve the operation of residential treatment settings." International Journal of Mental Health, 1973, 2(2): 81-93.

Feibleman, J. K. "Theory of integrative levels." British Journal of Philosophical Science, 1954, 5: 59-66.

Feigl, H. & Scriven, M., eds. *The foundations of science and the concepts of psychology and psychoanalysis.* Minneapolis: University of Minnesota Press, 1956.

Fein, R. *Economics of mental illness.* New York: Basic Books, 1958.

Feldman, A. S. & Tilly, C. "The interaction of social and physical space." American Science Review, December, 25: 877-84.

Felix, R. H. "Community mental health." American Journal of Orthopsychiatry, 1963, 33: 788.

Fellin, P. "The standardized interview in social work research." Social Casework, 1963, 44: 81-85.

Festinger, L., Gerard, H. B., Hymovitch, H., Kelly, H., & Rosen, B. "The influence process in the presence of extreme deviates." Human Relations, 1952, 5: 327-346.

Fine, S. *Guidelines for the design of new careers.* Kalamazoo, Mich.: W. E. Upjohn Institute for Employment Research, 1967.

Fishbeing, M. & Ajzen, I. "Attitudes and opinions." Annual Review of Psychology, 1972, 23: 487-544.

Fishburn, C. *Decision and value theory.* New York: John Wiley, 1964.

Fischer, E. "Altruistic attitudes, beliefs about psychiatric patients, and volunteering for companionship with mental hospital patients." Proceedings, Annual Convention of American Psychological Association, 1971, 6: 343-344.

Fischer, G. H. The role of cost-utility analysis in program budgeting. Cited by D. Novick (ed.), *Program budgeting.* Washington, D.C.: Government Printing Office, 1964.

Fisher, G., King, J., & Shernoff, E. "Do-it-yourself computer reports in the medical record department." Medical Record News, June 1972, 43(3): 31-38.

Fleiss, J. L. & Zubin, J. "On the methods and theory of clustering." Multivariate Behavioral Research, 1969, 4(2): 235-250.

Fletcher, C. R. "Measuring community mental health attitudes by means of hypothetical case descriptions." Social Psychiatry, 1969, 4: 152-156.

Fontana, A. "Familial etiology of schizophrenia: Is scientific method possible?" Psychological Bulletin, 1966, 66: 214-227.

Forehand, G. A. & Gilmer, B. H. "Environmental variation in studies of organizational behavior." Psychological Bulletin, 1964, 62: 361-382.

Forst, B. E. An analysis of alternative periodic health examination strategies. Cited in W. A. Niskanen, A. C. Harberger, R. H. Haveman, R. Turvey, & R. Seckhauser (eds.), *Benefit-cost and policy analysis 1972.* Chicago: Aldine, 1973.

Foster, C. D. & Beesley, M. E. "Estimating the social benefit of constructing an underground railway in London." Journal of the Royal Statistical Society, 1967, 126.

Foster, R. J. "Acquiescent response set as a measure of acquiescence." Journal of Abnormal and Social Psychology, 1961, 63: 155-160.

Foucault, M. *[Madness and civilization: A history of insanity in the age of reason]* (R. Howard, trans.). New York: Pantheon, 1965.

Fournet, G. "Cultural correlates with attitudes, perception, knowledge and reported incidence of mental disorders." Dissertation Abstracts, 1967, 28 (1B), 339: 74, 78.

Fraiberg, S. "Some aspects of residential casework with children." Social Casework, April 1956, 37(4): 159.

Frank, G. H. "The role of the family in the development of psychopathology." Psychological Bulletin, 1965, 64: 191-205.

Frank, J. D. "Common features account for effectiveness." International Journal of Psychiatry, 1969, 7: 122-127.

Frankel, H., Grant, J. D., Milligan, J., & James, M. "Technical report: Developing new career ladders, with appropriate educational components, in the administration of justice." Unpublished manuscript, Social Action Research Center, Oakland, California, 1969.

Franks, C. M., ed. *Behavior therapy: Appraisal and status.* New York: McGraw-Hill, 1969.

Freeman, H. E. "A note on the prediction of who votes." Public Opinion Quarterly, 1953, 17: 288-292.

Freeman, H. E. "Attitudes toward mental illness among relatives of former patients." American Sociological Review, 1961, 26: 59-66.

Freeman, H. E. & Sherwood, C. "Research in large scale intervention programs." Journal of Social Issues, 1965, 21(2): 11-28.

Freeman, H. E. & Simmons, O. "Mental patients in the community: Family settings and performance levels." American Sociological Review, 1958, 23: 147-154.

Freeman, H. E. & Simmons, O. "Social class and posthospital performance levels." American Sociological Review, 1959, 24: 345-351.

Freeman, H. E. & Simmons, O. "Feelings of stigma among relatives of former mental patients." Social Problems, 1961, 8: 312-321.

Freeman, H. E. & Simmons, O. *The mental patient comes home.* New York: John Wiley, 1963.

French, J. W., Ekstrom, R. B., & Price, L. A. *Manual of kit for reference tests for cognitive factors.* Princeton: Educational Testing Service, 1963.

Fried, M. "Effects of social change on mental health." American Journal of Orthopsychiatry, 1964, 34: 3-28.

Fried, M. Social differences in mental health. In J. Rosa, A. Antonovsky, & I. K. Zola, *Poverty and health: A sociological analysis.* Cambridge, Mass.: Harvard University Press, 1969.

Friedman, H. "Magnitude of experimental effect and a table for its rapid estimation." Psychological Bulletin, 1968, 70: 245-251.

Fromm, E. *The sane society.* New York: Holt, Rinehart & Winston, 1955.

Fuchs, V. R. *The service economy.* New York: National Bureau of Economic Research, 1968.

## G

Galbraith, J. K. "Economics as a system of belief." American Economic Review, 1970, 60: 469-478.

Galle, O. R., Gove, W. R., & McPherson, J. M. "Population density and pathology: What are the relations for man?" Science, 1972, 176.

Galtung, J. *Theory and methods of social research.* Oslo: Universitetsforloget; London: Allen & Unwin; New York: Columbia University Press, 1967.

Gannon, C. A. "Consumer demand, conjectural interdependence, and location equilibrium in simple spatial duopoly." Papers of the Regional Science Association, 1972, vol. XXVIII.

Gans, H. J. *The urban villagers.* New York: Free Press, 1962.

Garber, B. *Follow-up study of hospitalized adolescents.* New York: Brunner/Mazel, 1972.

Gardiner, P.C. *The application of decision technology and Monte Carlo stimulation to multiple objective public policy decision-making: A case study in California coastal zone management.* Unpublished doctoral dissertation, University of Southern California, 1974.

Gardner, E. A. & Babigian, H. M. "A longitudinal comparison of psychiatric service." American Journal of Orthopsychiatry, October 1966, 36(5): 818-828.

Gardner, E. A., Miles, H. C., Iker, H. C. & Romano, J. "A cumulative register of psychiatric services in a community." American Journal of Public Health, August 1973, 53(8).

Gardner, E. A., Miles, H. C., Bahn, A. K. & Romano, J. "All psychiatric experience in a community." Archives of General Psychiatry, October 1963, 9.

Gardner, J. W. *Self renewal: The individual and the innovative society.* New York: Harper & Row, 1964.

Gardner, J. W. & Gardner, H. "A note on selective imitation by a six-week-old infant." Child Development, 1970, 41: 1209-1213.

Garfinkel, H. *Studies in ethnomethodology.* Englewood Cliffs, N.J.: Prentice-Hall, 1967.

Gartner, A. *Do paraprofessionals improve human services: A first critical appraisal of the data.* New York: New Careers Development Center, New York University, 1969.

Gartner, A. "The use of the paraprofessional and new directions for the social service agency." Public Welfare, 1969, 27(2): 117-125.

Gaviria, B. & Pratt, D. F. *Problem-oriented medical records: Instruction manual for problem-oriented recordkeeping in psychiatric services.* Albany, New York: Veterans Administration Hospital, 113 Holland Ave., January 1973.

Gaylin, W. "What's normal?" New York Times Magazine Section, Sunday, April 1, 1973: 14, 54, 56, 58, 59.

Geismar, L. L. & LaSorte, M. A. "Research interviewing with low-income families." Social Work, 1963, 8(2): 10-13.

Gelfand, S. & Ullman, L. P. "Change in attitudes about mental illness associated with psychiatric clerkship training." International Journal of Social Psychiatry, 1961, 7: 292-298.

Georgiou, P. "The goal paradigm and notes towards a counter paradigm." Administrative Science Quarterly, September 1973, 18: 291.

Gergen, K. J. *The psychology of behavior exchange.* Reading, Mass.: Addison-Wesley, 1969.

Gershenson, C. P. "Residential treatment of children: Research problems and possibilities." Social Service Review, September 1956, 30(3): 268-275.

Gerth, H. H. & Mills, C. W., eds. *From Max Weber.* New York: Oxford University Press, 1946.

Gilandas, A. "Implications of the problem-oriented record for utilization review and continuing education." Hospitals and Community Psychiatry, January 1974, 25(1).

Gilbert, D. C. & Levinson, D. "Custodialism" and "humanism" in staff ideology. In D. J. Levinson & R. H. Williams (eds.), *The patient and the mental hospital.* Glencoe, Ill.: Free Press, 1957.

Gilbert, D. C. & Levinson, D. Role performance, ideology, and personality in mental hospital aides. In M. Greenblatt, D. J. Levinson, & R. H. Williams (eds.), *The patient and the mental hospital.* New York: Free Press, 1957.

Gilbert, J. P., Light, R. J., & Mosteller, F. Assessing social innovations: An empirical base for policy. In C. A. Bennett & A. Lumsdaine (eds.), *Central issues in social program evaluation,* in press.

Gillespie, W. I. Effect of public expenditures on the distribution of income. Cited by R. A. Musgrade (ed.), *Essays in fiscal federalism.* Washington, D.C.: Brookings Institution, 1965.

Gillis, L. & Keet, M. "Factors underlying the retention in the community of chronic unhospitalized schizophrenics." British Journal of Psychiatry, 1965, 111: 1057-1067.

Gilmer, B., Miller, J. O., & Gray, S. W. *Intervention with mothers and young children: Study of intra-family effects.* Nashville, Tenn.: DARCEE Demonstration and Research Center for Early Education, 1970.

Gintis, H. "Consumer behavior and the concept of sovereignty." American Economic Review, 1972, 62: 267-278.

Giovannoni, J. M. & Eullman, L. P. "Conceptions of mental health held by psychiatric patients." Journal of Clinical Psychology, 1963, 19: 398-400.

Gladwin, T. "Social competence and clinical practice." Psychiatry, 1967, 30(1): 30-43.

Glaser, E. M. et al. *Utilization of applicable research and demonstration results.* Washington, D.C.: Final report to Vocational Rehabilitation Administration, DHEW, Project RD-1263-G, 1966.

Glaser, E. M. & Ross, H. L. *Increasing the utilization of applied research results.* Final report to the National Institution of Mental Health (Grant No. 5 R12 MH 09250-02). Los Angeles, Calif.: Human Interaction Research Institute, 1971.

Glaser, E. "Knowledge transfer and institutional change." Professional Psychology, November 1973: 434-444.

Glaser, W. A. "Experiences in health planning in the United States." Prepared for a Conference on Health Planning in the United States, Columbia University, June 4-6, 1973. (Mimeograph).

Glass, G. V. "Analysis of data on the Connecticut speeding crackdown as a time-series quasi-experiment." Law and Society Review, 1968, 3(1): 55-76.

Glass, G. V., Tiao, G. C., & Maguire, T. O. "Analysis of data on the 1900 revision of the German divorce laws as a quasi-experiment." Law and Society Review, 1969.

Glasscote, R. M., Sossex, J. N., Cumming, E., & Smith, L. H. *The community mental health center: An interim appraisal.* Washington, D.C.: Joint Information Service of APA, 1969.

Glueck, B. C. & Luce, G. "The computer as psychiatric aid and research tool." Mental Health Program Reports, No. 2, DHEW Public Health Service, February 1968, 353-372.

Glueck, B. C. & Glueck, S. *Unravelling juvenile delinquency.* Cambridge, Mass.: Harvard University Press, 1968.

Glueck, B. C., Rosenberg, M., & Stroebel, C. "The computer and the clinical decision process." American Journal of Psychiatry, 1967, 124(5).

Glueck, B. C. et al. "Computers in psychiatry." Psychiatric Annals, December 1972, 2(12).

Godel, K. *Godel's theorem: On formally undecidable propositions.* New York: Basic Books, 1963.

Goff, C., Osborne, G., Campbell, K., & Fletcher, M. "Preliminary report on the use of the PARS scale by Oregon's community mental health clinics." Unpublished manuscript, 1971.

Goffman, E. *Asylums.* Garden City, N.Y.: Doubleday-Anchor, 1961.

Goffman, E. *Stigma: Notes on the management of a spoiled identity.* Englewood Cliffs, N.J.: Prentice-Hall, 1963.

Goldenberg, I. *Build me a mountain.* Cambridge, Mass.: MIT Press, 1971.

Goldin, G. J., Margolin, K. N., & Stotsky, B. A. "The utilization of rehabilitation research: Concepts, principles, and research." *Northeastern Studies in Vocational Rehabilitation,* 1969, No. 6.

Goldman, A. E. "The group depth interview." Journal of Marketing, 1962, 26: 61-68.

Goldman, T. A., ed. *Cost-effectiveness analysis.* New York: Frederick A. Praeger, 1967.

Goldstein, A. P. *Therapist-patient expectancies in psychotherapy.* New York: Pergamon Press (Macmillan), 1962.

Goldstein, J. H. The effectiveness of manpower training programs: A review of research on the impact on the poor. In W. A. Niskanen et al. (eds.), *Benefit-cost and policy analysis 1972.* Chicago: Aldine, 1973.

Goltz, B., Sternbach, R. A., & Rusk, T. N. "A built-in evaluation system for a new community mental health center. Unpublished manuscript.

Goodwin, L. "On making social research relevant to public policy and national problem solving." American Psychologist, 1971, 26(5): 431-442.

Gordon, A. "Mental health: A time of change." Physician's World, 2973, 1: 41-44.

Gordon, I. J. *A home learning center approach to early stimulation.* Gainsville, Fla.: University of Florida, Institute for Development of Human Resources, College of Education, 1971.

Gordon, I. J. *An early intervention project: A longitudinal look.* Gainsville, Fla.: University of Florida, Institute for Development of Human Resources, College of Education, 1973.

Gordon, J. *The poor of Harlem: Social functioning of the underclass.* New York: Office of the Mayor, Interdepartmental Neighborhood Service Center, 1965.

Gotkin, L. G. & Goldstein, L. S. *Descriptive statistics: A programmed textbook.* New York: John Wiley, 1964.

Gottfredson, D. M. & Ballard, K. B. "Offender classification and parole prediction." Unpublished manuscript, Institute for the Study of Crime and Delinquency, Vacaville, California, 1966.

Gottfredson, L. M. "Research—Who needs it?" Research Report, Department of Institutions, State of Washington, 1969, 2: 11-17.

Gouldner, A. "The sociologist as partisan: Sociology and the welfare state." American Sociologist, 1968, 3: 103-116.

Gouldner, A. *The coming crisis of Western sociology.* New York: Basic Books, 1970.

Gove, W. R. & Fain, T. "The stigma of mental hospitalization." Archives of General Psychiatry, 1973, 28: 494-500.

Grad, J. & Sainsbury, P. "Mental illness and the family." Lancet, 1963, 1: 544-547.

Grad, J. & Sainsbury, P. Evaluating a community care service. In H. Freeman & J. Farndale (eds.), *Trends in the mental health services.* New York: Macmillan, 1963.

Grad, J. "Psychiatric social workers and research." British Journal of Psychology and Social Work, 1964, 7: 147.

Grad, J. & Sainsbury, P. "Evaluating the community psychiatric service in Chichester: Results." Milbank Memorial Fund Quarterly, 1966, 44(1): 246.

Grad, J. & Sainsbury, P. "The effects that patients have on their families in a community care service: A two year follow-up." British Journal of Psychiatry, 1968, 114: 265.

Grad, J. & Crocetti, A. Interviewing in psychiatric field surveys. In P. Sainsbury & N. Kreitman (eds.), *Methods of psychiatric research.* London: Oxford University Press, 1974.

Graham, G., Jr. "Effects of introductory and abnormal psychology courses on students' attitudes toward mental illness." Psychological Reports, 1968, 22: 448.

Graham, J. R., Allon, R., Friedman, I., & Lilly, R. S. "The ward evaluation scale: A factor analytic study." Journal of Clinical Psychology, 1971, 27: 118-122.

Graham, J. R., Lilly, R. S., Allon, R., & Friedman, I. "Comparison of the factor structures of staff and patient responses on the ward evaluation scale." Journal of Clinical Psychology, 1971, 27: 123-128.

Gralnick, A. *The psychiatric hospital as a therapeutic instrument.* New York: Brunner/Mazel, 1969.

Grant, J. D. & Grant, J. "New Careers Development Project: Final report." Unpublished manuscript, Institute for the Study of Crime and Delinquency, Sacramento, California, 1967.

Grant, J. D. The offender as a correctional manpower resource. In F. Riessman and H. I. Popper (eds.), *Up from poverty.* New York: Harper & Row, 1968.

Grant, J. D. "Delinquency prevention through participation in social change (new careers in the administration of justice)." Paper prepared for Delinquency Prevention Strategy Conference sponsored by the Juvenile Delinquency Task Force of the California Council on Criminal Justice, Santa Barbara, February 1970.

Grant, J. & Grant, J. D. Client participation and community change. In D. Adelson and B. L. Kalis (eds.), *Community psychology perspectives in mental health.* San Francisco: Chandler, 1970.

Grant, J. D. & Grant, J. Contagion as a principle in behavior change. In H. C. Rickard (ed.), *Unique programs in behavior readjustment.* Elmsford, N.Y.: Pergamon Press, in press.

Grant, J. D. & Rodriguez, M. "Final report: Beyond the opportunity structure." Unpublished manuscript, Social Action Research Center, Oakland, California, 1970.

Grant, R. L. & Maletsky, B. M. "Application of the weed system to psychiatric research." Journal of Psychiatry in Medicine, 1972, 3.

Grant, J. *Natural and political observations. Made upon the Bills of Mortality.* Baltimore: Johns Hopkins Press, 1939. (Originally published, 1662.)

Gray, S. W. & Klaus, R. A. "The early training project: The seventh-year report." Child Development, 1970, 41: 909-924.

Gray, W., Duhl, F., & Rizzo, N. *General systems theory and psychiatry.* Boston: Little, Brown, 1969.

Green, L. W., Gustafson, H. C., & Begum, A. I. "Validity in family planning surveys: Disavowed knowledge and use of contraceptives in a panel study in East Pakistan." Paper presented at the annual meeting of the Population Association of America, 1968.

Greenblatt, M., Moore, R., Albert, R., & Solomon, M. *The prevention of hospitalization.* New York: Grune & Stratton, 1963.

Greenleigh Associates. *Diagnostic survey of the tenant households in the West Side urban renewal area of New York City.* New York: Greenleigh, 1965.

Greenwood, E. *Experimental sociology: A study in method.* New York: King's Crown Press, 1945.

Griffith, J. R. *Quantitative techniques for hospital planning and control.* Lexington, Mass.: Lexington Books, 1972.

Gross, B. M. *The managing of organizations: The administrative struggle.* London: Free Press of Glencoe, 1964.

Gross, B. M. *The state of the nation: Social system accounting.* London: Tavistock Publications, 1966. (Also in R. M. Bauer, *Social indicators.* Cambridge, Mass.: MIT Press, 1966.)

Gross, B. M., ed. "Social goals and indicators." Annals of the American Academy of Political and Social Science, 1967, 371: Part 1, i-iii; 1-177; Part 2, i-iii; 1-218.

Gross, B. M., ed. *Social intelligence for America's future.* Boston: Allyn & Bacon, 1969.

Gruenberg, E. M., ed. "Evaluating the effectiveness of mental health services." Milbank Memorial Fund Quarterly, 1966, 44(2): 353.

Guilford, J. P. *Psychometric methods* (second ed.). New York: McGraw-Hill, 1954.

Guilford, J. P. *Personality.* New York: McGraw-Hill, 1959.

Guilford, J. P. *The nature of human intelligence.* New York: McGraw-Hill, 1967.

Guion, R. M. *Personnel testing.* New York: McGraw-Hill, 1965.

Gula, M. *Agency operated group homes: A casebook.* Washington, D.C.: Children's Bureau, 1965.

Gulo, E. V. & Fraser, W. "Students attitudes toward mental illness." College Student Survey, 1967, 3: 61-63.

Gurel, L. *Correlates of psychiatric hospital effectiveness.* Intramural Report 64-5, Psychiatric Evaluation Project, Veterans Administration Hospital, Washington, D.C., 1964.

Gurin, G., Veroff, J., & Feld, S. *Americans view their mental health.* New York: Basic Books, 1960.

Guttentag, M. Evaluation of social legislation. In F. F. Korten, S. W. Cook, and J. I. Lacey (eds.), *Psychology and the problems of society.* Washington, D.C.: American Psychological Association, 1970.

Guttentag, M. "Models and methods in evaluation research." Journal for Theory of Social Behavior, 1971, 1(1): 75-95.

Guttentag, M. "Subjectivity and its use in evaluation research." Evaluation, 1973, 1(2): 60-65.

Guttentag, M. & Snapper, K. J. "Plans, evaluations, and decisions." Evaluation, 1974, 2(1): 58-64; 73-74.

Guttmacher, S. & Elinson, J. "Ethno-religious variation in perceptions of illness." Social Science and Medicine, 1971, 5: 117-125.

Guttman, L. "An approach for quantifying paired comparisons and rank order." Annals of Mathematical Statistics, 1946, 17: 144-163.

# H

Haber, L. D. "Evaluating response error in the reporting of the income of the aged: Benefit income." Proceedings of the Social Statistics Section, American Statistical Association, 1966: 412-419.

Hagburg, E. "Validity of questionnaire data: Reported and observed attendance in an adult education program." Public Opinion Quarterly, 1968, 32: 453.

Hage, J. & Aiken, M. *Social change in complex organizations.* New York: Random House, 1970.

Haley, J. *Strategies of psychotherapy.* New York: Grune & Stratton, 1963.

Halleck, S. L. "Psychiatry and the status quo." Archives of General Psychiatry, 1968, 19: 257-265.

Hallowitz, E. & Riessman, F. "The role of the indigenous nonprofessional in a community mental health neighborhood service center program." American Journal of Orthopsychiatry, 1967, 37: 766-778.

Halperin, M. H. *Why bureaucrats play games.* Washington, D.C.: Brookings Institution, 1971. (Reprint No. 199)

Halpert, H. P. "Public acceptance of the mentally ill." Public Health Reports, 1969, 84: 59-64.

Hanoch, G. "An economic analysis of earnings and schooling." Journal of Human Resources, 1967, 2: 310-329.

Hansen, M. H. & Hurwitz, W. N. "The problem of non-response in sample surveys." Journal of the American Statistical Association, 1946, 41: 517-529.

Hanson, R. H. & Marks, E. S. "Influence of the interviewer on the accuracy of survey results." Journal of the American Statistical Association, 1958, 53(283): 635-655.

Harburg, E., Schull, W. J., Schork, M. A., Wigle, J. B., & Burkhardt, W. R. *Stress and heredity in Negro/White blood pressure differences.* Progress report to National Heart Institute, 1969.

Hare, P. A. "Interview responses: Personality or conformity?" Public Opinion Quarterly, 1960, 24: 679-685.

Hare, P. A. & Davie, J. S. "The group interview." Sociology and Social Research, 1954, 39: 81-87.

Harman, H. H. *Modern factor analysis.* Chicago: University of Chicago Press, 1967.

Harre, R. & Secord, P. *The explanation of social behavior.* Oxford: Blackwell & Mott, 1972.

Harrison, B. "Public service jobs for urban ghetto residents." Good Government, 1969: 1-20.

Hartmann, E. L., Isaacson, M. L., & Jurgell, C. M. "Public reaction to public opinion surveying." Public Opinion Quarterly, 1968, 32: 295-298.

Hatry, H. P., Winnie, R. E., & Fisk, D. M. *Practical program evaluation for state and local government officials.* Washington D.C.: Urban Institute, 1973.

Hauck, M. & Steinkamp, S. *Survey reliability and interviewer competence.* Urbana: University of Illinois Press, 1964.

Hauser, P. M. & Duncan, O. D., Eds. *The study of population.* Chicago: University of Chicago Press, 1959.

Havelock, R. G. *Planning for innovation through dissemination and utilization of knowledge* (Office of Education, Dept. of HEW Contract No. OEC-3-7-070038-2143). Ann Arbor, Mich.: Center for Research on Utilization of Scientific Knowledge, Institute for Social Research, University of Michigan, 1969.

Havelock, R. G. *A guide to innovation in education.* Ann Arbor: Center for Research on the Utilication of Scientific Knowledge, Institute for Social Research, University of Michigan, 1970.

Havelock, R. & Markowitz, E. *A national problem-solving system: Highway safety research and decision-makers.* Ann Arbor: University of Michigan, 1971.

Havelock, R. & Lingwood, M. *R. & D. utilization and functions: An analytical computation of four systems.* Ann Arbor: Institute for Social Research, University of Michigan, 1973.

Haveman, R. H. The ex-post evaluation of navigation improvements. In W. A. Niskanen, A. C. Harberger, R. H. Haveman, R. Turvey, & R. Seckhauser (eds.), *Benefit-cost and policy analysis 1972.* Chicago: Aldine, 1973.

Haveman, R. H. & Margolis, J., eds. *Public expenditures and policy analysis.* Chicago: Markham, 1970.

Havighurst, C. C. "Regulation of health facilities and services by 'Certificate of Need.' " Virginia Law Review, October 1973, 59: 1143-1232.

Haworth, L. "The experimental society: Dewey and Jordan." Ethics, 1960, 71(1): 27-40.

Hayakawa, S. E. The language of social control. In E. P. Hollander and R. G. Hunt (eds.), Current perspectives in social psychology (second ed.). New York: Oxford University Press, 1967.

Hayes, D. & Grether, L. "The school year and vacation: When do students learn?" Paper presented at the Eastern Sociological Convention, New York, 1969.

Hays, W. L. Statistics for psychologists. New York: Holt, Rinehart & Winston, 1963.

Hearings (Serial No. 93-39) Before the Subcommittee on Public Health and Environment and the Committee on Interstate and Foreign Commerce. Oversight over the administration of the community mental health centers. House of Representatives, 93rd Congress, May 9 and June 15, 1973.

Hearings on a Bill to Provide for Assistance in the Construction and Initial Operation of Community Mental Health Centers. Before the Subcommittee on Interstate and Foreign Commerce, March 26, 27, 28, 1963.

Heaton, E. R. "Increasing mail questionnaire returns with a preliminary letter." Journal of Advertising Research, 1965, 5: 36-39.

Hebb, D. O. The organization of behavior. New York: John Wiley, 1949.

Heber, R., Garber, H., Harrington, S., & Hoffman, C. Rehabilitation of families at risk for mental retardation. Madison, Wisconsin: Rehabilitation Research and Training Center in Mental Retardation, University of Wisconsin, 1971.

Heilbroner, R. Between capitalism and socialism. New York: Random House, 1970.

Hennes, J. D. "The measurement of health." Medical Care Review, 1972: 1268-1288.

Henry, J. "Types of institutional structures." Psychiatry, February 1957, 20: 47-60.

Henry, J. P., Meehan, J. P., & Stephens, P. M. "The use of psycho-social stimuli to induce prolonged hypertension in mice." Psychosomatic Medicine, 1967, 29: 408-432.

Hersch, C. "Social history, mental health and community control." American Psychologist, 1972, 27: 749-754.

Hertzig, M. E., Birch, H. G., Thomas, A., & Mendez, O. A. Class and ethnic differences in responsiveness of preschool children to cognitive demands. Society for Research in Child Development, 1968, 33(1). (Monograph).

Herzog, E. Some guidelines for evaluative research. Washington, D.C.: U.S. Department of Health, Education and Welfare, Children's Bureau, 1959.

Herzog, E., Newcomb, C. H., & Cisin, I. H. Double deprivation: The less they have the less they learn. In S. Ryan (ed.), A report on longitudinal evaluations of preschool programs. Washington, D.C.: Office of Child Development, 1972.

Herzog, E., Newcomb, C. H., & Cisin, I. H. "But some are poorer than others: SES differences in a preschool program." American Journal of Orthopsychiatry, 1972, 42: 4-22.

Herzog, E., Newcomb, C. H., & Cisin, I. H. Preschool and postscript: An evaluation of the inner-city program. Washington, D.C.: Social Research Group, George Washington University, 1973.

Hess, R. D., Shipman, V. C., Brophy, J. E., & Bear, R. M. The cognitive environments of urban preschool children. Chicago: University of Chicago Graduate School of Education, 1968.

Hess, R. D., Shipman, V. C., Brophy, J. E., & Bear, R. M. The cognitive environments of urban preschool children: Follow-up phase. Chicago: University of Chicago Graduate School of Education, 1969.

Hicks, J. R. Value and capital (second ed.). London: Oxford University Press, 1946.

Hilleboe, H. E., & Barkhuus, A. "Health planning in the United States: Some categorical and general approaches." International Journal of Health Services, 1971, 1(2): 134-148.

Hinkle, L. E. "Ecological observations of the relation of physical illness, mental illness, and the social environment." Psychosomatic Medicine, 1961, 23(4): 289.

Hinkle, L. E. "The concept of stress in the biological and social sciences. Scientific Medicine and Man, 1973, 1: 43.

Hinkle, L. E. Journal of Chronic Disease, 1959, 10: 46.

Hinrichs, H. & Taylor, G. *Program budgeting and benefit-cost analysis.* Pacific Palisades, Calif.: Goodyear, 1969.

Hirsch, J. & Borowitz, G. "The tyranny of treatment." Paper read at American Psychiatric Association Convention, Hawaii, May 8, 1973.

Hirsch, W. Z. "Cost functions of an urban government service: Refuse collection." Review of Economics & Statistics, 1965, 47: 87-92.

Hirsch, W. Z. *The economics of state and local government.* New York: McGraw-Hill, 1970.

Hirschi, T. & Hanon, S. *Delinquency research.* Glencoe, Ill.: Free Press, 1967.

Hitch, C. J. & McKean, R. N. *The economics of defense in the nuclear age.* Cambridge, Mass.: Harvard University Press, 1960.

Hobbs, N. "The process of reeducation." Paper presented at the first annual workshop for the Staff of Project Re-Ed., in Gatlinburg, Tenn., September 1, 1963.

Hobbs, N. "Helping disturbed children: Psychological and ecological strategies." American Psychologist, 1966, 21: 1105-1115.

Hochstim, J. R. "A critical comparison of three strategies of collecting data from households." Journal of the American Statistical Association, 1967, 62: 976-989.

Hodges, W. L., McCandless, B. R., & Spicker, H. H. *The development and evaluation of a diagnostically based curriculum for preschool psychosocially deprived children.* Washington, D.C.: U.S. Office of Education, 1967.

Hoenig, J. & Hamilton, M. *The desegration of the mentally ill.* London: Routledge & Kegan Paul, 1969.

Hoff, W., Stewart, P., Gross, S. B., & Malcolm, J. C. "Home Health Aide Pilot Training Project: Final evaluation report." Unpublished manuscript, Alameda County Health Department, Oakland, California, 1968.

Hollingshead, A. B. & Redlich, F. C. *Social class and mental illness.* New York: John Wiley, 1958.

Holmes, T. & Rahe, R. "The social readjustment rating scale." Journal of Psychosomatic Research, 1967, 11: 213-218.

Holtzberg, J. D. & Gerwitz, H. "A method of altering attitudes toward mental illness." Psychiatric Quarterly Supplement, 1963, 37(1): 56-61.

Homans, G. C. "Social behavior as exchange." American Journal of Sociology, 1958, 63: 597-606.

Homans, G. C. *Social behavior: its elementary forms.* New York: Harcourt, Brace & World, 1961.

Homme, L. *How to use contingency contracting in the classroom.* Urbana: University of Illinois Press, 1969.

Homme, L. & deBaca, P. D. "Contingency management on the psychiatric ward." Unpublished manuscript, January 1966.

Homme, L. & Tosti, D. T. "Contingency management and motivation." National Society of Programmed Instruction Journal, 1965, 4(7): 1-3.

Honigfeld, G. *Problem-oriented psychiatric records–manual and automated.* Orangeburg, N.Y. Information Sciences Division, Research Center, Rockland State Hospital, 1972.

Horn, J. S. *Away with all pests.* New York: Monthly Review Press, 1969.

Horngren, C. T. *Cost accounting.* Englewood Cliffs, N.J.: Prentice-Hall, 1967.

Horowitz, I. L. *The new sociology.* New York: Oxford University Press, 1964.

Horst, P. *Psychological measurement and prediction.* Belmont, Calif.: Wadsworth, 1966.

Houston, T. R. The behavioral sciences impact-effectiveness model. In P. H. Rossi and W. Williams (eds.), *Evaluating social programs: theory, practice, and politics.* New York: Seminar Press, 1972, pp. 51-65.

Houts, P. & Moos, R. "The development of a Ward Initiative Scale for patients." Journal of Clinical Psychology, 1969, 25: 319-322.

Hovland, C. L., Lumsdaine, A. A., & Sheffield, F. D. *Experiments on mass communication.* Princeton: Princeton University Press, 1949.

Howard, E. "How to be serious about innovating." Nation's Schools, April 1967, 79: 89-90, 130.

Hu, T., Lee, M. L., & Stronsdorfer, E. W. "Economic returns to vocational and comprehensive high school graduates." Journal of Human Resources, 1971: 25-50.

Hull, C. L. *A behavior system.* New Haven: Yale University Press, 1952.

Humphries, N., Ed. *Vital statistics: A memorial volume of selections from the reports and writings of William Farr.* London: Sanitary Institute, 1885.

Hunt, C. McV. *Intelligence and experience.* New York: Ronald Press, 1961.

Hunter, A. "The ecology of Chicago: Persistence and change, 1930-1960." American Journal of Sociology, 77(3): 425-444.

Husek, T. R. "Persuasive impacts of early, late, or no mention of a negative source." Journal of Personality and Social Psychology, 1965, 2: 125-128.

Husek, T. R. & Bobren, H. "The relative importance of labels and behavior descriptions in determining attitudes toward labeled behavior." Psychological Record, 1964, 14: 319-325.

Husek-Rosen & Associates. "Evaluation design for the education aides program of the Los Angeles city school districts." Unpublished manuscript, Los Angeles, 1970.

Hutcheson, B. R. & Krause, E. A. "Systems analysis and mental health services." Community Mental Health Journal, 1969, 5(1): 29-45.

Hutschneker, A. "The stigma of seeing a psychiatrist." New York Times, November 20, 1973: 39.

Hyman, H. H. *Survey design and analysis.* New York: Free Press, 1955.

Hyman, H. H., Cobb, W. J., Feldman, J. J., Hart, C. W., & Stember, C. H. *Interviewing in social research.* Chicago: University of Chicago Press, 1954.

Hyman, H. H. & Wright, C. R. Evaluating social action programs. In P. F. Lazarsfeld, W. H. Sewell, & H. L. Wilensky (eds.), *The uses of sociology.* New York: Basic Books, 1967.

Hyman, H. H., Wright, C. R. & Hopkins, T. K. *Applications of methods of evaluation: four studies of the encampment for citizenship.* Berkeley: University of California Press, 1962.

**I**

IBM. *The multi-state information system for psychiatric patients.* IBM Data Processing Division, 1133 Westchester Avenue, White Plains, New York, GK20-0607-0, April 1973.

Iguchi, M. T. & Hohnson, R. C. "Attitudes of students associated with participation in a mental health hospital volunteer program." Journal of Social Psychology, 1966, 68: 107-111.

*Infant education research project.* Washington, D.C.: U.S. Office of Education, Booklet No. OE-37033.

Isard, W., Bramhall, D., et al. *Methods of regional analysis: an introduction to regional science.* Cambridge, Mass.: MIT Press, 1960.

Iscoe, I. "Community psychology and the competent community." American Psychologist, 1974, 20: 607-613.

Ittleson, W. H., Proshansky, W. M., Rivlin, L. G., Winkel, G. H., & Dempsey D. *An introduction to environmental psychology.* New York: Holt, Rinehart & Winston, 1974.

**J**

Jackson, D. M. & Messick, S. "Response styles in the MMPI: Comparison of clinical and normal samples." Journal of Abnormal and Social Psychology, 1962, 65: 285-299.

Jackson, E. F. "Status consistency and symptoms of stress." American Sociological Review, 1962, 27: 469-480.

Jackson, J. Toward the comparative study of mental hospitals: Characteristics of the treatment environment. In A. F. Wessen (ed.), *The psychiatric hospital as a social system.* Springfield, Ill.: Charles C. Thomas, 1964, pp. 35-87.

Jackson, J. "Factors of the treatment environment." *Archives of General Psychiatry,* 1969, 21: 39-45.

Jacob, P. E. & James F. "Values and their function in decision making." American Behavioral Scientist Supplement, May 1962.

Jamison, D., Fletcher, D., Suppes, P., & Atkinson, R. "Cost and performance of computer-assisted instruction for education of disadvantaged children." Paper presented at the National Bureau of Economic Research Conference on Education as an Industry, Chicago, June 1971.

Janowitz, M. Foreword. In D. Street, R. D. Winter, and C. Perrow, Organization for treatment. New York: Free Press, 1966.

Jenkins, D. H. Force field analysis applied to a school situation. In W. C. Bennus, K. D. Benne, & R. Chin (eds.), The planning of change: Readings in the applied behavioral sciences. New York: Holt, Rinehart & Winston, 1962, pp. 238-244.

Jensen, A. R. "How much can we boost IQ and scholastic achievement?" Harvard Educational Review, 1969, 39: 1-123.

Johanssen, W. J. "Attitudes toward mental patients: A review of empirical research." Mental Hygiene, 1969, 53: 218-228.

Johanssen, W. J., Redel, M. C., & Engel, R. G. "Personality and attitudinal changes during psychiatric nursing affiliation." Nursing Research, 1964, 13(4): 343-345.

Johnson, L. & Reid, J. An evaluation of ten years' work with emotionally disturbed children. Seattle: Ryther Child Center, 1947.

Johnson, N. L. & Smith, H. New developments in survey sampling. New York: Wiley-Interscience, 1969.

Johnson, R., Dokecki, P. R., & Mowrer, O. H., eds. Conscience, contract, and social reality. New York: Holt, Rinehart & Winston, 1970.

Joint Commission on Mental Illness and Health. Action for mental health. Final report of the Joint Commission on Mental Illness and Health, 1961. New York: Basic Books, 1961.

Joint Economic Committee. The analysis and evaluation of public expenditures: The PPB system. 91st Congress, First Session, 1969.

Joint Economic Committee. Economic analysis and the efficiency of government. 91st Congress, Second Session, 1970.

Jones, E. E. Ingratiation. New York: Appleton-Century-Crofts, 1964.

Jones, K. J. "Problems of grouping individuals and the method of modality." Behavioral Science, 1968, 13: 496-511.

Jones, S. J. & Moss, H. A. "Age, state, and maternal behavior associated with infant vocalizations." Child Development, 1971, 42: 1039.

Judd, R. C. "Telephone usage and survey research." Journal of Advertising Research, 1966, 6: 38-39.

# K

Kagan, J. On cultural deprivation. In D. C. Glass (ed.), Environmental influences. New York: Rockefeller University Press, 1968.

Kagan, J. Change and continuity in infancy. New York: John Wiley, 1971.

Kahana, B. & Kahana, E. "Changes in mental status of elderly patients in age-integrated and age-segregated hospital milieus." Journal of Abnormal Psychology, 1970, 75: 177-181.

Kahn, A. J. Studies in social policy and planning. New York: Russell Sage Foundation, 1969.

Kahn, H. & Bruce-Briggs, B. Things to come: Thinking about the 70s and 80s. New York: Macmillan, 1972.

Kahn, R. & Mann, F. Developing research partnerships. In G. J. McCall and J. L. Simmons (eds.), Issues in participant observation: A text and reader. Reading, Mass.: Addison-Wesley, 1969.

Kahn, R. L., Wolfe, D. M., Quinn, R., & Rosenthal, R. A. Organizational stress: Studies in role conflict and ambiguity. New York: John Wiley, 1961.

Kain, J. F. An analysis of metropolitan transportation systems. In T. A. Goldman (ed.), Cost-effectiveness analysis. New York: Frederick A. Praeger, 1967.

Kamisar, Y. "The tactics of police-persecution oriented critics of the courts." Cornell Law Quarterly, 1964, 49: 458-471.

Kane, R. P. & Chambers, G. S. "Seven year follow-up of children hospitalized and discharged from a residential setting." American Journal of Psychiatry, May 1961, 117: 1023.

Kanfer, F. H. & Phillips, J. S. Contract psychology: An operational approach to the problems of conscience and self-control. In R. Johnson, P. R. Dokecki, & O. H. Mowrer (eds.), Conscience, contract, and social reality. New York: Holt, Rinehart & Winston, 1970.

Kanfer, F. H. & Phillips, J. S. The learning foundations of behavior therapy. New York: John Wiley, 1970.

Kantor, M. B., ed. Mobility and mental health. Springfield, Ill.: Charles C. Thomas, 1965.

Kaplan, A. The conduct of inquiry: Methodology for behavioral science. San Francisco: Chandler, 1964.

Kaplan, B. H., ed. Psychiatric disorder and the urban environment. New York: Behavioral Publications, 1971.

Kaplan, S. R. & Roman, M. The organization and delivery of mental health services in the ghetto: The Lincoln Hospital experience. New York: Prager, 1973.

Karnes, M. B. Research and development program on preschool disadvantaged children: final report. Washington, D.C.: U.S. Office of Education, 1969.

Karnes, M. B. & Badger, E. E. Training mothers to instruct their infants at home. In M. B. Karnes, Research and development program on preschool disadvantaged children: Final report. Washington, D.C.: U.S. Office of Education, 1969, pp. 249-263.

Karnes, M. B., Hodgins, A. S., & Teska, J. A. The effects of short-term instruction at home by mothers of children not enrolled in a preschool. In M. B. Karnes, Research and development program on preschool disadvantaged children: Final report. Washington, D.C.: U.S. Office of Education, 1969, pp. 197-203.

Karnes, M. B., Hodgins, A. S., & Teska, J. A. The impact of at-home instruction by mothers on performance in the amelioration preschool. In M. B. Karnes, Research and development program on preschool disadvantaged children: Final report. Washington, D.C.: U.S. Office of Education, 1969, pp. 205-212.

Karnes, M. B., Studley, W. M., Wright, W. R., & Badger, E. D. "Educational intervention at home by mothers of disadvantaged infants." Child Development, 1970, 41: 925-935.

Karnes, M. B., Teska, J. A., Hodgins, A. S., & Badger, E. D. "Educational intervention at home by mothers of disadvantaged infants." Child Development, 1970, 41: 925-935.

Karnes, M. B., Zehrbach, R. R., & Teska, J. A. An ameliorative approach in the development of curriculum. In R. K. Parker (ed.), The preschool in action. Boston: Allyn & Bacon, 1972.

Karno, M. & Edgerton, R. "Perception of mental illness in a Mexican-American community." Archives of General Psychiatry, 1969, 20: 233-238.

Katz, D. "Do interviewers bias poll results?" Public Opinion Quarterly, 1942, 6(2): 248-268.

Katz, D. & Kahn, R. L. The social psychology of organizations. New York: John Wiley, 1966.

Katz, E. "The social itinerary of technical change: Two studies on the diffusion of innovation." Human Organization, 1961, 20: 70-82.

Katz, J., Kunofsky, S., Patton, R. E., & Allaway, N. C. "Cancer mortality among patients in New York mental hospitals." Cancer, 1967, 20(12): 32-43.

Katz, M. M., Lowery, H. A., & Cole, J. O. Behavior patterns of schizophrenics in the community. In M. Lorr (ed.) Explorations in typing psychotics. New York: Pergamon Press, 1967.

Katz, M. M. & Lyerly, S. B. "Methods for measuring adjustment and social behavior in the community: 1. Rationale, description, discriminative validity, and scale development." Psychological Reports, 1963, 13 (Monograph supplement 4-V13).

Kaysen, C. "Data banks and discovery." Public Interest, 1967, 7: 52-60.

Keeney, R. L. "Utility functions for multi-attributed consequences." Management Science, 1972, 18: 276-287.

Keeney, R. L. "Multiplicative utility functions." Technical Report No. 70, Operations Research Center, MIT, Boston, 1972.

Kellam, S. G., Goldberg, S. C., Schooler, N. R., Berman, A., & Shmelzer, J. L. "Ward atmosphere and outcome of treatment of acute schizophrenia." Journal of Psychiatric Research, 1967, 5: 145-163.

Kellam, S. G., Shelzer, J. L., & Berman, A. "Variation in the atmospheres of psychiatric wards." Archives of General Psychiatry, 1966, 14: 551-570.

Keller, S. "The social world of the urban slum child." American Journal of Orthopsychiatry, 1963, 33: 823.

Kelley, F. "Relatives' attitude and outcome in schizophrenia." Archives of General Psychiatry, 1964, 10: 389-394.

Kelly, G. The psychology of personal constructs (Vols. I and II). New York: W. W. Norton, 1955.

Kelman, H. The effect of a brain-damaged child on the family. In H. G. Birch (ed.), Brain damage in children. Baltimore: Williams & Wilkins, 1964.

Kelman, H. The social consequences of social research. In H. Kelman, A time to speak: On human values and social research. San Francisco: Jossey-Bass, 1968.

Kennedy, J. J. "The eta coefficient in complex anova designs." Educational and Psychological Measurement, 1970, 30: 885-889.

Kennedy, R. F. Thirteen days. New York: W. W. Norton, 1969.

Kephart, W. M. & Bressler, M. "Increasing the responses to mail questionnaires: A research study." Public Opinion Quarterly, 1958: 22: 123-232.

Keppel, G. Design and analysis: a researcher's handbook. Englewood Cliffs, N.J.: Prentice-Hall, 1973.

Kiesler, C. A., Collins, B. E., & Miller, N. Attitude change: A critical analysis of theoretical approaches. New York: John Wiley, 1969.

Kildegaard, I. C. "How consumers misreport what they spend." Journal of Advertising Research, 1965, 5: 51-55.

Kilpatrick, F. P., ed. Explorations in transactional psychology. New York: New York University Press, 1961.

Kincaid, H. V. & Bright, M. "Interviewing the business elite." American Journal of Sociology, 1957, 63: 304-311.

King, J. A. & Smith, C. G. "The treatment milieu and prediction of mental hospital effectiveness." Journal of Health and Social Behavior, 1972, 13: 180-194.

King, J. T., Lee, Y. C. P., & Vissacher, M. B. "Single versus multiple gage occupancy and convulsion frequency in C H mice." Proceedings of the Society of Experimental Biological Medicine, 1955, 88: 661-663.

Kinsey, A. J., Pomeroy, W. B., & Martin, C. E. Sexual behavior in the human male. Philadelphia: W. B. Saunders, 1948.

Kiresuk, T. J. & Sherman, R. E. "Goal attainment scaling: A general method for evaluating comprehensive community mental health programs." Community Mental Health Journal, 1968, 4: 443-453.

Kirk, R. E. Experimental design: Procedures for the behavioral sciences. Belmont, Calif.: Wadsworth, 1968.

Kirk, S. A. Early education of the mentally retarded. Urbana: University of Illinois Press, 1958.

Kirk, S. A. The effects of early education with disadvantaged infants. In M. B. Karnes, Research and development program on preschool disadvantaged children: Final report. Washington, D.C.: U.S. Office of Education, 1969.

Kish, G. B. & Hermann, H. T. "The Fort Meade alcoholism treatment program: A follow-up study." Quarterly Journal of Studies on Alcohol, 1971, 32: 628-635.

Kish, G. B., Solberg, K., & Uecker, A. "The relation of staff opinions about mental illness to ward atmosphere and perceived staff roles." Journal of Clinical Psychology, 1971, 27: 284-287.

Kish, G. B. & Stage, T. "College student mental hospital volunteers: Any benefits to the student or to society?" Journal of Community Psychology, 1973, 1: 13-15.

Kish, L. "Some statistical problems in research design." American Sociological Review, 1959, 24: 328-338.

Kittrie, N. N. *The right to be different: Deviance and enforced therapy.* Baltimore: Johns Hopkins Press, 1971.

Kivlin, J. E. "Contributions to the study of mail-back bias." Rural Sociology, 1965, 30: 322-326.

Klarman, H. E. Syphilis control programs. In R. Dorfman (ed.) *Measuring benefits of government investments.* Washington, D.C., 1965.

Klaus, R. A. & Gray, S. W. "The early training project for disadvantaged children: A report after five years." Monographs of the Society for Research in Child Development, 1968, 33 (4, Serial No. 120).

Klee, G., Spiro, E., Bahn, A., & Gorwitz, K. An ecological analysis of diagnosed mental illness in Baltimore. In R. Monroe, G. Klee, & E. Brody (eds.), *Psychiatric epidemiology and mental health planning.* Psychiatric Research Report No. 22, American Psychiatric Association, 1967, pp. 107-148.

Kleffel, D. *A statistical information program for utilization review in extended care facilities.* DHEW Publication No. HSM 72-6500, 1972.

Klein, D. C. *Community dynamics and mental health.* New York: John Wiley, 1968.

Klein, H. D. "The Missouri story, a chronicle of research utilization and program planning." Paper presented at the National Conference of Social Welfare, May 1968.

Klein, W., Levine, M., MacLennan, B., Walker, W., & Fishman, J. R. "Leadership training for new careers: The non-professional counselor, supervisor, and trainer." Unpublished manuscript, Institute for Youth Studies, Howard University, undated. Reprinted by Information Clearinghouse, New Careers Development Program, University Research Corporation, Washington, D.C.

Klerman, G. "Current evaluation research on mental health services." American Journal of Psychiatry, 1974, 131: 783-787.

Klett, S. L., Berger, D. G., Sewall, L. G., & Rice, C. E. "Patient evaluation of the psychiatric ward." Journal of Clinical Psychology, 1963, 19: 347-351.

Kliewer, D. "From aftercare to community care." Final report, Mid-Kansas Rural Aftercare Demonstration. Prairie View Mental Health Center, Newton, Kansas, 1970.

Knop, E., Thompson, M., & Falk, R. F. "Education and job success in a new careers program." Unpublished manuscript, New Careers Research, General College and Minnesota Center for Sociological Research, University of Minnesota, 1969.

Kobler, A. & Stotland, E. *The end of hope: The life and death of a hospital.* New York: Free Press, 1964.

Kobrynski, B. & Miller, A. "The role of the state hospital in the care of the elderly." Journal of the American Geriatrics Society, 1970, 18(3).

Koehler, W. *The place of value in a world of facts.* New York: Liveright, 1938.

Koerner, J. D. *The Parsons College bubble.* New York: Basic Books, 1970.

Kogan, L. "The electrical recording of social casework interviews." Social Casework, 1950, 31: 371-378.

Kolmer, M. & Kern, H. "The resident in community psychiatry: An assessment of changes in knowledge and attitudes." American Journal of Psychiatry, 1968, 125: 698-702.

Komarovsky, M. *Blue collar marriage.* New York: Random House, 1964.

Konopka, G., Kamps, F., Wollinga, J., & Hovda, P. "Implications of a changing residential treatment program." American Journal of Orthopsychiatry, 1961, 31(1): 17-39.

Korkes, L. *The impact of mentally ill children upon their parents.* Unpublished doctoral dissertation. (Dissertation Abstracts, June 1959, 3391.)

Kraft, I., Fushillo, J., & Herzog, E. Prelude to school: An evaluation of an inner-city school program. Children's Bureau Research Report No. 3. Washington, D.C.: Children's Bureau, 1968.

Kramer, M. "Mental health statistics of the future." Eugenics Quarterly, 1966, 13(3).

Krasner, L. & Ullmann, L. P., eds. *Research in behavior modification: New developments and implications.* New York: Holt, Rinehart & Winston, 1965.

Kraus, A. S. & Lilienfeld, A. M. "Some epidemiologic aspects of the high mortality rate in the young widowed group." Journal of Chronic Diseases, 1959, 10(3): 207-218.

Krause, M. S. "Construct validity for the evaluation of therapy outcomes." Journal of Abnormal Psychology, 1969, 74: 524-530.

Kreitman, N., Sainsbury, P., Morissay, J., & Scrivener, J. "Reliability of psychiatric assessments: an analysis." Journal of Mental Science, 1961, 107: 887.

Kroeber, A. Cultural and natural areas of native North America. Berkeley: University of California Press, 1939.

Krutilla, J. V. & Eckstein, O. Multiple purpose river development. Baltimore: Johns Hopkins Press, 1968.

Kulik, J., Martin, R., & Scheibe, K. "Effects of mental hospital volunteer work on students' conceptions of mental illness." Journal of Clinical Psychology, 1969, 25: 326-329.

## L

Laing, R. D. The divided self. Chicago: Quadrangle Books, 1960.

Lamb, H. R. & Goertzel, V. "Discharged mental patients—Are they really in the community?" Archives of General Psychiatry, 1971, 24: 29-34.

Lamb, H. R., Heath, D., & Downing, J. J., eds. Handbook of community mental health practice. San Francisco: Jossey-Bass, 1969.

Lander, B. Towards an understanding of juvenile delinquency. New York: Columbia University Press, 1954.

Lander, J. & Schulman, R. "The impact of the therapeutic milieu on the disturbed personality (Hawthorne Cedar Knolls School, Hawthorne, New York). Social Casework, May 1960, 41(5).

Langner, T. S., Gersten, J. C., Eisenberg, J., Greene, E. L., & Herson, J. H. Children under stress: Family and social factors in the behavior of urban children and adolescents. New York: Columbia University Press, 1973.

Langer, T. S., Greene, E., Herson, J., Demson, J., Goff, J., & McCarthy, E. "Psychiatric impairment in welfare and non-welfare city children." Paper presented at the American Psychological Association Convention, September 1969.

Lansing, J. B., Ginsberg, G. P., & Bresten, K. An investigation of response error. Urbana: University of Illinois Press, 1961.

LaPiere, R. T. "Attitudes vs. actions." Social Forces, 1934, 13: 230-237.

Larson, P., Beldin, N., & Falk, R. F. "A critique of agencies in the Minneapolis new careers program." Unpublished manusacript, New Careers Research, General College and Minnesota Center for Sociological Research, University of Minnesota, 1968.

Larson, P., Bible, M., & Falk, R. F. "Down the up staircase: A study of new careers dropouts." Unpublished manuscript, New Careers Research, General College and Minnesota Center for Sociological Research, University of Minnesota, 1969.

Laska, E., Logemann, G. W., & Weinstein, A. S. "The multi-state information system for psychiatric patients." Transactions of the New York Academy of Sciences, December 1971, 33(8): 780-790.

Laska, E., Weinstein, A., Logemann, G., Bank, R., & Breuer, F. "The use of computers at a state psychiatric hospital." Comprehensive Psychiatry, December 1967, 8(6).

Lasky, D. I. & Dowling, M. "The release rates of state mental hospitals as related to maintenance costs and patient-staff ratio." Journal of Clinical Psychology, 1971, 27: 272-277.

La Sorte, M. A. "The caseworker as research interviewer." American Sociologist, 1968, 3(3): 222-225.

Lawton, M. P. "Correlates of the opinion about mental illness scale." Journal of Consulting Psychology, 1964, 28(1): 94.

Lawton, M. P. "Personality and attitudinal correlates of psychiatric-aid performance." Journal of Social Psychology, 1965, 66: 215-226.

Lawton, M. P. "Institutions for the elderly: Theory, content, and methods for research." Gerontologist, 1970, 10: 305-312.

Lawton, M. P. Ecology and aging, In L. Pastalan and D. H. Carson (eds.) *Spatial-behavioral relationships in the aged.* Ann Arbor: University of Michigan Press, 1970.

Lawton, M. P., Lipton, M. B., & Cohen, J. "Criteria for the evaluation of mental health programs." National Institute of Mental Health Grant, MH-17473. Norristown State Hospital, Norristown, Pennsylvania, 1974.

Layard, P. R. G., ed. *Cost-benefit analysis.* London: Penquin, 1972.

Lazarsfelf, P. F. & Rosenberg, M., eds. *The language of social research.* New York: Free Press, 1955.

Lazarsfelf, P. F. & Thielens, W., Jr. *The academic mind.* New York: Free Press, 1958.

Leavitt, H. J. Applied organization change in industry: Structural, technological and humanistic approaches. In J. G. March (ed.), *Handbook of organizations.* Chicago: Rand McNally, 1965.

Lederer, H. "How the sick view their world." Journal of Social Issues, 1952, 8: 4-15.

Lee, E. S. "Socio-economic and migration differentials in mental disease." Millbank Memorial Fund Quarterly, 1964, 41: 249-268.

Lee, R. D., Jr. & Johnson, R. W. *Public budgeting systems.* Baltimore: Johns Hopkins University Press, 1973.

Lefton, M., Angrist, S., Dinitz, S., & Pasamanick, B. "Social class, expectations and performance of mental patients." American Journal of Sociology, 1962, 68: 79-87.

Lehmann, S. "Personality and compliance: A study of anxiety and self-esteem in opinion and behavior change." Journal of Personality and Social Psychology, 1970, 15(1): 76-80.

Lehmann, S. "Selected self-help: A study of clients of a community social psychiatry service." American Journal of Psychiatry, 1970, 126: 1444-1454.

Leighton, D. C., Harding, J. S., Macklin, D. E., Macmillan, A. M., & Leighton, A. H. *The character of danger.* New York: Basic Books, 1963.

Lemert, E. L. Social structure, social control and deviation. In M. Clinard (ed.), *Anomie and deviant behavior.* London: Free Press, 1964.

Lemkau, P. *Mental hygiene in public health.* New York: McGraw-Hill, 1955.

Lemkau, P. Planning mental health programs for New York City. In Milbank Memorial Fund, *Programs for community mental health,* New York, 1957.

Lemkau, P. Evaluation of the effect of changes in environmental factors, with special attention to public attitudes toward mental health and mental illness. In J. Zubin and F. Freyhan (eds.), *Social psychiatry.* New York: Grune & Stratton, 1968.

Lemkau, P. & Crocetti, G. "An urban population's opinion and knowledge about mental illness." American Journal of Psychiatry, 1962, 118: 692-700.

Lenski, G. E. & Leggett, J. C. "Caste, class and deference in the research interview." American Journal of Sociology, 1969, 65(5): 463-467.

Lerman, P. "Evaluating studies in institutions for delinquents: implications for research and social policies." Social Work, 1968, 3: 55-64.

Levenstein, P. "Cognitive growth in preschoolers through verbal interaction with mothers." American Journal of Orthopsychiatry, 1970, 40: 426-432.

Levenstein, P. *Verbal interaction project.* Mineola, New York: Family Service Association of Nassau County, 1972.

Levenstein, P. "But does it work in homes away from home? Theory into Practice, 1972, 11: 157-162.

Lenvenstein, P. & Levenstein, S. "Fostering learning potential in preschoolers." Social Casework, 1971, 52: 74-78.

Levenstein, P. & Sunley, R. "Stimulation of verbal interaction between disadvantaged mothers and children." American Journal of Orthopsychiatry, 1968, 38: 116-121.

Levin, A. *The satisficers.* New York: McCall, 1970.

Levin, H. M. "A cost-effectiveness analysis of teacher selection." Journal of Human Resources, 1970, 5: 24-33.

Levin, H. M. A new model of school effectiveness. In *Do teachers make a difference?* Washington, D.C.: U.S. Department of Health, Education and Welfare, 1970.

Levine, A. S. "Cost benefit analysis and social welfare program evaluation." Social Service Review, June 1968, 42(2): 173-183.

Levine, M. S. & Pearl, A. "Designs for the evaluation of training programs: training report C.S. Number 13." Unpublished manuscript, Center for Youth and Community Studies, Howard University, 1965.

Levine, R. A. & Williams, A. P., Jr. Making evaluation effective: A guide. Santa Monica, Calif.: RAND Corporation, 1971.

Levy, E. "Long term follow-up of former in-patients at Children's Hospital of the Menninger Clinic." American Journal of Psychiatry, June 1969, 125: 1633-1639.

Levy, L. & Rowitz, L. The ecology of mental disorder. New York: Behavioral Publications, 1973.

Levy, R. A. "Six-session outpatient therapy." Hospital and Community Psychiatry, 1966, 17: 340-343.

Lewin, K. Resolving social conflicts: Selected papers on group dynamics. New York: Harper & Row, 1948.

Lewin, K. Self-hatred among Jews. In G. Lewin (ed.), Resolving social conflicts. New York: Harper & Row, 1948.

Lewin, K. Field theory in social science. New York: Harper & Row, 1951.

Lewin, K. Feedback problems of social diagnosis and action. In W. Buckley (ed.), Modern systems research for the behavioral scientist. Chicago: Aldine, 1968.

Lewis, C. I. Mind and the world order. New York: Scribners, 1929.

Lewis, I. L. & Cleveland, S. E. "Nursing students' attitudinal changes following a psychiatric affiliation." Journal of Psychiatric Nursing, 1966, 4: 223-231.

Lewis, V. & Zeichner, A. "Impact of admission to a mental hospital on the patient's family." Mental Hygiene, 1960, 44: 503-509.

Lewis, W. W. Project Re-Ed: The program and a preliminary evaluation. In C. Rickard (ed.), Unique Programs in Behavior Re-Adjustment. Elmsford, N.Y.: Pergamon.

Li, J. C. R. Statistical inference (Vol. II): The multiple regression and its ramifications. Ann Arbor: Edwards Brothers, 1964.

Lidz, T., Hotchkiss, G., & Greenblatt, M. Patient-family-hospital interrelationships: Some general considerations. In M. Greenblatt, D. Levinson, & R. Williams (eds.), The patient and the mental hospital. New York: Free Press, 1957.

Liebow, E. Tally's corner. Boston: Little, Brown, 1967.

Life, August 11, 1972: 31.

Lifson, M. W. Value theory. In J. M. English (ed.), Cost-effectiveness: The economic evaluation of engineered systems. New York: John Wiley, 1968.

Likert, R. & Bowers, R. G. "Organizational theory and human resource accounting," American Psychologist, 1969, 24: 585-596.

Lindblom, C. E. The policy-making process. Englewood Cliffs, N.J.: Prentice-Hall, 1968.

Lindzey, G. & Aronson, E., Eds. The handbook of social psychology. Reading, Mass.: Addison-Wesley, 1968.

Linn, L. S. "State hospital environment and rates of patient discharge." Archives of General Psychiatry, 1970, 23: 346-351.

Linn, M. "Of wedding bells and apron strings: A study of relatives' attitudes." Family Process, 1966, 50: 100-103.

Linn, R. L. "Development and evaluation of several programmed teaching methods." Educational and Psychological Measurement, 1969, 29(1): 129-146.

Linsky, A. "Who shall be excluded: The influence of personal attributes in community reaction to the mentally ill." Social Psychiatry, 1970, 5: 166-171.

Linton, T. "The education model: A theoretical monograph." Journal of Special Education, 1971, 5(2): 155-190.

Lippitt, R. "The use of social research to improve social practice." American Journal of Orthopsychiatry, 1965, 35(4): 663-669.

Lippitt, R. & Havelock, R. Needed research on research utilization. In Research implications for *educational diffusion.* East Lansing: Department of Education, Michigan State University, 1968.

Lipsky, M. "Toward a theory of street-level bureaucracy." Paper presented for presentation at 1969 Annual Meeting of the American Political Science Association.

Lipton, H. & Klein, D. C. Training psychologists for practice and research in problems of change in the community. In D. Adelson and B. Kallis (eds.), *Community psychology and mental health.* San Francisco: Chandler, 1970.

Little, I. M. D. *A critique of welfare economics* (second ed.). London: Oxford University Press, 1957.

Lord, F. M. "The relation of the reliability of multiple-choice tests to the distribution of item difficulties." Psychometrika, 1952, 17: 181-194.

Lord, F. M. "A theory of test scores." Psychometric Monographs, 1952, No. 7.

Lord, F. M. "An approach to mental test theory." Psychometrika, 1959, 24: 283-302.

Lord, F. M. "Large-scale covariance analysis when the control variable is fallible." Journal of the American Statistical Association, 1960, 55: 307-321.

Lord, F. M. Elementary models for measuring change. In C. W. Harris (ed.), *Problems in measuring change.* Madison: University of Wisconsin Press, 1962.

Lord, F. M. "A paradox in the interpretation of group comparisons." Psychological Bulletin, 1967, 68: 304-305.

Lord, F. M. "Statistical adjustments when comparing pre-existing groups." Psychological Bulletin, 1969, 72(5): 337-337.

Lord, F. M. & Novick, M. R. *Statistical theories of mental test scores.* Reading, Mass.: Addison-Wesley, 1968.

Lorei, T. "Prediction of length of stay out of the hospital for released psychiatric patients." Journal of Consulting Psychology, 1964, 20: 358-363.

Lorr, M. & Hamlin, R. M. "A multimethod factor analysis of behavioral and objective measures of psychopathology." Journal of Consulting and Clinical Psychology, 1971, 36: 136-141.

Lorr, M., Klett, C. J., McNair, D. M., & Lasky, J. J. *Inpatient multidimensional psychiatric scale.* Palo Alto, Calif.: Consulting Psychological Press, 1963.

Lorr, M., McNair, D. M., & Goldstein, A. P. A comparison of time limited and time unlimited psychotherapy. In A. P. Goldstein, K. Heller, & L. B. Sechrest (eds.), *Psychotherapy and the psychology of behavior change.* New York: John Wiley, 1966.

Los Angeles Unified School District. "Evaluation reports: Economic Opportunity Act programs 1968-1969." Unpublished manuscript, Los Angeles, 1969.

Loughmiller, C. *Wilderness road.* Austin: Hogg Foundation for Mental Health, University of Texas, 1965.

Lowinger, P. & Dobie, S. "What makes the placebo work?" Archives of General Psychiatry, 1969, 20: 84-88.

Luborsky, L. "Clinician's judgments of mental health." Archives of General Psychiatry, 1962, 7: 407-417.

Lubove, R. *The professional altruist.* New York: Atheneum, 1965.

Lyden, F. & Miller, E. *Planning, programming, budgeting: A systems approach to management.* Chicago: Markham, 1968.

Lynn, L. E. "Notes from HEW." Evaluation, 1972, 1(1): 24-28.

Lynn, L. E. "A federal evaluation office?" Evaluation, 1973, 1(2): 56-59, 92, 96.

# M

Maass, A. *Design of water resource systems: new techniques for relating economic objectives, engineering analysis and government planning.* Cambridge, Mass.: Harvard University Press, 1962.

Mabel, S. "Outcome of patients taking over a 'critical' staff function." Hospital and Community Psychiatry, 1972, 22: 25-28.

Maccoby, E. E. & Maccoby, N. The interview: A tool of social science. In G. Lindzey (ed.), *Handbook of social psychology* (Vol. I). Reading, Mass.: Addison-Wesley, 1954.

MacDonald, G. *The epidemiology and control of malaria.* London: Oxford University Press, 1957.

MacDonald, G. "The dynamics of helminth infections, with special reference to schistosomes." Transactions of the Royal Society of Tropical Medicine Hygiene, 1965, 59(5): 489-506.

Mack, R. P. & Myers, S. Outdoor recreation. In R. Dorfman (ed.), *Measuring benefits of government investments.* Washington, D.C.: Brookings Institution, 1965.

Mackie, R. R. & Christensen, P. R. *Translation and application of psychological research.* Technical Report 716-1. Goleta, California: Santa Barbara Research Park, Human Factors Research, Inc., 1967.

MacMahon, B. & Pugh, T. F. *Epidemiology: Principles and methods.* Boston: Little, Brown, 1970.

MacNaughton-Smith, P. "The classification of individuals by the possession of attributes associated with a criterion." Biometrics, June 1963.

Maguire, L. M. *Observations and analysis of the literature on change.* Philadelphia: Research for Better Schools, Inc., 1970.

Maidlow, S. T. & Berman, H. "The economics of heroin treatment." American Journal of Public Health, 1972: 1397-1406.

Malinowski, B. *Argonauts of the western Pacific.* New York: E. P. Dutton, 1922.

Maluccio, A. N. "Residential treatment of disturbed children: A study of service delivery." Child Welfare, 1974.

Maluccio, A. N. & Marlow, W. D. "Residential treatment of emotionally disturbed children: A review of the literature." Social Service Review, June 1972, 46(2): 230-250.

Mandel, J. "Flammability of children's sleep-wear." Standardization News, May 1973, 26: 11.

Mandelbaum, D. G. "Soldier groups and Negro soldiers." Psychological Review, 1959, 66: 269.

Mandelbaum, M. "Societal facts." British Journal of Sociology, 1955, 6: 305-317.

Mandelbrote, B. & Folkard, S. "Some factors related to outcome and social adjustment in schizophrenia." Acta Psychiatrica Scandinavica, 1961, 37: 223-235.

Manis, J. G., Hunt, C. L., Brawern, M. J., & Kercher, L. C. "Public and psychiatric conceptions of mental illness." Journal of Health and Human Behavior, 1965, 6: 48-55.

Manis, M., Houts, P. S., & Blake, J. B. "Beliefs about mental illness as a function of psychiatric status and psychiatric hospitalization." Journal of Abnormal and Social Psychology, 1963, 67: 226-233.

Mann, F. C. & Neff, F. W. *Managing major change in organizations.* Ann Arbor, Mich.: Foundation for Research on Human Behavior, 1961.

Manniche, E. & Hayes, D. P. "Respondent anonymity and sata matching." Public Opinion Quarterly, 1957, 21(3): 384-388.

March, J. G., Ed. *Handbook of organizations.* Chicago: Rand McNally, 1965.

March, J. G. & Simon, H. A. *Organizations.* New York: John Wiley, 1958.

Margenau, H. *The nature of physical reality.* New York: McGraw-Hill, 1950.

Marglin, S. A. *Approaches to dynamic investment planning.* New York: North-Holland, 1963.

Marglin, S. A. "The social rate of discount and the optimal rate of investment." Quarterly Journal of Economics, 1963, 77: 95-112.

Marmor, T. R. *The politics of Medicare.* London: Routledge & Kegan Paul, 1970.

Maroney, R. J. "Program milieu and treatment effectiveness." Paper presented at the annual meeting of the American Psychological Association, Washington, D.C., September 1969.

Marris, P. & Rein, M. *Dilemmas of social reform.* London: Routledge & Kegan Paul, 1967.

Marrow, A. J. *The practical theorist: The life and work of Kurt Lewin.* New York: Basic Books, 1969.

Marrow, A. J. Ed. *The failure of success.* New York: Amacon, 1972.

Marshall, A. W. & Goldhamer, H. "An application of Markov processes to the study of the epidemiology of mental disease." American Statistical Association Journal, March 1955.

Maslow, A. H. "Toward a humanistic biology." American Psychologist, 1969, 24: 724-735.

Maslow, A. H. *The farther reaches of human nature.* New York: Viking, 1971.

Mason, W. & Brady, J. V. The sensitivity of the psychoendocrine systems to social and physical environment. In D. Shapiro (ed.), *Psychobiological approaches to social behavior.* Stanford: Stanford University Press, 1964.

Matsushima, J. "Communication and cottage parent supervision in a residential treatment center." Child Welfare, December 1964, 43(10): 529-534.

May, J. J. *Health planning: Its past and potential* (Health Administrative Perspectives No. A5). Chicago: Center for Health Administration Studies, 1967.

May, P. R. A. *Treatment of schizophrenia.* New York: Science House, 1968.

Mayer, M. & Blum, A., Eds. *Healing through living.* Springfield, Ill.: Charles C Thomas, 1971.

Mayo, C., Havelock, R., & Simpson, D. "Attitudes towards mental illness among psychiatric patients and their wives." Journal of Clinical Psychology, 1971, 27: 128-132.

McClelland, W. A. "The process of effecting change." Presidential address to the Division of Military Psychology, American Psychological Association, San Francisco, September 1968.

McCord, J. & McCord, W. "A follow-up report on the Cambridge-Somerville youth study." Annals of the American Academy of Political and Social Science, 1959, 332: 89-97.

McCullough, P. "Training for evaluators–Overview." Supplemental material presented to the NIMH sponsored conference on program evaluation in Washington, D.C., April 1974.

McDill, E. L., McDill, M. S., & Sprehe, J. *Strategies for success in compensatory education: An appraisal of evaluation research.* Baltimore: Johns Hopkins Press, 1969.

McGee, R. K. "The relationship between response style and personality variables." Journal of Abnormal and Social Psychology, 1962, 64: 229-233.

McGregor, D. *The human side of enterprise.* New York: McGraw-Hill, 1960.

McGuire, W. J. "Some impending re-orientations in social psychology: Some thoughts provoked by Kenneth Ring." Journal of Experimental Social Psychology, 1967, 3: 124-139.

McGuire, W. The nature of attitudes and attitude change. In G. Lindzey & E. Aronson (eds.), *The handbook of social psychology.* Reading, Mass.: Addison-Wesley, 1968.

McKeachie. W. J. Research on teaching at the college and university level. In N. L. Gage (ed.), *Handbook of research on teaching.* Chicago: Rand McNally, 1963.

McKeachie. W. J. "Student ratings of faculty." AAUP Bulletin, 1969, 55: 439-444.

McKinlay, J. B. "Some approaches and problems in the study of the use of services: An overview." Journal of Health and Social Behavior, 1972, 13(2): 115-152.

McNabb, N. A. *POR in developmental disabilities: Preliminary instructions manual for problem-oriented recordkeeping in developmental disabilities services.* Monroe Developmental Services, Rochester, N.Y., August 1973.

McNemar, Q. "A critical examination of the University of Iowa studies of environmental influences upon the I.Q." Psychological Bulletin, 1940, 34: 63-92.

McNemar, Q. *Psychological Statistics* (fourth ed.). New York: John Wiley, 1962.

McPartland, T. S. & Richart, R. H. "Social and clinical outcomes of psychiatric treatment." Archives of General Psychiatry, 1966, 14: 179-184.

Mechanic, D. *Mental health and social policy.* Englewood Cliffs, N.J.: Prentice-Hall, 1969.

Mendel, W. "Concepts of effective intensive short-stay treatment programs." Denver, December 15-17, 1965.

Mendel, W. M. "Effects of length of hospitalization on rate and quality of remission from acute psychotic episodes." Journal of Nervous and Mental Disease, 1966, 143: 226-233.

Menz, F. D. "Economics of disease prevention: Infectious kidney disease." Inquiry, 1971: 3-18.

Menzel, H. A. "Scientific communication: Five themes from social science research." American Psychologist, 1966, 21: 999-1004.

Merewitz, L. Cost overruns in public works. In W. A. Niskanen et al. (eds.) Benefit-cost and policy analysis 1972. Chicago: Aldine, 1973.

Merton, R. *Social theory and social structure.* Glencoe, Ill.: Free Press, 1957.

Meyer, J. "Attitudes toward mental illness in a Maryland community." Public Health Reports, 1964, 79: 769-772.

Meyer, V. & Chesser, E. S. *Behavior therapy in clinical psychiatry.* Baltimore: Penguin, 1970.

Michaux, W., Katz, M., Kurland, A., & Gansereit, K. *The first year out: Mental patients after hospitalization.* Baltimore: Johns Hopkins Press, 1969.

Middleton, J. "The prejudices and opinions of mental hospital employees regarding mental illness." American Journal of Psychiatry, 1953, 110: 133-138.

Milbank Memorial Fund. *Decentralization of psychiatric services and continuity of care.* New York: Milbank Memorial Fund, 1962.

Miles, H. C. & Gardner, E. A. "A psychiatric case register: The use of a psychiatric case register in planning community mental health services." Archives of General Psychiatry, June 1966, 14: 571-580.

Miller, E. G. & Rice, A. K. *Systems of organization* (Tavistock pamphlet No. 3). London, 1967.

Miller, G. "Psychology as a means of promoting human welfare." American Psychologist, 1969, 24: 1063-1075 .

Miller, J. G. "Living systems: Basic comments concepts." Behavioral Science, 1965, 10: 193-237.

Miller, J. "The nature of living systems." Behavioral Science, 1971, 16(4): 277-301.

Miller, L. W., Kaplan, R. J., & Edwards, W. "JUDGE: A laboratory evaluation." Organizational behavior and human performance, 1969, 4: 97-111.

Miller, M. "The Waukegan study of voter turnout prediction." Public Opinion Quarterly, 1952, 16: 381-398.

Miller, N. W. "Analytical studies of drive and reward." American Psychologist, 1961, 16: 739-754.

Miller, R. G., Jr. *Simultaneous statistical inference.* New York: McGraw-Hill, 1965.

Mills, C. W. *The sociological imagination.* New York: Oxford University Press, 1959.

Mills, C. W., Ed. *Images of man: The classic tradition in sociological thinking.* New York: George Braziller, 1960.

Mills, E. *Living with mental illness: A study in East London.* London: Routledge & Kegan Paul, 1962.

Minneapolis Public Schools. "Teacher aide program—A research report." Unpublished manuscript, Special School District No. 1, Minneapolis, Minn., 1967. (Reprinted by New Careers Information Clearinghouse, New Careers Institute, University Research Corporation, Washington, D.C.)

Minneapolis New Careers Program. "University component: A summary of the program and its second year's objectives." Unpublished manuscript, Minneapolis, 1969.

Mischel, W. *Personality and assessment.* New York: John Wiley, 1968.

vonMises, L. *Human action: A treatise on economics.* New Haven: Yale University Press, 1949.

Mishler, E. G. & Scotch, N. A. "Sociocultural factors in the epidemiology of schizophrenia: A review." Psychiatry, 1963, 26: 315-351.

Mohring, H. Urban highway investments. In R. Dorfman (ed.), *Measuring benefits of government investments.* Washington, D.C.: Brookings Institution.

Monkman, M. *A milieu therapy program for behaviorally disturbed children.* Springfield, Ill.: Charles C Thomas, 1972.

Moore, C. L. & Jaedicke, R. K. *Managerial accounting.* Cincinnati: South-Western Publishing, 1967.

Moos, R. *Ward atmosphere scale: Preliminary manual.* Stanford, Calif.: Stanford University Medical Center, 1969.

Moos, R. "Size, staffing, and the psychiatric ward treatment environment." Archives of General Psychiatry, 1972, 26: 414-418.

Moos, R. *Ward atmosphere scale manual.* Stanford, Calif.: Department of Psychiatry, Stanford University, 1973.

Moos, R. & Houts, P. "The assessment of the social atmosphere of psychiatric wards." Journal of Abnormal Psychology, 1968, 73: 595-604.

Moos, R. & Insel, P. M., eds. *Issues in social ecology.* Palo Alto, Calif.: National Press Books, 1974.

Moos, R. & Schwartz, J. "Treatment environment and treatment outcome." Journal of Nervous and Mental Diseases, 1972, 154: 264-275.

Moos, R., Shelton, R., & Perry, C. "Perceived ward climate and treatment outcome." Journal of Abnormal Psychology, 1973, 82: 291-298.

Mora, G. et al. "A residential treatment center moves toward the community mental health model." Child Welfare, December 1969, 48(10): 585-590.

Morgan, J. S. Managing change. New York: McGraw-Hill, 1972.

Morissey, J. D. "The Chichester and district psychiatric service." Milbank Memorial Fund Quarterly, 1966, 44(1): 28.

Morissey, J. D. & Sainsbury, P. "Observation on the Chichester and district mental health service." Proceedings of the Royal College of Medicine, 1959, 52: 12, 1061.

Morris, D. & Tweeten, L. "The cost of controlling crime." Annals of Regional Science of the Western Regional Science Association, 1971, 5: 33-49.

Mosher, L. & Gunderson, J. "Special report on schizophrenia: 1972." Schizophrenia Bulletin, NIMH, Issue 7, Winter 1973.

Moss, H. A. "Sex, age, and state as determinants of mother-infant interaction." Merrill-Palmer Quarterly, 1967, 13: 19-36.

Mosteller, F. & Tukey, J. W. "The uses and usefulness of probability paper." Journal of the American Statistical Association, 1949, 44: 174-212.

Moynihan, D. P. "The professionalization of reform." Public Interest, 1965, 1.

Moynihan, D. P. Maximum feasible misunderstanding. New York: Free Press, 1970.

Moynihan, D. P. "Policy vs. program in the '70's." Public Interest, 1970, 20: 90-100.

Mudd, E. H. & Froscher, H. B. "Effects on casework of obtaining research material." Social Casework, 1950, 31: 11-17.

Murnaghan, J. H., Ed. "Ambulatory medical care data: Report of the Conference on Ambulatory Medical Care Records." Medical Care, 1973, 11, Supplement.

Murphy, J. F. Multi-attribute utility analysis: An application in social utilities. Career Education Project Technical Report (74-1), July 1974, Providence, R.I.

Murphy, L. B. "Problems in recognizing emotional disturbance in children." Child Welfare, 1963: 473-487.

Murray, H. A. Explorations in personality. New York: Oxford University Press, 1938.

Musgrave, R. A. The theory of public finance. New York: McGraw-Hill, 1959.

Musgrave, R. A. "Cost-benefit analysis and the theory of public finance." Journal of Economic Literature, 1969, 7: 797-806.

Musgrave, R. A. & Musgrave, P. B. Public finance in theory and practice. New York: McGraw-Hill, 1973.

Mushkin, S. J. "Health as an investment." Journal of Political Economy, 1962, 70: 129-142.

Mushkin, S. J. "Evaluations: Use with caution." Evaluation, 1973, 1(2): 30-35.

Myers, J. & Roberts, B. Family and class dynamics in mental illness. New York: John Wiley, 1959.

Myers, J. K. & Schaffer, L. "Social stratification and psychiatric practice: A study of an out-patient clinic." American Sociological Review, 1954, 19: 307-310.

Myers, J. R. & Bean, L. L. A decade later: A follow-up of social class and mental illness. New York: John Wiley, 1968.

Myers, R. J. "Accuracy of age reporting in the 1950 United States census." Journal of the American Statistical Association, 1954, 49: 826-831.

# N

National Center for Health Statistics. Vital and health statistics, series 11: Data from the National Health Survey. Washington, D.C.: Department of Health, Education and Welfare.

National Committee on Employment of Youth. "An evaluation of the Public Service Careers Program for the Manpower Career Development Agency." Unpublished manuscript, New York, 1969.

National Committee on Employment of Youth. "Models of sub-professional employment. I. The community action program model." Unpublished manuscript, New York, 1967.

National Committee on Employment of Youth. "Where do they go from here? A study of the roads and roadblocks to career mobility for paraprofessionals working in human service agencies." Unpublished manuscript, New York, 1970.

National Council on Crime and Delinquency. "Beyond the opportunity structure." Proposal submitted to National Institute of Mental Health, MH 14345-01, 1967.

National Institutes of Health. *Manual of statistical presentation.* DRG Statistical Items, January 1970, Number 10.

National Institute of Mental Health. *Community mental health center data systems: A description of existing programs.* Public Health Service Publication No. 1990, 1969.

National Institute of Mental Health. *Statistical notes.* Rockville, Maryland: Biometry Branch, Survey and Reports Section (series).

National Science Foundation. *Knowledge into action: Improving the national use of the social sciences.* Report of the Special Commission on the Social Sciences of the National Science Board. Report N S13 69-3, Washington, D.C.: Government Printing Office, 1969.

National Science Foundation. *Federal technology transfer.* Washington, D.C., 1973.

Navarro, V. & Parker, R. D. Models in health services planning. In W. W. Holland (ed.), *Data handling in epidemiology.* London: Oxford University Press, 1970.

Nelson, C. A. "An integrated management information system." Hennepin County MH/MR Area Program, Minneapolis, Minnesota, June 1973.

Nelson, R. H., Singer, M. J., & Johnsen, L. O. "Community consideration in the evaluation of a children's residential treatment center." Proceedings, 81st Annual Convention, American Psychological Association, 1973, pp. 951-952.

Nelson, R. H., Singer, M. J. & Johnson, L. O. "The application of a residential treatment evaluation model." Unpublished manuscript, 1974.

Neser, W. B., Tyroler, H. A., & Cassel, J. "Stroke mortality in the black population of North Carolina in relation to social factors." Paper presented at the American Heart Association Meeting on Cardiovascular Epidemiology, New Orleans, 1970.

Nesselroade, J. R. & Reese, H. W., Eds. *Life-span developmental psychology.* New York: Academic Press, 1972.

New Careers Newsletter. "Evaluation." New Careers Development Center, New York University, 1968, 2(6): 5.

New Careers Newsletter. "Job coaches reduce turnover." New Careers Development Center, New York University, August 1967: 8.

New Careers Newsletter. "Kansas psychiatric aides move for better service and new careers." New Careers Development Center, New York University, 1968, 2(2): 1.

New Careers Newsletter. "The politics of mental health." New Careers Development Center, New York University, 1969, 3(2): 1.

New York State Temporary Commission To Revise the Social Service Law. "Report on the preliminary recommendations on social services and income maintenance of the Temporary State Commission To Revise the Social Service Law." Albany, December 1972.

New York University, Graduate School of Social Work, Center for the Study of Unemployed Youth. "Summary of proceedings: workshop on nonprofessional careers for disadvantaged youth." New York, December 1966.

Newsweek, August 7, 1972: 12-16.

Nicholls, W. L., II. "Dimensions of interviewer performance in the survey." Paper presented at the 60th meeting of the American Sociological Association. 1965.

Nichols, R. C. & Meyer, M. A. "Timing postcard followups in mail questionnaire surveys." Public Opinion Quarterly, 1966, 30: 306-307.

Niskanen, W. A., Harverger, A. C., Haveman, R. H., Turvey, R., & Seckhauser, R., Eds. *Benefit-cost and policy analysis 1972.* Chicago: Aldine, 1973.

Northrup, F. S. *The logic of the sciences and the humanities.* New York: Macmillan, 1947.

Novikoff, A. B. "The concept of integrative levels and biology." Science, 1945, 101(2618): 209-215.

Nuffield Provincial Hospitals Trust. *Medical history and medical care.* London: Oxford University Press, 1971.

Nuckolls, C. B., Cassell, J., & Kaplan, B. H. "Psycho-social assets, life crises and the prognosis of pregnancy." American Journal of Epidemiology, 1972, 95: 431-441.

Nunnally, J. C. *Popular conceptions of mental health: Their development and change.* New York: Holt, Rinehart & Winston, 1961.

Nunnally, J. C. *Psychometric theory.* New York: McGraw-Hill, 1967.

Nunnally, J. C. *Introduction to psychological measurement.* New York: McGraw-Hill, 1970.

Nunnally, J. C. Research strategies and measurement methods for investigating human development. In J. Nesselroade & H. Reese (eds.) *Life-span developmental psychology.* New York: Academic Press, 1972.

Nunnally, J. C. *Educational measurement and evaluation* (second ed.). New York: McGraw-Hill, 1972.

## O

Office of the Secretary of Defense, Assistant Secretary of Defense (Manpower). Guidance paper: Project one hundred thousand. Washington, D.C., March 31, 1967. (Mimeograph).

Ohlin, L., Coates, R., & Miller, A. "Radical correctional reform: A case study of the Massachusetts youth correctional system." Harvard Educational Review, 1974, 44: 74-111.

Olendzki, M. C. *Welfare medical care in New York City: A research study.* Unpublished Ph.D. dissertation, University of London, 1965.

O'Neill, H. W. "Response style influence in public opinion surveys." Public Opinion Quarterly, 1967, 31: 95-102.

Operations Research Incorporated. "Manpower evaluation study." Proposal prepared for the Office of Economic Opportunity in response to RFP No. RPP/E-69-20, November 1968.

Orlans, H. *Contracting for knowledge.* San Francisco: Jossey-Bass, 1973.

Orne, M. T. "On the social psychology of the psychological experiment." American Psychologist, 1962, 17: 776-783.

Overall, B. & Aronson, H. "Expectations of psychotherapy in patients of lower socioeconomic class." American Journal of Orthopsychiatry, 1964, 33: 421.

Overall, J. E. & Klett, C. J. *Applied multivariate analysis.* New York: McGraw-Hill, 1972.

Ozarin, L. & Taube, C. "Psychiatric inpatients: Who, where and future." American Journal of Psychiatry, 1974, 1313: 98-101.

## P

Panzetta, A. F. "The concept of community." Archives of General Psychiatry, 1971, 25: 291-297.

Pappenfort, D. M., Dinwoodie, A., & Kilpatrick, D. M. *Population of children's residential institutions in the United States.* Chicago: University of Chicago Center for Urban Studies, 1968.

Pappenfort, D. M., Kilpatrick, D. M., & Roberts, R. W., Eds. *Child caring: Social policy and the institution.* Chicago: Aldine, 1973.

Parker, S. & Kleiner, R. J. *Mental illness in the urban Negro community.* New York: Free Press, 1966.

Parry, H. J. & Crossley, H. M. "Validity of responses to survey questions." Public Opinion Quarterly, 1950-51, 14: 61-80.

Parsons, T. *The social system.* New York: Free Press, 1951.

Parsons, T. & Fox, R. "Illness, therapy and the modern urban American family." Journal of Social Issues, 1952, 8: 31-44.

Pasamanick, B., Scarpitti, F. R., & Dinitz, S. *Schizophrenics in the community.* New York: Appleton-Century-Crofts, 1967.

"Patients' families protest liberal laws on commitment." Psychiatric News, July 18, 1973: 19.

Paul, B. D. Interview techniques and filed relationships. In A. L. Kroeber et al. (eds.), *Anthropology today.* Chicago: University of Chicago Press, 1953.

Paul, G. L. *Insight vs. desensitization to psychotherapy: An experiment in anxiety reduction.* Stanford: Stanford University Press, 1966.

Paul, G. L. "Strategy of outcome research in psychotherapy." Journal of Consulting Psychology, 1967, 31(2): 109-117.

Pearl, A. "New careerists probe their para-professions: Reports on higher education." Western Interstate Commission for Higher Education, November 1969.

Pearl, A. & Riessman, F. *New careers for the poor: The nonprofessional in human service.* New York: Free Press, 1965.

Perl, L. J. "Family background, secondary school expenditure, and student ability." Journal of Human Resources, 1973, 8: 156-180.

Perrow, C. "The analysis of goals in complex organizations." American Sociological Review, 1961, 26: 854-866.

Perry, S. E. & Wynne, L. C. "Role conflict, role definition, and social change in a clinical research organization." Social Forces, 1959, 38(1): 62-65.

Person, P. H. *A statistical information system for community mental health centers.* PHS Publication No. 1863, 1969.

Peters, C. C. & Van Voorhis, W. R. *Statistical procedures and their mathematical bases.* New York: McGraw-Hill, 1940.

Peterson, D. R. *The clinical study of social behavior.* New York: Appleton-Century-Crofts, 1968.

Pettigrew, T. F. *A profile of the Negro American.* Princeton: D. Van Nostrand, 1964.

Phillips, D. L. "Identification of mental illness: Its consequences for rejection." Community Mental Health Journal, 1967, 3: 262-266.

Phillips, D. L. "Public identification and acceptance of the mentally ill." American Journal of Public Health, 1966, 55: 755-763.

Phillips, D. L. "Rejection: A possible consequence of seeking help for mental disorders." American Sociological Review, 1963, 28: 963-972.

Phillips, D. L. "Rejection of the mentally ill: The influence of behavior and sex." American Sociological Review, 1964, 29: 679-687.

Phillips, L. D. *Bayesian statistics for social scientists.* New York: Thomas Y. Crowell, 1973.

Pigou, A. L. *A study in public finance* (third ed.). London: Macmillan, 1951.

Piliavin, I. "Conflict between cottage parents and caseworkers." Social Service Review, March 1963, 37: 17-25.

Pitt, R. "The concept of family burden." Paper presented at the annual meeting of the American Psychiatric Association, 1969.

Piven, F. F. & Cloward, R. A. *Regulating the poor: The functions of public relief.* New York: Pantheon, 1971.

Plasman, F. B. "The medical record—The basis for an automated information system." Medical Record News, June 1972, 43(3): 15-21.

Pless, I. B. "Chronic illness in childhood: The role of lay family counsellors." Presented at the Health Services Research Conference, Chicago, December 8-10, 1971.

Polanyi, M. A society of explorers. In M. Polanyi, *The tacit dimension.* New York: Doubleday, 1966.

Polanyi, M. "The growth of science in society." Minerva, 1967, 5: 533-545.

Pollack, M., Levenstein, S., & Klein, D. "A three-year posthospital follow-up of adolescent and adult schizophrenics." American Journal of Orthopsychiatry, 1968, 38: 94-109.

Polsky, H. W. Changing delinquent subcultures: A social psychological approach. In H. W. Polsky, D. S. Claster, & C. Goldberg (eds.), *Social system perspectives in residential institutions.* East Lansing: Michigan State University Press, 1970.

Polsky, H. W. *Cottage six: The social systems of delinquent boys in residential treatment.* New York: Russell Sage Foundation, 1962.

Polsky, H. W. & Claster, D. S., in collaboration with Goldberg, C. *The dynamics of residential treatment: a social system analysis.* Chapel Hill: University of North Carolina Press, 1968.

Polsky, H. W., Claster, D. S., & Goldberg, C., Eds. *Social systems perspectives in residential institutions.* East Lansing: Michigan State University Press, 1970.

Polsky, H. W. & Kohn, M. "Participant observation in a delinquent subculture. American Journal of Orthopsychiatry, October 1959, 29: 737.

Pomeroy, W. B. "The reluctant respondent." Public Opinion Quarterly, 1963, 27(2): 287-293.

Popper, K. *Conjectures and refutations.* London: Routledge & Kegan Paul; New York: Basic Books, 1963.

Porter, A. C. *The effects of using fallible variables in the analysis of covariance.* Unpublished Ph.D. dissertation, University of Wisconsin, June 1967. (University Microfilms, Ann Arbor, Michigan, 1968.)

Porter, A. C. "Comments on some current strategies to evaluate the effectiveness of compensatory education programs," and "Comments on the Westinghouse-Ohio University study." Two memoranda prepared for Robert D. Hess for use at the Symposium on the Effectiveness of Contemporary Education Programs in the Early Years: Reports from Three National Evaluations and Longitudinal Studies. Annual Meeting of the American Psychological Association, Washington, D.C., August 31, 1969.

Pratt, S. "Systematic philosophy and organizational change: The perspective of contract psychology." Paper presented as part of the symposium on the Social-Behavioral Scientist as Mental Hospital Superintendent. American Psychological Association, Washington, D.C., September 1967.

Pratt, S. "Administrative theory and involuntary commitment." Paper presented at symposium on Involuntary Hospitalization–A Service or Disservice for the Hospitalized Patient? American Orthopsychiatric Association, Detroit, Michigan, April 1972.

Pratt, S. "Contract-systems approach to community actualization." Paper presented at the 4th International Congress of Social Psychiatry, Jerusalem, Israel, May 1972.

Pratt, S. "Contract therapy: Work and creativity." Paper presented at the 4th International Congress of Social Psychiatry, Jerusalem, Israel, May 1972.

Pratt, S., Scott, G., Treesh, E., Khanna, J., Lesher, T., Khanna, P., Gardiner, G., & Wright, W. "The mental hospital and the treatment field." Monograph No. 8, Journal of Psychological Studies, 1960, 11. (Also published in *Research on the psychiatric hospital as a social system.* Third Annual Conference, Social Science Institute, Washington University, St. Louis, 1961, 53-122.

Pratt, S. & Tooley, J. "Action psychology. I: Action psychology and social action. II: Some metatheoretical and epistemological considerations. III: Some methodological considerations and the research contract." Journal of Psychological Studies, 1967, 15(3). (Whole-issue monograph).

Pratt, S. & Tooley, J. "Human systems actualization through 'participative organization'–A strategy of contract-systems psychology." Paper presented at the Conference on Behavioral Modification as a Function of Social and Interpersonal Factors, Kent State University, April 1969.

Pratt, S. & Tooley, J. "Mental hospitals as active partners in total community actualization." Paper presented at the 7th Annual John W. Umstead Series of Distinguished Lectures, Man, Systems, and Mental Health: Complexity, Dynamics and Viability. North Carolina Department of Mental Health, Raleigh, February, 1970.

Pratt, S. & Tooley, J. Toward a metataxonomy of human systems actualization: The perspective of contract psychology. In A. H. Mahrer (ed.), *New approaches to personality classification.* New York: Columbia University Press, 1970.

President's Committee on Juvenile Delinquency and Youth Crime. *Training for new careers: The Community Apprentice Program.* Washington, D.C.: Government Printing Office, 1965.

Pressman, J. L. & Wildavsky, A. *Implementation.* Berkeley: University of California Press, 1973.

Prest, A. R. & Turvey, R. "Cost-benefit analysis: A survey." Economic Journal, 1965, 75: 683-735.

Price, D. O. & Searles, R. "Some effects of interviewer-respondent interaction on responses in a survey situation." Proceedings of the Social Statistics Section, American Statistical Association, 1961: 211-221.

Proshansky, H. M., Ittelson, W. H., & Rivlin, J. C., Eds. *Environmental psychology.* New York: Holt, Rinehart & Winston, 1970.

Provus, M. Evaluation of ongoing programs in the public school system. In R. W. Tyler (ed.), *Educational evaluation: New roles, new means.* Chicago: University of Chicago Press, 1969.

Pryer, M., Distefano, M., & Marr, L. "Attitude changes in psychiatric attendants following experience and training." Mental Hygiene, 1969, 53: 253-257.

Psacharopoulos, G. *Returns to education.* San Francisco: Jossey-Bass, 1973.

Pulier, M., Honigfeld, G., & Laska, E. *Psychiatric record-keeping: an analysis of current trends.* Information Sciences Division, Research Center, Rockland State Hospital, Orangeburg, New York 10962, 1972.


# Q

Quade, E. S. *Analysis for military decisions.* Chicago: Rand McNally, 1964.


# R

Rabkin, J. G. "Opinions about mental illness: A review of the literature." Psychological Bulletin, March 1972, 77(3).

Radin, N. "The impact of a kindergarten home counseling program." Exceptional Children, 1969, 36: 251-256.

Radin, N. "Three degrees of maternal involvement in a preschool program: Impact on mothers and children." Child Development, 1972, 43: 1355-1364.

Radin, N. & Glasser, P. H. "The use of parental questionnaires with culturally disadvantaged families." Journal of Marriage and the Family, 1965, 27: 373-382.

Radin, N. & Weikart, D. "A home teaching program for disadvantaged preschool children." Journal of Special Education, Winter 1967, 1: 183-190.

Raiffa, H. *Decision analysis: Introductory lectures on choices under certainty.* Reading, Mass.: Addison-Wesley, 1968.

Raiffa, H. *Preferences for multi-attribute alternatives* (Memorandum RM-5968-DOT/RC). The RAND Corporation, April, 1968.

Rainwater, L. & Yancey, W. L. *The Moynihan report and the politics of controversy.* Cambridge, Mass.: MIT Press, 1967.

Ralph, D. E. "Attitudes toward mental illness among two groups of college students in a neuropsychiatric hospital setting." Journal of Consulting Psychology, 1968, 32: 98.

Ramsey, G. V. & Seipp, M. "Attitudes and opinions concerning mental illness." Psychiatric Quarterly, 1948, 22: 428-444.

Ramsey, G. V. & Seipp, M. "Public opinions and information concerning mental health." Journal of Clinical Psychology, 1948, 4: 397-406.

Rashkis, H. A. "Cognitive restructuring: Why research is therapy." AMA Archives of General Psychiatry, June 1960, 2: 34, 612.

Ratcliffe, H. L. & Cronin, M. T. I. "Changing frequency of arteriosclerosis in mammals and birds at the Philadelphia Zoological Garden." Circulation, 1958, 18: 41-52.

Rawnsley, K., Loudon, J. B., & Miles, H. L. "Attitudes of relatives to patients in mental hospitals." British Journal of Preventive and Social Medicine, 1962, 16: 1-15.

Redick R. "Residential treatment centers for emotionally disturbed children, 1968." Statistical Note No. 11. (NIMH, OPPE, Nov. 1969).

Redick, R. & Johnson, M. NIMH Statistical Note No. 100. February 1974, U.S.D. H.E.W.

Redl, F. "Strategy and techniques of the life space interview." American Journal of Orthopsychiatry, January 1959, 29: 1-18.

Redl, F. & Robinson, G. W. "Child psychiatry: Hospital aspects." Mental Hospitals, 1956, 7: 38-41.

Redl, F. & Wineman, D. *Children who hate: The disorganization and breakdown of behavior controls.* Glencoe, Ill.: Free Press, 1951.

Redlich, F., Dollard, J., & Newman, R. "High fidelity recording of psychotherapeutic interviews." American Journal of Psychiatry, 1950, 107: 42-48.

Redlich, F., Hollingshead, A., & Bellis, E. "Social class differences in attitudes toward psychiatry." American Journal of Orthopsychiatry, 1955, 16: 60.

Reid, J. H. & Hagan, H. R. *Residential treatment of emotionally disturbed children.* New York: Child Welfare League of America, 1952.

Reinhar, U. E. "Proposed changes in the organization of health-care delivery: An overview and critique." Milbank Memorial Fund Quarterly, Spring 1973, 51: 169-222.

Reisman, D., Cohen, M., & Pearl, B., eds. *Mental health of the poor.* New York: Free Press, 1964.

"Relationships among (sic) parent ratings of behavioral characteristics of children." National Center for Health Statistics, Series 11, No. 121, October 1972.

Report of Commission Testing. *Righting the balance, I.* New York: College Entrance Examination Board, 1970.

Resnick, M. B. & Van De Riet, V. *Summary evaluation of the Learning to Learn program.* Gainsville: University of Florida, Department of Clinical Psychology, 1972.

Reznikoff, M. "Attitudes to psychiatric nurses and aides toward psychiatric treatment and hospitals." Mental Hygiene, 1963, 47: 354-360.

Reznikoff, M., Gynther, M. D., Toomey, L. C., & Fishman, M. "Attitudes toward the psychiatric milieu: An inter-hospital comparison of nursing personnel attitudes." Nursing Research, 1964, 13: 71-72.

Rheingold, H. L. The social and socializing infant. In D. A. Goslin, *Handbook of socialization theory and research.* Chicago: Rand McNally, 1969.

Rheinstein, M. "Divorce and the law in Germany: A review." American Journal of Sociology, 1959, 65: 489-498.

Ribich, T. *Education and poverty.* Washington, D.C.: Brookings Institution, 1968.

Rice, A. K. *The enterprise and its environment: A systems theory of management organization.* London: Tavistock Publications, 1963.

Rice, C. E., Klett, S. L., Berger, D. G., Sewall, L. G., & Lemkau, P. V. "The Ward Evaluation Scale." Journal of Clinical Psychology, 1963, 14: 251-258.

Rice, D. P. The direct and indirect cost of illness. In *Federal Programs for the development of human resources: A compendium of Papers Submitted to the Sub-committee on Economic Progress,* 1968: 469-490.

Rice, S. A. "Contagious bias in the interview." American Journal of Sociology, 1929, 35(3): 420-423.

Richardson, E. L. Address before the Institute of Medicine. Washington, D.C., May 10, 1972. (Mimeograph)

Richardson, E. R. "Conversational contact." Evaluation, 1972, 1(1): 9-16.

Richardson, S. A., Dohrenwend, B. S., & Klein, D. *Interviewing.* New York: Basic Books, 1965.

Ridker, R. G. *The economic costs of air pollution.* New York: Praeger, 1967.

Riecken, H. W. *The volunteer work camp: A psychological evaluation.* Reading, Mass.: Addison-Wesley, 1952.

Riecken, H. W., Boruch, R. F., Campbell, D. T., Caplan, N., Glennan, T. K., Pratt, J., Rees, A., & Williams, W. *Experimentation as a method for planning and evaluating social innovations.* New York: Seminar Press, 1975.

Rieger, N. & DeVries, A. "The child mental health specialist: A new profession." American Journal of Orthopsychiatry, 1974, 44: 150-158.

Riessman, F. *The culturally deprived child.* New York: Harper, 1962.

Riessman, F. "The revolution in social service: The new nonprofessional." Unpublished manuscript, Mobilization for Youth, New York, November 1963.

Riesmann, F. "Strategies and suggestions for training nonprofessionals." Unpublished manuscript, Albert Einstein College of Medicine, New York, 1966.

Ring, K. "Experimental social psychology: Some sober questions about some frivilous values." Journal of Experimental Social Psychology, 1967, 3: 113-123.

Ring. S. & Schein, L. "Attitudes toward mental illness and the use of caretakers in a black community." American Journal of Orthopsychiatry, 1970, 40: 710-716.

Rivlin, A. *Systematic thinking for social action.* Washington, D.C.: Brookings Institution, 1971.

Roberts, A. O. H. & Larsen, J. K. *Effective use of mental health research information.* Final report for National Institute of Mental Health, Grant No. R01 MH 15445. Palo Alto, California: American Institutes for Research, January 1971.

Robin, S. E. "A procedure for securing returns to mail questionnaires." Sociology and Social Research, 1965, 50: 24-35.

Robins, L. H. & Murphy, G. E. "Drug use in a normal population of young Negro men." American Journal of Public Health, 1967, 57: 1580-1596.

Robinson, J. & Smith, G. "The effectiveness of correctional programs." Journal of Research in Crime and Delinquency, 1971, 17: 67-80.

Rodman, H. & Kolodny, R. L. Organizational strains in the researcher-practitioner relationship. In A. Gouldner and S. M. Miller (eds.), *Applied sociology: Opportunities and problems.* New York: Free Press, 1965.

Roeher, G. A. "Effective techniques in increasing response to mailed questionnaires." Public Opinion Quarterly, 1963, 27: 299-302.

Roen, S. R. & Burns, A. J. *Community adaptation schedule.* New York: Behavioral Publications, 1968.

Rogers, E. M. *Diffusion of innovations.* New York: Free Press, 1962.

Rogers, E. M. & Shoemaker, F. F. *Communication of innovations: A cross-cultural approach.* New York: Free Press, 1971.

Rogler, L. & Hollingshead, A. *Trapped: Families and schizophrenia.* New York: John Wiley, 1965.

Rogow, A. *The psychiatrists.* New York: G. P. Potnam's Sons, 1970.

Rootman, I. & Lafave, H. "Are popular attitudes toward the mentally ill changing?" American Journal of Psychiatry, 1969, 126: 261-265.

Roper, L. "Summary of the Ellsworth affair." Oregon Psychological Association Newsletter, December 1970, 17(2): 9-18.

Rose, A. M. "Needed research on the mediation of labor disputes." Personnel Psychology, 1952, 5: 187-200.

Rose, C. "Relatives' attitudes and mental hospitalization." Mental Hygiene, 1959, 43: 194-203.

Rosen, G. "Social aspects of Jacob Henle's medical thought." Bulletin of the Institute for the History of Medicine, 1937, 5: 509-537.

Rosenberg, M., Glueck, B. G., Jr., & Stroebel, C. F. "The computer and the clincial decision process." American Psychiatric Association, 1967.

Rosenthal, G. D. *The demand for general hospital facilities.* Chicago: American Hospital Association, Hospital Monograph Series No. 14, 1964.

Rosenthal, R. "On the social psychology of the psychological experiment: The experimenter's hypothesis as unintended determinant of experimental results." American Scientist, 1963, 51: 268-283.

Rosenthal, R. *Experimenter effects in behavioral science.* New York: Appleton-Century-Crofts, 1966.

Rosenthal, R. & Jocobson, L. *Pygmalion in the classroom.* New York: Holt, Rinehart & Winston, 1968.

Rosenthal, R. A. & Weiss, R. S. Problems of organizational feedback processes. In R. A. Bauer (ed.), *Social indicators.* Cambridge, Mass.: MIT Press, 1966.

Ross, H. L. & Campbell, D. T. The Connecticut speed crackdown: a study of the effects of legal change. In H. L. Ross (ed.), *Perspectives on the social order: Readings in sociology.* New York: McGraw-Hill, 1968.

Rossi, P. Practice, method and theory in evaluating social action programs. In J. L. Sundquist (ed.), *On fighting poverty: Perspectives from experience.* New York: Basic Books, 1969.

Rossman, P. & Miller, D. "The effect of social prejudice on hospitalized adolescents." American Journal of Psychiatry, 1973, 130: 1029-1030.

Rothenberg, J. *Economic evaluation of urban renewal.* Washington, D.C.: Brookings Institution, 1967.

Rothman, D. J. *The discovery of the asylum.* Boston: Little, Brown, 1971.

Rowntree, G. & Pierce, R. M. "Birth control in Britain, part I: Attitudes and practices among persons married since World War I." Population Studies, 1961, 15: 3-31.

Rubin, E. Z. & Simson, C. B. "A special class program for the emotionally disturbed child in school: A proposal." American Journal of Orthopsychiatry, 1960, 30(1): 144-153.

Ruesch, J. & Brodsky, C. M. "The concept of social disability." Archives of General Psychiatry, 1968, 19: 394-403.

Rulon, P. J., Tiedeman, D. V., Tatsuoka, M. M., and Langmuir, C. *Multivariate statistics for personnel classification.* New York: John Wiley, 1967.

Rutter, M. "The influence of organic and emotional factors on the origins, nature, and outcome of childhood psychosis." Developmental Medicine and Child Neurology, 1965, 7: 518-528.

Ryan, W. *Distress in the city.* Cleveland: Case Western Reserve University Press, 1969.

## S

Saenger, G. "Patterns of change among treated and untreated patients seen in psychiatric community mental health clinics." Journal of Nervous and Mental Disease, 1970, 150: 37-50.

Sainsbury, P. "Community psychiatric services and the general practitioner." Journal of the Royal College of General Practitioners, 1969, Supplement 3, 17.

Sainsbury, P. "Medical research council clinical psychiatry unit." Psychological Medicine, 1971, 1: 429.

Sainsbury, P. "Suicide, opinions and facts." Proceedings of the Royal Society of Medicine, 1973, 66: 579.

Sainsbury, P. "Suicide and depression." British Journal of Psychiatry, 1968, Special publications 2(2).

Sainsbury, P. "Incidence rates and the evaluation of services." Abstract 289, 5th World Congress of Psychiatry, Mexico City, 1969.

Sainsbury, P. "Social and community psychiatry." American Journal of Psychiatry, 1969, 125: 1226.

Sainsbury, P. "The social relations of suicide." Social Science and Medicine, 1972, 6: 189.

Sainsbury, P., Costain, W. R., & Grad, J. "The effects of a community service on the referral rates and admission rates of elderly psychiatric patients." Psychiatric Disorders in the Aged, 1967, 23. Proceedings of the World Psychiatric Association Symposium, London.

Sainsbury, P. & Grad, J. Evaluation of treatment and services, in Nuffields Provincial Hospital Trust. *In Burden on the community.* London: Oxford University Press, 1962.

Sainsbury, P. & Grad, J. "The effects of community care on the family of the geriatric patient." Journal of Geriatric Psychiatry, 1970, 4: 23.

Sakamoto, Y. "A study of the attitude of Japanese families of schizophrenics toward their ill members." Psychotherapy and Psychosomatics, 1969, 17: 365-374.

Salsbery, D. L. In P. M. McCullough, *Accounting guidelines for mental health centers and related facilities.* Boulder, Colo.: Western Interstate Commission for Higher Education, 1971.

Sampson, H. Messinger, S., & Towne, R. "Family processes and becoming a mental patient." American Journal of Sociology, 1962, 68: 88-96.

Samuelson, P. A. *Economics* (eighth ed.) New York: McGraw-Hill, 1970.

Sanazaro, P. J. Federal health services research and development under the auspices of the National Center for Health Services Research and Development. In E. E. Flock and P. J.

Sanazaro (eds.), *Health services research and R & D in perspective.* Ann Arbor: University of Michigan, Health Administration Press, 1973.

Sanford, N. "Psychology in action: Research with students as action and education." American Psychologist, 1969, 24: 544-546.

Sanford, N. "Whatever happened to action research?" Journal of Social Issues, 1970, 26(4): 3-23.

Sanford, N. & Comstock, C. *Sanction for evil: Sources of social destructiveness.* San Francisco: Jossey-Bass, 1971.

Sarbin, T. R. & Mancuso, J. C. "Failure of a moral enterprise: Attitudes of the public toward mental illness." Journal of Consulting and Clinical Psychology, 1970, 35: 159-173.

Sarbin, T. R. & Mancuso, J. C. "Paradigms and moral judgments: Improper conduct is not disease." Journal of Consulting and Clinical Psychology, 1972, 39: 6-8.

Sashkin, M., Morris, W. C., & Horst, L. "A comparison of social and organizational change models: Information flow data use processes." Psychological Review, 1973, 80: 510-526.

Sattler, J. M. & Leppla, B. W. "A survey of the need for children's mental health facilities." Mental Hygiene, 1969, 53(4): 643-645.

Saunders, D. R. "Moderator variables in prediction." Educational and Psychological Measurement, 1956, 16: 209-222.

Savage, L. J. Subjective probability and statistical practice. In M. S. Bartlett (ed.), *The foundation of statistical inference.* London: Methuen Company, Ltd, 1962.

Sawyer, J. & Schechter, H. "Computers, privacy, and the National Data Center: The responsibility of social scientists." American Psychologist, 1968, 23: 810-818.

Schachter, S. "Deviation, rejection and communication." Journal of Abnormal and Social Psychology, 1951, 46: 190-207.

Schaefer, E. S. *Progress report: Intellectual stimulation of culturally-deprived parents.* Bethesda, Md.: National Institute of Mental Health, 1968.

Schaefer, E. S. Need for early and continuing education. In V. H. Denenberg (ed.), *Education of the infant and young child.* New York: Academic Press, 1970.

Schaefer, E. S. "Parents as educators: Evidence from cross-sectional longitudinal and intervention research." Young Children, 1972, 27: 227-239.

Schaefer, E. S. & Aronson, M. Infant education research project: Implementation and implications of the home-tutoring program. In R. K. Parker (ed.), *The preschool in action.* Boston: Allyn & Bacon, 1972.

Schank, R. L. & Goodman, C. "Reactions to propaganda on both sides of a controversial issue." Public Opinion Quarterly, 1939, 3: 107-112.

Schatzman, L. & Strauss, A. "Social class and modes of communication." American Journal of Sociology, 1955, 60: 329-338.

Scheff, T. J. "The role of the mentally ill and the dynamics of mental disorder: A research framework." Sociometry, 1963, 26: 436-453.

Scheff, T. J. *Being mentally ill.* Chicago: Aldine, 1966.

Schelling, T. C. The life you save may be your own. In S. B. Chase (ed.), *Problems in public expenditure analysis.* Washington, D.C.: Brookings Institution, 1968.

Schick, A. "From analysis to evaluation." Annals of the American Academy of Political and Social Science, 1971, 394: 57-71.

Schlaifer, R. *Analysis of decisions under uncertainty.* New York: McGraw-Hill, 1969.

Schmuck, R. Social psychological factors in knowledge utilization. In T. L. Eidell and J. M. Kitchel (eds.), *Knowledge production and utilization in educational administration.* Eugene: Center for the Advanced Study of Educational Administration, University of Oregon, 1968.

Schneider, J. B. "The spatial structure of the medical care process." RSRI Discussion Paper Series, No. 14. Philadelphia: RSRI, 1967.

Schoenheimer. R. *Dynamic steady state of body constituents.* Cambridge, Mass.: Harvard University Press, 1942.

Schoggen, M. and Schoggen, P. *Environmental forces in home lives of three-year-old children in three population sub-groups.* Nashville, Tennessee: George Peabody College for Teachers, Demonstration and Research Center for Early Education Papers and Reports, 5(2), 1971.

Schon, D. A. *Beyond the stable state.* New York: W. W. Norton, 1971.

Schorer, C. E., Lowinger, P., Sullivan, T., & Hartlaub, G. H. "Improvement without treatment." Diseases of the Nervous System, 1968, 29: 100-104.

Schrager, J. "A focus for supervision of residential staff in a treatment institution." Bulletin of the Menninger Clinic, March 1954, 18: 64.

Schroder, D. & Ehrlich, D. "Rejection by mental health professionals: A possible consequence of not seeking appropriate help for emotional disorders." Journal of Health and Social Behavior, 1968, 9: 222-232.

Schulberg, H. C. & Baker, F. "Program evaluation models and the implementation of research findings." American Journal of Public Health, 1968, 58(7): 1248-1255.

Schulberg, H. C., Sheldon, A., & Baker, F. *Program evaluation in the mental health fields.* New York: Behavioral Publications, 1969.

Schultz, T. W. "Capital formation by education." Journal of Political Economy, 1960, 68: 571-583.

Schultze, C. L. *The politics and economics of public spending.* Washington, D.C.: Brookings Institution, 1968.

Schumach, M. "Halfway houses for former mental patients create serious problems for city's residential communities." New York Times, January 12, 1974: 31.

Schumach, M. "D.S. checking Creedmoor and its release of patients." New York Times, January 23, 1974: 37.

Schuman, H. "The random probe: A technique for evaluating the validity of closed questions." American Sociological Review, 1966, 31: 218-222.

Schwartz, C. "The stigma of mental illness." Journal of Rehabilitation, 1956, 21: 7.

Schwartz, C. "Perspectives on deviance: Wives: definitions of their husbands' mental illness." Psychiatry, 1957, 20: 275-291.

Schwartz, M. What is a therapeutic milieu? In M. Greenblatt, D. G. Levinson, & R. H. Williams (eds.), *The patient and the mental hospital.* New York: Free Press, 1957.

Schwartz, M. & Schwartz, C. G. "Problems of participant observation." American Journal of Sociology, 1955, 15: 343-353.

Schwartz, R. D. "Field experimentation in sociological research." Journal of Legal Education, 1961, 13: 401-410.

Schwartz, R. D. & Orleans, S. "On legal sanctions." University of Chicago Law Review, 1967, 34: 274-300.

Schwartz, R. D. & Skolnick, J. H. Televised communication and income tax compliance. In L. Arons and M. May (eds.), *Television and human behavior.* New York: Appleton-Century-Crofts, 1963.

Schwitzgebel, R. L. "Behavior instrumentation and social technology." American Psychologist, 1970, 25: 491-499.

Scotch, N. A. "A preliminary report on the relation of socio-cultural factors to hypertension among the Zulu." Annals of the New York Academy of Science, 1960, 85: 1000.

Scotch, N. A. "Sociocultural factors in the epidemiology of Zulu hypertension." American Journal of Public Health, 1963, 52: 1205-1213.

Scott, W. R. Field methods in the study of organizations. In A. Etzioni (ed.), *A sociological reader on complex organizations.* New York: Holt, Rinehart & Winston, 1969.

Scriven, M. The methodology of evaluation. In S. Tyler, R. M. Gagne, & M. Scriven (eds.), *Perspectives on curriculum education.* Chicago: Rand McNally, 1967.

See, P. *The labeling and allocation of deviance in a southern state: A sociological theory.* (Dissertation Abstracts, 1968, 29(2A): 687-688.)

Sehdev, H. S. "Adapting the Weed system to child psychiatric records." Hospital and Community Psychiatry, January 1974, 25(1): 31-32.

Sehmais, A. *Implementing nonprofessional programs in human services.* New York: Center for the Study of Unemployed Youth, Graduate School of Social Work, New York University, 1967.

Seidenberg, R. "Drug advertising and perception of mental illness." Mental Hygiene, 1971, 55: 21-31.

Sells, S. B. "An interactionist looks at the environment." American Psychologist, 1963, 18: 696-702.

Selowsky, M. An attempt to estimate rates of return to investment to infant nutrition. In W. A. Niskanen, A. C. Harberger, R. H. Haveman, R. Turvey, & R. Seckhauser (eds.), *Benefit-cost and policy analysis 1972*. Chicago: Aldine, 1973.

Selvin, H. "A critique of tests of significance in survey research." American Sociological Review, 1957, 22: 519-527.

Selye, H. "The general adaptation syndrome and diseases of adaptation." Journal of Clinical Endocrinology, 1946, 6: 117.

Seward, G. H. *Psychotherapy and culture conflict in community mental health*. New York: Ronald Press, 1972.

Shapiro, S. & Eberhart, J. C. "Interviewer differences in an intensive interview survey." International Journal of Opinion and Attitude Research, 1947, 1(2): 1-17.

Shaw, C. R. & McKay, H. D. *Juvenile delinquency in urban areas* (second ed.). Chicago: University of Chicago Press, 1969.

Sheldon, A. & Baker, F. *Systems of medical care*. Cambridge, Mass.: MIT Press, 1970.

Shepard, H. A. Changing interpersonal and interagency relationships in Organizations. In J. C. Marsh (ed.), *Handbook of organizations*. Chicago: Rand McNally, 1965.

Sherwood, S. The impact of home care service programs. In T. O. Bjerts (ed.), *Housing and environment for the elderly*. Washington, D.C.: Gerontological Society, 1973.

Sherwood, S., Greer, D. S., Morris, J. N., and Sherwood, C. C. *The Highland Heights experiment: A final report*. Washington, D.C.: Government Printing Office, 1973.

Shevky E. & Bell, W. *Social area analysis*. Stanford: Stanford University Press, 1955.

Shevky, E. & Williams, M. *The social areas of Los Angeles: Analysis and typology*. Berkeley and Los Angeles: University of California Press, 1949.

Shewhart, W. A. *Statistical method from the viewpoint of quality control*. Washington, D.C.: Graduate School, Department of Agriculture, 1938.

Shlien, J. M. "Time-limited psychotherapy: An experimental investigation of practical values and theoretical implications." Journal of Consulting Psychology, 1957, 4: 318-322.

Short, J. F., Jr. & Strodtbeck, F. L. *Group process and gang delinquency*. Chicago: University of Chicago Press, 1965.

Shostrom, E. L. *Man, the manipulator: The inner journey from manipulation to actualization*. New York: Abingdon Press, 1967.

Shubin, M., Ed. *Game theory and related approaches to social behavior*. New York: John Wiley, 1964.

Shyne, A. W. Research on child-caring institutions. In D. M. Pappenfort, D. M. Kilpatrick, & R. W. Roberts (eds.), *Child caring: Social policy and the institution*. Chicago: Aldine, 1973.

Sidman, J. & Moos, R. "The relationship between psychiatric ward atmosphere and helping behavior." Journal of Clinical Psychology, 1973, 29: 74-77.

Sieveking, N. & Doctor, R. "Student attitudes toward physical, psychological and social problems." Proceedings of the 77th Annual Convention, American Psychological Association, 1969, 4: 855-856.

Sliver, H. "The residential treatment of emotionally disturbed children: An evaluation of fifteen years' experience." (Hawthorne Cedar Knowws, Hawthorne, N.Y. and Bellefaire, Cleveland, Ohio). Journal of Jewish Communal Service, Winter 1961, 38(2).

Silverman, D. *The theory of organizations*. New York: Basic Books, 1971.

Simon, A. J. "Residential treatment of children: Unanswered questions." Social Service Review, 1956, 30: 26.

Simon, A. J. & Gershenson, C. P. "Residential treatment of children." Social Service Review, September 1956, 30(3): 260-275.

Simon, H. A. *Administrative behavior*. New York: Free Press, 1947.

Simon, J. *English sanitary institutions*. London: Cassell, 1890.

Simon, J. L. "The price elasticity of liquor in the United States and a simple method of determination." Econometrica, 1966, 34: 193-205.

Simon, J. L. *Basic research methods in social science: The art of empirical investigation.* New York: Random House, 1969.

Sinnett, E. R., Stimpert, W. E., & Straight, E. A. "Five-year follow-up of psychiatric patients." American Journal of Orthopsychiatry, 1965, 35: 573-580.

Skeels, H. M. "Adult status of children from contrasting early life experiences." Monographs of the Society for Research in Child Development, 1966, 31, Serial No. 105.

Skeels, H. M. & Dye, H. B. "A study of the effects of differential stimulation on mentally retarded children." Proceedings and Addresses of the American Association on Mental Deficiency, 1939, 44: 114-136.

Skeels, H. M., Updegraff, R., Wellman, B. L., & Williams, H. M. "A study of environmental stimulation: an orphanage preschool project." University of Iowa Studies in Child Welfare, 1938, 15, No. 4.

Skipper, J. K., Jr., & Ellison, M. E. "Personal contact as a technique for increasing question-naire returns from hospitalized patients after discharge." Journal of Health and Human Behavior, 1966, 7: 211-214.

Skodak, M. & Skeels, H. M. "A final follow-up study of 100 adopted children." Journal of Genetic Psychology, 1949, 75: 86-125.

Sjoberg, G., Brymer, R., & Farris, B. "Bureaucracy and the lower class." Sociology and Social Research, 1966, 50: 325-327.

Sjoberg, G. & Cain, L. D., Jr. Negative values, countersystem models, and the analysis of social systems. In H. Turk & R. L. Simpson (eds.), *Institutions and social exchange: The sociologies of Talcott Parsons and George C. Homans.* Indianapolis: Bobbs-Merrill, 1971.

Sjoberg, G. & Nett, R. *A methodology for social research.* New York: Harper & Row, 1968.

Sjoberg, G. & Vaughan, T. R. The sociology of ethics and the ethics of sociology. In E. Tiryakian (ed.), *The phenomenon of sociology.* New York: Appleton-Century-Crofts, 1971.

Slate, S. Service support programs developed for Highland Heights residents since its develop-ment to fall 1972. In S. Sherwood, D. S. Greer, J. N. Morris, & C. C. Sherwood, *The Highland Heights experiment: a final report.* Washington, D.C.: Government Printing Office, 1973.

Smith, A., Traganza, E., & Harrison, G. "Studies on the effectiveness of anti-depressant drugs." Psychopharmacology Bulletin, March 1969: 1-53.

Smith, C. G. "Mental hospitals: A study in organizational effectiveness." Notre Dame, Ind.: University of Notre Dame Department of Sociology and Anthropology, 1971. (Mimeo-graphed).

Smith, D. K. "Correcting for social desireability response sets in opinion-attitude survey research." Public Opinion Quarterly, 1967, 31: 87-94.

Smith, D. M. "A theoretical framework for geographical studies of industrial location." Economic Georgraphy, April 1966.

Smith, E. V. "Field interviewing of problem drinkers." Social Work, 1959, 4: 80-86.

Smith, J. J. "Psychiatric hospital experience and attitudes toward 'mental illness.' " Journal of Consulting and Clinical Psychology, 1969, 33: 302-306.

Smith, J. O. *Social research in a psychiatric setting: The natural history of a research project.* Unpublished dissertation, Ohio State University, 1969.

Smith, K. R., Miller, M., & Golladay, F. L. "An analysis of the optimal of inputs in the production of medical services." Journal of Human Resources, 1972, 7: 208-225.

Smith, L. C., Hawley, C. J., & Grant, R. L. "Questions frequently asked about the problem-oriented record in psychiatry." Hospital and Community Psychiatry, January 1974, 25(1): 17-22.

Smith, M. B. "Toward a scientific and professional responsibility." American Psychologist, 1954, 9: 513-516.

Smith, M. B. School and home: Focus on achievement. In A. H. Passow (ed.), *Developing programs for the educationally disadvantaged.* New York: Teachers College Press, 1968.

Smith, M. S. & Bissell, J. S. "Report analysis: The impact of Head Start." Harvard Educational Review, 1970, 40: 51-104.

Smith, W. R. "Police-community relations aides in Richmond, California." Unpublished manuscript, Survey Research Center, University of California at Berkeley, 1967.

Snapper, K. J. & Peterson, C. "Information seeking and data diagnosticity." Journal of Cognitive Psychology, 1971, 87: 429-433.

Snedicor, G. W. Statistical methods (fifth ed.). Ames: Iowa State College Press, 1956.

Snedicor, G. W. & Cochran, W. G. Statistical methods. Ames: Iowa State University Press, 1967.

Snow, J. On the mode of communication of cholera (second ed.) London: J. Churchill, 1855. (Reprinted as Snow on cholera. New York: Commonwealth Fund, 1936.)

Soar, R. S. "An integrative approach to classroom learning." NIMH Project No. 5-R11MH01096 to the University of South Carolina and 7-R11MH 02045 to Temple University, 1966.

Soar, R. S. Follow-through classroom process measurement and pupil growth (1970-71). Gainesville, Fla.: University of Florida College of Education, 1972.

Soar, R. S. & Soar, R. M. "Pupil subject matter growth during summer vacation." Educational Leadership Research Supplement, 1969, 2: 577-587.

Sobol, M. G. "Panel mortality and panel bias." Journal of the American Statistical Association, 1959, 54: 52-68.

Solomon, R. W. "An extension of control group design." Psychological Bulletin, 1949, 46: 137-150.

Somers, G. G. & Stromsdorfer, E. W. "A cost-effectiveness analysis of in-school and summer Neighborhood Youth Corps: nationwide analysis." Journal of Human Resources, 1972, 7: 446-459.

Sommer, R. "Letter-writing in a mental hospital." American Journal of Psychiatry, 1958, 115: 514-517.

Sommer, R. "Visitors to mental hospitals: A fertile field for research." Mental Hygiene, 1959, 43: 8-15.

Sonquist, J. A. & Morgan, J. N. "The detection of interaction effects: A report on a computer program for the selection of optimal combinations of explanatory variables." Unpublished manuscript, University of Michigan, 1964.

Sorensen, J. E. & Phipps, D. W. Cost-finding and rate-setting for community mental health centers. Association of Mental Health Administrators, 2901 Lafayette Avenue. Lansing, Michigan, December 1971.

Spearman, C. " 'General intelligence' objectivity determined and measured." American Journal of Psychology, 1904, 15: 201-293.

Special Commission on the Social Sciences. Knowledge into action: Improving the nation's use of the social sciences. Washington, D.C.: National Science Foundation, 1969.

Sperry UNIVAC Computer Systems. Series 70, program application, statistical system, BMDP series. Systems Publications, Building 24-1, Cinnaminson, New Jersey, January 1973.

Spiegel, D. & Younger, J. "Ward climate and community stay of psychiatric patients." Journal of Consulting and Clinical Psychology, 1972, 39: 62-69.

Spiegel, J. & Bell, N. The family of the psychiatric patient. In S. Arieti (ed.), The American handbook of psychiatry. New York: Basic Books, 1969.

Spitzer, R. L. & Endicott, J. "Automation of psychiatric case records." International Journal of Psychiatry, 1970-71, 9: 604-621.

Spitzer, R. L. & Endicott, J. "An integrated group of forms for automated psychiatric case records." Archives of General Psychiatry, June 1971: 24.

Spitzer, S. & Denzin, N. The mental patient: Studies in the sociology of deviance. New York: McGraw-Hill, 1968.

Spitzer, S., Morgan, P., & Swanson, R. "Determinants of the psychiatric patient career: Family reactions and social work intervention." Social Service Review, 1971, 45: 74-85.

Sprigle, H. Learning to learn program. In S. Ryan (ed.), A report of longitudinal evaluation of preschool programs. Washington, D.C.: Office of Child Development, 1972.

Stanford Research Institute. Implementation of a planned variation in Head Start: preliminary evaluation of planned variation in Head Start according to follow-through approaches *(1969-70)*. Washington, D.C.: Office of Child Development, U.S. Department of HEW, 1971.

Stanford Research Institute. *Longitudinal evaluation of selected features of the national follow-through program*. Washington, D.C.: Office of Child Development, U.S. Department of HEW, 1971.

Stanley, D. T., Mann, D. E., & Doig, J. W. *Men who govern: A biographical profile of federal political executives*. Washington, D.C.: Brookings Institution, 1967.

Stanton, A. H. & Schwartz, M. S. *The mental hospital*. New York: Basic Books, 1954.

Star, S. "The public's ideas about mental illness." University of Chicago, National Opinion Research Center, 1955. (Mimeographed).

Stein, Z., Susser, M., & Guterman, A. "Screen programme for the prevention of Down's syndrome." Lancet, 1973, 1(7798): 305-310.

Stevenson, I. "The challenge of results in psychotherapy." American Journal of Psychiatry, 1959, 116: 120-123.

Stieber, J. W. *Ten years of the Minnesota Labor Relations Act*. Minneapolis: University of Minnesota, Industrial Relations Center, 1949.

Stinchcombe, A. L. *Constructing social theories*. New York: Harcourt, Brace & World, 1968.

Stinchcombe, A. L. "Environment: The cumulation of events." Harvard Educational Review, 1969, 39: 511-522.

Storrow, H. A. "The measurement of outcome in psychotherapy." Archives of General Psychiatry, 1960, 2: 142-146.

Stotland, E. & Kobler, A. L. *The life and death of a mental hospital*. Seattle: University of Washington Press, 1965.

Stouffer, S. A. The point system for redevelopment and discharge. In S. A. Stouffer, et al., *The American soldier. Volume II: Combat and its aftermath*. Princeton: Princeton University Press, 1949.

Stouffer, S. A. et al. *Measurement and prediction*. (Vol. IV) Princeton: Princeton University Press, 1950.

Street, D., Vinter, R. D., & Perrow, C. *Organization for treatment: A comparative study of institutions for delinquents*. New York: Free Press, 1966.

Struening, E. L. & Cohen, J. "Factorial invariance and other psychometric characteristics of five opinions about mental illness factors." Educational and Psychological Measurement, 1963, 23: 289-298.

Struening, E. L., Lehmann, S., & Rabkin, J. G. Context and behavior: A social area study of New York City. In E. B. Brody (ed.), *Behavior in new environments*. Beverly Hills: Sage Publications, 1970.

Struening, E. L. & Peck, H. B. The role of research in evaluation. In R. H. Williams & L. D. Ozarin (eds.), *Community mental health*. San Francisco: Jossey-Bass, 1968.

Struening, E. L., Rabkin, J. G., Cohen, P. Raabe, G., Muhlin, G., & Cohen, J. "Family ethnic and economic indicators of low birth weight and infant mortality: a social area analysis." Annals of the New York Academy of Sciences, 1973, 218: 87-107.

Struening, E. L., Rabkin, J. G., & Peck, H. B. Migration and ethnic membership in relation to social problems. In E. B. Brody (ed.), *Behavior in new environments*. Beverly Hills: Sage Publications, 1970.

Strupp, H. H. & Bloxom, A. L. "Preparing low-class patients for group psychotherapy: development and evaluation of a role-induction film." Journal of Consulting and Clinical Psychology, 1973, 41: 373-384.

Suchman, E. A. *Evaluative research: Principles and practice in public service and social action programs*. New York: Russell Sage Foundation, 1967.

Suchman, E. A. "Evaluating educational programs." Urban Review, 1969, 3(4): 15-17.

Sudman, S. "Quantifying interviewer quality." Public Opinion Quarterly, 1966-67, 30: 664-667.

Sudman, S. *Reducing the cost of surveys*. Chicago: Aldine, 1967.

Suits, D. B. "Use of dummy variables in regression equations." Journal of the American Statistical Association, 1957, 52: 548-551.

Sullivan, H. S. *The interpersonal theory of psychiatry.* New York: W. W. Norton, 1953.

Sullivan, H. S. *The fusion of psychiatry and social science.* New York: W. W. Norton, 1964.

Summers, G. F. & Hammonds, A. D. "Effect of racial characteristics of investigator on self-enumerated responses to a Negro prejudice scale." Social Forces, 1966, 44(4): 515-518.

Sundquist, J. L. & Davis, D. W. *Making federalism work.* Washington, D.C.: Brookings Institution, 1969.

Suppes, P. & Morningstar, M. "Computer-assisted instruction." Science, 1969, 166: 343-350.

Suppes, P. & Morningstar, M. *Evaluation of three computer-assisted instruction programs.* Stanford: Psychology Series, 1969.

Susser, M. W. & Watson, W. *Sociology in medicine.* London: Oxford University Press, 1962.

Suttles, G. D. *The social construction of communities.* Chicago: University of Chicago Press, 1972.

Swanson, R. & Spitzer, S. "Stigma and the psychiatric patient career." Journal of Health and Social Behavior, 1970, 11: 44-51.

Sween, J. & Campbell, D. T. "A study of the effect of proximally auto-correlated error on tests of significance for the interrupted time-series quasi-experimental design." Available from author, 1965. (Mimeographed).

Swingle, P. "Relatives' concepts of mental patients." Mental Hygiene, 1965, 49: 461-465.

Swinyard, E. A., Clark, L. D., Miyahara, J. T., & Wolf, H. H. "Studies on the mechanism of amphetamine toxicity in aggregared mice." Journal of Pharmacological Experimental Therapy, 1961, 132: 97-102.

Syme, S. L., Borhani, N. O., & Buechley, R. W. "Cultural mobility and coronary heart disease in an urban area." American Journal of Epidemiology, 1965. 82: 334-346.

Syme, S. L., Hyman, M. M., & Enterline, P. E. "Some social and cultural factors associated with the occurrence of coronary heart disease." Journal of Chronic Disorders, 1964, 17: 277-289.

Syme, S. L., Hyman, M. M., & Enterline, P. E. "Cultural mobility and the occurrence of coronary heart disease." Health and Human Behavior, 1965, 6: 173-189.

Szasz, T. S. *The myth of mental illness.* New York: Hoeber-Harper, 1961.

Szasz, T. S. *Law, liberty and psychiatry.* New York: Macmillan, 1963.

Szasz, T. S. *Ideology and insanity.* Garden City, N.Y.: Doubleday Anchor Books, 1970.

# T

Taietz, P. "Conflicting group norms and the 'third' person in the interview." American Journal of Sociology, 1962, 68: 97-104.

Taylor, D. & Alpert, S. *Continuity and support following residential treatment.* New York: Child Welfare League of America, 1973.

Taylor, J. A. "A personality scale of manifest anxiety." Journal of Abnormal and Social Psychology, 1953, 48: 285-290.

Tharp, R. G. "Community intervention: A behavioral approach." Symposium presented at the American Psychological Association Annual Convention, Honolulu, September 1972.

Tharp, R. G. & Wetzel, R. J. *Behavior modification in the natural environment.* New York: Academic Press, 1969.

Thistlethwaite, D. L. & Campbell, D. T. "Regression-discontinuity analysis: An analysis to the ex post facto experiment." Journal of Educational Psychology, 1960, 51: 309-317.

Thomas, G. "Community-oriented care in children's institutions." Second year interim report on project funded by the Office of Child Development, Grant No. OCD-CB-106, conducted by the Regional Institute of Social Welfare Research, University of Georgia, 1260 South Lumpkin Street, Athens, Georgia 30601, 1972.

Thomas, L. *The lives of a cell.* New York: Viking Press, 1974.

Thompson, J. D. *Organization in action.* New York: McGraw-Hill, 1967.

Thompson, I. G. Suicide and mortality in depression. In R. Fox (ed.), *Proceedings of the Fifth International Conference for Suicide Prevention,* Vienna I.A.S.P., 1970.

Thorndike, R. L. "Regression fallacies in the matched group experiment." Psychometrika, 1942, 7: 85-102.

Thorndike, R. L. & Hagan, E. *Measurement and evaluation in psychology and education.* New York: John Wiley, 1961.

Tillman, W. A. & Hobbs, G. E. "Social background of accident free and accident repeaters. American Journal of Psychiatry, 1949, 106: 321.

Tilly, C. Feagin, J. R., & Williams, C. "Rent supplements in Boston." Joint Center for Urban Studies of the Massachusetts Institute of Technology and Harvard University. 1968. (Mimeographed).

Titmus, R. M. *Problems of social policy.* London: H.M.S.O., 1950. (Quoted by E. W. Howard, "The effects of social stimuli on the response to stress." Psychological Reviews, 1959, 66: 269.

Toch, H. "Change through participation (and vice versa)." Unpublished manuscript, School of Criminal Justice, State University of New York at Albany, 1969.

Tolor, A. "Opinions about mental illness and political ideology." American Journal of Psychiatry, 1973, 130: 1269-1272.

Torgerson, W. *Theory and methods of scaling.* New York: John Wiley, 1958.

Tornqvist, L. "An attempt to analyze the problem of an economical production of statistical data." Nordisk Tidsskrift for Teknisk Okonomi (Vol. 37), 1948.

Tribe, L. H. Policy science: Analysis or ideology? In W. A. Niskanen, A. C. Harberger, R. H. Haveman, R. Turvey, & R. Seckhauser (eds.), *Benefit-cost and policy analysis, 1972.* Chicago: Aldine, 1973.

Trieschman, A. E., Wittaker, J. K., & Brendtro, L. T. *The other 23 hours.* Chicago: Aldine, 1969.

Tringo, J. L. "The heirarchy of preference toward disability groups." Journal of Special Education, 1970, 4: 295-306.

Tripodi, T., Epstein, E., & MacMurray, C. "Dilemmas in evaluation implications for administrators of social action programs."

Tryon, R. C. "Identification of social areas by cluster analysis." University of California Press, Publications in Psychology, 8(1): 1-100.

Tryon, R. C. "Predicting group differences in cluster analysis: The social area problem." Multivariate Behavioral Research, 1967, 2: 453-475.

Tryon, R. C. "Comparative cluster analysis of social areas." Multivarate Behavioral Research, 1968, 3(2): 213-232.

Tryon, R. C. & Bailey, D. E. *Cluster analysis.* New York: McGraw-Hill, 1970.

Tulkin, S. R. & Cohler, B. J. "Child rearing attitudes on mother-child interaction among middle and working class families." Paper presented at the 1971 meeting of the Society for Research in Child Development.

Tulkin, S. R. & Kagan, J. "Mother-child interaction: social class differences in the first year of life." Proceedings of the 78th Annual Convention of the American Psychological Association, 1970: 261-262.

Turner, R. & Wagenfeld, M. "Occupational mobility and schizophrenia: An assessment of the social causation and social selection hypotheses." American Sociological Review, 1967, 32: 104-113.

Tyroler, H. A. & Cassel, J. "Health consequences of culture change: The effect of urbanization on coronary heart mortality in rural residents of North Carolina." Journal of Chronic Diseases, 1964, 17: 167-177.

## U

Ullmann, I. *Institution and outcome: A comparative study of mental hospitals.* New York: Pergamon, 1967.

Ullman, L. P. & Krasner, L., eds. *Case studies in behavior modification.* New York: Holt, Rinehart & Winston, 1965.

United States Army Finance School. *Statistical presentation.* Fort Benjamin Harrison, Indiana, July 1963.

United States Congress, Senate, Committee on Government Operations, Subcommittee on Executive Reorganization and Government Research. *Federal role in health: report pursuant to Senate resolution 390.* 91st Congress, April 30, 1970, Senate Report 91-801.

United States Department of Health, Education, and Welfare. The influence of interviewer and respondent psychological and behavioral variables on the reporting in household interviews. Prepared by C. F. Cannell, F. J. Fowler and K. H. Marquis. *Vital health statistics,* 1968, series 2, number 26.

University of Minnesota. "Cultural education specialists." Unpublished manuscript, Office of New Careers, February 1969.

University of Minnesota. "Up the up staircase: Impressions of the new careerists as a student." Unpublished manuscript, Office of New Careers, June 1969.


# V


Van Arsdol, M., Jr., Carmiler, S., & Schim, C. "The generality of urban social areas indexes." American Sociological Review, June 1958, 23: 277-284.

Van De Riet, V. *A sequential approach to early childhood and elementary education.* Bainesville, Florida: University of Florida Department of Clinical Psychology, 1972.

Vanhounds, H. M. *An automated community mental health information system.* Region 3B Management Information, Adolf Meyer Center, Decatur, Illinois.

Vaughan, G. M. & Corballis, M. C. "Beyond tests of significance: Estimating strength of effects in selected anova designs." Psychological Bulletin, 1969, 72: 204-213.

Vayda, A. P. "An ecological approach to cultural anthropology." Bucknell Review, 1969, 17: 112-119.

Vernallis, F. F. & St. Pierre, R. G. "Volunteer workers' opinions about mental illness." Journal of Clinical Psychology, 1964, 20: 140-143.

Veterans Administration Report to the House of Representatives Committee on Veterans Affairs. Washington, D.C., 1969.

Vinter, R. & Janowitz, M. "Effective institutions for juvenile delinquents: a research statement." Social Service Review, June 1959, 33: 118.

Von Mering, O. & King, S. H. *Remotivating the mental patient.* New York: Russell Sage Foundation, 1957.


# W


Wachs, S. & Kumagai, T. G. "Physical accessibility as a social indicator." Socio-Economic Planning Science, October 1973, 7: 437-456.

Walk, D. "Suicide and community care." British Journal of Psychiatry, 1967, 113: 1381.

Walker, H. M. & Lev, J. *Statistical inference.* New York: Holt, Rinehart & Winston, 1953.

Wallace, S. R. "Criteria for what?" American Psychologist, 1965, 20: 416-417.

Wallace, W., Ed. *Sociological theory.* Chicago: Aldine, 1969.

Ward, D. A. Evaluation of correctional treatment: Some implications of negative findings. In S. A. Yefsky (ed.), *Law enforcement science and technology.* London: Academic Press, 1967.

Ward, D. A. & Kassebaum, G. G. *Women's prison.* Chicago: Aldine, 1965.

Ward, D. A. & Kassebaum, G. G. On biting the hand that feeds: Some implications of sociological evaluations of correctional effectiveness. In C. H. Weiss (ed.), *Evaluating action programs: Readings in social action and education.* Boston: Allyn & Bacon, 1972.

Warren, M. Q. "Correctional treatment in community settings: A report of current research." Paper presented at the III International Congress on Criminology, Madrid, Spain, September 1970.

Warren, M., Neto, T., Palmer, R., & Turner, K. *Community treatment project: Fifth program report: An evaluation of the community treatment for delinquents.* Sacramento: California Youth Authority, 1966.

Warren, R. L. "The interorganizational field as a focus for investigation." Administrative Science Quarterly, December 1967, 12: 396-419.

Warren, R. "The social context of program evaluation research." Paper presented at the Ohio State University Symposium on Evaluation in Human Service Programs, June 1973.

Waters, M. & Northover, J. "Rehabilitated long stay schizophrenics in the community." British Journal of Psychiatry, 1965, 111: 258-267.

Watson, G. & Glaser, E. M. "What we have learned about planning for change." Management Review, 1965, 54(11) 43-46.

Wattenberg, E. "Progress report on education, first fiscal year ending June 30, 1968." Unpublished manuscript, Minneapolis New Careers Program, University of Minnesota, 1968.

Wattenberg, E. "Special curriculum for university new careers program in the General College." Unpublished manuscript, Office of New Careers, University of Minnesota, 1970. (Reprinted by New Careers Information Clearinghouse, University Research Corporation, Washington, D.C.)

Watts, H. W. "Graduated work incentives: An experiment in negative taxation." American Economic Review, 1969, 59: 463-472.

Webb, E. J., Campbell, D. T., Schwartz, R. D., & Sechrest, L. B. *Unobtrusive measures: Nonreactive research in the social sciences.* Chicago: Rand McNally, 1966.

Weber, G. H. "The use of the conference method in the in-service training of cottage parents." International Journal of Social Psychiatry, Summer 1957, 3: 49.

Weber, G. & Haberlein, B. *Residential treatment of emotionally disturbed children.* New York: Behavioral Publications, 1972.

Weed, L. L. *Medical records, medical education, and patient care.* Cleveland: Press of Case Western Reserve University, 1969.

Weeks, A. *Youthful offenders at Highfields: an evaluation of the short-term treatment of delinquent boys.* Ann Arbor: University of Michigan Press, 1968.

Weick, K. Systematic observational methods. In G. Lindzey and E. Aronson (eds.), *The handbook of social psychology.* Reading, Mass.: Addison-Wesley, 1968.

Weick, K. Interlocked behaviors: The elements of organizing. In K. Weick, *The social psychology or organizing.* Reading, Mass.: Addison-Wesley, 1969.

Weick, K. The enacted environment. In K. Weick, *The social psychology of organizing.* Reading, Mass.: Addison-Wesley, 1969.

Weikart, D. P. *Preschool intervention: A preliminary report of the Perry Preschool Project.* Ann Arbor, Michigan: Campus Publishers, 1967.

Weikart, D. P. "A comparative study of three preschool curricula." Paper presented at the biannual meeting of the Society for Research in Child Development, Santa Monica, California, March 1969.

Weikart, D. P. et al. *Longitudinal results of the Ypsilanti Perry Preschool Project.* Ypsilanti, Mich.: High/Scope Educational Research Foundation, 1970.

Weikart, D. P., Kamii, C. K., & Radin, M. "Perry preschool progress report." Ypsilanti, Mich.: Ypsilanti Public Schools, 1964.

Weikart, D. P., Rogers, L., Adcock, C., & McClelland, D. *The cognitively oriented curriculum.* Washington, D.C.: National Association for the Education of Young Children, 1971.

Weinberg, E. *Community surveys with local talent: A handbook.* Chicago: University of Chicago, National Opinion Research Center, 1971.

Weinberg, S. K., Ed. *The sociology of mental disorders.* Chicago: Aldine, 1967.

Weinstein, A. S., Hanley, A. T., & Strode, R. L. *Services to the mentally disabled of the Metropolitan Hospital community mental health catchment area in New York City.* USDHEW-HSM Contract 42-72-53, New York State Department of Mental Hygiene, 44 Holland Avenue, Albany, New York, 1972.

Weinstein, A. S. & Maiwald, A. "Trends in the New York State mental hospital population, admissions and length of stay." *The Willard State Hospital Centennial Symposium.* Hanover, New Jersey: Sandoz Pharmaceuticals, in press.

Weinstein, A. S. & Patton, R. E. "Trends in chronicity in the New York State mental hospitals." Paper presented at the American Public Health Association meeting, Philadelphia, Pennsylvania, November 10, 1969. (Mimeographed).

Weisbrod, B. A. *Economics of public health: Measuring its economic impact on diseases.* Philadelphia: University of Pennsylvania Press, 1960.

Weisbrod, B. A. Preventing high school dropouts. In R. Dorfman (ed.), *Measuring benefits of government investments.* Washington, D.C.: Brookings Institution, 1965.

Weisbrod, B. A. Income redistribution effects and benefit-cost analysis. In S. B. Chase, Jr. (ed.), *Problems in public expenditure analysis.* Washington, D.C.: Brookings Institution, 1968.

Weiss, C. H. "Validity of welfare mothers' interview responses." Public Opinion Quarterly, 1968, 32(4): 622-633.

Weiss, C. H. "The politicalization of evaluation research." Journal of Social Issues, 1970, 26(4): 57-68.

Weiss, C. H. *Evaluation research: Methods of assessing program effectiveness.* Englewood Cliffs, N.J.: Prentice-Hall, 1972.

Weiss, C. H. "Between the cup and the lip." Evaluation, 1973, 1(2): 49-55.

Weiss, C. H. "The politics and evaluation research meet." Evaluation, 1973, 1(3): 37-45.

Weiss, R. S. & Rein, M. "The evaluation of broad-aim programs: a cautionary case and a moral." Annals of the American Academy of Political and Social Sciences, 1969, 385: 133-142.

Weiss, R. S. & Rein, M. "The evaluation of broad-aim programs: Experimental design, its difficulties, and an alternative." Administrative Science Quarterly, 1970, 15: 97-109.

Weiss, R. S. & Rein, M. The evaluation of broad-aim programs: difficulties in experimental design and an alternative. In C. H. Weiss (ed.), *Evaluating action programs.* Boston: Allyn & Bacon, 1972.

Weller, L. & Luchterhand, E. "Interviewer-respondent interaction in Negro and white family life research." Human Organization, 1968, 27(1): 50-55.

Werner, D. Measuring the motive. In National Institute of Mental Health, *Experiment in culture expansion,* 1963.

Werts, C. E. & Linn, R. L. "Analyzing school effects ANOVA with a fallible covariate." Educational and Psychological Measurement, 1971, 31: 95-104.

Whatley, C. "Social attitudes toward discharged mental patients." Social Problems, 1958-9, 6: 313-320.

White, O., Jr., & Sjoberg, G. The emerging "new politics" in America. In M. D. Hancock and G. Sjobert (eds.), *Politics in the post-welfare state.* New York: Columbia University Press, in press.

Whittaker, J. K. & Trieschman, A. E., Eds. *Children away from home: A source book of residential treatment.* Chicago: Aldine-Atherton, 1972.

Wholey, J. S., Scanlon, J. W., Duffy, H. G., Fukumoto, J. S., & Vogt, L. M. *Federal evaluation policy.* Washington, D.C.: Urban Institute, 1970.

Whyte, W. F. *Street corner society.* Chicago: University of Chicago Press, 1955.

Wicker, A. "Attitudes versus actions: The relationship of verbal and overt behavioral responses to attitude objects." Journal of Social Issues, 1969, 25: 41-78.

Wilcocks, C. *Aspects of medical investigation in Africa.* London: Oxford University Press, 1962.

Wildavsky, A. *The politics of the budgetary process.* Boston: Little, Brown, 1964.

Wilder, J. F. "Day care versus inpatient hospitalization: A controlled study." American Journal of Psychiatry, April 1971, 127: 1381.

Wilder, J. F., Leven, G., & Zwerling, I. "A two year follow-up evaluation of acute psychotic patients treated in a day hospital." American Journal of Psychiatry, 122: 1095.

Wiley, W. W. Six steps to new careers. *Methods for manpower analysis, Number 3: a systems approach to new careers.* Kalamazoo, Michigan: W. E. Upjohn Institute for Employment Research, 1969. (Reprinted by National Institute for New Careers, University Research

Corporation, Washington, D.C., as *Comprehensive health services–Career development issues,* 1970, No. 1.)

Wilkins, L. T. *Social deviance: Social policy, action, and research.* Englewood, Cliffs, N.J.: Prentice-Hall, 1965.

Wilkins, L. T. *Evaluation of penal measures.* New York: Random House, 1969.

Willems, E. P. & Raush, H. L., Eds. *Naturalistic viewpoints in psychological research.* New York: Holt, Rinehart & Winston, 1969.

Williams, A. Cost-benefit analysis: Bastard science? and/or insidious poison in the body politic? In W. A. Niskanen, A. C. Harberger, R. H. Haveman, R. Turvey, & R. Seckhauser (eds.), *Benefit-cost and policy analysis 1972.* Chicago: Aldine, 1973.

Williams, D. H., Jacobs, S., Debski, A., & Revere, M. "Introducing the problem-oriented record on a psychiatric inpatient unit." Hospital and Community Psychiatry, January 1974, 25(1): 25-28.

Williams, E. J. *Regression analysis.* New York: John Wiley, 1959.

Williams, J. A., Jr. *Interviewer-respondent interaction: A study of bias in the information interview.* Unpublished Ph.D. dissertation, University of North Carolina at Chapel Hill, 1963.

Williams, J. & Williams, H. M. "Attitudes toward mental illness, anomia and authoritarianism among state hospital nursing students and attendants." Mental Hygiene, 1961, 45(3): 418-424.

Williams, O. P. *Metropolitan political analysis.* New York: Free Press, 1971.

Williams, R. H. & Ozarin, L. D. Eds. *Community mental health.* San Francisco: Jossey-Bass, 1968.

Williams, W. & Evans, J. W. "The politics of evaluation: The case of Head Start." Annals of the Academy of Political and Social Science, September 1969, 385 : 118-132.

Wilner, D. M., Walkley, R. P., Pinkerton, T. C., & Tayback, M. *The housing environment and family life.* Baltimore: Johns Hopkins Press, 1962.

Wilson, J. C., Fishman, J. R., & Mitchell, L. E. "An assessment of technical assistance and training needs in new careers projects being sponsored by the United States Training and Employment Service, Manpower Administration, United States Department of Labor." Unpublished manuscript, National Institute for New Careers, University Research Corporation, Washington, D.C., 1969.

Wilson, J. Q. "The bureaucracy problem." Public Interest, 1967, 6: 3-9.

Wilson, J. Q. "The urban unease." Public Interest, 1968, 12: 26.

Wilson, R. A. "Anomie in the ghetto: A study of type race and anomie." American Journal of Sociology, July 1971, 77(1).

Windle, C. & Volkman, E. M. *A working model for mental health program evaluation.* November 1973.

Wineman, D. "The life-space interview." Social Work, January 1959, 4(1): 3-18.

Winer, B. J. *Statistical principles in experimental design* (second ed.). New York: McGraw-Hill, 1971.

Wing, J. K. & Hailey, A. M. *The evaluation of a community psychiatric service.* London: Oxford University Press, 1972.

Wing, J., Monck, E., Brown, G., & Carstairs, G. M. "Morbidity in the community of schizophrenic patients discharged from London mental hospitals in 1969." British Journal of Psychiatry, 1964, 110: 10-21.

Wohlwill, J. F. & Carson, D. H. *Environment and the social sciences.* Washington, D.C.: American Psychological Association, 1972.

Wolf, E., Luke, G., & Han, H. *Scheidung und Scheidungsrecht: Grundfragen der Ehescheidung in Deutschland.* Tubigen: J.C.B. Mohrm, 1959.

Wolff, H. G. "Life stress and bodily disease." Research Papers for the Association of Nervous and Mental Disorders, 1950, 29: 3-1135.

Wolfowitz, J. "Remarks on the theory of testing hypotheses." New York Statistician, March 1967, 18(7).

Wolins, M., Ed. *Successful group care: Explorations in the powerful environment.* Chicago: Aldine, 1974.

Wood, E. C., Rakuskin, J. M., Morse, E., & Singer, R. "Interpersonal aspects of psychiatric hospitalization." Archives of General Psychiatry, 1962, 6: 46-55.

Wright, C. R. & Hyman, H. H. The evaluators. In P. E. Hammond (ed.), *Sociologists at work.* New York: Basic Books, 1964.

Wright, F. Observational child study. In P. Mussen (ed.), *Handbook of research methods in child development.* New York: John Wiley, 1960.

Wright, F. H. & Klein, R. A. "Attitudes of hospital personnel and the community regarding mental illness." Journal of Counseling Psychology, 1966, 13: 106-107.

Wynee, L., Ryckoff, I., Day, J., & Hirsch, S. "Pseudomutuality in the family relations of schizophrenics." Psychiatry, 1958, 21: 205-220.


# Y

Yamamoto, K. & Dizney, H. F. "Rejection of the mentally ill: A study of attitudes of student teachers." Journal of Counseling Psychology, 1967, 14: 264-268.

Yarrow, M., Clausen, J., & Robbins, P. "The social meaning of mental illness." Journal of Social Issues, 1955, 11: 33-48.

Yarrow, M., Schwartz, C., Murphy, H., & Deasy, L. "The psychological meaning of mental illness in the family." Journal of Social Issues, 1955, 11: 12-24.

Yuchtman, E. & Seashore, S. "A system resource approach to organizational effectiveness." American Sociological Review, December 1967, 32: 891-903.


# Z

Zlotowski, M. & Cohen, D. "Effects of change in hospital organizations upon the behavior of psychiatric patients." Paper presented at the meeting of the Eastern Psychological Association, Atlantic City, April 1965.

Zolik, E. S., Lantz, E. M., & Sommers, R. "Hospital return rates and pre-release referrals." Paper presented at the 75th Annual Convention, American Psychological Association, Washington, D.C., 1967.

Zwerling, I. & Wilder, J. F. "An evaluation of the applicability of the day hospital in treatment of acutely disturbed patients." Israel Annuals of Psychiatry and Related Disciplines, 1961, 2: 162-185.

# ABOUT THE AUTHORS AND EDITORS

LEE GUREL is Director of the Division of Manpower Research and Development of the American Psychiatric Association and was formerly Director of the Program Evaluation Staff of the Veterans Administration Department of Medicine and Surgery. He received his Ph.D. in 1952 from Purdue University and is author or co-author of nearly one hundred publications in a wide range of subject matter areas. He is also President-Elect of the District of Columbia Psychological Association and past president of the Division of Psychologists in Public Service of the American Psychological Association.

GIDEON SJOBERG is currently Professor of Sociology at The University of Texas at Austin. He is author of *The Preindustrial City* (1960) and (with Roget Nett) *A Methodology for Social Research.* He edited *Ethics, Politics and Social Research* (1967) and co-edited (with M. Donald Hancock) *Politics in the Post-Welfare State* (1972). He is currently completing a book with Ted R. Vaughan on "The Sociology of Ethics." His primary interests are in the sociology of ethics; the relationship between social theory and research procedures; bureaucracy; and life styles.

JEROME ROTHENBERG is Professor of Economics at the Massachusetts Institute of Technology, and a Fellow of the Joint Center for Urban Studies of MIT and Harvard University. He is the author of several books, including *The Measurement of Social Welfare* (1961, Prentice-Hall), and the forthcoming *An Econometric Model of the Metropolitan Housing Market.* His present research in progress is in the fields of modeling urban housing markets, alternative types of pollution policy, housing allowance programs, urban highways and community disruption, the economics of solid waste disposal, and an evaluation of public policy for metropolitan development.

HENRY M. LEVIN is Associate Professor in the School of Education and on the Affiliated Faculty of the Department of Economics at Stanford University. Prior to going to Stanford in 1968, he served as a research associate in the Economic Studies Division of the Brookings Institution. He is a specialist in the economics of human resources, the economics of education, and in government finance. He has published several books and a large number of articles on cost-effectiveness analysis, financing education, the production of education, and the evaluation of social problems.

PETER SAINSBURY is Director of Research at the Medical Research Council's Clinical Psychiatry Unit and Consultant Psychiatrist at Graylingwell Hospital since 1957. Previously he was research assistant to Sir Aubrey Lewis at the Institute of Psychiatry. His present research interests include evaluation of services, suicide and its prevention, epidemiological studies, and psychophysiology.

STEVE PRATT was, before his recent untimely death, Professor of Community Psychology at Wichita (Kansas) State University. He had received his Ph.D. in clinical psychology from Purdue University. He published extensively in professional journals, consulted with state, government, and institutional agencies, and lectured widely at scientific meetings. His major research work was in the fields of mental hospital theory and models, and the development of a new theoretical system called "contract psychology," capable of synthesizing the social-behavioral sciences, value theory, epistemology, and action-research methodology.

MERLE CANFIELD has for the past five years served as Program Evaluation Coordinator at Prairie View Mental Health Center in Newton, Kansas. His interest in mental health studies and behavioral science began while he was in the Navy. He studied at Ft. Hays State College and at Colorado State University (Ft. Collins). He has worked with the mentally retarded at Wheatridge State Home and Training School in Colorado and at Jacksonville State Hospital in Illinois in hospital program development and research.

M. POWELL LAWTON is Assistant Director of Program Research at Norristown State Hospital and Director of Behavior Research at the Philadelphia Geriatric Center. He graduated from Haverford College and received his Ph.D. in clinical psychology from Columbia University.

JACOB COHEN is currently Professor of Psychology and Chairman of the Quantitative Psychology Area of New York University's Graduate Psychology Department. He previously worked extensively with the Veterans Administration, his research interests including practice and research in clinical psychology and later quantitative research methodology in the behavioral sciences. In addition to many articles and chapters in books, he has authored an introductory statistics text, and a handbook entitled *Statistical Power Analysis for the Behavioral Sciences* (1969, Academic Press). In collaboration with Patricia Cohen, he will be co-author in mid-1975 of a textbook/manual entitled *Multiple Regression/Correlational Analysis for the Behavioral Sciences* (Lawrence Erlbaum Associates.)

ROBERT B. ELLSWORTH is Chief of Research Service at the Veterans Administration Hospital in Salem, Virginia. His primary research areas include evaluation of the effectiveness of psychiatric hospital and mental health center programs, and identification of the psychosocial characteristics of effective programs. His past interests have included the creation of therapeutic roles for nonprofessionals and the relationship between staff attitudes and behavior. He is presently coordinating a large-scale, multi-hospital study entitled "Characteristics of Psychiatric Programs and Their Relationship to Treatment Effectiveness."

RODERICK P. DURKIN is currently Director of Education and Training at Manhattan Childrens' Treatment Center and Director of Sage Hill Camp, Inc. He received his Ph.D. in social psychology from Columbia University, and has conducted a variety of research and demonstration projects sponsored by the U.S. Office of Education, the Office of Child Development, and the U.S. Department of Labor in the context of a summer camp and follow-up program for poverty and/or disturbed children.

ANN BOTSFORD DURKIN received a B.A. from Barnard College and an M.A. in philosophy from Tufts University. She has worked on a variety of research and social action projects and is currently a graduate student in social work at Adelphi University.

RICHARD N. BRANDON is a professional staff member of the U.S. Senate Budget Committee. His experience with the mental health service system was largely gained as director of Systems Analysis and Planning for the New York City Department of Mental Health and Mental Retardation Services, from 1969 to 1972. He has had urban policy experience working with the Health and Welfare Committee of Philadelphia's City Council, and has been a community planning board member in that city. He has also been a research fellow in the Department of Political Science of the University of Pennsylvania.

JUDITH G. RABKIN received her Ph.D. in clinical psychology from New York University. She has served as psychological consultant at Lincoln Hospital of the Albert Einstein College of Medicine, and as staff psychologist at the Jewish Family Service. Since 1969 she has been Associate Research Scientist in the New York State Department of Mental Hygiene, working in the Epidemiology of Mental Disorders Research Unit.

DOLORES E. KREISMAN is Associate Research Scientist with the New York State Department of Mental Hygiene and a participant in the Community Research Program located at New York University.

VIRGINIA D. JOY is Senior Research Scientist with the New York State Department of Mental Hygiene and on the faculty of New York University. She is collaborating with Dolores Kreisman on a longitudinal study of symptom tolerance in the families of schizophrenics. She and Ms. Kreisman are also doing research on the interaction of symptom tolerance and labeling in an experimental setting and in a questionnaire study of the general public.

URIE BRONFENBRENNER is Professor of Human Development and Family Studies, and Professor of Psychology at Cornell University. He received his Ph.D. from the University of Michigan, and was honored with the 1975 American Educational Research Association Award for distinguished contribution to the field. He previously was affiliated with the University of Michigan and the Veterans Administration, and is Director of the FCD Program of Research on the Ecology of Human Development. He is Consulting Editor for both the *Journal of Personality and Social Psychology* and for *Soviet Psychology*.

THOMAS W. BICE is Professor of Sociology at Washington University in St. Louis. He received his Ph.D. from Purdue University in 1969. His major areas of research interest are health planning and regulation, and health behavior.

ROBERT L. EICHHORN is Professor of Sociology at Purdue University and Director of the Health Services Research and Training Program. He spent two years with the National Center for Health Services Research and Development, serving as chief of the Social Analysis Branch, director of Special R & D Division, and associate director for Program Planning and Development.

DENISE A. KLEIN is currently employed in the Department of Sociology at Purdue University as Senior Research Associate. She received a B.A. from Antioch College in 1965.

JOAN GRANT is Project Director with the Social Action Research Center in Berkeley, California. Her research interests include the development and study of new careers for offenders and paraprofessional mental health workers. She has contributed a chapter to *New Careers for the Poor.*

J. DOUGLAS GRANT is President of the Social Action Research Center in Berkeley, California. Previously he was chief of research for the California Department of Corrections. He is co-author of *Agents of Change: A Study in Police Reform,* and he contributed a chapter to *New Careers for the Poor.* His major research areas are new careers for offenders, and the study of paraprofessional mental health workers.

MARCIA GUTTENTAG is President of the Division of Personality and Social Psychology of the American Psychological Association. A developmental social psychologist at the Harvard University Graduate School of Education, she was formerly Professor of Psychology at the Graduate Center, CUNY, and Director of the Harlem Research Center. She has served as evaluation consultant to UNESCO, the Office of Child Development, the National Institute of Mental Health, and other federal agencies. She was chairwoman of the Task Force on the Evaluation of Training in Community Mental Health, for the National Institute of Mental Health. She is co-author of the *Evaluation of Training* and many chapters and articles on evaluation, in addition to being a past president of the Society for the Psychological Study of Social Issues. She is currently engaged in a national evaluation study of women and mental health.

ELMER L. STRUENING is currently Director of the Epidemiology of Mental Disorders Research Unit, Psychiatric Institute, New York State Department of Mental Hygiene, and Associate Professor, Columbia University. From 1965-1969 he was Director of Research, Lincoln Hospital Mental Health Services, Albert Einstein College of Medicine. His research interests include the methodology and application of social area analysis, the structure of attitudes, the social epidemiology of mental disorders, and the methodology of evaluation research.

# AUTHOR INDEX

# SUBJECT INDEX

H
62
H 2454 /
Vol. II / 18, 13 7                CAMROSE LUTHERAN COLLEGE
                                        LIBRARY